Twentieth-Century Literary Criticism

Guide to Gale Literary Criticism Series

When you need to review criticism of literary works, these are the Gale series to use:

If the author's death date is: **You should turn to:**

After Dec. 31, 1959
(or author is still living)

CONTEMPORARY LITERARY CRITICISM

for example: Jorge Luis Borges, Anthony Burgess,
William Faulkner, Mary Gordon,
Ernest Hemingway, Iris Murdoch

1900 through 1959

TWENTIETH-CENTURY LITERARY CRITICISM

for example: Willa Cather, F. Scott Fitzgerald,
Henry James, Mark Twain, Virginia Woolf

1800 through 1899

NINETEENTH-CENTURY LITERATURE CRITICISM

for example: Fedor Dostoevski, George Sand,
Gerard Manley Hopkins, Emily Dickinson

1400 through 1799

LITERATURE CRITICISM FROM 1400 TO 1800
(excluding Shakespeare)

for example: Anne Bradstreet, Pierre Corneille,
Daniel Defoe, Alexander Pope,
Jonathan Swift, Phillis Wheatley

SHAKESPEAREAN CRITICISM

Shakespeare's plays and poetry

Antiquity through 1399

CLASSICAL AND MEDIEVAL LITERATURE CRITICISM

for example: Dante, Homer, Plato, Sophocles, Vergil,
the Beowulf poet

(Volume 1 forthcoming)

Gale also publishes related criticism series:

CHILDREN'S LITERATURE REVIEW

This ongoing series covers authors of all eras.
Presents criticism on authors and author/illustrators
who write for the preschool to junior-high audience.

CONTEMPORARY ISSUES CRITICISM

This two-volume set presents criticism on
contemporary authors writing on current issues.
Topics covered include the social sciences,
philosophy, economics, natural science, law, and
related areas.

ISSN 0276-8178

Volume 20

Twentieth-Century Literary Criticism

**Excerpts from Criticism of the
Works of Novelists, Poets, Playwrights,
Short Story Writers, and Other Creative Writers
Who Died between 1900 and 1960,
from the First Published Critical Appraisals
to Current Evaluations**

Dennis Poupard
Editor

Marie Lazzari
Thomas Ligotti
Associate Editors

Gale Research Company
Book Tower
Detroit, Michigan 48226

STAFF

Dennis Poupard, *Editor*

Marie Lazzari, Thomas Ligotti, *Associate Editors*

Paula Kepos, Serita Lanette Lockard, *Senior Assistant Editors*

Sandra Liddell, Jay P. Pederson, Joann Prosyniuk, Laurie A. Sherman, *Assistant Editors*

Sharon R. Gunton, Phyllis Carmel Mendelson, *Contributing Editors*
Melissa Reiff Hug, *Contributing Assistant Editor*

Lizbeth A. Purdy, *Production Supervisor*
Denise Michlewicz Broderick, *Production Coordinator*
Eric Berger, *Assistant Production Coordinator*
Kathleen M. Cook, Maureen Duffy, Sheila J. Nasea, *Editorial Assistants*

Victoria B. Cariappa, *Research Coordinator*
Maureen R. Richards, *Assistant Research Coordinator*
Daniel Kurt Gilbert, Keith E. Schooley, Filomena Sgambati,
Vincenza G. Tranchida, Valerie J. Webster, Mary D. Wise, *Research Assistants*

Linda M. Pugliese, *Manuscript Coordinator*
Donna Craft, *Assistant Manuscript Coordinator*
Maureen A. Puhl, Rosetta Irene Simms, *Manuscript Assistants*

Jeanne A. Gough, *Permissions Supervisor*
Janice M. Mach, *Permissions Coordinator, Text*
Patricia A. Seefelt, *Permissions Coordinator, Illustrations*
Susan D. Battista, *Assistant Permissions Coordinator*
Margaret A. Chamberlain, Sandra C. Davis, Kathy Grell, Josephine M. Keene,
Mary M. Matuz, *Senior Permissions Assistants*
H. Diane Cooper, Colleen M. Crane, Mabel C. Schoening, *Permissions Assistants*
Margaret Carson, Dorothy J. Fowler, Helen Hernandez, Anita Williams, *Permissions Clerks*

Frederick G. Ruffner, *Publisher*
Dedria Bryfonski, *Editorial Director*
Christine Nasso, *Director, Literature Division*
Laurie Lanzen Harris, *Senior Editor, Literary Criticism Series*
Dennis Poupard, *Managing Editor, Literary Criticism Series*

Library of Congress Catalog Card Number 76-46132
ISBN 0-8103-2402-4
ISSN 0276-8178

Computerized photocomposition by
Typographics, Incorporated
Kansas City, Missouri

Printed in the United States

Contents

Preface   7

Authors to Be Featured in *TCLC*, Volumes 21 and 22   11

Additional Authors to Appear in Future Volumes   13

Appendix   433

Cumulative Index to Authors   449

Cumulative Index to Nationalities   499

Cumulative Index to Critics   503

Arnold Bennett 1867-1931 15

Herman Broch 1886-1951 44

Dino Campana 1885-1932 81

Sheila Kaye-Smith 1887-1956 . . . 91

Velimir Khlebnikov
   1885-1922 121

Ferenc Molnár 1878-1952 154

Benjamin Péret 1899-1959 180

Horacio Quiroga 1878-1937 . . . 205

Raymond Roussel
   1877-1933 224

John Ruskin 1819-1900 256

Marcel Schwob 1867-1905 317

Lincoln Steffens 1866-1936 331

George Sterling 1869-1926 367

Virginia Woolf 1882-1941 390

Preface

It is impossible to overvalue the importance of literature in the intellectual, emotional, and spiritual evolution of humanity. Literature is that which both lifts us out of everyday life and helps us to better understand it. Through the fictive lives of such characters as Anna Karenina, Jay Gatsby, or Leopold Bloom, our perceptions of the human condition are enlarged, and we are enriched.

Literary criticism can also give us insight into the human condition, as well as into the specific moral and intellectual atmosphere of an era, for the criteria by which a work of art is judged reflects contemporary philosophical and social attitudes. Literary criticism takes many forms: the traditional essay, the book or play review, even the parodic poem. Criticism can also be of several types: normative, descriptive, interpretive, textual, appreciative, generic. Collectively, the range of critical response helps us to understand a work of art, an author, an era.

Scope of the Series

Twentieth-Century Literary Criticism (TCLC) is designed to serve as an introduction for the student of twentieth-century literature to the authors of the period 1900 to 1960 and to the most significant commentators on these authors. The great poets, novelists, short story writers, playwrights, and philosophers of this period are by far the most popular writers for study in high school and college literature courses. Since a vast amount of relevant critical material confronts the student, *TCLC* presents significant passages from the most important published criticism to aid students in the location and selection of commentaries on authors who died between 1900 and 1960.

The need for *TCLC* was suggested by the usefulness of the Gale series *Contemporary Literary Criticism (CLC)*, which excerpts criticism on current writing. Because of the difference in time span under consideration *(CLC* considers authors who were still living after 1959), there is no duplication of material between *CLC* and *TCLC*. For further information about *CLC* and Gale's other criticism series, users should consult the Guide to Gale Literary Criticism Series preceding the title page in this volume.

Each volume of *TCLC* is carefully compiled to include authors who represent a variety of genres and nationalities and who are currently regarded as the most important writers of this era. In addition to major authors, *TCLC* also presents criticism on lesser-known writers whose significant contributions to literary history are important to the study of twentieth-century literature.

Each author entry in *TCLC* is intended to provide an overview of major criticism on an author. Therefore, the editors include approximately twenty authors in each 600-page volume (compared with approximately fifty authors in a *CLC* volume of similar size) so that more attention may be given to an author. Each author entry represents a historical survey of the critical response to that author's work: some early criticism is presented to indicate initial reactions, later criticism is selected to represent any rise or decline in the author's reputation, and current retrospective analyses provide students with a modern view. The length of an author entry is intended to reflect the amount of critical attention the author has received from critics writing in English, and from foreign criticism in translation. Critical articles and books that have not been translated into English are excluded. Every attempt has been made to identify and include excerpts from the seminal essays on each author's work. Additionally, as space permits, especially insightful essays of a more limited scope are included.

An author may appear more than once in the series because of the great quantity of critical material available, or because of a resurgence of criticism generated by events such as an author's centennial or anniversary celebration, the republication of an author's works, or the publication of a newly translated work or volume of letters. Generally, a few author entries in each volume of *TCLC* feature criticism on single works by major authors who have appeared previously in the series. Only those individual works that have been the subjects of vast amounts of criticism and are widely studied in literature classes are selected for this in-depth treatment. Virginia Woolf's *Mrs. Dalloway* is an example of such an entry in *TCLC,* Volume 20.

Organization of the Book

An author entry consists of the following elements: author heading, biographical and critical introduction, principal works, excerpts of criticism (each followed by a bibliographical citation), and an additional bibliography for further reading.

- The *author heading* consists of the author's full name, followed by birth and death dates. The unbracketed portion of the name denotes the form under which the author most commonly wrote. If an author wrote consistently under a pseudonym, the pseudonym will be listed in the author heading and the real name given in parentheses on the first line of the biographical and critical introduction. Also located at the beginning of the introduction to the author entry are any name variations under which an author wrote, including transliterated forms for authors whose languages use nonroman alphabets. Uncertainty as to a birth or death date is indicated by a question mark.

- The *biographical and critical introduction* contains background information designed to introduce the reader to an author and to the critical debate surrounding his or her work. Parenthetical material following many of the introductions provides references to biographical and critical reference series published by Gale, including *Children's Literature Review, Contemporary Authors, Dictionary of Literary Biography, Something about the Author,* and past volumes of *TCLC.*

- Most *TCLC* entries include *portraits* of the author. Many entries also contain illustrations of materials pertinent to an author's career, including holographs of manuscript pages, title pages, dust jackets, letters, or representations of important people, places, and events in an author's life.

- The *list of principal works* is chronological by date of first book publication and identifies the genre of each work. In the case of foreign authors where there are both foreign language publications and English translations, the title and date of the first English-language edition are given in brackets. Unless otherwise indicated, dramas are dated by first performance, not first publication.

- *Criticism* is arranged chronologically in each author entry to provide a useful perspective on changes in critical evaluation over the years. All titles by the author featured in the critical entry are printed in boldface type to enable the user to ascertain without difficulty the works being discussed. Also for purposes of easier identification, the critic's name and the publication date of the essay are given at the beginning of each piece of criticism. Unsigned criticism is preceded by the title of the journal in which it appeared. When an anonymous essay is later attributed to a critic, the critic's name appears in brackets at the beginning of the excerpt and in the bibliographical citation. Many critical entries in *TCLC* also contain translated material to aid users. Unless otherwise noted, translations within brackets are by the editors; translations within parentheses are by the author of the excerpt.

- Critical essays are prefaced by *explanatory notes* as an additional aid to students using *TCLC.* The explanatory notes provide several types of useful information, including: the reputation of a critic; the importance of a work of criticism; the specific type of criticism (biographical, psychoanalytic, structuralist, etc.); a synopsis of the criticism; and the growth of critical controversy or changes in critical trends regarding an author's work. In many cases, these notes cross-reference the work of critics who agree or disagree with each other. Dates in parentheses within the explanatory notes refer to a book publication date when they follow a book title and to an essay date when they follow a critic's name.

- A complete *bibliographical citation* designed to facilitate location of the original essay or book by the interested reader follows each piece of criticism. An asterisk (*) at the end of a citation indicates that the essay is on more than one author.

- The *additional bibliography* appearing at the end of each author entry suggests further reading on the author. In some cases it includes essays for which the editors could not obtain reprint rights. An asterisk (*) at the end of a citation indicates that the essay is on more than one author.

An appendix lists the sources from which material in each volume has been reprinted. It does not, however, list every book or periodical consulted in the preparation of the volume.

Cumulative Indexes

Each volume of *TCLC* includes a cumulative index to authors listing all the authors who have appeared in *Contemporary Literary Criticism, Twentieth-Century Literary Criticism, Nineteenth-Century Literature Criticism,* and *Literature Criticism from 1400 to 1800,* along with cross-references to the Gale series *Children's Literature Review, Authors in the News, Contemporary Authors, Contemporary Authors Autobiography Series, Dictionary of Literary Biography, Something about the Author,* and *Yesterday's Authors of Books for Children.* Users will welcome this cumulated author index as a useful tool for locating an author within the various series. The index, which lists birth and death dates when available, will be particularly valuable for those authors who are identified with a certain period but whose death date causes them to be placed in another, or for those authors whose careers span two periods. For example, F. Scott Fitzgerald is found in *TCLC,* yet a writer often associated with him, Ernest Hemingway, is found in *CLC.*

Each volume of *TCLC* also includes a cumulative nationality index. Author names are arranged alphabetically under their respective nationalities and followed by the volume numbers in which they appear.

A cumulative index to critics is another useful feature in *TCLC*. Under each critic's name are listed the authors on whom the critic has written and the volume and page where the criticism may be found.

Acknowledgments

No work of this scope can be accomplished without the cooperation of many people. The editors especially wish to thank the copyright holders of the excerpted criticism included in this volume, the permissions managers of many book and magazine publishing companies for assisting us in securing reprint rights, and Anthony Bogucki for assistance with copyright research. We are also grateful to the staffs of the Detroit Public Library, the Library of Congress, University of Detroit Library, University of Michigan Library, and Wayne State University Library for making their resources available to us.

Suggestions Are Welcome

In response to various suggestions, several features have been added to *TCLC* since the series began, including: explanatory notes to excerpted criticism that provide important information regarding critics and their work; a cumulative author index listing authors in all Gale literary criticism series; entries devoted to criticism on a single work by a major author; and more extensive illustrations.

Readers who wish to suggest authors to appear in future volumes, or who have other suggestions, are cordially invited to write the editors.

Authors to Be Featured in *TCLC*, Volumes 21 and 22

Henri Bergson (French philosopher)—One of the most influential philosophers of the twentieth century, Bergson is renowned for his opposition to the dominant materialist thought of his time and for his creation of theories that emphasize the supremacy and independence of supra-rational consciousness.

Sadeq Hedayat (Iranian novelist)—Considered the most important prose writer in modern Persian literature, Hedayat has been compared to Edgar Allan Poe and Franz Kafka for his gruesome outlook on the human condition and for the often fantastic quality of his works.

James Hilton (English novelist)—Hilton was the author of *Goodbye, Mr. Chips* and *Lost Horizon*, two of the most popular and well-loved works of twentieth-century English fiction.

Julia Ward Howe (American poet and biographer)—A famous suffragette and social reformer, Howe was also a popular poet who is best known as the composer of "The Battle Hymn of the Republic."

T. E. Hulme (English poet)—A major influence on the work of T. S. Eliot, Ezra Pound, and other important twentieth-century poets, Hulme was the chief theorist of Imagism and Modernism in English poetry.

Ilya Ilf and Evgeny Petrov (Russian novelists and short story writers)—Among the most prominent humorists of post-Revolutionary Russia, Ilf and Petrov collaborated on numerous works satirizing the weaknesses of Soviet society. Their humorous but pointed stories and novels earned them a reputation as "the Soviet Mark Twain."

Henry James (American novelist)—James is considered one of the most important novelists of the English language and his work is universally acclaimed for its stylistic distinction, complex psychological portraits, and originality of theme and technique. *TCLC* will devote an entire entry to critical discussion of his novella *The Turn of the Screw*, which is considered one of the most interesting and complex short novels in world literature.

Sarah Orne Jewett (American novelist and short story writer)—One of the foremost American writers of regionalist fiction, Jewett is known for her sympathetic depiction of the characters and customs of nineteenth-century rural Maine.

Sinclair Lewis (American novelist)—A prominent American novelist of the 1920s, Lewis is considered the author of some of the most effective satires in American literature. In his most important novels, which include *Main Street*, *Babbitt*, and *Arrowsmith*, he attacked the dullness, smug provincialism, and socially enforced conformity of the American middle class. *TCLC* will devote an entire entry to critical discussion of *Main Street*.

Thomas Mann (German novelist)—In novels characterized by irony and a deep, often humorous, sympathy for humanity, Mann singlehandedly raised the German novel to an international stature it had not enjoyed since the time of the Romantics. In his most important novel, *The Magic Mountain*, Mann explored such themes as the nature of time, the seduction of the individual by disease and death, and the conflict between the intellect and the spirit. *TCLC* will devote an entry to critical discussion of this work, which is considered the twentieth century's foremost representative of the German bildungsroman.

Dmitri Merezhkovsky (Russian novelist, philosopher, poet, and critic)—Although his poetry and criticism are credited with initiating the Symbolist movement in Russian literature, Merezhkovsky is best known as a religious philosopher who sought in numerous essays and historical novels to reconcile the values of pagan religions with the teachings of Christ.

Gustave Meyrink (Austrian novelist and short story writer)—Considered one of the foremost twentieth-century novelists of the supernatural, Meyrink was also a figure of controversy during his lifetime for his satirical short stories ridiculing contemporary social and political institutions. His most important works utilize elements of Christian and Jewish mysticism, Eastern philosophy, and occultism to depict an individual's quest for spiritual knowledge.

Munshi Premchand (Indian novelist and short story writer)—A major figure in twentieth-century Indian literature, Premchand is credited with being the first author writing in the Hindi language to eschew the Hindi literary traditions of fantasy and romance in favor of realistic depictions of Indian life. Premchand was strongly influenced by the teachings of Mahatma Gandhi, and his works often express ethical concerns and the need for widespread social reform in his homeland.

Kenneth Roberts (American novelist)—Roberts's works, many of which are set in New England during the American Revolution, are considered among the best historical novels in American literature.

Bernard Shaw (Irish dramatist, critic, novelist, and essayist)—Considered the greatest dramatist of the English language since Shakespeare, Shaw revolutionized English theater by disposing of the romantic conventions of the "well-made" play and instituting a theater of ideas firmly grounded in realism. In *Man and Superman*, which he called "a dramatic parable of Creative Evolution," Shaw described his theory of a life-force that guides the evolution of humanity. *TCLC* will devote an entire entry to critical discussion of this work.

Oswald Spengler (German philosopher)—Spengler rose to international celebrity in the 1920s on the basis of *The Decline of the West*, a controversial examination of the cyclical nature of history. Although frequently deprecated by professional historians, *The Decline of the West* became one of the most influential philosophical works of the twentieth century.

Olaf Stapledon (English novelist)—An important influence on the works of C. S. Lewis, Arthur C. Clarke, and Stanislaw Lem, Stapledon was the author of what he described as "fantastic fiction of a semi-philosophical kind." Today, critics regard his novels as among the most significant and accomplished examples of science fiction and speculative writing.

Leslie Stephen (English biographer and critic)—A distinguished man of letters, Stephen is ranked among the most important literary critics of the late nineteenth century.

August Strindberg (Swedish dramatist and novelist)—One of the most influential modern dramatists, Strindberg was a major exponent of Naturalist drama who later developed an experimental style that is recognized as a forerunner of Expressionism, Surrealism, and the Theater of the Absurd.

Leon Trotsky (Russian essayist and political philosopher)—A leader of the Bolshevik Revolution in Russia, Trotsky was also a historian, biographer, and one of the most influential political theorists of the twentieth century.

Beatrice and Sydney James Webb (English social writers)—Prominent members of the progressive Fabian society, the Webbs wrote sociological works significant to the advent of socialist reform in England and influenced the work of several major authors, including H. G. Wells and George Bernard Shaw.

Oscar Wilde (Anglo-Irish dramatist, novelist, and poet)—A crusader for aestheticism, Wilde was one of the most prominent members of the nineteenth-century "art for art's sake" movement. *TCLC* will devote an entire entry to his play *The Importance of Being Earnest,* which is considered his best and most characteristic work as well as the apogee of drawing-room farce.

Owen Wister (American novelist)—Considered the founder of modern fiction about the Old West, Wister is best known as the author of *The Virginian,* a novel that established the basic character types, settings, and plots of the Western genre.

Emile Zola (French novelist, dramatist, and critic)—Zola was the founder and principal theorist of Naturalism, perhaps the most influential literary movement in modern literature. His twenty-volume series *Les Rougon-Macquart* is one of the monuments of Naturalist fiction and served as a model for late nineteenth-century novelists seeking a more candid and accurate representation of human life.

Additional Authors to Appear
in Future Volumes

Abbey, Henry 1842-1911
Abercrombie, Lascelles 1881-1938
Adamic, Louis 1898-1951
Ade, George 1866-1944
Agustini, Delmira 1886-1914
Akers, Elizabeth Chase 1832-1911
Akiko, Yosano 1878-1942
Aldanov, Mark 1886-1957
Aldrich, Thomas Bailey 1836-1907
Aliyu, Dan Sidi 1902-1920
Allen, Hervey 1889-1949
Archer, William 1856-1924
Arlen, Michael 1895-1956
Attila, Jozsef 1905-1937
Austin, Alfred 1835-1913
Austin, Mary 1868-1934
Bahr, Hermann 1863-1934
Bailey, Philip James 1816-1902
Barbour, Ralph Henry 1870-1944
Barreto, Lima 1881-1922
Benét, William Rose 1886-1950
Benjamin, Walter 1892-1940
Bennett, James Gordon, Jr. 1841-1918
Benson, E(dward) F(rederic) 1867-1940
Berdyaev, Nikolai Aleksandrovich
    1874-1948
Beresford, J(ohn) D(avys) 1873-1947
Bergson, Henri 1859-1941
Bialik, Chaim 1873-1934
Binyon, Laurence 1869-1943
Bishop, John Peale 1892-1944
Blackmore, R(ichard) D(oddridge)
    1825-1900
Blake, Lillie Devereux 1835-1913
Blum, Leon 1872-1950
Bodenheim, Maxwell 1892-1954
Bowen, Marjorie 1886-1952
Byrne, Donn 1889-1928
Caine, Hall 1853-1931
Cannan, Gilbert 1884-1955
Chairil, Anwar 1922-1949
Chand, Prem 1880-1936
Churchill, Winston 1871-1947
Coppée, Francois 1842-1908
Corelli, Marie 1855-1924
Croce, Benedetto 1866-1952
Crofts, Freeman Wills 1879-1957
Cruze, James (Jens Cruz Bosen) 1884-
    1942
Curros, Enriquez Manuel 1851-1908
Dall, Caroline Wells (Healy) 1822-1912
Daudet, Leon 1867-1942
Davidson, John 1857-1909
Davis, Richard Harding 1864-1916
Day, Clarence 1874-1935
Delafield, E.M. (Edme Elizabeth Monica
    de la Pasture) 1890-1943

Deledda, Grazia 1871-1937
Deneson, Jacob 1836-1919
Devkota, Laxmiprasad 1909-1959
DeVoto, Bernard 1897-1955
Douglas, (George) Norman 1868-1952
Douglas, Lloyd C(assel) 1877-1951
Dovzhenko, Alexander 1894-1956
Drinkwater, John 1882-1937
Drummond, W.H. 1854-1907
Durkheim, Emile 1858-1917
Duun, Olav 1876-1939
Eaton, Walter Prichard 1878-1957
Eggleston, Edward 1837-1902
Erskine, John 1879-1951
Fadeyev, Alexander 1901-1956
Ferland, Albert 1872-1943
Feydeau, Georges 1862-1921
Field, Rachel 1894-1924
Flecker, James Elroy 1884-1915
Fletcher, John Gould 1886-1950
Fogazzaro, Antonio 1842-1911
Francos, Karl Emil 1848-1904
Frank, Bruno 1886-1945
Frazer, (Sir) George 1854-1941
Freeman, R. Austin 1862-1943
Freud, Sigmund 1853-1939
Froding, Gustaf 1860-1911
Fuller, Henry Blake 1857-1929
Futabatei, Shimei 1864-1909
Gladkov, Fydor Vasilyevich 1883-1958
Glaspell, Susan 1876-1948
Glyn, Elinor 1864-1943
Golding, Louis 1895-1958
Gosse, Edmund 1849-1928
Gould, Gerald 1885-1936
Guest, Edgar 1881-1959
Gumilyov, Nikolay 1886-1921
Gyulai, Pal 1826-1909
Hale, Edward Everett 1822-1909
Hall, James Norman 1887-1951
Harris, Frank 1856-1931
Hawthorne, Julian 1846-1934
Heijermans, Herman 1864-1924
Hernandez, Miguel 1910-1942
Hewlett, Maurice 1861-1923
Heyward, DuBose 1885-1940
Hope, Anthony 1863-1933
Hudson, W(illiam) H(enry) 1841-1922
Huidobro, Vincente 1893-1948
Hviezdoslav (Pavol Orszagh) 1849-1921
Ilyas, Abu Shabaka 1903-1947
Imbs, Bravig 1904-1946
Ivanov, Vyacheslav Ivanovich 1866-
    1949
Jacobs, W(illiam) W(ymark) 1863-1943
James, Will 1892-1942
Jammes, Francis 1868-1938

Jerome, Jerome K(lapka) 1859-1927
Johnson, Fenton 1888-1958
Johnston, Mary 1870-1936
Jorgensen, Johannes 1866-1956
King, Grace 1851-1932
Kirby, William 1817-1906
Kline, Otis Albert 1891-1946
Kohut, Adolph 1848-1916
Korolenko, Vladimir 1853-1921
Kubin, Alfred 1877-1959
Kuzmin, Mikhail Alexseyevich 1875-
    1936
Lamm, Martin 1880-1950
Lawson, Henry 1867-1922
Ledwidge, Francis 1887-1917
Leipoldt, C. Louis 1880-1947
Lemonnier, Camille 1844-1913
Lima, Jorge De 1895-1953
Locke, Alain 1886-1954
Long, Frank Belknap 1903-1959
Louys, Pierre 1870-1925
Lucas, E(dward) V(errall) 1868-1938
Lyall, Edna 1857-1903
Maghar, Josef Suatopluk 1864-1945
Manning, Frederic 1887-1935
Maragall, Joan 1860-1911
Marais, Eugene 1871-1936
Martin du Gard, Roger 1881-1958
Masaryk, Tomas 1850-1939
McClellan, George Marion 1860-1934
McCoy, Horace 1897-1955
Merezhkovsky, Dmitri 1865-1941
Meyrink, Gustave 1868-1932
Mirbeau, Octave 1850-1917
Mistral, Frederic 1830-1914
Monro, Harold 1879-1932
Moore, Thomas Sturge 1870-1944
Morley, Christopher 1890-1957
Morley, S. Griswold 1883-1948
Mqhayi, S.E.K. 1875-1945
Murray, (George) Gilbert 1866-1957
Nansen, Peter 1861-1918
Nobre, Antonio 1867-1900
Nordhoff, Charles 1887-1947
Norris, Frank 1870-1902
Obstfelder, Sigborn 1866-1900
O'Dowd, Bernard 1866-1959
Ophuls, Max 1902-1957
Orczy, Baroness 1865-1947
Owen, Seaman 1861-1936
Page, Thomas Nelson 1853-1922
Papini, Giovanni 1881-1956
Parrington, Vernon L. 1871-1929
Peck, George W. 1840-1916
Phillips, Ulrich B. 1877-1934
Pickthall, Marjorie 1883-1922
Pilnyak, Boris 1894-1937

Pinero, Arthur Wing 1855-1934
Pontoppidan, Henrik 1857-1943
Prem Chand, Mushi 1880-1936
Prévost, Marcel 1862-1941
Quiller-Couch, Arthur 1863-1944
Randall, James G. 1881-1953
Rappoport, Solomon 1863-1944
Read, Opie 1852-1939
Reisen (Reizen), Abraham 1875-1953
Remington, Frederic 1861-1909
Riley, James Whitcomb 1849-1916
Rinehart, Mary Roberts 1876-1958
Ring, Max 1817-1901
Roberts, Kenneth 1885-1957
Rohan, Kada 1867-1947
Rohmer, Sax 1883-1959
Rolland, Romain 1866-1944
Rozanov, Vasily Vasilyevich 1856-1919
Saar, Ferdinand von 1833-1906
Sabatini, Rafael 1875-1950
Saintsbury, George 1845-1933
Sakutaro, Hagiwara 1886-1942
Sanborn, Franklin Benjamin 1831-1917
Santayana, George 1863-1952

Sardou, Victorien 1831-1908
Schickele, René 1885-1940
Seabrook, William 1886-1945
Seton, Ernest Thompson 1860-1946
Shestov, Lev 1866-1938
Shiels, George 1886-1949
Skram, Bertha Amalie 1847-1905
Smith, Pauline 1883-1959
Sodergran, Edith Irene 1892-1923
Solovyov, Vladimir 1853-1900
Sorel, Georges 1847-1922
Spector, Mordechai 1859-1922
Spengler, Oswald 1880-1936
Squire, J(ohn) C(ollings) 1884-1958
Stavenhagen, Fritz 1876-1906
Stockton, Frank R. 1834-1902
Subrahmanya Bharati, C. 1882-1921
Sully-Prudhomme, Rene 1839-1907
Sylva, Carmen 1843-1916
Thoma, Ludwig 1867-1927
Trotsky, Leon 1870-1940
Tuchmann, Jules 1830-1901
Turner, W(alter) J(ames) R(edfern) 1889-1946

Vachell, Horace Annesley 1861-1955
Van Dine, S. S. (William H. Wright) 1888-1939
Van Dyke, Henry 1852-1933
Vazov, Ivan Minchov 1850-1921
Veblen, Thorstein 1857-1929
Villaespesa, Francisco 1877-1936
Wallace, Edgar 1874-1932
Wallace, Lewis 1827-1905
Walsh, Ernest 1895-1926
Webb, Mary 1881-1927
Webster, Jean 1876-1916
Weil, Simone 1909-1943
Whitlock, Brand 1869-1927
Wilson, Harry Leon 1867-1939
Wolf, Emma 1865-1932
Wood, Clement 1888-1950
Wren, P(ercival) C(hristopher) 1885-1941
Yonge, Charlotte Mary 1823-1901
Zecca, Ferdinand 1864-1947
Zeromski, Stefan 1864-1925

Readers are cordially invited to suggest additional authors to the editors.

(Enoch) Arnold Bennett

1867-1931

(Also wrote under pseudonym of Jacob Tonson) English novelist, critic, journalist, essayist, and dramatist.

A prolific fiction writer and influential literary critic during his lifetime, Bennett is credited with popularizing among English novelists of the early twentieth century the techniques of such French realist authors as Gustave Flaubert and Guy de Maupassant. His reputation today rests almost exclusively on the novels *The Old Wives' Tale* and *Clayhanger*, realistic works set in the Five Towns pottery district of Bennett's youth. Displaying the evocative details, precise language, and meticulous organization that are characteristic of his fiction, these novels seek to illuminate the beauty and drama that he found in the everyday lives of ordinary people.

Bennett was born into a middle-class family near Hanley, one of the Midlands towns of North Staffordshire that he would later use as the setting of his Five Towns novels and stories. His father was a solicitor, and when Bennett was eighteen he went to work as a clerk in his father's office, intending to earn a law degree. However, he considered North Staffordshire intellectually stifling and left home for London, where he again served as a law clerk. While Bennett had published short stories in local newspapers in his home town, it was not until he won a prize for one of his stories in *Tid-Bits* that he began seriously to consider fiction writing as a career. This inspired him to write the story "A Letter Home," which was published in the *Yellow Book* in 1893. The same year he accepted an assistant editorship with the small periodical *Woman*, writing recipes, fashion hints, and advice to the lovelorn in addition to book and theater reviews. He became editor of *Woman* in 1896, and also contributed reviews to other journals, including the *Academy* and, later, the *New Age* and the *Evening Standard*.

Bennett's first novel, *A Man from the North*, was published in 1898 and was followed four years later by *The Grand Babylon Hotel* and *Anna of the Five Towns*. These early novels received mixed, though largely favorable reviews, and Bennett's popular reception was such that established literary journals sought his critical opinion in their columns. He moved to France in 1902 and for the next decade lived and worked in Paris and Fontainebleau. Devoting himself exclusively to writing, he conscientiously adhered to a self-imposed daily word quota which yielded an unusually large body of work. With rapidity and apparent ease he produced an average of one novel per year for twenty years, and in addition wrote literary and theatrical criticism, short stories, essays, pocket philosophies, and several dramas. As a literary critic Bennett was catholic in his tastes and proved prophetic in his anticipation of future greatness for many younger writers, most notably D. H. Lawrence. Along with other writers he was employed as a propagandist for the British government during the First World War, and some weeks before the war's end was named Director of Propaganda. His literary reputation declined along with his popularity in the postwar years, resurging only briefly with the publications of *Riceyman Steps* and *Lord Raingo*, which were perceived by critics as literary achievements comparable to the earlier Five Towns novels. In November of 1930 he contracted

typhoid fever on a visit to France and died of the disease in March of the following year.

Bennett considered the realistic works of such French writers as Flaubert, Maupassant, and the brothers Edmond and Jules de Goncourt superior to the Victorian novel. In *A Man from the North* he scrupulously imitated the characteristics of his French models: narrative objectivity, detailed characterization and settings, and an essentially materialistic view of life. He also credited the Irish novelist George Moore with awakening him to the "romantic nature of the district I had blindly inhabited for twenty years," and although Bennett never again lived in his home province, his best works grew out of fictional renderings of the Midlands region. *The Old Wives' Tale* and *Clayhanger* remain the most popular and widely studied of the Five Towns series, which was begun in 1902 with the publication of *Anna of the Five Towns*.

When *The Old Wives' Tale* was published in 1908, Bennett's reputation as a meticulous craftsperson and highly respected, influential literary critic was well established. With the appearance of this novel, he was additionally acclaimed as one of England's foremost contemporary novelists, and critics compared him to H. G. Wells, John Galsworthy, and Joseph Conrad, novelists then at the forefront of English fiction. *The Old Wives' Tale* is an objectively realistic portrayal of provincial life which explores the beauty of the Five Towns pottery district and the individual triumphs and tragedies of the protagonists Constance and Sophia Scales. Following their lives from childhood to death, the novel is meticulously structured to evoke the passage of time, and, like the later novel *Clayhanger*, displays Bennett's fascination with social organization and human relationships. Factual information is dispassionately reported by a detached narrator. Discussing this detachment in Bennett's works, Rebecca West noted that he established "democracy among perspectives." Bennett deliberately avoided espousing Victorian attitudes and values in his fiction, and most critics acknowledge that the absence of moralizing and sentimentality in Bennett's works distinguishes them from the writings of most of his contemporaries. H. L. Mencken, however, found that the irony and aloofness which serve this end are also responsible for rendering Bennett's novels "empty of the passion that is, when all is said and done, the chief mark of the true novelist." Virginia Woolf's essay "Mr. Bennett and Mrs. Brown" (see *TCLC,* Volume 5) began a critical tradition that heralded Bennett's technical dexterity but condemned his characters as lifeless creations, asserting that he looks "never at life, never at human nature." However, in a discussion of the impersonal school of realism, William J. Scheick utilizes *Anna of the Five Towns* to argue that although Bennett does not make use of the humanist and realistic value systems usually regarded as "requisite to a tragic view of humanity," the author does not "quite extricate himself from the humanist heritage of the nineteenth century," and Scheick suggests that "Bennett cares while trying not to care too much."

In addition to these serious works, Bennett also published novels that he conceived in a lighter vein, including such satires as *Buried Alive* and *The Card.* Many critics who had hailed *The Old Wives' Tale* and *Clayhanger* as masterpieces of English realism objected to Bennett's periodic publication of more fanciful works. *Buried Alive,* for example, which satirizes the English court system, the excesses of modern life, and human folly in general, was condemned—along with *The Glimpse, The Ghost,* and other Bennett works—by W. D. Howells, who asserted that "apparently he has found a comfort, or a relaxation, or an indemnification in writing a bad book after writing a good one." Some critics accused Bennett of writing such works, which were often completed within two or three months, solely for money and without regard for artistic concerns. Bennett, who liked *Buried Alive* far better than the critics or the reading public did, recorded in his journal that he undertook the work midway through the writing of *The Old Wives' Tale* to earn quick money to pay debts. He added, however, that "it is all pretty good," and upon rereading the novel a year later wrote, "I don't think I have ever read a funnier book than this." Bennett did not like all of his humorous works this well, but he did take pride in himself as an honest craftsperson, whatever the theme or treatment. *The Card,* he remarked, was not of any "real distinction, . . . but well invented, and done up to the knocker, technically, right through." This story of a charming young man who exploits those around him in order to rise in station is filled with whimsical extravagances of egoism as the protagonist plots his path to success, and was praised by critics for its clever humor and characterization—although some critics charged Bennett with promoting unscrupulous actions—and the work was popular among the reading public as well. Bennett defended his option to write serious or fanciful novels as he chose, affirming that he considered himself a pragmatic artist who "while respecting himself, will respect the idiosyncracies of his public." Kinley E. Roby, noting the complex and often contradictory elements in both

Bennett's personality and his works, has argued that "it is a mistake to pretend that Bennett's poor novels are of a different kind than the best ones. To do so is to assume . . . that they are without value, and that Bennett wrote seriously only on occasion. . . . They are all products of a single imaginative process."

Contemporary critics have suggested that Bennett's prolificacy was responsible in part for the fluctuating quality of his works, and that monetary concerns often dictated his treatment of material. Bennett's last novel, *The Imperial Palace,* depicts the behind-the-scenes workings of a luxury hotel, and many critics regard it as the culmination of the novelist's self-indulgence in the copious compilation of information for its own sake. Recent critics who recognize the coherence of theme, plot, and characterization that render *The Old Wives' Tale* and *Clayhanger* superlative literary creations contend that his lesser works are often humorous and entertaining, and display technical skills that render them superior to other works of their kind. Donald D. Stone has stated that "the author of *The Old Wives' Tale* is surely the finest realist of his generation, yet his best novels draw upon more than realism, are indebted to something beyond the realist's world of time and place and causality. For Bennett is also . . . a poet who . . . through force of empathy, the ability to see the world through his characters' eyes, transmutes the everyday material reality that is his starting point into something rich and strange."

(See also *TCLC,* Vol. 5; *Contemporary Authors,* Vol. 106; *Dictionary of Literary Biography,* Vol. 10: *Modern British Dramatists, 1900-1945;* and Vol. 34: *British Novelists, 1890-1929: Traditionalists.*)

PRINCIPAL WORKS

Journalism for Women (essay) 1898
A Man from the North (novel) 1898
Anna of the Five Towns (novel) 1902
The Grand Babylon Hotel (novel) 1902
The Gates of Wrath (novel) 1903
Leonora (novel) 1903
A Great Man (novel) 1904
Sacred and Profane Love (novel) 1905; also published as
    The Book of Carlotta, 1911
Tales of the Five Towns (short stories) 1905
The Ghost (novel) 1907
The Grim Smile of the Five Towns (short stories) 1907
Buried Alive (novel) 1908
How to Live on Twenty-Four Hours a Day (essays) 1908
The Old Wives' Tale (novel) 1908
The Glimpse (novel) 1909
*Clayhanger (novel) 1910
Helen with the High Hand (novel) 1910
The Card (novel) 1911; also published as *Denry the
    Audacious,* 1911
*Hilda Lessways (novel) 1911
The Matador of the Five Towns (short stories) 1912
Milestones [with Edward Knoblock] (drama) 1912
**The Great Adventure (drama) 1913
The Price of Love (novel) 1914
*These Twain (novel) 1916
Books and Persons (essays) 1917
The Pretty Lady (novel) 1918
The Roll-Call (novel) 1918
Judith (drama) 1919
Lillian (novel) 1922

Mr. Prohack (novel) 1922
Riceyman Steps (novel) 1923
Elsie and the Child (short stories) 1924
The Bright Island (drama) 1925
Lord Raingo (novel) 1926
The Imperial Palace (novel) 1930
The Journals of Arnold Bennett. 6 vols. (journals) 1971

*These works were published as *The Clayhanger Family* in 1925.

**This drama is an adaptation of the novel *Buried Alive*.

[W. D. HOWELLS] (essay date 1911)

[*Howells was the chief progenitor of American realism and the most influential American literary critic during the late nineteenth century. He was the author of nearly three dozen novels which, though neglected for decades, are today the subject of growing interest. He is recognized as one of the major literary figures of the nineteenth century: he successfully weaned American litera- ture away from the sentimental romanticism of its infancy, earning the popular sobriquet "the Dean of American Letters." Through realism, a theory central to his fiction and criticism, Howells sought to disperse "the conventional acceptations by which men live on easy terms with themselves" that they might "examine the grounds of their social and moral opinions." To accomplish this, according to Howells, the writer must strive to record de- tailed impressions of everyday life, endowing characters with true- to-life motives and avoiding authorial comment in the narrative. Criticism and Fiction (1891), a patchwork of essays from his column the "Editor's Easy Chair" in* Harper's Magazine, *is often considered Howells's manifesto of realism, although, as René Wellek has noted, the book is actually "only a skirmish in a long campaign for his doctrines." In addition to his perceptive criti- cism of the works of his friends Henry James and Mark Twain, Howells reviewed three generations of international literature, urging Americans to read the works of Emile Zola, Bernard Shaw, Henrik Ibsen, Emily Dickinson, and other important authors. In the following excerpt, he distinguishes Bennett's "real and true" works, among which Howells includes* The Grim Smile of the Five Towns, The Old Wives' Tale, *and* Clayhanger, *from his "romantic novels," which include* The Grand Babylon Hotel, Buried Alive, *and* The Gates of Wrath.]

There are two or three of [Arnold Bennett's] books which we have not read, and which we cannot classify, but apparently he has found a comfort, or a relaxation, or an indemnification in writing a bad book after writing a good one. It is very curious; it cannot be from a wavering ideal; for no man could have seen the truth about life so clearly as Mr. Bennett, with any after doubt of its unique value; and yet we have him from time to time indulging himself in the pleasure of painting it falsely. (p. 633)

The mass of Mr. Bennett is wrought over with close detail, which detracts nothing from its largeness, though in his latest work he has carried largeness to the verge of immensity, with- out apparently reflecting that immensity may be carrying large- ness too far. If he does not break under it himself, his reader may; though it is only honest to say that we are not that sort of reader. In fact, **Clayhanger** has left us wishing that there were more of it, and eager, or at least impatient, for the two other parts which are to complete the trilogy promised; an enemy might say threatened; but we are no enemy, and we rather admire the naïve courage of the author in giving so brave a warning, especially at a moment when the reader may be

doubting whether he can stand any more of Hilda. For ourselves we will say that we can stand a great deal more of Hilda, and that we should like very much to know how or why, having just engaged herself to Clayhanger, she should immediately marry another man. We should like to have the author's ex- planation. We are sure that it will be interesting, that it will be convincing, even if it is not satisfactory. That is his peculiar property: to be convincing if not satisfactory, and always to be interesting. We would not spare the least of his details, and as we have suggested, his mass is a mass of details, not only superficially but integrally.

If it shall be demanded how, since he is a mass of details, his work can also be epical, we will say that the central motive of his fiction—that is, his good fiction—is the collective life of those Five Towns, and that his fiction revolves round this, falling back into it by a force as of gravitation, when it seems finally thrown off from it. It is epical, not with the epicality of the Odyssey, but of the Iliad, and its hero is a population of Achaian homogeneity; yet it is not Homeric so much as it is Tolstoyan, and its form, its symmetry, its beauty is spiritual rather than plastic. For this sort of epical grandeur, which we find in high degree in Mr. Bennett's true fiction, the supreme Russian gave once for all the formula when he said, "The truth shall be my hero," and it was not necessary for the Englishman, when he took the Five Towns for his theme, to declare that he was going to act upon it; you could not read a dozen paragraphs of his book without seeing what he meant to do, what he was already about. Tolstoy's inspiration was his sense of the es- sential equality of men, and the essential value of every human being, who in any scheme of art must be as distinctly recog- nized as every other, whether prominently shown or not. Some- thing must be said or done to let you into the meaning of every soul in the story; none could be passed over as insignificant; each presence contributed to the collective effect, and must be proportionately recognized. Life may seem to consist of a few vast figures, of a few dramatic actions; and the representation of life may reflect this appearance; but for the artist there can be no seeming except as the result of being, and his design, in fiction at least, must be so Pre-Raphaelite that the reader can always see the being within the seeming. The nakedness of humanity under its clothes must be sensible to the painter or he will not be able to render the figure, even if apparently it is no more part of the drama than a table or a chair; really, it can never help being part of the drama.

We do not say that the perception of this is always evident in what Mr. Bennett does, or the consciousness of it; but we do say that without it, latent or patent, his work would lack mas- tery, the mastery which we feel in it. He has by means of it made his Five Towns, just wherever or whatever they are, as actually facts of the English map as if their names could be found in the gazetteer. The towns are so actual, in fact, that we have found their like in our own country, and when reading the **Grim Smile** of them, we were always thinking of certain American places. Of course one always does something of this sort in reading a book that convinces, but here was a book that studied unexpected traits of English life, and commended them so strongly to our credence that we accepted them for Amer- ican, for New England, for Connecticut. Afterward in reading more of the author's work, say **The Old Wives' Tale** and **Clay- hanger,** we were aware of psychical differences in those man- ufacturing-town, middle-class English people from our own, which we wish we could define better than we shall probably be able to do. Like our own they are mostly conscientious, whether still sunk in their original Dissent, or emancipated by the Agnostic motions of modern science; they are of a like Puritan conscience with our own New-Englanders; they feel, beyond the help of priest or parson, their personal responsibility for wrong-doing. But it appears that they accept Nature rather more on her own terms and realize that human nature is a part of her. They do not prize respectability less; they prize it rather more; but they do not stretch accountability so far as our Puritanized wrong-doers; they know when to stop atoning, when to submit, and, without any such obsolete phrasing, leave the rest to God. (pp. 633-35)

Of the sort of vital detail in which the author abounds it would be only too easy to multiply instances, but we will take only one, one so luminous, so comprehensive, that it seems to us the most dramatic incident, like, say, a murder, or an elopement, or a failure in business, could not be more so, or so much so, in so little space. When Sophia, in *The Old Wives' Tale,* after her long sojourn in Paris, had come back to her sister in one of the Five Towns, and they were both elderly, ailing women, they were sitting one night waiting for supper. "The door opened and the servant came in to lay the supper. Her nose was high, her gaze cruel, radiant, and conquering. She was a pretty and an impudent girl of about twenty-three. She knew she was torturing her old and infirm mistresses. She did not care. She did it purposely. . . . Her gestures as she laid the table were very graceful, in the pert style. She dropped forks into their appointed places with disdain; she made slightly too much noise; when she turned she manœuvred her swelling hips as though for the benefit of a soldier in a handsome uniform."

Here is not only a wonderful bit of detail, a pinch of mother earth precious beyond rubies, but a cosmical implication in which a universe of circumstance and condition and character is conveyed. Here is not only a lesson in art beyond the learning of any but the few honest men and women presently writing fiction, but an illustration of the truth which commonplace detail alone can give. It is at once intensely realistic and insurpassably imaginative, as the realistic always and alone is; but more than anything it is interesting and poignantly pertinent to the affair in hand, which is not to ascertain or establish the excellence of Mr. Arnold Bennett's work, but to put the reader upon the trial of a psychological inquiry often, not to say constantly, engaging the curiosity of the Easy Chair, and moving it to speculation which it has had no great difficulty in keeping trivial, at least in appearance. We mean the question of that several self, which each of us is sensible of in his own entity, without much blushing, or, in fact, anything but a pleasing amaze, but which he perceives in others with stern reprobation as involving a measure of moral turpitude.

We have already noted not only the wide disparity, but the absolute difference of nature in the two varieties of Mr. Arnold Bennett's fiction, parallel in time and apparently of like deliberate intention. So far as our knowledge of it goes, and we do not say it goes the whole way or quite inclusively, every alternate book of his is ungenuine in material, false in make, and valueless in result, so far as any staying power with the reader is concerned. We can think of but one such story which seems to summon a measure of reality to the help of its structural hollowness; in *A Great Man* there is something like human comedy in the unhuman farce; a good deal of living detail in the persons and situations from time to time forces your faith in the general scheme of make-believe. It is an amusing book; it is good farce; but it is essentially farce, and things do not happen in it, but are made to happen. For the rest, we may

safely say, the author's different books are as unlike as so many peas: peas out of the pod, and peas out of the can; you have but to taste, and you know instantly which is which.

It is not less than wonderful, the difference in the product which is apparently always green peas; we use the figure respectfully and for its convenience, and not in any slight of a writer whose serious performance no one can pass us in prizing and praising. Since Tolstoy is gone, and Björnson is gone, and Flaubert, and Zola, and the Goncourts, and Frank Norris, and all the early naturalists are gone, and we have no more books from Perez Galdós or Palacio Valdés, there is no writer living in whose reality we can promise ourselves greater joy than Mr. Bennett. For one thing, we can instantly know it from his unreality; we lose no time in doubt; the note of truth or the note of untruth is struck with the first word; in one case we can securely lend our whole soul to listening to the end; in the other, we can shut the book, quite safe from losing anything.

But again the question is not so much aesthetical or ethical (the one always involves the other) as psychological. Apparently there are two selves of the one novelist who are simultaneously writing fiction entirely opposed in theory and practice. Can there, outside of the haunts of the Advertising Muse, be any possible comparison between *The Gates of Wrath,* say, and *The Old Wives' Tale,* say? If we are right in holding that there can be none, then is not it within the force of hypnotic suggestion to constrain the self of Mr. Bennett writing such books as *The Gates of Wrath* to write such books as *The Old Wives' Tale,* and to do this invariably? The self which we here propose to constrain may reply that it addresses an entirely different public, which does not care for *Old Wives' Tale,* but wants *Gates of Wrath,* and continually more of them. To any such argument we should return that a public of this sort is profitably negligible; and in our contention we believe we shall have the earnest and eager support of that self of Mr. Bennett's which writes only, and can write only, *The Old Wives' Tale,* and the like, and to which we are now looking impatiently for the two remaining parts of the *Clayhanger* trilogy.

Of course there is always the chance that there may be two Mr. Arnold Bennetts, rather than two selves of one. Or it may be that there is a pseudo-Mr. Arnold Bennett who is abusing the name of a master to foist his prentice inventions upon the public. . . . [We] may say that the genuine Mr. Arnold Bennett writes with a directness which is full of admirable consciousness. Slowly, carefully, distinctly, he accumulates the evidences of situation and character, and then sets them forth so steadily, so clearly, that your mind never misgives you as to their credibility. In the long stretches of time covered by the action, the persons of the drama grow up from childhood to youth, from youth to age, and when they die it is no more theatrically than when the immense majority of the race daily attests its mortality. More important than all this, it is shown how each seed of character bringeth forth fruit of its kind, and does not turn into some other kind because of the weather, the drought, the frost, the tempest; no nature is changed in a single night from black to white, or the reverse. We do not allege instances because the books are all instance, but what is certain, without any such trouble, is that here once more, and in the years that we might have feared would be years of famine, we have a harvest of fiction, such as has not been surpassed in any former season, and the field of it is so wide that no one of wholesome appetite need hunger. Whether the reaper shall finally stand out against the sky as vast as the reapers of other days, does not matter. Probably he will not. Along with other in the direction of St. Luke's Church. The music seemed to linger a long time in the distance, and then it approached, growing louder, and the Bursley Silver Prize Band passed under the window, at the solemn piece of the Handel's Dead March. The effect of that dirge, heavy with its own beauty and with the vast weight of harrowing tradition, was to wring the tears from Constance's eyes; they fell on her aproned bosom, and she sank into a chair. And though the cheeks of the trumpeters were puffed out, and though the drummer had to protrude his stomach and arch his spine backwards, lest he should tremble over his drum, there was majesty in the passage of the band. The boom of the drum, desolating the interruptions of its melody, made sick the heart, but with a lofty grief; and the dirge seemed to be weaving a purple pall that covered every meanness.

The bandsmen were not all in black, but they all wore crepe on their sleeves, and their instruments were knotted with crepe. They carried in their hats a black-edged card. Cyril held one of these cards in his hand. It ran thus:

Sacred to the memory
of
Daniel Povey
a Town Councillor of this town
judicially murdered at 8 o'clock in the morning of 8th February 1888
"He was more sinned against than sinning."

In the wake of the band came the aged rector, bareheaded, and wearing his surplice over his overcoat, his thin white hair was disarrayed by the chill breeze that played in the sunshine; his hands were folded on a gilt-edged book. Churchwardens and sidesmen followed. And after these, in a procession that had apparently no end, came the unofficial multitude, nearly all in black mourning, and all, save the more aristocratic, carrying

Holograph copy of Bennett's manuscript of The Old Wives' Tale.

kinds of heroes, the author-hero has probably gone forever. At least, in the interest of literature, we hope so. (pp. 635-36)

[W. D. Howells], "Editor's Easy Chair," in *Harper's Monthly Magazine*, Vol. CXXII, No. 730, March, 1911, pp. 633-36.

HENRY JAMES (essay date 1914)

[*As a novelist James is valued for his psychological acuity and complex sense of artistic form. Throughout his career, James also wrote literary criticism in which he developed his artistic ideals and applied them to the works of others. Among the numerous conceptualizations he formed to clarify the nature of fiction was his definition of the novel as "a direct impression of life." The quality of this impression—the degree of moral and intellectual development—and the author's ability to communicate this impression in an effective and artistic manner were the two principal criteria by which James estimated the worth of a literary work. James admired the self-consciously formalistic approach of contemporary French writers, particularly Gustave Flaubert, whose approach contrasted with the loose, less formulated standards of English novelists. On the other hand, he favored the moral concerns of English writing over the often amoral and cynical vision which characterized much of French literature in the second half of the nineteenth century. His literary aim was to combine the qualities of each country's literature that most appealed to his temperament. After considering various fictional strategies, James arrived at what he thought the most desirable form for the novel to take. Basically objective in presentation—*that is, without the intrusion of an authorial voice—the novel should be a well-integrated formal scheme of dialogue, description, and narrative action, all of which should be received from the viewpoint of a single consciousness, or "receptor." In James's novels this receptor is usually a principal character who is more an observer than a participant in the plot. Equal in importance to the artistic plan of a novel is the type of receptor a novelist chooses to use. The type demanded by James's theory possesses a consciousness that will convey a high moral vision, a humanistic worldview, and a generally uplifting sense of life. James's criteria were accepted as standards by a generation of novelists that included Ford Madox Ford, Joseph Conrad, and Virginia Woolf. In the following excerpt, James discusses what he calls the "saturation" of significant detail in Bennett's novels.]*

The new or at least the young novel is up and doing, clearly, with the best faith and the highest spirits in the world; if we but extend a little our measure of youth indeed, as we are happily more and more disposed to, we may speak of it as already chin-deep in trophies. The men who are not so young as the youngest were but the other day very little older than these: Mr. Joseph Conrad, Mr. Maurice Hewlett and Mr. Galsworthy, Mr. H. G. Wells and Mr. Arnold Bennett, have not quite perhaps the early bloom of Mr. Hugh Walpole, Mr. Gilbert Cannan, Mr. Compton Mackenzie and Mr. D. H. Lawrence, but the spring unrelaxed is still, to our perception, in their step, and we see two or three of them sufficiently related to the still newer generation in a quasi-parental way to make our whole enumeration as illustrational as we need it. Mr. Wells and Mr. Arnold Bennett have their strongest mark, the aspect by which we may most classify them, in common—even if their three named contemporaries are doubtless most interesting in one of the connections we are not now seeking to make. The author of *Tono-Bungay* and of *The New Machiavelli*, and the author of **The Old Wives' Tale** and of **Clayhanger,** have practically launched the boat in which we admire the fresh play of oar of the author of *The Duchess of Wrexe*, and the documented aspect exhibited successively by *Round the Corner*, by *Carnival* and *Sinister Street*, and even by *Sons and Lovers* (however much we may find Mr. Lawrence, we confess, hang in the dusty rear). We shall explain in a moment what we mean by this designation of the element that these best of the younger men strike us as more particularly sharing, our point being provisionally that Mr. Wells and Mr. Arnold Bennett (speaking now only of them) began some time back to show us, and to show sundry emulous and generous young spirits then in the act of more or less waking up, what the state in question might amount to. We confound the author of *Tono-Bungay* and the author of **Clayhanger** in this imputation for the simple reason that with the sharpest differences of character and range they yet come together under our so convenient measure of value by *saturation*. This is the greatest value, to our sense, in either of them, their other values, even when at the highest, not being quite in proportion to it; and as to be saturated is to be documented, to be able even on occasion to prove quite enviably and potently so, they are alike in the authority that creates emulation. It little signifies that Mr. Wells's documented or saturated state in respect to a particular matter in hand is but one of the faces of his *generally* informed condition, of his extraordinary mass of gathered and assimilated knowledge, a miscellaneous collection more remarkable surely than any teller of "mere" tales, with the possible exception of Balzac, has been able to draw upon, whereas Mr. Arnold Bennett's corresponding provision affects us as, though singularly copious, special, exclusive and artfully economic. This distinction avails nothing against that happy fact of the handiest possession by Mr. Wells of immeasurably more concrete material, amenable for straight and vivid reference, convertible into apt illustration, than we should know where to look for other examples of. The author of *The New Machiavelli* knows, somehow, to our mystified and dazzled apprehension, because he writes and because that act constitutes for him the need, on occasion a most desperate, of absorbing knowledge at the pores; the chronicler of the Five Towns writing so much more discernibly, on the other hand, because he knows, and conscious of no need more desperate than that particular circle of civilisation may satisfy.

Our argument is that each is ideally immersed in his own body of reference, and that immersion in any such degree and to the effect of any such variety, intensity and plausibility is really among us a new feature of the novelist's range of resource. (pp. 318-20)

All revolutions have been prepared in spite of their often striking us as sudden, and so it was doubtless that when scarce longer ago than the other day Mr. Arnold Bennett had the fortune to lay his hand on a general scene and a cluster of agents deficient to a peculiar degree in properties that might interfere with a desirable density of illustration—deficient, that is, in such connections as might carry the imagination off to some sport on its own account—we recognised at once a set of conditions auspicious to the newer kind of appeal. Let us confess that we were at the same time doubtless to master no better way of describing these conditions than by the remark that they were, for some reason beautifully inherent in them, susceptible at once of being entirely known and of seeming delectably thick. Reduction to exploitable knowledge is apt to mean for many a case of the human complexity reduction to comparative thinness; and nothing was thereby at the first blush to interest us more than the fact that the air and the very smell of packed actuality in the subject-matter of such things as the author's two longest works was clearly but another name for his personal competence in that matter, the fulness and firmness of his embrace of it. This was a fresh and beguiling impression—that the state of inordinate possession on the chronicler's part, the mere state as such and as an energy directly displayed, *was* the interest, neither more nor less, *was* the sense and the meaning and the picture and the drama, all so sufficiently constituting them that it scarce mattered what they were in themselves. Of what they were in themselves their being in Mr. Bennett, as Mr. Bennett to such a tune harboured them, represented their one conceivable account—not to mention, as reinforcing this, our own great comfort and relief when certain high questions and wonderments about them, or about our mystified relation to them, began one after another to come up.

Because such questions did come, we must at once declare, and we are still in presence of them, for all the world as if that case of the perfect harmony, the harmony between subject and author, were just marked with a flaw and didn't meet the whole assault of restless criticism. What we make out Mr. Bennett as doing is simply recording his possession or, to put it more completely, his saturation; and to see him as virtually shut up to that process is a note of all the more moment that we see our selected cluster of his interesting juniors, and whether by his direct action on their collective impulse or not, embroiled, as we venture to call it, in the same predicament. The act of squeezing out to the utmost the plump and more or less juicy orange of a particular acquainted state and letting this affirmation of energy, however directed or undirected, constitute for them the ''treatment'' of a theme—*that* is what we remark them as mainly engaged in, after remarking the example

so strikingly, so originally set, even if an undue subjection to it be here and there repudiated. Nothing is further from our thought than to undervalue saturation and possession, the fact of the particular experience, the state and degree of acquaintance incurred, however such a consciousness may have been determined; for these things represent on the part of the novelist, as on the part of any painter of things seen, felt or imagined, just one half of his authority—the other half being represented of course by the application he is inspired to make of them. Therefore that fine secured half is so much gained at the start, and the fact of its brightly being there may really by itself project upon the course so much colour and form as to make us on occasion, under the genial force, almost not miss the answer to the question of application. When the author of **Clayhanger** has put down upon the table, in dense unconfused array, every fact required, every fact in any way invocable, to make the life of the Five Towns press upon us, and to make our sense of it, so full-fed, content us, we may very well go on for the time in the captive condition, the beguiled and bemused condition, the acknowledgment of which is in general our highest tribute to the temporary master of our sensibility. Nothing at such moments—or rather at the end of them, when the end begins to threaten—may be of a more curious strain than the dawning unrest that suggests to us fairly our first critical comment: ''Yes, yes—but is this *all*? These are the circumstances of the interest—we see, we see; but where is the interest itself, where and what is its centre, and how are we to measure it in relation to *that*?'' Of course we may in the act of exhaling that plaint (which we have just expressed at its mildest) well remember how many people there are to tell us that to ''measure'' an interest is none of our affair; that we have but to take it on the cheapest and easiest terms and be thankful; and that if by our very confession we have been led the imaginative dance the music has done for us all it pretends to. Which words, however, have only to happen to be for us the most unintelligent conceivable not in the least to arrest our wonderment as to where our bedrenched consciousness may still not awkwardly leave us for the pleasure of appreciation. That appreciation is also a mistake and a priggishness, being reflective and thereby corrosive, is another of the fond dicta which we are here concerned but to brush aside—the more closely to embrace the welcome induction that appreciation, attentive and reflective, inquisitive and conclusive, is in this connection absolutely the golden *key* to our pleasure. (pp. 324-27)

The Old Wives' Tale is the history of two sisters, daughters of a prosperous draper in a Staffordshire town, who, separating early in life, through the flight of one of them to Paris with an ill-chosen husband and the confirmed and prolonged local pitch of the career of the other, are reunited late in life by the return of the fugitive after much Parisian experience and by her pacified acceptance of the conditions of her birthplace. The divided current flows together again, and the chronicle closes with the simple drying up determined by the death of the sisters. That is all; the canvas is covered, ever so closely and vividly covered, by the exhibition of innumerable small facts and aspects, at which we assist with the most comfortable sense of their substantial truth. The sisters, and more particularly the less adventurous, are at home in their author's mind, they sit and move at their ease in the square chamber of his attention, to a degree beyond which the production of that ideal harmony between creature and creator could scarcely go, and all by an art of demonstration so familiar and so ''quiet'' that the truth and the poetry, to use Goethe's distinction, melt utterly together and we see no difference between the subject of the show and the showman's feeling, let alone the showman's manner, about it. This felt identity of the elements—because we at least consciously feel—becomes in the novel we refer to, and not less in *Clayhanger,* which our words equally describe, a source for us of abject confidence, confidence truly *so* abject in the solidity of every appearance that it may be said to represent our whole relation to the work and completely to exhaust our reaction upon it. *Clayhanger,* of the two fictions even the more densely loaded with all the evidence in what we should call the case presented did we but learn meanwhile for that case, or for a case of what, to take it, inscribes the annals, the private more particularly, of a provincial printer in a considerable way of business, beginning with his early boyhood and going on to the complications of his maturity—these not exhausted with our present possession of the record, inasmuch as by the author's announcement there is more of the catalogue to come. This most monumental of Mr. Arnold Bennett's recitals, taking it with its supplement of *Hilda Lessways,* already before us, is so describable through its being a monument exactly not to an idea, a pursued and captured meaning, or in short *to* anything whatever, but just simply *of* the quarried and gathered material it happens to contain, the stones and bricks and rubble and cement and promiscuous constituents of every sort that have been heaped in it and thanks to which it quite massively piles itself up. Our perusal and our enjoyment are our watching of the growth of the pile and of the capacity, industry, energy with which the operation is directed. A huge and in its way a varied aggregation, without traceable lines, divinable direction, effect of composition, the mere number of its pieces, the great dump of its material, together with the fact that here and there in the miscellany, as with the value of bits of marble or porphyry, fine elements shine out, it keeps us standing and waiting to the end—and largely just because it keeps us wondering. We surely wonder more what it may all propose to mean than any equal appearance of preparation to relieve us of that strain, any so founded and grounded a postponement of the disclosure of a sense in store, has for a long time called upon us to do in a like connection. A great thing it is assuredly that *while* we wait and wonder we are amused—were it not for that, truly, our situation would be thankless enough; we may ask ourselves, as has already been noted, why on such ambiguous terms we should consent to be, and why the practice doesn't at a given moment break down; and our answer brings us back to that many-fingered grasp of the orange that the author squeezes. This particular orange is of the largest and most rotund, and his trust in the consequent flow is of its nature communicative. Such is the case always, and most naturally, with that air in a person who has something, who at the very least has much to tell us: we *like* so to be affected by it, we meet it half way and lend ourselves, sinking in up to the chin. Up to the chin only indeed, beyond doubt; we even then feel our head emerge, for judgment and articulate question, and it is from that position that we remind ourselves how the real reward of our patience is still to come—the reward attending not at all the immediate sense of immersion, but reserved for the after-sense, which is a very different matter, whether in the form of a glow or of a chill. (pp. 329-32)

> Henry James, "The New Novel," *in his* Notes on Novelists, with Some Other Notes, *Charles Scribner's Sons, 1914, pp. 314-61.**

H. L. MENCKEN   (essay date 1919)

[*From the era of World War I until the early years of the Great Depression, Mencken was one of the most influential figures in American letters. His strongly individualistic, irreverent outlook on life and his vigorous, invective-charged writing style helped establish the iconoclastic spirit of the Jazz Age and significantly shaped the direction of American literature. As a social and literary critic—the roles for which he is best known—Mencken was the scourge of evangelical Christianity, public service organizations, literary censorship, boosterism, provincialism, democracy, all advocates of personal or social improvement, and every other facet of American life that he perceived as humbug. In his literary criticism, Mencken encouraged American writers to shun the anglophilic, moralistic bent of the nineteenth century and to practice realism, an artistic call-to-arms that is most fully developed in his essay* "Puritanism as a Literary Force," *one of the seminal essays in modern literary criticism. A man who was widely renowned or feared during his lifetime as a would-be destroyer of established American values, Mencken once wrote:* "All of my work, barring a few obvious burlesques, is based upon three fundamental ideas. 1. That knowledge is better than ignorance; 2. That it is better to tell the truth than to lie; and 3. That it is better to be free than to be a slave." *In the following excerpt, Mencken discusses the merits and limitations of Bennett's novels.*]

Of Bennett it is quite easy to conjure up a recognizable picture by imaging everything that Wells is not—that is, everything interior, everything having to do with attitudes and ideas, everything beyond the mere craft of arranging words in ingratiating sequences. As stylists, of course, they have many points of contact. Each writes a journalese that is extraordinarily fluent and tuneful; each is apt to be carried away by the rush of his own smartness. But in their matter they stand at opposite poles. Wells has a believing mind, and cannot resist the lascivious beckonings and eye-winkings of meretricious novelty; Bennett carries skepticism so far that it often takes on the appearance of a mere peasant-like suspicion of ideas, bellicose and unintelligent. Wells is astonishingly intimate and confidential;

"The Old Self and the Young Self," a caricature of Bennett by Max Beerbohm. Old Self: "All gone according to plan, you SEE." Young Self: "MY plan, you know." Reproduced by permission of Eva Reichmann.

and more than one of his novels reeks with a shameless sort of autobiography; Bennett, even when he makes use of personal experience, contrives to get impersonality into it. Wells, finally, is a sentimentalist, and cannot conceal his feelings; Bennett, of all the English novelists of the day, is the most steadily aloof and ironical.

This habit of irony, in truth, is the thing that gives Bennett all his characteristic color, and is at the bottom of both his peculiar merit and his peculiar limitation. On the one hand it sets him free from the besetting sin of the contemporary novelist: he never preaches, he has no messianic delusion, he is above the puerile theories that have engulfed such romantic men as Wells, Winston Churchill and the late Jack London, and even, at times, such sentimental agnostics as Dreiser. But on the other hand it leaves him empty of the passion that is, when all is said and done, the chief mark of the true novelist. The trouble with him is that he cannot feel with his characters, that he never involves himself emotionally in their struggles against destiny, that the drama of their lives never thrills or dismays him—and the result is that he is unable to arouse in the reader that penetrating sense of kinship, that profound and instinctive sympathy, which in its net effect is almost indistinguishable from the understanding born of experiences actually endured and emotions actually shared. Joseph Conrad, in a memorable piece of criticism, once put the thing clearly. ''My task,'' he said, ''is, by the power of the written word, to make you hear, to make you feel—it is, above all, to make you *see*.'' Here seeing, it must be obvious, is no more than feeling put into physical terms; it is not the outward aspect that is to be seen, but the inner truth—and the end to be sought by that apprehension of inner truth is responsive recognition, the sympathy of poor mortal for poor mortal, the tidal uprush of feeling that makes us all one. Bennett, it seems to me, cannot evoke it. His characters, as they pass, have a deceptive brilliance of outline, but they soon fade; one never finds them haunting the memory as Lord Jim haunts it, or Carrie Meeber, or Huck Finn, or Tom Jones. The reason is not far to seek. It lies in the plain fact that they appear to their creator, not as men and women whose hopes and agonies are of poignant concern, not as tragic comedians in isolated and concentrated dramas, but as mean figures in an infinitely dispersed and unintelligible farce, as helpless nobodies in an epic struggle that transcends both their volition and their comprehension. Thus viewing them, he fails to humanize them completely, and so he fails to make their emotions contagious. They are, in their way, often vividly real; they are thoroughly accounted for; what there is of them is unfailingly life-like; they move and breathe in an environment that pulses and glows. But the attitude of the author toward them remains, in the end, the attitude of a biologist toward his laboratory animals. He does not *feel* with them— and neither does his reader.

Bennett's chief business, in fact, is not with individuals at all, even though he occasionally brings them up almost to life-size. What concerns him principally is the common life of large groups, the action and reaction of castes and classes, the struggle among societies. In particular, he is engrossed by the colossal and disorderly functioning of the English middle class— a division of mankind inordinately mixed in race, confused in ideals and illogical in ideas. It is a group that has had interpreters aplenty, past and present; a full half of the literature of the Victorian era was devoted to it. But never, I believe, has it had an interpreter more resolutely detached and relentless— never has it had one less shaken by emotional involvement. Here the very lack that detracts so much from Bennett's stature

as a novelist in the conventional sense is converted into a valuable possession. Better than any other man of his time he has got upon paper the social anatomy and physiology of the masses of average, everyday, unimaginative Englishmen. One leaves the long series of Five Towns books with a sense of having looked down the tube of a microscope upon a huge swarm of infinitely little but incessantly struggling organisms— creatures engaged furiously in the pursuit of grotesque and unintelligible ends—helpless participants in and victims of a struggle that takes on, to their eyes, a thousand lofty purposes, all of them puerile to the observer above its turmoil. Here, he seems to say, is the middle, the average, the typical Englishman. Here is the fellow as he appears to himself—virtuous, laborious, important, intelligent, made in God's image. And here he is in fact—swinish, ineffective, inconsequential, stupid, a feeble parody upon his maker. It is irony that penetrates and devastates, and it is unrelieved by any show of the pity that gets into the irony of Conrad, or of the tolerant claim of kinship that mitigates that of Fielding and Thackeray. It is harsh and cocksure. It has, at its moments, some flavor of actual bounderism: one instinctively shrinks from so smart-alecky a pulling off of underclothes and unveiling of warts.

It is easy to discern in it, indeed, a note of distinct hostility, and even of disgust. The long exile of the author is not without its significance. He not only got in France something of the Frenchman's aloof and disdainful view of the English; he must have taken a certain distaste for the national scene with him in the first place, else he would not have gone at all. The same attitude shows itself in W. L. George, another Englishman smeared with Gallic foreignness. . . . George has put his sniffs into *Blind Alley;* Bennett has got his into **The Pretty Lady.** I do not say that either book is positively French; what I do say is that both mirror an attitude that has been somehow emptied of mere nationalism. . . . What the Bennett story attempts to do is what every serious Bennett story attempts to do: to exhibit dramatically the great gap separating the substance from the appearance in the English character. It seems to me that its prudent and self-centered G. J. Hoape is a vastly more real Englishman of his class, and, what is more, an Englishman vastly more useful and creditable to England, than any of the gaudy Bayards and Cids of conventional war fiction. Here, indeed, the irony somehow fails. The man we are obviously expected to disdain converts himself, toward the end, into a man not without his touches of the admirable. He is no hero, God knows, and there is no more brilliance in him than you will find in an average country squire or Parliament man, but he has the rare virtue of common sense, and that is probably the virtue that has served the English better than all others. Curiously enough, the English reading public recognized the irony but failed to observe its confutation, and so the book got Bennett into bad odor at home, and into worse odor among the sedulous apes of English ideas and emotions on this side of the water. But it is a sound work nevertheless—a sound work with a large and unescapable defect.

That defect is visible in a good many of the other things that Bennett has done. It is the product of his emotional detachment and it commonly reveals itself as an inability to take his own story seriously. Sometimes he pokes open fun at it, as in **The Roll-Call;** more often he simply abandons it before it is done, as if weary of a too tedious foolery. This last process is plainly visible in **The Pretty Lady.** . . . One is arrested at the start by a fascinating statement of the problem, one follows a discussion of it that shows Bennett at his brilliant best, fertile in detail, alert to every twist of motive, incisively ironical at every step—

and then, at the end, one is incontinently turned out of the booth. The effect is that of being assaulted with an ice-pick by a hitherto amiable bartender, almost that of being bitten by a pretty girl in the midst of an amicable buss.

That effect, unluckily, is no stranger to the reader of Bennett novels. One encounters it in many of them. There is a tremendous marshaling of meticulous and illuminating observation, the background throbs with color, the sardonic humor is never failing, it is a capital show—but always one goes away from it with a sense of having missed the conclusion, always there is a final begging of the question. It is not hard to perceive the attitude of mind underlying this chronic evasion of issues. It is, in essence, agnosticism carried to the last place of decimals. Life itself is meaningless; therefore, the discussion of life is meaningless; therefore, why try futilely to get a meaning into it? The reasoning, unluckily, has holes in it. It may be sound logically, but it is psychologically unworkable. One goes to novels, not for the bald scientific fact, but for a romantic amelioration of it. When they carry that amelioration to the point of uncritical certainty, when they are full of "ideas" that click and whirl like machines, then the mind revolts against the childish naïveté of the thing. But when there is no organization of the spectacle at all, when it is presented as a mere formless panorama, when to the sense of its unintelligibility is added the suggestion of its inherent chaos, then the mind revolts no less. Art can never be simple representation. It cannot deal solely with precisely what is. It must, at the least, present the real in the light of some recognizable ideal; it must give to the eternal farce, if not some moral, then at all events some direction. For without that formulation there can be no clear-cut separation of the individual will from the general stew and turmoil of things, and without that separation there can be no coherent drama, and without that drama there can be no evocation of emotion, and without that emotion art is unimaginable. The field of the novel is very wide. There is room, on the one side, for a brilliant play of ideas and theories, provided only they do not stiffen the struggle of man with man, or of man with destiny, into a mere struggle of abstractions. There is room, on the other side, for the most complete agnosticism, provided only it be tempered by feeling. Joseph Conrad is quite as unshakable an agnostic as Bennett; he is a ten times more implacable ironist. But there is yet a place in his scheme for a sardonic sort of pity, and pity, however sardonic, is perhaps as good an emotion as another. The trouble with Bennett is that he essays to sneer, not only at the futile aspiration of man, but also at the agony that goes with it. The result is an air of affectation, of superficiality, almost of stupidity. The manner, on the one hand, is that of a highly skillful and profoundly original artist, but on the other hand it is that of a sophomore just made aware of Haeckel, Bradlaugh and Nietzsche.

Bennett's unmitigated skepticism explains two things that have constantly puzzled the reviewers, and that have been the cause of a great deal of idiotic writing about him—for him as well as against him. One of these things is his utter lack of anything properly describable as artistic conscience—his extreme readiness to play the star houri in the seraglio of the publishers; the other is his habit of translating platitudes into racy journalese and gravely offering them to the suburban trade as "pocket philosophies." Both crimes, it seems to me, have their rise in his congenital incapacity for taking ideas seriously, even including his own. (pp. 36-45)

The public, with its mob yearning to be instructed, edified and pulled by the nose, demands certainties; it must be told definitely and a bit raucously that this is true and that is false. But there *are* no certainties. *Ergo,* one notion is as good as another, and if it happens to be utter flubdub, so much the better—for it is precisely flubdub that penetrates the popular skull with the greatest facility. . . . Moreover, there is probably no hidden truth to be uncovered. Thus, by the route of skepticism, Bennett apparently arrives at his sooth-saying. That he actually believes in his own theorizing is inconceivable. He is far too intelligent a man to hold that any truths within the comprehension of the popular audience are sound enough to be worth preaching, or that it would do any good to preach them if they were. No doubt he is considerably amused *in petto* by the gravity with which his bedizened platitudes have been received by persons accustomed to that sort of fare, particularly in America. (pp. 46-7)

So much for two of the salient symptoms of his underlying skepticism. Another is to be found in his incapacity to be, in the ordinary sense, ingratiating; it is simply beyond him to say the pleasant thing with any show of sincerity. Of all his books, probably the worst are his book on the war and his book on the United States. The latter was obviously undertaken with some notion of paying off a debt. Bennett had been to the United States; the newspapers had hailed him in their sideshow way; the women's clubs had pawed over him; he had, no doubt, come home a good deal richer. What he essayed to do was to write a volume on the republic that should be at once colorably accurate and discreetly agreeable. The enterprise was quite beyond him. The book not only failed to please Americans; it offended them in a thousand subtle ways, and from its appearance dates the decline of the author's vogue among us. . . . His war book missed fire in much the same way. It was workmanlike, it was deliberately urbane, it was undoubtedly truthful—but it fell flat in England and it fell flat in America. There is no little significance in the fact that the British government, in looking about for English authors to uphold the British cause in America and labor for American participation in the war, found no usefulness in Bennett. Practically every other novelist with an American audience was drafted for service, but not Bennett. He was *non est* during the heat of the fray, and when at length he came forward with ***The Pretty Lady*** the pained manner with which it was received quite justified the judgment of those who had passed him over.

What all this amounts to may be very briefly put: in one of the requisite qualities of the first-rate novelist Bennett is almost completely lacking, and so it would be no juggling with paradox to argue that, at bottom, he is scarcely a novelist at all. His books, indeed,—that is, his serious books, the books of his better canon—often fail utterly to achieve the effect that one associates with the true novel. One carries away from them, not the impression of a definite transaction, not the memory of an outstanding and appealing personality, not the after-taste of a profound emotion, but merely the sense of having witnessed a gorgeous but incomprehensible parade, coming out of nowhere and going to God knows where. They are magnificent as representation, they bristle with charming detail, they radiate the humors of an acute and extraordinary man, they are entertainment of the best sort—but there is seldom anything in them of that clear, well-aimed and solid effect which one associates with the novel as work of art. Most of these books, indeed, are no more than collections of essays defectively dramatized. What is salient in them is not their people, but their backgrounds—and their people are forever fading into their backgrounds. (pp. 47-9)

This constant remainder, whether he be actually novelist or no novelist, is sufficient to save Bennett, it seems to me, from the swift oblivion that so often overtakes the popular fictioneer. He may not play the game according to the rules, but the game that he plays is nevertheless extraordinarily diverting and calls for an incessant display of the finest sort of skill. No writer of his time has looked into the life of his time with sharper eyes, or set forth his findings with a greater charm and plausibility. Within his deliberately narrow limits he had done precisely the thing that Balzac undertook to do, and Zola after him: he has painted a full-length portrait of a whole society, accurately, brilliantly and, in certain areas, almost exhaustively. The middle Englishman—not the individual, but the type—is there displayed more vividly than he is displayed anywhere else that I know of. The thing is rigidly held to its aim; there is no episodic descent or ascent to other fields. But within that one field every resource of observation, of invention and of imagination has been brought to bear upon the business—every one save that deep feeling for man in his bitter tragedy which is the most important of them all. Bennett, whatever his failing in this capital function of the artist, is certainly of the very highest consideration as craftsman. Scattered through his books, even his bad books, there are fragments of writing that are quite unsurpassed in our day—the shoe-shining episode in *The Pretty Lady,* the adulterous interlude in *Whom God Hath Joined,* the dinner party in *Paris Nights,* the whole discussion of the Cannon-Ingram marriage in *The Roll-Call,* the studio party in *The Lion's Share.* Such writing is rare and exhilarating. It is to be respected. And the man who did it is not to be dismissed. (pp. 50-1)

H. L. Mencken, "Arnold Bennett," in his Prejudices, *first series, Alfred A. Knopf, 1919, pp. 36-51.*

VIRGINIA WOOLF (essay date 1925)

[Woolf is considered one of the most prominent literary figures of twentieth-century English literature. Like her contemporary James Joyce, with whom she is often compared, Woolf is remembered as one of the most innovative of the stream-of-consciousness novelists. Concerned primarily with depicting the life of the mind, she revolted against traditional narrative techniques and developed her own highly individualized style. Woolf's works, noted for their subjective explorations of characters' inner lives and their delicate poetic quality, have had a lasting effect on the art of the novel. A discerning and influential critic and essayist as well as a novelist, Woolf began writing reviews for the Times Literary Supplement *at an early age. Her critical essays, which cover almost the entire range of English literature, contain some of her finest prose and are praised for their insight. Along with Lytton Strachey, Roger Fry, Clive Bell, and several others, Woolf and her husband Leonard formed the literary coterie known as the "Bloomsbury Group." In the following excerpt from an essay first published in* The Common Reader *(1925), Woolf expresses her dissatisfaction with Bennett's novels, grouping them with those of H. G. Wells and John Galsworthy.]*

Mr. Wells, Mr. Bennett, and Mr. Galsworthy have excited so many hopes and disappointed them so persistently that our gratitude largely takes the form of thanking them for having shown us what they might have done but have not done; what we certainly could not do, but as certainly, perhaps, do not wish to do. No single phrase will sum up the charge or grievance which we have to bring against a mass of work so large in its volume and embodying so many qualities, both admirable and the reverse. If we tried to formulate our meaning in one word we should say that these three writers are materialists. It is because they are concerned not with the spirit but with the body that they have disappointed us, and left us with the feeling that the sooner English fiction turns its back upon them, as politely as may be, and marches, if only in the desert, the better for its soul. Naturally, no single word reaches the centre of three separate targets. In the case of Mr. Wells it falls notably wide of the mark. And yet even with him it indicates to our thinking the fatal alloy in his genius, the great clod of clay that has got itself mixed up with the purity of his inspiration. But Mr. Bennett is perhaps the worst culprit of the three, inasmuch as he is by far the best workman. He can make a book so well constructed and solid in its craftsmanship that it is difficult for the most exacting of critics to see through what chink or crevice decay can creep in. There is not so much as a draught between the frames of the windows, or a crack in the boards. And yet—if life should refuse to live there? That is a risk which the creator of *The Old Wives' Tale,* George Cannon, Edwin Clayhanger, and hosts of other figures, may well claim to have surmounted. His characters live abundantly, even unexpectedly, but it remains to ask how do they live, and what do they live for? More and more they seem to us, deserting even the well-built villa in the Five Towns, to spend their time in some softly padded first-class railway carriage, pressing bells and buttons innumerable; and the destiny to which they travel so luxuriously becomes more and more unquestionably an eternity of bliss spent in the very best hotel in Brighton. . . . (pp. 208-09)

We have to admit that we are exacting, and, further, that we find it difficult to justify our discontent by explaining what it is that we exact. We frame our question differently at different times. But it reappears most persistently as we drop the finished novel on the crest of a sigh—Is it worth while? What is the point of it all? Can it be that owing to one of those little deviations which the human spirit seems to make from time to time Mr. Bennett has come down with his magnificent apparatus for catching life just an inch or two on the wrong side? Life escapes; and perhaps without life nothing else is worth while. It is a confession of vagueness to have to make use of such a figure as this, but we scarcely better the matter by speaking, as critics are prone to do, of reality. Admitting the vagueness which afflicts all criticism of novels, let us hazard the opinion that for us at this moment the form of fiction most in vogue more often misses than secures the thing we seek. Whether we call it life or spirit, truth or reality, this, the essential thing, has moved off, or on, and refuses to be contained any longer in such ill-fitting vestments as we provide. (pp. 210-11)

Virginia Woolf, "Modern Fiction," in her The Common Reader, *first and second series, Harcourt Brace Jovanovich, Inc., 1948, pp. 207-18.**

THE JOURNEYMAN [PSEUDONYM OF J. MIDDLETON MURRY] (essay date 1926)

[Murry was a noted magazine editor and influential literary critic during the first half of the twentieth century. A longtime contributor of literary criticism to the Times Literary Supplement, *he was the last editor of the distinguished review the* Athenaeum *before its absorption by the* Nation, *and founding editor of the* Adelphi. *Murry was also the husband of short story writer Katherine Mansfield, whose letters and journals he published after her death. Considered a perceptive and romantic critic whose work reveals his "honesty to the point of masochism," he has contributed important studies on the works of Mansfield, John Keats, Fedor Dostoevski, William Blake, and his intimate friend, D. H.*

Lawrence. In the following excerpt, Murry discusses Bennett's criticism.]

Arnold Bennett was the first really to welcome Tchehov in England. He first realised, and publicly declared, the significance of Tchehov. This is what he wrote on March 18th, 1909, on two volumes of Tchehov's stories then for the first time translated into English:—

> To read them, after even the finest stories of de Maupassant or Murray Gilchrist, is like having a bath after a ball. Their effect is extraordinarily one of ingenuousness. Of course, they are not in the least ingenuous, as a fact, but self-conscious and elaborate to the highest degree. The progress of every art is an apparent progress from conventionality to realism. The basis of convention remains, but as the art develops it finds more and more subtle methods of fitting life to the convention or the convention to life—whichever you please. Tchehov's tales mark a definite new conquest in this long struggle. As you read him you fancy that he must always have been saying to himself: "Life is good enough for me. I won't alter it. I will set it down as it is." Such is the tribute to his success that he forces from you. . . .
>
> We have no writer, and we have never had one, nor has France, who could mould the material of life, without distorting it, into such complex forms to such an end of beauty. . . .

Those were astonishing words to have written about Tchehov in 1909. They are plumb in the middle of the note. Whatever more there is to be said about Tchehov—there is more: I myself have tried to say some of it—that judgment stands absolutely firm. Time will not invalidate a single syllable. Thus to *place* a new and wholly original author on his first appearance is the very perfection of criticism.

Time after time, in matters no less important, Arnold Bennett has done this thing—beautifully, with the exquisite justice of art. . . . I have been reading *Books and Persons* again. I read those little essays first when they appeared in the brilliant *New Age* of fifteen to twenty years ago: I read them again in 1917: now for the third time.

They seem to me better than ever they did. Therefore I will not hesitate to declare that Arnold Bennett was far and away the finest critic before the war. I say *was*, I say *before the war*. Not because anything better is now being done—nothing nearly so good is being done. But because Arnold Bennett himself has declined. *Books and Persons* was written in his prime—the vigour, the clarity, the precision of the prime is evident on every page. The rest of us critics seem muddlers, or pedants, or, at best, apostles of well-meaning woolliness by the side of the Arnold Bennett of 1908-10.

But that Arnold Bennett no longer exists, or exists only in flashes. Arnold Bennett the critic we now have makes mistakes—many of them. His over-estimate of André Gide's *Dostoevsky* was prodigiously wrong: so, too, his extraordinary exaggeration of the merits of the Sitwell family. There is no arguing these matters: those judgments betray a failing eye. Not but what the old lion can do wonders still, when he turns in his sleep. *Riceyman Steps* was a fine book; yet not so fine as the work of Bennett in his prime. The circle of his scope had shrunk; his radius diminished: one felt the effort, while one applauded it. (pp. 565-67)

Arnold Bennett is now taken in. Taken in by books, taken in by life. It comes to the same thing in the end. I read *Books and Persons* and wonder how such a man, vital, honest to the marrow, swift, unerring, could come to be taken in. Of all fates the last one would have prophesied for him. But who could have prophesied the War? And, if some could, who could have foretold that precisely those who could prophesy it were those who would find themselves cast aside by it. Only those who were annihilated by the War have really survived it—lived on into something new, or the promise of something new.

With these Arnold Bennett is out of touch. He is aware of their existence only as figures on the horizon, wildly gesticulating against the sky. He does not believe that they possess any significance, because nothing has happened in himself to correspond with what they are. Therefore, *il se paye de Sitwells*. If it were a joke, it would not matter; but it is deadly serious. Bennett will be honest to the end of his days. When he is taken in, he *is* taken in—heart and mind and soul.

There is nothing in the whole pandemonium of modern literature that I regret more profoundly than this. I can spare Shaw, I can spare Wells—strange to say that, considering what his sheer genius is and what his books once meant to me, but I can spare Wells, without a pang—but the sense that Bennett is past the best gives me a real pain. Bennett has not Wells's genius, nor Shaw's talent; but he represented something finer than they. He represented honesty of an order that neither of his great peers possessed. He was, and is (I doubt not) more of a *man* than they. One trusted Bennett in a way one would never trust Shaw or Wells. His word was his bond. I am not speaking of personal qualities: I have never met any of these three men: but of the quality of their writings, their thought and their judgments. Of the three I am convinced Bennett was the courageous one. I admire courage: I admire honesty: I admire generosity. All these three things Bennett had in abundance. And he was a fine writer. . . . (pp. 567-68)

The Journeyman [*pseudonym of J. Middleton Murry*], *"Autour D'Arnold Bennett," in* The Adelphi, *Vol. III, No. 8, January, 1926, pp. 565-70.*

REBECCA WEST   (essay date 1931)

[*West is considered one of the foremost English novelists and critics to write during the twentieth century. Born Cecily Isabel Fairfield, she began her career as an actress—taking the name Rebecca West from the emancipated heroine of Henrik Ibsen's drama* Rosmersholm—*and as a book reviewer for the* Freewoman. *Her early criticism was noted for its militantly feminist stance and its reflection of West's Fabian socialist concerns. Her first novel,* The Return of the Soldier *(1918), evidences a concern that entered into much of her later work: the psychology of the individual. West's greatest works include* The Meaning of Treason *(1947), which analyzes the motives of Britain's wartime traitors—notably, William Joyce ("Lord Haw-Haw")—and* Black Lamb and Grey Falcon *(1942), a record of the author's 1937 journey through Yugoslavia. West's literary criticism is noted for its wit, its aversion to cant, and its perceptiveness. Of her own work, West has commented: "I have always written in order to discover the truth for my own use, on the one hand, and on the other hand to earn money for myself and my family, and in this department of my work I hope I have honoured the truth I had already discovered. I have like most women written only a quarter of what I might have written, owing to my family responsibilities. I dislike heartily the literary philosophy and practice of my time, which I think has lagged behind in the past and has little relevance to the present, and it distresses me that so much contemporary work is dominated by the ideas (particularly the political and religious ideas) of the late eighteenth or nineteenth century, and those misunderstood.'' In the following excerpt, West discusses Bennett's importance in early twentieth-century English literature.]*

Arnold Bennett was indubitably great. I do not mean that he was a great writer, for about that, owing to the peculiar circumstances of his literary career, it is not easy to be sure. But as a character in a novel written by a great writer at his best was great, so was Arnold Bennett. He could not be compared properly with Fielding, or Dickens, or Balzac, but he could be compared with Squire Western, or Mr. Micawber, or Lucien de Rubempré. He was positive as they were, positive as the creations of mere nature rarely are. (p. 5)

Arnold Bennett wanted to do everything and to be everything. That determined his personal life and his literary career; and in that latter sphere it led to the curious result that he succeeded in being nearly everybody in turn. Incredible as it may seem, he successively occupied the positions in English literature which are roughly comparable to those in America occupied by—at their zenith—S. S. Van Dine, Sinclair Lewis, James Huneker, Theodore Dreiser and William Lyon Phelps. These analogues are not exact. The parallel between Arnold Bennett and Sinclair Lewis lies in nothing profound, but simply in the fact that both turned back from the metropolis and set themselves to a patient evaluation of provincial life, and gained great applause thereby. But the range of names does suggest the astonishing diversity of eminences between which he journeyed in his life-time. It is not less astonishing that in the spaces between his enjoyment of these eminences he was not eminent at all. He was as unequal as Wordsworth—a writer whom he resembled more closely than the hasty might suspect.

He had the first necessity for a novelist in his insatiable appetite for life. He loved every phenomenon which the world presented to him and grudged no expense of time and energy in studying it. Also he had the right emotional dynamo: what he saw he loved. The phenomena which the world was presenting to him at the moment when he began writing were those which composed life in the Five Towns: the amalgam of always patient and occasionally heroic and occasionally contemptibly supine endurance of routine and tedium, of staunchness and obstinacy, of preference for the uncolored stuff that lasts over the colored stuff which wears into holes, which is characteristic of English provincial life. He looked on this and saw that it was good. He saw, too, and here he was in advance of his age, that its physical setting was good: that the plumes of flame with which the factories brush the night sky, that snowdrops pushing their naive whiteness through the oily blackness of a sooty garden in front of a little house in a row, that the lights and shadows in a mean little room are as gloriously beautiful to the artist's eye as the Parthenon against a blue sky.

This was nearly a revelation at this time. There are many reasons why Shaw and Wells and Galsworthy and Bennett should be honored; but chief among them is the difference between the state of English literature when they started to write and its state today. The English novel of the '90s was deplorably frivolous. The outstanding personality in English fiction since the passing of Dickens, Thackeray, Trollope and George Eliot was Robert Louis Stevenson; and it was his personal tragedy that he was under the thrall of an imaginary commitment to the graceful and discreet and limited. (pp. 12-14)

The age was hungry for more solid food. Thomas Hardy, discouraged by the outcry over *Jude,* had shut up shop as a novelist. George Moore was working away, but he was so great that there was always bound to be a slight uneasiness between him and his generation. His way was not theirs; he was teaching them a new way. They were bound to feel a certain shyness, suspicion, resentment, envy. Henry James was doing superb work, but all the same he was (being essentially timid) subscribing to the heresy of the age and was not honestly with those who wanted sounder doctrine. The so-called esthetic movement of the '90s had promised much, but it had vanished, partly on account of trouble with the police, but largely because it knew too little about esthetics. Its literature was noisy but empty of content like a drum. It was no wonder that the one writer who insisted on being earnest, George Gissing, received a homage from the young which is well nigh incredible in view of the drab incompetence of his writing. The situation was deplorable.

Then there came Shaw, Wells, Galsworthy and Bennett. And Bennett's was in a sense the most easing advent. The other three came to give good writing which, however, they entangled in the nexus of modern and anti-capitalist thought. But Bennett stood for a purer liberation. He stood for the emancipation of the phenomenon, for the establishment of democracy among the perceptions. A novel need not depict nice people, it need not inculcate an established system of morality, it need not be loyal to any standard of delicacy. Simply it must celebrate life. He piled up book after book of sober, unevasive studies of provincial existence, till the world took notice and saw that a barrier had been built up between it and the floods of romanticism that had threatened to wash it away. True that at first he had to attract their attention by writing thrillers of a new kind, as glossily efficient and abounding in gadgets as a modern bathroom. It is not sufficiently remembered that he invented the modern type of detective story that is half an adventure story. The business had been begun by Conan Doyle, who showed one Sherlock Holmes and Watson peering down on the tobacco ash; but not till *The Grand Babylon Hotel* did one have a detective story that showed the crime being committed, that gave the rapture of the flight as well as the chase. As always, Arnold Bennett had to have everything.

He wrote better and better. *Whom God Hath Joined* is possibly still the best novel ever written about divorce; there is a scene beside a canal, a prehensile woman being detached, which is a masterpiece. *Leonora* is a beautiful study of maturity. In their day both were not only good but daring. One did not write about divorce, for it was too full of sensuous possibilities; and for the opposite reason one did not write about a woman of forty. Financial ease came to him and he went to live in France, and in that country, where traditions grow thick-trunked and deep-rooted like old oaks, he found the reinforcement of the spirit that many find there. Then he traveled on to the point where he wrote *The Old Wives' Tale.*

That was his highest point. It is high enough to establish in itself his claim to greatness. It is certain that his work will puzzle posterity, for the reason that in the years after the production of his masterpiece he applied no standard to his artistry save the single test of quantity. He was utterly without power of self-criticism, and he would issue his worst in the confident illusion that it was simply different in kind from his best. It is quite possible that by the end of his life his grossly and obviously bad books outnumberd his good; and scholarly posterity by the time it has waded through half a dozen *Lillians* and

Pretty Ladies will have had a pretty tough time. But when they come on *The Old Wives' Tale* they will know why we count him a king among writers.

I have said that there was a certain resemblance between Wordsworth and Arnold Bennett; and here it is most manifest. For it is a lifting from the earth of the web of false values which gentility and romanticism have thrown over it, and a recognition of the true colors of the things that grow upon it. Knights pricking o'er the plain are tragic and glorious; but so too are linendrapers in Bursley. Maidens tied to trees by wicked kings touch the heart; but so too do two Five Town wenches named Constance and Sophia. There is now no longer any need to stress this point, any more than there is to stress Wordsworth's case for the abolition of the specialized poetic vocabulary. But the desire to prove this point when that was necessary wrought up both these men to a pitch of excitement that enabled them to extend their power to as near the human limits as their generation could. Arnold Bennett used his power of empathy to enter into each of his characters in turn, to imagine how each of them would have reacted to all of their experiences. He analyzed each moment that was thus presented him till he squeezed the last drop of significance from it, he synthesized the results of his analysis with his dogged determination to get the right relationship between his thought and the reader's attention, so that once read it is retained. It has the peculiar strength of something that is cut back to the primitive roots of being. The degree to which these people are civilized means merely that they have stepped out of the chiaroscuro of the jungle into a clear light where it can be seen more plainly what birth and love and death meant to them. And at the same time, as "Jacob Tonson" in the London weekly, *The New Age,* he indorsed with his criticism all the other writers of his time who claimed the same right to range with daring and seriousness through the whole of life. He inspired a whole generation of writers just as Huneker did in America.

He came near to reaching that standard again in *Riceyman Steps;* but not, I think, in the Clayhanger trilogy. His novels declined in quality for a variety of reasons, most of which were paradoxically rooted in his virtues. For one thing, the ambition to know everything defeated itself. I only came to know him during the last sixteen years of his life, and he then struck me as being at once one of the most observant and unobservant persons I have ever known. He would remember the order of the shops in an unimportant street in a foreign city for years; but he was curiously blind about human beings. He would know a man and a woman for years and see them constantly without realizing that they were engaged in a tragical love affair; he could meet a man shaken by a recent bereavement and notice nothing unusual about him till he was told. I am told that this was amazingly unlike him in his youth and indeed all the earlier books bear proof of an extremely penetrating vision regarding his fellow creatures. The plain fact was, I suppose, that there is a limit to the powers of human attention and memory, and that he had touched it. (pp. 15-19)

> *Rebecca West, in her* Arnold Bennett Himself, *The John Day Company, 1931, 21 p.*

KINLEY E. ROBY (essay date 1972)

[*In the following excerpt, Roby examines some of Bennett's views on the purpose of fiction and discusses his critical reputation.*]

[Bennett] wished to be thought of—perhaps wished to think of himself—as a practical man of affairs who ran his writing business much as one would run any other business, with a maximum of efficiency for the greatest possible profit. In his pocket philosophies he consciously set himself forward as a man of common sense, and it is that quality above all others that shines through them. It was the true Midland wisdom breaking out in him. "Money'll do owt," the Five Towns say. "It will not," the skeptic replies. "Then it will do all that wants doing," Five Towns respond. Bennett was quite willing to allow people to think that it was a guinea that most stimulated his imagination. His first serious attempt at writing, for example, was in competition for a cash prize, which he won.

It is that picture of Bennett that has persisted. He is remembered as a kind of soulless writing machine—what his publisher Newman Flower called a "mechanized biscuit factory"—that clicked away very efficiently for a specified number of hours each day, turning out books, articles, and reviews. Once the day's task was completed, the machine rose, donned an evening suit made by the King's tailor, and went out to dine with the nabobs of London's literary world. In company he was charming, if a bit overpowering; and his wit was spiced with a carefully cultivated stammer. The picture created is of the "card," and as amusing as it is, it has two weaknesses: It leaves out most of the man and all of his art. He is not to be disposed of so easily. There was nothing simple about Arnold Bennett; he abounded with contradictions. (pp. 5-6)

He wrote rapidly, but he was serious about what he wrote, especially about his novels. "The novel," he said, "has no rival at the present day as a means for transmitting the impassioned vision of life." "The novelist," he said, "is he who, having seen life, and being so excited by it that he absolutely must transmit the vision to others, chooses narrative fiction as the liveliest vehicle for the relief of his feelings." The charge that Bennett wrote mechanically is denied by his views on the nature of fiction. "First class fiction," he insisted, "is and must be autobiographical." Not being able to invent a "psychology," the artist must depend on himself, on what he has seen and felt. "Good fiction is autobiography dressed in the colors of all mankind."

On the other hand, writing was still a business. Bennett said that he had no rspect for the artist who, having turned out a marketable piece of work, allowed it to be passed over because it was not properly placed before the buyers. He even deplored the fact that custom prevented his taking on such a well-paying task as that offered Shaw, H. G. Wells, and himself simultaneously by Harrods' stores. Wells and Shaw took the "high line" in their refusal to write advertising copy, insisting that they were "priests and prophets" who could not be paid for their opinions. Bennett also declined but with great reluctance. (p. 7)

His character was complex and sometimes contradictory. So was his writing. It is not possible to discount any of it as being purely commercial—if by *commercial* one means containing nothing important of the man or of his art. On the other hand, it is not possible to say even of his best work that it was done with no concern for the market. Bennett put something of himself into everything that he wrote. Articles, pocket philosophies, fantasias, and the great novels all contain an essential part of the man.

Bennett was a professional writer. To him, such a writer "labors in the first place for food, shelter, tailors, a woman, European travel, horses, stalls at the opera, good cigars, ambrosial evenings in restaurants; and he gives glory the best chance he can.'' For some readers of his own time and for more later, this attitude put Bennett in the Philistine camp, aligned him with ''the breed without the law.'' For Bennett it meant simply that his position in relation to art and to the world was clear. He was the enemy of the esthete: ''The notion that art is first and the rest of the universe nowhere is bound to lead to preciosity and futility in art.''

In the early years of Bennett's career, George Stuart had tried to force him to distinguish between art and nonart and to put nonart away from him. Bennett refused. He was engaged in the business of writing for a living. He was much more responsive to the urgings of Eden Phillpotts, who persuaded him to write a serial. The result was *The Ghost,* which Bennett did not think very well of but which brought in some welcome money. For a period of seven years he edited a magazine called *Woman.* During that time, he wrote book reviews and articles on fashions, cooking, and domestic economy for the magazine under such names as Gwendolyn and Sal Volatile. He was doing what he could with what he had and doing it well, but his ambition was to be an independent writer. In 1900 he chucked the magazine; moved into the country with his mother, his sister, and his ailing father; and turned to full-time writing.

Between 1900 and 1914 Bennett published nineteen novels, three collections of short stories, six pocket philosophies, and had three of his plays produced. In addition he turned out a host of book reviews and articles, some of which he wrote for the *New Age* under the name of Jacob Tonson. The ''Books and Persons'' series was extremely influential in its time, although Bennett derived very little in the way of financial benefit from it. Dame Rebecca West has said that she and a great many other young writers and intellectuals looked forward to the appearance of the Jacob Tonson pieces with eager anticipation, finding in them a liveliness and freshness of viewpoint that was missing from the rest of contemporary criticism. (pp. 10-11)

Those fourteen years both shaped Bennett's attitudes towards the art of writing and confirmed many of his convictions about it. First, the world was there to be lived in: As Bennett asserted in *The Author's Craft,* ''The artist who is too sensitive for contacts with the non-artistic world is thereby too sensitive for his vocation.'' He had come to terms with his conscience on two counts. Wells had accused him of having no ''passion for justice.'' Bennett agreed. It was not an artist's business to champion causes. It was his business ''to keep his balance amid warring points of view.''

He also came to terms with the public's conservative tastes in literature. He said that an author should compromise. ''The artist who will have the public only on his own terms is either a god or a conceited and impractical fool.'' He saw the relationship between the author and his public as a bargain in which the artist had a responsibility as well as the public. ''The sagacious artist,'' he said, ''while respecting himself, will respect the idiosyncracies of his public.'' As to the danger that such compromising might turn the writer into a ''popularity hunter,'' Bennett acknowledged the possibility, but thought that it would probably not occur if the writer had ''anything to say worth saying.'' In any case, the writer who wished to gain a hearing could not ignore the realities of his profession. ''The public,'' he said, ''is a great actuality, like war. . . . You can do something with it, but not much.''

Not every critic was able to accept Bennett's compromise. William Dean Howells, for example, found it very difficult to explain to his own satisfaction how Bennett could write so well

at one time and so badly at another. He observed that Bennett ''found a comfort or a relaxation or an indemnification in writing a bad book after writing a good one'' [see excerpt dated 1911]. (pp. 11-12)

[Howells'] admiration led him to conclude that ''no man could have seen the truth about life so clearly as Mr. Bennett, with any after doubt of its unique value.'' But Howells is pained to note at the same time that ''we have him [Bennett] from time to time indulging himself in the pleasure of painting it falsely.'' Howells concluded that, at times, Bennett deliberately subverted his art. Wells once criticized Bennett in much the same terms. Referring to *Sacred and Profane Love,* he said, ''There never was a woman like your woman [Carlotta], but no end of women journalists and minor actresses have imagined themselves like her.'' Bennett replied that ''no character in any novel is more than a hint of the real thing. . . . All that I would claim for Carlotta is that now and then she does what a real woman would do.''

Howells' conclusion is wrong. That is not to say that Bennett never wrote a weak novel. He wrote many of them. But it is a mistake to pretend that Bennett's poor novels are of a different kind than the best ones. To do so is to assume that the ''bad'' novels can be ignored in an evaluation of Bennett's writing, that they are without value, and that Bennett wrote seriously only on occasion and possessed in reference to his craft, as F. L. Lucas said so maliciously of Browning, ''the conscience of a pavement artist.''

It is probably closer to the truth to say that Bennett's novels are uneven in conception and in execution but that they are all products of a single imaginative process. Furthermore, it is clear that Bennett was sometimes wrong about the quality of his books. *The Glimpse,* for example, is a very weak novel; but Bennett thought it ''much too good'' and ''much too spiritual'' for the *Black and White* magazine, in which it was serialized in 1908. When it came out in book form, he was puzzled that so few people wrote to him praising the novel. Bennett actually thought that some of *The Glimpse* was as good as the best he could do. He was also satisfied with *The Pretty Lady.* Few readers have found it good. Walter Allen has called it ''a triumph in vulgarity'' [see excerpt in *TCLC,* Vol. 5]. Of this aspect of Bennett's talent, Rebecca West has said that there was a certain similarity between Bennett and Wordsworth in their inability to be objective about the quality of their own work. Bennett, she said, ''was utterly without the power of self-criticism, and he would issue his worst in confident illusion that it was simply different in kind from his best.''

Those who were writing about Bennett's art in the closing years of the Edwardian era were more interested in what Bennett was doing with the novel form and with the technique of the novel than in making excuses for his failures. It was generally conceded that he was a leader among the writers of the new novel. He shared the position, in Henry James's view, with Joseph Conrad, Maurice Hewlett, John Galsworthy, and H. G. Wells. In ''The New Novel, 1914'' [see excerpt dated 1914], James placed Wells and Bennett in the vanguard of the innovators and suggested that they were the literary parents of that younger group of writers—Hugh Walpole, Gilbert Cannan, Compton MacKenzie, and D. H. Lawrence—whom Virginia Woolf would later call the Georgians. (pp. 12-14)

James felt that the essential interest which Bennett's writing held was the degree to which Bennett was in possession of his material. The meaning and the drama in the writing sprang from this sense of possession. The details present in the writing in such quantity were justified by the fact that Bennett had them at his command, that they were interesting in themselves, and that they were their own meaning. (p. 15)

There were those who had doubts about what Bennett was doing. H. G. Wells wrote to Bennett in 1905 to protest that Bennett was "always taking surface values.... For some unfathomable reason," he said, "you don't penetrate." Bennett defended himself by saying "You will never see it, but in rejecting surface values you are wrong. As a fact they are just as important as other values." In another place he said, "I have never yet been able to comprehend how ... spirit can be conceived apart from matter."

Henry James followed his praise of Bennett's work in "The New Novel, 1914" with a biting attack on the "saturation" technique.... Referring to *Clayhanger,* he said that bringing together such impressive quantities of facts about life in the Five Towns may satisfy the reader for a time but will not permanently satisfy him. Eventually he will ask, "But is this all? These are the circumstances of the interest—we see; we see; but where is the interest itself, where and what is its center, and how are we to measure it in relation to *that*?"

He concluded that the reader who expected more from Bennett's novels than a view of "the stones and bricks and rubble and cement and promiscuous constituents of every sort" that had been heaped there would be disappointed. The reader was certainly not to expect a "pursued and captured meaning." James appears to have overlooked the judgment implicit in all of Bennett's major novels that life is meaningless. The "captured meaning" James sought and did not find is simply that life is without meaning. In taking such a view of the human experience, Bennett anticipated a major theme in English and American literature that came to maturity in the post-World War I years and has persisted into the present.

Naturally, Bennett did not see his method as a "promiscuous" heaping of rubble. For him details were the building stones of the novel and were the products of a precise and highly disciplined process of observation. "Good observation," he said, "consists not in multiplicity of detail, but in the coordination of detail according to a true perspective of relative importance, so that a finally just general impression may be reached in the shortest possible time."

His justification for making the detailed observations and recording them lay in his conviction that "all physical phenomena are interrelated, that there is nothing which does not bear on everything else." You may profess not to be interested in meteorology, he said, but you are. "For an east wind may upset your liver and cause you to insult your wife." In a more serious tone he added, "No human phenomenon is adequately seen until the imagination has placed it back in its past and forward into its future."

There is no doubt that Bennett was a master of detail. At his best the minutiae, which is both a texture and a context in the novels, takes on a vividness and an intensity generally found only in poetry. In *The Old Wives' Tale* Bennett describes the death of an elephant. The animal is dragged away from the Wakes' ground, where it met its death, and is ultimately hacked to pieces for souvenirs. The elephant is generally taken to be a symbol of Victorian England. It is also a curiosity with such a power to attract that Mrs. Baines, Constance, and Mr. Povey leave the ship together—an unprecedented event—in order to look at it. But it is first and finally, vividly and intensely, an

elephant. What locks the incidents surrounding its demise into life is not the death of Mr. Baines but the detail of the string of boys who appear the following day at Mr. Critchlow's chemist shop and who say to that fierce old man, "Please a pennoth o' alum to tak' smell out o' a bit o' elephant."

Wells and James were wrong about Bennett's technique. It is not an acceptance of surface values in place of more important values. Nor is it a mechanical piling up of "rubble." Bennett was carrying out a large design with considerable fullness of treatment. James seems to have failed to grasp this fact. As a consequence he also failed to see the details in relation to the design. Detail in Bennett's novels reproduces the facade which life throws up in the form of fancy waistcoats and glittering restaurants, as well as the grime of the Potteries. Detail creates the context within which the human drama takes place.

It is a context which largely defines the nature and the direction of the dramatic action. In addition, detail has emotional and psychological significance. It is possible to say that the emotional lives of Bennett's characters draw their force from the heavily "documented" context and are a product of the amassing of detail. The past of every life described has so powerful a force, gained from the sheer totality of its rendering, that the future seems to be foreordained by it. The context or facade is for Bennett the reality of life. There is nothing behind it, no guiding principle, no cosmic purpose. It is in this sense that life in Bennett's novels is meaningless.

The sense of inevitability created by Bennett in the lives of his characters gives to his writing a distinct emotional tone. The tone is one of melancholy, perhaps even disillusionment. (pp. 15-18)

[The] absence of passion in his characters is evidence of Bennett's own profound distrust or fear of that emotion and accounts, at least in part, for the melancholy quality of his writing. In the last analysis there is nothing in his novels to relieve the tedium of existence. It is possible that he wrote too close to life and, as Northrop Frye has suggested, the reality achieved became a "self-defeating process," bringing into action "some mysterious law of diminishing returns."

Passion in the Five Towns, as in E. A. Robinson's New England, appears to have been "a soilure of the wits." Even in *Don Juan de Marana* Bennett was unable to create the illusion of true passion. He thrust it away like a contamination, and the play becomes an oddly academic discussion of the possibility of defending the indulgence of passion as the pursuit of an ideal. Passion remains off-stage and, of course, loses the argument.

Personal courage, shrewd good sense, the capacity for folly, the ability to endure are all found in Bennett's characters in varying degrees. But a *passionate* attachment to anything in life—with the exception of money in the cases of the two misers Ephraim Tellwright and Henry Earlforward—is not to be found in his writing. (pp. 18-19)

Bennett's characters, at crisis points in their lives, tend to deny something to themselves or to be deprived of something. Their greatest achievements appear to be their renunciations. Sophia Baines's refusal to become Chirac's mistress is a case in point. Anna Tellwright's submission to her father is another. The monk Sanchez in *Don Juan de Marana* says that "wisdom is to find the next duty and to do it." That duty is, very likely, going to be unpleasant. Bennett's characters do not, as a rule, have a great talent for catching hold of what he referred to as ''that gewgaw known as happiness.'' (p. 20)

Kinley E. Roby, in his A Writer at War: Arnold Bennett, 1914-1918, *Louisiana State University Press, 1972, 326 p.*

DAVID LODGE   (essay date 1977)

[*Lodge is an English novelist, critic, and dramatist. The following excerpt is from his* The Modes of Modern Writing, *in which he "considers some fundamental questions of literary theory and critical practice, illustrated by a wide range of modern texts," among them Bennett's* The Old Wives' Tale.]

[Pursuing a] somewhat morbid theme, let us take as a classic instance of an execution described in a realistic novel, Chapter iii, Book III of Arnold Bennett's *The Old Wives' Tale* . . . , entitled 'An Ambition Satisfied'. This follows closely upon the elopement of Sophia, the more wilful and adventurous of the two sister-heroines, with Gerald Scales, a commercial traveller who has inherited a small fortune, and whose superficial sophistication has dazzled Sophia and blinded her to his essentially weak and coarse-grained character. Scales in fact intended to seduce Sophia and to take her to Paris as his mistress, but when Sophia, sensing danger, insists on being married before proceeding beyond London, Gerald capitulates. The couple spend their honeymoon in Paris and for a while all goes well: Gerald, who is familiar with the country and the language, enjoys showing the worldly, dazzling capital of Louis Napoleon to his innocent and provincial bride, buying her Parisian dresses and taking her to expensive restaurants patronized by the *demi-monde*. Sophia's disillusionment in her husband begins one night when he becomes involved in a drunken quarrel at the Restaurant Sylvain, causing her considerable embarrassment and anxiety. . . . However, she rationalizes her criticisms of his conduct, and when the next day he announces his intention of satisfying 'a lifetime's ambition' by witnessing an execution, she agrees to accompany him and his friend Chirac. . . . The town is Auxerre and the condemned is a young man called Rivain, convicted of murdering his elderly mistress: the case had been eagerly discussed at the Restaurant Sylvain, where Gerald met Chirac.

For Sophia the experience is a deepening nightmare. At each stage of the journey she becomes more and more uncomfortably aware of the unpleasant emotion and excitement generated by the impending execution, and of the unsavoury character of those who are attracted by the spectacle. She is in fact being led unawares into a sadistic and sexual orgy. By a series of evasions and subterfuges, Gerald installs her not in the respectable hotel he had promised but in a seedy establishment overlooking the very square where the execution is to take place the next morning, paying for the dingy bedroom a grossly inflated price. . . . At supper that evening, Sophia is alarmed and repelled by the greedy, noisy and licentious behaviour of the company. 'All the faces, to the youngest, were brutalized, corrupt, and shameless.' . . . Gerald, eventually 'somewhat ashamed of having exposed his wife to the view of such an orgy', takes her to the bedroom and leaves her, explaining that he does not intend to go to bed. Sophia lies awake, depressed by the events of the day and disturbed by sounds reaching her from every part of the hotel, some of which are obviously sexual, though with sadistic connotations: 'long sighs suddenly stifled; mysterious groans as of torture, broken by a giggle. . . .' Suddenly she is startled by a noisy commotion in the square—

the first signs of the crowd gathering to witness the execution. Against the promptings of her better self, she 'yielded to the fascination and went to the window'. It is dawn, and the windows of the other buildings around the square are already filled with spectators. 'On the red-tiled roofs, too, was a squatted population.' Down below the police are engaged in pushing back

a packed, gesticulating, cursing crowd . . . as the spaces of the square were cleared they began to be dotted by privileged persons, journalists or law officers or their friends, who walked to and fro in conscious pride; among them Sophia descried Gerald and Chirac, strolling arm in arm and talking to two elaborately clad girls who were also arm in arm.

Then she saw a red reflection coming from one of the side streets of which she had a vista.

This comes from a lantern on the wagon, drawn by a gaunt grey horse, that brings the components of the guillotine to the square. The crowd bursts into a ferocious chant as the 'red columns' of the guillotine are erected and its mechanism tested;

> *Le voila!*
> *Nicolas!*
> *Ah! Ah! Ah!*

('Nicolas' is evidently a familiar name for the guillotine deriving from its first victim, Nicolas Jacques Pelletier.) To Sophia's dismay the executioner's party retires to the hotel where she herself is situated, and occupies a room on the same floor. The excitement in the square increases.

In a corner of the square she saw Gerald talking vivaciously alone with one of the two girls who had been together. She wondered vaguely how such a girl had been brought up, and what her parents thought—or knew! . . . Her eye caught the guillotine again, and was held by it. Guarded by gendarmes, that tall and simple object did most menacingly dominate the square with its crude red columns. Tools and a large open box lay on the ground beside it. . . .

She loses sight of Gerald and then, fearing that he might return to the room and find her at the window, she returns to bed, vowing that she will remain there until he comes back. She is awakened from a doze by

a tremendous shrieking, growling and yelling: a phenomenon of human bestiality that far surpassed Sophia's narrow experience. . . . 'I must stay where I am,' she murmured. And even while saying it she rose and went to the window again and peeped out. The torture involved was extreme, but she had not sufficient force within her to resist the fascination. She stared greedily into the bright square. The first thing she saw was Gerald coming out of a house opposite, followed after a few seconds by the girl with whom he had previously been talking. Gerald glanced hastily up at the facade of the hotel, and then approached as near as he could to the red columns . . . the racket beyond the square continued and even grew louder. But the couple of hundred persons within the cordons, and all the inhabitants of the windows, drunk and sober, gazed in a fixed and sinister enchantment at the region of the guillotine, as Sophia gazed. 'I cannot stand this!' she told herself in horror, but she could not move; she could not move even her eyes. . . . Then a gigantic passionate roar, the culmination of the mob's fierce savagery, crashed against the skies. The line of maddened horses swerved and reared, and seemed to fall on the furious multitude while the statue-like gendarmes rocked over them. It was a last effort to break the cordon and it failed.

From the little street at the rear of the guillotine appeared a priest, walking backwards and holding a crucifix high in his right hand, and behind him came the handsome hero, his body all crossed with cords, between two warders, who pressed against him and supported him on either side. He was certainly very young. He lifted his chin gallantly, but his face was incredibly white. Sophia discerned that the priest was trying to hide the sight of the guillotine from the prisoner with his body, just as in the story she had heard at dinner.

Except the voice of the priest, indistinctly rising and falling in the prayer for the dying, there was no sound in the square or its environs. The windows were now occupied by groups turned to stone with distended eyes fixed on the little procession. Sophia had a tightening of the throat, and the hand trembled by which she held the curtain. The central figure did not seem to her to be alive: but rather a doll, a marionette wound up to imitate the action of a tragedy. She saw the priest offer the crucifix to the mouth of the marionette, which with a clumsy unhuman shoving of its corded shoulders butted the thing away. And as the procession turned and stopped she could plainly see that the marionette's nape and shoulders were bare, his shirt having been slit. It was horrible. 'Why do I stay here?' she asked herself hysterically. But she did not stir. The victim had disappeared now in the midst of a group of men. Then she perceived him prone under the red column, between the grooves. The silence was now broken only by the tinkling of the horses' bits in the corners of the square. The line of gendarmes in front of the scaffold held their swords tightly and looked over their noses, ignoring the privileged groups that peered almost between their shoulders.

And Sophia waited, horror-struck. She saw nothing but the gleaming triangle of metal that was suspended high above the prone, attendant victim. She felt like a lost soul, torn too soon from shelter, and exposed for ever to the worst hazards of destiny. Why was she in this strange, incomprehensible town, foreign and inimical to her, watching with agonized glance this cruel, obscene spectacle? Her sensibilities were all a bleeding mass of wounds. Why? Only yesterday, and she had been an innocent, timid crea-

ture in Bursley, in Axe, a foolish creature who deemed the concealment of letters a supreme excitement. Either that day or this day was not real. Why was she imprisoned alone in that odious, indescribably odious hotel, with no one to soothe and comfort her, and carry her away?

The distant bell boomed once. Then a monosyllabic voice sounded sharp, low; she recognized the voice of the executioner, whose name she had heard but could not remember. There was a clicking noise. . . .

She shrank down to the floor in terror and loathing, and hid her face and shuddered. Shriek after shriek, from various windows, rang on her ears in a fusillade; and then the mad yell of the penned crowd, which, like herself, had not seen but had heard, extinguished all other noise. Justice was done. The great ambition of Gerald's life was at last satisfied. . . .

It might be felt that in the last paragraph but two in this extract, the one beginning 'And Sophia waited . . .', Bennett has to some extent spoiled his effect by spelling out explicitly and somewhat clumsily what has already been adequately implied. Certainly, any sensitive reader will have apprehended, either analytically or intuitively, that the execution at Auxerre is experienced by Sophia as a violation, both literal and symbolic, of her selfhood, and is therefore an 'objective correlative' for her disillusionment in Gerald as lover and husband. In its way the episode fills up a conspicuously vacant space in the narrative—the absence of any description of Sophia's initiation into sex. In the Restaurant Sylvain, Sophia's face is described as 'so candid, so charmingly conscious of its own pure beauty and of the fact that she was no longer a virgin, but the equal in knowledge of any woman alive'. But the context, contrasting Sophia's 'baby's bonnet' and 'huge bow of ribbon' with the 'violently red lips, powdered cheeks, cold, hard eyes, self-possessed arrogant faces, and insolent bosoms' of the Parisiennes . . . makes it clear that Sophia's 'knowledge' is of a very superficial or self-deceiving kind. Real knowledge comes later, at Auxerre. Or, to put it another way, the execution brings to a crisis Sophia's suppressed suspicions about her husband's weakness of character simultaneously with her suppressed feelings of having been sexually outraged by him. Of course it is not only Sophia who is suppressing these feelings but also Bennett. But it is obvious that if Bennett, in the manner of a present-day novelist, had described the sexual side of the honeymoon in detail, it would have been as trauma for Sophia: everything we are told about her and Scales compels this deduction. The reticence of Edwardian taste, or Bennett's own reticence, led him to transfer this trauma to the execution (though without leaving the bedroom). Possibly this was to the book's advantage.

The expedition to Auxerre is steeped in a thickening atmosphere of sexual licence and degradation from its genesis in the Restaurant Sylvain to its climax in the square, where Gerald is flagrantly unfaithful to his new bride under her very eyes (whether or not Sophia realizes, or allows herself to realize, the full implications of Gerald's emergence from the house opposite with the girl he has picked up in the square is not entirely clear—she reflects later on his 'fatuous vigil of unguessed licence . . .'—but she certainly feels betrayed). It is because she is herself emotionally alienated to an agonizing degree that Sophia is unable to achieve any sympathetic imaginative connection with the prisoner Rivain. . . . [She] is not struck by the poignant contrast between her own freedom and the prisoner's fate. On the contrary, she sees him as 'a doll, a marionette wound up to imitate the action of a tragedy' because she feels herself to be equally deprived of free will, unable (as that antepenultimate paragraph makes clear) to account for her own actions and her own situation. But this does not lead to anything like the penitent and therefore spiritually liberating identification with the condemned man. . . . (pp. 27-31)

The references to the red rooftiles, the red lantern and the four references to the red columns of the guillotine have already been quoted. One might add that the furnishings of Sophia's hotel bedroom are 'crimson'. Although these references are entirely literal they acquire considerable connotative force. . . . Clearly Bennett's 'red' has nothing to do with the redeeming blood of Christ any more than Rivain's 'incredibly white face' has anyting to do with the 'white seal' of Christ. There is no possibility of transcendence in Bennett's materialist vision, either for Sophia or for Rivain—who butts the offered crucifix away with his head. Transcendence is hardly present even in a negative or demonic form: though the crowd's roar is 'devilish' we cannot say with much conviction that the red in this scene is the glow of hellfire.

Red is the colour of passion, of sexual love, of sexual sin (the courtesan in the Restaurant Sylvain wears a vermilion cloak in case there should be any doubt that she is a scarlet woman), the colour of blood (which is shed at deflowerings as well as beheadings) and of the erect male sexual organ. We need look no further to explain why Sophia's gaze keeps returning with horrified fascination to the 'red columns' of the guillotine which 'had risen upright from the ground' (as though by their own volition) and beside which she observes 'a large open box'— presumably a receptacle for the head, but also a classic female symbol in Freudian dream analysis. At the climax it is surely not only Rivain's head, but Sophia's maidenhead, and by extension her inviolate self, that lies 'prone under the red column' (*column* now significantly changed from the plural to the singular) 'between the grooves' (the analogy with female genitalia is striking) awaiting the brutal and irreversible stroke. Which she does not in fact see, does not need to see, before she 'shrank down to the floor in terror and loathing, and hid her face, and shuddered'. If there are any doubts about the validity of this reading they should be dispelled when we turn to the next section of the same chapter, where Gerald returns in a state of shock from the execution, and the contempt of Sophia, now beginning to rally, is expressed with veiled allusion to detumescence: 'Not long since he had been *proudly conversing* with impudent women. Now in *swift collapse,* he was as *flaccid* as a sick hound and as disgusting as an aged drunkard' (. . . my italics; perhaps it is worth pointing out that 'proud' can mean swollen by sensual excitement and 'conversation' can refer to sexual intimacy). (pp. 31-2)

Phallic guillotines are not the kind of thing we expect to find in realistic fiction, surely? But if there is any truth in the Freudian account of the mind, there is of course no reason why such things should not appear in the literary rendering of 'reality'. The point is simply that in realism we have to look very hard for them, we have to go down very deep to find them, because 'in reality' they are hidden, latent, suppressed. Sophia is not *conscious* of the full significance the 'red columns' have for her, and prehaps Bennett himself is not. Realism is a mode of writing derived from consciousness rather than the unconscious, the daylight rather than the nighttime world, the ego

rather than the id: that is why it is such an excellent mode for *depicting* repression.

But in describing *The Old Wives' Tale* as a realistic novel we should be thinking in the first place of the justice it does to the individual experience of a common phenomenal world. In the chapter just reviewed we should be responding to the vivid evocation of the atmosphere in Auxerre on the eve of the execution, the graphic description of the events in the square, and the convincing portrayal of how a young, innocent, provincial English bride reacts to these things—always assuming we considered that Bennett had succeeded in doing what he was trying to do. 'Yes, that's what it would have been like— yes, that's how she would have behaved', is on one important level the kind of response Bennett is seeking to elicit from the reader. (p. 32)

In his preface to the novel Bennett makes an observation on the effect of authenticity in the Auxerre episode which bears interestingly on some of the questions raised in our enquiry: . . .

> Mr Frank Harris, discussing my book in *Vanity Fair,* said it was clear I had not seen an execution (or words to that effect), and he proceeded to give his own description of an execution. It was a brief but terribly convincing bit of writing, quite characteristic and quite worthy of the author of *Montes the Matador* and of a man who has been almost everywhere and seen almost everything. I comprehended how far short I had fallen of the truth! I wrote to Mr Frank Harris, regretting that his description had not been printed before I wrote mine, as I should assuredly have utilized it, and, of course, I admitted that I had never witnessed an execution. He simply replied: 'Neither have I.' This detail is worth preserving, for it is a reproof to that large body of readers, who, when a novelist has really carried conviction to them, assert off hand: 'O, that must be autobiography!'

In this last remark we encounter a recognition of the realist's paradoxical situation: that one hundred per cent success in creating an illusion of reality is a kind of failure, in that it denies him a recognition of his artistry. But there is in fact some confusion of categories here. No one could suppose that the Auxerre chapter as presented was 'autobiographical' . . . , because this would imply that Bennett was a woman. For the chapter is not really about the execution of Rivain but about Sophia's experience of it, an experience which partly overlaps with the common experience of all those present (the guillotine was red, the gendarmes struggled to control the crowd, the crowd roared the chant about Nicholas, etc.) but is largely peculiar to Sophia, determined by her personality, her physical angle of vision and her emotional situation. In this latter aspect of the experience—what is peculiar to Sophia—we can discriminate between the conscious (e.g. her observation of Gerald's movements) and the unconscious (e.g. the sexual significance of the guillotine) but it is clear that they are connected. Even if Bennett had been present at a guillotining, then, he couldn't possibly have experienced it in the same way as Sophia. . . . If Bennett's rendering of Sophia's experience of the event 'carries conviction', therefore, it must be an imaginative achievement on his part. Only the 'public' part of the chapter could possibly be autobiographical—i.e., remembered rather than researched or invented. But there is no way in which a novelist like Bennett can reveal which of these methods he has used at a particular point, no way in which he can indicate the seams joining together recalled, researched and imagined material, without violating the conventions of his mode and destroying his 'realism'.

In the scene that immediately follows the execution, however, Bennett finds a way of drawing attention to the fictiveness of his narrative without violating the illusion of historical veracity he has created. Gerald is brought back to the bedroom by Chirac in a state of shock: 'his curiosity had proved itself stronger than his stomach'. The arrival of the landlady to collect the price of the room, even more inflated than Gerald had admitted, completes Sophia's disillusionment. Surveying Gerald's ignoble, prostrate and dormant figure, she reflects:

> Such was her brilliant and godlike husband, the
> man who had given her the right to call herself
> a married woman! He was a fool. With all her
> ignorance of the world she could see that no-
> body but an arrant imbecile could have brought
> her to her present pass.

Sophia's rage gives her the strength to act independently. From this moment begins her recovery from her disastrous elopement with Gerald (a heroic recovery, but also a tragic one, based on the acquisition of money and the denial of eros). She takes from Gerald's coat an envelope containing £200 in English banknotes and sews them into the lining of her skirt, reasoning that he will assume he has lost them.

> With precautions against noise, she tore the
> envelope and the letter and papers into small
> pieces, and then looked about for a place to
> hide them. A cupboard suggested itself. She
> got on a chair, and pushed the fragments out
> of sight on the topmost shelf, *where they may
> well be to this day.* (. . . my italics)

What is the force of that last phrase? . . . The novelist has deliberately overreached himself in his realistic enterprise. By the excessiveness of his claim that Sophia and Gerald belong to real history he reminds us that they belong to fiction. He thus makes explicit what is, according to Roland Barthes, always implicit in the realistic novel: 'giving to the imaginary the formal guarantee of the real, but while preserving in the sign the ambiguity of a double object, at once believable and false.' (pp. 33-5)

> *David Lodge, "Arnold Bennett: 'The Old Wives'
> Tale'," in his* The Modes of Modern Writing: Met-
> aphor, Metonymy, and the Typology of Modern Lit-
> erature, *Cornell University Press, 1977, pp. 27-35.*

GLORIA G. FROMM   (essay date 1982)

[*In the following excerpt, Fromm discusses the importance of windows and visual perception in* The Old Wives' Tale.]

When [Arnold Bennett] finally began to write *The Old Wives' Tale,* four years after the idea had occurred to him in Paris, he was newly married to Marguerite Soulié, living in Fontainebleau and reading Wordsworth's *Prelude* with "intense pleasure".... They were married . . . in July 1907. By Christmas he had finished the first part of *The Old Wives' Tale;* and he took his wife "home" to the Potteries for a holiday visit. But during January and February, instead of going on with his large novel, he wrote the whole of another, much smaller (and hu-

Bennett in his later years.

morous) novel, **Buried Alive.** By August *The Old Wives' Tale* was duly finished, but before the end of the year Bennett had also written (among other things) the story called **"The Matador of the Five Towns."** it ought not to be surprising that when looked at together the two novels and the story form an emotional unit.

The action proper of *The Old Wives' Tale* begins with the two young Baines girls at the showroom window watching Maggie, the family's oft-engaged but still unmarried servant, set out on her one free afternoon a month. They are astonished and fascinated by the glimpse they get of her, masquerading (in their eyes) as an independent being, in new clothes, performing the feat of arriving at the top of St. Luke's Square to a rendezvous with a man. And she is not even wearing gloves.

The position at the window, looking out, is both characteristic and crucial. Yet no one seems to have registered the importance *within* Bennett's fiction of the habits of observation and notetaking that are associated with the techniques of the realist. Indeed, without its various windows *The Old Wives' Tale* might no longer stand up—not only its actual windows with observers posted at them but the figurative windows on the world that we connect with Henry James's celebrated image of the house of fiction. It occurs in the preface to *The Portrait of a Lady,* a novel in which Isabel Archer paid dearly for not taking note of certain signs suggesting there was more between Gilbert

Osmond and Madame Merle than met Isabel's unpractised eye. In Arnold Bennett's portrait of two ladies—whose initial vantage point from the shop window in Bursley recalls the "office" (Isabel's favorite room) in the Albany house—the results of limited vision are equally devastating. And ironically,, observation is as central an activity in the later novel as it was in the earlier.

If, for example, the girls' paralyzed father is not watched in his bed every moment of the day or night he will slip out of position and strangle himself. This is precisely what happens when Mrs. Baines and Constance go off to look at the dead circus elephant along with everyone else in Bursley except the disdainful Sophia. And she, spotting the handsome Gerald Scale through the bedroom window, leaves her father alone to descend into the shop and flirt with the young man. As a matter of fact, Sophia's first glimpse of Gerald, a few months before, had also been through a window, which is how—one is tempted to say—Bennett tips the scale against Baines life. But it was also the way things were learned in the tight quarters of mid-Victorian England, perhaps even the way desires formed.

From its beginning to its end, Sophia's doomed relationship with Gerald is marked at every stage by the act of observing. Before their elopement and the insight it provided her into his character, Sophia spends most of her time polishing the image she retains of his beauty and keeping a dazzled eye out for his infrequent appearances. Once they are married, she watches Gerald through increasingly cynical eyes in order, for the most part, to keep herself informed if not to outwit him. So a casual practised glance nets her his £200 windfall and ultimately provides her with the means not only to survive but also to prosper when he finally disappears. But she actually spies on him as well, following him through the streets of Paris and taking in—with passionate interest that is also contempt—every gesture he makes, as though to exorcise his image by filling her eyes to surfeit. Indeed, at the center of their fundamentally sham marriage is an orgy of spectation: the public execution at Auxerre of the handsome young murderer Rivain, which drives the huge crowd to a kind of onanistic frenzy reaching its climax with the click of the guillotine. Crouching in terror beneath the window of her hotel room, Sophia hears both the click and the "mad yell of the penned crowd," but she averts her eye. Her sense of revulsion is complete when Gerald enters, immediately after, in a state of collapse, "as flaccid as a sick hound." The marriage, as well as Rivain, has been dealt its death blow.

It is well-known how the episode at Auxerre fits neatly into the structural plan of the novel, with its English counterpart the provincial affair of Daniel Povey. But it has not been noted how powerfully the scene works below the surface, dramatising with unusual clarity Sophia's indirect, always parochial and increasingly withdrawn, anti-physical relation to life. This is how, indeed, she manages to survive for the next thirty years, remote and single, withstanding every siege of her personal life. And then, as if in punishment, she is shocked into participation, into empathy, into "a pure and primitive emotion" by the unexpected sight of Gerald's old dead body. Too surprised to invoke her usual protective distance, she is in touch, before she realizes it, with the aged, toothless, shrunken, burned-out corpse lying on the bed, and the contact virtually kills her. She comes down to young Povey's car shattered, unable to speak. For she cannot bear to live with, much less to communicate to anyone else, the knowledge finally thrust upon her after a lifetime spent avoiding it: the primacy of flesh. Her

defenses penetrated at last, she has had her first genuinely sensual experience—violated by a dead body. But it has happened this way because the pitifully reduced Gerald had once been so devastatingly attractive to her inexperienced eyes, looking through that narrow window on the world in St. Luke's Square, a window which was never to widen.

An exemplum? Yes. But Bennett's lesson was even profounder than he knew. It embraced Constance, indeed the Poveys as well, whose own relationship to life had a corresponding insularity and prudishness. Again it is in the manner of dying that the essential style of the life is bared. So Sam Povey, his own shell broken into one night by the pebbles cast up at his window, embraces his cousin's cause, becomes a 'maniaque,' and dies. Or might it not be more accurate to say that for the first time in his life he is startled out of himself and into touch with the rest of the world, which is what Bennett surely tells us when he has the awakened Sam perceive "with a wild surmise" the dim naked forms of Daniel's employees moving in the preternatural darkness of the bakery yard. One needs to bear in mind the place Daniel had always occupied in Sam's crude, undeveloped, flickering imagination. Not only did Daniel seem superior socially but his life struck Sam as more daring and more passionate—and ultimately more valauble than his own. There is no doubt of the strong erotic element in Sam Povey's identification with his proud reckless cousin, an identification Constance observes but cannot understand, for the feelings involved are alien to her own thoroughly tamed sensibility.

By contrast what kills Constance is not a desire for the release of dangerous feelings but the compelling and blind need of the Baineses (and of course an entire class, as Paul Siegel has noted in *Clio*) for permanence and stability. 'No change, no change,' is her futile cry in the midst of a changing world; and violating her own established mode she goes out to cast her vote against the inevitable Federation—and to catch pneumonia, as Bennett himself, years later, in the process of violating all his own rules, would come down with a fatal case of typhoid fever.

The Old Wives' Tale seems to me to illustrate that in the universe of Bennett's imagination a person is damned for letting loose and equally damned for not—unless he happens to be Mr. Critchlow, the "fabulously senile" chemist of St. Luke's Square, the eternal onlooker who takes in everything and gives up nothing. Bennett referred to him in one of his letters . . . as his "favourite" and "recurring" character. Just as Kipps, as a type, cropped up in Wells's novels, so did Critchlow in his own, he said, no doubt because, like Kipps for Wells, he was the perennial image to Bennett of what he might have been. Cautious yet outspoken, self-contained, all-seeing, ironic, morose, Critchlow is the only character in *The Old Wives' Tale* who never takes the slightest risk, who acts only when it is safe to do so, and lives on and on. He provides the clue to the underlying theme of the novel, illustrated over and over again as though it were being hammered home to Bennett himself: the utter precariousness of ordinary existence. The operating terms, Bennett seems to feel, may shift at any moment and instead of being on the sidelines safely watching (as you thought you were), you are in the fray itself, propelled into it by that unknown part of you always lurking beneath the surface in Bennett's world and suddenly come to life. So one keeps forever on the lookout—only to catch sight of destiny through a window or in the overheated shadowy darkness of a bakery yard. For Bennett dangers seemed to lurk everywhere—cankers as well as cancers, a tremor of the lip here, a rending of the veil there. And one would expect such a master of phenomena as Bennett to have devised ways to protect himself from what he saw. (pp. 25-8)

Bennett's literary method is customarily ascribed to his youthful reading and endorsement of nineteenth century Russian and French realism and perhaps a novel or two of George Moore. But it was, after all, his own temperament—"formed and unchangeable" at birth, or so he seemed to believe—that led him to them and led him also to conclude that if "humanity walks ever on a thin crust over terrific abysses" (as he says it does in *The Old Wives' Tale*) and life is unpredicatable and perilous, then one kept life at bay by concentrating on how things worked. In this way, at least one knew what was happening even though very little could ever be prevented. Yet it made sense to wrap oneself in such knowledge anyway, as though in a protective cocoon. For behind the material world he seemed so adept at bending to his will was for him an implacable uncontrollable universe pictured in **"The Matador of the Five Towns"** as "swinging and whirling as usual" no matter what went on at ground level. (pp. 28-9)

Gloria G. Fromm, "Remythologizing Arnold Bennett," in Novel: A Forum on Fiction, Vol. 16, No. 1, Fall, 1982, pp. 19-34.

WILLIAM J. SCHEICK (essay date 1983)

[*Scheick is an American editor, essayist, and critic. In the following excerpt he discusses the realistic style and tragic theme of* Anna of the Five Towns, *comparing Bennett's novel with George Gissing's* The Unclassed.]

That George Gissing and Arnold Bennett wrote fiction in the "realistic" mode is a commonplace observation of academic scholarship, as is the tendency of this scholarship to classify their novels in the category of realism identified as literary naturalism. This association of Gissing and Bennett obtains most apparently when we recognize in their fiction the influence of Balzac, Flaubert, Zola, and Tolstoy. The association is reinforced, moreover, by Gissing's and Bennett's similar artistic experiments with objectivity, frankness, and amorality in narrative point of view as well as by their mutual evocation (albeit different in degree of intensity) of a sense of determinism and pessimism. Granting for the moment the accuracy of this comparison, the fact remains that Bennett's novels differ from Gissing's in the experience they give the reader. Although their fictional techniques certainly share the basic traits of literary naturalism, Bennett's manner seems to evince a quality somewhat at variance with the determinism and pessimism characteristic of Gissing's works.

In some subtle way Bennett appears to be, as it were, more present in his fictional narrative, perhaps somewhat more engaged than Gissing by his protagonists. To remark this difference of degree, so tentatively suggested here, is not to imply that Gissing is absent from his novels; on the contrary, critics have been inordinately fond of pointing to similarities between such characters as Edwin Reardon of *New Grub Street* (1891) and their creator. Nevertheless, in Bennett's fiction the reader detects a certain elusive quality of authorial presence that distinguishes his novels from Gissing's fiction. This distinction can be brought into clearer focus if we consider the nature of authorial compassion informing Bennett's *Anna of the Five Towns,* begun in 1896 and published in 1902, and Gissing's

Unclassed, first published in 1884 and revised in 1895. (p. 293)

The influence of "Gissing . . . and the impersonal school" was noted by H. G. Wells in his ambivalent reaction to Bennett's *Anna of the Five Towns.* One of Bennett's best novels, *Anna* correlates the disfigurement of the Bursley terrain by human industrialization, the degeneration of religious revivalism to mercenary ventures, the transformation of a religious person into a misanthropic miser, and the destruction of a young woman's yearning for something ideal by her eventual acceptance of a loveless marriage. Anna Tellwright, the protagonist of Bennett's novel, experiences the conversion of her "vague but intense longing skyward" into a stoical endurance of the fate "that a woman's life is always a renunciation." Anna's destiny parallels the changes in the Bursley landscape and in the lives of its inhabitants; the inevitableness of this correspondence imparts a pesimistic undertone ot Bennett's novel, which manifests such other traits of literary naturalism as narrative frankness, amorality, and objectivity.

Bennett especially controls narrative objectivity. When, for example, Anna learns of Price's suicide, the result of his hopeless indebtedness to her, the narrative voice veers the reader's response away from sentiment by deflating Anna's sense of guilt: "She forgot that she had disliked the dead man, that he had always seemed to her mean, pietistic, and two-faced. She forgot that in pressing him for rent many months overdue she and her father had acted within their just rights—acted as Price himself would have acted in their place." . . . A similar restraint on the reader's emotional engagement, managed by narrative objectivity, occurs in the account of the death of Sarah Vodrey, the Prices' good-hearted and loyal housekeeper: "The next day [she] died—she who had never lived save in the fetters of slavery and fanaticism. After fifty years of ceaseless labour, she had gained the affection of one person, and enough money to pay for her own funeral." . . . (pp. 305-06)

The control of sentiment in such passages certainly augments their irony. Literary irony can be extremely frigid, expecially in nautralistic fiction. Bennett, however, avoided both icy irony and torrid sentimentality; he sought an objectivity between these extremes. While always ready to defend *Anna* against accusations of either sort, Bennett was particularly sensitive to the classification of his novel as an example of "the impersonal school," as Wells had remarked, and as lacking any emotion, as George Sand had noted. Responding to Sand, Bennett insisted, "The book is impassioned & emotional from beginning to end. Every character . . . is handled with intense sympathy." Controlled management of emotion is, in fact, a significant feature of the narrative voice of Bennett's novels generally; it is especially prominent in his *Old Wives' Tale,* published in 1908, the year Bennett remarked in his journal: "I can and do look at suffering with scientific (artistic) coldness. I do not care, I am above it. But I want to hasten justice, for its own sake," so suffering "prompts me to support social reforms." This dual reaction recalls Gissing's equally ambivalent position in *The Unclassed,* between detached observation of irremediable human suffering and implicit desire to alleviate this misery through social reform. But whereas Gissing's compassion is Schopenhauerian, Bennett's is Christian-humanistic and romantic. Bennett cares while trying not to care too much.

In *Anna* Bennett achieves this position partly by employing the "prospect" of romantic convention. That is to say, the narrative voice takes the reader to some height where the reader can be "above it" all and attain a wider perspective than that of each of the individual characters in the novel. Of the five instances of this technique in *Anna*, the most significant occurs about midway in the book when the protagonist, vacationing on the Isle of Man, walks along "the high coast-range which stretches peak after peak," surmounts "the limit of habitation," and from this "prospect" experiences a vision of beauty momentarily satisfying her "intense longing skyward":

> It was the loveliest sight her eyes had ever beheld, a panorama of pure beauty transcending all imagined visions. It overwhelmed her, thrilled her to the heart, this revelation of the liveliness of the world. Her thoughts . . . seemed to lose their pain. It was as if she had never been really unhappy, as if there was no real unhappiness on the whole earth. . . .

This supreme moment, epitomizing Bennett's use of the "prospect," clarifies the implications of an early instance of this manner in the novel: "Look down into the valley from this terrace-height where love is kindling, embrace the whole smoke-grit amphitheatre in a glance, and it may be that you will suddenly comprehend the secret and superb significance of the vast Doing which goes forward below." . . . (pp. 306-07)

The secret is that life is comprised of a dynamic dualism. Most evident is "the unending warfare of man and nature": "so ruthless is his havoc of her, so indomitable her ceaseless recuperation." . . . Within this large encounter occur the many dualities (real or imagined) of human experience: life/death, spirit/body, joy/sorrow, love/hate, success/failure, expectation/disappointment, rise/fall, the beautiful/the ugly. Like Gissing in *The Unclassed*, Bennett in *Anna* emphasizes the rise-and-fall rhythm of these dualities of human existence, a condition no one can modify for escape. The narrative voice of *Anna* is "above it all" because it speaks of life from a "prospect" permitting identification with, at the same time as distance from, humanity. As Bennett wrote in his journal in 1896, the "essential characteristic of the really great novelist [is] a Christ-like all-embracing compassion"; Christ, who "fraternized with sinners" . . . , was at once of and above humanity, and so, in Bennett's opinion, is the ideal artist.

Although they mutually endorse compassionate objectivity in fictional narrative, Gissing's attitude is somewhat more detached than Bennett's. Whereas Gissing too recognized the applicability of certain characteristics of pure Christianity to artistic compassion, he believed Schopenhauer's philosophy to be the true success of pure Christianity . . . ; herein lies the degree of difference between Gissing and Bennett concerning authorial compassion. Bennett is slightly more ambivalent than Gissing about the hopelessness of the human condition. Though they both paraculturally avoid any overt suggestion of social amelioration or of human adjustment to an increasing degeneration of the quality of life, Bennett evinces a vein of nostalgia which implies that something vital in the human self has been stifled and that something valuable (at least potentially) in human culture has been lost. This trace of nostalgia, intimating a certain loss of human dignity, informs Bennett's equation of Christ and the artist. Whereas Gissing's compassion, derived from a philosophical overview of humanity, consists of a profoundly sympathetic yet detached observation of the *pathos* of the human condition, Bennett's compassion, derived from a paracultural "prospect," consists of a nostalgically sympathetic yet ambivalently detached observation of the *tragedy* of the human condition. This difference between them is suggested in Bennett's citation of *The Nether World* (1889) as an

example of Gissing's limitation as a novelist: "There are a dozen wistful tragedies in this one novel . . . but the dark grandeur which ought to have resulted from such an accumulation of effects is weakened by a too impartial diffusion of the author's imaginative power."

So Bennett thought he had in his own work achieved a greater sense of tragedy than had Gissing; but that the degree of difference between Gissing's pathos and Bennett's tragedy is small is accidentally suggested in a complaint by D. H. Lawrence: "I hate Bennett's resignation. Tragedy ought really to be a great kick at misery. But *Anna of the Five Towns* seems like an acceptance." Lawrence was responding to the elements of pathos in *Anna* that led Wells to associate this book with Gissing's novels. *Anna*, however, does not evince the same degree of pathos evident in *The Unclassed* because Bennett's narrative veers somewhat more toward tragedy. This variance in degree of authorial compassion is a minor concern per se, but it led to a significant artistic difference between the architectonic patterns of these two novels, a difference which accounts for the reader's sense of a certain elusive quality distinguishing *Anna* from *The Unclassed*. In *The Unclassed* Gissing's Schopenhauerian perception of the relentless and impersonal cycles of humanity's hopelessly miserable existence—the pathos of the human condition—is structurally expressed as a fixed nodal even through which the narrative loops three times. In *Anna* Bennett's ambivalent paracultural view of how the intrinsic dualisms of existence frustrate the human self's innate yearning for something transcendent—the pathos and the tragedy of the human condition—is structurally expressed as a triangle, along the three points of which the narrative rises and falls. (pp. 307-08)

[The] structure of *Anna* evinces the five-part pattern [Gustav] Freytag attributed to tragic drama: introduction, rise, climax, fall, and catastrophe. In *Anna* three events comprise, as it were, the points of this triangular structure. In contrast to Ida's "first great grief" in *The Unclassed*, the initial event in Anna's life occurs when she "realize[s] for the first time that she [is] loved"; "this was one of the three great tumultuous moments of her life." . . . The events of the novel then "rise" until about midway in the book when the second major episode of Anna's life occurs: she accepts a proposal of marriage and has a "prospective" vision on the Isle of Man: "amid laughter and tears the brief and unique joy of Anna's life began." . . . This emotional peak, what H. G. Wells described as "the top of the book," is followed by a "fall" in the narrative that ends with Anna's climactic realization that she is not only lovable but also capable of loving, a painful discovery that "she loved another man" . . . followed by her dutiful acceptance of a life of renunciation in a loveless marriage.

The "fall" and climax of *Anna* arrive somewhat more rapidly than the "rise" and emotional peak of the book, which feature disturbed several of Bennett's contemporaries. Although he refuted this criticism publicly, Bennett on an earlier occasion in his journal confessed his own discontent with the swift ending of *Anna;* and later in *Cupid and Commonsense* . . . , an adaptation of *Anna*, he even created a contrived and comic conclusion. . . . Bennett's difficulty concerned pace, not consistency with structural configuration; for the conclusion of *Anna* conforms perfectly to the Freytagian triangle of tragic drama.

Anna's final "renunciation" . . . differs from Ida's in *The Unclassed*. Ida appears to possess an innate character, by means of which she preserves something akin to human dignity throughout her various tribulations. But Ida evinces the dignity of the stoical Schopenhauerian saint, who is largely disengaged from aspiration, expectation, and general concupiscence; whereas in contrast, innately "simple" Anna evinces the dignity traditionally associated with a meaningful sacrifice of personal desire. Even if Anna's enunciation in fact servs no purpose, Bennett attributes to it an ironic poignancy derived from a nostalgic recollection of humanistic values. The reader senses not only the inevitable hopelessness of Anna's story but also at the same time the faint implication that in some ideal time, either in the lost past or in prospective human vision, Anna's life might have gone differently: not that she or anyone else in the novel could ever have transcended the dualities of life, but taht she could have been happier, could have lessened in the self gap between yearning and fulfillment. In an oblique way Anna's "intense longing skyward" (the dignity of which is implicitly reinforced during her ecstatic moment on the Isle of Man) grants heroic status to her acceptance of duty in violation of her spirit, as if the pattern of her experience, in some sense, corresponds to the "grim [and] . . . heroic" struggle between mankind and nature. . . . (pp. 309-10)

Whereas Bennett's Christian-humanistic compassion treats Anna's renunciation as a sacrifice, even though it occurs in a world devoid of the values which would make her action tragic, Gissing's Schopenhauerian compassion treats Ida's and Osmond's renunciation merely as a stoical acceptance of the pathos of human existence. Gissing and Bennett share a paracultural attitude toward human life, but Bennett is somewhat more ambivalent and so cannot quite extricate himself from the humanist heritage of the nineteenth century. Bennett's compassion grants humanity more intrinsic worth than does Gissing's compassion; and this difference registers most prominently in the structure of their novels. In *The Unclassed* Gissing's perception of the pathos of the human condition is expressed in his use of a single initial episode as a fixed structural node through which the narrative cyclically passes three times. Bennett's view of life accords with Gissing's perception of pathos, but in *Anna of the Five Towns* he applies the rise-and-fall structure of tragic drama to convey the faintest hint of tragedy while at the same time indicating the absence of the religious or humanistic value systems requisite to a tragic view of humanity. This variation in structure accounts for the different impressions these two books give the reader, a major variation resulting from a relatively minor difference in authorial compassion. (p. 310)

> *William J. Scheick, "Compassion and Fictional Structure: The Example of Gissing and Bennett," in* Studies in the Novel, *Vol. XV, No. 4, Winter, 1983, pp. 293-313.**

DONALD D. STONE (essay date 1983)

[*In the following excerpt, Stone discusses some of the major characteristics of Bennett's work.*]

Bennett's chief character trait is his dualism. . . . Despite the tendency to self-repression in his personal life which his biographers and friends have pointed out, Bennett allowed his romantic side an outlet in his novels—in his depictions of "cards," for example (enterprising individuals who bend circumstances to their ends in defiance of reality), but also in his portraits of bleakly-situated protagonists who employ their imagination to remake the world they live in. For all the authorial fidelity to objective reality, nothing and no one are as

they initially appear in a Bennett novel. To this sense of the doubleness of identity and things we owe Bennett's continual insistence on the beauty that is to be found in commonplace reality and on the bravery that underlies the daily lives of ordinary people. "To find beauty, which is always hidden," he told himself; "that is the aim . . . My desire is to depict the deeper beauty while abiding by the envelope of facts." (p. 19)

Bennett's avowed intention in *Anna of the Five Towns* . . . was twofold: to write "a sermon against parental authority" (a supremely modern theme) and to show the fictional possibilities of his native Five Towns. His detailed study of a small industrial town—"*mœurs de province* it will be"—would be painstakingly French in manner, with the technique of the Goncourts applied to a subject reminiscent of Balzac's *Eugénie Grandet* (with its dutiful daughter victimized by her lover and her miser-father). The novel would show all the ugliness and oppressiveness of life in a Potteries town, complete with a guided tour of one of the factories, and would show the few ways in which the inhabitants dealt with their lot—through Wesleyan revival meetings, church functions, walks through the park, sewing meetings, and, for the lucky, occasional flights from the town in the form of vacation or reverie. Yet while Bennett's French admirer Georges Lafourcade noted the French influence in the book's concrete depictions of provincial life ("It would have won a literary prize in France," he remarks condescendingly), he was annoyed to find a less honorable literary ancestor: "The book has all the sluggishness and something of the atmosphere of a novel by George Eliot." Written long before his revaluation of Eliot, *Anna* does reveal that Bennett, for all the modernism of his technique, was less than modish in his insistence on the atmosphere of "beauty" to be found in his ugly setting and especially in his affection for his heroine—indeed, for all the major characters in the book. One might call *Anna* a French novel undermined—or saved—by authorial love.

Turgenev provided Bennett with the inspiration here. The Russian novelists received his highest praise throughout his life: "They are not frightened by any manifestation of humanity," he affirmed in 1927. Moreover, the author of *Fathers and Sons, On the Eve,* and *The Sportsman's Notebook* was the first to show Bennett how ordinary life could be transformed through art and love. In his description of the ramshackle Kirsanov estate, near the beginning of *Fathers and Sons,* for example, Turgenev indicates how what the peasants mock as the "Will-o'-the-wisp Farm" is seen as something Arcadian by its inhabitants. Similarly, the force of authorial affection transforms Bazarov from a boorish, self-righteous medical student into a heroic figure whose fate is profoundly moving. In Bennett's novel, too, an unheroic, submissive young woman is proved capable of heroism and an ugly world is made to seem picturesque and even beautiful. In 1898, while working on *Anna,* Bennett expressed himself "convinced that there is a very real beauty underneath the squalor & ugliness of these industrial districts"; and in the novel he writes thus of the Five Towns:

> They are mean and forbidding of aspect—
> sombre, hard-featured, uncouth; and the va-
> porous poison of their ovens and chimneys has
> soiled and shrivelled the surrounding country
> till there is no village lane within a league but
> what offers a gaunt and ludicrous travesty of
> rural charms. Nothing could be more prosaic
> than the huddled, red-brown streets; nothing

more seemingly remote from romance. Yet be
it said that romance is even here—the romance
which, for those who have an eye to perceive
it, ever dwells amid the seats of industrial manufacture, softening the coarseness, transfig-
uring the squalor, of these mighty alchemic
operations.

Bennett's characteristic dualism runs through the entire passage
(of which the quotation above is a small section). He is both
objectively modernist in his description of the "prosaic" ugliness and romantic in his evocation of a mysterious nature
which sends forth "sooty sheaves" in defiance of man's efforts
to "disfigure" her. Nature and man are involved in an "unending warfare," Bennett contends in the manner of a French
naturalist, whereby each disfigures the other; but the imagination allows one to "transfigure" both. The key phrase is
"romance is even here . . . for those who have an eye to
perceive it": one is irresistibly reminded of Wordsworth's view
of the imaginative mind which half creates what it perceives.
Thus, when Anna Tellwright expresses delight at her first sight
of Liverpool harbor—"it was all too much, too astonishing,
too lovely"—Bennett by no means intends us to look down
on his seemingly naive heroine. ("They call Liverpool the slum
of Europe," her prospective suitor, Henry Mynors, responds. . . .) From Turgenev Bennett learned to cherish the
point of view that sees beauty where others see it not. Bennett's
first great novel pays tribute to Anna's poetic sensibility, her
ability to transform the world through vision in opposition to
that world's attempt to contain her spirit.

Like Eliot's Dorothea Brooke, Anna is initially described as
having been born out of her time and in the wrong place: hers
"seemed a face for the cloister, austere in contour, fervent in
expression, the severity of it mollified by that resigned and
spiritual melancholy peculiar to women who, through the error
of destiny, have been born into a wrong environment." . . .
The habit of submission is ingrained in Anna, not as a result
of her religious ardor (it is a sign of Anna's integrity that she
cannot give herself over to a religion she does not fully believe
in), but as a result of her father's hold on her. Ephraim Tellwright belongs to what Bennett sardonically describes as "the
great and powerful class of house-tyrants, the backbone of the
British nation" . . . ; yet Anna's reaction to him is dual. Up
to her twenty-first birthday, at the point the novel begins, he
has been the "chief figure" in her life, "that sinister and
formidable individuality, whom her mind hated, but her heart
disobediently loved." . . . Anna's native Bursley is dominated
by patriarchal figures, whether they be parental autocrats, industrial masters, or a Methodistically-inclined heavenly Father;
and Anna's main action in life (as we see it in the novel) is to
leave her father's house and marry Mynors, the ambitious industrialist. On the way to that act, however, she is required to
assert herself in two unforeseen ways: against her faith and
against her father. Incapable of giving way to the emotional
fervor of the Methodist revival meeting, Anna blames herself
for her sinful pride; but Bennett lets us see that Anna is in fact
saved by her "just and unshakeable self-esteem" . . . , by her
honesty in regard to herself and her situation. (pp. 24-7)

But in refusing to accept through religion the means of transcending Bursley, Anna allies herself with her antireligious
creator, who points to other means by which relief is to be
attained. The symbolic center of the novel is Anna's kitchen,
her refuge from Bursley and its grim religion, its narrow materialism, and its ugly surroundings. Bennett devotes three pages

of description to this single "satisfactory apartment in the house"
with its atmosphere of order and tradition. Half his description
is devoted to the oak dresser, which "a dynasty of priestesses
of cleanliness" had polished to such a smoothness that its
"surfaces were marked by slight hollows similar in spirit to
those worn by the naked feet of pilgrims into the marble steps
of a shrine." . . . In this respect Anna is a surrogate artist, the
Bachelardian housewife who shines her cherished household
objects until they attain "a new reality of being, and . . . take
their place not only in an order but in a community of order"
[*The Poetics of Space* by Gaston Bachelard]. Poets and women,
suggests Bachelard, build houses from within, shelters of civilization that provide refuge against the world of disharmony
and discontent lurking outside.

Bennett was annoyed when a friend, charging that *Anna* had
been written in too detached (that is, French naturalist) a spirit,
cited the kitchen scene as a proof that his characters were treated
like "animals at the Zoo."

> The book is impassioned & emotional from
> beginning to end [Bennett replied]. Every char-
> acter . . . is handled with intense sympathy. But
> you have not perceived the emotion. Your note
> on the description of Anna's dresser is a clear
> proof of this. The whole thing, for some reason
> or other, has gone right past you. You are look-
> ing for something which you will never get in
> my fiction, or in any first-rate modern fiction—
> the Dickens or Thackeray grossness. I "let my-
> self go" to the full extent; but this does not
> mean that I shout and weep all over the place.

And, in fact, the kitchen scene reveals, with brilliant economy,
the poignance of Anna's situation; her refuge is also a kind of
prison. The irony of Mynors' remark to Anna that he associates
her with her kitchen becomes apparent at the end of the novel
when she leaves her father for a man she realizes to be a kindlier
and younger version of Tellwright. However, for Bennett's
reader to realize the poignance of her situation—indeed, for
the reader to feel the heroism of Anna's position when she
reacts against father and religion—that reader must become as
observant as Anna or Bennett. The majority of people, as
Bennett contends in *The Author's Craft,* are incapable of such
feats of perception: "We all go to and fro in a state of the
observing faculties which somewhat resembles coma. We are
all content to look and not see." Bennett's friend who failed
to see the author's force of sympathy—kindliness based on
observation, to repeat the maxim from *The Author's Craft*—is
not unlke those holders of the "general opinion" in the novel
to whom Anna seems "a cold and bloodless creature." . . .
(pp. 28-9)

What distinguishes Anna from the other members of the Five
Towns is the quality of her perception, a perception that deepens in the course of the novel. Anna alone seems aware of
"the repulsive evidences of manufacture" . . .—not just the
material ugliness but, more important, the materialist codes of
Bursley society which prize money above all things and which
support a religion designed to keep workers and women in their
place. Anna initially idealizes Mynors for his good qualities,
and she especially envies him "his sex. She envied every man.
Even in the sphere of religion, men were not fettered like
women." . . . She discovers in time that the possession of such
mastery involves the loss of something precious. When, on her
twenty-first birthday, her father signs over to her her mother's
property, Anna is baffled by her enormous wealth. The Bursley

banker predicts that the "naive and unspoilt" young woman will "harden like the rest" . . . ; but Anna keeps her distance from the world of getting and spending. Unlike her father, for whom "the productivity of capital was . . . the greatest achievement of social progress," Anna, who has "some imagination" . . . , is troubled by the money. She refuses to see it as something of importance despite its obvious value to her father, to Mynors, or to the wretched father and son, Titus and Willie Price, whom Anna learns to be the defaulting tenants of a ramshackle factory she now owns. In *Clayhanger* Bennett speaks of "the vast unconscious cruelty which always goes with a perfect lack of imagination"; but Anna, with her kindly imagination, finds herself disturbingly allied with the "rich, powerful, autocratic" hounds, and she realizes, when she sees the effects of her father's harassment of the Prices, the human implications of the text, "Blessed are the meek, blessed are the failures, blessed are the stupid, for they, unknown to themselves, have a grace which is denied to the haughty, the successful, and the wife." . . . (pp. 29-30)

Bennett's heroine learns the value of love when she discovers the truth of her maternally inspired feeling for Willie Price, yet is obliged to renounce it. She has a "revelation of the loveliness of the world" . . . on her visit to the Isle of Man, but is forced to settle down in ugly Bursley. She does renounce her inheritance, in effect, by passing it from fatherly to husbandly control; and, most important, she does stand up to her father when she destroys the forged note which Willie has given her in lieu of his rental payment. The result of that "audacious and astounding impiety" in her father's eyes . . . is that she is cut off forever from him. . . . Anna stoically resigns herself, since "experience had taught her this: to be the mistress of herself." . . . (pp. 30-1)

Instead of being a detached examination of wasted lives in teh Potteries, the novel is about the small forms of heroism permitted people in impossible positions, and it is about the transforming power of imagination and love. For Anna, the discovery of love's existence is momentous: "She saw how miserably narrow, tepid, and trickling the stream of her life had been, and had threatened to be. Now it gushed forth warm, impetuous, and full, opening out new and delicious vistas. She lived; and she was finding the sight to see, the courage to enjoy." . . . Anna's initial sense that Mynors will liberate her from the worst of her serflike status under her father is not entirely unjustified: Mynors is capable of appreciating the "picturesque" perspective from outside his factory window . . . , and he is romantic enough to cherish the plate Anna paints when he shows her around his factory. But her inability to love him as she loves Willie is based on her knowledge that he too belongs among the hounds, not the hares. The fact that Mynors is one of the successful of Bursley ("that symbol of correctness and of success") makes him one of the masters, one of the "Pharisees," who will never be able to feel with the weak and downtrodden on their level. . . . Anna's feeling for Willie, by contrast, puts them on the same level, although only in her eyes as it turns out. For Willie is incapable of being saved through love, and the discovery that his love for Anna is reciprocated pushes him over the edge. Although Anna is sustained, in the end, by a "vision" of Willie "pursuing in Australia an honourable and successful career," . . . Willie has in fact followed his father's example. Titus Price's suicide—a "theatrical effect," as Bennett calls it, and which Anna sees as "something grand, accusing, and unanswerable" . . .—is one form of confronting one's fate; but Anna eschews such

dramatic gestures. Her heroism rests in her ability to accept her lot and thereby transcend it.

Anna accepts because she is a loving character, and in a similar manner Bennett regards his creations with boundless generosity of affection. Paying tribute to Bennett's "insatiable appetite for life," Rebecca West declared, "What he saw he loved" [see excerpt dated 1931]. The Sutton family, Anna's uppercrust friends, are treated with amused affection rather than the satire which Bennett's friend H. G. Wells would surely have employed—and at the other end of the social spectrum, the Prices' overworked servant, Sarah Vodrey, is allowed her moment of glory. But it is, above all, in the figure of the surly miser Tellwright that we see Bennett's ability to write with candor as well as authorial fondness. Tellwright is a monster, but he is also a superb comic creation. Like Balzac, Bennett loves his monsters, although he humanizes them in a manner that Balzac was incapable of. One can see why Anna both loves and fears her father, not why Eugénie should love old Grandet. Typically, for a Bennett novel, Tellwright is perceived by others in a mistaken fashion: "To the crowd . . . he was a marvelous legend." . . . Up close, he is a tyrant to his family, a tyrant not by independent choice or system but out of habit and failure of imagination. "If you had told him that he inflicted purposeless misery not only on others, but on himself, he would have grinned . . . vaguely aware that he had not tried to be happy, and rather despising happiness as a sort of childish gewgaw." Lacking all capacity for "joy" and thus creating "a melancholy gloom" at home (which Anna and her sister Agnes seek to assuage by means of polish or a potted mignonette), Tellwright fails to notice "that his heart lightened whenever he left the house, and grew dark whenever he returned; but he was incapable of the feat [of self-analysis]. His case, like every similar case, was irremediable." . . . Anna's terror when she forgets to buy bacon for her father's breakfast is vividly conveyed—and indicates the momentousness of her later act of defiance. Nevertheless, Bennett, in giving the most significant stage directions and the best bits of dialogue to Tellwright, creates a figure who makes the reader, no less than Anna, reluctant to make moral judgment in the miser's presence. And we are never allowed to forget that we are seeing Tellwright, most of the time, through Anna's eyes. It is her mixture of fear and reverence that makes him so forbidding a character, but that also makes his rejection of her so poignant an event.

Bennett's focusing on the characters and events in Bursley as seen through Anna's point of view is the most distinctive aspect of his art: in *Anna of the Five Towns,* as in the more famous novels *The Old Wives' Tale* and *Clayhanger,* these things have significance because the characters invest them with significance. Once we step away from Constance Povey, we see her from the point of view of others, "a stout old lady with grey hair and a dowdy bonnet." But in her mind, and in that of the reader, Constance remains youthful, resourceful, romantic—albeit in less obvious ways than the self-conscious romanticism of her sister Sophia. (A source of irony in *The Old Wives' Tale* is the fact that the "romantic" sister who goes to Paris becomes a model of good sense, while the stolid sister who stays home has an adventurous streak which is finally the cause of her death.) In Bennett's second novel we are shown the father, the suitor, and the simple-minded lover from Anna's point of view, and this allows them qualities that could scarcely be projected sympathetically in a French naturalist novel where the point of view is invariably flawed or misguided. For what a feeling heart sees has its own validity: a tyrannical father is still one's father, and the uncouth lover is the man one loves. In this way, Bennett reveals his Romantic origins and provides the premise for the most extraordinary of his novels, *Riceyman Steps*. (pp. 31-4)

Riceyman Steps . . . , written when he had fallen "under the whips of les jeunes" (as he observed to his friend André Gide), . . . reveals, I think, the fullest measure of Bennett's genius. Here he drew upon his mastery of the uses of point of view and upon his considerable generosity of spirit to produce a *tour de force:* the sordid world of a miserly bookseller who starves his wife and himself to death is transformed into a prose poem in celebration of the human and artistic spirit. In this book the underlying theme of *Anna, The Old Wives' Tale,* and *Clayhanger* reaches its ultimate expression: the world redeemed by love and imagination. There is no need, he shows, for one to go the Isle of Man or Paris or even the Imperial Palace Hotel in search of romance; romance exists in the most unlikely of places, in the heart of Gissing's "nether world," Clerkenwell.

Coming from a novelist who was tagged, early in his career, as a documentary realist, *Riceyman Steps* is an uncommonly literary book. Bennett's original idols, Turgenev and the French naturalists, have given way to Stendhal, Chekhov, and, above all, Dostoevsky; and one can detect traces of the psychologist of love, the master of "absolute realism" (Bennett's description of Chekhov), and the most probing and forgiving of the Russians in Bennett's novel. To Gide, Bennett expressed his ambition of "getting so near the truth, and getting there beautifully," as had Stendhal and Dostoevsky, although he felt that he "could never do anything equal to that." In *Riceyman Steps* he came very close indeed to a Dostoevskian richness of empathy. Bennett viewed the author of *The Brothers Karamazov* as the "greatest sympathiser of all"; his "nature had for human imperfections that universal, Christ-like uncondescending pity which should be the ideal of all novelists." Along with the Dostoevskian power of empathy in *Riceyman Steps* there exists a measure of Dostoevsky's humor. Henry Earlforward, Bennett's miser-hero, is related to one of those Dostoevskian comic monsters—Marmeladov in *Crime and Punishment,* for example—who is never denied our sympathy in spite of his worst excesses. Furthermore, the book's subplot, which involves the charwoman Elsie's wait for the return of her wayward lover Joe, recalls Dostoevsky's "White Nights."

There is also a strong element of literary self-parody in the book: Elsie's amazing devotion to her employers, the Earlforwards, makes Anna's devotedness to her father seem trifling by comparison; and in place of Anna's theft and destruction of Willie Price's forged document, Bennett gives us Elsie's theft of sixpence from the Earlforward safe—an act which destroys the miser's "foundations of faith" and precipitates his death. In the miserly couple's clinging to the "mystery" of one another, Bennett seems to be burlesquing the sentimental excesses of the Edwin Clayhanger-Hilda Lessways relationship; and in Earlforward himself, descendant of a line of misers in Bennett's fiction, Bennett appears to be indulging in a parody of his own proneness to inflated rhetoric and to be mocking certain of his own weaknesses: his meticulousness, his orderliness, and his faith in willpower. James Hepburn has provocatively argued that in *Riceyman Steps* Bennett goes beyond documentary realism—despite the novelist's claim that the miser and his shop were based on actual Southampton models which he transplanted to Clerkenwell. Although he read up on Clerkenwell and studied a book about misers for various details, Bennett ultimately turned to his imagination for the main

points. In doing so, however, he also returned to the world of nineteenth-century English fiction. Elsie, for example, inevitably reminds us of one of Gissing's dutiful characters. His comment that "in some magic way she had vanquished the difficulties of a most formidable situation by merely accepting and facing them" . . . echoes Bennett's description of Gissing himself, made over two decades earlier: "He is neither gay nor melancholy; but just, sober, calm, and proud against the gods; he has seen, he knows, he is unmoved; he defeats fate by accepting it. (pp. 34-6)

The grimness of *Riceyman Steps* may suggest Gisisng, but the quirky humor of the book is Dickensian, as are certain significant details in the book. Earlforward's cluttered bookstore, for example, is a reincarnation of that "dark greasy shop" in Clerkenwell where Mr. Venus accumulates his precious junk, while Earlforward himself is akin to the fantastic misers whom Boffin enjoys reading about in the same novel, *Our Mutual Friend*. (Dickens might have written Earlforward's bizarre query to the vacuuming crew that has removed the dust from his shop: "Do you sell it? Do you get anything for it?" . . . The heaps of dust have obvious symbolic value in both *Our Mutual Friend* and *Riceyman Steps*.) Bennett, nonetheless, expressed a lifelong dislike of Dickens, citing his ignorance, exaggerations, and lack of a sense of art or beauty. The modern critical sense that certain Bennett characters—such as Earlforward or Tellwright—are Dickensian in their comic grotesquerie would have horrified him. One is speaking, hence, not in terms of influence but of temperamental affinities—above all, in the two novelists' mutual determination to recreate the world according to the whims and needs of the imagination.

Imaginary recreation of the world is not only Bennett's object in *Riceyman Steps* but also the occupation of his major characters. However, while he is aware of the terrible squalor overlying the strange beauty of his subject, they are blind to all but what their limited perspectives perceive as beautiful. The fortyish bookseller Henry Earlforward and his stolid cleaningwoman Elsie are described initially in terms of their mixture of insensitivity and extravagance: "An ecnhantment upon these two human beings, both commonplace and both marvelous, bound together and yet incurious each of the other and incurious of the mysteries in which they and all their fellows lived! Mr. Earlforward never asked the meaning of life, for he had a lifelong ruling passion. Elsie never asked the meaning of life, for she was dominated and obsessed by a tremendous instinct to serve." . . . Earlforward's "strange passion" and Elsie's "tremendous instinct" are the contending values of the novel, as they were in *Anna of the Five Towns:* the malignant power of money and the saving power of love. But Bennett refuses to bring the book down to earth by intruding moral judgments. Elsie and Earlforward and Violet Arb, the widow whom Earlforward marries and locks up within his shop, see life form a narrow but magical perspective that lifts them above their Clerkenwell setting. What they don't know, oddly enough, saves them.

As middle-aged lovers, Henry and Violet regard one another with an incomprehension that is romantic rather than pathetic. From the beginning, we learn that he is "subject to dreams and ideals and longings" . . . ; at the sight of Violet, he is attracted to her embodiment (in his eyes) of "life, energy, downrightness, masterfulness." . . . She is, to be sure, a "sensible" woman (sensible in her sharing of many of his frugal habits), but she is also magnificently "feminine." "Forceful, she could yet (speaking metaphorically) cling and look up. And also she could look down in a most enchanting and disturbing way.'' . . . From her point of view, the miser's defects are a source of delight: ''His slight limp pleased and touched her. His unshakable calmness impressed her. Oh! He was a man with reserves, both of character and of goods. Secure in these reserves he could front the universe. He was self-reliant without being self-confident. He was grave, but his little eyes had occasionally a humorous gleam . . . In brief, Mr. Earlforward, considered as an entity, was nearly faultless.'' . . . In her state of presumed helplessness, he seems ''a rock fo defence, shelter, safety!'' . . . Earlforward, smitten, yearns to ''share with her sympathetic soul his own vision of this wonderful Clerkenwell,'' where they have neighboring shops. He wishes to tell her the romantic history of the district, including the fact that here, in the middle Ages, ''the drama of Adam and Eve [was] performed in the costume of Adam and Eve to a simple and unshocked people. (Why not? She was a widow and no longer young.) And he would point out to her how the brown backs of the houses which fronted on King's Cross Road resembled the buttressed walls of a mighty fortress, and how the grim, ochreish unwindowed backs of the houses of Riceyman Square (behind him) looked just like lofty, mediaeval keeps.'' . . . One can no more mock these curious fancies and romantic descriptions than one can mock Anna's astonishment at the sight of Liverpool harbor: in Bennett's novel, Clerkenwell becomes a kind of Eden and the middle-aged lovers reenact the story of Adam and Eve. Under their unprepossessing exteriors, they are primal beings.

To Violet, Henry is a chivalrous protector (she sees ''chivalry'' even in his choice of wedding present to her, a safe for her securities), while to the inexperienced bachelor she is ''the most brilliant, attractive, competent, and comfortable woman on earth; and Mr. Earlforward was rapidly becoming a hero, a knight, a madman capable of sublime deeds. He felt an heroical impulse such as he had never felt.'' . . . Presuming to know the characters better than they know each other, the sagacious reader is likely to remember the prenuptial blindness of Lydgate and Rosamond in *Middlemarch*—''Each lived in a world of which the other knew nothing''—and suspect that grave disillusionment is in store. But the Earlforwards married are not altered by experience; their points of view remain colored by their original romantic preconceptions, and no realization of annoying discrepancies can change them. . . . (pp. 37-9)

The most extreme case of redemptive blindness in the book is that of Elsie, who becomes the Earlforwards' maidservant after their marriage. Victimized by her employers and her occasionally brutal boyfriend Joe (who has been traumatized by his experience in the war), Elsie is the most downtrodden example of the ''priestess'' class mentioned in *Anna of the Five Towns;* yet she sees nothing wrong with her situation. For the first time in her life having a bedroom and a bed to herself, Elsie is unable to see the room as the ''cold,'' ''bare,'' and ''small'' thing that it is: ''It was ugly, but Elsie simply could not see ugliness.'' For her, possession of the room affords a delusive security equivalent to that which the Earlforwards have found in one another. Unaware of the injustice of her circumstances, Elsie has ''no glimmer of realization that she was the salt of the earth! She thought she was in a nice, comfortable, quiet house, and appointed to live with kindly people of superior excellence.'' . . . Elsie's role in the novel gives her a superficial resemblance to the legion of devoted servants in English fiction, but the deliberately exaggerated nature of her devotedness (Bennett was annoyed at the sentimental public which saw in

her the domestic servant of its dreams), plus her too-obviously symbolic function as life force—each morning she ''breathed the breath of life into the dead nocturnal house'' . . .—lift her above mere sentimentalism. She is at once archetype and self-parody. With her voracious appetite and her masochistic streak, she incarnates the opposing pulls of the novel, simultaneously toward and away from life. Rather than serving as an ''innocent'' foil to her employers, she embodies *in extremis* their own dual natures.

To see Elsie as the life force opposed to the Earlforwards' death instinct does an injustice to Bennett's remarkable achievement in *Riceyman Steps.* Just as she has her perverse strain (her clinging to Joe parallels Violet's clinging to Henry in defiance of her own early advice to Elsie: ''What do you want with men?'' . . ., so too do Henry and Violet have a life force and romantic streak that survive all the horrors of their self-imposed penury. The reader's first glimpse of Henry Earlforward—a man ''in the prime of life,'' whose ''vitality'' is suggested by his ''rich, very red lips'' . . .—is the image that Violet never loses sight of. Similarly, for him she always remains the ''girlish'' yet ''masterful'' woman who has sexual ''experience'' . . . on her side to bring him. During the course of their marriage, which lasts barely over a year, both husband and wife waste away, of cancer and undernourishment respectively; yet he sees in her, even when emaciated, a ''romantic quality perceptible in no other woman,'' while she, despite grievances against him, ''wanted to fondle him, physically and spiritually; and this desire maintained itself not without success in opposition to all her grievances, and, compared to it, her sufferings and his had but a minor consequence.'' . . . From their point of view, they alone are safe—unlike the ''pathetic creatures'' whom they see thronging the streets in search of vain pleasures, ''sheltered in no strong fortress'' such as theirs. Neither Henry's miserliness nor his increasingly withered features can alter her vision. After pondering the fate of the helpless outsiders, Violet, unaware of her own helplessness, regards her good fortune in having such a protector in a manner which invests her with grandeur as well as pathos. (pp. 39-41)

And it is thus that the author of *Riceyman Steps* transmutes and transcends realism: by focusing on his characters' reworking of reality, he enables us to see with their eyes and accept as beautiful what to an objective outsider can only seem sordid or comic-pathetic. Bachelard's insight into the poet's recreation of reality applies both to Bennett as novelist and to his characters as surrogate poets. Among the strongest images of permanence which the poetic imagination clings to, notes Bachelard, are images of the house as nest: a secure world built from within, whereby ''facts'' are altered by the ''values'' which the poet applies to them. Violet's initial impression of Earlforward's home (over the bookshop) fills her with doubts and fears concerning the man she will marry. The ''gloomy shop'' has ''the air of a crypt''; ''the dirt and the immense disorder almost frightened her.'' . . . Yet she is ''fascinated'' as well as filled with ''terror'' by the house and its revelation of Earlforward; and she is attracted by the challenge of bringing order and life and warmth to the house and its master. ''What could she not do with him? Could she not accomplish marvels?'' . . . Her association of husband and house ironically echoes Henry Mynors' linking of Anna with her kitchen: the male admires the woman who will bring order to his life; the woman is delighted by the challenge to bring order to her husband's life. However, despite an initial brave attempt to transform the house (as her wedding present to Henry, Violet arranges to have it vacuumed), all returns to its original state.

A year after the marriage the dust has resettled in place, and even Elsie is dimly aware that something must be done. "The atmosphere of the sealed house," notes Bennett, "was infected by the strangeness of the master, who himself, in turn, was influenced by it. Fresh air, new breath, a great wind, was needed to dispel the corruption. The house was suffocating its owners." . . . (pp. 41-2)

Like Woolf's Mrs. Ramsay, Violet makes a valiant effort to impose order upon disorder; but her husband is intractable, life is intractable, and corruption conquers in the end. Nevertheless, she does make an impression on her husband—his romantic letter to her is proof of that—and he in turn confirms her in the view that they are safe within the house. Once out of that delusive safety she dies; and Henry, tormented by the loss but incapable of realizing his contribution to it, makes a pathetic and heroic effort to disregard his own frail state. "Animated by the mighty power of his resolution to withstand fate he felt strong—he *was* strong." . . . Before his final collapse, he dresses himself in one of his new blue suits and returns downstairs to his business: "Work! Work! The reconstruction of his life!" . . . (His work ethic is a wry parody of Bennett's own obsessiveness.) Henry dies a surrogate artist, and much of the shock of the ending comes from the intrusion, after the Earlforwards' deaths, of the outside world offering a commonplace version of, and passing conventional judgment on, the characters and events the reader has absorbed through unconventional and unmoralistic eyes. (p. 42)

Bennett's accomplishment is to make the reader share the vision of his characters—and hence to regard as impertinent the attempts of the outside world to make its judgment on the basis of physical appearance or to evaluate the story with conventional complacency. (p. 43)

> *Donald D. Stone, "The Art of Arnold Bennett:.Transmutation and Empathy in 'Anna of the Five Towns' and 'Riceyman Steps'," in* Modernism Reconsidered, *edited by Robert Kiely with John Hildebidle, Cambridge, Mass.: Harvard University Press, 1983, pp. 17-45.*

ADDITIONAL BIBLIOGRAPHY

Bequette, M. K. "The Structure of Bennett's Trilogy." *The Arnold Bennett Newsletter* 2, No. 1 (Winter 1976): 9-17.
    Discussion of Clayhanger trilogy as "the first serious British experiment with the novel sequence." Bequette reasons that the books which make up the trilogy—*Clayhanger, Hilda Lessways,* and *These Twain*—should be studied as a unit in order to experience the full impact of the work's sophisticated artistry and remarkable structural achievement.

Broomfield, Olga R. R. *Arnold Bennett.* Boston: Twayne Publishers, 1984, 163 p.
    Biographical and critical study primarily concerned with Bennett's ten most notable novels. Broomfield uses Bennett's works, facts about his personal life, and his own views about his works to argue for his inclusion among experimentalists in English fiction during his era, challenging the long-held view that he was a "dated traditionalist preoccupied with superficialities."

Buitenhuis, Peter. "Arnold Bennett: The Propagandist versus the Novelist." *CLIO* V, No. 2 (Winter 1976): 151-74.
    Discussion of Bennett's role as an important propagandist for the British government during World War I and the effect this work had upon his literary production.

Chesterton, G. K. "The Mercy of Mr. Arnold Bennett." In his *Fancies versus Fads,* pp. 101-09. New York: Dodd, Mead and Co., 1923.
    Critique of Bennett's views on social justice.

Cowley, Malcolm. "Random Reflections." *The Literary Review* I, No. 37, May 21, 1921.
    Positive review of Bennett's book of essays *Things That Have Interested Me.*

Drabble, Margaret. *Arnold Bennett.* New York: Alfred A. Knopf, 1974, 397 p.
    Critical biography.

Greene, Graham. "The Public Life." *The Spectator* 156, No. 5618 (28 February 1936): 362.
    Review of *Arnold Bennett's Letters to his Nephew Richard Bennett.*

Harding, J. N. "The Puritanism of Arnold Bennett." *The Contemporary Review* CLXXX, No. 1028 (August 1951): 107-12.
    Examines the importance of religious conduct in *The Old Wives' Tale* and *Clayhanger.* Harding contends that although Bennett was an agnostic, he reflected upon his religious past—through the portrayal of both truly religious and hypocritical characters—in his early works, but abandoned this practice to the detriment of later works.

Hepburn, James G. *The Art of Arnold Bennett.* Bloomington: Indiana University Press, 1963, 247 p.
    Critical study.

Hicks, Granville. "Mr. Bennett Lets Us Down." *The Nation* CXXXI, No. 3417 (31 December 1930): 736.
    Negative review of *The Imperial Palace.*

Howells, W. D. "Editor's Easy Chair." *Harper's Monthly Magazine* CXXVI, No. 755 (April 1913): 796-99.
    Discussion of *Those United States.*

Hynes, Samuel. "The Whole Contention between Mr. Bennett and Mrs. Woolf." In his *Edwardian Occasions: Essays on English Writing in the Early Twentieth Century,* pp. 24-38. New York: Oxford University Press, 1972.*
    Examines the conflict over literary ideals between Woolf and Bennett, as well as the effect of Woolf's critiques of Bennett on later criticism of Bennett's work.

Jameson, Storm. *The Georgian Novel and Mr. Robinson.* London: William Heinemann, 1929, 75 p.*
    Compares *The Old Wives' Tale* with Charles Dickens's *David Copperfield* and Virginia Woolf's *Mrs. Dalloway.*

MacCarthy, Desmond. "A Question of Standards." In his *Humanities,* pp. 194-97. London: MacGibbon & Kee, 1953.
    Critique of the quality of Bennett's judgments in his weekly book review column in the *Evening Standard.*

Mencken, H. L. "Some New Books." *The Smart Set* LXXI, No. 3 (July 1923): 140.
    Review of *Lillian.*

Murry, J. Middleton. "Mr. Bennett Functions." *The Athenaeum,* No. 4735 (28 January 1921): 96.
    Negative review of *Things That Have Interested Me.*

Pilkington, Frederick. "Methodism in Arnold Bennett's Novels." *The Contemporary Review* CLXXXIX, No. 1082 (February 1956): 109-15.
    Examines Bennett's intimate understanding of Methodist fellowship and the importance of his "unsympathetic, and often libellous, attacks on Methodism" to the Five Towns novels. Pilkington uses *The Old Wives' Tale* and *Anna of the Five Towns* to illustrate the effect of Bennett's Methodist upbringing on his portrayal of religion.

Roby, Kinley E. "Arnold Bennett's Social Conscience." *Modern Fiction Studies* XVII, No. 4 (Winter 1971-72): 513-24.

Examines Bennett's propagandist writings during World War I, contending that he was not always aloof and dispassionate in his opinions.

Shaw, Bernard. "Arnold Bennett." In his *Pen Portraits and Reviews by Bernard Shaw*, pp. 43-52. London: Constable and Co., 1932.
Parody of Bennett's style written in response to Bennett's assertion in *The Author's Craft* that plays are easier to write than novels because they are shorter.

Swinden, Patrick. "Time and Motion." In his *Unofficial Selves: Character in the Novel from Dickens to the Present Day*, pp. 120-57. New York: Barnes & Noble, 1973.*
Bennett, Ford Madox Ford, George Moore, and others are discussed in a chapter concerning English realist fiction. Swinden regards *The Old Wives' Tale* as a combination of methods in which, by "softening and diffusing naturalist inclinations with impressionist handling of specific scenes, Bennett wrote a masterpiece."

Swinnerton, Frank. *Arnold Bennett: A Last Word*. London: Hamish Hamilton, 1978, 120 p.
Personal appreciation based on reminiscences and interviews.

Van Doren, Carl, and Van Doren, Mark. "Prose Fiction." In their *American and British Literature since 1890*, pp. 164-211. New York and London: Century Co., 1925.*

Discussion of Bennett's life and works.

Wells, H. G. "Edifying Encounters, Some Types of *Persona* and Temperamental Attitude." In his *Experiment in Autobiography*, pp. 509-43. New York: Macmillan Co., 1934.*
Several pages devoted to the friendship between Wells and Bennett, recalling their artistic and personal differences and similarities.

West, Rebecca. "Mr. Bennett Chooses a Difficult Theme." *The Literary Digest International Book Review* 11, No. 2 (January 1924): pp. 109, 160.
Positive appraisal of *Riceyman Steps*.

Wilson, Edmund. "Post-war Shaw and Pre-war Bennett." *The New Republic* LXXI, No. 914 (8 June 1932): 92-4.*
Article includes a review of *The Journal of Arnold Bennett: 1896-1910*. Wilson discusses Shaw's Fabianism and Bennett's position as "more or less the glorifier of the commercial and organizational side of capitalism."

[Woolf, Virginia]. Review of *Books and Persons*. *The Times Literary Supplement*, No. 807 (5 July 1917): 319.
Praises the timeliness and vivacity of Bennett's collected reviews.

Young, Kenneth. *Arnold Bennett*. Harlow, England: Longman Group, 1975, 54 p.
Biographical and critical study.

Hermann Broch

1886-1951

Austrian novelist, novella and short story writer, essayist, critic, and dramatist.

One of the foremost figures in modern Austrian literature, Broch is often compared to James Joyce and Thomas Mann for his contribution to the development of the twentieth-century novel. Heavily influenced by the work of philosophers Immanuel Kant and G.W.F. Hegel, he coined the term "epistemological novel" to designate the fictional works in which he propounded his metaphysical theories. Broch is also known as a technical innovator whose experiments in narrative form and technique, particularly in his novel *Der Tod des Vergil (The Death of Virgil)*, represent what George Steiner has called "the only genuine technical advance that fiction has made since *Ulysses*."

The eldest son of a successful textile manufacturer, Broch was born in Vienna in 1886. Despite an early interest in philosophy and the natural sciences, he was expected to enter the family business, and his education was geared toward a career in industry. Upon completion of secondary school in 1903 he attended the Vienna Institute for Weaving Technology and a textile school in Alsace-Lorraine, from which he graduated in 1906 with a degree in textile engineering. He entered his father's business in 1908 and progressively assumed more responsibility in the management of the mills while pursuing his interest in philosophy and mathematics, studying at home to compensate for his lack of formal education in these areas. In 1913 he published his first essays in liberal literary journals, and during the next ten years he published a series of essays in which he began to explore the theories of values and of history that became the basis of his later fiction. Having succeeded his father as supervisor of the family business, Broch also functioned for much of this period as what he mockingly called "a captain of industry," serving on industrial advisory councils, directing a local military hospital, and acting as a government-appointed mediator in labor disputes. In time Broch's preoccupation with philosophical research began to conflict with his business obligations, especially after he had registered at the University of Vienna as a candidate for a doctorate in philosophy. In 1927 he sold the family mills—probably for a combination of economic and personal reasons—thereafter devoting himself fully to his studies. At the University of Vienna he was exposed to the leading proponents of logical positivism, a philosophical movement that disregarded ethics and metaphysics in an attempt to limit philosophy to those areas of inquiry subject to mathematical proof. Broch rejected the tenets of this movement, maintaining that in disregarding the nonrational aspects of existence, logical positivism evaded what he saw as the obligation of philosophers to explore human experience in its totality. By 1928 he had left the University and abandoned philosophy, convinced that solutions to metaphysical questions were more likely to be found in literature, a discipline he considered better suited to dealing with the nonrational elements of life. His first fictional work, a three-volume novel entitled *Die Schlafwandler (The Sleepwalkers)*, combined an intricate plot with chapters of philosophical theory to explore the moral and spiritual fragmentation of European

society before World War I, in what Ernestine Schlant called "Broch's defiant answer to the logical positivists." Critically acclaimed, the novel established Broch as a major voice in modern fiction; unfortunately, the work's complexity and the disastrous economic situation in Germany, where it was published, limited its popular success.

After the publication of *The Sleepwalkers* Broch published no major works until *The Death of Virgil* in 1945, writing steadily but limiting himself to essays, introductions, reviews, short stories, and fragments of more ambitious projects. Left without income after the sale of the textile mills, Broch found it necessary to neglect what he considered his most meaningful works in order to complete assignments that were more lucrative. His writing was additionally hindered by distress over developments in Nazi Germany, which prompted doubts about the role of literature in a world of political and social upheaval. Upon Germany's annexation of Austria in 1938 Broch was arrested by the Gestapo, apparently through the efforts of a postal employee who brought Broch's extensive correspondence with liberal public figures to the attention of authorities. Broch was released several weeks later and through the intervention of prominent friends secured an exit visa, which allowed him to emigrate to the United States via England and Scotland. He immediately became involved in refugee activities, devoting most of his time to securing affidavits for potential immigrants, collecting funds, and petitioning the United States government for the humane reconstruction and democratization of Germany at the conclusion of the war. He also pursued a variety of literary projects, including three novels, numerous political essays and proposals, and a study of mass hysteria and political psychology. Many of Broch's writings remained incomplete or unpublished at the time of his death in 1951.

Although Broch considered himself primarily a philosopher, not a novelist, it is through his fiction that he has achieved acclaim. Rejecting aestheticism, Broch's novels reflect his ethical concerns and scientific interests while exploring the social and philosophical theories introduced in his essays. *The Sleepwalkers,* for example, is based on Broch's theory of the cyclical nature of history, which postulates two-thousand-year cultural eras culminating in a period of "disintegrating values"—in this case the years preceding World War I—when the unifying value structure of a society has broken down and a new system has not yet evolved. In volumes subtitled "Romanticism 1888," "Anarchy 1903," and "Objectivity 1918," Broch depicted the lives of three representative characters at critical stages in the process. In accordance with his assertion that "cataclysms in the world necessitate a cataclysm in poetic creativity," the novel is radical in style and intent, attempting to transcend the limitations of the nineteenth-century psychological novel by seeking metaphysical patterns behind psychological behavior. Hannah Arendt has observed that each volume ends abruptly, concluding "not when the characters' private invented destinies have been played out, but when the historical essentials of the given period are established." The abstract function of characters in *The Sleepwalkers* has prompted criticism of Broch's artistry, with some critics maintaining that the work is overly schematized through the manipulation of characters to illustrate various facets of his theory. Broch, however, valued narrative artistry only when it served his essential concern with the attainment of an elevated vision surpassing both individuals and historical epochs. Toward this end Broch was willing to sacrifice aesthetic interests to experiment with techniques that he believed could approach such a vision in a work of prose literature. Among these techniques are the deliberate use of outmoded narrative styles, lengthy interpolations of philosophical discourse, and manipulations of reader perspective based on Broch's study of Albert Einstein's theory of relativity. According to Theodore Ziolkowski, it was with the last of these techniques that Broch succeeded in creating an ideal perspective through a final amalgam of several limited perspectives which reflect the fundamental nature of the Einsteinian universe, a universe in which the act of observation itself necessarily distorts what is observed and thus forms a barrier between truth and human apprehension of truth. Discussing this narrative device in *The Sleepwalkers,* Ziolkowski writes: "With Broch . . . no premium is placed upon the role of narrator as such; we are not enjoying a cozy community of irony as we do with Goethe or Thomas Mann, for instance, because it is only at the end of three volumes that we even realize that there is a supreme narrator or observer uniting the many mediate subject voices." In the opinion of many critics, the expression of this "supreme" perspective is most effectively and most artistically achieved in *The Death of Virgil.*

Like *The Sleepwalkers, The Death of Virgil* concerns the end of a cultural epoch, depicting the last day and night in the life of the poet during the declining years of the Roman Empire. According to Walter Baumann, Broch "decided that Virgil could be used as a persona through which the very structure of all such end phases could be expressed." The novel was begun shortly before the author's arrest and imprisonment and was completed after his emigration to America; Broch commented that it "was not written as a 'book,' but (under Hitler's threat) as my private discussion with death." In addition to his reflections on the nature of death, the novel incorporates the author's concerns about art, which he eventually came to consider an immoral evasion of reality and ethical responsibility. The book's central conflict concerns Virgil's decision to burn the *Aeneid,* which he intends to destroy in symbolic repudiation of art and of a life devoted to aestheticism rather than charity. The novel is written entirely as an interior monologue, in a style described by Aldous Huxley as one "whose enormously long sentences and cadenced repetitions suggest the continuous, unanalyzed nature of the reality they describe." Some commentators criticize this technique as verbose and repetitious; John O'Hara, for example, calls *The Death of Virgil* "one of the most exasperatingly tedious great works in any language." Such commentators as Robert Martin Adams, however, attribute much of the novel's success to this narrative style. Adams ranks *The Death of Virgil* among the great novels of the twentieth century, observing that the book follows James Joyce's *Finnegans Wake* "unreservedly in making language a subject in itself at the expense of usurpation of its expressive functions."

Broch's three remaining novels reflect his interests and theories in much the same way as *The Sleepwalkers* and *The Death of Virgil;* however, these works are generally considered to be of lesser literary merit. *Die Unbekannte Grösse (The Unknown Quantity),* concerns the intrusion of the irrational forces of love and death into the life of a young mathematician, shaking his previously unquestioning reliance on rationality. Critics dismiss this work as Broch's least successful, maintaining that the novel's conflict between rational and irrational forces is too schematically drawn. *Die Schuldlosen (The Guiltless),* which consists of eleven loosely related stories set in Germany between World War I and World War II, is Broch's most overtly political novel, portraying various protagonists whose collective indifference to social and political issues facilitates Adolf Hitler's rise to power. *Der Versucher* presents a symbolic representation of the same events, depicting the rise to power of a demagogue in a remote Austrian village. According to critics, Broch conceived the novel as a synthesis of his theories of mass psychology, demagoguery, and the disintegration of values; he wrote to his publisher, "I know that the meaning of my life lies in this work." He composed three separate versions of the novel over a period of sixteen years, but only the first was completed by the time of his death. Although many critics contend that the novel's complex aims are not successfully integrated into the narrative in any of the versions, Ziolkowski maintains that the unfinished novel "represents, next to Thomas Mann's *Doctor Faustus,* the most profound fictional portrayal of the rise of irrationalism in Germany during the Hitler era."

Critics often refer to Broch as "a writer in spite of himself" whose fascination with philosophy was at odds with his talent as a prose writer. Throughout his life, Broch considered the importance of his work to lie in his purely philosophical writings and in the philosophical significance of his fiction. Commentators, however, who find little originality in his philosophical theories, rank Broch among the most important novelists of the twentieth century for his technical and thematic achievements in *The Sleepwalkers* and *The Death of Virgil.*

PRINCIPAL WORKS

Die Schlafwandler (novel trilogy)   1931-32
  [*The Sleepwalkers,* 1932]
Die Unbekannte Grösse (novel)   1933
  [*The Unknown Quantity,* 1935]
**Den sie wissen nich, was sie tun* (drama)   1934
James Joyce und die Gegenwart (speech)   1936
Der Tod des Vergil (novel)   1945
  [*The Death of Virgil,* 1945]
Die Schuldlosen (novel)   1950
  [*The Guiltless,* 1974]
Gesammelte Werke. 10 vols.   (poetry, novels, essays,
    treatise, and letters)   1953-61
***Der Versucher* (unfinished novel)   1953; published in
    Gesammelte Werke
Short Stories (short stories)   1966
*Hugo von Hoffmansthal and His Time: The European
    Imagination, 1860-1920* (criticism)   1985

*This work comprises the novels *Pasenow; oder, Die Romantik 1888,
Esch; oder, Die Anarchie 1903,* and *Hugenau; oder, Die Sachlichkeit
1918.*

**This work was published as *Die Entsühnung* in 1936.

***This work was written between 1935 and 1951.

EDWIN MUIR   (essay date 1932)

[*Muir was a distinguished Scottish novelist, poet, critic, and translator. With his wife Willa, he translated a variety of German
works unfamiliar to the English-speaking world, including,* The
Sleepwalkers *and works by Gerhart Hauptmann and Franz Kafka.
Throughout his career, Muir was intrigued by psychoanalytic
theory, particularly Freud's analyses of dreams and Jung's theories of archetypal imagery, both of which he often utilized in his
work. In his critical writings, Muir was more concerned with the
general philosophical issues raised by works of art—such as the
nature of time or society—than with the particulars of the work
itself, such as style or characterization. In the following excerpt,
he discusses how* The Sleepwalkers *derives its narrative structure
from its philosophical ideas.*]

The Sleepwalkers (Die Schlafwandler) is a trilogy, the separate
volumes of which have appeared consecutively and at intervals
in Germany. The first is entitled ***Pasenow, or Romanticism*** and
the action is laid in 1888; the second is ***Esch, or Anarchy, 1903;***
the third, ***Huguenau, or Realism, 1918.*** The action in each of
the volumes is quite short, approximately a year. Nor does the
book resemble in other ways the ordinary trilogy, which is
generally concerned with the history of successive generations
of the same family, as for instance *The Forsyte Saga.* In ***Pasenow*** the action takes place partly on a large estate on the
Polish border of Prussia and partly in Berlin, and it consists
largely of the perplexities of Joachim von Pasenow, a romantic
young officer of aristocratic family who sees the old traditions,
the old security of life losing their reality, and cannot come to
terms with the new ways which insist on forcing themselves
on his notice and determining his way of looking at the world.
The second volume, on the other hand, gives a picture of lower-
middle-class, working-class, and Bohemian life in the Cologne
and Mannheim of 1903, with a glimpse of the socialist and
trade union movement which was becoming powerful then.
Only two of the characters in ***Pasenow*** come into this volume,

and they have already assumed a rather legendary aspect. Edouard
von Bertrand, a former friend of Joachim's, who deserted his
class to go into business and is now a very rich man, and
Ruzena, Joachim's mistress, who has fallen on evil days (she
appears only for a few minutes). Esch, the hero of this volume,
is an incarnation both of the confusion of the age and of its
frantic and muddle-headed desire to put things right and achieve
a new order. The old security to which Joachim von Pasenow
clung so desperately is no longer effectively in existence; Esch
does not know where he stands; even the most respectable and
solidly established things turn out, when he looks at them, to
be unstable or unjust or corrupt: confusion everywhere. With
the third volume we are in 1918, the last year of the War. The
scene is the little Rhineland town of Kur-Trier. Now appears
the man who in Herr Broch's eyes is the typical representative
of the age: Huguenau, the realistic business man, without prejudices, without morality, without culture, and without any
traditions save those of his specialized occupation. The old
security has almost completely vanished; even Esch's struggles
to find some trace of a just and reasonable order in the world
have lost their reality, have deteriorated into a despairing battle
with shadows; and nothing much remains but the naked and
almost meaningless actuality, in dealing with which Huguenau,
the man without prejudices, is alone perfectly at home. In this
volume where all the implications immanent in the first two
volumes are resolved Joachim von Pasenow and August Esch
again appear; the heroes of the three volumes are thrown together in the petty daily life of a small provincial town. But
no satisfactory solution of their relation to one another is possible, and it is violently ended in the few days of the German
Revolution, when Esch is killed and Joachim von Pasenow's
car is wrecked by the mob and he himself loses his wits.
Huguenau remains triumphant.

This is a bald account of the structure of the trilogy. But in
spite of the skill that is obvious in that structure, for instance
the changing of the social setting from the first to the second
and from the second to the third volumes, giving one the feeling
of witnessing the development not merely of a family but of
a civilization, and at the point in each case where that development can be most clearly seen in operation, what I have said
thus far of the structure of the book tells one very little about
it, for that structure merely repeats the lines of a more essential
structure, a structure of imaginative thought to which all the
action has a strict relation and which itself amounts to a philosophy of history. To make clear the relation of this philosophical structure to the action of which the triology consists
I shall draw upon the best known illustration I can find. The
formal structure of *The Divine Comedy* is clear, logical, and
satisfying in itself. But we know that implicit in it is the structure of mediaeval theological thought, and that without the
existence, the support, of the edifice of mediaeval thought it
could not have been what it is. In his book on Dante, Mr. T. S.
Eliot has made admirably clear that to enjoy *The Divine Comedy* as a poem it is not essential that we should accept its body
of ideas, though it is necessary that we should understand them.
The same is true of Herr Broch's trilogy. It can be enjoyed,
it is true, but not enjoyed rightly, if one ignores altogether the
philosophical conception informing it and giving it shape; but
its full significance can be seized only if one understands that
conception, which is not an afterthought or a moral tacked on
to the story, but is immanent in the action and determines the
development.

As there is no other modern novel of which, so far as I know,
this is true, it will be advisable at this point to make a distinction

before going on to outline Herr Broch's underlying conception. His trilogy, for example, is not a propagandist work; he does not use fiction as a means for making certain views prevail against certain other views, as Mr. Shaw does in his plays and Mr. Wells does in his novels. Nor are his ideas introduced in the form of philosophical dialogues on matters in general, such as the dialogues which Mr. Aldous Huxley writes with so much intelligence and skill. The vice of such dialogues in a novel is that they are rarely necessarily in character; the thoughts put in the various interlocutors' mouths could be exchanged without making any essential difference. There are no dialogues of that kind in *The Sleepwalkers;* the characters do not talk to amuse, or enlighten, or persuade us; they talk about their own concerns and in a style that fits their natures. Herr Broch's thought is implicit not in what they say, but in the destinies he gives them and the world in which he sets them; it is silent for the most part, until in the last volume he gives it explicit and formed expression in a philosophical essay consisting of nine chapters which appear at intervals throughout the volume. When these chapters come at last they have the effect of a crystallization towards which all the preceding action has been working; they are the legitimate expression of the logical content of the work, a content which has throughout been immanent and could only in this way and at this point be given a clear intellectual formulation.

The chapters in which the ideas are developed are given the heading of *Disintegration of Values.* Leaving out all the proofs and qualifications, Herr Broch's thesis is this: that ever since the dissolution of the mediaeval synthesis a disintegration of values has been going on which today has almost worked itself out. This process could not have been avoided and cannot be stopped until it has reached its conclusion; and it was rendered necessary by the bankruptcy of the mediaeval logic itself, by the fact that mediaeval theological thought, a closed deductive system, could not resolve its own antinomies, and so had to allow the reason to start anew from the fact of the empirically given world, or rather from the multitude of facts presented by that world. The world of mediaeval thought rested on the Christian God; all knowledge, all value, all experience, were given their place in the mediaeval hierarchy solely by reference to God as the ultimate Reality; and all thought ended in Him. But when the mediaeval synthesis was dissolved the Christian God was no longer left enthroned as the finite-infinite, heavenly-earthly bourne of all human aspiration and thought; man's goal was now projected into the infinite, and there no longer remained any ultimate symbol in which all human values converged and were bound together, any meaning that was more binding than the meaning of each value individually. But as these values could no longer find a final common point at which to come to rest, they had to run on parallel to each other, driven on by their own immanent logic, until each became autonomous, each resolved to break its own record, as the author expresses it. So military technique becomes a thing in itself, business a thing in itself, art a thing in itself, getting rich a process in itself, even revolution an end in itself: each governed by its own laws, each regardless of its neighbouring values, and each reaching its *reductio ad absurdum* in a state where only a business man can understand business and only a painter can tell what a picture is about. This process is what Herr Broch means by the "disintegration of values", and the state I have just described is, according to his analysis, the state of the modern world. The logic which drives on those parallel and autonomous value systems is characterized by a complete ruthlessness, by what the author calls "an almost metaphysical lack of consideration for consequences"; and the end towards which it makes is a world in which the old bonds which united men are destroyed, and human understanding is almost impossible, so fatally are men entangled in separate values that ignore each other and cannot comprehend each other. It is a state in which the isolation of the individual grows more and more intense and the value of human life progressively contracts until all that it covers effectively is an occupation or a *métier*.

But though *The Sleepwalkers* ends with the consummation of this process, though the author pursues his analysis of the disintegration of our time to its conclusion, his book is not an incitement to despair, but far rather a confession of faith. As he sees it the process is a painful but necessary historical liquidation; but when it is consummated the Platonic idea is fated to return; the unity of humanity must be restored because the very laws of the reason, the needs of the human soul, make it inevitable.

This is a very bald summary of an historical and philosophical essay filled with the most subtle and exact thought. My purpose, however, is merely to give a sufficient outline of it to make comprehensible the main conception from which the triology derives its structure; for the whole book follows, or rather imaginatively incarnates, this conception of the disintegration of values. It does this so thoroughly that each of the three volumes, recording different moments in the process, has a separate form of its own. The ostensible plot of *Pasenow* is straightforward, and consists simply of the solution in action of various perplexities in the hero's mind, these being symbolized by his relations to his friend Bertrand, which he never understands, and his feelings towards his mistress Ruzena and his future wife Elisabeth, which he also never understands. But the dying tradition to which he clings has still sufficient strength to step in and round off the plot with neatness: for he marries Elisabeth. This volume is a miracle of delicate suggestion, of suggestion so subtle and fine that it produces an impression of magic. In *Esch* human relations are by no means simple; in his struggle to establish order the hero involves himself in all sorts of confusion and absurdity, and although in the process he does achieve something—not what he desires, but still something—he becomes a comic figure, a figure surrounded by a rarefied humour not unlike that of Franz Kafka. In this book it would be difficult to say what the plot is, for cause and effect work in a peculiar idiosyncratic way, as if in the general dislocation of things reason itself had got a twist. The method is still suggestion, but it is used to open up sudden abysses beneath the action and to show us states of mind never before, I think, explored by any other novelist, states of mind in which the seeds of the future seem to be growing in darkness. The action may be called deliberately arbitrary; it is irrational, but irrational in a particular methodical way, with an irrationality which resembles that of a child who wishes to bring order into the world, but all of whose attempts are defeated by a quite naïve and predetermined ignorance. In *Huguenau* there is hardly any action at all; the lives of the characters run in the main parallel to one another, converging only now and then, unfruitfully or disastrously; and a catastrophic event from outside, the outbreak of the Revolution, is needed to unite for a moment their destinies.

In all these three volumes there is felt by the characters a dim perception of two things: that the world is becoming a more and more homeless place, more and more insensible to their desires, their deepest needs, and that a way of salvation must be found; a consciousness of the dehumanization of the world

Advertisement for Die Schlafwandler (The Sleepwalkers). *Courtesy of Buchhaendler-Vereinigung: Archive für Geschichte Buchwesens.*

and of the need for redemption: there are the two motives which run through the lives of the characters in **The Sleepwalkers,** the two motives which recur again and again in countless variations throughout the trilogy. One of these motives is finally rounded off, as we have seen, in the essay on *Disintegration of Values* in the third book. The other is given its final expression in the same volume in a curious section, also in chapters scattered at intervals through the text, entitled *Story of a Salvation Army Girl in Berlin*. It is a separate story, with no attempt at realism of presentation, cutting across the parallel strands of the narrative. It is altogether outside the story in a world of its own; it is indeed on the very frontier of the book, where one imagines the author wished it to be. Part of it is written in a sonnet sequence, part in prose. In these poems the aspiration for salvation felt by the characters is raised to a different plane, where it serves as a counter theme to the theme of disintegration. It will be seen that the pattern is extremely complicated; but it is an ordered and deliberate complication, the complication of a musical composition which works out in harmony.

From this account one may gain some impression of the extraordinary formal elaboration and harmonious balance of this astonishing work. I can give no idea of the profundity and exactitude of the author's psychology, for I should have to cite examples, extract scenes or whole characters, and the book is so closely knit that such a thing is almost impossible. Herr Broch's psychology may be called deductive as against the inductive psychology, for instance, of Proust. Proust began with certain sensations or feelings and followed them as far as

they would take him; and in the end by this means we know that he achieved a metaphysic of his own, as the last volume of his colossal work shows. Herr Broch starts from an extremely comprehensive, profound, and exact knowledge of the human heart and mind, from certain universal emotions and thoughts which all human beings must feel and think, rather than from what one particular character will feel or think. But, as they are felt and thought by the various figures in this trilogy, these emotions and thoughts take on the most subtle individual modifications, and are pursued, on the opposite route from that of Proust, to their most secret and almost invisible manifestations. Herr Broch is certainly a very great psychologist, and at his best the effect he produces on one's mind is that of pure illumination. He lays bare desires so secret that only by the road he has pursued could he have reached them, desires more secret than could ever have been discovered by a writer like Proust who started from the given concrete data of sensation, and the limits of whose exploration were determined by that fact. It is as if Herr Broch were taking us within the mind itself and from there were showing us horizons of which we have only dreamed before.

This, I think, is the essential thing to be said about his trilogy. As for the subtle harmonies of his style, I can convey no idea of them, nor of the consummate skill with which he presents a scene or suggests an atmosphere, nor of the exquisite finish which he has given to all the separate parts of a balanced and majestic whole. But I have tried at least to show that he has made a new contribution to the modern imagination and incidently to the modern novel, widening the scope of both. (pp. 664-68)

Edwin Muir, "Hermann Broch," in The Bookman, New York, Vol. LXXV, No. 7, November, 1932, pp. 664-68.

FRED T. MARSH (essay date 1935)

[*In the following excerpt, Marsh reviews* The Unknown Quantity.]

Hermann Broch is the author of the trilogy *The Sleepwalkers*. . . . That was an extraordinarily ambitious work containing romantic, realistic and grotesque episodes and tales woven into the three novels along with much metaphysical and historical matter, and including fragments of a difficult epistomological essay scattered through the book. It was a study of our times and its background in strange symbolic form, times which Herr Broch finds chaotic because individualistic, amorphous and spasmodic in action. In his asides he goes back to the break-up of a world society that followed the Protestant Reformation.

The new novel [*The Unknown Quantity*] is much slighter and wholly entertaining, though compounded out of serious matter. But we are left as much in the dark as to its ultimate meaning as we were by *The Sleepwalkers*. Just as in the earlier work we felt there must be something more to its intention than Spenglerian acceptance of a world in decay, so in this book we feel there should be something more than the point that love and science are not incompatible. But if there is we have missed it.

Of Hermann Broch we are told that he did not begin to write until he was forty-six. Previously he had built up a prosperous industry while pursuing his youthful interest in science and metaphysics. *The Unknown Quantity* shows his interest in modern scientific theory and this background makes interesting reading to the layman. The hero, Richard Hieck, is an able young scientist who has turned from pure mathematics to physics, and during the course of the novel makes another switch to astronomy. His lean, ascetic face is in contrast to his big, awkward body, and the conflict that develops within him is the conflict between the scientist who has lived an almost monastic life and the man who is both physically powerful and socially sensitive.

Richard's family had always been a strange family, the result of these two conflicting sides of life—the ascetic and the sensual. His father before his death had been a strange, weird, unknowable man, given to silence and star-gazing. Mysteriously and with few words and actions he dominated the house. The mother was a peasant girl, by nature hearty and attractive. Now since the father's death she is gradually recapturing her true nature, emerging from the years of repression. Richard's sister, Susanne, is like him, possessed of a big healthy body dominated by an ascetic ideal. She is a devout Catholic and intends to become a nun. The younger brother, Otto, is the esthete, the sensuous youth, about whom hovers the lingering odor of decadence. The story shifts back and forth between Richard's home and the university.

At home Otto is planning to get hold of some of his mother's money with the help of his friend, Karl. At the university Professor Weitprecht, the absent-minded mathematical genius who is scarcely more than an unembodied mind, is cracking up and Richard is working on his papers. In the home circle Susanne grows more devout, the mother blooms and takes an interest in the boy, Karl. Otto takes to staying out nights, worrying his brother, while evil thoughts, suspicions and desires fester his mind. At the university Richard finds himself taking a personal interest in two of his girl assistants. He shows Ilse Nydhalm over the observatory. He goes swimming with Erna Magnus. He has a discussion with the able but cynical and worldly mathematics colleague, Dr. Kapperbrunn, who has none of the rapt intensity of Richard and tells him he ought to go in for mountain climbing or, with his physique, take to felling trees.

Richard is going through a period of inner turmoil which comes to a climax when Otto, after a quarrel with him, dashes from the house, grabs his bicycle and rides madly forth to his death. Richard emerges from the pain of the tragedy with a new outlook. His devotion to science is not lessened, but he knows that all of life cannot be reduced to ordered form. The unknown quantity, the life of impulse and affection finding its highest expression in love, remains.

Fred T. Marsh, "Love Is Unknown Quantity to Science," in New York Herald Tribune Books, May 12, 1935, p. 7.

ALDOUS HUXLEY (essay date 1945)

[*Known primarily for his dystopian novel* Brave New World *(1932), Huxley was a British-American man of letters who is considered a novelist of ideas. The grandson of noted Darwinist T. H. Huxley and the brother of scientist Julian Huxley, he was interested in many fields of knowledge, and daring conceptions of science, philosophy, and religion are woven throughout his fiction. Continually searching for an escape from the ambivalence of modern life, Huxley sought a sense of spiritual renewal and a clarification of his artistic vision through the use of hallucinogenic drugs, an experience explored in one of his best-known later works,* The Doors of Perception *(1954). In the following excerpt, he favorably reviews* The Death of Virgil.]

Of Virgil, as of most of the other great men of antiquity, we know astonishingly little. His father was a yeoman farmer, but the boy was given the best education then available in the provinces. Proceeding to Rome as a budding poet, he soon made friends and acquired patrons. Rich and powerful men, such as Pollio, Maecenas and Augustus, solved all his economic problems for him; poets, such as Horace and Varius, were his intimates. People liked him for his gentleness and modesty and praised him for that reverent loyalty to friends, country and religious tradition, which the Romans dominated *pietas*. He never married, and the Neapolitans, among whom he lived for some time, gave him the nickname of Parthenias, or "the Virgin." Quoting ancient traditions, his fourth-century commentator, Donatus, states that "his desire was more inclined to boys," and also that he "most pertinaciously" refused Varius's offer of a share in the favours of the latter's mistress, Plotia Hieria.

As an artist, Virgil was in the last degree painstaking and conscientious. It took him more than ten years to write the *Aeneid*, and when he had finished, he retired to Athens with the intention of giving three more years to a final revision. Unhappily Augustus, who was also traveling in Greece, insisted on his returning to Rome with the imperial retinue. Virgil obeyed—with fatal consequences. At Megara he took sunstroke, lay mortally sick during the subsequent sea voyage and died a few days after landing at Brindisi. On his death bed he left instructions that the *Aeneid* was to be destroyed, but Augustus set the will aside and the poem, though imperfect in its author's eyes, was published and became the national epic of Rome.

On this exiguous biographical foundation, and within a times-pan no more extensive than the final two or three days of Virgil's life, Hermann Broch has reared a massive and elaborate work of art [*The Death of Virgil*], in which historical narrative is strangely combined with what may be called lyrical philosophy. To readers of his first novel, *The Sleepwalkers* . . . , Broch's current preoccupation with metaphysics will not seem at all surprising. For that remarkable book owed its power and its rather disquieting beauty to the fact that it existed, as it were, on two incommensurable planes, that beneath the solid and convincing characters, moving within their well constructed narrative, there lay the half-divined implication of "the absolutely other." In Virgil these implied depths are brought more explicitly to the surface. The fundamental theme of the book is Gnosis or, as Mr. Broch calls it, "perception"—the immediate knowledge of divine reality—and the conditions of such knowledge. These conditions are easy to formulate, hard to fulfill; for nobody can live to Reality who has not died to Self. On his death-bed Virgil comes to this understanding. Instead of becoming a saint he has been content to remain a mere genius; has lived irresponsibly for beauty instead of for charity. In an act of repentance and atonement he decides to sacrifice the symbol and, in a sense, the very substance of his offending selfhood—the *Aeneid*.

The narrative portions of the book describe the sick man's efforts to make his three best friends, Plotius Tucca, Varius and Augustus, understand the reasons for this decision. But Plotius is too much the good citizen and average sensual man to be able to grasp what Virgil is talking about, Varius is too much the professional esthete; Augustus is too firmly convinced that subordination to his new totalitarian state is man's highest duty and final end.

This incomprehension is displayed against a background of that which is not comprehended—the divine ground of all being. And here, of course, the literary problem becomes really interesting. Any competent writer can turn out a historical novel, but who can give artistic expression to metaphysical reality? Traditional language describes the world in terms of discrete entities acting upon one another in space and time. That is why, when they wish to describe a continuum, mathematicians have to use a special calculus radically different from common speech. Spiritual reality is not merely a continuum; it is out of space and time. Language is therefore doubly inadequate to its description. In order even to hint at its nature, men have had to resort to paradox, hyperbole, negation.

Mr. Broch's solution to this old semantic problem consists in a style whose enormously long sentences and cadenced repetitions suggest the continuous, unanalyzed nature of the reality they describe, and in which the great predominance of adjectives and substantives over verbs gives the impression of something that timelessly is, rather than of something that acts and becomes within the world of successive events. This stylistic device is fully successful where it is used in comparatively brief passages that alternate contrastingly with passages of straight narrative. But there are, unfortunately, two long sections of the book where Mr. Broch makes use of it for many pages at a stretch. The result is bewildering. It is as though a sculptor had carved a vase bas-relief with no flat spaces between the figures. But these defects—the consequences of an excess of intellectual wealth—should not blind us to the fact that *The Death of Virgil* is a very remarkable work. To make the best

esthetically speaking, of both worlds is the hardest of all literary tasks. . . . Mr. Broch has come very near to success.

Aldous Huxley, "Why Virgil Offered a Sacrifice," in New York Herald Tribune Weekly Book Review, *July 8, 1945, p. 5.*

WALDO FRANK   (essay date 1945)

[*Frank was an American novelist and critic who was best known as an interpreter of contemporary civilization, particularly that of Latin America. A socialist and supporter of various radical groups in the United States, he was a founding editor of the* Seven Arts (1916-17), *a leftist, avant-garde magazine of literature and opinion. One of Frank's most significant works of criticism,* Our America (1919), *derides the "genteel tradition" in American letters and is considered an influential work in its support of realism in the nation's literature. In the following excerpt, Frank assesses the artistic achievements and failures of* The Death of Virgil.]

The Death of Virgil [is] a story that consciously and powerfully attempts to deepen the bases of the novel in its destined role of modern tragedy, modern epic, modern poem. The story is simple. Virgil, secure in Rome's glory but sick unto death in flesh and soul, returns with the Emperor Augustus from Athens to Brundisium. His fever brings spiritual clarity; he finds the synthetic art of his still unpublished but already famous *Aeneid* unworthy of survival. In a night of lucid delirium, he descends to the sources of his life and of human fate; and in the morning emerges with the resolve to burn his manuscript. Two court poets of Rome, Plotius Tucca and Lucius Varius, visit him and he tells them his grim purpose. Failing to dissuade him, they bring the bad news to Augustus who has already enlisted the *Aeneid* as a political weapon of imperial consolidation. Augustus comes to his old friend, and they argue. Augustus sees the political structure of Rome as an end in itself; his empire, to his pragmatic eye, is universal since it embraces the limits of the known world; and without temporal end, since he cannot see beyond the values of *Pax Romana*. Of this fulfilled greatness, Virgil's poem is the symbol; the poet cannot destroy what has become a part and function of Rome. Virgil's vision (the conventional medieval legend of the poet, which Dante used) is of the ancient world's death and transfiguration. Imperial Rome has assembled the "body"; a savior dimly descried will bring rebirth in Holy Rome. The emperor, the practical man, does not know what Virgil is talking about, and suspects his fever. But he wins the argument. Virgil promises not to destroy the poem; Augustus may take it back with him to Rome. Virgil dictates his will to his two friends. The fourth and final part of the story, called "Air—the Homecoming," is a long prose-poem of nearly fifty pages, which describes the poet's dissolution backward to primal pantheistic sources.

This is the story; its substantial elements are less simple. In the first part, we see the imperial fleet, the *Völkerchaos* of the Latin town, the harmonies and discords of Virgil's complex relations—since he is peasant, court-poet and mystic seer—with the people, with his art and with imperial Rome. All this is done superbly. The man on the boat, hearing the parasitic talk on deck, the painful journey on the litter through Brundisium's Misery Street, the counterpoint of the poet's sensibilities and thoughts, create a plastic, dense, organic substance, rich in smells, colors, dynamic motions. By contrast, the Egypt in Mann's *Joseph* is synthetic. The second part, called "Fire—the Descent," delivers the poet through a delirious and revealing night. It is a huge psychological tapestry, in which the poet's immersion in the ineffable is all too fragilely graphed by the street noises, the talk of drunken brawlers through the open window of his sickroom, and by the presence of the adoring slave-boy, Lysanias, who is designed to concretize Virgil's conflict of aspiration as poet and seer with the official role that Rome has thrust upon him. The prose strains and sweats, gyres and convulses, to attain the inexpressible *Ding-an-sich* ["thing in itself"]. It is full of words that the translator has Englished, as un-space, un-dimension, un-symbol, un-art, un-remembrance: words aimed dialectically to portray, beyond the thesis and antithesis of phenomena, life's essence. The German language lends itself better than ours to these excursions into the ineffable: one reason why it produced Kant and Hegel, and so few good prose writers. . . . The wordy mountains of "un-words," embed a series of Hölderlinesque odes on human fate which should have inspired the author to eliminate the slag of many pages. The personality of Virgil fitfully emerges, is lost, reappears. Probably this is the condition of personality in delirium and euphoria from which pain, the slaveboy's presence, the street-noises, spasmodically drag the poet back. But even if we admit this naturalistic justification of the scene's immense verbosity, it could with benefit have been cut by at least fifty pages.

Part Three gives us again sharp, objective portraits: the two poet friends, the court physician, the remarkably glimpsed Syrian slave (prophetic Jew?) and finally the tough, shrewd, gracious Augustus, whose delineation sheds convincing light, not only on Rome's synthetic culture but on the modern magnate. Yet here too, the same lack of measure militates against success. Of all the long line of German prose, I can name no story-teller who achieves organic proportion in the novel: not Goethe (so controlled in *Faust* and the lyric), not Mann, who succeeds best in the *novelle*, not Schnitzler, whose plays are full of grace: not one, except the Bohemian Franz Kafka. In this immense dialogue between emperor and poet (no wonder Virgil died), the arguments are marred by repetition, by want of evolution, and by occasional insertions of hind-thought ideas, which sound more like twentieth-century Roman Catholicism charading its source than like Roman paganism prophesying its future. Throughout this part, Virgil is supposed to oscillate between clarity and fever. Broch legitimately exploits this ambiguous state to fuse his hero's memories and visions with the actual scene. Characters physically in the room merge with others no longer present, and with still others, like Virgil's lover, Plotia, who are always absent. Broch's aim in this device is to paint more sharply the symbolic values of his persons. But to succeed, both the flesh and the symbol must be firm. A good universal must be sharply particularized. Plotia, Lysanias remain vague conveyancers of value because the artist's hand in drawing them wavers and fumbles.

In the final part, which describes what Broch would perhaps name Virgil's return into "the All"—called "Air"—symbol of ubiquity, Virgil is no longer present; therefore the process of his dissolution is not esthetically achieved. You cannot stage a disappearing act without the presence of what is to vanish. What we do have is a beautiful prose-poem, reminiscent of Lautréamont and Rimbaud: a vision of a unitary passage of the soul back to primeval beginnings, before man, and then before the beast: a pantheist exordium of life to which the dying poet returns. Resplendent in itself, this part has only an ideal nexus with the story. Where it fails, the success of the last cantos of Dante's *Paradiso* makes clear. Throughout the *Divina Commedia*, the focal dynamic attitude has been the poet's search; the stages of his journey have been the anatomy of his salvation;

and the final mystic scene is the ultimate goal where the motion becomes rest. Broch's story centers on Virgil's drama; his dissolution and transfiguration in death should have remained within its matrix.

The distinctions between the novel as poem and the prose-poem may help us to judge *The Death of Virgil* as a work of art. Too often the magnificent weight of thought, the vast vistas of vision, fail to be *contained* within the characters and the events that should embody them; they burst out into subjective passages (prose-poems) or dissolve into wordy inarticulation. Broch's strength as artist seems to be less than his ambition as mystic. One cannot pile up gigantic verbalisms into the expression of the infinite and the eternal (the Jewish Merkabah writers vainly tried it). The best literary mystics, from Ezekiel to Saint John of the Cross, and from Blake to Kafka, convey the experience of the limitless in concise, often humble pictures. They dimension their sounds with silence. Broch's book is *not* silent enough.

But whatever its comparative failures, *The Death of Virgil* has far more importance than most literary "successes." It hugely transcends the shallow "realistic" vision of life which has debauched the modern novel. Rejecting the thin one-dimensional prose which most reviewers misname "clear," it invents an organic prose sentence (even longer than Proust's) which, like Proust's, is an immediate unity of complex states. It boldly approaches the novel as the modern tragic poem: the freest and most potential medium by which the contemporary writer may reveal life whole. (pp. 226-28)

> *Waldo Frank, "The Novel as Poem," in* The New Republic, *Vol. 113, No. 8, August 20, 1945, pp. 226-28.*

HERMANN J. WEIGAND (essay date 1953)

[*Weigand was an American educator and critic specializing in German and medieval literature. He is also the editor of the 1965 Taschenbuch Verlag edition of* Die Schuldlosen. *In the following excerpt, Weigand discusses the stylistic and thematic heterogeneity of the stories that make up* Die Schuldlosen *and examines the work's central characters.*]

Few men of letters have been personally loved and revered like Hermann Broch. Reducing the sphere of his private wants to an unbelievable minimum, he radiated a warmth and tolerance and sympathy so rare as to be unforgettable. His seeing eye, set in the face of a raven, had a quality of timeless wisdom that neutralized specific curiosity regarding his private past and even his literary development. For such things, so far as they mattered, there would be plenty of time, it seemed, in years to come. Did he not say with a chuckle that he would live to be a hundred? Then came the stunning shock, on a late May morning in 1951: he was dead.

Die Schuldlosen had appeared half a year before. Like his *Death of Virgil,* this book weaves a spell of incantation that dissipates the transparent film of sense reality and pushes beyond into a domain of not unreal but super-real timeless multi-dimensionality, while on the hither side of the transitional zone of sense it induces a heightened awareness of ourselves as bodies and explores the descent into the dark and silent subsensory depths of organic life. But unlike that of the earlier prose epic, the organization of this work is disconcertingly intricate. It is like a puzzle, to be played with, and perhaps solved, given unlimited time. Queries addressed to the author would be in order, it seemed, only after the direct approach of meditating on the work, of listening to its heartbeat, of wheedling it into yielding up its secrets, had been patiently tried. Meanwhile the time for asking questions had run out.

The focus—that is where the difficulty begins. A novel, in the form of eleven stories set in three groups punctuated by decades—1913, 1923, 1933; each group preceded by a block of verse, heterogeneous in the style and mood of its elements; the while preceded by an elusive rabbinical parable and followed by an account of how the work came into being: five stories independently conceived and published between 1917 and 1934, retouched and fused into an interlocking series by the addition of six new stories written in a burst of productivity during the summer of 1949; the old stories reshuffled with the new to destroy the chronological sequence of their origin; the compilation presenting itself as a foreshortened, condensed symbol of the temper of three decades viewed under the aspect of eternity, piecework and totality in one—an intellectual jig-saw puzzle and symbol of mankind in a world-moment of acutest crisis—that is what Hermann Broch aimed to achieve in *Die Schuldlosen.*

The heterogeneity of the elements is evident, as regards the stories, the styles of presentation, and the literary themes and intellectual currents and influences that come to the fore. Of the eleven stories, eight form a unified cluster centering around Andreas, while the three that remain, though concerned with figures that also have a functional significance in the Andreas stories (Zacharias, the ''Bee-Father,'' Hildegard), are offered without any overt relation to the central figure. Stylistically, the influence of Joyce seems to predominate in the stories, even though the stream-of-consciousness method is never carried to the degree of choking off articulate communication. They include, as a matter of fact, some magnificent examples of the art of story telling. Two of the stories, on a superficial level of reception, read like unadulterated satire in the manner of Heinrich Mann. Portions of the ''Voices'' numb us with the shrill and deafening frenzy of the expressionistic generation. The use of Freudian complexes and symbols abounds. We find ourselves involved in situations of Kafka's devising and overwhelmed by existentialist anxieties that suggest preoccupation with Heidegger and perhaps Kierkegaard. A radical skepticism as concerns the status of art and the artist in the contemporary world reveals a close contact of Hermann Broch's thinking with Thomas Mann's most persistent theme. The emotional climate of the nineteenth century is exposed as deeply committed to ''Kitsch'' (**''Seelenlärm''**). The realization that only deepest involvement in evil may restore the integrity of the self when it has become the prey of blind impulse has a Dostojevskian ring (**''Zerline''**). There are numerous echoes of Rilke's voice. There is what looks like a startling affirmation of Stefan George's view of human destiny as evolving in cycles of two thousand years, until one remembers that Broch arrived at it independently by way of his *Tod des Vergil;* and the name of Einstein is thrown into the discussion to remind us that, like the inner world of experience, man's picture of the outer world of physical reality has also undergone a pandynamic transformation.

Within the framework of *Die Schuldlosen* eight stories are concerned with Andreas. To say that they are linked by a common biographical thread is to understate their interconnection. ''They are all one dream,'' Hermann Broch maintained. This is certainly true, but the reader is not likely to suspect this fact before he has come to the end of the cycle, and then he will look for a key that will give him access to the logic that pervades the

Dust jacket for the first edition of Die Schuldlosen (The Guiltless). *Courtesy of Buchhaendler-Vereinigung: Archive für Geschichte Buchwesens.*

tissue of the dream. How will the faint tracery of the early stories coalesce into a pattern with the eerie magic and the blinding flash of the dénouement? The key is found in the realization that the Andreas cycle conforms to the structure of tragedy in terms of a definition that I came upon in a very stimulating essay. According to Helen Adolf tragedy involves ''the unfolding into time and space of something that, seen from above, has already happened and therefore preexists in the mind of the author.'' The Andreas cycle asks to be read as such a tragedy. It unfolds into time and space in the later stories, notably in **''Erkaufte Mutter''** and **''Steinerner Gast.''** But the initial story, **''Mit leichter Brise segeln,''** is a symbolic anticipation of the whole constellation of Andreas' life and death. Here the son, in his one-sided attachment to the mother image, is challenged by the antagonistic image of the father as the eternal (and eternally just) slayer-avenger. The whole drama is fought to a tragic conclusion on the purely mental plane of Andreas' imaginative experience; on that inner plane, moreover, it is experienced as something that has already happened. It is both anticipation and recurrence. Within the shadowy domain of the inner consciousness all the motifs that come into play in the later stories are presented as preformed and preexisting.

The second story of the Andreas cycle, **''Verlorener Sohn,''** lays the groundwork for Andreas' tragic involvement. It is concerned with incidents that, outwardly considered (or objectively considered), are casual and inconsequential. However, the presentation of these commonplace incidents is surcharged at every turn with symbol and commentary that envelop them in an atmosphere of portent and tragic tension. This atmosphere does not emanate from the incidents as such, it is arbitrarily superimposed upon them, rather, by a quality of second sight inherent in the seeing eye of the author. To experience its spell, the reader has to cooperate actively and allow himself to be submerged in a sort of hypnotic trance: he must share in the author's dream on the author's terms. It is very remarkable to find that the concluding paragraph of this story, again in purely symbolic terms, foreshadows Andreas' suicide under its double aspect of stern expiation and gentle exoneration. . . . There will be a total fusion of justice and mercy in the end!

Thus the cycle has meaning only insofar as the action has already happened and preexists in the mind of the author.

This, then, is the key to the understanding of the cycle. But, as is the case with every key, it is a potential instrument that manifests its efficacy only by being put to use. If this key is to be more than an empty formula we must put it to use by a very concentrated rereading of the Andreas stories. Only then will it unlock the enigma of the cycle.

To present so strange a composition, not to a small community of followers but to the general reading public, involves an uncommon degree of self-confidence. An author whose position in the literary world is established beyond doubt can afford to take risks: the weight of his accepted production will compel attention to any work of his, no matter how difficult of approach. Hermann Broch had not come to be accepted in this fashion. A great deal of lip-service was rendered to his monumental prose symphony, *The Death of Virgil,* the work which expresses the essence of Broch, regardless of what he wrote before and what he might have written after, but its reputation was still in the making. Many readers entered the charmed circle of the *Virgil* willing to submit to the spell of its eternal melody only to find sooner or later that the ordeal of sustained imaginative participation exceeded their powers of endurance. Outward circumstances might well have produced a decisive change. Hermann Broch was in the front line of nominees for the Nobel Prize. "Jeder bekommt ihn, wenn er nur alt genug wird" ["Everyone gets it if he simply becomes old enough"], he would say with ironic self-depreciation, but the award was an eventuality with which to reckon. Hermann Broch died too soon.

As in the *Death of Virgil,* as in the unpublished *Bergroman* (climaxed by a bizarre ritual slaying in propitiation of the mountain deity), so in *Die Schuldlosen* Hermann Broch's eternal melody comes to the fore. No ear, however obtuse, can fail to hear that eternal melody, which is ever the same despite infinite variations. I call it a melody, because it is a central personal experience and a message to humanity that cannot be formulated in rational language. It becomes articulate only in the language of poetry, where every element of speech is altered, apprehendable only as music, as the cosmic vibration of a human medium. It expresses and communicates the mystic's sense of totality, the fusion of the moment with eternity, of life with death, the merging of the individual with the All, the coincidence of all opposites in the abyss of Godhead. This melody is sounded on the first page of the parable in the Rabbi's cryptic utterance: "Des Herrn Sprache . . . ist Sein Schweigen, und Sein Schweigen ist seine Sprache. Sein Sehen ist Blindheit,

und Seine Blindheit ist Sehen. Sein Tun ist Nicht-Tun, und Sein Nicht-Tun ist Tun" ["The language of the Lord . . . is his silence, and his silence is his language. His vision is blindness, and his blindness is vision. His action is inaction, and his inaction is action"]. It is heard again and again throughout the stories in passages teeming with abstract negative compounds. . . . The same melody, heard in terms of a weird music, strikes Andreas' ear amid the crashing sounds of the woodcutter's axe, as the blind grandfather-deity approaches to demand of him a reckoning which turns into a boon. . . . Any attempt on my part to elucidate in rational terms Hermann Broch's eternal melody, central experience, and insistent message would be futile: only clichés could emerge. There is a negative side, however, which must not be overlooked: man's ear has tended to become deaf to the eternal melody; the fact of guilt has all but blocked its perception. Man's deepest guilt is his "Urgleichgültigkeit," his arch-indifference to the postulate of the inner unity of the self. Andreas penetrates to the core of this "Ur-Schuld" ["arch-guilt"] in his confession, after devious attempts at dodging and building up fictions of guilt at more superficial levels. The scene is a highly original variant of Ibsen's Peer Gynt and the Button-Moulder. The title of the book, *Die Schuldlosen,* assumes a deeply ironic aspect, of course, in view of the fact that one so innocent of malice as Andreas should be overwhelmed by a sense of that collective guilt from which no man is exempt and that it should fall to his lot to perform an act of symbolic expiation in the full freedom of a metaphysical choice.

I shall not recapitulate in any detail the story of the central figure, Andreas, whom we first meet in a Paris café as a young, recently orphaned Dutchman endowed with the sixth sense of the entrepreneur in whose hand every business venture turns to profit. We find him again at the height of the German inflation, after a decade of successful globetrotting, drifting into a middle-sized German city. There things shape up for him in such a way that he, who had come as a temporary lodger into the home of an ageing baroness, soon finds himself installed in the role of adopted son and provider. But while this change of status is still in the making, fate has closed in upon Andreas by enmeshing him in quickest succession in two erotic entanglements, the first representing the perfect realization of a man's idyllic wish-dream, while the second involves a ghastly psycho-physical ordeal and a bloody tragedy. (Hermann Broch referred to Andreas' night with Hildegard as "the most nauseating love story ever written.") After another ten years' interval, we have a final glimpse of Andreas, now grotesquely transformed into an obese and inert animal mass, indicating, it would seem, complete and irrevocable surrender to the aimless activity of a routine existence. But the unpredictable happens. As he sits on that winter afternoon in the cold of the open window, swathed and padded, ringed by concentric layers of fat, shuffling his accounts, a wave of Reality somehow manages to penetrate through the multiple armor to the very core of his self. He listens; contact with the All is reestablished; the blinding clarity of super-reality is upon him. There is a prolonged moment of ultra-conscious self-examination in terms of the Whole. Judge and defendant in one, he comes to understand, he confesses, he passes judgment on himself, he is absolved. Then he puts a bullet through his temple.

The structural identity that obtains between Hermann Broch and Andreas is not subject to challenge. Broch is Andreas, as he is Vergil in his hour of death. Like his author, the individual Andreas is an introvert with hypersensitive antennae that record the interplay of invisible waves that shuttle between points of the multi-dimensional space-time frame of the self. Modern photography, with its luminous tracery of the movements of a violinist's bow in physical space, supplies a simple visual analogy for the infinitely complex invisible dynamics of perception and association on all the levels of memory and consciousness and organic sensation in the matrix of the self. Where Andreas' experience is concerned, Broch heightens our awareness of its dynamics, conjuring up a luminous tracery of its pattern before the inner eye. The other characters, except for the Grandfather, who is also Broch, are peripheral and seen from without. Andreas is seen from within. The incidents that add up to the shadowy outline of Andreas' biography are, of course, purely fictional, but his way of experiencing life is Broch's own, Andreas is "entscheidungsschüchtern" ["indecisive"] . . . and "schicksalsgläubig" ["fatalistic"]. . . . These key terms formulate the bond that unites the author's self with its fictional projection in his hero. And to a marked degree, not so easy to define, this identity extends to the complexes that govern the organization of Andreas' experience—the father complex (negative), the mother complex (positive), and the complex of insecurity and anxiety. But these complexes, assuming their autobiographical roots, loom also as universal symbols of conflicting age-old drives in the self, and it is by virtue of these complexes that the individual Andreas comes to be felt in the end as a symbol of mankind.

As for the Grandfather, he exists on a surrealistic level. Complementary to Andreas and his experience of the unfathomable complexity of life, he is the principle of unity—totality, made concrete in one of Broch's most characteristic acts of creation. Psychologically he is the super-ego, the voice of conscience. Religiously speaking, he is the divine spark in man—"das Absolutheitsfünklein" that is never quite extinguished. This is clearly his function in that final appearance of his where he induces Andreas to stop hedging and stand squarely face to face with his conscience. What makes him so eerie a figure is the fact that he assumes his surreal status almost imperceptibly—unlike Peer Gynt's Button-Moulder, who reveals himself as an emissary from the Beyond in unmistakable fashion, so that henceforth our footing is secure on the supernatural level to which we have shifted. Throughout the dialectic colloquy between Andreas and his visitor, on the other hand, the specks never cease to dance before our eyes. This blind, white-bearded, white-maned adamantine dynamo of cosmic song hails from the same region of the mythopoeic imagination as Lysanias, the swarthy peasant youth from Andes in the *Virgil,* who turns into Hermes-Telesphoros, the divine guide of souls. Both figures start on a level of reality and transcend it later. There is a hint, to be sure, in the elevated lyrical tone of the **"Ballade vom Imker,"** of the transformation that the ex-artisan, turned wandering teacher and "Bienenvater" ["bee-keeper"], is destined to undergo. And if we recall the veneration accorded the bee in ancient myth we realize that the wanderer's association with the bee is designed to invest him with a divine aura. How many other areas of myth have contributed to the figure of the blind singer, I could not venture to say. But I happened upon one—certainly not fortuitous—correspondence too remarkable to overlook. The old man's final appearance is prepared for by a weird music that deliberately conjures up in the reader the strains of the finale of Mozart's *Don Giovanni* (a resurgence of the Don Juan motif, enigmatically baffling as concerns the plot of the story). Blended with this music the crashing blows of a wood-cutter's axe are heard. All this is symbolic, of course, of the hour of destiny having arrived. But this is exactly the situation in the Finnish folk-epic *Kalevala,* where Kullervo, the child, who is at the same time a giant-god, fashions an axe

to fell the forest. In Karl Kerényi's account of the divine "Holzfäller" ["woodcutter"] we read: "Das Roden wird in fürchterlichem Ausmasszuerst durch diese Axt, sodann—wie es dem Geiste der finnischen Epik noch mehr entspricht—durch magischen Gesang vollbracht" ["The clearing is accomplished to a terrible extent first by this ax, then—still further in accordance with the spirit of the Finnish epic—by magical song"]. Kerényi's name was never mentioned in our conversations, but among Hermann Broch's papers, deposited in Yale, there is his report to a publisher on another manuscript of Kerényi's to show, if external proof were needed, how intimately familiar Broch was with the interpretation of myth as practiced by Carl Gustav Jung and his school.

The story, **"Steinerner Gast,"** in which Andreas faces his hour of destiny is, in my opinion, one of Hermann Broch's very greatest pieces of writing. This warrants calling attention to a companion piece that expresses a variant of the same situation in another medium. It is an intimate lyric poem of thirty-five lines, in the first person, entitled **"Der Urgefährte,"** and in the cryptic condensation of its code language it is perhaps the most beautiful formulation of Hermann Broch's wisdom. What interests us here is the visionary setting to which the poet tells of himself as awakening: a dark room into which snow has drifted; a silent, frozen river outside; the door ajar and, limned in its frame, the figure of a man who has been absent on a long journey. He is instantly recognized. There he stands, clothed in ice, the shepherd, the ageless, ancestral companion come to summon the sleeper to the stern journey. With his coming the substantiality of existence is dissolved along with the outlines of the words that grope for new affinities. . . . (pp. 323-31)

In our approach to *Die Schuldlosen* we have limited our concern to those figures that are linked with the author by a deep bond of identification. When I said above, however, that the other figures are seen from without, whereas Andreas and the Grandfather are seen from within, I was guilty of an unavoidable over-simplification. The fact is that all of them, whether limited and arrogant like Zacharias, tortured like Philippine, undeveloped in her loveliness like Melitta, vacuous like the old Baroness, voraciously uninhibited in their animal instincts like Zerline, or rigidly sclerotic like Hildegard—they all have moments of levitation, when the divine spark re-fuses the chain of being, when their eyes are opened to the perception of a reality that transcends the limits of their isolation. In those moments they are Hermann Broch. More successfully than Andreas, more in the spirit of his Vergil, Hermann Broch divests himself of his particular name in order to be known by all names from A to Z, from Andreas to Zacharias, in order to feel the bond of identification with everything human. (p. 331)

Hermann J. Weigand, "Hermann Broch's 'Die Schuldlosen': An Approach," in PMLA, *68, Vol. LXVIII, No. 3, June, 1953, pp. 323-34.*

SIDONIE CASSIRER   (essay date 1960)

[*In the following excerpt, Cassirer discusses Broch's early philosophical and critical essays.*]

Hermann Broch was already in his forties when his first novel, part of the trilogy *Die Schlafwandler,* appeared in 1931. One continuing result of the prominence which this work brought to Broch has been an almost complete neglect of his few earlier writings. (p. 453)

There are various reasons for this seeming lack of interest in Broch's early writings. Most of these works, consisting of eleven fairly short non-fictional items—many of them extended book reviews as well as a poem and an amusing short story, and all written between 1913 and 1920—were published in magazines of short duration or sporadic publication dates, so that they are not easily accessible. Search is also made difficult because Broch often signed his initials only, particularly in the case of reviews. In addition, when the first bibliography of his work was compiled in 1950-51, Broch wanted it to be selective, since it was intended to reintroduce him to the Austrian public. Because of political developments and the war, his books had been practically unobtainable and even his major novel, *Der Tod des Vergil,* was almost unknown in Austria. In these circumstances Broch did not regret the omission of some of his early and less finished writings in the first bibliography.... If, however, one wants to grasp the remarkable unity and continuity of Broch's thought in his work as a whole, these early publications are indispensable reading.

Most of the early works start out as critical reviews and end as philosophical essays. Broch would not permit himself a judgment without rational examination. His tendency to explain and modify, to examine and synthesize often interferes with his brilliant gift for quick formulation. This constant check and interpretation of intuition stems undoubtedly from Broch's desire for precision, but ironically enough it often results in an ambiguous and even abstruse style.

Broch's standards of judgment emerge quite clearly in these articles. In general, he rejects all thought and art which he considers grounded in "materialism," while all real achievement, intellectual, spiritual, and moral, must have its source in philosophical idealism. Broch never clearly defines the two concepts and equates in effect realism, positivism, materialism, and naturalism, while he conceives "idealism" in its widest sense as an attitude towards truth which seeks to transcend material reality. Fortunately for the Broch scholar, Broch in his critiques devotes much more space to his own ideas on art and the artist than to the writers and the works on which he comments.

The very first article, **"Philiströsität, Realismus, Idealismus der Kunst"** [published in the Austrian magazine *Der Brenner*] . . . , is based on the distinction between "the two great categories of thought" idealism and realism, and follows a polar structure characteristic of much of Broch's art and thought in general. This article is a reply to Carl Dallago, who was an ardent admirer of Nietzsche, a poet of the Tyrolean locale, an essayist and frequent contributor to *Der Brenner,* and the author of a book *Philister* (1912). Dallago had deplored that Thomas Mann, as he felt, had lost his touch as an artist and had become a philistine.

In his answer Broch defines philistinism as a particularly vicious form of realism. Like the realist, the philistine neglects to think in terms of philosophical analysis.... The difference between the realist and the philistine is one of degree, the latter being "a realist of the purest order." . . . The philistine takes an active part in promoting a narrow, materialistic view of ideas and values. When he castigates the philistine writer and with him the religious and the political fanatic, Broch evidently directs himself against the *Bildungsphilister,* a person who mistakenly considers himself educated and who has become the butt of contempt, particularly with Nietzsche.

A philistine, Broch further maintains, can never be a true artist because he lacks an original vision and instead stresses only

technical perfection. On the other hand, realism is also deficient from the point of view of ethics because it leaves no room for the autonomous search for ethical principles. Like a lower form of life, realism lacks a scale of values and is ruled by deterministic laws.... Broch's definition also contains a note of oblique social criticism. While Broch concedes that the group mentality characteristic of realism serves its purpose in maintaining the continuity of society, he blames the "Generationengedächtnis" ["memory of generations"] for fostering undesirable as well as beneficial aspects of social living. He holds this unindividuated form of group mind responsible for "Sympathie, Rassenhass, die Instinkte des Einzelnen, des Volkes, Art und Leben, Institution und Schichtung der Gesellschaft" ["sympathy, racism, the instincts of the individual, of the masses, birth and life, institutionalization and stratification of society"].... What emerges, in fact, in Broch's first published work is the outline of his criticism of the "Spiesser" ["Philistine"] as he appears in the figure of the schoolteacher Antigonus in **"Eine Methodologische Novelle"** ... and, almost thirty-five years later, in the lyrics of the novel *Die Schuldlosen.*

It is significant, in view of Broch's later questioning of the value of art, that in this essay he places art below mysticism and philosophy in the hierarchy of steps that lead to the knowledge of truth. In fact, basing himself on Schopenhauer's esthetics, Broch contends that the artist cannot be a pure idealist, since he deals with the object world, but that, contrary to the philistine, the artist has the ability to transcend the world of materialism to perceive behind the object its "platonic idea," and to manifest his vision in matter. He disagrees with Mann's opinion as expressed in *Der Tod in Venedig* that philosophical sceptical thought is cynicism and in conflict with artistic creativity; that, furthermore, philosophy is an "abyss" which, if Aschenbach's case is typical, can lead to the destruction of art. Thinking in terms of Kantian idealism Broch rejects Mann's narrow view of philosophy: "dies ... ist 'angewandte' Philosophie und eine solche gibt es ebensowenig wie 'angewandte' Kunst ..." ["this ... is 'applied' philosophy, and there is no more such a philosophy than there is 'applied' art"].... If the sceptical, agnostic attitude of philosophical idealism should ultimately interfere with artistic productivity, such a development in the artist—away from art and towards mysticism— becomes "eine weitere Vertiefung des Menschen; kein Sturz in den Abgrund, sondern hellste Auflösung des Seins" ["a great deepening of the man; not a tumble into the abyss, but rather the clearest resolution of being"]. It is characteristic of Broch that he measures art, philosophy, and mysticism in terms of the benefit to the development of the individual personality. He implies that this individualism rests on the cognition of a supra-individual truth. The experience of pure consciousness through mysticism or philosophy surpasses the esthetic experience in what Broch would have called "Erkenntniswert" ["cognitive value"]. Even before Broch had published a line of fiction himself, we find here the expression of his life-long reservation about art which is partly responsible for his tortured and equivocal attitude towards his own work.

In his critique of Mann's novella Broch warmly praises in particular the conscious artistry of *Der Tod in Venedig:* "Ich glaube ... in der Novelle eine ganz ausserordentliche Anspannung des künstlerischen Wollens erblicken zu können und darin auch die Ursache ihrer hohen Vollkommenheit" ["I believe ... one can discern in the novella a wholly extraordinary exertion of artistic intent, and therein the root of its sublime accomplishment"].... The action is a brilliant translation of the law of logic as it is embodied in the main character, Aschenbach, into "the seemingly accidental happenings of material reality." . . . Consistent with his view that the basic esthetic principle of balance can be interpreted also as a "law of nature," Broch describes the structure of the work in terms of a state of dynamic equipoise achieved by the balanced interplay of physical forces. . . . In order to emphasize further the dynamic order of Mann's *Novelle* he also compares its esthetic structure to that of a pyramid or dome "striving towards infinity."

The image of "ein geschlossenes, im Gleichgewicht schwebendes Gebilde" ["a closed formation suspended in balance"], which Broch uses here for the first time, represents a kind of *Urerlebnis,* an archetypal experience, the blueprint of a vision of fluidity and balance that was to haunt him all his life. . . . In his novels and in the short stories, most prominently in **"Vorüberziehende Wolke,"** he returns to this vision of dynamic balance in a variety of scenes and situations. Although the personal relationship between Broch and Thomas Mann always remained within the bounds of respectful distance after their first meeting in 1932, Broch's tribute to the author of *Der Tod in Venedig* could hardly have been personal and sincere than in this praise of the harmony and mastery of this work in his favorite terminology.

Both **"Philiströsität"** and Broch's second article **"Ethik"** point to a phase of Broch's intellectual development which so far has not received attention by Broch scholarship: his early preoccupation with Kant. In his distinction between idealism and realism Broch repeatedly bases himself on Kant and on critical idealism as a frame of reference for all philosophical thinking. His allusions to Kant in **"Philiströsität"** had been incidental. In **"Ethik"** he deals more directly with Kantian philosophy.

"Ethik," too, is a review, a spirited attack on Houston Stewart Chamberlain as author of the book *Immanuel Kant*. It sounds as if Broch wanted to retrieve Kant from the clutches of his emotional and racist admirer Chamberlain. His efforts to remain impersonal in this polemic are not very successful. He points out that Kant was led by his rigorous and objective investigations to a position of "heroic scepticism." He implies that Chamberlain based his thinking on unexamined premises and, as a result, produced a philosophy of "commonplaces of feelings and experience." Kant was original and concerned with the realm of pure thought. Chamberlain remains "weltgebunden," "körpergebunden" ["bound to the earth," "bound to the body"] and never transcends the rationalizations of a group of smug and self-satisfied literati. The great philosopher and the great mystic approach the search for truth with humility. . . . He indirectly accuses Chamberlain of indulging in a sentimental pseudo-mysticism that merely produced "Kitsch." Broch states that Kant's philosophy resigns itself wisely to delimiting truth by the study of the laws of logic and thought ("Denkformen"). It does not and cannot rigidly define content. The reader infers that Chamberlain's interpretation of Kant in terms of a racist outlook violates the methods of objective inquiry and forces truth into a dogmatic straightjacket. Most serious of all, Broch emphatically insists that the aim of all intellectual, spiritual, and artistic achievement is ethics, and he indirectly impugns Chamberlain's intellectual integrity.

While Broch in **"Ethik"** shows himself in agreement with basic aspects of Kantian philosophy—the postulation that mind orders and unifies empirical experience, the methods of logical formalism and the concept of a supra-individual, supra-empirical "pure consciousness" are among them—he was already familiar with Husserl, to whom he refers as "scharfer Denker"

["sharp thinker"] . . . and professes to be aware of the limitations of Kantianism when applied to modern problems. It would be difficult to miss, however, the deeply personal note in Broch's defense of Kantianism as a basis for all subsequent developments in philosophical thinking; in his denunciation in the name of Kant's rigorous intellectuality of "mystische Gefühlsurteile," "materiale Theorien," and "willkürliche Provisorien" ["mystical judgments based on emotion," "material theories," and "arbitrary stipulations"]; in his admiration for Kant's quest for truth which led Broch for the first time to link the depth of rational thinking with the wisdom of mysticism. . . . Broch's tribute to Kant, besides being an indirect blow against Chamberlain, also represents his personal intellectual and ethical credo. It is the sum total of his insistence that the inquiring mind must proceed with intrepidness and exactness and that it must remain objective. In reading over these first two essays one gets the impression that Kant was a *Bildungserlebnis* for Broch and that Broch's knowledge of Kant rests not only on study but on a meeting of minds. Therefore the philosophy of critical idealism and, particularly, Kant's ethics—or perhaps more precisely Kant's own ethical attitude—could provide a kind of general orientation in Broch's personal development which in no way restricted his own thought. (pp. 453-56)

In one important respect **"Philiströsität"** and **"Ethik"** constitute two sides of a coin: while Broch in his first article had emphasized the lack of individualism in the philistine, he stresses in the second the indispensability of individualism for any form of "geistiges Leben" ["spiritual life"]. . . . He develops this idea through his remarks on "solitariness." The term "Einsamkeit" ["solitariness"] becomes the persistent leitmotif of **"Ethik."** Broch regards the realization of man's "terrifying" and "unalterable" solitariness as the key to human existence. It is "die einzige und gewaltigste Tragik des Menschseins" ["the single and most powerful of tragedy of humanity"] . . . , but it is also "the source and touchstone of all intellectual and spiritual pursuits (alles Geistigen)." . . . Broch singles out the elements of "Einsamkeit" in the chief aspects of Kant's philosophy: in his critical method which accepts scepticism as "the source and zero point of all philosophy" . . . ; in his concept of truth which rests on the "eternal loneliness and unity of the ego"; and, finally, in Kant's ethics. The aim of this ethics is "to strengthen man in facing his solitariness" . . . and, in so doing, it alone enables him to live as "geistiger Mensch" ["spiritual man"]. But this rigorous individualism, far from constituting an escape from society, becomes the very basis of social living. For Broch, logic is the basis of ethics. Unethical action seen in this light is primarily an infraction of the intellect and its search for truth. "Wer das Gesetz seines Denkens—nur dieses und kein anderes—verletzt, ist unmoralisch; er wird zum Wahnsinningen und zum Verbrecher" ["He who breaks the law of his reason—only this and no other—is immoral; he will become a madman and a criminal"]. . . . Crime is essentially wrong thought or complacency towards the search for knowledge. The truthfulness of the autonomous ego which cannot lie to itself thus becomes the source of social ethics. (p. 457)

In 1913 *Der Brenner* started a literary inquiry to vindicate Karl Kraus, who had been attacked by the press as the result of a lecture sponsored by the editors of *Der Brenner*. Thomas Mann, Arnold Schoenberg, Oskar Kokoschka, and many other writers and artists were approached for this public defense and Broch joined his testimony to theirs. His admiration of Kraus, though genuine, is tempered somewhat by his respect for the "solitariness'' of the creative artist and thinker, which makes him doubt the appropriateness of a public denonstration such as the *Brenner* inquiry.'' . . . Broch wrote two open letters, the one on behalf of Kraus and one in 1918, **"Die Strasse."** . . . Both reveal a deep-seated fear of ''the masses.'' In **"Die Strasse"** he is critical of the demonstrations of the socialist workers in the streets of Vienna following the downfall of the imperial government and the declaration of peace. In the Kraus letter he speaks out against the intellectual audiences listening to Kraus's lectures in Vienna. His own experience in attending these gatherings of Kraus devotees leads him to say that nothing is as horrible as the crowds who wrongly think they understand but, in reality, only express ''vulgar enjoyment'' of the ''surface'' of Kraus's humor. His strong condemnation in **"Die Strasse"** of the political masses for dragging the eternal ideals of freedom and justice into the vulgar arena of politics differs from the Kraus letter only in degree. Both letters stem from the same source: Broch's idealism and his belief in the autonomous ''solitary'' thinking ego which alone is capable of appreciating intellectual and artistic achievements and alone can produce true social ethics. Seen against the background of these two letters, particularly **"Die Strasse,"** the figure of the fastidious maiden lady in the story **"Vorüberziehende Wolke"** . . . appears not only as social satire but as a satire of Broch's own antipathy to the masses.

After the articles in *Der Brenner* Broch did not publish for several years. *Der Brenner* itself temporarily became a victim of the war in 1915. Broch undoubtedly had to devote more time to his father's textile business, of which he became acting director in 1915. Personal documents also indicate that Broch, at least formally, had been entrusted with the supervision of a military hospital in Teesdorf in 1915 as part of his homeguard duties. Towards the end of the war Broch held official and semi-official positions concerned with various aspects of management and labor relations. He tells in his autobiography that this practical work provided him with valuable experience but

A letter from Broch to his friend and editor Daniel Brody.

also strengthened his desire for theoretical studies. Indeed, since his work brought him frequently to Vienna he could keep in personal contact with other writers and artists, and the years 1916-19 proved to be a productive literary period for Broch as well. Two articles, **"Zum Begriff der Geisteswissenschaften"** . . . and **"Konstruktion der Historischen Wirklichkeit"** . . . , show his preoccupation with the philosophy of history. A publisher's announcement of monographs in preparation even lists a ''Theory of Values'' by Broch which, however, seems never to have seen the light of print. Paul Schrecker, who knew Broch well, also recalls having seen at that time a longer manuscript by Broch in the field of symbolic logic. These studies evidently were lost or were reworked in Broch's later essays. (pp. 458-59)

In his two philosophical essays Broch attempts a critique of the positivist approach to history. In **"Zum Begriff der Geisteswissenschaften"** he maintains that positivism cannot be ''philosophically'' exact, i.e. possess objective validity, because it is dependent on phenomena, on facts and quantities, while objectively valid inquiry depends on the intellectual framework, the system, given to phenomena by the prior activity of the mind. He then turns to the example of Dilthey as the most distinguished representative of ''Geisteswissenschaft'' [''the humanities''] and examines how it was possible for Dilthey to produce significant work in spite of his professed positivistic approach. He finds the answer in Dilthey's gift of artistic vision, of ''Erschauen,'' that is, in an individual quality and not in a generally valid method. Dilthey's achievements, he concludes, were solely due to his personal genius and hence he could not found a school. His imitators inevitably remained journalistic.

What is historical reality, and how can we understand a period through an objective method rather than personal intuition? These are the questions which occupy Broch in **"Konstruktion der historischen Wirklichkeit."** To the first one he answers that only ethical aims and ideals constitute the significant forces that shape and express a period. . . . Having narrowed history and its essential data in this way, Broch suggests by way of answer to the second point that the historian must inquire into the values of the ethically conscious individual of a period. This type of historical research has an objective basis. Ethos, Broch reiterates, is subordinate to Logos and therefore the mind can provide a bridge of understanding between one period and another. On the other hand, ethical aims and actions take in also non-rational factors and Broch hopes therefore that an analysis of the values of a period might incidentally yield clues also to these indefinable forces. The solution Broch offers, beneath a web of reasoning so intricate that it may have led this and many another reader astray, sounds oversimplified. But even from this sketchy outline it is easy to see that this essay forms a kind of prelude to *Die Schlafwandler.* Here Broch succeeded in combining personal artistic vision and objective analysis in treating a historical period by inquiring into the values of its typical representatives.

As contributor to *Summa* Broch also found time to continue his work as literary critic. Within the short space of a year (1917-18) he published three articles on such disparate personalities as Zola, Heinrich v. Stein, and Morgenstern. In every case Broch makes basic philosophical assumptions similar to those of the earlier works.

Broch's article **"Zolas Vorurteil,"** in its attack on naturalism and its preference for Dostoyevski, follows a trend characteristic of German and Austrian writers at the time. More interesting is Broch's reasoning. He ascribes Zola's strong points to his innate genius, to his unusual gift for apprehending and transcribing reality. These qualities are vitiated by Zola's materialism, that is, by his equating of reality and truth, two terms between which Broch, as an idealist, draws a sharp distinction. "Oh, nie," he exclaims, "war die Wahrheit (nicht die Wirklichkeit) in schlechteren Händen als hier, da sie an diesen gewaltigsten Unkünstler der Literatur geriet" ["Oh, never was truth (not reality) in worse hands than here, where it fell into those of this most violent un-artist of literature"]. . . . Zola's inability to portray individuals, his sentimentality whenever he deals with personal emotions are also directly traceable to his materialism. But for Broch Zola presented an ethical even more than an esthetic problem: as a Jew he felt impelled to admire Zola's act of moral courage during the Dreyfus Affair, an admiration that was shared by a large part of the non-Jewish German intelligentsia, yet as a philosophical idealist he questioned the intellectual basis of Zola's ethical stand. It is typical of Broch that he merely hints at this, probably the focal point of the entire article, in the following ambiguous sentence which could refer either to Zola's famous letter or to the strain of social criticism that pervades all his novels: "Zolas Grösse: das fürchterliche j'accuse, das aus der kausalen Wirklichkeit seines Objektes klingt und sein Werk durchhallt" ["Zola's greatness: that dreadful j'accuse that rings from the causal reality of his subject and penetrates his work"]. . . . . In his evaluation of Zola, Broch seems to imply that there existed a fundamental incongruity between Zola's spontaneous thought and action and the absence of a satisfactory philosophical basis for his ethics as well as his esthetics. Broch's criticism of Zola thus comes to a rather inconclusive ending. The reader is left with the impression that Broch was not able to resolve the problem of Zola, an impression confirmed by the frequent reappearance of Zola's name in Broch's later critical writings. In **"Das Böse im Wertsystem der Kunst"** . . . , for example, he cites as an illustration of "Kitsch" not one of the myriad inane love stories but Zola's *Quatre Evangiles.* (pp. 459-60)

To be sure, Broch's logical constructions in [his critical] articles tell us little about the characteristic aspects of naturalism or satire, about the uniqueness of Zola or Morgenstern or any of the other writers he discusses, since he essentially limits himself to the position that the shortcomings of these authors are the result of a professed or recondite positivist outlook. Yet, reading these articles one also becomes aware of an undercurrent of social and ethical consciousness. Three of the five men on whom he chose to write, Chamberlain, Zola, and v. Stein, had, or at least Broch associated them with, political ideologies. The fourth review, on Thomas Mann, is indirectly a criticism of Carl Dallago, one of those well-meaning but confused followers of Nietzsche who with the best intentions and high personal integrity saw war mainly as a means to overcome the almost obese philistinism of his period. In his ideas on satire it is furthermore Karl Kraus, not Morgenstern, to whom Broch gives highest praise. Karl Kraus, however—although Broch does not mention that aspect of his writings—was well known for his courageous stand before and during the war against the pen-brandishing journalists who advanced the causes of a red-blooded nationalism and of war.

These early articles constitute in a sense the rough draft of the critique of his time which Broch then perfected in *Die Schlafwandler* and in subsequent works. His chief concern, as far back as his first writings, was ethical, even social, although this is not immediately apparent here, since Broch believed that wrong action was merely an outgrowth of wrong thinking and of the absence of thought. Hence for him the problem of intellectual integrity represented the key problem. Basing himself on Kant, he stated that social as well as individual ethics are founded on the dignity of the autonomous intelligible ego and he was convinced that all achievement, whether in politics, art, scholarship, or philosophy must be directed towards a humanism predicated on the intellectual integrity of the individual. This criticism of the intellectual climate of his time, the expression of his belief in the ideal of "Menschentum, Menschlichkeit in der Einsamkeit des Geistes—Ethik" ["humanity, humanness in the solitariness of the spirit—ethics"] . . . represents the first step in the gradual formulation of his ultimate ethos of "Anständigkeit" ["decency"] voiced in the divine command: "Sei fromm um Meinetwillen, selbst ohne Zugang zu Mir; das sei dein Anstand, die stolze Demut, die dich zum Menschen macht. Und siehe, das genügt" ["Be pious for My sake, without access to Me; this be your moral, the proud humility that makes you human. And behold, that will suffice"]. (pp. 461-62)

　　　　Sidonie Cassirer, "Hermann Broch's Early Writings," in PMLA, 75, Vol. LXXV, No. 4, September, 1960, pp. 453-62.

D. J. ENRIGHT　(essay date 1966)

[*Enright is an English man of letters who has spent most of his career abroad, teaching English literature at universities in Egypt, Japan, Berlin, Thailand, and Singapore. The author of critically respected works in a variety of genres, he is best known for his poetry, which is conversational in style and often reflects his humanistic values in portraits of Far Eastern life. According to William Walsh, "Enright is a poet with a bias toward light and intelligibility," and his critical essays are frequently marked by sardonic treatment of what he considers culturally pretentious literature. In the following excerpt, he criticizes* The Death of Virgil *as a ponderous and unfocused work of fiction.*]

Hermann Broch's enormous trilogy, ***The Sleepwalkers*** . . . , begins with old Herr von Pasenow, an excellent short sketch of character both physical and moral. It ends with a long and rebarbatively abstract epilogue, the tenth installment of a sequence of similar disquisitions on the "Disintegration of Values" which sadly weaken the impact and hardly clarify the significance of the third part of the trilogy. ***The Death of Virgil*** . . . constitutes a marked advance, or prolongation, in the direction indicated by the philosophizing parts of the earlier work, though with this difference: that the reflections of the dying Virgil, while equally abstract, are largely unargued, they proceed less by logic than by what alas is called "poetry," sometimes reminding us of *Thus Spake Zarathustra,* but rarefied, diluted, and inflated, lacking in pointedness and in Nietzsche's dubious yet undoubted excitement.

Formally ***The Death of Virgil*** has been described more or less aptly by a number of admirers. Thus Hannah Arendt calls it an "uninterrupted flow of lyrical speculation leading through the last twenty-four hours of the dying poet" [see excerpt dated 1949]. (H. M. Waidson estimates it at eighteen hours: to me both estimates *seem* highly conservative.) And George Steiner has said that the book "represents the only genuine technical advance that fiction has made since *Ulysses.*" But few critics, so far as I know, have attempted to ascertain the success, as distinct from the intention, of the novel, and the usefulness, rather than the nature, of the technique. Two questions are provoked by the descriptions I have just quoted. Could it be that what a flow of lyrical speculation needs is precisely to be interrupted from time to time by the unlyrical and the known? And can a technical advance be "genuinely" an advance if its prime effect is to produce unreadability? But then, the argument of *The Death of Virgil* is so abstract, assertive yet evasive, so highflown and yet so narrow in compass, that one hardly feels inclined to study it with the closeness that a critical appraisal would require. It is safer to exclaim, "A great European novel!" and leave it at that. Which, fair enough, will serve to warn off the great majority of potential readers.

In form *The Death of Virgil* consists of almost continuous interior monologue, in sentences so long that their beginnings are forgotten before their ends are known. The monologue is interrupted by a conversation between Virgil and Augustus of a length and earnestness which no sick man could possibly sustain, and a scene with Virgil's friends which, modest as it is, seems to me much nearer the sublime than anything else in the work. The book's speculative profundity can be indicated by a few quotations. "What we seek is submerged and we should not seek it as it mocks us by its very undiscoverability." Or "Only he who is able to perceive death is also able to perceive life." Broch's prose poetry is rather similar to Rilke's poetry deprived of most of what makes it poetry, or occasionally reminiscent of the more sanctimonious or portentous lines of *Four Quartets*. ". . . The evil of man's imprisoned soul, the soul for which every liberation turns into a new imprisonment, again and again." The style is heavily paradoxical. "Shadowily projecting the formless into form, and floating between non-being and being . . ." ". . . this always known yet never known goal." It is the old Germanic taste for picturing the unpictureable, defining the indefinable, uttering the unutterable. . . . For one who aims at "the word beyond speech," Broch displays a most remarkable fluency in the written word.

Even the highest and most subtle speculation must have something to speculate about. The main subject for speculation here, the meatiest bone in a voluminous soup of words, is art, beauty, or poetry—and those grave doubts about the propriety of art which loom large in German writing, from Goethe and before to Thomas Mann and after. Striving "to build up the imperishable from things that perish," art is "pitiless toward human sorrow." Beauty is cruelty, "the growing cruelty of the unbridled game . . . the voluptuous, knowledge-disdaining pleasure of an earthly sham-infinity. . . ." The poet is "unwilling to help," unable to help; "shy of communion and locked in the prison of art," he depicts kings, heroes and fable-shepherds: but real human people, the men and women in the street whose curses Virgil hears from his sick-bed—these mean nothing to him. The poet therefore is a "perjurer," he perjures reality. In itself the idea is certainly worthy of attention, but the argument spins in claustrophobic circles, for the most part swathed in language which you cannot get your fingers round, so that before long it comes to seem hardly more meaningful than (say) the assertion that coffee-drinking is a cause of cancer. Is poetry really *that* bad? *How* bad is that bad? Are poets worse than mass-murderers? What poetry? Which poets? "The concern of art was how to maintain equilibrium, the great equilibrium at the transported periphery, and its unspeakably floating and fugitive symbol, which never reflected the isolated content of things but only their interconnections, this being the only way in which the symbol fulfilled its function, since it was only through this interconnection that the contradictions of existence fell into a balance, in which alone the various contradictory trends of the human instincts were comprehended. . . ."

It might seem high irony indeed to read immediately thereafter that "the gracebearing savior was one who has cast off from himself the language of beauty . . . he has pushed on to simple words . . . the simple language of spontaneous kindness, the language of spontaneous human virtue, the language of awakening." This, perhaps, is Virgil's prefiguration of the language of Christ. The habitual language of *The Death of Virgil*—with all due respect to the author, who wrote the book while a refugee from Nazi Germany—is undeniably one of those Germanic languages which Günter Grass assaults in *Dog Years:* it is a way of almost not saying anything. Broch is obviously a conscious victim of this un-Christlike verbalism, and not a linguistic miscreant. His very diagnosis is symptomatic. Remembering Erich Heller's comment that Thomas Mann's *Doctor Faustus* is "its own critique, and that in the most thorough going manner imaginable," we might cleverly propose that *The Death of Virgil* too is a thorough-going critique of itself. But then it will surely have to be admitted that the discrepancy between the vastness of the critique . . . and the slightness of what is being criticized is disconcertingly pronounced.

"Peasants are the real people," says Virgil in one of his few undecorated statements. Poets aren't people at all: by striving to rise above, they fall below. And so Virgil desires to burn his *Aeneid*. Virgil is made to regret his poetry—and made to regret it in Broch's ineffable poetic prose. . . . Happily Caesar, to whom the work is dedicated, does not wait for the things that are his to be rendered unto him: he takes them. Augustus orders the manuscript to be carted off in a chest. What Broch thinks of this behavior—collusion between art and the State?—it is impossible to say. And Virgil has no choice but to make his will and die. (pp. 19-20)

    D. J. Enright, "Uttering the Unutterable," in The New York Review of Books, *Vol. V, No. 11, January 6, 1966, pp. 19-20.*

THEODORE ZIOLKOWSKI   (essay date 1967)

[*An American educator and critic, Ziolkowski is best known as the author of* The Novels of Hermann Hesse *(1965) and as the editor of numerous English translations of Hesse's works. He is also the author of the biographical and critical study* Hermann Broch *(1964). A professor of German language and literature, Ziolkowski contends that literature cannot be studied from a single national perspective; accordingly, throughout his career he has promoted the value of comparative literary studies. In the following excerpt, Ziolkowski discusses Broch's incorporation of relativity theory into his fiction, particularly into the narrative technique of* The Sleepwalkers.]

"For about thirty years," Broch wrote in 1949, "I have been wrestling with the question of the *observer in the field of observation*—a question that first occurred to me in connection with the theory of relativity and from which I have learned that positivistic means afford no satisfactory solution." It would be no exaggeration to say that the theory of relativity, and specifically the problem of the observer, supplied one of the central and most meaningful metaphors of Broch's thought. This preoccupation is soon apparent to anyone who peruses his letters and essays. Time and again his thinking on the greatest variety of topics—from ethics and epistemology to aesthetics and literary criticism—is reduced to the phenomenon of the observer in the field of observation.

This obsession with relativity is conspicuous on various levels of his fiction as well. Most superficially, it provides subject matter, atmosphere, and means of characterization. A rather amusing example occurs in the early novel—Broch's least impressive work—*The Unknown Quantity*. . . . The short novel relates a critical year in the life of a young mathematician, Richard Hieck. Hieck's passion for orderliness and clarity have led him to mathematics, which he regards as an ''island of decency'' in the midst of a world of uncertainty and irrationality. In the course of the novel, love and death encroach upon the mathematically ordered world of young Dr. Hieck, undermining the categories according to which he had attempted to live and showing that the important matters of life are often not accessible of rational explanation. (The novel is in one sense an attack on logical positivism.)

One evening Hieck invites a girl friend, who is also a mathematician, to visit the observatory where he works. Neither of the two feels at ease. Hieck, taking refuge in shop-talk, begins to expatiate on ''the Einsteinean macrocosm.'' He hustles her through the observatory, talking about such topics as ''the cosmogony of the relativity theory.'' But all his efforts to remain objective and impersonal somehow fail. ''They stepped outside. Richard had again taken up his lecture and now arrived at Einstein's hypothesis concerning curved space, whose expansion and restriction is supposed to condition the movement of the great stellar systems.'' But through all his pontifications the girl senses that ''here the cosmos was being exercised for something that had rather little to do with mathematical formulation—for something that stood, supercosmic, powerful, behind any precise expressibility.'' Despite all Richard's rationality, the irrational—the ''unknown quantity'' of the title—intrudes into his life: love. The irony of the intellectual whose elaborate systems turn out to be no defense against the power of emotion is delightful. And it is brought forth in a scene built around the theory of relativity.

In his last novel, *The Innocents* . . . , Broch once more exploited the theory of relativity as a means of ironic characterization. In Chapter Seven the still unnamed hero A. has a conversation with the mathematics teacher Zacharias. (Their initials are supposed to indicate the great disparity between the complete emotional lability of A. and the irrational commitments of Zacharias.) The two men have met, during the 'twenties, at an assembly protesting against the theory of relativity. A. is present not out of any strong conviction—he tends to be indifferent about everything—but he approves intuitively of the theory of relativity because he feels that it reflects his own moral relativism. Zacharias has a more complex attitude. As a Social Democrat he is theoretically in favor of Einstein because the theory of relativity implies liberalism and progress. As a mathematician, however, the theory ''repelled him because of its difficulty,'' and he opposes its acceptance in the academic curriculum of the high schools. ''Precisely that had to be prevented, irrespective of its correctness or incorrectness. How could one practice the profession of teaching if one were compelled to learn continually new material? Wasn't it the same as giving the pupil a free hand in posing impertinent questions fraught with embarrassment? Didn't the teacher have a well founded claim to a certain conclusiveness of knowledge?''

Such passages are amusing and symptomatic of Broch's interests, but they prove very little. Anyone can use the theory of relativity for ironic characterization. In Aldous Huxley's *Point Counter Point* Illidge is ''sadly worried'' by Einstein and Eddington, but for reasons precisely opposed to those of his counterpart Zacharias. As a scientist, namely, Illidge feels that he should accept the theory of relativity, ''but his principles

make him fight against any scientific theory that's less than fifty years old.'' Likewise, when Joyce, in *Finnegans Wake,* speaks of ''the dime-cash problem'' and the ''whoo-whoo and where's hairs theorics of Winestain,'' we laugh knowingly and appreciate the pun. But the references remain wholly superficial and tell us nothing about the impact of the theory of relativity on Joyce and Huxley. Broch is of interest, by contrast, precisely because his concern with relativity goes far beyond its casual use for plot or atmosphere, which can be found in dozens of twentieth-century novels. In Broch's works the theory of relativity has pierced to the very structural heart of his fiction. He does not merely use theory of relativity as subject matter. He attempts to reshape the principles of narrative so as to reflect this important turning-point in modern science. He wants, as a novelist, *to look at reality as the scientist does*. This is an important distinction, for it separates Broch from two groups of writers frequently cited as evidence of the impact of science—or more specifically, relativity—on fiction.

Many writers of our century have produced novels about science. I will mention only two successful and well known examples: C. P. Snow's *The Search* (1934) and Heinrich Schirmbeck's *If Thine Eye Offend Thee* (1957). Both of these novels deal with physics in an informed and sophisticated manner. C. P. Snow, of course, is himself a scientist of international repute; Schirmbeck is a former science reporter with a firm grasp of modern physics and cybernetics. Their novels are informative and technically accurate; they are good, if not great, fiction. But in both cases—and this is the important point—the novels are written in the traditional style of nineteenth-century narrative. Apart from the subject matter there is nothing in these works to indicate that they are ''modern.'' The radicalization of subject matter has had no impact whatsoever upon the style and structure. Though theory of relativity is mentioned repeatedly, it does not have the least bearing on the authors' approach to their fiction.

There are writers like Kafka and Joyce, on the other hand, whose fiction in its radicality often seems to reflect certain developments in modern science. But since the authors themselves are at most casually acquainted with the scientific innovations of the century, there can be no question of a conscious attempt to adapt scientific discoveries to the exigencies of fiction. Joyce makes puns on the name of Einstein and the time-space problem. Kafka, in some of his works, depicts a physical reality that seems to reflect conceptions of relativity (e.g. the landscape of *The Castle* or the temporal system of *The Country Doctor*). In both cases it is sometimes helpful to call on terms borrowed from relativity theory to characterize the literary phenomenon—but always with the explicit awareness that we are using the terms strictly as illuminating metaphors and in no technical sense! For neither Kafka nor Joyce was attempting consistently to apply the principles of relativity to fiction. In the one case, then, we have scientific modernity of content without modernity of form; in the other case modernity of form without a corresponding scientific intent. Most twentieth-century writers fit into one of these two categories.

A few writers, however, have combined both aspects: a detailed knowledge of science and an experimental sense capable of producing new literary forms. In recent years one thinks of Lawrence Durrell or Alain Robbe-Grillet. During the 'twenties and 'thirties in Germany a group of writers emerged whom it is now fashionable to designate as *poetae docti:* writers who exploited their scientific training in order to produce fiction or poetry of a radically new sort—Gottfried Benn, Alfred Döblin,

Robert Musil. Of all these, none was more consistently radical than Hermann Broch. In Broch we have a writer with the technical competence to comprehend the full implications of the theory of relativity. At the same time, he had the literary ability and ambition to conceive new techniques whereby those scientific insights could be made fruitful for literature. Only in such cases, I believe, are we justified in speaking of the influence of relativity theory in literature. In C. P. Snow and Heinrich Schirmbeck it remains pure subject matter; in the case of Joyce and Kafka, relativity theory can supply terms that are useful in criticism, but the terms remain metaphors. In Broch's works, however, the principles of relativity have had a profound impact on the structure of the works themselves, helping to reshape the very form of the modern novel.

Broch has been called, appropriately, a writer *malgré lui* ["in spite of himself"] since he came to literature late in life and only after he had concluded that literature offered better possibilities as a vehicle of philosophy than the logical positivism that dominated most philosophical thinking of the 'twenties. By the same token he could be called a mathematician manqué. As a boy, Broch felt himself strongly fascinated by physics and mathematics. But family pressures forced him into technical studies so that he could eventually take over the family textile mills near Vienna. During these years of practical training Broch got no closer to his intellectual love than business and insurance mathematics. But as soon as he became reasonably independent, around 1910, he undertook his studies again and, with the help of friends and tutors from the University of Vienna, kept up as well as possible with the exciting advances in physics and mathematics during the age of relativity, collecting in the process a three-thousand volume library of mathematical and philosophical works. By the early 'twenties Broch was familiar with the theory of relativity in professional detail. In 1929, when he enrolled as a special student at the University of Vienna, he came under the influence of such scholars as the mathematician Hans Hahn and the philosopher Moritz Schlick, two of the founders of the Viennese school of logical positivism. This exposed Broch to the philosophical implications of relativity theory and, at the same time, precipitated his disenchantment with academic philosophy. Since philosophy, he felt, had reneged on its responsibility to treat human problems and dealt only with matters accessible of mathematical proof, the traditional questions of philosophy had to take refuge in literature. This attitude explains Broch's remark about the insufficiency of positivism in the letter cited in the first paragraph; and it helps to explain the ironic approach to a character like Richard Hieck, who believes at first that pure rationalism can cope with all situations that arise in life. And finally: this epistemological conception of literature accounts for Broch's efforts to translate the theory of relativity into literary terms.

The primary problem, of course, was to find a means of rendering the theory of relativity, or some aspect of it, in a form adequate for fictional representation. This is a problem that obsessed Broch constantly in his letters and essays from 1930 on. Interestingly, his reflections on relativity and fiction revolve from the very beginning around the phenomenon of Joyce. In 1930 Broch wrote to a friend that *Ulysses* is "a totally inconsiderate book" inasmuch as it completely ignores the reader. In every work of art, he argues, there is "the Platonic idea of an 'effect'"; hence incomprehensibility must be regarded as an ethical defect in any work. He justifies this view by establishing "a kind of parallel to the ideal observer who has entered relativity theory as an argument (proving thereby, moreover, that there are no isolated intellectual phenomena

and that whatever holds true in one area—physics, for instance—must also be found in another fashion in aesthetics and everywhere else)."

This passage contains two points of relevance. First, the parenthetical remark reveals the synoptic thinking so characteristic of Broch. Indeed, for him there are no isolated intellectual phenomena. As a result, the theory of relativity—or at least its ideal observer—shows up in all phases of his work: from this system of ethics to his theory of knowledge. For this reason Broch strikes us as having an immensely consistent mind. We find the same guiding principles throughout his work, fictional and theoretical alike.

Secondly, this early passage shows us that Broch was already concerned with the practical question of execution: namely, how is it possible to render the ideal observer in fiction? In this letter of 1930 Broch approaches the problem from the point of view of the reader. This, as he says, is ethically important; the writer must make himself comprehensible to an ideal observer—the reader—who receives the "effect" of the work. But it is not a very helpful idea from the standpoint of composition. Broch soon worked out another possibility of application, and it was again in connection with Joyce that he formulated his idea. In an important essay on **"James Joyce and the Present"** . . . he talked at length about relativity. But it will be noticed that the ideal observer is no longer thought of as being an idealized reader, for the reader is a factor beyond the control of the writer. Rather, it is an ideal narrator built, as it were, into the work of art itself and hence subject to narrative control. *Ulysses*, Broch contends,

> surely has nothing to do with the theory of relativity; the term is not mentioned a single time in the novel. And yet it can be argued with some justification that the epistemological essence of the theory of relativity is given in the discovery of the logical medium within the physical sphere of observation. What I mean is this. Classical physics was content to observe and to measure the phenomena to be studied; it took into consideration the means of observation, the act of viewing, only insofar as this observation contained sources of error—whether through the insufficiency of the human sensory organs or that of the earthly measuring instruments. The theory of relativity has discovered, however, that there is a source of error beyond the error in principle: namely the act of viewing itself, the observation in itself. It concluded, therefore, that in order to avoid this source of error, the viewer and his act of viewing, an ideal observer and an ideal act of viewing, must be drawn into the field of observation. In short, a theoretical unity of physical object and physical subject must be created.

After we have recovered from our astonishment at finding a passage of this sort in an ostensibly literary essay on Joyce, we note that Broch's statement is a very precise recapitulation of the principle of the observer in the theory of relativity. Then Broch continues:

> It is no insult to the theory of relativity if we draw a parallel to literature. The classical novel was content with the observation of real and psychic circumstances of life and was content

to describe them with the means of language. The main requirement was simply: to view a piece of nature through a temperament. You portrayed something and, to this end, used language as a ready-made instrument. What Joyce does is essentially more complicated. In his work we constantly sense an awareness that one cannot simply put the object into a sphere of observation and describe it. Rather, the *subject* of representation, that is the "narrator as idea," and no less the language with which he describes the object of representation, belong there as means of representation. What he is trying to create is a unity of object of representation and means of representation in the broadest sense.

Broch's language, as is all too often the case in his essays, is unnecessarily ponderous. And the difficulty of grasping what he is driving at is aggravated by the fact that he develops his ideas in an essay ostensibly about Joyce, who would probably have been astonished to find his novel discussed in these terms. In fact, the whole passage makes more sense if it is read as a commentary on and as a theoretical justification of Broch's own novel, *The Sleepwalkers.* . . . Since it was his first work; since it had a relatively long period of composition (from 1928 to 1932); and since Broch wrote it during the very period when he was working out his ideas regarding relativity and the ideal observer, *The Sleepwalkers* is a particularly revealing document in this connection. Moreover, the essay on Joyce merely states a general principle; the application of that principle is still a technical matter that varies from text to text and that can best be determined by a close textual analysis. Let us consider two examples.

On the surface the first volume of the trilogy, *Pasenow or Romanticism,* seems to be a rather traditional narrative related very much in the style of the realistic novel of the later nineteenth century. The plot, certainly, is one that can be found in many novels in England, France, or Germany around the turn of the century: a young officer falls in love with a girl from the lower classes, but ultimately throws her over in order to marry a lady of his own social class. Broch makes a surprisingly original and fascinating novel of this trivial plot, with implications that are of particular interest for depth psychology. But we are concerned here with the style of the work. It turns out that we become very uncomfortable as we read. The narrative, which begins so innocently, seems to shift and change its focus under our very eyes. At no point do we find a narrative voice with which we can identify as we do in the traditional realistic novel.

> In the year 1888 Herr von Pasenow was seventy, and there were people who felt an extraordinary and inexplicable repulsion when they saw him coming towards them in the streets of Berlin, indeed, who in their dislike of him actually maintained that he must be an evil old man. . . . When he gazed in the mirror he recognized there the face that had returned his gaze fifty years before. Yet though Herr von Pasenow was not displeased with himself, there were people whom the looks of this old man filled with discomfort, and who could not comprehend how any woman could ever have looked upon him or embraced him with desire in her

> eyes; and at most they would allow him only the Polish maids on his estate, and held that even these he must have got round by that slightly hysterical and yet arrogant aggressiveness which is often characteristic of small men. Whether this was true or not, it was the belief of his two sons, and it goes without saying that he did not share it.

Anyone who looks closely at this passage will see what Broch has done. Although the paragraph contains certain statements of simple fact, every statement containing any sort of ethical judgment is conditioned by the intrusion of a *subject* of observation who makes his comment on the *object* of observation, Herr von Pasenow: "there were people who"; "When he gazed in the mirror"; "there were people whom"; "they would allow . . . and held that"; "it was the belief of his two sons." The seeming "objectivity" of the realistic novel has given way to the relativity of the modern point of view. The entire first part is narrated consistently in this manner. Although there is no personal narrator, every observation is tied somehow to an observing subject, to a "narrator as idea." This narrator, who enters the narrative field of observation (as Broch puts it), has no existence outside the language of the novel. The "people who" cease to be as soon as that particular sentence ends. They have an existence, so to speak, only within the "system" of that particular statement. This technique differs radically, of course, from the various types of narrator known to traditional fiction: omniscient, personal, first-person, Jamesian, and so forth. It is a structural and stylistic innovation that emerged directly from Broch's preoccupation with the theory of relativity and from his attempt to find a fictional means of representation for the ideal observer of relativity.

The first part of the novel describes an episode from the life of a Prussian junker in 1888. In the second volume the scene shifts, fifteen years later, to the industrial proletariat of the Rhineland. (Here, by the way, a different narrative principle is exploited: instead of a variety of points of view brought to bear on a simple action, we find a single point of view brought to bear on a complicated action.) The third part, finally, carries us fifteen years further along in history to a small town on the banks of the Mosel where the central characters of volumes one and two are brought together with the hero of volume three in the main action of the plot. But more than this: in the third part we have not merely one central narrative, but roughly half a dozen parallel plots in the manner of Dos Passos, each representing a different "narrator as idea."

When he had reached this stage of composition, in the summer of 1931, Broch decided to reshape the third volume radically. Into the narrative strands he interpolated sections of a lyric poem written by a young man named Bertrand Müller, who otherwise appears in none of the episodes of plot. And counterposed against these are ten chapters of a theoretical digression on the theory of values. To make a long story short: by the end of volume three it becomes apparent to the reader that Bertrand Müller is also the author of the philosophical treatise. Since, in turn, the essay refers to incidents in the narrative strands and thus embraces them, Bertrand Müller becomes, by extension, the author of the entire novel—not only of volume three, but by implication of volumes one and two as well. As a result, the narrative of the first two volumes turns out to be subjectively colored by what we learn of the narrator toward the end of volume three. Broch has introduced the "narrator as idea" into the narrative in a form different from that of part one.

This entire play with narrative point of view can be understood only as a corollary to the epistemological theory that Broch developed during the 'twenties and then set down in the theoretical essays of the novel. According to Broch's first thesis, "history is composed of values, since life can be comprehended only in the category of value—yet these values cannot be introduced into reality as absolutes, but can only be thought of in reference to an ethically-motivated value-positing subject." Through the cumbersome language we perceive a theoretical justification of the stylistic technique of volume one, where every value was linked to a "value-positing subject." The second thesis goes on to define the value-positing subject more closely: it cannot be imagined concretely, but "only in the isolation of its selfhood." At this point Broch is no longer talking about the stylistic subjects of volume one, but the more general "value-positing subject" of the entire novel, Bertrand Müller. In order to determine the precise relationship between these two sets of subjects, we must look at Broch's third thesis, which concludes that the entire world is "a product of the intelligible Self." We have, in other words, a relative reality that we can experience and an intelligible Self (or ideal observer) that, existing in its isolation, cannot be experienced. Then how do we get to know it? This is where the value-making subjects of part one come in. The world, namely, is what Broch calls "a relative organization" since it is produced not directly but only mediately by the intelligible Self. The intelligible Self (the ideal observer) posits other value-making subjects (the stylistic subjects of part one, for instance), "which in their turn reflect the structure of the intelligible Self and fashion their own value-products, their own world-formations." These intermediate value-subjects, then, play an immensely important double role. As we saw in our analysis of the opening paragraph, they relativize the reality as it is perceived in the novel, for every value-judgment is linked to one of their innumerable points of view. And at the same time they reflect, in their multiplicity, the structure of the Intelligible Self (the ideal observer).

This last function comes rather as a surprise, for up to this point in the novel—within fifty pages of the end—we had not been aware of the presence of the Intelligible Self. Only now do we begin to understand why Broch found it necessary to introduce the seemingly obtrusive lyrical sections and the theoretical essays into his narrative: Bertrand Müller represents the Intelligible Self, the ideal observer, the ethical center of the novel; the three-stage process is now complete. According to Broch's epistemology, the Intelligible Self posits Value-making Subjects who in turn fashion their own world Formations. In the terms of the novel: Bertrand Müller posits Stylistic or Structural Points-of-view which in turn fashion their own Fictional World. The reader, however, is not aware of this process until the end of the novel. For this reason Broch's technique must be distinguished from the device, say, of the personal narrator so common in fiction from Boccaccio to Thomas Mann.

There, namely, the narrator is a token of authenticity; he represents the voice of the community with which we are expected to identify ourselves and from whose point of view we are expected to regard the action. Once we accept the narrator's voice, we can settle back and view the action "objectively," for we have a fixed standpoint—even if it is an unusual one, like the idiot Benjy in Faulkner's *The Sound and the Fury* or the dwarf Oskar Matzerath in Günter Grass' *The Tin Drum*. With Broch, however, no premium is placed upon the role of narrator as such; we are not enjoying a cozy community of

irony as we do with Goethe or Thomas Mann, for instance, because it is only at the end of three volumes that we even realize that there is a supreme narrator or observer uniting the many mediate subject voices. By then we have already become acquainted with the narrator *within* the fictional world he represents—we see him inside the sphere of observation, so to speak, before we learn that he is the observer. When we finally learn that this figure is the narrator of the entire action, we are forced to perform an act of mental translation in order to rearrange everything we have learned in the light of this new information. Everything that seemed to be "relatively" stable reality is suddenly relativized again by the intrusion of this ideal observer, who has been there all the time without our knowledge. What we have taken to be absolute reality is revealed as a relative system dependent upon this novel's "intelligible Self," Bertrand Müller. Broch has succeeded in translating the theory of relativity into fictional terms by making the reader *experience* the relativization of the world.

In his subsequent novels Broch continued to be obsessed with the problem of the ideal observer and with the "narrator as idea," finding in each case a different solution. But in no novel is his consistency of thought and style more evident than in *The Sleepwalkers*, which contains in its theoretical chapters theory of relativity that informs the structure and style of the work. In the light of Broch's achievement I believe that we should be cautious in using the term "relativity" loosely in connection with literature. We should distinguish strictly between works that display relativity of content without relativity of form (Snow, Schirmbeck) and those that display relativity of form without explicit intention (Kafka, Joyce). And we should reserve the term "relativity in fiction" to those works in which the author's *technical competence* has been catalyzed by his *conscious intent* in order to *reshape fictional reality* in such a manner as to reflect the way in which men experience the world in the age of relativity. (pp. 365-76)

Theodore Ziolkowski, "Hermann Broch and Relativity in Fiction," in Wisconsin Studies in Contemporary Literature, *Vol. VIII, No. 3, Summer, 1967, pp. 365-76.*

ERICH KAHLER   (essay date 1969)

[*A Czech-born sociologist, philosopher, and literary historian who emigrated to the United States and taught at Princeton, Kahler was a personal friend of Broch. In the following excerpt, he discusses the innovative aspects of Broch's fiction.*]

The artistic rank of an author cannot be established without considering his innovative contributions, that is, the extent to which he advanced the development of forms of art relevant to his time. The innovative quality of a work of art is intimately connected with the artist's ability to grasp the ever new, ever changing reality of the human condition, to give it original, precisely adequate expression, and to create a new style for this new reality. Truth is always new.

Hermann Broch's first literary work, *Die Schlafwandler* [*The Sleepwalkers*] . . . consists of three novels: *Pasenow or Romanticism,* *Esch or Anarchy,* and *Huguenau or Factuality.* The trilogy describes an entire era, and with it the unfolding of a universal social and psychic crisis. This, however, is not its actual innovation; such description had been undertaken before by various great authors of the 19th century, most prominently by Balzac and Zola. But what had not been done before was to use different narrative styles for each of the three phases of the crisis, and this without losing the specific author's original quality.

The first novel takes place in 1888; it is Broch's version of a novel by Theodor Fontane—an organized, coherently progressing action in the narrative style of the 19th century, but without a trace of parody, depicting the atmosphere of a period already undermined by destructive forces. The second novel describes the situation in the year 1903 when the established life structures were visibly crumbling; the style used here is naturalistically abrupt. The third novel finally illustrating the year 1918, shows the completely disintegrated, chaotic condition after World War I, that uncontrolled mixture of fragmented rational and irrational behavior, of cynically business-like factuality and brutal emotionality. It shows the disruption of all intrinsic communication among people, and the psychic, even physical derangement of the self. As a further innovation, the third novel in its entirety is interspersed with historical and philosophical interpretations of this universal process of dissolution, a "disintegration of values."

In Broch's last book, *Die Schuldlosen* (. . . *The Guiltless*), a collection of loosely connected stories, the accent is shifted to one of radical morality. The *Sleepwalkers* who are not yet aware of the great crisis in which they are involved, who are its objects, turn into the hypocritically *Guiltless* who shun the responsibility for what is happening—a responsibility to themselves as well as to their fellow men. They evade this responsibility with indifference, and eventually meet their judgment.

The three novels written by Broch between his first and his last work, carry out this transformation in which a process of human nature becomes a trial at the day of reckoning. In the center of this development at the crossroads of human responsibility stands his main work: *Der Tod des Vergil (The Death of Virgil)*. In this extraordinary work, one of the greatest though most difficult works of world literature, it is impossible to point to individual innovations; in its entirety it is unprecedented and original. In it we find the universal crisis in which and with which Broch has grown up, turning inward, from an external objective of observation into an issue of personal destiny. This crucial experience is carried to such depth that it touches upon the ultimate question and innermost problem of human existence: the affinity of life and death.

People become aware of this problem particularly in times of great crisis. What is death but a transformation of life and what is a great crisis, a world crisis such as ours, but an immense transformation of life. There is much dying in such crises. Human beings perish in vast numbers, but so do values, institutions, life structures, whether we admit it or not. Thus, during the Thirty-Years'-War, Baroque literature was obsessed and preoccupied with the idea of dying, with premonitions of death and the futility of temporal existence; all of life was viewed and taught solely as a preparation for dying. Consequently, it is not incidental when by the end of the 19th century the death motif again begins to figure predominantly in literature and philosophy. Not in the same manner, to be sure, as in the religiously inclined Baroque period where the individual soul, being spiritually prepared for death, was assured of eternal life. At the "fin de siècle"—which encompasses more than just the end of a century—there is no spiritual solace any more, death emerges undisguised, as a fact of life, indeed, as an elucidating element of temporal existence itself. The "fin de siècle" begins with Schopenhauer, Richard Wagner, Kierkegaard. It dawns in the writings of some French symbolists, in their wooing of death. In his great story, *The Death of Ivan*

Iljitsch Tolstoi for the first time describes death as the key to earthly life, as illuminating true existence. . . . Rilke was totally preoccupied with the problem of death. "Everybody," he says in *Malte Laurids Brigge,* "carries his death in himself, as a fruit carries its seed." Thomas Mann, finally, in *Death in Venice, The Magic Mountain,* and *Doctor Faustus* deals with death as being intimately linked with life.

But none of these authors, above all nobody who loved life as much as Hermann Broch did, went so far in his inquiry, in his blasphemous curiosity, indeed in his love of life, as this writer who tried to descend to death in the midst of life, who tried to *live* death by means of an imagination that went up to and almost beyond the limits of the humanly conceivable. Living through the great crisis, which is still with us today, contemplating profoundly the nature of the crisis and within it the meaning of his own death which he felt approaching, Broch was thrust into the conception of this work. He followed the Orpheic descent to the shadows with a relentless realism, far beyond the realm of individual humanity into a cosmic sphere, into a community of all creatures, to arrive at the source of all being where death becomes transformation of life and creation.

Experiencing the descent into one's innermost self, descent to the point of transcending oneself, onto the borderline where extinction becomes regeneration—this kind of experience has been the core of all mysteries and mysticism. With Broch, however, the old mystic experience took a new turn and reached a new scope in that it is not a communion with God any longer. Where is God, who is God? He has become neutral, nonparticipant, the Unknowable, the Unexperiencable, the one who cannot be approached and whose messages never reach us; this is the way Kafka endured and expressed it in many parables. God is the one who does not answer us, "whose response is silence" "der uns anschweigt," as Rilke once burst out in bitterness; who ignores our prayers, as Broch himself has God declare in a poem at the end of his novel *The Guiltless:* "No prayer should be addressed to Me, as I don't hear it. Be pious for My sake even without access to Me, let this be your propriety, your proud humility which makes you a human being. . . . For as far as I am, and as far as I am existing for you, I implanted into you the nonpresence of my nature, the extremest exterior into your innermost being."

Indeed, for Broch there is no communion with God any more. The mystic union takes place between the individual and his innermost, deepest self, his *id* which merges with the basic elements of life that are universal and common to all. Here, in Broch's crucial experience, psychoanalysis has become a mystical process. The ego transcends to the id, indeed, to a deeper, a transpersonal stratum of the id, that is, to its unfathomable cosmic sources. Virgil, on his deathbed, is striving for an awareness and clarification of the common nature of life, and hence he comes to realize that in the pursuit of artistic perfection he has missed the principal duty of the human being, the care of the good of his fellowmen.

This specific quality of Broch's vision, the mystic penetration of death and the tracing of individual existence into the generic id, results in a very unusual quality of his style: His characters speak a vigorous, robust language, very much corresponding to their personalities and their social status, be they servants, peasants, or businessmen; often they speak almost in dialect. Broch is a master when it comes to specific characterizations. But then, suddenly the narrative reaches a culmination point where a character will express not only his ego but his self, not only what he is aware of but the essence of his personality.

Without break or caesura the id begins to express itself. Along with this transformation, however, the tone is changed and raised imperceptibly to a heightened diction, without losing the naturalness and spontaneity of expression. This is how unintentionally the lyricism of Broch's prose develops. There is an effortless interchange between the simplest, everyday idiom and the most sublime, poetical language.

Actually, *The Death of Virgil* is a long poem. It became a poem because its lyricisms flow naturally from the state of mind of the dying poet, Virgil. The book describes the last eighteen hours of Virgil, beginning with his return from Greece and arrival in Brundisium with the fleet of Emperor Augustus, and ending with Virgil's death in the imperial palace on the following day. It describes these final hours by means of an inner monologue: all events are seen from Virgil's inner experience, even factual occurences, as when Virgil is carried through the streets of the harbor, when the odors from the docks, the storehouses, and the shacks come upon him, when the crowd closes in on him, and the women yell down to him from their windows—even then everything appears as it is perceived by the most delicate sensorium of the ailing poet. His feverish condition is used in an ingenious way to show how reality was momentarily sharpened and intensified for him and at the same time preserves a lasting transcendence. In a delirious state the border-line between hyperacute reality and phantasmagoria is blurred. Factual phenomena alternately appear and disappear, coming much closer to such heightened sensibility than under normal conditions. The outer world presents itself to the consciousness with such extreme, obscene nakedness that it is constantly on the point of falling apart, of dissolving a multitude of hallucinations, memories, premonitions, dream waves, and vanishing into the unfathomable. Inner and outer life are turbulently mixed. The new analysis of the disintegration of self, started by Broch in *The Sleepwalkers,* is continued here in his description of the condition of fever: erosion of consciousness, of perception of bodily consistency. The world of appearances is in perpetual flux and particular limbs develop an independent life of their own. Interspersed between, however, there are moments of lucid clarity such as normal consciousness can never attain. His whole life, the failure of his life, is made transparent in a flash. This is the condition of the ailing Virgil, and it is under these ever-changing and intensified aspects that the narrative unfolds. The inner monologue is presented in the third person; this facilitates the transition from the self to the id, and it is only through this device that the process of dying could be finally pursued to the cosmic sphere.

But the man who is dying here is not an ordinary man, he is a poet, and a poet living in a world shaken by great crisis, in an era of fundamental transformation of life similar to ours; tending in the opposite direction though, in that it saw the decline of paganism and the rise of Christianity, while today Christianity seems to disintegrate into a variety of pagan movements. He is a poet moreover who had come to the painful realization that, having spent himself in the service of art, he has neglected the essential duty of his age which was human and moral.

The fulfillment of this task was Broch's most urgent problem, which beclouded his last years and caused him much suffering. Paradoxically, his greatest book, to which he applied his most accomplished artistry, proclaimed the end of art as a salvation of humanity. After the completion of this work he intended to renounce any artistic effort and to devote himself exclusively to science, whose strict discipline and verifiable results he

expected to exert a convincing power. He was, however, not allowed to conclude his tragic career the way he wanted to, as a scientist. Apparent circumstances aiding an innermost necessity forced him to round out his artistic work, thus giving it its organic end and moral apotheosis: *The Guiltless.*

In Virgil's last hours, in this hardly controllable state of delirium, when it takes the greatest effort to hold his ego together, yet when a sudden awareness of himself and his world overwhelms him as never before, in this condition Virgil takes stock of himself and of his relations to the figures in his life, among them the ruler of the world, his sovereign and closest friend, the Caesar Augustus. The climax of this inner reckoning, the point where it reaches out once more into the outer world, is the great discussion with Augustus, who visits him and with whom he argues about the work of his life even as he strives for a clarification of man's significance and obligation in this era of change. He wants to destroy the "Aeneid" because he deems it invalid and meaningless—not artistically but humanly meaningless—when measured against what he should have done with his life. He wants to destroy it as an act of atonement for the neglect of his human obligation, as anticipatory death, as an act of submersion into anonymity. But Augustus finally wrests the work from him; Virgil relinquishes it—as a last gift of friendship, of love between man and man.

What is happening here at last, in the mirror of this book, is a threefold transformation: transformation of the world, of the soul, and of the body, which is death. But death is here experienced in such local intensity that it rises beyond individual and physical death into a sphere of cosmic transformation: it has become an oversized model of the process of dying. This disintegration of consciousness, and with it the disintegration of the human body, takes the form of a reversal of the biblical process of creation: the mind, the self, the body sinks gradually back, passing through the animal, the vegetable, the mineral, and the cosmically material spheres, reuniting with all of them and, after looking back once more, like Orpheus, spanning the entire range of creation with a single, simultaneous glance, it slips away from him into the realm of the divine logos, the humanly inexpressible. (pp. 186-92)

Erich Kahler, "The Epochal Innovations in Hermann Broch's Narrative," in Salmagundi, *Nos. 10 & 11, Fall, 1969 & Winter, 1970, pp. 186-92.*

ROBERT ALTER (essay date 1971)

[*An American scholar, Alter has published highly respected studies of Stendhal, American Jewish writers, and the picaresque novel. In the following excerpt, originally published in* Commentary *in October 1971, he examines the treatment in Broch's works of a theme that recurs in much of twentieth-century fiction: the legitimacy of art in modern society.*]

Children of a dark century, we tend to look into our literature as in a glass darkly. The glass itself, in our most recurrent images of it, is thought of as cracked and splintered and skewed so that through its own violent fashioning it may mirror more faithfully the twisted confusion of faces that modern reality has assumed. If we ask ourselves how writers have been able to go on making poems and plays and novels while mankind runs amok, irresistibly bent, it often seems, on the simultaneous destruction of its own past and its own future, our most common answer is that literature has served as a uniquely sensitive seismograph of the age's disasters, or, indeed, as a warning-system for disasters still to come. (p. 3)

If much of the major literature of our century has turned upon some historical or moral abyss, it is also true that literature in this period has been turned in upon itself to an unprecedented degree. *The Trial, Women in Love,* and *The Sound and the Fury* are, of course, exemplary works of the years of deepening inner trouble that followed World War I, but just as exemplary, in a very different way, are Valéry's *Le Cimetière marin,* Wallace Stevens's *Harmonium,* Joyce's *Ulysses;* and the Thomas Mann who wrote *The Magic Mountain* in these years would also work, both early and late in his career, on *Felix Krull,* a radiant portrait of the artist as protean master of experience. Mann's example should suggest that the impulse to look into the depths has often been intertwined with the impulse of the artist to reflect on the processes of making art. Proust's patient evocation of the growth of an artist's consciousness through time concludes with a whole cultural order in ruins and the reverberation of German bombs in the salons of the Faubourg Saint-Germain. Conversely, Sartre's *Nausea,* which begins with a traumatic exposure of its protagonist to the formless abyss of the absurd, ends on a resolution to transcend meaningless existence by, of all things, writing a novel.

There are, to be sure, certain escapist or elitist tendencies in this recurrent preoccupation of modern writers with art as the subject of art. To cite a relatively recent example, the French New Novel of the fifties and early sixties, for all the insistence of its manifestoes that it sought to confront a world stripped of predetermined value, represented a retreat of the imagination from history after four decades of historical trauma, and thus reduced the novel to a laboratory of narrative technique. Elsewhere, however, literary art has often been driven to reflect on itself out of the deepest inner necessity, recapitulating its own past through complex strategies of allusion, imitation, and parody; brooding over its own nature and ends; exploring its connections with all that is not art—in order to make literature still possible in a world that threatens to overwhelm it, and through the assertion of literature's prerogatives to keep alive as well the idea of a more humanly livable world.

The two major works of Hermann Broch offer an instructive paradigm of this dialectical relationship between the literary consciousness of history and the literary consciousness of art. His trilogy, *The Sleepwalkers,* written in Austria on the eve of Hitler's ascent to power, moves step by careful step, from 1888 to 1918, toward what Broch himself calls the "disintegration of values" of European civilization. The darkening historical landscape is appropriately reflected in the shifts of narrative texture from one part of the novel to the next. The poignant muted lyricism of the 1888 section gives way in the middle volume, set in 1903, to a harsher satirical mode of representation in which a discursively meditative narrator views the sexual and commercial shenanigans of the characters as despairing acts of creatures hungering for an unattainable salvation. The last volume, set in the closing months of World War I, is deliberately disjointed, moving back and forth nervously among different, barely related stories, interweaving verse-narrative with the prose, interpolating chapters of a historical-philosophical essay on the decay of European values in the modern age. It is Broch's contention here that with the breakdown of an overarching system of values, competing "partial systems," representing different techniques, interests, spheres of life, tend to absolutize their own values and thus to translate destructive unreason into social and political action

on an unprecedented scale. "There arises a specific commercial kind of thinking, or a specific military kind of thinking, each of which strives toward ruthless and consistent absoluteness, each of which constructs a deductive *schema* of plausibility to suit itself, each of which has its 'theology' or its 'private theology.'" Forty years after the writing of these words, they seem at least one likely way of explaining the various kinds of mentality that could invent a Final Solution, a global strategy of overkill, and "plausible" scenarios for the pacification of Southeast Asia. Yet the very sharpness of Broch's analysis has the effect of cutting the ground from under him as a novelist. Like most ambitious writers, Broch clearly wants to make literature work as an art of the whole—pulling all characters and events into an orchestrated system of values, seeing individual lives and life at large in a unified field of vision. But how can an art of the whole function among the broken pieces of an age of partial systems? Not at all, one is led to infer from the end of *The Sleepwalkers,* where the novel, caught in the toils of imitative form, seems to confess the inability of the literary imagination to produce coherence in an incoherent world.

I have underscored the predicament of the novel-form implicit in *The Sleepwalkers* because it helps make clear why Broch's later work, *The Death of Virgil,* is both a logical development in his own career and, for all its seeming peculiarity, part of an important current in twentieth-century literature. Viewed superficially, the writing of such a book looks like an act of mere withdrawal: a major European novelist, in exile in America, at the very moment when his native continent is in flames, turns his back on two thousand years of history to re-create in an elaborate poetic novel the death of a Roman poet. Obviously, there are many ways of talking about so anomalous a book: as the longest lyric poem in the German language, as the closest approximation in fiction to the formal effects of music, or—in connection with the predicament of the novel raised by *The Sleepwalkers*—as a threatened literary art undertaking a sweeping review of its own resources and limits, of its own ontological grounds. The choice of the historical setting, then, is doubly apt, because it allows the writer to focus on an archetype of the European poet with an intense introspective purity, and because the whole novel thus implies the relationship between the act of writing and the cultural past that is so central to the problematics of literature in an age of disintegrating values. Broch is careful not to project too crudely the troubles of his own time onto Virgil's, but, like Yeats, he thinks of history as a series of two-thousand-year cycles, and so can see a structural correspondence between Virgil's age and ours as periods of critical transition. Accordingly, he suggests that already for Virgil poetic invention had become a self-conscious, self-skeptical act; that the Latin poet was already isolated from the people, the people itself become a potentially anarchic mob; that great political forces were changing the face of the known world and making imperious demands on the writer to be their voice. "Oh, Augustus," Virgil calls out at one point in his long colloquy with the emperor, "the ground is shaking . . . nothing shook for Homer or his heroes."

What is perhaps most impressive about Broch's oceanic meditation on poetry is the way it avoids easy resolutions, swinging back and forth in great dialectic movements between doubt and affirmation. The dying Virgil knows how the calling of poetry has kept him apart from other men, always self-bent on the fashioning of his own edifice of fame, but as an artist he will not relinquish the idea of "an affiliation with the human community, which was the aim of real art in its aspiration toward humanity," and his own luminous poetic consciousness in this novel of the living and the dead finally demonstrates how art can reach outward from the prison of the self to embrace mankind. Virgil is haunted by a still more troubling fear that his whole life has been only a game with words, that all words can do is to embellish, imperfectly duplicate, and thus falsify reality. "Nothing unreal is allowed to survive," he announces to his dismayed friends in order to explain his decision to burn the *Aeneid.* The major part of the novel is caught up in the backward and forward surge of debate over this harsh resolution. In the end, Virgil leaves the manuscript of the *Aeneid* in Caesar's possession, whether out of uncertainty, or inclination to compromise, or sheer fatigue, or some glimmering hope that his epic may not after all be entirely unreal.

Language, the dying poet perceives, is an instrument of treacherous duplicity, forever tempting us to take the resonant word for the thing itself. Yet if all reality, as Virgil tells Augustus, "is but the growth of perception," language remains the necessary medium for the realization of perception, and cadenced language shaped into images is our chief means of making the world around us real, binding the fragments of transient experience into a ring of lasting significance: "Human life was thus image-graced and image-cursed; it could comprehend itself only through images, the images were not to be banished, they had been with us since the herd-beginning, they were anterior to and mightier than our thinking, they were timeless, containing past and future, they were a twofold dream-memory and they were more powerful than we."

Perhaps it begins to be clear why this self-consciously "literary" novel was no self-indulgence for Broch. He began working on it not long before his months of imprisonment by the Nazis and his subsequent departure from Austria in 1938, and his very choice of this subject at that time and place suggests how the nightmare of history has driven much modern literature back upon itself, led it to rehearse the process of literary creation in order to discover what use literary creation might conceivably have in a world of nightmares. The chief use of literature that emerges from *The Death of Virgil* is as the one road of escape from what Broch calls the "herd-experience"— that primordial condition in which each individual creature cowers before the menace of death in his animal aloneness, crowding against the bodies around him for the surface warmth and solace of sheer physical closeness. Language, as the unique human instrument, and poetry, as the most complex ordering of language, lift man beyond the herd by placing his consciousness in touch with others, with the collective consciousness of mankind, with the shared human experience of the past back to its evolutionary beginnings, through all these allowing man to project an image of the future out of his trapped moments of existential dread. Sounds and colors and shapes have timeless quality, always present as materials for the artist, but language is the one artistic medium that develops perceptibly through historical time, bearing the marks of past uses upon it, and thus literature is before all the others the memory-laden art, the one that resumes its past in the very act of exploiting its full resources for the expression of the present. In "An Apology for Literature," . . . Paul Goodman formulated this essential operation of the literary imagination with a fine lucidity: "Man is the animal who makes himself and the one who is made by his culture. Literature repeats the meaning and revives the spirit of past makings, so they are not dead weight, by using them again in a making that is occurring now." The possession of a past, then, is a necessary condition for the imagining of the future; the vaster and more varied the past, the richer the possibilities of the future will be.

Viewed in these terms, the very end of *The Death of Virgil* is not an outrageous self-assertion of poetry but a resonant culmination of Virgil's long inner journey. The poet's fantastically restless, image-spawning mind having explored the far reaches of personal and collective memory, Broch creates for him an apotheosis which fuses the Western literary memory of two great moments of creation, the first chapter of Genesis and the first chapter of John, memory thus triumphantly passing into renewal. The Logos here is not an embodiment or intermediary of the Divinity but is in itself the generating nub of existence, the image of the fulfilled perfection of language making reality, toward which all the imperfections of earthly poetry aspire: "The word hovered over the universe, over the nothing, floating beyond the expressible as well as the inexpressible, and he, caught under and amidst the roaring, he floated on with the word . . . ; it was the word beyond speech." It is characteristic of Broch that this assumption of the poet into eternity did not end his own inner dialogue on the worth of literature. Haunted by the revelations of the Nazi horrors, he resolved in his last years to abandon literature for the direct action of politics and the chaste precision of mathematics. Nevertheless, circumstances led him to rewrite for publication two earlier works, *The Tempter* and *The Innocent,* and it seems clear that there was some inner necessity as well that impelled him again to the making of fiction. (pp. 4-9)

HERMANN BROCH

———

JAMES JOYCE
UND DIE GEGENWART

———

Rede zu Joyce's 50. Geburtstag

H
R
V

HERBERT REICHNER VERLAG

WIEN-LEIPZIG-ZÜRICH

1936

Title page of James Joyce und die Gegenwart. *Courtesy of Buchhaendler-Vereinigung: Archive für Geschichte Buchwesens.*

Robert Alter, ''Defenses of the Imagination,'' in his Defenses of the Imagination: Jewish Writers and Modern Historical Crisis, *The Jewish Publication Society of America*, 1977, pp. 3-22.*

JAMES HARDIN   (essay date 1974)

[*Hardin is an American educator and critic who has written extensively on German literature and literary figures. In the following excerpt, he discusses Broch's fictional expression of his theories of mass psychology in* Der Versucher.]

Hermann Broch's largely neglected writings on mass psychology, contained chiefly in his *Massenpsychologie: Schriften aus dem Nachlass* . . . are of considerable significance in elucidating certain aspects of his novels. Particularly important is the relationship between Broch's theories of mass psychology and his work *Der Versucher.* . . .

Broch first mentioned his intention of writing what he termed a ''religious novel'' in 1932, but actual work on the book began apparently only in 1935. In 1936 the first version was completed, under various working titles: *Bergroman, Demeter, Bauerroman* among others. The final title *Der Versucher* was chosen by Felix Stössinger, who in 1953, on the basis of the *Nachlass* [''literary bequest''], produced not a critical edition but a compilation of the three versions of the novel which Broch had developed over a period of almost twenty years. (p. 24)

The consistency of Broch's outlook as reflected in the *Bergroman* during its long gestation is confirmed by a study of the *Massenpsychologie,* which appeared in 1953. . . . That Broch had already developed many of his basic and enduring views on mass psychology as early as 1935 is proven by a comparison of the first version of the *Bergroman* with *Massenpsychologie.* While the chronological relationship between the theoretical writings and *Der Versucher* at first glance appears to show that the novel is antecedent to the theory, in fact both works drew on ideas which Broch had begun to develop prior to 1933. The usefulness of the theoretical writings in *Massenpsychologie* is that they reveal Broch's views on mass psychology much more clearly and thus constitute a kind of commentary on the action and motivation of *Der Versucher.* That the novel requires such a commentary, owing to obscurities in motivation and characterization, also implies something about its quality, as we shall have occasion to note.

It seems advisable to recapitulate the action of *Der Versucher,* as it is relevant here. Marius Ratti, a vagabond with political ambitions and a gift for rhetoric, settles in Kuppron, a remote, superstitious Austrian village. In a manner which parallels Hitler's rise to power, Ratti gains control of the villagers through his intuitive gauging of their collective insecurity. Symbolically and subliminally, he offers them salvation from their fear of death, and in return demands absolute power. His methods of assuaging the ubiquitous fear of death lead ultimately to an orgy culminating in the sacrificial collective murder of a young girl. He carries out his schemes against the opposition of a somewhat unconvincingly portrayed mother figure, Mutter Gisson, who dies toward the end of the novel, and in spite of the efforts of the narrator of the work, a country doctor.

Broch began *Der Versucher* in 1934 and had still not completed a final version in 1951, the year of his death. This fact reflects in part the complexity of the artistic goals involved. Broch was attempting to work into the novel not only his theories of demagogy and mob psychology, but also a modern version of the Demeter myth. In addition, he was interested in including his complex ideas on the disintegration of values (*Wertzerfall*), as he had done in the *Schlafwandler* trilogy in the early 1930's. This was certainly a problematic undertaking, possibly beyond the capabilities of the most gifted novelist, but in some respects the disparate aims harmonize, both philosophically and aesthetically, while in others there is no successful synthesis.

Broch's well-known concept of the disintegration of values, rather uncritically accepted until recently, had an important bearing on his theories of mass psychology, since he felt that in periods of cultural and moral decay—e.g. his own time— man is particularly vulnerable to the ploys of the demagogue. Virtually all the figures of *Der Versucher* (except kindly old Mutter Gisson, who gives the impression of having just stepped out of a romantic *Märchen* [''fairy tale'']) have lost their faith in a universal system of values which might free them from their anguish, and they find themselves in a state of what Broch called ''spiritual panic.'' They can no longer communicate; each speaks the language of and lives according to the ''logic'' of his own system of values. Having lost contact with their fellow men, his characters feel that the entire outer world is hostile to them. This state of affairs is discussed in *Massenpsychologie,* where Broch writes that man attempts to counteract such a mental zero point by ''Ich-Erweiterung,'' ego-expansion, a process which can take either a positive or a negative turn. In its most extreme negative form, the individual attempts to make the whole external world his own material possession. This is the psychotic behavior of a Hitler. On the other hand, positive ''Ich-Erweiterung'' involves cognition of the outer world in a spiritual, loving, and symbolic manner. This low-key mysticism, a typical ingredient of German and Austrian literature of the early twentieth century—one thinks of Rilke or Werfel—leads according to Broch to ultimate peace of mind and knowledge of the cosmos. This is the course followed by Mutter Gisson. The action and the message of *Der Versucher,* then, are reflected in the conflict between Ratti's materialism and the idealism embodied in Mutter Gisson and the doctor.

Broch contends in his essays that an ethically unstable and fearful group of people is dangerously susceptible to the lure of the irrational. In times of transition from one value-system to another, man's innate existential anguish is obviously more acute than during periods of metaphysical security. A pervasive collective *Angst* may manifest itself in the specific fear of individuals or groups who seem to represent a threat to the majority, and can lead to the attempt, by whatever means, to eliminate them. Also, in the endeavor to improve their lot, people generally only create a new system of absolute values, which can actually bring about the reversion to an irrational, primitive religion with its attendant magical symbols, totemism, and gruesome ritual. This is precisely what occurs in *Der Versucher.* Marius virtually hypnotizes his victims. (pp. 24-6)

But Ratti himself, even more than the villagers, is prey to ethical and spiritual insecurity; his anguish is paradoxically evidenced in his ''will to power.'' Behind a projected façade of self-confidence he conceals a pathological fear of death; it is rather broadly hinted that this is the reason for his aimless, uprooted life when a minor figure of the novel remarks ''Wer wandert, der läuft vor dem Tod davon'' [''He who wanders is fleeing death'']. . . . Ratti attempts to grasp the disturbing mystery of death by the sacrifice of a young girl named Irmgard, who apparently finds him more convincing than the reader does, and seems almost to relish being led to the inevitable slaughter. The other villagers, although their credulity does not have the same consequences as Irmgard's does, are just as easily fooled by Ratti's huckster tricks and pseudomysticism. Ratti is genuinely obsessed with death. "Das höchste Wissen ist das Wissen um den Tod" ["The highest knowledge is the knowledge of death"] . . . , he tells the doctor, but the latter sees the superficiality of his grasp of the death-problem and compares it with what he vaguely characterizes as the natural wisdom of Mutter Gisson: "Ihr [Mutter Gissons] Wissen um den Tod ist das Wissen um das Leben, um das sichtbare, das fühlbare Sein, nicht aber um unvorstellbare Allgemeinheiten, mit denen der Un-Mann [Ratti] seinen männlichen Glauben predigt und verheißt" ["Her (Mutter Gisson's) knowledge of death is the knowledge of life, of visible, tangible being, not of unimaginable generalities with which the un-man (Ratti) preaches and promises his manly beliefs"]. . . . (p. 27).

There are other indications of a deep-seated fear in Ratti. In his essays, Broch theorizes that man reacts in one of two ways to the feeling of anguish: he surrenders abjectly to his fear, or he feigns courage, counteracting his anxiety by extreme self-assertion, striking out at even minor threats to himself. This last obviously applies to Ratti. He attacks not only Christianity in general, but also a harmless insurance agent named Wetchy, whose meek passivity presents only a trifling barrier to his plans. Also, while he claims to be Mutter Gisson's enemy, and ruthlessly directs a hate campaign against her, it is quite apparent that he is powerfully drawn towards her and yearns for the security which she represents. In this respect he is very similar to Andreas in Broch's *Die Schuldlosen*. Ratti repeatedly refers to Mutter Gisson simply as "Mutter," and one is tempted to see in this a "Freudian slip." He implores her to accept him and to grant him her magical knowledge of nature and man. . . . In an encounter with Irmgard, he suddenly buries his hands and face in a bag of grain lying at his feet—one thinks of the Demeter myth—and cries out "Oh, Mutter!". . . . In Jungian terms (which are appropriate, as Broch was unquestionably influenced by Jung's thought) Ratti is the "lost son," illustrating as an archetype the mother complex. But in *Der Versucher* the son's search takes on additional significance. Ratti—who is clearly another of those psychotic fictional representatives of modern man cast out into an absurd world—has lost faith in all traditional value systems and is seeking desperately some new system or knowledge to free him of his anguish. His search for the mother is linked to his quest for a new value system.

The doctrines advanced by Ratti (including an attack on modern technology, advocacy of a return to simple, Germanic ways, male comradeship, and revolt against the Mother-principle) are irrational and patently contradictory. Nonetheless, he succeeds in fooling and exploiting the villagers, and becomes temporarily the dictator of Kuppron. This scheme of events reflects Broch's conviction that demagogic power rests more on imaginary than on actual bases. According to *Massenpsychologie,* the ethical insecurity of the masses can be eliminated by supplying even an irrational system of values. In this connection Broch distinguishes between "open" and "closed" systems of thought. . . . The former rest on logical bases, while the latter include false premises and cannot withstand logical scrutiny from an external vantage point. Broch states, perhaps naively, that in order to convince individuals living in an open system of the truth and necessity of political, social, or metaphysical values, these truths need only be opened to view in an organized and objective manner. However, when the masses

are to be convinced of the truth of a closed system of thought, no objectivity may be permitted. In *Der Versucher* the two conflicting systems of thought are represented primarily by Marius and Mutter Gisson. Both have irrational elements, as Mutter Gisson is a kind of beneficent witch. Her knowledge, her ethic, however, is basically simple, unpretentious, open, in keeping with her character. Of Marius and his followers, however, the doctor writes: . . . "vielmehr ist er wie einer, der bloß die Regeln eines kalten, starren und abstrakten Spieles gelernt hat und meint, sie seien die alles Menschentums . . ." ["he is much more like one who has simply learned the rules of a cold, rigid, and abstract game and believes that they should be those of all mankind"]. . . . Unfortunately, as is apparent in the action of the novel, man in his anguish is all too ready to accept such a limited view of the world. Broch writes in his essay **"Die mythische Erbschaft der Dichtung,"** "der Mensch—und darin gleicht der moderne all seinen Vorfahren—ist weit lieber abergläubisch als wissend, und er folgt lieber dem falschen Propheten, als daß er die Stimme des echten zu hören gewillt ist." ["man—and in this modern man resembles all his ancestors—is far more willingly superstitious than knowing, and he would rather follow a false prophet than hear the voice of a true one"].

Marius is adept at finding and exploiting hidden sources of *Angst* among the villagers. He is preternaturally sensitive to abnormal or unhappy familial relationships, and when he discovers a situation of this sort in the Wenter family, he exploits it in a way which leads to a tragic outcome. Wenter and his wife feel that their marriage has been a failure. They hope to find in their personal relationship with Ratti a substitute for their missing happiness. . . . Ratti thus becomes acquainted with and then seduces, but only in a figurative sense, their daughter Irmgard, who is to become the sacrificial lamb. Irmgard sees in him the father, Wenter the brother. Others in the village are motivated by submerged feelings of anguish and isolation. One, Gilbert Sabest, hopes to find in Marius a friend and a kind of soldierly comradeship for which he desperately longs. Donat, the blacksmith, also desires a male comradeship, adventure, and unrestricted freedom . . . , and Broch apparently intended him to represent that large group of Germans who have a penchant for hiking and soldiering. Superstition and fear play the main part in the conversion of an oafish peasant named Johanni, who has the notion that a "spell" has been cast on his plow-horse by the "foreigner" Wetchy (who was born in the city). Johanni's muddled obsessions and Donat's simple faith and Germanic *Treue* ["loyalty"] are representative of the dark, fearful soil in which Marius' doctrines take root and thrive.

Another factor which contributes psychologically to Ratti's success in uniting most of the village behind him is the invention of a "cause," in this case the opening of an abandoned mine in the mountain near Kuppron in hopes of finding gold. On the surface the plan has little merit, for everyone knows that the mine has long ceased to be productive, but it becomes apparent that gold, and the mountain itself, serve to awaken atavistic desires in the villagers. . . . The plan to open the mine . . . is really an expression of [Ratti's] longing for absolute knowledge and his desire to impart it to the villagers. Yet he speaks of his followers with contempt, and addresses the doctor, his enemy, as an equal. He holds before the villagers the prospect of finding a treasure in the mountain, a kind of Nibelungen hoard, but the entire action is really an allegory of the conquest of death.

Although the attempt to reopen the mine ultimately fails, Ratti gains a peculiarly brutal victory in the sacrificial murder of Irmgard. The murder should be regarded in the light of Broch's theory, possibly stemming from Jung, that when the masses find themselves in a period of extreme stress and resultant ethical insecurity, an archaic collective level of their mentality may surface. Such a process can lead to a lynching, a pogrom, or a human sacrifice. No one is immune to such regressive drives, for even the doctor—surely intended by Broch to represent the forces of reason and humanity—is carried away by the obscene dancing of the mob prior to the murder; the intoxicating, Dionysiac fluting of the dance, which had begun sedately enough, robs him temporarily of all capacity for self-control, although his impaired moral judgment still functions residually. . . . And later, when the mob screams ''das Opfer, das Opfer'' [''the sacrifice, the sacrifice''], the doctor admits with horror and disgust that he may also have cried for blood. . . . (pp. 27-30)

In his *Massenpsychologie* Broch refers to human sacrifice as a form of ''Angstbefreiung'' [''liberation from fear'']; this is the obvious purpose of the murder of Irmgard. We find frequent allusions during the sacrifice scene to the anguish of the villagers, and the death ritual represents a horribly misguided attempt to allay this fear. Before the murder, Marius himself appears convinced that human sacrifice will put an end to his anguish, and Wenter, one of Ratti's most rabid supporters, also speaks vaguely of a rebirth through sacrifice. This hope is dashed. . . . [While] fear and anguish have proved to be Ratti's most important psychological weapons, their reemergence after the sacrifice also exposes the superficiality of his ideology, even on its own depraved level.

A less sensational, but equally vicious method employed by Ratti to control the villagers is his use of the agent as a scapegoat for their repressed hatreds and anxieties. Wetchy is viewed with resentment and distrust by the rest of the community because he is the only Protestant in Kuppron (although it appears likely that Broch, himself Jewish, intended Wetchy to represent a Jewish minority). He is of Hungarian extraction and is virtually the only person in the village other than the doctor who does not earn his living from the soil. He is small and sickly, obviously not the robust sort who might fit into the narrow, earthy atmosphere of a provincial Austrian village. He is a creature of the city, as Ratti is quick to point out . . . , and none of the villagers, not even the doctor and Mutter Gisson, can avoid feeling some involuntary but deep-seated aversion toward him. . . . Ratti immediately makes Wetchy his target; for he recognizes that the anguish of the villagers can be channeled into resentment of the persecuted minority. (This point is also made by Broch theoretically.) In the end, Wetchy is savagely beaten by Marius' stormtroopers and leaves Kuppron, an incident more effective than the murder of Irmgard because the sacrifice scene is not so convincingly portrayed and motivated.

Although *Der Versucher* is the best example, Broch's theories are reflected in the other novels as well, particularly in *Der Tod des Vergil*. During his terrifying passage through the teeming streets of Brundisium, Virgil becomes aware of the anguish of the masses and their desperate readiness to accept any new leader who will promise them salvation. Likewise, he recognizes that the proletarian throngs, like the inhabitants of Kuppron, are all too ready to substitute Dionysiac frenzy and blood lust for courageous, direct confrontation with their own anguish. . . . (pp. 30-1)

In conclusion, I would not argue that Broch's theories of mass psychology are original, nor even that *Der Versucher* is a successful novel. Broch's emphasis on the disintegration of values and the anguish produced by the fear of death is probably the most original aspect of his theory of mass psychology, although here too one can speak at most of affinities with existential philosophers such as Kierkegaard and Heidegger. The significance of mass-psychological phenomena in recent history, however, makes Broch's theory and the literary treatment of it in *Der Versucher* worthy of more than passing interest. (p. 31)

> *James Hardin, ''Hermann Broch's Theories on Mass Psychology and 'Der Versucher','' in* The German Quarterly, *Vol. XLVII, No. 1, January, 1974, pp. 24-33.*

ROBERT MARTIN ADAMS   (essay date 1977)

[*An American educator and critic, Adams is the author of works on religion, opera, and a variety of literary topics, including the highly regarded* Stendhal: Notes on a Novelist *(1959). In the following excerpt, he examines aspects of Broch's fiction that demonstrate an affinity with the works of James Joyce.*]

[Hermann Broch] was an articulate man, with strong feelings about the destiny of the European novel and European culture in general; like many middle-Europeans of his age and milieu (1920s Vienna), he felt that with the war something solid and important had fallen out of the center of things, and that the very existence of the artist-poet-*Dichter* had thereby been called into question. Joyce, as the most intricate and resourceful writer of the age, was a crucial figure for Broch, partly as a symptom of a world-condition, partly as evidence of a possible set of responses to that condition. Apart from many private and occasional references to the work on Joyce, Broch on at least one occasion made explicit public profession of his views on Joyce's achievement. It is a complex declaration of abstract principles, compounded with deep admiration not only for *Ulysses* but also for *Finnegans Wake*, and yet tempered with some misgiving. It was published as a somewhat belated tribute on the occasion of Joyce's fiftieth birthday, as *James Joyce und die Gegenwart* . . . ; and, like everything Broch wrote, it's a curiously suggestive document. The abstract principles center around that by-now-familiar topos, the disintegration of the object (illustrated with examples from modern painting and modern physics); the admiration is primarily for Joycean polyphony and symbolic ingenuity; the misgivings are chiefly over the increasing privacy and incommunicability of the Joycean universe, in which language as a subject in itself has usurped over representation and communication. Joyce turned the polyphonic novel from an ethical course into an aesthetic one; Broch in his own work undertook to return that novel to what he understood as its proper course.

Of these various considerations, those involving specific fictional techniques might be expected to carry over most directly into Broch's own fiction; but on the whole they didn't, at least not in any explicit or obvious way. A reader without previous mental preparation could, I think, very well read straight through the trilogy of *The Sleepwalkers* . . . and that immense lyrical-historical-epical romance, *The Death of Virgil* . . . without thinking more than momentarily and peripherally of Joyce. But in fact there's very good reason to think of him more than occasionally and more than casually.

The three novels of *The Sleepwalkers* are carefully dated at fifteen-year intervals, 1888, 1903, and 1918; they trace (or, rather, imply) a developing state of moral and physical entropy, in which a general system of categorical and universal values is splintered and disintegrated to the point where even its absence is no longer remarked. Joachim von Pasenow, the central figure of the first novel, is a Prussian officer vaguely and sleepily aware of a moral code and his own relation to it. He is partly and momentarily led away from it, from his duties to the uniform, to his ancestral estates, and to his destined bride; the chief instigators of this restlessness are his dark, sensual, semi-literate Hungarian mistress, and his cynical, sophisticated friend, Eduard von Bertrand. But he is not led very far; as Eduard prophesies, not without a broad streak of disdain, he returns after a fleeting flirtation with the wide world and its disintegrated values to his traditional pre-fabricated role: he manages his estate, serves obediently the military machine of his country, and marries the expected girl, the blonde (not to say pallid) Elisabeth, heiress of a nearby squire. The final unit of the first novel underlines, in the author's person, Bertrand's contempt for these shallow and childish persons. Between docility and timidity, Joachim and Elisabeth go through the form of a chilly marriage, and the author dismisses them with perfunctory contempt:

> Nevertheless after some eighteen months they had their first child. It actually happened. How this came about cannot be told here. Besides, after the material for character construction already provided, the reader can imagine it for himself. . . .

So much for Joachim and Elisabeth; and in fact with these words the lady disappears from the trilogy for good, while her husband turns up in the third volume, thirty years later, under a wholly different configuration; if it weren't for his name one would hardly recognize him as the same neutral, negative person that he was in the first novel.

These transparent and unassertive characters, who amount to so little in themselves, nonetheless make up an interwoven counterpoint of voices which is greater than the sum of its parts—and here we start to sense, among these sleepwalkers, the looming presence of a pattern that transcends their conscious intentions and in fact their consciousness as a whole. In a first and wholly negative evidence, the characters as they advance through the trilogy become more and more transparent and ghostlike. Pasenow in the final novel is literally possessed by an idea; Esch, the obsessed bookkeeper who is the central figure of the second novel, is increasingly, throughout it and through the third, the solitary inhabitant of his own fantasy; and though Eduard von Bertrand reportedly commits suicide toward the end of the second novel, he reappears, modified almost unrecognizably, as an itinerant philosopher, lecturer, and seeker of spiritual light, midway through the third. There are intimations that he may be a type of Christ; they are buried intimations, but they are reinforced by the fact that the third novel brings us into the presence of an authentic Lazarus-figure. More positive if less portentous than these intimations of occult import is a persistently skewed and twisted turn to the logic of the characters' represented thoughts. One distorting force is evidently an unsystematic and unobtrusive stream of symbolism that runs just under the surface of the narration. Hats, beards, walking-sticks, uniforms, and hunting are just a few of the trappings with symbolic import; they disturb, perceptibly if only subtly, the flow of thought—without, for all that, constituting a strongly present mythical pattern, such as one finds beneath the surface of *Ulysses*. Finally, Broch's trilogy makes

constant use of leitmotifs—recurrent verbal units, used in a variety of circumstances with a variety of different meanings, to strike a resonance between various parts of the book and to suggest musical harmonics heard outside the characters or between them—harmonics for which they are only in the vaguest way intentionally responsible. And these various subsurface devices, working against the increasingly diaphanous surface of Broch's trilogy, give to it a streaming, semi-visionary character loosely akin to that of *Ulysses,* with its fading and increasingly transparent characters, set in an increasingly transparent and timeless cosmos.

Yet though he might have picked up many of these concepts and techniques from a perusal of *Ulysses,* though consideration of them suggests strong affinities with Joyce's work, one can easily overstate the case. Very little of what we might want to call Joyce's contribution to Broch was distinctive to Joyce. Leitmotifs and symbolism, hostility to literal realism, a sense of social chaos and human debility—these a Viennese author did not have to learn from an Irish novelist. On a much humbler level of reflection, Broch's English left a good deal to be desired, and he must always have known Joyce, as it were, through a veil. And that is the sense of Joyce's presence that one gets from *The Sleepwalkers*—like so many other things in the trilogy, the knifeblade aspect of Joyce's mind, with his Aristotelian fondness for particulars and specifics, is sensed only through a veil and at a middle distance.

The Sleepwalkers provides one exception to the rule of simple-minded characters possessing relatively little inwardness; that is Eduard von Bertrand, who seems to act from deeper layers of reflection, and with greater awareness of philosophic considerations, than any of the other persons. Characteristically mysterious and almost perversely dialectical is his abrupt declaration of eternal passion for Joachim's intended Elisabeth—a piece of lovemaking *à l'allemand,* abrupt, metaphysical, and prefaced by an eternal farewell. Evidently he wishes to imprint on her mind, before she enters on the soggy business of domesticity, intimations of a higher and more spiritual potential. And this is very much the sort of light that in the third volume of the trilogy we find him trying to shine through the murky world of the war years, when he has been metamorphosed somehow into Bertrand Muller, PhD, with a double preoccupation for the Wandering Jew Ahasuerus, and for a Salvation Army girl in Berlin, named Marie. Both these somewhat unlikely figures evidently represent for Bertrand (and, transparently, for Broch himself) a kind of light in the darkness. And the mythic pattern that emerges from the trilogy, visible chiefly in retrospect, is essentially the emergence of this prophetic vision from the ever-darkening greed and vulgarity of an age whose standards are set by cold-blooded sharks like Huguenau. He is essentially an Alsatian Snopes; by the end of the trilogy he has triumphed not only over the weak and decent Joachim von Pasenow but also over a chief actor of the second novel, the intermediate figure August Esch. Esch's moral light is not, to begin with, particularly dazzling; as a commercial bookkeeper he feels, more in irritation than exaltation, that moral as well as business books should balance out. Injustice upsets him as a piece of divine inaccuracy; but as the horizons of the world lower and darken around him, this fretful and anxious morality deepens into an evangelical vision. Because society is so deeply sunk in filth and blind selfishness, only something like a Second Coming can possibly bring about its redemption. But, as seems to be the rule in Broch, the redeeming power works from behind the characters and in some sense against them, rather than through them. Villainous Huguenau manages to gain command over senile Major von Pasenow and to dispose of Esch with a bayonet in the back. The trilogy can then conclude on a reverberant prophetic note from the Book of Revelations: the cycle of history having reached its nadir, the dialectic demands that at this point some transcendent, unifying, regenerative principle is bound to make itself felt—as, duly, it does.

Even so perfunctory and schematic a sketch of *The Sleepwalkers* cannot fail to suggest major areas of sharp difference from the art of Joyce. Broch's work has an overriding moral and didactic dimension that Joyce's work largely lacks, it invokes traditional symbols and creeds in an unequivocal way that Joyce doesn't, and its characters are thinned out close to insubstantiality without acquiring the temporal dimension of archetypes. Disintegration and ironic simultaneity are supposed to be expressed in the final novel by the interweaving of several narrative strains with choral interludes and lay sermons, but the effect of densely intertwined realities, as in "Proteus" and "Penelope," doesn't rise out of Broch's essentially disparate narrative strands. Yet behind the veil of difference, one senses in Broch as in Joyce the emergent figure of the Eternal Return, haunted by that mythical nomad of millennial cycles, the Wandering Jew, and murmuring the intricate, polyphonic music of history.

The appropriate form of the modern novel was Broch's unremitting concern. He worried the question continually, writing and rewriting each of his books till the overlay of first, second, and third intentions, combined with an aspiration for Germanic profundity, sometimes created an opacity verging on muddle. Yet there can be little doubt that his troubles with the form of fiction stemmed very largely from an overflowing of poetic vision, the massive if unusual problem of too much. *The Death of Virgil* is more successful fiction than *The Sleepwalkers* because it gives way more fully to this excess and follows the *Wake* more unreservedly in making language a subject in itself at the expense of usurpation of its expressive functions.

Historically speaking, the death of Virgil was not far removed in time from the death of Ovid, and Broch in planning his book evidently contemplated for a while building it around the author of the *Metamorphoses* and the *Fasti*. Either figure would have served his fictional purpose, for both were poet-mages, makers and reworkers of legend who found themselves at odds with the imperial society for which they wrote. Both lived at the moment of the world's most gigantic transition, when within the accomplished political *pax romana* was being born the new Christian principle of peace. It was a fact of which both poets, though specifically ignorant, showed themselves intuitively, poetically, uneasily aware—or were at least supposed to have done so. Virgil perhaps won out because in the fourth eclogue he was long reputed to have hailed the birth of the savior; because his reputed wish to burn the *Aeneid* implied a wide range of speculative possibilities; and because his death at Brundisium, in the heart of the empire while attending the emperor, lent some dramatic coloring to a novel which, as Broch planned it, was bound to have a minimum of episode.

The external action of *The Death of Virgil,* reduced to its elements, amounts to very little. Virgil returns from Greece to Brundisium deathly ill of a fever; carried on a litter through the squalid port, he is lodged in a room of the imperial palace by the special care of a mysterious boy Lysanias (through whom one is invited to sense the figure of Hermes *psychopompos*). There, in a feverish trance, he reviews and arraigns his career, accusing himself of having betrayed to aestheticism gifts that should have been turned to ethical ends—the civilizing of the Roman urban masses, for instance. This meditation leads to the clear imperative that the *Aeneid* must be burnt, as an act of spiritual betrayal. The third, and in many ways the least successful, section of the book is an argument between the dying poet and the emperor over the burning of the *Aeneid*, an argument all too protracted in the light of the reader's unflagging confidence that it can turn out only one way. The fourth and final unit is an imaginative sea-journey taken by the soul of Virgil backward up the stream of history, pre-history, and the period before human or animal or vegetable life toward the original and ultimate darkness.

By comparison with *The Sleepwalkers, The Death of Virgil* is largely uncluttered with characters, social impedimenta, and the dramatic conventions that their presence imposes. This is certainly all to the good. The long, lyrical, inward meditations of Virgil are written in streaming, intricately attenuated, and almost unstructured sentences, rising now and again to hymns of lyric questioning and affirmation which are surely among the most affecting things Broch ever wrote. The four sections of the book are associated respectively with "Water," "Fire," "Earth," and "Air"; in one sense, these designations may appear arbitrary, but in the sense that they make up a complete cosmos, they are not. The speculations of dying Virgil run constantly to the transcendent spiritual unity beyond the cosmic unity beyond the aesthetic unity—to the fullness of inward communion which, for a mind in this life and in the year 19 B.C., is "not quite here but yet at hand."

Toward intimations of this rarefied nature the prophetic mind of the dying poet, by summoning all its energies and sensitivities, can partially and momentarily rise. It does so rise, on the stream of an interior monologue more unbroken and more self-generative than anything even in the *Wake*. The language is extraordinarily insubstantial because it uses so many negative abstract nouns, so many oxymorons, so many adjectives and adjectivals in place of nouns, so many linked, repetitive participles in place of independent verbs—and conversely uses so few concrete nouns and so few active verbs within its enormously drawn-out, strongly rhythmical sentences. Yet, paradoxically, the prose is not only attenuated but opaque, as if designed to delay or impede insight by a series of immediate obstacles to conceptualization, while offering as an incitement to go behind the words only a distant diaphanous shadow of an indefinable phantom. Throughout *The Death of Virgil,* words serve to withhold movement as they do in Beckett, but not in order to sustain and verify individual existence, rather to keep the narrator on dialectical tenterhooks between the perception of everything and of nothing. The end of Virgil's voyage is found in the resonant silence of the Logos itself, which puts an end to all human speech as it stuns the human mind with the enormity of its presence:

> —bursting out of the nothing as well as out of the universe, breaking forth as a communication beyond every understanding, breaking forth as a signficance above every comprehension, breaking forth as the pure word which it was, exalted above all understanding and significance whatever, consummating and initiating, mighty and commanding, fear-inspiring and protecting, gracious and thundering, the word of discrimination, the word of the pledge, the pure word.

(pp. 137-45)

The oratorical and prophetic qualities of this diction, to say nothing of its Platonic luminosity, set it altogether apart from any prose of Joyce's devising. But the imaginative process by which Virgil's consciousness advances down a stream of language toward diffusion into a cosmos of light, air, and vacancy is like nothing so much as the processes of the *Wake*. In neither instance do we deal with anything like a deliberate program for the novel; neither author wrote in response to anything but his own deepest intuitions, and as a result neither book is of the common measure. Almost in defiance of his literary programmatics, Broch wrestled like a musclebound Titan with the traditional themes of German romanticism and German philosophy, as Joyce wrought like a blind forger of patterns in the underground caverns of language. There is very little question of influence, but in the hazier fields of affinity one might wander widely for a long time. (p. 145)

> *Robert Martin Adams, "Döblin, Broch," in his* AfterJoyce: Studies in Fiction after "Ulysses," *Oxford University Press, 1977, pp. 134-45.**

ERNESTINE SCHLANT   (essay date 1978)

[*A German-born American educator and critic, Schlant is the author of* Die Philosophie Hermann Brochs *(1971) and* Hermann Broch *(1978), the most comprehensive biographical and critical study in English of Broch to date. In the following excerpt from that work, she examines the principal themes and techniques of* The Sleepwalkers.]

The Sleepwalkers falls into three parts: *1888—Pasenow or Romanticism; 1903—Esch or Anarchy;* and *1918—Huguenau or Matter-of-Factness.* At first glance, the three parts present three distinct units, each of them commanding a separate style. It has been suggested that *Pasenow* is reminiscent of Fontane's realism and his relativistic perspective, *Esch* of naturalism (by virtue of the choice of milieu and characters), and *Huguenau* of expressionism due to the apocalyptic-utopian emotionalism and the disjointed presentation. Yet Broch is not interested in re-creating styles practiced at specific historical periods in order to present "authentic" imitations; he uses them as a critique of the style and, by extension, of the period. By limiting himself to historically conditioned modes of perception and expression, he demonstrates the limits of that period, as well as why and how the characters in the novel were confined by experience and language within the horizons of their epoch. Insensitivity to this metacritical frame results in misinterpretation when, for example, Broch is seen as promulgating the very attitudes and ideas which he inspects critically and rejects with reasons stated. *Huguenau* for example, is a critique of messianic expressionism rather than its recreation.

The continuity and interrelatedness of the three parts is assured through a complex web of symbols and images, through the metamorphoses of recurring images, and the use of lietmotivs. While working on *The Sleepwalkers,* Broch repeatedly mentioned the importance of the "rational-irrational polyphony" and imputed the delay in the completion of the novel to the difficulty of achieving a balanced architecture. Above all, however, his theory of value holds the three tableaux together, places them in a meaningful relationship to each other, and provides, through the sequence of disintegrating value systems, a philosophy of history.

The three episodes span the reign of Emperor William II, beginning with his ascension to the throne in 1888 and ending with his abdication in November, 1918. Although each episode encompasses a relatively static historical period from spring to fall of the same year, the consecutive tableaux suggest movement and provide the intended historical perspective. For each temporal shift, there is a corresponding shift in geography and in social class. From Berlin and the surrounding Mark Brandenburg, the heartland of Wilheminian Prussia with its Junker class, the move is to Mannheim and Cologne with is urban proletarian petit-bourgeoisie; and from there, in the last part, to a small town on the Mosel River with a stable middle class, impoverished wine growers, and temporary inhabitants brought there through the war and gathered around the army hospital. It may well be that "the movement in the trilogy from Prussia through the Rhineland to the Mosel valley represents a symbolic progression from Eastern romantic mysticism to Western rationalism"; but then, rationalism must be understood as the driving force of positivism, and therefore of the disintegration of the formally cohesive social bonds. The hypertrophy of rationalism is then exemplified by the revolution—revolution being, in the Brochian context, the ultimate consequence of the fragmentation of values, leading via anarchy to total freedom, and concomitantly to the outbreak of the irrational. The location of the "nameless, medieval little town" in the vicinity of Trier may be an allusion to Karl Marx, who was born there in 1818, exactly one hundred years before the events of *Huguenau*. That *Huguenau* takes place on Marxist territory is further suggested by the one-day pseudorevolution at the end of the novel, when the medieval city hall, the last architectural remnant of an "integrated" age, goes up in flames and the prison gates are thrown open.

The hero of the first part of the novel is Joachim von Pasenow, second son of a family belonging to the landed gentry in Western Prussia. In accordance with tradition, he is destined for a military career, while his older brother Helmut must take over the estate. Although Helmut would prefer the military and Joachim the country life, neither of them can think of alternatives to the tradition of which they are part. Helmut is killed in a duel and thus dies the "death in the field of honor" properly reserved for the military. This alleged usurpation of Joachim's military role forces Joachim to quit the service and take over the management of the estate. As the elder von Pasenow's eccentricities develop into insanity, he in turn sees Joachim's new role as an usurpation of the dead Helmut's career.

The archetypal triangle situation of the Pasenow males (a father blessing one son, Helmut, while cursing the other, Joachim) is complemented by an even more common triangle: a young man, Joachim, is torn between two women. According to Victorian convention, one is fair, proper, and virginal, as her name indicates: Elisabeth. The other is dark, exotic, and erotic: Ruzena. Joachim is the easy victor without battle in the male triangle. It is much more difficult for him to extricate himself from the dark charms and explosive demands of the show girl Ruzena and to enter into the expected marriage with Elizabeth, daughter of a neighboring estate owner and member of the same social class.

The first part of the novel emphasizes the conventionality, indeed triviality, of events. The protagonists, however, lack this perspective, and experience their lives and the events surrounding them as complex and ambivalent.

On occasion this ambivalence causes excitement, but more often fear, to which the characters respond by withdrawing into habitual and conventional patterns of behavior and thought. The openness inherent in ambivalence, and the sensation of incipient freedom from the habitual, signal the moment when breakthroughs into new systems become possible. That these moments are rarely taken advantage of—indeed, cannot be taken advantage of due to the social, psychological, and cognitive "boundaries" of the individual—demonstrates the restrictive interaction between man and his society, or more precisely, between man and the specific historical period in which he lives.

At the beginning of the novel, Joachim seems well established in his military career. A few months and several cataclysmic events later (after the death of his brother, his affair with Ruzena, and his father's insanity), the first part of the trilogy ends on Joachim and Elisabeth's wedding night, their future secure as landed West Prussian gentry.

Esch, the hero of the second part, follows a similar pattern. Like Joachim, he is thirty years old, experiences an extreme and intense period of dislocation (geographically as well as spiritually and financially), and settles into marriage at the conclusion of the cataclysmic events. Having lost his job as a bookkeeper in Cologne, Esch finds employment as a store clerk in the Mannheim dockyards. He rents a room from the customs inspector Balthasar Korn, who wants him to marry his sister, Erna. At a Cabaret, Esch encounters Ilona, who poses for the knife-thrower Teltscher-Teltini. Esch quits his job to "redeem" Ilona from her dangerous act and organizes ladies' wrestling matches. When the enterprise fails, he returns to Cologne and marries Mutter Hentjen, a tavern keeper from his past, in the late fall of the same year, 1903.

The helplessness which Joachim felt is here intensified into frustration and rage. For Esch, an "impetuous man" . . . , ambiguities of existence are radicalized into either/or propositions since he is much less protected by social convention and upbringing than Joachim. Esch views himself as an orphan, "free" of parents . . . ; born in Luxemburg, a "free" country . . . , he is "free" to go wherever jobs take him. When the world does not make sense (as, for instance, when he is fired from his job), the lack of a system of conventions, which could absorb his fears, causes him to fly into rages. His actions illustrate Broch's view that the loss of guiding value systems entails immediate translation of spontaneous impulses into action. The anger and rage, which lead to the beatings of Mutter Hentjen, are not indications that Esch is a vicious person, but rather demonstrate that his unchecked emotions need to be "tamed" into rational systems in which events "make sense." There is an obvious parallel between Freud's theory of civilization as sublimation of potentially dangerous eruptions of the id and Broch's view of civilization, in which spontaneous, nonrational impulses are absorbed and thereby defused in value systems (and the more comprehensive the value system, the fewer the instances of "free," that is, nonrational, elements in it).

Although the disintegration of value systems has progressed considerably from Joachim to Esch, Esch still relies on one system to explain events: bookkeeping. Radicalized, he experiences the daily incongruities as metaphysical injustices; and the bookkeeping, designed to set accounts straight, correspondingly assumes cosmic dimensions. Since a balancing factor is needed to set the accounts straight, Esch wants to sacrifice himself in order to "redeem" the world of its injustices. This "sacrifice" is conceived as an archaic fertility rite, where fertilizing the barren earth (Mutter Hentjen and Ilona both do not have children) will initiate a new cycle of cosmic order. Broch deliberately combines bookkeeping and sexuality as redemptive forces to characterize Esch. In Esch, he dissects the

anatomy of the irrational before it is channeled into rational systems.

In Broch's opinion, the irrational is the most personal, since it has not yet been structured by extraneous systems. The refurbishing of this enormous reservoir with continuously erupting irrational impulses is due to man's innate awareness and fear of death. (Indeed, Broch maintains that sense of time and, with it, of death is one of the characteristics which make man human and distinguish him from the animal.) It is for the sake of investigating areas such as this, that Broch turned from philosophy to literature, from positivism to metaphysics. Yet the irrational sphere that contains man's knowledge about death cannot be clearly segmented from the rational, since even the most archaic attempts to exorcise this fear are expressed in some kind of rational structures. For this reason, religion is interpreted as a primary attempt to cope with death. And for the same reason, the breakdown of value systems releases impulses which cannot remain free (that is, irrational), but immediately fuse into a "private theology." This "private theology" is an individual's makeshift solution to structure the personal universe.

An example is provided in the scene in which Esch first sees Ilona pose for the knife-throwing Teltscher-Teltini. Esch's physical and metaphysical aspirations fuse in and act of mental acrobatics that is equal to Teltscher-Teltini's knife-whirling artistry.

> Esch could almost have wished that it was himself who was standing up there with his arms raised to heaven, that it was himself being crucified, could almost have wished to station himself in front of that gentle girl and receive in his own breast the menacing blades. . . . Indeed the thought of standing up there alone and forsaken where the long blades might pin one against the board like a beetle, filled him with almost voluptuous pleasure. . . . It was the fanfare of the Last Judgment, when the guilty were to be trodden underfoot like worms; why shouldn't they be spitted like beetles? Why, instead of a sickle, shouldn't Death carry a long darning-needle, or at least a lance?
>
> (pp. 41-6)

Here, Esch is only beginning to warm up to the system of cosmic checks and balances, yet his misapprehended redeemer fixation is Broch's excellent device to demonstrate the use of imagery and symbols epistemologically. It shows the extent and the limitations of the character's emotional and intellectual capacities and underlines Broch's conviction that even the irrational forces can manifest themselves only in a personal and historical guise. Esch combines Christian imagery and symbols (devoid of their "logical context," that is, their function within the Christian value system) with the logic of bookkeeping to shape his own religion—a mystical mathematics which is at most capable of accommodating a "protestant" sectarianism.

At this point, it may be appropriate to focus upon the distinction between the cognitive and epistemological function of a symbol. When Esch speaks about the Anti-Christ, he indicates the limits of his cognitive system, the boundaries of his cognitive faculties; hence "the Anti-Christ" serves to describe Esch in his cognitive context. The epistemological theory that encompasses this "phenomenon Esch" explains why Esch is caught at this cognitive level at this historical point. It embeds the individual incident in an historical analysis of the past, and shows why Esch is incapable of choosing any other alternative that might point into the future.

In keeping with the requirement that each historical period is limited by its particular "style of thought," Broch presents each protagonist in the epistemologically appropriate pattern. The triangle relationships in which Joachim is caught are easily recognizable and border on a cliché, emphasizing that Joachim moves very much in conventional patterns, even when he experiences them as acute personal crises. Within one specific historic period and within one specific social class, only a limited range of experiences is possible. This practice exemplifies in fiction Broch's understanding of the Kantian "conditions of possible experience."

Since Esch lives in an environment where traditional structures have considerably eroded and the irrational is no longer absorbed into existing value systems, he unknowingly reenacts primordial events where sexual practices become religious rites meant to establish a cosmic order. At the same time, Esch's being-in-history occurs in the form of an interaction with archaic, barely recognizable irrational shadows. Broch chooses prehistorical fragments of myths in order to explicate Esch's battle in which he confronts, with mystic ardor and sectarian zeal, the most sinister female triad imaginable. The constellation of Mutter Hentjen, Ilona, and Erna represents the negativity of all mother-goddess myths. Dead, immovable, barren, Mutter Hentjen presides behind her counter and under the picture of her dead husband over a dark tavern. Under this aspect, she is Persephone, queen of the dead, raped and brought to the nether world by her husband (Hades). No amount of symbolic mathematics on Esch's part—his demand that she remove Herr Hentjen's picture from behind the bar or his desire to make her pregnant—can return her to fertility and life. But she is also an archaic Aphrodite: the Aphrodite of brothels, the patroness of saleable love, who knows how to avail herself of her sexuality. She despises the men in the restaurant, but is compassionate with the waitresses who serve the men's desires. Anger and rage are her most prevalent moods . . . , suppressed into stiffness when she presides over her dark, cavernous world.

Ilona is the second figure in this negative trinity. She has much in common with Mutter Hentjen. The two women, who never meet, are described in similar terms: both are indifferent, mute, immovable, with heavy bodies and expressionless, puffy faces; both have been "killed" in their encounter with men . . . and cannot have children. But Ilona is less restrained than Mutter Hentjen, who is literally and symbolically held together by her tight corset and stiff coiffure. Ilona is on intimate terms with death and mutilation, posing in the posture of crucifixion night after night for the whirling knives of the cabaret performer Teltscher-Teltini. Bloodthirsty avenger and victim in one, she embodies the sinister Kali-aspect of a merciless archaic code:

> She bore a scar on her neck and she felt that the man to whom she had been unfaithful that time had been justified in trying to kill her. If Korn had been unfaithful to her, however, she would not have killed him, but merely thrown vitriol at him. Yes, in matters of jealousy such as apportionment of punishment seemed to her fitting, for if one possessed another, one would want to destroy, but if one merely employed another one could content oneself with making the object unfit for use. . . . Once a man had killed himself because of her; it had not touched

her very deeply, but she liked to remember it. . . .

(pp. 46-8)

Erna Korn is the spinster sister of Balthasar Korn, with whom Ilona has an affair while in Mannheim. Erna appears as the very opposite of Ilona: a calculating tease, skinny, quick, talkative, and nasty, but she, too, bears the negative marks of what constituted the virginal aspect in a positive triad. She and Ilona are presented as "sisters," complementing as "daughters" the mother aspect of Mutter Hentjen. Esch's confrontation with this archaic female triad in modern guise points to the danger inherent in the breakdown of value systems: "private theologies" pave the road toward a rebarbarization of previously overcome stages of social and religious evolution.

Erna is marketing her (long lost) virginity as a commodity for the highest bidder; and finally catches the "chaste Joseph" Lohberg, owner of a cigar store. Here an epiphenomenon spins off the central mythological constellation of the female triad, insofar as Erna, the shrewd nonvirgin, becomes pregnant by Esch, making the "chaste Joseph" believe he is the father. The shift from the female triad to the mother-holy infant myth alludes to a historical progression; in the *Bergroman (Mountain Novel)* Broch will make a more detailed use of this technique of indicating successive time frames. Seen here in the context of Esch's erotic mysticism, the unborn child becomes the hope for opposing the Anti-Christ and redeeming the world. This cruel parody of the holy family serves as an indication of Esch's attempt to organize the world in religious terms, but at the same time criticizes his delusions. The transfer of orthodox religious doctrine and imagery to a secular, petit bourgeois, profane setting produces a freakish hybrid, meaningful only to Esch. What clearer verdict could be spoken over Esch's misconceptions?

The *éminence grise* of **The Sleepwalkers'** first two parts is Eduard von Bertrand. Acquainted with Joachim von Pasenow when they both attended military school, he quit military service to become an export-import merchant. Fifteen years later, he is the president of the Mannheim shipping company where Esch finds temporary employment. Free from convention and from the emotional lethargy that characterizes Joachim, Bertrand represents to Joachim excitement as well as danger, the very qualities inherently connected with "freedom." Joachim's ambivalent, even contradictory attitudes are crystalized in his reactions to Bertrand, whom he sees, on the one hand, as "agent provocateur," mocking his attachment to tradition, and on the other hand, as a physician, helping Joachim straighten out his affair (which means terminating the affair with Ruzena in a "gentlemanly manner" by paying her off).

The difference in social class between Esch and Bertrand is too great for them ever to meet on approximately equal terms. Yet after Esch's redeemer aspirations fail, Bertrand becomes for him the cause of everything that is wrong. And since Bertrand's alleged homosexuality is the only bit of hearsay evidence Esch can get hold of, he fastens his sexual-mystic indignation on this source of cosmic putrefaction. In a surreal dream sequence, he travels to Bertrand's retreat in Badenweiler and confronts him in a garden of Eden-Gethsemane, acting Judas to an Anti-Christ whose suicide will not redeem the world and balance the cosmic records.

Bertrand is relativized in the first two parts of the novel through the subjective perspectives of the characters (Joachim, Ruzena, Esch, etc.) who project their dreams and unconscious fears on him. Because of their helplessness and incompetence in worldly matters, he seems of superior mind and character. In the third part of the novel, the theory of value will interpret the occurrences of the entire novel in an historical frame. It is here that the verdict over Bertrand and his kind is spoken. Broch emphasized Bertrand's elusive quality in his role as reflector and catalyst of events (though Bertrand's range, too, is limited to the specific historical periods in which he acts). In a letter to his publisher of June 24, 1930, Broch guards against too concrete a rendition of this protagonist: "After much thought and many experiments, I have come to the conclusion that the figure of Bertrand must not be 'made flesh' any further. This too is a preparation of what is to follow: this figure, though still acting and speaking normally despite a slight turn toward the abstract, is nowhere 'described' in the proper sense of the word." (pp. 48-9)

In *Huguenau,* a third "possible experience" of the same basic pattern is offered: the period of dislocation starts in early spring and ends in late fall with the protagonist's return to a more stable environment, exemplified as in the two previous instances, in marriage. In this final instance, the interim quality of the period under inspection is even further stressed: Huguenau is on vacation. The vacation starts when he deserts the army in Flanders in the spring of 1918 and ends as he returns to his native Colmar, town of the Isenheim Altar, equipped with proper military papers, in November of the same year. He spends his "vacation" in a small Mosel town in the vicinity of Trier, where he meets with Joachim von Pasenow, the town's military commander, and Esch, now a local newspaper publisher. He establishes credibility by posing as the agent of an imaginary conglomerate, interested in buying Esch's newspaper. When this "adequate child of his time" . . . is caught in the outbreak of unrest at the conclusion of the war, he feels free, in the ensuing chaos, to enact the archetypal Oedipus situation: he kills Esch and seduces/coerces Frau Esch. After this climactic episode, content and without misgivings, he returns to the life of an industrious and successful petit bourgeois. En route, he delivers Major von Pasenow, who had literally lost his mind when his car turned over and burned during the minirevolution, to a military hospital in Cologne.

Huguenau consists of about three hundred pages—almost as long as the first two parts together. It is composed of a number of narratives that run parallel to the major plot and portray Hannah Wendling, a young doctor's wife in the town; the orphan Marguerite, drifting in and out of the Esch household; the mason Gödicke who had been buried in the trenches; the doctors, nurses, and convalescent soldiers at the hospital. In addition, ten essays on the disintegration of values and the "Story of the Salvation Army Girl" in Berlin, apparently unconnected with the events in the little Mosel town, are interspersed. The fragmentation of a previously continuous narrative "enacts" the theme of the novel from the structural point of view. The conventional requirements of the novelistic genre are exploded as bits and pieces of narrative, essays, lyrical prose and poetry, drama, and samples of specialized prose such as business letters and newspaper articles, follow each other in unmediated directness.

In keeping with his theory that each historical era has unique characteristics, Broch showed how even this seeming chaos is informed by one overriding concept. He explained this to Daisy Brody in a letter of July 23, 1931, a few months before the publication of *Huguenau:*

> The book consists of a series of stories which are all variations of the same theme, i.e. man's confrontation with loneliness—a confrontation due to the disintegration values . . . These individual stories, interwoven like tapestry, present various levels of consciousness: they rise out of the wholly irrational (story of the Salvation Army Girl) to the complete rationality of the theory (disintegration of values). The other stories take place between these two poles on staggered levels of rationality.
>
> (pp. 49-50)

Broch did not mention that "the staggered levels of rationality" in the novel as a whole also implied a time factor, that is, a progression in time toward disintegration. Yet such an "historically limiting factor," in which certain events are possible only within a specific historical parameter, again acknowledged Broch's interpretation of the Kantian "boundaries of reason." Since the delineation of these boundaries of reason preoccupied Broch in all his intellectual endeavors, it should not surprise that he wanted to show in fiction, too, limitations inherent in the medium. He formulated this endeavor in the "narrator as idea." Deeply impressed by James Joyce's *Ulysses* and its "scientific objectivity," he drew upon the theory of relativity to explain Joyce's technique and implicitly his own aspirations as a novelist. In analogy to the theory of relativity, where "an ideal observer and an ideal act of observation must be included in the field of observation" . . . , he realized "that one cannot simply place an object under a lightbeam and describe it, but that the subject of representation, hence the 'narrator as idea,' and no less language, with which the object of representation is described, are part of the means of representation." . . .

The "narrator as idea" is Broch's contribution to the theory of the novel in the twentieth century. In distinction to the traditional techniques of narrative perspective (omniscient, first person, personal perspectives, etc.) the "narrator as idea" is present in any device which draws attention to the fact that the novel is a deliberate, "scientific" construct, expressing not only narrative content but cognizance of stylistic and technical limitations as well as those of perspective. With the presentation of the "narrator as idea" Broch made a major contribution to the arsenal of novelistic techniques. (p. 51)

> *Ernestine Schlant, in her* Hermann Broch, *Twayne Publishers, 1978, 192 p.*

RENÉ WELLEK   (essay date 1985)

[*Wellek is an American scholar and the author of* A History of Modern Criticism, *a major, comprehensive study of the literary critics of the last three centuries. Wellek's critical method, as demonstrated in* A History *and outlined in his* Theory of Literature, *is one of describing, analyzing, and evaluating a work solely in terms of the problems it poses for itself and how the writer solves them. For Wellek, biographical, historical, and psychological information is incidental. Although many of Wellek's critical methods are reflected in the work of the New Critics, he was not a member of that group, and rejected their more formalistic tendencies. In the following excerpt, Wellek reviews* Hugo von Hofmannsthal and His Time.]

Thomas Mann, Rainer Maria Rilke, and Franz Kafka are the twentieth-century German writers who have made a deep impression in this country. But the three prominent Austrian writers of this century—Hugo von Hofmannsthal, Robert Musil, and Hermann Broch—have never found a wider audience.

Hofmannsthal is mainly known as the librettist of six operas by Richard Strauss: *Elektra, Der Rosenkavalier, Ariadne auf Naxos, Die Frau ohne Schatten, Die ägyptische Helena,* and *Arabella.* His extensive work as a novelist and essayist was translated only when the Bollingen Foundation published *Selected Prose* (1952), the first of three volumes of Hofmannsthal's writing. Broch wrote its introduction. . . .

At first, Broch certainly thought of Hofmannsthal as a *fin de siècle* aesthete, a type he had come to detest. But while reading Hofmannsthal in preparation for writing his introduction, Broch changed his mind. He became more and more interested in Hofmannsthal as a representative figure of his time and as a person whose ancestry and background resembled his own. (p. 75)

While preparing for the Bollingen Foundation's commission, Broch decided to write a monograph on the nineteenth century and on Austria in particular—and only then to focus on Hofmannsthal. But he had to interrupt this project when the Foundation pressed him for the introduction to *Selected Prose.* Broch wrote a literary-critical account of Hofmannsthal's prose writing; it was published in English translation in 1952, after Broch's early death in New Haven, Connecticut (on May 30, 1951). The bulk of the larger project, the monograph, appeared in 1955, in German, in a collection of Broch's essays that included a postscript by Hannah Arendt. Another chapter from the monograph, entitled "The Tower of Babel," was first printed only in 1975.

For *Hugo von Hofmannsthal and His Time,* [editor] Michael P. Steinberg has assembled all this material and translated it into English. . . .

Authorized by some letters of Broch's, Mr. Steinberg subtitles this volume "The European Imagination, 1860-1920" to indicate that Broch goes back in history and discusses Europe as a whole. (The exact dates are in no way justified by the text, however.) Broch begins with a wholesale condemnation of the nineteenth century as "one of the most miserable periods of world history," basing his disapproval on its lack of a single architectural style: the rapid succession of false Baroque, false Renaissance, and false Gothic. Broch sets his condemnation of nineteenth-century architecture in a general concept of history, popular at the time, which traced the decay and disintegration of man in the modern period from the Middle Ages. This concept of decay pervaded German thought in many versions. Although Oswald Spengler's *Untergang des Abendlandes (The Decline of the West)* is the best known, Egon Friedell's *Kulturgeschichte der Neuzeit (Cultural History of Modern Times)* is closer to Broch's discussion, since Friedell did not believe that a complete catastrophe would come to Western civilization but cherished the hope of its rebirth, a return to an integrated society and a whole man. (p. 76)

Broch states his idea forcefully, first in general terms and then with application to Austria. He gives it a sharply anti-bourgeois point. The bourgeois combined rationalism and hedonism, which together cover the general misery of civilization with decoration. Broch sees, however, that the realistic novel of nineteenth century aimed at totality. In terms strongly reminiscent of Lukács's *Theory of the Novel,* Broch surveys the writings of Balzac, Dickens, and Zola and then, surprisingly, recognizes another exception to his general condemnation of nineteenth-century art: the theater, where the art of acting kept alive a sense of style. Broch then describes the reaction against the failures of nineteenth-century art as a turning away from dec-

oration. This turning away begins with Impressionism, which, according to Broch, discovered the medium as reality and returned art to the fully irrational sphere, particularly in the work of Van Gogh and Cézanne.

Broch was convinced that the world of art expresses the irrational but that it still conveys knowledge, even giving us metaphysics. "Without a grasp of reality there is no genuine art." In his own development, Broch had begun as an engineer and a student of positivistic philosophy; he then turned to fiction writing because he had arrived at the conviction that only art can convey and express the true essence of reality. *The Sleepwalkers* and *The Death of Virgil* are philosophical novels which combine poetry and philosophy. Only toward the end of his life did Broch return to straightforward speculation, to an immense project on mass psychology. In an autobiographical sketch he even disparaged his fictional writings. His judgment here seems overly harsh, even if we may come to the conclusion that his novels are, at times, an unhappy hybrid of philosophy and art.

While Broch admired Impressionism for returning art to its wellspring in man's irrational essence, he also believed that it paved the way for the *l'art pour l'art* movement of the late nineteenth century. *L'art pour l'art,* for Broch, meant an indifference to social reality and a cult of cruelty. Broch finds both in Baudelaire, who with his followers paved the way for the darkest anarchy of the twentieth century. Although *l'art pour l'art* was anti-decorative, it did not descend to the unconscious, did not create a new myth, a new totality. Broch discusses the ideal of totality in Melville and Tolstoy, claiming that the Russian novel broke through the limits of *l'art pour l'art* and opened the door to a new ethical work of art; nevertheless, he argues, it did not itself create a new myth. Even Joyce ultimately failed, according to Broch, although Broch had earlier hailed Joyce as the representative of a new age, as the creator of a new novel of simultaneity, of an epic totality. This section of the book, on general European culture, ends with only a vague hope for a reconciliation of art and ethics in a new myth.

In the second section of the book Broch narrows his focus to Germany, Austria, and Vienna. The reflections on the vacuum of German art become more concrete. Wagner, characterized as an "unmusical genius of music and an unpoetic genius of poetry," and Nietzsche are both made responsible for the shameful events of the Nazi period, even though they might have disavowed them. Vienna of the early twentieth century is described as a town of museums, alive only in the theater. Broch draws a picture of the Emperor Franz Josef as a totally isolated man who lived in solitude while the aristocracy engaged in the pursuit of fugitive pleasures—all the while expecting catastrophe. The bourgeoisie, aping the upper classes, was no better. In Broch's view Vienna was the capital of *Kitsch* and *Gemütlichkeit;* to him this implies a wisdom that senses demise and accepts it. "Nevertheless," Broch writes, "it was operetta wisdom, and under the shadow of the approaching demise it became spectral . . . and developed into Vienna's gay apocalypse." Broch's picture here seems grossly overdrawn. Even the Emperor, old and struck by the tragedies of his family, was not that isolated. He had his friendship with Katharina Schratt and was a jovial companion of officers, hunters, and stableboys during his long months in his villa at Ischl. The ordinary Vienna burgher rarely had premonitions of the end until the later stages of the War.

Finally we arrive at Hofmannsthal. We are told the story of his ancestry, his assimilation into the Catholic aristocracy, and his religious crisis (which possibly made him contemplate entering the Franciscan order). Hofmannsthal was a prodigy. Even in the Gymnasium he published poetry and was an instant success. Broch recognizes that the youthful Hofmannsthal was not an aesthete but an artist who was searching for an ethical center. It is true that he lived in a dream world, but even the earliest poems and plays circled around the theme of life and death; their deliberate impersonality was only an attempt by Hofmannsthal to hide his struggle for self-transcendence. Broch contrasts Hofmannsthal with Stefan George and Rilke, who thought of themselves as priests of a religion of art. Hofmannsthal, in contrast, found an objective style in his work for the theater. Broch sees this turn as the result of what he calls "the second assimilation." Hofmannsthal identified with both the Austrian aristocracy and with the people, the folk (a fairy-tale entity, in Broch's view). Hofmannsthal searched for an individual style but found it only in his last drama, *The Tower*. Here Broch comments for the first time on Hofmannsthal's "only too well-known" fictional letter, written under the name of "Lord Chandos" [see excerpt dated 1902 in *TCLC*, Vol. 11], which expresses despair about language. This despair led him to appeal to the magic of music, according to Broch. Broch is upset by his collaboration with Richard Strauss; he suspects the proximity of Wagner and sees Hofmannsthal's turn to the theater as a surrender to the "vacuum of values." Thus Hofmannsthal became, for Broch, a symbol of a disappearing Austria, of its disappearing aristocracy and disappearing theater—"a symbol in the vacuum, not of the vacuum." Here the original manuscript of *Hofmannsthal and His Time* breaks off.

It was at this point that Broch composed the introduction to *Selected Prose*. Here he again expounds Hofmannsthal's impersonality concept, his desire to suppress the ego, his anti-expressionism. "Confession is nothing, knowledge is everything," Hofmannsthal writes; that is, knowledge means a complete identification with the object. Broch quotes the Sanscrit "tat van asi"—"I am you"—which he, like Hofmannsthal, learned from Schopenhauer. But this idea implies mysticism, ecstasy, the inability of the artist to ever identify with his object, confined as he is to the enmity and incomprehensibility of things. Hofmannsthal made a compromise between these views. He pronounced an injunction against lyric poetry but felt that poetry could flourish on the stage and in narrative.

Broch characterizes Hofmannsthal's extremely varied narrative prose in general terms—as visual, as an enchantment with landscape. The alps, the plains of the Po, Venice, the motifs of travel and water dominate in it, while Hofmannsthal's protagonists remain childlike in a fairy-tale atmosphere. Speaking in the tradition of German aesthetics, Broch sees in allegory a dangerous process of petrification. But Hofmannsthal, according to Broch, broke through to beautiful simplicity with *The Woman Without a Shadow*, a fairy tale which Broch rightly considers one of Hofmannsthal's most successful works. Still, Hofmannsthal felt obliged to return to the theme of childhood in *The Tower*. Broch alludes to this play several times admiringly, but finds no occasion to discuss it in detail. He turns rather to Hofmannsthal's essayistic work, praising particularly the travel sketches, *The Moments of Greece,* where Hofmannsthal, who disapproved of confessional poetry, came closest to speaking of himself. (pp. 77-80)

Broch's chapter entitled "The Tower of Babel" looks like another attempt to rewrite the Hofmannsthal monograph. It is

obviously later than the chapters printed first in 1955. It expounds the very same argument in somewhat different terms. We hear first of the *fin de siècle* style as a form of rococo. Broch alludes to the fashion for Japanese art and to the Vienna *Sezession*. He also discusses, again, French Impressionism, which he says produced two trends in the other arts. Impressionism in music appeals by its brightness in contrast to the gloom of Wagner's music. Symbolism in literature is the fairy-tale of the period. In Maeterlinck it approaches pantomime and leads to the dancing of Isadora Duncan. According to Broch, Vienna did not care for symbolism, either in dance or painting.

On all these issues Hofmannsthal was a typical Viennese. He was touched by the new trends—Impressionism and symbolism—but remained a traditionalist who wanted to do things better. For Broch, *Der Rosenkavalier* is a comedy ennobling the style of Da Ponte, the librettist of *Don Giovanni, Le Nozze di Figaro,* and *Cosi fan tutte.* About the time of *Rosenkavalier* many new trends were evident in the arts. Arnold Schönberg and his pupil Alban Berg were renovating Viennese music. There was Futurism in painting, which seems to Broch inferior. Cubism, he admits, was a real technical novelty, but its effect on literature seems to Broch minimal. The great novelists of the time—Thomas Mann, Henry James, Marcel Proust—were solidly upper class and bourgeois, since language puts a constraint on the artist. Only Joyce broke the yoke. Joyce's *Ulysses* and *Finnegans Wake* are described as the *summa* of all ages. But then Broch says that they reduce man to his most primitive universal traits. "His two-leggedness is left, all knowledge useless, useless everything that man knows about himself." Surprisingly (Broch's conversion to Hofmannsthal's greatness must have been then complete) Broch now states that Hofmannsthal exceeds Proust in poetic, though not in psychological, wealth and that in Hofmannsthal's compassion for humanity he is more poetic than Joyce, who did not know compassion.

Broch's section on "ethical art" ranges widely over social art from Ibsen to Hauptmann and Gorky and again discusses the relation between art and ethics (Broch avoids the term "morality"). He holds fast to the view that art must remain autonomous but again rejects the inflated claims of Nietzsche and Stefan George, saying that they lead to dehumanization. Hofmannsthal's *Everyman*, a rewriting of the English mystery play, was a call for a return to Christianity. But it and the *Great World Theater* were transformed by Max Reinhardt into almost blasphemous spectacles for the philistine rabble. Broch sees hope in the ethical art of satire, alluding to Karl Kraus. He still believed that the development of art (not its non-existent progress) serves ethical progress and that it could ultimately avert the world catastrophe. He trusts the conjunction between the naturalism of satire and the anti-naturalism of avant-garde painting—their common faith in the ethical and hence in the divinity of man. Hofmannsthal is forgotten. He would not fit on either side.

Obviously, *Hofmannsthal and His Time* is a bewildering panorama. In spite of some final expressions of hope, it paints a picture of unrelieved gloom, of the disintegration of man, the decadence of art, the end of the great tradition. Broch understandably felt the end of the world of his youth acutely. He believed in the *Zeitgeist*, the integrity of every period, and judged it from a lofty ethical and artistic point of view. The condemnation of the nineteenth century and of Vienna of the *fin de siècle* seems to me too sweeping. The phrase "gay apocalypse" ignores the continuity of life of the masses, who were hardly affected by the frivolity of the upper crust and who were aware of the impending disaster only when the outbreak of the war brought it home to everybody. The accomplishments of the time in the arts keep their enduring value whatever the objections to individual figures and works may be. It may be an excessively sober and commonsense conclusion to say that one should avoid two extremes. One must avoid the sentimental glorification of Old Vienna and old Austria-Hungary nurtured by a century-and-a-half-old propaganda, which ignores the sins of the monarchy and the German ruling classes against what they called "nationalities." However great the accomplishments, quite unrelated, of writers living in Vienna—Freud and Wittgenstein (both neglected by Broch), Hofmannsthal, Musil, Broch, Karl Kraus, and others—other centers of the time could compete very well: Paris, Petersburg, and London certainly. On the other hand, one must also avoid embracing Broch's view of a complete "vacuum of values" which can be defended only by a philosophy of history which prophesies decay and doom. (pp. 80-1)

René Wellek, "Hofmannsthal's World," in The New Criterion, *Vol. 4, No. 4, December, 1985, pp. 75-81.**

ADDITIONAL BIBLIOGRAPHY

Arendt, Hannah. "Hermann Broch: 1886-1951." In her *Men in Dark Times*, pp. 111-51. New York: Harcourt, Brace, & World, 1968.
   Analyzes Broch's philosophy of life and art.

Baumann, Walter. Review of *Short Stories*, by Hermann Broch. *Seminar: A Journal of Germanic Studies* 2, No. 2 (1966): 62-4
   Commends the collection as an excellent introduction to Broch's major works.

———. "The Idea of Fate in Hermann Broch's *Tod des Vergil*." *Modern Language Quarterly* XXIX, No. 2 (June 1968): 196-206.
   Considers Virgil's struggle to overcome fate to be the novel's key theme.

Breuer, Robert. "Hermann Broch: Poet and Philosopher." In *International Literary Annual No. 2*, edited by John Wain, pp. 159-69. New York: Criterion Books, 1959.
   Biographical and critical essay.

Casey, Timothy J. "Questioning Broch's *Der Versucher*." *Deutsche Vierteljahrsschrift für Literaturwissenschaft und Geistesgeschichte* 47, No. 3 (1973): 467-507.
   Examines the principal themes and techniques of *Der Versucher*.

Cohn, Dorrit Claire. *"The Sleepwalkers": Elucidations of Hermann Broch's Trilogy*. Paris: Mouton & Co., 1966, 179 p.
   Detailed analysis of what the author considers the most enigmatic elements of *The Sleepwalkers*: its complex narrative structure, the character Bertrand, the "Ahasverus" poem, and the sleepwalk symbol.

———. "Laughter at the Nadir: On a Theme in Hermann Broch's Novels." *Monatshefte* LXI, No. 2 (Summer 1969): 113-21.
   Demonstrates how "Broch uses laughter as the symbolic orchestration of the void between historical epochs, when old values are dying and new ones have not yet been born."

Hardin, James N., Jr. "The Theme of Salvation in the Novels of Hermann Broch." *PMLA* 85, No. 2 (March 1970): 219-27.
   Examines how savior figures in Broch's novels embody his dualistic philosophy of salvation, which "reconciles the mystical and empirical, the rational and irrational extremes within man's psyche and in his external environment."

Hatfield, Henry. "Squaring the Circle: Hermann Broch's *The Sleepwalkers*." In his *Crisis and Continuity in Modern German Fiction*, pp. 109-27. Ithaca: Cornell University Press, 1969.
   Praises Broch's intention and achievement in *The Sleepwalkers* but denies that the trilogy is a completely successful work of art.

Herd, E. W. "Hermann Broch and the Legitimacy of the Novel." *German Life & Letters* n.s. XII, No. 4 (July 1960): 262-77.
   Discusses Broch's doubts about the legitimacy of literature as a form of expression and analyzes the technical innovations with which he hoped to transcend the limitations of the traditional novel in order to better express the "totality of human experience."

———. "The Guilt of the Hero in the Novels of Hermann Broch." *German Life & Letters* XVII (1964): 30-9.
   Examines the recurring theme of guilt in Broch's novels, noting similarities among his central characters in their evasion of ethical responsibility.

Horrocks, David. "The Novel as History: Hermann Broch's Trilogy—*Die Schlafwandler*." In *Weimar Germany: Writers and Politics*, edited by A. F. Bance, pp. 38-52. Edinburgh: Scottish Academic Press, 1982.
   Considers Broch's philosophy of history "of questionable validity" and criticizes its effect on the artistic quality of *Die Schlafwandler*, citing a tendency for "the characters to become mere puppets, manipulated by the author to illustrate this or that point from the theory."

Isaacs, J. "Culture, Chaos, and Order." In his *An Assessment of Twentieth-Century Literature: Six Lectures Delivered in the B.B.C. Third Programme*, pp. 105-32. Port Washington, N.Y.: Kennikat Press, 1951.*
   Cites *The Sleepwalkers* and *The Death of Virgil* in a discussion of major twentieth-century novels primarily concerned with life at the end of a cultural era, asserting that "although his themes are chaos, disintegration and hysteria, Mr. Broch is almost the only optimist among all the great writers of this century."

Kurz, Paul Konrad. "Hermann Broch's Trilogy *Die Schlafwandler*: Contemporary Criticism and Novel of Redemption." In his *On Modern German Literature*, translated by Sister Mary Frances McCarthy, Vol. I, pp. 105-30. University: University of Alabama Press, 1970.
   Discusses Broch's indictment of his era and treatment of the salvation theme.

Lehner, Fritz. "Hermann Broch." *Life and Letters Today* 15, No. 6 (Winter 1936): 64-71.
   Discusses Broch's exploration in *The Sleepwalkers* of "the gravity of our time."

Modern Austrian Literature: Special Hermann Broch Issue 13, No. 4 (1980): 1-235.
   Contains essays in English and German by eleven critics, including Theodore Ziolkowski ("Broch's Image of Vergil and its Context"), Mark Bernheim ("Style: Abstraction and Empathy in Hermann Broch's *Die Schlafwandler*"), and Alice von Kahler ("Broch als Übersetzer").

Mueller, William R. "Waiting for the Logos." In his *Celebration of Life: Studies in Modern Fiction*, pp. 251-72. New York: Sheed & Ward, 1972.
   Views *The Sleepwalkers* as "a microcosmic portrait of a Western civilization which has its roots in Athens and Jerusalem, has become a 'lost generation,' and may look forward to a glorious rebirth only when the Logos (Greek and Christian) once again becomes the informing Value of all values."

O'Hara, J. D. Review of *The Guiltless*, by Hermann Broch. *New York Times Book Review* (21 April 1974): 4.
   Praises *The Guiltless* as a "thoroughly satisfactory and valuable" work, noting that Broch's "ironic humor leaves no character untouched, while baroque elaborations of thought lurk beneath the social and often comic surface."

Osterle, Heinz D. "Hermann Broch, *Die Schlafwandler*: Revolution and Apocalypse." *PMLA* 86, No. 5 (October 1971): 946-58.

Considers *Die Schlafwandler* "one of the great counterrevolutionary works of this century," arguing that "the function of its apocalyptic symbolism . . . is to provide a basis for its eminently conservative rhetoric."

Rabaté, Jean-Michel. "Joyce and Broch; or, Who Was the Crocodile?" *Comparative Literature Studies* 19, No. 2 (Summer 1982): 121-33.*
Analyzes Broch's utilization of and departure from James Joyce's narrative techniques.

Rosenfeld, Paul. *"The Death of Virgil."* Chimera III, No. 3 (Spring 1945): 47-55.
Favorable review.

Schlant, Ernestine. "Hermann Broch and Modern Physics." *Germanic Review* LIII, No. 2 (Spring 1978): 69-79.
Assesses Broch's knowledge of current scientific research and discusses how he incorporated into his fiction the philosophical implications of contemporary developments in physics and mathematics.

Schoolfield, George C. "Notes on Broch's *Der Versucher.*" *Monatshefte* XLVIII, No. 1 (January 1956): 1-16.
Investigates the sources of *Der Versucher,* including local Austrian history, classical mythology, current events, and mass psychology.

———. "Broch's *Sleepwalkers:* Aeneas and the Apostles." *James Joyce Review* 2, Nos. 1-2 (Spring-Summer 1958): 21-38.*
Demonstrates that Virgil's *Aeneid* is retold four times in *The Sleepwalkers.*

Simpson, Malcolm R. *The Novels of Hermann Broch.* Bern: Peter Lang, 1977, 113 p.
Discusses Broch's major fiction.

Strelka, Joseph. "Hermann Broch: Comparatist and Humanist." *Comparative Literature Studies* XII, No. 1 (March 1975): 67-79.

Explores the ways in which *The Death of Virgil* expresses both the author's theory of literature and his humanistic values.

Thomas, R. Hinton. "The Novels of Hermann Broch." *Cambridge Journal* VI, No. 10 (1953): 591-604.
Contends that Broch exploited "the remarkable technical resources of the modern novelist—to a great extent evolved, in a spirit diametrically opposed to his own, as a way of imparting significance in the absence of conviction—or of any purpose beyond art itself—in the service of moral and human values."

Untermeyer, Jean Starr. "Midwife to a Masterpiece." In her *Private Collection,* pp. 218-77. New York: Alfred A. Knopf, 1965.*
Personal recollection of the author's collaboration with Broch on the English translation of *The Death of Virgil.*

Weigand, Hermann J. "Broch's *Death of Virgil:* Program Notes." *PMLA* XLII, No. 2 (June 1947): 525-54.
Analyzes the novel's principal themes and techniques.

White, John J. "Broch, Virgil, and the Cycle of History." *Germanic Review* XLI, No. 2 (March 1966): 103-10.
Demonstrates how *Die Schuldlosen,* "set in the twentieth century, uses the two-thousand year cycle of history artistically to point back to the world of antiquity, to highlight a situation similar to our own," while *Der Tod des Vergil,* "set in the first century B.C., uses the same cyclic concept to point forward to our own age."

Ziolkowski, Theodore. *Hermann Broch.* New York: Columbia University Press, 1964, 48 p.
Informative introduction to Broch's life and works.

———. "Hermann Broch: *The Sleepwalkers.*" In his *Dimensions of the Modern Novel: German Texts and European Contexts,* pp. 138-80. Princeton: Princeton University Press, 1969.
Comprehensive discussion of *The Sleepwalkers,* including its composition, literary influences, and theoretical basis.

Dino Campana

1885-1932

Italian poet and prose writer.

Campana was an Italian lyric poet whose works combine elements of Futurism, in particular the reaction of that movement against the romanticism of late nineteenth-century Italian culture, with influences from various nineteenth-century Italian and foreign poets, including Giosuè Carducci, Walt Whitman, and Arthur Rimbaud. While Campana is often included in critical discussion of the Futurist poets and essayists, especially F. T. Marinetti, Piero Jahier, Clemente Rèbora, and Camillo Sbarbaro, some critics have pointed out that he should not be thought of as part of the Futurist movement, nor was he ever considered such during his life and career. Rather, Campana served a "Futurist apprenticeship," in the words of Italian poet and critic Eugenio Montale, during the course of his development as a lyric poet, and his work is distinguished by a broader European rather than an exclusively Italian perspective.

Campana was born in Marradi to an elementary school principal and his wife. He was a precocious child and excellent student who, biographers report, early exhibited the signs of mental instability that led to his youthful reputation as "that strange son of the school superintendent." After his primary and secondary schooling in Marradi and Florence, Campana studied chemistry at the University of Bologna, but in 1907 was dismissed from the school because of wild behavior and dangerous, unsupervised experiments that often resulted in unplanned explosions. After his expulsion from the university, Campana began a period of international peregrination that took him first to South America, where he worked as a fireman, a miner, a gaucho, and as a doorman at a Buenos Aires nightclub. On returning to Europe he joined a gypsy caravan at Odessa and travelled with them for several years. Many of his poems address or mention a young gypsy woman who is regarded alternately with attraction and repulsion, love and fear, pity and loathing. Throughout his travels Campana was frequently jailed for his public displays of aberrant behavior, often manifested in violent verbal and physical attacks upon passersby. As it became increasingly obvious that his erratic actions were not within his control, he was more often committed to mental institutions for periods of observation and given such treatment as was available at the time.

By 1913 Campana had returned to Marradi. He undertook courses of chemistry and pharmaceutical science at the universities of Bologna, Genoa, and Florence, but abandoned his studies without earning a degree. Late in 1913 Campana took the manuscript of *Canti orfici (Orphic Songs),* his sole collection of poetry, to Giovanni Papini and Ardengo Soffici, editors of the avant-garde Florentine literary and political journal *La voce.* When Soffici lost the only copy of the manuscript, Campana rewrote the text and had the book published by a local Marradi printer. Lacking the means of distribution afforded authors whose works are brought out by publishing houses, Campana took to selling his book of poetry on the streets and at sidewalk cafés. Also in 1913 Campana joined the Italian army; he advanced to the rank of captain before he was discharged on grounds of mental derangement. In his increasingly infrequent lucid stages, he would seek work. During one such

period he met and fell in love with the poet and novelist Rina Faccio, who wrote under the name Sibilla Aleramo. Their published letters, written between 1916 and 1918, chronicle Campana's gradual descent into final and irrevocable madness. Campana wrote no poetry after 1916; in 1918 he was committed to the Castel Pulci asylum in Florence, where he spent the remaining fourteen years of his life, at one point telling a doctor: "I was a writer once but had to give it up, being of unsound mind. I don't connect ideas. I don't follow . . . ."

Canti orfici has undergone numerous editions since the single publication that Campana himself oversaw. Campana's close friend Bino Binazzi edited a second edition of the *Canti* while Campana was still alive, including some poems that did not appear in the first edition; and subsequent editions have added further poetry and prose culled from Campana's manuscripts and notebooks. *Canti orfici* is a collection of highly personal lyric poems. Despite frequent critical comparison of Campana's poetry with that produced by the Futurists, many English-language critics also note several significant differences. For example, although the repetition, broken syntax, and irregular punctuation characteristic of Futurist poetry are also found in Campana's work, John Frederick Nims has pointed out that Campana differs from the Futurists in his heavy reliance on often ambiguous adjectives, a poetic nuance that was anathema to Futurist writers. Nims and Caroline Mezey have further contended that the erratic elements in Campana's poetry, though similar to Futurist stylistic devices, actually stem from the disordered character of Campana's mind and not from the Futurist influence. Critics find that when he is at his best, as in such lyrics as ''Giardino autunnale'' (''Autumn Garden'') and ''L'invetriata'' (''The Window''), Campana achieves a lucidity of imagery and color unsurpassed by other early twentieth-century Italian poets. However, because his poems are often the intensely personal reflections of Campana's ''spiritual confusion,'' the imagery and internal references are sometimes so obscure as to be meaningless to readers.

Although he has never been widely known outside of his own land, within post-World War I Italian literature Campana is highly regarded as one of that country's most distinctive and original poets. He utilized aspects of major trends in European literature, including the radicalism of the most avant-garde movements, as well as elements from the classical tradition of Italian poetry, to create works that Nims called ''too idiosyncratic to be imitated''; poetry that, when unmarred by what I. L. Salomon terms ''the marks of his insanity'' which ''are like stigmata on the corpus of his work,'' is unequalled for its color, clarity of imagery, and musical lyricism.

PRINCIPAL WORKS

Canti orfici (poetry) 1914
   [*Orphic Songs,* 1968]
Inediti (poetry and prose) 1941
Taccuino (notebook) 1949
Lettere di Dino Campana e Sibilla Aleramo (letters) 1958
Taccuinetto faentino (notebook) 1960
Le mie lettere sono fatte per essere bruciate (letters) 1968
Fascicolo marradese inedito (notebook) 1972
Opere e contributi (poetry and prose) 1973
Il più lungo giorno (poetry) 1974

*This work has appeared in numerous revised and enlarged editions with supplementary poetry and prose added.

DINO CAMPANA   (letter date 1914)

[*The following excerpt is taken from a letter Campana wrote to Giuseppe Prezzolini after Prezzolini had assumed editorship of* La voce *and before Campana learned that former editor Ardengo Soffici had lost the manuscript of* Canti orfici.]

Distinguished Mr. Prezzolini,

I address myself to you, eminent Sir. I am a poor devil who writes as he feels: perhaps you will be willing to listen. I am that specimen who was introduced to you by Mr. Soffici at the Futurist Exhibition as a misfit, a so-and-so who from time to time writes something worthwhile. I write prose-poems and poetry: no one wants to publish me and I need to be published; in order to prove to myself I exist and to keep on writing I need to be published. I add that I deserve to be published since I feel that that bit of poetry I know how to create has a purity of accent that is little common among us today. I am not ambitious but I think that after having been tossed about the world and mangled by life, my word despite its wit has a right to be heard. . . . I prefer to send you my oldest and frankest poems, old in metaphor yet intricate in form; however you will

hear a spirit that frees itself—I wait in complete trust—in homage I revere you.

> *Dino Campana, in a letter to Giuseppe Prezzolini on January 6, 1914, in his* Orphic Songs, *translated by I. L. Salomon, October House Inc., 1968, p. 27.*

EUGENIO MONTALE   (essay date 1942)

[*Montale was an Italian poet, critic, and translator in the humanist tradition who is often regarded as the most important poet in modern Italian literature. For his small but highly respected body of poetry, his many important critical studies, and his translations of world literary masterpieces into Italian, Montale received the Nobel Prize for literature in 1975. In the following excerpt, originally published in the Italian journal* L'Italia che scrive *in September, 1942, Montale offers a retrospective view of Campana's career. The Lacerbians referred to in the excerpt are the contributors to and editors of the noted avant-garde literary and political journal* Lacerba *that appeared between 1913 and 1915.*]

The publication of an entire volume of uncollected writings by Dino Campana [*Inediti*] and the republication of the *Canti Orfici* in a more accurate edition than the previous (1928) one offers a good pretext in several respects for re-examining the work of a poet who has not been forgotten. . . . The poet of Marradi was not unappreciated; and if, in his opinion, help and assistance of a more concrete nature did not accompany this appreciation before he was struck by an incurable ''spiritual confusion,'' he was not alone in suffering such a fate. Much is granted to dead poets, little to the living: especially to the living with the troublesome nature of Campana. Proud, sick, and restless as he was, who could have calmed him and brought him peace? Strictly speaking, we repeat, there was no lack of appreciation. When Campana published in *Riviera Ligure,* between November 1915 and May 1916, the five poems which [Campana's friend and editor Bino] Binazzi added to the 1928 edition of the *Canti Orfici* . . . , the curiosity that had been aroused by the *Canti Orfici* showed no signs of abating. . . . In 1917 I myself came to know a group of student officers who were confirmed ''Campanians'' in the barracks of the Palazzo della Pilotta in Parma. . . . But in 1918 Campana was placed permanently in a sanatorium, and it was then that his myth was born. Since then, articles on the *Canti Orfici* have followed one after another, among the most notable of which for me are those by Solmi, Gargiulo, Contini, and Bo. . . . In these writings one can see plainly the double interpretation of Campana which was already latent in his earliest critics, and which finally attained perfect clarity of expression in Contini's essay. Is Campana a *visual* or a *visionary* poet? A recent rereading of the *Canti Orfici* has convinced me—let me say right off—that the horns of this dilemma are anything but irreconcilable: for it is true that Campana's critics who are least inclined to mysticism and irrationalism concede him ''illuminations pushed to the point of myth'' (Gargiulo) and deny that in Campana it is possible to speak of simple impressionism (Contini); while on the other hand the most astute interpreter of the poet's ''uncontrollable night'' (Carlo Bo) has expressed himself in phrases and images (''a poetry that did not have the time to flower, or did so only with the too-early, cruel assistance of its fruits'') which reveal at least one limit of this poetry.

The observation, which is easy enough to make even if it were not confirmed by personal recollection, that Campana was soon noticed by the establishment, must not lead one to think that the rumor-mongers of the moment (futurists, Lacerbians, etc.) paid much attention to the author of the *Canti Orfici.* They may have taken him for one of their own, but at a proper distance; and Campana himself did not regard them with great sympathy. Still, the poet did not sprout like a mushroom in an atmosphere unprepared to receive him. One of the interests of the uncollected work just published (about sixty poems, along with various notes, aphorisms, pensées, etc.) is precisely that they allow us to relate Campana better to his times and shed light on his futurist apprenticeship. An apprenticeship about which there had always been explicit and implicit doubts. Today the weakest parts of the *Inediti* (*Unpublished Writings*), and especially of the forty-four poems in the recently discovered notebook, convince us that the poet began and developed anything but precociously, in an atmosphere red-hot with isms. The list of poems that contain striking traces of the work in Marinetti's first anthology of 1912 would not be short. They range from a "tentacular" Marinetti-Buzzi ambience (**"O poesia poesia," "Oh l'anima vivente," "Umanità fervente sulla sprone,"** etc) to an Art Nouveau-style symbolism, somewhere between Lucini and D'Annunzio (**"Convito romano egizio"** and others). There are also signs of the "loutish" Palazzeschi (**"Prosa fetida"**) sometimes combined with the scene-painting of Rosai (**"Notturno teppista"**). . . . But the group also contains poems which will be significant when set next to those of the *Orfici*: **"Donna genovese," "Il ritorno," "Sulle montagne,"** for example. There is also the typical Campanian musical *Stimmung* a little bit everywhere (**"A un angelo del Costa," "Furibondo," "Une femme qui passe"** . . .) which we shall see later in *La chimera*. As well as that vast Mediterranean sense of space which is typical of certain of Campana's efforts, here, naturally, not without a great deal of D'Annunzio.

Are they juvenile poems? Up to a point. In all probability, the poems in the notebook were written between 1912 and 1914 when the poet was between twenty-seven and twenty-nine. Perhaps they were all transcribed quickly and at once, making use of recent experiences (recollections of his trip to America in March-November 1913) as well as others less recent, so that they wouldn't be lost. It's impossible to know for certain. The most achieved poems of the *Orfici*, the only ones that stay in one's memory, are almost all here; or their musical germ is here. Campana seems to have included them in the *Orfici* without looking at the notebook again. And when we remember that after the manuscript of the *Orfici* was lost Campana rewrote it very speedily, it is possible to conclude that the rewriting-transcribing of the parts of the notebook included in the *Orfici* must also have been rapid: rapid, and followed, if not by a repudiation, then certainly by dissatisfaction and disinterest. Clearly the notebook was put away for what Campana thought would be forever. We know nothing of the manuscript of the *Orfici* that was lost; nor how far the recopied manuscript followed the old one in the prose it contained. But we can conclude that here too Campana had worked *ex novo* and quickly, if it is true that they represent the maturest part, in a stylistic sense as well, of the book. Campana saved only a small part of the earlier poems represented wholly or in part by the notebook—clearly the best part, thus proving himself a perceptive critic of himself. In any case it is clear that—whether from memory or not—Campana took the verse part of the *Orfici* from his notebook. He cut the poems, pruning and lightening them. The idea of a "European, musical, colorful" poetry was a product of Campana's education as well as an instinct; but it clearly had been accompanied or preceded by an experimentation, still somewhat inert and passive, with the new isms then in the air. Official Futurism, too, like the innovators at the turn of the century, had claimed that it was "breaking the glass," clearing the air. Campana, however, had chosen subtler masters than

those followed by his temporary mentors. He instinctively rejected the more mechanical, cataloguing aspect of the free verse that was then fashionable, and went—as the facts confirm—to the truest sources of the movement, from Whitman to Rimbaud. For himself, in art and life, he related an issue of style to an issue of conscience, and he was aware that in his time and place his was a new and different voice. But we should be careful not to attribute too much conscious reflection to a man who, due to the tragic and precarious state of his health, was the poet of a brief, perhaps extremely brief, period. One of the charms of Campana's poetry certainly lies in its obscurity, which was anything but intentional, but which the poet's illness protected and favored. It is a poetry—here I share the opinion of Solmi—"which can hardly be separated from the feverish atmosphere which constitutes its source." Gargiulo seems to feel otherwise; he points out the poet's obscurities and declares that "nothing, on the page, authorizes us to make biographical deductions as to the causes of this defect: on the page we can only attribute it, as in similar cases, to the profundity or 'ineffability' of its inspiration." It is not entirely clear what similar cases Gargiulo has in mind. The reference to ineffability makes one think of Ungaretti; but it is well known that in Ungaretti the danger of obscurity is accepted, even theoretically, as the inevitable counterpart of a risky desire for pure poetry which is much less apparent in Campana. Ungaretti, who has qualities all his own which distinguish him from his epigones and imitators, clearly shares the taste for the fragment understood as a new genre, perhaps the only genre of our time, a legitimate and self-sufficient expression of the lyric *moment*, the product of a poetics which does not wish to mix the necessarily brief and flashing apparitions of poetry with elements of a different, voluntary nature. Up to a point, Campana shares in this climate: among his obscure intentions one can make out a demiurge, the ritualism of the conjurer of poetry which probably never would have been satisfied on the plane of pure lyric. His is a poetry in flight, which always disintegrates at the point of completion: its development would have been unpredictable, to say the least. For the idea of what would have followed, that is, the idea of a later, *different* Campana is somehow unthinkable to us, and even unlikely. And in fact no one has dared to confront it, very few have considered Campana as a promising poet, cut off by an evil fate.

It has been observed that Campana was in better trim in prose than in poetry. This is an accurate observation, but it cannot

Left to right—Campana's mother, Campana, his younger brother, and father.

be forced. Campana the poet per se lacked time, application, and continuity, i.e., the very conditions which allow a poet, when he is not an *enfant prodigue* (as he was not), to perfect his instrument. Still, Campana's verse, even that part which is most open to classicizing movements, often justifies itself as a type or a variety of his prose. If it is important in a poet to cultivate the point of contact or coincidence between instinct (physiology) and technique, a close examination would permit us to observe the scant difference, which is not always a difference in tone, that lies between these two modes. Nevertheless, it remains true that—whether or not he cultivated them—Campana achieved the conditions of spontaneity in which he was able to express himself more often and more easily in his prose writings: writings which run from the lowest, most diaristic tone, to the most elevated, which is not always his most poetic. It also seems probable, if not certain, that Campana was very unsure of his verse, since when he wrote or rewrote the prose sections of the *Orfici,* though he did not omit the poems in the notebook, he made a strict selection from them, and revised them with great insight. As to the selection itself, we have already seen that apart from the few exceptions indicated, it was made with extreme clearsightedness. . . . (pp. 61-6)

["**Boboli**"] is the most detached and perfect of Campana's lyrics: but such crystallization is rare for him. More often the poet seems tempted by *Lied,* even if it is a stuttering *Lied,* verging on the inexpressible. . . . (p. 68)

Elsewhere much greater ambitions, compositional as well as musical, prevail: "**La chimera**," "**Immagini del viaggio e della montagna**," "**Viaggio a Montivideo**," "**Genova**"—thematically valuable, but only in places. Nevertheless, these poems show the direction which Campana the poet was consciously planning to take: the path from his most Lacerbian poems ("**Batte botte**"), passing close to the rhythmical experiments of Palazzeschi—with that breath rising to a double alexandrine time . . . which hoped to arrive at a complete coloristic-musical dissolution of poetic discourse. (p. 69)

An urgency of content flashed into the uncontrollable night; the energetic will and voluptuousness of a nomad, a "tramp" who knew Whitman and Rimbaud and experimented with his poetry as an activity that was indivisibly both aesthetic and voluntary, moral; "song of himself"; *"saison en enfer"*; Lacerbian and Vocean free verse and autobiography; diffuse neoclassical echoes—De Robertis has mentioned Carducci, and the idea of a traditional poet destroyed by sickness or bad training has also been suggested here and there—echoes not only of Carducci but of D'Annunzio, which for my part I would not want to separate from the more personal and obscure nature of Campana's "barbarous" message, from that idea of an Orphic poetry which is not confined to the title of his book and cannot be considered irrelevant to his conception of himself as a latter-day Germanic rhapsode, seduced and dazzled by the bright lights of the Mediterranean—all of this appears in flashes in the few pages of the *Canti Orfici.*

Let us pause for a moment at this "Orphism," which Campana's book certainly makes no effort to define. It coincides with the rise of a metaphysical painting in Italy (Carrà, De Chirico) of whose existence and intentions Campana could not have been unaware. Like the early De Chirico, he evokes powerfully the ancient cities of Italy: Bologna, Faenza, Florence and Genoa shine forth in his poems and inspire some of his greatest moments. Is this barbarous or if you will antique aspect another indication perhaps of his latent Carduccianism,

which is even more apparent in the openings of some couplets? Possibly; but it seems to me that Campana's Orphism and his illusion that he was a latter-day *poeta germanicus* lost in the lands of the south coincide in his intentions and even in his achievements. I do not wish to make Campana into a German poet except metaphorically, or into a theoretician of racism, but it was clearly not by chance that he dedicated the first edition of the *Orfici* to the "tragedy of the last German in Italy," and that in his dream of barbarism—which may have been nothing more than his incorrigible conviction that he was an ancient—there was actually a suggestion of an ideological and moral nature. The disparate pensées *(Storie)* published in the recent *Inediti* includes several curious allusions to this: "The creator of French impressionism is the *gaulois,* a scoundrel who has become self-aware through democracy, a slave, incapable of abstract, i.e., aristocratic, ideas. The human odor of the *gaulois* is what makes France uninhabitable for delicate sensibilities.—Nietzsche." Other remarks follow which are also useful in interpreting his poetry: "To flow over life, this would be necessary, this is the only possible art" [Montale adds in a footnote: "Here Campana is translating from the *Gay Science* of Nietzsche."], and there are other references to Nietzsche and Wagner. But there is little, too little for one to make out anything like Campana's "thought." We do not know precisely how much German the poet knew: certainly it must have been among the five languages which he claimed to know well. . . . He probably knew little or nothing of George, and the Orphic Rilke came after his book; perhaps he had some awareness of Hölderlin's Greece; with Nietzsche he had a secure and often obsessive familiarity. In any case it is obvious that his sense of escape, "that investigation of dimension, that spatial tension" (Contini) was not achieved—at times, it is true—without the help of a language which vies with German in its abstract capacities, an unfocused language, blunt at the edges, capable of halos and iridescences, of an "extremely bloated and never definite" speech (Bo); the one language which could render the *Stimmung* of "**La chimera**," "**Notte**," and many other fragments—at times, even, in the notebook, in fragments of fragments, of a more or less Futurist intonation. Is Campana a *poeta germanicus,* then? And why not, if we remain in the realm of metaphor and admit that Campana instinctively excavated for himself, out of our language, a language entirely his own? I have said "excavated" but actually it is not the notion of an excavation that best describes Campana. We should think instead of actual leaps in the air, of rapid immersions in a different element, unfamiliar to the poet himself.

> Dal ponte sopra la città odo le ritmiche cadenze mediterranee. I colli mi appaiono spogli colle loro torri a traverso le sbarre verdi ma laggiù le farfalle innumerevoli della luce riempono il paesaggio di una immobilità di gioia inesauribile. Le grandi case rosee tra i meandri verdi continuano a illudere il crepuscolo. Sulla piazza acciottolata rimbalza un ritmico strido: un fanciullo a sbalzi che sfugge melodiosamente. Un chiarore in fondo al deserto della piazza sale tortuoso dal mare dove vicoli verdi di muffa calano in tranelli d'ombra: in mezzo alla piazza, mozza la testa guarda senz'occhi sopra la cupoletta. Una donna bianca appare a una finestra aperta. È la notte mediterranea.

[From the bridge above the city I hear rhythmic Mediterranean cadences. To me, the hills look barren with their towers through the green bars but below the innumerable butterflies of the lights fill the landscape with a stillness of inexhaustible joy. The huge reddish houses among the green mazes continue to elude the twilight. A rhythmic shout echoes on the cobbled piazza: a child fleeing melodiously, by fits and starts. A brightness beyond the desert of the piazza rises tortuous out of the sea where green alleys of mold set in snares of shadow: in the midst of the piazza, the eyeless severed head keeps watch from the little cupola. A white woman comes to an open window. It's Mediterranean night.]

There may be something of De Chirico here, but dissolved in a Zarathustrian intoxication. Note that this is not an extreme example, but one of those which loses least in being taken out of context. Let us see again, still choosing from among the average examples, whether it is painting or music that dominates in apparently descriptive observations of this sort:

> Tre ragazze e un ciuco per la strada mulattiera che scendono. I complimenti vivaci degli stradini che riparono la via. Il ciuco che si voltola in terra. Le risa. Le imprecazioni montanine. Le roçce e il fiume.

> [Three girls and a donkey, coming down the muletrack. Lively compliments from the roadmen lining the way. The donkey who rolls on the ground. Laughter. Mountain curses. The rocks and the river.]

Is everything here? So it seems. But it is obvious that not even an extensive series of examples could make our metaphor visible, material. And yet we don't know what other key to offer to new readers of the *Orfici* than the recommendation that they take this poet's music in its native form, which is alive here and there throughout his work and especially in those mythic sketches—the return, the Mediterranean night, the figure of Michelangelo, the backgrounds of the "divine primitive Leonardo"—when Campana pauses at the threshold of a door that doesn't open, or now and then opens only for him.

Beyond this, beyond these escapes not only into space but also into the dimensions of a language which is born anew within another foreign, passive language entirely unaware of its latent capacity for transformation—and I am not referring to the language of Marinetti or the more human language of Soffici—Campana's notebook would seem to have little lasting interest for us, and the objections of many of his critics would seem more than legitimate.

Campana has nothing to fear from a selection which would preserve his truest gift: his *diversity* of tone. It's true: the message of the *voyant* may leave us unconvinced, vague as it is; in his work "we are given to encounter neither the cultural drama nor the explosive religious anxiety of a Hölderlin" (Solmi); nor, let us add, the blaze of light of a Blake, nor the subterranean thematic unity of a Rimbaud. It is easy to admit that Campana was working toward structures and perspectives that were very different from those to be found in the *chimismi* of his time [the translator of Montale's essay adds in a footnote that "a *chimismo* is the complex of chemical processes which together make up a physiological function. *Chimismi lirici* was the title of a well-known book by Soffici published in 1915."], but it is also clear that he was not a lyric poet in the exclusive

sense, *tout entier à sa proie attaché*. The sense of limitation, of obstacle, is rare in him; he was fought over and visited by too many abstract possibilities; his own notion of a musical, colorful European poetry sounds a bit vague today. The poet has need of a decisiveness of an almost physical nature, the impossibility of expressing himself in any other way. And this decisiveness, which at a certain point coincides with an artist's greatest spontaneity, we find above all in Campana's prose. If it were not repugnant to reduce to shreds a spirit who aimed at total expression and yet has left us with such a fragmentary picture of himself, we might be inclined to abridge Campana's work, which is already so short, limiting it to a few incorruptible pages in which we feel it is impossible to deny that the poet of Marradi had a voice very different from the others of his time. An anthology which would include, for example, **"La notte," "La Verna," "Firenze," "Scirocco," "Piazza," "Sarzano," "Faenza,"** a few of the nocturnes, some of the poems already mentioned, and a few other fragments and pensées. Is it little? Is it poetry in prose and therefore base in tone? Let's forget the "therefore," I don't believe it necessarily follows. Dino Campana, who, as Cecchi has said, "passed like a comet," may not have exercised "an incalculable influence," but the traces of his passing are anything but buried in sand. There was nothing mediocre in him; even his errors we should not call errors but inevitable collisions with the sharp corners that awaited him at every step. The collisions of a blind man, if you will. Visionaries, even if they happen to be "visual" like our Campana, are inevitably the most artless, the blindest of creatures on this earth. (pp. 69-74)

> *Eugenio Montale, "On the Poetry of Campana," in his* The Second Life of Art: Selected Essays of Eugenio Montale, *edited and translated by Jonathan Galassi, The Ecco Press, 1982, pp. 61-74.*

EDWARD WILLIAMSON (essay date 1951)

[*In the following excerpt from a discussion of some major developments in post-World War I Italian poetry, Williamson notes Campana's place within modern Italian literature.*]

In the years just before and after the first world war the 'little magazine' played an important role [in the development of Italian poetry]. The *Voce* (1908-16) was an early rallying point for the advance guard, which later found means of publication in *Lirica* and *Lacerba* and carried on a lively polemic with the contributors to *Ronda* (founded 1919) under the leadership of Vincenzo Cardarelli, today the editor of *La Fiera Letteraria*. Cardarelli advocates what he calls neoclassicism, by which he means setting up Leopardi as a standard for poetic practice; he converted the *Ronda* into the 'return to order' review. Whatever the announced issues and programs, the real accomplishment of the *Voce-Ronda* writers was a subtilizing of the poetic material considered in the abstract. In the course of their work occurred, by progressions individually almost imperceptible, a shift of climate which killed off the eloquence, the extrapoetic elements, which supported and made popular much of the poetry of Carducci and Pascoli, and destroyed even the anecdotic descriptive structure of *crepuscolarismo*. This progressive erosion of the narrative and logical elements was accompanied, as it naturally would be in so self-conscious a culture as the Italian, by a series of critical skirmishes. At first the opponents spoke of fragmentism, a belated observation, as fragmentism had for some time dominated both poetry and prose. The defenders countered with theories of pure poetry borrowed from the French. Looking back on the polemic, one might say the Italian concept of lyrism, brought to a high theoretic perfection by Croce, was swamped by two notions imported from France: atomism and analogy. Atomism, or what might be called blitz-poetry, was the theory which the French had distilled from Poe's dictum that poetry must correspond to the flash of inspiration, and as inspiration is brief so poetry must be. This view received in Italy support from a popular misunderstanding of Croce's doctrine of lyric intuition. (The exaltation of Leopardi by the anti-atomists was their way of asserting that inspiration does not necessarily come in flashes but may be a long and steady illumination with a corresponding length of poetry.) Analogy is, of course, as old as poetry, but the word is used in a restricted sense by the moderns and requires the suppression of mediating terms and the systematic gestation of new metaphors within the key metaphor. The explanation of the first process by Pierre-Quint in *Le comte de Lautréamont et Dieu* has had a wide diffusion in Italy; the passage from simile (Mon âme est *comme* un oiseau) ["My soul is *like* a bird"] through symbol (Mon âme *est* un oiseau) ["My soul *is* a bird"] to ellipsis (Cet oiseau . . .) ["This bird . . ."]. Theoretic understanding of the second process, successively generated analogies, has chiefly been gathered by observation of the practice of Mallarmé, Rimbaud, and Valéry. That poetry dominated by these theories will be more European than Italian is evident. It is the mode in which the poets now dominating Italian literature have chosen to write.

Its first authentic voice was that of Dino Campana, whose *Canti orfici*, published in 1914, had almost the effect of revelation on slightly younger writers. It has been several times republished and has acquired an increasing reputation among readers and exerted a continuing influence over young poets. In recent years interest in Campana has brought about the editing of three volumes of material he did not choose to publish; while the list of men who have written studies of his work is almost an honor roll of critics, and includes also poets like Montale and Solmi. Campana was a personality in a way that later Italian poets—chiefly professorial and intellectual—have not been. Sbarbaro thus describes a visit: "My family barely tolerated him because of his lice. In the evening he had an almost maidenly modesty about taking off his clothes. Hospitality was quickly irksome to him, and by the third day he would have no more of it. I watched him go off, stubborn, with his vagabond's gait, toward Sottaripa. For his only baggage he had in his pocket *Leaves of Grass*." The circumstances of Campana's life (he died in an insane asylum and his years before confinement were passed in vagabondage), his frequent use of 'poetic prose,' and his striving for a poetry which would be a primary emotional experience shorn of intellectual categories and hence a first-hand contact with reality, have led most critics to compare him with Rimbaud, but the luminous landscapes which are glimpsed through the broken architecture of his verse are purely Italian: they are peaceful landscapes where archaic figures stand in attitudes of immemorial rite. . . . (pp. 165-68)

> Edward Williamson, "Contemporary Italian Poetry," in Poetry, Vol. LXXIX, No. 3, December, 1951, pp. 159-81.*

FREDI CHIAPPELLI   (essay date 1958)

[*In the following excerpt, Chiappelli provides a critical introduction to Campana.*]

Absolute poverty and the absolute contemplation of poetry were to be the destiny of a man so completely free from any sub-

Holograph copy of a page from Campana's manuscript of Il più lungo giorno. *Courtesy of the Literary Estate of Dino Campana.*

mission to matter and so taken up with the importance of feeling and of expressing himself. The need that turned Campana into a sufferer, a nomad, a sick man, was not the result of negligence or incapacity: it was the price paid by him daily for a disengaged autonomy of the spirit, which was intent on rediscovering and re-establishing the forces, values and intensity of its own world. In this way, poverty, even though it ruined Campana's health and, hence, his physical life, did not prejudice his nature; that nature which, with fateful insight, described itself in the few pages of his that are left to us. It is not purely by chance that the first edition of the *Canti orfici* . . . ends with the words: "They were all torn—and cover'd with—the boy's blood," as if to suggest the immense price exacted by this poetry. And, in a letter of May 1916 to Emilio Cecchi, we read: "If, dead or alive, you still give a thought to me, I beg you not to forget the final words *They were all torn and cover'd with the boy's blood,* which are the only important ones in the book. The quotation is from the *Song of Myself* by Walt Whitman, whom I adore." (pp. 3-4)

The *Canti orfici* consist of some fanciful prose-passages (e.g. *La notte*), and others based on actual reminiscences (e.g. *La Verna*), alternating with poems: *I notturni* (a group of seven poems), *Varie e frammenti* (two poems), *Genova* (a long poem in seven parts). Its poetic world is a unitary one. This is all the more marked, in that in neither the prose nor verse passages does the author attempt to achieve an external completeness or an explicit declaration of motives and relationships. It is the most elementary poetic world possible, recreated in an expression capable of dealing with the greatest psychological complexity: "in the voice of the element we hear all things," as we read in the **Inediti**. . . . The poetic image, evoked by a direct contemplation of the elements—and nourished by the thousand and one currents of the feelings, senses, dreams, taste, and culture—becomes a coherent transfiguration of experience and, at the same time, an interpretation of its most hidden meanings (hence "orfici"). Moreover, what is more important, it rises up to an autonomous life of its own, which is particularly intense and secure, and beautiful precisely because of the complexity and rarity of its architecture.

Some readers may find certain textual difficulties disconcerting. With regard to this, we may point out that, if Campana is difficult to understand, he is so rather in inspiration than in expression. As [Mario] Luzi said of the *hermetic* poets, obscurity of meaning must be accepted "as the price to be paid by someone who is destined to bring to light all that is most hidden and least defined in the real life of man." Campana, who heard *all things* in the voice of the element, could not have done otherwise than wish to express all things. Here, I should like to offer the analytical example of an image in which nothing but figurative complexities appear. It is an image taken from the poem that brings the book to a close—**Genova:**

Per i vichi marini nell'ambigua
Sera cacciava il vento tra i fanali
Preludii dal groviglio delle navi.

Along the sea-alleys in the ambiguous
Evening the wind hunted between the street-lamps
Preludes from the clutter of ships.

This is merely the image of the wind, at nightfall, in the port of Genoa. However, the evocation of the wind, conceived as a force laden with preludes, and which pursues preludes (namely, the conjunction of the idea of music with the idea of movement and violence) is not in itself an easy image (it will be noticed that it already bears a style; it is already poetic); and it is further complicated by the picturesque image of the "clutter of ships," and by the choice of the vague, suggestive time of twilight, "the *ambiguous* evening," the moment when evening is about to be transformed into night. This choice and determination of the hour introduce and sketch out, as it were, a cold shiver in this image animated by the wind, and prolong it in the alleyways of the port. And, over the whole, there also hovers a motif indicated at the very beginning, though indirectly, that of the *smell* of the sea: "Along the sea-alleys." These elements rise up all together, they intermingle one with the other, like sensation in the imagination, and create a complex reality, which the poet succeeds in capturing in its entire significance.

Campana's world includes, without boundaries, both dreams and reality, so that his transports always appear boundless. The association of things and images, immobility and movement, segment and arabesque, proceeds spontaneously from his poetic fantasy. It is a complex world, but one of substantial unity, which is revealed in the freedom with which the poet moves therein, and which is reflected in his language. This is essentially unitary, even in cases of interruption and repetition, and especially in its general categories: "in the *Canti orfici*, Campana nearly always aimed at imposing an impetuous movement

on his composition, and, in this impetus, at unifying both rhythm and syntax [De Robertis, *Scrittori del 900* (1943)].

The fact of having fixed their attention solely on the more sensational elements in Campana's world—for example, the images or impulses of movement—may have suggested to critics certain unsatisfactory comparisons with other poets, e.g., D'Annunzio, even as the atmosphere surrounding them may have brought Baudelaire to mind. The latter was certainly of interest to Campana, in his internal compositions, which are the most structured. But what really matters is the poet's sure ability in this world of his, composed of nature and dreams; his natural ability to dominate it, sweep through it and retain vast, serried sections of this in each image.

The moment when Campana's mind roams unhampered through time and space is for him the moment of creation: "Recollections of gipsy-girls, of distant loves, sounds and lights: moments of weariness in love, sudden weariness on the bed of a distant tavern *another adventurous cradle of certainty and regret*" (**La notte,** in **Canti orfici**): from fact to feeling and its transfiguration, we have only a poetic interval wherein nothing is inert, and which opens up vistas along the horizon of the ineffable. We find expressed here the almost unbelievable docility with which this spirit submitted itself to a poetic inspiration that was always unitary and classical, whether it proceeded from the most elementary experience of nature or (immediately and even simultaneously) from the artist's most troubled unrest: "And here are the rocks, layer upon layer, monuments of a lonely tenacity, which console the heart of man. And my fugitive destiny has seemed sweet to me, in the fascination of the distant mirages of happiness that still smile upon the blue mountains: and in hearing the murmur of the water beneath the bare rocks, which is still fresh from the depths of the earth. And so, I am made aware of a sweet music in my memory, without remembering a single note of it: I know that its name is parting or reunion." (**La Verna,** in **Canti orfici**).

One of the aspects of this "greatness" of soul may be the synthetic quality of some images conceived at immense distance, such as, "and the shadows of human labor bent there over the cold hills (poggi algenti)" of the famous verse from **Chimera**; or, in prose, the telescopic form of a town: "Tilted fanfare, arabesque amidst the meadows, Berne." Another aspect of this same "greatness" is the immediate sense of intimacy present in the most complex and dazzling metaphor; as in another famous passage from **Chimera:** "But for your maidenly head / Reclined, that I, nocturnal poet, / Kept vigil over the vivid stars in the depths of the sky," or in the summit of solitude represented by the image of the alpine peaks known and understood in their most secret myth: "I watch the white rocks, *the mute fountains of the winds.*" The taste for color and harmonic notations, which is in any case a fully conscious one in Campana, is exalted by freedom (and led on to surprising effects that have caused critics to speak of "vision"). The poet told Dr. Pariani . . . that he had wished to create "a colored musical European poetry" that had "the sense of colors, which previously did not exist in Italian poetry."

The variable metric forms, constantly adapted to the fullness of his fanciful period, must also be understood as another manifestation of this same "greatness." A qualitative prosody, which was also described by Campana in a judgment on Luisa Giaconi: "A stanza liberated from the multiform chain with two or three elementary cases of assonance expresses a purer love of light and form."

I think it necessary to specify that the vehemence of Campana's poetic transports has nothing whatever to do with the progress of madness or psychic hypertension. On the contrary, it represents an extreme concentration of the individual's powers, a considerable detachment from the chains of matter, and hence a capacity of the spirit, in its intensely free unity, to obey the slightest impulse with great impetus. . . . [The] most delicate and intricate texture of feeling and sensation can be preserved in a strong, sure expression, as in the image of the preludes of wind. Similarly in this picture, where the freedom and obedience of the spirit to the slightest presence of life, the sense of the infinite in action, the clarity of tone and sculptural quality of figuration, all contribute to form a like creative power and to illumine a classical, conclusive centrality of feeling:

> a bunch of withered flowers in the corner with
> a large sign on the window-panes, and I stood
> on tiptoe watching the panes, to see whether
> my love was there, and she was not.
>
> The roadway was dark and narrow at the corner
> of the large square.
>
> Repetition. Why describe all that? And yet,
> however withered the bunch of flowers, I felt
> a great peace descend upon me. . . .
>
> (pp. 6-10)

The absolute volatility and freedom of Campana's spirit . . . were impelled by love to dizzy heights of alternating happiness and pain. Even the intimacy of the most secret feeling takes on an aspect of violence, the surge towards further horizons: "Although I have hardly shaken hands with you, O apprehensive beauty, I see you here silhouetted against my thoughts and the landscape." His rare moments of transport towards happiness remind one of that movement of flight towards illusion, and conglomerations of light and natural reflections on man's shadow, which is characteristic of the *Notturni* (especially *Chimera*). . . . The signs of despair alternate with these and become more frequent. It is impossible to tell whether it was passion that irritated and precipitated the poet's illness, or whether it was the illness that vitiated and devastated his passion. . . . The increasingly convulsive signs of madness were interrupted by moments of calm, when the man tried to take a grip on himself, looked about in order to overcome his wretchedness, and attempted to find a job. . . . Nevertheless, his fate was already sealed. (pp. 10-12)

On January 28, 1918, at the age of thirty-two, Campana had to be taken to the asylum of Castel Pulci. He remained there fourteen years, until his death on March 1, 1932, from "acute primitive septicaemia, or direct virulent microbial infection of the blood."

Of Dino Campana there remain the *Canti orfici*, the small volume of the *Altri scritti,* and some letters, which, I hope, will some day be published. His poetic task, one of the most resolute in modern poetry, tended towards an ever-new totality of art, creating figures in which man's life, the colors and forms of nature, the expanses of time and space, of inner existence, reveal their mutual values, in constant movement and composition: sufficient signs remain of these to prove their classical quality. There even remains an elementary definition of them, a formula pronounced with ascetic precision in one of the phrases the sick poet told his doctor: "I put memories into the Italian landscape." (p. 12)

Fredi Chiappelli, "An Introduction to Dino Campana," translated by J. A. Scott, in Italian Quarterly, *Vol. 2, No. 2, Summer, 1958, pp. 3-15.*

JOHN FREDERICK NIMS   (essay date 1960)

[*Nims is an American poet, critic, translator, and educator. He is particularly noted for the ironic wit displayed in his poetry and for the skill and sensitivity of his translations of foreign poetry. Nims's* Sappho to Valéry: Poems in Translation *(1971) is widely acclaimed for its adherence to the spirit and tone of the translated works. In the following excerpt, Nims provides a line-by-line explication of "Giardino autunnale" ("Autumn Garden"), one of Campana's most famous poems.*]

"Giardino Autunnale"

> Al giardino spettrale al lauro muto
> De le verdi ghirlande
> A la terra autunnale
> Un ultimo saluto!
> A l'aride pendici
> Aspre arrossate nell'estremo sole
> Confusa di rumori
> Rauchi grida la lontana vita:
> Grida al morente sole
> Che insanguina le aiole.
> S'intende una fanfara
> Che straziante sale: il fiume spare
> Ne le arene dorate: nel silenzio
> Stanno le bianche statue a capo i ponti
> Volte: e le cose già non sono piú.
> E dal fondo silenzio come un coro
> Tenero e grandioso
> Sorge ed anela in alto al mio balcone:
> E in aroma d'alloro,
> In aroma d'alloro acre languente,
> Tra le statue immortali nel tramonto
> Ella m'appar, presente.
>
> (Canti orfici. . . .)

High over the Futurist bandstands and across the wan sky of the Crepuscolari, the poetry of Dino Campana flashed in 1914 like the wildest of meteors. Driven since he was fifteen by a nervous compulsion, the bronze-haired blue-eyed roustabout had wandered over much of the world, *Leaves of Grass* in his pocket; he had been in and out of jail and of the asylum that finally claimed him, had himself peddled his crudely printed *Canti orfici*—whose very title, *Orphic Songs*, suggested mystery, magic, revelation. Campana lived for poetry; when close to him, said Cecchi, one could feel it like an electric shock or a high explosive. His own work, too idiosyncratic to be imitated, provided the young writers with a new sense both of the freedom poetry might enjoy and of its pictorial and musical possibilities—all richly realized in his **"Autumn Garden."**

The setting is the Boboli Gardens in Florence. (1) *To the spectral garden to the laurel shorn* (2) *Of the green garlands* (3) *To the autumn earth* (4) *A last greeting!* There should be commas after *garden* and *garlands:* the fever of Campana's thought is frequently impatient of punctuation. In this he resembles the Futurists (whose poetry, he objected, lacked music); but he is unlike them in relying heavily on the adjective, often taking a chance on those that in terms of communication seemed a bad risk in the context. Here *muto* is such a word; it means "silent," but in the poem, as an earlier version proves, it stands for "pruned" or "shorn." The laurel are *mute* of their garlands because with clipping they have lost some of their murmur or rustle. Campana may have been thinking too of Dante's *luogo d'ogni luce muto,* "a place devoid [mute] of all light." His farewell to the waning garden continues with a violent change of color: from spectral grey to bitter red. (5) *To the dry hillsides,* (6) *Harsh, reddened in the final sunlight* (7-8) *The faraway* [*sound of*] *life cries, troubled with gruff rumblings:* (9) *Cries to the dying sun* (10) *That fills with blood the flower-beds.* As the passage is steeped in keener red, emotion goes well beyond literal meaning: the sun is *in extremis,* is a dying sun; its blood is on the place of innocence; and life from the city below, clamorous and confused in its purposes, is invoking a dying god. Shrill color turns to shrill sound, as if for a moment that crimson had a voice: (11) *A brass band is heard* (12) *That lifts ear-splitting*—a single piercing blast, it seems, because all is immediately muted to a twilight silence: *the river vanishes* (13) *Between its gilded sands* ["ne le" for the usual "nelle"—like "de le," etc., above—is a rather literary touch]: *in the silence* (14) *Stand the white statues at the bridgehead* (15) *Turned: and things exist no longer.*

Always fond of studding his poems with references to works of art, Campana makes this the most portentous image of the poem. As everything fades in his evening vista, the statues stand out like illusions on the bridges over the Arno—in their unearthly whiteness, against the russet and dim gold, seeming to belong to another order of reality. Called immortal in line 21, they are already like gods. *Volte* ("turned") gives them a life and volition of their own: to turn to or away from something is a gesture charged with drama. We are not told what the statues mean in the poem: they impress by their very presence; they seem the tutelary deities of the scene, supreme and unchanging, as everything else loses its form in the gathering darkness. The firm shapes of day no longer exist. (Thought, feeling, and imagery here recall Hopkins' "Spelt from Sibyl's Leaves," also about disintegration at the end of the day.) (16) *And from the deep silence, as it were a chorus* [the subject is the phrase "come un coro"] (17) *Tender and vast* (18) *Arises and yearns upward to my balcony,* the rampart or terrace in the park. This chorus is the voice with which the whole scene cries out to him. In the welter of sensations, each flowing into each like the twilight forms, images of color and sound now give way to the more immediate images of smell: (19) *In the* [*sharp*] *fragrance of laurel,* (20) *The fragrance of laurel bitter and languorous,* (21) *Among the immortal statues in the sunset,* privileged to survive the day and its undoing, (22) *She appears to me, present.*

The sudden revelation refocuses the entire poem, makes it meaningful in a way we had not previously suspected. This is no farewell to a mere garden, but to a girl he loved—whose apparition, we now see, has been anticipated by the mystic statues over the river: she is the goddess of the scene and the motive of the poem. Appearing so abruptly, for a moment she seems a stranger. But everything the poem has said is about her or the poet's relation to her: the farewell to a ghostly garden, a dying year, a dying sun; the scarlet land, the flower-beds running blood, the music snatched abruptly into silence, the golden river gone, the olympian statues turned, the thrilling cry of all that stricken world, the fragrance sweet and bitter. What they constitute is a definition of lost love. (pp. 298-99)

John Frederick Nims, "Dino Campana (1885-1932)," in The Poem Itself, *edited by Stanley Burnshaw & others, Holt, Rinehart and Winston, 1960, pp. 297-99.*

CARLO L. GOLINO (essay date 1961)

[*In the following excerpt from a discussion of trends in post-World War I Italian poetry, Golino mentions Campana's contributions to Italian lyric poetry.*]

Futurism ran its course quickly; but if life was not entirely in the future as it had claimed, a return to the past was also impossible. This was becoming more and more evident not only in relation to the arts and literature but on a moral plane as well. Italian culture, it seemed, had to be integrated in all its manifestations into the life of the nation if it was to have a true significance. A new magazine appeared, a new banner was raised, a new impetus was found. The same Giuseppe Prezzolini who several years before had founded [the periodical] *Leonardo* with [Giovanni] Papini now founded *La Voce.* It was 1909, the year of the futurist manifesto. *La Voce* quickly attracted the attention and the support of the best minds of Italy. Prezzolini's first and foremost credo was action—at all times, at all costs—and this rage for action was shared by a great many. The perplexity that followed the collapse of futurism was quickly overcome by the possibilities proclaimed by *La Voce,* and the response was general. Thus, among the *vociani* we find G. Papini, A. Palazzeschi, C. Sbarbaro, P. Jahier, C. Rèbora, and D. Campana, to mention but a few; their names represent a list of the major poets of the time. It would be difficult to speak of a poetics of the vociani, for theirs was a heterogeneous group and the poetical solution that each one of them found for their common problem varied appreciably from one to the other. What united them and gave their movement a certain cohesion was their common desire for a renewed awareness of social and spiritual questions and of moral responsibility. Futurism provided a point of departure and the vociani borrowed freely from it, but added a new kind of dedication. In poetry the results were as varied as the individual solutions to moral problems, but some sort of pattern did emerge in the preference for strongly impressionistic imagery, brief fragmentary compositions, a pervasive use of analogy, and a great freedom in versification. (pp. xi-xii)

The anguished need for moral self-justification reached a pitch of exasperation in the tragic personality of Dino Campana. None of the poets of *La Voce* achieved the lyric purity of Campana, but his recurring mental derangement, which became permanent in the last part of his short life, precluded any possibility of a personal solution of the problem. The tormented life of Campana found its only relief in outbursts of lyricism, which, when they corresponded to moments of mental lucidity, have no equal in twentieth-century Italian poetry. But more often, his beclouded poetry is only a harmony of words and a race of images. It is nonetheless beautiful, even when it is marred by the obscurities of an infirm mind. Campana roamed over Europe and South America and engaged in the strangest assortment of occupations. He was continually in and out of jails and mental institutions—always poor, alone, urged on only by his devouring anguish. Campana is a modern poet, as are all the other poets of *La Voce,* with whom he shares the credit for having given a sound meaning to the reforms of the futurists and for opening the way to a new life for Italian poetry. (p. xiii)

Carlo L. Golino, in a preface to Contemporary Italian Poetry: An Anthology, *edited by Carlo L. Golino, University of California Press, 1962, pp. vii-xxi.**

I. L. SALOMON (essay date 1968)

[*Salomon is an American poet, critic, and translator. In the following excerpt from the introduction to his translation of Cam-*

pana's poetry, he briefly discusses some aspects of Campana's work. Unexcerpted portions of the essay provide biographical information.]

Dino Campana . . . , the poet of **Orphic Songs (Canti Orfici)** was the wild man of Italian poetry in 1914 on the eve of The Great War. He is as important to 20th century poetry as, say, Lorca or Mayakovsky. His poems and prose-poems are unique. They read as if they were thrown into the wind in an ecstasy of violence. They reflect the disintegration of a man.

Campana has been compared to Rimbaud. His **Orphic Songs** lacks the cohesiveness of the poems in *The Drunken Boat* or the prose-poems in *The Illuminations*. There are affinities: fantastic fervor, a fine frenzy of poetic image, metaphors in transfiguration. In their lives there are only surface resemblances: each rebelled against the provincialism of his upbringing. At odds with the world, each was more at odds with himself. In search of answers to imponderables, each roamed the cities of the world. (p. 13)

In rebellion against the bourgeoisie and in his desire to embrace "pure idealism," Campana dedicated **Orphic Songs** to Kaiser Wilhelm II in 1914. Although he subtitled his book 'The Last German in Italy,' he recognized the seeds of subversion and destruction in Nietzsche and in Wagner. Not too long after, he disclaimed his dedication in "Franco-Italian Proletarian Song": *Italy / I love you with immeasurable aching.* (pp. 13-14)

In breaking the fetters of an enslaving culture, the poet Dino Campana delighted only a handful of the avant-garde of his generation. Right at its heels there was another, the oncoming young, who in every age are outraged at their stultified elders. The imperishable young as the years went by took to heart this poetry written at white heat from memory. For all its a-grammatical and ungrammatical structure, its hiatuses and unfilled brackets (as if a thought were blown away never to be recaptured), this was a poetry for Italy's youth. They could feel it in their bones. Their Campana had created his own aesthetic and developed a sense of tone-color never before experienced in Italian poetry. Throughout his work there were key words integral to his sense of sound, words singularly his own: *taciturn, nocturnal, ambiguous, dizziness, serene* and their cognates. Here was a poetry unshackled and unchecked, nothing in it dependent on tricks and techniques. Here was no Futurist fathering of a word like ROSA, its tone-color indicated by a repetition of letters: frrrrrr/iiiiiiiii/frrrrrr. To Dino, Futurist verse was false, without harmony, mere improvisation. His own was a confluence of color and harmony. He denied he owed anything to Rimbaud, who in the sonnet, "Voyelles" had assigned arbitrary colors to each vowel. In Dino's poetry there was an other-worldly music and unearthly splendor so like the dark landscape of Thule, Poe's ultimate dim dreamland. If Poe's imaginative vision infused **Orphic Songs,** Whitman left an even stronger mark in a few phrases directly translated: *Faint creaking of cordage* became *un dolce scricchiolìo,* just as *hankering, gross, mystical, nude* found an altered variant in *Nude mystical*

up high hollow, and *O book! fulfil your destiny!* had its counterpart in *O sea prepare my destiny.*

Pre-dating Eliot in "The Waste Land," Dino assaulted the sensibilities of the pedants by abusing their notions on the structure of sentences. Absence of punctuation heightens the aberrant syntax. . . . (pp. 18-19)

From the very first Dino's poetry had the ingredients the young were after. In **"The Chimera,"** written during his university days and printed in a Bolognese student folio, there is a mixture of sensual yearning in sensuous language, the mystery of the unknown, and the deification of unfulfilled desire, grievous to the girl and to the poet. . . . (p. 20)

There is a sense of loneliness and abandonment in his poetry as if in a brutish world, halved by the light of madness and the dark of sanity, he groped for the cold asylum of eternity. (p. 21)

The marks of his insanity are like stigmata on the corpus of his work. (p. 22)

> *I. L. Salomon, in an introduction to* Orphic Songs *by Dino Campana, translated by I. L. Salomon, October House Inc., 1968, pp. 13-22.*

ADDITIONAL BIBLIOGRAPHY

Golino, Carlo L. "Notes on the Poets: Campana, Dino." In *Contemporary Italian Poetry: An Anthology,* edited by Carlo L. Golino, p. 216. Berkeley: University of California Press, 1962.
    Calls Campana "a fundamental influence on the development of Italian poetry."

Mezey, Caroline. "Dino Campana's Return from Belgium: Four Unpublished Documents." *The Modern Language Review* 78, No. 4 (October 1983): 830-37.
    Reprints the texts of official reports by Italian police and Italian and Belgian medical authorities chronicling instances of Campana's public displays of aberrant behavior and noting his incarceration in mental institutions. In an introductory essay, Mezey stresses the importance of considering Campana as mentally ill and not merely as an "eccentric Bohemian" artist.

Nims, John Frederick. "Dino Campana." In *The Poem Itself,* edited by Stanley Burnshaw, p. 297. New York: Holt, Rinehart and Winston, 1960.
    Line-by-line translation and explication of Campana's "L'invetriata" ("The Window") and "Giardino autunnale" ("Autumn Garden"). See the excerpt dated 1960 in the entry for Nims's explication of "Autumn Garden."

Riccio, Peter Michael. "Campana, Dino." In his *Italian Authors of Today,* pp. 139-46. 1938. Reprint. Freeport, N.Y.: Books for Libraries Press, 1970.
    Noncritical biographical sketch noting the adversities suffered by Campana.

Sheila Kaye-Smith

1887-1956

English novelist, short story writer, poet, autobiographer, biographer, critic, and essayist.

A popular English novelist between the First and Second World Wars, Kaye-Smith is best known for her distinctive portrayal of the land, people, and history of Sussex. She was a realist who presented both the beauty and harsh reality of rural life as she communicated the simple lives and complex psychology of her characters. Her successful representation of subjects and themes which had long been the sphere of male writers became the basis of her reputation as "the woman who could write like a man." Although she was aware of literary trends and familiar with a broad range of literature, she was largely a traditionalist who derived most of the material and inspiration for her works from her experience as a native of Sussex and her gradual conversion to Roman Catholicism. Known as a great storyteller, regional novelist, and social historian, Kaye-Smith depicted not only a small portion of England, but basic human experiences and conflicts common to all people.

Kaye-Smith was born in St. Leonards-on-Sea, near Hastings, Sussex. A highly imaginative child, she displayed an early talent for storytelling as well as a deep love for the country. Accompanying her father, a country doctor, as he visited patients and spending many summers on farms helped to shape her active imagination; later in her life these experiences provided material for *The Children's Summer* and *Selina Is Older*, two autobiographical novels based on her childhood. At the age of nine Kaye-Smith entered Hastings and St. Leonards Ladies' College, where she studied for the nine years which comprised her formal education and acquired a love of books which lasted throughout her life. As she did not attend church regularly during her childhood, most of her knowledge of Christian theology was derived from Victorian classics of religious instruction. In her autobiography, *Three Ways Home*, Kaye-Smith states that her parents' way of explaining God and religion in terms of morality and good conduct stifled her interest in the supernatural aspects of Christianity. Kaye-Smith's three childhood ambitions—to live alone in the country, to become a famous author of novels about rural life, and to become "extremely High Church"—were all realized, with some variations, in her adult life.

Her first novel, *The Tramping Methodist*, was published when she was twenty-one, and her second, *Starbrace*, appeared shortly afterward. Both of these works display Kaye-Smith's storytelling talent, as well as ideas, techniques, and views of life that were largely derived from her reading. Her portrayal of such characters as highwaymen, outlaws, rogues, and vagabonds, and her presentation of some sordid, brutal subjects, was surprising in light of her sheltered existence, her shy disposition, and her limited knowledge of the world. Following the publication of these two novels, Kaye-Smith gained some independence from her parents. She visited London and began to circulate among literary people, to be influenced by different ideas and styles, and to include these experiences in her novels. *Spell Land* reflects her enthusiasm for newly acquired religious and philosophical ideas, and autobiographical concerns similarly inform *Three against the World*. Her early works were

Photograph by E. O. Hoppe

uneven in quality and tended toward melodrama and sentimentality. Not long after the publication of *Three against the World*, which was poorly received, Kaye-Smith met W. L. George, an author who significantly affected her career. He gave her the idea for *Sussex Gorse*, her first successful novel, and several years later his suggestions led to *Joanna Godden*, her best-known work. George advised Kaye-Smith to adopt a more realistic, less sentimental approach to her stories, and to develop in them a strong sense of locale as well as more faithful characterizations of rural men and women. Kaye-Smith's success with these elements drew much critical acclaim.

Although her career spanned two world wars as well as major social and technological changes, Kaye-Smith had little interest in contemporary affairs and usually kept the events and issues of her time out of her novels. In addition, for most of her life Kaye-Smith remained aloof from society, had few close friends, and according to her friend G. B. Stern, "revelled in solitude." However, her two novels following *Sussex Gorse* gave some expression to her responses to World War I. *The Challenge to Sirius*, which deals only indirectly with the war by being set in part in America during the Civil War, expressed her desire to escape from the war and illustrated her feeling of remoteness from God. Her ability to face the war more directly underlies *Little England*, published near the end of World War I, in which she depicted the repercussions of the war on some country people. Although Kaye-Smith had been an agnostic for some time, during this period she was again attracted to Anglo-Catholicism and in 1918 she became a convert.

Although very happy with her decision, she did not let her experience overflow into her novels. Thus, in *Tamarisk Town, Green Apple Harvest,* and *Joanna Godden* she remained objective toward the religious beliefs of her characters, only occasionally hinting at her position. However, in *The End of the House of Alard* Kaye-Smith wrote an Anglo-Catholic story which made her position obvious. This novel became a bestseller in England and America, and Kaye-Smith enjoyed financial success for the first time in her career. While she seldom revealed herself in her novels, there is more self-disclosure in her largely unknown poetry, such as the collections entitled *Willow's Forge, and Other Poems* and *Saints in Sussex.* Regarding her poetry, Coulson Kernahan states that in it she "allowed . . . the expression of a profoundly spiritual, if mystical, order of mind and a singularly original and attractive personality."

In 1924 Kaye-Smith married Reverend Theodore Penrose Fry, a High Anglican Church rector, and they moved to London where she continued to write for five years. *Shepherds in Sackcloth,* written toward the end of that time, is a sympathetic portrayal of a poor clergyman and his wife and is her last novel written as an Anglican. In 1929, having become gradually disillusioned with Anglo-Catholicism, she and her husband converted to Roman Catholicism and moved to a farm in Sussex, where Kaye-Smith did religious work among Catholics in her district for the rest of her life. About two years after moving to the farm, she produced her last major novel, *The History of Susan Spray, the Female Preacher;* she continued to write prolifically until the end of her life, but these later novels are largely undistinguished. During this period she also appeared occasionally as a speaker in England and America. Kaye-Smith died at home on January 14, 1956.

Rural Sussex is the setting of most of Kaye-Smith's regional novels. She depicts the country as both the background for her characters and as something which motivates, conditions, and causes conflicts in their lives. Her descriptions of the country evoke the beauty within nature as well as the dirt, sweat, and struggle that are part of working on the land. She has often been compared with Thomas Hardy for their deep kinship with specific regions of the English countryside, their portrayal of locale as an influence on human character, and their tragic vision. However, whereas Hardy was deterministic and fatalistic, Kaye-Smith's artistic vision reflected hope. Critics find that she portrayed both human nature in general and Sussex inhabitants in particular with deep understanding and fidelity. Described by Dorothea Walker as "stories based on human need," her novels present protagonists who are strong-willed, purposeful individuals. Within her powerful narratives, Kaye-Smith studied the nature and effects of ambition, class differences, and religion in the lives of her characters, most of whom are farmers and their families.

Kaye-Smith's most successful novels were published between 1916 and 1931. *Sussex Gorse* is the story of an ambitious nineteenth-century landowner, Reuben Backfield, who, in his obsessive determination to tame and develop several hundred acres of gorse-grown land, becomes cruel and ruthless, rejects traditional values and norms of behavior, and sacrifices all human relationships to accomplish his goal. In *Tamarisk Town,* the only one of these novels to be set in a town, Kaye-Smith

examines another ambitious man, Edward Monypenny, who accomplishes his dream to develop and popularize a seaside resort. Although his ambition is all-consuming for many years, Monypenny is more vulnerable to human love than is Backfield, and he is considered a more complex character than his predecessor. *Joanna Godden* presents an ambitious female landowner who becomes prosperous in a traditionally male domain through her hard work and courage. Kaye-Smith depicts the trials, mistakes, and triumphs of this strong woman as she struggles with fellow farmers who deem her a competitor rather than a colleague, with people outside of her social class, and with the conflicting desires for both career and family. *The End of the House of Alard* portrays the attempts and failures of a post-World War I aristocratic family to maintain its traditions. The novel deals with two intertwining themes—the effects on the Alards of the succession of lower-class farmers into the ranks of the gentry, and the conflict between Low and High Church Anglicanism. In *Susan Spray* Kaye-Smith analyzes the life of a nineteenth-century woman who struggles, like Godden, to fit into a traditionally male role, that of a preacher. Her motivation stems from her desire to be free of the standard, subordinate roles of women and from her feeling of superiority. Within her are mingled genuine religious feelings and an egocentric desire for power, and although she succeeds in her own estimation—by becoming a powerful preacher—she becomes a superstitious, hypocritical person in the process. Critics find that none of Kaye-Smith's novels after *Susan Spray* maintained the realism and power of her most successful work, and her popularity declined after World War II.

Although Kaye-Smith's talent as a storyteller and her fine descriptive ability were noted by critics of her very first novel, with the appearance of *Sussex Gorse* the realistic aspects of Kaye-Smith's work were recognized as exceptional. In discussing her objectivity toward and competent handling of subjects and themes uncommon among women writers, as well as her remarkable ability to create convincing, striking male characters, early critics often described Kaye-Smith as having a "masculine" outlook and an ability to write "like a man." Kaye-Smith's successful presentation of harsh, grim aspects of life—generally without compromise, sentimentality, or exaggeration—also contributed to this characterization of her work. Although more recent criticism discusses these traits as inherent qualities of good writing, the earlier phraseology reflects widely held assumptions of her time about the nature and abilities of women as well as the usual subject matter of popular women writers.

While it is clear that Kaye-Smith was inspired by the concrete and intangible realities of the land, people, and history of Sussex, critics disagree regarding the effect of her regionalism on her development and reputation as a novelist. Some critics emphasize that within this framework she produced beautiful, evocative prose and a significant body of fiction that immortalized a portion of England. Additionally, it is noted that Sussex provided material for her portrayal of both elemental nature and fundamental human truths, making her work timeless. On the other hand, some critics consider Sussex a limited source of material from which to derive characters and situations, and view her regionalism as cause for the repetitive and ephemeral qualities of her work, and for the decline in her reputation. However, the essence and importance of what she accomplished through her best work is reflected in Patrick Braybrooke's statement that "Miss Kaye-Smith has achieved a great deal; she is a novelist worthy of and in a secure position in the front rank. And perhaps this is so because she is both human and yet a severe critic when she likes, able to be remorseless when such treatment is necessary. In a word, perhaps the best description of her art, is that it is not only art, but very Rational art.''

(See also *Dictionary of Literary Biography,* Vol. 36: *British Novelists 1890-1929: Modernists.*)

PRINCIPAL WORKS

The Tramping Methodist　(novel)　1908
Starbrace　(novel)　1909
Spell Land　(novel)　1910
Isle of Thorns　(novel)　1913
Three against the World　(novel)　1914; also published as *The Three Furlongers,* 1914
Willow's Forge, and Other Poems　(poetry)　1914
John Galsworthy　(criticism)　1916
Sussex Gorse　(novel)　1916
The Challenge to Sirius　(novel)　1917
Little England　(novel)　1918; also published as *The Four Roads,* 1919
Tamarisk Town　(novel)　1919
Green Apple Harvest　(novel)　1920
Joanna Godden　(novel)　1921
The End of the House of Alard　(novel)　1923
Saints in Sussex　(poetry)　1923
The George and the Crown　(novel)　1924
Anglo-Catholicism　(essay)　1925
Joanna Godden Married　(short stories)　1926
Iron and Smoke　(novel)　1928
Shepherds in Sackcloth　(novel)　1930
The History of Susan Spray, the Female Preacher　(novel)　1931; also published as *Susan Spray,* 1931
The Children's Summer　(fictional autobiography)　1932; also published as *Summer Holiday,* 1932
The Ploughman's Progress　(novel)　1933; also published as *Gipsy Waggon: The Story of a Ploughman's Progress,* 1933
Gallybird　(novel)　1934
Selina Is Older　(fictional autobiography)　1935; also published as *Selina,* 1935
Rose Deeprose　(novel)　1936
Three Ways Home　(autobiography)　1937
Talking of Jane Austen [with G. B. Stern]　(criticism)　1943; also published as *Speaking of Jane Austen,* 1944
The Lardners and the Laurelwoods　(novel)　1947
Mrs. Gailey　(novel)　1951
The View from the Parsonage　(novel)　1954
All the Books of My Life　(criticism)　1956

THE ATHENAEUM　(essay date 1908)

[*In the following excerpt, the critic offers a positive review of* The Tramping Methodist.]

It is an uncommon pleasure to meet so promising a first novel as [*The Tramping Methodist.* Miss Sheila Kaye-Smith] has the gift of impregnating her story with the atmosphere of the period, and has contrived to give a wonderfully life-like picture of rural life in Kent and Sussex at the close of the eighteenth century. Eight years after the death of Wesley, the kindled fire

of Methodism was striving for the souls of the people in direct antagonism in these country by-ways to the neglect and callousness of the Established Church. Humphrey Lyte, himself the son of a Sussex parson, turns in disgust from his father's practices, and, becoming a Methodist, tramps the roads of the southern counties, and preaches in the villages in company with a friend. The rustic peace of the story is rudely interrupted by the tragic circumstances of Humphrey's romance, which lead him to be arrested for murder and within sight of the gallows, his innocence being attested through a series of dramatic incidents which are finely handled. The conclusion—in which Humphrey and his love set off to tramp the roads together as man and wife, is written, as indeed is the whole book, with considerable beauty and pathos.

A review of ''The Tramping Methodist,'' in The Athenaeum, No. 4225, October 17, 1908, p. 469.

THE NORTH AMERICAN REVIEW　(essay date 1916)

[*In the following excerpt, the critic discusses the merits and flaws of* Sussex Gorse.]

Sussex Gorse, by Sheila Kaye-Smith, is a story of the sort that is usually called strong and impressive, and it deserves the somewhat faint praise which these terms in common usage imply. It also no doubt deserves the disparise which is implied in the equally uncritical terms monotonous and depressing. The story is discerningly realistic; it is big and typical; it persuades and pleases with its genuine flavor of earth, and with its true atmosphere of English peasant life. On the other hand, there is monotony enough in the tale, and there is a lack of sentiment for which a kind of robust earthiness does not perhaps wholly make up. The author has taken no pains to relieve possible tedium. She allows the persons of her story to talk as no doubt they would talk, and to repeat phrases as no doubt they would repeat them in real life. The rural vocabulary in *Sussex Gorse* is not extensive. Things are ''hemmed bad,'' or ''tedious little,'' or ''lamentable long'' or ''justabout good,'' without much variation throughout the book. As a means of arousing and holding interest the author relies upon the largeness of her theme, and upon the power of an exceptionally clear and vigorous style. But if you like the talk of very honest simple, sometimes muddleheaded folk, and if you have pleasure in frank description, you will be pleased with the details of the story.

The plan of the novel is exceedingly simple. As a boy Reuben Backfield became filled with the ambition to conquer Boarzell Moor: he would buy this waste land and lay it under cultivation. As a man, Reuben fought a long bitter fight with the Moor. In order that he might have soldiers to help in the battle, he married and begot sons and daughters. His wife died, and he married again. His second wife deserted him. Another woman who understood him, but who would have thwarted his ambition, he resolutely put out of his life. One by one his children, crushed by the tyranny of ''the farm,'' deserted him. . . . Reuben was hated, deserted, betrayed, bereaved, and he seems to have felt no emotions save pride and anger. . . . At sixty this splendid animal was in his prime. At eighty-five, he had conquered, and had not a soul to love him. He died a happy man.

The question as to whether this story is really big and impressive or merely little and depressing must be decided with reference to its meaning. If there is grandeur in the spectacle of a human being so immersed in nature that he moves on his way with the resistless force and with the callousness to suffering of Nature herself, then the story in all its monotony is big—the horizon widens to contain the thought, and the farmhouse becomes a castle. But if this be not true, if Reuben must be regarded as merely a poor obsessed creature who has missed the best in life because Nature drugged his higher thought-centers, then the story is not big but sordid—not even tragically sordid, for Reuben died happy.

Nature, not man, is the hero of the story. It is Nature in Reuben that triumphs over Boarzell and over the little short-lived Kingdoms of love and happiness that his children raised.

A breaking down of the distinction between Man and Nature—such seems to be the essential meaning, impressive or not, of this forceful story. (pp. 943-44)

> *A review of "Sussex Gorse," in* The North American Review, *Vol. CCIV, No. 733, December, 1916, pp. 943-44.*

W. L. GEORGE (essay date 1918)

[*A French-born English fiction writer, journalist, and critic, George is best known for* A Bed of Roses *(1911), a novel about the life of a prostitute. After this first and very successful effort as a novelist, George became stereotyped as a writer specializing in sexuality and the problems of women. From his own viewpoint, critics did him an injustice by overlooking what he considered the serious sociological and psychological interest of his works in order to focus on their sexual elements. A supporter of various liberal causes, most notably the rights of workers and women, George believed that writers should devote themselves to topics relevant to their own time and place. As Kaye-Smith wrote of his work: "It may not live forever, but at least it lives now." In the following excerpt, George, who significantly influenced Kaye-Smith's career, discusses aspects of her writing which were considered masculine during her time, compares the heroes in several of her novels, and appraises her writing.*]

I do not know whether this is a compliment, but I should not be surprised if a reader of, say *Starbrace*, or *Sussex Gorse*, were to think that Sheila Kaye-Smith is the pen-name of a man. Just as one suspects those racy tales of guardsmen, signed "Joseph Brown" or "George Kerr" of originating from some scented boudoir, so does one hesitate before the virility, the cognisance of oath and beer, of rotating crop, sweating horse, account book, vote, and snickersnee that Sheila Kaye-Smith exhibits in all her novels. This is broader, deeper than the work of the women novelists of to-day, who, with the exception of Amber Reeves, are confined in a circle of eternally compounding pallid or purple loves. One side of her work notably surprises, and that is the direction of her thoughts away from women, their great and little griefs, towards men and the glory of their combat against fate. Sheila Kaye-Smith is more than any of her rivals the true novelist: the showman of life. (pp. 94-5)

[There] is in her a sort of cosmic choler restrained by a Keltic pride that is ready to pretend a world made up of rates and taxes and the nine-two train to London Bridge. Afire within, she will not allow herself to "commit melodrama." (pp. 95-6)

Sheila Kaye-Smith has given expression to the county that from the Weald spreads green-breasted to meet the green sea. In all the novels is the slow Sussex speech, dotted with the kindly "surelye", the superlative "unaccountable"; women are "praaper", ladies "valiant", troubles "tedious." It has colour, it is true English, unstained of Cockneyism and American. It is the speech of the oasthouse, of the cottage on the marsh,

of the forester's hut in Udimore Wood, where sings the lark and rivulets flow like needles through the moss. (pp. 96-7)

Her Sussex is male: it is not the desiccated Sussex of the modern novelist, but the Sussex of the smuggler, of the Methodist, the squire; the Sussex where men sweat and read no books. Old Sussex, and the Sussex of to-day, which some think was created by the L. B. & S. C. Railway, she loves them both, and in both has found consolation, but I think she loves best the old. It was old Sussex made her first novel, *The Tramping Methodist.* Old Sussex bred its hero, Humphrey Lyte. He was a picaresque hero, the young rebel, for he grew enmeshed in murder and in love, in the toils of what England called justice in days when the Regent went to Brighton. But Lyte does not reveal Sheila Kaye-Smith as does *Starbrace*. Here is the apologia for the rebel: Starbrace, the son of a poor and disgraced man, will not eat the bread of slavery at his grandfather's price. You will imagine the old man confronted with this boy, of gentle blood but brought up as a labourer's son, hot, unruly, lusting for the freedom of the wet earth. Starbrace is a fool, disobedient; he is to be flogged. He escapes among the smugglers on Winchelsea marsh, to the wild world of the mid-eighteenth century. It is the world of fighting, and of riding, of blood, of excisemen, of the "rum pads" and their mistresses, their dicing and their death. Despite his beloved, Theodora Straightway, lady who fain would have him gentleman, Starbrace must ride away upon his panting horse, Pharisee. Love as he may, he cannot live like a rabbit in a hutch; he must have danger, be taken, cast into a cell, be released to die by the side of Pharisee, charging the Pretender's bodyguard at Prestonpans. All this is fine, for she has the secret of the historical novel; to show not the things that have changed, but those which have not.

Starbrace is, perhaps, Sheila Kaye-Smith's most brilliant flight, but not her most sustained. She has had other adventures in literature, such as *Isle of Thorns,* where Sally Odiarne wanders with Stanger's travelling show, hopelessly entangled in her loves, unable to seize happiness, unable to give herself to the tender Raphael, bound to good-tempered, sensual Andy, until at last she must kill Andy to get free, kill him to escape to the sea and die. But she finds God. . . . (pp. 97-9)

Sheila Kaye-Smith has not surrendered to life, though the weakness of her may be found in another book, *Three Against the World,* where the worthless Furlonger family can but writhe as worms drying in the sun. The vagary of her mind is in such work as criticism: she has published a study of John Galsworthy, which is judicial, though not inspired. But she was destined for finer tasks. Already in *Spell Land,* the story of a Sussex farm where lived two people, driven out of the village because they loved unwed, she had given a hint of her power to see not only man but the earth. She has almost stated herself in *Sussex Gorse.*

I have read many reviews of this book; I am tired of being told it is "epic." It is not quite; it has all the grace that Zola lacked in "La Terre", but if the beauty is anything it is Virgilian, not Homeric. The scheme is immense, the life of Reuben Backfield, of Odiam, inspired in early youth with the determination to possess Boarzell, the common grown with gorse and firs, the fierce land of marl and shards where naught save gorse could live. The opening is a riot, for the Enclosures Act is in force, and the squire is seizing the people's land. In that moment is born Reuben's desire; Boarzell shall be his. He buys some acres, and his struggle is frightful; you see his muscles bulging in his blue shirt, you smell his sweat, you hear the ploughshare gripped with the stones, teeth biting teeth. For Boarzell Common is old, crafty and savage, and would foil man. Reuben is not foiled; he can bear all things, so can dare all things. . . .

He gives all to Boarzell, to fighting it for seventy years, sometimes victor, sometimes crushed, for Boarzell is evil and fierce. . . . (pp. 99-101)

There are faults, here and there, degraded clichés; Sheila Kaye-Smith loves the stars too well, and often indulges in horrid astronomic orgies; there is not enough actual combat with the earth; the author intervenes, points to the combat instead of leaving at grips the two beasts, Reuben and Boarzell. She has not quite touched the epic, yet makes us want to resemble the hero, fierce, cruel, but great when old and alone, still indomitable. And one wonders what she will do, what she will be. (p. 102)

I do not know whether she will be great. It is enough that to-day she is already alone. (p. 103)

> *W. L. George, "Three Young Novelists," in his* Literary Chapters, *Little, Brown, and Company, 1918, pp. 74-103.**

K. M. [KATHERINE MANSFIELD]　(essay date 1919)

[*Mansfield was an important pioneer in stream-of-consciousness literature and among the first English authors whose fiction depended upon incident rather than plot, a development that significantly influenced the modern short story form. Throughout 1919 and 1920, Mansfield conducted a weekly book-review column in* The Athenaeum, *a magazine edited at the time by her husband, John Middleton Murry. In the following excerpt, Mansfield reviews* Tamarisk Town, *commenting on the landscape and characterization in the novel.*]

Were Miss Kaye-Smith a painter, we should be inclined to say that we do not feel she has yet made up her mind which it is she wishes most to paint—whether landscape or portraits. Which is it to be? Landscape—the blocking-in of a big difficult scheme, the effort required to make it appear substantial and convincing, the opportunity it gives her for the bold, sweeping line—it is plain to see how strongly this attracts her. Portraits—there is a glamour upon the human beings she chooses which fascinates her, and which she cannot resist. Why should she not be equally at home with both? What is her new novel *Tamarisk Town* but an attempt to see them in relation to each other? And yet, in retrospect, there is her town severely and even powerfully painted, and there are her portraits, on the same canvas, and yet so out of it, so separate that the onlooker's attention is persistently divided—it flies between the two, and is captured by neither.

Her theme is the development of a small Sussex town into a select seaside resort, patronized by the wealthy and aristocratic, not on account of its natural beauties alone, but because of the taste and judgment with which its reformation has been achieved. There is a time when it seems established in its enchanting prosperity for ever, but the hour of its triumph contains the seeds of its downfall. Very gradually, and then more swiftly, it is attacked by vulgarians, who are allowed to have their way, until at the end, wretched, shoddy, decayed little place that it is become, it is the scene of a brawl between drunken trippers. *Sic transit gloria Marlingate.*

It is, of course, absurd to imagine that Marlingate could grow, come to flower, blow to seed, without the aid of man, and yet at the moments when Miss Kaye-Smith is least conscious of the forces that govern it, she is at her happiest. Wandering at will in the Assembly Rooms, in the beautiful little Town Park, along the white, gleaming parade, in the woods at French Landing, her style is very natural and unforced, and, until the beginning of the disintegrating process, her touch is light. But, after all, this is only the landscape half. Let us examine the "portraits." The chief is Edward Monypenny, creator of Marlingate, who, at the age of twenty-eight, is in a position powerful enough to determine the future of the town. This curious young man, with his shock of white hair, coal-black eyes and black side whiskers, is, for all his cynical aloofness, in love with Marlingate; we are to believe that, until he meets with the little wild governess, he has never known what it was to feel for anything more responsive than a new block of houses or a bandstand. But she, Morgan, Morgan le fay, running out of the wood with dead leaves in her hair, very nearly makes havoc of his resolute ambition in the old, old way. . . .

It is a matter for wonder that, in spite of all the many pages describing the progress of their guilty love, in spite of the tremendous pains taken by the author to depict the agonies of Monypenny upon his discovering that sweet Morgan le fay holds in contempt, nay hates, his beloved Marlingate, and the other tremendous pains taken to show Morgan's despair upon realizing that Edward will not flee with her to foreign parts—we are never once moved by these two creatures. Marionettes they are, and marionettes they remain, jigging in a high fierce light that Miss Kaye-Smith would convince us is the fire of passion, until the last puppet-quarrel and the last glimpse of the heroine, "half under the water, half trailing on the rock . . . something which, from the top of the cliff, looked like a dead crimson leaf." This extreme measure is for love of Monypenny, who, at first, is properly grateful for his freedom. Again he is a man like a town walking, until one day he is filled with the idea that his first love is fattening upon the dead body of his second love, and that, after all, a woman is more to be desired than bricks and mortar. This starts working passion number three—he will kill that which killed her, and so have his revenge.

Here, to our thinking, the book ends. All that is going to happen has happened; we are at the top of the hill. Below us lies Marlingate, in its prosperity, "lying there licked by the sun," and gazed upon by the man who has made it, and is about to unmake it. But the author is, if we may be pardoned the expression, "as fresh as when she started." New characters appear—a wife for Monypenny, a little wooden son who has time to grow up and marry the daughter of Morgan le fay (so like, yet so unlike) and to live his father's history all over again before Marlingate is destroyed. And the years roll by, unbroken, heavy, like waves slapping against the promenade, the vulgar pier, before Miss Kaye-Smith is content to leave Marlingate to its fate.

How does it happen that a writer, obviously in love with writing, is yet not curious? This is the abiding impression left us by Miss Kaye-Smith; she is satisfied to put into the mouths and the hearts and minds of her characters the phrase, the emotion, the thought that "fits" the situation, with the result that it does not seem to matter whether they speak, feel or think. Nothing is gained by it. They are just where they are. The plot's the thing—and having decided upon it she gets her team together and gives out the parts. There is but to speak them. And into the hand of Morgan le fay she thrusts a scarlet umbrella, she throws a cherry cloak about her and clothes her in a scarlet dress—and sets her going.

K. M. [Katherine Mansfield], "A Landscape with Portraits," in The Athenaeum, *No. 4663, September 12, 1919, p. 881.*

MALCOLM COWLEY   (essay date 1920)

[*Cowley, an American critic, has made several valuable contributions to contemporary letters with his editions of important American authors (Nathaniel Hawthorne, Walt Whitman, Ernest Hemingway, William Faulkner, F. Scott Fitzgerald), his writings as a literary critic for the* New Republic, *and above all, with his chronicles and criticism of modern American literature. Cowley's literary criticism does not attempt a systematic philosophical view of life and art, nor is it representative of a neatly defined school of critical thought. Rather, it focuses on works—particularly those of "lost generation" writers whom he knew—that Cowley believes personal experience has qualified him to explicate and that he considers worthy of public appreciation. The critical approach Cowley follows is undogmatic and is characterized by a willingness to view a work from whatever perspective—social, historical, aesthetic—that the work itself seems to demand for its illumination. In the following excerpt, Cowley discusses* The Challenge to Sirius *and* The Four Roads, *asserting that* The Four Roads *is the superior of the two works.*]

Modern art subsists to a remarkable extent by taking in its own washing. Novelists adopt poets for heroes, who write sonnets on pictures, for which musicians compose orchestral settings. Painters contribute fantastic portraits of all these folks and become in turn the heroes of new novels; the circle is complete. . . . It is true of course that an occasional hero is free from the taint of art; he is always different, however, from the mass of men, having at least the artistic sensibilities. Sometimes an author dives into the sea of life and grasps an authentic, unliterary experience; at such occasions we have reason to be grateful. Sheila Kaye-Smith has made the plunge and returned tightly clutching a bit of soil.

No wonder she prizes her discovery, for the soil is not merely the background of her novels; it serves also to motivate the actions of her characters; in fact the earth of Sussex might be called the chief of her dramatis personae. It is not by oversight that her heroes are never allowed to love a woman very strongly. The real affection is for the ground itself. No more is it accidental that Miss Kaye-Smith grows impassioned only when she describes a landscape, analyzing her characters as coldly as if they were mathematical theorems. She has laid claim to a corner of England, but her ownership is one of the soil alone; with the ways of its inhabitants she has little sympathy.

There is, on the border of Kent and Sussex, a district of hillocks and spongy pastures, with farms caught in a web of little, twisting lanes. . . . It is this country which she has chosen for her own. At first she confined herself to it rigorously. Later she has dared occasional expeditions into the outer world, but she has not yet learned to keep her footing on other ground than Sussex.

Especially is this evident in *The Challenge to Sirius.* The novel is long and inchoate, bound together only by the fact that it is the biography of Frank Rainger; while he, in turn, is convincing only when he moves against a south-English background. Rainger spends his boyhood and adolescence in the Isle of Oxney, "a little pip of a county wedged between Sussex and Kent." There he returns, a man in his fifties, to marry his first love and settle down. The interval is taken up with a London sojourn—of which Miss Kaye-Smith gives a brilliant and thoroughly second-rate account—a history of the Civil War from

Pittsburg Landing to Atlanta, and a final interlude of eleven years in Yucatan.

An English view of the War of the Rebellion is always fascinating to the American reader. Here Miss Kaye-Smith is safe but not inspired. She wisely lays stress more on the general features of the campaigns than on the reactions of the individual soldier; these remain somewhat of a closed book to women. She is less discreet when she gives herself free rein on Southern landscapes. Evidently she has gained her knowledge of them through textbooks of botany. Frank, escaping from the Union forces, makes his way through a jungle of Indian pipe and sumach. He hides from his pursuers behind a pokeberry bush! and at last floats down the Suwanee River, breathing in the heavy scents of orange-flowers, syringa, oleander, and myrtle, and watching the delicate palm-fronds outlined against the stars. . . . It is beautiful, it is exotic, but it reminds one more of Chateaubriand than of Georgia. More real is the portrait of the planter-at-arms, Zollicoffer, and especially that of Lorena Middleton; she is a pressed flower of the Old South.

The scenes in the Isle of Oxney show more accuracy. Tom Coalbrun and his lumpish brother Dave; Maggie, whom Frank Rainger loves mildly and persistently—"She was habit and hunger like his daily bread"—these people are depicted patiently, exactly, and with a skill which Miss Kaye-Smith surpasses only in her descriptions of the fields of marl which are their livelihood. It is from the style, however, that the volume derives much of its worth. This quality is one of which our generation seems almost unconscious. We know that George Moore writes good prose—he has told us so himself. Critics trumpet the perfection of Conrad in our ears. Appreciation of the cadenced beauty which characterizes *The Challenge to Sirius,* however, rests on no publicity methods. The ideas which Miss Kaye-Smith expresses are often banal—she is naively indifferent to her own platitudes—but the sentences that clothe them are hammered in bronze; each one perfect, each sufficient to itself.

The flux and reflux of sentences such as these makes beautiful the prose of *The Four Roads.* Here the subject is Sussex in wartime. One hears at first the boom of ghostly artillery across the Channel as a dissonance in the usual hum of afternoon. Later it grows louder, threatening to destroy utterly this peaceful countryside. Sussex triumphs over the guns; with the young men killed, there is left another generation to grasp the warm plough-handles that the fathers had dropped. The victory, however, is precarious, and the new Sussex is not the peaceful county of Victoria's reign that sowed and reaped and voted Tory to keep the prices up.

As a novel *The Four Roads* is almost everything that its precursor was not. The real hero is a village instead of one man; despite this fact, the story is distinctly of a single piece. One does not pick many flaws; neither does one grow especially enthusiastic. Tom Beatup and his solid, maternal Thyrza; Tom's younger brothers; Jerry, the scapegrace son of the Nonconformist parson and a gypsy woman from Ihornden: all these characters are delineated with infinite understanding but without real sympathy. Miss Kaye-Smith, near as she is to the heart of Sussex, is a stranger to its people, much like the woman of Ihornden who married there and died and was a friend only to the wild twisting roads. Or she is like the Frank Rainger of the earlier volume, who, she says, "had sunk into the fibre of Moon's Green like a nail embedded in the live trunk of an oak. He would always be different in substance from his surroundings."

This charge of lack of sympathy can hardly be brought against her portrait of the Reverend Mr. Sumption. A gaunt, lonely Baptist, he too was a stranger to the folk among whom he lived. His son, his flock, his faith: one after another the war deprives him of these; finally he discovers salvation in physical labour. On a few such characters as this, on her style, and above everything else, on her feelings of kinship with a few square miles of Sussex earth, Miss Kaye-Smith can justly base a claim to a rank beside the dozen or half-dozen best novelists of her generation.

Yet if she ranks with the Young Englishmen, she is not one of them. There is a peculiar datelessness about her work that separates her from the experiments and bustling tract-novels of her contemporaries. I do not mean by this that she is not a very modern young woman, nor to hint that she does not possess perfect acquaintance with the literary movements of the last decade. At times she writes two or three paragraphs of Galsworthy; there is a chapter in **The Four Roads** that is utterly Wellsian; but these passages seem excrescences. At their best her novels partake of the timelessness of the subject; she is Sussex rather than Victorian or Georgian. The limits of her development are of the same nature; her art is bounded not so much by her understanding, by her technique, as geographically by the River Rother and the Royal Military Canal. (pp. 259-62)

Malcolm Cowley, "The Woman of Ihornden," in The Dial, *Vol. LXVIII, No. 2, February, 1920, pp. 259-62.*

R. BRIMLEY JOHNSON (essay date 1920)

[*In the following excerpt, Johnson offers a comparative study of some early twentieth-century women novelists and their understanding of human nature, discusses the "masculine" traits of Kaye-Smith's writing, and surveys her novels through* Little England.]

[Sheila Kaye-Smith's masculine intellect is] a feature which cuts more deeply than the mere form of such stories as the **Challenge to Sirius** and **Tamarisk Town** where . . . the narrative is told exclusively from the man's outlook.

In the predominance of local colour, the dependence upon place, for example, she leaves the feminine manner. Miss Macaulay, indeed, has the academic manner and touches Cambridgeshire—but incidentally. The London of others is no more than the natural centre of intellect and society: country surroundings are merely illustrative of a character-type: Miss Sidgwick uses France and Germany to accentuate race distinctions.

Miss Kaye-Smith is mainly inspired by locality: elsewhere the stimulus came from thought and emotion. The fact indicates a deeper difference: she works from study and observation, while they depend upon experience, instinct, and emotion. In the conventional sense, therefore, she is more professional (here approaching Miss Sidgwick), not attempting the new realism; and, manlike, she leans to melodrama. It is a similar distinction to that observed between George Eliot—who took up subjects—and Fanny Burney or Jane Austen—who revealed themselves. The class of subject resembles, most obviously, Hardy's: and, in this sense, most of our contemporary novelists do not take up a subject at all—outside Life and Truth. They merely express themselves, and their point of view.

In treatment, again, she is more brutal, or masculine, than any of her contemporaries—save possibly, Mrs. Mordaunt. She spares us no details of dung and sweat from the farmyard:

being apparently convinced that the romance of the countryside needs strong meat from the realist. She is frankly rustic in speech.

It is a commonplace of social reformers that the sordidness of village life is no less repulsive than a slum-street. We have long left behind us the innocent milkmaids of the pastoral. But it is nevertheless, a matter for criticism that Miss Kaye-Smith has not quite escaped that fondness for dirt—which characterises the school: and we are haunted, at times, by the suspicion that she has "got up" her localities from books and hearsay, without having herself "lived" them. Here is a little too much "scenery" for the village drama.

I cannot, for instance, quite believe in the **Isle of Thorns,** wherein the melodrama is perilous. Sally has *really* lost some of her natural instincts and inherited refinement. The adventurer, too often, descends to the level of one to the manner born. Seeking colour or romance, she loses her soul and her imagination altogether. Andy, at times, does violence to one half of his double nature; degenerating to the "impossibles": and Raphael tolerates cheerfully what a man of his nature could, and would, have avoided. Yet the story-scheme was to glorify adventure, to idealise the born rebel, the man, or woman, who keeps a child's heart; but it just misses the poetry and the imagination (with which R. L. Stevenson has clothed the tramp)—the glow of youth, which remains beautiful—and we suspect she misses because she has studied, and not lived.

It is perhaps, in her studies of the "old" Sussex that we should rather look for Miss Kaye-Smith's sincerity in local colour; for she is an adept (as, again, have been few women) at the historical novel. Humphrey Lyte, in the picturesque **Tramping Methodist**—of the Regency days—is a true rebel; and so, above all, is **Starbrace,** that fine fool of a man, the swaggering comrade of smugglers, who would ride away from his lady love; choosing rather the glorious risks of free adventure in a world of turmoil, finding his death in battle against the Pretender at Prestonpans.

Tamarisk Town, again, does not betray the midnight oil. Here we have town life replacing the village; and—for whatever reason—the draughtsmanship is both finer and more assured. The book is, mainly, a study in egoism: revealing that struggle which is the chief mainspring of drama, between a man's personality and his ambition, between what himself is and the impression he longs to stamp on the public, between his vision and his work. It is the more subtle, and more dramatic because, in this case, we recognise Vision on both sides of his nature. Practically, and as others see the man, Councillor Moneypenny was an idealist. If his outlook was parochial and his aims paltry, they at least reveal a steady imagination and iron will. It was he alone who could visualise Marlingate as it might be—a select and prosperous resort, developed with taste, for a defined purpose, tempting the best people: not a get-rich-quick affair, but a sound, steadily progressive, investment. It was he alone who had the intelligence, the far-seeing courage, the instinct for selection, which could clothe his ideal in bricks and mortar. His, too, the personality to prevail over his fellow councillors who were at once more cautious and (once they caught a glimmer of his idea) more crude and impatient.

To this obsession of the solitary dreamer, we find opposed a contrary vision:—that of Morgan le Fay, the elfin woman: for whom the old town, asleep in its haunting beauty, offers a very different appeal. She is jealous, too, of her man's absorbing materialism, his passion for the child of his brain. Let him persist at his peril. He may build Marlingate—at the cost of her love and his own Soul. But she has come too late, he has plotted and planned too long. When behold (as she had warned him) there slips into his heart a full realisation of what his choice meant, the thwarted egoist turns furiously upon himself; once more rousing the full force of his immense will-power—now turned demoniac—to the destruction of all he had wrought in his pride.

Marrying carelessly—in all the bitterness of a dead soul—his solitary old age is yet further tortured by witnessing a repetition of the same struggle in his only son. The boy, having inherited the old man's first enthusiasms, is left in the dark before the stern destructiveness of the new policy. He, too, loves Marlingate; and to him also, comes the love of a maiden—for whom the town of his dreams has no inward significance. Reversing, as we feel inevitably, his father's decision, he finds new happiness in wider fields: breaking the chains implanted by childhood memories; winning at once the freedom of his own soul and the reward of unselfish love. He is the smaller egoist, and the bigger man.

Here we see Miss Kaye-Smith at work upon a slight variant of the theme that inspired (three years before) her almost epic *Sussex Gorse;* where, again, Reuben Backfield loses everything for fierce love of the Boarzell acres—the savage common of gorse and furze, of marl and shards:

> It lay in a great hush, a great solitude, a quiet
> beast of power and mystery. It seemed to call
> to him through the twilight like a love forsaken.
> There it lay: Boarzell—strong, beautiful, de-
> sired, untamed, still his hope, still his battle.

In the mad frenzy of possession, he is sustained through seventy years of desperate fighting; careless even of human sacrifice, losing almost without a pang, every man and woman linked to him by natural affection. Gone from him were his brother Harry, his two wives, his six sons, and his two daughters; gone, too, others with whom the human bond of love was yet closer. Yet he must fight on.

Here is the true passion for Mother Earth (as she has hinted it, also, in *Spell Land*); if it be fiercely consecrated to one tiny spot thereon. Such is the sacrifice that our gods demand.

It is, however, the *Challenge to Sirius* which is most typical of Miss Kaye-Smith at her best: at once most completely masculine and most sincere. There is a sentence, which reveals its essential philosophy, to be found in Mrs. Mordaunt's *The Pendulum* . . . :

> People so often wonder why a man is not faith-
> ful to a woman for whom he undoubtedly cares;
> and yet it seems that an affection like this pro-
> duces its own vacuum—a vacuum ready to be
> filled for the most part, by the antithesis of its
> former occupant. Or, again, he is like a man
> but partially recovered from a bad illness, sen-
> sitive, liable to catch another.
>
> (pp. 83-9)

Miss Kaye-Smith, indeed, permits her Frank two infidelities. In the first case, the digression is little more than episode, the first stirring of youth's young blood, wholly physical, and without any lasting effect on character: the almost inevitable consequence of an untutored lad from the country being tossed suddenly into the very centre of an ill-regulated London circle of Bohemian failures in life: men and women with no higher

ambition among them than "defying the law because it *was* a law"; prompted in all their talk and action, by an unreasoning hostility to convention and morality.

But, on the other hand, we find real romance and manly passion combined in the love of his manhood; Lovena, the fair American—a true woman and, for at least much of his character, a true mate. Experience here elevates Frank instead of degrading him: it is not infatuation, but inspiration.

Wherefore the final return, nearing the end of life, to the familiar nature atmosphere of boyhood; the final marriage with the sweetly simple-minded and primitive woman to whom he had given his child's heart; assumes for us the significance of a symbol. Maggie, in fact, is a true child of nature, the very spirit of Country Life: with all its dumb fancies and brooding imaginations, linked to a shrewd, elementary, materialism. Whence we see in Frank's delayed loyalty to her, that strange return to the atmosphere of our childhood, its tastes, its instincts, and its dreamings; which lies at the root of character, and, not infrequently, brings with it the highest happiness and content.

Finally, Miss Kaye-Smith has captured a similar truth in her tragic war-novel, *Little England,* where the world's upheaval is used, with dramatic concentration, for the revealing of the rustic; with his sternly limited imagination, his slow but single-minded determination, and his inarticulate pathos. In the two young men (one a plain hero, the other a coward and failure) who go to the front: in the brother who manfully shoulders the whole responsibility of the old farm, breaking up new land to feed the nation; or in the sister whose crude love story is so curiously complicated by khaki inroads; Miss Kaye-Smith has skilfully linked the permanent in life and nature to what was, temporarily, engraved thereon by the catastrophe. However much (and there was far more in villages than in town life) went on normally, however often men and women loved, married, or died, were faithful or faithless; the surface was changed, and the depths were stirred. She does not attempt, here, any psychological analysis: she does not discuss social, or international, policy: but she does use, legitimately and dramatically, the conditions which were disturbing the whole world. It is a fragment of genuine human history, a record of great artistic value; which could only have been seen and drawn by one who was very much alive at that particular period.

Thus we find that Miss Kaye-Smith (at her best) uses her own—more conventional—methods of observation towards the inner vision with which women are mainly concerned. If far more realistic—in the old sense—than most, she is still a realist. What we find new in contemporary fiction, indeed, cannot be destined to cover the whole field, to be adopted by all. Like other genuine forward movements, it will leaven the lump, influencing, no doubt, those who do not fall in line, those—even—who, as a matter of judgment, are hostile.

On the other hand, we do not expect many women-writers to follow Miss Kaye-Smith. She is too masculine: but as there is nothing in her work which counters the most characteristically feminine ideals; there is, also, a certain passionate sympathy and tenderness, which the men of her school seldom, if ever, attain.

Sussex remains, as it were, her private park. She has caught that mysterious personality which does, in fact, distinguish the folk and atmosphere of one English county from life spent over the boundary. Probably we can all recognise the man from Manchester, or the Cornish man; but a far subtler instinct becomes necessary for differentiation between counties that are adjacent; members of one group. There are groups within groups: one town on the East Coast differeth from another. And in Miss Kaye-Smith we recognise that inner vision, that imaginative sympathy (perfected by Thomas Hardy) which has grown into one particular corner of our Mother Earth. Here, inevitably, we find silent kinship with nature, and an understanding of primitive man: which is the inheritance of those not caught in the whirl of progress, not limited by London life. Miss Kaye-Smith, obviously, knows something—it may be much—about the "new" theories of art and morality, on which the intellectuals of an over-cultivated society are always busying themselves: but she has chosen to leave such matters alone. For her the Vision of youth trembles under the firmament, sunny or clouded, among the green fields or the golden crops. Always it savours of the soil. Whence her message: and that, too, has its meaning—towards the discovery of Truth—for the most sophisticated of us. The background remains eternal. (pp. 89-93)

> *R. Brimley Johnson, "Sheila Kaye-Smith," in his* Some Contemporary Novelists (Women), *1920. Reprint by Books for Libraries Press, 1967; distributed by Arno Press, Inc., pp. 83-93.*

LOUISE MAUNSELL FIELD   (essay date 1922)

[*In the following excerpt, Field reviews* Joanna Godden.]

So much of the fiction offered us of late has dealt with the manners and morals—or perhaps it might be closer to accuracy to say lack of morals—of the extremely up-to-date and extremely sophisticated, that to meet with such an unsophisticated and old-fashioned person as Sheila Kaye-Smith's new heroine, [the title character of] *Joanna Godden,* is quite a pleasant change. Joanna had lived all her life at Little Ansdore, one of the farms lying amid the marshes near the Sussex coast. It was about three miles from the town of Rye, on the land from which the sea receded generations ago, turning Rye from a port into an inland town. The novel begins on the day Joanna Godden came into possession of Little Ansdore; it ends some seventeen years later, when, after much achievement and some failure, she suddenly finds herself—"On the threshold of an entirely new life—her lover, her sister, her farm, her home, her good name, all lost. But the past and the future still were hers," and with them the one thing she has always wanted most of all.

It is a thoroughly realistic novel, this study of farm life in the district known as the "Three Marshes," between the years 1897 and 1914. There are comparatively few long descriptions, either of the farm or of the surrounding country, but one gets the very sight and smell of the sea farm on the marsh amid the water-courses, a farm mostly of pasturage "dappled over with the big Kent sheep." We see it in the "soft, golden glow" of the hot Summer morning, as well as in the early hours when the mists lie heavy over the land, and the marsh wears "its strange, occasional look of being under the sea." The stir and bustle of the busy farm life in which Joanna reveled, the anxieties of lambing time, the gossip at the Woolpack Inn, which in its old-fashioned way provided many of the opportunities offered by the modern country club in the matters of food and scandal—all these are presented with the sureness of complete familiarity, with quiet self-confidence and the skill which conceals all traces of effort. Yet they are but a deftly painted, clearly detailed background for the full-length portrait of Joanna herself, the book's central figure, and its reason for being.

She is drawn with a fidelity, a glow and vividness, an absence of either idealization or exaggeration which are truly remarkable. Generous, warm-hearted, impulsive, courageous, quick to forgive, far-sighted and adventurous along certain lines, lavish both with her love and with her money, she is also exacting, domineering, cocksure, flamboyant, redolent of swank and swagger. . . .

It is the story of the central portion of her life the book tells, from the day when, to the horror of the conservative farmers roundabout, who all held strong opinions as to what was and what was not a woman's business, she declared her intention of managing her farm herself. Her trials, her mistakes, and the triumphs which presently transform her into "Squire Joanna Godden" and a power in the neighborhood are related with verisimilitude and an abundance of quiet humor. But it is her emotional life which is of primary importance. In the admirable handling of Joanna's simple, yet in its way complicated, psychology is the author's greatest success. Her development, her headlong, undisciplined impulses, her lack of understanding, or of any control over her own mental processes, are unfolded clearly and convincingly. The young woman of 23 who "smacked" her 10-year-old sister one minute and hugged her the next, develops logically into the woman of 40 who faced so bravely the consequences of her last and disastrous love affair. For always at the root of her character is the conscience, the keen sense of right and wrong, which, though comic in some of its manifestations, is nevertheless sturdy and brave. Joanna is one of the memorable women of fiction, vivid, faulty, human, real through and through. Big and bouncing and buxom, with a touch of the barbaric, warm and glowing, impulsive and passionate, always convinced that she knew what was best, not only for herself but for every one else, and ought therefore to manage other people's lives for them, she radiates vitality from first to last.

This glow and radiance of Joanna, who was so like a big, golden flower, somewhat dims the other characters, yet they have been well and carefully drawn. Arthur Alce, the faithful lover who let Joanna manage his life for him, with results very far from satisfactory, and Ellen, the little sister to whom "submission was an effective weapon of her warfare," and who "despised Andore for its very splendors," and the flaunting colors and swaggering magnificence Joanna adored, are especially well done. One of the most noticeable things about the book is its evenness of excellence—an evenness which is the result of a carefully, conscientiously cultivated talent. The reader remembers it rather as a whole than for any outstanding scene or flash of insight. It is an admirable novel, balanced, interesting, artistic, in many ways a notable addition to the many noteworthy tales of rural life in England.

> *Louise Maunsell Field, in a review of "Joanna Godden," in* The New York Times Book Review, *February 5, 1922, p. 14.*

L. P. HARTLEY   (essay date 1923)

[*Author of the acclaimed novel trilogy* Eustace and Hilda (1944-47), *Hartley was an English novelist and short story writer whose fiction is unified by the theme of the search for individuality and meaning in the post-Christian era. In his examination of moral dilemmas he is often compared to Nathaniel Hawthorne, while his effective use of symbolism and close attention to craft and plot unity evoke frequent comparisons to the works of Henry James. A literary critic as well, Hartley contributed reviews for many years to the* Saturday Review, Time and Tide, *the* Spectator, *and other periodicals. In the following excerpt, he offers a mixed appraisal of* The End of the House of Alard.]

As its title implies, the hero of Miss Sheila Kaye-Smith's latest novel [*The End of the House of Alard*] is not a person but an abstract entity, a god of the countryside that has outlasted its function and become its own parasite. To maintain the impoverished estate of the Alards, "the largest in East Sussex," the living representatives of the family are one by one joylessly sacrificed. From the outset the movement of the story sets towards tragedy, recognizably and inevitably. . . .

The End of the House of Alard is a painful book, almost devoid of humour and of the sense of free-will. Of self-will, dogged and unrewarding, there is plenty; there is even, in the passage where Jenny makes love to the farmer, Ben Godfrey, a sensible loosening of bonds, a spontaneous motion of personality, like water finding its way down hill. But the other characters give an effect of stress, of thwarted development, as though the half-hearted economy practised at the manor had lodged itself in their natures. One could not, perhaps, expect them to be otherwise, torn as they were between competing loyalties. It is both a merit and a shortcoming of the book that, such is the force with which its predicament imposes itself on the mind, any action, however inconsistent, on the part of any of the characters, can be justified simply by reference to it. Not that Miss Kaye-Smith is guilty of inconsistency in her delineations; her people are convincing enough as far as they go, as far as their inter-dependence will let them go. But they do not, all of them at least, go very far. They are easily recognizable; one can tell almost at once that Sir John Alard is rude and witty and autocratic, that Peter is stolid, selfish, neurotic and sentimental, Gervase tender and rebellious, Stella Mount high-principled and passionate, Rose Alard spiteful, narrow-minded and mean. They are not imperfectly realized and yet they have a flatness that makes them, as one reads, live on the page rather than in the imagination. It is the same with the dialogue, which is always good and yet often recalls the way people talk in a book. It illustrates but does not illuminate. . . .

Just as the Alards suffered under the mortmain of their ancestors, so, one feels, their history is clogged by its chief assumption—the assumption that a family could be found, in these days, to live steadfastly and stupidly in the past, and feed on the memory of past importance. Miss Kaye-Smith does everything possible with such a theme. No one could read *The End of the House of Alard* without interest or without emotion; but the interest is the interest we feel in a problem deftly worked out, and the emotion is the emotion that necessarily arises from the skilful handling of tragic events, not from the direct apprehension of their reality.

> *L. P. Hartley, in a review of "The End of the House of Alard," in* The Spectator, *Vol. 131, No. 4968, September 15, 1923, p. 358.*

A. ST. JOHN ADCOCK   (essay date 1923)

[*An English author of numerous works, many of which concern the city of London, Adcock served as editor of the London* Bookman *from 1923 until his death in 1930. In the following excerpt, Adcock asserts that Kaye-Smith has been the most successful woman to date at portraying men and discusses both her writing style and her ability to create convincing, authentic characters of both sexes.*]

Talking of Charlotte Brontë, in a novel of Sheila Kaye-Smith's that goes back to mid-Victorian days, a hairy young man, with

a moustache, in addition to the whiskers of the period, agrees that she is crude and outlandish, and adds, "That always comes when women write books. They're so frightened of being called feminine that they bury what talent they may have under a mountain of manliness—and manliness for them consists entirely of oaths and violence and scarlet sin."

Whether you agree or disagree with him, the hairy young critic was expressing an opinion that was common among his contemporaries, who have handed it down to a large number of their successors. It was probably half true, and is not so true now as it was. The women novelists now who specialise in scarlet sin have no particular use for oaths and violence. Moreover, though it would be easy to name several who have a tendency to colour their pages with sin of all colours, there is nothing exclusively masculine in that and their novels remain essentially feminine. It would be easy to name others who are much addicted to violent scenes and characters, but I doubt whether that is any conscious attempt on their part to be manly—on the contrary, it arises from an inherent, very feminine admiration of that barbaric strength and muscular vigor which the average woman is supposed to find so splendid and so attractive in the average man. It is such an orthodox feminine conception of the ideal male that its presence in a story almost inevitably betrays the sex of the author.

All which means no more than that the woman novelist quite legitimately does her best to draw a man, as the man novelist does his best to draw a woman, and she succeeds nearly as often; and no woman novelist, past or present, has been more uniformly and extraordinarily successful in this difficult application of her art than Sheila Kaye-Smith. It is usual for the male author to excuse his artistic shortcomings by insisting that woman is a mystery and it is impossible to comprehend her; but it seems likely that he may himself be as much of a mystery to woman and that is why, in fiction, the men she depicts so often seem like women in masquerade. (pp. 143-44)

But the men in Miss Kaye-Smith's novels are the real thing; they are the unqualified male in whom male readers unhesitatingly recognise their kind. Not because they are harsh or brutal, though some of them are that; not because they are susceptible to the lure of the other sex and masterfully override the laws of conventional morality, though some of them do that; not because they are heavy drinkers and lusty fighters with their fists, though some of them are this and some that; but simply because in their general habits, their ordinary everyday behaviour, in what they say no less than in what they think, they are obviously of the masculine gender. It is easy to create an illusion that your character is a man if you call him a soldier and describe him as acting with vigour or daring; but take this fragment of conversation, chosen at random from *The Challenge to Sirius,* between Frank Rainger and the retired studious Mr. Bellack. Frank is the son of an embittered gentleman who has withdrawn from the struggle of life; he works, from choice, on the farm where he and his father live, and goes daily to the Rectory to take lessons with Mr. Bellack, but has come to hesitate between his love of working on the land and a desire to go away somewhere and know more of life, and asks his tutor to advise him:

> 'The question is which is the best: happiness or experience? If it's experience, you had better get out of this hole as quickly as possible; if it's happiness, you had better stay where you are.'

'Which do you think it is, sir?'

'My good boy, how can I tell you? Personally I would rather you did not go to London and take your chances there, as I feel that, though you have brains and certain rudimentary gifts, it is not the kind of life you are cut out for, and that you will probably fail and be wretched. On the other hand, never renounce what seems to you a good opportunity and a fine experience because an old chap like me hints at trouble ahead. Besides, your father would rather see you starve as a journalist than grow fat as a farmer. Perhaps he is right—perhaps I am.'

'Did you ever have to make a choice of your own, sir?'

'Certainly I did, and I chose to be Rector of Wittersham with an income of two hundred a year, no congenial society, a congregation of hop-sacks, and for my sole distraction the teaching of a muddle-headed boy who, at the age of nineteen, is still undecided as to how he shall live the rest of his life.'

'So you chose wrong, I reckon.'

'How do you reckon any such thing? You don't know what my alternative was. Besides, you may be sure of this, no matter which way you choose you will never definitely know whether you were wrong or right. The great question of all choosers and adventurers is "Was it worth while?"—and whatever else you may expect of life, don't expect an answer to that'.

Now if there had been nothing to indicate who the boy was talking with you would know at once he was not talking to a woman, for there is a man's way of thinking, a man's manner, even a man's voice in all that Mr. Bellack says. There is always this subtle, easy, truthfully realistic presentation of Miss Kaye-Smith's male characters, of the mild, unassertive, commonplace, as well as the aggressive and more virile of them. Her rustic clowns are as roughly human and racy of the soil as Hardy's. Robert Fuller, half animal, half saint, in *Green Apple Harvest;* Monypenny, the practical idealist of *Tarmarisk Town,* who, ambitious to develop and popularise a seaside resort, triumphs over all obstacles, carries his schemes through, rises to wealth and dignity, and, sacrificing to his ambition the woman he loves, finds himself lonely and unhappy on his height and turns remorsefully and madly to destroy all he has so laboriously built; Miles, in *Starbrace,* with his strangely varying moods, his strength and pitiful weaknesses; the stern, harsh, ruggedly heroic Reuben Backfield, in *Sussex Gorse,* wholly given over to his desperate, indomitable fight for the possession of a wild, unfruitful common; Mr. Sumption, the dour, pathetic Baptist minister in *Little England,* a graphic, poignant revelation of what the war meant in a rural community, and one of the two or three great novels of that era—these and, in their differing class and degree, all the men who belong to her stories are real, authentic, humans—are men in flesh and bone and spirit, easy, natural, alive.

Her women are drawn with a knowledge that is apparently as minutely exact and is certainly as sympathetic. If I had to single out her most remarkable study in feminine temperament and psychology, I think I should say Joanna Godden; but her ex-

plicit interpretations of women are not so unusual as her understanding of men. She knows their businesses as thoroughly as she knows them. If, like Coalbran or Backfield, they are farmers and working on the land, she is not contented with vivid generalities but makes the varied, multifarious circumstance of farming and cattle raising, and the whole atmosphere and environment that has moulded their lives part of her story. When Monypenny devotes himself to the development of Tamarisk Town you are not asked to take anything for granted but are shown how he financed his scheme, acquired land, carried out his building operations, how the borough was formed, and the elections conducted—you follow the growth of the place through its various stages, and Monypenny's own story grows with and through it. It is this acquaintance with practical detail, this filling in of all essential surroundings that help to give the novels their convincing air of realism. (pp. 145-49)

[Miss Kaye-Smith's] first two novels are of the eighteenth century; one or two are of mid-Victorian times; the rest are of our own day. Occasionally she brings her people to London, but nearly always they are at home in Kent or Sussex. In *The Challenge to Sirius* and *The End of the House of Alard* they are on the borderland of the two counties; but mostly her scenes are in the county where she was born. In her books she has become its interpreter and made it her own. She has put something of her love of it and of the rugged lives and passions of its folk into the poems in *Willow Forge,* and *Saints in Sussex;* but her best poetry is in her novels. If you compare her with some of her leading women contemporaries you have a sense of as much difference between them as there is between collectors of insects and the hunter of big game. Those others take you into a study and scientifically exhibit curious specimens under a microscope; she is too warmly human for such pedantries and takes you where there is sky and grass and a whole ordinary world full of mortal creatures and shows you them living and working in the light of common day. I believe the secret of her power is largely in her complete unselfconsciousness; she has no affectations; the charm and strength of her style is its limpid simplicity; she seems, while you read, to be merely letting her characters act and think; to be thinking of her work and never of her own cleverness; as if she were too sure and spontaneous an artist to be even aware of the fact. (pp. 149-50)

A. St. John Adcock, "Sheila Kaye-Smith," in his Gods of Modern Grub Street: Impressions of Contemporary Authors, *Sampson Low, Marston & Co., Ltd., 1923, pp. 143-50.*

G. B. STERN   (essay date 1925)

[*Stern was a close friend of Kaye-Smith and her collaborator on two studies of Jane Austen. In the following excerpt, Stern discusses the heroines in Kaye-Smith's novels, emphasizing the differences between women who were victims of men's plans and those who, like Joanna Godden, had significant ambitions and abilities outside of romance.*]

The heroines of Sheila Kaye-Smith's novels pass before me slowly, one by one, as in a procession. Shadows, at first; but they grow stronger; their outlines clearer. It is almost inconceivable that the creator of those first unreal, bloodless puppets, Ruth of *The Tramping Methodist,* Theodora of *Starbrace,* Maggie and Lorena of *The Challenge to Sirius,* should also be the creator of—Joanna Godden; most of her readers will cry exultantly, as this brilliant buxom woman-farmer, with the ambitions of a man, and a woman's soul, tender and white and hidden as the inside of a horse-chestnut in October, pauses for a moment in the centre of the stage along which the procession is trooping; pauses, conscious that she, of all the others, is likeliest to live and be remembered. Joanna Godden!—but quite alone in my own corner, unheard, perhaps, in the universal shout of admiration, I shall be piping the name of my own favorite, Morgan Wells, who was loved by the mayor of Tamarisk Town.

Ruth, Theodora, Emily—no, they died quickly, for they were woven painfully, laboriously, out of the author's mind, never from pure inspiration. She had as yet no interest in drawing women. Her men, from the beginning, were full-fledged, full-blooded, lusty creatures, with will and force and personality that swept the story along to its usual tragic end; for the early Sheila Kaye-Smith revelled in tenebrous glooms and horrors. In six or seven novels her heroines, though differing a little in individuality from book to book, were yet entirely subservient; to use stage jargon, their appointed part was to "feed" the man; to serve him, to help him towards achievement or failure.

The first attempt, a gallant but unsuccessful one, to create a heroine who should not be entirely of plasticine, was in *Isle of Thorns.* Sally Odiarne was unsuccessful because she was cheap and tawdry, and smelt of the Chelsea studio, whereas she was meant to be modern, vivid, and adventurous. Yet in her you might recognize that dawning interest in woman as a separate entity from man, that was to lead presently to Morgan Wells, Joanna Godden, and Stella Mount. In *Three against the World* the wistful little school-girl, Tony, is hardly a bright enough candle to draw the eye in a book which in itself was so far below the standard of all the other books to come, that we marvelled at that masterpiece, *Sussex Gorse,* published directly afterwards. *Sussex Gorse* enshrines no one heroine, but a group of women who are all interesting, except Alice Jury, who might officially claim the title of heroine, but reveals herself as merely bright and ladylike, and what, in our childhood, we used to call "preachy-preachy." It is pleasant, even luxurious, nowadays, to dwell on these inadequate figures among Sheila Kaye-Smith's characters; while saving up, as a child saves up the currants from the cake, our knowledge of her successes in the future. Naomi, the wife of Reuben Backfield, who patiently has to bear him son after son until she sinks under the weight and dies, might be taken as symbolical of the author's queer sadic delight in showing woman the victim of ·man's more cosmic ambitions. We have had this theme sounded before; it was to be sounded again, even after Naomi had been sacrificed to the great boor, Boarzell. Maggie, in *The Challenge to Sirius,* was equally sacrificed to Frank's lust for travel and experience. Morgan, in *Tamarisk Town,* saddest victim of all to Moneypenny's frantic desire to be sponsor of a fashionable seaside town. Finally, in *The End of the House of Alard,* Stella Mount had to be set aside to suffer, while the last squire clung obdurately to his last lands. It is of significant interest that never once does the ambition of the man, to which is sacrificed the heart and individuality of the woman, take the form of art. Most women novelists are especially fond of showing art as an altar, and love the votive offering; but all these lusty strenuous adventurers go stumbling and swinging after the soil and the stars, fighting, and religion, and the soil again.

The most vivid little sketch of a woman in Miss Kaye-Smith's earlier novels is in *Sussex Gorse*—Reuben Backfield's second wife, Rose; pretty Rose, with her longings for trivial jollities, and happiness that was all of the flesh. Rose was altogether sensual, and altogether charming; she belongs to the group who find their joy in things they may touch, in things they may see, most certainly in lips they may kiss. There is something in all of us that responds to the irresponsible heroine. Not so many books ahead, in *The End of the House of Alard,* we are to discover, in Stella Mount, a perfect blend of the heroine who loves spiritual things, and the heroine who loves material things; but then, they were still sharply divided; the author had not yet conceived the subtle art of mingling body and soul. In her next book after *Sussex Gorse, The Challenge to Sirius,* we encounter again one of those terrible lapses into gentility; Lorena, a ladylike young woman with a pale pure profile, and that ingratiating type of thin Italian voice at the piano, which one associates, somehow, with a swanlike neck and drooping eyelids.

Then we pass on into *Little England.* There are three women in *Little England:* Thyrza, Ivy, and Nell; country women, and farm women. Thyrza was well done; she was a maternal woman; you could picture her always with both lover and child lying softly in the crook of her arm. And so, indeed, we leave her, in the last lines of this, the most tender of all Sheila Kaye-Smith's books; and find ourselves face to face with *Tamarisk Town.*

I have often marvelled whence exquisite Morgan le Fay came dancing down into the author's mind. She is less a heroine, in the familiar sense of the word, than the spirit of all intangible romance and beauty, that sometimes steals very near to a man, and then, when he puts out his hand for it, melts away again. For Edward Moneypenny, Mayor of Marlingate, was after solid and yet frangible things. His dream and his ambition were municipal translations of Reuben Backfield's; Reuben had desired to tame the untamed moor and grow oats upon its stoniest crest; Moneypenny dreamed and schemed for a fair town beside the sea, and to this end he sat upon town councils, and examined maps for the erection of an esplanade and a band-stand. Morgan Wells was a little governess who married another town councillor, after Moneypenny had set her aside; developed graciously into a Lady of the mid-Victorian Period; and then threw herself down from the edge of a cliff into the sea, because Moneypenny had broken through her spells, and she could not bear to live and watch his love grow worldly-cold. The deep interest of this portrait is that suddenly, quite suddenly and perfectly, Sheila Kaye-Smith has realized woman-alive! It was a paradox that her first real woman should hardly be a woman at all, but the embodiment of her creed that a woman in man's life stands for something that takes him away from his appointed task, whatever that may be. Morgan stands for the wild woods, and the wild sea; when she dies, halfway through the book, the pages die with her, and become dead and flabby. She lives again in the end, when we realize that she, and not the town, has triumphed; that all his life long, Moneypenny has lacked her, as a man who cannot live by roofs and chimneys alone.

It is impossible, in a few lines, to recall the many pictures of Morgan le Fay, delicate brilliant pictures, that we carry away with us, a precious freight, from the reading of *Tamarisk Town.* Leave her then for her great contrast, Joanna Godden.

Between the two, lay *Green Apple Harvest,* but in *Green Apple Harvest* no woman matters vitally except Gipsy Hannah, who, again voicing and re-emphasizing the creed, is less of an individual than a symbol of the warm flesh. It is curious how many of the women, though none of the men, in these novels, could take part in old morality plays, as abstract virtues or vices.

But Joanna Godden, beyond all doubt or argument, is neither victim, spirit, temptation, nor is she submissive in any way to a man's central figure. She, for the first time in all this procession of heroines, is the actual book itself, from beginning to end; a woman who, with all her domineering will and mind and energies, was bent on becoming a farmer, and was beaten again and again by being too much woman; and who finally, at the end, became a heroine, in the word's finest aspect, in that she was given strength for a renunciation beyond that of man in any of the books. For not only did she renounce her farm and her lands, but also her deeply valued respectability, and her hope of marriage with "the little singing clerk," so that she might devote all that was left of her life to her illegitimate child. Joanna was symbolic of nothing; she was very much flesh and blood, with her hot, practical speech; her pride in glowing colors, and fine clothes, and good eating; in the smack of vulgarity in nearly all her doings. At times, when Joanna was most loudly trying, one could sympathize quite poignantly even with the priggish and refined younger sister, Ellen Godden. Yet we love Joanna, and grant her literature's immortality, for two simple strong reasons; that she was human, and that she blundered.

"What you are doesn't matter in love, but it matters in marriage." So spoke Ernley Munk, with a flash of wisdom, in *The George and the Crown*—and that is why the heroine of Sheila Kaye-Smith's latest novel is not the principal woman character, the ubiquitous Belle Shackford, an untidy, beautiful blowse, without much meaning to her emotional gestures, selfishly grabbing at love's physical warmth and possession, caring little whom she sacrificed, and with no ideals to turn passion's fire and flame into steadfast starshine; but Rose Falla, the child whom Daniel Sheather marries during his brief sojourn in Sark. Rose is like an exquisite tender gift, to us as well as to her husband. And when he loses her, we sigh, bereaved as he is; more bereaved, indeed, for Daniel finds comfort again: "Was it indeed true, then, that the woman of his dream who sat in an inn stable with her child upon her knee, was not Belle, nor even Rose, but just any woman, every woman, whose heart was warm and whose eyes were kind?"

Again and again, in the last group of Sheila Kaye-Smith's books, we have been startled by achievement which her early books taught us to believe could never be hers. Stella Mount is the reply to those who, while admitting Morgan to be an elfin sprite of the woods, and Joanna a strapping woman of the soil, yet asserted that she had not the power to present to us a normally attractive, human girl of her own class. The unspoken challenge was accepted, and the result was the heroine of *The End of the House of Alard*. . . . [Stella] was ardently religious, but her religion did not make her dreary, for hers was also a gay, yet eminently decent, outlook on the world; she is, indeed, in spirit, the very best type of the gallant modern girl; when her heart is broken, she can still crank up the engine of her father's motor-car, because she knows it has to be done. Her naïve lack of respect for the dignity of the Alard family was delicious; though she had enough imagination to love the home of the Sussex squires, which was crumbling into financial ruin; enough human recklessness not to worry if it did crumble, so long as she and Peter might marry and "be together always," which was her sweeter substitute for "live happy ever after." (pp. 204-08)

> G. B. Stern, *"Letters and Comment: The Heroines of Sheila Kaye-Smith,"* in The Yale Review, Vol. XV, No. 1, October, 1925, pp. 204-08.

ELIZABETH A. DREW   (essay date 1926)

[*In the following excerpt, Drew discusses the relationship between the characters in Kaye-Smith's fiction and the agrarian world which shapes their lives, comparing this characteristic of her work with the novels of Emily Brontë and Thomas Hardy.*]

[Mere] keenness of observation and delicacy of descriptive skill are not enough in themselves to make a real "novel of the soil"; nor is the mere statement of elemental truths about the immutable earth and the essential reality of peasant life. These things have got to be felt with a passion which fuses character and background so indissolubly that the story cannot be thought of apart from the setting: it must be created from the earth, not constructed against a background of a certain locality, however carefully and even lovingly that background may have been observed and reported: it must have something of the quality which makes us conscious of the moors in every line of *Wuthering Heights,* though they are never directly described, something of the quality which makes it impossible to think of Tess, or Bathsheba Everdene, apart from Wessex. (pp. 125-26)

[We] have this sense of truth of human character which cannot be thought of apart from the soil it springs from in the work of Sheila Kaye-Smith. There are writers about the country whose genius burns sometimes with an intenser heat and a brighter light, but none which have such a clear and steady flame. Her general outlook is quiet, sane, generous and richly human, but she knows the passions which leave the mind bled of all thought, the heart bled of all feeling: she can create the aching misery of Dan Sheather in *The George and The Crown* when he has lost Belle Shackford, or the mystic intensity of Robert Fuller in *Green Apple Harvest,* or the agony of Mr. Sumption when he knows Jerry is dead, in *Little England,* as well as the tenderness of the love between Rose and Handshut or Robert and Bessy in *Sussex Gorse* or that between Joanna and the child Ellen in *Joanna Godden.* And unlike most writers about the countryside (and about most things in present-day fiction, alas) she has humour. She can show us the aesthete asking the tremendous old farmer, Reuben Backfield, if he has ever heard Pan's pipes; or show us Reuben himself asked to speak at a recruiting meeting, and replying by an address urging the Sussex farmers to stay at home and grow more grain; or Joanna Godden, in a burst of generous good will, giving (unasked) permission to the vicar to confirm all her farm hands. But her greatest artistic achievement has been in her creation of "the spirit of the land" in the characters of Reuben and Joanna. There *is* something epic and almost superhuman in the figure of Reuben, ruthless as the winds that blustered over Boarzell, hard as the stones that covered it, wiry as the gorse roots that twisted in its marl, dedicating his life to the purpose of owning the moor, "that great beast of power and mystery . . . strong, beautiful, desired, untamed," in the certainty that by craft, by strength, by toughness, man could fight the nature of a waste as well as of a beast: in that picture of him stopping his plough to shake his fist at the land on whose hard and sterile scab he is trying to grow grain: wading through blood and tears to his conquest of the soil: tearing women and the love of children out of his life as he tears the gorse from his beloved land: battling with seasons, elements, earth and nature, challenging God and man to prevent him accomplishing his quest— and finally triumphing.

And if *Sussex Gorse* is the epic of human hardihood, of masculine single-mindedness, *Joanna Godden* is the epic of woman's strength, of the stability and steadfastness of character which incarnates the vitality and simpleness of the land itself.

Joanna has no education and no sophistication, she is tactless and bumptious, she has a loud voice, a truculent manner, and a barbaric taste in dress, yet she remains one of the most lovable personalities in modern fiction. She is "like a plot of marsh earth, soft, rich, and alive," so healthy, so vigorous, and with such glowing warmth and generosity of heart. (pp. 127-29)

Then in contrast to her early stalwart good-heartedness and unquenchable belief in herself and the rightness of her standards, comes her own passionate experience and its distressful sequel, and Joanna "looking like a great, broken, golden sunflower in her despair," coming back to Ansdore to confess her folly to the superior Ellen, to renounce her beloved farm, to fall on her knees and pray:

> Oh please God forgive me. I know I have been wicked, but I'm unaccountable sorry. And I'm going through with it. Please help my child—don't let it get hurt for my fault. Help me to do my best and not grumble, seeing as it's all my own wickedness: and I'm sorry I broke the Ten Commandments.

And finally, nearly forty years old, to turn her back on the life and the heritage which have made her what she is: her lover, her sister, her farm, her home, her good name, all lost; but holding in her heart, as her dear fields held, the imperishable quality of solidity and endurance, a certain elemental and unshakable faithfulness. (pp. 131-32)

> *Elizabeth A. Drew, "Yokel Colour," in her* The Modern Novel: Some Aspects of Contemporary Fiction, *Harcourt Brace Jovanovich, 1926, pp. 117-32.**

PATRICK BRAYBROOKE (essay date 1927)

[*In the following excerpt, Braybrooke discusses Kaye-Smith's narrative artistry in* The End of the House of Alard.]

It is perhaps a little melancholy to have to record the fact that a good deal of Miss Kaye-Smith's work is grim. There is certain enjoyment discernible in this grimness, as though the author took pleasure in revealing that side of life which is hard and utterly uncompromising. I find this hard strain very evident in one of Miss Kaye-Smith's most noteworthy books, **The End of The House of Alard.** But let it be said at once, and said quite emphatically, that the grimness of the story is a very good reason for the high artistic level of this particular work. It may be that it is in large part the background of **The End of The House of Alard** that postulates the austerity of the story. The open country, by its very contempt of man, is naturally reserved and austere, unconcerned, callous, and this atmosphere logically conveys itself to Miss Kaye-Smith. (p. 13)

In dealing with the characters in **The End of The House of Alard,** Miss Kaye-Smith adopts, for the most part, a rather detached attitude to them. Perhaps this is a very marked characteristic of her art. Yet, and this is the clever dualism of the author, though she is detached from her characters, Miss Kaye-Smith invests them with the warm attributes of flesh and blood. Her characters possess more than anything else, an excellent degree of naturalness. Possibly in this way Miss Kaye-Smith gives us the key to her well-deserved popularity and her high position in the world of fiction writers. There seems to be very little conscious effort about her; we feel that once the tale is started, the author has merely followed an easy passage until the last word is written. Particularly is this so in the book I am writing of. **The End of The House of Alard** moves with a

delightful ease; it has an easy air of conscripting the reader's attention without making him a little angry; that conscription has been applied to his attention.

Through the whole of the book we are made to feel sorry for the Alards; they are the participators in such an unequal fight. They fight an internal relentless foe, they seem to demonstrate the absolute truism, that we can usually fight anything and anybody with some chance of success, except *ourselves.* The end of the noble house of Alard is brought about by the Alards. It is in this that Miss Kaye-Smith harps on the tragic, for of all the tragedies that pursue a family, the most tragic is that tragedy which makes a family, as it were, end itself. (pp. 15-16)

In **The End of The House of Alard** the author deals with that essential kind of culture which the unthinking are very prone to call pure and simple snobbery. The head of that most worthy house is delightfully drawn. Miss Kaye-Smith almost uncannily gets at the disgust of Sir John that his sons should so degrade themselves as to earn any money! Miss Kaye-Smith brings out this rather typical characteristic when she describes the reception that Gervase gets at the hands of his father, when he brings in the first earned money to wit, no less than five whole and intact shillings.

> The sarcasm that greeted his first return on Saturday afternoon with his five shillings in his pocket was equalled only by his own pride.

Sir John is naturally irritated, for the earning of such money is something that is the beginning of the end, or at least the beginning of a new point of view, and old aristocrats do not readily accept new points of view. They are scornful of conservatism, the backbone and mainstay of aristocracy.

> "We can launch out a bit now," said Sir John at luncheon. "Gervase has come to our rescue, and is supporting us in our hour of need."

Again this culture or snobbery of the Alards is brought out pungently enough when Stella remarks that the Alards are not poor, as they keep so many motor cars and servants. But that is exactly why they are poor. They cannot adapt themselves. Perhaps Miss Kaye-Smith is a little hard on the old people, for it is morally impossible for certain people to realise that new conditions have arrived, that old boats must be burned, that life must continue, but continue along a different path; a path, it may be, choked with thorns, where it had been decked with sweet-smelling roses. (pp. 17-18)

Miss Kaye-Smith has a clever way of creating dialogue that deals with difficult questions, and she is particularly good at showing the difference in the masculine and feminine point of view with regard to a problem that is both sordid and delicate. The example of this art, that I quote, is where Sir John and Lady Alard argue about the disquieting but popular practice of adultery. Always an unpleasant subject, because adultery, sometimes harmless enough in itself, brings out all the self-complacency in those admirable people who are perfectly moral for fear of the consequences.

Adultery comes to the Alard family with something of the shock that such an event has on all families which consider themselves free from the ordinary weaknesses of mankind. Miss Kaye-Smith seems to be a little shocked and annoyed by the self-satisfaction of the Alard family.

Peter was genuinely shocked—the Alards did not appear in the divorce court.

Sir John, while admitting that adultery is a "nasty mess," has no dislike of talking about it quite openly in front of his wife and daughters. The dialogue is again natural and reasonable.

> "That would be a nasty mess, wouldn't it, sir?" said Peter.
>
> "Not such a nasty mess as my daughter being held up in all the newspapers as an adulteress!"
>
> "Oh, John!" cried Lady Alard, "what a dreadful thing to say before the girls."

There is a good deal of perception in these remarks. There is a certain weakness about Lady Alard, a vague temerity which makes her quail before her bullying and authoritative husband. Sir John Alard cares for nothing really except his good name; Lady Alard is more concerned for the morals of her daughters. Miss Kaye-Smith brings out the fundamental difference in viewpoint with discrimination and skill. She shows again and again in her works this understanding of the eternal difference that persists and always will persist between the two sexes. It is this understanding that makes her fiction so valuable and created with such a lively realisation of human nature. Sir John is perturbed about the adultery of one of his daughters from purely selfish motives, the dragging down of his good name; Lady Alard is chiefly upset that such a thing should happen to one of her own children. It is the everlasting and essential unselfishness of motherhood.

I shall proceed some distance to another incident in the history of this unfortunate Alard family. It concerns the death of George Alard, the son of the family who is a clergyman.... (pp. 19-20)

I think on careful consideration that the description of the death of George Alard has a right to be selected as a fine piece of writing and a picture of the art of Miss Kaye-Smith at her best.

There is nothing so easy for a novelist as to exaggerate when writing of any real and essentially deep moment in life. The description of many death scenes written by novelists give the impression of a very conscious effort to produce something highly melodramatic. They appear to be written with more regard for drama than for truth, perhaps very largely because some novelists do not seem to realise that death is drama and need never be *made* into drama. A death scene should work out its own salvation, it should take the situation in its own hands and lead the novelist along, very gently it may be, or with a violence that may leave him terrified and exhausted.

I think that the reason Miss Kaye-Smith has written such a fine and moving picture of the death of George Alard, is that she has allowed the scene to work its own way through. The author gets all the confusion of sudden death, the frantic ringings of bells, the hurried calling of a sleeping house into activity, the desperate attempt to stave off death by the calling in of a doctor, the terrible coming of the priest and the last preparations to send forth the soul equipped with some kind of spiritual and metaphysical armour. (p. 21)

In all her work, Miss Kaye-Smith shows a certain coldness and aloofness to her characters. Yet this is a strength and not a weakness. A somewhat detached attitude is, I think, quite admirable for a novelist. The novelist can better be a critic, if he adopts a detached air. One of the reasons why Miss Kaye-Smith's characters stand out is that she submits them to a penetrating gaze, a certain amount of disdainful approval; yet a reasonable amount of sympathy is lavished on them at the same time. She seems to understand their difficulties. Particularly well does she deal with the insoluble problem of class consciousness. This is very well brought out when Miss Jenny Alard is having the difficult experience of falling in love with someone who is in a totally different social position to her. (p. 24)

Miss Alard meets the farmer with whom she is falling in love, and there at once arises in her a very complicated conflict. The surge of love that threatens to overwhelm her is modified by a feeling of something that is almost revulsion, a feeling that she cannot overcome with any ease the traditions of her class. This conflict makes her adopt a cold and haughty manner towards the man she really wants to love. Very significantly does Miss Kaye-Smith deal with this intricate piece of psychology. I think a quotation will show this.

> "Good-morning Miss Alard. You've come a long way so early."
>
> "Yes, I was coming to Fourhouses—it struck me that you might be willing to sell one of those collie pups you showed me yesterday."

Cold and calm words, when the heart is bursting with love, but the lips so often do not convey the emotions of the heart. The heart is not shy, it has no bashfulness, but lips are more reserved, for, to a woman, her lips can never lie, once she has relieved them of any restraint.

> This was not how she had meant to speak. She knew her voice was clipped and cold. Hang it! she might have managed to break through the wall on this special occasion. First words are the most significant, and she had meant hers to have a more than ordinary warmth, instead of which they had a more than ordinary stiffness.

And there is a very good reason, the curse or blessing, as you wish, of class consciousness, the culture or snobbery, as you wish, of a different bringing up. And a woman is usually far more class conscious than a man. It is easier for a squire to love a shop girl than for the daughter of a squire to love a farmer. If it is asked why this should be so, perhaps it is that a man at times does not look beyond sex, whereas a woman nearly always has wider vision, unless she has become utterly abandoned and has no thought beyond the physical gratification of the moment.

> But it was no good trying—she would never be able so to get rid of the traditions of her class and of her sex as to show this young man that she loved him—if indeed she really did love him.

But a little later, when love has swept aside all worry about tradition, Jenny Alard, in many ways a tiresome superficial character, gives herself utterly. Miss Kaye-Smith records her progress carefully. The climax is admirable; having got exactly what she wanted, Miss Alard bursts into tears, she is "so silly," she is like so many millions of other silly women, so silly because she wants the kisses of her lover, the physical attractions of his near presence. I do hope Miss Kaye-Smith is not laughing at Miss Alard and her lover from the land, but I rather think she is! (pp. 24-6)

Miss Sheila Kaye-Smith can be defined as a relentless writer, pursuing her characters, exposing their weaknesses with a grim determination that leaves their very souls open to a minute inspection. She has no mercy at times, which is a reason why Miss Kaye-Smith has reached such a distinguished position in the art she has chosen. Not very far from the end of the book, when the unfortunate House of Alard is heading towards its inevitable ruin, the author draws a remorseless picture of Sir John Alard, a picture that is a vivid scrutiny under which the arrogant and bullying baronet might well quiver, could he see his own soul placed upon the rack constructed by a clever and uncompromising writer of fiction.

> Indeed, of late Sir John had grown alarmingly eccentric. His love of rule had passed beyond the administration of his estate and showed itself in a dozen ways of petty dominion. He seemed resolved to avenge his authority over the three rebellious children on the two who had remained obedient.

The "sympathetic" response to their father proves nothing, for Miss Kaye-Smith so naïvely implies that any excitement might cause poor Sir John to have another stroke. And such an occurrence might be the sudden end of the Alard House.

With an untiring energy Miss Kaye-Smith hurries us along to the climax of the tragedy of the House of Alard. There is the death of the old baronet, then the deplorable suicide of Peter, the social suicide when Jenny marries a farmer.

It is all very sad, this end of an old English family. Miss Kaye-Smith is gloomy and grim, she delights in her own pessimism, she is definitely proud of her occasional bursts into cynicism, perhaps she is not so conscious of how "beautifully" she can write when she chooses.

The two last lines in the book are dire tragedy. There is a pathetic hopelessness about them.

> "Oh, Father," sobbed Doris. "Oh, father—oh, Peter!... What would you have done if you had known how it was going to end?"

Miss Kaye-Smith, in my opinion, is one of the cleverest women writers of to-day.

The End of The House of Alard seems to me to indicate quite a number of her qualities, her capacity for constructing a tragedy, her ability to write something in one sentence, bringing in, in a few words, an intense drama. Her dialogue seems to indicate a certain aloofness, yet an ardent wish to be accurate in the cause of Realism. If Miss Kaye-Smith is rather "cruel" to some of her characters, it is because she has a passionate regard for truth. Platitudes creep into her work, but like many platitudes, they are well worth while. Generally speaking, Miss Kaye-Smith is pessimistic, which is a reason why we feel that she will never despair of humanity.

Again, Miss Kaye-Smith has very high powers of writing about love without wallowing in sex or passing it by as though love can be divorced from sex. Her women love, love; but they like a pound of flesh with it, her men love women both physically and spiritually.

Miss Kaye-Smith has achieved a great deal; she is a novelist worthy of and in a secure position in the front rank. And perhaps this is so because she is both human and yet a severe critic when she likes, able to be remorseless when such treatment is necessary. In a word, perhaps the best description of her art, is that it is not only art, but very Rational art. (pp. 27-9)

> Patrick Braybrooke, "Miss Sheila Kaye-Smith," in his Some Goddesses of the Pen, 1927. Reprint by Books for Libraries Press, 1966; distributed by Arno Press, Inc., pp. 13-29.

COULSON KERNAHAN   (essay date 1928)

[*In the following excerpt, Kernahan discusses Kaye-Smith's poetry.*]

[According to Theodore Watts-Dunton]: "Poetry is like the knickerbockers of a growing boy—it has become too small somehow; it is not quite large enough for the growing limbs of life. The novel is more flexible; it can be stretched to fit the muscles as they swell."

Is that the reason, one wonders, why Miss Sheila Kaye-Smith has published many lengthy novels, but only two slender volumes of verse? Had her work in poetry been well known when Watts-Dunton so wrote ... one might not unreasonably suppose that Watts-Dunton had Miss Kaye-Smith directly in mind. That, however, is out of the question, for no volume of poems by her appeared within his lifetime.

Into the issue raised by Watts-Dunton, be it heretical or orthodox, I shall not enter; but as the early and experimental work, in poetry, of a woman of such genius as Sheila Kaye-Smith is of exceptional interest, I propose first to turn the pages of her first published book of poems (*Willow's Forge* ...) to illustrate, by quotation and comment, how deep, even then, was her religious faith, how profound her pitifulness for life's outcasts, and how original and individual were both her outlook and her order of mind.

The reader may be the more interested in such an examination of Miss Kaye-Smith's beginnings in poetry when I add that she once said to me that her poems were the expression of an inner self, which she did not reveal in her novels nor even to her friends. ... (p. 132)

What I have to say of *Willow's Forge* will be concerned with the subject of the different poems, not with the technique. Such early work it would be ungenerous to judge by too high or too critical a standard of poetry. That [the title-poem] is a Sussex poem is fitting when one is writing of the novelist-poet whose name is as inseparably associated with Sussex, as is the great name of Mr. Thomas Hardy with Wessex. The fascination which the eerie has for the young poet is already evident. (p. 133)

As I have said of this that the fascination which the "eerie" has for the young poet is already evident, another early and eerie poem, "The Ballad of the Quick and Dead," may be instanced. In "Willow's Forge," a woman sees the ghost of the man she had loved, the man who had loved her. In "The Ballad of the Quick and Dead," a man sees the ghost of the woman he had loved. Love for him she had none, all her love being given to one who had proved himself to be a false lover. In "Willow's Forge," the man who loved and was loved died of a broken neck—by hanging. In "The Ballad of the Quick and Dead," the woman died of a broken heart, for she had been first betrayed, and then deserted. (p. 135)

To a critic who remarked of ["Willow's Forge" and "The Ballad of the Quick and Dead"]: "As poetry, they are ordinary," I replied that, whatever they might or might not be as poetry—in grimness of subject, and in weird imaginativeness, so far from thinking them "ordinary," I thought them *un*-ordinary, and in no way resembling the smoothly-running, generally sentimental, and prettily-imitative work of most young poets, even of some who have since come to fame. (p. 137)

In *Willow's Forge* is a poem on the warring of the senses against the spirit. Miss Kaye-Smith is a Churchwoman, an Anglo-Catholic, was one of the speakers at the Anglo-Catholic Congress, and contributed to the *Guardian* a remarkable sermon, for a sermon, in effect, it was, with the striking title, **"Forgive us our Righteousness."** In poems, hymns, and religious utterances by Anglo- and Roman Catholics, as well as by members of other Communions, such expressions as "this vile body" are not uncommon, but, in one of T. H. Gill's well-known hymns, so far from describing the body as "vile," he would have it held sacred, for to "Oh! mean may seem this house of clay," he adds, "Yet, 'twas the Lord's abode." (p. 144)

Sheila Kaye-Smith thinks of this body of ours neither as "vile," nor as "holy," but, more humanly, as the soul's fellow-pilgrim to Bunyan's Celestial City; as the fellow-fighter and ally of the soul against Bunyan's Apollyon. She does not picture the body as a never-stumbling fellow-pilgrim. Many times, but for the soul's upholding hand, the body had fallen, and dragged its fellow-pilgrim down with it, the two to perish among the quicksands. She does not show the body as the stoutest of fellow-fighters and allies, but as fearful and wavering—half-minded, sometimes, itself to go over, and to betray its ally to the enemy, and as brought to a sense of right and duty only by the sternest disciplinary measures. Of herself, however, she does not say, "The spirit is willing, but the flesh is weak." She knows that the spirit, too, may weaken against assailants, other than those that would assail the flesh, and that there are times when the spirit turns for succour to its ally, the body.

In human nature there is, as has been said, something of the angel and of the animal. Of all animals the best beloved of man is the dog. The animal, even in a fierce dog, may be so trained and controlled—and by a timid woman—that none need fear him. But let his mistress be attacked by a brutal assailant, and the dog will fly at the assailant's throat. So, under spiritual assault, Miss Kaye-Smith believes that the body, that which is "animal" in us, should thus spring to the defence of its fellow-pilgrim and fellow-fighter, the soul. She believes, too, that only as fellow-pilgrims, can soul and body arrive at and enter the Celestial City; only by and through the body, no less than by and through the soul, can the victory—which both must share—be theirs. And because she believes that victory will crown the end, Miss Kaye-Smith entitles her remarkable poem **"To my Body—A Thanksgiving."**... (pp. 145-46)

We come now to Miss Kaye-Smith's only other volume of poems, *Saints in Sussex*.... To her later and so more mature work I shall pay the compliment of testing it by a high standard.

The range of the poems is wide, but not a few are religious, even ecclesiastical, in subject.... (p. 147)

[There is a] very marked mystical element in Miss Kaye-Smith's work. Mysticism has been defined by Dean Inge as "the attempt to realize the presence of the living God in the soul and in Nature, or, more generally, as the attempt to realize in thought and feeling the immanence of the temporal in the eternal and the eternal in the temporal." Of another poet than Miss Kaye-Smith I had occasion to write elsewhere:

There are truths so entirely spiritual, so high, and so heavenly, that, in human speech, they can be expressed, if at all, only symbolically. Or perhaps I should say that they can only be hinted at, rather than actually expressed. Some readers, this hinted word, this play of a broken light upon an elsewhere mist-shrouded sea—so strangely stirs, and lends such farness to their sight, that, beyond this broken light upon deep waters, a new horizon opens. Though the unseen remains unseen, they stand trembling on the very verge of vision.

Similarly Miss Kaye-Smith would, I think, admit that she, too, has striven by means of symbolism to express certain thoughts too ethereal, certain truths too spiritual, to be translated into common speech. With the exception of Miss Evelyn Underhill, I know no woman-poet of to-day in whose work the mystical element is so evident as in Miss Kaye-Smith's. One of her masters is clearly Jakob Boehme, who

> ...learned the secrets
> And signs of all the sky,
> And wrought the Magnum Opus
> Of holy Alchemy.

Another is surely that visionary, William Blake, who saw "a tree full of angels in Peckham" (of all places on earth), and whose methods his disciple sometimes adopts. Just as Blake imagines Christ in England:

> And did those feet in ancient times
> Walk upon England's mountains green,
> And was the Holy Lamb of God
> On England's pleasant pastures seen?

so Sheila Kaye-Smith imagines the Magdalen and her Saviour in Sussex.... (pp. 153-54)

[Miss Kaye-Smith's] aim is to show that were Christ to revisit our earth His presence and preaching would have the same effect upon a Magdalen of to-day as His presence and preaching had upon the greatly forgiven, because greatly loving, Magdalen of whom we read in the New Testament.

I agree. But in seeking thus to relate the past and the present, and to relate also the holy things of long ago to the human needs of the life of to-day, a poet so intensely reverent and spiritually-minded as Sheila Kaye-Smith cannot be too careful in the choice of word or phrase.

I hope she will change the wording in future editions of *Saints in Sussex,* and that she will find an alternative to a line so prosaic as ...

> The Preacher has brought Magdalene to His mother.

An alternative might also be found in the poem, following that last quoted, for the word "smudgy," as applied to the sky, in the line

> A smudgy, sweet, grey sky.

One thinks of a smudge as relatively small rather than as large, whereas "sky" suggests a sense of space.

But "praise is more important than judgment," said Mr. Le Gallienne once, adding that "it is only at agricultural societies that men dare sit in judgment upon the rose." As, in a sense, myself a literary agriculturist, my task was at first to cast a critical eye over the roses of Miss Kaye-Smith's growing, and to mark where here a petal was imperfect, where there an ill-formed leaf might be clipped away, or where her flower of song seemed to me to be marred by the setting. (pp. 155-56)

Like George Eliot, Miss Kaye-Smith is a born novelist. But, again, as in the case of George Eliot, one is less sure—the lyric note is so often missing—that she is a born poet. Nor, with the exception of Emily Brontë, do I recall an instance of a great woman novelist who was also a born poet. The four opening and haunting lines (repeated at the poem's end) of her love poem **"Immortality"** come near, however, to capturing the lyric note, for which in other work of hers, we listen, often vainly. The poem is all the more interesting for the reason that it appeared not in **Saints in Sussex,** but in her first and so experimental volume—**Willow's Forge.** (p. 160)

Some of Miss Kaye-Smith's poems, those written for a saint's day or other holy day of the Church especially, have a quaint and mediaeval stiffness, as if purposely patterned to be in keeping with the stiffly embroidered stole or vestment worn by priests when celebrating the Sacrament. If crude the poems be, the crudity strikes one as intentional, and as if she had before her when at work some such specimen of early Italian ecclesiastical art as one sees in the National Gallery, or as forming the diptych, triptych, or reredos of altars of Catholic or Anglo-Catholic churches. Other poems are as distinctly twentieth century, as when she writes:

> All pageantry with colours,
> All poetry with words,
> Wait those blazoned motor 'buses
> In their fiercely panting herds.
>
> (p. 164)

Whatever the period or the subject, individuality, and so originality, we find in Miss Kaye-Smith's work. She may pen ballads of love or of pity, hymns for holy days, or (a quaint contrast!) "cant songs," as the lays of the "rumpads," or smugglers of a long-ago Sussex, were called (there is a section entitled "Cant Songs" in one of her volumes), but though some may be rough-cast, none is commonplace. Thus far "the swing of her arm," to borrow a figure of speech from a letter by Dante Gabriel Rossetti, "is freer in prose than in verse." (pp. 167-68)

Whether Miss Kaye-Smith will steal a march upon her critics by making the like surprisingly rapid advance as a poet which she has already made as a novelist and as a speaker, one hesitates to say on the evidence of two slim volumes of verse. As a novelist she is the possessor of genius, and her poems may be said to be the complement of her novels, for in them, as has already been said, she has allowed, as she does not allow herself in her novels, the expression of a profoundly spiritual, if mystical, order of mind and of a singularly original and attractive personality. (pp. 168-69)

> *Coulson Kernahan, "Sheila Kaye-Smith as a Poet," in his* Five More Famous Living Poets: Introductory Studies, *1928. Reprint by Books for Libraries Press, 1969; distributed by Arno Press, Inc., pp. 131-73.*

T. S. MATTHEWS   (essay date 1931)

[*In the following excerpt, Matthews favorably appraises the characters in* Susan Spray, *but considers the novel generally out of date.*]

Sheila Kaye-Smith long ago staked a claim for herself in Sussex, and she has been cultivating her garden there ever since. There are various reasons for gardening, but Candide's is perhaps not so very different from the suburbanite's: the world has been too much with both of them. Miss Kaye-Smith eludes the vexatious questions of her own day by simply disregarding them; the action of **Susan Spray** takes place two generations ago, in early Victorian times. If we were Communists we should doubtless call Miss Kaye-Smith a good example of the ostrich school; to which Miss Kaye-Smith might well retort that she never had any intention of being a journalist. The news she has chosen to report is of a kind not much affected by the passage of time or legislation. Her scene is rural England, her people poor or middling well-to-do farmers. . . .

Sheila Kaye-Smith writes about her people with discernment, sympathy, sometimes with ironic detachment. She is no Thomas Hardy, but she does a good job. The general effect, however, is one of old-fashionedness: her news is news that men have heard before. And, like Housman and the oracle, you may think it sound good sense but it really doesn't help you very much. In this day and age, the Sheila Kaye-Smith kind of novel does actually seem curiously out of date. You need not go so far as to call her an ostrich, but you cannot help feeling she has missed the train. (p. 157)

> *T. S. Matthews, "Novels as News," in* The New Republic, *Vol. LXVIII, No. 877, September 23, 1931, pp. 157-58.**

CALVERT ALEXANDER   (essay date 1935)

[*In the following excerpt, Alexander discusses Kaye-Smith's achievements and her promise as a Catholic author, citing* Gallybird *and* Superstition Corner *as notable efforts in creating Catholic novels.*]

"Never before in the history of English literature," says Francis Talbot, S.J., in the preface to *Fiction by Its Makers*, "have there been so many brilliant Catholic novelists." The statement is, I think, quite accurate, as the enumeration of such names as those of Maurice Baring, Compton Mackenzie, Sir Philip Gibbs, Sheila Kaye-Smith, Montgomery Carmichael, Enid Dinnis, Peadar O'Donnell, Francis Stuart, Frank Spearman, Kathleen Norris, Edith O'Shaughnessy, Evelyn Waugh, James B. Connolly will indicate. Still it must be said that the abundance of first-rate workers in this field notwithstanding, the status of the contemporary novel is one more of promise than of actual achievement.

There is achievement, of course; much of it. But it bears little proportion to the possibilities indicated by the richness of the talent, on the one hand, and the promise of a newer and higher type of fiction envisioned by the Catholic ideal, on the other. For the doctrines of Christ which have so powerfully altered human nature and life have also changed our conceptions of the novel which deals with life and human nature. This must be so. And it is admitted by our most competent artists. Many of them have never written what might be called a Catholic novel in the full and complete sense, a novel, that is to say, of life illuminated by Faith. But they are working toward this goal and if many of them reach it we shall be able to speak of classical Catholic novels as we speak of classical Catholic poetry. (p. 332)

[Miss Kaye-Smith] has developed her art in isolation from Catholicism. By dint of long and patient observation she has become the recognized voice of a people without Catholic consciousness, and the laureate of a land which remembers only dimly the monks of Canterbury. The well-beloved Sussex of Miss Kaye-Smith, which has given to her quite as much as she has given to it, will, one feels, be the greatest obstacle in the way of her production of a Catholic novel. For, unlike poetry, the novel demands something more than that the author himself be steeped in Catholicity. It would seem to require also that the material be Catholic, that the people whose lives he interprets be firmly rooted in generations of Catholic tradition. And this is particularly true of the sort of fiction Miss Kaye-Smith writes. . . .

Religion and the things of the spirit have never been absent in any of her novels, although none of them may properly be called novels of Grace. Her excellence consists in the skill with which she delineates simple nature and the fundamental emotions of people who live close to the soil. It is this that has caused many critics to predict for her works a longer life than those of other contemporaries whose talents lie in the portrayal of things less elemental and human. Not a few of her novels, notably *Joanna Godden* and *Sussex Gorse,* impress one as tremendous achievements which future generations may place side by side with the great classics. She is today certainly one of, if not the most distinguished of English women novelists. She has few equals even among the men. (pp. 341-42)

[In a footnote, Alexander adds: As this book goes to press Miss Kaye-Smith is receiving unstinted praise from the critics for her two most recent books, *Superstition Corner* and *Gallybird.* And they are both Catholic novels, not specifically by reason of the presence in them of some Catholic characters, but by reason of the realistic picture the author gives of the progressive moral and intellectual distintegration of a family which has rejected the Faith and its fonts of supernatural aid. The family is that of the Alards whose extinction Miss Kaye-Smith recorded in *The End of the House of Alard.* . . . She now retraces the early history of that family in the sixteenth and seventeenth centuries in two historical novels that are distinguished not only by the author's accustomed art and subtle penetration into the fundamental things of human nature, but also by an equally subtle understanding of the relation of grace to that human nature, and of the rank weeds of superstition, fear, and ineffectiveness which must spring up when grace is uprooted.] (p. 342)

Calvert Alexander, "The Novel," in his The Catholic Literary Revival: Three Phases in Its Development from 1845 to the Present, *1935. Reprint by Kennikat Press, Inc., 1968, pp. 332-53.**

SHEILA KAYE-SMITH (essay date 1937)

[*In the following excerpt from her autobiography* Three Ways Home, *Kaye-Smith discusses the success of* Joanna Godden, *the critical response to her overt disclosure of her religious views in* The End of the House of Alard, *and how her work changed during and after the writing of* Alard.]

Joanna Godden was published in the Autumn of 1921, and was received in a manner that made it at first my biggest success and later my heaviest burden. Most authors find that sooner or later they write a book which their readers never allow them to forget. As far as I am concerned, *Joanna Godden* is that book. Though in many ways, I think, inferior to *Green Apple Harvest* and even to *Little England,* and in some ways inferior to *Sussex Gorse* and *Tamarisk Town,* it did something to my

literary reputation which no earlier book was able to do in quite the same way. . . . Its appeal was mainly to those with some share of the novelist's outlook—Joanna is essentially a "novelist's heroine" and since the days of *Adam Bede* it has always been easy to hit a certain section of the public with a little love child. I do not wish to appear ungrateful, but when one has written more than twenty novels it is sometimes trying to be known as the author of only one of them.

It is equally trying to hear *Joanna Godden* sighed over as the last novel I wrote before religion spoilt me as a novelist. The contrast between it and *The End of the House of Alard* is commonly put down to religion. I had taken to Anglo-Catholicism in the interval and according to the rather naïve views of authorship held by some readers and even by some critics, immediately sat down to write about it.

Actually *Joanna Godden* is full of clues to the author's religious position. Apart from the sympathetic portrait of Lawrence Trevor, the Anglican monk, there are several allusions to Catholic customs and ideas. Joanna's morality, too—her attitude towards divorce and illegitimacy—is definitely Catholic and Christian. Certainly the book's religion is more explicit, if less dominating, than in *Green Apple Harvest,* and would almost certainly have been recognized for what it was had *Joanna Godden* been published after instead of before *The End of the House of Alard.* As things were it aroused comment, and for fifteen years the novel has been held up to me as an example of the excellent work I used to do in the days before I became mixed up with religion.

From that point of view, perhaps, I was unwise to write *The End of the House of Alard.* When it first appeared a far-sighted friend said to me: "Now, whatever you may write for the rest of your life, you will always be suspected of religious propaganda." This I have found true; if Sussex is a label, religion is a dye and there is no getting rid of it. The public does not necessarily object to propaganda, but it likes the propaganda to propagate something it wants, like divorce, not something like Catholicism which it does not want and largely disapproves of. Criticism at once ceases to be candid, for the majority of critics so dislike the colour of one's thoughts that they refuse to look at any beauty there may be in the form that embodies it, whereas the minority whose view one is expressing can see no possible defect in that expression. (pp. 149-52)

Actually religion provides nearly as many good situations as the sex-instinct—there are endless combinations, permutations, frustrations and deviations which the novelist can use, and its effect on character (either by its growth or by its thwarting) makes something new in the way of psychological interest. I myself had used it many times before I wrote *The End of the House of Alard*—in *The Tramping Methodist,* in *Spell Land,* in *Isle of Thorns,* in *Sussex Gorse,* in *Sirius,* in *Green Apple Harvest,* in *Joanna Godden;* in fact I do not think that there is a novel of mine where it does not make some appearance—except *Tamarisk Town,* in the middle of which I found it.

The difficulty about its appearance in *Alard* is that it is professedly and obviously in a form in which I myself believe. The sensational Methodism or the conventional Anglicanism of the earlier books could not possibly carry any propaganda with them. Obviously I did not believe in these things as I wrote them, or if I did my belief was static and self-centred rather than dynamic and missionary. In *Alard* I was definitely challenging and proclaiming, and here—speaking from a religious as well as from an artistic point of view—my error lay.

I am not of course suggesting that an author should not write about what he personally believes, but that he should realize that to do so involves more dangers than to write about what he personally feels, since he is likely to find himself interfering in his own creation, destroying the balance of that transcendence and immanence which makes for an ordered literary cosmos. Actually I did realize this, but not so fully as I might, and I was too confident of my own power to overcome the difficulty. I did not grasp the fact which ought to have been obvious, that I had always been an imaginative rather than a reproductive writer, and that it was dangerous to start right away like this from a point well outside my imagination. (pp. 153-54)

[The] story of the Alards had been suggested to me by the news that the heiress of a certain large and important Sussex family had entered a convent. The idea came to me of writing the history of that family's last two generations as I had heard it from my father. It must be a more common history than I imagined, for the only local family that did not recognize itself in the book was the one I had in mind.

The religious interest was not, then, extraneous to my subject; it was the root from which the whole thing had started, and I was necessarily committed to it in some way. My failure did not lie in my inability to keep out an obsessive or incongruous idea, but rather in my treatment of that idea, which was not objective enough. I voiced it in dialogue rather than expressed it in action, and I did not sufficiently mix it with the other ingredients of my story—I was altogether too personal and exuberant. Up till then I had never gone to life for my novels, but now I had gone to it for much more than my ''plot.'' For the first time I was writing from actual fact and experience— much of it my own. I was ''in'' this novel all through. Hence possibly its selling qualities, for artistic detachment does not as a rule make for big sales. *The End of the House of Alard* sold as no novel of mine has sold before or since. (pp. 156-58)

[My] friend's prophecy was being fulfilled, and I saw that my work was henceforth to be judged in the light of my critics' religious susceptibilities. I am not for a moment suggesting that *Alard* did not deserve at least a great deal of what it got; my objection is that the book's inferiority to its predecessors was almost universally put down to the religious element in it. Few critics who did not protest against this criticized it on other grounds.

Actually it is open to criticism in a number of ways. The swift and sudden collapse of the family may perhaps be paralleled in life—though I telescoped two generations to bring it about— but it is too hurried and forced as I have written it. There is also a fatal lack of inevitableness about the story, which should have swooped down on its ending instead of creaking to it mechanically at its author's obvious contrivance. But of these faults as well as of others it can be said that I have done worse things in earlier novels, and yet in each case managed to write a better book. The fundamental criticism which truly accounts for *Alard's* inferiority to, say, *Green Apple Harvest* or *Sussex Gorse,* was made by only one writer—the Rev. C. C. Martindale in the *Dublin Review.*

Writing of the South American scene in *Sirius* he states his belief

> that she could similarly know almost anything, provided she had so soaked herself in it that she reacted as nearly as possible by instinct, and not consciously. . . . What, then, is the

strange lack of comment in these books, such that when for once she does introduce her own appreciation she makes one jump? It certainly is not that she does not feel, but (can one say it without being rude?) she is far at her best, and wisely allows herself to be so, when she is not *thinking*. Take *The House of Alard*. To start with, the whole book is a thesis. . . .

He then goes on to examine the weakness of that thesis, and the faults of observation and characterization by which I try to prove it.

> These instances are accumulated to justify our surmise that in this novel Miss Kaye-Smith is not letting herself go to that uncanny second self in virtue of which she wrote her first admirable novels, and which was hardly a *thinking* self at all. . . . And this is a great pity. We can quite imagine that Miss Kaye-Smith thinks she *has* been more 'personal' in this last novel— that there is more of herself in it; well, yes, of that conscious self which was just what did *not* make the amazing success of her work so far.

This is, I think, the truth, and fully accounts for the difference between *Alard* and the earlier books; but I am not sure if the reviewer realized that the process he described was to a certain point inevitable—that a time was bound to come when I should no longer write from unconscious instinct but from conscious thought and observation. It is fatally easy to attribute any falling off in an author's work to some external event such as marriage or conversion to religion, losing sight of the fact that the deterioration may be equally due to inner changes of personality and consciousness. Of course external events may produce these changes, but equally such changes take place of themselves as one grows older. No one seems to look to the simple explanation of Anno Domini. Authors grow up, grow middle-aged, grow old. They pass out of their adolescent dreams, though perhaps they manage to retain them longer than most people, and enter on a new and adult relationship to life.

Now this, I think, is what had happened to me. Hitherto I had been, psychologically speaking, adolescent. I had spun *Joanna Godden* out of the same web of day-dream and fantasy that had made *The Tramping Methodist*. The later book is more definitely shaped by external knowledge and acquired literary skill—I did not write in a trance—but it is equally the work of that ''uncanny second self'' of which Father Martindale speaks, and which somehow when I came to write *Alard* had disappeared into the background, where it has remained ever since. There was no question of ''not letting myself go to it.'' It just was not there.

This growing up process may have been hastened by religion, which often brings on psychological maturity by its unifying effect on the personality. Or it may have been brought about by the shock of my contact with fundamental realities in my father's death. Or it may simply have been due to the fact that I was now over thirty. I do not blame the subject of *Alard* for its onset. It is true that I had chosen an external happening in the world of facts, but there is no valid reason why my imagination should not ultimately have taken hold of this as it took hold of the stories of *Sussex Gorse* and *Joanna Godden,* both of which came from an outside source, or of the story of *Green Apple Harvest* which was based on the actual life of a preacher who at one time roamed the borders of Kent and Sussex with an eccentric gospel. The fact that I myself was consciously in the book may have hastened the withdrawal of my unconscious, but it cannot be solely responsible for it, or the next book to *Alard,* from which I was entirely detached, would have shown a return to the old position. Actually it did not. No book of mine since *Joanna Godden* has been written from that anteroom of consciousness which is in some of us so much more richly stored than consciousness itself. I sometimes fear that I shall never write so well with this new, unified personality as I did with a personality that was (shall we say?) a trifle split. In some authors to grow up may be an advantage, just as some people—most, in fact—are pleasanter as grown-ups than as children. But with others it is the contrary. (pp. 158-62)

I have to learn a new method of writing, just as I have to learn a new method of religion. In religion I have to learn to look not outwards but inwards, and in my writing I have to learn to look not inwards but outwards. Before I became a Catholic my religion was largely concerned with external observances, with services, ritual and beauty; now I have to do without much that I used to consider essential, and worship in a manner more closely akin to Little Bethel than I should have thought edifying ten years ago. When I began to write I could find within myself all the material I needed, bright with the star-dust with which the unconscious gilds even the dullest gingerbread; now I have to resign myself to the fact that the cupboard of this internal Mother Hubbard is bare, and I must take my imagination out into the highways.

Actually the change in my writing has been more fundamental than the change in my religion, but it is less obvious because there is here no change in externals. I still write about Sussex and shall probably continue to write about Sussex—the setting of *Rose Deeprose* in the Kentish weald means nothing at all, for East Sussex is far more like West Kent than it is like West Sussex. But even Sussex has suffered a change, and my feeling for it has become far more detached and external, and at the same time more detailed and intimate, than it used to be in the days when I lived in the town and the country northward of Brede was just a rare and glorious adventure. Living in the midst of it, sharing its life, its farms and fields a part of everyday experience, I can no longer see it in the same shining light as when it was for me excitement, holiday, wish and dream. But I am more than ever dependent on absolute familiarity with my background if I am to move my creatures freely against it, having lost that "uncanny second self" which was once able to take me more or less successfully to Yucatan. (pp. 255-56)

Sheila Kaye-Smith, in her Three Ways Home: An Experiment in Autobiography, *Harper & Brothers Publishers, 1937, 258 p.*

MARK LONGAKER AND EDWIN C. BOLLES (essay date 1953)

[*In the following excerpt, Longaker and Bolles discuss the limitations of Kaye-Smith's regionalism.*]

Sheila Kaye-Smith has been hampered by the self-imposed restriction of her regionalism. It is not too hard for a novelist to follow Dickens and to find ample new material in the variety of cities, but to follow Hardy where the simplicity and conservatism of country life severely limit the possibilities of character and situation is another matter—especially as in Sheila Kaye-Smith's case Sussex is the eastern frontier of Hardy's country and offers none of the differences in racial stock, occupation, and environment that would be found in, say, Staf-

fordshire or Westmoreland. Consequently as her work progressed, the monotony of her themes became more evident along with a straining to distinguish character by peculiarity or quaintness. Possibly like Jane Austen, whom she admires, she has been afraid to venture beyond what she knows well (How long, by the way, could Jane Austen have gone on writing novels about her little world?), but possibly also her talents would have developed more fully with greater scope. Joanna Godden and Susan Spray are both memorable characters and the novels have real warmth of local color and a passionate feeling for the land. (pp. 358-59)

Mark Longaker and Edwin C. Bolles, "Sheila Kaye-Smith," in their Contemporary English Literature, *Appleton-Century-Crofts, Inc., 1953, pp. 358-59.*

ROBERT O. BOWEN (essay date 1955)

[*In the following excerpt, Bowen offers a negative review of* The View from the Parsonage, *discussing flaws in the novel's narrative technique, characterization, structure, and theme.*]

The element which distinguishes twentieth century prose is its fine style, the particularity of diction and rhythm in which its authors have cast each his own special vision of the world. Time was that language of a truly particular nature was suitable only to the poet, and the prose writer was expected to produce a standard form, a kind of journalism really. He was expected to withhold his personal sensitivity and to write from a kind of artistic anonymity, thus keeping from his writing not only his personal opinions but also his opinions as an artist; whereas the poet spoke often through the first person, not personally but sensitively. The twentieth century prose master writes as poets of the past have written; the major characters of his fiction are ideal projections of his own artistic nature. In the prose art of this century we find, therefore, within stylistic texture itself, a sense of a special vision of the world, a distinct statement of faith. Hemingway, Faulkner, Mann, Wolfe—what distinguishes such men is the separate vision of each, as portrayed in their various styles.

As for Sheila Kaye-Smith's language in *The View from the Parsonage,* she not only fails to produce a prose that conveys a sense of a particular view—she fails to bring her clerical narrator alive.

The novel is a long, dull, sentimental, pretentious, Victorian tale told by the old Anglican minister of a backwater community. The man had originally selected this living because it had "called to him with promises of healing for his trampled heart." The diction promised in this line continues in rather the same vein except when a peasant of the regional setting speaks. Then one finds an unwitting likeness to a bit of John P. Marquand's fine literary satire in *Wickford Point*—the absurdly stilted narration of the Harvard teacher's novel.

The View from the Parsonage opens with a hackneyed and somewhat irrelevant scene which is never fully accomplished. On page two this scene fades without having proliferated; and for more than twenty-five pages one is dragged through a conglomerate historical background which demonstrates Sheila Kaye-Smith's research abilities, one supposes, but hardly her dramatic skill. Seldom can one make legitimate value judgments about language forms, but regarding this book one can say simply that the narrative technique is wrong. The characters—a love-lorn, young, Anglican clergyman; a gone-Roman, ex-Anglican clergyman; a gone-atheist, ex-Anglican clergyman; the latter's daughters, one of whom eventually becomes a Sister Clare after sowing some sophisticated oats, the other who becomes a conscious hypocrite after having her moment of spiritualism—the characters are types, and they remain types, at times almost caricatures.

They are the sort of characters that Dickens produced. Dickens, however, succeeded with them admirably because, no matter how artificial their construction was, they hustle into his stories with such Gargantuan vitality that we cannot deny them. We may quibble about the sentimental foundations of *Bleak House;* we cannot, though, deny that it carries us along. What Dickens knew well and many of his imitators know not at all is that the type is more suitable to the dramatic action of the stage than to the novel's frequently introspective bent. Because of this, Dickens' novels are rich in external drama. Sheila Kaye-Smith fails in *The View from the Parsonage* not because her characters exhibit Dickensian artificiality, but because she includes in the book few if any real scenes, and of the scenes that we do see most are not calculated to produce the best effect with the problem at hand. For instance, when the clerical narrator and a young lady friend travel together to France to fetch back two fleshly erring lambs, the only scene in many pages is a would-be comic bit concerning the Gallic inability to understand why the two travellers do not share a bed. This is hardly comic-relief; it seems rather to be evidence that the author had not yet, on page 203, decided on quite what the shape of her story was. There is this hesitancy, this shuffling away from the significant element, at each turn of the story.

The air of indirection is not limited to a few inconsequential scenes. The entire production is strewn with uncorrelated elements. Characters enter as though for a major reason and then drift off to limbo like the comrades of ocean voyages. One of the major figures is disposed of in a casual second marriage which leads to his apparent murder. There is no structure to give this action meaning. It simply happens as in life. In fact, a great deal of the action in this book happens in the same disorganized way that things happen in life.

Nor can one ascribe the accidental nature of the story to some new theory of art without running into an inconsistency in another direction. The character motivation is limited to such quaint drives as *generosity, loving-kindness,* and the like. Now it is hard to believe that a writer who finds the foundations of character in these naive conceptions has given us an over-all dramatic form of such subtlety that we did not perceive it. The over-simplified motivations mentioned here are themselves a serious flaw in the book, especially so in an age when psychology and other studies have given the articulation of twentieth century vision a complexity that earlier writing generally lacked. Too, it is one thing for Dante to find sublimity in his love of God; it is quite another for Sheila Kaye-Smith to think that she has explained a person when she speaks of his ''loving-kindness.'' Dante's conception of God was not, after all, a very simple matter.

The attitude toward religion which one finds in the novel is what might be expected: there is no suggestion of a statement of faith in the actual writing. We know in about which direction Hemingway's faith lies from reading him; we know about what Faulkner's faith must be; we get no such help from Sheila Kaye-Smith. In all parts of the novel, whenever matters of faith enter, the narrator shifts as though with that English fear of broaching religious discussion lest someone be offended. The Catholic Church is handled with about the philosophical depth that marks the usual Oursler or Douglas product. The

significant transition of spiritual stability in the major character—from a free-thinking, free-loving, young divorcee to a fervent Sister Clare—is ignored completely. In point of fact, there is no one place in the book where an internal development is handled with force, although the major advantage of written language over other art forms is its ability to present such internal matters.

In the end it seems that through all the confusion of narrative direction and the lack of disposal of characters and the non-fruition of bits of drama the story is not really *about* anything in particular. For instance, one character is somewhat telepathic, and for a time we feel that this will lead to some insight into the relation of spiritualism and religion, but no; the handling of this remains on the synopsis level, unviable as solid fiction. Again, one entire family is Catholic, living in, of course, anti-Roman England; but we get little or no experience of being a Roman Catholic in England. The truth is that the English Catholic is nearly always an exceptionally fine member of the Church, conscious of the national attitude against his faith and set on publicly proving the good effect of that faith in himself. There is no reason to believe from reading *The View from the Parsonage* that Sheila Kaye-Smith felt that Catholicism was intrinsically different from any other religion or, for that matter, that religion was ultimately different from any other basis for human behavior. The figure which one feels should be the focus of much insight and feeling, the old free-thinker, is presented to us in but a few scenes, these much under-done, and we never get from him any new or even particularly significant attitude about the real drama his position apparently symbolizes, the loss of religion by many in the modern world.

In all honesty one must conclude that this book creates the impression that it was written about what might have been an interesting group of people involved in a significant problem but that its narrator had no understanding of the human experience involved. She not only withholds her judgment in sectarian matters; she offers no suggestion of the particular way which she feels the materials she handles should be viewed—except perhaps the suggestion that one should be well-mannered, which can hardly be considered a significant contribution. (pp. 135-37)

Robert O. Bowen, "Sheila Kaye-Smith Signifying Little," in Renascence, *Vol. VII, No. 3, Spring, 1955, pp. 135-37.*

E. D. PENDRY (essay date 1956)

[*In the following excerpt, Pendry discusses* Joanna Godden, The Lardners and the Laurelwoods, *and* Mrs. Gailey *as they illustrate changing social orders and reflect Kaye-Smith's attitudes toward class differences.*]

A woman-novelist . . . who made her name before the war but who, though still writing, is now rather unjustly neglected, is Sheila Kaye-Smith. One would get a very false impression of her social outlook if one were to read only her autobiographical *Kitchen Fugue*. . . ; here she declares her impatience with socialism and with the British working-man and his family. Her own Victorian parental home was prosperous and well-staffed with servants. . . . Perhaps the most offensive feature of the book is that she treats her wartime efforts at cooking as an eccentric adventure when it is in fact merely one of the daily occupations of countless women—who, however, do without three daily helps.

It is all the more surprising to find that, in her novels, she describes lives she has not shared with insight and impartiality. She sees class-differences as the material of tragedy, on both sides. Thus, in her distinguished early novel *Joanna Godden* . . . Joanna makes a great financial success of farming on the marshes through her own hard work and courage, but is brought low by her associations with people of unfamiliar classes. She falls in love with a member of the local gentry who dies; from generosity and wilfulness she buys her own sister an education which makes her into an alien being; and at the close she is left heart-broken and pregnant by a middle-class city-clerk. Class-differences are the implicit theme in two recent novels of good quality—*The Lardners and the Laurelwoods* . . . and *Mrs. Gailey* . . . . The first, as the title suggests, is about two families who become socially connected. The Laurelwoods are wealthy middle-class, who for many years spent their summer holidays at Idolsfold as lodgers in the house of the farming Lardners. The visits came to an end when the delicate relationship of employer and employed was upset at several levels—between the children, between the adolescents, and finally between the parents. *Mrs. Gailey* illustrates Sheila Kaye-Smith's unusual ability to keep up with the times—though it may perhaps be questioned whether her continuing belief in the incompatibility of the classes is still valid even by her own evidence. In the Sussex country-district, which she inevitably takes as her setting, only the vestige of an earlier and stricter social order remains. Mrs Winrow, the lady of the manor, is an embittered latter-day Mrs Dalloway; she and her kind are in decline:

> They're clinging to a state of things that's over and done with. That's what scares them—they're afraid they won't have anything left. Think of how Mrs. Winrow used to live before the war— before both the wars—with plenty of money, plenty of servants, everything easy, all the tenants looking up to her and flattered if she asked them to a servants' ball. Now it's all changed.

Sheila Kaye-Smith depicts in miniature that period during and after every war when social life is greatly disturbed, and many strange people rise briefly to the top before sinking out of sight once more. One such person is Mrs Gailey herself, who becomes secretary to Mrs Winrow's philanthropic daughter, Leslie. Coming from a respectable working-class family, she has acquired a saloon-bar sophistication (which never deceives Mrs Winrow for a moment) in the company of shiftless men, including her late husband. Apparently hard-bitten and hedonistic, she preserves a kind of battered innocence which makes her still the prey of any gay deceiver. Mrs Gailey and Charley Vine, a farming tenant of Mrs Winrow's who became a major during the war, are parvenus who are unwittingly responsible for Leslie's suicide. Without the intrigues of the first, which are in harmony with the views of a more insecure, harder and more fiercely competitive society, and the suavity of the second, cultivated in accordance with higher class standards he has not properly assimilated, Leslie would have lived. To this extent the social opinions of Iris Winrow are vindicated. (pp. 59-62)

E. D. Pendry, "Pride and Sensibility," in her The New Feminism of English Fiction: A Study in Contemporary Women-Novelists, *Kenkyusha Ltd., 1956, pp. 46-66.**

GLEN CAVALIERO (essay date 1977)

[*An English poet, critic, and former Anglican cleric, Cavaliero is a member of the Faculty of English at Cambridge. A well-read critic, he is the author of acclaimed studies of the works of E. M. Forster, John Cowper Powys, and of the rural tradition in the early twentieth-century English novel. In the following excerpt, Cavaliero discusses Kaye-Smith as a novelist of rural life.*]

[Sheila Kaye-Smith's] early novels are historical romances, but *Spell Land* . . . , with its sub-title 'The Story of a Sussex Farm', shows where her real interest lay. It is a depressing book, melodramatic and full of moral attitudinising. *Isle of Thorns* . . . is more determinedly modern, and embarrasses as a result—a note of high-pitched idealism (the hero ensuring that the girl he loves does a spell in prison for the manslaughter of his rival) being matched with a would-be sexual outspokenness—an uncomfortable mixture. These novels were, the author confesses, made up as they went along: the decisive factor in her literary growth was her friendship with the novelist W. L. George, who 'taught me to plan beforehand in great detail—almost down to paragraphs; then having got my blueprint absolutely clear, to follow it closely in a single script which would need only slight revision'. This accounts both for the novels' readability and for their rather machine-made air. Impeccably paragraphed, each chapter subdivided into short sections, the books move forward simply, easy to take up and easy to put down. (pp. 72-3)

But at their best Sheila Kaye-Smith's novels, though they do not surprise, have the merit of an honest and faithful reporting on experience. Her Sussex is realistically presented, her subject matter being for the most part the lives and ambitions of small farmers; and, although she has a love for old customs and traditions, she accepts the twentieth-century world without complaint (in this an exception among rural writers) though not without criticism. In *The End of the House of Alard* . . . , one of her more popular and more stereotyped novels, she portrays an ancient aristocratic family adapting to change through the various compromises and revolts of the younger generation. The eldest son, putting the estate before personal inclination, deserts his true love and marries money. The theme is Trollopian though the resolution—suicide—is not. One of the daughters turns down the man she loves because he is not good enough for the family, while her younger sister marries a local farmer and has to adjust her life accordingly. The youngest son becomes a garage hand and, later, a monk: on his accession to the title he decides to sell the estate. There is a constant stress on the stultifying nature of mere conformity to tradition, a serious questioning of such values as family loyalty. But in the sequel, *The Ploughman's Progress* . . . , Gervase Alard's altruistic action comes in for sharp criticism. As one of the independent farmers writes to him,

> You took the land away from the squires to give it to the yeomen, but I don't suppose you will be broken-hearted to hear that the yeomen have found your gift too expensive and have in their turn handed it over to the speculative builder (on the edges) and to desolation (in the midst).

This book, a thoughtful treatment of the changing agricultural conditions of the time, is a characteristic rural novel of the 1930s; but the conventional incidents and characterisation make it compare unfavourably with the less obviously polished work of A. G. Street and Adrian Bell.

In other novels we find the invocation of a more intangible reality (the kind of reality at which Hugh Walpole more uncertainly hints).

He looked out to sea, and saw the path that the light had trodden from the moon. The low soft roar, the blurred horizon, the phosphorescent break of the waves on the beach were a comfort to him in the strangeness of his disembodied town. His little refuge between the sea and the woods had betrayed him—his bit of time had crumbled—but its eternal boundary remained, the great whole of which Marlingate was a part, and to which its ghost, so restless and trembling tonight, belonged, the deep from which it was taken and to which it would return. [*Tamarisk Town*]

This sense of an underlying physical order that can be spiritually apprehended is a feature of several of the novels, as it is of those of Eden Phillpotts. It is the final comfort of the defeated hero of *Spell Land,* and an abiding one to the ferocious protagonist of *Sussex Gorse.* The latter novel is the nearest that Sheila Kaye-Smith comes to writing the kind of work parodied and criticised in [Stella Gibbons's] *Cold Comfort Farm.* It is the story of Reuben Backfield, a Sussex farmer who surrenders his life to an obsession, his determination to buy up and subdue to the plough the piece of upland called Boarzell Heath. To this he sacrifices everything—wife, children, honour and love. The story anticipates Mary Webb's *Precious Bane,* but, whereas Gideon Sarn is defrauded in the hour of his triumph, and his wrong-headed choice proved false, Reuben Backfield wins through. There is something satisfying about his refusal to conform to the expected moral pattern: throughout the book one waits for the apparently inevitable defeat, only to find at the end that he regards the havoc he has wrought as well worth while. It is an interesting departure from his creator's general approach (one which she again derived from the advice of W. L. George) and a corrective to the relentless intensity of other parts of the novel. Reuben is seen as being almost a force of nature; and he has a good deal more vigour than most of Eden Phillpotts's characters in this vein. (pp. 73-4)

Sheila Kaye-Smith's writing has the merit of evoking not only a contemplative's feeling for landscape but also the actual feel of working the land. *Joanna Godden* is a faithfully drawn picture of a young woman farmer; indeed, it contains more than the portrait of Joanna herself, and portrays a whole community, the other marsh farmers, the clergy, the labourers, the squires, as well as the impact of the world of the town, above all the world of social fashion as mediated through Joanna's younger sister Ellen, whom she succeeds in educating into a way of thought and feeling hostile to all that the farm stands for. The world of the farm is the world of honesty, of work as a source of life and not simply as a means towards it: it represents the positive in the author's scale of values. In a characteristic passage she portrays both Joanna and that for which she stands:

> Father Lawrence came to see her one April day when the young lambs were bleating on the sheltered innings and making bright clean spots of white beside the ewes' fog-soiled fleeces, when the tegs had come down from their winter keep inland, and the sunset fell in long golden slats across the first water-green grass of spring. The years had aged him more than they had aged Joanna—the marks on her face were chiefly weather marks, token of her exposure to marsh suns and winds, and of her own ruthless ap-

plications of yellow soap. Behind them was a little of the hardness which comes when a woman has to fight many battles and has won her victories, largely through the sacrifice of her resources. The lines on his face were mostly those of his own humour and other people's sorrows, he had exposed himself perhaps not enough to the weather and too much to the world, so that where she had fine lines and a fundamental hardness, he had heavy lines like the furrows of a ploughshare, a softness beneath them like the fruitful soil that the share turns up.

This is beautifully done: two worlds of experience are here related and shown to be complementary. Sheila Kaye-Smith's own Christian convictions are, however, subdued to a more general concern with the values of a Christian humanism—her study of religious fanaticism in *Green Apple Harvest,* for example, has more to do with its effects on her pitiful protagonist than with the rights and wrongs of his belief. Where her own specific convictions obtrude they are ecclesiastical, as in the portrait of the young Anglo-Catholic priest in *The End of the House of Alard* and of the older one in *Shepherds in Sackcloth . . . ,* which are sympathetic accounts of the impact made by the Oxford Movement in the country districts.

It is, however, in the study of farmers and their families that Sheila Kaye-Smith excels. Her Sussex is a place where people work, their lives making for health and sanity in spite of the complications wrought by human temperament. In *Iron and Smoke . . . ,* a story of the marriage between the daughter of a northern industrial magnate and a southern squire who loves his land more than his wife and family, industrialism is seen as the enemy, and the book ends on a note of triumph with the breaking of the General Strike. The author clearly has sympathy with the magnate's rebellious son when he says,

> The trouble's deeper—in the earth itself. She has set her curse upon us for digging into her heart for our wealth, when she gladly gave us her surface for our necessity. It's the work itself that's impossible, apart from any housing or wages. If we paid our miners sixty pounds a week and gave them palaces to live in, they would still be a rebellious race, because they live and work at enmity with nature.

But this is a superficial distinction; and one has only to read Lawrence's account of the miners in *Sons and Lovers* to perceive the limitation. When Paul has to leave home to go to work he sees that 'the valley was full of corn, brightening in the sun. Two colleries, among the fields, waved their small white plumes of steam.' The juxtaposition is not a contrast; and seen like that it shows up Sheila Kaye-Smith's opposition between mining and farming as being, however humanitarian in impulse, an artificial one.

In the straightforward portrayal of men and women at work she is on surer ground. . . . [The title character of *Joanna Godden*], with her high spirits, her impulsive affections, her ambition and love of property is a characteristic early twentieth-century heroine, a type that begins with Bathsheba Everdene and ends with Scarlett O'Hara. The feminist movement had as one of its principal literary results these portraits of a capable but feminine woman in a man's world. (pp. 75-8)

[A] familiar style of farming family is portrayed in *Little England.* The fortunes of the Beatup family and their neighbours in the First World War is coloured by a vein of patriotic fervour that is, however, commendably restrained. As an observant, sympathetic, unpatronising picture of very ordinary people it is among the most likable of Sheila Kaye-Smith's books, and is representative of all her best qualities. . . . This novel is the author's least romantic book, a straightforward chronicle of an English hamlet. Its virtues—skilful balancing of incidents and character analysis, humanity and credibility are characteristic. Its weakness is more a matter of limitation, a deficiency in imaginative force, so that situations tend to drift into storybook resolutions; and in any great sense of change and history. But limitations can be more deadly than faults. As Edwin Muir observed, 'Her imagination is loose and general, she lacks that intensity which is the same thing as exactitude.'

Sheila Kaye-Smith's Sussex labours under a particularity that limits its relevance; and her own powers were insufficient to overcome that limitation: the novels remain provincial in significance while metropolitan in presentation. Sussex is simply the place where the stories happen, and, lovingly described though it is, and evocatively as its place-names are used, it does not seem to have any particular meaning in itself. (The account of Romney Marsh in *Joanna Godden* is so vivid, however, as almost to cancel out this criticism.) The author's kindly if ironical understanding flickers over her characters, but it needs a mind of the rare warmth and sympathy of a George Eliot to combine this with intensity of feeling. Ultimately the work of Sheila Kaye-Smith, however workmanlike and humane, fails to kindle the imagination; its tendency is less to heighten its subject than, very slightly, to belittle it.

But only very slightly. And it is a novelist worthy of respect who composed the following letter [in *Little England*] from a village youth who has deserted from the trenches.

> Dear Father,
> By the time you get this I will be out of the way of troubling you any more. I am in great trouble. Mr. Archie said perhaps not tell you, but I said I would rather you knew. It is like this. I kept away in——last time we went up to the trenches, with a lady friend, you may have heard of. Beatup says he told you. Well, I am to be shot for it. I was court-martialled and they said to be shot. Dear Father this will make you very sorry, but I cannot be helped, and I am not worth it. I have been a very bad son to you, and done many wicked things besides. Things always were against me. Mr. Archie is sitting with me tonight, and he says he will stay all night, as I am feeling very much upset at this great trouble. I am leaving you my ring made out of a piece of Zep and my purse, only I am afraid there is no money in it. Please remember me to Ivy Beatup, and say if it had not been for her I should not be here now. I think that is all.
>
> ever your loving son,
> Jeremiah Meridian Sumption
>
> P.S.—The pardry says Jesus will forgive my sins. Thank you very much, dear father, for those fags you sent. I am smoking one now.

(pp. 78-9)

Glen Cavaliero, "Literary Regionalism: Hugh Walpole, Sheila Kaye-Smith," in his The Rural Tradition *in the English Novel, 1900-1939,* Rowman and Littlefield, 1977, pp. 66-80.**

DOROTHEA WALKER (essay date 1980)

[Walker is an American educator and critic specializing in women's studies. In the following excerpt, she summarizes the importance of Kaye-Smith's work.]

Perhaps the life work of Sheila Kaye-Smith might best be summed up by the remark of Hugh Walpole that "it has been Sheila Kaye-Smith's virtue . . . to make her novels timeless." Because she probes the psychological depths of human needs, she presents characters who appear as real people, caught up in forces which either aid or hinder them in their growth toward human maturity. The human needs which form these forces do not change with changes in a societal view. The need for acceptance as an individual, the need for freedom to reach one's potentiality, the need for community with one's fellow human beings—all these reside deep within human nature. By showing the basis for these human needs and by picturing the constructive or destructive use to which they are put, Sheila Kaye-Smith provides insight into the core of life—human relationships.

Ample evidence exists that her novels were extremely popular in their time. Unfortunately, other techniques and other visions supplanted the solid, expert, professional technique wedded to a hopeful vision that remained central to the talent of Sheila Kaye-Smith. But copies of her books are still available in libraries, and apparently they are read. Many should be reprinted, and not only because they are good stories, but because they provide insight into this time and every time.

Sheila Kaye-Smith always tells a good story. From the time she was a tiny girl, stories were part of her. Her imagination pulled together memories, observations, and intuitions, resulting in artistry. Her stories contain well-plotted action as well as expertly motivated characters. The effect is to draw the reader into the circle of which she writes, so that the characters step from the printed page into the reader's consciousness. (p. 152)

Miss Kaye-Smith's critical acclaim rests on her use of Sussex as locale, her conversion to Roman Catholicism, and her supposed ability to write like a man. But each novel can be taken as an entity. The locale, the religion, the objectivity, the power, the breadth of vision—all serve to point to a vision which sees life in a certain way. This way is based in part on the tragic vision, in which each individual brings about his or her own destruction through a tragic error. Added to this is the Judeo-Christian tenet, in which love of self and love of neighbor must be manifest before maturity as a human being can be reached, plus an existential view of existence in which action precedes essence, so that her protagonists become by doing. Added to these fundamentals is a questioning of them, particularly in the characterization of Reuben in *Sussex Gorse*. Although she does not take sides in the struggle of her protagonists for selfhood against the formidable forces arraigned against them, she conveys the idea that good and evil depend upon sanctions outside the individual. When a character fails to accept these sanctions, which are rooted in love, he or she falls, in her view, even though he or she may see himself or herself as successful, as, for example Reuben Backfield and Susan Spray.

Thus, there is paradox in her characterizations as there is in life. She has no easy answers to the problem of existence. But, then, Sheila Kaye-Smith does not attempt to write religious tracts. She presents stories based on human need, and she succeeds in making this need understandable to her readers. To read **Sussex Gorse** and **Tamarisk Town** is not only to experience the effect of a driving ambition, but also to understand the need through which this driving ambition comes into being as well as the lack of moral/ethical considerations which helps create the human monster. **Joanna Godden** and **Susan Spray,** although stories of women, have no propaganda to preach. The reader can find in these women characteristics which pertain to both sexes. The contradictions which make up human existence can be experienced through reading **The End of the House of Alard** and **The View from the Parsonage.** And most important of all, that which keeps the human race apart, instead of together in community, can become part of one's consciousness through reading **The Lardners and the Laurelwoods** and **Mrs. Gailey.**

The other novels of Sheila Kaye-Smith are likewise important and satisfying to the reader, because all pertain in some way to the struggle all human beings must engage in as part of a growth to maturity. Although there are certain basic principles of human activity which appear important to Miss Kaye-Smith and although she writes of a certain locale, all of the novels are different. Even though the theme may be similar in two or more novels, as pointed out above, a different view of the conflict brings added insight into the struggle.

Despite the fact that some critics complain of a certain detachment in her writing, this detachment is fortunate because it allows her to write with an objectivity which would not be possible if she clearly supplied her own value system. This is not to say that there are no moral/ethical values present in the novels. As noted above, her vision is based upon traditional values of Western culture. Yet her objectivity allows the reader room to interpret motivation, development, and conclusion based on his or her own values, provided, of course, that these values generally agree with the traditional values as noted above.

Sheila Kaye-Smith appears to have lived a happy and productive life. She created herself through her writing and through her acceptance of the religion of which she felt herself part. The creation of self appears as an important aspect of her novels. Undoubtedly her awareness of this as the fundamental goal of every human being underlay not only her novels, but her life as well. The self she created shows forth in her autobiographical works as well as in her novels. She did not wear her religion on her sleeve, but the values she apparently lived by and the values that appear in her novels are those basic Judeo-Christian ones whose core is the creative power of love.

Sheila Kaye-Smith has enhanced English literature, not only by preserving a section of England for immortality, but also by preserving fundamental human values which might help her readers in their own creation of self. For this she deserves their gratitude. (pp. 152-54)

> *Dorothea Walker, in her* Sheila Kaye-Smith, *Twayne Publishers, 1980, 169 p.*

JANET MONTEFIORE   (essay date 1982)

[*In the following excerpt from an essay written in 1982, Montefiore discusses* Susan Spray, *maintaining that the characterization of the heroine—her nature, formative experiences, vocational and psychological development—is the source of this novel's success.*]

Susan Spray is a remarkable novel by a writer who deserves resurrection: Sheila Kaye-Smith, once celebrated as the "Sussex novelist", and now almost forgotten. Her novels have two major narrative virtues: they go with a "passionate swing" (her own phrase), and they combine a strong sense of place (usually but not invariably East Sussex) with a feeling for English social history. **Susan Spray,** like her other novels, is saturated in concrete social detail, from the soup made of stolen turnips eaten by the starving farm labourers (the effect of the Corn Laws), to the description of the open country near London in the 1860s where the cottage roofs are dirty and "the little untidy farms seemed nothing but poultry shops". The novel has another virtue surprising to those who know its author only vaguely as a "rural writer": psychological complexity. This, rather than the plotting, is the source of its success. Susan's story is absorbingly told (given a certain lushness of style) and the reader is kept in suspense right up to the last page, but it suffers from an excess of coincidence; the architectonics of narrative are not Sheila Kaye-Smith's strong point (as Forster observed apropos of **Sussex Gorse**). The novel rests on the character of its heroine, whose motives are explored with detached, ironic sympathy.

Susan Spray is a success story—with a twist, the twist being religion. In **Three Ways Home** Sheila Kaye-Smith names the "three things that have meant most to me" as "the country, my writing and my religion", and she argues that religion is an important theme for novelists:

> It may be suppressed, inhibited or misdirected, after the manner of other human instincts, but it is still there, colouring human life for good or evil. . . . Actually religion provides nearly as many good situations as the sex-instinct . . . and its effects on character (either in its growth or its thwarting) make something new in the way of psychological interest.

However unpromisingly put, this manifesto is valid for herself: Sheila Kaye-Smith's best energies as a novelist were engaged by the religious psychology and experience of simple people. It is clear too that the idea of a female *preacher*, not merely a public speaker, laid hold of her imagination.

The novel was inspired, she says, by "the visit to England of a notorious American evangelist" (presumably Aimée Semple MacPherson, also the original of Mrs Ape in Waugh's *Vile Bodies*); and Susan Spray owes little to any literary predecessors. She is a preacher in a poor Protestant sect, like Dinah Morris in *Adam Bede*, and she has a beautiful voice like Verena Tarrant in *The Bostonians,* but there the resemblances end. In her literal-minded grasping of the Word, she is a product of Bible Protestantism—(the sect to which she belongs, the Colgate Brethren, actually take their doctrine of the Gate of Salvation from a pun on their founder's name: "The True Gate, the Golden Gate, the Holy Gate, the Colgate").

As a woman she is a product of the mid-nineteenth century: brought up in the bitter poverty of a farm labourer's family in the Hungry Forties (the bleak chapters dealing with her childhood are the best writing in the book); vain and anxious to dress the part of preacher (she is constantly hungry for clothes); an ambitious and successful woman whose social and literal mobility is symbolised by travelling first class on the new railway across Sussex, but still a big fish in a very little pond, she is convincingly presented *not* as a "typical Victorian" but as someone who could only have become the person she is in the particular time she is born into. The detached sympathy with which she and her congregations are treated is especially impressive, given that the author was a convert to Roman Catholicism; there is almost no mention of Rome and no trace of Chestertonian patronage in the handling of the Colgate Brethren.

As with *Joanna Godden,* the story of *Susan Spray* rests mainly on its heroine. Susan's character is a remarkable study in self-deception. She has a genuine imaginative capacity, a talent for religious feeling and an apprehension of the power of language, enhanced by Bible Protestantism. But her ability, as child and woman, to enthrall a congregation is founded on, at best, hallucination; her sermons have less to do with the needs of the Brethren than with her own desires and jealousies. These things Susan chooses, with increasing success, not to know. She begins in falsehood by protecting the privacy of her experience from the violation inherent in utterance by embroidering it, and ends virtually unable to tell right from wrong. But the falsity of her visionary speech has a truthful double in her genuine dreams and nightmares, which express the self-knowledge she refuses when awake in the only self-knowledge available to her: the language of Revelations. These dreams, only obliquely related to her life, have an authentic beauty and terror: in them she is at the mercy of the signs she articulates so confidently in her oratory.

Susan is a farm labourer's daughter, born in a class and sex normally doomed to silence. Her refusal, from childhood up, of the constraints of ''woman's destiny'' stems from the intuition that preaching is her vocation. The language of the Bible becomes for her the language of her being. She is not born with this mastery: as a child consoling her orphaned siblings, she is ludicrous.

> ''They're angels, wud crowns on their heads and harps in their hands, and their faces are like coals of fire and their feet like brass, and they cease not day and night crying Holy, Holy.''

> This unexpected picture of their parents made the young Sprays thoughtful for a while.

> ''Wot have they got to eat?'' asked Elis at last!

But by the end of the novel, while Susan's behaviour has become progressively more dishonest, her speech has gained in beauty and authority. She can hold an audience spellbound when she compares herself to a cornfield beaten down by rain and ''an empty pond all trodden and fouled by cattle''.

Susan's preaching is the true essence of her personality, and it is seen in different ways by each of her lovers. Her first, indulgent husband, who lets her preach without interference but with little interest, hears only music in her voice: ''for him her preaching was nothing but words spoken in a sweet husky voice by adorable lips.'' Her third husband takes her at her own value as the voice of inspiration, and becomes her acolyte. However, the intelligent but sexist Clarabut (the only lover, incidentally, who arouses her sexually) is thoroughly hostile to her preaching—or even speaking. (pp. ix-xii)

Susan rightly perceives Clarabut's potent sexuality and her own response to it as a threat to her vocation. This contradiction leads her to question the institution of patriarchal marriage:

> ''I can't marry you—not unless you'll come and live at Lambpool and let me go on with my preaching.''

''I told you I could never do that.''

''Why shouldn't you? Why shouldn't you? Why shouldn't you give up your notions instead of me giving up mine? Your work ain't worth what mine is—it's earthly and mine's heavenly.''

''But, my darling child, I am a man and you are a woman.''

''What difference does that make?''

The woman's questions have a resonance now that her creator probably did not intend. Susan's lifelong resentment and avoidance of the constrictions of her female lot are treated by her creator without much sympathy as a refusal of necessary destiny. (Unfortunately, when it comes to female sexuality, Sheila Kaye-Smith's line is regrettably close to Judith Starkadder in *Cold Comfort Farm:* ''Tes the hand of nature, and we women cannot escape it.'') But Susan Spray, despite her power of speech, would in any case make a very unsatisfactory feminist heroine. She is not a nice woman, nor a heroic one: vain, selfish, greedy of money and recognition; jealous of her sister Tamar, vindictive towards her and wilfully self-deceived. ''I've never seen you do a kind action,'' Clarabut accuses her, ''and I've seldom heard you speak a kind word.'' But Clarabut the rationalist has never seen the whole of Susan. She is, as he says a ''humbug'', but not a confidence-woman, and she never deceives herself entirely. The contradictions and half-truths of her nature are the fascination of the narrative. (pp. xii-xiii)

> *Janet Montefiore, in an introduction to* The History of Susan Spray: The Female Preacher *by Sheila Kaye-Smith, Virago, 1983, pp. ix-xiii.*

RACHEL ANDERSON (essay date 1982)

[*In the following excerpt, Anderson discusses the religious themes in Kaye-Smith's work and in the work of her contemporaries, considers the dilemma of choosing between domestic and professional fulfillment as faced by Joanna Godden, and points out the merits and limitations of the novel* Joanna Godden.]

Religion as it features in [Sheila Kaye-Smith's] writing closely parallels the quasi-religious themes and messages of the popular romantic novelists of her time. Just as in the romances of Florence Barclay, Elinor Glyn or Ethel M. Dell, in her novels too, we see men and women being stirred up by enthusiasms, moods and passions which are of both an earthly and a heavenly nature. As the *Publisher's Circular* had declared twenty years earlier, ''Of all forms of fiction, the semi-religious is the most popular.''

''Actually,'' wrote Sheila Kaye-Smith,

> religion provides nearly as many good situations as the sex-instinct—there are endless combinations, permutations, frustrations and deviations which the novelist can use, and its effect on character (either by its growth or by its thwarting) makes something new in the way of psychological interest.

Nowhere are the plots of her novels as silly as those of Ethel M. Dell or Florence Barclay through her use of a restricted emotional vocabulary—thrill, throb, mother, breast, heart and home—to convey emotional or spiritual intensity, is similar. Nor was she the first popular writer to be driven by her evangelising zeal to place God as a character in a novel. God, angels, divine phallic visions, had all been used to effect in Marie Corelli's erotic-spiritual quests. However, Sheila Kaye-Smith was the first to allow the Almighty to speak in a specially reconstructed Sussex idiom: "I am your God—döan't you know Me?" the Almightly calls down to an agricultural worker about to commit suicide in *Green Apple Harvest*. . . . (pp. xii-xiii)

> Did you think I was away up in heaven, watching you from a gurt way off? Didn't you know that I've bin with you all the time?—that every time you looked out on the fields or into your kind brother's eyes or at your baby asleep in his bed you looked on Me?. . . Why wöan't you look and see how beautiful and homely and faithful and loving I am?

In these displays of respectable moral passion, her aim was to be "challenging and proclaiming". She was writing, not of pantheism, or nature worship, but about "Catholicism—God in all things, no matter how simple and seemingly insufficient. It is the ground of the sacramental system, through which by the operation of the Holy Ghost nature gives birth to that which the whole world cannot contain."

Lack of a sense of proportion is, paradoxically, her biggest limitation as she sows the seeds of her great themes across huge literary fields. Most writers get to a point where they realise that there is something that they cannot achieve. Bad and middling writers don't have this limitation, for the genuine desire to improve the world combines with an unswerving belief that, by the power of their pens, they are doing so.

As in the case of any writer who hovers uncertainly on the borderline between being a good bad writer, and a bad good writer, the critics of the time couldn't make up their minds about her. Frank Swinnerton said *Tamarisk Town* . . . was "a noble failure". Another critic concluded that though she had the power to present sometimes masterly prose "yet greatness is excepted", while, in contrast, the *Westminster Gazette* confirmed, in 1924, that she was "one of the very few novelists now writing who have quite definitely achieved greatness". (pp. xiii-xiv)

Joanna Godden . . . was sometimes cited as an example of the good books Sheila Kaye-Smith wrote before being overtaken and spoilt by religion. She was at pains to point out that her religious viewpoint, though less explicit and dominating than in subsequent books, was already perfectly apparent in *Joanna Godden*, in such details, she said, as "the sympathetic pen-portrait" of Father Lawrence, the Anglican monk. Like its predecessors, *Sussex Gorse* . . . and *Tamarisk Town*, it is the study of an ambitious landowner but, unusually, she is a woman—a sheepfarmer on the Romney and Walland Marshes in Kent. (p. xiv)

Popular romantic heroines of the twenties, whether large or small, were uncertain whether they wished to be liberated from man or dominated by him; to choose true love inevitably meant to choose male domination. Joanna Godden, though she yearned for love, though she dreamed of a giant shepherd surrounded by giant sheep, who would seize hold of her and crush her, was not in her waking mind able to accept such a domination.

She is an unsophisticated woman who has never been as far as London. Her trials of courtship are acted out within the narrow confines of the gaunt, wind-bitten marshland, beneath doom-laden skies, on soggy soil. Sheila Kaye-Smith writes untiringly about fogs, mists, smoke, water, mud and wind. She writes about sheep-tick, sheep-dipping and root crops. The descriptive prose is tight-packed with swarth, swart, sward, tussocks, shards, lumps of marl and wealden clay. The rustic oafs, whose curious but authentic names the author selected from local tombstones and parish registers, stumble about a landscape spattered with genuine place-names and locations which the author took from the map. There is, however, something more powerful about the novel than the author's fascination for the ring of ancient surnames, and her passing interest in quaint country customs.

A story, as E. M. Forster coldly pointed out in a lecture in 1927 *(Aspects of the Novel)*, can have only one merit—that of making the audience want to know what happens next, and conversely only one fault: that of making the audience not want to know what happens next. In *Joanna Godden*, even if we are unmoved by the author's sanctimonious generalisations about life and death, we are nonetheless driven to turn the pages of her story. We must know how Joanna will secure the future she deserves. As she rejects or mislays suitor after suitor, we begin to grow restless. Is the author stringing us along to a predictable conclusion of early spinsterhood?

Then, Sheila Kaye-Smith delivers her surprise. She makes Joanna do something completely out of character so that even as the novel ends on its ambiguous note, we are once more wondering what on earth will happen next to this impossible woman. For Joanna is caught up in a universal dilemma which the passage of forty years, and a women's liberation, can do little to resolve.

As a reasonably well-off (though not well-to-do) landowner, Joanna was free, as are most women today, to choose between domestic or professional fulfilment. She was, however, limited to one or other of these options, not both. She attempted to enter and succeed in a traditional man's world. Thus, she is not a colleague in farming, but a competitor. As a woman, she must work harder, must succeed more remarkably, than any of her fellows. "'Oh God!' She mourned to herself—'why didn't you make me a man?'" Today, the dilemma Joanna faces still faces many women who attempt to succeed with a traditional masculine career. Total fulfilment of a business ambition does not allay the yearnings for maternal fulfilment.

Possibly, the heroine's inability to settle to any man reflected the author's own ignorance of men and marriage. At any rate, at the time of writing *Joanna Godden*, Sheila Kaye-Smith was thirty-four and single, and she conveys with tenderness and conviction, the pain and indeed the actual physical ache of Joanna's unresolved desires. As many women do, Joanna misinterprets her broodiness as a succession of minor and major ailments, from rheumatism to consumption and cancer, before recognising her real problem. The evocation of the middle-aged virgin, waiting in bed in her sensible cotton nightgown buttoned to the neck, is fresh, vital and, in its prudish way, even erotic.

Middling bad writers may fail in their more grandiose schemes to explain and resolve the whole human condition. But in communicating some of the personal anguish of women, they manage to write with intensity, passion and above all honesty. As Virginia Woolf, in defence of women writers, explained in a lecture in 1929:

> The whole character of women's fiction at the present moment is courageous; it is sincere; it keeps closely to what women feel. It is not

bitter. It does not insist upon its femininity. These qualities are much commoner than they were, and they give even to second- and third-rate work the value of truth and the interest of sincerity.

(pp. xv-xvii)

Rachel Anderson, in an introduction to Joanna Godden *by Sheila Kaye-Smith, 1983. Reprint by Doubleday & Company, Inc., 1984, pp. xi-xviii.*

ADDITIONAL BIBLIOGRAPHY

Boynton, H. W. "Challenge and Quest." *The Bookman,* New York XLIV, No. 2 (April 1919): 184.
    Discusses theme and style in *The Challenge to Sirius.* Boynton finds Kaye-Smith's style vivid and eloquent but at times inappropriate to the subject.

Braybrooke, Patrick. "Sheila Kaye-Smith and Her Realism." In his *Some Catholic Novelists: Their Art and Outlook,* pp. 179-206. New York: Bruce Publishing Co., 1931.
    Examines *Sussex Gorse, Joanna Godden,* and *Tamarisk Town* as illustrations of Kaye-Smith's use of realism, and *The Tramping Methodist* as a blend of romanticism and realism, a portrait of conversion, and a demonstration of Kaye-Smith's ability to describe both beautiful and horrifying aspects of life. Braybrooke asserts that "she is a great novelist because her characters are 'great' people. They live with great force in her fiction, they are almost, not quite, great enough to live OUTSIDE of fiction."

Connors, Joseph B. "Instead of Pets." *Renascence* IX, No. 3 (Summer 1957): 213-14.
    Reviews Kaye-Smith's last work, *All the Books of My Life,* finding it informative and enjoyable.

Dalglish, Doris N. "Some Contemporary Women Novelists." *The Contemporary Review* CXXVII (January 1925): 82-3.*
    Considers the invented circumstances in Kaye-Smith's novels to be excessive, resulting in unrealistic situations that make it difficult for the reader to sympathize with the characters. Dalglish also states that Kaye-Smith's artistic ability is limited by her failure to clearly define and reveal herself in her work.

Ellis, Stewart Marsh, "A Novelist of Sussex: Miss Sheila Kaye-Smith." In his *Mainly Victorian,* pp. 470-73, 1925. Reprint. Freeport: Books for Libraries Press, 1969.
    Recalls Ellis's discovery of Kaye-Smith's work prior to her wide recognition, and reprints an article he had written in 1914 in which he discusses Sussex, some authors who had written about Sussex, and Kaye-Smith's success at portraying the beautiful landscape of this part of England. Ellis also reviews *Starbrace* and *Isle of Thorns,* deeming *Starbrace* the best of her first four novels, describing the work as "one of the most vivid and picturesque accounts in fiction of the highwayman."

Hopkins, R. Thurston. *Sheila Kaye-Smith and the Weald Country.* London: Cecil Palmer, 1925, 225 p.
    Compares the characters and scenes from Kaye-Smith's novels with the actual people and countryside of Mid-Sussex, East-Sussex, and Romney Marsh. Hopkins quotes from Kaye-Smith's works to illustrate their fidelity to life in this region of England.

Krutch, J. W. "Woman Freed." *The Nation* CXIV, No. 2957 (8 March 1922): 291-92.*
    Compares Joanna Godden with heroines in three other novels by female contemporaries of Kaye-Smith. Krutch points out that, with the exception of Joanna Godden, all the heroines are defeated by their inclination toward passivity and toward justification and fulfillment in a relationship with a man. He states, "Sheila Kaye-

Smith has in her book reached full maturity as a novelist and has both the sympathy to understand and the detachment to see clearly."

Lawrence, Margaret. "Matriarchs." In her *The School of Femininity,* pp. 210-18, 236-38. 1936. Reprint. Port Washington, N.Y.: Kennikat Press, 1966.
    Defines a matriarch as "a woman whose emotional center is in her regard for arranging and rearranging the affairs of people around her," and categorizes a group of twentieth-century women writers, one of whom is Kaye-Smith, as matriarchal. According to Lawrence, the work of a matriarchal writer is noticeably organized, is inspired by a desire to restore or improve society, and is a study of a group—usually a family or community. She summarizes *Susan Spray,* analyzing the title character and asserting, "It is, for all its literary power, a grave study of matriarchal danger."

Mackenzie, Margaret. "The House that Sheila Built." *Thought* VI, No. 1 (June 1931): 108-18.
    Discusses the architecture and atmosphere of Kaye-Smith's home as reflections of qualities in her novels. Mackenzie describes Sussex and its influence on her writing, attributing Kaye-Smith's greatness as a writer to her focus on things that endure and to her fidelity to life.

Mais, S. P. B. "Sheila Kaye-Smith." In his *Why We Should Read,* pp. 157-68. London: Grant Richards, 1921.
    Discusses what Mais finds attractive in Kaye-Smith's works, quoting extensively from *Sussex Gorse* and *Green Apple Harvest.* Mais praises the breadth of Kaye-Smith's outlook, her perception of the beauty of Sussex, the dignity and music of her prose style, her accurate sense of history, and her characterization of people from various eras.

Malone, Andrew E. "The Novelist of Sussex: Sheila Kaye-Smith." *The Fortnightly Review* n.s. CCX (2 August 1926): 199-209.
    Explains how Kaye-Smith's realistic depiction of the farm and of farmers' struggles, aspirations, and achievements differs from previous fictional treatment of these subjects, noting that her convincing portrayal suggests actual experience as a farmer. Malone states, "She has, in common with Thomas Hardy, that imaginative sympathy which finds kinship with silent nature and an understanding with primitive man."

Maxwell, J. R. N. "Sheila Kaye-Smith." *America* XLIV, No. 14 (10 January 1931): 339-41.
    Survey of Kaye-Smith's career, providing synopses and appraisals of some of her major works and emphasizing her realistic portrayal of farm life. Maxwell describes her as a "novelist of character and natural backgrounds, a weaver of rhythmical paragraphs that rise and fall with the swelling undulations of her own Sussex hills."

Pritchett, V. S. "Warnings." *The Spectator* 144, No. 5299 (18 January 1930): 99-100.
    Ambivalent review of *Shepherds in Sackcloth.* Pritchett cites Kaye-Smith's depiction of a clerical atmosphere and of clergymen as a merit of this work, but faults her use of characters to represent a case in religious controversy, noting that "she does this with rather suspicious melodramatic effect."

Quigley, Jane. "Miss Sheila Kaye-Smith." *The Fortnightly Review* 120, No. DCLXXXII (1 October 1923): 593-99.
    A general discussion of Kaye-Smith, focusing on her career, qualities of her writing, her personality, and her home. Of Kaye-Smith's works, Quigley states, "Even her most severe critic must own that she knew how to tell a story, and that her books are eminently readable on that account apart from everything else."

Roberts, R. Ellis. "Sheila Kaye-Smith." *The Bookman* (London) LXII, No. 378 (March 1923): 269-71.
    Asserts that in great literature characters possess the illusion of reality, whereas in second-rate literature characters seem to exist primarily to serve the author's overall purpose. Roberts argues that, based on this distinction, many of Kaye-Smith's novels qualify as great literature, and he commends her for devoting herself

''to understanding the lives and the work of working men and women.''

Stack, Mary. ''Sheila Kaye-Smith, Novelist.'' *The Commonweal* XXI, No. 12 (18 January 1935): 335-36.

Mixed appraisal of Kaye-Smith's work, concluding that ''she has all gifts in abundance, but greatness is excepted.''

Stern, G. B. ''Sheila Kaye-Smith.'' In her *And Did He Stop and Speak to You?*, pp. 74-92. Chicago: Henry Regnery Co., 1958.

Discusses Kaye-Smith's works, personality, tastes, and spiritual development. Regarding her autobiographical novels *The Children's Summer* and *Selina Is Older,* Stern notes that ''they provide a vivid blueprint for her whole career in theological adventure; the embryonic writer, too, is seen making significant discoveries.'' Stern also relates how she and Kaye-Smith came to collaborate in writing *Talking of Jane Austen* and *More Talk of Jane Austen.*

Swinnerton, Frank. ''The Younger Novelists: Sheila Kaye-Smith.'' In his *The Georgian Scene: A Literary Panorama,* pp. 288-90. Murray Hill: Farrar & Rinehart, 1934.

Discusses Kaye-Smith's tragic vision of life, her career, and her reputation. Swinnerton describes her novels as ''models of construction,'' ''dramatic narratives, which stood of their own accord as excellent, honorable work,'' and expresses his admiration for their ''great sincerity.''

Weygandt, Cornelius. ''The Neo-Georgians: Sheila Kaye-Smith.'' In his *A Century of the English Novel,* pp. 434-35. New York City: Century Co., 1925.

Acknowledges the dramatic intensity and large effects in Kaye-Smith's works, but, unlike most critics, contends that her work does not demonstrate an intimate knowledge of either the land or community of Sussex.

Wilson, Edmund. ''A Long Talk about Jane Austen.'' In his *Classics and Commercials: A Literary Chronicle of the Forties,* pp. 196-203. New York: Farrar, Straus and Co., 1950.*

Discusses *Speaking of Jane Austen,* an informal critical work by Kaye-Smith and G. B. Stern, pointing out Kaye-Smith's particular interest in the historical background of Austen's novels and Stern's primary focus on the characters in her works. Wilson states, ''The book . . . contains a good deal that will be interesting to those interested in Jane Austen, though neither Miss Stern nor Miss Kaye-Smith, it seems to me, really goes into the subject so deeply as might be done.''

Velimir (Vladimirovich) Khlebnikov

1885-1922

(Born Viktor Khlebnikov; also transliterated as Velemir; also Xlebnikov and Chlebnikov) Russian poet, short story and novella writer, dramatist, essayist, and diarist.

Khlebnikov was a founder and leading member of Russian Futurism, a literary movement of the early twentieth century whose adherents sought to revitalize poetry by rejecting traditional aesthetic principles. A diverse group with disparate literary aims, the Futurists were united primarily by their repudiation of the past and by their devotion to the "self-sufficient word," a concept subordinating content to form through technical innovations in order to direct attention to language itself. The Futurists hoped thereby to revivify language rendered clichéd by everyday usage and permit the expression of a fresh vision of the world. Khlebnikov's poetic experiments with the relationship between sound and meaning earned him a reputation as one of the movement's most brilliant practitioners and theoreticians, declared by Futurism's most prominent member, Vladimir Mayakovsky, to be "a Columbus of new poetic continents."

Khlebnikov was born in 1885 in the Astrakhan region of Russia, an area near the Caspian Sea populated by Russians and a mixture of central-Asian peoples. The Khlebnikov family lived in various cities on or near the Volga River during Khlebnikov's childhood and youth, and commentators attribute his lifelong fascination with Asian cultures to his experiences in these areas. His parents were members of the middle-class intelligentsia who stressed the importance of both literature and the natural sciences in Khlebnikov's education; under their influence Khlebnikov first began writing poetry and prose while a student in secondary school. In 1903 he entered the University of Kazan as a student of mathematics, where he read avidly, took part in revolutionary activities, and continued to write. Five years later he enrolled at the University of St. Petersburg, where his diverse interests led him to change his major from mathematics to biology, to Sanskrit, and finally to Slavic studies, after which he abandoned formal education entirely in order to devote himself to literature. His first published work, a fragment entitled "Iskushenie greshnika," appeared in the journal *Vesna* in 1908. Through the magazine's managing editor, Vasily Kamensky, Khlebnikov became associated with the modernist poets whose avant-garde experiments gradually evolved into Futurism. Khlebnikov first brought critical attention to the group in 1910 with "Zaklyatie smekhom" ("Incantation by Laughter"), a poem composed entirely of derivations of the word "laugh." Futurism quickly rose in prominence after 1910, and between 1910 and 1916 Khlebnikov became one of the movement's central figures through the publication of numerous volumes of poetry and prose, pamphlets of literary and historical theory, and contributions of poetry, fiction, dramas, and essays to approximately twenty-five Futurist miscellanies.

Khlebnikov, however, had little interest in the Futurists' growing fame or in the publication of his works, the majority of which were pieced together by his friends from manuscript fragments and published without his assistance. His attention was engaged by a variety of other projects, including philological research, mathematical calculations to discover patterns

in history, and what Vladimir Markov has described as "various semifantastic projects, developing or resembling ideas by Pythagoras, Leibnitz, Fourier, and Nikolay Fyodorov, for reforming practically all aspects of human life." A utopian visionary, Khlebnikov was obsessed with the prospect of a world in which humanity lived in peace and the comfort resulting from scientific advances. To foster his vision, he formed the utopian "Society of Presidents of the Globe," composed of leading figures in science and the arts. While other prominent Futurists toured the country in flamboyant road shows and engaged in behavior and polemics intended to scandalize conventional mores, Khlebnikov shunned public appearances and undertook solitary journeys. According to acquaintances, he crossed and recrossed Russia incessantly, carrying a pillowcase full of poetry and mathematical calculations. In 1916, while visiting his home province of Astrakhan, Khlebnikov was unexpectedly drafted into the Russian army. Horrified by military life, he wrote to a friend, "I am a dervish, a yogi, a Martian, anything but a private of a reserve regiment." He was liberated by the Revolution of 1917, which he initially welcomed both because the upheaval secured his release from hated army life and because he viewed the establishment of a new order as a step toward the realization of his utopian vision. According to critics, however, Khlebnikov gradually became disillusioned with the Revolution, and his later poetry expresses ambivalence toward the events of 1917. Khlebnikov resumed his itinerant way of life and continued to write prolifically, but he published little after the Revolution. He spent the rest of his life in poverty, chronically malnourished and often ill, and died in 1922.

Although Khlebnikov wrote successfully in a variety of genres, he has gained renown primarily for the short poetic works in which he conducted his linguistic experimentation. Maintaining that "word creation is the enemy of the literary petrification of language," Khlebnikov sought to restore the communicative power of the word through the creation of thousands of neologisms in experimental sketches and complete poems such as "Incantation by Laughter." According to Victor Erlich, his favorite method of word-formation involved the dissolution of "familiar words into their morphological components, which he then reshuffled at will and reintegrated into new verbal units, poetic neologisms." Although Khlebnikov's coinages generally have no denotative value, they retain numerous connotations, unlike the nonsensical neologisms of Futurist Alexey Kruchonykh, which represent an attempt to free poetic language from all constraints of meaning. Instead, Khlebnikov sought to reverse the usual relationship between a word and its referent. Erlich writes: "In 'practical' language the sign is obviously subordinated to the object to which it points. In Khlebnikov's 'trans-sense' verse the object appears, if at all, as a faint echo of the sign; it is overshadowed by the whimsical interplay of the word's potential meanings." Khlebnikov's experimentation with what he called "trans-sense" language included not only the creation of neologisms, but also the search for a universal language. Convinced that linguistic adaptation was crucial to world harmony, he wrote: "Trans-sense language is the embryonic future language of the universe. Only it can unite men. Rational languages are already disuniting men." His attempts to create such a language were based on the theory, now discounted by modern linguists, of a fundamental correspondence between sound and meaning, and his efforts centered primarily on the isolation of language sounds expressing pure, abstract ideas.

In addition to his short, experimental poetry, Khlebnikov wrote over thirty long poems which are gradually attaining the critical regard formerly limited to his experiments. More conservative than his shorter works, Khlebnikov's long poems often demonstrate an affinity with Russian epic poetry of the eighteenth century. At the same time, they contain such experimental elements as neologisms, dialectisms, and unconventional grammar and syntax. According to B. Yakolev, Khlebnikov's principal themes constitute "a chaotic mixture of idealistic mysticism and anarchistic Utopianism," and critics often note a disparity in his longer poems between primitive, emotional elements and rational, intellectual elements. Fascinated by Slavic folklore and mythology, Khlebnikov idealized nature and primitive life in such works as "I i E," a love story set in Russian prehistory, and lamented the loss of ancient, pagan virtues in "Lesnaya toska," an idyll set in a mythological world. In contrast to the primitivism of these works stands the rationalism of such poems as "Ladomir" ("Goodworld"), in which he depicted a utopia achieved through progress in science and technology. Many of his poems concern historical events and figures and contain dates and mathematical formulas, reflecting his fascination with history and the laws of time. "Nochnoi obysk" ("The Night Search"), for example, which was written in 1921 and depicts the search of a bourgeois apartment by Communist soldiers during the Revolution, is headed by the epigraph "$3^6 + 3^6$." According to R. D. B. Thomson, the num-

bers represent Khlebnikov's mathematical formulation of events counteracting the original impulse of the Revolution and signify his growing ambivalence toward the new order. Praised for its complex rendering of the clash between old and new cultures, "The Night Search" is considered one of Khlebnikov's best poems.

Khlebnikov was also the author of numerous dramas and works of prose fiction, which, unlike his poetry, have received little critical attention. Stylistically and thematically diverse, these works combine traditional and experimental elements in much the same way as his longer poems. Dissatisfied by the limitations of traditional genres, Khlebnikov also combined poetry, fiction, dramas, and essays in a form he called the "supertale." The supertale was usually composed of separate, previously completed works; Khlebnikov described his creation as being "constructed from independent pieces, each with its own god, its own faith, and its own code." Critics observe that in many of the supertales the actual relationship between the components is indiscernible, a lack of cohesion that Nikolai Khardzhiev attributes to "Khlebnikov's tendency to destroy the established ways of temporal and local fixation and thus to create a multiplicity of stylistic and thematic levels." However, in *Deti vydry* and *Zangezi*, which commentators consider his most successful supertales, Khlebnikov effectively combined disparate parts into an integrated whole: *Deti vydry* comprises historical essays and depictions of various historical eras in what has been called "an artistic synthesis of Khlebnikov's mathematical exploration," and *Zangezi* presents the poet's most important philosophical, historical, mathematical, and linguistic ideas through the philosopher Zangezi, who appears in each section of the work.

The unusual nature of Khlebnikov's life and works has perpetuated what Viktor Shklovsky describes as "a legend of a silent eccentric, a perpetual wanderer, an idiot, and a genius." Indeed, during his lifetime critical appraisal of Khlebnikov was divided between those who considered him one of the most brilliant poets of the twentieth century and those who considered him a lunatic. His admirers rank him among the world's most skillful linguistic innovators and poetic craftsmen; however, the obscurity of his works has limited his readership to a small, select audience. In 1926 D. S. Mirsky predicted that Khlebnikov's poetry would never be read by anyone but poets and philologists, and as late as 1960 Vladimir Markov observed that Khlebnikov was "still an enigmatic and elusive poet, worshipped by a few, dismissed as a crank by some, and ignored by the majority." In recent years, however, Khlebnikov's works have become the subject of increasing critical attention, and two sizable English translations of his poetry and prose have increased the availability of his works to English-speaking readers.

PRINCIPAL WORKS

Mirskonca [with Alexey Kruchonykh]   (dramatic sketch) 1912
   [*The World in Reverse* published in *The King of Time*, 1985]
Izbornik stikhov   (poetry)   1914
Oshibka smerti   (drama)   1921
Zangezi   (prose and poetry)   1922
   [*Zangezi* published in *The King of Time*, 1985]
Sobranie proizvedenii. 5 vols.   (poetry, prose, letters, and diaries)   1928-33
Stikhotvoreniia i poemy   (poetry)   1960

Snake Train (poetry, prose, dramas, and essays) 1976
The King of Time: Selected Writings of the Russian Futurian
(poetry, prose, dramas, and essays) 1985

Translated selections of Khlebnikov's poetry have appeared in the following publications: Bowra, Cecil Maurice, ed., *A Second Book of Russian Verse*; Burlyuk, David, ed., *Color and Rhyme*, No. 31; *Hip Pocket Poems*, No. 2; *Hip Pocket Poems*, No. 4; Kaun, Alexander, ed., *Soviet Poets and Poetry*; Lindsay, Jack, ed., *Russian Poetry 1917-1955*; Reavey, George, and Slonim, Marc L., eds., *Soviet Literature*; and Yarmolinsky, Avrahm, ed., *A Treasury of Russian Verse*.

DAVID BURLYUK, ALEXEY KRUCHONYKH, VLADIMIR MAYAKOVSKY, AND VELIMIR KHLEBNIKOV (essay date 1912)

[*The following excerpt is from the Futurist manifesto* "A Slap in the Face of Public Taste," *originally published in 1912.*]

To those who read our New First Unexpected.

We alone are the *face of our Time*. Time's clarion blares forth in us, in our art of words.

The past is stifling. The Academy and Pushkin are more incomprehensible than hieroglyphs. Overboard from the steamship of modernity with Pushkin, Dostoyevsky, Tolstoy, and others, and others!

He who will not forget the *first* love, will not know the last. Who, then, is so gullible as to direct his last love to the perfumed lechery of Balmont? Can the audacious spirit of Today find therein its reflection? Who, then, is so craven as to hesitate in pulling the paper armor off the black frockcoat of warrior Bryusov? Are the dawns of unknown beauty thereon?

Wash your hands that are sticky with the filthy slime of books written by those innumerable Leonid Andreyevs.

A summer villa by the river, is all that's desired by these Maxim Gorkys, Kuprins, Bloks, Sologubs, Remizovs, Averchenkos, Chornys, Kuzmins, Bunins, and others, and others. Fate metes out such a reward to tailors.

From the height of skyscrapers we look down on their paltriness.

We command to honor the rights of poets:

1. To an enlargement of the poet's vocabulary by arbitrary and derivative words—neologisms.

2. To an insurmountable hatred for the language used previously.

3. With horror to thrust aside from their proud brows the wreath of cheap fame made out of your bathhouse brooms.

4. To stand firmly on the rock of the word "we" amid the sea of hisses and indignation.

If, for the time being, even our lines still retain the foul brands of your "common sense" and "good taste," across them already flutter the Heat-lightnings of a New Oncoming Beauty of the Self-Sufficient Word. (pp. 16-17)

> *David Burlyuk, Alexey Kruchonykh, Vladimir Mayakovsky, and Velimir Khlebnikov, "A Slap in the Face of Public Taste," translated by Alexander Kaun,*

in Soviet Poets and Poetry *by Alexander Kaun, University of California Press, 1943, pp. 16-17.**

VLADIMIR MAYAKOVSKY (essay date 1922)

[*Mayakovsky was the leading artistic voice of the Russian Revolution of 1917. Noted for his ability to create utilitarian literature without compromising artistic standards, he wrote critically respected poetry and dramas extolling the common worker and the Revolution. In addition, Mayakovsky was a central figure of Russian Futurism. The Futurist poets sought to destroy traditional poetic precepts through disregard for metonymic and grammatical convention and through the use of bizarre imagery, invented vocabulary, and techniques borrowed from avant-garde painting, such as irregular typefaces, offbeat illustrations, and authors' handwriting. Mayakovsky's poetry is marked by powerful rhythm and hyperbolic imagery, and, according to D. S. Mirsky, "is very loud, very unrefined, and stands absolutely outside the distinction between 'good' and 'bad' taste." During the last years of his life Mayakovsky lost favor with Soviet officials, who maintained that his poetry was too individualistic and that the avant-garde tenets of Futurism were incompatible with Soviet ideology. Nevertheless, after his death in 1930 he was praised by Joseph Stalin as "the greatest Soviet poet," and he remains one of Russia's most popular authors. In the following excerpt from a eulogy originally published in the journal* Krasneya nov *in 1922, Mayakovsky summarizes Khlebnikov's poetic technique.*]

Khlebnikov's poetical fame is immeasurably less than his significance.

For every hundred readers, fifty considered him simply a graphomaniac, forty read him for pleasure and were astonished that they found none, and only ten (futurist poets and philologists of the "OPOYAZ" [Organization for the Study of Poetic Language]) knew and loved this Columbus, this discoverer of new poetic continents that we now populate and cultivate.

Khlebnikov is not a poet for consumers—they can't read him. Khlebnikov is a poet for producers.

Khlebnikov never completed any extensive and finished poetic works. The apparent finished state of his published pieces is most often the work of his friends' hands. We chose from the pile of his discarded notebooks those that seemed most valuable to us and we published them. Often the tail of one draft was pasted to an extraneous head, to Khlebnikov's cheerful astonishment. You couldn't let him have anything to do with proofs: he would cross out everything completely and give you an entirely new text.

When bringing something in for publication, Khlebnikov usually remarked, "If something isn't right, change it." When he recited his poems he would sometimes break off in the middle of a sentence and indicate simply "et cetera."

In this "etc." is the whole of Khlebnikov: he posed a poetic task, provided the means for its solution, but the use of this solution for practical purposes, this he left to others.

The story of Khlebnikov's life is worthy of his brilliant literary constructions; it is an example to real poets and a reproach to hacks.

What about Khlebnikov and poetic language?

For the so-called new poetry (our latest), and especially for the symbolists, the word is the raw material for the writing of verses (expressions of feelings and thoughts)—a raw material, the texture, resistance, and treatment of which was unknown. This raw material the new poets dealt with intuitively, first in

Drawing of Khlebnikov by Vladimir Mayakovsky, 1916. Reproduced by permission of VAAP.

one poem and then in another. The alliterative accidents of similar-sounding words were taken to be an internal cohesion, and to signify an unbreakable relationship. The established form of a word was considered to be permanent and some poets tried to fit it over things that went far beyond the verbal material itself.

For Khlebnikov, the word is an independent force which organizes the raw material of thoughts and feelings. Hence the delving into roots, into the source of the word, into the time when the name corresponded to things—when there were only ten root words, but new words appeared as case modifications of the root (declension of the root, according to Khlebnikov). For example, *byk* ("bull")—that which hits—*byot; bok* ("side")—the place *where* it hits. Or *lys* ("bald")—that which the forest (*les*) becomes; *los* ("elk"), *lis* ("fox")—those who live in the forest.

Take Khlebnikov's lines

> Lesa lysy.
> Lesa obezlosili. Lesa obezlisili.
> (The forests are bald / bare.
> The forests are elkless. The forests are foxless.)

These lines may not be broken apart. They are an iron chain.

The word as we think of it now is a completely arbitrary thing useful for practical purposes. But a word in its proper poetic function must express a wide variety of nuances of meaning.

Khlebnikov created an entire "periodic table of the word." Taking the word in its undeveloped unfamiliar forms, comparing these with the developed word, he demonstrated the necessity and inevitability of the emergence of new words.

If the existing word *plyas* ("dance") has a derivative *plyasunya* ("dancer"), then the growth of aviation, of "flying" (*lyot*), ought by analogy to yield the form *letunya* ("flier"). And if the day of christening is *krestiny*, then the day of flying is, of course, *letiny*. There is, of course, no trace here of cheap Slavophile slapping together of roots. It is not important that the word *letunya* is for the present neither necessary nor established in usage. Khlebnikov is simply revealing the process of word formation.

Khlebnikov, however, is a master of verse.

I've already said that Khlebnikov did not have any finished compositions. In his last piece, *Zangezi,* for example, you clearly feel that two different variants have been published together. But in studying Khlebnikov you must take into account fragments of poems that contribute to the solution of poetic problems.

In all Khlebnikov's things you are struck by his unprecedented skill. He could not only quickly write a poem upon request (his mind worked on poetry twenty-four hours a day), but he could also give things the most unusual form. He wrote a very long poem, for instance, that's simply a palindrome; it may just as easily be read from right to left as from left to right:

> Koni Topot. Inok.
> No ne rech, a cheren on.
> (Horses, Clapping, Monk.
> But no speech, black he is.)

This, of course, is just a deliberate trick, the result of an excess of poetic inventiveness. But Khlebnikov was very little interested in trickery: he made things neither for self-display nor for the market.

Philological work brought Khlebnikov to a kind of poetry that develops a lyrical theme through variations on the root of a single word.

His best known poem, **"Zaklyatie smekhom" ("Incantation by Laughter"),** published in 1909, is a favorite of poets, innovators, and parodists, and of critics too:

> O laugh it up you laughlets! . . .
> That laugh with laughs
> That laugherize laughily.
> O laugh it out so laughily . . . the laugh
> of laughish laugherators.
> (O, zasmeytes, smekhachi,
> Chto smeyutsya smekhami,
> Chto smeyanstvuyut smeyalno,
> O, issmeysya rassmeyalno smekh
> Usmeynykh smeyachey. . . .)

Here the one work *smekh* ("laughter") yields *smeyevo*, the "country of laughter," and the sly *smeyunchiki* ("laughers"), and *smekhachi* (perhaps "laughlets")—by analogy with *silachi* ("athletes").

In comparison with Khlebnikov how verbally wretched is Balmont when he attempts to construct a poem using only the word *lyubit* ("to love"):

> Love, love, love, love,
> Madly love love itself.

(Lyubite, lyubite, lyubite, lyubite,
Bezumno lyubite, lyubite lyubov.)

This is mere tautology. Mere word poverty. And this is offered as a complete definition of love! Khlebnikov once submitted for publication six pages of derivations of the root *lyub* (''love''). It couldn't be published because the provincial typographer didn't have enough of the letter ''l.'' (pp. 83-6)

In the name of preserving a just literary perspective, I consider it my certain duty to publish in my own name and, I do not doubt, in the name of my friends the poets Aseev, Burliuk, Kruchonykh, Kamensky, and Pasternak, the statement that we considered and do consider him one of our masters in the art of poetry, and a most magnificent knight in our poetic battles. (p. 88)

> *Vladimir Mayakovsky, ''V. V. Khlebnikov,'' translated by J. Rosengrant, in* Major Soviet Writers: Essays in Criticism, *edited by Edward J. Brown, Oxford University Press, 1973, pp. 83-8.*

OSIP MANDELSTAM   (essay date 1923)

[*Mandelstam was one of the leading figures of the Acmeist movement in early twentieth-century Russian poetry. Led by Nikolay Gumilev, Anna Akhmatova, and Mandelstam, the Acmeists reacted against the earlier school of the Russian Symbolists, whose works they criticized as abstract, diffuse, and alienated by mysticism from the beauty and value of the physical world. The Acmeists established a poetics that demanded concise and concrete renderings of physical reality, emphasizing a neo-Classic formalism that contrasted with what they considered the loose transcendental verbiage of the Symbolists. In the following excerpt from a 1923 essay criticizing the influence of Church Slavonic on the language of Russian poetry, Mandelstam praises Khlebnikov's colloquial style.*]

Whenever I read Pasternak's *My Sister Life,* I experience the sheer joy of the vernacular, the colloquial language, free from the superficial influences of salon speech, the common everyday tongue of Luther after the strained and, although intelligible (of course, intelligible), unnecessary Latin, that which had once been a trans-sense language, but which to the great chagrin of the monks, had long since lost its trans-sense quality. That is just how the Germans in their tile-roofed houses rejoiced when, for the first time, they opened their new Gothic bibles still smelling of printer's ink. And reading Khlebnikov can be compared to a still more magnificent and instructive event, to a situation in which our language, like a righteous man, could have and should have developed, unburdened and undesecrated by historical necessity and adversity. Khlebnikov's language is so completely the language of the laity, so completely secular, that it seems as if neither monks, nor Byzantium, nor the literature of the intelligentsia had ever existed. His speech is the absolutely secular and worldly Russian language resounding for the first time in the history of Russian letters. If we accept this view, there is no need to regard Khlebnikov as a sorceror or shaman. He projected different paths of development for the language, transitional and intermediate paths, but the historically unprecedented path of Russia's oral fate was realized only in Khlebnikov's work. It took hold there in his trans-sense language which was no more than those transitional forms which failed to conceal themselves beneath the hard crust of meaning created by a properly and piously developing language. (p. 417)

> *Osip Mandelstam, ''Some Notes on Poetry,'' translated by Jane Gary Harris, in* Russian Literature Triquarterly, *No. 6, Spring, 1973, pp. 415-18.**

YURY TYNYANOV   (essay date 1929)

[*Tynyanov was a highly respected Russian critic of the Formalist school, who, along with Nikolai Stepanov, initiated the first publication of Khlebnikov's collected works. In the following excerpt from an essay originally published in the collection* Arkhaisty i novatory *in 1929, Tynyanov discusses Khlebnikov's poetic innovations.*]

Speaking of Khlebnikov, you can avoid mentioning symbolism and futurism, and you don't have to mention trans-sense language (*zaum*) either. Because up till now such an approach has led not to a discussion of Khlebnikov, but of ''something or someone and Khlebnikov'': ''Futurism and Khlebnikov,'' ''Khlebnikov and Trans-Sense Language.'' ''Khlebnikov and Mayakovsky'' are rarely linked (but they have been), and ''Khlebnikov and Kruchonykh'' are often mentioned together.

This approach proves a false one. In the first place, both futurism and trans-sense language are not at all simple quantities, but rather complex names that cover a variety of phenomena, lexical units unifying various matters—something in the nature of a surname that serves not only people related to one another but others who happen to have the same last name.

After all, it's no accident Khlebnikov called himself *budetlyanin* (not futurist), and it is no accident that this word has not stuck.

In the second place—and this is the main point—at different times generalizations will be made according to different indicators. Generally speaking, there is no such phenomenon as a personality ''in general,'' a man ''in general'': in school his age is the standard; in a military company, his height. Military, medical, and class statistics will reckon the same person in different columns. Time passes—and time alters all generalization. And finally a time comes when there is a demand for the man himself. Writings on Pushkin treated him as a poet of romanticism, and Tyutchev as a poet of the ''German School.'' Reviewers could grasp this approach more readily, and textbooks found it more convenient.

Trends split up into schools; schools attenuate into groups.

But at this point Russian poetry and Russian literature must take a good look at Khlebnikov himself.

Why? Because suddenly a certain ''and'' of much greater proportions has come to light: ''Modern Poetry *and* Khlebnikov'' and a second ''and'' is already ripening: ''Modern Literature *and* Khlebnikov.''

When Khlebnikov died, one extremely cautious critic, perhaps just out of sheer caution, called all his work ''clumsy attempts at revitalizing language and verse'' and in the name ''not only of literary conservatives'' declared Khlebnikov's ''unpoetic poetry'' unnecessary. Of course, it all depends on what the critic understood by the word ''literature.'' If by ''literature'' we should understand the periphery of literary and journalistic production and empty-headed, cautious ideas, he is correct. But there is a profound literature engaged in a harsh struggle for a new vision that has had its fruitless successes, made the conscious ''mistakes'' it needed to make, had its decisive uprisings, negotiations, battles, and deaths. And the deaths in this business are real, not metaphoric: the deaths of men and of generations.

It is a common notion that a teacher prepares for his students' acceptance. In point of fact just the opposite occurs: appreciation and acceptance of Tyutchev were prepared for by his pupil Fet and by the symbolists. What had seemed bold but unwarranted in Tyutchev in Pushkin's time, to Turgenev seemed illiterate, and Turgenev corrected Tyutchev. The poetic periphery was leveling the center. Only the symbolists restored the real meaning of Tyutchev's metrical "illiteracy." Likewise, Rimsky-Korsakov—musicians say—corrected the "illiterate" and "gawky" Moussorgsky whose music to this very day has been published only in part. Such "illiteracies" are illiterate, only in the sense that a phonetic transcription of language is "illiterate" when compared to Grot's orthography. Many years pass while a principle ferments—subterranean and hidden—and at last it emerges onto the surface not as a "principle," but as a "phenomenon."

Khlebnikov's voice has already made itself heard in modern poetry: it has already created a ferment in the poetry of some; it has held private consultations with others. Students prepared the way for the acceptance of their teacher. The influence of his poetry is an accomplished fact. The influence of his lucid prose is a matter for the future. (pp. 89-90)

Khlebnikov said:

> It is for me, a butterfly, who has flown
> Into the room of a man's life,
> To leave the handwriting of my dust
> On the stern windows, like an inmate's autograph.

Khlebnikov's handwriting really resembled the dust a butterfly strews: the child's prism, the infantilism of the poetic word—revealed in his poetry not with "psychology," but in the very elementary, the briefest segments of words and phrases. The child and the savage were new poetic personalities who had suddenly mixed up the fixed "norms" of meter and word. A child's syntax, the infantile "look!," the sudden arbitrary shifts in the category and sense of certain words—all of this was part of a frank and outright struggle with the empty literary phrase, with literary clichés that were far removed from people and from the contemporary moment. It's useless to apply to Khlebnikov the seemingly very significant word "searches." He didn't "search," he "found."

Therefore, his individual verses have the quality of simple discoveries, just as simple and irreplaceable as certain lines of *Evgeny Onegin* were in their time:

> How often later we regret the loss of
> What we first discarded.

Khlebnikov's was a new vision. A new vision takes in various subjects simultaneously. Thus not only do these subjects "begin life in verse," according to Pasternak's remarkable formula, but they live also in the form of epic poetry.

And Khlebnikov is our only epic poet of the twentieth century. His short lyrical pieces are that same butterfly's handwriting, sudden, "infinite" notations that continue on into the distance, observations that enter into an epic, either themselves, or in a related form.

At the most crucial moments in an epic, the epic emerges out of the fairy tale. That's how *Ruslan and Lyudmila* emerged, determining Pushkin's approach to the epic and to the versified

tale of the nineteenth century; that's how Nekrasov's *Who is Happy in Russia?*, the democratic *Ruslan*, also emerged.

A pagan fairy tale was Khlebnikov's first narrative poem. Khlebnikov gave us a new "light poem" in the pre-Pushkin, eighteenth-century sense of this term, the almost anacreontic *Tale of the Stone Age (Skazka o kamennom veke)*, a new bucolic idyl: *Shaman and Venus (Shaman i Venera)*, *The Three Sisters (Tri sestry)*, and *Sylvan Sadness (Lesnaya toska)*. Of course, those who read *Harmonious World*, *Razin's Boat (Ustrug Razina)*, *Night Before the Soviets (Nochyu pered sovetami)*, and *Zangezi* will consider those other poems mere youthful things. But this doesn't lessen their importance. Such a pagan world—close at hand, bustling nearby, inconspicuously blending with our village and town—could be constructed only by an artist whose own verbal vision was new, childlike, and pagan:

> Sky-blue flowers
> Threaded by Lada into the buttonhole.

Khlebnikov didn't collect themes assigned to him from outside himself. It's unlikely that such a term—assigned theme, an assignment—existed for him. An artist's method, his personality, and his vision grow into themes by themselves. Infantilism, a primeval pagan attitude toward the world, and an ignorance of modern man naturally lead to paganism as a theme. Khlebnikov himself "predicts" his own themes. You must give consideration to the strength and completeness of this relationship to grasp how Khlebnikov, a revolutionary of the word, "predicted" the Revolution of 1917 in his article on numbers.

Futurism's bitter word battles, which demolished any notion of a gradual, happy, and planned evolution of "the word," of poetic language, were, of course, no accident. Khlebnikov's new vision, like a pagan's and a child's mixing the big and the little, could not reconcile itself to the fact that the solid, confining literary language does not hit on the most important and intimate thing, that this important, incessant thing is driven off by the literary language's "wrappings" and declared accidental. Now for Khlebnikov, the accidental became art's primal element.

And so it is in science also. Small mistakes, "accidents," explained by the older scientists as errors due to imperfect experiments, serve as stimuli for new discoveries: what had been explained as an "imperfect experiment" turns out to be the action of unknown laws.

Khlebnikov the theoretician becomes the Lobachevsky of the word: he does not find minor shortcomings in old systems, but discovers a new order, which results from the accidental displacement of those systems.

The new vision—very intimate, almost infantile (the "butterfly")—turned out to be a new order of words and of things.

People hastened to oversimplify his language theory—luckily it was called "trans-sense language"—reassuring themselves that Khlebnikov had created a "meaningless sound speech" *(zvukorech)*. This is inaccurate. The whole essence of his theory is that he transferred the center of gravity in poetry from the issue of sound to that of meaning. For him no sound is uncolored by meaning, and the questions of "meter" and "theme" do not live separate existences. "Instrumentation," which had had the function of a kind of onomatopoeia, in his hands became a weapon to alter meaning, to revive a word's long-forgotten kinship with its near relatives, and to find new grounds for kinship with words that heretofore had been strangers.

The "dreamer" did not separate his daily existence from dreaming, life from poetry. His vision became a new order, and he himself a "transport engineer of artistic language." "There are no transport engineers of language," he wrote. "Who would travel from Moscow to Kiev via New York? And yet what line of modern poetic language is free from such trips?" He preaches the "explosion of the language of silence, of the deaf-and-dumb layers of language." Those who think his language is "meaningless" do not see how a revolution is simultaneously a new order. Those who talk of Khlebnikov's "nonsense" should reconsider this question. It is not nonsense, but a new semantic system. Not only was Lomonosov "nonsensical" (this "nonsense" provoked Sumarokov's parodies), but there are parodies (many of them) of Zhukovsky in which this poet—whose work is now used as a primer for children—is ridiculed for his "nonsense." Fet was sheer nonsense to Dobrolyubov. All poets, even those who only partially altered the semantic system, have been declared nonsensical, but were later understood, not all by themselves, but because their readers rose to the level of the new semantic system. Blok's early verses were not easily "comprehensible," but who does not "comprehend" them now? But those who nevertheless wish to locate the Khlebnikov question's center of gravity precisely on the issue of poetic nonsense should read his prose: *Nikolay, The Hunter Usa Gali (Okhotnik Usa-Gali), Ka,* and so forth. This prose, semantically as clear as Pushkin's, will convince them that "nonsense" is not at all the issue, but a new semantic system, and that this system with different material yields different results—from Khlebnikov's trans-sense language, (meaningful, and not nonsensical) to the "logic" of his prose. (pp. 92-6)

[An] exact, authentic transcript of human conversation, without any authorial elucidation, will seem meaningless. Khlebnikov's variable verse lines (first an iamb, then a trochee, a masculine ending followed by a feminine) contribute even to traditional verse language a variable semantic content, a special kind of sense.

Khlebnikov's verse is certainly not a linguistic collage. Rather it is modern man's intimate language, given as though accidentally overheard, with its abruptness, its mingling of a high style and domestic details, together with that sharp precision that modern science has given to language. At the same time it contains the infantilism of the modern city-dweller. We have commentaries on his poem **"Gul-Mulla"** by a man who knew Khlebnikov during his sojourn in Persia—and each fleeting image turns out to be perfectly exact, not "retold" in a literary fashion, but created afresh.

Before the tribunal of Khlebnikov's new system literary traditions have been laid wide open. An enormous displacement of traditions results. Suddenly the ancient *Tale of Igor's Campaign* proves more modern than Bryusov. Pushkin enters the new system, not in hard, unchewed clumps that stylists like to flaunt, but transformed:

> Apparently that's how the sky wished
> To serve mysterious Fate,
> So as to instill in all who exist
> A cry for love and bread.

Lomonosov's and Pushkin's odes, the *Tale of Igor's Campaign,* and the "Sobakevna" section from **"The Night before the Soviets"** that echoes Nekrasov, are unrecognizable as "traditional": they have been incorporated into a new system.

Khlebnikov was able to produce a revolution in literature for the very reason that his system was not a closed literary one. His system gives meaning to the language of verse and the language of numbers, to chance conversations on the street, and to events from world history; for him the methods of literary revolution and historical revolution were similar. His long historical poem on numbers may not be scientific, and his angle of vision may be only a poetic one, but *Harmonious World,* **"Razin's Boat," "The Night before the Soviets,"** the sixteenth fragment of *Zangezi,* and *The Night Search (Nochnoi obysk)* may be the most important of all verses on the Revolution.

> If the fist concealed a knife,
> While vengeance dilated wide the pupils of her eyes,
> It's Time that set up a howl: "Give!"
> While dutiful Fate answered: "Aye, aye, sir!"

Poetry is similar to science in its methods—this is what Khlebnikov teaches us.

It must be like a scientific discovery that meets the facts. And this means that, when faced with the accidental, it must reorganize itself so that the accidental ceases to be accidental.

The poet who regards the word and verse as objects, the importance and usage of which he has known for a long time (and so they have begun to bore him), will regard an everyday object as a hopelessly old acquaintance however new the object may be. The role of poet requires that a man regard things either looking down from above (satire), or looking up from below (ode), or with his eyes shut (song). Then, too, poets who write for magazines also have an "aside" look, an "in general" look.

But Khlebnikov looks at things the way a scientist, penetrating into a process and its movement, regards phenomena—he views them from the same level. He has abandoned traditional poetic roles.

He finds nothing in poetry dilapidated (from the "ruble" to "nature"). He doesn't write of things "in general." He does have a personal thing. It courses on, correlated with the entire world, and is, therefore, valuable.

For him there are no "base" things.

His village poets don't view villages like a condescending urbanite sitting in his summer cottage. (How much smugness there is in our village lyric, in these village ditties about rye and blue-eyed homesteaders. They're not reminiscent of Karamzin—no chance of that. They're reminiscent of Volf's children's books: there the pictures of children presented them as pint-size little men with large heads, but without moustaches.) The same holds true for the East: the East in **"Gul-mullah's Trumpet" ("Truba Gul-mully")** isn't European: there's no condescending interest, no exaggerated respect. On the same level—that's how the dimensions of themes change, and how they are reappraised.

This is possible only when the word itself is regarded as something like an atom, with its own processes and its own structure.

Khlebnikov is not a word collector, not a property owner, and not a wise guy seeking to startle. He looks upon words as a scientist, and he reappraises their dimensions.

And so Khlebnikov's poetic personality was constantly changing: the wise man of Zangezi, the pagan of the forest, the child-poet, Gul-mullah (the priest of flowers), and the Russian dervish, as they called him in Persia, was, at the same time, also an engineer of the word. (pp. 96-8)

No school and no trend can claim this man. His poetry is just as inimitable as that of any poet. And you can learn from him, only first trace the paths of his development and his starting points, first study his methods. Because in his methods is the ethic of the new poet. This is the ethic of attention and fearlessness: attention to the ''accidental'' (but actually characteristic and real), which is overwhelmed by rhetoric and blinded by habit; the fearlessness of the honest poetic word which goes onto the paper without any literary ''wrapping paper''—the fearlessness of the right word that has no substitute, and is ''not panhandled from the neighbors'' as Vyazemsky put it. And what if this word is childish, if sometimes the most banal word is the most honest of all? But this is precisely Khlebnikov's daring—and his freedom. Without exception, all the literary schools of our time live by prohibition: you can't do this, you can't do that, this is banal, that is ludicrous. Khlebnikov existed in a state of poetic freedom which in every given case was a matter of necessity. (p. 99)

> *Yury Tynyanov, ''On Khlebnikov,'' translated by Charlotte Rosenthal, in* Major Soviet Writers: Essays in Criticism, *edited by Edward J. Brown, Oxford University Press, 1973, pp. 89-99.*

Drawing of Khlebnikov by Porfiry Krylov, 1922. Reproduced by permission of VAAP.

MAURICE BOWRA   (essay date 1944)

[*Bowra, an English critic and literary historian, was considered among the foremost classical scholars of the first half of the twentieth century. He also wrote extensively on modern literature, particularly modern European poetry, in studies noted for their erudition, lucidity, and straightforward style. In the following excerpt, he discusses the ways in which Khlebnikov reconciled intellectual and emotional elements in his poetry.*]

Vladimir Khlebnikov . . . was a strangely compounded character. On the one hand he was a creative philologist, a man who loved words so well and had so fine a feeling for his own language, that he was always experimenting with it, inventing new words, trying old words in new combinations, feeling his way to some essential, primitive Russian which should be more expressive than the time-worn instrument of contemporary literature. On the other hand he was a prophet of the primitive and the irrational, of all those apprehensions and suspicions which uncivilised man feels because he cannot rationalise them. Khlebnikov was extremely superstitious in his own life and felt most at home among primitive peoples or in stories of men and women who are not moved by reason. The combination of such characteristics is uncommon, but it was well suited to Futurism which both claimed an interest in the creation of new words and denied the rational nature of man. Marinetti had called for 'the word at liberty' and claimed the superiority of intuition to intelligence. Khlebnikov in his own way agreed with him. He wished to change his language not so much because he was tired of it as because he was by temperament an experimental philologist; he would have little to do with the civilised and rational way of looking at things because he was at heart uncivilised and primitive, a Slav who wished to get back to the soul of his race before Christianity and Westernisation had imposed their patterns on it, a man of letters who enjoyed displaying his skill at catching and conveying all the stranger shadows which pass over the human consciousness.

With an equipment like this Khlebnikov could hardly expect to be a popular poet. Nor was he. He is important because he exerted a considerable influence on other poets and because his poetry is, despite its oddities, valuable for its own sake. It took him time to find subjects which suited him, and his early work has an experimental character. He invented words, he played with roots and formations, and in his **"Oath by Laughter"** he created a whole poem of newly coined derivatives from the Russian word for 'laughter,' *smekh*. It is a brilliant *tour de force*, amusing and wonderfully ingenious. Indeed the new words look strangely convincing to a foreigner. But as yet Khlebnikov's difficulty was to find subjects suited to this philological inventiveness, and it is not surprising that he sought out themes extremely remote from the modern world, in the Stone Age or the old Slavonic world. His manner varies with his subjects, but tends to be impressionistic and even telegraphic. His treatment of syntax can be seen from his use of proper names as imperatives:

> Farm-house at night—Genghiz Khan!
> Rustle, grey birches.
> Red sky at night—Zarathrustra!
> But blue sky—Mozart!

His Futurism, despite its primitive emotions, still keeps a highbrow air. There is a discord between his emotions and his intellect which he has not fully solved.

The solution was found for him by the War and the Revolution. Like other Russian poets, Khlebnikov viewed the war with horror and the Revolution with rapturous joy. If the first simplified his manner for him and drove him to express himself in a noble, austere manner, the second awoke in him an ecstatic excitement in liberty and a sense of vast new prospects opening to the future. While other poets saw the revolution as a tragic event needed to purify Russia, Khlebnikov, who had been sent to prison for political reasons when a student, saw a new, vivifying force which should animate Russia to great activities and creation. In the first thrill of it he wrote poems which are almost like songs:

> Now naked comes Liberty walking
> And on hearts scatters flowers of love;
> We march on in step with her, talking
> Like old friends to the skies above.
>
> We are fighters whose hands never quiver
> When they bang on a resolute shield.
> There and here, and for ever, for ever
> The people its power shall wield.
>
> From the windows let singing girls praise us,
> Of age-old campaigns are their songs,
> Of the Sun, whose true service obeys us,
> Of the People, to whom rule belongs.

A great simplification has taken place in Khlebnikov's style. The neologisms and learned, literary references have gone; the syntax is easy and straightforward. What remains is the vivid use of imagery to convey excited states of mind.

The Revolution demanded and created other emotions than this, and in his poems from 1917 to his death in 1922 Khlebnikov found a proper field for his talents in a new kind of heroic theme. The poet Gumilev said of him, 'Many of his verses seem to be the fragments of a great epic which has never been written.' Khlebnikov wrote several poems which breathe a heroic spirit of rebellion. In some he touches on the present; in others he deals with themes from the past which were relevant to his time. His poem on Stenka Razin is a fine attempt to catch the spirit of the old rebel, who is the type of natural man asserting his rights:

> And Razin's choked ' I listen'
> Rises up to the hills of day
> As a red flag flies on a roof-top
> And tells of troops on the way.

So too Khlebnikov used the figure of a wise philosopher in **"Ladomir"** to tell of the far-reaching aspirations which the revolution woke in him for a Utopian future when men should be in harmony with nature and with each other:

> You shall set up on earth a spool
> Where the thunder is only a wire
> And with streams and dragonflies
> Sing the girl of your desire,
> A sign that all is levelled
> Between labour and idleness.

He held such hopes of the revolution, and he died before they could be disappointed.

Khlebnikov was fully aware of what the revolution meant in horror and destruction, and his poems about it were characteristically sincere. He recognised the facts, but believed that something incalculably magnificent would arise from them. The mixture of his intellectual grasp and his high hopes is well displayed in **"I believe, sang the guns,"** It is a vision of the revolutionary scene in which the powers of new gods are revealed, and it hints at horrors of revenge and brutality:

> The god of the pavements,
> Painted in yesterday's blood,
> In the briars of fresh graves,
> In the bandages of sniping armies,
> Looks from public places at night
> With the large eyes of death,
> In a frame of cobble-stones.
> The picture of a grim god
> On a grey board
> Set up by the hands of the days
> Hangs over the capital.

Khlebnikov dwells on the storm of destruction and the passions which drive it, on the death-sentences given in cellars, on the shattering of glass by bullets, on the eyes staring 'like two gun-barrels,' on the noise of an alarm in the sky. Then he rises to his close:

> The poplar we felled, the poplar in salvoes
> Fell to the ground in leaves of lead
> On the crowds, on the public places!
> The poplar we felled, crashed, fell
> Covering with death's leaves the faces of many.
> All night long screams the iron rattle,
> And stars croak over the roof of the death-chamber.
> The night is blacker than pitch. . . .
> Multitudes of stars, multitudes of birds
> Suddenly rise in the air.
> I have startled them.

In this way Khlebnikov not only said what he felt about the revolution but found a means to reconcile his own conflicting gifts. In a highly sensitive and intellectual style he wrote about the primitive feelings which were at the root of his nature. (pp. 71-4)

> *Maurice Bowra, "Futurism and Poetry," in* The Cornhill Magazine, *Vol. 161, No. 961, January, 1944, pp. 68-79.**

VICTOR ERLICH   (essay date 1952)

[*Erlich is a Russian émigré educator and critic who has written extensively on Russian literature. In the following excerpt, he discusses Khlebnikov's "trans-sense" language.*]

For the spokesmen of prerevolutionary Russian Futurism, subject matter was a minor consideration. . . . Attention was focused on the outward form or sensory texture of the linguistic symbol rather than on its communicative value, on the sign rather than on its object. Indeed, a deliberate attempt was made to loosen the bond between the two, to emancipate the word, as Kruchonykh put it, from its "traditional subservience to meaning."

This revolt against meaning found its expression in the slogan of "trans-sense language" (*zaumny i yazyk*). The most extreme proponents of this notion were Kruchonykh and V. Kamensky. They tried to write verse composed solely of arbitrary combinations of sounds, and they advertised their accomplishments as vastly superior in expressiveness and vigor to Pushkin's and Lermontov's feeble attempts.

If these rather crude experiments with nonsense syllables could be dismissed as an example of Bohemian extravagance, V. Khlebnikov's poetic discoveries attest to a much higher degree of artistic maturity and linguistic virtuosity. A "tireless pathfinder of language," Khlebnikov was too keenly aware of the organic relationship between sound and meaning to become the apostle of pure euphony. His verse, obscure and elliptic though it is, cannot, contrary to the widely held belief, be described as completely devoid of "sense." It is rather, to quote Jakobson's acute study of Khlebnikov, poetry with a "toned-down" semantics. The basic unit of Khlebnikov's bizarre idiom is not the individual sound, nor the syllable, but the morpheme; the latter, be it a root or an affix, is bound to have a certain, at least a potential, meaning. Khlebnikov's avowed, though obviously unattainable, goal was to "find, without breaking out of the bewitched circle of the roots, the philosopher's stone of the mutual transformations of Slavic words, to fuse freely the Slavic words." His favorite procedure was to break down the familiar words into their morphological components, which he then reshuffled at will and reintegrated into new verbal units, poetic neologisms. One of Khlebnikov's poems, **"Incantation by Laughter,"** is based on an astoundingly ingenious play with formants; it consists almost entirely of newly coined derivatives from the root *smekh* (Russian for "laugh").

The use of poetic neologisms is typical of Khlebnikov's attitude toward language. The words he invented were always certain to carry a number of connotations, however vague and embryonic; but they did not have, as a rule, any denotative value. As products of the poet's linguistic fancy, they clearly did not correspond or refer to any identifiable aspect of objective reality. One is reminded, in dealing with his bold innovations, of the fruitful distinction made by Husserl between the "meaning" of the word and its "object." Speaking in Husserlian terms, one could say that many of Khlebnikov's verbal formations have an approximate "meaning" but are apparently free from the "object." The semantic value of the newly coined word does not bear any direct relation to extralinguistic reality. It is contingent upon purely linguistic factors, notably the components or the inner structure of the sign and upon the general semantic aura provided by the context. The meaning of the poetic neologism is flexible, oscillating, dynamic. The slogan of the "self-sufficient word" thus became a reality. The customary relation between the linguistic symbol and the referent was reversed. In "practical" language the sign is obviously subordinated to the object to which it points. In Khlebnikov's "trans-sense" verse the object appears, if at all, as a faint echo of the sign; it is overshadowed by the whimsical interplay of the word's potential meanings. (pp. 67-9)

> Victor Erlich, "Russian Poets in Search of a Poetics," in Comparative Literature, Vol. IV, No. 1, Winter, 1952, pp. 54-74.*

VLADIMIR MARKOV   (essay date 1960)

[*Markov is a Russian-born American educator and critic specializing in modern Russian poetry. Considered by Helen Muchnic "one of the most perceptive, scholarly, and original" critics of modern Russian literature, Markov is the author of the first comprehensive study of Russian Futurism and of the highly regarded study* The Longer Poems of Velimir Khlebnikov (1962). In the following excerpt, he surveys Khlebnikov's longer poems.]

A separate edition of all Khlebnikov's longer poems (*poemy*) could be a fine introduction to his work. They form a world of their own within his work, and they are more revealing and representative of his true poetic nature than either his ambitious "supertales" (*sverkhpovesti*), to which he attached so much

importance, or the numerous experimental sketches which were extolled beyond their real importance by his admirers. There is much more unity, spontaneity and organic development in these poems than in any other literary category attempted by Khlebnikov. In them he displays his true originality, supreme artistry and infinite variety. In short, it is in his *poemy* that Khlebnikov shows what he really is: a major Russian poet and a giant of twentieth-century poetry.

Three of Khlebnikov's "little tragedies," the ballads **"Maria Vetsera"** (*Mariya Vechora*), **"Juno's Lover"** (*Lyubovnik Yunony*) and **"Alchak"** already contain many features which are characteristic of his longer poems. These seem to be early works, probably written around 1908, and they prepare for and anticipate his *poemy* in many respects.

Possibly the earliest genuine *poema* by Khlebnikov is his **"The Tsar's Bride"** (*Tsarskaya nevesta*), presumably written in 1908, which forms a curious finale to the popular tradition of romantic poems portraying Ivan the Terrible and his time. At the beginning of this tradition stands Lermontov's "Song of the Merchant Kalashnikov" (1837), and the period of its greatest popularity is linked with the name of Alexey K. Tolstoy. Despite the associations with L. Mey evoked by the title, Khlebnikov's work is based on a different source, "The Tsarina Maria Dolgoruky" by A. A. Navrotsky (1839-1905), a forgotten third-rate poet of the seventies (a fact never noted by Khlebnikov scholars). Its five episodes remind one of five acts in some Russian opera, presented, however, as though seen through the eyes of a child. In this poem Khlebnikov already appears as a mature artist with an original technique. The melodramatic story is charmingly touched with infantilism, and the scene where the heroine is drowned is full of strange beauty.

"Malusha's Granddaughter" (*Vnuchka Malushi*), written in 1909, marks a shift by Khlebnikov to more ancient times and away from the centers of Russian empire, Moscow and Petersburg. This trend towards decentralization meant much to him. Partly based on the Primary Russian Chronicle and filled with pagan Slavic mythology, which will play an important part in Khlebnikov's later *poemy*, this work is placed in the time of Prince Vladimir and in some respects resembles Pushkin's "Russlan and Ludmilla." Though obviously a part of the contemporary symbolist infatuation with Russian paganism (see works by A. Remizov, S. Gorodetsky and K. Balmont in 1907-08), **"Malusha's Granddaughter"** belongs to the older and greater tradition of the "Russian" poem of the eighteenth and nineteenth centuries, which includes the names of Radishchev, Vostokov, Zhukovsky, Batyushkov, Pushkin (see his plan of "Mstislav") and Katenin. The poem shows the poet's first-hand familiarity with the Old Russian language. The second part of the poem rather surrealistically brings the heroine to the Petersburg of the twentieth century, and it ends with a bitter satire on contemporary university education.

"Malusha's Granddaughter" marks the beginning of the period of Khlebnikov's life and work which may be called the Petersburg period. It extends from 1908, when he enrolled in the University of Petersburg, to 1916, when he was drafted. Although, biographically, Khlebnikov visited many places and traveled continuously during that time, he kept returning to Petersburg's literary life. In a few *poemy*, the city appears directly (**"Malusha's Granddaughter," "The Crane"**) or indirectly (**"The End of Atlantis"**).

Another *poema* of 1909, **"The Crane"** (*Zhuravl*) is a surrealistic Petersburg fantasy, worthy of a place in the Pushkin-

Gogol Dostoevsky-Bely tradition. Though it pays tribute to Symbolism in its Brysov-like atmosphere of apocalyptic urbanism, its main theme, the revolt of inanimate objects, anticipates Mayakovsky whose "Vladimir Mayakovsky" (1913), "Mystery-Bouffe" (1918) and "150,000,000" (1919-1920) are direct offshoots of **"The Crane,"** both thematically and rhythmically. A similar eschatological mood permeates **"The Serpent Trains"** (*Zmei poezda*), written in 1910, with its vision of a monstrous dragon devouring the passengers on a train who are hardly aware of the danger. This interesting example of Khlebnikov's didactic Symbolism with its "return to nature" message is always overlooked by critics and scholars. It is reminiscent of Alexey K. Tolstoy's "The Dragon" and of Dante's *Commedia*.

Also in 1910, Khlebnikov wrote a *poema* which constitutes an exception among the rest because it is based on neologisms. His preoccupation with the coining of new words is well-known, but it is rather surprising to find only one long poem reflecting this tendency. This poem was entitled, presumably not by the author, **"The War, the Death"** (*Voyna-smert*), and it is again exceptional among Khlebnikov's epics because of its essentially lyrical character. In fact, it is reminiscent of the grandeur of the eighteenth-century ode, and its partly obscure message consists of dark prophesies. The title is a misnomer since many images have revolutionary rather than martial connotations. The poem shows Khlebnikov's profound disillusionment and his regrets about his country's being split into two irreconcilable political camps.

In 1911 begins what can be termed the flowering of primitivism in Khlebnikov's work. Prehistoric background attracts him now, and in **"The Forest Maiden"** (*Lesnaya deva*) we find a kind of Russian Stone Age with naked lovers surrounded by primeval forests. The protagonists are part of nature: they even lack names. The poem begins with a passionate tryst, but ends in a duel of two rivals and the death of one of them. Nevertheless, this does not deprive the poem of a unique lightness and charm. Its nearest equivalent in the arts would be the paintings of Henri Rousseau.

The Stone Age of **"I and E"** (*I i E*) is less abstract, and Khlebnikov even adds some mythological and anthropological details in his attempts to portray prehistoric society, its religion and priesthood, its hunting and fishing ways. There is a rare poetic enchantment in this story of two lovers who seek death but find happiness and glory. From several points of view this poem may be considered one of Khlebnikov's early masterpieces. Its metrical balance, the subtlety with which the poet puts together the episodes, the diversity of his primitivistic technique, and unusual freshness and lightness make it one of his best achievements.

The first of Khlebnikov's *poemy* to appear in a separate edition was written by him in collaboration with Alexey Kruchonykh in 1912. This grotesque picture of a card game in hell, played by devils and sinners, is entitled **"A Game in Hell"** (*Igra v adu*) and has its source in Pushkin's "Sketches to the *Faust*-work" (1825).

A return to tragedy, while still retaining the primitivistic flavor, can be observed in another *poema* of 1912, **"The End of Atlantis"** (*Gibel Atlantidy*). The two protagonists in this work, a priest and a slave girl, personify rationalism and instinct. After the priest, provoked by the girl, kills her, revenge begins, and the poem ends in the eschatological spectacle of a flood. There is something of the somber beauty of Pushkin's "Bronze Horseman" in this poem's tragically fantastic atmosphere, in the predominance of classical outline, and, finally, in the description of the flood. Its verse is more stabilized and its composition shows a simplicity and finish rare in Khlebnikov's poetry.

After the Atlantis poem, peace and idyllic life are restored in Khlebnikov's *poemy*, and this can be found in purest form in **"A Villa and a Wood-Goblin"** (*Vila i leshy*). There is very little action in this Russian version of "L'Après-midi d'un faune," and the greater part of the poem consists of the mischievous coquettish Slavic nymph's rondo-like teasing of a lazy, old wood-goblin. This is interspersed with a description of a hot day. In contradistinction to the preceding poem, it looks like a draft lazily sketched on a hot day similar to the one described in the poem.

The next idyll, written also in 1912 and entitled **"A Witch-Doctor and Venus"** (*Shaman i Venera*) has much in common with the preceding *poema*. Here Venus, tired of the West, appears in the cave of an old, impassive Siberian witch-doctor, who remains unmoved by her feminine subtlety. This is a twentieth-century mock-heroic poem with stress on absurd contrast, nonsense and irrelevance. The poem is full of logical contradictions, grotesque exaggeration, tautological constructions and literary parody.

The ties of Russian Futurism with the eighteenth century have been noted by several scholars, but there have never been any studies of this relationship. In earlier poems one could observe Khlebnikov within such eighteenth-century traditions as the mock-heroic poem, the "Russian" poem, and the high ode. In **"Khadzhi-Tarkhan"** (1913), Khlebnikov's tribute to his native city of Astrakhan, he resurrects another genre largely neglected during the nineteenth century: the descriptive poem. It is a succession of landscapes, historical episodes and meditations on history, which follow each other in seemingly haphazard fashion. It is also a poem of vast spaces and great distances, occasionally extending Russia to the borders of India, ancient Egypt, and Assyria. These great vistas, in combination with a kind of golden languor which covers all like patina, make the poem an inimitable work deserving the name of masterpiece. Its verse moves like the Volga it describes, which begins and ends the poem and is felt throughout the entire poem. Also masterful are his use of epithets, condensation of meaning in a single line, variety of color and the force and precision of some of his images.

There is more tired blood in **"Rustic Friendship"** (*Selskaya druzhba*), probably written in 1913. This is a romantic poem whose plot is based on mystery and whose locale is in the Western part of Russia. It imitates, in fact almost parodies, the Russian Byronic poems of the 1820's and the 1830's, although hand in hand with this there are distinct elements of icon-painting which hardly blend with complexly constructed similes and other tropes and elaborate rhyming patterns.

The shorter **"Rural Enchantment"** (*Selskaya ocharovannost*), while still an idyll, marks a turn towards realism both in the portrayal of protagonists and in a wealth of detail of everyday life, which sometimes makes the poem resemble a Dutch painting. For the first time, a Khlebnikov *poema* is not a romantic reproduction of history or a mythological fantasy but a slice of contemporary life, devoid, however, of any social element. It builds an excellent bridge from Khlebnikov's early "passéism" to his attempts "to face reality" after the Revolution of 1917.

The first six *poemy* written after the Revolution belong to what may be called the Kharkov period in Khlebnikov's life (1919-20). They are tied to each other not only thematically or stylistically but also geographically. In many respects Khlebnikov continues to write in Kharkov in his old idiom, but attempts to abandon or to modify the old habits are also discernible. He turns more and more to the nineteenth-century tradition in his rhyme, verse melody, imagery and sound. Lyricism and meditation take the place of illogical primitivism and persiflage. Now he posits problems and tries to solve them on other than an esthetic level. Contemporary events now appear directly in Khlebnikov's works, but all these new elements appear more or less shyly and the old manner still prevails.

"A Night in a Trench" (*Noch v okope*), written in 1919, is a typical work of Khlebnikov's intermediate period. One finds in it remnants of the early periods, a growing conservatism, some important new elements, and starting points for the development of subsequent Soviet poetry. The theme is the Revolution and the Civil War of 1917-20, but historical details do not contradict a certain timelessness added to the whole by the fact that the ancient Scythian stone statues watch the battle between the Reds and the Whites. The epic, non-realist cavalry attack is reminiscent in spirit, if not in content, of the *Igor-Tale*. Although the poet's Communist sympathies here are unmistakable, Khlebnikov's presentation is a far cry from the familiar clichés of Soviet poetry about the Civil War. This difference becomes even more clear with Khlebnikov's portrayal of Lenin, multi-dimensional, unorthodox and very much superior to that of Mayakovsky, not to mention the pathetic endeavors of lesser poets.

"A Stone Woman" (*Kamennaya baba*) is a little sister of the preceding *poema;* a lyrical variation on the same theme unjustly neglected even by Khlebnikov's admirers. It is the same battlefield with ancient statues, except that there is no battle, and a poet, "the last painter of the unheard-of terror on earth," bewails the death of thousands in the Civil War, as Khlebnikov did in the earlier **"The War, the Death."** The second part of the poem, however, is a magnificent dance, a "blue hopak," which reaches universal proportions, sparkling with richness of color, meter and rhyme.

The most important *poema* of the period is, in my opinion, **"The Poet"** (*Poet*). Here Khlebnikov deepens his favorite genre of idyll and achieves a synthesis of the primitivism of his early work with the classical elements which now come to the fore. The splendid introductory lines, mixing heaviness and lightness, give a picture of autumn which turns out to be a part of an elaborate simile of the colorful spring carnival which opens the poem. **"The Poet"** is written with quiet nonchalance in the use of rhyme and rhythmic variations. However, the poem's carnival is only a background to the three lone and sad figures: the poet, the water nymph (*rusalka*), and the Mother of God. Paganism, Christianity and poetry are clearly the outcasts in the post-revolutionary world of crowds and science.

Echoes of crisis and disillusionment are still heard in **"The Sylvan Sadness"** (*Lesnaya toska*), Khlebnikov's last mythological poem and last idyll. Written in the form of an operatic libretto, this is primarily a poem of sound, but under this display of sonic splendor there is deep sadness, and it is the poet's sadness, since none of the fantastic creatures that populate the poem is sad. It is Khlebnikov's farewell to his beloved world of pagan mythology, a yearning for a paradise lost, and there is irony in the arrival of the morning at the end of the poem. The morning is too simple, too realistic, too trivial and

it drives away all those likable villas, water nymphs and wood-goblins.

With the disappearance of pagan mythology, paganism remains still in Khlebnikov's watercolor-like **"Three Sisters"** (*Tri sestry*), his shortest *poema*. Here, in the portraits of his three friends, one finds water nymphs and ancient Slavic amazons who only pretend to be women of our century. This pantheistic idyll may be an escape on the part of the poet from the grim realities of the Civil War. It is unusually lyrical and puts unusual stress on religious imagery, which, in its complexity, stands in contrast to the simplicity of conception and style.

The last, and longest, of the Kharkov poems, **"Ladomir,"** is an ambitious work which was meant to be an encyclopedia of Khlebnikov's ideas on and dreams about the future of mankind. It has been called "the sum total of Khlebnikov's poetry" (Tynyanov), and is a rather belated, really Futurist work by a poet whose love for the past had tended, until then, to make him a contradictory figure, with the exception of his one poem about the future: the grim fantasy **"The Crane."** Whereas Khadzhi-Tarkhan was a city of beloved past, Ladomir is the name of the city of the future, where universal harmony is achieved and technological and scientific progress helps mankind towards its ultimate happiness. Khlebnikov the Utopian, the author of fantastic projects, a revolutionary, a rationalist idyllist, displays here the infinite variety and richness of his outlandish ideas and gives poetic realization to his numerous dreams. The poem appears to be a disorderly succession of passages, with a chaotic mixture of past and future, repetitious and overly long; but in this conglomeration there is a distinct direction and movement. It is like a procession, multicolored, heterogeneous, but advancing step by step. This loud picture of the future which can be identified with socialism, containing anti-religious passages and poster-like denunciations of the tsarist past, could not fail to produce bravos on the part of the Soviet critics. But it is even more interesting in its maintaining the tone of the eighteenth-century ode, echoing the ideas of the philosopher Nikolai Fyodorov (1828-1903) and the mathematician Nikolai Lobachevsky (1792-1856), playing with proper names, dialect words and slang as well as making moderate use of his own "trans-rational language" (*zaum*). In many respects, in this *poema* Khlebnikov seems to be taking his last inventory before saying good-bye to the old devices.

The ten poems written after Kharkov, form a definitely new stage in Khlebnikov's development. Contemporary themes dominate now. Even more than that, most poems of this time are about what Khlebnikov actually saw. The previous fantasies give place to a clear vision of things before him. One may call it "realism" if one likes, but the very intensity of this realism makes one remember Dostoevsky's famous words about being "a realist in a higher sense." Primitivistic technique is now abandoned almost completely; direct vision reigns instead of literary controversy, game or dream as was the case before. The very fact of Khlebnikov's wanderings through Caucasus and Iran during these years (1920-1921) may partly account for this fact: he was alone in the wide world, far from the literary circles of Moscow and Petrograd.

However, **"Razin,"** the first draft of which was written when Khlebnikov was still in Kharkov, is more in the old tradition of a literary game. It is probably the longest palindromic poem in the world, in which each of its 408 lines also reads backwards. Though an exception among Khlebnikov's *poemy*, **"Razin"** is only an attempt to enlarge upon what Khlebnikov tried to do before on a smaller scale. It can also be easily placed in the context of Russian Futurism, Russian folklore and the now still largely ignored baroque tradition. But for Khlebnikov it was more than a verbal exercise. It was a comparison of two destinies, Stepan Razin's and his own, which are identical, but which are moving in opposite directions. It is also a series of magnificent tableaux depicting Razin's story. Despite the fact that the palindromic structure seems bound to hamper the natural flow of poetic emotion, some parts are seething with energy, and the poem's consonantism is naturally and properly rough, barbaric, and picturesque.

One of Khlebnikov's supreme masterpieces is **"Gul-mullah's Trumpet"** (*Truba gul-mully*), the poetic diary of his visit to Persia with the Red Army in 1921. Hardly anything in Russian poetry approximates it in directness of poetic vision. It develops simultaneously on the symbolic and on the realistic levels, and all details seen by the poet have the quality of being seen for the first time, with eyes wide open. Khlebnikov had dreamt about the Orient all his life, and here it was right before him. The poem sings all the way through as befits the fulfillment of a life-time dream. These jottings-down are full of a special kind of lyricism which leaves reality's outlines and colors intact but makes them more intense than in "real life." Pure enjoyment of this kind can only be found in the works of European poets on their first visits to Italy.

The next three *poemy* form what sometimes is called Khlebnikov's "triptych of retribution" (a theme which attracted Khlebnikov long before the Revolution), and they are all about the Russian Revolution of 1917. They are essentially unfinished drafts, and between two of them it is even hard to draw a line: they are two versions of the same plan. The post-Kharkov period gave birth to Khlebnikov's best and worst poetry. These three are among the most unsuccessful ones, full of propagandistic crudities and even betraying a certain lack of interest on the part of the author. The meaning of the Revolution is simple for Khlebnikov: the nobility and the rich pay for their past sins. This theme sounds clearly in the long-winded **"The Night Before the Soviets"** (*Noch pered Sovetami*), which is a conversation between a nervous noblewoman (kind, compassionate and even with a leftist political past, but doomed and destined to pay for the crimes of her ancestors) and her old housekeeper who does not spare her mistress's feelings by prophesying that she will be hanged. The greater part of this work is taken up by the old woman's story of her grandmother, who was ordered by her master to breast-feed young puppies. This part is unbearably long, written in a slipshod manner and contains too much of cheap melodrama. The only interesting element is the influence of the poet N. A. Nekrasov. The second poem, **"The Washerwoman"** (*Prachka*), is a disorganized mass of raw material, but it is perfectly clear that Khlebnikov's idea of the real forces of the Revolution is far from the orthodox Soviet viewpoint. For him the Revolution is made by and for the *Lumpenproletariat,* and he portrays in detail the beggars and the underworld who, before the rebellion, found shelter amid piles of warm horse dung at the city dump in Petersburg. The other side of the conflict is presented in **"The Present"** (*Nastoyashchee*), the most finished and successful work of the triptych. The old regime is symbolized in the Grand Duke, who is presented as a tragic figure, somewhat naïve, but unquestionably noble in his stoic acceptance of the retribution. In striking contrast is the second part, a series of choruses after the Grand Duke's monologue. It is extremely rich in inflections and declamatory forms which anticipate many later attempts by Soviet poets (*e.g.,* Ilya Selvinsky's phonetic experiments and songs in Mayakovsky's "It's Good!").

The theme of **"A Night Search"** (*Nochnoi obysk*) is still the Revolution as retribution, but it is a far cry from the triptych. In fact, it is the peak of Khlebnikov's tragic art. This is a picture of a search by revolutionary sailors of a bourgeois apartment, during which they shoot a young officer and are later burned alive by his mother. No other Soviet poet would dare to write this tale in which a Red learns courage from a White and uses it in a Nietzschean combat with God, of which the outcome remains an enigma. Khlebnikov, in a truly tragic, objective way, takes no sides. He only shows how metaphysical symbols grow out of a "real life" incident, how the old sailor's drunken babbling is transformed into a mystic vision and how both Whites and Reds find death in the fire of anarchistic uprising. The eschatological finale could hardly be expected from the author of rationalistic utopias.

On the other hand, **"The Coast of Slaves"** (*Nevolnichy bereg*) is Khlebnikov's most abortive work, an uninteresting propagandistic melodrama, written without inner conviction. It is a pacifist poem about the soldiers of World War I who are selected in a manner similar to that used by slave traders and who later return home as cripples.

Among the late poems, **"Razin's Boat"** (*Ustrug Razina*) occupies a place similar to that of **"Ladomir"** in the Kharkov period. After having established a new style, Khlebnikov suddenly returns here to old standards and devices. Having struck a tragic note in the works on contemporary themes, he relaxes in the old primitivism applied to history. The dynamism of the poems on the Revolution gives way here to static portraiture and stylized description. It is rather "classic" in its brevity and semantic compactness, forming a contrast to the "romantic" outbursts, repetitions, and ramifications of poems like **"A Night Search."** The verse of the old days is used instead of the free rhapsodic lines of the other late poems. But it is also unquestionably a work of the late period in its violence and premonitions of death, its greater integration of old devices into the texture and its two passages where the 1921 famine is projected upon the seventeenth century of Razin. The *poema* follows the plot of the popular song *"Iz-za ostrova na strezhen,"* which seems to be its real source rather than A. K. Tolstoy and the historical songs about Razin which are usually mentioned by scholars. Moreover, the song's four-foot trochee is also the dominant meter of the poem. The poem is saturated with sound and is full of most interesting alliterative effects.

The last two *poemy* of Khlebnikov occupy a special place among the works of the late period. Clearly, a new period is entered with these two poems, a period which was destined, however, to remain undeveloped because of the poet's death six months later. Its originality consists mainly in a new use of free verse. . . . Both poems were written in Moscow in 1922. **"The Coup d'Etat in Vladivostok"** (*Perevorot v Vladivostoke*) uses the entrance of Japanese troops into Vladivostok for its theme and is based on his friend, the poet Aseev's, stories of his sojourn in the Far East in 1918-19. Khlebnikov's enthusiasm for the East never included Japan. This time the poet obviously shows his fascination while observing Oriental evil as embodied in the figure of a Japanese soldier, and he lavishes some of his most elaborate imagery on this soldier.

The second poem, **"The Blue Chains"** (*Sinie okory*) is Khlebnikov's longest and, in parts, most obscure. It also uses Aseev's stories about the Far East, but most of it describes or hints at events and small details of the poet's frequent visits to the country home of the Sinyakov sisters in the Ukraine (three of these sisters are portrayed in his poem **"Three Sisters"**).

Khlebnikov's theories on the repetition of historical events are also an important part of the work. As a whole, it is one vast synthesis of Khlebnikov's efforts in more fields than one. His life, his dreams, his theories and his art are here merged in one, and the poem moves like a big river, from association to association, changing shape under way. It is astonishingly optimistic and full of healthy, though not necessarily subtle, humor. The life affirmation has never been so strong or exuberant in the otherwise stylized, archaistic, theoretical, or tragic works of Khlebnikov, and one is surprised to find this serenity in a sick man who, after years of privations, is disillusioned upon his arrival in Moscow, shortly before his terrible death.

The doors opened by Khlebnikov in his last poems, especially in rhythm and imagery, attracted no one. Russian poets had only begun to cultivate the results of his early, primitivistic work (N. Tikhonov, Zabolotsky) when the heavy hand of Socialistic Realism halted the natural evolution of Russian literature. The discovery of Khlebnikov's late achievements may be the task of a distant future. Khlebnikov refuses to become the past of Russian poetry even in this manner. (pp. 339-51)

> *Vladimir Markov, "The Literary Importance of Khlebnikov's Longer Poems," in* The Russian Review, *Vol. 19, No. 4, October, 1960, pp. 338-70.*

RENATO POGGIOLI (essay date 1960)

[*Poggioli was an Italian-born American critic and translator. Much of his critical writing is concerned with Russian literature, including* The Poets of Russia: 1890-1930 *(1960), which is considered one of the most important examinations of this literary*

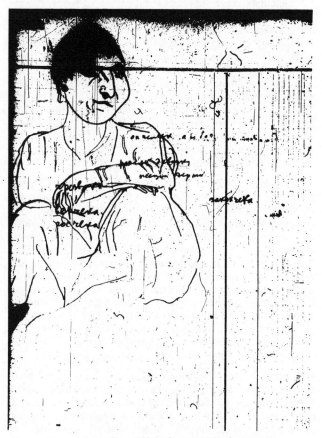

Page from Khlebnikov's notebooks.

era. In the following excerpt from that work, Poggioli examines the principal themes of Khlebnikov's poetry and his linguistic experimentation.]

Khlebnikov was the most important figure which Russian Futurism produced. Majakovskij acknowledged more than once the merits of Khlebnikov. Immediately after the latter's death, Majakovskij described him as "the most magnificent and blameless knight in our poetic struggle . . . the Columbus of new poetic continents later settled by us" [see excerpt dated 1922]; and subsequently paid many other similar tributes to the memory of that master. Even writers of very different literary and political tastes qualified their critical reservations with an unbounded admiration for the originality and integrity of the work of Khlebnikov. For instance, "several of his lines," said Nikolaj Gumilev, "seem like the fragments of an unwritten epic." (p. 256)

In spite of its label, the poetry of Khlebnikov is not Futuristic in the literal sense of the word. This is no less true from the standpoint of ideas and feelings than from the standpoint of form and technique. Khlebnikov looked at modern life with a sense of aversion, and worked hard at his experiments and research, while the other Futurists were often satisfied with announcing the most radical innovations in resounding manifestoes, or in rhetorical proclamations. Khlebnikov's indifference toward modern themes, toward the most attractive or repulsive aspects of contemporary existence, is proved by contrast by his deep interest in Slavic mythological lore, which inspired several of his poems; or more generally, by his longing for all those forms of primordial or ancestral life which are the field of study of the archaeologist and the anthropologist.

In Khlebnikov's work there breathes a kind of pantheistic inspiration à la Walt Whitman, but his own is an escapist pantheism, out of tune with the present, going backward into the past, and trying to find the regained paradise of primitive innocence in the darkness of prehistory. Also from this viewpoint his poetry has little to do with the international movement to which he gave his allegiance. One should suppose that Futurism was bound to unfold in Russia as one of the last and most extreme literary manifestations of the Westernizing tendency, while in the West it was nothing else than an unconscious variation of the nineteenth-century idea of progress, from which it derived the myth symbolized by the very term "Futurism." Yet, despite such expectations, Russian Futurism turned out to be a uniquely Russian creation. As for Khlebnikov himself, he was from his very beginnings one of the most consistent Slavophiles in the history of Russian poetry: he even anticipated the ideology built up after the Revolution by a group of *émigré* scholars on the claim that Russia and Siberia are an ethnographic and geopolitical unit, forming the sixth continent of Eurasia.

Khlebnikov's utopia is regressive and retrospective, and it repudiates our own steel or iron age for a mythical age of gold, even for a stone or wooden age. His sentiment and imagination constantly turn back to the time when the forests and plains of European and Asiatic Russia were still inhabited by the spirits of the trees and the waters. This nostalgia is expressed in pieces like **"Woodland Anguish"** or **"The Vila"** (the Slavic name for a wood nymph); or even in the poem entitled **"The Shaman and Venus,"** which combines barbaric and classical mythology, and in which the goddess of love offers herself not to a hero or demigod, but to a Mongol, to a Siberian sorcerer. And Khlebnikov's repudiation of modern life is tragically stated in the poem **"The Crane,"** with its monstrous mechanical bird wrecking the world as a vengeance of the machine upon man.

It would be wrong to interpret too literally the numerous poems which Khlebnikov devoted to historical subjects: their themes are never ends in themselves, but rather media through which the poet turns our attention toward what is archaic and prehistoric in life and man. This effect is generally produced by employing anachronisms, because, as we read in one of the poet's tales, "there are no barriers within time. . . ; consciousness joins together the different ages. . . ." These violations of chronology, this conversion into other categories of the dimension of time, are applied by Khlebnikov not only to the collective experience of mankind, but to the individual himself. That tale is **"The World Upside Down,"** reversing the biography of the protagonist, and rehearsing his life from grave to cradle.

As shown by the judgment of Gumilev, quoted above, the impersonal, almost choral solemnity of Khlebnikov's poetry has led a few critics to assert the epic character of his inspiration. But in the poet's imagination the mythical element is stronger than the heroic one; and his conception of nature as in a state of permanent flux, as a steady renewal of the first day of creation, as an everlasting conflict between the human and the cosmic, between creatures that are like things and things that are like creatures, suggests, rather than the epic, the theogonic character of his inspiration. This character can be easily recognized also in the poems which Khlebnikov wrote under the impact of the war and the Revolution. Except for one piece or two written in the spirit of Majakovskij's "marches," all these poems look at those two historical events as if they were cosmic catastrophes, elementary cataclysms. The military and revolutionary struggle is seen as a new Titanomachy, as a conflict between upper and nether gods, as the eternal warfare between the animistic forces of the universe. History, again, is reduced to prehistory; war, to a telluric outburst; the Revolution, to a metamorphosis. The tragic breath of the gods of destruction and death transforms the cosmos into chaos, and the earth into a Gehenna.

Sometimes Khlebnikov seems to conceive of revolution as a palingenesis, as in the poem **"Liberty for All"**: but even here, significantly enough, he asks for the resurrection of the natural deities of the primitive mythology of the Slavs. In **"Death Feast"** he describes the burning of the corpses on a modern battlefield as if it were an ancient ritual, an archaic funeral pyre, while the uncontrolled forces of nature, symbolized by two great Russian rivers, are considered as more powerful than that fire which man has learned to use and to control. Thus, in Khlebnikov's poetry the fragile order of man is forever upset by the revolt of the elements. This can be seen in the beautiful poem describing a fusillade in the dark streets of a city, in the autumn or early winter of 1917. We do not see the people who are killing, but only those who are being killed; we hear only the voice of the guns. The shots themselves, rather than a man-made curse, are a wind of fire, a rain of lead. The bullets are like cruel sprites engendered in the obscure recesses of the material world. Human beings are either their blind victims, or their blind instruments, never their conscious agents. The very act of slaughter is described as the cutting down of a poplar tree's branches and trunk.

Nothing is more significant than this identification of war and murder with the falling of leaves, with the felling of a tree; in brief, with autumn and winter. Here Khlebnikov shows once more his tendency to translate the events of human history into the phenomena of natural history, to interchange epochs and seasons, to introduce within the microcosm the laws and pro-

portions of the macrocosm. The methods mentioned above, tending toward indifferentiation and anachronism, the same attempt to establish metaphysical and metahistorical categories, are to be found also in his linguistic revolution, in his verbal reform. In this, too, he remains independent of the mainstream of the literary movement to which he belongs. While the average Futurist starts from the traditional vocabulary to shape his strange words, and from conventional grammar to postulate his final denial of syntax, Khlebnikov looks into the storehouse of popular and national speech in order to find ancient and eternal roots and to rebuild a new tongue on the ideal chain of pure forms and perfect words. The neologisms and barbarisms so frequent in normal Futurist idiom are replaced in this poet's work by archaisms and Slavonicisms, more often reinvented than found anew. It is by means like these that Khlebnikov seems literally to fulfill the poet's task as defined by Mallarmé: *donner un sens plus pur aux mots de la tribu* ["to give a purer meaning to the words of the tribe].

As a philologist, Khlebnikov is especially interested in the primitive stage of the linguistic evolution. It is there that he tries to find the embryo or the shell, the secret of the genesis of language, or even of creation itself, since he is one of those who believe that "in the beginning was the Word." He states his purpose in the following terms: "Without breaking the links of the roots, to find the philosopher's stone of the reciprocal interchange of all Slavic words, freely dissolving them into each other; such is my conception of the word. The Word per se, outside of life, and beyond its vital uses." The notion of the poetic word as an entity completely divorced from history and culture, this reversal of the idea of language as a token conventionally accepted and exchanged by man, are conceptions that may be found also in Mallarmé, although it is quite probable that Khlebnikov was unaware of the relationship.

The poet tried to put into practice the doctrines of the theorist, by testing them in the crucible of his art. This is what he did with a poem like **"Incantation** [or "Conjuration"] **by Laughter,"** by which he sought to achieve the lyrical catharsis of an etymological unit. In this poem, where one does not find even one of the forms of the verb "to be," all words are without exception derived from the Russian and Slavic root meaning "to laugh." This root is used in all its existing forms or possible variants: nouns and verbs, adjectives and adverbs, cases and aspects, tenses and moods, derivatives and compounds; and also in new words convincingly invented by the poet with the aid of several prefixes and suffixes. Because of this reduction of the poem to only one word-idea, the experiment from the linguistic standpoint has an exclusively phonetic and morphological character. As a work of art, it aims successfully at achieving a poetic equivalent of that kind of musical composition called "theme with variations." As a psychological or anthropological document, the poem is, however, as Roman Jakobson has observed, also an act of verbal witchcraft, working, as its title indicates, like a charm or spell.

Khlebnikov's linguistic and experimental interests relate his work to the critical theories of the Formalist school. But the poet, besides being a born philologist, was also an arbitrary and mystical one, as was the case with some of the Symbolists. He was obsessed by the ancient myth of the universal tongue, of an adamic or edenic language, which he dreamed of reaching again through methods reminiscent of those employed by the French René Ghil. Valerij Brjusov had been the only one in Russia to pay any attention to René Ghil and his "scientific poetry," which, rather than scientific, was cabalistic. Khlebnikov thought, however, of poetry as a means for discovering the secret of language itself, and stated his position in the following terms: "After having realized that the roots are but ghosts hiding the alphabet's strings, to find the universal identity of all tongues: this is my second conception of the word."

It is evident that by letters of the alphabet Khlebnikov meant not only the sounds, but also the signs representing them; like many poets of his time, he wanted not only to speak or sing, but also "to paint with words." This led him to experiment not only with merely verbal, but also with nonverbal, signs; his research in the field of general symbolism is a poetic anticipation of modern semantics. His early verbal exercises had been a clever manipulation of the doctrine of the "transmental tongue," as shown by the predominance of phonetic values, if not of onomatopoeic effects. But while we have been led to compare the compositions of other "transmental" poets to a kind of nonsense verse, we must say that these experiments by Khlebnikov are charged, even overcharged, with meanings of every sort, not merely verbal, but graphic and ideographic too. They are dominated by a system of allusions in which there also appear, like hieroglyphics, historical references and iconic symbols. Yet even these are reduced to the common denominator of linguistic structure, playing at the same time the roles of grammatical functions and of myths.

Thus, in the opening lines of a short piece without title, which begins with the words "Villa by night," Khlebnikov takes three proper names belonging to the cultural and historical tradition (Genghis-Khan, Zarathustra, Mozart) and treats them as if they were the roots of three verbs. By a sleight-of-hand change of the closing letter of each, he turns those names into three imperatives; and, along with the three noun-objects of the lyric's landscape (the villa, the nocturnal darkness, the blue sky), he throws those verbal forms into the chaos of the poem as agents of that mytho-poeic metamorphosis which is the ultimate aim of his art. The strangeness and arbitrariness of such methods may be equally approved or reproved, and their importance may be too easily overrated. But we must not stop at the technical details per se. What counts is that by means of a given device the poet has shown us an insight into a world of his own, where human reality and historical events become qualities of things, where life and history are lowered, or raised, to the condition of nature itself. It is for visions of this kind, not only for his daring use of language, that the poet Khlebnikov, far more than Andrej Belyj, whose novels have been so often compared to such a work as *Ulysses*, reminds us of Joyce and of his creations, especially of *Finnegans Wake*. (pp. 257-63)

Renato Poggioli, "The Poets of the Advance Guard," in his The Poets of Russia: 1890-1930, Cambridge, Mass.: Harvard University Press, 1960, pp. 238-75.*

VLADIMIR MARKOV (essay date 1962)

[*In the following excerpt, Markov discusses the classification of Khlebnikov's works by genre and examines his prose works, dramas, and "supertales."*]

In analyzing Khlebnikov's work, three aspects of his creative personality must be considered and, whenever possible, kept separate. His artistic work includes short and long poems, prose fiction, and dramas. Although some of these were never finished, or are extant only in rough draft, they were all specifically written for either publication or performance, and must therefore be distinguished from pure experiments, such as so-

lutions of or attempts to solve complex poetical problems. The latter were not meant for publication and were considered by Khlebnikov himself as pure laboratory work. Finally, there are numerous pieces of wayward character, which include Utopian projects, mathematical analyses of history, and, to some extent, philological essays. The boundaries separating these three aspects of Khlebnikov's intellectual activity are sometimes blurred, because he often tried to introduce experiment into his nonexperimental works and to apply his theories in artistic writings. He himself considered the third aspect the most important, and seldom emphasized the first one. Yet experiment and application of theories, though reflected in Khlebnikov's poetic writings, are not necessarily a determining factor. There is no agreement among critics as to how much importance should be ascribed to Khlebnikov's theories.

It is also somewhat difficult to classify Khlebnikov's artistic output. It is true to some extent that "Khlebnikov's works destroy the habitual idea of genre, so that often verse cannot be separated from prose, short lyrical poems [*stikhotvorenija*] from epics [*poèmy*], epics from dramas; small pieces have the appearance of fragments, or of sketches [*zagotovki*] for larger works." But one should not drive the point too far; Khlebnikov's artistic work may be divided into five main groups.

Although some critics thought highly of Khlebnikov's prose, it is probably the least known and least explored part of his work. Its influence on Olesha and on Tynyanov has been suggested. Khlebnikov's first writing and his first published work were in prose. His early prose includes "neologistic" works like **"Pesn miryazya"** (**"A Song of the Peaceful One"**), and stylizations like **"Uchilitsa"** (**"A Coed"**), which are often surrealistic in technique. There are also stories about men of nature, such as **"Okhotnik Usa-Gali"** (**"The Hunter Usa Gali"**) and **"Nikolay"** (**"Nicholas"**), which are written with classical simplicity, and autobiographical sketches like **"Oktyabr na Neve"** (**"October on the Neva"**). His three most important prose works are the short novel **"Ka"** (**"Ka"**. . .), set in Egypt in 1378 B.C., the short novel **"Esir"** . . . , which deals with Russia's Indian connections and may be considered Khlebnikov's masterpiece; and the story **"Malinovaya shashka"** (**"The Crimson Saber"**. . .), a psychological study.

Among Khlebnikov's dramatic works, the following are noteworthy. The stylized *Snezhimochka* (*Snow Maiden* . . .) was influenced by Ostrovsky's *Snegurochka* (*Snow Maiden*) and by Blok's plays. Another stylization, *Devy bog* (*The Maidens' God* . . .), is more ambitious in its attempt to show the pure Slavic element. More interesting is the whimsical *Chortik* (*The Little Devil*. . .), combining Blok, Trediakovsky, and the second part of Goethe's *Faust,* and built around a satire on the [magazine] *Apollon* and its circle. In *Markiza Dezes* (*Marquise Desaix* . . .), a satire ends in a surrealistic metamorphosis; here Khlebnikov tries conventional verse shaped on his study of Griboedov. *Mirskontsa (The World Upside Down)* is a primitivistic work with palindromic action; it uses Ostrovsky's diction, but is more reminiscent of Kozma Prutkov's nonsense plays. In *Gospozha Lenin* (*Mrs. Lenine*) there is a Maeterlinck touch; and *Oshibka smerti* (*Death's Mistake* . . .), is a curious example of a symbolist work written when the symbolist movement had long been dead.

Khlebnikov's overpublicized short experimental poems should probably be deëmphasized for the sake of balance in the study of his work. Sometimes it is difficult to distinguish between a finished short poem, a mere fragment, or an experimental sketch. Nevertheless, it is this kind of poetry that is usually presented in anthologies, headed by the inevitable **"Zaklyatie smekhom"** and **"Bobeobi."** This one-sided approach has affected even criticism and scholarship abroad, where statements like "... [Khlebnikov] was above all an experimenter and innovator in rhyme, meter, and vocabulary" are common.

Much less attention has been given to Khlebnikov's most ambitious genre, the "supertales" (*sverkh-povesti*), probably because the approach to them is difficult. They are worthy of consideration, however, for they bear a direct relation to the problem of defining Khlebnikov's longer poems, or epics (*poèmy*). The supertales are sometimes incorrectly placed in the category of the longer poems, whereas in them Khlebnikov was actually striving to combine all his genres in one vehicle.

Khlebnikov himself defined the supertale in the preface to *Zangezi:* "The supertale, or transtale [*zapovest'*], is constructed from independent pieces, each with its own god, its own faith, and its own code." Although Khlebnikov defines the components of a supertale as "independent pieces," and also as "primary tales" (*povesti pervogo porjadka*), he never explains how the components are put together. More often than not, the parts serve a common purpose or follow the same idea, but even then the general impression of a rather arbitrary combination is created. Khardzhiev wrote that the "bringing together in a cycle of works written at different times and belonging to different genres results from Khlebnikov's tendency to destroy the established ways of temporal and local fixation [*priuročivanie*] and thus to create a multiplicity of stylistic and thematic levels." To a great extent this is true, although here the familiar note about Khlebnikov the destroyer is again overstressed. The explanation may be simpler. Khlebnikov's work was important in the development of the tendency of modern Russian poets to revive major genres which had deteriorated during the nineteenth century and had become virtually extinct during the reign of symbolism. Khlebnikov's ambitious attempt to create the supertale shows that he was not completely satisfied with his own more or less traditional major genres. He strove for a "super-major" genre, which loomed before his eyes as a cycle created from heterogeneous material united on an unspecified level.

Khlebnikov's first supertale was **"Deti vydry"** (**"The Otter's Children"**), composed of the independent works of 1911-1913. It is divided into six "sails" (*parusa*), combining verse and prose, narrative and drama. Khlebnikov deliberately mixed epochs of history, and emphasized his favorite ideas on Russo-Asiatic ties. In form there is a certain similarity to the romantic comedy of Ludwig Tieck, as for example, when dramatic characters become a part of the audience. **"Deti vydry"** has been called "an artistic synthesis of Khlebnikov's mathematical exploration."

Slightly different in its organization is **"Voyna v myshelovke"** (**"The War in a Mousetrap"**). Here the thematic principle is clearer than in any other supertale; all parts are united by the antimilitaristic mood and by Khlebnikov's favorite ideas on the state of time. Because Khlebnikov used only verse in this work, some editors classified it as a *poèma*. Actually, however, it consists of individual short poems written in 1915-1917, and combined by the poet into one work in 1919. To place it among the *poèmy* would create substantial difficulties, both chronological and evolutionary. **"Voyna v myshelovke"** is entirely outside the clear and natural development of Khlebnikov's *poèma* from **"Selskaya ocharovannost"** (**"Rural Enchantment"** ...), to *Noch v okope* (*A Night in a Trench*...). All the twenty-eight short poems in **"Voyna v myshelovke"** had been printed be-

fore, whereas in the final supertale as many as five of the original short poems may appear as one "chapter." This demonstrated that after a lapse of time Khlebnikov frequently regarded his finished pieces as fragments of larger works.

Although there is little justification for it, **"Tsarapina po nebu"** (**"A Scratch on the Sky"**) is sometimes also classified as a *poèma*. Written in 1920 in Kharkov, it was an attempt by Khlebnikov to apply his linguistic theories. The work consists of several fragments. Some of the fragments are written partly in the "language of stars" [another term for Khlebnikov's trans-sense language], or contain what Khlebnikov called *zvukopis'* (sound-writing); some, written in free verse and filled with mathematical formulas, expound Khlebnikov's ideas on history; some resemble a treatise on semantics. Khardzhiev has correctly classified the work as a supertale. **"Vlom budushchego,"** a fantasy in dramatic form embodying Khlebnikov's ideas on time, also comes close to being a supertale.

The unfinished supertale **"Syostry-molnii"** (**"The Sisters, the Lightnings"**) has a rather complicated history. It was started in 1915-16, but was not completed until 1921. Divided into *parusa* (sails), like **"Deti vydry,"** it is concerned with reincarnation. The middle "sail" is the soliloquy of a soldier who is crucifying Jesus. Some fragments, printed ... separately (e.g., the Picasso-like **"Chu, zashumeli vdrug oblaka"**), were obviously meant to be additional "sails" of **"Syostry-molnii."**

"Azy iz uzy" (**"A's from Propolis"**?), which was written in 1920 [and reworked in 1921], ... and **"Shestvie oseney Pyatigorska"** (**"A Parade of the Pyatigorsk Autumns"**) ... are supertales similar to **"Voyna v myshelovke"**; that is, they are cycles consisting of short poems originally written separately. The former comprises the short Asiatic poems and the latter is a lyrical cycle of landscape poetry, unified by the locality described in it.

Zangezi ... is Khlebnikov's last, most important, and probably most successful supertale. In it he attempted all possible kinds of poetic language, and presented most of his ideas. The integration of the component parts into one work is more skillful than in earlier supertales. The last part (*ploskost'*) of *Zangezi* is a dramatic poem, or rather a morality play, *Gore i smekh (Grief and Laughter)*, written about 1920. Originally Khlebnikov toyed with the idea of using his poem **"Nochnoy obysk"** as the final part of *Zangezi*. (pp. 25-9)

This brief survey of supertales is included for the purpose of separating them and their components from ... the *poèmy*, the long poems of epic proportions. Khlebnikov obviously regarded them as different genres even though he used *poèmy* (as he used prose or dramatic works) as components of his supertales. It is significant, however, that the *poèmy* finally chosen by him to be parts of supertales are experimental in nature or are concerned with the application of his linguistic, historical, or philosophical theories. In all likelihood, Khlebnikov considered the supertale the ultimate vehicle for his experimentation. (p. 29)

Vladimir Markov, in his The Longer Poems of Velimir Khlebnikov, *University of California Publications in Modern Philology, No. 62, University of California Press, 1962, 273 p.*

VAHAN D. BAROOSHIAN (essay date 1974)

[*Barooshian is an American educator and critic specializing in Russian literature. In the following excerpt, he examines simi-*

Holograph copy of a poem by Khlebnikov.

larities and differences between Khlebnikov's poetry and that of
the Russian Symbolists and analyzes the poem "Žuravl'" ("The
Crane").]

As a theoretician of Russian Futurism, Xlebnikov's linguistic
experiments with *zaumnyj jazyk* (trans-sense language) fall into
two basic categories: (1) the creation of neologisms from Slavic
morphemes by analogy with other words, and (2) the creation
of a universal language. Xlebnikov expressed his 'attitude toward the word' as follows:

> To find, without breaking the circle of roots,
> the philosopher's stone for transforming all
> Slavic words one into another—this is my first
> attitude toward the word. This self-contained
> word is beyond daily life and everyday uses.
> Having observed that roots are only spectres
> which conceal the strings of the alphabet, to
> find the unity of world languages in general,
> constructed of units of the alphabet—this is my
> second attitude toward the word. The road to
> the world of trans-sense language.

With regard to the creation of neologisms (Xlebnikov's concern
for a universal language will be dealt with in another context),
Xlebnikov employed prefixes, suffixes, and infixes in the work
that bestowed fame on him, **"Zakljatie smexom"** (**"Incantation by Laughter"**). . . . Related to this category were Xleb-

nikov's numerous creations of neologisms by replacing the
initial consonant of a substantive with another consonant. For
example, he would replace the consonant "k" in the word
knjaz' 'prince' with the consonant "m" and create the word
mnjaz', which Xlebnikov defined as "thinker". He wrote in
this connection: "If we have a pair of words such as *dvor*
["courtyard"] and *tvor* ["creature"] and we know of the word
dvorjane [the noblemen], we can create the word *tvorjane*—
creators of life." (pp. 23-4)

Xlebnikov's linguistic experiments were designed to enrich
poetic language and to expand the range of poetic expression.
"Word creation", Xlebnikov remarked, "is the enemy of the
bookish ossification of the language, and, inasmuch as this is
supported by the fact that in the country . . . language is being
created every instant . . . this right carries over into living
literature". The Russian Symbolists, to be sure, made numerous linguistic experiments, but only so as to lend their work
a suggestive atmosphere, enabling them "to transcend the limits of reality", by means of vague hints and associations; so
that their experiments were "a means of materialization, of
unveiling 'contacts with other worlds'". To a certain extent,
this may be said of Xlebnikov. Unlike the Symbolists, however, Xlebnikov was concerned with linguistic technique *per
se*. His technique, moreover, was of "a rational and logical
character", in part a conscious effort to create new paths to a
scientific linguistic system.

Passionately dedicated as he was to determining 'national destinies' and to the 're-creation' of humanity—both Symbolist
notions—Xlebnikov set himself two basic tasks which claim
brief discussion.

Curiously, Xlebnikov devoted almost all his life to research
on numbers, and not to poetry. For Xlebnikov, history was not
the result of the efforts of men to impose their will on events,
or the result of human conflict, human interaction or human
activities, but the result of mathematical laws or cycles; and
Xlebnikov firmly believed that these were discoverable by, and
amenable to, mathematical formulae. Xlebnikov simply could
not live in an unpredictable and irrational and illogical world;
and he was determined to discover "the rules to which national
destinies are subject". But where and with which event does
one begin? Since there were no criteria for selecting historical
events and for assigning significance or irrelevance to them,
selection was perforce arbitrary. Xlebnikov therefore had to
manipulate selected events until he reduced them to a scheme
in which a number or formula appeared often enough to permit
him to embrace other events. After years of lucubration, intensive research in libraries and endless wandering about Russia
in an effort to sense the rhythms of history, Xlebnikov discovered that three hundred seventeen (years) was the magic
number that separated turning points in history. He concluded
and predicted that the year 1917 marked "the fall of a state",
which for Xlebnikov meant Russia.

Xlebnikov's chronic obsession with, and perhaps mystical belief in, numbers as the magic key to the structure of history
and reality are central to an understanding of his poetry. This
obsession with numbers was poetically productive. Poetry for
Xlebnikov was often an outlet for, or the handmaiden of, his
mathematical and historical theories, as well as a medium for
their creative application. These theories not only shaped to a
large degree his view of art as description of an historical era
or event, but also enriched and informed most of his poetry;
they shaped its epic orientation and led Xlebnikov to explore
specific periods of Russian and world history. Markov points

out that "There is more unity in Xlebnikov's verse than in his themes, which were as disorganised and varied as the reality surrounding him."

Xlebnikov explored historical eras to escape from reality. . . . Since Xlebnikov believed that the past would inevitably merge with the future, he also contemplated and explored historical eras to discover which era would merge with that future. **"Car-skaja nevesta"** (**"The Czar's Bride"** . . .) deals with Ivan IV; **"Vnučka Maluši"** (**"Maluša's Granddaughter"** . . .) concerns the era of Prince Vladimir; **"Lesnaja deva"** (**"The Forest Maiden"** . . .) and **"I i È"** (**"I and E"** . . .) have their settings in prehistory; **"Marija Večora"** (**"Marie Vetsera"** . . .) is based on the suicide of the Austrian archduke Rudolf and his mistress Marie Vetsera in 1889, an event to which Xlebnikov seems to have attached considerable importance in constructing his mathematical theories of history. **"Deti vydry"** (**"The Otter's Children"** . . .), which Xlebnikov considered one of his greatest works and which has been regarded as one of the artistic syntheses of Xlebnikov's "mathematical explorations", combines historical eras and introduces key historical figures: Marx, Justinian I, Darwin, Hannibal, Sten'ka Razin, Hus, Pugačev, Copernicus and others. Stepanov perhaps rightly observes that Xlebnikov's "historical and philosophical hypotheses are not only the themes of his poetry, but also their semantic base [*kostjak*], which permeates all the imagery and themes". This in part explains the plotless and fragmentary nature of Xlebnikov's poetry and accounts for the presence of historical data and numbers and mathematical formulae in his work. In **"Gibel' Atlantidy"** (**"The Death of Atlantis"** . . .), Xlebnikov pointed out the significance of numbers and their relation to events and nature. That Xlebnikov had Czar Nicholas II as "king" is conceivable: . . .

> The grim marches of soldiers,
> The murder of the king by lance
> Are subject to numbers, like the sunset,
> The rain of stars and the blue fields.
> The years of war, the coming of the plague
> I have added and subtracted in my head.
> And respect for numbers
> Grows, leading the brooks to the channel. . . .

While the Russian Symbolists spoke of re-creating and transforming humanity 'artistically', Xlebnikov attempted to achieve this *linguistically*. And this was his second major project: to create a universal language of consonants so as to restore the lost unity of men. Quite conceivably, Xlebnikov was prompted to this fantastic task by the human violence and carnage which he saw in history. "Trans-sense language is the embryonic future language of the universe. Only it can unite men. Rational languages are already disuniting men." Xlebnikov believed that, in the state of primitive reality, men spoke one language, when "savage understood savage". Languages, however, "betrayed their glorious past" and began to "serve the cause of discord". And Xlebnikov once asked: "What is better, a universal language or universal slaughter?" To Xlebnikov's vision of universal harmony, this universal language was central. In **"Ladomir"** (**"World Harmony"** . . .) Xlebnikov spoke of remaking "the languages of the world into a unified language of mortals", and in his view the Futurists "had given their oath to destroy languages".

Xlebnikov's idealization of, and intense yearning for, a primitive world and a mythical universal language can be seen as a kind of corollary to the Symbolist ideas of Vjačeslav Ivanov and Belyj, for whom art and language were the key to some 'other' reality and a kind of religious activity, or at least a substitute for it. This intense longing may have been a form of escape from, and a negative protest against, reality. This at least was true of the Russian Symbolists.

Before discussing one of Xlebnikov's works and some features of his poetic practice, it would be useful here to give a summary, however brief, of the Symbolist orientation of his poetry. Xlebnikov's poetry, rich in ideas and in mythological allusions, exhibits an extraordinary thematic and linguistic range. As noted, he has an abiding concern with historical eras and *dramatis personae;* he yearns for the past and antiquity, and is almost religiously devoted to the east. For Xlebnikov, poetry was not an end in itself, or a 'realistic' description of reality, or an obsession with the 'I', but a means of exploration and discovery of, and innovation in, style, language, and new forms. Because he saw poetry as a symbolic language and because of his supreme linguistic command, Xlebnikov often consciously eschewed logical or precise selection of poetic language. The notion of the 'right' word in poetry was alien to him as it was to many Symbolists. The operative principle in poetic word selection was often the 'wrong', or 'illogical', or 'trans-sense', or 'automatic' word. Hence the deformation of language and distortion of phenomena in his poetry. For poetry, in Symbolist esthetics, is the art of a seer who seeks analogies between things; it is an intellectual, cryptic, and elliptical art of words, a complex of sound relationships and their suggestive and evocative ability; it is an art which requires of the reader that he unravel or decipher its deliberate or calculated mystery. Some of these aspects will be seen in Xlebnikov's poetry.

One of Xlebnikov's early works, **Žuravl'** (**"The Crane"** . . .) will now be examined. The work appears to be a synthesis of the real and dream worlds. One may also consider it a surrealistic allegory. Gumilëv has remarked in this regard that Xlebnikov "is a visionary. His imagery is convincing by its absurdity, his thoughts by their paradox. It seems that he dreams his poems and then writes them down, preserving the entire incongruity of the course of events." In the **"Crane"**, the city of St. Petersburg revolts against man and is transformed into a crane. The crane evolves from an "iron hook" which "gallops along the river in a certain whirlwind". Chimneys become animate and "raise their necks". The crane takes on movement and begins to "rush toward things with hitherto unknown strength, like a prisoner who rushes to meet his beloved". The crane takes on further shape as the "iron and cunning chambers" of the city, "in a certain fierce fire, like a flame arising from heat", form the crane's legs. Then chimneys become animate and fly, "imitating the movements of a worm". Parts of trains form the crane's veins. Nature joins in the revolt as the railroads become uprooted by "the motion of pods ripened in the autumn". The crane then comes to wreak savage destruction on the city with the assistance of its inhabitants, who come to worship and offer sacrifices to the crane. Finally, the crane performs its ritualistic and grotesque victory dance, "like a savage over the corpse of a vanquished enemy", and disappears.

By equating the city with the grotesque, or by treating the city grotesquely, Xlebnikov was continuing the tradition of the Symbolists—especially Blok, Belyj, Brjusov—who treated the city in similar terms. They, too, saw the city as sordid and menacing. Moreover, by viewing the transformation of the city as inevitable—"according to some ancient design"—and by alluding to the evolutionary process of the crane—"And the hook forms the hand of the bird, a vestige of that time when it knew life as a four-footed animal''—the work may be considered as Xlebnikov's vision of the way mechanical civilization will fuse with ''primitive'' reality—the crane. Finally, the work may be viewed as nature's revenge upon urban civilization.

Jakobson has pointed out that **"Žuravl'"** is a 'realized' metaphor. The 'plot' of the work is to develop the primary metaphor—the transformation of the ''machine'', the city, into a ''crane''. Hence the double meaning of the word *žuravl'*. Stepanov notes that Xlebnikov achieves the realization of the 'basic' metaphor by means of structural shifts, whose aim is to violate the usual correlation and static nature of things. 'Secondary' metaphors and similes contribute to the unfolding of the 'basic' metaphor. For example: . . .

The chimneys . . . imitating the movements of a worm. . . .

The bridge . . . imitating the movement of an iceberg. . . .

The railroads . . . lacing like snakes into a wattle fence. . . .

From the graves the dead flew to him [the crane]
And covered the iron skeleton with flesh.

The poetic devices and themes in **"Žuravl'"** invite particular study, for they seem to constitute Xlebnikov's contribution to both the poetry and the prose of the 1920's. The work contains a number of Symbolist features: an aura of vagueness produced by the use of indefinite pronouns (*kakoj-to*) and by the work itself, which seems to require an imaginative effort to fill in, so to speak, the details; the ''occasional passages of high diction'', which are reminiscent of Vjačeslav Ivanov; the use of colloquialisms, which has a great deal in common with Andrej Belyj's use; and the use of sound repetitions that were cultivated by the Russian Symbolists.

Xlebnikov uses in **"Žuravl'"** devices and themes that were perhaps peculiar to Futurism. First, the theme of the ''revolt of things'' to which Xlebnikov makes direct reference: . . .

Even Koščej was not more angry
Than will be, perhaps, the revolt of things.

Secondly, the emphasis on concrete phenomena is also a Futurist feature. Third, 'deformation of reality' is the device of 'making-it-strange', which is a 'semantic shift', a means of transferring an object to a ''sphere of new perception''. Xlebnikov alludes to street-cars which form part of the crane thus: . . .

Beetle-shaped vehicles,
Whose aim is to sail over the lightning-charged waves,
Painted in red and yellow stripes
Form the bird's backbone.

Markov notes the appearance of 'wrong' words in Xlebnikov's poetry. This may very well be a literary device. One of the cardinal features of Xlebnikov's poetry, the odd word creates 'strangeness' within a familiar context. 'Strangeness' may also be a way of arousing perception. For example, instead of the word ''tears'', Xlebnikov uses ''devout dewdrops''. . . . Finally, there are a number of mythological and folklore motifs in the work which Xlebnikov used when treating contemporary themes: the sacrifices and prayers to the crane; the animation of inanimate objects; the allusion to Koščej, and to the ''stern and gloomy maidens who fly, tugging their garments, like melodies of the wind's forces''.

To diversify his poetry, Xlebnikov used a 'cubist' device which afforded him maximum flexibility and variation—the shift. This may be characterized as a radical mixing of mutually exclusive poetic categories. Xlebnikov deftly and successfully applied the shift to most of his poetry. That he borrowed this device from cubist painting is unmistakable. It extends not only to the structure of the plot, as in **"Žuravl'"**, but to meters, tenses, rhymes, genres, and to levels of language.

According to Markov, ''the salient feature of Xlebnikov's poetry is the mixing of traditional meters, with one meter predominant, usually iambic tetrameter''. While Xlebnikov initially mixed accentual and free verse in **"Žuravl'"**, in many of his works he used iambic tetrameter as the metrical base and ''violated'' it by ''constant metrical shifts''.

Xlebnikov's experiments with epic genres and his use of the 'didactic poem' link him with Lomonosov and Deržavin. One of Xlebnikov's major achievements was experimentation with his creation of new poetic genres, which were neglected by the Russian Symbolists because traditional genres suited their aims. His most daring innovation was the 'supertale' which consisted of a cycle of works, such as tales, stories, poems, and mathematical, historical and linguistic treatises. **"Vojna v myšelovke"** (**"The War in a Mouse Trap"** . . .), **"Zangezi"** (**"Zangezi"** . . .), **"Carapina po nebu"** (**"A Scratch on the Sky"** . . .) and others belong to this category. In **"Deti vydry"**, also a 'supertale', Xlebnikov mixed prose, drama, poetry and narrative because one genre apparently could not embrace the extraordinary sweep of his historical interests. Xardžiev notes that Xlebnikov's mixing of genres stemmed from his ''tendency to destroy the traditional framework of temporal arrangement and therefore to create multiple stylistic and thematic planes''. (pp. 24-34)

In conclusion, Xlebnikov was clearly influenced by, and was sympathetic to, the literary and art movements of his time—Symbolism, Acmeism, Cubism. Yet Xlebnikov also reacted against certain tendencies which he detected in literature and poetry. He was repelled by the despair and negation and melancholy in the works of Arcybašev, Andreev, Remizov, Merežkovskij and Sologub. Xlebnikov saw only ''horror'' and ''death'', not ''beauty'' in their works. For Xlebnikov, Russian literature affirmed nothing: Brjusov ''cursed'' the past. As for the Symbolists as a whole, Xlebnikov considered them slavish imitators of Western Symbolism and therefore utterly devoid of national roots. By introducing it into Russia, the Russian Symbolists seemed to Xlebnikov to be feeding ''poison'' to Russian youth.

Finally, Xlebnikov's life and work point to the conclusion that he brought to fruition poetic and linguistic tendencies within Symbolism and gave new direction to them. His ultimate link with Symbolism appears to be that he saw in *numbers* reflections of the 'other' reality. Torn by the chaos, irrationality, human discord and violence of history, Xlebnikov dedicated his life to the discovery in language of conceptual structures that would unify men. Until his tragic death in 1922 of malnutrition, Xlebnikov remained totally and unflinchingly committed to the enchanting Symbolist notions of human solidarity and universal harmony. In view of all his supreme efforts towards their realization, Xlebnikov was not cheated. For the epitaph on his coffin reflected his deepest and loftiest aspiration: ''The President of the Universe'' (a typically Symbolist gesture). (pp. 36-7)

Vahan D. Barooshian, ''Velimir Xlebnikov,'' in his Russian Cubo-Futurism, 1910-1930: A Study in Avant-Gardism, *Mouton, 1974, pp. 19-37.*

EDWARD J. BROWN (essay date 1976)

[*Brown is an American educator and critic who has written extensively on post-Revolution Soviet literature. Notable among his
studies is* Russian Literature since the Revolution (1963), *which
some critics consider the standard work on the period. In the
following excerpt from an introduction to* Snake Train, *Brown
offers a general discussion of Khlebnikov's works.*]

Mayakovsky maintained that Khlebnikov was not a poet for
"consumers," that is, for readers of poetry [see excerpt dated
1922]. "They can't read him," he said. Those who knew him
and appreciated him in his own day were almost exclusively
Futurist poets or philologists, and they, again in Mayakovsky's
words, "knew and loved this Columbus, this discoverer of
new poetic continents that we now populate and cultivate." It
was not only philistines that Khlebnikov affronted, but also
the lovers and "consumers" of poetry. If he had been a hermetic poet of the established type, one whose sibylline lines
carry the shadow of arcane meanings, a Russian Rimbaud or
even a Russian Symbolist, poetry lovers would never have
complained that he was "incomprehensible." Difficulty in a
poet was hardly an embarrassment in the early years of the
century; it could be a positive advantage. But Khlebnikov's
verse is not hermetic in the usual sense, nor does it bear the
imprint of Symbolist poetics. It's true that scholars have found
traces of Bely, Vyacheslav Ivanov, Balmont, and other Symbolists in Khlebnikov's work, and there can be no doubt that
Khlebnikov, like Mayakovsky, owed something to the Symbolists. But the fact that a poet's adolescence was spent in the
Symbolist stream, and that even his mature work shows evidence of the experience, does not argue an affinity with that
school. On the contrary: Khlebnikov's major effort was to expel
the influence. He uses language not as a vehicle for transcendental experience, but to discover the world. It may seem a
paradox, but the fact is that by comparison with the Symbolists
he is much too simple and clear. This world, our own world,
is vividly present in his poetry and in his prose. His *Menagerie*
is populated by real animals apprehended by a human intelligence of Slavic origin and Russian education whose associations are idiosyncratic, but startling in their clarity and beauty.
Naturally the parrots when he enters accost him in Russian
with their choral salutation, "Idiot! Idiot!" (and why not in
Russian?) and the "eagles look up at the sky, expecting a
thunderstorm" when they hear the cannon that announces
noontime every day. And all the animals imprisoned in the zoo
lose their marvelous potential, like a copy of the *Tale of Prince
Igor* caught in the pages of a religious manuscript.

The world in Khlebnikov's poetry is palpable and real, though
it often asserts itself in dreamlike gibberish. Very real also are
the building materials of poetry, the units of language. Khlebnikov offers the reader the somewhat rare experience of handling those materials himself and contemplating their nature
and use. His most famous poem, **"Incantation by Laughter"**
(**"Zaklyatie smekhom"**) offers precisely such an experience
with the materials of the Russian language. Based, as everyone
knows, on a rich multiplicity of prefixes and suffixes used with
the root word for laughter (*smekh*), it serves as a working model
of the Russian language. Moreover it reveals, without any
distractions of meaning or reference, certain essentials of poetic
device: repetend, assonance, rich alliteration, a variety of
rhythmic intonations. It is a perfect example of what Jakobson
once called the "poetic" function: the focus on the message
for its own sake. (pp. 11-13)

Khlebnikov's experiments with language had important theoretical implications. He entertained a philosophy of language
which postulated a single, original and universal tongue whose
primeval riches lay concealed under the fixed habits—which
vary from one language to another—of grammar, syntax and
conventional spelling. He offers the following on his search
for the universal language.

> To find, not breaking the circle of roots, the
> touchstone of all Slavic words, the magic by
> which one may be transformed into another—
> to freely fuse together Slavic words, such is
> my first approach to the word. This self-valuing
> word stands beyond ordinary life and what's
> useful for it. Observing that the roots are only
> a phantom, beyond which stand the strings of
> the alphabet, I took as my second approach to
> the word the task of finding the general unity
> of the world's languages, built out of the units
> of the alphabet.

The search for a universal trans-sense language may seem nonsense to strictly empirical linguists, but the idea has a long
history and also an affinity with certain important trends in
modern thought about language. (p. 13)

The German critic Walter Benjamin, writing in 1923 on the
theory and problems of translation, admits . . . to a search for
something analogous to Khlebnikov's universal language. A
determined foe of literalism in translation, Benjamin makes
the following points:

> . . . no case for literalness can be based on a
> desire to retain the meaning. Meaning is served
> far better—and literature and language far
> worse—by the unrestrained license of bad
> translators. . . . Fragments of a vessel which are
> to be glued together must match one another in
> the smallest details, although they need not be
> like one another. In the same way a translation,
> instead of resembling the meaning of the orig-
> inal, must lovingly and in detail incorporate the
> original's mode of signification, thus making
> both the original and the translation recogniz-
> able as fragments of a greater language, just as
> fragments are part of a vessel.

Benjamin's position is that at a deep level of linguistic activity
all human languages are one, and that the pure translator's task
is to "release in his own language that pure language which
is under the spell of another . . . ," and thus to establish a
concrete link with "the word as such," the universal language.

It's quite natural that translators should face the problem of
linguistic universality, since their craft presupposes the existence of an essential community among all the separate languages. Khlebnikov himself was conscious of the linguistic
problem, and even while not engaged in actual translation he
did attempt to convey in certain of his poems what Benjamin
might call the "mode of signification" of other languages. He
maintained that in *Maidens' God (Devii bog)* the linguistic principle is Slavic, in *Ka* African, in *Otter's Children (Deti Vydry)*
Asian. It may be true that his procedures were arbitrary and
subjective, but the work was nonetheless an attempt to achieve
community among widely distant and sharply separated language systems. The problem and its implications are still with
us in the debates of modern linguistic schools.

Khlebnikov's experiments with the Russian language, viewed
from a wider perspective, are actually an effort to discover

how language itself "grows" and "works." His "delving" into roots, as Mayakovsky put it, was a search for the source of the word, a return to the time when the "name corresponded to things," when there were only ten root words, but new words appeared as case modifications of the root. (pp. 14-15)

Khlebnikov attempted a special kind of language discovery in the play *World from the End (Mirskontsa)*, in which the dialogue involves at least two distinct types of language. There is first an exact transcription, without punctuation marks, of rapid colloquial speech, an oral language articulated casually and subject only to the habits of conversation. The result, as often happens in Khlebnikov, has the effect of a language newly discovered, and is the precise antithesis of conventional dramatic dialogue in which statements are not made in imitation of actual speech, but are structured artificially to reveal character, motivate action, or advance the plot. The dialogue in that play then drifts imperceptibly into rhyming couplets which suggest the stylized lines of classical theater, but at the same time the rhyming proverbs of common Russian speech. The language of the play in both its aspects is a parody of dramatic style; it offers at one extreme a colloquial idiom too simple and natural for the conventional theater, and at the other a highly artificial rhymed speech. (pp. 16-17)

Khlebnikov's "questioning" of the accepted forms of language took the shape also of a search for purely mathematical formulas which would reveal the laws of history and of human development. The urge to abandon the "word" for numerical symbols whose sense is precise and not subject to the vagaries of connotation may at first sight seem paradoxical in a poet, especially in Khlebnikov, but his "mathematical" pursuits are, I believe, simply one aspect of his search for an ultimate, or "universal" language.

The categories of the human reason as Kant classified them are subject to severe modification in the work of Khlebnikov. The play *World from the End* is an experiment with literary time which has the effect of a motion picture film run backwards: it begins with the funeral of Polya, the husband, and ends with Polya and Olya, his wife, riding past in baby buggies holding toy balloons in their hands. Time reversal in the form of memories, flashbacks, dreams and the like is of course commonplace in literature. Shifts in the apprehension of time in which a few brief moments seem to last forever, while much longer periods have only momentary duration are also fairly common. But in Khlebnikov, as Jakobson has pointed out, such shifts are not motivated by a particular literary situation but are given for their own sake. Khlebnikov, in other words, deals directly with the time dimension, a problem which has long agitated the human intelligence, and which, as Henry James has pointed out, is a "terrible" and frightening problem for the novelist. Khlebnikov's procedures have the effect of "cancelling out" the problem as a philosophical concern and simply treating it as one of the elements in an esthetic experience. Analogous procedures lead to a poetic displacement of space, and a montage-like association of separate spatial planes, without movement in time or strict causal sequence—consider for instance the structure of the story *Ka*. Khlebnikov effects a "simultaneity" of action which, like his experiments with time, may be compared to the techniques of the modern film in which rapid movements of the camera produce an interconnection of diverse persons, places, and situations, without logical motivation (Eisenstein, Antonioni).

Nikolai Stepanov, one of the principal Soviet authorities on Khlebnikov, makes the point that at first sight his works give an impression of chaos, seem to consist of the "fragments" of a magnificent edifice in a state of destruction. "And yet," he goes on to say, "attentive rereading makes the thought, the architectural plan which unites the fragments, stand forth more and more clearly." . . . "Estrangement" is the essence of such a poetic art; or, again drawing on Shklovsky, Khlebnikov reveals poetic form to us by destroying it. Yet he is never deliberately complex or tricky. His lines come to us simply and deeply out of the very source of poetry itself in the unpredictable operations of the human imagination.

Minds wedded to the obvious question Khlebnikov's sanity, and philistines of course reject him with amusement or anger. Yet those who say that the man was crazy may be pointing to something important in the nature of modern art; indeed there is psychiatric evidence to support analogies between the linguistic behavior of psychotic patients and of many modern poets. . . . A contemporary of the Futurists, the psychiatrist E. P. Radin, wrote a study entitled *Futurism and Madness* (1914) in which he compared Futurist poetry to the actual writing of committed schizophrenics—with astonishing results. The compulsion to coin new words from existing roots (as in **"Incantation by Laughter"** and many other things), to use existing words in meaningless combinations ("to laugh with laughs" for instance), to create totally new sound configurations which receive special emotional significance ("when I wrote the words of Ikhnaton before his death 'manch! manch!' they produced on me an unbearable effect," said Khlebnikov), all of these things characterized the writing of paranoid schizophrenics. Radin draws no clear conclusions from his evidence, and yet that evidence does suggest an essential kinship between Khlebnikov's work and certain verbal manifestations of lunacy. Both madmen and Khlebnikov violently shift the established forms of language and both thereby lead us into a direct experience of the speech process itself. Just as "dark" is the opposite that enables us to apprehend "light," so the quality of Khlebnikov's poetry that many experience as linguistic opacity actually illuminates the language phenomenon. . . . Perhaps we can come closer to appreciating Khlebnikov and much of modern art if we heed the surrealist André Breton, who said, "A poem must be a debacle of the intellect. It cannot be anything else."

The [collection *Snake Train*] offers translations of a number of Khlebnikov's prose works, a body of writing which has not yet received its full due. The critic Yury Tynyanov, writing in 1929, said of Khlebnikov that "the influence of his poetry is an accomplished fact. The influence of his lucid prose is a matter for the future" [see excerpt dated 1929]. It's doubtful that Russian literature has been deeply affected by that "lucid prose," although the work of Yury Olesha, in its metaphoric directness, shows some evidence of the reading of Khlebnikov. Indeed Olesha has paid glowing tribute to Khlebnikov and recommended him highly as a model and teacher: . . .

> Khlebnikov's prose is a model of the art of picturing. . . . I consider *Menagerie* a masterpiece. "The stag is pure terror, blooming like a massive rock," such ought to be the academic authority for writers of prose. Proletarian writers call upon their followers to learn from the classics: Turgenev, Tolstoy.
>
> All lies! Self-destruction!
> Only from Khlebnikov!

(pp. 17-21)

Menagerie is undoubtedly a masterpiece, but probably the summit of Khlebnikov's prose is the long story *Ka*. . . . It is another experiment with time in which the narrative consciousness moves freely through the history of ancient Egypt but is still aware without embarrassment of contemporary things: a Sikorsky airplane, the artist Filonov, Andrée's balloon. Ka is the "phantom of the soul, its double, an envoy to those people dreamed by his snoring master." Time offers no obstacles to him: "he intersects time." And again: "Ka makes himself as comfortable in the centuries as in a rocking chair. Isn't it true that one's consciousness assembles the different ages as if they were chairs in a parlor?" The narrative viewpoint is subject to subtle and at times very poignant shifts: Ka is not simply the "phantom of the soul" represented by an Egyptian word and setting, but also the narrator's "soul"; at other times he is associated with particular objects, for instance the beach stone upon which a girl writes Japanese "tankas." The story is rich with verbal invention: the apes' language is a special case of trans-sense language, as are the last words of Ikhnaton before his death. The great religious reformer is murdered by the priests, and again by a merchant, a modern one. Time is made to yield its stubborn hold on the mind, as in the following passage which concerns the artist Filonov:

> We were avoiding trains and kept hearing the roar of a Sikorsky. We hid from both of them and learned to sleep while walking. Our feet kept going in a certain direction independently of the sleep department. The head slept. I met a certain artist and asked whether he was going off to war. He replied: "I am also waging a war, only not for space but for time. I am sitting in a trench and wresting from the past a scrap of time. My task is just as onerous as that undertaken by those who fight for space."

Vladimir Markov points out that while Khlebnikov's prose is lucid and economical he "occasionally indulges in rhythmic prose or in an imitation of scientific prose, or mixes his narrative prose with drama and verse" [see entry in Additional Bibliography]. At times the prose offers the barest elements of meaning, and statement so simple that it seems a brilliant revelation of matters that might have escaped attention, as in this exchange with a scholar of the year 2222:

> . . . He commissioned me to draw up a description of man. I filled in all the questions and presented a brief account. "Number of eyes—two; number of fingers and toes—twenty." He rested his thin gleaming skull on a spectral finger. We discussed the advantages and disadvantages of that number. "Do these numbers ever change?" he asked, giving me a piercing look with his big, intelligent eyes.
>
> "These are the maximum numbers," I replied. "The fact is, that there are people with one hand or foot. The number of such people will increase noticeably in 317 years."
>
> (pp. 22-3)

But Khlebnikov's prose is also capable of poetic rhythms or complex linguistic speculation, or elaborately careful numbered statement. As a matter of fact it is a virtuoso performance, the main purpose of which would seem to be to demonstrate infinite possibilities in the medium.

The work of Khlebnikov presents a number of sharp paradoxes. Much of it deals with the distant past, with the vocabulary and idiom of old Russia, Russian folklore, figures from Russian history, and in *Ka* the present and the deep past fully coexist in the experience of the narrator. At the same time he produced utopian fantasies which forecast a future of harmony, wealth, and peace under the benevolent rule of the human reason. His dreams of the future have suggested to some critics an affinity with Chernyshevsky, whose heroine in *What Is To Be Done?* dreams of a happy socialist future for all of mankind, though of course there are cataclysmic differences in form between the two writers. The long poem *Goodworld* (*Ladomir* . . .) tells of a city of the distant future which derives its name from the Slavic roots for harmony (*lad*) and peace (*mir,*) and the future he foresees is one of universal health and happiness under the aegis of science. It is a time when the non-Euclidian mathematician Lobachevsky's curve "adorns the cities," and even death is controlled and regulated. And when "Hiawatha's skull adorns the summit (head) of Mont Blanc" revolutionary science and primitive pastoral virtue have joined to create a new Europe. I have already alluded to Khlebnikov's "mathematical" interests, and to his efforts to find numerical formulas that would express the laws of historical development. The paradox presented by the scientific concerns of a writer whose work is also a revolutionary assault on the rational categories is expressed very well by Nikolai Stepanov:

> His historical and philosophical hypotheses serve not only as a semantic skeleton forcing attention upon itself through every image and idea. Khlebnikov introduces into those poems material scientific in its form: mathematical calculation, historical facts and dates. In order to explain the sense of Khlebnikov's work one must have some concept, at least in general terms, of his theoretical hypotheses. Khlebnikov was a utopian and a fantastical dreamer. His "social utopias" on the cities of the future . . . are "scientific" to the same extent that the utopias of Thomas More or Campanella are scientific.

But the rational "skeleton" of which Stepanov speaks is embedded in surrealistic poems which do represent, in Breton's phrase, "a debacle of the intellect." Stepanov speaks of the "associative" structure of the story material in the narrative poems, of the way separate thematic links are "strung together" without logical motivation, and he quotes the happy comment of Gumilev on Khlebnikov: "His images are convincing by their absurdity, his thoughts by their paradox. It's as though he dreams his poems and then writes them down, preserving all the incongruity of the course of events."

The unique contribution of Khlebnikov to modern literature is a body of work which in a sense "examines" the rational processes by the simple device of departing from them in the direction of "free" association, dream symbols, accidental sound coincidences much like the material of dreams (*vremya,* "time," has in the realm of dream association as also in poetic etymology a relationship to *bremya,* "burden"), the linkage of disparate events with no regard for causality, and direct tampering with the time sense. Khlebnikov, who died in 1922, is in the forefront of that modern experimentation in all forms of art which both questions and enhances the human perceptive experience. (pp. 23-6)

Edward J. Brown, in an introduction to Snake Train: Poetry and Prose *by Velimir Khlebnikov, edited by*

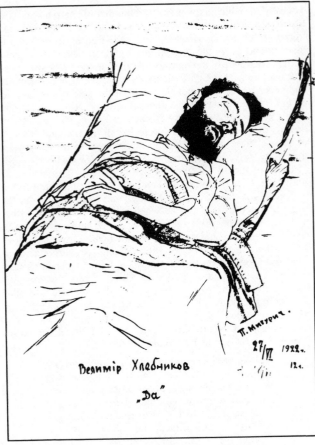

Khlebnikov on his death bed.

Gary Kern, translated by Gary Kern & others, Ardis, 1976, pp. 11-26.

BORIS THOMSON (essay date 1978)

[*In the following excerpt, Thomson examines the theme of the past in Khlebnikov's poetry. Translations in the entry are by Thomson.*]

Khlebnikov's first approach to the theme of the past occurs in his poem *The End of Atlantis (Gibel' Atlantidy. . .)*. The work is set in a future rationalist Utopia, which has discovered the secret of immortality, and is dedicated to continual progress; in this world the past seems to have no place. As the High Priest says, rather smugly: . . .

[The descendants, proud of their science, had forgotten the ruined cemeteries. What if we had forgotten and lost touch with the gait of four legs!]

However, his assurance is challenged by a slave-girl who presents irrationality as the necessary complement to his crude scientism ('I am your consonance', she tells him). Driven by her logic to an act of irrationality the High Priest kills her and thus prepares the way for a new outbreak of chaos. A flood ensues, which destroys Atlantis, while the head of the slave-girl appears over the waters as a vengeful Medusa: . . .

[And lo, among the constellations, undulating with / like black grass-snakes, a face of ven-

geance and retributions, a head severed with knives.]

In the immediate context of the poem this apparition may seem to represent the triumph of the irrational, and the same unusual (for Khlebnikov) rebellion against science, and even numerology, can be found in other works of 1912, such as **'Hearts more transparent than a vessel' ('Serdtsa, prozrachney, chem sosud')** and the 'Titanic' section of *Otter's Children (Deti vydry);* but, as we shall see, the image can also be taken as referring to the past.

The most remarkable and influential instance, however, of Khlebnikov's complex attitude to the past is to be found at the end of his revolutionary trilogy of November 1921. This consists of three narrative poems, *Night before the Soviets (Noch' pered Sovetami)*, *The Present (Nastoyashcheye)* and *Night Search (Nochnoy obysk)*. As their titles suggest, they are all set at night, and there is an implied temporal progression within them, 'before, during, after'. Each part of the trilogy contains a clash between representatives of the old order and the forces of the revolution.

In the first of the three poems, a 'Lady' is being prepared for bed by her old nurse, who relates the story of her family's humiliations at the hands of their masters. In the central episode an old peasant-woman, the grandmother of the nurse, is forced to put her own son from her breast in order to suckle one of her owner's puppies. When her son grows older he kills the dog and is flogged almost to death for it. The complaints and recriminations of the old woman break out finally into open threats to her mistress: 'They will hang you tomorrow'. In the second poem the reflections of an elderly Grand Prince are contrasted with the violence of the first days of the revolution, and at the end the insurgents burst in to murder him and rape his daughter.

In each poem the past, its aristocracy (they are old and the revolution is young), its culture, its religion, its values, are swamped under the tide of retribution, and the development of the imagery emphasizes its historical logic. Humiliated even by the hounds of their masters, the people have become hunting-dogs themselves; the blue eyes of the oppressed peasants evolve into the blue of the sea which has spawned the revolutionary sailors.

In the final poem, however, the events and the imagery take a different direction. *Night Search* is prefaced by a mysterious epigraph, '$3^6 + 3^6$'. In his *The Boards of Fate (Doski sud'by)* Khlebnikov explained that the powers of three are associated with the reversal of historical trends and events, and he gave as an example the following: 'Tsarist debts acknowledged by Soviet Russia 6/xi 1921, $3^6 + 3^6 = 1458$ days after the beginning of Soviet power 10/xi 1917, when they were reduced to nil'; the poem *Night Search* is dated 7 November-11 November 1921. In other words the poem is concerned with the reversal of the original revolutionary impulse, celebrated in the first two poems of the trilogy, and brought about by the Soviet government's decision to accept liability for the debts incurred by its Tsarist predecessors. So much may be clear; the actual working out of this theme, however, is not so simple.

At the beginning of *Night Search* a band of Red sailors enters a middle-class apartment in search of loot and class-enemies. The son of the house, a White, fires a shot at the sailors but misses; in the search he is soon caught; he is stripped naked and then shot before the eyes of his mother and sister. The sailors pun grimly on his name, Vladimir: . . . .

[Curled up on the floor he possesses peace (*Vla-deet Mir*om; the phrase could also be translated 'he possesses the world') And doesn't breathe.]

The pun at first seems ornamental, but as the poem unfolds, it reveals a functional significance.

The White boy accepts his fate with schoolboyish heroism. He laughs at the sailors and asks to be shot without a blindfold and facing his executioners: . . .

[Will you shoot me in the forehead then?]

His request is granted and his last words are: . . .

[Farewell, fool! Thanks for your shot.]

His acceptance of death and his insolent courage make a deep impression on the sailors, and one of them continues to reflect on it: . . .

[The swine! He laughs even after death.]

In a long monologue, he three times goes over the events leading up to the execution; he becomes increasingly aware of the wanton destructiveness of his actions, and of the reproach in the eyes of the ikon. But he too refuses to submit: he challenges God as the White boy had challenged him: . . .

[Will you shoot me in the forehead then? You shoot me in the forehead, you virginal god. You have seven shots, you with your great blue eyes. And I shall say thank-you for your letters and your love. . . .

I want to fall dead on the spot, and the fatal fire to fall on me from the ikon corner. I want the black muzzle to appear from there so that I can say to Him 'Fool' in the face of death, as that boy shouted it at me, laughing easily into the twin barrels of death. I burst into his life and killed him like a dark god of the night, but I was overcome by his clear laughter, ringing with the crystal of youth. Now I want to overcome God with the same laughter and the same strength, though I feel gloomy and depressed. And confused.]

In the final lines he seems to have achieved his ambition. He sees the fire break out, and coolly strikes the pose he has sought: . . .

[We're on fire! Help! Smoke! But I am calm and unruffled. I stand and twirl my moustache, just as I should. Savior! you're a fool!]

but somehow the gesture seems of 'dubious value' as Vladimir Markov has suggested. It is partly that the atmosphere of the two passages is quite different. In the first case the tone is foolhardily heroic, in the second it is grim and fatalistic. What had been instinctive and natural for the White boy is achieved by the Red sailor through will-power and deliberate emulation, and the contrast between the sudden heroism of the boy and the obsessive ambition of the old sailor serves still further to weaken the impact of the second death. Thus the verbal repetitions serve to suggest the differences rather than the similarities between them.

This strange and unexpected ending is paralleled by some equally strange changes in the imagery: the blue eyes that had been associated with the peasants and the revolutionaries are now given to the Christ in the ikon. The ikon is desecrated but it is no longer helpless; it is allowed to answer back, as it does with the final fire. The 'sinister old woman' of the opening lines of *Night before the Soviets* seems to reappear in the final lines of *Night Search* as the immediate agent of the fire. Finally even the dog image is reinterpreted in the piano-smashing episode. . . .

[Who of the brothers can play? That we can . . . Just belt it with the stock or the rifle butt . . . Watch, brothers, trot along here, there'll be some racket and thunder and singing . . . and a wail, as if a puppy were whimpering in a ditch, a puppy forgotten by everybody. And suddenly the ominous roar of cannons arises, and someone's laughter, someone's underwater, Lorelei laughter. They crowded round. The chatter of the strings, the laughter, the quiet laughter of the strings. Belt it with your rifle butt!]

The puppy has here lost its earlier associations of power and brutality; it is treated as a victim, and is even linked once again with the culture of the past. Like the dying White boy, even in destruction it laughs at the Red sailors; it is compared to a Lorelei/*rusalka,* and later in the poem the reproachful eyes of Christ in the ikon survive the sailor's bullet and recall the same 'Lorelei with cloudy, powerful eyes.'

The tone too changes dramatically from the coarse speech, violent actions and staccato rhythms of the first half to an impersonal mode of narration, imprecise ('someone's'), almost mystical in its serenity. And even though the elements of destruction soon return as the piano is thrown out of the window ('that box with a puppy moaning in it', as one of the sailors comments scornfully), this vision of a different set of values remains unassailable, and finally, in the closing lines, emerges as the dominant element.

To some extent, of course, the poem is concerned with the self-destructiveness of the revolution; the images that were originally associated with the people finally turn against them. But at a deeper level it is concerned with the problem of the values of the past. It is seen at its crudest in the epigraph, with its reference to the Soviet government's acceptance of the financial obligations of the Tsars, an apparent betrayal, at least in the eyes of Khlebnikov. But in the poem itself, the murdered White youth and the smashed piano come to life again and inspire the revolutionaries, however grudging, to emulation. It is extraordinary to discover that these apparently discredited values can, in spite of everything, still 'provide a standard and model beyond attainment'.

The ironies of the poem deepen the more we read it. In the first two poems of the cycle, the representatives of pre-revolutionary Russia are old, and the revolutionaries are young; in *Night Search* the White is a youth, and his killer an older man, named Starshoy (elder). The old sailor's cry to the dead boy 'possess the world' (or, at first reading, it might be merely, 'possess peace') turns out to be truer than he knew; for the White youth does seem to have spirited away with him a whole world of values in art and human conduct. But why should these values still be desirable and enviable? Can the revolution then never be free of its past?

Khlebnikov's *Night Search* offers no answers, but it captures with the diagrammatic simplicity and moral complexity of true myth the ambivalent attitude of Soviet Russia to its past, a mixture of love and envy, admiration and hatred, a confused impulse to emulate and acquire it, but also to master and destroy it. (pp. 79-83)

Boris Thomson, *"The Secret of Art: Two Soviet Myths," in his* Lot's Wife and the Venus of Milo: Conflicting Attitudes to the Cultural Heritage in Modern Russia, *Cambridge University Press, 1978, pp. 77-97.**

RONALD VROON (essay date 1983)

[*Vroon is the author of* Velimir Xlebnikov's Shorter Poems: A Key to the Coinages, *a detailed analysis of the linguistic principles behind Khlebnikov's neologisms and the relationship of his coinages to the Russian language. In the following excerpt from that work, he discusses Khlebnikov's theories of language.*]

As a poet Xlebnikov took a surprisingly prosaic view of language in the sense that he most often stressed its communicative, as opposed to aesthetic, function. At the same time his approach was decidedly diachronic: he was far less concerned with the static structure of language than with its past and its development. His preoccupation with the past led him to accept the monogenesis theory of language. Initially this position was reflected in his concern with the family of Slavic languages and his desire to bare their common roots:

To find, without breaking the circle of roots, the philosopher's stone (*volšebnyj kamen'*) for transmuting all Slavic words, the one into the other—to freely melt down Slavic words—that was my first approach toward the word. . . .

Eventually it formed the basis for his concept of *zaum'* ("transsense," "transrationality"), the foundation for a universal language:

Seeing that roots are merely phantoms behind which stand the strings of the alphabet, to discover the overall unity of all the world's languages, a unity formed from the units of the alphabet—such was my second approach to the word. The path leading to a universal transrational language. . . .

Naturally Xlebnikov's monogenetic view was emotionally colored by his own primitivist conceptions of this *Ursprache*. It was the language, not only of primitive man, but of all nature. There was, and is, a language of the stars, and a language of the earth. This ancient language united all men, and its purity guaranteed mutual understanding. "At one time," Xlebnikov claims, "when words broke down enmity and made the future transparent and calm, languages . . . united men 1) of the cave, 2) of the village, 3) of the tribe, the kinship group, 4) of the state, into one rational world. . . . The savage understood the savage and set aside his blind weapon." . . . (pp. 8-9)

Concomitant to this particular view, as one might expect, is the poet's belief that primeval language was invested with real power. The language of prehistoric man was also the language of the gods, as well as the language of the forces of nature. When Xlebnikov argues against allowing the infidel of foreign words to enter the temple of his language . . . , his claim is based on the concept of sacred language. We are naturally tempted to draw parallels here between Xlebnikov's primitivism and what Ernst Cassirer calls "word veneration" in various mythologies, a vision of the word as a source of creation and power. The poet's discourse on the similarities between transrational language and the incomprehensible liturgical writings

of the world's great religions, to which believers attribute the power to move "the hearts of gentle men" . . . would seem to support the analogy. But it cannot be sustained against the background of Xlebnikov's intrinsic rationalism. He is a visionary, but not a mystic. Language had power, and has power, not by virtue of its primal existence ("In the beginning was the Word, and the Word was with God, and the Word was God") but because it is a repository of wisdom. Language is knowledge. In one of his earliest essays Xlebnikov writes:

The simplest language saw only the play of forces. Perhaps in the mind of ancient man these forces simply rang with the language of consonants. Only the advance of science will permit us to divine all the wisdom of language, which is wise because it was itself part of nature. . . .

Elsewhere he adds, "It appears that language is just as wise as nature, and only with the advance of science are we learning to read it. . . . The wisdom of language preceded the wisdom of science." . . . The wisdom of language is such that it is even suitable for solving abstract problems—analyzing the nature of light, for example, or ascertaining the character of good and evil. This supposition is oddly reminiscent of Benjamin Lee Whorf's thesis that the structure of language reflects the speaker's cosmological perceptions. Xlebnikov, too, is asserting that linguistic structures reveal, and by implication affect our perception of the world around us. The difference, of course, is that the poet believes language in its original form to be a repository of absolute knowledge: perceptional relativism, to the extent that it is acknowledged at all, is a consequence of linguistic diversity, which for the poet was symptomatic of evolutionary disintegration.

Also implicit in Xlebnikov's claim is a denial that the linguistic sign is arbitrary; he repeatedly asserts that there is a kind of identity between the signifier and the signified. I say "a kind of" because Xlebnikov never insists on the "essential identity between the word and what it denotes." The identity is iconic, as we discover in the poet's reflections on *zaum'*:

Hence the concept of language as a game of dolls; in this game dolls for all the world's things are sewn out of scraps of sound. People who speak the same language take part in this game. For people who speak another language these dolls of sound are merely a bunch of sound-scraps. Thus a word is a doll of sound, and a dictionary a bunch of toys. But language naturally evolved from a few basic units of the alphabet; consonants and vowels were the strings in this game of dolls of sound. And if one takes a combination of such sounds in arbitrary order—for example, *bobeobi*, or *dyr bul ščel*, or *manč'! manč'! či breo zo!*—such words do not belong to any particular language, but at the same time they say something, something elusive, but nonetheless something real. . . .

The gods in *Zangezi* are frightened away by the transrational monologue of the hero, not because of any inherent power of the word stemming from its sacral origins, but because of the knowledge that surfaces when thick layers of semantic convention are brushed away.

In order to understand more fully the power of the word one must be aware of the psychology of language as Xlebnikov perceives it. The word, he says, is a face with a hat slung low over the forehead: the mental precedes the verbal and aural. . . . Once the link is established between the verbal and the mental, the power of the word is established, and its power is truly awesome, for "the word controls the brain, the brain—the hands, and the hands—the state." . . . That is why the poet frequently refers to words, and more specifically to their semantic distillation in the form of consonants, as a "conducting wire of fate." "The word is tripartite in nature: sound, mind, and a path for fate." . . . The initial consonant is a "wire, a channel for the currents of fate" whereby we "hear the future in indistinct murmurings." . . . (pp. 9-10)

Unfortunately, language as we know it today has "betrayed its glorious past." . . . It has grown petrified and lost touch with its original meaning. In view of the ancient power of the word, the consequences have been fateful. The original language of mankind has disintegrated into several mutually unintelligible languages, which has led to misunderstanding (the distortion of knowledge) and enmity. . . .

Here we see the theoretical foundations of Xlebnikov's anti-symbolist and xenophobic stance. If the poet is expected to wrestle with languages, to "lay siege to their secrets," . . . it is enough that he has to deal with his own language in its present state of dissolution without having to put up with the Babel of foreign influences. The symbolists are a harmful influence, not because of their symbolism, but because they idolize the West and reject their Russian roots, both linguistically and culturally:

> All the robust, full-fleshed words of the Russian language were banished from the pages of (the symbolist journal) *Vesy*. Their *Vesy* is a dog on its back, waving its paws at the West, yelping about its total innocence before the yellow wolf-hound. . . .

The symbolists are also accused of profaning the language and contributing to its petrification by working with the language merely as craftsmen:

> It would be totally senseless to enter into verbal battle with these men of verbal industry. One has to pick them up like traitors with a hand protected by a glove, and then the Russian literary field will be rid of these spiders. . . .

Eventually Xlebnikov became less chauvinistic in his views; Viktor Gofman is quite correct in asserting that Xlebnikov used a large number of foreign words, including those borrowed from languages outside the Slavic family, but the majority of these borrowings occurred after he had formulated his ideas of a universal language. Nonetheless when he did manifest an interest in a key to all languages his attention was focused on the East—Persia, India, Japan—and not the West.

Despite the deficiencies that Xlebnikov detects in present-day languages as opposed to the pristine language of the prehistoric past, he is still convinced that it retains many of its primeval features. Language is still wise, language is still powerful, but its wisdom has to be rediscovered and its power once again exploited. This is where the poet, the word-maker, finds his true function. He discovers his model in the linguistic activity of that amorphous entity known as "the people."

Here we must make a brief digression into the nature of Xlebnikov's *narodnost'* ("folk impulse"), not because that quality is so often attributed to the poet (it is not) but because it is so

frequently used in discussing his early coinages. Nikolaj Xardžiev, for example, cites passages from **"Svjatogor Mound"** and **"Our Foundation"** to buttress the claim that the poet's early word creations find their antecedent in folk poetry. But we must be careful not to lend too literal an interpretation to Xlebnikov's words. This is what he has to say:

> And will we remain deaf to the voice of the earth: "Give me lips! Give me lips!" Or will we continue to parrot Western voices? . . . Will Russian wisdomry (*umnečestvo*), which has always thirsted for the truth, repudiate the right it has been granted by the will of the people, the right to create words. . . .
>
> (pp. 10-12)

Only a few of Xlebnikov's published works consistently employ the derivational means of folk poetry, among them **"Kak vo lodočke . . ."** . . . and **"Komu skazaten'ki . . ."**. . . . A fairly large number of affixes have a pronounced colloquial flavor, but the coinages in which they appear seldom give the context the air of folk poetry. Of course there may be markedly folkish works in Xardžiev's possession which would fill in the picture, but until they are made available for critical scrutiny we must conclude that as far as word creation is concerned, attempts to imitate folk forms are not the rule in Xlebnikov's poetry. What the poet probably had in mind in the passage from **"Svjatogor Mound"** quoted above was the *principle* of word creation, most productive in the rich flow of peasant speech. In his wanderings across Russia he had every opportunity to acquaint himself with these riches, as the abundance of dialectisms in his poetry clearly demonstrates. In fact they often pose a problem to the critic because there are numerous cases where a word registered as a dialectism in some dictionary might just as well be construed as an unintentionally homonymic coinage. Of course the poet did not have to wander about Russia in search of colloquial models for his coinages. He was familiar with, and obviously borrowed from, Dal''s *Tolkovyj slovar'*, which provided him with hundreds of examples of word creation in folk speech, not to mention the words coined by Dal' himself.

In fact there is no need to search for neological antecedents in folk poetry to justify Xlebnikov's claim that his own coinages were made in the spirit of the vernacular; he provides us with another, more convincing rationale. We have already spoken of language's ties with nature in Xlebnikov's conception. But nature is not limited to the voice of the earth or the murmur of the pines. It is, says Xlebnikov, "the soul of the people." . . . This is the key to Xlebnikov's "folk" approach. The language of the people is far less petrified than the language of books. Its fluidity is manifested in the freedom with which words are created. It provides the poet with a model. If he can master the method, he too can bring new life to language:

> Just as modern man stocks the depleted waters of rivers with schools of fish, so language-making (*jazykovodstvo*) gives one the right to stock the impoverished waves of the language with new life, with extinct or non-existing words. . . .
>
> (pp. 12-13)

The difference between the people and the poet is that the latter approaches the problem of renovating the language and, more specifically, of creating new words, in a more methodical and scientific manner. It is the application of science, says Xlebnikov, which permits us to learn what language has to say, to fathom its wisdom. . . . Of course Xlebnikov's science is subjective and altogether suspect from our perspective, but it does imply a very real methodology of creation. Moreover this science is syntonic with its poetic environment, which is reason enough to examine it.

Given, then, that the use of coinages (together with archaisms and dialectisms) is one of the primary means of linguistic renovation, how exactly does the poet proceed? The answer to that question is found in the structure of the language and the word itself as revealed by the poet's scientific method. Here Xlebnikov resorts to metaphorical description. Each metaphor reveals something of his view of the word's structure. First, and most obvious, is the metaphor of the linguistic tree. The words of the language are like the leaves of a tree which are fed by the roots of the language. The roots, says the poet, are of God, and the words of man. . . . By implication, then, one can return to the language of the gods by returning to the roots of the language. Sometimes the poet uses "root" rather loosely to mean not the base, but the primary meaning of the word:

> Besides the sound-leaves and root-thought in words (via the initial sound) there runs the thread of fate, and consequently it [the word] has a tubular structure. . . .

Here Xlebnikov is curiously close to Saussure's concept of the sign, which consists of the sound-image or *signifiant* (*zvuko-list'ja*) and the concept or *signifié* (*korne-mysel*). Paradoxically the term *korne-mysel* is a reflection of Xlebnikov's insistence on some sort of inner relationship between sound and meaning, a point vigorously disputed by the Swiss linguist.

While the metaphor of roots and branches accentuates the word's past and its evolution, the next image proffered by the poet, the word as a butterfly or moth, leads us into a field that has very few antecedents in linguistic scholarship because it stresses word potential. In a sense this is the very essence of Xlebnikov's futurism. It reveals the true dynamism of his theoretical approach. In the previous metaphor the word's past is treated as something hidden below the surface of the word, and its present as something that has the visibility of broad leaves. In the metaphor of the butterfly, the present is a visible shell or cocoon; what is hidden from view are the curled wings of the future. Language is a dynamic structure and the poet's primary concern is to study the process of its coming-into-being, and to participate in that process:

> . . . Cannot the Russian people permit itself the luxury . . . of creating language? . . . One who knows the Russian countryside knows of words which are formed for an hour and have the life span of a butterfly. . . .

(pp. 13-14)

The poet's involvement in the very process he is studying is underscored by the use of the metaphor in another context:

> For me, a butterfly who happened to fly
> Into the room of human life,
> To leave the script of my wing-dust
> On the stark windows like a captive's signature
> On the harsh glass panes of fate,
> How dull and gray
> Is the wallpaper of human life!
> The transparent "No" of the windows!
> I have already worn off my blue glow, the patterns of
>   dots,
> My azure wing-storm, my first freshness.

> The wing-dust is gone, the wings have withered and
>   grown transparent and brittle.
> Wearily I beat against man's window. . . .

No wonder the believers cry out, "Sing us self-sufficient songs! Tell us about El! Read in transrational speech. Speak of our terrible age in words of the Alphabet!" . . . There is an intriguing similarity between the uncertainty principle in quantum mechanics and the poet's attempt to study derivational processes in language: his involvement in that process alters the very dynamics of what is being investigated. In the end, of course, the most important thing is the poet's participation, a fact recognized by Mandel'štam when he said, "Xlebnikov works over words like a mole, and in the process he has dug passages in the earth for the future, for a whole century. . . .".

Another highly suggestive metaphor, or rather, chain of metaphors, can be found in the poet's first volume of verse, *Tvorenija (Creations)*. Here Xlebnikov states laconically, "Slovo—pjal'cy; slovo—len; slovo tkan'" ("The word is a tambour; the word is flax; the word is fabric"). . . . This series of comparisons is certainly open to a variety of interpretations, but against the background of Xlebnikov's coinages one chain of meanings stands out: the word is a construct whose components include: 1) meaning (the ready cloth or fabric), 2) sound (the material from which the fabric is woven), and 3) the rules governing the combination of threads of sound into fabrics of meaning (the tambour or frame). Consequently the fashioning of new words may involve 1) the alteration or rearrangement of the semantic units of language; 2) the free selection and combination of the sound materials that make up the word; 3) modification of the rules that govern their combination. Xlebnikov exercised all these options in his neology.

One of the images that frequently arises when Xlebnikov tries to justify his word-making is silence and dumbness. For Majakovskij it is the streets which are tongue-tied and turn to the poet for aid. For Xlebnikov it is the language itself which needs a voice, and word creation provides the necessary medium:

> Word creation is an explosion of language's silence, the deaf-and-dumb layers of language. By replacing one sound with another in an old word we immediately create a path leading from one valley of language to another, and like engineers we blaze trails of communication in the land of words across the mountain crests of the silence of language. . . .

New words give names to concepts which have been smothered or masked by superficial meaning. The "language of the stars" permits one to name "concepts of units of the mind" . . . which have been silenced in the passage of the centuries.

But word creation also has a very practical communicative function. It guarantees mutual understanding and is conducive to the acquisition of true knowledge. It unites men where ordinary language divides them, and therefore it can serve as a guarantor of peace. Self-sufficient speech (*samovitaja reč'*) is a "bridge to the self-sufficient kingdom (*samovitoe carstvo*)" . . . , where war and Babel are both anachronisms.

It should be clear from all I have said that Xlebnikov is vitally concerned with meaning. I have stressed—perhaps even belabored—this point because most of the misunderstanding of Xlebnikov's poetics is based on the false presumption that the poet is concerned almost exclusively with sound as such and the word as such. Nonetheless there is a streak of aestheticism running through his works that must be acknowledged. Initially that aestheticism seemed to be a response to the mysticism of the second generation of symbolists, as was the aestheticism of the acmeists:

> Do not all means also wish to be ends? Here are the paths for the beauty of the word to follow, apart from its ends. The tree that forms a hedge itself produces flowers. . . .

In his reflections **"On Contemporary Poetry"** . . . Xlebnikov sets his own aestheticism in a historical context. In the history of the literary language, he says, there are times when the sound element dominates and times when the conceptual element comes to the fore. Sometimes sound is the satellite circling the concept, and sometimes the concept is the satellite circling sound. For all those who follow the path of experimentation, the factor of sound assumes prominence, not to the detriment of meaning, but rather to its fuller embodiment. This was true of Lomonosov, who posited theories that sound very much like a defense of transrationalism, and it was true of Xlebnikov. The tree of language, he says, must flower first if it is to bear fruit.

There is one last aspect of Xlebnikov's aestheticism directly related to his most radical forms of word creation which should also be mentioned. In his own theoretical declarations Xlebnikov constantly presents the poet as a revolutionary and prophet whose task is to recreate language as such, not merely poetic language. The creation of *zaum'*, a universal language, is the poet's ultimate goal. Yet Xlebnikov was primarily a poet, not a theoretician, and he was forced to admit that *zaum'*, for all its merits, could never really serve as a medium for poetic expression. That is why, for example, he says that once a universal language takes hold "languages will remain the property of art and will be freed from their insulting burden." . . . The word, he asserts, "will no longer be used for everyday affairs, but for the sake of the word itself." . . . But until that goal is achieved, the word retains all the complex functions we have discussed, and word creation will remain a sacred obligation. (pp. 14-16)

> *Ronald Vroon, in his* Velimir Xlebnikov's Shorter Poems: A Key to the Coinages, *Department of Slavic Languages and Literatures, The University of Michigan, 1983, 251 p.*

PAUL SCHMIDT (essay date 1985)

[*In the following excerpt, Schmidt discusses the principal themes and techniques of Khlebnikov's works.*]

Khlebnikov creates poems by playing with the relationship between the morphological and phonological structures of language and meaning: he makes frequent use of forms that tend to produce maximum ambiguity, such as neologisms, homonyms, puns, and nonsense. The structure of a word could be examined, Khlebnikov found, and its latent meanings laid bare; new words could be created on the models of existing ones. Much of Khlebnikov's writing, therefore, has to do with the texture of language, with poetry as *made words*. His puns and neologisms are attempts to lay bare the meanings that may be hidden in the worn-out language of every day.

Khlebnikov was convinced of the magic power of words. In the story **"K"** he writes: "I believe that before a major war the word *pugovitsa* [button] has an especially frightening meaning, since the war—even though as yet undreamed of—lurks

in that word like a conspirator, a harbinger lark, because the root of the word is related to *pugat'* [to frighten]." Now in fact the two words are not related historically, but that is precisely the point. This kind of derivation, which linguists refer to as folk etymology, was for Khlebnikov the point of entry into the hidden net of coincidences and poetic correspondences that Baudelaire first wrote of, but that for Khlebnikov are more systematic and profound. For him they reveal the workings of destiny because they point the way to the future. Just as magic words are intended to bring about a desired future, so these unexpected glimpses of "magic" patterns hidden beneath the ordinary surface of language can offer us a vision of the world to come. In a preface written in 1919, Khlebnikov comments that "little things are significant when they mask the start of the future. . . . Whenever I saw old lines of writing grow dim and their hidden content become the present day, then I understood. The future is creation's homeland, and from it blows the word-god's wind." We touch here upon the profoundest function of poetry. Familiar language suddenly opens up, and in it something unexpected is revealed. The unexpected is always the future; it appears to us at the edges of meaning, in a moment of illumination that is simultaneously a denial of the ordinary rational use of language. Words refuse to be ideas, part of the world of human reason, which is always the world of the present. They open up the unknown, the unnamed—the world of the future. This is Khlebnikov's great perception. He is able to take a word by itself as a palpable living thing and, by working with it, make it yield new forms and new meanings. (pp. 13-14)

The magic possibilities of language are constantly alive for Khlebnikov. He is always conscious of the wonders that are revealed in permutations in the *form* of words. Puns, palindromes, word derivations, above all the creation of new words: these are fields of experimentation for him, and the experiments pass into his poems. The most famous is **"Incantation by Laughter,"** permutations of the word *laugh* into a weird scenario full of prehistoric chortles.

Beyond purely linguistic transformation, Khlebnikov works with many of the patterns of folk poetry. One frequent presence in his writing is the old Russian folk device of the riddle: the "enormous arboreal monster," for instance, is a lascivious garden swing, hung from the branch of a tall tree. And other poems are full of wonders: flute-playing tigers, peripatetic frogs, singing bones, the transformation of the stricken deer into the conquering lion.

This sense of the vitality of the natural world is part of Khlebnikov's heritage from Russian folklore. The magical inhabitants of the Slavic forest—the *rusalka*, the *leshy*, the *vila* (river mermaid, goblin, forest enchantress)—all populate his poetry and his imagination. Khlebnikov's earliest attempts at poetry were rooted in the revival of the old Slavic tradition that was a side branch of Russian Symbolism: attractive experiments with folk languages, folk patterns even, poems as reflections of the intricate embroideries and wood carvings of peasant culture. These are the same influences that are reflected in the other arts, in Stravinsky's *Sacre du printemps* and *Les Noces* and in Goncharova's designs for Diaghilev. (p. 19)

[In the poems published between 1914 and 1916] Khlebnikov's cosmic vision begins to grow. The correspondences between elements of the natural world suddenly expand to include abstract phenomena like numbers and the movement of the stars and planets; history echoes in sounds drifting on the water; the names of the great creators of human culture resound in the wind and rain. The folkloric patterns in Khlebnikov blend with his studies in the sciences; the magical, pagan, Slavic forest culture and the abstract conception of mathematics fuse metaphorically:

> I see right through you, Numbers.
> I see you in the skins of animals
> coolly propped against uprooted oaks.

In a similar way the legendary city of Kitezh in *The Tables of Destiny* rises magically from the bottom of a lake and transforms itself into a long equation whose powers and superscripts rise like crenellated towers and glitter, reflected in the water.

Khlebnikov seems to have heard within himself not just one voice but hundreds, and was able to make out beneath their clamor the pure sounds of language forming themselves into patterns, resonating with the "sounding string of humanity." Khlebnikov was searching for the voice of Time itself, sounding in language. (p. 27)

In 1921, in connection with his activities as a civilian publicist with the military on the southern front, Khlebnikov suddenly got the chance to go to Persia as a journalist and lecturer with the Red Army. In mid-April he sailed for Enzeli, ecstatic at the sun and sea, and the opportunity finally to be in the East he had felt a part of for so long. He stayed for a time as a tutor in the house of a Talysh Khan and explored coastal and inland villages, tanned and long-haired, dressed in native robes, living on handouts. "I told the Persians," he wrote, "that I was a Russian prophet."

All the poems that relate to his sojourn in Persia are full of excitement and events: the thrill of travel, exotic landscapes, the turmoil of revolution—Khlebnikov mentions the exploits of his friend, the revolutionary sailor Boris Samorodov—possible experiments with drugs. But above all, his time in Persia seems to have confirmed his sense of vocation. His poem "Night in Persia," with its reference to the Mekhdi (Mahdi), the Islamic messiah, is filled, like Pushkin's "Prophet," with wonder at the divine visitation that turns a poet into a spokesman for the ineffable.

The pull of Asia was very strong in Khlebnikov, partly as a result of his upbringing near the Caspian and partly as a corrective for what he considered the excessive Western European influence on Russian culture—an attitude documented in manifestos like "!Futurian!" But even more important is Khlebnikov's vision of the land mass of Asia as the center of the world of the Future, when Slavic culture would join with the cultures of Islam, Hinduism, and Buddhism to form an unshakable foundation for a regenerated planet. (p. 39)

The Civil War of 1918-1920 meant massive disruption of the Russian economy, and in the summers of 1920 and 1921 there was disastrous drought. Like many Russians during this time, Khlebnikov wandered from place to place and suffered hunger, deprivation, and disease.... [The poems from his notebooks dated 1920-21] differ in style from his earlier work—these are simpler, freer, perhaps not yet fully worked. They provide one of our most moving documents of that tragic period of Russian history. (p. 46)

The years 1920-1922 were a time of enormous hardship in Russia, but also years of an enormous surge of creativity in all the arts. "I remember shaking with excitement all the time," Sergei Eisenstein wrote, thinking of his work in the theater during those years. For Khlebnikov too this was the period of his greatest achievement. In the midst of privation and the upheaval of civil war and famine, he had his most prophetic visions of the future. They found shape in essays like "**The Radio of the Future**" and "**Ourselves and Our Buildings,**" in the grandiose conceptions of *Zangezi* and *The Tables of Destiny,* and in a series of remarkable, mature poems: powerful, direct, inspired by vision and a sense of the accomplishment of his own destiny. (p. 53)

Khlebnikov writes in 1919: "In *Mrs. Laneen* I wanted to discover the 'infinitesimals' of artistic language." ... [Many of his fictions,] plays and prose, are in a sense attempts to make that discovery: What are the building blocks of artistic creation, Khlebnikov asks, and how can they be fitted together? How, in particular, does the accumulation of details go to create the perception of an event? ... [Two] small plays, *Mrs. Laneen* and *The World in Reverse,* seem like sketches for more elaborate treatment, but both are strictly schematic and derive from theater experiments of the time: they are attempts at interior monologue, following the experiments of Maeterlinck in *The Intruder, Interior,* and *The Blind,* and especially of Evreinov, whose monodrama, *The Performance of Love,* similar in style to *Mrs. Laneen,* was published in 1910 in the same journal as Khlebnikov's poems "**Incantation by Laughter**" and "**The Tangled Wood.**"

The fantasy "**K**" is, in its own way, a compendium of the devices of science fiction written well before the development of that genre but, for all its hallucinatory details, is a first-person narration describing the perceptions of the narrator, as are *Mrs. Laneen* and "**October on the Neva.**" The fact that one is fantasy, one a play, and the other a historical memoir is less important than the basic matter of what and how we perceive and record. Khlebnikov addresses the question of what constitutes an event—in history as well as in personal, emotional life—and at what level of perception we might possibly distinguish the objective from the subjective.

"**Nikolai**" is also a first-person narration, but here, as in "**Usa-Gali,**" Khlebnikov writes more conventionally, as he focusses on the vital question, for him, of man's relationship to his natural environment. The presentation of two such "natural" men, in a traditionally objective narrative frame that distances us from them and their behavior and thus offers them as models, points to Khlebnikov's intense concern for a world in danger of destruction. (pp. 61-2)

Human beings have long perceived the workings of destiny—the grand pattern of the mover of the universe—in coincidence, in accident, in the moment of perception of a problem previously unsuspected. So did Khlebnikov. Destiny was his prime concern. The category of those who study the workings of the universe is unclear—Lucretius and Dante may be scientists, just as Newton and Einstein may be poets. Khlebnikov was both. For him, the shift in sound that produces a shift in meaning was a shift in the structure of the universe. That the shift of a vowel made the Russian word for sword (*mech*) become the word for ball (*miach*) gave Khlebnikov a vertiginous sense of the power of language to influence the natural world. The shift of a consonant was all that distinguished *inventors* from *investors* or *explorers* from *exploiters*—and suddenly there appears the image of a struggle between *N* and *S*, between *R* and *T*. The movement of consonants became a metaphor for political and economic conflict.

To many of his readers this seemed, and seems, like nonsense. But we must be careful to distinguish, as he did, between nonsense and *beyonsense* (*zaum,* in Russian). The word *zaum* was part of the Futurist vocabulary, used by different poets in different ways. In Khlebnikov the word must be seen first as a function of its root, the word *um:* intellect, intelligence, reason, the rational faculty of the mind. *Um* implies the creation of "pilings," the foundations of the man-made structures that must sooner or later destroy the mind's unity with the natural world. *Um* also implies the separation of thinking man from the natural stuff of language: the shape, sound, and color of words. The opposite of *um* is magic, magic words, the part of language that contains a power inaccessible to the intellect and is always opposed to it. It is here that poetry stands—but poetry had been weakened during the nineteenth century, especially in Russia, by positivism and historicism. So Khlebnikov attempts a radical corrective: to reclaim a power for poetry by reaching back beyond (*za*) intellect (*um*), to the roots of language.

The "strange wisdom" of language perceived in this way, he writes . . . in the fragmentary essay **"On Poetry,"** "may be broken down into truths contained in separate sounds: *sh, m, v,* etc. We do not yet understand these sounds. We confess that honestly. But there is no doubt that these sound sequences constitute a series of universal truths passing before the pre-dawn of our soul." The purpose of beyonsense is to return to poetry a status as life-sustaining communication, relieved of worn-out words, those "clumps of intellect, stacks of sense, / a wagon train of dead ideas." Beyonsense was to make language ready for the future.

The tone of [many of Khlebnikov's essays] . . . is aggressive, polemical, aimed at the established older generation of Symbolist writers—Briusov, Balmont, Merezhkovsky—and their journal *Libra*. It is the tone of an impatient young man, aware of his Russianness and concerned to defend it against Western influences. **"!Futurian!"** attacks the wave of European influence that Symbolism represented in Russia. **"The Word as Such"** defends Russian Futurism from the prior claims of Italian Futurism. In **"The Trumpet of the Martians"** and **"An Appeal by the Presidents of Planet Earth,"** the voice of the younger generation makes a more sweeping claim: in 1916 Khlebnikov with his friend and disciple Grigory Petnikov founded the Society of 317, intended to be an association of creative scientists, writers, and thinkers from various countries who would form a world government and oppose the evils wrought by political states. Soon Khlebnikov's name for himself and his group of friends evolved into the Presidents of Planet Earth, "inventor / explorers" who took a stand against the "investor / exploiters" of this world.

The most astonishing of these pieces are the visions of the future, where Khlebnikov predicts some of modern technology's most compelling achievements. His essay **"The Radio of the Future"** foresees the global communication network of present-day television, while **"Ourselves and Our Buildings"** and **"A Cliff Out of the Future"** describe with accuracy and a certain amount of wit the wonders of late twentieth-century urban architecture and city planning. **"To the Artists of the World"** envisages a universal written language.

All these projects are universal in scope, and they aim at the same restructuring of the world as did the 1917 Revolution— which, we must always remember, echos at the margins of all these texts. But Khlebnikov's projects attempt to set humanity free from the tyranny of history and causality; they could not compete with an ideology organized on those very premises. (pp. 113-15)

It was in mathematics that Khlebnikov found his dominant metaphor. The presence of Time in poetic rhythm eventually forced him to look for the rhythms that sounded beneath the conventional ones, to seek meaning in the cyclical patterns of the universe. Number was the key. On February 25, 1911, the twenty-six-year-old poet wrote to his brother Alexander: "I am making a diligent study of numbers and have discovered quite a few patterns. I intend to keep going and work it all out completely, though, until I get some answers as to why it all behaves this way." That diligent study was to become almost an obsession, as Khlebnikov tried to work out an all-embracing system of correspondences between languages and the "language of the stars," between human behavior and the movement of the universe.

Khlebnikov traces the origins of this enterprise to the Russian defeat in the Russo-Japanese War. In a brief memoir written in 1919 he states: "I wanted to discover the reason for all those deaths." We come, then, to the perception that lies at the source of philosophical speculation and of all the great poetic structures of human culture. "I had not thought death had undone so many," Dante marvels. For Khlebnikov, trained as a mathematician, the free play of numbers offered the possibility of circumventing the disasters of history. To study the past in order to envisage the future is no new idea; what is new here, however, is the conception—unrelated to the cabalistic tradition—of numbers as the unifying force that creates, in some predictable way, the relationships within which we perceive meaning.

Khlebnikov tries to explain the subjective universe that we as human beings inhabit as a function of the objective universe of classical mathematics, a world of unique entities with inherent properties and fixed relationships among them: to make numbers explain and influence human behavior in the same way that human language does. He attempts to reconcile an abstract, self-contained system like mathematics with the human world of ambiguity and the pervasive presence of metaphor. His attempt, no matter how it may be judged objectively, is a powerful metaphoric act, an act of poetry on an awesome scale. And although poetry was his means to this attempted end, Khlebnikov is by no means a mystic. He saw himself rather as a prophet, a discoverer, in the line of Aryabkatta, Leibniz, Lomonosov, and Lobachevsky: thinkers with a vision of the whole, creators of new forms that would penetrate the surface of phenomena and yield a new art that might change the human condition.

In a wry little poem printed in 1914, Khlebnikov describes concisely the underlying principle of his view of history, the idea of an equilibrium produced by the shift from positive to negative states:

> The law of the see-saw argues
> That your shoes will be loose or tight,
> That the hours will be day or night,
> And the ruler of earth the rhinoceros
> Or us.

It is this notion of an equilibrium to be found in a shift from positive to negative, from victory to disaster, that underlies *The Tables of Destiny*. This work was to be Khlebnikov's crowning achievement. Like Poe's *Eureka*, it is a strange, seemingly "unpoetic" finale to a life's work. It was intended to document in seven sections . . . the operation of this law of the see-saw, now called the Laws of Time. (pp. 167-68)

Khlebnikov manipulates conventional poetic forms in surprising ways. Basic to his style is the notion of what he called a "supersaga"—a number of seemingly discrete texts put together to form a whole. *Zangezi* is the most extraordinary of these strange hybrids, "an architecture composed of narratives," as Khlebnikov puts it in his introduction.

The supersaga works against the notion of the discreteness of a particular composition; it points to the fact of any artist's work as a continuous on-going whole, a constant reconsideration of a few basic themes. It also makes us reexamine our sense of the way things hang together, the way we as readers make sense of a text. The apparent difficulties of a text like *Zangezi*—unexplained references, seemingly illogical and nonsensical juxtapositions—are deliberate attempts by its author to create a text where our experience of the world will not serve, but where we are forced, as children are, to perceive an unknown world.

Khlebnikov valued the writing of children; in their work he saw human creativity before reason and intelligence had been at work, before the oppositions skill—clumsiness and good-bad are learned. In the innocence of such work Khlebnikov thought he could make out the quality of what all writing would be like "in the Future," when these oppositions and *um*, the dualistic reasoning power that creates them, have dissolved. His own use of alogical, primitive, nonrational "languages" attempts to recapture the childhood experience, the creation of a new world, the discovery of new continents.

The hero of Khlebnikov's theater piece, his alter ego, is the prophet Zangezi, conceived somewhat in the spirit of Nietzsche's Zarathustra. Like the young Khlebnikov—and like those other young forest heros, Hiawatha and Siegfried—Zangezi understands the language of the birds. But he understands the powers of language in its broadest senses—and the various "planes" of *Zangezi* catalogue and exemplify some of the possible languages that connect the universe: the language of the gods, the beyonsense language *zaum*, the language of the stars in Plane Eight, where each letter and sound of the alphabet is in fact an arrangement of points in space ("Alphabet is the echo of space!"), the declension of intellect in Plane Nine, sound-writing in Plane Fifteen, fragments of popular speech in Planes Sixteen and Seventeen, the grand movement of numbers as history in Planes Eighteen and Nineteen, and finally, in Plane Twenty, in a pure theatrical metaphor, a scene from some fantastic medieval morality play, the crystallization of all human endeavor in the struggle of Laughter with Death. (pp. 189-90)

Zangezi is in many ways Khlebnikov's summation of his own work. It is a presentation of his ideas and poetic style joined in an edifice like some fabulous cathedral, whose bewildering juxtapositions of mosaics and frescoes will tell, if they are read correctly, the story of a transcendent faith in the human spirit. (p. 190)

Paul Schmidt, in editorial comments in The King of Time: Selected Writings of the Russian Futurian *by Velimir Khlebnikov, edited by Charlotte Douglas, translated by Paul Schmidt, Cambridge, Mass.: Harvard University Press, 1985, 255 p.*

JOSEPH BRODSKY (essay date 1986)

[*Brodsky is a Russian poet and critic who emigrated from the Soviet Union in 1972 and became an American citizen in 1977. His early poems were considered morally and politically subver-*

sive by the Soviet government, which exiled him for a time to labor at a remote collective farm. Nevertheless, Brodsky's eventual flight from a repressive communist society was also an estrangement from the Russian culture of which he felt a rightful part, as well as a separation from the language necessary to his vitality as a poet. This latter deprivation is an especially poignant one for Brodsky, who has stated his view of poetry as a relief from the horrors and absurdities of life and the meaningless vacuum of death. In a line from one of his most admired poems, "Gorbunov and Gorchakov," he states: "Life is but talk hurled into the void." This temperament, along with the often philosophical cast of his poetry, has led critics to link Brodsky with the modern school of existentialism, an affiliation supported by the important influence played by such precursors of existentialism as Søren Kierkegaard and Fedor Dostoevski in forming Brodsky's artistic vision. Brodsky's work has been well-received by English and American critics, many of whom have called him the greatest living Russian poet. In the following excerpt, he discusses the influences of Futurism, philology, and the social events of the early twentieth century on Khlebnikov's works. In an unexcerpted portion of this essay, Brodsky details what he considers the deficiencies of Paul Schmidt's translations of Khlebnikov's work in The King of Time.]

Of all the "isms" this century coined, Futurism's life span proved to be the shortest. That is owed to the future's overnight tendency to encroach on the present. In literature this process is more palpable than in other arts, because of its incurably semantic nature. To be evaluated, an utterance must make sense. To survive, it must contain a grain of truth, be that a psychological, social, scientific, philosophical, or metaphysical truth; it also has to be stylistically distinct. Short on the former and very drastic on the latter, Velimir Khlebnikov's work is a phenomenon of towering incoherence, and that is what perhaps ultimately justifies its label.

Born in 1885, Khlebnikov died at the age of 37 of typhus, which he contracted on one of his seemingly aimless wanderings through the land in which his entire adult life was spent. He was a foot and railroad-car man as much as a writer. From under his dead head a pillowcase was extracted, filled with heaps of his manuscripts: poems, plays, short stories, literary manifestos, treatises. . . . [His collected] output runs to six volumes, and the word that comes to mind considering his works' quantity and quality is exactly this: mileage.

He was a product of an era now famous for its hysterical, apocalyptic pitch, for its millenarian sensibility: the era marked by the turn of the century, Halley's comet, social utopianism, the carnage of the Great War, the collapse of the social order in a minimum of three European countries, the Russian Revolution, the Civil War, cinema, flying machines, and starvation. In Russia, however, it was also a period of great upsurge in religious philosophy, as well as in poetry and philology. Khlebnikov's work fell prey to all those, or vice versa; but first and foremost he was a philologist and a visionary. Naturally, this wasn't a matter of training, for at the university Khlebnikov studied physics and biology; it was a matter of vocation.

The proximity between philology—from the Greek "philo" (love) and "logos" (word or reason)—and the art of letters is such that often an individual who practices one mistakes his occupation for the other. Thus Roman Jakobson in his youth wrote poetry (which was, as a matter of fact, every bit as Futuristic as anything produced by Khlebnikov). Khlebnikov, however, was not prepared, either by his temperament or by the circumstances of his life, to make a distinction. He set out to reach two goals—first, to collect, and thereby to purify and to create, the Russian language, a process that he felt was as yet unfinished by history; and second, to discover the rhythm of world history. If for the first task he resolved to poke in the dictionaries of the Slavic peoples (Montenegrins and others, to use his own words), the latter required plain arithmetic, and he in fact came up with the figure 317—the number of years that constituted the interval with which similar cataclysmic events changed the world.

Both tasks demanded stretching, as well as squeezing. The material of the first, however, was more pliable, and it yielded far more attractive, far less embarrassing results. Russian is a highly inflected language. A word in Russian gets changed not only by gender, number, and its grammatical function in the sentence; it is also modified by prefixes, suffixes, and infixes. This is what everyone does, but Khlebnikov went to town with it. At times his verse sounds like what birds presumably heard from St. Francis. Under his pen, nouns, verbs, adjectives, adverbs, and prepositions undergo mutations as mind-boggling as those of a cell hit by immense radiation. Beautiful or grotesque, the results are often memorable, if only because the trophy of a word's meaning is paid for with the casualties of his mutilated grammar.

About 80 percent of Khlebnikov's verse and prose are utterly unpalatable and incomprehensible. The remaining 20 percent are diamonds of an unparalleled splendor, although the trouble of extracting them from the mud heap of the rest is formidable. (p. 32)

Joseph Brodsky, "The Meaning of Meaning," in The New Republic, *Vol. 194, No. 3, January 20, 1986, pp. 32-5.*

ADDITIONAL BIBLIOGRAPHY

Baran, Henryk. "Xlebnikov and the Mythology of the Oroches." In *Slavic Poetics: Essays in Honor of Kiril Taranovsky*, edited by Roman Jakobson, C. H. Van Schooneveld, and Dean S. Worth, pp. 33-9. The Hague: Mouton, 1973.
Investigates Khlebnikov's adoption of themes and motifs from the mythology of the Oroche, an Asian tribe inhabiting the Amur River region near China in the southeastern Soviet Union.

———. "Xlebnikov and the *History* of Herodotus." *Slavic and East European Journal* 22, No. 1 (Spring 1978): 30-4.*
Examines several works in which Khlebnikov adapted Herodotus's renderings of Scythian history, observing that "motifs associated with the Scythians—bravery, patriotism—could not fail to attract Xlebnikov, who constantly sought to explore cultures which he regarded as healthier than that of modern Russia."

Cooke, R. F. "Image and Symbol in Khlebnikov's 'Night Search'." *Russian Literature Triquarterly*, No. 12 (1975): 279-94.
Examines Khlebnikov's use of imagery to depict the protagonist's inner conflict.

———. "Magic in the Poetry of Velimir Khlebnikov." *Essays in Poetics* 5, No. 2 (September 1980): 15-42.
Discusses magical and mythological motifs in Khlebnikov's poetry, focusing in particular on the numerous incantations in his poems.

De Jonge, Alex. "President of the Terrestrial Globe." *Times Literary Supplement*, No. 3912 (4 March 1977): 252.
General discussion of the works in *Snake Train*.

Jakobson, Roman. "Modern Russian Poetry: Velimir Khlebnikov [Excerpts]." In *Major Soviet Writers: Essays in Criticism*, edited by Edward J. Brown, pp. 58-82. London: Oxford University Press, 1973.*
Excerpts from Jakobson's 1921 analysis of Khlebnikov's poetic language, which is now considered a classic essay in formalist literary criticism.

Lönnqvist, Barbara. *Xlebnikov and Carnival*. Uppsala, Sweden: Almqvist & Wiksell, 1979, 166 p.
Detailed analysis of the poem "Poet."

Markov, Vladimir. *Russian Futurism: A History*. Berkeley and Los Angeles: University of California Press, 1968, 467 p.*
Comprehensive study of Russian Futurism, examining the movement's origins, theories, major figures, and most notable works, with numerous references to Khlebnikov.

Mirsky, D. S. "The Rise of Futurism." In his *Contemporary Russian Literature: 1881-1925*, pp. 266-70. New York: Alfred A. Knopf, 1926.*
Brief critical essay focusing on the primitive mysticism of Khlebnikov's works, arguing that "his vision of the primitive world was not the pageant of Gumilev's mythology, nor the virtuous simplicity of Rousseau: what he was after was not natural man, but magical man."

Pomorska, Krystyna. "Futurism as a Poetic School." In her *Russian Formalist Theory and Its Poetic Ambience*, pp. 77-118. The Hague: Mouton, 1968.*
Analyzes the poetic theories and practices of Khlebnikov and other prominent Futurists.

Slonim, Marc. "After the Symbolists." In his *Modern Russian Literature from Chekov to the Present*, pp. 211-33. New York: Oxford University Press, 1953.*
Briefly characterizes Khlebnikov's works, noting that his "savage onslaught on syntax and grammar had a truly rebellious and anarchical tone."

Thomson, R. D. B. "Khlebnikov and $3^6 + 3^6$." In *Russian and Slavic Literature*, edited by Richard Freeborn, R. R. Milner-Gulland, and Charles A. Ward, pp. 297-312. Cambridge, Mass.: Slavica Publishers, 1976.*
Discusses the complex attitude toward the past expressed in Khlebnikov's poems concerning the Revolution.

Vroon, Ronald. "Velimir Khlebnikov's 'Razin: Two Trinities': A Reconstruction." *Slavic Review* 19, No. 1 (March 1980): 70-84.
Maintains that the poem is an unfinished fragment and proposes a possible conclusion based on analysis of the text as well as examination of Khlebnikov's life and other works.

———. "Velimir Khlebnikov's 'I esli v "Xhar'kovskie ptitsy"' . . .': Manuscript Sources and Subtexts." *Russian Review* 42, No. 3 (July 1983): 249-70.
Detailed analysis.

Zavalishin, Vyacheslav. "The Futurists." In his *Early Soviet Writers*, pp. 68-90. New York: Frederick A. Praeger, 1958.*
Discusses the ideological and stylistic changes in Khlebnikov's poetry after the Revolution, maintaining that he abandoned nonrepresentational poetry in order to express his growing antipathy toward the new order.

Ferenc Molnár

1878-1952

(Born Ferenc Neumann) Hungarian dramatist, novelist, short story and novella writer, essayist, and autobiographer.

The author of light comedies praised for their charm and technical excellence, Molnár was the first Hungarian dramatist to achieve international acclaim. His plays often depict relationships between men and women, generally portraying men as victims of their scheming but irresistible partners. His most successful play, *Liliom,* gained fame through its adaptation by Richard Rodgers and Oscar Hammerstein as the musical *Carousel.*

Molnár was the second son of a successful Budapest physician, Mór Neumann, and his wife, Jozepha Wallfisch. As was usual among the Hungarian upper class, he was educated by private tutors until the age of nine. He then entered a Calvinist secondary school, where he printed his own periodicals and staged his first play at the age of fourteen. Upon completion of secondary school in 1895, Molnár studied law at the University of Budapest and at the Swiss University in Geneva. During this period he published articles and feuilletons in Hungarian newspapers and wrote his first novellas and short stories. In 1896 Molnár returned to Budapest, abandoning his law studies to become a full-time journalist. His essays and sketches for leading newspapers were praised for their originality and stylistic excellence, and Molnár was quickly accepted into Budapest's most prominent literary circles, where he earned a reputation as a brilliant conversationalist. In 1901 he published his first novel, *Az éhes város.* Generally disparaged by critics, the novel was immediately popular with readers and became a Hungarian bestseller. Molnár eventually turned to drama, the genre for which he became famous, and his first professionally produced play, *A doktor úr (The Lawyer),* was staged in 1902. This and subsequent productions of Molnár's plays were overwhelmingly successful with audiences. While gaining renown as a dramatist, he continued to be extremely prolific in other genres. According to S. N. Behrman, Molnár's self-imposed literary program for the twenty years preceding World War I required the completion of "a feuilleton or a short dialogue for the papers every day, a short story every week, and a play and a novel every year." He became a celebrity as the result of both the popularity of his works and the scandalous nature of his numerous love affairs, several of which resulted in highly publicized marriages. Molnár's personal relationships were often dramatized in his works; according to Clara Györgyey, "the gossip-hungry Budapest populace stormed the theaters to watch the new developments in the playwright's private life."

At the outbreak of World War I, Molnár was sent by the Budapest daily *Az Est* to accompany Austro-Hungarian troops into battle. His resulting reports, which were also published in the *London Morning Post* and the *New York Times,* were praised for their realistic portrayal of the horrors of war. After 1920 Molnár lived a life of luxury and celebrity, residing in the finest hotels of Budapest, Vienna, Karlsbad, Venice, and Nice. Acclaimed throughout the world, he was decorated with the French cross of the Legion of Honor and was received by President Calvin Coolidge. By 1937, however, the growing threat of war began to affect Molnár's enthusiasm for life. He

became subject to bouts of anxiety and depression and abandoned society life for semiseclusion. He emigrated to the United States in 1941, a move which biographers note had a temporary rejuvenating effect on the author, who rapidly completed a series of plays and short stories. In 1943, however, a massive heart attack and news about the atrocities of the war combined to destroy Molnár's emotional equilibrium. According to Györgyey, "he became apathetic, morose, a misanthrope." In 1947 his despondency was compounded by the suicide of Wanda Bartha, his longtime secretary and companion. Molnár immersed himself in his writing, maintaining that "there is only one consolation on earth, and that is work." His plays and novels from this period, which critics find uncharacteristically melancholy and didactic, are not as highly regarded as his earlier works. After a period of failing health, Molnár died of stomach cancer in 1952.

Molnár's plays reflect his central preoccupations, frequently depicting theater life, the aristocracy, and, most often, relationships between the sexes. Many contain fantastic or supernatural elements, such as *Az ördög (The Devil),* which was the first of his dramas to achieve acclaim outside of Hungary. *The Devil* portrays the efforts of the title character to encourage a young woman to leave her husband for the man she loves. Like many of his works, the play dramatizes a conflict from

Molnár's personal life. According to acquaintances, it was written as a challenge to his mistress and precipitated a duel with her jealous husband that led to a jail sentence for Molnár. Critics note that the play demonstrates Molnár's interest in psychology; most agree with Behrman's assessment that the character of "the devil is merely the materialized subconscious of the troubled and vacillating characters." In *A testőr (The Guardsman)*, *Játék a kastélyban (The Play's the Thing)*, and three one-act plays published together as *Szinház*, Molnár again portrayed domestic triangles while addressing another of his favorite themes: the relationship between illusion and reality and their intermingling in the world of the theater. In *The Guardsman*, perhaps the best known of the group, an actor masquerades as a Russian guardsman to test his wife's fidelity. Despite an ostensible reconciliation between the characters, an ambiguous resolution leaves the audience uncertain of the wife's loyalty, and the play concludes on a note of cynicism. The characters are typical of Molnár's comedies: the woman is beautiful, fickle, and cunning, while the man is jealous, somewhat befuddled, and ultimately defeated by the woman. As Joseph Reményi and others have noted, in Molnár's plays "man generally suffers because of a woman and the woman almost never suffers because of a man." *Előjáték Lear Királyhoz (Prologue to "King Lear")*, the most successful of the *Szinház* plays, is based on a situation similar to that in *The Guardsman*: a husband discovers his wife's infidelity and attempts to confront her lover, an actor who is costumed as King Lear. The actor takes advantage of the dignity of his role and the husband finds it impossible to chastise him, lamenting, "My wife's seducer hides from me behind the mask and stands in the guise of a majestic figure, an unhappy mythical king and father whose fate has often stirred me . . . I'm paralyzed." Györgyey observes that "Molnár adorns the Shakespearean characters with so much authority that the play's actual characters are compelled to admit their own lack of substance and, after being deflated, they scramble off into their dim, makeshift reality." In such works as *A hattyú (The Swan)* and *Olympia*, Molnár treated the theme of jealousy in a different setting, satirizing the snobbishness of the aristocracy in their romantic liaisons. *The Swan*, one of Molnár's most popular plays, has often been praised for its sparkling dialogue and subtle characterization.

In *Liliom*, widely acknowledged to be his finest play, Molnár once again combined the theme of love with elements of the supernatural. The plot concerns a carnival barker whose rough exterior conceals a gentle heart, yet who is nevertheless unable to refrain from inflicting pain on his loved ones. After his death and fifteen years in purgatory, Liliom is allowed to return to earth to visit his family and redeem himself by doing one good deed. He fails, slapping his daughter in exasperation when she refuses a gift; however, the blow does not hurt the child, whose mother explains: "It has happened to me too . . . it is possible, dear, that someone may beat you and beat you and beat you— and not hurt you at all." Critics identify the play's protagonist with the author, who demonstrated similar qualities of cruelty and remorse, and view *Liliom* as Molnár's public apology to his first wife and tribute to her endurance. The play has been variously interpreted as commentary on the fate of the outcast unable to conform to society, on the futility of the struggle for salvation of a man predestined to damnation, and on the nature of love, which penetrates beyond externals and endures all abuse. Critics attribute Molnár's artistic success in *Liliom* to his rejection of facile entertainment in favor of sincere exploration of eternal truths. According to John Gassner, "*Liliom* is a play of rare beauty, one of the most gratifying romantic plays of the twentieth century."

Molnár wrote fourteen novels, the majority of which are even more overtly autobiographical than his plays. According to Györgyey he used the genre as therapy for his personal traumas, writing a novel "each time he suffered a deep wound—genuine or imagined—in the forever-raging combats with the 'weaker sex'." His novels are therefore dominated by troubled sexual relationships and often end in tragedy. At the time of their publication, Molnár's novels were almost invariably popular with readers but attacked by critics, who considered them superficial and lacking in artistic merit. The single exception was *A Pál utcai fiúk (The Paul Street Boys)*, which was acclaimed by both critics and readers as a classic of juvenile literature. *The Paul Street Boys*, which is also unique among Molnár's novels for its nonsexual subject matter, successfully combines naturalistic descriptions with a sentimental theme to depict the heroic sacrifice of a schoolboy, and is praised for its insight into the psychology of children. Molnár was also the author of numerous short stories, which are notable primarily for their skillful use of dramatic dialogue.

Although Molnár's plays continue to be popular with audiences all over the world, critical opinion is divided as to their literary value. While some critics praise his works for their brilliant dialogue and technical craftsmanship, others dismiss them as insignificant and superficial, maintaining that Molnár sacrificed artistry to commercial ends. Some commentators, however, contend that Molnár aspired to be an entertainer, not an artist. He readily achieved this goal in twenty-four plays of wit, charm, and sophistication, becoming the most popular Hungarian dramatist of the first half of the twentieth century.

(See also *Contemporary Authors*, Vol. 109.)

PRINCIPAL WORKS

Magdolna és egyeb elbeszélések (novella and short stories)
   1898
Az éhes város (novel) 1901
Egy gazdátlan csónak története (novel) 1901
   [*The Derelict Boat* published in *"Eva"* and *"The Derelict Boat,"* 1924]
A doktor úr (drama) 1902
   [*The Lawyer* published in *The Plays of Ferenc Molnár*, 1929]
Éva (novel) 1903
   [*Eva* published in *"Eva"* and *"The Derelict Boat,"* 1924]
A Pál utcai fiúk (novel) 1907
   [*The Paul Street Boys*, 1927]
Az ördög (drama) 1907
   [*The Devil*, 1908]
Muzsika (short stories) 1908
Rabock (novel) 1908
   [*Prisoners*, 1924]
Liliom (drama) 1909
   [*Liliom*, 1921]
A testőr (drama) 1910
   [*The Guardsman*, 1924; also published as *The Guardsman*, 1978]
A farkas (drama) 1912
   [*The Tale of the Wolf* published in *The Plays of Ferenc Molnár*, 1929; also published as *The Wolf*, 1975]
Kis hármaskönyv (short stories) 1914
Farsang (drama) 1916
   [*Carnival* published in *The Plays of Ferenc Molnár*, 1929]

Úri divat   (drama)   1917
   [*Fashions for Men* published in *"Fashions for Men" and
   "The Swan,"* 1922]
A hattyú   (drama)   1921
   [*The Swan* published in *"Fashions for Men" and "The
   Swan,"* 1922]
Szinház: Előjáték Lear Királyhoz, Marshall, Az ibolya
   (dramas)   1921 [first publication]
   [*A Prologue to "King Lear," Marshall,* and *The Violet*
   published in *The Plays of Ferenc Molnár,* 1929]
*Égi és földi szerelem   (drama)   1922
   [*Heavenly and Earthly Love* published in *The Plays of
   Ferenc Molnár,* 1929]
A vörös malom   (drama)   1923
   [*Mima* published in *The Plays of Ferenc Molnár,* 1929]
Husbands and Lovers   (dialogues)   1924
Az üvegcipő   (drama)   1924
   [*The Glass Slipper* published in *The Plays of Ferenc
   Molnár,* 1929]
A gőzoszlop   (novel)   1926
   [*The Captain of St. Margaret's,* 1945; also published as
   Captain Magnificent, 1946]
Játék a kastélyban   (drama)   1926
   [*The Play's the Thing* published in *The Plays of Ferenc
   Molnár,* 1929]
Molnár Ferenc művei. 20 vols.   (dramas, novels, and short
   stories)   1928
Olympia   (drama)   1928
   [*Olympia,* 1928]
The Plays of Ferenc Molnár   (dramas)   1929
A jó tünder   (drama)   1930
   [*The Good Fairy,* 1932]
A zenélő angyal   (novel)   1933
   [*Angel Making Music,* 1935]
A cukrászné   (drama)   1935
   [*Delicate Story* (revised edition), 1941]
Őszi utazás   (novel)   1939
   [*Autumn Journey,* 1942]
Panoptikum   (drama)   1944
   [*Waxworks,* 1952]
**Isten veled szivem   (novel)   1947
   [*Farewell My Heart,* 1945]
***Companions in Exile   (autobiography)   1950
Stories for Two   (short stories)   1950

*This work is a dramatic adaptation of the novel *The Derelict Boat.*

**This work was first published in an English translation.

***This work was first published in English from the unpublished
   Hungarian manuscript.

O.W. FIRKINS   (essay date 1909)

[*Firkins was an American educator and critic whose works include
studies of Jane Austen and William Dean Howells. In the following
excerpt, he discusses the title character of* The Devil.]

It is a notable fact that two of the great successes in recent or,
more properly, current plays, have owed their motive and interest to the supernatural, and in both cases it has been a variant
of the old-time traditional supernaturalism that has achieved
the success. *The Servant in the House* and *The Devil* are distinguished . . . by their appeal to the modern taste; yet they

are almost equally distinguished from the usual type of modern
work by the use of ancient and, in part, at least, outworn
traditions as the instrument of this appeal. (p. 438)

The moral tendency of the English play [*The Servant in the
House*] admits of no dispute; the same cannot be affirmed of
the Hungarian drama which agrees with it in its bold appro-
priation of the old time supernaturalism to the service of current
sentiments and purposes. Not that there is very much purpose
in *The Devil;* it is suggestive, rather, of reckless caprice or
audacious trifling. Its author may, for aught I know to the
contrary, be the exemplar of all the private and domestic virtues, but there is an aroma in his work that suggests the man
to whom one would sooner commit any other charge than the
care of a young and handsome female relative. Yet there is
often as wide a gulf between character and intentions on the
part of an author as there is between intention and result in the
composition of the work. Whatever the writer may have felt
or meant, it is hard to see how *The Devil* as it stands can be
reckoned an immoral play. The principle of evil appears in
person, and, in the course of twenty-four hours, succeeds in
luring or rather goading two weak but well-meaning persons
into the commission of a sexual crime. An offense of this sort
is surely not recommended to general imitation by its ascription
to the direct promptings of the author of all evil, particularly
when that author is himself unprepossessing. Moreover, there
is a peculiar ignominy in the state to which the lovers are
finally reduced which makes it all but impossible, not merely
to approve or share, but even to credit their felicity. One can
see how a man who is neither a churl nor a rake might envy
the illicit joys of a Lancelot and Guinevere, a Paolo and Francesca, perhaps even an Armand and Camille; but it is hard to
see how even a Don Juan or Lovelace, how any one, in fact,
short of a Caliban, could feel anything but contempt for the
state of those two benighted puppets, harried and hustled into
a crime equally wanting in the dignity of a clear resolve or the
strength of an unprompted impulse. Few men would care to
be sentenced to this form of happiness, and to make vice contemptible is a more effective deterrent than to make it terrible
or revolting.

Passing on to the subject of our main inquiry, we ask ourselves
what old or new variety of devil the drama offers for our study.
In the first place, we note in the person in question the faintness
of the tincture of the supernatural. Beyond a few passing allusions, which are mere credentials, the presentation of his
card to the audience, so to speak, there is nothing in his language or his acts beyond the power or the malignity of an able
and depraved human being. The effects of the acts and words
are another matter, on which an observation must be made later
on; but aside from the momentary dallyings with his biography
and his domicile, the devil says and does nothing impossible
to human nature. Here, again, one wonders if in the ascription
of these vices a mere human agent would not have given them
an emphasis which they cannot possess in a being in whom
vice is the basis and staple of existence. When bad things are
done by the Prince of Darkness, we say to ourselves as Luther
is said to have done when he heard the fiend stalking about
the house at night, 'Oh, it's only the devil,' and resume our
interrupted labors. The calling in of a supernatural being to
carry out an artist's designs in a way of brutality and iniquity
seems a needless and undeserved reflection on the proved efficiency of man himself in those directions. The author of this
play has had the wisdom to lay aside the jugglery and trickery
which amused Marlowe in his *Faustus* and even the mature
and serene Goethe in his *Faust,* but is not the retention of the

old name or mask, when the character and conduct have become thoroughly humanized, itself a juggle which might well follow the rest to the lumber room?

The devil of the contemporary play is not a great literary figure, but he has points of contact with originality. In his make-up we find a trace of Pandarus, Chaucer's Pandarus, without the good humor and the naïveté, a trace of Falstaff in his coarse but prodigal vitality, and rather more than a trace of the Goethean Mephistopheles in his mocking wit and his curious blending of gusto and insouciance. He is one of the temperamental devils, with a strong animal basis which, however, serves less to shape his own conduct than to direct the cynical and sensual philosophy in which his active though narrow mind finds its main sustenance and delectation. He is not only a self-sufficient but a self-sufficing personage, for whom the quarry is of less account than the chase, and the chase itself hardly more important than the trimness of his own figure in the hunting jacket. He is a happy devil; indeed it must be said of the devils in general from the uncomplaining and contented Satan of the Scriptures to the lively and sportive Mephistopheles of *Faust,* that they have kept up their spirits under adverse circumstances in a fashion worthy of the admiration and the imitation of the saints. But the devil of the recent play is distinguished, even in this cheerful company, for high spirits and unruffled self-content. He has, indeed, no excuse for not being happy; he likes himself, and he is always successful.

It is no surprise to find that he belongs to the class of loquacious demons. The motto, 'Let losers talk,' has always found one of its main applications in the chief loser in the first and greatest of all games that was played for the lordship of the universe. The talking propensity did not show itself at once. The Satan of the Bible is an industrious and self-contained workman, conspicuous mainly by his modesty and self-reserve, uttering hardly more than two or three hundred words during the course of his recorded operations. But later on he was captivated by the romantic splendor of his own unique and startling role in the great drama of the earth and heavens. He ceased to be a workman in the fatal moment when he found that he was a personage. The capture of souls became a mere incident in the life of a being whose main function was the exploitation of his own distinctions and peculiarities. The Satan of the *Paradise Lost* finds an assuagement even of the mournful gloom and the burning marl in the dexterities of his superb rhetoric. Byron's Lucifer showed his parentage in his vivid sense of the effectiveness, from a picturesque and literary standpoint, of his own situation and attitude. The Mephistopheles of Goethe's poem is as happy to find an audience as a victim. He clings to Faust with a tenacity which suggests less an avarice of souls than obtuseness on the part of his normal associates in hell to the piquancies of a corrosive wit. Had his victorious enemy cut out his tongue, further damnation would have been superfluous. The devil who now interests us is of the same talkative and self-exploiting breed. The peopling of the inferno is with him only a secondary object; what he really likes to do is to sun himself in the admiration of the shuddering but cringing human race. He is interested in the trapping of men and women; but if it came to a choice between a soul and a bon mot the soul would be regretfully but unhesitatingly relinquished.

The purpose of his witticisms is to bring out the frailties and bestialities of human nature, to perform an analysis of man's spirit which shall leave only the sediment, in other words, the mud. As the composition of dust into man was the congenial work of the divine spirit, so the resolution of man into slime is the converse office of the devil. It may be remarked in passing that all this unction in probing human weakness is out of keeping with the character of an authentic Satan. The being who had played the game for thousands of years would be as little likely to revel in the infirmities of man as a veteran angler to chuckle over the gullibility of fishes.

There is one further point of interest in the supernatural element in *The Devil*. . . . The devil's triumph, as we have seen, is absolute; but he is far from being a profound or even an adroit tempter. Many a half-fledged Lothario would smile at the clumsiness, not to say perversity, of his methods. If one had a wife who had to be tempted by somebody, there is no one whom one could more cheerfully see installed in the role of Don Juan than this supposed embodiment of wiliness and dexterity. The persons whom he wishes to bring under the domination of the senses are generous idealists; and the strategy which he adopts is the ruthless exposure of all that is earthy and bestial in the passion that allures them. Dealing with characters with whom drapery and disguise are imperative, he pursues the plan of uncompromising disillusion. In the details of the action, his choice of means is equally impolitic. He appears in a place where his presence is suspicious and vexatious, he bullies and insults the persons whose trust and good will it is indispensable to gain, he incurs the needless hate of half a dozen leading persons in a society in which his footing is a matter of moment to his own purpose, he suggests indecorums which are also puerilities to a well-bred and self-respecting woman, he dictates a letter in which the contradiction between the assumed and the actual purport would be clear to an intelligent child, he works in short for the undoing of his own cause with a zeal that might furnish a model to evangelists and missionaries? How, then, does he succeed? The answer is simple enough: He is the devil. He reveals a contempt for methods which implies a command of the results. We are left to suppose that there is some emanation from his personality, some supernatural efflux, which reinforces the feeble inducements, or offsets the powerful deterrents, which his policy offers to the consummation of his will. (pp. 443-46)

[The] only means by which we can account for the ruin of two persons in twenty-four hours . . . by the use of resources so clumsy or insufficient is the supposition that these persons act under a supernatural coercion, under a temporary displacement, in other words, of those conditions of free will and rational motive which are the foundations both of ethics and drama. The assumption of any such marvelous potency is the negation of true art. The introduction of a force that is both unknown and unlimited, in seeming to broaden the scope of art, really leaves it helpless: for with the unknown, recognition, the first of esthetic pleasures, is impossible; and with the unlimited, artistic skill, that is to say the evolution of a result within fixed limits, is equally out of the question. What interest could there be in watching a game of chess in which the moves were new and unknown to the spectator, or, again, what interest could attach to a game in which every piece was allowed to move anyhow or anywhere? The great literary artists have shown a wise reserve in their handling of the supernatural. They suspend the laws of matter in favor of their superhuman entities; but they keep inviolate the laws of mind. The ghost in Hamlet and the witches in Macbeth appear and vanish under conditions unknown to the laws of physics, but their words operate upon the mind of the ambitious thane and the brooding prince in precisely the same way that the words of common human beings (if believed to be supernatural) would operate. They produce no moral effect which might not equally have been produced by successful imposture. Human will and human motives remain normal in their presence.

The narratives of the four Gospels in the New Testament, if we take them as they stand, afford a curious instance of the distinction between physical and what we may perhaps call moral miracles. The suspensions of the laws of matter are incessant, but they are unaccompanied with any deflection or displacement in the laws of mind. Bodies are healed by superhuman methods, but minds feel, will, and act according to natural and familiar laws. In fact, the object of the physical anomalies is to obviate the need of moral ones; miracles are performed to render belief rational, in other words, to enable men to believe in obedience to, not in dissonance with, their psychology, their human constitution. With the descent of the Holy Ghost in the Acts of the Apostles, the moral miracle comes into play. We admit the physical marvel in narrative and drama, because we instinctively feel that in ordinary fiction matter is the secondary consideration, and a little toying or tinkering with its possibilities leaves the essential psychological interest intact. But in a narrative where, as in some of Poe's and Verne's, the material or physical problem should be uppermost, the introduction of an external miracle would be felt to be as obtrusive and destructive as a psychological somersault in other work. (pp. 447-48)

> *O. W. Firkins, "The Supernatural in Two Recent Plays," in* Poet Lore, *Vol. XX, No. 6, November-December, 1909, pp. 438-48.*

LUDWIG LEWISOHN   (essay date 1921)

[*A German-born American novelist and critic, Lewisohn was considered an authority on German literature, and his translations of Gerhart Hauptmann, Rainer Maria Rilke, and Jakob Wassermann are widely respected. In 1919 he became the drama critic for the* Nation, *serving as its associate editor until 1924, when he joined a group of expatriates in Paris. After his return to the United States in 1934, Lewisohn became an advocate for the Zionist movement, and served as editor of the Jewish magazine* New Palestine *for five years. Many of his later works reflect his humanistic concern for the plight of the Jewish people. In the following excerpt, Lewisohn favorably reviews* Liliom.]

Franz Molnar's *Liliom*—the "Roughneck"—. . . illustrates with extraordinary force and freshness the plasticity of dramatic form. Instead of a play in three acts or four we have here a dramatic "legend in seven scenes and a prologue." To emphasize this matter of form is to recall, of course, the unteachableness of the human mind. Despite the theater of the Hindus, the Greeks, the medievals, the Elizabethans, the moderns, your average director, critic, playwright believes that the form of the drama is now immutably fixed. He has substituted a dead formula for a living reality and guards that formula with belligerent ardor. Therefore to us, at this moment, the very form of *Liliom* has a special and exhilarating charm.

That form was used in a tentative way by Hauptmann in *Elga*. It was deliberately cultivated by Frank Wedekind from whose works the Hungarian Molnar undoubtedly derives it. It seeks to substitute an inner for an outer continuity, successive crises for a single one, and to blend chronicle with culmination. It takes the crests of the waves of life as the objects of its vision. The last wave merges into the indistinguishable sea. Film technique may be said to have influenced this form or even the chronicle method of Shakespeare. But it does not select its episodes to tell a story. They must unfold the inner fate of souls. In Wedekind and the expressionists the scenes are not

only symbolical from the point of view of the entire action but also in their inner character, and little attempt is made to preserve the homely colors of life. What makes *Liliom* so attractive is that Molnar has avoided this extreme. He has used the expressionist structure and rhythm; the content of his scenes is beautifully faithful to the texture of reality.

Poor Liliom, barker for a merry-go-round in an amusement park, what is he but once more the eternal outcast, wanderer, unquiet one? He hasn't been taught a trade; he can't settle down as a care-taker; he isn't canny like the excellent Berkowitz. But he loves Julie. She weeps over his worthlessness and he strikes her—strikes her out of misery, to flee from self-abasement, to preserve some sort of superiority and so some liking for himself. She is to have a child and something cosmic and elemental tugs at the bully's heart. Are love and fatherhood only for the canny ones, the treaders in the mill, the hewers of wood? This is the conflict that destroys him. He is, viewed in another fashion, Everyman, and the little play, which has its shoddy, sentimental patches, is a sort of gay and rough and pitiful Divine Comedy. Liliom did not ask to be born with those imperious instincts into a tight, legalized, moral world. Society demands so much of him and gives him nothing wherewith to fulfil those demands. The world process has not even given him brains enough to think himself beyond demands and restrictions. He struggles with his body and nerves. His mind is docile. He believes that he is a sinner; he doesn't doubt that there are police courts in heaven as there are on earth, that there are cleansing, purgatorial fires, and a last chance, maybe, to be good. But neither the fires of hell nor his belief in them have power to change the essential character with which the implacable universe brought him forth. His notion of an expiatory action is to steal a star from the sky for his little daughter. He is Liliom still, and the joke is on the order with which man has sought to snare the wild cosmos. The joke is on a man-made world and a man-made heaven, because both that world and that heaven have used force. The joke is not on Julie. Julie has used love. "There are blows that don't hurt; oh, yes, there are blows that you don't feel." Love does not feel the blows. Love does not demand nor coerce nor imprison. Paradise is in the heart of love. For the sake of that ending you forgive Molnar the shoddy, sentimental little patches, for the sake of that moment which is beautiful, which is indeed great.

> *Ludwig Lewisohn, in a review of "Liliom," in* The Nation, *Vol. CXII, No. 2914, May 11, 1921, p. 695.*

FRANK W. CHANDLER   (essay date 1931)

[*Chandler was an American educator and the author of several studies of modern drama. In the following excerpt, he discusses some of Molnár's best-known plays.*]

Although Molnár could have won his spurs in fiction, he was diverted by the larger rewards of the theater. Out of Hungary, he is known as a dramatist only. He is facile, versatile, romantic, unconcerned with social or political problems. Except in *Liliom* he shows little depth. Proof of his easy superficiality may be found in his treatment of an old idea in *The Devil*. Here he follows Goethe afar off, introducing the Prince of Darkness as a polite go-between in evening dress. When a trustful husband leaves his wife to pose for an artist with whom she has earlier been in love, the Devil emerges from a high-backed chair to incite the artist to resume the old romance. That night he piques the lover's jealousy, making it appear that

Olga has come to meet the gentleman Devil clad only in a cloak, "like a classic goddess, like a modern Monna Vanna." When the artist demands that she doff the cloak, the lady proves to be fully dressed; but the trick has served its purpose in awakening Karl's passion. Then the Devil prompts Olga to send Karl a love letter. He seems to comply when she bids him destroy it; but when, vacillating, she wishes it back, he returns it unharmed, declaring that he had burned instead his tailor's bill. As she snatches the letter, and with it goes to give herself to the artist, the Devil, following, listens at the door, and rubs his hands in triumph.

All that has happened is little enough. A claptrap Mephistopheles forces together a couple, who, without him, might have remained honest. Olga is happily wed, and the artist is already beloved by two other women. One is a devoted model, who laments that she is like a little railway station at which the mighty train stops only a moment in passing. The Devil is pleasantly humorous. In a different connection he observes that, "If women wrote time-tables, they would tell all the hours at which the trains didn't start, and all the places at which you must not stop to get to your destination." Asked if he be a man of the world, he answers, "Of many worlds"; and he insists that, "The real wife is always the other man's wife," and that, "They may fire cannon out of respect, but pistols?—no!—; that's love every time."

An immense gap separates this play from that which followed. *Liliom* is a masterpiece. It employs what was then the new technique of expressionism to touch the heart and to emphasize a significant idea. The rudest exterior may conceal a tender nature. It is characteristic of human perversity to injure those we love. Molnár, who had married the daughter of a journalist, was divorced by her within two years. In his play he would justify himself against his wife's charge that once he had struck their little girl. His hero is far ruder than he, a bully employed as barker and "bouncer" for a Budapest merry-go-round. Liliom, "the lily," fascinates a little servant maid, who becomes his willing victim, though warned against him by the police. She endures his ill-treatment, does the work that he is too lazy to do, and is content that he exults with new pride when she tells him that she is to make him a father. Thereupon, Liliom rebuffs the flashy proprietress of the merry-go-round, who has discharged him in jealousy and would now urge his return. But, to a fresh temptation, he is more open. Needing money for the baby that is coming, he succumbs to the suggestion of a tramp that they rob a factory cashier. "But why use a knife?" asks Liliom. "Only if the cashier wants it," retorts the Swallow. "People are so queer that they refuse to give up their money without dying."

Beneath an archway in a railroad embankment, Liliom, waiting for the cashier, loses at cards his share of the prospective booty, and, as he quarrels with the Swallow, is surprised by his intended victim. The Swallow twists away, but Liliom, though he scales the embankment, is cornered by the police, and stabs himself. Carried dying to Julie, he can do no more than beg her, for the sake of their unborn child, to marry the old carpenter who has offered to make her his bride. Only when Liliom has expired does Julie kneel at his side and speak her mind: "Sleep, Liliom, sleep! . . . You bad, quick-tempered, rough, unhappy, wicked—dear boy;—sleep peacefully, Liliom; they can't understand how I feel. . . . You treated me badly—that was wicked of you—; but sleep peacefully, Liliom! . . . I love you."

At this point, the naturalistic drama turns romantic as two solemn personages lead the dead man out into a serio-comic heaven before the celestial police magistrate. Here suicides are being tried, and each is accorded the privilege of returning to earth to do whatever he had left undone. Liliom declines to return, scoffs at the others, and with chest thrown out marches into the flames to be purged for fifteen years, at the end of which time he will be allowed one day to visit his wife and child.

With the last act, the period of probation is over, and Liliom, come to earth for his one day of grace, stands outside the house of Julie and her daughter. As the little girl turns from him in fear when he declares that her father was a bad man, he calls her back to offer her a star that he has stolen on his way down to earth. At her refusal to kiss him, he slaps her. Then, overcome by shame, he is led away by the celestial policemen, while Julie, summoned by the girl's cry, stares after him, startled by his resemblance to the dead man. The child is perplexed, for the blow that the stranger struck sounded loud yet did not hurt. The mother explains the riddle: "It is possible, dear, that some one may beat you and beat you and beat you,—and not hurt you at all." In short, a steadfast, simple heart like that of Julie cannot feel the blows dealt by the perverse and inexpressive love of one like Liliom.

Note the poetic combination here of realism and idealism, the rough humor, the pathos, the rare character portrayal, and the setting forth of a truth universal. How often, Molnár seems to say, do we injure those we care for, our love by some black magic employing the terms of hate! How impossible, then, to judge of rude and vagabond natures merely by their deeds! The quiet and submissive beauty of Julie's soul contrasts with the violence and obstinacy of Liliom's unmoral personality. In technique the supernatural and the natural mingle perplexingly. Heaven appears as the child-like conception of the untutored hero, but evidently it exists, also, as something outside of his view of it. The final scenes cannot be explained as the vision or dream of any one character. Herein the procedure is that of Wedekind in *The Awakening of Spring*.

Molnár, having sought to propitiate his angry wife in *Liliom*, proceeded in *The Guardsman* and *The Wolf* to dilate upon his affair with Irene Varsanyi. It was for Irene that he had written *The Devil*, wherein he may be seen challenging her to leave her prosaic husband. That husband, the manufacturer Szecsi, soon reclaimed her, and Molnár began to speculate in dramatic wise as to whether it was he or Szecsi for whom she really cared. In *The Guardsman*, he tells the story of an actress yearning for a fresh romance after six months of marriage. Her actor husband, suspecting her, announces that he must leave town to perform at a distance, but plots to return in disguise as a guardsman of the Russian embassy. If she refuse to yield to the guardsman, he will be delighted; if she succumb, he will enjoy in the person of another the love she no longer accords him in his own. When she receives him as the guardsman in her ante-room at the opera, he is torn between jealousy and pride in acting well his assumed rôle. Next day, he returns in his own person and extorts from his wife a half-confession. Then, reassuming his guardsman's costume, he thinks to confound her. But she declares that she has known his identity all along. She had continued to flirt in order to fool him. Is this true? The husband is more perplexed than before. He observes her at the piano playing Chopin with that far look in her eyes, and duplicates the first scene of the play as the curtain falls upon the last. A critic friend can only observe that, after all this pother, the precious pair are just where they were to begin with. The last act here should have been enriched by some further turn of the plot. It is all a bit too thin.

In *The Wolf,* acted in English as *The Phantom Rival,* Molnár shows Irene Varsanyi's husband perturbed by the question as to whether a man to whom she had once given her affections may still hold them. Says Molnár, a woman will revert in longing to her first lover, however happy she may be with her husband, and he adds that the safest cure for such longing is to bring her face to face with that lover. . . . For husbands half the danger lies, not in reality, but in the perfervid fancy of their romantic wives. Confront these wives with reality if you would banish your phantom rivals.

There is little novelty in the theme of a royal princess beloved by a man of the people, but Molnár, in *The Swan,* was not so romantic as to show the princess sacrificing her future, or the commoner running dire risks to make her his own. Instead, he laughs at the struggle of a royal mamma to effect a good match for a dutiful daughter. To this end she has invited to her castle a crown prince. But for four days he has proved only distantly polite. As a last resort, the mother bids Alexandra make the prince jealous by paying marked attention to her brothers' tutor. The tutor, exalted by these unusual signs of favor, grows assertive and insults the royal guest. When the prince threatens him, Alexandra, stepping between them, gives the tutor an impulsive kiss by way of protecting him. Apparently the royal match is ruined. But Alexandra's jovial uncle, a priest, saves the day, explaining to the prince's mother that the girl merely pitied the tutor in his defenceless state. To the girl herself, grown suddenly romantic, he shows how foolish would be her proposal to resign her royal pretensions. Not love but bravado and compassion led her to kiss the tutor. As Alexandra, convinced, upbraids the youth, the penitent prince interposes to protect him, just as she had protected him the night before, and, burlesquing her action, kisses and forgives him. "Alexandra!" he exclaims; "last night you made handsome amends for a blunder of mine. I ask you now to stay at my side through life. And when I am at fault, be always as courageous as you were then." They have not contrived a love match, he admits; but they will attain to something more beautiful still, love that comes after marriage, a "love which comes later and endures longer."

The title of the play is explained in a speech by the prince's mother, who bids Alexandra keep in mind the dignity of her position. "Remember that your sainted father used to call you his swan. Think often what it means to be a swan, gliding proudly, majestically, where the moon gleams on the mirror of the water, gliding always in the purple radiance and never coming ashore. For when a swan walks, my daughter, when she waddles up the bank, then she painfully resembles another bird."

There is a pleasing mixture in this play of the idyllic and the satiric. The tutor's talk of the stars and of his village and his sister catches the audience, as does the humorous tolerance of Father Hyacinth, and the matrimonial anxiety of Beatrice and her fussy sister, Symphorosa. The dialogue throughout is sparkling, and the exposition is easily achieved by means of the bantering gossip of Alexandra's young brothers. The supper scene is especially admirable in its by-play of *double entendre,* followed by the insult, the withdrawal of Beatrice, and the succeeding calm as Father Hyacinth counsels the tutor and the princess. No sooner has the tutor confessed his love than a fresh storm breaks with the return of the prince, who denounces

the tutor and provokes the osculatory defence of Alexandra. After this capital scene leading up to the apparent wrecking of her royal future, it required real art for the dramatist in the last act to continue without a sense of anticlimax, uniting the spirited little minx with her indulgent prince.

The Swan was more popular than *Fashions for Men.* Yet the latter develops an interesting notion, namely, that, in the long run, generous innocence will conquer guile. With Lowell, Molnár holds to the aphorism, "Be noble, and the nobleness which lies in other men, sleeping but never dead, shall rise in majesty to meet thine own." His hero is what the Germans call a "simple fool,"—an innocent, like Parsifal, without the medieval trappings. He is proprietor of a fashion-shop. He will hear no evil, speak no evil, see no evil. He treats his customers and clerks like friends, and permits his chief salesman to walk away with his wife and fifty thousand kronen. Thus thrown into the hands of a receiver, Peter quits his shop to serve as manager on the estate of a count. But good nature makes him unduly indulgent here to the workmen; and his virtue leads him to protect that of his former assistant, who has thought to win wealth by going to the count. So far does Peter interfere in the count's advances to little Paula that he is presently sent back to his shop in Budapest on the pretext that his salesman has returned the borrowed kronen. Though Peter discovers the ruse, he continues his shop-keeping and wins the affection of Paula, ready now to abandon her scheme of seeking advancement by unworthy dependence. Then the rascal who had robbed Peter of wife and money reappears, down and out, complaining that sympathy for the saintly Peter is so general that no one will give him a job. For once, Peter is inclined to neglect an opportunity to be noble. But Oscar, nothing daunted, takes advantage of a rush of business to step behind the counter and resume his former place, and Paula arrives to take her chair as cashier. She will marry Peter when he has secured a separation from his fugitive wife; but she stipulates that Oscar must go. "Take a dozen pair of socks," says the generous Peter. "I have," retorts Oscar, departing. An amusing minor character here is Philip the drudge, who, although he has witnessed the last act of *Lohengrin* sixteen times, has never been able to leave the shop early enough to behold the entrance of the swan. (pp. 438-46)

Less successful than *Liliom,* but repeating the mood of that masterpiece, is *The Glass Slipper,* a study of low life brightened by the character of its heroine. Irma is the drudge of a Budapest boarding-house. Endowed with a Barriesque imagination, she loves in all humility the landlady's star boarder, a middle-aged cabinet-maker. But the landlady is determined to marry him. After the wedding, the bride carries on with a younger lover, and when the groom remains deaf to the warnings of little Irma, the latter in despair is ready to throw herself into an evil profession. Caught in a raid upon the establishment of a Hungarian Mrs. Warren, she is haled to court. In spite of the circumstances of her arrest, the pure soul of Irma at last impresses its charm upon the cabinet-maker. Already he is disillusioned by his abortive marriage with the vicious landlady. Irma and he will go away together, a strange Cinderella and a stranger prince.

In itself, the story is ugly and improbable. But the heroine redeems it, especially as she is shown in the first act. In setting the table for the cabinet-maker, she kisses the glass from which he will drink and the napkin with which he will wipe his dear mouth. In arranging his room, she sniffs with intoxication his smoking jacket, and caresses his pillow. He is her "beautiful angry aviator" whom she pictures dropping down from the clouds. What if he orders her about in harsh monosyllables? Is he not her Prince Charming? In the later acts, this whimsical, sad, gay child has grown piteous and lovelorn. At last she would drown body and soul in sin as a way of committing suicide. When she is rescued by her adored old cabinet-maker, we wonder if she will find the heaven on earth that she expects. If so, it will be only because, in her dreams, she may wear a glass slipper, and not because of any virtue in the fellow himself. The landlady is admirably drawn,—a wicked shrew secretly yearning to be decent. Once she had loved the cabinet-maker for a week when he was ill; now, after living with him for years, she has betrayed him for a younger man. And yet she knows that the latter is only professing to love her in order to escape paying his board-bill. Here is what Noel Coward has called "heartbreaking beauty" built up from a sordid theme and squalid surroundings. The tenderness and understanding of what is fine in human nature atones in part for the overemphasized brutality.

On the whole, Molnár is a gifted, facile, highly imaginative writer, apt at transforming his personal experience into effective works of art. Except in *Liliom,* he has shown no special depth of thought, although there, in his conception of a love that is no less love for being cruel and inarticulate, he demonstrates his originality. In that play, also, he has carried forward the new tendency to mingle the naturalistic with the fantastic, just as, in *The Glass Slipper,* he combines crass realism with dreamy idealism, and reveals primitive natures as somehow brightening their clay with a spark of divinity. (pp. 451-53)

> *Frank W. Chandler, "Hungarian and Czech Innovators," in his* Modern Continental Playwrights, *Harper & Brothers, 1931, pp. 438-64.**

S. N. BEHRMAN (essay date 1946)

[*Behrman was one of twentieth-century America's most successful authors of comedies of manners. Praised by Joseph Wood Krutch for their "intelligence, wit, tolerance, and grace," his plays combine urbane characters, witty dialogue, and sophisticated settings with moral and social criticism, often exploring the conflict between zealous idealism and tolerant acceptance. Behrman was also an essayist, biographer, and screenwriter whose works include a film adaptation of* Liliom *(1930). In the following excerpt, originally published in the* New Yorker *in 1946, he examines the principal themes and techniques in Molnár's best-known works.*]

Molnar's theatre is unique in our time, because it is an endless self-exploration. Shaw started with a fixed idea—Fabian socialism—which he has masterfully stuffed down the throats of his audiences while they were agape with laughter. Maugham, quite objectively and with dazzling craft, describes the society he has observed about him. O'Neill deals in cosmic symbols. But Molnar's theme is himself and he has taken his society right along with him over the footlights and confided to it expansively in stage whispers. Unlike the novel, the theatre has rarely been autobiographical; Molnar's plays are the great exception. His Budapest was preeminently a theatre town; the cafés bubbled with gossip, personal and professional; the intrigues from its bohemias overflowed onto the stage from the restaurants and boudoirs. When Molnar, who was always engaged in feuds, lampooned some current enemy in a play, the audience knew whom he was transfixing and watched the victim's expression in the stalls, much as a Boston audience stared at Alexander Woollcott during a performance there of *The Man Who Came to Dinner.* When, in a play, Molnar allowed himself

to run through the statistics of an actress's infidelities, the audience was in on the count. His own life became so inextricably involved in the theatre that it was probably inevitable that he should develop, singlehanded, a theatre about the theatre itself. This genre has become popular with playwrights in England and in America, but Molnar invented it. Living in a zone in which reality and illusion overlap, he finally developed a category of plays in which he gave up all attempt to divide the two worlds and used as his theme their very indivisibility.

It may be gathered from reading his plays that Molnar loves artists, the poor, and royalty. *Liliom,* his finest play about the poor, is also a prime example of his self-analysis. Molnar's friends say that Liliom *is* Molnar. They point out the hero's, and Molnar's, constitutional inability to avow love, and the hero's vacillation between cruelty and repentance, reflecting the dualism in Molnar's own nature—the combination of the impulse to suffer and the impulse to make suffer. There is in *Liliom,* besides, a deep feeling and tenderness for the dispossessed. "Budapest was wonderful for a few," Molnar says now, in his exile in New York, where he has lived since 1940, "but for the vast majority it was something else." He has put that "something else" into *Liliom* and into his other proletarian plays, as well as into *The Paul Street Boys,* one of his best-known novels. A member of a persecuted minority, Molnar has always felt a sympathy for the underprivileged. *Liliom* had censorship trouble in England on the score that it was sacrilegious. For that matter, Molnar has never had—except for one play, *The Swan,* a comedy about royalty—much success in England. The psychological reasons for the British coolness to Molnar are perhaps traceable. The passion of love, as a dramatic subject, went out of the English theatre after Shakespeare; to treat seriously of love in the wide open spaces of the proscenium, before a lot of strangers, seems to the English a violent breach of taste. In the Budapest theatre the audiences not only encouraged the discussion but felt cheated if they could not identify the characters. (pp. 216-17)

The interpenetration of life and the theatre in Budapest reached some sort of incestuous climax when Molnar's theatre began feeding upon itself and he wrote his series of theatre plays, among them *The Guardsman, The Play's the Thing, The Violet,* all three eventually produced in New York, and *A Prologue to "King Lear,"* which has not been done here and is probably the best of the lot.

"Is there anything," says the Critic to the Actor in *The Guardsman,* "that you can't believe if it's necessary?" The Actor has just allowed his wife, the Actress, to persuade him that the Russian guardsman was not at her apartment the afternoon before, although, since the guardsman was actually the Actor himself in a disguise, he knows very well he was there, and the Critic's rhetorical question serves as still another illustration of the half-world between reality and fantasy in which actors live. Later, when the Critic upbraids the Actor for crying over his wife's willingness to be unfaithful with the character he has impersonated, he whimpers, "I can't help it. I'm so used to shedding real tears on the stage that I can't always restrain them at home."

In Molnar's *A Prologue to "King Lear,"* one of the characters is an actor cast in the role of Lear. He cries when the husband of the wife he has been pursuing comes backstage to accuse him of dallying with her; the husband is unconvinced by his tears, and the actor says:

> Anyone can cry. But to us it is like the throat
> to the man who swallows knives. We practice

crying so long that it no longer pains us; else acting would destroy us. Do you know where the fault lies? In that crying fails to move us even when we might relish the pain of tears. That is why I find no relief—in crying privately.

When Molnar wrote *The Guardsman,* he was told by friends that no one would accept the fact that a wife wouldn't recognize her own husband, no matter how ingenious the vocal and physical makeup. Molnar brushed this argument off; he said, "The theatre exists to lie—except in essentials. If an audience will accept a bit of painted canvas as a forest, they'll accept this. They'll believe she didn't recognize him because I say she didn't." Technically, *The Guardsman* is a model of dexterity. Molnar tosses off this thin and perilously unbelievable story with great ease. In the midst of a quarrel between the Actor and his wife, Molnar innocently introduces a theatre-loving creditor who comes to the Actor's home to dun him for a bill. The Actor puts him off with a couple of passes for the following night to the show in which he is playing. The Actor's quarrel with his wife rises in intensity. The creditor departs, but a few minutes later sends back a message; he has found out that the Actor won't be appearing the next night and is returning the tickets because he doesn't want to see someone else in the role. The message is tossed into the Actor's rising spiral of emotion, and at the top of it he hears himself declaring, "I say, you know it's mighty decent of a simple fellow like that to refuse to go to the theatre when I'm not acting. Believe me, that makes me feel good." A moment later he is back writhing in his unhappiness. (pp. 222-24)

In *A Prologue to "King Lear,"* Molnar gives the shadow characters created by Shakespeare so much authority that the so-called actual characters have to acknowledge their own lack of substance and scramble off, beaten, into the dim makeshift of reality. (p. 227)

Molnar remembers wistfully the reign of Franz Josef. His affection for the Emperor was not snobbish; it was a matter of temperament. He loved the imperial climate because it was exceedingly mild. Franz Josef, so Molnar seems to feel, was an amiable monarch who had no prejudices and who believed in living and letting live. "Why shouldn't men of my generation be monarchists?" Molnar has inquired. "The first time we got drunk, the first time we made love, the first time we painted the towns of Vienna and Budapest red, there was an emperor on the throne. What is more natural than that we should believe we would again be able to make love, again get drunk with impunity, again be able to paint the town red, if only there was an emperor back on the throne?" This is to regard the Emperor as a kind of Voronoff and is perhaps expecting too much of him.

Molnar's infatuation with royalty is responsible for a series of plays, the most famous of which is *The Swan,* a satire on the mechanics of dynastic marriage. The head of a dethroned family, an energetic and frustrated woman whose passion it is to get her family back in the royalty business, is entertaining in her household the young heir apparent to a throne, in the hope that he will marry her young daughter. The young man is maddeningly indifferent. In the household is an attractive young man who has been engaged as tutor for the princess. The dowager mother conceives the idea of having her daughter flirt with the tutor in an attempt to make the visiting heir apparent jealous. Once this banality has been stated (Molnar even allows one of his characters to comment on it), it is treated with

remarkable freshness and feeling. The attitude of the mother toward the tutor is exactly the attitude of Higgins toward Eliza Doolittle in *Pygmalion*—that the subject's own feelings about the experiment are not to be taken into consideration. No one will ever see a more dehumanized scene than the one in *Pygmalion* in which Higgins and Pickering come back home with Eliza after her successful début at the Duchess's garden party. They never speak to Eliza; they simply discuss her as if she were not in the room and, between yawns, tell each other what a bore the experiment was. Such a scene could have been written only by a man temporarily crazed by a passion for phonetics. Molnar's princess is far more human; when she sees the suffering in the eyes of her guinea pig, she forgets her bargain with her mother, breaks down, and tells all. She loves the tutor, who loves her, too, and the memorable second-act curtain comes down with her kissing him publicly. This was also Molnar's kiss, blown to a princess who was as susceptible to unpremeditated love as were his own plebeian friends in the cafés. (pp. 229-30)

In Molnar's novels and plays, people on the fringes of misery clutch at the hope of love, the hope of happiness, but there is always the intimation of morality. Since Budapest was the capital city of the borderland between the East and the West in Europe, a borderland in which bitterly opposed ideologies have often clashed and in which there has always been war or the threat of war, it is no wonder that Molnar has divided his attention between gaieties now vanished and death. In his serious plays, the characters are irked by love, but they are also beckoned by death. In many of his amorous triangles, the third figure is hooded.

In this country, Molnar is scarcely known as a novelist at all, but in Europe he has a considerable reputation. Possibly his most celebrated work there is a novel, *The Paul Street Boys.* In it, too, death plays an important role. It is a story of juvenile street-gang warfare. Molnar is vastly interested in children. He has said that of all human beings, children are the most cruel, but *The Paul Street Boys* is no *Innocent Voyage.* For one thing, these children are mostly very poor. They are nevertheless cruel enough, especially to one of their number, a boy who is terrified by the fighting in which his companions are engaged. This boy, eroded by the sense of his inadequacy, by his loss of face with his comrades, embarks on a daring adventure beyond his physical equipment. He falls ill as a result of it. The book is populated only by children until the final chapter, when the boy is brought home mortally ill. The boy's father, Nemecek, is a tailor. As the boy lies on his deathbed, an impatient customer comes into the shop to try on a suit. From the next room, the boy's final delirium, as he lives over again the titanic battles fought in a vacant lot, comes through to the father while he is trying to please the fussy customer. This is the kind of counterpoint that occurs over and over in Molnar's plays and with which, when he is at his best, he manages to convey a sense of the erratic, grotesque, and comic interplay of ordinary life. Molnar's awareness of poverty is intimate and personal, just as Shaw's is abstract. Shaw is undoubtedly justified in bracketing himself with Shakespeare as the other great playwright of the English language, but Shakespeare is a bit more realistic with his poor characters than Shaw is, and so, for that matter, is Molnar. The poor in Shaw's plays have never missed a meal; they are like his well-off characters except that they drop their aitches. But Molnar's have a salivary reality; you feel their glandular reflexes while they stare through plate glass shop windows at the confectionery. It is the difference between *Das Kapital* and Dickens. The tailor in *The Paul Street Boys* goes to work at once on the brown jacket his customer orders; the thought comes into his mind that the money he gets for it will pay for his child's coffin. While he sews, he does not permit himself to look at the bed in the next room, because "he was afraid that a glance in that direction would discourage him and would make him fling everything—Mr. Csetneky's brown jacket—to the floor, and then throw himself beside his darling child." When the child has died, the tailor goes to the bed and sinks beside it, weeping: "But even now," Molnar writes, "he was not unmindful of Mr. Csetneky's handsome brown jacket; he slipped it off his knee, so as to prevent it from being stained by tears." Molnar understands the pressure on people who have to go on making a living even when they are dying. (pp. 232-34)

S. N. Behrman, "Playwright," in his The Suspended Drawing Room, *Stein and Day Publishers, 1965, pp. 191-253.*

JOSEPH REMÉNYI   (essay date 1946)

[*Reményi was a Hungarian-born American man of letters who was widely regarded as the literary spokesman for America's Hungarian community during the first half of the twentieth century. His novels, short stories, and poetry often depict Hungarian-American life, and his numerous translations and critical essays have been instrumental in introducing modern Hungarian literature to American readers. In the following excerpt, Reményi discusses the technical expertise and thematic shallowness demonstrated in Molnár's works.*]

To understand Molnar's fame it is not enough to discuss him as the author of "well made" plays in the sense of Victorien Sardou, or as a writer of experimental plays. In relationship to his complete works, it is somewhat out of proportion to emphasize his importance as a playwright and to be half-hearted about his work as a writer of short stories and novels. Some critics take the attitude that his narratives are more readily subjected to legitimate literary criticism than his plays; they are especially fond—and many readers share this fondness—of his sketches and children stories. In his stories Molnar could not avoid the technique of dramatic dialogues which is his congenital manner of expression. When one considers his total output, one becomes aware that his narratives contain some of his most salutary qualities, though their plot is about as slight as that of his plays, and characterization seems too deliberate. Many of his stories are, what reviewers call, "light fiction."

Deeper roots are missing in Molnar. Even his affections seem to emanate from sunbaked pavements, or from the inexpensive sentimentalism of expensive households. He can portray pure joyousness and some of his stories rightfully take their place among the better works of his contemporaries; nevertheless the cross-section of his prose writings and of his plays appears to be outside of a world that gains its strength from vital roots. He disapproves of slapstick methods in every form of expression, yet often neither in style nor in psychology does he get close to the organic reality of human happiness and unhappiness. Paradoxically one could say that he made artificiality natural, and that his talent is such that it symbolizes calculated sensations with the illusion of spontaneity. He is so rational in his fundamental self that when he becomes irrational one immediately senses in the fantastic atmosphere of his stories and plays the concealed directives of a cerebral intelligence. To be great in a creative sense it is not enough to be a magician of anecdotical or picaresque imagination or of the lively and piquant contrasts of reality and unreality. Molnar is neither unusually complex, nor unduly involved, although these assumptions made him fashionable for some time. In his sense of values he reveals the luxury of the spirit that sparkles like a diamond, but does not have the weight of an intellectual jewel. He is glib, at times ingratiating or scintillating; he can only enter into the soul of certain people and depict certain characteristics; his complicated scenes and incidents seem brilliant because of his bent for the unexpected. In conjunction with all this one might say that Molnar relies upon contradictory psychology, hence employs fictional and dramatic tricks that can be successful only with a superior technique.

Molnar seldom tries the patience of the reader or of the audience; nevertheless, he rarely produces sufficient aesthetic anticipation in *literary* critics. He was preeminently identified with the capricious moods of twentieth-century Hungary's plutocratic and urban middle class society. Apart from the fact that he remained a stranger to the ploughman of his country, he lived and wrote in an environment in which the "castle in the air" and the "make believe" psychology of the political and literary past were replaced by determinants of human existence that resorted to mechanical means, commercial schemes and disguised artificialities infringing on the purity of art. Times were becoming ominous; some values of the past were debatable; the responsibility of objectivity was diminishing; misgivings about transitory critical yardsticks were well founded. Yet one could not do away with the fact that progress removed many social and political handicaps of bygone days, and that in Hungary, more than ever before, greater numbers of people aligned themselves with what is styled the "modern spirit." Molnar was instrumental in creating public interest in the diverse tastes and thrills of urbane writing. Even when criticized, he did not suffer from a lack of patronage; his novels, stories, sketches sold well, many of his plays ran for a long time. He supplied demands and created demands. To measure him thus means to give him credit for a recreational intelligence and inventiveness that had its conspicuous aesthetic flaws, but it also had attributes of subtleness, grace and delight. There is a quite sensible proportion between his admirable traits and his pseudo-literary predilections. Too bad that much of the praise bestowed upon him was either effusion or the policy of "literary politics."

In some of his stories literature as an art form is satisfactorily represented. What aestheticians call "things known in the marrow" and "trusted intuition," are qualities that affected the substance and composition of his best stories. For example *Pal Utcai Fiuk (Paul Street Boys)* is such a moving story in its internal and external psychology, that it confirms the view of those who contend that, with more critical conscience, Molnar probably could have developed into a novelist of first order. The novel was published in 1907, and has been translated, like most of his works, into English and other languages. It is a juvenile story. Because of the youthful impulses that are blended in the book, it had a similar effect upon the Hungarian public, as Edmondo de Amicis' *Cuore (Heart)* had upon the Italian public. In many ways, of course, the story of the nineteenth century Italian writer differs from Molnar's novel. In the novel of the Hungarian writer the hero is a boy called Erno Nemecsek, the son of a janitor in the ninth district of Budapest, "member of the Putty Club, a captain of the Paul Street *grund*" (a vacant city lot used for a playground.) The *grund* "to the child of Budapest is his open country, his grassland, his plains. To him it spells freedom and boundlessness, this plot of ground that is hedged about by a rickety fence on one side, and by rearing walls stabbing skyward." The characters are mostly boys, shown in their enthusiasm, pranks, exuberance, nobility, and folly. The *grund* is the battlefield of youth, of mischievousness and wholesome ambitions, of tiny pleasures and self-willed forces. Erno Nemecsek symbolizes heroic sacrifice; he symbolizes the community spirit in the world of schoolboys. Foremost in his thought is the duty to his friends, to his club, to the society he belongs. The description of his dying moments and of his death reveals the very best of Molnar's creative spirit and power. The writer's insight into the soul of boys, the interaction of instinctive and conscious deeds, his sympathy with their breathless and brave hopes, plans, and dreams, is communicated to the reader with an economy of words, suggesting poetry and credibility. Things, episodes and events are in proper relief. Molnar does not adorn youth with a halo but tries to understand it. The quality of the novel justifies its estimation as a matter of literary significance.

Although some of his other stories were lauded by critics and readers, their value, with some exception, lies rather in their potential artistry, than in the full realization of their artistic potentialities. Next to *Paul Street Boys* and other children stories and sketches, his *A Haditudosito Naploja (The Diary of a War Correspondent)* and the story, "Szentolvajok" ("Coal Thieves") should be mentioned. They thrust upon the discerning reader the feeling that Molnar's narrative ability is sometimes superb. Yet despite the dazzling techinque with which children and adults, egotists and altruists are portrayed, much of his fictional and journalistic work is of minor importance. In fact, his voluntary and involuntary departure from authentic art for the sake of superficialities is almost incomprehensible. He is always a civilized writer, a self-assured author, but too often uninspiring or merely tainted with the color of creative intention. It is worth noting that much of his work culminated in short-run glory, though he has stories which seem like a joyride on the imaginative road of destiny. One must bear in mind that his defects are particularly manifest when one expects more than mere amusement. His stories have the logic of the *routinier*, who knows how to embroider self-evident symbols with gay, satirical, and whimsical threads. *Az éhes város (The Hungry City)*, *Éva (Eva)*, *Egy gazdátlan csónak története (The Story of a Derelict Boat)*, *Rabock (Prisoners)*, *Andor (André)*, and other novels, have a Budapest or a provincial background; this same background is noticeable in his stories and sketches, like *Muzsika (Music)*, *Pesti Erkolcsok (Morals of the City of Pest)*, *Az Orias es Egyeb Elbeszelesek (The Giant and Other Stories)* and in the rest of his fictional writings. *The Captain of Saint Margaret's*, which is the story of an imposter, published in 1945 in New York, is consistent with the Budapest background of his earlier stories. Molnar combines European and American experiences in the middle aged protagonist of his recent novel, *Farewell, My Heart*, originally published in English, but written in Hungarian. There is nothing new about the love-complex of an aging man; it is a commonplace occurrence to have substitute-emotions and to experience their extension as an illusion of profound feelings. It is a fabricated story, the product of the impure medium of unconvincing artificiality; an evidence of the writer's striving for effects by all means. The saving grace of the novel is Molnar's dramatic sense which dominates the external psychology of the plot. Many of his tales contain the segment of an artificial society. Unfortunately Molnar wrote too much to the exclusion of that which has permanent value. This habit of his gave rise to charges that he yielded too quickly to an effortless manner of writing. Animosity reached him from those who blindly denied his ability.

As a rule his women characters have psychological advantages over the male; it does not seem to make much difference whether they are fickle or truthful. These advantages are instinctual and at times detrimental to the pride and dignity of the male. Their coyness and cunningness intrigue Molnar. His women characters are travesties of George Bernard Shaw's "life force." Critics remarked that in his fictional world man generally suffers because of a woman and the woman almost never suffers because of a man. Jealousy is one of his paramount topics. Next to this the problem of adolescence. The colloquial speech he uses is that of Budapest salons or sidewalks; it lacks euphoniousness, even when it serves so-called poetic emotions. His vocabulary seems like an uprooted or adulterated Hungarian language. Molnar developed a dramatically intense and concise vocabulary which knows how to play on the sentimentalism and sense of humor of the middle class. Much of his work is sheer routine, interspersed with a neat turn of phrase, embellished with a captivating *apercu*, enriched with an ironic twist that rewards the reader's interest, though characterization may not be entirely satisfactory. In a country of geraniums he seems to distribute perfumed paper-flowers among those who are pleased with this sort of gift. His stories do not lack probability, not because they are realistically reliable, but because Molnar was careful enough to produce a congruous contact between his characters and their surroundings. The symbolic attributes of his art are easily recognizable. Regardless of whether he writes about infidelity or enforced faithfulness, about gentlemen who are distinguished or about distinguished spirits not related to "gentlemen," whether he makes certain experiences attractive or shows them in their nakedness, his good people and his rogues, his parents and children, his husbands, wives and suitors, seem unable to resist Molnar's individual manner of expression which often deteriorates into mannerisms.

In his dual capacity as a prose stylist and as a playwright Molnar's verbal qualities are more or less on the same level. His puns and maxims, expressed with the virtuosity of associative wit, leave the impression of a writer whose facility for well arranged cleverness did not derive from an aesthetic feeling for words. In twentieth century Hungary, a country that was in the process of urbanization, to pass smart observations and phrases on readers and audiences seemed an extraordinary achievement. It was not to Molnar's advantage to have imitators who presumably represented modernity whereas they merely sought and enjoyed sensationalism in some form or other. Of course, Molnar cannot be blamed for the adulation of his fervent followers. The latter were overawed by his international market value, and were inclined to ignore his creative character which genuine literary critics never denied, but measured according to the aesthetic value of his works, and not according to the mobility of his spirit, and smoothness of his words and the prerequisites of expediency. Few people question the amusing qualities of Molnar's plays, but in many instances it is evident that their merit is incompatible with the lofty or ostentatious gestures of appreciation he received from his numerous admirers. There was a time when the Hungarian theatrical world accepted him without mental reservation. His plays, sometimes on the borderline of the grotesque and the fantastic, were of uncommon interest inasmuch as they were permeated with irrealities that seemed the prime movers of false and honest plots. In a world of growing materialism this groping for "originality" through verbal stunts and through a preference for fanciful mystifications, indicated a craving of the public for extravagant excitements which, within the limits of the stage, Molnar was able to satisfy. In the bedlam of modern life, in the pursuit of bliss which, however, was pretty much a longing for palliatives of unimaginative loneliness impatient with its own restlessness, Molnar, accustomed to the practice of dispelling one's doubts and worries with sentimentality or fun, fulfilled a task that in the hands of an unskilled or poorly skilled playwright would have been a solely extraneous experience, but with him it frequently meant stimulation from which the audience could draw a recreational satisfaction of a better sort.

At times Molnar turned to "poetic designs," but the result was not a poetic creation, merely a theatrical *tour de force*. In its artistic merit such a play was not far above his usual plays. In tone and atmosphere most of his plays are dated; they almost suggest a period piece of stage literature. This proves how shortlived "modernity" can be. His variations on one theme—for instance, man desires woman, woman is the tempter, she almost succumbs to the machinations of man, but ultimately reverts to her bourgeois moral code, or the subject of the obsession with money and social position and all the indiscretions and ramifications of such state of mind—are less exciting and seem to suggest less delight than they used to. Because of the structural lucidity of some of his plays and his consistent attachment to the theater, in all probability Molnar's ties with the stage will ever remain strong. This is, at least, the Hungarian opinion about him. His greatest defect seems to be that he never wrestled with destiny in that sense that one envisions in connection with the spiritually heroic struggle of major playwrights. Dramatized love-affairs, or semi-mystical concerns with the meaning of life, the recurring theme of what is real in acting and what is masque-like in reality, have their commendable dramatic possibilities, but the method that Molnar employed sufficed only for the entertaining effects of such problems, avoiding at the same time their total presentation in a tragic, tragicomic, and comic sense. Molnar occasionally made grand use of his skill, less so of his creative ability.

Years ago unequivocal approval was given to his play, *Liliom,* which he called a legend in seven scenes. Praises were heaped upon him by competent critics. There were those who considered this play a masterpiece. Meanwhile, however, the question arose whether the principle of sincerity and insincerity, as a creative postulate, could be applied to the kind of plays that Molnar wrote. His art, even *Liliom,* is a compound of ingeniousness, technique, pleasing and inventive imagination expressed effectively. But is this play, surpassing anything he has done, truly great? Is it really "poetic" or is it a charming fable raised to the level of exceptional theatrical art? (pp. 1189-94)

Liliom is a tender, touching, impressive play, yet on the whole a bit artificial. Molnar, like Gerhardt Hauptmann in some of his plays, fused naturalistic and romantic elements into the construction and psychology of this play, which seems like a conspiracy between ingenuity and poetry. Many were unprepared for this kind of a theatrical experience. To dramatize is to externalize, but not at the expense of the internal perspective of a conflict. Underneath Molnar's sentiments there is sentimentality; his "transcendental" imagination has nothing to do with the *naivete* of an angelic spirit. His wisdom is not that of a childlike poet, but of a charitable cleverness participating in the plight of mortality and hopes of eternity. No doubt, some of Molnar's one act skits and brief dialogues are small literary *objets d'art,* and *Liliom* is close to being perfect; but some of his full length plays are merely skillfully or less skillfully pieced together, therefore negligible as literary products. In the preface to the first volume of *Continental Plays,* Thomas H. Dickinson,

the editor, says that "the art of the theater is an art of artifice." Thus Molnar is not only a writer of the theater, but a theatrical writer, that is a persistent player of a game which, without the aid of artifice, would not recognize the *raison d'être* of its own being. In consequence a conscientious evaluation of his complete works precludes unreserved approval; so much of his work is transparent, so much merely perplexing by turning from the surface of the obvious to the surface of the less obvious. So much is a mere spectacle to those who like to sit in the comfortable chair of a theater and forget the daily troubles of their existence. Molnar's ethics of goodness are plausible; nevertheless they seem to be prescribed as a spiritual medicine by a sophisticated doctor. There are too many cracks in the architecture of his less competent plays. Perhaps Molnar had no choice in the matter, as he gave what he was able to give. Yet *Liliom* and some of his other plays and in parts his fiction, short stories and sketches reveal an ability which promised creative eminence that was more than mere pliancy for spirited amusement. In Molnar's heyday it seemed that his usual indifference to the acute social problems of his times—though a reference occasionally turns up in his prose and theatrical works—was not a sign of creative inadequacy; it was said by his apologists that he was only being true to the type of the entertaining writer he happened to be, and that the manner of his writings suited his purpose. A rather flimsy excuse, and I am inclined to believe that Molnar himself would refuse this. What makes *Liliom* outstanding compared with his other plays is that in this play, despite an incongruousness with the heavenly symbol of everlasting blessedness and the evident "playful" character of the play, Molnar tried to take stock of imponderables which showed an honest quest for truth transcending the horizon of his credulous plays.

Molnar's plays have comic and tragicomic, romantic and bizarre elements. Critics agree that his later plays, implying a desire for new forms of expression, reveal a lack of control over his material. It is also possible that he tired of repetition, but the result was a somewhat vague sense of form, instead of a new dramatic way of producing unity. His interest in the subconscious, in the varying manifestations of the mind and the heart, his sometimes reliable insight into the pathetic and ludicrous motives of human conduct, showed Freudian influence. He followed the literary tendency of his times which was to unmask the spiritual and moral maladies of man with psychoanalytical methods. But there is no magnitude in his outlook. When the curtain falls, not only the lights go out in the theater, but after a certain time the light of the spirit dims, that is the allusions, over-refinements, the currents of wit that one experienced for a whole evening, linger only faintly in the consciousness of the mind. Preposterous, timid, incredible, well mannered, cunning and braggart characters appear in these plays, mirroring the writer's versatility; yet they are distorted by Molnar's habit of making use of psychological tricks. In *Az Ördög (The Devil)* the sharply outlined psychology of Mephistopheles is related to the psychology of relative truth applied to women. The devil as the protagonist of duplicity, temptation, malignity, and other attributes of falseness and underhandedness is a traditional subject of literature. Molnar's approach was fortunate in its gayness, subjecting the audience to an experience of pleasure with smiles and laughter. In *A testör (The Guardsman),* a characteristic play of masquerade psychology, jealousy is the central theme; a stereotyped subject wittily expressed and consistent with Molnar's view that women are likely to outwit men. Molnar likes to write about stagefolks and in *The Guardsman* one observes the elasticity and limitations of such characters.

There is undoubtedly much good talk in Molnar's plays, for example in *Játék a kastélyban* [*The Play's the Thing*] where again stage-folks are the *dramatis personae,* unfolding the idea that the play is the thing; or in *A hattyú (The Swan)* where the jealousy theme finds a new intonation defying psychological obstacles with graceful and vivacious dialogues. The plot of *Olympia,* based on intrigue, the amusing improbabilities of *Az üvegcipő (The Glass Slipper),* are realized with well coined phrases, though there is a difference of merit in these two plays, *The Glass Slipper* being the better one. The Schlemil-like protagonist of *Úri divat* [*Fashions for Men*], the proprietor of a fashion shop, is a sentimentally drawn character; he could be as well a product of William Saroyan's fancy. Both writers weaken their case of artistic authenticity by stubbornly repeating truisms. In *A vörös malom (The Red Mill)* Molnar endeavored to be poetic and spectacular. This play (the author calls it a "morality play") lacks coherence and the kind of satirical morality and allegorical reliability that one observes in the fifteenth and sixteenth century drama. In the play the devils retain the writer's wit in their earthly and infernal destiny, but otherwise are quite unconvincing devils. Molnar's attention was not concentrated on inward experiences. *Jozsi (Joe), A farkas (The Wolf), Farsang (Carnival), Égi és földi szerelem (Heavenly and Earthly Love),* and the rest of Molnar's plays merit more or less the same terms of evaluation that were used in the preceding critical estimates.

Most of Molnar's plays are potential movie scenarios, and several have been successfully transplanted to the screen. In no small degree this explains Molnar's reputation. Yet such plays seem stepchildren of his unquestionable talent. They are creative illusions drowned in the water of expressionistic or pseudo-romantic experimentations. In spite of their "modernity" they suggest a remoteness from actualities; and what makes them seem dated is not only that nothing is sooner out of date than that which is merely up to date, but they display an emotional state that in a world undergoing constant change is consciously or unconsciously related to a small and passing section of human destiny. Molnar's subtle and delicate instincts, his tact and fantasy, could not make one forget the defects of his plays, especially of the later ones. One detects qualities of the real playwright in most of his plays, but one also notices that the author was caught in the web of his own cleverness. Whatever is vivid, astute and pleasing in his short skits and in his other plays proves convincingly that it is justifiable to speak about Molnar's meritorious contribution to the Hungarian stage. It is evident that he has the ability to sustain suspense, to portray the intimate inconsistencies of human nature reflected in the conduct of "polite" society and in the conduct of the underprivileged; he knows how to capture amusing images of human conflicts in the behavior of "royal" and less royal characters. Several of his plays could be the libretto of a twentieth century Offenbach. Within the framework of his contrived plots he sometimes reveals a remarkable gift for dramatization of shattered ideals and ridiculous schemes. But it would be an overestimation to seek hidden meanings in his plays. Their symbols, notwithstanding complicated inferences, do not answer and do not attempt to answer unanswerable questions.

With time enthusiasm for Molnar's plays diminished, but the view remained, that this individualist of the stage, will not be entirely discounted by future Hungarian readers and audiences. His lack of deep convictions and great passions, expressed, as a rule, in brief sentences, will probably continue to narrow the interest in his work; yet it is possible that he will have a renaissance, the readers and audiences will find relief from revolutions and worries in his stories and plays. (pp. 1195-98)

In any case it should be stressed that Molnar could give body to unimportant or temporary ideas and whims. Scattered throughout his stories and plays, including those that were "best sellers" and "hits" and highly acclaimed by trade criticism (theatrical magazines, theatrical columns of daily newspapers, popular weeklies), one finds flashes of a unique temperament. Molnar was not endowed with the Apollonian calm of the classicist, nor with the Dionysian frenzy of the nonconforming romanticist; nevertheless this juggler of epigrammatic wit and fun, this expert of studied simplicities, who often turned to the undifferentiating flexibility of amusing and "naughty" situations, marked a progress of the Hungarian stage. This progress imposed no first rate imaginative sensitivity and receptivity upon the public, but it was irreconcilable with the hackneyed manner of many publicly recognized writers. The intricacies of Molnar's art, his dramatic dialogues spiced with ripost, are distinct qualities for which praise must be given; on the other hand, despite his devotion to fiction and to plays throughout a long and pragmatically successful life, and his custom to maximize stage-effects, despite his cultivated taste, the sum total of his work amounts to the change from a traditional play-technique to a relatively new one. Prospero's lines in Shakespeare's *Tempest,* "We are such stuff as dreams are made on," were, of course, applicable to his art; in fact, while he did not possess the fabulous riches of creative imagination, in the controversies over his significance critics generally agreed that Molnar owed much of his success to a certain airy quality which gave his discriminating readers and audiences a surcease when they were annoyed by excessive theatrical tricks in his plays and in his stories. His international fame brought him to the top of the theatrical world, proving that as an "export" writer of plays he entertained not only audiences of various nations, but called their attention to a Danubian country in which people speak and write a language that, although philologically and poetically isolated, can be used splendidly for the expression of universal sentimentality, gaity, illusionism, and ingenuity. (pp. 1198-99)

Joseph Reményi, "Ferenc Molnar, Hungarian Playwright," in PMLA, *61, Vol. LXI, No. 4, December, 1946, pp. 1185-1200.*

EMRO JOSEPH GERGELY   (essay date 1947)

[*Gergely is an English educator and critic. In the following excerpt, he discusses the plays in which Molnár employed fantastic elements.*]

Molnár's plays of imagination and fancy at once set him apart [from other Hungarian dramatists of the early twentieth century]. While the imaginative dramas of the others consist almost entirely of period plays and melodramatic pieces, Molnár's are with one exception versatile treatments of the supernatural, at their best poetically symbolic and mystically poignant. The single exception is *Carnival,* a representation of Budapest life in the late 1850's which recreates a historical period in Hungary's relations with Austria. In the half dozen others Molnár gains his supernatural effects by methods that clearly indicate his versatility and establish his superiority. In *The Devil* the dramatist represents Satan as an apparently normal man but gives him omnipotence and makes him a symbol of the perverseness in each of the other characters. But in *Mima,* Satan is presented without disguise in the very midst of Hell, surrounded by lesser devils feeding the flames of a realistic inferno in medieval style. In *Liliom* scenes shift from the sordid hovel of urban poverty to the court of justice in the other world, and earthly characters mingle eerily with departed spirits. The unearthly effects in *Launzi*, however, result from an intense psychological analysis of the pathology of insanity and from bold use of ordinary stage properties as symbols. Another method of attaining supernatural effects is exemplified by *The Phantom Rival,* in which the retrospections of a romantic wife blossom out in vivid dream scenes on the stage. In *The Good Fairy,* in a fanciful epilogue, the preternatural effects thin out into mere subtleties.

The intriguing symbolism implicit in the character of Satan in *The Devil* lifts the play above its somewhat ordinary satire of social conventions. The story of Molnár's original, *Az ördög,* concerns Jolán, the pretty young wife of a rich elderly merchant. She has successfully smothered a youthful first love for János, an artist. Years later János, having become famous, is commissioned by the rich husband to paint Jolán's portrait. The resulting opportunity for intimate association between the two proves a strong temptation, which provides the Devil (Dr. Kovács) his chance. He gradually intensifies their rekindled love by constant references to it, by convincing arguments, by breaking up the proposed marriage between János and his fiancée, and by slyly manipulating circumstances to make the final yielding very convenient. So closely do the words of this Satan approximate the subconscious thoughts and emotions of the characters that his speeches in effect become asides, furnishing a clever medium for Molnár's penetrating satire on the emotional processes of persons involved in a triangle in "smart" society. With the exception of the Devil, the characters are the usual social figures. The lovers have just the right amount of restraint and virtuous intention to gain our sympathy. Elza, whom the young wife has selected to marry the artist as a last minute gesture to save herself, proves a good foil, by offering the opportunity for a safe but uninspired marriage in contrast to the hazardous but thrilling romantic liaison. The husband is the commonplace, unsuspecting spouse. The artist's model and mistress, Cinka, brings the touch of continental sophistication.

Yet *The Devil* is not predominantly a play of social criticism; the focus is rather upon the omnipotent personality of the Devil. From his first, unexplained entrance he establishes himself as more than a flesh-and-blood personality. He displays omniscience in his knowledge of intimate details in the lives of all the other characters; he anticipates their thoughts; he controls their actions by subtly breaking their inhibitions and recharting their plans. We must accept him as the symbol of the dual personality within each human being. Thus, the play reaches into the psychic, and may be characterized as an analytical study of the impulse of evil in man, with the Devil an allegorical, supernatural character. However, in spite of its suggestion of the Faust theme and Satan's philosophic commentaries (less numerous in the adaptations), the play does not quite attain its possibilities because it lacks sustained seriousness and nobility of motive. (pp. 11-13)

[In *The Devil*] Satan on earth appears to have an advantage over mankind. But in Molnár's fantastic satire *A vörös malom (The Red Mill),* adapted by David Belasco as *Mima,* Satan is paradoxically confounded in his own realm by man. Molnár's prospectus of the piece suggests its fanciful method and satirical-moral intent. "Every human mood enters into the dramatic action—some humorous, some serious, some fantastic in the extreme. The . . . scenes are strung together in mutual action,

and while this is a play of Hell in Hell, it nevertheless is a morality play." This kernel of morality around which the elaborate theatrical situations are built is the incorruptibility of man: no matter how depraved he becomes, the last spark of virtue can never be entirely extinguished and will flame up at the most unexpected moment to save him. Hell's chief engineer, Magister, has invented a "psycho-corruptor" that, he claims, will in the course of an hour transform the best specimen of mankind into an evil doer. To test the machine before the Devil and his court, Magister, after some difficulty, finds a thoroughly good man on earth—János, a simple peasant—and kidnaps him from his cottage door for the purpose. The machine rapidly breaks down every virtue János possesses. He gambles, commits adultery, lies, attempts to kill his fellow man in a duel, denies his wife and unborn child, betrays his constituents in politics, floats worthless stocks, marries and betrays a virtuous young lady for her wealth, and finally with merciless hardness is about to cause the death of the woman who has betrayed him. Just then she mentions that once, in a virtuous moment, she sent a dried-up violet to his mother. János is touched and forgives her. This remnant of goodness in him at the moment of his deepest sinfulness confounds Magister, and the intricate corrupting machine falls into ruins. Freed from its power, János joyfully goes back to his faithful wife, waking up at his rustic cottage as though from a dream.

The features of the play are its quality of fancy, despite the apparent realistic theatrical paraphernalia, its penetrating excursions into the criticism of life, and the undercurrent of silent laughter beneath the serious morality theme. (pp. 17-18)

Liliom, the title of both the original and the adaptation, not only identifies the hero but characterizes him in the Hungarian vernacular of the day. It represents an odd paradox—the sarcastic but somewhat affectionate application of the name of a flower, the lily, to the "tough" of the city's lower life. The title, therefore, has some symbolic significance in suggesting the spark of fundamental goodness in the character. The story deals with the influence of genuine love upon the lives of the two main characters: Liliom, a barker for Mrs. Muskát's carousel in a Budapest amusement park, and Juli, a humble maid-of-all-work. (p. 24)

The play has three noteworthy features: the flexibility of its meaning, the effective mixture of its raw realism and daring fancy, and the odd looseness, yet perfect coherence, of its structure.

The American critics reveled in the many possible interpretations. Some pointed to the love story as an argument that love penetrates below the external signs of mischief, absorbing even wickedness, or that a woman will love completely even though the man is not worthy. Others, looking deeper, saw the ethical, sociological implications: the sad fate of the outcast, from whom society expects conformity yet gives nothing in return; the tragedy of two souls with a true vision of what life should be, trying to fit themselves into unyielding reality; the reclamation of a "bum" (although to some the ending indicated the futility of a man predestined to damnation even trying to save his soul); and the bitter satire of man's helplessness in the face of the unknowable—as Liliom puts it, "It's all the same to me who was right—It's so dumb. Nobody's right— but they all think they are right. A lot they know!" Still others emphasized the character study, which demonstrates the strangely paradoxical makeup of human nature—the tangled mixture of good and evil in us, the perversity with which our actions can misinterpret our hearts. Nor did the more objective materials of the play escape notice: the picture of the life of the under-privileged, the indirect criticism of worldly justice in the courts, and the bits of religious custom, folklore, and fairy tale.

This richness of meaning is brought into relief by the quick, subtle gradations from realism to fancy. Almost every scene begins with the disarming simplicity of casual realism and grows, sometimes swiftly, sometimes leisurely, into romance or fantasy—a metaphysical heaven, or a whimsical reincarnation. Thus we have in the first scene a sordid quarrel among uncouth characters leading slowly into the romance of Juli and Liliom, as they rise out of themselves to accept their love. In the second scene, the squalor of drab domesticity is swept clean by the spontaneous, primitively noble cry of Liliom, "I'm to be a father!" In the fifth scene, the few simple details of the delivery of the wounded Liliom to Juli rapidly give place to his pathetic last words, as dying he seems to express what living he could not—and the scene ends still another level removed from the realistic when two heavenly policemen take the dead Liliom away. Most striking of all, in scene seven, into the midst of the prosaically well-ordered life of Juli and her now sixteen-year-old daughter comes Liliom, neither as a ghost nor as himself, but as a beggar, whom Juli does not recognize—not objectively—yet she is touched somehow, supernaturally, by the same sympathetic chord that brought them together when he was alive. Of such juxtaposition of realism and fantasy in the same scene, the best example is the embankment episode. Liliom and Ficsur await the coming of the cashier. As they rehearse the holdup, Liliom remarks with childlike naïveté on the romance of the unending railroad tracks, of the power in the locomotive, of the secret conversations in the telephone wires, of the little bird that looks at him. Here, as elsewhere, the effect is gained by the contrast not only of situation but of the two natures within Liliom himself. The result of such interplay of realism and fancy is a continual titillation of the senses. One is never left on a dead level of the prosaic, yet every flight of fancy is established by the speech and action of real, plain, folk characters.

Since Molnár is more of a dramatic craftsman than a philosopher, one must judge the structure of the play not as an accidentally happy falling together of episodes in the life of a "tough," but rather as having a designed unity. By discarding the conventional division into acts, Molnár obtains through his seven scenes a fluent continuity, the central interest of which is not what happens, but what happens to Liliom. Love does not change his character fundamentally; it does not kill his pride. But his love for Juli does disturb his sense of values. He gives up success as a "tough" for failure on a higher level of life. Each scene is built up with all Molnár's skill in handling subtle climaxes and contrasts. (pp. 24-6)

The other-worldly quality of *Launzi*, adapted by Edna St. Vincent Millay, consists not so much in supernatural as in unnatural or pathological elements. Molnár's original, *Égi és földi szerelem (Heavenly and Earthly Love)*, is a tragedy of the disillusionment of youthful ideals; its chief interest is the microscopic, almost morbid, study of the inception and growth of insanity in the mind of the heroine, Lonti. Lonti and her mother, Ella, live in suburban Budapest. Ella has been divorced from her husband, Ivan, who as a struggling music teacher could not satisfy her extravagant tastes. She finds happiness as mistress of Aribert, a wealthy industrialist. Lonti loves a sensitive young idealist, Imre. This young man, however, becomes passionately enamored of her mother, proofs of which attachment Lonti meets on several occasions. Disillusioned and finally convinced that Imre can not sincerely return her love, Lonti tries to commit suicide but is dragged alive from the river. Gradually she sinks deeper and deeper into the hallucination that she is an angel in heaven, and that those around her are merely the people on earth who are thinking of her at the moment. Her end comes when she steps out of a tower window, attempting to follow some Christmas carolers dressed as angels.

The tragedy lies in the inability of Lonti to withstand the shock of her double disillusionment. Imre's preference of lust for the mother to a more wholesome love for the daughter breaks Lonti's faith in the power of the spiritual element in love; and Ella's momentary encouragement of Imre shows Lonti that her mother was not altogether sincere even in discarding the faithful Ivan for the richer Aribert. Thus, left without support of her ideals and frustrated in her attempt at solution by suicide, Lonti finds consolation in a pretense at a living death that becomes more and more real to her as time goes on.

The playwright's treatment of Lonti's insanity deserves comment because of the effective way in which he traces the growth of the madness from seemingly inconsequential trifles to a climactic break and the consequent disintegration of reason. Early in the play Lonti is about to try on a set of angel's wings for the tableau and ball she plans to attend. Just at that moment she first overhears Imre declare his love to her not-unwilling mother. These wings play an increasingly important role from this point until the end of the play when Lonti tries to soar with them out of the tower window. The hallucination begins quite innocently, with the dreamy contemplation of the wings as symbolic of escape from an imperfect world. But when Lonti returns from the ball still wearing them and sees Imre in her mother's bedroom in an abandon of passion, suggestions of escape into make-believe come to her. When she parts from Ella at dawn to go to her father, Ivan, her mind is already playing with death and the bier. Although violently agitated within, Lonti appears abnormally self-controlled; when she is rescued from the river this self-control becomes the keen and all-too-calm alertness of a nerve-strained constitution. The next step comes with her fantastic test of Imre's love by pretending to be a corpse on the funeral bier; this is a truly mad gesture, yet the purpose behind it gives it reason. But the moment Imre admits that he can not love her, Lonti passes beyond the borders of sanity—for a short time into violent madness and thence into the settled, pathetic hopelessness of mental decay. Thus the dramatist, using such tangible materials as a pair of angel's wings, a funeral bier, and the custom of Christmas caroling, and following psychologically sound principles, makes convincing the subtle process of the disintegration of a mind.

Another theme that enriches the play is the clash of youthful ideals with the compromises of maturity. Both Lonti and Imre succumb to the materialistic forces of life. Lonti breaks under her absolute philosophy that seeks death rather than accept compromises in life. Imre, with all his poetic, visionary zeal against the sordid, immoral materialism represented by Aribert, is swept away by physical love. In the end he even makes Lonti's suffering futile by entering into a prosaic marriage. As the original title suggests, the conflict is between idealistic love, such as that of Lonti for both Imre and her mother, and sensual love, represented by the relationship between Ella and Aribert and by Imre's passion for Ella. Molnár's habitual satire is unusually well restrained in this play; we are not inclined to mistrust his pathos here. The tone of seriousness is consistent. And although the dramatist's specific materials are often fanciful, the tragedy progresses through the subtle fluctuations of Lonti's diseased mind and reaches imaginative, poetic significance in the heroine's last stages of insanity. (pp. 27-9)

In *Launzi* Molnár probed the intricacies of madness; in *The Phantom Rival* he explored the workings of the subconscious mind, but in a much lighter manner. The original, *A farkas (The Wolf)*, has for its theme the idealization in middle age of a youthful first love. Vividness is gained by crystallizing the romantic daydreams of a bored wife into scenes in which reality and fancy are piquantly mingled. The pattern of the plot is that of the domestic triangle. Dr. Kelemen, lacking heroic charm and romantic glamor, hopes to hold Vilma, his attractive wife, through his wealth and position. His ever present jealousy becomes inflamed at the appearance of Vilma's first love, Szabó, especially when he discovers that she has preserved that young man's parting love letter of years ago. However, Vilma's idealized envisionings of the return of her first love are rudely upset by the totally unheroic figure he presents in their actual interview. In the end, Dr. Kelemen wins a new confidence in his own desirability as a husband and Vilma returns sensibly to her domestic responsibilities.

The real technical achievement of the play is the development of the dream from the disarming phrases of the love letter that Vilma treasures. Seeking escape from the unwarranted, self-abasing jealousy of her husband, Vilma sighs over the promises in the letter that her first love will return to claim her—as a victorious soldier, as a world famous artist, as a powerful international diplomat, or perhaps only as a humble servant. The dream reveals her lover in each guise, to the obvious disadvantage of her husband. When she awakens, with the dream of his greatness still fresh in her mind, she is confronted by the real Szabó, who has come on a business errand to her husband. It does not take her long to discover that he is even more prosaic and less capable and noble than Dr. Kelemen. It is during the four dream scenes that the play rises above the trite marital-triangle theme. The author uses many artistic and psychological devices to create the illusion: the pursuit element of dreams and the accompanying flight, with its maddening hesitation; the occasional incoherent passage; the slightly exaggerated rhetoric of each hero-lover; the absurdly abrupt yet neatly dovetailed transitions from soldier to diplomat to singer to lackey; the growing realization of the impossibility of it all—and finally a knock on the door, which breaks the sleep and the illusion. (pp. 31-2)

Less substantial in theme and less sure in execution than any of the other fanciful or supernatural plays, *The Good Fairy*, adapted by Jane Hinton from Molnár's play of the same name *A jó tünder,* is built around the intuitive sense of goodness possessed by Lu, the extremely naïve heroine. She acts only on impulse, but that impulse is always directed toward someone else's benefit. A humble usher at a neighborhood movie, she has dreams of wealth and position. At a tea-dance she meets Konrad, a rich American who becomes enamored of her. But she can not bring herself to accept his offer of a life of ease as his mistress; she pretends to be a respectable married woman who might be persuaded to love, but not for profit. From the telephone directory she selects at random the name of a lawyer, Dr. Sporum, as her "husband." To overcome Lu's scruples about selling herself, Konrad offers to engage him for some legal work, thereby only indirectly remunerating her. She thus sees a way of playing the good fairy by turning Konrad's generosity into help for Dr. Sporum, who turns out to be a struggling attorney of forty-eight, whose honest rejection of

shady cases and politics has left him barely scraping together an existence. The temptation of this proposition is too strong for him, and he accepts the commission, thus making possible Lu's acceptance of Konrad's love. At the last minute, however, the impressionable Lu yields to the importunities of a head-waiter that she avoid the contaminating love of the commercial-minded Konrad. She therefore breaks the Konrad rendezvous and instead spends the night with the headwaiter, who offers her marriage. Konrad, piqued more by Lu's change of heart than by her breach of contract, withdraws his patronage from Dr. Sporum, who thereby regains his self-respect. In a fanciful epilogue we see the entire group gathered at dinner on the tenth anniversary of Lu's marriage—not to the headwaiter, but to a state secretary whom Konrad has made his general European manager, evidently at Lu's request. Lu seems to have been the good fairy to them all; they have prospered in some magical way through the illogical but instinctively guided flights of the "fairy."

Although one is tempted by Molnár's cynical thrusts here and there to suspect satire as his motive, the general tone of the play creates a fanciful atmosphere. Lu may act like a petty racketeer in playing one lover against another, and Dr. Sporum may lull his protesting conscience to sleep by disillusioning legal logic; but the play holds consistently to its imaginative theme of how a woman with a genuine desire to see other people happy but having no sense of moral values, can with all her blundering still be led intuitively to happiness for herself and others. The illusion is created in two ways: by the subtle delineation of Lu as an insubstantial, almost symbolic character, and a few structural devices. Lu constantly refers to herself as a fairy, destined to bring good luck through her possession of the magic of life. "I make mistakes," she says, "only when I think. . . . I have no logic, only instinct." True, the author characteristically breaks over into the ridiculous occasionally, as in Lu's generous willingness to allow everyone to undress her that people may enjoy her pretty figure. But we do not suspect her of being a poser; she has a sincere desire to do good and acts with unselfish abandon. Only a spark of self-sacrifice could motivate her scruples against selling herself without someone else benefiting. In the end, she remains slightly impersonal, other-worldly, a symbol of a force in life. Molnár achieves this impression by several mechanical means. At the end of Act I, for instance, as Lu is leaving, a door opens of itself, she whisks out, and the door slowly, mysteriously closes. The main dramatic device used to create the fanciful impression is the epilogue. Introduced in the typical Molnáresque style, wherein the audience is given a little lecture on play ending, the epilogue has a dream-like disregard for time and definiteness. Lu chides each guest for being a half hour late, an hour, two hours, when it is apparent that only a few minutes elapse before the last one arrives. Lu greets each with an embrace—the headwaiter, Dr. Sporum, Konrad, and the Secretary; each one we mistake for her husband. Lu herself flutters around all of them like a spirit that has guided them all to this spot and is responsible for their destiny. Whatever meaning the epilogue may have must be left to the individual interpretation.

On the whole this play lacks conviction. As pure comedy it entertains, but its attempt to do more leaves one dubious; as symbolism, it lacks depth and moral soundness and sureness in execution. The dramatic devices employed seem shallow and artificial beside Molnár's masterful control of them in other plays. (pp. 34-6)

These imaginative dramas of Molnár which have a special supernatural flavor have been largely responsible for his being classed as an expressionist. In them may readily be found the characteristics usually associated with the expressionist school—symbolism, abstraction, fantasy, and an almost morbid analysis of abnormal psychological states. Yet two counter traits in Molnár may also be noted. He is careful to establish his fantasy or symbolic illusion by realistic treatment; and he has an unmistakable sense of humor, a geniality which, along with the satire, makes the plays palatable, though, as some would have it, less profound.

The single play included in this classification which has no supernatural quality is *Farsang (Carnival)*. It belongs here because of the symbolic use of the diamond which the heroine finds at the ball. The powerful forces motivating the admirably portrayed heroine, Kamilla, and the social pattern in which she challenges love can not be completely understood without an appreciation of the period Molnár intended as his setting. His direction in the original, "Budapest during the late Fifties of the past century," has historical significance that makes the social background clear and the story plausible. The dramatist painstakingly builds up Kamilla's character, even sacrificing rapidity of action to establish her complete personality. She is a beautiful young woman, wholesome, cool, and with the wild exultation of a healthy outdoor person. But intellectually and emotionally she is sleeping, waiting for something or someone to awaken her. She is married to Oroszy, a masterful country gentleman, much older than she. Each year they go together to Budapest during the carnival season to take part in the social activities. Here she is continually surrounded by young admirers, but only one of them appeals to her—Miklós, who has loved her for two years. A stirring event takes place. At the grand state ball she finds a priceless diamond which has dropped from the princess' crown. But instead of giving it up to the police she submits to the magic of its beauty and the symbolism of its power and challenges Miklós to flee with her and the jewel if he loves her, no matter what the consequences. Miklós does not measure up to such abandon; rather, he suggests divorce or an illicit but guarded romance. To her his proposal represents the very things she hates—the hypocritical conventions of an urban society that does not have the courage to be natural. She has been awakened, but only to learn that the dream was better. She drops the diamond where it is easily found and goes back to her wholesome husband.

The period of the late 1850's reflected the national mood that prevailed after the unsuccessful Hungarian revolution of 1848. The carnival season itself is not restricted to that time, for it is still a custom of Hungary, although its features, like those of the royal ball, have changed considerably. But Molnár has injected into the play at several points the anti-Austrian sentiment of the landed Hungarian gentry. Kamilla repeatedly expresses her disgust at the public's self-abasement before the Austrian royal family, who condescend to make an appearance at the ball. "I despise the whole scene . . ." she says. "Why do they come here to sparkle—to make themselves envied—why do they stir up the ordinary citizens?" Even the diamond represents more than a clever theatrical symbol to bring the love test to a crisis; through Kamilla's decision to keep it, it becomes a symbol of her revolt against the whole elaborate social structure built around the court. Molnár also draws a contrast between the sturdy Magyar element in Hungarian social life which the Oroszys represent and the decadent "salon" type of intercourse that developed in Budapest under French and Austrian influence, represented by its perfumed young men and characterized by its thinly refined conversational wit, its highly mechanized conventions, and its routine of card playing,

elaborate private suppers, formal dances, dueling on the slightest provocation, and romantic love-making. Kamilla may seem crude in expressing her preference for gypsy music rather than the opera, for the circus rather than the theatre, and for sleep rather than all-night parties; but hers is the expression of the Magyar national spirit seeking to develop its culture through its own slow process of refinement rather than having foreign conventions thrust upon it. (pp. 36-8)

[Molnár's] social criticism emphasizes the class distinctions of his native country; but in all his depictions, from the rustic peasant and city roustabout to the arrogant royal princess, his sophistication and satire are directed against the evil forces in life. Even in plays like *The Devil, The Guardsman,* and *The Play's the Thing,* in which virtue does not entirely triumph, the satirical laughter calls attention to human weaknesses rather than condones them. In his lighter comedies his craftsmanship makes up for the lack of content. However, when his dramatic art and his penetrating commentary on life are combined, as in *Liliom* or *The Swan,* he reaches full stature. (p. 59)

Emro Joseph Gergely, "Ferenc Molnár," in his Hungarian Drama in New York: American Adaptations, 1908-1940, *University of Pennsylvania Press, 1947, pp. 10-60.*

LYNTON HUDSON   (essay date 1949)

[*In the following excerpt, Hudson discusses the characteristic themes and techniques of Molnár's plays.*]

Molnár has a well-deserved reputation as a *raconteur* and a wit. Once an interviewer asked him to explain his development as a dramatist. He replied, "It is the same as a cocotte's. First I did it to please myself, then I did it to please my friends, and now I do it for money." It is not necessary to take this too seriously or to attempt to trace a descending curve of inspiration. But it is an unusually frank admission that he has at times pandered to the public taste for stage tricks and frivolous amusement, for which he can cater with such ease; that he has yielded to the temptation which besets every modern dramatist—increasingly because of the allurements of the films—to write more of what the managers require of him and less of what he requires of himself. How many successful playwrights would admit as much so boldly?

However, the moralist in Molnár died very hard, though he never indulged this tendency so openly as in *The Red Mill.* This is in structure as well as substance a morality play. Its forty scenes begin where *Liliom* ended, in heaven, where Lucifer strikes a wager with the Almighty that he can ruin the best of men. The choice of the perfect man is left to God, and the Devil corrupts his innocence with the time-honoured instruments of corruption—gold and woman. Alongside the moralist is the abstract thinker. He is less easily kept under control. Sometimes one thinks that Molnár has caught the Pirandellan germ and doubts the reality of the human individual. Being so intensely a man of the theatre, he is supremely conscious of the theatricality of life. He would, I think, agree with Evreinov when he says: "Eliminate those moments when you are not posing or acting, or watching others posing or playing rôles themselves. Eliminate those moments when you see this or that in your dreams, the author and director of which is your subconscious ego. Eliminate all the theatrical, ceremonial sides of your life, the games of your past and present childhood, your buffoonery, your imitation of your acquaintances. Eliminate your reading of plays and novels, which represent nothing else than artificially re-enacted life. Eliminate your hours of hypocrisy, hours devoted to social duties and conventionalities, the stream of hours displaying your 'good breeding,' and you will see that there is so little in our lives that is not theatre, in the broad sense, that most of us would exclaim: 'Every minute of our lives is theatre!' ... We play constantly; we invent a new world by transforming ourselves. In life, illusion is just as essential as on the stage and therefore the most important of all stages is in the soul.'' That is why the actor figures so constantly in Molnár's dramatis personæ. There is, if you care to look for it, a symbolism underlying that brilliant comedy *The Guardsman,* and wherever Molnár brings an actor on the stage you detect his fundamental contempt of the Komödiant, of that side of our nature which eternally falsifies the truth.

It is difficult to select a typically Molnár play. What indeed are the idiosyncrasies of Molnár comedy? A Molnár play is cardinally a duologue, commentated by the philosopher, the old *raisonneur* of the French theatre, who is seldom absent from Molnár's plays. The actor, the actress, and the playwright in *The Guardsman* are a simplification of this form. The play is built round a broadly comic idea. It is technically skilful and theatrically effective. Molnár understands what is self-evident to so few modern playwrights, except the French, that the theatre should be theatrical, just as drama should be dramatic and art artistic. It has, unobtruded and kept well below the surface, some universal truth. And it combines astonishingly sophisticated comedy with a broader element of farce. In the language of the wine merchant's catalogue, a vintage Molnár is a dry sparkling wine, having both body and aroma.

Let us sample the first one-act play in the trilogy characteristically entitled *Theatre.* It is called *A Prologue to King Lear.*

The scene is the stage of the theatre immediately before the curtain rises on a performance of *King Lear.* The actors and actresses are taking up their positions ready for the curtain to go up. The dressers are giving the final adjustment to their robes, the coiffeur the final curl to their false beards. On to the stage rushes a little, excited man in street attire. He is a professor of mathematics. Tempestuously he insists on speaking with one of the actors whom he knows by name only. He has just made a discovery which has convinced him that his wife has been carrying on a clandestine affair with this actor, who turns out to be the impersonator of King Lear. Amid a scene of appalled excitement as the minutes tick away, the professor, undeterred by every effort to expel him from the stage, persists in having it out with the seducer, whose very appearance is disguised by the whiskered make-up of his part. Pedantically, in precise mathematical terms, jabbing his pencil to mark each point in the direction of his rival, the professor marshals his evidence like a proposition of Euclid. Majestically, grandiloquently, in almost Shakespearian language, the actor, now half identified with his rôle, rebuts the accusations, while a stage fireman (always present in the wings of Continental theatres) acts as Greek chorus and, like a radio commentator at a heavy-weight championship, sums up the rounds. Finally the professor's logic is extinguished by this bravura of rodomontade and he withdraws confounded and convinced of the absurdity of his ungenerous suspicions. Quickly the actors group themselves. The *trois coups* resound. The curtain rises for the performance.

The absurdity of the situation, the ludicrous contrast between the cuckold professor's colloquial pedantry and the grandiose, highfalutin indifference of the actor, must be at once apparent. The flash of wit which enlivens the argument must be imagined.

Molnár is always conscious of the theatre. His characters are always great acting parts; they offer the actor and the actress tremendous opportunities. Anyone who has seen the Lunts in *The Guardsman,* of which they also made a film, cannot fail to realize the delight of acting them. (pp. 122-25)

Lynton Hudson, ''Dulce est desipere ...,'' in his Life and the Theatre, 1949. Reprint by Roy Publishers, 1954?, pp. 111-25.*

HENRY POPKIN (essay date 1953)

[*In the following excerpt, Popkin disparages the plays in* Romantic Comedies *for their superficiality.*]

[Molnar] is the stockbroker's playwright, the man to invest in for a quick turnover. The artful, superficial plays collected in *Romantic Comedies* are mostly American versions of some old commercial products. The Hungarian master has some genuine skill at farce, a skill which is visible in *President,* but in that amusing sketch of a high-pressure business man who invents a new identity for a cabdriver, Molnar seems almost to be giving away his trade-secrets. Is this not how the commercial playwright assembles his characters? A bank account with the right amount of money in it, a name, some stock attitudes on politics and on Einstein—and we have our tailor-made man. It is amusing to watch Molnar's President creating his mannikin. It is less amusing to see the end-products of Molnar's similar activity in the rest of the plays.

Naturally, a worldly son of Budapest has some worldly attitudes. He is cynical about human motives—not so cynical as ever to forego a happy ending, but just cynical enough. This contradiction becomes one of the playwright's little jokes, but the trouble is, it is a real contradiction. In any consistent comic world, it simply cannot be that everyone is rotten but that everything always turns out all right, unless we are in the super-cynical world of Brecht's *Good Woman of Sezuan,* where the gods depart urging the good woman to continue to be virtuous in a world where virtue is impossible. But Brecht's comic universe is beyond the modest intention of Molnar's plays. The cynicism of *Waxworks* and *The Good Fairy* is a merely naughty cynicism. This is Molnar's most notable characteristic, this tendency to play at being serious and then suddenly to pull off the false beard and shout: ''Bless you! I'm really on the side of the box-office after all.'' In fact, one of his characters, in *Anniversary Dinner,* actually does pull off a false beard and reverse the course of events. The play itself provides a shining instance of cliché sentimentality and surface seriousness. A self-made man is celebrating an anniversary with his wealthy friends. A detective enters to arrest him for debt. His false friends fall away from him, swear they never trusted him, and wish they had never known him in the first place. The detective rips off his whiskers and reveals himself as Cousin Rudy, come to play a little joke. The false friends are exposed and our anniversary celebrants are disillusioned, but Molnar still maintains his balance between the pessimism of characterization and the optimism of plotmaking. Everyone is a scoundrel, but no evil can befall.

Molnar has the same way of playing both ends against the middle in his attitude toward the nobility. He finds aristocrats worthless, ''conceited, haughty and hypocritical,'' inhabitants of a ''waxworks,'' but he loves the titillation of crossing class lines. The best example of this cross-eyed view of the upper classes is probably *The Swan,* ... but both *Waxworks* and *Actor from Vienna* exhibit the standard pattern.

The author of these **Romantic Comedies** had one of the best brains for the mechanics of drama. One might add, "But when he thinks, he is a child," except that he never pretends for very long to be thinking. The critic may extrapolate ideas, observe that they do not fit together, and discover what he knew from the beginning, that these ideas do not satisfy the most elementary requirements for the comedy of ideas. Every*one* is bad, but every*thing* is good. The aristocrats are vicious, but, my, they *are* aristocratic! Of course—no one ever accused Molnar of being a thinker. (pp. 507-09)

> Henry Popkin, *"Three European Playwrights,"* in The Sewanee Review, *Vol. LXI, No. 3, Summer, 1953, pp. 507-14.**

EDMUND WILSON   (essay date 1966)

[*Wilson, considered America's foremost man of letters in the twentieth century, wrote extensively on cultural, historical, and literary matters, including several seminal critical studies. He is often credited with bringing an international perspective to American letters through his widely read discussions of European literature. Wilson was allied to no critical school; however, several dominant concerns serve as guiding motifs throughout his work. He invariably examined the social and historical implications of a work of literature, particularly literature's significance as "an attempt to give meaning to our experience" and its value for the improvement of humanity. Although he was not a moralist, his criticism displays a deep concern with moral values. Another constant was his discussion of a work of literature as a revelation of its author's personality. However, though Wilson examined the historical and psychological implications of a work of literature, he rarely did so at the expense of a discussion of its literary qualities. Perhaps Wilson's greatest contributions to American literature were his tireless promotion of writers of the 1920s, 1930s, and 1940s, and his essays introducing the best of modern literature to the general reader. In the following excerpt from his "Notes from a European Diary," he discusses* The Glass Slipper, Fashions for Men, *and* The Devil.]

I have read in Hungarian three of Molnár's comedies: *Az üvegcipő* (**The Glass Slipper**), *Úri divat* (done on Broadway as **Fashions for Men**), and *Az ördög* (**The Devil**). I did not care much for the first of these, though it has its amusing patches. I am told by Molnár's widow, Lili Darvas, that Molnár declared it was based on his early relations with her—which seems to me, on Molnár's part, something of a piece of impertinence, comparable to the statement by Bernard Shaw that the relations between Higgins and Eliza in *Pygmalion* were based on his own relations with Mrs. Patrick Campbell. The Irma of **The Glass Slipper**—Miss Darvas insists that she was not very good in this part—is a pathetic but impudent little slavey who devotedly waits upon and is hectored by a middle-class maker of furniture (perhaps a joke by Molnár about his own craft). The J. M. Barrie side of Molnár—the Barrie of *A Kiss for Cinderella*—is too much in evidence here: the poor, quaint, and wistful little girl who is designed to bring on smiling tears. And the last act is terribly padded—as is likely to be the case with Molnár—with unnecessary characters and incidents contrived to fill out the evening. The furniture manufacturer, as we have clearly foreseen from the start, will marry the little girl.

Úri divat is, however, much better—is, in fact, it seems to me, something of a comic masterpiece. The first and last acts take place in a shop which—as one would not gather from the Broadway translation of the title, which really means "Clothes for the Quality"—deals in women's clothes as well as men's. In the first act, a terrible triangular crisis is going on between the owner of the shop and his wife and a scoundrelly assistant. The situation is just about to come to a head, but this is always being postponed or interrupted by the necessity of looking after the customers, and the shopkeepers and their assistant are always being forced to alternate between serious personal scenes and obsequious professional ones in which they have to try to please these customers. The dramatist exploits, to great comic effect, the social discriminations, with their corresponding usages and honorifics, of the old Hungarian society: the *nagyságos asszonyom* and *uram* (appropriate to the middle class), the *méltóságos asszonyom* and *uram* (appropriate to certain officials), the *méltóságos báró* and *kegyelmes gróf* (when it is necessary to deal with a title), as well as the formulas of abject deference with which the language of such people as the shopkeepers was encumbered in addressing their social superiors. . . . It is not at all surprising that this comedy should have had no success on Broadway. Only the great popularity of Molnár's plays in the United States in the twenties could have led to the folly of attempting it. The force of the comedy partly depends on the contrast between the language that the shopkeepers use to the customers and the language that they use to each other, and the former almost entirely evaporates, I find, in looking up the translation, when all the gentlemen are addressed as "sir" and all the ladies as "madam." Then there have to be nuances of deportment in relation to the elderly Count, the Nervous Gentleman, the Noble Lady, the Shy Lady, the Anxious Lady, the Efficient Lady, the Dissatisfied Lady, and the Patient Lady. The whole play is really a study in the shopkeeper's profession—some have the qualifications, some do not—in a city such as old Budapest. It reminded me of the shopkeepers in Karlsbad, in my childhood, who would greet one, if one stopped to look into the window, with a bow and an *"Ich habe die Ehre"* ["I have the honor"]. The play has a curious resemblance to an Elizabethan comedy—Thomas Dekker's *The Honest Whore*—of which the subplot depends on a similar character: a linen draper so meek and subservient that he will stand for any insolence from his customers and from any provocation on the part of his contemptuous wife. I was struck by a typically Magyar reaction in the case of a Hungarian lady in Cambridge, Massachusetts, to whom I gave *Úri divat* to read. "That man is a fool!" she said. "Such people ought to be exterminated! The people who always submit do just as much harm as the aggressive people." I suggested that the character was amusing. "He is not amusing at all!"

I was not able to see this play in Budapest. Nowadays it would never do. The gentle, self-effacing shopkeeper who allows himself to be swindled by his wife and his shop assistant but who emerges as almost a saint, with the love of his once discontented but later adoring cashier, to return to his Heaven-sent vocation could hardly today be tolerated as even a comic hero. But I did see another play of Molnár's which had for me a special interest. Ferenc Molnár made his first international reputation through a comedy called **The Devil,** which was produced in Budapest in 1907 and reached America the next year in—I learn from S. N. Behrman's chapter on Molnár in his book *The Suspended Drawing-Room*—no less than four simultaneous productions: two in English, one in German, and one in Yiddish. I did not see either Edwin Stevens or George Arliss in the title role but only a road company in Red Bank, New Jersey. The play had such a sulphurous reputation that—I was then thirteen—it rather frightened me, and I was curious, in Budapest, to find out what all the fuss had been about.

There was a very creditable revival going on in the repertory of the Vigszínház (the Comedy Theatre), where the play had been first produced, and I took the precaution of reading it first in order to be able to follow it. Two young people, a boy and girl, have been brought up, as protégés and hangers-on, in the house of a rich family. They had always loved one another, but the girl has married the rich man's son and the boy has become a successful painter, who has been having an affair with his model but is engaged to a society girl. János, the young man, and his former sweetheart have now been seeing each other on social occasions, but no move has been made to revive the past. The husband of Jolán, the young woman, however, a stock odious husband of the period, a pretentious parvenu, stupidly unaware of the inflammable situation, brings his wife to the painter's studio and insists on his painting her in décolleté. For this, she has to take off her blouse. The husband then leaves her with the artist, and, after a scene in which the two young people intimately discuss their old love, the painter leaves the young woman alone. Shyly and hesitantly, she makes herself unbutton the blouse, and as she is about to hang it on a throne for models which is standing with its back to the audience, she suddenly screams and drops it. The Devil appears from the throne, where he says he has been asleep, and politely hands her the blouse: "*Pardon*, Madam. You have dropped something." All this I remember quite clearly, but I could not have been interested in the rest, for what happened after these first provocative scenes I found that I had almost completely forgotten. I could only remember the Devil, in a later act, walking past a window and flashing the red lining of his cloak at a moment when Jolán is struggling with her temptation. I cannot imagine that the long speeches in which the Devil expounds his immoral moralities were not cut for the productions in English. It is worth noting that *Man and Superman* was first produced in New York in 1905, and that there had hardly been time in the theatre for Shaw to have set a precedent. In any event, the "diabolonian ethics," as Shaw called it, was prevented from outraging the audience by his sending them out of the theatre reassured by an ending which, if not quite conventional, was calculated to gratify the ladies. And Molnár's Devil, for all his ostensible cynicism, is bringing Boy and Girl together. The scruples that Jolán feels about succumbing to János and that are steadily combatted by the Devil are of so purely conventional a character—since her husband does not deserve her and there are no children to complicate matters—and János's relations with his fiancée are based on such mistaken motives that the Devil seems right to discourage them. His role is very much like that of the old gentleman in George Arliss's *Disraeli* or one of those other romantic comedies, who disentangles the young lovers' difficulties and ultimately effects their union. As someone said to me in Budapest, Molnár's Devil—especially as played by a stout actor of amiable appearance and of by no means towering stature—really should have been called Onkel Teufel ["Uncle Devil"]. But the play—unlike such trade goods as *Disraeli*—does have some psychological interest: the Devil is more or less made to represent the hidden impulses of sincere passion which are at war with the social exactions.

One of the cleverest scenes is that in which Jolán is made to write a letter for the purpose of telling János that he must never see her again. She hesitates as to how to go about it: she is aiming, she tells herself, at something extremely severe, "brief and dry and final." But the Devil is there and takes over. He dictates a flaming epistle in which he makes her declare that her friend must never see her again, because if he did their love would go up in a holocaust, they could never control themselves, they would kiss as they had never kissed before. "What have I written?" she asks, in a daze. Says the Devil,

"Something very severe, calculated to banish him." This is followed by some hanky-panky about the delivery of the letter, which the Devil does not at first give János and which János tears up without reading it, thus sparing the woman the embarrassment of her overheated avowal. But they finally go into the bedroom together, and the Devil, after listening at the door, turns to the audience and announces, "*Voilà!*" . . . The artist, in the meantime, has made things all right for an audience of the early nineteen-hundreds by announcing that Jolán is his "future wife." (pp. 118, 121-22, 124)

*Edmund Wilson, "Notes from a European Diary,
1963-64: Budapest," in* The New Yorker, *Vol. XLII,
No. 15, June 4, 1966, pp. 88-139.**

CLARA GYÖRGYEY   (essay date 1980)

[*Györgyey is a Hungarian-born American educator, translator, and critic whose publications include the most comprehensive study in English of Molnár's life and works. In the following excerpt from that study, she discusses Molnár's fiction and evaluates his career.*]

Of the twenty volumes of his *Collected Works*, published in 1928, Molnár designated only two collections as short stories: *Muzsika* (*Music* . . .) and *Kis hármaskönyv* (*Three in One* . . .). Some of these stories had previously been published in newspapers and included in other volumes; some served as drafts for plays ("**Bedtime Story**" is *Liliom*'s outline), and novels ("**The Steampillar**" is the basis of *The Captain of St. Margaret's*). (pp. 53-4)

Both volumes deal primarily with urban people: bankers, artisans, Bohemians, and women of all types, from princess to prostitute. The tone is again anecdotal, satirical, and the dramatic dialogue is the main form of expression. The writer shows remarkable narrative ability in his realistic characterization and in his manner of controlling the plot with unerring technique and with the logic of a *routinier*. As critic J. Remenyi observes, "Molnár could give body even to seemingly unimportant or temporary ideas and whims; . . . he was an expert of carefully studied simplicities that he turned into universal complexities" [see excerpt dated 1946].

The form of delivery varies: confessions written in letter form; extended anecdotes; formal novellas with dramatic dialogues; some embody momentary emotions or whims, and others elaborate on background and personality development. Molnár is always a meticulous writer but in his *bona fide* short stories he seems to use more symbolic language and more poetic devices than in his feuilletons. (p. 54)

The short stories' style reflects Molnár's dazzling playwriting skills; to delineate both characters and atmosphere authentically, he often uses the colloquial talk of the Budapest salons and streets. He writes in a clear style, using a dramatically intense and concise vocabulary which is interspersed with picturesque phrases and whimsical symbols and is embellished with irony. He quickly establishes contact with the readers by addressing them directly, and is capable of making the fantastic seem real, the insignificant horrendous, the artificial natural, without becoming overly complex.

Like the dialogues, the short stories also feature women as chief protagonists. These sensual and powerful females make men prisoners of their desires, keeping them in perpetual excitement by fomenting their jealousy. Women provide both sexual ecstasy and reasons for doubt. Generally, man suffers on account of a woman but a woman seldom suffers because of a man. In the game of sexes, the gallant, insecure men observe the rules, but women do not; they sadistically enjoy trampling upon their partners' pride and dignity. In both his plays and stories jealousy is one of Molnár's paramount subjects.

The other frequent topic is the portrayal of the suffering of the poor and the losers. A cavalcade of servants, derelicts, streetwalkers, starving artists, orphans, and beggars is shown with compassion and understanding. Molnár keeps balance by his sense of proportion and his naturalistic description of the setting.

Molnár's first short-story collection, *Music,* contained eighteen diverse tales of varying length. The contemporary critic Miksa Fenyő considered it important because this volume of short prose, he claims, included the author's best novellas, which "exude lovable witticism, light and facile wisdom . . . instead of placing foul ideals on the pillory, Molnár exposes life's physical flaws: its blisters, freckles, chewed-up nails and baldness." (pp. 54-5)

For the second short-story collection, *Three in One,* Molnár borrowed the title from old almanacs which used to contain a calendar, record of past events, and miscellaneous tales. His volume has thirty short stories, impressions and commentaries. Their subject matters do not deviate considerably from the earlier stories: capricious, strong, and selfish females and their often-humiliated male counterparts trying to surmount their weaknesses. In addition, Molnár attacks provincialism and narrow-mindedness; contrasts honesty with corruption, rich with poor, pure with evil, reworking some of his newspaper articles on a loftier plane. The impressions and commentaries are rapid-fire vignettes of various Budapest types: foxy lawyers, cunning gamblers, tempestuous actresses caught in humorous or sorrowful imbroglios. (pp. 59-60)

[Like] Molnár's dramatic works, his short stories both in *Music* and in *Three in One* are always entertaining. They often end in anticlimatic jest he is fond of appending to the more pathetic or serious scenes so that people do not feel their essential bitterness. In the opinion of a Hungarian-American scholar, George Halasz, Molnár's tales are "sugarcoated laxatives for the soul, delicious and always effective." The artistic excellence of a few masterpieces minimize the disappointing impact of the somewhat weaker, trivial tales in both collections. In the shadow of his towering dramatic accomplishments, Molnár's narrative ability, too, merits praise: in fact, some of his short stories belong among the classics of the genre.

Molnár had no intention of becoming either a playwright or a novelist. While attending law school in Geneva, however, he met Péter Heim, an erudite, enthusiastic Francophile, who talked about Maupassant, Zola, and Flaubert, and who so inspired Molnár that he started to write short stories and prepared outlines for a novella, *Magdolna.* (pp. 61-3)

During 1898 and 1899, he returned to Western Europe, which he considered "the Mecca of modern novelists." While traveling in Switzerland, Germany, and France, he completed *The Hungry City* and began *The Derelict Boat.* (p. 63)

Subsequently Molnár wrote twelve novels, half of which were published between 1901 and 1907, and the rest at uneven intervals in the following forty years. At the time of their publication these books were widely popular, yet in literary histories Molnár's name is missing among the Hungarian novelists:

he is listed only as the author of the "immortal" juvenile story *The Paul Street Boys.* Some scholars contend that with more critical conscience and deeper penetration into substance, Molnár could have developed into a novelist *par excellence;* his early prose revealed a potential for creative eminence "but the lure of money and success proved stronger than the call of a true artist, so he eventually sank into prosaic mediocrity." Ultimately, in this genre, too, Molnár remained faithful to his artistic credo: he aspired solely to be an entertainer. Treading on this path, he continued the Hungarian realistic narrative tradition of the late nineteenth century, but he had no significant links with any fashionable literary movements of the period. As an avid reader, he was familiar with and an admirer of the works of Zola, Maupassant, Dumas, France, Rolland, Keller, Tolstoy, and Dostoevsky, but their works rather more inspired than influenced his prose. Molnár's novels indeed reflected the trends of literature that held sway in Europe at the time; namely, Naturalism, Neo-Romanticism, Impressionism, and the Freudian psychoanalytical views. But he utilized the tenets of these new styles only when and insofar as they suited his purpose.

At the time when Molnár began writing novels, the discussion of sexual relationship was taboo in Hungarian letters. Previous writers rendered it only in a diluted form. Molnár severed the ties with the prudish past and made sex the topical center of his novels and dramas. Since Freudianism was at its initial stage, it was not conscious Freudianism but mere intuition that made Molnár a pioneer in this field. He realized that this universal subject offered countless variations. Thus, almost every Molnár novel is an appraisal from a different angle of the incessantly raging battle of the sexes. The only notable exception is *The Paul Street Boys,* in which sensuous love played no role.

Molnár's first major novel, a *roman à clef,* was published in 1901 and its controversial reception ironically forecast his fate as an artist. *The Hungry City* had a bombshell effect; it provoked venomous attacks from both the literary critics and the leaders of the Establishment. At the same time, the book reaped an unprecedented popular success and made the little-known Budapest reporter a nationwide celebrity.

Molnár's bold, sincere novel was written in the style of a pamphleteer and presented an impressive catalogue of those human frailties, social ills, and economic inadequacies that used to occupy the columns of young liberal journalists of the time. In the opinion of a leading contemporary critic. Aladár Schöpflin, the novel was "saturated with overzealous, sometimes juvenile enthusiasm, and exaggerations of an idealistic novice-novelist eager to put across a social message. Still, it portended a promising writer."

Paul Orsovai, the novel's hero, is the prototype of the Hungarian white-collar worker: a young, struggling bank clerk without vice or talent whose sole ambition is to make the world forget his low-class Jewish origin and be accepted by Budapest society. When he contracts bronchitis and his doctor orders a change of climate, Paul leaves for an Adriatic resort on borrowed money. At Abbazia he meets Elly Hutchinson, a wealthy American girl traveling in Europe with her father. After a brief, listless courtship, he finds himself married to one of the world's greatest fortunes. When Budapest hears of Orsovai's extraordinary good luck, the whole city is overcome by frenzy and prepares a hero's welcome. "People became hysterical; engulfed in greed, ministers, businessmen, even the clergy, plotted and planned, schemed and conspired toward one end: to get hold of his money. Upon arrival home, they gave Paul the loudest ovation in recent history.''

Unseen and unheralded, a poor Italian dock-worker, Ambrosio Posi arrives by the same train, looking for work. Failing to cheer for the celebrity, he is promptly arrested for vagrancy. From here on Posi's penniless, hapless existence runs oddly parallel with the luxuriant, aimless life of the overnight nabob.

No sooner is Paul settled in his new home than he is besieged by sycophants from all walks of life intent on begging, stealing, or bribing him out of the Hutchinson millions. For money he can buy everything: membership into exclusive literary societies and clubs, titles and privileges that place him among the country's elite.

But, as the cliché goes, not even Midas's fortune can buy happiness; shortly Elly realizes that Paul married her only for money. Disgusted by his shallowness and the naked avarice of the city, she decides to divorce him. Anna, the only woman Paul ever loved, is also lost: she now lives in marital bliss, and even his most tempting offers fail to win her from her husband. Deserted by Elly, longing for Anna, the disconsolate hero commits suicide a day before he is to be elected representative in the Parliament. His body is taken to the city morgue and there, once more, fate links him with another lonely mortal, Posi, whose starved body is also brought in that same night. The two men, who lived a world apart, seemed to share their unhappiness, caused by too much money or the lack of it.

The Hungry City, though not published in English, is perhaps one of Molnár's most sincere, noncynical, unpretentious works. It is also his most sustained effort at social satire; but the writer does not fully exploit the rich possibilities latent in his theme, nor does he succeed in creating a ''burlesque of the *Bildungsroman*'' as was his plan. Molnár failed primarily in the portrayal of the protagonist, Julien Sorel's Hungarian alter-ego. Instead of depicting the complete downfall and ruin of this immoral social climber, and pursuing his career to the bitter end by showing how the money-craving city deserts its penniless son, Molnár resolved the conflict by a convenient suicide. The characterization of the two Americans is also superficial and unrealistic: they do not seem to have language problems in Hungary and Elly's quick adjustment to a strange culture seems improbable at best.

Instead, though the book expands on a cavalcade of sharply drawn minor characters, caricatures of corrupt statesmen, cunning politicians, seamy businessmen, demoralized judges, bribed editors, and immoral bishops. Molnár's stylistic idiosyncrasies are geared to convey more energy than reflection. The large array of people who tumble through Orsovai's life are more remarkable than remarked upon and make the book cluttered with irrelevant details. Events and people swirl like unanchored pinwheels, often to dazzling effect, but most portraits remain rough-and-ready sketches only. Perhaps the character of Ambrosio Posi is an exception. The destitute Italian is presented with straightforward realism; both his personality and predicament are credible and genuinely moving.

Even the description of Budapest, Molnár's native sphere, is hurried and somewhat uneven. What made the novel an instant bestseller was the satiric and often hilarious characterization, the arrogantly outspoken critical tone and the fluent style, but this also reduced it to a typical period piece because ''only contemporary readers could revel in trying to identify who the disguised fictional figures were in real life.'' Incidentally, not even the most meticulous scholars can recognize the characters

today. Thus, the novel's salutory qualities lie rather in its potential artistry than in the full realization of its artistic potentialities.

In view of Molnár's fascination with women it was not surprising that most of his novels centered around female protagonists modeled after his lovers. The author frequently transposed his private conflicts into his art, but his novels appeared even more conspicuously autobiographical than his plays. In fact, Molnár used this genre as self-cure for his occasional depression. Each time he suffered a deep wound—genuine or imagined—in the forever-raging combats with the ''weaker sex,'' he turned to prose. During his career Molnár seemingly wrote novels either to find solace and purge himself through reliving some dramatic events in his life, as in *Andor* or *Autumn Journey;* or to repent publicly for the pains he had inflicted by immortalizing the injured partners into romantic heroines, as in *The Derelict Boat, The Green Hussar,* and others. These fictitious ladies, unlike their devious, domineering counterparts in the short stories and dialogues, were presented as victims of love and circumstances beyond their control. Thus, Molnár's early narrative works were devoid of humor and generally considered tragic. (pp. 63-7)

The Derelict Boat, published less than a year after *The Hungry City,* was unanimously well received. This short, poetic novel, a psychological study of an adolescent girl's first love, proved Molnár an accomplished prose artist. Eighteen years later, when he elaborated it into a play, *Heavenly and Earthly Love,* the book became popular in Hungary again and later attracted foreign publishers as well.

The simple plot focuses on fifteen-year-old Pirkó Wald, a precocious, highly sensitive, and slightly neurotic girl. She spends summer vacation with a friend on the *Margitsziget,* in mid-Danube between Buda and Pest. There she meets Andy Tarkovics, a thirty-two-year-old cynical, Bohemian journalist. The young girl, impressed by Andy's age, looks, and sophistication, falls desperately in love with him, savoring the soul-searching and suffering of hidden and unrequited love. He is bemused by the girl's attention and ''adult philosophizing''; their conversations grow in length and intensity and so does her adulation. However, when Pirkó feels she is about to win his heart, her flamboyant, sensuous mother returns unexpectedly from Paris. It soon becomes apparent that Andy's attention to Pirkó was only a pretext: his real object was to get closer, through the daughter, to Mrs. Wald, the only woman the journalist ever loved. The utterly devastated girl sneaks out one stormy night, dressed in a long white gown, unties a rowboat, and lets herself be swept off by the raging waves. At dawn, perplexed oarsmen of a nearby barge spot the derelict boat and discover the tragedy.

Despite its brevity, *The Derelict Boat* has complexity that lends itself to multileveled interpretation. The novel, it has been said, was inspired by actual experience. Whether or not this assertion is true, one thing is certain: Tarkovics's character contains many traits of Molnár. He, too, was a carefree journalist defying authorities, scoffing at the gods and old values. The hero, like his creator, was an unconventional cynic and a Heine enthusiast, perpetually seeking pleasure. The womanizer social lion Molnár was also rumored to have prompted the suicide of a lovelorn lady. And the book's bucolic setting was his favorite haven; he sought refuge on the island periodically every year.

The novel's significance lies not in the autobiographical curiosities but in its poetic style. Molnár makes use of familiar literary allusions to create a melancholy mood throughout. Pirkó's tragic purity reminds us of Hauptmann's Hannele; her drowning in a resplendent white dress brings to mind Ophelia's death; she rocks herself onto the other shore of the River Styx (the Danube), summoned by luring sounds coming from the billows, as was Wagner's Senta. Pirkó's wailing: "I do want to suffer, it's so good for me!" could have been uttered by Goethe's Ottilie or any other romantic heroine. These devices and the theme lend the story a romantic aura even though characterization and the descriptive parts are realistic, showing touches of Naturalism.

The presentation of Pirkó's personality and her tragic plight is resonant with Freudian echoes: a fatherless girl's infatuation with a much older man, hatred and jealousy for the mother, and an almost clinical analysis of a neurotic teen-ager's mounting anxieties. The psychological profile of the adolescent in transition is drawn with systematic, nearly scientific precision. The reader can follow the process as the tormented, confused soul is at first torn between, then falls victim to, the most profound opposites. Like her peers, Pirkó knows no moderation. But her emotions are not simply extreme, they are pathological: her passion borders on the manic and her sadness edges close to depression. If we read the novel as a confrontation between filial attachment and sensuous love, we may find that the book's translator, Emil Lengyel, underscores the heroine's motivation when he observes; "The soul of this young girl vibrates more readily to every little affection because she is a delicate instrument, created to respond to every melody of love's symphony."

The structure is clear and firm: the first part shows how love has ripened into an all consuming passion in her soul. The second part is an intense, dramatic narration which explains and leads to Pirkó's tragic fall. Demonstrating Molnár's psychological insight, this essentially romantic story can be regarded as a small masterpiece. (pp. 67-9)

Published in 1907, Molnár's most celebrated work of prose, *The Paul Street Boys,* has since made many eyes grow misty all over the world. This poignant story of two juvenile street gangs became a classic and has remained one of Hungary's most popular books. (pp. 71-2)

The book is about a group of youngsters and their "gang"— a microcosm of society. Their country is the playground on Paul Street where they reconstruct the world of adults. In reality, this vacant lot, called "the *grund,*" is owned by a lumber company, but the boys feel they possess in it a miraculous piece of land which, according to their mood and the requirement of the game, is continually changing in their imagination from mountains to prairies, from ocean beach to blood-drenched battlefields. "To the child of Budapest [the *grund*] is his open country, his grassland, his plains. To him it spells freedom and boundlessness, this plot of ground that is hedged about by a rickety fence on one side, and by rearing walls stabbing skyward on the others." The Paul Street gang is headed by Bóka, "the fair and humane general," and the members are colonels, captains, and lieutenants. Besides the guard's dog, the only other private is Ernő Nemecsek, the book's diminutive hero. The wretched youth is forever taunted and never gains his ends because "to most people [he] was thin air; like the figure one in arithmetic, he neither multiplied nor divided things. No one paid attention to him. He was an insignificant, lean and weak-kneed youngster. It was probably this very inferiority which made him an ideal victim." There are always notations against him in the gang's Black Book, but nothing serious even

as things go in this strict "military organization." The little loser, never discouraged, keeps striving to earn an officer's cap.

One day he detects Feri Áts, the feared leader of the Red Shirts, the rival gang, stealing their flag. This is an open declaration of war. As both groups begin preparation for the attack, Geréb, Bóka's antagonist among the Paul Street Boys, decides to defect and join the other gang. Nemecsek discovers the foul play and follows the traitor to the enemy's headquarters. There, hiding on a tree, he overhears Geréb betraying their tactics, and the subsequent strategy meeting of the Red Shirts. In a dramatic moment, mustering extreme courage, he reveals himself to the whole gang, each member of which is older, stronger, and tougher than himself. This heroic deed earns him respect among the big boys, but still the spy has to be punished. The frail boy bravely endures three "forced plunges" in the icy water of a nearby pond and catches pneumonia.

On the day of the battle, the gravely ill little private escapes from bed, and the sudden appearance of a figure wrapped in blankets in the fight's crucial moment causes such confusion that the almost-beaten Paul Street Boys win. The hero collapses. Bóka and Áts bring him home and together they keep vigil at his deathbed. Nemecsek dies happily after having been promoted to the rank of captain, never knowing that his "country," the *grund,* is forever gone: construction is about to begin; a new apartment building will be erected on the empty lot.

Nemecsek symbolizes heroic sacrifice; the fragile, downtrodden little fellow endows with true community spirit the world of teen-agers. Even in his last moments the duty to his friends, to his *grund,* to his club, to this society are foremost on his delirious mind. Before his death, the little private metamorphoses into a true hero and leaves a legacy for all young boys to strive for.

The description of his dying moments demonstrates Molnár's remarkable creative ability, sensitivity, and artistic power. Nemecsek's father is a poor tailor. As the boy lies mortally ill, a customer comes to try on a suit. From the next room, the youth's final agonizing hallucination, as he lives over again the gigantic battle fought on the *grund,* comes through to the grief-ridden father while he is painstakingly trying to please a fussy customer. This kind of counterpoint conveys a sense of grotesque, pathetic, and ironic interplay of ordinary life; in such techniques the writer is at his best. When the child dies, the tailor sinks beside the bed, weeping, "But even now," Molnár writes, "he was not unmindful of Mr. Csetneky's handsome brown jacket; he slipped it off his knee, so as to prevent it from being stained by tears."

The book is populated with realistically portrayed children playing adults; they are deadly serious, and so is Molnár in recounting their genuine nobility, innocence, idealism, love of freedom, camaraderie, loyalty, and also their inherent cruelty. The gang life is an allegory: the troubled childhood incapsulates the problem-ridden age. The *grund* is a metaphor for their insatiable yearning for freedom; it is the battlefield of youth, mischief, ambitions, of small pleasure and self-willed forces.

The passages depicting the gang war are interwoven with images of Romanticism of the Indian Wars (fortress, lantern, dungeon, tomahawk), echoing both the strong Cooper craze in Hungary at that time, and Molnár's admiration for Mark Twain. Critics often compare this work with *Tom Sawyer* and *Huckleberry Finn,* as well as with Edmondo de Amicis' *Cuore* because of the similar effect they had on the public.

Throughout the novel, Molnár maintains balance and credibility: the precise, realistic descriptions counterbalance the sentimentality of the theme. He also measures out Romanticism and Naturalism carefully, keeping episodes, dialogues, and descriptions in proper balance. The writer's insight of young people's psyche is communicated to the reader in a succinct, poetic style.

During the last two years of World War I, overcome by anguish and disillusionment, Molnár wrote his longest (621 pages) and darkest novel, *Andor,* allegedly based on the life of Sándor Mester, editor of the *Pesti Napló.* After a mixed reception, the book was soon forgotten and no English translation has been made. Recently, however, Marxist critics reevaluated its ideological significance and revived the public's interest. Of more importance is the novel's difference from other works. It is Molnár's most detailed portrayal of a male protagonist's futile attempt to free himself from his congenital enervation and gain control over his future.

The protagonist's life parallels in many respects the author's own life, and Molnár seems to have projected his character into the novel for therapeutic reasons. Unfortunately, he failed to sustain the reader's interest in the hero's inane, idle existence. (pp. 72-5)

Fifteen years elapsed before Molnár wrote another novel. During the intervening period his mood grew increasingly gloomier. Fame and fortune notwithstanding, the onetime debonair socialite turned into a morose introvert. Advancing in age, bereft of his native city, Molnár registered the social changes even more concernedly than before. He sensed the gradual collapses of his old world and the looming of a new cataclysm. Engulfed in nostalgia for his youth, his beloved Budapest, and all the glory of yore, Molnár turned to the narrative genre and found it again the most auspicious vehicle for alleviating his depression and providing temporary solace. He wrote *A zenélő angyal (Angel making Music . . .), A zöld huszár (The Green Hussar . . .),* and *Őszi utazás (Autumn Journey . . .),* in memory of the resplendent past. In these novels, his customary irony and humor appeared less often than anguish and pathos. The tone was subdued; the mood, overly melancholy; and most characters were tragic or rejected.

Angel making Music was the most successful of the three. The peregrinating author moved the locale of his new book to a frequented favorite stopover on his sojourns: the romantic city of Venice, an especially appropriate setting for a sad love story. Indeed, the overly luxuriant environment and its hothouse atmosphere served as convenient artistic means by which Molnár set the mood and tone. Although combining elements of travelogue and detective story, the novel essentially manifested the author's unabating interest in youth and the feminine psyche. The book was an instant success in Hungary and Italy; its English version also received favorable reviews.

Ultimately this is a one-woman novel. The writer focuses on his heroine's internal conflicts, using other characters and the milieu as props in a psychological drama. A prosperous Hungarian banker's daughter, Irma Lietzen, is vacationing in Venice with her parents. The highly emotional young girl, affected by the romantic surroundings, falls in love with the first man she meets, who happens to be her father's local secretary. Aurél, an expatriate, is bright, earnest, and subserviently polite. The novel's first part is a poetic exploration of how Irma's affection—though utterly devoid of carnality—develops into an all-consuming rapture. The pivotal episodes take place in

the second part when the young clerk fails to return her devotion. He prefers the wholesomely sensuous, mature Judith, Mrs. Lietzen's nurse. The two "servants of the rich" soon become lovers. Unrequited love and jealousy all but unhinge Irma's mind and she behaves like a maenad overcharged with schemes of vengeance. She smuggles her mother's diamond brooch into Judith's suitcase to incriminate the unsuspecting girl who is getting ready to escape with Aurél. The last part of the book recounts the proceeds of a nerve-wracking investigation and Irma's agonizing soul-searching. She is beset by twinging guilt, but is too proud to confess. In the end, truth triumphs: the exalted, selfish girl remains alone, and her slandered rival is exonerated and marries Aurél. As the family is leaving Venice, Irma asks to stop at Church Frari. Kneeling before Bellini's *Madonna,* she stares at Judith's favorite painting. When she spots the chubby cherubs with the flute near the Madonna, Irma breaks down and within a few minutes undergoes a complete change. This is the prolonged climax of the tale.

Underneath the multilayered insouciance and suppressed physical desires, she begins to feel a sudden upsurge of sexuality. She realizes that the angel making music is the symbol of women's primordial wish to bear a child. "Her face lit up . . . there . . . there was the fat little music-making angel-child blowing on his flute. A sweet warmth surged through her." Irma discovers Judith's secret, the painting's magic, and her purpose in life.

Molnár's characterization is naturalistic; nothing is withheld: the heroine in close-up stands naked with her physical and metaphysical blisters ruthlessly exposed. Molnár's achievement is that he made this rather superficial character oddly vulnerable, even touching, despite her abominable machinations. The others remain only entertaining cameos: the weak, doting father; the snobbish, hypochondriac, parvenu mother; and the scrupulously honest, warm, feminine Judith. Aurél comes across as a featureless, average youth.

Molnár is eloquent in depicting the setting, the glory of Venice. With realism and rarely displayed artistry, using rich similes and metaphors, he revives the semi-Oriental splendor, the exuberance of Renaissance and Baroque art and architecture, and the golden blue magnificence of "the city of pedestrians." "San Giorgio Maggiore burned red in the sun. As if, from centuries of sunshine, the walls and the green cornices of the brick tower had acquired the burnt, brownish red skin-color of the old fishermen and gondoliers. . . . The Laguna—that distant, sprawling, waveless, false sea—was blue now. The sky still more blue, almost steel blue in the heat. These Latin blues are not afraid of the German word *Kitsch,* they dare to be just as blue as they fancy."

The descriptive parts reflect the artist, who had lived in the city for some time and knew it intimately. The language blends with the setting; it is translucent and sparkling like Venetian glass beads; gently coiling like the canals; facile, lacy, like the Gothic steeples; and miraculously sustained like the buildings on the lagunas.

Concurrent with his adoration of Venice, Molnár's nostalgia for his homeland rises from the pages. During conversations, people keep reminiscing, recalling memories of Budapest and making comparisons: the canals with the Danube, Italian luxury liners with Hungarian steamships, the gondoliers' serenading with Gypsy music, the spicing of Veal Parmesan with *Wiener*

Schnitzel. All through the book the reader can unmistakably sense the author's yearning for his country.

The style is also in harmony with the novel's rich, velvety texture. Irma's outbursts and internal monologues are complex and vibrant with neurotic images. In the direct characterization, however, the language is calm and transparent. Unfortunately, there is a complete change in atmosphere and a break in style in the last part when the police begin investigating the alleged theft. The shift is awkward because Molnár as a sleuth sounds dissonant and a bit sensational. It appears to be a rather cheap and easy form of denouement of a truly artistic and entertaining case history of a young girl's love, or the collision between Platonic love and sensuous passion. (pp. 77-80)

Molnár's novels are characterized by stylistic brilliance, cleverly calculated plots, meticulous structure, realistically portrayed characters, and authentic settings. His tone is urban and self-assertive, revealing both his journalistic training in the consistently economic use of words, and his playwriting talent in his fluid dramatic dialogues. In the often autobiographical, character-oriented novels, there are no villains, only erring human beings. A genuinely entertaining but by no means universal novelist, Molnár may be evaluated at his best on the basis of *The Paul Street Boys,* a belletristic masterpiece. (p. 82)

"Molnár! Author, stage-director, dramatist, poet: Ferenc Molnár. Today, whether at home in his beloved Hungary, or here, in America, a name to reckon with." Thus exclaimed David Belasco in 1929, echoing many other critics around the world. Through his plays, Molnár broke out of the literary isolation of his native land, and achieved international fame by amusing audiences everywhere for five decades. Instead of pretending to convey social messages or extreme profundity, this prolific, facile, imaginative writer aimed merely to entertain by transforming his personal experience into effective works of art.

Molnár had no significant links with any fashionable literary movements of his time; he stood alone, but dipped freely into the literary wealth of the past. He utilized the tenets of Naturalism, Neo-Romanticism, Expressionism, and the Freudian psychoanalytical concepts, but only when and insofar as they suited his purpose. In his prose, he was inspired by the works of Zola, Maupassant, Dumas, Tolstoy, and Dostoevsky. In his dramas, he at first continued the tradition of the French boulevard authors—Capus, Bataille, Bernstein, and Bernard; later, Wilde, Shaw, Hauptmann, Schnitzler, and Pirandello left the deepest impression upon him. By fusing the realistic narrative and stage tradition of Hungary with Western influences into a cosmopolitan amalgam, Molnár emerged as a versatile artist whose style was uniquely his own.

As a Hungarian journalist, he valued keen observation, precise description, suave mischief, and wit. His easy-flowing, urbane, vibrant short stories are poetic and meticulously structured, reflecting his consummate skill with dialogue. Although his novels are characterized by stylistic brilliance and cleverly calculated plots, thematically their range is rather narrow, and in content largely empirical. While his mostly autobiographical novels are only interesting period pieces, *The Paul Street Boys* emerges as a masterpiece.

Molnár, a natural-born playwright, demonstrated mesmerizing, unerring dramatic instincts, originality, dazzling technique, and craftsmanship, and it was in this field that he rendered his major contribution. In his graceful, whimsical, sophisticated drawing-room comedies, he provided a felicitous synthesis of Naturalism and fantasy, Realism and Romanticism, cynicism and sentimentality, the profane and the sublime. He delivered his invariably interesting plots with accurate dramatic timing, through witty, sparkling, and spicy dialogues. According to Robert Brustein, his civilized plays enjoy universal appeal because of their "champagne quality: they are healthy, bubbly, and refreshing; they suit the taste of a general public everywhere." Molnár wrote elegant, satiric dramas on manners, human frailties, and illusions; he portrayed suave, lovesick gentlemen and perfumed, cunning women, or thugs and simple servants, all engaged in the battle of the sexes. Out of his forty-two plays, *The Devil, Liliom, The Swan, The Guardsman,* and *The Play's the Thing* endure as recognized classics of the world of drama.

His artistry shines most brightly in his technique. He was an undisputed expert of stagecraft. The inextricable fusion of his life with the theater gave him theatrical versatility and vast knowledge of all the tricks of the stage. The ease and vigor of his innovative talent, the ability to construct plays faultlessly, the discipline and sense of dramatic proportion, make him one of the finest theatrical craftsmen of his era.

He once stated that he wrote only what was natural to him. Perhaps that is why his work was enormously successful during and after his life, both with the simple reader or audience and knowledgeable critics. He is superb as an observer, a technician, a storyteller, and a humorist. He does not conceal his ideas in obscure language, pseudosymbolism, forced social consciousness, or intellectual aloofness. His brilliance is one that not only entertains but also enlightens.

His tremendous national and international fame inspired scores of Hungarian playwrights—Elemér Boross, László Fodor, Lajos Biró, László Bús-Fekete, Ernő Vajda, Attila Orbók, and Imre Földes, among others—to follow his style of playwriting. The export plays of these perhaps not always conscious imitators achieved temporary success abroad, especially in the United States, but their popularity died rapidly. The interest in Molnár's work, however, has not abated. His place in the world of drama is secure—most of his plays are still relevant and are being performed all over the world.

Molnár's long and turbulent life was one of hard and incessant work. For over fifty years he transposed his inner conflict into his literary work; writing was his oxygen, elixir, and self-therapy. Though not all his creations are masterpieces, few are carelessly done. He wanted primarily to be an entertainer, not a preacher or propagandist. He succeeded. By his special skill, he provided the public with escape, gaiety, and an illusory world in which conflicts were fun and amenable to solution. Perhaps not a Hungarian Molière, but certainly a Hungarian Noel Coward, Molnár deserves respect as a stage magician who, "with a flourish, lifted us up to the sky." A true artist, he contributed prodigally to the literary heritage of the world by spreading truth and joy among his fellow men. (pp. 172-74)

> *Clara Györgyey, in her* Ferenc Molnár, *Twayne Publishers, 1980, 195 p.*

ADDITIONAL BIBLIOGRAPHY

Burke, Kenneth. "Little Men." *New York Herald Tribune Books* 4, No. 12 (4 December 1927): 4.
    Favorable review of *The Paul Street Boys.*

Gassner, John. "Hauptmann's Fellow-Travelers and the Expressionist Eruption." In his *Masters of the Drama*, pp. 467-94. New York: Dover Publications, 1940.*

> Brief discussion of Molnár's career. Gassner observes that Molnár's dramas are characteristic of turn-of-the-century Hungarian theater, which "won wide acceptance abroad and belongs to dramatic history as one popular way of coping with life—that is, by sugar-coating it."

Greene, Graham. Review of *Angels Making Music*, by Ferenc Molnár. *The Spectator* 153, No. 5545 (5 October 1934): 498.

> Favorable review maintaining that "Herr Molnár is a distinguished dramatist, and the dialogue has an enviable point and economy."

Kronenberger, Louis. "Un-American Love." *New York Herald Tribune Books* 2, No. 88 (6 June 1926): 11.

> Favorable review of *"Eva"* and *"The Derelict Boat,"* stressing the typically European aspects of the novels' plots and characters.

Krutch, Joseph Wood. "Two Comedies." *The Nation* 119, No. 3096 (5 November 1924): 501-02.*

> Considers *The Guardsman* "unimportant," maintaining that "the piece was never more than a bit of ingenious theatricality."

Middleton, George. "The End of the Adventure: Molnár, Schnitzler, Brieux." In his *These Things Are Mine: The Autobiography of a Journeyman Playwright*, pp. 363-73. New York: MacMillan, 1947.*

> Personal reminiscence of the author's meetings with Molnár.

Nathan, George Jean. *"Miracle in the Mountains:* April 25, 1947." In his *The Theatre Book of the Year: 1946-1947*, pp. 373-76. New York: Alfred A. Knopf, 1947.

> Praises the play's quaintness and charm while acknowledging the conventionality of its plot.

———. *"The Play's the Thing:* April 28, 1948." In his *The Theatre Book of the Year: 1947-1948*, pp. 358-60. New York: Alfred A. Knopf, 1948.

> Favorable review praising Molnár's skillful handling of the "play within a play" theme.

Stragnell, Gregory. "A Psychopathological Study of Franz Molnár's *Liliom*." *The Psychoanalytic Review* IX, No. 1 (January 1922): 40-49.

> Considers *Liliom* "a tragedy of souls unable to fit into the world of reality," maintaining that the central characters "were goaded on by infantile trends which came out one time in this way, one time in that way, but always there was an endeavor to relive symbolically the days of childhood and yet never knowing what it was all about."

Trilling, Diana. Review of *Farewell My Heart*, by Ferenc Molnár. *The Nation* 161, No. 6 (11 August 1945): 139-40.*

> Negative review maintaining that Molnár's topical references to World War II do not enrich "either the emotional or social texture of Mr. Molnár's book, but, instead, [appear] as something of an offense against taste."

Wilson, Edmund, Jr. Review of *Liliom*, by Ferenc Molnár. *The New Republic* XXVI, No. 335 (4 May 1921): 299.

> Observes that the play's "theme is slight and rather sentimental, but it is handled so deftly and so lightly and redeemed with such sharpness and wit that the result is a drama of considerable dignity."

Benjamin Péret

1899-1959

French poet, essayist, short story writer, and editor.

Péret was a central figure in the Surrealist movement and a principal advocate of the movement's techniques and ideas. His highly original poetry is characterized by surprising imagery and irrationality, and displays an iconoclastic contempt for social and religious institutions. While André Breton was the author of the 1924 *Manifeste du surréalisme (Manifesto of Surrealism)* which inaugurated the movement, it was Péret who most successfully utilized the prescribed Surrealist literary technique, psychic automatism, in the creation of both poetry and prose. His work is considered by most critics to be the best example of Surrealist literary theories in practice.

Péret was born in the village of Rézé, in western France. Although little information is available concerning Péret's early life, it is known that his parents separated when he was two years old, that he was raised by his mother, and that he joined the army in 1917. Péret, like many of his contemporaries, was deeply affected by his experiences during the First World War, which contributed to his enormous distaste for modern society. When the war ended, Péret moved to Paris and there met Breton, whose writings he admired and who was at that time editor of the journal *Littérature*. Together, Péret and Breton became active in the Dada movement, which had been brought to France from Zurich by its founder, Tristan Tzara. Dadaism was one of the first artistic responses to the horror and disillusionment inspired by World War I and was a profoundly nihilistic movement, asserting absolute meaninglessness and holding all of civilization in contempt. From 1920 to 1922, Péret participated in Dada "events," including the mock trial of ultraconservative novelist Maurice Barrès, during which Péret goose-stepped about wearing a German uniform and a gas mask. In 1921, his first volume of Dadaist poetry, *Le passager du transatlantique,* was published. Péret and Breton, however, quickly tired of the unproductive negativity of that movement, and when Breton broke away in 1922, planning to synthesize the lessons of the early twentieth century into a more positive credo, Péret followed. When the first issue of Breton's *La révolution surréaliste* was published in December of 1924, Péret served as an editor of the journal. Péret and Breton shared great mutual respect and they remained close friends throughout their lives.

Péret's concerns, however, were not confined to the realm of literature, and his revolutionary political beliefs created much conflict in his life. In 1927, one year before the publication of his first major volume of poetry, *Le grand jeu,* Péret joined the French Communist party. That same year, he married a Brazilian woman, and in 1929 they returned to her homeland. Two years later, Péret was imprisoned and expelled from Brazil because of his continuing communist activities. From 1936 to 1938, he fought on the side of the Republican forces in the Spanish Civil War. In Paris at the beginning of the German occupation, Péret was again imprisoned for his communist sympathies, but he obtained his release by paying ransom to the occupation forces and eventually escaped to Mexico in early 1941.

Photograph by Man Ray, 1934. Copyright, Juliet Man Ray, 1986

Although several volumes of Péret's poetry had been published between 1929 and 1940, they were largely collections of works written before politics had come to dominate his life. The period of exile in Mexico allowed Péret to return to poetic endeavors, and he became very interested in native Latin American folklore, which he considered to be the product of primal, prerational, and hence more poetic states of awareness. During this portion of Péret's life, his works began to reflect his anthropological interests: he wrote several important essays, including *La parole est à Péret (Magic: The Flesh and Blood of Poetry)* and *Le déshonneur des poètes (The Dishonor of Poets),* regarding the nature and function of poetry which exhibit a distinct cross-cultural perspective; he compiled an anthology of ancient Latin American mythology, *Anthologie des mythes, légendes et contes populaires d'Amérique;* and he wrote many short stories in the form of legends. Péret returned to Paris in 1948, where he continued to write until his death in 1959.

While many authors joined the Surrealists only to later decamp, Péret adhered to the tenets of Surrealism throughout his career, rejecting rationality and using automatic writing to some extent in all his creative works. This technique, invented by Breton, involved the writer's surrendering himself to a vacant, trancelike state of mind which was thought to bypass the repressive, rational conscious mind and free the subconscious to control the creative process. Based upon psychoanalytic theory, in which Breton was well versed, this technique produced a literature hailed by the Surrealists as the portal to a larger reality, accessible only when all levels of consciousness, including the dream state, could function freely and simultaneously. Péret's devotion to automatic writing created consistency throughout the body of his work. With his intellect deliberately suppressed, he wrote emotionally forceful poetry which is filled with humor, as in his poem "Vive la revolution": "He was beautiful like fresh glass / Beautiful like the smoke from his pipe / Beautiful like the ears of a donkey that brays / Beautiful like a chimney / Which falls on the head of a policeman."

Péret's poetry is typically concerned with what he calls "sublime love" and "the marvelous." Sublime love is Péret's term for that emotional state which transports the individual to a higher level of awareness and is therefore the opposite of carnal love, which is simply a limiting physical impulse. Péret's concept of the marvelous, however, is more difficult to define, since he believed it was something to be experienced and not discussed. For him, the marvelous is not an attribute of objects but a mode of perception in which all levels of awareness participate fully to reveal the ultimate value of objects or events in a way that transcends the barriers of custom, subjectivity, and dogmatism. Both of these phenomena, then, are facets of the expanded consciousness which the Surrealists believed would intensify and enrich the individual's experience of existence. Conversely, Péret was contemptuous of those institutions he viewed as impediments to intellectual and emotional freedom, particularly governments and the church. So great was Péret's hatred for these institutions that he devoted an entire volume of poetry, *Je ne mange pas de ce pain-là*, to their vilification. However, since Péret believed strongly that literature should never be made to serve any ideological master, the majority of his works are neither laudatory nor censorious, but simply expressions of his inner voice given free reign.

Since the Surrealist school stressed a radical break with all that had come before, the art it produced was never intended to appeal to critics or the general public. Surrealist works were typically published in small numbers by firms which were run by other Surrealists or individuals who were sympathetic to their cause. It is therefore not surprising that Péret's work received little attention during his lifetime. Among other Surrealists, however, Péret was revered for his ability to apply the theories of the movement faithfully and successfully. Recent critical interest in the entire Surrealist movement reaffirms their opinion; Péret's work has been praised for its humor and power, and he is considered by many critics to be the most important Surrealist poet.

PRINCIPAL WORKS

Le passager du transatlantique (poetry) 1921
Immortelle maladie (poetry) 1924
Dormir, dormir dans les pierres (poetry) 1926
Le grand jeu (poetry) 1928
De derrière les fagots (poetry) 1934
A Bunch of Carrots (poetry) 1936
Je ne mange pas de ce pain-là (poetry) 1936
Je sublime (poetry) 1936
Remove Your Hat (poetry) 1936
La parole est à Péret (essay) 1943
　　[*Magic: The Flesh and Blood of Poetry* (partial
　　　translation) published in journal *View*, 1943]

"La pensée est UNE et indivisible" (essay) 1944;
　　published in journal *VVV*
　　["Thought is ONE and Indivisible" published in journal
　　　Free Union libres, 1946]
Le déshonneur des poètes (essay) 1945
　　[*The Dishonor of Poets* published in journal *Radical
　　　America*, 1970]
Main forte (short stories) 1946
Feu central (poetry) 1947
"Notes on Pre-Colombian Art" (essay) 1947; published
　　in journal *Horizon*
La brebis galante (short story) 1949
Air mexicain (poetry) 1952
Anthologie de l'amour sublime [editor] (poetry and prose)
　　1956
Le gigot, sa vie et son oeuvre (short stories) 1957
Histoire naturelle (prose) 1958
*Anthologie des mythes, légendes et contes populaires
　　d'Amérique* [editor] (folklore) 1960
Péret's Score / Vingt poèmes de Benjamin Péret (poetry)
　　1965
Oeuvres complètes. 2 vols. (poetry, short stories, and
　　essays) 1969-71
A Marvelous World (poetry) 1985

ANDRÉ BRETON (essay date 1940)

[*Breton was a French poet, prose writer, and critic who is best known as the founder of Surrealism. One of the most influential artistic schools of the twentieth century, the Surrealist movement began in 1924 with Breton's* Manifeste du surréalisme. *Strongly influenced by the psychoanalytic theories of Sigmund Freud, the poetry of Arthur Rimbaud, and the post-World War I movement of Dada, Breton proposed radical changes in both the theory and methods of literature. He considered reason and logic to be repressive functions of the conscious mind and sought to draw upon the subconscious through the use of automatic writing, a literary technique closely related to the psychoanalytic technique of free association. Breton's theories, however, reached far beyond the limits of literature; he considered Surrealist art a means of liberating one's consciousness from societal, moral, and religious constraints, thereby enriching and intensifying the experience of life. While Breton's creative works are considered by most critics to be uneven, his importance as a literary theorist remains unquestioned. In the following excerpt from his* L'anthologie de l'humour noir (1940), *Breton praises Péret's work.*]

I weigh my words as I say that Benjamin Péret affords the best example I know of the *foolproof detachment* needed to emancipate language, as he has done from the start. He alone has fully realised on the *word* an operation corresponding to the alchemical operation of 'sublimation' which consists of provoking the 'ascension of the subtle' by its 'separation from the dense'. The *dense*, in this realm, is that crust of exclusive signification with which usage coats all words and which leaves practically no play to their associations outside of cases in which immediate or accepted utility confines them in little groups, solidly supported by routine. The narrow space which opposes itself to every new introduction of relations between significative elements today held between words ceaselessly amplifies the zone of opacity which alienates man from nature and from himself. It is there that Benjamin Péret intervenes as a liberator.

Before him, in fact, the greatest of poets shored themselves up with excuses for having seen 'very frankly, a mosque in place of a factory' [Rimbaud] or needed to assume a challenging attitude while affirming that they saw 'a fig eating a donkey' [Lautréamont]. They seemed, while offering such passwords, to retain the feeling of having committed a crime, of profaning human consciousness, of infringing on the most hallowed taboos. With Benjamin Péret, on the other hand, such 'guilty conscience' is done away with, censorship is abolished, one pleads one's case with the countersign 'all is permitted'. Words and what they designate, freed once and for all from domestication, never before enjoyed such liberty.

Natural objects need not drag behind manufactured objects in this parade; each rivals the other in availability. We are absolutely through with rubbish and dust. Manic joy has returned. It is all in the magic of a glass of white wine:

> this wine which is only white to make the sun come up
> because the sun runs its hands through its hair.

Everything is free, everything is poetically liberated by the vigorous reassertion of a generalised principle of mutation, of metamorphosis. No longer restricted to the celebration of 'correspondences' as great but unfortunately intermittent gleams, one need only orient oneself, one moves only by an uninterrupted realisation of *passional accords*.

I am speaking now very close to a light that, day by day across thirty years, has embellished my life. Humour gushes here as from a geyser. (pp. 195-96)

> *André Breton, "'Anthology of Black Humour',"*
> *translated by Stephen Schwartz, in his* What Is Sur-
> *realism? Selected Writings, edited by Franklin Rose-*
> *mont, Monad, 1978, pp. 188-96.**

BENJAMIN PÉRET   (essay date 1945)

[*In the following excerpt from* The Dishonor of Poets, *originally published in 1945 as a response to a famous French Resistance anthology of sentimental nationalist verse entitled* The Honor of Poets, *Péret explains his concept of the function of poetry and the role of the poet in society.*]

If one searches for the original significance of poetry, today concealed behind the thousand tawdry ornaments of society, one realizes that it is the veritable breath of man, the source of all knowledge, and knowledge itself in its most immaculate aspect. The entire spiritual life of humanity since the beginning of its consciousness is condensed in poetry; in it palpitates the highest creations and, soil forever fertile, it holds perpetually in reserve the colorless crystals and the harvests of tomorrow. Tutelary divinity with a thousand faces, it is here called love, there freedom, and elsewhere science. It remains omnipotent: it rushes forth in the mythical tales of the Eskimo, blazes in a love letter, machine guns the execution squad shooting the worker who breathes his last sigh of social revolution, and therefore of freedom; it sparkles in the discovery of the scholar; faints, anemic, as the most stupid productions make use of it; and its memory, a eulogy which would like to be funereal, still pierces the mummified words of the priest, its assassin, to whom the faithful listen in seeking it, blind and deaf, in the tomb of dogma where it is no more than fallacious dust.

Its innumerable slanderers, true and false priests, more hypocritical than the priesthood of all churches, false witnesses of all time, accuse it of being a means of evasion, a flight from reality, as if it were not reality itself, its essence and its ex-

altation. Incapable of conceiving reality in its totality and its complex relationships, they want to see it only in its most immediate and sordid aspect. They perceive only adultery without ever feeling love; the bomber planes without remembering Icarus; the adventure novel without understanding the permanent, elementary, and profound poetic aspiration which its vain ambition is to satisfy. They scorn dreams in favor of reality as if dreams were not one, and the most overwhelming, of its aspects; they exalt action at the expense of meditation as if the first without the second was not a sport as insignificant as any other sport. Formerly, they opposed the spirit to matter, their god to man; today they defend matter against the spirit. Finally, they have put intuition in the aid of reason without recollection of the source of reason.

At all times the enemies of poetry have been obsessed with submitting it to their immediate ends, to crush it with their god. . . . For them, life and culture are summed up in useful and useless, it being understood that the useful takes the form of a pick-axe wielded for their benefit. For them poetry is only a luxury of the rich, the aristocrat or the banker, and if it should want to make itself "useful" to the masses, it must be resigned to the "applied," "decorative", "household" arts, et cetera.

Instinctively, they feel poetry is the fulcrum demanded by Archimedes, and fear that if it is overturned, the world might fall on top of them. Thus their ambition to revile it, to take away from it all efficacy, all exalting value, in order to give it the hypocritically consoling role of a sister of charity.

But the poet does not have to maintain for others an illusory hope, human or celestial, or appease the spirits by inflating them with an unlimited confidence in a father or leader, against whom all criticism becomes sacrilege. Quite the contrary, it is for the poet to pronounce the forever sacrilegious words and permanent blasphemies. The poet must first of all be conscious of his nature and place in the world. An inventor for whom discovery is only the means of attaining new discoveries, he must struggle ceaselessly against the paralyzing gods who strive to maintain man in his servitude, both the social authority and the divinity, which mutually complete each other.

He will therefore be revolutionary, but not among those who oppose only the tyrant of today, inauspicious in their eyes because he offends their interests, but who extol the excellence of tomorrow's oppressor, whose servants they already are. No, the poet struggles against all oppression: in the first place that of man by man, and the oppression of his thought by religious, philosophical, and social dogmas. He fights so that man may attain an ever more perfectible knowledge of himself and the universe. It does not follow that he desires to put poetry in the service of a political action, even revolutionary. But his very nature as a poet makes him a revolutionary who must fight on all fronts: that of poetry by the means proper to it, and on the field of social action, without ever confounding the two fields of action for fear of re-establishing the very confusion which it is its task to dissipate, consequently ceasing to be a poet, which is to say, revolutionary. (pp. 15-16)

> *Benjamin Péret, "The Dishonor of Poets," trans-*
> *lated by Cheryl Seaman, in* Radical America, *Vol.*
> *IV, No. 6, August, 1970, pp. 15-20.*

MARY ANN CAWS   (essay date 1964)

[*Caws is an American critic and educator who is noted for her prolific contribution to the study of the Dada and Surrealist move-*

Photograph of André Breton, Paul Eluard, Tristan Tzara, and Péret in 1922.

ments and for her translations from the works of the most significant figures of those movements. In the following excerpt, Caws discusses some prominent characteristics of Péret's poetry.]

André Pieyre de Mandiargues thinks it improbable that Péret will be widely read, while at the same time he maintains: "No one else can now or in the future presume to represent fully and purely Surrealist poetry." . . . Péret is the most faithful poet to Surrealism because he is never untrue to its theory; he is the only one constantly at ease in automatic writing. . . . It is said that he sat for hours in noisy cafés scribbling page after page which he corrected little, if at all. In his spontaneous writing, image follows image with no apparent effort on the part of the poet. The reader is conscious neither of strain nor of exaggeration, only of a flow of images all consistent with a world in which the poet is at home. In reading Breton, one is always aware of a certain solemnity which evokes admiration rather than participation. One feels less distant from Péret whose universe is less difficult to enter.

One reason for the accessibility of Péret's poems is that, in spite of their difficult appearance, they do have a structure, sometimes exterior, sometimes interior. The most obvious external regularity of this poetry is its logical sentence form: if one went to such and such a place, one would find such and such to be true; when A happens, B happens, and for that reason. . . . The poem may also be built around similar sounds (the famous "Les Enfants du quadrilatère" which Breton included in his *Petite Anthologie de l'humour noir* is formed mostly of "r's" and "l's") or held together by a specific style. **"Samson"** of **Le Grand Jeu** is an epic in rhythm as the poetry

of Saint-John Perse: "Or nous delégués par les sceptres. . . . Arrivez sources de ma main et réchauffez les ossements des glaciers." . . . Many of Péret's poems are complete within themselves and not open to continuation; the final words are unmistakably final. And after a gloomy group of images, one finds: "Cheerful, isn't it?", and after the mention of a general (called Bernadette) who likes castles without windows, "Oh la la." His stories are, like non-Surrealist stories, bound into an at least recognizable framework by events; and they are not reversible. Things happen, time passes, and the end is obviously different from the beginning. Mme Lannor is hanged from the obelisk on the Place de la Concorde, for instance, and Pulcherie, whose highest aspiration has been to ride in a car, does so at last. On the other hand, the poem or story can be left open:

> car les tulipes soupirent comme des gants bleus
>   abandonnés
> sur un billard
> car les billards s'ennuient comme des locomotives
> car
>
> [for the tulips are sighing like blue gloves left
> on a billiard table / for the billiard balls grow
> bored like locomotives / for. . . .]

But here there is an implied invitation to continue the poem in the same pattern of repetition.

Repetition is in fact a characteristic device of Péret. It can be more complicated—when, for example, three times in the poem there is a group of three lines, each of these lines beginning in the same way—or less so—as in the regular alternation:

> Donne-lui quelques sous
> son chapeau sera trop petit
> Donne-lui deux cravates
> il mentira tous les jours

[Give him a few pennies / his hat will be too small / Give him a couple of ties / he will lie every day. . . .]

or:

> Petite vaisselle
> *aboutira*
> Beurre d'oiseau
> *grandira*
> Pelle de sel
> *patinera.* . . .

[Little dishes / *will succeed* / Bird butter / *will grow* / Salt scoop / will *glide.* . . .]

Occasionally, the repetition is a basic one in which each line begins with the same word. In the most interesting poems, Péret (or Péret's hand, according to the purists) either works gradually into the pattern until the end, where all the accumulated attributes of the repeated noun are absorbed by it:

> Aujourd'hui je regarde par tes cheveux
> Rosa d'opale du matin
> et je m'éveille par tes yeux
> Rosa d'armure . . .
> Rosa de fumée de cigare
> Rosa d'écume de mer faite cristal
> Rosa

[Today I am looking with your hair / Rosa of morning opal / And I am waking through your eyes / Rosa of armor . . . / Rosa of cigar smoke / Rosa of sea foam made crystal / Rosa. . . .]

or he begins by the repetitions ("Mon . . . Mon . . .") and concludes very simply: "Je t'aime (**"Allô,"** *Je Sublime*)." It is not only a matter of surface ingenuity, for inside this pattern exist the same *interior* connections between the parts as in the wanderings of an intelligent mind.

For instance, both the poems just mentioned have such interior links, but they are not evident except on close reading. The first describes the remarkable fusion that takes place in love as seen by a Surrealist, a fusion of senses and of personalities. The second poem is centered about a group of liquid images: "inondé," "vin," "Rhin," "écume," "pluie," "étang," "se noyer," "cascade," "puits" ["flooded," "wine," "the Rhine," "foam," "rain," "pool," "to drown oneself," "waterfall," "well"].

And poems are clearly distinguishable from each other by the feeling peculiar to each. There are silly poems for sheer amusement, poems like **"Voyage de découverte,"** . . . where we read: "Un bas-seul ne dure pas longtemps / mais c'est assez quand on est seul / dans le bas du seul-seul;" and there are desolate ones, such as **"La Semaine pâle,"** . . . a poem full of words like "égaré," "perdu," "disparu," "s'éloigna," "passa," "séparaient" ["bewildered," "lost," "vanished," "alienated," "expired," "separated"]. To be sure, it is unremarkable for a poet to vary his tone; what is more significant is that the work of a genuine Surrealist can present such believable

distinctions of feeling. At first glance, "spontaneous" writing may seem all alike; it is not. After digesting a fair amount of Péret, a reader is touched by sad tomatoes tempted to suicide, and even by tears of mayonnaise on "de trés vieux vestons / des vestons extrêmement vieux" ["very old jackets / jackets extremely old"]. . . .

But in general, the universe which Péret presents to us is a more humorous one, where rubber tears when they fall only hurt the concierge. Here there is nothing dull or drab to mar the bright colors. . . . There are birds of all colors and varieties, enormous cherries, oranges and sun. On all sides there is quantity and variety: objects are constantly multiplying or increasing in size. A baobab becomes ten baobabs, one boa constrictor becomes six thousand. Three spaniels in a car grow with each roll of the tires and then the car itself grows enormous. One thing leads to another—a chimney to a cave which enters a second cave. And some need others to accompany them here, if nowhere else: there is to be no laugh without a hat by it nor flowers without smoke. A few of Péret's titles suffice to give an accurate picture of his world: **"Que font les olives," "Sans tomates pas d'artichauts," "Un oiseau a fienté sur mon veston salaud."** (The last poem concerns Paul Claudel, always a target for the Surrealists because of his lack of humor and surfeit of self-righteousness.) To be content in this world of poetry, one has to be willing to see as freshly as Péret such things as these:

> . . . les plus profonds soupirs
> qui se camouflent parfois en bains de lait
> orageux comme un mouton
> parfois en brute épaisse
> qui rêve de dentelles
> comme un haricot au clair de lune

[the deepest sighs / which disguise themselves sometimes as milk baths / sometimes as a hulking beast / dreaming of lace / like a bean in moonlight. . . .]

A child's imagination and curiosity are all that is required; this is often the case in Surrealism. Péret's stories, collected under the title *Le Gigot, sa vie et son oeuvre* demand, perhaps even more than his poetry, the proper attitude on the part of the reader. Heroes and heroines have ridiculous names: Glouglou and Pulcherie, Zacharie Artichaut, M. Détour, Macarelle, and M. Sucre—who melts in water. The action is equally ridiculous and sufficiently lively to counteract any claim that Surrealist writing is static. A frequent element in these highly animated children's stories is the chase, always fantastic like that of Aglaé pursuing the baobab in a bus: both the bus and the baobab fly, dive underground, and multiply. There is another absorbing drama in which music students, once split in two, and now reconstituted, slaughter crowds of bystanders until God and his angels fall to earth in a hailstorm, breaking up a passing procession. Consistent with this sustained naiveté is the recurrence in both the stories and the poems of certain aspects which most particularly appeal to Péret; more predominant even than the cherry trees, the elephants, and the sardines, are mustaches, pipes, and especially toes—perhaps because they are closely associated with humans, or perhaps simply because Péret likes them. There is even a short epic entitled **"Aventures d'un orteil."** People are frequently seen taking off their toes, generally those on the left foot, or having flowers sprout from them. (From a pedantic standpoint, the fact that stinging nettles are also common may corroborate the Surrealist claim that words spring as *auditive* entities directly into the mind; "ortie" resembles "orteil," and it is possible that Péret's inner ear delights in these sounds.)

Breton cannot *play* in any light sense, whereas Péret plays enthusiastically, and possibly the titles *Le Grand Jeu* and *Je sublime* should be considered as part of this play. He is even capable of mocking a word to which all the Surrealists pay homage. When the man-automaton invented by Jacquet-Droz sits down to write, his first word is "merveilleux." After the inventors have properly admired this feat, the automaton finally runs in and knocks over his inventor. Jacquet-Droz, flat on the ground, benevolently calls, "Merveilleux! Merveilleux! Merveilleux! Merveilleux!" (Of course one might interpret this story seriously, as the miraculous overwhelming the human, but that seems out of keeping with its tone, and Péret always writes in a style appropriate to his mood.) Péret's world is obviously full of the marvelous, but he takes it all no more and no less seriously than the staircase he mentions which a person ascends by sticking an arrow into himself, marking the floor he wants. At any moment the writer may belittle the whole vision with: "What's more, I don't know why we're talking about that." . . .

At his funniest, he is straightfaced, treating everything on the same level: "But the world is made in such a way that it's more scandalous to live with a sardine-butterfly than alone in a carafe." . . . Rather than reveling in the strangeness of his world, he takes it for granted and enjoys being there. After all, "any old salad bowl falling from the fifth floor / on an old lightning rod" can be counted on to tremble as it falls. Fleas look for ears forgotten in taxis and hard-boiled eggs spy at keyholes, while statues dissolve "into a cream of elephants / determined to try anything in order to escape from the catacombs." . . . Interspersed with these unconventional phenomena are such clichés as "a lot more could be said about that" and "but we haven't got that far yet" to show that is really all part of the same world, nothing being any more fantastic or any duller than anything else. Péret *likes* playing with language; in **"Les Malheurs d'un dollar"** Baba has to speak without verbs because she has been floating for so long on a pond in a bowler hat. . . . Because of this unfailing lightness his poetry never spills into sentimentalism; he keeps a sufficient distance from the poem to reflect on it as merely another object. After a poem full of words like "guttapercha" and "majordome," he says (with reason): "It all has a queer sound." . . .

This is not to say that Péret treats *everything* lightly. When it is a matter of poetry itself, he is adamant. Being the purest source of knowledge, poetry must be protected against all constriction and all reduction. In *Le Déshonneur des poètes* Péret levels a violent attack against all those who, in the name of authority of any kind, try to force poetry to serve as propaganda or to be useful like home economics: "They scorn dreams for the sake of their reality, as though dreams were not one of reality's aspects—indeed its most staggering, they exalt action at the price of meditation, as though the former without the latter were not a sport—insignificant like all sports." Poetry must continue to pronounce blasphemous words since it is in essence revolution. Heretics question the bases of myth and thus prevent the collective exaltation of a people from hardening into *dogma;* priests are the assassins of poetry. In contrast with the lyric optimism of certain passages where he speaks of "la naissance des eaux claires" ["the birth of clear waters"] and "le séjour de l'aube derrière la montagne" ["the sojourn of the dawn on the other side of the mountain"], or where men finally draw together, **"Celui qui . . ."** leading up to

"Tous et tant d'autres qui. . . ." Péret's vicious poems stand out all the more sharply. He makes fun of the monarchy:

> Pue pue pue
> Qu'est-ce qui pue
> C'est Louis XVI l'oeuf mal couvé

[Stink stink stink / What stinks / It's Louis XVI / the badly-hatched egg . . .]

the government:

> Un Poincaré jaune malgré tout
> se grattant le foie

[A Poincaré yellow in spite of it all / scratching his liver . . .]

and the army:

> Pour rappeler mon ruban
> je me suis peint le nez en rouge
> et j'ai du persil dans le nez
> pour la croix de guerre
>
> Je suis un ancien combattant
> regardez comme je suis beau

[To remind you of my ribbon / I've painted my nose red / and I'm wearing parsley in it / for the croix de guerre / I'm a veteran / see how handsome I am. . . .]

Nothing escapes his mockery, neither "La Marseillaise," nor the pope. Poetry has no country since it belongs to all places and is, like freedom, its own religion.

Man, says Péret in **"A l'intérieur de l'armure,"** is basically noncourageous; he makes gods and then, afraid of them, takes refuge in armor; that is, whatever authoritative structure best suits him. Life is outside that armor and beyond that authority; the business of poetry is to open the armor: "Ouvrons les armures. Ouvrons toutes les armures" ["Let us open the armor / Open all the armor"].

Of course poetry must itself be free. Spontaneous writing is a succession of images unhampered by stylistic *concern*. It cannot be judged by logical criteria nor appreciated by authoritarian minds. It must be approached on its own terms and not on those provided by a discipline exterior to it. Above all Péret deplores the loss of the capacity for pleasure, "that ever blossoming rose without which life would be nothing more than a poisoned thorn." "Literature" may have little place for this kind of naive pleasure, but poetry depends on it.

Only invertebrates need inflexible shells, and Péret's universe has the inner cohesive structure of a unique vision. The reader gradually becomes aware of certain consistencies in tone and theme so that the interior, and in some cases exterior, connections between his images make poetic sense. The elements which form these images are all familiar, even if the relations into which they naturally enter here would in any other world be improbable. But the special quality of Péret's poetry is that even non-Surrealists should be able to enjoy it. (pp. 105-11)

Mary Ann Caws, "Péret—Plausible Surrealist," in Yale French Studies, *No. 31, May, 1964, pp. 105-11.*

MARY ANN CAWS (essay date 1966)

[*In the following excerpt, Caws explores Péret's conception of l'amour sublime ("sublime love") as a liberating and purifying influence, comparing it to André Breton's conception of l'amour fou ("mad love"). Caws contrasts l'amour sublime to the ingrained codes of conventional society, particularly those derived from the teachings of the Catholic church and its representative, the priest.]*

For Péret, the priest, with his "paroles momifiées" ["mummified words"], is the assassin of liberty and the defender of the "répugnante morale d'hypocrisie, de bassesse et de lâcheté qui a cours dans la société actuelle" ["repugnant hypocritical morality of baseness and cowardice which circulates in present society"]. If the worst indignity to the human mind is to *penser en prêtre* ["think like a priest"], it is because the church puts an illusory heavenly paradise, at dime-store prices ("à des tarifs d'Uniprix"), before the eyes of a man, like a carrot before a donkey, so that he cannot see the possibility of an always perfectible "paradis relatif humain" ["relative human paradise"]. Péret's particular accent is distinguished by a recurring insistence on a sharply uncompromising human dignity and a fierce attack on anything that might detract from that dignity or from the liberty which makes it possible—hence his refusal, in the name of all men, of "religious myths." The priests have to think like dualists, deliberately intensifying the split between poetry and reason in order to protect the existing moral and physical structures on which they depend. In their conventional conception, the body is separate from the mind, science from poetry, reality from the dream. A structure based on such convention must therefore be violently opposed by those who, like the surrealists, believe in the eventual *union* of all things; so when Péret says that a human being is the direct opposite of the social man, he speaks for all the surrealist revolutionaries. To the religious myth, the surrealists oppose the "mythe exaltant" ["exalting myth"] of poetic vision, based on a strong sense of human ambivalence and an equally strong confidence that the poet, endowed with the magic power of the sorcerer and the imaginative liberty of the insane, can overcome that ambivalence. He is called upon to answer the innate "besoin du merveilleux" ["need for the marvelous"] felt by ordinary men everywhere and to eliminate, in Breton's words, "l'idée déprimante du divorce irréparable de l'action et du rêve" ["the depressing idea of an irreparable divorce between actions and dreams"].

The surrealist is always aware of such oppositions and separations, and many surrealist works center around aesthetic contrasts of light and dark or philosophic contrasts of subjective belief and objective reality. Breton's most characteristic essays describe the way in which chance encounters demonstrate the necessary link between the inner human desire and the outward world of realisation. Péret's essays are based on other contrasts: the dry bread of slaves and the succulent feast of masters, costume jewelry or poetry "à dix sous" ["for ten cents"] and the "merveilleux poétique" ["poetic marvelous"], "poètes" and "amuseurs," ["entertainers"], "le cri de l'angoisse humaine" ["the cry of human anguish"] and the "chant d'allégresse" ["song of joy"], the dark underground recess we live in at present and the "lumière éblouissante" ["resplendent light"] of the Eldorado we can be lifted to by the power of poetry. The poet who replaces the priest in the new myth is more a *seer* in Rimbaud's sense than a creator. . . . Only those with this sort of poetic vision and intense hatred of social convention are capable of the *comportement lyrique* ["lyrical behavior"] essential to surrealist love, "lyrique" applying equally to poetic sensitivity and to unprosaic love. Eluard's famous phrase *L'amour la poésie* perfectly describes the sentiment at the heart of the surrealist revolution; Breton adds to

it *La liberté* (often citing Hugo in this connection and reminding us how closely the surrealist revolution is linked to the romantic.)

The important place held by the concept of love in surrealism is partially explained by the hope centered in the female or irrational element as the only possible liberating force from the overmechanized masculine world and, on the other hand, by the resort to eroticism as a purely surrealist domain, a "théâtre d'incitations et de prohibitions" ["theater of incitements and prohibitions"]. It is certainly not a simple question of the scabrous used for its antisocial shock value, although of course that is part of it (see Péret *La Brebis galante, Les Rouilles encagées,* etc.) Breton quotes from Lubicz in the preface to the EROS surrealist exhibition of 1960: "Si les sens de la pudeur et de l'esthétique doivent être niés en érotique, les sens de la vie et du sacré ne peuvent pas être niés sans, en même temps, provoquer la négation même de l'érotique"["If the sense of decency and the sense of aesthetics must be denied in the erotic, the sense of life and of the sacred cannot be denied without, at the same time, provoking the negation of the erotic itself"]. The ordinary concept of the beautiful must be deliberately denied in surrealist love. Just as in the surrealist image, the distance between the two elements or the improbability of their encounter gives shock value to the union. It takes a poet to recognize the face of love under its masks, and poetry, says Péret, is the only filter capable of separating from the multitude the elected, those endowed with the *grâce d'aimer* ["grace to love"]. The *insolite* ["unusualness"] to which the poet is sensitive can have nothing in common with the beauty ("esthétique") easily perceived by prosaic men. This is not to be confused with the school of thinking which finds beauty chiefly in ugliness: the philosophical "désir" of the surrealists is a sort of vital force ("sens de la vie") working under the sterile and prudish exterior of the normal world, a sudden consciousness of necessity, of hidden questions answered in unpredictable ways. Péret admired Breton particularly for his emphasis on this type of love:

> Plus que tout autre, André Breton a reconnu dans l'amour le centre explosif de la vie humaine qui a le pouvoir de l'illuminer ou de l'enténébrer, le point de départ et d'arrivée de tout désir, en un mot, l'unique justification de la vie.
>
> [More than any other, André Breton has recognized love as the explosive center of human life, having the power to illuminate or darken, and the point of departure and arrival for every desire; in a word, the unique justification of life. . . .]

Here again light contrasts with dark: "illuminer," "enténébrer." More than anything else in the writings of Breton and Péret, their essays on love oppose the luminous quality of surrealist love to the murky life of the non-elect. In *L'Amour fou* Breton speaks of fire, of sparks, of crystalline salt cubes, of transparency and of his perfect glass chain, of a bright dizziness; Péret, in his *Amour sublime,* of the "irisation" of the world (by love), of "scintillement," of "vertigineuse illumination."

But it is here also that the essential difference lies: Breton says that his house of "sel gemme" ["rock salt"] was "inhabitable" ["uninhabitable"] and that he could never live at his "point sublime": "Il eut d'ailleurs, à partir de là, cessé d'être sublime et j'eusse, moi, cessé d'être un homme'' [''Besides, it would then cease to be sublime, and I myself would then cease to be man'']. He can only make it visible for others. *Les Vases communicants* and *L'Amour fou* are descriptions of surrealist love from the inside, from the world which remains ''de l'autre côté'' [''on the other side''] from the rational world; the ''amour fou'' can be lived, but the ''point sublime'' can only be shown.

Péret, however, sees his *amour sublime* as the *reachable* summit of desire, in lofty contrast to the ''bassesse'' [''baseness''] of the social condition as it is to the ''grossièreté'' [''coarseness''] of purely sensual love. Breton's implicit contrast between *l'amour fou* and reasonable love considers two things to be imagined on the same plane if at opposite poles, whereas *l'amour sublime* is a deliberate use of vertical imagery. Péret's fascination with the hard geometrical precision of the diamond and of the ''point-limite'' is a strong reminder of Breton's ''point sublime'' and his ''éloge du cristal'' [''eulogy of crystal''], but Péret carries the geometrical sharpness farther than Breton. It has often been remarked that all Breton's work is built on a dialectical process—in his picture of dream and reality as two ''vases communicants'' [''communicating vessels''] he presents a kind of fluidity and interchange which the perfect crystalline structure he speaks of does not have. Péret never gives any place to this sort of flexible compromise: for him, even poetry is a ''lieu géométrique'' [''geometric place''] and only a being with the poetic spark can possibly aspire to the other ''lieu géométrique'' which is ''l'amour sublime.'' Rigidity of spirit, asceticism and sacrifice are the basis for the harsh purity of this *perfect* love, in which the lovers exalt each other in an always symmetrical movement, ''jusqu'à constituer un complexe à la fois religieux et magique'' [''to the point of constituting a complex at once religious and magical'']. . . . He will not tolerate an impure ambivalence of sentiment, such as the simultaneous aversion and desire Baudelaire felt for Jeanne Duval, to enter his magic universe of sublime love. . . . (pp. 205-08)

In Péret's collection *Je Sublime* . . . there are two poems whose throwaway titles mock their inner complexity, **''Allo''** and **''Clin d'oeil.''** The first does not sound at all like a love poem until the end, when all the apparently heterogeneous images are seen in retrospect as defining in quite subtle ways the feeling of the poet for the woman loved:

> Mon avion en flammes mon château inondé de vin du Rhin
> mon ghetto d'iris noir mon oreille de cristal . . .
> ma cassette de soleil mon fruit de volcan
> mon rire d'étang caché où vont se noyer les prophètes distraits . . .
> mon revolver de corail dont la bouche m'attire comme l'oeil d'un puits
> scintillant
> glacé comme le miroir où tu contemples la fuite des oiseaux-mouches de ton regard
> perdu dans une exposition de blanc encadrée de momies
> je t'aime
>
>> [My airplane in flames my castle flooded with Rhine wine / my ghetto with black rainbow my ear of crystal . . . / my casket of suns my fruit of volcanos / my laugh of a hidden pond where deranged prophets go to drown themselves . . . / my coral revolver whose muzzle attracts me like the eye of a well / scintillating / frozen like

the mirror in which you contemplate the humming-birds' flight of your gaze / lost in an exhibition of white surrounded by mummies / I love you.]

Here the images do not serve as adjectives to *describe* her; she *is,* rather, all these things. The choppiness of the beginning leads to the final long complex image with its shifting perspectives and to the simple revelation, which could have been banal at the poem's beginning, but is not at its end. Breton's poem spoke of ''shoulders of champagne and fountains of princely heads under the ice''; Péret's has an abundance of Rhine wine echoed later by an ''inondation de cassis,'' a black foam of hair followed by a rain of red grasshoppers, and a hidden pond followed by a sparkling well iced over. The world seems very full, though it consists in reality of only one being; it has snails, mosquitoes, birds of paradise, gazelles and butterflies, opals and turquoise, grapes and onions, all in twenty lines. Péret's personal exuberance is transformed directly into poetry.

''Clin d'oeil'' situates itself immediately as a straight-forward love poem:

> Des vols de perroquets traversent ma tête quand je te vois de profil
> et le ciel de graisse se strie d'éclairs bleus
> qui tracent ton nom dans tous les sens. . . .
>
>> [Flights of parrots go through my head when I see you in profile / and the sky of grease streaks itself with blue lightning / which traces your name in all directions. . . .]

The birds are brightly colored and the sky becomes so in a highly emotional vision which has nothing extraordinary about it. But the poem moves quickly toward a remarkable sort of surrealistic intersubjectivity,

> où les seins aigus des femmes regardent par les yeux des hommes
> Aujourd'hui je regarde par tes cheveux
> Rosa d'opale du matin
> et je m'éveille par tes yeux
> Rosa d'armure
> et je pense par tes seins d'explosion. . . .
>
>> [where the pointed breasts of women gaze through the eyes of men / Today I gazed through your hair / Rosa, opal of the morning / and I awakened through your eyes / Rosa of armor / and I think through your breasts of an explosion. . . .]

Surrealism wages war on the principle of *identity* and values love precisely for its destruction of egoism, as *Le Grand Jeu* and *Je Sublime* make way for *L'Amour fou* and *L'Amour sublime.* Again the end is simple, and the last line assumes in itself all the accumulated qualities of the other lines:

> Rosa de forêt noire inondée de timbres-poste bleus et verts
> Rosa de fumée de cigare
> Rosa d'écume de mer faite cristal
> Rosa
>
>> [Rosa of the black forest deluged with blue and green postage stamps / Rosa of cigar smoke / Rosa of the foam of a crystal sea / Rosa.]

As in Péret's other poem, the images reflect each other; the greens and blues of the stamps are the colors of the parakeets, and the smoke and foam are changed into the clarity of the crystal as the blue flashes of her name make bright streaks in the greasy sky. Breton's woman absorbs in herself all the things that were used to describe her—"Ma femme à ..." ["My woman with ..."]. This is, after all, the normal way to speak: "aux yeux de savane" ["with eyes of the savanna"] has exactly the same kind of sense as "aux yeux bleus" ["with blue eyes"]. Rosa is, however, not described as *having* shoulders of champagne: she is *of* morning opal, etc. Breton's catalogue of attributes is very different from Péret's perception of coalescence. It is as if there were a certain comfortable distance, a breathing space, between the elements of Breton's universe, between the poet and the woman, the woman and her qualities. Péret's poetry leaves none, since the poet wakes up *through* her eyes, and since she is literally part of that which in most poems she would only resemble.

In Péret's poem of 1942, **"Où es-tu,"** the complexity comes not in the woman but in the poet loving her.

> Je voudrais te parler cristal fêlé hurlant comme un chien
>   dans une nuit de draps battants
> comme un bateau démâté que la mousse de la mer
>   commence d'envahir
> où le chat miaule parce que tous les rats sont partis. . . .

> [I would like to tell you of cracked crystal howling like a dog in a night of thrashing bedsheets / like a dismasted ship that sea-foam begins to overflow / and where a cat yowls because all the rats have left. . . .]

Here the initial uncertainty lies in the "cristal fêlé"—to whom does it apply, the person addressed or the poet? Since Péret so often thinks of Baudelaire, we tend to remember his "Cloche fêlée" and assume that the poet feels himself in some way damaged. The rest of the poem bears out this supposition; "Je voudrais te parler comme ..." introduces two more sets of catastrophic descriptions. After the howling and the sinking, there is a tree overturned in a storm, a series of ripped-out telephone wires, the noise of a door being broken-in, a subway train stalled, a toe with a splinter, a sterile vine, a cold hearth, a deserted café. The form becomes more and more intricate until there are seven clauses depending one on the other, linked less awkwardly than one would expect by a line of utterly banal words: "Avec ... dans ... pareil à ... dans ... qui ... que ... où ... comme ... dans ... qui ... que ... où ..." ["With" ... "in" ... "like" ... "in" ... "who" ... "that" ... "where" ... "like" ... "in" ... "who" ... "that" ... "where" ..."]. But the surface is totally smooth and leads to a deceptively quiet end after all the images of negation and violence:

> Je te dirais simplement
> que je t'aime comme le grain de blé aime le soleil
>   se levant en haut de sa tête de merle.

> [I would simply say to you / that I love you as the grain of wheat loves the sun / rising above its blackbird's head.]

Which leaves a question still—why should he want to speak *as* those negations when what he is saying is so positive? Is it for humility? Isn't the grain of wheat small enough and the blackbird black enough to make a sufficient contrast to the rising sun? The blackbird's head brings another switch of per-

spective and identity: is the wheat deliberately making of itself a dark object, destructive *of itself,* drawn to the sun in an attraction of opposites? In this case, the "simplement" becomes heavily sarcastic. Or is it all a purely poetic transposition of planes? "Je te dirais" holds no hope of being able to speak the love *in reality* and the "Où es-tu" of the title implies the absence even of the person spoken to, if speech were possible. Ironically, the poem comes from a group called *Un point c'est tout.* Like so many of Péret's titles, it cuts away the ground from under all interpretations and placing a definitive end right at the beginning, which is as unreasonable and as intelligent as surrealism itself. (pp. 210-12)

>   Mary Ann Caws, "Péret's 'Amour Sublime'—Just
>   Another 'Amour fou'?" in The French Review, Vol.
>   XL, No. 2, November, 1966, pp. 204-12.

HERBERT S. GERSHMAN   (essay date 1969)

[*Gershman was an American critic and educator who specialized in French literature of the nineteenth and twentieth centuries. In the following excerpt, he contrasts Péret's imaginary world with that of Lautréamont (Isidore Ducasse), a nineteenth-century poet who was highly admired by the Surrealists and whose* Chants de Maldoror *(1868) is a series of nightmarish prose poems expressing rebellion against God and society.*]

To the surrealists Lautréamont had seen through the forest of symbols which surround us into the glory that lies just beyond the *dérèglement de tous les sens.* The *Chants,* however, are less visions of perfect moments, a preview of Proust's *moments privilégiés,* than scenes of unreal horror that might have been enacted by an early Caligari, scenes which, if [André] Breton was willing to accept as authentic, he had no intention of imitating. Only Péret, of the early surrealists, rose to this challenge and attempted a synthesis of the technique of automatism, carefully controlled so as to give the desired end result, with the content of the Gothic novel: a combination of deliberate sensory and logical confusion with a matching subject. All this in an impeccable syntax.

> —Die, deaf horn!
> —Die, eel soap!
> —Die, head paper!
> —Die, flighty elephant!

> Such were the cries which echoed inside the tin tube where two virgins and their shadow were sleeping. With arms raised to heaven, they begged the arsonists to spare the roots of the beech tree which had given birth to them. The younger of the virgins, whose brow was a wine cellar reserved for the purest alcohols, those which the philosopher extracts from fur coats after they have shielded a woman's shoulders from indiscreet glances of a winter's night similar to a picture book Christmas when booted Russians hunt wolves in vegetable gardens bristling, for decorative effect, with frozen brushes and mannequins who nonetheless. . . .

This is the wonderland of a child's picture book where reigns the wicked witch, a land where animal horns may turn deaf, eels wash (or [savon d'anguille] is it simply soap made of eels?), skulls are the source of paper (or [papier de crâne] is the paper *for* the skull?), and elephants are fickle. Not really very wicked or dangerous when compared with either of the world wars between which this falls, or when held up to the mischievous works of a Sade or a Lautréamont. On the surface this is far more a pampered child's version of what is dreadful in the world about him. For adults, on the other hand, Péret's tales are neither terrifying nor amusing. His chambers of false horrors are indeed so anodyne that there arises the suspicion he wanted it that way, that he was deliberately engaged in writing new fables for old children, as [Robert] Desnos and [Jacques] Prévert were to do years later in their *Chantefables* and *Paroles*. (pp. 43-4)

For those tired of logic, of reason, of lockstep consensus, Péret offers an enchanted land where houses are built in a twinkle, and one goes from candy swords to prodigious bicycle races. Much may happen in this aloof dream world, but it is all harmless, for it doesn't really "engage" us as would, say, tangible reality. Things become people, women are always at the ready, nothing is burdensome, and should you be injured you can always change into something else. (p. 46)

In this dream world, which could serve as a model for a film to delight the young and disturb the rest of us, the heart reigns supreme. The standard tools of comprehension are of little avail. Nonetheless, the human animal is sufficiently resilient to assimilate even the strangest of human artifacts, however odd they may appear at first sight. In a sense this is the glory of surrealism and its major contribution to literature. Having obliged us to recognize the irrational in the world, it challenges the smug and obliges the sedate to redraw the boundaries of reality. From the time of symbolism to the present a certain type of art has become more and more of a private affair, the author writing less for a public, even the restricted one of fellow authors, than for himself. Art, at this point, becomes a form of self-knowledge requiring new techniques and a new logic, in much the same way that life then is identified with spontaneity and action, rather than with the idea of progress. Is this very different from Tristan Tzara? For both Tzara and the old-line surrealists art-for-a-public was to be replaced by art-for-truth (subjective truth, *bien entendu!*), with each artist dipping his own siphon into the unconscious well and marveling at the bubbles which rose to the surface, individual bubbles reflecting a collective consensus. Where Tzara saw psychoanalysis as a "dangerous illness, [for it] puts the antireal penchants of man to sleep" and shores up a declining middle class, Breton perceived the possibility of turning psychoanalytic techniques away from integrating the "patient" into society and toward a new revolutionary self-awareness. In Péret, as in Tzara before him, the content is sufficiently amorphous so that the reader is encouraged to restructure the poem (or story) according to the dictates of his ever-solicited caprices. The end result, as Breton foresaw, was "an unprecedented freedom of expression," one that, according to one critic, "does not aim to bridge the distance between the real and the surreal; it places us unequivocally in the realm of the latter."

In Péret's universe, as occasionally in [Stéphane] Mallarmé's, disembodied words have a reality all their own. Had not Breton insisted that "man was given language so that he might use it surrealistically"? Péret would not have it any other way. The one pitfall is to *explain*, to reduce the complex unknown to a simple known, this in spite of the fact that **"Thought is ONE and indivisible."** Although no mystic, Péret has a mystic's unconcern for categories: all is one and one is all. Where he differs is in placing the Godhead in poetry, surrealist poetry, to be sure. In that Wonderland where whim and chance are the reigning monarchs, Alice-Péret, the wanderer from beyond, will describe glass sternums polished by cellar sunlight and a turquoise titmouse beating its wings in cream. (pp. 46-7)

Herbert S. Gershman, "The Early Literature of Surrealism," in his The Surrealist Revolution in France, *The University of Michigan Press, 1969, pp. 35-79.**

FRANKLIN ROSEMONT (essay date 1970)

[*Rosemont is an American poet and critic who is one of the leading figures among the present-day generation of Surrealist writers. In the following excerpt, he praises Péret for his imagination and devotion to the cause of human freedom.*]

The most vital and revolutionary currents in modern poetry owe much to Benjamin Péret. The appearance of his work in English translation is especially welcome since Péret's characteristic agressivity, revolt, and humor, as well as his admirably incurable passion for all that is marvelous, are precisely the qualities most lacking in poetry in the English language in this century. (One would have to go to Blake's *Island in the Moon* or to certain works of Lewis Carroll: *The Hunting of the Snark,* for example, or the songs of the gardener in *Sylvie and Bruno,* to approach, in English, the poetic universe of Péret.) André Breton, in his *Anthologie de l'Humour Noir* [see excerpt dated 1940], has described the great poetic advance made by Péret. Before him the greatest poets in the French language had been able to see only "a mosque in place of a factory" (Rimbaud) or to see "a fig eating a donkey" (Lautréamont). Moreover, ". . . they seem to hold to the sentiment that they are committing a violation, that they are profaning human consciousness, that they are infringing on the most sacred of taboos. With Benjamin Péret, to the contrary, this sort of 'bad conscience' is done away with, censorship no longer exerts itself, one pleads that 'all is permitted.'" For example:

> I call tobacco that which is ear
> and the mites take their chance to throw themselves on
>   the ham
> hence a remarkable fight between the springs
> flowing from gingerbread
> and the spectacles that prevent blind men from seeing
>   clearly. . . .

It must be emphasized that Péret is, far more than is generally thought, a poet of love. But love for Péret has nothing to do with conventional pseudo-amorous sentimentality nor the vile platitudes of so-called "popular" music: it is, rather, the most decisive and thoroughgoing individual human experience, comprising the most delirious and overpowering moments of one's life: love which is wild, succulent, corrosive, frenzied, violently opposed to the last shred of Christian morality and to every other conceivable social constraint; love which, in a single glance, is capable of reinventing, from scratch, one's conception of life.

The poetry of Benjamin Péret, with its rapid and violent metamorphoses, its wild shattering flights, like a Roman candle, into the blue sky of appearances, and its mad plunges, like an uncontrollable bathysphere, into the deepest sea of dreams, seems to me especially well-equipped to disperse the stale mythological fog that still obscures man's desperate glance into the future, and to restore to man a truer vision of his infinite capacities for transforming the world. Long before reaching the second line, Péret has established the dictatorship of the imagination and rigorously enforces the revolutionary terror of the convulsively beautiful image.

The same may be said for another category of Péret's work, his considerable number of tales which are in fact really inseparable from the rest of his poetic practice. It goes without saying that these "prose" works are entirely independent of the various insignificant devices of fiction—plot, character development, setting, et cetera—literary gadgets which Péret turns against themselves in the service of a superior order of imaginative activity. Thus these narratives do not meet the ordinary definitions of a "short story", any more than the longer tales—some of which are of book length, and divided into chapters—may accurately be called "novels". The effect of these tales is like a fresh breath of pure oxygen in a musty room: one feels a certain exhilaration, a sense of expansiveness; one feels freer, surer of oneself, perhaps slightly dizzy—but it is a dizziness quite distinct from intoxication: it is the feeling of looking over a cliff at a great height which one is delighted to have reached. It is to Péret's everlasting credit that he continually reaches such heights, as far as possible from the mundane, that he does so without effort, and that he takes the reader along with him on these lyrical expeditions.

Alongside and allied with his poetry and tales is Péret's theoretical work, the importance of which, for surrealism, is immense. In *La Parole est à Péret, Le Déshonneur des Poètes,* **"Thought is ONE and Indivisible,"** and **"Noyau de Comète,"** Péret explores, with verve and lucidity, the origins and development of the poetic faculties, their applications, implications, and ramifications. Always emphasizing the liberatory essence of poetry, always defending the subversive primacy of love in the gamut of emotions, always celebrating the revolt of the mind against its jailers, he traces the trajectory of myths and legends, the perversions of religious mystification, the interrelationships between poetry and society, between poetry and revolution. These texts testify with burning clarity to Péret's relentless devotion to the cause of breaking the social, cultural, and psychological fetters which reduce the imagination to misery and degradation. "The poet of today," he wrote, "has no other choice than to be a revolutionist or not to be a poet."

It was Péret's rare genius to be able to speak of revolutionary poetry and revolutionary politics equally from within. But let us hasten to add, to avoid confusion on a fundamental point, that Péret consistently refused any false, arbitrary, superficial syntheses of these two complementary but independent planes of revolutionary activity. Unlike many current so-called "cultural revolutionaries", including the ideologists of various "avant-garde" sects who boast of having "surpassed" surrealism, and who proclaim that they are able to "solve" the problems of poetry and revolution, and all problems, with the mere application of a few convenient "anti-artistic" formulas, Péret disdained such evasive pretensions and invariably approached the burning questions of human freedom with full recognition of their complexity and diversity. The cause of the liberation of the mind (surrealism) and the cause of proletarian revolution (marxism) are not at all, in the eyes of Péret, reducible to abstract philosophical schemes or readymade slogans. They represent, rather, concrete and miraculous moments in the struggle for the total liberation of man. "These two activities", as Jean Schuster has written, "for him, surely, were but one. But the lucidity of his consciousness permitted him to understand that an objective conciliation was premature. That is why, belonging to these two very close but separate movements, he strictly forbade himself to bend the course of one in terms of the essential principles or circumstantial imperatives of the other. That is why, in all serenity, he served, on two planes, revolutionary truth." (pp. 6-8)

Franklin Rosemont, "An Introduction to Benjamin Péret," in Radical America, *Vol. IV, No. 6, August, 1970, pp. 1-13.*

J. H. MATTHEWS (essay date 1975)

[*Matthews is a Welsh critic and educator who has written extensively on the Surrealists. In the following excerpt from his book-length study of Péret's life and works, he discusses Péret's poetic principles.*]

Péret's opposition to inherited poetic forms was imperious, uncompromising, and unrelenting. Yet it rested upon no concerted plan for replacing old forms with new ones. Everything, it seems, followed naturally from his dismissal of the reflective process in favor of the spontaneity that automatism guarantees. There is nothing unexpected in this. More worthy of notice, surely, is the fact that Péret was not able to identify his poems as his own when he heard them read aloud. Those of us who think of the work of Benjamin Péret as instantly recognizable, in content and structure too, may feel it paradoxical that this should have been so. But, for that very reason, Péret's reaction is particularly deserving of attention.

As Breton foresaw when first advocating its use, verbal automatism by no means precludes individuality in writing. All the same, the effect of natural impulse, in giving form to the language of Surrealism, is quite different from the implementation of a literary technique, deliberately applied. Failure to recognize his own work was symptomatic of a profoundly characteristic trait in Péret: his complete freedom from a proprietary attitude toward his writings. This trait is important to notice, since in one respect at least it made Benjamin Péret unique among the first-generation Surrealists.

Paul Eluard's creative urges tended to centralize poetic experience upon the satisfaction of demands making themselves felt within himself. All that is typical of his Surrealist poetry testifies, therefore, to a rearrangement of elements borrowed from the world of familiar reality and brought together in a new order, under the influence of the poet's private needs. Much the same may be said of André Breton, who in his verse habitually fell into the role of intermediary between the reader and the world of the surreal. The first-person mode in well-known poems like his "Vigilance" and "Ode à Charles Fourier" is no more significant in this connection than the possessive pronouns that recur throughout his "L'Union libre." Authority rests everywhere with the poet, whose posture before the world that his work depicts accounts for the way he makes us see things. As for Robert Desnos, with the verbal experiments of *L'Aumonyme* (1923) and *Langage cuit* (1923) behind him, he, too, resorted to the first-person perspective in *A la Mystérieuse* (1926) and *Les Ténèbres* (1927). Louis Aragon, of course, was aggressively egocentric in all his Surrealist verse. In a sense, then, all these early Surrealist poets turned to an approach that was essentially traditional in character. They challenged their readers to accept the viewpoint of the writer, to see the world as his experience made him see it, and hence to share in the emotional excitement and imaginative release engendered by that experience. This is to say that the presence of the poet, to which the distinctive tone of his voice makes us sensitive, justifies all that he has to show us. We are brought face to face with a creative sensibility animated by personal feelings that, in the best tradition of lyrical poetry, inspired Eluard, for example.

Péret has something different to offer. For the most part, his work eludes the controls normally imposed upon the creative process by the poet's need to satisfy the demands of an ego ever ready to display itself for the admiration of others. A special kind of modesty pervades his writings. Characteristically, he declines to take up a central position in his poems. Instead, he either celebrates the beauty of woman in texts where he is content to bear witness to the miracle of love, or he evokes a world which to some of his readers must appear impertinent or frivolous, precisely because he betrays no inclination to relate what he shows us to the familiar by way of a personal reaction. Typically, beneath the title **"Mémoires de Benjamin Péret,"** he opens one of his poems with the words:

Un ours mangeait des seins
Le canapé mangé l'ours cracha des seins
Des seins sortit une vache
La vache pissa des chats
Les chats firent une échelle

A bear was eating breasts
The sofa eaten up the bear spat out breasts
From the breasts emerged a cow
The cow pissed cats
The cats made a ladder. . . .

Whether we understand *canapé* as a sofa or as a slice of bread fried in butter (or even, preferably, as both at the same time— this is Péret's universe, not the world we are accustomed to see about us), we still face the fact that nothing in the opening of **"Mémoires de Benjamin Péret"** or in the rest of the poem seems to keep the promise of its title, according to the traditions of confessional poetry. (pp. 29-31)

Because he did not feel possessive about the things he wrote, Péret was all the better able to assume the role of witness to poetic manifestation, as he understood the term, and so to become, beyond question, the most faithful of the "modest *recording instruments*"—as Breton's 1924 manifesto described the Surrealists. Quite indifferent to the mannerisms that, in his opinion, pass for style, Péret was always at liberty to start anew and to discover in his poems the prompting of verbal automatism in the very process of consigning them to paper. (pp. 31-2)

On the subject of poetry, Benjamin Péret wrote as though he felt he had only to remind his audience of self-evident truths that needed neither discussion nor defense, too fundamental to meet serious objection. The tone is stern in *Le Déshonneur des poètes* but by no means as aggressive as might be expected of a man who showed no reluctance to admit to the following peculiarities: "detests priests, cops, Stalinists, and tradespeople." And so a distinctive feature of the texts in which Péret speaks of the essential characteristics of poetry is the mingling of apparently banal statements with others, given no more stress or development than the former, that are very difficult to follow sometimes and that lie at the source of Péret's motivation as a poet. What, for instance, does he mean when, on the first page of *Le Déshonneur des poètes,* he calls poetry "the source of all knowledge and that knowledge itself in its most immaculate aspect?" Students of Surrealism will have no trouble recognizing the orthodoxy of Péret's basic principles, seen from the standpoint of Surrealism, which from its inception equated poetic action with the act of cognition. But this still does not take us all the way to our ultimate goal: definition of the contribution that Péret's idea of poetry led him to make within the framework of Surrealism. We shall come much nearer to that goal if we begin by facing a question important enough to Péret to provoke him, against custom, into personal reminiscence in *La Parole est à Péret.* This is the question of the significance of the marvelous and, specifically, of what, in Péret's estimation, it represents in poetry.

La Parole est à Péret provides a convenient and reliable starting point for an examination of what may be termed, very approximately, Péret's theory of the marvelous. This text shows how far he is willing to go on the theoretical plane and lets us know unequivocally at which point he is prepared to stop. "It is expected no doubt that I will define the poetic marvelous. I shall take good care not to do so. It is of a luminous nature that does not suffer competition from the sun: it disperses shadows and the sun dulls its brilliance. The dictionary, of course, confines itself to giving its dry etymology in which the marvelous can be recognized with as much difficulty as an orchid preserved in a herbarium. I shall try only to give a suggestion of it". . . .

To Benjamin Péret, obviously, the important thing is not defining the marvelous so much as experiencing it, acknowledging its ever-presence and its disruptive effect: "However, the marvelous is everywhere, hidden from the eyes of the vulgar, but ready to explode like a time bomb." Returning to emphasize this point, he equates the marvelous with life itself—"on condition though that it does not render life deliberately sordid as society strains its ingenuity to do with its schools, religion, law-courts, wars, occupations and liberations, concentration camps, and horrible material and intellectual wretchedness." It is only now that having linked the marvelous to the spirit of anticonformity, Péret alludes to his period of confinement at Rennes.

He reports that one day he discovered the window of his cell had been painted over. In each of its four panes, he could now make out an evocative shape. From day to day these pictures would appear to change, only one of them seeming invariably the same: the figure 22, which had convinced him he would be freed on the 22nd of a month as yet unknown. After his release—it occurred on July 22, 1940—Benjamin Péret tried his hand at painting window panes, but without producing interesting results. The marvelous cannot be manufactured, he now realized: "It grabs you by the throat. A certain state of 'vacancy' is needed for the marvelous to deign visit you."

This statement is of the greatest importance, sparing us the temptation to set off in the wrong direction, in our search for the meaning of the marvelous in his work. Within Surrealism, Benjamin Péret does not rank as the most admirable of poets just because he was the one who most closely and most consistently respected the recommendations concerning automatic practices set forth in the *Manifeste du surréalisme.* Such a claim to fame would rest upon the notion of poetry as mere technique, as a recipe available to all but applied best by the writer best equipped to follow it most faithfully. In this connection, we cannot overstress Louis Aragon's remark that if one writes idiotic things according to the Surrealist method, they are no less idiotic for that. The automatic method was promoted within the Surrealist movement as a means of releasing inspirational resources, not as an excuse for forgiving those in whom these resources proved to be inadequate. Thus Péret did not gain preeminence among the Surrealist poets merely by his willingness to rely on automatism, but because automatic writing enabled him to offer a perspective upon reality that was uniquely his. It would be futile to try analyzing his work in the hope of learning how to write like Péret. As

Péret understood and practiced it, poetry lies in a viewpoint upon the world, not in a method for dealing with it. And it is in probing the idea of the marvelous that we have most chance of explaining what that viewpoint was and how it is communicated through his writings.

Allusions to the marvelous remain discreet in *La Parole est à Péret*. And there are none at all to be found in the pages, written in São Paulo in August, 1955, added to the 1942 text so that it could preface Péret's *Anthologie des Mythes, légendes et contes populaires d'Amérique*. This is because in his mind poetry and the marvelous are one. Speaking of the former necessarily means referring to the latter, especially when poetry is being discussed in its revolutionary function:

> It fell to romanticism to find the marvelous once again and to endow poetry with a revolutionary significance that it still retains today and that allows it to live an outlaw existence, but to live all the same. For the poet—I'm not speaking of amusers of every sort—cannot be acknowledged as such if he does not oppose the world in which he lives with total nonconformism. . . .

Coming after a succession of statements that insist upon the inevitably revolutionary role of poetry, these words establish the basis for our appreciation of Péret's writings: that the marvelous is a sign of social and moral anticonformity, signaling unyielding resistance to accepted social modes of thought and feeling. It measures the poet's difference, his distance from a society by which he does not seek acceptance. This is the sense in which we are to take the declaration in *La Parole est à Péret* to the effect that the poet of today has "no other resource than to be a revolutionary or not to be a poet." Fulfilling this role meant, to Péret, "ceaselessly plunging into the unknown." This is to say that "there are no gilt-edged investments, but risk and adventure renewed indefinitely." Only in this way, Péret was convinced, can the poet call himself a poet and "claim to take a legitimate place in the very forefront of the cultural movement, where he can earn neither praise nor laurels but strike with all his might to level the barriers raised time after time by stupidity and routine." Indeed the poet's situation as an outsider is proof of his authenticity: "The curse thrown at him by present-day society already indicates his revolutionary position; but he will shed his obligatory reserve in order to see himself placed at the head of society when, completely turned upside down, it has recognized the common origin of poetry and knowledge and when the poet, with the active and passive cooperation of everyone, creates the exciting marvelous myths that will send the whole world to the assault of the unknown."

These words, with which *La Parole est à Péret* comes to a close, may appear more enthusiastic than persuasive. To be given their full weight, they need to be considered in the light of a basic assumption upon which the whole essay rests: that mankind has "a thirst for the irrational" which, as we would expect, Péret bitterly regretted seeing channeled by religious faith. It seemed logical to Benjamin Péret that eliminating religion would result in releasing the need for the irrational, *"les élans irrationnels"* being latent in all men. It appeared to him no less logical that, in men deprived of the irrational, this need would find satisfaction through the marvelous, and not through the—to him—false substitute of religious faith.

Now it is possible to comprehend why all the information we have gathered so far concerning the poetic marvelous found its

way into an essay intended to present an anthology of myths, popular legends, and folktales. It was Péret's belief that in earlier days man could think "only in the poetic mode," and that, in consequence, he could "penetrate perhaps intuitively farther" into himself and into nature, "from which he was scarcely differentiated," than the rationalist thinker who starts out from book learning in his attempt to dissect nature. A point upon which *La Parole est à Péret* insists, therefore, is that rationalist thought is mistaken, in holding poetry in contempt. . . . (pp. 32-6)

Falling chronologically between *La Parole est à Péret* and *Le Déshonneur des poètes,* Benjamin Péret's 1944 article ["**La Pensée est UNE et indivisible**"] establishes the continuity of his thought beyond a shadow of a doubt. It opens with a reference to the eighteenth century as, in France, the century of rationalist thought and hence as a period that saw only one poet worthy of mention—the Marquis de Sade, who revolted against the essential postulates of the era in which he lived. As Péret's text speaks of it, Sade's revolutionary role—and hence, of course, his claim to the rank of poet—was to challenge the eighteenth century's effort to replace one mode of blind faith, religion, with another, no less fallacious in Péret's estimation: reason.

True, the so-called Age of Enlightenment had eliminated God, "the obstacle to all knowledge." But, having substituted another deity, it had to be opposed. And opposition could come, in Péret's view, only from a poet. Sade merits the title of poet, therefore, not as a writer of verse—Péret's ideas in broadening the application of the term well beyond limitations of a literary nature were entirely consonant with Surrealist teaching—but because he met criteria specified in *Le Déshonneur des poètes:* "An inventor for whom discovery is but the means for attaining a new discovery, without respite he must fight the paralyzing gods bent on keeping man in servitude to social powers and divinity that complement one another. He will therefore be a revolutionary. . . ."

Behind Péret's confidence in the poet as a revolutionary lies trust in political convictions of no particular kind, faith in no plan for social reorganization of utopian character. Rather, his reliance on the poet as the agent of revolution reflects unshakable trust . . . in poetry as "the source and crown of all thought." Under reason's tutelage, however, poetry is subject to distortion. This is because, evidently, the marvelous, "heart and nervous system of all poetry," has been rejected. Where reason has not been "cast down from its celestial throne," the marvelous will always be treated in this fashion, Péret believed. And so this is why the peculiar accent of the individual poet's voice—even of his own voice—impressed Benjamin Péret not at all. He was attentive, instead, to intimations of a collective impulse to challenge the world of reason through the release of imaginative forces that he took to be universal in effect. Hence his abiding interest in myths, folkore, and legend, all of which pay homage to the salutary power of imagination, without taking into account the contribution made by individuals in testifying to that power. In Péret the imaginative liberation of natural phenomena, as the substance of poetry, occurred all the more readily, it would seem, because the writer was subject to no inclination to disrupt the familiar universe in order to satisfy selfish desires. It was Eluard who, as a Surrealist, was most frequently given to citing Lautréamont's dictum, "Poetry will be made by all, not one." But it was Péret who most consistently worked in the light of the principle that Eluard invoked.

Alluding to a poem by Paul Eluard, ''Liberté,'' said to have been dropped over occupied France during leaflet raids by the Royal Air Force, Péret does not deign to mention it by name, when closing *Le Déshonneur des poètes*. His comments render exact identification superfluous: ''Any 'poem' that exalts a 'liberty' deliberately undefined, when it is not decorated with religious or nationalist attributes, first ceases to be a poem and then constitutes an obstacle to the total liberation of man, for it deceives him by showing him a 'liberty' that conceals new chains. On the other hand, from every *authentic* poem emanates a breath of liberty, total and efficacious, even if that liberty is not evoked in its political and social aspect, and, in this way, contributes to the effective liberation of man.''

In a world dominated by reason, the position of the poet is necessarily that of an adversary. More precisely, for its disruptive nature, that which Péret termed in 1944 ''poetic intuition'' continues to be regarded with enmity. Hence, to Péret's mind, the discredit under which prophetic intuition has fallen among the ''blind followers of rationalist thought.'' Thus poetry as described in *Le Déshonneur des poètes*—''understood as total liberation for the human mind''—is a commodity for which there is no demand, and the poet has no place in society as long as he ''fights to attain a forever perfectible knowledge of himself and the universe.''

Of necessity, the poet must resist accepting the scale of values established by conscious reality, as described in Péret's essay [**''La Pensée est UNE et indivisible''**] . . . : ''the rational product of absurd and horrible social constraints.'' This means that the poet must recognize consciousness as ''always in the wrong from the point of view of the necessities of man and of his development,'' while the unconscious is to be acknowledged as ''the seat of desire, the sovereign phoenix engendered indefinitely from its own ashes.'' To be able to do this, the poet has to realize that the unacceptable values are the ones perceived ''through the deforming prism of rationalist education,'' which treats intuition as a caretaker, when in reality, according to Péret, it is ''the engineer who directs operations, the only man of science, the great inventor, the creator of reason itself.''

At the source of Péret's argument lies the hypothesis that reason has usurped the power rightly belonging to intuition and now uses that power to crush intuition. Reestablishing the supremacy of intuition means, therefore, recognizing that intuition gave rise both to reason and to unreason. Abolition of all gods, including reason, entails understanding that ''there is no thought without intuition, that is to say, without second sight, no intuition without thought.'' Thus the hypothesis upon which **''La Pensée est UNE et indivisible''** rests calls for reducing the role of reasoned thought and increasing that of poetic intuition. Such is the generally accepted trust in reason, however, that presuming to question its universal validity may appear an open invitation to madness and disorder. Thus, attaining the balance demanded by Benjamin Péret in 1944 can pass for evidence of imbalance, or at least an unacceptable predisposition toward it. As Louis Aragon once put it:

> The marvelous opposes what exists mechanically, what *is* so much it isn't noticed any more, and so it is commonly believed the marvelous is the negation of reality. This rather summary idea is conditionally acceptable. It is certain the marvelous is born of the refusal of *one* reality, but also of the development of a new relationship, of a new reality that this refusal has liberated.

Responsiveness to the marvelous, as Péret's theoretical writings speak of it, is quite impossible until we appreciate that the refusal emphasized by Aragon stands for something very different from escapist fancy. Intuition opposed to rationalist thought, finding encouragement in a spirit of liberty that takes no account of the social, moral, and political customs of contemporary society is the prime element in the marvelous as we shall see it celebrated in Péret's poetic writings. Here the marvelous confronts us with a variety of inherited and inculcated prejudices and predispositions, all of them unacceptable from the standpoint of poetry, as Péret understood it. Does then the marvelous lose, in the process, its ability to elicit the wonder, pleasure, excitement, joy, and dread that were so much a part of the folk literature Péret admired? Hardly. This is a question that can be asked with some degree of seriousness only by someone who knows nothing about the direction Péret's theories led him to take and who is unacquainted with the universe of the marvelous to which his imagination supplied the key. (pp. 37-41)

No Surrealist more consistently than [Péret] showed so little inclination to reason with his audience, on their ground and in terms of their choosing. All the same, one thing is clear, both in Péret's published declarations on the subject of poetry and in the poetic texts he has left behind. As the direct consequence of voluntary choice, his work represents his persistent willingness to accept a calculated risk. At all times Péret gave precedence to hallucinated and hallucinating visions, liberated in creative consciousness by the uncensored flow of imaginative inspiration, with which he never ceased to identify authentic poetic expression. (p. 155)

In its phenomenal richness, Benjamin Péret's work epitomizes some of the central ambitions of Surrealism, typified in some of the most characteristic features of the Surrealists' poetic program. Love, humor, imagination, invective, all find expression through his writings with special acuity, so that if future generations were to have access to the work of no other Surrealist than he, they would have to hand evidence reliable enough for them to form an accurate impression of the major themes of Surrealist poetry. And indeed, ever since the inception of Surrealist activity none of these themes, as Surrealists have used them, could have been defined adequately without reference to their development in Péret's work.

Benjamin Péret represents Surrealism as no other writer has done. But this does not mean that his work is to be considered valuable only for the fidelity with which it mirrors Surrealist aspirations and the ways they have been pursued. His work remains uniquely his own, his originality unquestionable and inimitable in its spontaneity. For in Péret's writings irrationality is an effect, not an aim provocatively pursued at the risk of alienating the public. Irrationality points to the ever-renewed triumph of the pleasure principle through a rectification of reality that, in Péret's opinion, it is the natural function of poetry to attain and the role of the marvelous to communicate. (pp. 157-58)

> *J. H. Matthews, in his* Benjamin Péret, *Twayne Publishers, 1975, 176 p.*

ELIZABETH R. JACKSON   (essay date 1976)

[*In the following excerpt, Jackson examines the dominant qualities of Péret's poetic world.*]

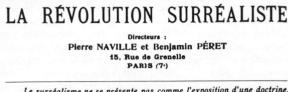

LA RÉVOLUTION SURRÉALISTE

Directeurs :
Pierre NAVILLE et Benjamin PÉRET
15, Rue de Grenelle
PARIS (7·)

Le surréalisme ne se présente pas comme l'exposition d'une doctrine. Certaines idées qui lui servent actuellement de point d'appui ne permettent en rien de préjuger de son développement ultérieur. Ce premier numéro de la Révolution Surréaliste n'offre donc aucune révélation définitive. Les résultats obtenus par l'écriture automatique, le récit de rêve, par exemple, y sont représentés, mais aucun résultat d'enquêtes, d'expériences ou de travaux n'y est encore consigné : il faut tout attendre de l'avenir.

Nous sommes

à la veille

d'une

RÉVOLUTION

SURRÉALISME

Vous pouvez y

prendre part.

Le BUREAU

CENTRAL

DE RECHERCHES

SURRÉALISTES 15, Rue de Grenelle, PARIS-7·

est ouvert tous les jours de 4 h. 1/2 à 6 h. 1/2

Title page for La révolution surréaliste, *December 1, 1924.*

Fired with the enthusiasm of the Surrealist project to liberate the human spirit from social restraints and rational intellectual bonds, Péret and his poetic world is best viewed within the context of that literary movement's esthetic and psychological conceptual framework. He joined the group in 1920, its early formative stage and his appearance is signalled with an appropriate air of mystery in Breton's *Nadja*. What is most unusual, in that group where dissidence and defection were the rule rather than the exception, is that he remained within the inner circle, close to Breton until his death. Péret was less inclined to formulate abstractly modes and aims of poetic creation, but certainly he was influenced by the theoretical pronouncements of the others and indeed, although his poems never received wide public acclaim, they were and are most highly regarded by those sensitive to the Surrealist ideal, the "happy few" so to speak.

The central poetic aim of the Surrealists was both optimistic and ambitious. The tone of optimism is particularly striking in the *First Surrealist Manifesto* (1924) which sets forth the goal of reconciling objective experience with the inner world of feeling and thought. Breton's definition of "surréalité" is precisely this: "une résolution future de ces deux états rêve et réalité en apparence contradictoires" ["a future resolution of the two apparently contradictory states of dream and reality"]. In subsequent documents he elaborates on this basic tenet. The *Second Manifesto* (1930) widens the elements of experience to be reconciled to include life and death, the real and the imag-

inary, the past and the future, the communicable and the incommunicable. And in a particularly interesting later essay, *Situation surréaliste de l'objet* (1935), he approaches the question from the point of view of plastic arts posing the aim of expressing visually internal perception, that is, using concrete forms from the outside world but considering them and translating them as integrated by the imagination in an inner mental world. This, of course, excludes representational art and also relegates rational and speculative thought processes to the background presuming to render the pleasure principle stronger than the reality principle. Freud's influence is obvious.

As for the means to discover and approach this goal, both in general experience and in artistic creation, attention is focused on the thing itself, that inner world, conceived from the start interestingly in temporal terms, in terms of thought process. Discovering and expressing this thought process becomes the means to the end. The famous definition of the *First Manifesto* makes this quite clear:

> Automatisme psychique pur par lequel on se propose d'exprimer, soit verbalement, soit par écrit, soit de toute autre manière, le fonctionnement réel de la pensée. Dictée de la pensée, en l'absence de tout contrôle exercé par la raison, en dehors de toute préoccupation esthétique ou morale.
>
> [Pure psychique automatism by means of which we propose to express either verbally, in writing, or in some other fashion, what really goes on in the mind. Dictation by the mind, unhampered by conscious control and having no aesthetic or moral goals.]

Amplifying this premise, Breton endows this area of human experience with an ontological superiority and also mentions dreams and free association as its main manifestations. Later Breton conceded that some element of control would enter into the picture in art, saying, "Un minimum de direction subsiste, généralement dans le sens de *l'arrangement en poème*" ["A minimum of direction subsists, generally in the sense of *the arrangement into a poem*"]. This concession is of considerable importance for the critic since it introduces the key notion of structure.

Equally essential to the whole picture is the Surrealist's faith in language. Here, positions vary somewhat. Breton and Aragon manifest a striking, and suprisingly traditional, confidence in verbal forms and expression. Although they dismiss purely logical expression as insufficient (in poetry), there is no apparent doubt about words having meaning, about words accurately expressing thought and feeling. Breton has an almost teleological view in this respect: "le langage a été donné à l'homme pour qu'il en fasse un usage surréaliste" ["language was given to man so that he might put it to a surrealistic use"]. The method is simply to trust instinctive judgment, to let the words flow freely and one will unquestionably achieve the desired lucidity. Aragon, in his *Traité du style*, goes so far as to insist that Surrealist writing is fully coherent and rigorous. If the meaning flows from within and if each word can not be explained simply by its dictionary definition, each word is nonetheless irreplaceable and the text as a whole will exhibit interrelated content and form. Furthermore, one is invited to make value judgments. Says Aragon, "Si vous écrivez suivant une méthode surréaliste de tristes imbécilités, ce sont de tristes imbécilités. Sans excuses" ["If in following a surrealist method you compose pathetic imbecilities, they are still pathetic imbecilities. Without excuses"]. This, together with his and Breton's suggestion that logical and grammatical analyses of Surrealist texts should be enlightening, leaves the critic encouraged, of course, but indeed awed by the difficulty of the task given the atypical use of meaning within normal syntactical forms. Tzara was perhaps more honest in a sense, or at least more willing to admit the elusive nature of Surrealist language. The central figure of the early Dada movement, he himself recognized later that reducing poetry (words) to a simple succession of sounds had led to a dead end although it had served the important purpose of emphasizing the volatile nature of meaning, the "capacité de fuite de la signification des mots" ["the capacity of flight from the meaning of words"].

Péret, as we have already remarked, shared Breton's faith in language as an unambiguous vehicle for poetic thought, with an individual emphasis on primitive and popular forms of expression as revealing more of instinctive, unconscious grasp of the world. Such expression escapes, never having experienced, the dualistic conception which values logic more highly than reason. But aside from an expression of faith in language untouched by rationalism, Péret does not go into detail about practical matters of writing. He does, however, indicate something about the source of poetic inspiration and links it directly with experience. In his preface to the anthology of Latin American myths he describes it in terms of a sense of the marvellous which one can encounter at any time, any place and which is ready to explode like a time bomb if only one is sensitively tuned to the possibilities. Here is an example he gives:

> Ce tiroir que j'ouvre me montre, entre des bobines de fil et des compas, une cuillère à absinthe. A travers les trous de cette cuillère s'avance à ma rencontre une bande de tulipes qui défilent au pas de l'oie. Dans leur corolle se dressent des professeurs de philosophie qui discourent sur l'impératif catégorique. . . .

> [This drawer which I open shows me, among the spools of thread and the compasses, an absinthe spoon. Through the holes of that spoon a band of tulips marching the goose-step come to meet me. In their corolla are standing philosophy professors airing their views about the categorical imperative.]

The starting point is a very ordinary external perception, a simple drawer containing simple objects. The development springs from the free play of the imagination and contains its own truth. It is not absurd, it has its own reality—a "surréalité"

Further on in the same essay he discusses in detail the mechanism of the formation of images starting from an even simpler external perception. In 1940, in a prison at Rennes, a particular series of images occurred to him as he was lying on the floor, looking at a window which had just been painted over. He saw the face of François Ier, a bucking horse, a tropical landscape like those of le douanier Rousseau. These images would reappear and sometimes undergo transformations. What is interesting is the fact that Péret gives a symbolic interpretation for each image, all having to do, he said, with a "violent appétit de liberté tout naturel dans ma situation" ["violent craving for freedom that was completely natural in my circumstances"]. The images stem directly from his past experience: the portrait of François Ier suggested history books in school where as a

youngster he felt similarly imprisoned; the bucking horse symbolized his vain protests and recalled his service in an armored division in World War I; the tropical forest involved a more complicated chain of associations having to do with experiences in Mexico. The conclusions to be drawn from this explanation are important for the reader. If the raw material, the initial image for poetic expressions comes from the outside world, the force governing the formation of images is emotional in nature, personal of course. And the images have a particular symbolic meaning which also is very personal drawn from the life of the poet. Once again the reader is reassured to know that an apparently gratuitous series of images likely contains definite symbolic significance, but he is also faced with limitations. Since the source of imagery is so very personal, the reader can not ever expect to attain full comprehension. Yet that is true of all human communication in literature or in life.

This being the case, the practical course is simply to examine what is available, the poems. Since Péret himself (and the other Surrealists) stresses the importance of immediate experience as the starting point, it should prove illuminating to consider initially just how the outer world is reflected in his work. Immediately striking is the fact that the impetus for many poems is an event, or an idea, or a feeling. The collection, *Je ne mange pas de ce pain-là,* provides the most obvious examples of political situations and actions which serve as the subject of particular poems. The problem of the instability of the French franc, a Eucharistic Congress in Chicago. . . . [One instance] which is even more circumstantial is a poem entitled **"6 février"**. Here are some excerpts:

> Vive le 6 février
> grogne le jus de chique
> vêtu en étron fleurdelysé
> Que c'était beau
> Les autobus flambaient comme les hérétiques
>   d'autrefois
> . . .
> Vive le 6 février
> et vive le 7
> J'ai hurlé pendant deux jours
> A mort Cachin A mort Blum
> Et j'ai volé tout ce que j'ai pu dans les magasins
> dont je brisais les vitres

> [Long live the sixth of February
> grumbles the tobacco juice
> dressed in shit adorned with fleur-de-lis
> How fine it was
> Buses were burning like heretics in the old days
> . . .
> Long live the sixth of February
> and long live the seventh
> I shouted for two days
> Death to Cachin Death to Blum
> And I stole everything I could in the stores
> whose windows I broke.]

Although this poem contains its share of unexpected characters and actions ("grogne le jus de chique . . .") ["groans the tobacco juice"], it tells of a specific event including realistic details such as the burning of buses and even including the author's own actions.

Also personal in nature, and exhibiting a form with traditional overtones, is an early poem, **"Le Quart d'une vie"**, written possibly when Péret was around twenty-five, composed of twenty-six short stanzas. Although the syntactic sequences are nonsensical, although the imagery is simply playful and often gratuitous, there is a personal tone. The first persons, singular and plural recur; there are indications of time past, time present, and time future. A melancholy air, mainly ironic, is noticeable. It ends thus:

> . . .
> Sa destinée fut courte comme une sueur
> Ma soeur
> as-tu vu ma pipe
> Ma pipe est morte
> et mon grand oeil est sans saveur
>
> [His fate was as short as a sweat
> My sister
> have you seen my pipe
> My pipe is dead
> and my wide eye is dull.]

One is reminded of *Les Testaments* of Villon; and in certain ways the two poets do resemble each other. Both led a life of vagabondage, of protest against existing society. Both also had a taste for the vernacular, for the earthy and used it spontaneously and colorfully as a poetic idiom. Even if this poem (**"Le Quart d'une vie"**) was primarily intended as a satire of traditional forms, there remains a substratum of authentic sentiment which, perhaps unconsciously, attenuates the negative, destructive aim.

A good many of Péret's poems have as inspirational force a frame of mind or a subjective feeling. Some are dedicated to particular people and one of these, addressed to René Crevel, shows both a depth of understanding and an ability and urge to express feeling through poetry. Crevel was one of the original Surrealist group, of an unhappy temperament, who exhibited over a number of years self-destructive symptoms and who committed suicide by hanging. In the collection *De Derrière les fagots* . . . a poem, **"S'Ennuyer"**, starts with these lines:

> Quand les montagnes têtent les serpents qui les
>   étouffent
> et les bêtes de sang somment l'électricité
> d'aller se faire pendre ailleurs
> la poussière amalgamée sur les nouveaux-nés
> se fend de haut en bas. . . .
>
> [When the mountains suckle the snakes which are
>   smothering them
> and the thoroughbreds summon the electricity
> to go hang itself somewhere else
> the dust amalgamated on the new-born infants
> splits from top to bottom.]

The title is clearly not absurd, the tone of suffering and desperation announced at the outset is developed and reinforced. Péret, too, experienced moments of anxiety, of fear and expressed these quite personal subjective sensations directly in a number of poems mainly found in the collections dating in the thirties. From this period also come the most sensitive love poems, especially the collection *Je Sublime* where a vast range of feelings—tenderness, warmth, passion, total joyous absorption, abandon—all find a spontaneous poetic outlet. **"On Sonne"** is only one of a number which show the free, light play of such personal warmth. . . . In a sense, despite the nonsensical syntactic groupings, Péret's poetic expression often exhibits a more direct kinship with traditional lyric verse by virtue of its origins in personal sentiment, romantic in nature.

But, if frequently the initial inspiration for a poem is an idea, an event or a feeling, such a traditional characteristic is more than compensated for by the case with which the author launches into fantastic adventures. The title of his first published collection is, significantly, *Le Grand jeu*. A spirit of playfulness, a taste for the ridiculous and pinpricking humor prevail, more so than in his later works. Also, particularly in the stories which date from that period, and in most of his poems throughout his life there is a refreshingly childlike enthusiasm for adventure. The Surrealists in general admired Lewis Carroll and much of the curiosity and that author's taste for pursuing unlikely trails is very similar to the way Péret's imagination can be carried away on an escapade at the drop of a hat in even rather serious poems. The starting point, the initial image or situation may still well be grounded in something immediate, like the example he gave in his preface—the contents of a drawer; but there is no telling what may follow in the way of encountering strange characters, strange situations and strange actions. A passage from **"Soleil route usée . . ."** shows how this can happen even in the most anguished atmosphere:

> mais les orties ô mosaïque les orties demain auront des
>   oreilles d'âne
> et des pieds de neige
> et elles seront si blanches que le pain le plus blanc
>   s'oubliera dans leurs dédales
> Ses cris retentiront dans les mille tunnels d'agathe du
>   matin. . . .

Suddenly those frightful thistles are seen as about to sprout donkey ears, feet of snow thus to furnish a labyrinth where the white bread will wander, lose itself and cry out. Very often Péret will relate such a sequence of bizarre events in the future tense, usually introduced by a conditional or adverbial clause ("Si . . ."; "quand . . .") ["If . . ."; "when . . ."]. But although the interlude is posed as hypothetical, the situations are so vivid that they seem real or at least inevitable. There is another such passage in **"On Sonne"**:

> . . . je t'aime comme le coquillage aime son sable
> où quelqu'un le dénichera quand le soleil aura la forme
>   d'un haricot
> qui commencera à germer comme un caillou montrant
>   son coeur sous l'averse. . . .

Sun, rain, germination, although posed as a future condition, appear in the context as a natural and unquestioned occurrence. The action of that poem furthermore leads afar—ending happily on an island forested with blue trees, a haven for lovers. This characteristic of the poetic imagination of Péret is very different from that of Aragon who spoke scornfully of the trips of Baudelaire, Rimbaud, and Gide, considering freedom and flights of fancy an illusion, emphasizing that no paradise of any sort exists.

The sharp clear outside world not only usually furnishes the starting point for Péret's poems, it also provides characters, qualities, in short, situations which are very life-like except for the impossible subjects of action, relationships, and occurrences. Active figures, the heroes of Péret's universe can be almost anything. Occasionally they are people—mainly in the stories. Very often they are animals, birds or insects: herons, parrots, crows, mayflies, other little insects; the dog and the flea, heroes of **"A Mi-Chemin"**, reappear as actors in other poems too. Sometimes parts of the human body are the main characters as in a poem, **"Le Genou fendu"**, which starts out: "L'épaule indifférente / et la bouche malade / sont tombées sur les épines . . .'' [''The indifferent shoulder / and the sick mouth / have fallen on the thorns'']. But inanimate objects appear and also engage in action. Péret is especially fond of food, often vegetables—carrots, radishes, artichokes—and bread which plays such an important role in **"Soleil route usée"**. The title of the main collection of short stories is naturally, *Le Gigot, sa vie et son oeuvre.* In the case of animals and food, the tone in which Péret speaks of them is usually very fond, even affectionate. Natural phenomena are called upon frequently to act too: rainbows, the sun, rocks, stones. One poem starts impressively: ''Tandis que le rocher surplombant la mer / admirait sa mâle prestance . . .'' [''While the rock overhanging the sea / admired his manly bearing'']. That sardine can we read of in **"On Sonne"** often figures prominently. Even abstract nouns can perform: ''les nombres élevés'', ''les fractions infinitésimales'', and one which I like especially, ''les adverbes sauvages''.

Péret's world is packed with action. . . . It is also complete with qualities of color, sound, and smells. **"A Mi-Chemin"** is an example where smells were used to impress on the reader the idea of decay (''le vieux chien puait l'officier crevé''; ''une odeur vénéneuse de champignons d'église'') [''the old dog stank like a dead officer''; ''a poisonous odor of church toadstools'']. Colors are sometimes used specifically to paint a metaphysical atmosphere. This is the case in the long poem, **"Dernier malheur dernière chance"**, written in Mexico, and in **"Soleil route usée . . ."** where, in the first section, one line alone darkens the whole scene—''parce que tout est noir'' [''because all is dark''], and where in contrast the color white evokes the glacial, frozen stillness. One line of that poem is particularly interesting because both colors appear in a description: ''ce pain si blanc qu'à côté de lui le noir est blanc'' [''this bread so white that beside it the darkness is white'']. It is a sort of play of contrasts where opposites disappear or are in some sense fused. . . . Eluard who is well known for his own verbal color magic wrote an introduction for a collection of verse by Péret, signalling an image (from a poem with heated negative political import) which combined sound and color: ''le cri strident des oeufs rouges.'' His remarks include the comment that such clear images convey perfect understanding (''compréhension parfaite'') of things out of the ordinary, substituting for dull common sense a new sort of logic, ''liée à la vie non comme une ombre mais comme un astre'' [''connected to life not like a shadow but like a star''].

Not only Péret's images display this different sort of logic. His entire world, where reigns supreme that taste for simple surprise or biting absurd irony, that readiness to launch into strange adventures, that willingness to expose himself and to be guided by a dream-like state even though it may be a source of terror as well as ecstasy, this world is not in the least formless and arbitrary but on the contrary exhibits a structure of its own. (pp. 133-39)

With the passage of time in Péret's world the reader views not only familiar shifts of feeling and familiar or unfamiliar actions but changes far more radical in nature. These are changes of the very nature of the actors, the objects or the scenery. They involve transformation of the essence of being. Metamorphosis is an ordinary and an essential occurrence in his tales and poems. . . . In the second part [of **"Soleil route usée"**] a number of transformations take place, all in connection with the nettles. The author suggests that if you throw the nettles in the black man's throat, ''le nègre deviendra ortie et soutane son oeil perdu'' [''the black man will become a nettle and a priest who

has lost his eye'']. And after the copper bar shoots up high enough, the nettles, having unbeknownst to us turned into children, ''les orties ne seront plus ses enfants / mais les soubresauts fatals d'un grand corps d'écume'' [''the nettles will no longer be children / but the fatal spurtings of a great mass of foam'']. Finally the nettles are destined to have donkey ears and feet of snow and at that point they undergo a more unobtrusive but more definitive change becoming a labyrinth. (p. 147)

In the eyes of Péret metamorphosis has a particularly profound significance because for him it is allied with an inherent and tenacious optimism combined with the strong desire actively to contribute to a better world. He expresses these thoughts in a preface to a book devoted to the artist Toyen in connection with the spirit underlying her painting; but they are equally applicable to his own temperament and his own artistic production. The exterior world remains the source of art but it is only one element in the composition of a ''complete'' world, a better world. ''Toute l'oeuvre de Toyen,'' he says ''ne vise pas à autre chose qu'à corriger le monde extérieur en fonction d'un désir qui s'alimente et s'accroit de sa propre satisfaction'' [''The entire work of Toyen has no other purpose than to reform the external world in terms of a desire that nourishes itself and grows for its own satisfaction'']. Through metamorphosis, the changes wrought by the poetic imagination, a new world comes into being, one which is coherent and entirely new (''l'ensemble formant un monde entièrement neuf'') [''the whole forming a world entirely new'']. He even envisages in this essay the world of the artist as resembling that of the first creator of the universe, where from a state of chaos and of unstable forms a new existence takes shape. This is exactly what Péret took as explicit subject matter in *Histoire naturelle*. And a passage from the chapter on the vegetable kingdom of that book demonstrates his faith in a possible universal harmony:

> Rien ne permettait de supposer qu'un jour l'harmonie régnerait, lorsque le ciel parut s'éclaircir et l'orage s'éloigna . . . un arc-en-ciel étincela au-dessus de la terre fascinée. La végétation comprit et, sans se rechigner, chaque plante occupa sans bruit le coin qui lui était destiné.

> [Nothing gave one to suppose that one day harmony would reign, when the sky seemed to clear up and the storm disappeared . . . a rainbow sparkled above the fascinated earth. The vegetation understood and, in good grace, each plant occupied noiselessly the corner for which it was destined.]

Such an ambitious project, the creation of an entire cosmos from chaos is not, however, really the main aim of Toyen or Péret. It simply illustrates the latter's natural comprehensive optimism. More down to earth is his description of the source and development of poetic thought which was mentioned at the outset of this chapter, where he defines the ''merveilleux'' in terms of the imaginative possibilities inherent in simple objects such as the contents of a drawer. The essay on Toyen also emphasizes the fact that if the exterior world is not the only factor involved in the esthetic process it remains the starting point. The example he gives in this case is the perception of a bird's song which can lead to the resurrection of a submerged city. And the bird song is not a negligible factor. Fernand Alquié in his penetrating study, *Philosophie du surréalisme*, emphasizes the extent to which for the Surrealists, as opposed to the French Romantic movement, real life is in the here and now, close at hand (''la vraie vie est là'') [''true life is here'']. That bird song is important in and of itself. Certainly, in Péret's poems the creatures he tells about have a colorful and warm immediacy.

This does not exclude the possibility of dissatisfaction with the world as it is. In fact, Alquié poses just such dissatisfaction as being at the origin of metaphysical speculation in general. For Péret and the other Surrealists the revolt was directed on the one hand against the constraints and injustices of the existing social order and on the other hand against the limitations and insufficiencies of rational thought and expression. It is certainly true that there is a strong negative streak in Péret's work ranging from invective against all aspects of bourgeois society to a more subtle but clear aim to satirize and destroy rational patterns of thought. But if the revolt springs from a desire for a better life, that desire in the case of Péret in its positive form in the long run overshadows the flippant, bitter, and often simply destructive drive.

Ultimately what mattered the most to him was that sense of the "merveilleux", which for him represented as much an object of faith as a source of esthetic gratification. The contents of the drawer, the bird song are examples he took at random from his own experience. But such simple perceptions are at the basis of the best of which man is capable, what he calls "conscience poétique du monde" [''poetic consciousness of the world'']. In an article on superstition, he describes this consciousness, primitive in nature, at the origin of myths and of ritual (before it is corrupted by organized religion), as being both a belief and capacity for feeling. As example he gives "la mélancolie qui l'empoigne [l'homme] à la vue de la neige éteignant tout bruit, flocon à flocon" [''the melancholy that seizes him (man) at the sight of snow that, flake by flake, smothers all sound''] or "l'enchantement que lui procure le muguet de mai" [''the enchantment he derives from the May-lily'']. As important as the initial perception are the feelings spontaneously aroused and they run the gamut of man's innermost and powerful emotive capacities from the pleasant, "l'enchantement", to the disturbing, "l'épouvante" [''terror''], "l'angoisse" [''anguish''], as well as the less threatening, "la mélancolie".

This is very similar to Lévy-Bruhl's well-known concept of "participation mystique", which Jung incorporated in his theory of the archetypal imagination, whereby primitive man integrates and fits natural phenomena into his world view first by totally emotional identification in experience. In the case of Péret, the emphasis is esthetic, although there is also an underlying sense of faith; in addition he introduces the idea of mission. Political and social changes are necessary and inevitable to better the human condition; yet the ultimate salvation will include recapturing the freshness and freedom of the primitive imagination. He describes the artist's role in the following fashion:

> La véritable mission de l'artiste—peintre ou poète—a toujours consisté à retrouver en lui-même les archétypes qui sous-tendent la pensée poétique, à les charger d'une affectivité nouvelle, afin que circule entre ses semblables et lui-même un courant énergique d'autant plus intense que ses archétypes actualisés apparaitront comme l'expression la plus évidente et la plus neuve du milieu qui a conditionné l'artiste.

> [The true mission of the artist—painter or poet— has always consisted of rediscovering in him-

self the archetypes which underlie poetic thought, of charging them with a new affectivity, so that, between himself and his fellow-men will circulate a current of energy so intense that his archetypes made real will appear as the most obvious and the newest expression of the milieu which conditioned the artist.]

(pp. 151-53)

> *Elizabeth R. Jackson, "Le grand coeur de la nature," in her* Worlds Apart: Structural Parallels in the Poetry of Paul Valéry, Saint-John Perse, Benjamin Péret and René Char, *Mouton, 1976, pp. 133-57.**

JULIA FIELD COSTICH   (essay date 1979)

[In the following excerpt from her book-length study of Péret's works, Costich views Péret's works as products of a personal mythology, created of necessity after Péret had rejected all traditional systems of belief as well as their corollaries in literature.]

In the Surrealism of Benjamin Péret, a new myth emerges in which change is the ruling force. Many of Péret's writings are directly concerned with the subject of myth; he reacts against the dominant myths of Western European civilization and favors primitive or Third World myth. Revolt against prevailing myth and study of other examples of mythological expression are two tendencies in Péret's work which can be interpreted as a thesis and an antithesis which are continually reaffirmed throughout his life.

Everything written by Péret expresses revolt against the myths of the culture in which he lives; texts which do so most explicitly include the poetry of *Je ne mange pas de ce pain-là, Le Déshonneur des poètes,* and the important body of political writings, for the myths against which he speaks are political and military as well as religious. In honor of the myths of other peoples, which Péret collected in the *Anthologie des mythes, légendes et contes populaires d'Amérique,* he wrote **Air mexicain,** as well as the articles **"Notes on Pre-Columbian Art," "Remembrance of Things to Come," "Arts de fête et de cérémonie," "Du fond de la forêt,"** and the long essay published as *La parole est à Péret.* Automatism in the tales relates them to myth, for as Breton says with reference to automatic writing, "la confrontation des produits de cette écriture avait braqué le projecteur sur la région où s'érige le désir sans contrainte, qui est aussi celle où les mythes prennent leur forme" [''the collation of the products of this writing has focused the spotlight on the region where stands desire without constraint, which is also the place where myths take shape'']. According to Péret's own definition, his synthesis cannot be perfect because the society in which he lives is not completely free. In *La parole est à Péret,* he postulates the advent of a new generation of mythographers in a society oriented toward complete liberty, rather than structured for repression like the present society:

> Si l'homme d'hier, ne connaissant d'autres limites à sa pensée que celles de son désir, a pu dans sa lutte contre la nature produire ces merveilleuses légendes, que ne pourra pas créer l'homme de demain conscient de sa nature et dominant de plus en plus le monde d'un esprit libéré de toute entrave?

> [If the man of yesterday, knowing no thoughts beyond his own desires, could, in his struggle with nature, produce these marvelous legends,

what will the man of tomorrow not be able to create, conscious of his own nature and dominating the world more and more with a spirit freed from all constraint?]

Péret's primary revolt against myth is directed toward God, and is Promethean and to some extent Oedipal, for myth-directed revolt is in itself part of mythology. The structure of myth implies change and the replacement of one ruling force with another in an endless series; as [Marie Odile] Banquaert states, "le sacré appelle sa violation et confère la divinité à qui l'a osée" ["the sacred invites violation and confers divinity upon whoever dares do so"]. The word "divinité" is misleading in the context of Péret's work because Péret denies the existence of God in unmistakeable terms: "l'idée d'un fantôme aussi sinistre est déjà une offense à l'humanité. Que ceux qui y croient nous démontrent son existence. Ce n'est pas à moi de prouver que je n'ai pas assassiné ma concierge" ["the idea of such a sinister phantom is an offense to humanity. Let those who believe in it prove its existence. It is not up to me to prove I haven't killed my landlady"]. Because God does not exist outside the human imagination, religion is inadmissible in its theocentric form; for Péret, it is a gratuitous tool of oppression. The Christian religion is presented as having been rejected in **"Il était une boulangère,"** although one of the major characters is a Pope and the people will continue to frequent church buildings if given good reason. The populace is sensitive to the mythical potential of everyday objects, and miracles occur in the form of transformations of the ordinary to an extent which belies the apparent suppression of *le merveilleux quotidien*. . . . For Péret, valid myth is an expression of popular creativity, not the imposition of a credo by some higher power. Discovery and stimulation of the powers of the human imagination is his mythical premise.

This point of view has led in the past and present to various attempts to create religious myth without God or gods. Péret also rejects these religions. . . . As examples, he discusses the cults of Hitler and Stalin. Although he does not make the analogy, the structure of these "religions" is appropriate to the schema established by Péret in his **"Notes on Pre-Columbian Art"**:

> the appearance of the grandiose in art marks the end of the creative period of mythical poetry . . . when mythical poetry has lost its power to create divinities, it acquires the power to celebrate heroes and deify them.

The mystique and exaltation formerly attached to religious phenomena are transplanted into a context which is, in the two current examples, predominantly military. In the Mexican civilization analyzed in the **"Notes on Pre-Columbian Art,"** this is the time of the alliance of priest and warrior which "leads to the moment when fear and horror completely dominate."

Unless the Promethean figure can rid himself and his culture of the idea of a God or gods, as Prometheus himself failed to do, the result of revolt will be further repression rather than liberation. In psychoanalytical terms, the revolt against God is a dimension of revolt against the father and is thus Oedipal. According to Péret, this is a significant theme in myth; the incest taboo "ressuscité dans le mythe, projectant sur l'infini des cieux l'image fini du père assassiné" ["revived in myth, projecting on the infinity of the skies the finite image of the murdered father"]. In terms of Greek mythology, the assassination of the father is a necessary preliminary to the con-

struction of a new society: Zeus kills his father, Chronos, with the collaboration of his mother Gaea (Earth). Again, there is a danger to be averted by the study of ancient mythical models, for the society over which Zeus reigns is a military dictatorship with a hero-god as leader. By Péret's standards, the mythology of the Greeks suffers in contrast with that of the pre-Columbians because its events are calqued on social and political reality, which is a post facto basis for the myth. "The pre-Columbian Indian speaks to the imagination in terms of its own language," and this is for Péret more valid than "the Greco-Latin products which, by relegating imagination to a secondary place, overlook the principal source of all art." Within his revolt against God and religion, then, there is a fundamental revolt against the cultural premises of Western civilization. This is the rebellion of the Surrealist movement itself: "l'opposition entre surréalisme et religion n'est ni relative ni partielle mais absolue; l'enjeu de la lutte est l'homme tout entier, que la religion veut asservir, que le surréalisme veut libérer" ["the opposition of Surrealisme and religion is neither relative nor partial, but absolute; what is at stake in the struggle is the whole of mankind, which religion wishes to dominate and Surrealism wishes to free"]. This statement by Jehan Mayoux, derived from a study of Péret's work and life, is interesting in its use of the terms Surrealism and religion as alternative human choices or as adversaries in a war for man's mind.

Surrealism is itself a myth, but in a different dimension from that of older mythological expressions; it is an outline of a schema which leaves the filling in of details to the individual and, more importantly, to the people of the future. Péret's new myth of change differs from the mythology of Surrealism in general, as well as diverging from the myths proposed by individual Surrealists. As a myth, Surrealism can be shown to have its representative gods which, as is generally the case in myth, are abstract, for example dream, *le merveilleux quotidien*, madness, and childhood. The heroes, another important component of myth, are enumerated in the First Manifesto: many of these, like Rimbaud and Lautréamont, had existences which were markedly separated from the normal range of human experience, and they are much more highly valued as dead ancestors than they were as living poets. In the works of André Breton and Louis Aragon, the concept of mythology in the modern world acquires a specificity which leads to a creation that diverges from that of Péret. Breton saw the problem of prophecy in a mythic context, associating it with ancient examples: "la voix surréaliste qui secouait Cume, Dodone et Delphes n'est autre chose que celle qui me dicte mes discours les moins courroucés" ["the Surrealist voice that shook Cuma, Dodone and Delphi is the same one that dictates my least angry words"]. In the 1942 "Prolégomènes à un troisième manifeste du surréalisme ou non," Breton's mystical preoccupations of the period lead him to propose the existence of "les grands transparents," who would be the basis and justification of "un mythe nouveau." For Aragon, the idea of myth is also accompanied by supernatural creatures of his imagination:

> L'évolution de ma pensée était un méchanisme en tout point analogue à la génèse mythique. . . . Il m'apparut que l'homme est plein de dieux. . . . Ils sont les principes mêmes de toute transformation de tout. Ils sont la nécessité du mouvement. . . . Je me mis à concevoir une mythologie en marche. Elle méritait proprement le nom de mythologie moderne.
>
> [The evolution of my ideas was a mechanism in every way analogous to the genesis of

myths. . . . It appeared to me that man is full of gods. . . . They are the source of all transformation. They are the necessity of movement. . . . I began to conceive an ongoing mythology. It properly deserved the name of modern mythology.]

The association made by Aragon between myth, transformation, and movement is similar to Péret's use of these concepts, but the creation of explicitly designated divinities is foreign to Péret. Aragon, like Péret, connects myth and poetry, but the emphasis is on the former term when he states that "le mythe est la seule voix de la conscience" ["myth is the only voice of consciousness"].

Whereas Breton and Aragon base their mythologies on the perception of divine or supernatural creatures and discuss these beings in vaguely mystical terms, Péret presents his mythomimetic characters as living in the world, as potential incarnations of ourselves. Far from being "transparent," like Breton's hypothetical creatures, they encounter resistance in the world of things as do normal human beings. The great difference between Péret's characters and Breton's beings (among whom such a factual character as Nadja might be included) is found in their confrontation of the world and their overcoming it through the force of change. They do not float, detached and mysterious, through the world, and they are not subject, as is Nadja, to the banishment which is a corollary of their irreality.

Revolt against repressive mythology and creative aspiration toward a new mythology are combined in Péret's Surrealism. . . . The sources of the process which leads to the creation of a new myth are multiple, and they include the names cited in the First Manifesto as Surrealist. For Péret, there is no doubt that the myths of poets, in the exemplary manners of Rimbaud and Lautréamont, are sources and inspirations. *Les Chants de Maldoror* are moral and mythical revolt; Lautréamont is quoted in the context of a discussion of myth in *La parole est à Péret,* and the collaborative poetry which he demands in the *Poésies* is exemplified in Péret's collection of myths, legends, and popular tales: "la poésie doit être faite par tous. Non par un" ["poetry should be made by all. Not by one."] For Péret, myth and poetry are expressions of the same spirit; myth is the first state in which poetry appears "et l'axe autour duquel elle continue de tourner à une vitesse indéfiniment accélérée" ["and the axis around which it continues to turn with ever-increasing speed."] Again, this is a myth which is poetic, not religious. Being identified with poetry, it also participates in the components of poetic expression, most notably in dream. (pp. 177-83)

The importance of poetry as the original expression or mythic thought is re-emphasized in the **"Notes on Pre-Columbian Art"**: "poetry, therefore, precedes plastic art, for man uses his imagination before possessing the means permitting him to give a form to the creatures born of his desires and of his agonies." Poetry is the starting point both of the codification of myth and of the formulation of religion. Because of its basic status, it is also intrinsically connected with the rhythms and structures of ritual. (pp. 183-84)

Like the myths of the early Mexicans, the modern, synthetic myth suggested by Péret's work is based on the force of the imagination rather than on any rational social or political model. The following comparison between definitions of the Surrealist image and of mythical activity shows their similarity:

> In terms of narrative, myth is the imitation of actions near or at the conceivable limits of de-

sire . . . (it is) a world in which everything is potentially identical with everything else, as though it were all inside a single, infinite body [Northrop Frye, *Anatomy of Criticism*].

> Tout devient mobile et fusible, équivalent et interchangeable, aucune cloison ne sépare plus le concret de l'abstrait, l'univers physique de l'univers mental qui sont reliés par le magnétisme de l'image.

> [Everything becomes mobile and fusible, equivalent and interchangeable, no barrier any longer separates the concrete and the abstract, the physical universe and the mental universe, which are bound by the magnetism of image (Marc Eigeldinger, "Surréalisme et dynamisme de l'imagination").]

The motivational force of desire in myth becomes the force of change in the image; this interconnection is a primary element of Péret's myth. Both of the characterizations of the world of myth and image insist on the element of synthesis and identity; a typical example of this principle in Péret's work is the first line of **"Qui est-ce"** in *De derrière les fagots:* "J'appelle tabac ce qui est oreille." Actions within the context of myth or image are extreme, beyond the bounds of reason, like almost any activity in the poetry or tales of Péret: literally anything is possible.

When Péret undertakes the pan-mythical analysis of "L'Invention du monde" [a film by Jean-Louis Bédouin and Michael Zimbacca], he finds illustrations of these principles in such aspects of mythical behaviour as the mask, which ostensibly changes the nature of its wearer from man to animal, ancestor or god, and permits him a latitude of behavior which is otherwise not allowed. The mask, as he states, "dissimule et stimule," but eventually man becomes dissatisfied with the imitation of freedom and leaves on an adventure to seek the source of power: "l'homme veut devenir la force même" ["man wishes to become power itself"]. As Péret explains, drawing primarily on native American and Oceanic myth, snakes represent this power in its terrestrial manifestations, while birds are the symbolic incarnation of divine power. The expanded awareness which is the result of the voyage reveals to primitive man a "vie frémissante qui jaillit de toute part" ["quivering life which springs up everywhere"], and is not limited to his island, valley, or forest. In "L'Invention du monde," the remarkable images which conclude the journey to mythological understanding represent the burning change of a "monde en devenir" ["world in formation"] and the multiplicity of an animistic world-view. This multiplicity is everywhere characteristic of myth, which is "a new arrangement of elements" [Claude Levi-Strauss, *The Savage Mind*]. Hence, when Péret analyzes the *capoeira,* he poses the question "une lutte ou une danse?," "un ballet ou un rituel?" Finally, the myths of primitive man are based on the most important things in their lives:

> les mythes primitifs sont en grande partie des composés et des résidus d'illuminations, d'intuitions, de présages confirmés jadis d'une manière si éclatante qu'ils ont pénétrés d'un trait jusqu'aux plus grandes profondeurs de la conscience de ces populations.

> [primitive myths are in large part composites and residues of illuminations, intuitions, and presages confirmed long ago in a manner so

dazzling that they penetrated with one stroke to the very depths of the consciousness of those populations.]

According to this formula, these perceptions passed directly into the subconscious without being refracted by rational mental activity; they are, therefore, pure communications between the depths of man's mind and the world in which he lives.

The significance of names in myth is often a subject of discussion in scholarly treatment of primitive thought. Péret's speculations on the foundations of mythology in "L'Invention du monde" show that ancestors play an important role in the original perception of the world, so it is to be expected that the names of those who are dead would appear in the mythological context of the tales. These names are common and generally belong to royalty, military heroes, and political figures. They act as touchstones within reality for the action which might otherwise be situated by the reader in another county, if not another world. Ironically, these characters may appear, in contrast with their consecrated historical identities, as figures of fun; in a mythical context, they are demystified. Examples of this type of character are Napoleon, who appears in "**La Fleur de Napoléon**" and "**Ne pas manger de raisin sans le laver**," Waldeck-Rousseau, the "athlète" in "**Les Malheurs d'un dollar**," and Pope Pius VII, a major character in "**Il était une boulangère**." (pp. 185-87)

But the allusive role of proper names is minimized in these tales; they are words in the same sense as are common nouns, and all people tend to behave in similar ways. The analogy between human conduct and the behavior of words in their liberated state is especially striking in the examples of these historical figures.

Not all the characters in the tales have familiar names; when the name is not drawn from the category of ancestors, it is generally indicative of fantasy. Monsieur Séraphin, the earliest example of this current, shares the action in "**Au 125 du boulevard Saint Germain**" with the king of Greece and the President of the Republic; other fantasy names include several with humorous overtones, such as Zacharie Artichaut in "**Le Pont des Soupirs**" and Monsieur Détour, the mayor in "**Les Malheurs d'un dollar**." (p. 188)

These protagonists share many traits with mythical heroes, but they are definitely not gods for, like the new myth to which Péret alludes in *La parole est à Péret:*

> ces mythes seront dépourvus de toute consolation religieuse puisque celle-ci sera sans objet dans un monde orienté vers la poursuite de la toujours provocante et tentatrice chimère de la perfection à jamais inaccessible.

> [these myths will be deprived of all religious consolation since they will be without object in a world oriented toward the pursuit of the ever-provocative and tempting chimera of forever inaccessible perfection.]

There are, therefore, imperfect heroes, but they are heroes nonetheless in their extensive activities beyond the limits of normally perceived human experience. They are like the participants in the *capoeira:*

> les "adversaires" possédant cette agilité étrangère à toute effort dont chacun est susceptible lorsque le sommeil le possède et qui, le soleil

levé, porte cependant l'inconséquent à accuser les images de la nuit.

> [the "adversaries" possessing this effortless agility of which each is capable during sleep and which, on waking, still has the residual effect of accentuating the images of the night.]

This strength is outside the realm of sport, to which Péret's hostility is vehement; it is the power which exists when awareness of rational human limitations is overcome. The connection between sleep and death which Péret posits in *Immortelle Maladie* and *Dormir dormir dans les pierres* continues to be valid in the context of his mythic synthesis; as Phillip Wheelwright notes in his study of Heraclitus, "in the universe as Heraclitus envisages it there is nothing truly immortal in the literal sense— except, indeed, the endless process of mortality itself." Mortality is the immortal malady, and as such it is also an intrinsic physical process in Péret's myth of change.

The characters in the tales have the effortless influence of the participants in the *capoeira*. Waldeck-Rousseau in "**Les Malheurs d'un dollar**" is typical in his physical prowess which is explicitly athletic in his approach to the marvelous. . . . Like a surreal Paul Bunyan, he is beyond normal measure and quite unlike the political figure after whom he is named, but, unlike Breton's "grands transparents" or Aragon's phantom ideas, he is a real person with essentially human characteristics. (pp. 189-90)

Even when the character in question is not the protagonist, he participates in an elevated, super-human context. In "**La Dernière Nuit du condamné à mort**," the defense attorney for the condemned man, who is identified as Péret, is won over to his client's ambition, a Lautréamont-like *généralisation du crime.*" The non-human characters also act in the manner of the heroes of myth: the Amazon river in "**Il était une boulangère**" is told by Nicholas II that "tu as fait le monde avec tes cheveux qui sont ces mouches de sel visibles sur la peau des demoiselles à marier" ["you have made the world with your hair which is a beauty mark of salt visible on the skin of ladies about to be married"]. The river also realizes what must have been a common masculine aspiration of the era contemporary with the writing of the tale: he receives a love letter from the aging dancer Mistinguett. The heroic stature of the Amazon is, like that of most of the protagonists, vitiated in an encounter with an insuperable obstacle when Mistinguett refuses to acknowledge her communication with the Amazon. It is interesting to note that this personage is not *an* Amazon, as might be expected in a traditional mythical context, but rather *the* Amazon.

In the action of the tales, the protagonists display an affinity with the heroes of myth in that they influence and interact with the order of nature. The easy transition of the Amazon river from natural to human existence is one example of this phenomenon. Another is in "**Un Vie pleine d'intérêt**," where the lovers can act without fear of harm from the helpless Madame Lannor because of the strength of their love. . . . (pp. 190-91)

Despite the proliferation of events which resemble the results of magic in the tales, the use of ritual in explicit form is rare. The transformations and miraculous deeds which take place are spontaneous and unpredictable, not the results of a predetermined formulation of cause and effect. The one person in the tales who is a sorceress, Madame Daisy in "**Sur le passage d'un panier à salade**," says "répétez les paroles que je vais prononcer et faites les gestes que je vais faire" ["repeat the words I am going to say and make the gestures I am going to

make''']; she implies a traditional form of action which is atypical in Péret's work. Her prediction of the future is accompanied
by a further indication that she belongs to a rejected tradition
of classical mythology: the River Lethe runs through her apartment. Her feats exceed those normally expected of a seer, but
they belong to an entirely different realm from that of most of
the characters in the tales. It is significant that the terror of the
Lethe is domesticated and made part of the human urban setting; hence, it is removed from its original sacred context.
(p. 192)

The immense flexibility of the characters in the tales means
that, like figures in myth, they are able to exist in both supra-
and subterranean environments without losing their identities. . . . "La Fleur de Napoléon" is striking in its use of this
theme; both the Cid and Napoleon make descents into the
underworld and then, as if in parody of this action, make
investigations of their physical selves. For the Cid, the action
of descent begins with his kissing the photograph of Chimena
and setting out for his office. After passing through a door, he
goes down a staircase "et se trouva dans une vaste salle où
brillaient des milliers de cierges fichés le long des murs" ["and
found himself in a huge room where shone thousands of candles
fixed to the walls"]. Napoleon has a similar experience: he is,
of course, dead, and so he returns to his tomb. At once, he
exits in the other direction and is inundated by a shower of
rose petals. Then, followed by his entourage, he proceeds to
the center of the earth, but the location of the entrance to this
passageway is within himself. . . . (p. 193)

These examples show that the myth toward which Péret is
working is based on an integration of the human body with the
world; although not humanistic in the usual sense, it is based
on human rather than mechanical, scientific, or religious perceptions and phraseology. In his essay on Breton, Michel Beau-
jour proposes a definition of Breton's mythology which is also
largely valid as a description of that of Péret:

> le poète propose les bases d'une cosmologie
> renouvelée, où la vision anthropocentrique dont
> relèvent toutes nos démarches, se dépasserait
> dans une vision analogique au sein de laquelle
> la nature humanisée et l'homme matérialisé
> dialogueraient sans obstacle, dans une exaltante
> transparence.
>
> [the poet proposes the bases for a new cos-
> mology, in which the anthropocentric vision,
> upon which all our actions are based, will be
> made obsolete by an analogous vision in the
> heart of which humanized nature and materi-
> alized man will commune without obstacle, in
> exhultant transparence.]

Whereas Breton "propose les bases" for this mythology, Péret
illustrates it in a large and consistent body of work. The free
dialogue between man and nature is exemplified in *Histoire
naturelle,* for example, where man, in the form of the narrator's
on can shape the heart of nature while the natural elements
take human form and behavior. Yet in Péret's work, the interplay between "la nature humanisée et l'homme matérialisé"
always takes place in a situation which includes obstacles; the
traditional separation must be overcome at every turn. Péret's
mythology is always in process, on the way to perfection rather
than being the perfect expression of harmony, and it is thus
that it is a mythology of continual change.

Once the poet has found a means for perceiving and conveying
change, he explores the workings of this universal phenomenon. Like Heraclitus, Péret finds change to be intrinsic to the
phenomenal world, and the Heraclitean image of fire, which
is basic to this universe in flux, is common in his poetry and
prose. Change is depicted as a creative activity, both in serial
transformations brought about by an external agent and in autonomous metamorphoses. Like the Mayan pyramid which he
describes in the preface to his translation of *Le Livre de Chilám
Balám de Chumayel . . . ,* Péret orients himself in a manner
which not only allows him to intercept and interpret change,
but which also facilitates the externalization and communication of the appearance of change.

Throughout Péret's work, change is presented in the structure
of desire; it is the function of such collections as *Je sublime*
and *Un point c'est tout* to define and explore its implications
at every level of human existence. As in the earlier works, in
this poetry it is the special gift of the poet to be able to see
beyond the temporal and spatial limits of man's life on earth
and to find desire in the superhuman and the subhuman. Erotic
love, a basic form of desire, is extended to encompass and
effect the entire experiential world through the process of sublimation, which is intrinsic to Péret's definition of love. Desire
extends to history in the human search for unity among men
and with nature; this manifestation of desire appears in the
long poems *Air mexicain . . .* and *Dernier Malheur dernière
chance. . . .* It informs a political view which emphasizes the
attempts of desire to eliminate all obstacles to the free expression of the marvelous; *Je ne mange pas de ce pain-là* and
Le Déshonneur des poètes are most direct in their emphasis of
this requisite, which is a strong element in all of Péret's work.
The natural adversaries of the poet are those who have civilized
themselves out of natural processes and those who work to
keep others from free participation in the ecology of the marvelous. They represent the status quo in its widest manifestation, that is, those forces which maintain stasis in opposition
to the dynamic force of desire. Among these are established
religion and repressive government, which Péret sees as alienating men from their own natures and from Nature itself.

Once desire is described and evoked in its positive and negative
aspects, Péret proceeds even deeper in his exploration of change
in the world to define generation itself. Change is inherent in
Péret's view of the mythical process of creation; everything in
the world is both the product of transformations and potential
material for further change. The force of desire, which provides
the structure for change, is manifested in generative processes
through the humanization of natural forces. The human point
of view is the only possible vantage for the poet; the pretense
of scientific objectivity, which fails to account for change in
the observer, is abandoned for a continual redefinition of stance
on the part of both subject and object in mythic interaction. In
his attempts to formulate the ideal relationship between man
and the world, Péret studies primitive myth and legend and
finds in them guidelines which are less contaminated by the
civilized European tradition. Péret finds the openness and vitality of primitive beliefs to be a more satisfying and valid
response to the need for physical and metaphysical interaction
with the world than the religious and political dogmatism which
separates man from nature.

Myth is not only a manifestation of the past; more important,
myth is the product of creativity in Péret's work. The situation
of his poems and tales is a world in which super- and subterranean elements are fused, as are all states of being and

consciousness. It is a dynamic form of utopia in which the pleasure principle dominates in the omnipresence of food and the use of play as the primary form of action and interaction. The great ruling force in Péret's myth is not a social god like Quetzalcoatl or Zeus, whose powers are limited to action within worlds created before their arrival. Unlike earlier mythographers, Péret does not personify his omnipotent central concept; rather, he depicts it as it inheres in every action in human and natural life. From the shaping of the cosmos to the events of daily life, it is change which rules the world. Because many aspects of the work of change are not perceived in the normal context of human awareness, this mythology relies on the imagination as a sixth sense which unites the conscious with the unconscious, dream and death. The unified, expanded insight of the poet into the mythological structure of the world is expressed through poetry, the vehicle of the image, and through a prose which empties narrative forms of their dead content to revive them as expressions of poetic insight. The Surrealist works of Benjamin Péret reveal the significance and implications of the new myth of change. (pp. 194-97)

> *Julia Field Costich, in her* The Poetry of Change: A Study of the Surrealist Works of Benjamin Péret, *North Carolina Studies in the Romance Languages and Literatures, 1979, 217 p.*

MELMOTH, CLIVE BALL, ROGER CARDINAL, PAULINE DRAYSON, SALAH FAIQ, PAUL HAMMOND, CONROY MADDOX, MICHAEL RICHARDSON, JOHN WELSON, AND HAIFA ZANGANA   (essay date 1985)

[*In the following excerpt from "Trajectory of Passion," a manifesto by a group of neo-Surrealists, the authors cite Péret's values of personal and poetic liberty as a model for present-day literary and social revolutionists. Their statement begins with the following quotation from Péret's works: "He (the poet) rises up against everyone, including those revolutionaries who adopt an exclusively political stance, thereby arbitrarily isolating politics from the cultural movement at large, and who advocate the submission of cultural activities to the accomplishment of the social revolution."*]

The quotation comes from Péret's introduction to [*Anthologie des mythes, légendes et contes populaires d'Amérique,*] an anthology of American native myths, in which the surrealist poet voices his hope that poetry might become—like the shared mythology of a tribal society—an idiom accessible to the masses. If there is to be a realization of Ducasse's injunction that 'poetry must be made by all', writes Péret, it follows that it must be stripped of its artifices and snobberies and rendered available to everyone. Simultaneously, all men must be freed by social revolution of the oppressions of class society.

In the meantime, Péret admits, the poet finds himself rejected by society. He must therefore exert himself and speak out in words of authentic feeling. In so doing he will carry out an act of revolutionary proportions, smashing the ivory tower and communicating through that which is most profoundly shared by all men. But at the same time as he strikes a blow for the revolution, he must take care not to let his language become contaminated by a concern for its merely political connotations. He must, insists Péret, remain true to his own deep meanings and not allow his work to be channelled in the direction of superficial propaganda or publicity.

Péret's remarks are situated historically, at a time when he was becoming aware of the servile functionalism to which poetry was being reduced in the French Resistance: his tract *Le Déshonneur des poètes* ... was to be a more explicit attack on those who place art in the service of political expediency and thereby degrade it. Propaganda poetry in the name of nationalism is anti-surrealist, Péret maintains. An authentic poem, on the other hand, is one which releases a breath of true liberty; it is not reducible to a mediocre cause, but swells forth in anticipation of the effective liberation of mankind on an international scale.

While circumstances today and in the country in which we are living are different we would find it hard to disagree with Péret. We are now faced with a situation in which it is no less a matter of politics being infiltrated by fellow-traveling artists who coyly sport their political badge as a variant on the foppish flower of aestheticism. Elsewhere we see politics infiltrating art and reducing it to the level of a consumer product. This is often achieved by subtle modes of recuperation whereby the state machinery contrives to annex those expressions of revolt which might in other circumstances undermine its authority: by encouraging certain forms of dissent, by even paying for them, the state empties them of their force and meaning. They become counterfeit tokens, flimsy as cardboard.

In Britain, we are surrounded by mechanisms which take all too good care of us. The welfare state looks after our bodies and seeks also to look after our brains. Where artistic creativity is concerned, the authorities seek to make of it a commodity that can be controlled or even marketed. The creative act is the individual's instinctive right. Yet the definition of creativity as a function of the social system is an immediate annihilation of that right. The subsidies lavished on an artist by the Arts Council of Great Britain are handed over in the name of free expression: but the money he receives will act as an invisible frame running right round whatever he makes to ensure that its meaning is assimilated within the commodity system. Even if the work itself is not literally marketed, it is still 'wrapped' in a capitalist definition and therefore valued under the terms of that system. This is part of a process we call cultural imperialism.

To create in a revolutionary spirit must therefore be to refuse all pseudo-approval or support from that which seeks to divert the current of authentic energy. The poet must be a special sort of moralist, never collaborating with the enemy, anxious lest his work slip into zones where recuperation might become possible. Today we have to accept the historicization of the Dada revolt, its retrieval as a respectable museum-piece. We can watch sections of the haute bourgeoisie queuing up to gawp at the spectacle of their own duplicity in the films of Bunuel. Just a few weeks after the May Events of 1968, one could purchase on the Paris boulevards a memento of those Events in the form of a 'certified cobblestone', inscribed like a holiday souvenir. Already revolt had become spectacle.

We wonder if it is inevitable that the full original impact of an act of protest should be subject to the processes of time, and eventually fall prey to recuperation in some form or other. Against this possibility, the revolutionary artist must strive to maintain a space of authenticity in which his message will remain defiant to the maximum. Péret remains one of the rare poets whose work continues to stick in the throats of the recuperators. His watchword, to which he remained faithful throughout his life, should—today more than ever—be the watchword of all genuine poets: 'I won't eat of that bread.' ...

As surrealists we believe in a poetry which will stand in its own right and yet be a partner to the cause of social revolution.

In a profound sense, the revolutionary and the poet cannot be separated anyway. For what is poetry if not a revolutionary activity, what is revolution if not a poem in action? We maintain that the true poem is one which will change perceptions and thus contribute to the changing of material conditions in the real world. The inventions of a new language—'accessible, one of these days, to all the senses', as Rimbaud put it—must take its place on the revolutionary calendar on a par with all the other urgent operations of change. Occulted and enigmatic it may seem for the present, yet one day this language of lyricism, this language of praxis, will open up to all as a transparent flower.

Thus the poetry we seek cannot but be anarchist. It spells the formidable collapse of the structures which determine our present mentality and lull us into imagining that the monotony of our everyday lives is somehow 'natural'. The poet, writes Péret, is the integral nonconformist who stands at the extreme point of the cultural advance, striking out with all his strength so as to 'smash the barriers of habit and routine which keep on springing up'. His poem does not mince its words in the machine of monopoly rhetoric. Instead it rises on dragonfly wings in the morning of the metaphor, unlocking the gate in the city wall to reveal the fertile horizons of desire. Like the bolt of William Tell, like the bomb of Emile Henry, like the Vendome column at the hands of Courbet, its passionate trajectory carries it straight toward the integral expression and realization of liberty. And as Artaud said, 'all true liberty is black'.

> MELMOTH, Clive Ball, Roger Cardinal, Pauline Drayson, Salah Faiq, Paul Hammond, Conroy Maddox, Michael Richardson, John Welson, and Haifa Zangana, "Trajectory of Passion," in Exquisite Corpse, Vol. 3, Nos. 9-10, September-October, 1985, p. 10.*

ADDITIONAL BIBLIOGRAPHY

Balakian, Anna. *Surrealism: The Road to the Absolute*, pp. 148ff. New York: Noonday Press, 1959.
Critical survey of the Surrealist movement in art and literature.

Caws, Mary Ann. "Péret and the Surrealist Word." *Romance Notes* XI, No. 2 (Winter 1969): 233-37.
Explanation of how Péret's poetry reveals his attitude toward language.

————. "Benjamin Péret's Game and Gesture." In her *The Inner Theatre of Recent French Poetry*, pp. 75-105. Princeton: Princeton University Press, 1972.
Close textual analysis with emphasis upon the element of motion in Péret's poetry.

Costich, Julia F. "The Poem in a World of Change: Péret's 'Quatre à Quatre'." *Romance Notes* XV, No. 3 (Spring 1974): 410-15.
Discussion of the ongoing process of metamorphosis in Péret's poetry.

Courtot, Claude. "Introduction to the Reading of Benjamin Péret." *Radical America* 4, No. 1 (January 1970): 37-8.
Translated excerpt from a laudatory lecture on Péret.

Jackson, Elizabeth R. "Poésie activité de l'esprit: A Study of 'Atout trèfle' by Benjamin Péret." *French Review* XLIV, No. 6 (May 1971): 1036-47.
Textual analysis of one of Péret's poems.

————. Introduction and appendix to *A Marvelous World*, by Benjamin Péret, pp. xiii-xvi, 93-7. Baton Rouge: Louisiana State University Press, 1985.
Explanation of Péret's poetic theories.

Simic, Charles. "Péret." In *From the Hidden Storehouse: Selected Poems*, translated by Keith Hollaman, pp. 9-14. Oberlin: Oberlin College, 1981.
General discussion of Péret's work by a modern poet.

Horacio (Sylvestre) Quiroga

1878-1937

(Also wrote under pseudonym of Guillermo Eynhardt) Uruguayan short story writer, essayist, poet, dramatist, and journalist.

Considered one of Latin America's greatest short story writers, Quiroga is best known for stories portraying conflict between an individual and the natural hazards of the South American jungle. Strongly influenced by the works of Edgar Allan Poe, Quiroga's stories reflect the author's preoccupation with madness, terror, and death, and, like Poe's, are often narrowly focused in order to evoke a single mood or stunning effect.

Quiroga was born in 1878 in Salto, Uruguay, to an Argentine vice-consul and the daughter of a highly respected Salto family. Within three months of Quiroga's birth his father was accidentally shot and killed, and in 1895 his stepfather committed suicide. These deaths were the first in a series of bizarre tragedies that continued throughout Quiroga's life and to which critics attribute his obsession with violence and the macabre. During his school years Quiroga preferred travel literature and periodicals to his formal studies and distinguished himself at the University of Montevideo through his skill in photography, bicycling, and carpentry rather than scholarship. His first essays were published in Salto newspapers in 1897 under the pseudonym Guillermo Eynhardt, the hero of a nineteeth-century French novel. Two years later he founded *Revista del Salto,* a short-lived literary magazine featuring works influenced by Edgar Allan Poe and by *modernismo,* a literary movement that dominated Spanish American literature from approximately 1890 to 1910. Through their innovative use of language, meter, and rhyme, the *modernistas* revitalized Spanish literature, which had seen little change since the seventeenth century, and created a uniquely Latin American form. Influenced by literary Romanticism and French Symbolism, the *modernistas* characteristically rejected Naturalism and materialism in an attempt to create timeless works that avoided historical or topical issues. An artistic pilgrimage to Paris in 1900 afforded Quiroga an opportunity to attend *modernista* gatherings and to meet the leader of the movement, the Nicaraguan poet Rubén Darío, but Quiroga quickly became disillusioned with the Parisian literary community and a few months later returned to South America. Upon his return he founded the first *modernista* group in Uruguay, "El Consistorio de Gay Saber," and in 1901 he published his first book, *Los arrecifes de coral,* a collection of Decadent poetry and prose that was critically unsuccessful.

In 1902 Quiroga accidentally shot and killed Federico Ferrando, a member of "El Consistorio" and one of Quiroga's best friends. Shaken by the tragedy, Quiroga left Montevideo for Buenos Aires, where he was soon appointed by the Argentine government to a commission formed to study the ruins of ancient Jesuit settlements in Misiones, a jungle province in northern Argentina. The commission's research expedition had a dramatic effect on his life and career: captivated by pioneer life in the tropical virgin forest, Quiroga later made the area his home and the setting for many of his most famous stories. After an unsuccessful attempt to grow cotton in the Chaco

region of northern Argentina, Quiroga returned to Buenos Aires to write and teach secondary school. In 1910 he made a second journey to Misiones, now accompanied by his young wife, and the couple remained there for five years while Quiroga farmed and experimented with making charcoal and distilling orange liqueur. Marital discord, particularly arguments about childrearing, is believed to be the reason that Quiroga's wife committed suicide in 1915. After her death Quiroga returned to Buenos Aires and entered into the most prolific period of his literary career: between 1916 and 1926 he published six of his most popular story collections, numerous articles and essays, two series of weekly film reviews, and the drama *Las sacrificadas.* Quiroga's literary output declined significantly after 1926. Following his final move to the jungle in 1932, he explained to a friend, "The primitive violence of making, building, improving and adorning my habitat has made artistic creation seem—ah!—somewhat artificial." Failing health led to a constant preoccupation with death, reflected in the morbidity of his final story collection, *Más allá.* In 1937, after learning that he had cancer, Quiroga committed suicide.

While his early writings in *Los arrecifes de coral* reflected the aestheticism of *modernismo,* Quiroga gradually turned to the realistic technique for which he later became known. His second collection, *El crimen del otro,* depicts the abnormal and horrific, relying on careful attention to detail to evoke disturbed states of mind and achieve extremely vivid effects. The influence of Poe dominates the collection: the title story, in which the narrator states, "Poe was at that time the only author I read. . . . My head was completely filled with Poe," concerns two characters obsessed with the theme of madness in Poe's story "The Cask of Amontillado." As in the Poe story, one character inters the other alive. Quiroga's next works, the short story "Los perseguidos" ("The Pursued") and the novella *Historia de un amor turbio*, are among the earliest examples of his transformation of autobiographical episodes into fiction: Quiroga acknowledged that he was the model for the protagonist in *Historia de un amor turbio*, one of several pieces in which he portrayed a passionate affair between a young woman and an older man. These works also signify Quiroga's final renunciation of *modernismo* in favor of realism and psychological analysis influenced by the works of Fedor Dostoevski and Guy de Maupassant.

With the publication of the short story collection *Cuentos de amor, de locura y de muerte*, his first book to include stories set in the jungle of Misiones, Quiroga achieved widespread popularity and critical acclaim. These stories and those in the collections that followed are distinguished by their simple, direct depiction of the brutality of jungle life. Many portray a lone individual struggling for survival, often in conflict with nature, which is seen as an omnipotent and merciless force. Typical of these is "La insolación" ("Sunstroke"), in which the protagonist, who underestimates the power of the afternoon sun and overestimates his own strength, is felled by sunstroke while attempting to clear his cotton plantation. Death, or more specifically the experience of dying, is a recurring motif, as exemplified by "El hombre muerto" ("The Dead Man"), in which a man who has received a fatal machete wound struggles to accept his imminent death. Critics praise Quiroga's objective, unsentimental treatment of physical suffering and death, as well as his terse style, which heightens the effect of his stories by eliminating all extraneous detail. Animals are featured as protagonists in many of the Misiones stories, particularly in those collected in *Cuentos de la selva (South American Jungle Tales)*, fables for children that have been favorably compared to Rudyard Kipling's animal stories. In stories such as "Anaconda," Quiroga contrasted animal instinct with human reason, which he considered inferior to instinct and insufficient for survival in a natural environment. *Los desterrados*, considered by critics to be among Quiroga's best and most characteristic collections, comprises portraits of the "exiles" peculiar to the Argentine jungle: pioneers, drunkards, derelicts, day laborers, and eccentrics fleeing civilization. Some critics note that the objectivity with which Quiroga portrayed his characters heightens the reader's sympathy for their plight; these critics further contend that although Quiroga's works are not primarily concerned with social protest, stories such as "Los mensú" ("The Contract Workers") and "Una bofetada" ("A Slap in the Face") provide poignant social commentary on the exploitation of the South American contract worker.

Critics disagree about Quiroga's technical skill as a short story writer; while many praise his masterful utilization of the tenets set out in his "Decálogo del perfecto cuentista" ("Decalogue of the Perfect Short Story Writer"), others maintain that his stories are undisciplined and uneven in style. Most critics, however, agree that Quiroga's genius lay in the evocation of the atmosphere of Misiones and rank his stories, for their power and vividness, among Latin America's best.

PRINCIPAL WORKS

Los arrecifes de coral   (poetry and short stories)   1901
El crimen del otro   (short stories)   1904
Historia de un amor turbio   (novella and short story)   1908
Cuentos de amor, de locura y de muerte   (short stories)
    1917
Cuentos de la selva   (short stories)   1918
   [*South American Jungle Tales*, 1922]
Las sacrificadas   (drama)   [first publication] 1920
El salvaje   (short stories)   1920
Anaconda   (short stories)   1921
El desierto   (short stories)   1924
Los desterrados   (short stories)   1926
Pasado amor   (novella)   1929
Más allá   (short stories)   1935
Cuentos. 13 vols.   (short stories and novellas)   1937-45
Our First Smoke   (short story)   1972
El mundo ideal de Horacio Quiroga   (letters)   1975
The Decapitated Chicken, and Other Stories   (short stories)
    1976
"The Flies"   (short story)   1976; published in journal
    Review 76

Translated selections of Quiroga's short stories have appeared in the following publications: Colford, William E., ed., *Classic Tales from Spanish America;* Flores, Angel, ed., *Spanish Stories;* Flores, Angel, and Poore, Dudley, eds., *Stories from Latin America;* Haydn, Hiram, and Cournos, John, eds., *A World of Great Stories;* Jones, Willis Knapp, ed., *Spanish American Literature since 1888;* and Onís, Harriet de, ed., *Spanish Stories and Tales.*

ERNESTO MONTENEGRO   (essay date 1925)

[Montenegro was a Chilean short story writer, essayist, and critic. In the following excerpt, he discusses four of Quiroga's story collections.]

Like many a writer who has come into the literary world directly from the field of his life experiences, the Argentine-Uruguayan Horacio Quiroga appears more concerned with what he has to say than he seems to be with the way of expressing it, or at least this is the impression one gathers from his motley vocabulary, patched here and there with words whose meaning has been twisted or reversed, coming from the mouths of perfectly plain people and striking the reader with the stiff accent of the unutterable "printed" word.

His hasty schooling shows in ways more than one and has its counterpart in the frequent sleepy spells of the critical faculty. But when we say that no more uneven writer has been recently produced by a race which, like the Latin-American, has never been strong for literary discipline or, for that matter, discipline of any kind, we must hasten to add that the author's qualities are also as genuine as nature's—strength, power of rejuvenation, life at its source. His stories have much of that natural appeal one finds in the yarns of miners, sailors and tramps. Each page is like the skins of wild animals we see displayed in a hunter's lodge, testifying to the warm and bloody forms from which they were torn.

Horacio Quiroga's field of observation lies in the primeval land in the heart of South America; his characters are in the main primitive men of our own time. His favorite studies are concerned with the subconscious and the instinctive. Up in the settlements of the Argentine territories of El Chaco and Misiones, close to the sources of the Paraná River, and still half submerged in the exuberance of tropical life, men of all races are met in a fateful rendezvous where nature, the beast and the man pursue their three-cornered struggle.

To anticipate a glimpse of Quiroga's personality, let the American reader think of a literary descendant of Jack London and Rudyard Kipling, with some of the fire of the former and no little of the bluntness of expression of the latter, the whole animated by their individualistic philosophy; and now let him imagine this Creole Kipling-London confronted with the task of recording the progress of the European settler through one of the rough spots still remaining on the American Continent.

There Quiroga lived and struggled many years. His experiences were those of the typical frontiersman. There living was stripped to the bare necessities; but life remained pregnant with possibilities of conflict, hard luck, sudden fortune and all manner of bewildering situations. A good deal of the author's concern is with man's wits matched against the brute forces of nature. The same immemorial duel is renewed here in the efforts of a resourceful mind to conquer wealth single-handed; in the drifting adventurer going from place to place and from trade to trade, always on the downward course; now a frail bride trying, and succeeding, to cross the mighty river, with her invalid mate for sole companion; others burning their souls alive while distilling coal by-products in their handmade laboratory; finally, a snake-bitten fellow in a lonesome boat race in search of medical attention being overtaken by death. . . .

The nature aspect, however, is only one of many in the works of Horacio Quiroga. Essentially a short-story teller, or, more strictly, dealing in those "morceaux de vie" ["slices of life"] dear to Maupassant, in which fiction merely arranges facts in a dramatic sequence, he seems to hold a strong predilection for those states of mind not yet out of the twilight of reason or already drifting beyond the world of consciousness. Among the two-dozen-odd stories contained in [*Historia de un Amor Turbio, El Desierto, Cuentos de Amor, de Locura y de Muerte*, and *Anaconda*] there are no less than six which are concerned in one way or another with the release of the soul, either by the process of natural death, by weird accidents, or merely through pathological hallucinations and reveries. . . .

[A] sudden breaking away of spirit from the body, not by the unperceived disintegrating process of age, but in full possession of our faculties, like the bird brought down in full flight by the bullet from the hunter, furnishes the dramatic climax to no less than three stories by Quiroga. Sheer mystery comes back in other stories, carrying us from the mirages of the operating table and the mad fancies of brain fever, on to the speculations as to the life beyond.

Still, his stories are seldom gruesome and never lugubrious. Almost always a sardonic humor plays a light accompaniment to his more fearsome imaginings. He has something of that same emphatic sort of statement that swaggers through the stories of Kipling. That huge South American river, the Paraná, displays throughout it all a sombre, godlike majesty, and much in the same spirit as the Bret Harte editor who couldn't refrain from a melancholy pride in California, even when its bigness was expressed in disaster, Quiroga tells us once and again of the equally devastating achievements of flood and drought, of the malaria chill that shrivels the strongest nature, of the trop-

ical sun that kills the red ant before many seconds of exposure. We cannot help feeling . . . that the ferocious instinct of the creatures of the wild has been melodramatically blackened, and that, unless we receive report to the contrary from the last survivor escaping the wilderness, we must take, with a grain of skepticism, those innumerable serpents going after the life of man; river fishes whose bite is indescribably painful and necessarily mortal that lie in wait for the unwary fisherman; wild honey of paralyzing effects helping the hordes of black ants to "empty" the body of a traveler at a single charge, or that bloodsucking bug capable of draining out the life of a grown-up person in a few nights.

The animated geography of a zone fully as wide as Alaska is revealed to us in the character of a self-reliant, restive population. Touching on the territories where back in Colonial times the Jesuits built their theocratic, feudal empire, the Upper Paraná jungle still preserves the features of a life untamed by civilization. There prey the native tiger and the lion, the alligator and the vampire bat. To its forest comes the trader in search of the quebracho tree, a wood so dense it cannot float. And this formidable paradise is only a few days by steamer from the opulence and Parisian-like refinements of Buenos Aires. No wonder then that when the earlier stories of Quiroga began to appear in Argentine magazines their crude vigor startled the intellegentsia as the taste of raw meat would the palate of an epicure.

In his *Historia de un Amor Turbio (The Story of a Troubled Courtship)*, the longest piece of fiction by Quiroga we know of, he deals at some length with passions whose foundations lie on the immediate physical urge. The impossibility of renewal of a love awakening, by the mere appeal of youth and grace is again sternly emphasized in **"Silvina y Montt."** Perhaps one of the outstanding merits of Quiroga in this respect is that he does not try to lionize his characters; the situations may be exceptional, but the men and women affected by them are usually of the average paste. Unlike Western American novelists of the blood-and-thunder school, neither the heroes nor the heroines in Quiroga's books behave with anything approaching perfection, either for good or evil.

For a similar reason we notice little of the romantic (except when at his worst he becomes grossly melodramatic) in his love stories. Man's egotism and the instinctive wiles of women are displayed in his realistic idylls more like a traphunting pursuit than the fool's paradise we are offered in syndicated fiction and elsewhere. Which means that if any of his heroines confesses a previous affair, however inconsequential, the Spanish masculine pride in such matters plays havoc with their hectic passional duel.

In two of his love stories Quiroga introduces American "movie" people. **"Miss Dorothy Phillips, my wife"** is one in which the characters and the situations are even more absurd than the supposed dream furnishing matter to the performance. Grotesquely conceived as this story is, it is valuable at least as an example of the utter failure of an artist with good eyes for objective and introspective work, when trying to "locate" his subject in lands unknown.

Not so his animal stories. Here he is on solid ground. . . . In these modern fables—or shall I say animal folklore?—the satire is social rather than political, as was obvious in the Englishman's Jungle Books. But, whatever the differences in workmanship that exist between the English masterpiece and this South American version, acknowledgment should be made of the superior learning in natural history and more direct contact with his subject on the part of the Argentine-Uruguayan author.

Quiroga has made a special study of the snake in its bewildering varieties. His best work on this theme is **"Anaconda,"** a story in which he has plainly described under the guise of scientific terminology the struggle being carried on between the undisciplined, bold forces of savagery and the snares of civilization. Inclined as he is to study social conflicts in one or another form, Quiroga approaches the position of his contemporary the Spaniard Baroja by a certain detached, diffident outlook, which points to a pessimistic view of mankind and confesses by its very attitude a congenital distrust of idealistic or humanitarian nostrums of redemption.

> Ernesto Montenegro, "Horacio Quiroga, Literary Kin of Kipling and Jack London," in The New York Times Book Review, October 25, 1925, p. 10.

HORACIO QUIROGA (essay date 1927)

[*In the following excerpt, Quiroga presents his "Decalogue of the Perfect Short Story Writer," in which he delineates his literary principles.*]

I. Believe in the masters Poe, Maupassant, Kipling, Chekhov—as in God himself.

II. Believe that your art is an inaccessible peak. Don't dream of conquering it. When you are able to do that you will succeed, without knowing it yourself.

III. Resist imitation as much as you are able, but imitate if the influence is too strong. More than anything else, the development of the [author's] personality requires long patience.

IV. Have blind faith, not in your capacity for triumph, but in the ardor with which you desire it. Love your art as your sweetheart, giving it all your heart.

V. Never begin to write without knowing where you are going from the first word. In an accomplished story the first three lines have almost the same importance as the last three.

VI. If you wish to express this situation with exactitude: "a cold wind was blowing from the river," there are no words in the human language to express it, other than those mentioned. Once in command of the words do not concern yourself with observing whether they are consonant or assonant.

VII. Don't adjectivize unnecessarily. Whatever tails you stick on a weak substantive will be to no avail. If you find the precise substantive, it alone will have an incomparable coloring. But you must find it.

VIII. Take your characters by the hand and lead them firmly to the end, seeing only the road you mapped for them. Don't distract yourself, seeing what they cannot see or what is not important for them to see. Don't abuse the reader. A short story is a novel stripped of padding. Hold this as an absolute truth though it might not be one.

IX. Don't write under the domination of emotion. Allow it to die and evoke it later. If you are then capable of reviving it as it was, you are halfway along the road of art.

X. Don't think about your friends when you are writing, nor in the impression your story will make. Tell it as if the account had interest only for the limited environment of your characters, of which you could have been one. Only in this way is the *life* of the story obtained. (pp. 42-3)

> Horacio Quiroga, "The Decalogue of the Perfect Short Story Writer," in Review, No. 19, Winter, 1976, pp. 42-3.

HERMINE HALLAM-HIPWELL (essay date 1929)

[*In the following excerpt, Hallam-Hipwell reviews* Pasado Amor.]

Horacio Quiroga . . . is among the Argentine writers whose works are always interesting and typical of the Latin-American attitude toward literature. His prose is vivid and forceful, its simplicity contrasts pleasantly with the heavily pompous styles adopted by some of his contemporaries, and he has done much to bring before his Buenos Aires public the tragic beauty of the Chaco. In . . . **"Pasado Amor,"** Quiroga has chosen as background for his story the *mate* plantations of Misiones, the North-Eastern territory of the Argentine Republic bordering on the Brazilian forest lands and the Paraguayan desert. . . .

Morán, the hero of Quiroga's novel, is a *mate* planter. A widower who lost his wife in tragic circumstances after a short twelve months of married life, he is from a European's point of view a strange creature. And yet he is the counterpart of many characters in present-day Argentine fiction which points to his type being common in certain literary circles. For this man, brusque in his manner, with little of the romantic Latin-American characteristics which some writers safely in New

Galley page with Quiroga's corrections.

York or London would assure us are typical of the inhabitants of the South American republics, is undoubtedly an excellent study of a present-day Argentine. By turns an idealist and a materialist it is the conflict between his two natures—a conflict which supplies some seventy-five per cent of the plots used by Argentine writers—brought into being by his love for Magda Iñíguez, which holds the reader's attention.

Morán's love is the result of his two lonely years of wandering away from Misiones in an attempt to forget the tragedy of the lonely plantation. His return to Misiones in order to pick up the threads of his old life, brings about a haunting sense of his loss and a fierce desire to lose himself in his new love for the pure and childlike Magda. Tormented by his desire and the opposition of Magda's mother and brothers, Morán seeks consolation in the love offered to him by Alica Hontou, the humble laborer's daughter, but is unable to forget either the past or his new passion for Magda. The end of the book is tragic. Morán loses both Alicia and Magda and then leaves Misiones where once again he has had bitterness and despair as his daily companions. Horacio Quiroga has sketched his characters very simply yet this simplicity serves to heighten the sense of tragedy lying heavily over Morán and Magda's slightest acts. The life of the plantations, those clearings in the midst of the primeval forests with the river far away on the horizon and a tiny village supplying the needs of the planters, is described in all its monotonous beauty. The life is one of constant hardship under tropic skies with nature and man continually at war, and Quiroga knows his subject thoroughly.

Equally well does he know people of the Iñiguez type: proud Peruvians of the most fanatical and aristocratic character, accustomed to large properties and the subservience of countless native servants, and bitterly opposed to all innovations. They are an unpleasant family but cleverly delineated by the author, and in their midst Magda, the gentle and pure heroine, strikes, to the foreign reader, an incongruous note. This type is, however, popular with Argentine readers; their heroines are rarely women of character or determination, on the contrary they are fatalists, with an ingrained sense of the tragedy of life and love. . . .

This novel of Quiroga's is not by any means his best work, but it is a good example of the fiction being written at present in Argentina by Argentine writers.

> *Hermine Hallam-Hipwell, "A Recent Argentine Novel," in* The Saturday Review of Literature, *Vol. VI, No. 18, November 23, 1929, p. 456.*

JOHN EUGENE ENGLEKIRK (essay date 1934)

[*An American critic and educator, Englekirk was a professor of Spanish at the University of California from 1958 until his retirement in 1973, during which time he came to be regarded as one of the English-speaking world's leading authorities on Latin American literature. In the following excerpt, Englekirk notes the extent of Poe's influence on Quiroga's works.*]

No other Hispanic prose writer has so vividly expressed the spirit of Poe's tales as has Horacio Quiroga. In manner and in style, in the exotic and extraordinary temper of his themes, and in the wedding of psychological acumen to states of horror, of fear, and of the varying stages of monomania, this formidable *cuentista rioplatense* ["short story writer from the River Plate"] is constantly evoking those sensations and reactions that mark him as one of the most successful adherents to the Poesque genre of the short story. (pp. 340-41)

El crimen del otro is a collection of tales based entirely on themes of a fictitious nature, on themes inspired by the intense reading of the works of others. These literary influences are fairly visible in most of the stories. Of deep concern for us is the title-story, for it is the very vivid confession of what Quiroga's reading of Poe has meant in the development of his art. (p. 342)

The plot of Quiroga's tale centers about "The Cask of Amontillado." The narrator or hero, who describes himself as one of abnormal characteristics, is so fascinated by Poe's tale that his super-susceptible temperament leads him to confuse his friend, whose name is Fortunato, with the characters of the story. . . . Suddenly Quiroga's friend also shows an extraordinary interest in Poe. . . . Fortunato is especially attracted by Poe's theme of madness. . . .

Fortunato can speak of nothing but madness, and in much of what he says there are palpable recollections of Poe's thoughts on the subject. Quiroga senses with alarm that his friend is rapidly approaching a mental crisis, and he makes every possible effort to prevent his final breakdown, but with no permanent results. At last Fortunato becomes irrevocably mad, and Quiroga, fearing that his companion will be taken from him, plans to dispose of him at his own will. The carnival season reminds him of Poe's cunning intrigue against his Fortunato; Quiroga is seized with the mad idea of duplicating the diabolical feat. . . . At three-thirty in the morning, Quiroga and Fortunato leave the carnival for home. The former laments the fact that his friend is far too mad to realize what is happening to him or to offer any such resistance as does the victim of Poe. He leads Fortunato to the cellar and tries to persuade him to drop into a wide hole that is to be his tomb. But the madman resists in terror, whereupon Quiroga's joy assumes the satanical dimensions of Poe. In gentle tones and with a suggestive lowering of the hands, Quiroga induces him to believe the hole is a well. Fortunato reacts to the idea, descends, and curls up satisfied as Quiroga begins his fiendish task. Poe dominates the final scene. . . . (pp. 345-46)

No one can possibly question Quiroga's complete absorption of the Poe whose characteristics appealed most strongly to his own peculiar nature. Poe's theme of madness and his ability to portray its psychological development; his keenness in the depicting of analogous conscious states; his themes of life beyond the tomb, of dual personality, of the reality of dreams; his recourse to the strange, the weird, and rare as suitable subjects for his art, and the careful attention to detail for the highest possible effect so firmly imbedded themselves in Quiroga during his assimilative period that, from their inception on, his art was but the incessant purifying and mastering of qualities that later evolved as his own. Quiroga's love of extraordinary themes was an inherent characteristic; but one that was directed from its highly artificial course to the most artistic and more original manner of his later period through the direct, early influence of Poe. (p. 348)

Quiroga's *Historia de un amor turbio* appeared in 1908. The title-story is a novelette that treats of the mysterious psychological changes of love. The author's keen analysis of the hidden forces and inexplicable reactions of the human mind is one of his fundamental traits and one that may well have been nourished by contact with Poe's work. What recalls a more direct influence of Poe, however, is Quiroga's stress on the diabolical presence of *el otro* ["the other"] and its consequent effect on the lover. In this case *el otro* is the girl's former beau. Quiroga's recourse to this psychological force for the breaking up of their love affair is not without precedent in his own work, for his earlier "**El crimen del otro**" also was undoubtedly inspired in this particular by Poe's "William Wilson."

"**Los perseguidos**" is the only other work in this volume of 1908. It is decidedly Poesque and draws very heavily upon Poe's tales of monomania. Quiroga's portrayal of the maniac who suffers from the illusion of being pursued is well-drawn with bold lines à la Poe. The dissimulation of the monomaniac is reminiscent of that of Poe's superintendent in "The System of Dr. Tarr and Prof. Fether." Quiroga's description of how the hero is unconsciously being infected with the same mania results in many fine passages in which fear, mad joy, and other Poesque sensations are much in evidence; such passages occur when Quiroga, unwittingly exultant, pursues "the pursued" and when, in the silence of his room, he finally realizes that his obsession of a feeling of being watched is the work of his maniac friend. In all of this we find that Quiroga has applied his own psychological powers effectively in the depiction of literary types found in Poe.

After long years of constant self-development, during which time Quiroga gradually weaned himself from the literary influences that shaped his earlier works, he emerged, at last, as a master of the short story and as a truly original writer in his very popular volume of tales, *Cuentos de amor, de locura y de muerte*. . . . In this collection there is not a single tale but has as its salient feature the abnormal. For that reason, and because of a choice of themes that inevitably suggest Poe, the volume represents the harmonious blending of outer influences and of Quiroga's own self-asserting nature. From this point on, it will be increasingly unwise to claim, with any degree of certainty, that a tale has been definitely and directly influenced by the American author. The Uruguayan critic [Alberto] Zum Felde has stressed Quiroga's affinity to Poe as the basis for whatever Poesque reminiscences may be found in his work. . . . Zum Felde cannot overlook the fact, however, that Poe has been the unquestionable source of many of Quiroga's themes, and this even after his emancipation from Poe's immediate influence; nor can he deny that through Poe, Quiroga benefitted incalculably in the development of his style and technique.

The Poesque title of the volume does not prepare one for the very pleasant surprise of Quiroga's having applied his now mature manner to themes of his beloved Misiones. It is in this new source of inspiration that Quiroga rises to the culmination of his art. (pp. 349-52)

Quiroga departs from the realms of pure imagination into the tropical wastes of Misiones where, after his marriage in 1910, he established himself anew at San Ignacio. Here he uncovered untold treasures with which to bring into original and masterful display those characteristics that had, up to this time, been employed on imaginary themes of a decidedly Poesque trend. Death personified in the angered, defiant reptiles and in the pestilential fevers and burning sun of these torrid regions; madness due to infection by the starved, pillaging dogs of the peons and to the incessant pounding of the tropical torrents; the primitive motives and superstitions of these sun-warped natives; the blind, ceaseless struggle of man with a savage and relentless nature; and the fatality that seems to pursue all alike, furnish the illimitable expanse of background upon which Quiroga essayed his superb artistry. In many of these tales, despite the occasional touch of Wells or Kipling, there appear in new relief the horror and fear and madness of Poe.

"**A la deriva**" is one of those tales in which Quiroga makes a very effective impression in the narrating of a single common event of this human struggle against an implacable destiny. A man is bitten by a yararacusú, and when his homely antidote fails, he takes to his canoe to paddle for medical aid. The poison works rapidly, and Quiroga depicts with Poesque skill the steady approach of death over the solitary figure drifting further and further from his intended earthly destination and cure. (pp. 356-57)

Quiroga's proneness to themes of madness finds ample room for expression in the realistic setting of Misiones. One of his very best productions in this field is his tale "**El perro rabioso.**" Quiroga depicts with marvelous skill the reaction of the dog's victim to the increasing intensity of the madness. He suits his style and manner to the increasing tempo and violence of the man's affliction, so that his readers must follow him headlong into the incoherent ejaculations and ravings of his character. This madness, arising out of innumerable causes in the tropics, is likewise the theme of "**El simún**," a tale wherein a new arrival at Misiones, who is exceedingly bored by the monotony of the tropical rains listens to an account of the madness that comes to men in the Sahara from the dreaded *cafard*, the evil fruit of the desert wind, sirocco. Many passages, especially those in which the narrator is driven to the point of insanity by the chronic twist of his friend's head, something which he had been accustomed to seeing through twenty years of intimate friendship, are very reminiscent of Poe. (p. 361)

Quiroga never fully abandons the purely imaginary theme and background. In some of his most recent works the tales are so Poesque in subject and in style that one is convinced that Quiroga never fully emancipated himself from Poe's influence. It would seem from an examination of some of these tales that Quiroga had sought and derived renewed vigor and inspiration from Poe. This is particularly true of many stories of his *Anaconda* that appeared in 1921. So Poesque is "**La lengua**" that its constituent elements remind one of no less than three of Poe's tales. The dissimulation of Quiroga's hero not only recalls that element of his own tale, "**El crimen del otro**," and "The Cask of Amontillado" from which it originated, but also the cunning pretense portrayed in "The Tell-Tale Heart," with which "**La lengua**" has most in common. The tongue that gives rise to the mad obsession of the dentist finds its counterpart in the teeth of "Berenice" as well as in the evil eye of "The Tell-Tale Heart." Quiroga's story tells of how a young dentist sought revenge on a former friend who had ruined his profession by spreading calumnies and lies. He deliberately and cunningly wins back his friendship. At last, when he has induced the calumniator to allow him to pull an aching tooth, he has him in his power. The man has misgivings and a foreboding of what is to happen. But he finally opens his mouth and is suddenly bereft of his tongue. The unfortunate man swoons. The gloating dentist is drawn by some uncontrollable influence to open the victim's mouth and consider his revenge, whereupon he sees a little red tongue dart up through the blood. He cuts this out too, only to find two more springing up in its place, and so his madness multiplies. . . . (pp. 361-62)

There are but two tales in his last collection [*Los desterrados*] that are in any sense Poesque. "**El hombre muerto**" treats of the thoughts of a dying "cultivator misionero" ["farmer"] who mortally wounded himself with his own machete as he slipped in crossing a fence to rest. Quiroga's hero is very much like any of Poe's characters when face to face with death, cooly poised and reasoning, and in full control of his mental powers. . . . **"Los destiladors de naranja"** offers the familiar scene of horror in which a father under the influence of liquor kills his own daughter, mistaking her for a rat in the delirium tremens from which he is suffering.

Quiroga has fortified himself with Poe's magic art of availing himself of every possible means for creating the effect desired. From start to finish there is not a detail but that is in perfect harmony with the prevailing mood. That is why Quiroga, like Poe, can hold his reader's interest in tales that under another's pen would fail utterly; and that is why both artists succeed in making the most impassive react in every mental and physical fiber to the sensations of horror, of fear, of madness, and of terror that their tales impart. (pp. 366-67)

Poe's strong influence during the formative period of Quiroga's art is an unquestionable fact. In his later works Quiroga emerges, tale by tale, as an affinitive spirit of the North-American author. But even in many of the more recent products of his pen, the reader is very, very conscious, at times, of more than a mere resemblance to Poe. The foregoing consideration of the possible influences and very noticeable resemblances to Poe in all of Quiroga's work assumes a much greater significance when we observe that he is esteemed as the most outstanding short-story writer of the Rio de la Plata country and as one of the great authors of Hispanic-American literature. Many of the younger prose writers have been inspired and guided by Quiroga's genius. They must have sensed the Poesque spirit that has motivated their master's pen and, in turn, succumbed in some degree to the ever fresh inspiration of Poe himself. (p. 368)

> *John Eugene Englekirk, "Poe's Influence in Spanish America," in his* Edgar Allan Poe in Hispanic Literature, *Instituto de las Españas, 1934, pp. 152-417.**

JEFFERSON REA SPELL (essay date 1944)

[*In the following excerpt, Spell offers a survey of Quiroga's short stories.*]

Between Quiroga the man and Quiroga the writer there is an inseparable bond. In many of his stories, he himself, faithfully delineated, is the principal character, and events from his own life—his disappointments in love, his experiences in the wilds of the Chaco and Misiones, his scientific experiments—provide him with the narratives. Highly imaginative by nature, he reveals, like the true romantic that he was, his obsession for the supernatural, particularly the thought of an existence after death, on which hinges a goodly number of his stories. Although he was indifferent toward religion, his observations in certain essays and allegories on human conduct bespeak a truly high and noble soul. His writings during his youth and his last years reveal that his mind was often occupied with thoughts on insanity, suicide, and murder.

His fondness for such morbid subjects appeared at the outset of his literary career. That he was very deeply impressed by d'Annunzio's *Il Trionfo della Morte* is evident in **"El Guardabosque comediante"** (**"The Actor Forest-Guard"**) and **"Sin Razón, pero cansado"** (**"Without Reason but Tired"**), two stories in his first book, *Los Arrecifes de Coral* [(*Coral Reefs*)]. . . . This novel of d'Annunzio traces the progress of insanity in the protagonist, Giorgio Aurispa, who, bored with existence, murders his mistress and takes his own life. Under the spell of this book, the central figure in **"El Guardabosque comediante"** lets himself be devoured by a pack of wolves. There is no

reference to d'Annunzio's novel in **"Sin Razón, pero cansado"**; its influence, however, is evident, particularly in Luciano, a bored individual, who, like his prototype, Giorgio, murders his mistress when he tires of her.

Quiroga admits also, in his early writings, an absorbing passion for Poe, who, as Englekirk observes in his *Edgar Allan Poe in Hispanic Literature* [see excerpt dated 1934], had a very definite influence on him. **"El Crimen del Otro"** [(**"Another's Crime"**)], the title story of one of his collections, is admittedly inspired by "The Cask of Amontillado." The two characters in the story are insane; infatuated with Poe's tales, each reveals their effect on him; and, finally, one of them, following Poe's story, buries the other alive. Insanity is the theme of **"La justa Proporción de las Cosas"** (**"Things in Exact Proportion"**)— another story in the collection—and also of *Los Perseguidos* [(*The Haunted Ones*)]. The latter is unique in that it is a sort of case history, purportedly written by one suffering from a persecution complex, of another victim of the same malady. (pp. 162-63)

D'Annunzio and Poe were not the only writers that influenced Quiroga. In his youth in Montevideo he was one of the leaders of a group of admirers of modernism. Particularly in the sketches in *El Crimen del Otro,* such as **"La Princesa bizantina"** (**"The Byzantine Princess"**), Quiroga was endeavoring to write in the modernist manner and striving for effect through rhythmic and figurative language. In his third work, *Historia de un Amor turbio* [(*An Ill-Fated Love*)], he is not concerned with refinements of style but with psychological analysis. The influence of Dostoevski in this novelette Quiroga acknowledged some years later, and he added that the Russian was one of very few writers in whom he still retained an interest.

In all this early work, in which Quiroga was endeavoring to find himself, individuality was lacking; but nevertheless the direction his later work was to take, in technique and subject matter, is clearly indicated. Like his more mature productions, they are, first of all, impressionistic; for Quiroga aims primarily at creating in the mind of the reader a mood, to which the action of the story is entirely subservient. The prevailing tone is one of gloom, although, as in **"La Muerte del Canario"** (**"The Death of the Canary"**), there are occasional touches of humor. In the subject matter utilized to produce the desired effect, he shows a decided preference for mental abnormalities. Nor in his study of abnormal beings does he overlook himself, a by-no-means well-balanced person. This highly personal element that definitely characterizes Quiroga's writing appears very early. In **"Hashish,"** a sketch in *El Crimen del Otro,* he recounts an experiment upon himself with that narcotic; in **"Los Perseguidos,"** he himself appears by name as one of the abnormal characters, his recent journey to Misiones is mentioned, and his friend Lugones plays a minor rôle. (pp. 163-64)

The stories he wrote in Misiones between 1910 and 1916 brought him a very enviable reputation as a *cuentista* ["short story writer"]; and it was fifteen of the most representative that he republished in *Cuentos de Amor, de Locura y de Muerte* [(**"Stories of Love, Madness, and Death"**)]. According to content they fall roughly into three groups. **"Nuestro primer Cigarro"** (**"Our First Cigar"**), **"El Meningitis y su Sombra"** (**"Meningitis and its Delusion"**), **"Una Estación de Amor"** (**"A Season of Love"**), and **"La Muerte de Isolda"** (**"The Death of Isolde"**), have an intimate tone that connects them at once with Quiroga himself. The first of these is a humorous account of a boyish trick. The second reveals the wildly imaginative and romantic side of Quiroga's mind; it concerns a young girl who during a severe illness fell deeply in love with the narrator of the tale, but—and here the fanciful element enters—was conscious of her infatuation only when delirious. **"Una Estación de Amor,"** of which *Las Sacrificadas* [*(The Sacrificed)*] . . . is a dialogued version, is based without a doubt on his first disappointment in love—a very bitter experience which he seems to have nursed all his life. (pp. 164-65)

Four stories of a very morbid nature, in which critics have detected the influence of Poe, constitute the second group in the collection. Technically, these stories vary considerably. Two relate mere incidents: the suicide craze of a crew that had manned an abandoned ship, **"Buques suicidantes"** (**"Barks that Lure to Death"**); and the pining away of a young bride caused, as was discovered after her death, by a loathsome parasitic animal in her pillow, **"El Almohadón de Pluma"** (**"The Feather Pillow"**). The remaining two stories of this group, however, **"El Solitario"** (**"The Solitaire"**) and **"La Gallina degollada"** (**"The Beheaded Hen"**), come as near meeting the requirements of an artistic short story as anything that Quiroga wrote. Both are told in a very direct and straightforward manner; each creates a very definite mood; the plots, though simple, are well constructed, each having a very definite climax; and the characters—each facing an impending catastrophe—are well delineated. Particularly effective is the contrast, in **"El Solitario,"** between the poor, plodding, and patient jeweler, Kassim, and his vain, frivolous wife. He, sick and weak, worked long hours at his trade to gratify her whims; she, ungrateful and dissatisfied, continually rebuked him for their poverty. In time, too, she was possessed by an inordinate desire for gems which her husband's trade gave her an opportunity to see; on one occasion she became so envious of a beautiful diamond that Kassim was mounting on a scarf-pin as to fly into an ungovernable fit of anger, in which she unwittingly revealed her unfaithfulness. When calmer, she retracted what she had said; but Kassim, as if unmoved by it all, continued his work on the scarf-pin. When he finished it late in the night, he took it to her; then, as she lay asleep, he thrust it into her heart and quietly left the house. The most tragic story that Quiroga wrote, however, is doubtless **"La Gallina degollada,"** in which some idiot sons, imitating the cook whom they had seen behead a chicken, kill their sister, a beautiful child and the only normal one of the children. Both these stories have an urban background and derive dramatic effect from the startling ending and from the dialogue in which the characters reveal themselves; but in neither, as is true of all Quiroga's stories so far discussed, is the setting a vital factor.

On the other hand, the most important element of the seven stories which constitute the third group from this collection is setting or background. With these, twenty-two others—five in *El Salvaje* [*(The Savage)*], seven in *Anaconda*, two in *El Desierto* [*(The Wilderness)*], and three in *Los Desterrados* [*(Exiles)*]—must be considered, for all are concerned in one way or another with the Misiones territory that borders the Paraná River. . . . [Quiroga's] passion for the region—its climate, its topography, its animal life, the human derelicts that had taken refuge there—found expression in this group of stories, which constitute his greatest achievement and give him his main claim to distinction as a writer.

In reading these stories, one senses first Quiroga's own imaginative personality and next his very close personal contact with Misiones. Particularly real and vivid are the details in these stories in regard to climate, topography, and animal life. . . . True to life, also, are many of the events in those tales in which

Quiroga himself is the chief actor—such as **"Los Fabricante de Carbón"** (**"Charcoal Burners"**) and **"Los Destiladores de Naranja"** (**"The Distillers of Oranges"**), which bring to light certain of his unfortunate business ventures and which emphasize his love for scientific experiments. . . . (pp. 165-67)

So real as to be unforgettable are the people of the region, in some thirteen stories of this group. Some of these are types found along the Paraná River in the Misiones section. **"Los Mensú"** (**"Hired Hands"**), which is undoubtedly one of Quiroga's best stories, recounts the experience of two laborers who, after contracting to work in a lumber camp where they faced enslavement and death from malignant fever, succeeded in escaping and, after untold hardships on a raft on the Paraná at flood stage, reached the town of Posadas. The story is remarkable, too, for its unexpected ending. For the laborers, after spending their first night of freedom in a state of drunkenness, signed up the next morning for the very sort of work from which they had just escaped. . . . In other sketches and narratives of this group, types peculiar to the region appear, with all of whom Quiroga had doubtlessly come into direct contact: day laborers, particularly one that had probably worked on Quiroga's own farm (**"El Peón"**); an overbearing landlord who paid dearly for an act of arrogance—**"Una Bofetada"** (**"A Slap"**); European immigrants who had come to take up land in Misiones—**"Inmigrantes"** (**"Immigrants"**) and **"La Voluntad"** (**"Will Power"**); a promoter who, after repeated failures, is finally successful—**"El Monte negro"** (**"Black Mountain"**); an ailing and drunken justice of the peace, of whose corpse the widow had a photograph made, probably by Quiroga himself—**"La Cámara oscura"** (**"The Dark Room"**); and other human flotsam and jetsam that had found a haven in the region (**"Los Desterrados,"** **"Van Houten,"** and **"Tacuara-Mansión"**).

While there is abundant evidence of a keen power of observation in the remaining stories with a Misiones background, realism is somewhat held in check and a freer rein given to romance and imagination. These stories are **"El Salvaje,"** **"Anaconda,"** **"El Regreso de Anaconda"** (**"The Return of Anaconda"**), and possibly two short sketches, **"A la Deriva"** (**"Down Stream"**) and **"El Hombre muerto"** (**"The Dead Man"**), which are identical in theme and technique, and in having a dying man as a single character. (pp. 167-69)

The play of imagination is far greater in **"El Salvaje,"** which, despite the lack of unity between its first and second part, is to be numbered among Quiroga's most original tales. The background is the upper Paraná, above Iguazú Falls, a region of dense forests and heavy rainfall. Tired of civilization, an educated man—no other than Quiroga himself—had taken refuge there, set up a meteorological observatory, and begun sending in reports to Buenos Aires. According to those that he sent in one season, the rainfall was so excessive that an inspector was sent from the central office in Buenos Aires to verify his figures. Shortly after his arrival the rain began to fall as the man had never seen rain fall before, and he had to spend the night with the amateur meteorologist—a tall, thin, pale man with a long black beard and a strange look in his eyes that suggested an unbalanced mind. Rather uncommunicative at first, the meteorologist suddenly asked the inspector if he had ever seen a dinosaur, and when the newcomer acknowledged he had not, the refugee told a long, impossible story of his experiences with one there on the Paraná River. The next morning when the inspector was going down the river he was overcome by the humidity of the air and the stench of the forest after the deluge. This convinced him that the storyteller had experienced in a dream the reality of that past age as fully as if he had actually lived in it.

"La Realidad" (**"Reality"**), as the second part of **"El Salvaje"** is entitled, is a unit in itself and, despite the fact that it deals with the Tertiary period, one of the most dramatic stories that Quiroga wrote. The principal character is a tree-dweller; his habitat is a humid, forest-covered, tropical region such as that of the upper Paraná; and what happens to him—his progress from a herbivorous to a carnivorous animal, from a tree-dweller to a cave-dweller, and from insecurity to security after he accidentally pushed a huge stone against the entrance of the cave—is the story of several stages in the slow upward progress of man.

If one of Quiroga's best stories deals with primitive man, it is not at all strange that he also writes about animals. Two stories of the Misiones group, **"El Alambre de Pua"** (**"Barbed Wire"**) and **"Yaguai,"** show an intimate understanding of domestic animals. Of the animal kingdom, however, snakes fascinate Quiroga most. In many of his stories they appear, very realistically, as actual snakes. But in **"Los Cazadores de Ratas"** (**"Rat Hunters"**), **"Anaconda,"** and its sequel **"El Regreso de Anaconda,"** they are endowed with the power of speech and certain other human characteristics. **"Anaconda,"** his masterpiece, pictures the consternation that ensued when the snakes in a certain district in Misiones learned that their natural enemy, man, had invaded their kingdom. A group of scientists, the serpents discovered, had come to catch venomous snakes, which abounded in that region, in order to extract their poison and make with it a serum that would render their one dangerous weapon ineffective. Preferring to die rather than to submit to such degradation, the snakes convened to discuss means of combating the intruder. In the convention there were two factions, the poisonous and nonpoisonous snakes, whose leaders—a large cobra and Anaconda, a huge boa—moved as much by the natural enmity between them as by the differences in viewpoint, almost came to the point of attacking each other. The cobra's plan, that the snakes in a body should attack the men, was finally adopted; and Anaconda, putting aside personal prejudice, yielded to the general will. The result was disastrous, for the snakes were routed and many were killed. Then followed a terrific battle between the two leaders who had survived; and although Anaconda killed the cobra, she herself at the end of the struggle lay senseless from his deadly poison. The men saved her, however, as they saw in her an ally against the poisonous snakes; and she lingered among them for a year, "nosing about and observing everything," before she returned to her natural habitat further north.

She was in that region, along the upper Paraná, when Quiroga writes of her again—this time in **"El Regreso de Anaconda."** (pp. 169-71)

In these two stories, **"Anaconda"** and **"El Regreso de Anaconda,"** Quiroga appears at his very best. In nothing else that he has written can there be found such a large number of excellent qualities. Here, imagination and observation have joined hands to make them the little masterpieces that they are. The background, particularly the Paraná River at flood stage, is intensely individual. The stories themselves are told with dramatic effect. The characters, whose psychology and bodily movements have been recorded with masterly precision, are interesting for themselves, that is as snakes, not solely, as in nearly all animal stories, for the human characteristics that have been attributed to them. If there is a supreme quality of excellence in these two stories, however, it is the feeling of admiration and of compassion that Quiroga arouses for the great boa herself. The style is very effective, being simple, unadorned by figures of speech but rhythmical.

The only remaining stories with the Misiones background are eight fables (*Cuentos de la Selva para Niños*) [(*South American Jungle Tales*)] that deal with certain animals of that region. . . . The story of the lazy bee is the only one that has a definite moral: in general Quiroga's aim in these fables is primarily to amuse. In nearly all of them, nevertheless, certain moral values are presented more or less indirectly—for instance, the consequences of disobedience on the part of young animals of the forest, and the gratitude that some animals show man in return for kindness. Certain qualities of these stories—their easy-flowing, chatty style, and the free hand that fantasy takes—recall *Alice's Adventures in Wonderland*.

On the other hand, six apologues—five in *El Desierto* and one in *Más Allá* [(*The Great Beyond*)]—differ from the fables in that their purpose is not so much to amuse as to exemplify some philosophic truth. In **"Los tres Besos"** (**"The Three Kisses"**), the only one of the stories in which animals do not figure, he shows that a desire which is long deferred on account of some other consideration finally ceases to be a desire. . . . The tenor of [three of the] stories—**"Juan Darién,"** which has points of similarity with Kipling's "Tiger! Tiger!," **"El León"** (**"The Lion"**), and **"La señorita Leona"** (**"The Young Lioness"**)—is that animals are in many respects superior to man. In each story a wild animal, after coming under the influence of human civilization, abandons it for the animal kingdom.

Motifs of an ethical nature are to be found also in the **"Cuadrivio laico"** (**"The Lay Cuadrivium"**), which is the general title of four stories in *El Salvaje*. One of these, **"Reyes"** (**"Kings"**), may be dismissed at once, as it is only a short prose poem in the "modernista" manner. The remaining three, which are genuine narratives, are significant in that they contain the only references in all of Quiroga's works to any phase of the Christian religion. Slightly ironical, **"La Navidad"** (**"Christmas"**) and **"La Pasión"** (**"The Passion of Jesus"**) recall the style of certain stories of Anatole France; both claim to be incidents in connection with Jesus Christ. When Herod sought Jesus, says the first story, and threatened to slay all the infants of a certain age unless the place where He was born were revealed, Salome, a Jewish girl, disclosed that information to her Roman soldier-lover. Later, to the dismay of Saint Peter, Salome was admitted to Heaven on the ground that she had shown a great tenderness of heart in preferring the betrayal of her God to the death of so many innocent infants. . . . In the last story of the group, **"Corpus"** (**"Corpus Christi"**)—which tells of the persecution and burning, in Geneva at the time of Calvin, of a young German for having made an image of Christ—there is a ring of true feeling. For Quiroga, although unaffected by religion, hated intolerance in any form.

The material in the collections that has not been discussed up to this point is of a heterogeneous nature. Especially is this true in the case of *El Salvaje*, which contains an account of a man that was stung to death by his bees—**"La Reina italiana"** (**"The Italian Queen"**); an essay picturing a scene in Belgium during the World War—**"Los Cementerios belgas"** (**"Belgian Cemeteries"**), one of the few instances in Quiroga's writings of references to contemporary events; five brief narratives—**"Estefanía,"** **"La Llama"** (**"The Flame"**), **"Fanny,"** **"Lucila Strinberg,"** and **"Un Idilio"** (**"An Idyl"**)—all rather plotless, thin in substance, and, if not downright wildly imaginary, at least inconsequential; a humorous skit on the tactics of the Buenos Aires "masher"—**"Tres Cartas y un Pie" ("Three Letters and a Foot")**; and a tragic-comic account of a squabble between a man and his wife, probably based on an actual event in Quiroga's life, when their baby waked them at night by its crying—**"Cuento Para Novios" ("A Story for the Betrothed")**. Of the remaining items in *Anaconda*, there are two articles dealing with climatic phenomena of tropical Africa—**"El Simún"** [**("The Simoom")**] and **"Gloria tropical" ("Tropical Glory")**; a ludicrous tale of the sad experiences of a young man who married the daughter of an expert in dietetics—**"Dieta de Amor" ("The Diet of Love")**; and **"Miss Dorothy Phillips, mi Esposa" ("Miss Dorothy Phillips, My Wife")**, which, aside from being a rambling, highly fanciful story of a young Argentine who went from Buenos Aires to Hollywood and married his favorite "movie" star, contains much light satire on Hollywood actors and actresses. (pp. 172-75)

Of [Quiroga's] ill-fated love affair in Misiones in 1925 with Ana María, he has left a record in his novelette *Pasado Amor (Bygone Love)*, which is mainly of interest as his most personal and definite confessional. Many of the incidents in the life of the chief character, Morán, have been clearly established as autobiographical—his return to Misiones, where everything reminded him of his dead wife; his falling madly in love with Magdalena, whom he had known as a child; and the opposition of her family, who succeeded in thwarting him. Another character, perhaps fictitious, is Alicia Hontou, who took her own life because she was deeply in love with Morán but unable to attract him.

The characterization of Morán is nothing more than a delineation of Quiroga himself; intensity of feeling is the quality that distinguishes him. It reveals itself in that inner force that drove him to work hard physically at the things that interested him: the clearing and cultivation of his fields, boat making, rowing up and down the Paraná River with its dangerous rapids. Highstrung, over-wrought, verging on madness, in his love affair with Magdalena he acted more like an adolescent than a middleaged man. So immoderate is his sentimentality as to arouse disgust in readers.

In this work Quiroga pays more attention than usual to the setting. Here, it is the country itself, the "mate" fields and the Paraná River, and the people of the region, rather than the animals and snakes, with which he concerns himself. An insight is afforded into the lives of three families of different social levels and points of view. There are comments, too, on the public dances, on that inevitable social institution, the bar, and on labor unions—organizations which had come into existence since Quiroga's earlier residence there. Interesting in themselves, these details of manners and customs fail, however, to contribute to the artistry of the novel; rather than being fused with the story, they seem entirely extraneous.

To the troubles that marred the last years of his life—domestic dissensions, financial difficulties, and ill health—are traceable in a measure the somber themes that characterize in general his last collection of stories, *Más Allá*. In at least seven of its eleven stories the preoccupation of the author with death, suicide, insanity, and an existence beyond the tomb seems not only to indicate an unhealthy state of mind but to presage his own tragic end. (pp. 175-76)

Two short sketches, **"Las Moscas" ("Flies")** and **"El Hijo" ("The Son")**, present very vividly states of mind: the former, that of a man, who, having fallen and broken his back, knows by the large green flies that begin to swarm about him that death is nigh; and the latter, the mental anxiety of a father shaken by a premonition of the death of his young son. Both of these sketches are very similar in technique to **"A la Deriva"** and **"El Hombre muerto."**

A tone of levity, rather than of gloom, characterizes . . . [other] stories in *Más Allá*. Based on a lapse of memory, one of these, **"La Ausencia" ("A Case of Amnesia")**, has the best plot in the collection. Roldán Berger, an engineer, finds himself one day with no knowledge of the last six years of his life but engaged to a very beautiful and intellectual woman who had been attracted to him by a renowned philosophical work attributed to him. The matter-of-fact engineer would have broken the engagement at once, but his physician counseled otherwise. Terribly bored, after his marriage, by the intellectuals who pursued him, he confessed to his wife that he had not written the book. As he had succeeded in making himself loved for his own sake, she did not forsake him; instead, before an open fireplace, they tore the leaves from the book and cast them into the flames. (p. 177)

Quiroga's entire literary output is not extensive—one narrative in dialogue, two novelettes, and some ninety-six short stories, sketches, and articles. The total impact, too, of his work is slight. Thin in substance in general, it is on the whole not much better than the usual type of journalistic material that fills the pages of the literary supplement of Sunday editions of newspapers or of weekly periodicals such as *Caras y Caretas* and *El Hogar*, in which much of it appeared. The influence of Poe on Quiroga in regard to themes and motifs is indisputable, but not in regard to his short-story technique, for only a few of his stories—**"El Solitario," "La Gallina degollada,"** and **"Los Mensú"**—can be cited as examples of fair narration. His forte, however, does not lie in narration or in the analysis of human character. It is his ability to transfer to his pages the atmosphere of Misiones, the scene of so many of his joys and sorrows, that catches the attention of his readers and gives him distinction as a writer. Of the many stories that have Misiones as their background, those that are outstanding are very limited in number. For only in three—**"El Salvaje," "Anaconda,"** and **"El Regreso de Anaconda"**—does his genius find its highest expression. But they are enough to entitle him to international fame as a short-story writer. (p. 178)

Jefferson Rea Spell, "Renowned Short-Story Writer, Horacio Quiroga," in his Contemporary Spanish-American Fiction, *The University of North Carolina Press, 1944, pp. 153-78.*

JEAN FRANCO (essay date 1969)

[*Franco is an English critic and educator who has written and edited numerous studies of Latin American literature. In the following excerpt, she discusses Quiroga as a regional writer who skillfully used the background of the Chaco and Misiones regions as an important element in his stories.*]

An essential factor in good regionalist literature is that the natural environment should be more than a setting for a human drama. The great regional novels, *La vorágine, Canaima, Don Segundo Sombra*, are those in which the human drama and the environment are inseparable. This is also true of Quiroga's best stories. From his early model, Poe, he had learned to concentrate on human personalities at breaking-point. After settling in the tropics, he began to write stories in which individuals found themselves in extreme danger or hardship, for people tended to show their real worth when natural hazards enabled them to display qualities that would otherwise have lain dormant. In [*Cuentos de amor, de locura y de muerte (Stories of Love, Madness and Death), Anaconda, El salvaje (The Savage), Los desterrados (The Exiles)*] . . . , the situations are often as bizarre as those of Poe, but they arise out of the combination of human weakness and carelessness, accident and a pitiless natural environment.

In both the Chaco and Misiones, man cannot control nature. He can only study the environment and hope to survive by pitting his courage, tenacity and resourcefulness against the overwhelming natural hazards. An accident or a moment of carelessness can change a normal working day into a fierce struggle for life. It was this that fascinated Quiroga. Nowhere else could he have found situations in which chance or accident, human will and natural force were all to play their part. Even the best human beings have defects which an accident can convert into tragic flaws.

A great majority of Quiroga's stories, then, follow a similar pattern. The protagonist is never an intellectual. He is usually a pioneer, a farmer or labourer in the Misiones or Chaco going about his daily work. The accident happens: a snake bites him, the river waters rise, a long period of drought alters the conditions of life. Suddenly he becomes a lonely man fighting for life.

Two of Quiroga's best stories follow this pattern: **'A la deriva'** ['Drifting'] and **'Un hombre muerto'** ['A Dead Man']. In both these stories, a fatal accident occurs in the first few lines and the protagonist dies at the end. The death struggle forms the only theme or plot. But in neither story is the death quite 'accidental'. In **'A la deriva'** a man bitten by a deadly snake paddles frantically down-river to get help, but he had quarrelled with his nearest neighbour. His cries for help are not answered, and he floats helplessly away between the dark cliffs along the Paraná. The snake-bite was an accident, but the man had in a sense contributed to his own death when, years before, he had quarrelled with his nearest neighbour. In **'El hombre muerto'**, a man who is tired after a day's work in the banana plantations slips and falls on a machete knife. The entire drama consists of the attempts of the man's 'I' to retain its hold on reality until the final disintegration of the personality when the plantation, 'his' knife and 'his' horse cease to be 'his'. But again the accident arises out of the man's character. Obsessed with clearing his banana plantation, he had neglected to see to the handle of his knife which needed replacing and was overtired when the accident took place; and there is a certain dramatic irony in the fact that the plantation of which he is so proud indirectly brings about his death. . . . And we see how, though dying, the man still assumes that he is owner of the property, how his mind still cannot adjust to the idea of death but goes on making plans for the future, for repairing the wire fence. At the same time, notice that the author never presents any thought too complex for the mind of a simple farmer.

Though Quiroga is not directly concerned with society in his stories, criticism of social organisation is often implicit. For Quiroga, all man-made institutions are fallible, fragile and ultimately unimportant, when set beside the mightiness of nature but he expresses this view indirectly, often by showing the failure of human organisation when confronted with natural hazards. In **'Los fabricantes de carbón'** ['The Charcoal Burners'], two men plan to set up a charcoal-burning furnace in Misiones and the story ironically comments on their careful calculations—the structure of the furnace, temperatures, etc.—

and the natural and human elements which defy calculation. There is thus a conflict between human reason and will which seeks to plan, structure and control the environment, and nature which defies such control. This also helps to explain why Quiroga should so often choose animals as the protagonists of his stories, since their instinctual knowledge and acts are totally opposed to the willed and motivated actions of human beings. This conflict is the subject of **'Anaconda',** a story in which the snakes rise up to fight a war to the death with a group of men in charge of a laboratory which manufactures snake serum. The snakes instinctively defend the natural order. Men seek to destroy this in order to bring nature under their control. In this story, the humans win a victory, but usually defiance of nature brings punishment, as in **'La insolación'** ['Sun-stroke'] where Mr Jones drives himself pitilessly to clear his cotton plantation during a hot spell. His dogs instinctively realise that they must conserve their energy and rest in the shade whereas their master kills himself from sunstroke in his anxiety to get a job done. In stories such as this, nature is no passive element but an actively destructive force, a threat to human identity. . . . [One] cannot talk of a natural 'background'; here as in other stories natural hazards take on the role of the Fates in the Greek drama, visiting on the human protagonist the punishment his own nature has destined him for.

Though social protest has no place in Quiroga's stories, he does not avoid stories about economic exploitation. His attitude towards social organisation inevitably led him to see the dehumanising effect of the semi-slave conditions in which many labourers worked, and several of his most striking stories illustrate this. **'Los mensús'** is about two *mensuales*—labourers hired on a monthly basis—who contract debts in a company store, are forced to work off the debts on a plantation where they are ruthlessly driven to work even when ill, and who escape. One of them dies during the escape bid, the other finds his way to the river port, only to contract debts and start the same fatal trajectory once again. In **'Una bofetada'** ['A Blow'], Quiroga tells a monstrous story of hatred between a foreman and an Indian labourer. The foreman slaps the labourer, who harbours his hatred for years until circumstances put the foreman in his power. The Indian manages to disarm him of his gun and whip, and proceeds to beat the man to death along the lonely tracks beween the plantations. Often in Quiroga's stories the landscape has symbolic features, as in the following passage:

> Korner no longer moved. The *mensú* then cut the ropes of the raft and getting into the canoe, he tied an end to the stern of the raft and paddled vigorously.
>
> Despite the slightness of the drag on the immense mass of logs, the initial impulse was enough. The raft turned slightly, entered the current and then the man cut the end.
>
> The sun had gone in some time before. The burning atmosphere of two hours before had now a funereal freshness and quiet. Beneath the sky which was still green, the raft drifted and turned round; it entered into the transparent shadow of the Parguayan coast to reappear again in the distance as a mere black line.

The dead foreman has reached the end of life's journey. The *peon* he had once beaten is now triumphant but no emotion is shown other than the quiet preparations to float the body downstream. All the emotional content of the passage lies in the description of the twilight and the boat floating away down the river. The heat has died down, the hours of torment are over, the peace and coolness of death have come. It is precisely this objectification of the emotions that gives the story a power that many orthodox social-protest stories do not have. For here we are shown how men behave under humiliation and oppression and we are shown this without rhetoric.

Quiroga's most bizarre and probably his best collection is *Los desterrados [The Exiles],* particularly the section he called 'Los tipos' which gives sketches of characters whom he had known in Misiones. Here we meet the dregs of humanity, drunkards and dipsomaniacs who have come to end their lives away from social censure. These 'real-life' stories have more horror in them than the fantasy stories Quiroga wrote under the influence of Poe. One of the characters, for instance, dies of exposure after drinking wood alcohol out of a lamp; another dies in a dipsomaniac delirium; a labourer disappears and all that is ever found of him are his boots hanging from a tree. These lonely desperate men were probably not unlike Quiroga himself. . . . (pp. 217-22)

Quiroga's importance is not only his contribution to regional writing but also his contribution to the art of the short story. His **'Decálogo del perfecto cuentista' ['Decalogue of the Perfect Short Story Writer';** see excerpt dated 1927] stresses the need for economy and intensity and shows that he was conscious of the scope and limitations of the genre. He can certainly be counted one of the Latin-American masters of the genre. (p. 222)

> Jean Franco, *"Regionalism in the Novel and Short Story," in her* An Introduction to Spanish-American Literature, *Cambridge at the University Press, 1969, pp. 193-230.**

CHARLES PARAM   (essay date 1972)

[In the following excerpt, Param discusses what he believes to be the autobiographical nature of the theme of personal courage in eight of Quiroga's stories.]

Perhaps the two most obvious elements in Horacio Quiroga's tropical short stories are a Nature dangerous to man and a kind of fatalism. The conventional summary description of these stories has not changed down through the years, so powerful are the forces of Nature on the rampage and so pervading is the mood of fatalism. Alfred Coester, for example, wrote over forty years ago: "Nature is really the chief personage in his stories. It is she who defeats man and beast in their struggle for survival." (p. 428)

The common description of these stories might lead one to believe that they are principally a recognition of the power of Nature. Too, one might perhaps think that Quiroga used Nature to comment generally on the frailties of man. While this is possible, it is also a possibility that he used Nature only as a backdrop for the action and the action as a means for the revelation or development of the character of his personages. If this is the case, then man and not Nature is the most important aspect of many of his tropical stories. We believe that the latter is very possibly the case in regard to some of his stories, and we believe that the direction taken by his characters is dictated by the author's attitude toward a certain and specific point in his view of man. Our study here will deal with eight of those stories in which that specific point in Quiroga's works is evident.

The eight narratives to be studied here are the following: **"El simún," "El monte negro," "Los pescadores de vigas," "Los fabricantes de carbón," "Gloria tropical," "En la noche," "La voluntad,"** and **"Los inmigrantes."** Several of Quiroga's approximately 200 stories present animals as the chief characters in a tropical setting. There are approximately forty others, depending on how one classifies them, also set in the tropics or the desert, but dealing with men's struggles against a hostile environment in every aspect that such conditions include. These stories range from the fantastic to the comical, but most of them are somber in tone and demonstrate a serious attempt to achieve realism.

There exists in the eight stories we have singled out for study a common bond that sets them apart from the remainder of the tropical narratives. This common bond, courage, is found in strength in these eight tales where man is challenged by those hostile conditions arrayed against him. The protagonist, an ordinary man, goes far beyond the limits of ordinary human endurance and becomes, in defeat or in victory, a kind of superman. In seven of the eight stories there is a secondary character with whom to contrast the development of the protagonist as he becomes an extraordinary individual. In view of the large amount of autobiographical inspiration in Quiroga's works we believe that these stories of courage are vivid brush strokes in the portrait of Quiroga, the man and the artist.

It will be apparent upon reading these eight stories that man's destiny, his success or failure, is generally left up to himself. If he resists heroically he has at least a chance to achieve his goal. Courage, purpose, and self-discipline are required of him. There is a type of fatalism in the fact that with the exception of the husband and wife situation (**"En la noche"** and **"La voluntad"**), the employer and employee relationship, (**"El monte negro"**), and the business association, (**"Los fabricantes de carbón"**), the protagonist cannot count on others for significant help. A brief outline of the eight stories will show how those admirable human qualities of courage, purpose, and self-discipline distinguish some of Quiroga's many protagonists.

In **"El simún"** the visitor tells the reader of his negative reaction toward the eternal rains, the dull gray-green panorama, and the monotony of life in that isolated weather station. He is astonished at the tranquility with which the attendant, the Frenchman, lives under such circumstances. The latter tells him how his experience as a legionnaire in the Sahara Desert taught him to face Nature's onslaughts. He was defeated on that occasion, his career ruined, and a strong friendship with another legionnaire destroyed. He is determined not to be defeated again.

Braccamonte, in **"El monte negro,"** is determined to complete a most difficult project he has undertaken, the building of bridges and a road through an area swept by high waters, because his pride and self-respect will not let him quit. His partner reaches the point of deciding to abandon the work because he can no longer tolerate the floodwaters, the swarms of insects, and the inept workers. Only Braccamonte's most eloquent arguments persuade him to remain, and they manage to complete the project.

Candiyú, the *pescador* ["fisherman"] is **"Los pescadores de vigas,"** enters the raging waters of the Paraná at floodtide in order to fish out some very particular logs. These logs are to be traded to the secondary character, the Englishman, for an old phonograph. The logs, "palo rosa," will be used in the making of some furniture in the Englishman's house. Candiyú is successful; he defeats the waters, secures the logs, and gets his coveted phonograph. What makes the feat an extraordinary one is that Candiyú is crippled at the onset of the story, having been incapacitated by a serious illness and forced to "retire" from filching logs. The Englishman's failure to recognize Candiyú's feat is in sharp contrast to the latter's heroic success.

There is not a great deal of difference between Dréver and Rienzi, the partners in **"Los fabricantes de carbón."** Both struggle under the strain and handicap of extreme weather conditions, primitive tools, and inept laborers. Dréver suffers the greater burden, due to the serious illness of his small daughter. It is Rienzi, however, who cracks under the pressure; he suddenly and unexpectedly announces that he is leaving for home, for Buenos Aires, and the project is never completed.

"Gloria tropical," like **"El Simún,"** is set in two places, South America and Africa. Málter, assigned to work on an island off the African coast noted for its abundant vegetation and its deadly fever, goes to his new post confident that he will overcome all obstacles. Although warned not to over-exert himself and not to undertake any unnecessary projects, he nevertheless throws himself into his work, adding a garden to his activities. Weeds and other choking vegetation spring up again almost overnight after being eradicated; the fever strikes Málter; his duties press him; and finally, after fighting the incredible growth of unwanted plants and struggling to stay afoot even though he is growing weaker day by day, he is forced to return home. (pp. 428-29)

"En la noche" is a rarity among Quiroga's tropical stories in that the protagonist is a woman. She and her husband take their small boat into the flooded and raging Paraná in search of medical aid when a deadly poisonous reptile bites the man. The story of her heroic and successful efforts to save her husband's life, (fourteen hours at the oars), evokes amazement and admiration in the traveller, the secondary character, a man who previously had fearfully observed the rampaging river. (p. 430)

Bibikoff's wife, in **"La voluntad,"** fits the same mold. **"La voluntad"** has an additional interesting oddity: there are dual protagonists, as the husband and wife share equally in the conflict against hostile surroundings, living in abject poverty in an alien land. The narrator tells how Bibikoff, too ill most of the time to work, suspiciously eyes every man that appears at their humble farm. The wife, dull of countenance, work-weary, and ugly to gaze upon, does the farm work when Bibikoff cannot work, does her own household chores, and weaves baskets for sale in order to earn a few pennies. At the end of three years the couple, one at a time, returns to Russia, and the narrator finds in Bibikoff's original manuscript the reason for their stay in the tropics. Bibikoff, an officer in the Russian army, had boasted that he could survive anywhere in the world by the sweat of his brow and with no help from anyone. He did what he said he could do, by surviving three years of poverty that exceeded that of the humblest "mensú" ["contract worker"]. . . . The narrator is . . . unstinting in his praise of Bibikoff's wife, stating that the man had no reason to be jealous, for it was not passion that she aroused in the narrator, but the highest respect and admiration for her. She was unselfish, courageous, and devoted to her husband, willing to suffer anything for him. In this story it is the narrator who provides the contrast with the two protagonists.

The final story in this group where courage is the outstanding element is **"Los immigrantes."** The principals, a Polish couple

making their way through the tropics toward their new home, become separated from their party when the woman, pregnant and ill, cannot maintain the pace. When she becomes too ill to walk her husband carries her on his back. She dies, but he continues to carry her. . . . The story ends as the man, delirious and believing that they are at home again in Poland, dies with his wife's body beside him.

There are perhaps other stories in which courage has a role of some importance, but in these eight narratives it is the outstanding element. Man, then, is the important aspect of the stories, not Nature. Man's courage comes to the front when circumstances require it. This is not the case in many of Quiroga's stories.

Alberto Zum Felde has noted that "Lo fantástico, lo heroico, lo trágico" found virgin ground in Quiroga's fertile imagination. Quiroga, in striving for perfection in his art, attempted to create a character that would justify his own creative effort. (pp. 430-31)

In the eight stories discussed here man's enemy is principally Nature in her various angry moods as she affects man's endeavors. There are other stories in the tropical setting in which man's enemies are the creatures of Nature, such as poisonous reptiles and insects, wild animals, and man's own carelessness. There are still other narratives in which man's enemy is other men. In all these stories the protagonist has the opportunity to resist his enemy, but regardless of the element of resistance, the general rule seems to be that he cannot count on significant help from others. As we have stated previously, the exceptions are the husband and wife situation, the employer and employee relationship, and the business partner associations. In the husband and wife situation, however, there is a variation: the woman in **"A la deriva"** makes no effort to help her husband avoid death after being bitten by a poisonous snake, and the man dies. Close friendships are rare in Quiroga's tropical stories, and people helping one another in adversity are conspicuously absent. The majority of relationships are based on commercial interest, a desire for revenge, or mutual suffering at the hands of a "patrón." Possibly there is a connection between the author's life and this situation in his works, as a brief examination of Quiroga in relation to his associations with other people tends to indicate.

To establish the strength of the autobiographical impulse in Quiroga's works we should take note of these aspects of his life: his experiences with drugs, farming, love affairs, and caring for his motherless children in Misiones; his guilt complexes; his childhood memories; and his failures as an industrialist. Rodríguez Monegal finds these and other elements in Quiroga's life as material for many of his stories.

Rodríguez Monegal also notes a certain compassion, a tenderness, with which Quiroga regarded some of his characters. This tenderness has its roots in Quiroga's own nature and is expressed toward his characters in **"El desierto,"** and in regard to Van-Houten, João Pedro, Juan Brun, the unnamed man in **"El hombre muerto,"** and in *Cuentos de la selva*, the children's stories. . . . The critic sees Quiroga as two men, then: the master of horror and the master of tenderness. . . . [Pedro] Orgambide also sees a tender quality in Quiroga, a compassion for people that influenced some of his works, particularly the *Cuentos de la selva*. Orgambide states that these stories served to find again the innocence of Quiroga's own boyhood. . . . There is an undeniable atmosphere of compassion in the children's stories, and the father and children relationships in **"Los**

fabricantes de carbón" and **"El desierto"** are beautiful moments indeed. However, whether the author regarded with compassion the brawling, drinking, murdering, and generally shiftless characters in **"Los desterrados"** is a point the individual reader will have to decide for himself.

In regard to the eight stories with which our study is concerned, it would seem that there exists a type of compassion the author expresses toward the principals. But we believe that such compassion, or tenderness, does not result from those causes and sources noted by Orgambide and Rodríguez Monegal in relation to the points discussed in their studies. We believe that the "dark" side of Quiroga is responsible for the unique character of the protagonists in this limited number of stories. (pp. 431-32)

The indications are . . . that Quiroga was a very complex person. The courage exhibited by the protagonists of the eight stories discussed comes from the pessimistic side of Quiroga's nature; and of great importance in establishing this idea are Quiroga's known relationships with friends and his seeming frequent reluctance to treat strangers civilly. . . . Quiroga often reached out to his friends, but perhaps as many times he sat silent and incommunicative in their midst. This could indicate any of several things, but it is very possible that he was never really certain of the enduring qualities of those friendships. If this was the case, perhaps he was correct; there were only "unos cuantos compañeros de oficio" ['a few fellow members of the trade"] at his funeral. As the cancer he knew was eating his life away grew in size and in intensity of pain, Quiroga, in those last letters to friends, was reaching out to people he had known, calling for moral support. This is quite different from the situations in so many of his stories, where his protagonists had no one to whom to call and consequently had to face their crises alone.

The possibility that he might not have been certain of the steadfastness of the friendships he had formed might be a reason for the lack of close friendships in his stories in general. There is another possibility to consider, and it concerns the horror and tragedy that hovered about him and the people close to him. The best-known examples are the accidental death of his father by gunshot wounds, the paralysis and then suicide of his stepfather, the suicide of his wife, and still another shooting in which his own hand accidentally discharged the pistol that killed one of his best friends. Perhaps the element of tragedy, or the possibility of new tragedies, caused those many periods of silence as Quiroga sat in the midst of friends. His silence could have been a wall, a protective wall, that rose up about him to shield him from additional grief, should those associations become too intimate and then end in tragedy.

We have presented, then, these provocative possibilities that Quiroga never felt he could really count on his friends and that he subconsciously wished to avoid close friendships because of the reasons listed above. Whether either is true, it is apparent that he protected his fictional characters from the too-intimate as well as from the fair-weather friendship so common in real life. In addition, he rarely permitted his characters to help one another. In only one tropical short story does it occur that an "outsider" helps a principal character. (pp. 433-34)

By refusing to permit his characters to form strong friendships, and by refusing to allow them to help one another in adversity, Quiroga forced them to depend on themselves and their own resources. To let them all fail in their struggles, to refuse to permit any of them to act heroically at times, and to deny them courage, would be to deny that man in general, and Quiroga

himself in particular, is capable of standing on his own two feet. Quiroga created his characters, turned them out into a hostile world, deprived them of the comfort of mutual support, but he gave them the opportunity to prove their own worth. To some of them, to the protagonists in the eight stories we have discussed, he gave the courage, purpose, and self-discipline that made them extraordinary people. It would be difficult to deny that this is a manifestation of compassion, of tenderness, for some of his characters. Since the select people are found in some of his tropical tales, it would seem that the usual capsule or formula description of the tropical stories as a whole should be amended to reflect the element of man's courage, rather than to stress his usual defeat as he struggles against the forces of Nature in an unfriendly environment. (p. 434)

Charles Param, "Horacio Quiroga and His Exceptional Protagonists," in Hispania, *Vol. 55, No. 3, September, 1972, pp. 428-35.*

GEORGE D. SCHADE   (essay date 1976)

[*In the following excerpt from his introduction to* The Decapitated Chicken, and Other Stories, *Schade explores the themes and techniques of Quiroga's short stories.*]

Commentators have tended to discount the significance or merit of some of Quiroga's early works, such as the longish story **"The Pursued."** Recently this tale has received more favorable critical attention. [Margaret Sayers Peden, the translator of *The Decapitated Chicken, and Other Stories*] . . . , maintains that **"The Pursued"** is the most modern piece he wrote because of what it anticipates. It is undeniably one of Quiroga's more ambiguous and inscrutable stories, lending itself to various interpretations as it elaborates on the theme of madness.

Another early story, **"The Feather Pillow,"** first published in 1907, is a magnificent example of his successful handling of the Gothic tale, reminiscent of Poe, whom he revered as master. The effects of horror, something mysterious and perverse pervading the atmosphere, are all there from the beginning of the story, and Quiroga skillfully, gradually readies the terrain, so that we are somewhat prepared for, though we do not anticipate, the sensational revelation at the end. But this story takes on much more meaning and subtlety when we realize that the anecdote can be interpreted on a symbolical level: the ailing Alicia suffers from hallucinations brought on by her husband's hostility and coldness, for he is the real monster. (p. xi)

"Anaconda," which describes a world of snakes and vipers and how they battle men and also one another, is one of Quiroga's most celebrated stories. It moves at a more leisurely pace than the typical Quiroga tale, with spun-out plot, lingering over realistic details. The characters in this ophidian world are more compelling than believable, and the animal characterization is not perhaps as striking as that of some shorter narratives like **"Sunstroke."** But Quiroga, the fluent inventor at work, can almost always make something interesting happen. **"Anaconda"** lies on the ill-defined frontier between the long story and the novella and will gainsay those who think Quiroga sacrifices everything to rapid narrative. Consequently, it loses something of the dramatic intensity of other stories, despite its original title of "A Drama in the Jungle: The Vipers' Empire." The tight-knit, tense structure we can perceive in **"Drifting,"** **"The Dead Man,"** and many other Quiroga stories is considerably slackened here. On the other hand, Quiroga compensates for this by offering us a story of exuberant imagination, rich in irony, with abundant satirical implications about man and his behavior. Like the *Jungle Tales,* "Anaconda" will have a special appeal for children, but, unlike the former, it is essentially directed to a mature audience.

If we examine Quiroga's stories attentively, we will find moments full of vision concerning mankind, often illuminating a whole character or situation in a flash. Quiroga has an astute awareness of the problems besetting man on every side, not only the pitfalls of savage Nature but also those pertaining to human relationships. Man is moved by greed and overweening ambition, hampered by fate, and often bound by circumstances beyond his control. Quiroga penetrates the frontiers of profound dissatisfaction and despair felt by man. His vision is clear and ruthless, and his comments on human illusions can be withering. Yet it is man's diversity that emerges in these stories, his abjectness and his heroism. Though Quiroga never palliates man's faults and weaknesses, the heroic virtues of courage, generosity, and compassion stand out in many of his stories.

All this rich and multifarious human material is shaped and patterned into story form by a master craftsman. Quiroga was very conscious of the problems involved in the technique and art of the short story, and, like Edgar Allan Poe and other masters of the genre, he wrote about them. His most famous document on technique is what he dubbed a **"Manual of the Perfect Short Story Writer"** [see excerpt dated 1927], a succinct decalogue filled with cogent and compelling advice. The usual warnings stressing economy of expression are here: for instance, "Don't use unnecessary adjectives"; and also those concerned with careful advance planning: "Don't start to write without knowing from the first word where you are going. In a story that comes off well, the first three lines are as important as the last three." It is easy to find apt examples of the latter dictum in Quiroga's work: **"Drifting," "The Dead Man," "The Decapitated Chicken," "The Feather Pillow,"** and so on. . . .

The last commandment in Quiroga's decalogue to the person desiring to write perfect short stories is probably the most suggestive: "Don't think about your friends when you write or the impression your story will make. Tell the tale as if the story's only interest lay in the small surroundings of your characters, of which you might have been one. In no other way is *life* achieved in the short story." Quite rightly Quiroga emphasizes the word *life,* for it is this elusive and vital quality which lies at the core of his stories. The idea that the author or his narrator might be one of the characters is also significant, for he often was one of the characters, at least in some aspect, or felt that he was one of them.

Certainly in his best stories Quiroga practiced the economy he talks about in his manual and which is characteristic of good short-story writers. Almost every page will bear testimony to this laconic quality. It is a brevity which excludes everything redundant but nothing which is really significant. Wonderful feats of condensation are common, as in **"The Dead Man,"** where he shows his powers in dramatic focus on a single scene, or in **"Drifting,"** a stark story in which everything seems reduced to the essential, the indispensable. The brief opening scene of **"Drifting,"** where a man is bitten by a venomous snake, contains the germs of all that comes afterward. The language is terse and pointed, the situation of tremendous intensity, the action straightforward and lineal. Everything moves in an unbroken line from beginning to end, like an arrow to its target, to use Quiroga's phrase referring to technique in the short story. The title, too, is particularly appropriate: while the dying protagonist literally drifts in his canoe downriver seeking

aid, we see him helplessly adrift on the river of life, unable to control his fatal destiny from the moment the snake sinks its fangs into his foot.

In **"Drifting," "The Son," "The Dead Man,"** and other stories, Quiroga plays on a life/death vibration, juxtaposing the two. While the throes of death slowly diminish the protagonist of **"The Dead Man,"** Nature and the landscape surrounding him pulsate with life—the ordinary domestic quality of daily life he is so accustomed to—so that he cannot accept the fact of his dying. Our curiosity is kept unfalteringly alive by Quiroga's dramatic technique. At his finest moments Quiroga reaches and maintains a high degree of emotional intensity, as in the three stories cited above, which have in common their magnificent treatment of death. Quiroga flinches from none of the difficulties perhaps implicit in this theme. In his dealing with death he is natural and matter-of-fact; we find no mawkish romantic sentimentality, no glossing over of realistic attributes, and no gloating over ugly clinical details characteristic of naturalistic writers.

There is also much suggestion and implication, rather than outright telling, in Quiroga's best work. **"The Dead Man"** is probably the most skillful instance of this technique, but interesting examples abound throughout Quiroga's narratives. A case in point is the heartfelt story **"The Son,"** where the protagonist father, suffering from hallucinations, imagines that his young son, who went hunting in the forest, has had a fatal accident. The father stumbles along in a frenzy, cutting his way through the thick and treacherous jungle, seeking a sign of the boy. Suddenly he stifles a cry, for he has seen something in the sky. The suggestion, confirmed later by the boy's death at the end of the story, is that the father saw a buzzard.

Dialogue does not play a heavy role in Quiroga's work. Occasionally we listen to scraps of talk, but, in the main, his stories do not move by dialogue; they are thrust along by overt action. Exceptions to this rule are **"Anaconda"** and some other animal tales. A stunning example of Quiroga's handling of dialogue occurs in **"A Slap in the Face"** toward the end of the story where the peon wreaks his terrible revenge on Korner, beating the boss into a bloody, inert pulp with his riding whip. Here Quiroga contrasts most effectively Korner's silence, symbolical of his beaten condition, with the peon's crackling commands *Levántate* ("Get up") and *Caminá* ("Get going"), the only words uttered in the latter part of this violent, sadistic scene. The word *caminá,* repeated four times at slight intervals, suggests an onomatopoeic fusion with the sound of the cracking whip, another instance of Quiroga's technical genius—language functioning to blend auditory effects with content.

Narrative interest seems to prevail over other elements which often dominate in the short story, such as the poetical, symbolical, or philosophical. And Quiroga does not have a social ax to grind. But some of the most trenchant social commentary in Spanish American fiction can be perceived in his stories, particularly those concerned with the exploitation of Misiones lumberjacks, like **"Los mensú"** (**"The Monthly Wage Earners"**) and **"A Slap in the Face."** In these tales no preaching is involved. Quiroga is clearly on the side of the oppressed but does not express their point of view exclusively. Consequently, the reader draws his own conclusions, and the social impact is more deeply felt.

Setting, as well as narrative technique, is vitally important to Quiroga, because it is inseparable from the real, the ordinary, domestic, day-to-day experience of human existence. Quiroga's feelings are bound up in place, in his adopted corner of Argentina, Misiones province, rather than the urban centers of Buenos Aires or Montevideo, where he also lived. He is vastly attracted to the rugged jungle landscape, where the majority of his best stories take place.... And he makes us feel the significance of his setting, too—the symbolic strength of the rivers, especially the Paraná, and the power and hypnotic force of its snake-infested jungles. So does this dot on the map that is Misiones come throbbingly alive for us. It is not just a framework in which to set his stories but an integral part of them, of Quiroga himself, brimming over with drama and life.

In the best stories, . . . action is perfectly illustrative: the stories have not only movement but also depth. The apparent spareness allows for a greater complexity and suggestion. A fine short story should have implications which will continue to play in the reader's mind when the story is done and over, as we can attest in **"The Feather Pillow," "The Dead Man,"** and almost all the stories [in *The Decapitated Chicken*]. . . . We are struck at the end of **"A Slap in the Face"** by the dual function of the river, which provides the final solution. The peon thrusts the almost lifeless, despicable Korner onto a raft where he will drift inevitably to his death, while the peon takes off in a boat in the opposite direction toward haven on the Brazilian shore. Thus the river assumes the role of justice, meting out death to the guilty and life to the accused. **"Juan Darién"** is probably one of the most subtle and interesting stories Quiroga ever penned. Rich in suggestions, it opens up to us a world of fantastic reality in which the protagonist is a tiger/boy. At one point in the story Quiroga has the inspector say that truth can be much stranger than fiction. Interpretations of this story will vary, but the most rewarding one may well be that of Juan Darién as a Christ-like figure. (pp. xii-xvii)

The contemporary Argentine Julio Cortázar, a writer very unlike Quiroga but also topflight in the short-story genre, has pointed out perspicaciously Quiroga's best and most lasting qualities: he knew his trade in and out; he was universal in dimension; he subjected his themes to dramatic form, transmitting to his readers all their virtues, all their ferment, all their projection in depth; he wrote tautly and described with intensity so that the story would make its mark on the reader, nailing itself in his memory.

Quiroga's is an art that speaks to us clearly and passionately, charged with the emotion of his jungle setting. The action is usually of heroic simplicity. Quiroga does not transcribe life; he dramatizes it. His vision is fresh, intense, dramatic. He seems caught up in it, and so are we. (p. xviii)

> *George D. Schade, in an introduction to* The Decapitated Chicken, and Other Stories *by Horacio Quiroga, edited and translated by Margaret Sayers Peden, University of Texas Press, 1976, pp. ix-xviii.*

GEORGE GARRETT (essay date 1976)

[*Garrett, an American poet, novelist, short story writer, dramatist, and critic, explores in his fiction and poetry such Christian themes as the problems of retaining faith and values in a fallen world. Best known in the 1950s and 1960s for his poetry, Garrett's major work is generally agreed to be the novel* Death of the Fox *(1971), an imaginative treatment of the last two days of Sir Walter Raleigh's life. In the following excerpt, Garrett discusses the stories in* The Decapitated Chicken, and Other Stories.*]*

Quiroga's stories express an easy familiarity and intimate fascination with violence, physical suffering, and not so much

death as the experience of dying. . . . Violence, suffering and death are not conventionally treated by Quiroga. Writing as a veteran of hard experience, he is sophisticated and not in the least sentimental. Certainly in the later stories he is clear and matter-of-fact without being, in a literary sense, morbid. Although these stories deal with physical and psychological suffering in painful and cumulative detail, at no time does the suffering of a character become the occasion of an exercise in self-pity. Perhaps typical is the reaction of the worker in **"A Slap in the Face"** who, having waited years to revenge himself for a gratuitous injustice, whips his enemy into bloody insensibility and sends him off to his death on a river raft. He must also flee the country, and here is his final reaction and the end of the story:

> "I'm going to miss the old gang," he murmured, as he bound a rag around his exhausted wrist. And with a cold glance at the raft, moving toward inevitable disaster, he concluded, under his breath, "But *he'll* never slap anyone in the face again, the damned gringo!"

His own familiarity with pain and suffering and with the pain of others served to refine away all the crudity of self-pity in Quiroga. Paradoxically, because this is so, the rhetorical effect is to arouse a sense of compassion in the reader.

The quality of great worldly sophistication, seeming to come more from flesh and blood than from literature or literary conventions, makes Quiroga one of the rare and special few among our twentieth-century writers. . . . And one can see, by comparing Quiroga with, for example, Julio Cortázar, as Schade invites us to do [see excerpt dated 1976], that the technical example and influence of Quiroga is strong—strong in the cultivation of economy, of dramatic form, of clean (if not clear) construction. And one could well argue that his more "civilized" stories, mostly excursions in the gothic and to a degree influenced by Poe, set in an urban and middleclass milieu, stories like **"The Feather Pillow"** and **"The Pursued"** and [**"The Decapitated Chicken"**], are at least close kin to a certain kind of fiction and material which seems to have deeply interested (each in a different way) such gifted writers as Borges, Cortázar, Donoso, Fuentes, García Márquez, etc. That is to say, Quiroga's "civilized" tales seem (to the interested outsider) to be a part of the same general mythopoeic tradition as theirs. And, as such, they seem a little dated in comparison. But with the Misiones stories and with the superb animal stories (as good as the very best of Kipling's animal tales . . .) Quiroga is working in a dimension, and in a direct relation to experiential reality, which is unusual among any writers of our time. He comes close to certain North American writers, roughly of his own generation. . . . Yet unlike the best of the North Americans, Quiroga's aim always seems less instructive than evocative. The familiar North American stance, and certainly Hemingway's favorite, is the story of initiation of one kind or another. Very few people (excepting the reader) in a Quiroga story are introduced to anything new. Often they have to suffer greatly, but their suffering seldom surprises them at all. And the extent and force of their suffering is not (except in the early gothic tales) intended to surprise the reader.

Sometimes, in the stoical and sophisticated presentation of long suffering, Quiroga's stories remind me of some contemporary writing coming out of Eastern Europe, particularly some of the Russian dissidents. It is not a matter of style or design so much as his experience with an attitude towards suffering that links the work of Quiroga with very recent Russian work like Varlam

Shalamov's *Kolyma Stories* or the prose of Solzhenitsyn or Andrei Sinyavsky. Sometimes in the high refinement of simple language and in construction Quiroga's work may seem analogous in feeling to some of the best stories of Camus. But, aside from vague technical affiliations, the world of Quiroga's stories is at once more savage and simple. You can't build a philosophy out of it. Quiroga's world breaks minds and spirits as easily as it breaks bones.

By the same token, and in contrast, what can only be defined as a kind of heroism—ironically presented and often ridiculous and obsessive but nonetheless admirable in the expression of the power of the human spirit—is common in Quiroga's stories. In the story **"In the Middle of the Night,"** the narrator, who is himself in the process of being sorely and dangerously tested, encounters a man and his wife, small provincial merchants, and judges them negatively at sight: "Upstanding members of the bourgeoise, in short: their air of satisfaction and well-being was typical of that class, qualities assured at the expense of the work of others." What follows the encounter is a story out of their past, one of terrible suffering and endurance and, finally, triumph. When their remarkable story is finished, we return to the narrator whose complex and ambiguous reaction, not so much denying his first impression as modifying it, adding shadow to three-dimensional characterization, can be taken as representing the equally complex and ambiguous reaction asked of the reader by a Quiroga story. "And as we stood again looking at the dark, warm, rising river flowing by, I asked myself what ideal is to be found at the core of an action when it is separated from the motivations that have fired it, since my wretched merchants, unbeknown to themselves, had committed an act of heroism."

Quiroga's stories are not tricky or overt examples of virtuosity. They are clear, clean, direct, and polished to a beautiful simplicity. And yet they are extremely demanding. They are and will be most accessible to those readers (in any language into which they may be translated, since he has refined his language to the utmost clarity) who have had, in "reality" or in a fully developed and active imagination, the most and deepest meaningful experience. Among other things this greatly limits, where it does not altogether preclude, much direct influence upon the young and the inexperienced, whether as readers or as writers. It strictly limits the potential of his literary influence. Yet for the same reason, and in an irony that I suspect Quiroga would have appreciated, the experience he draws on and the sophistication of his treatment of that experience virtually guarantee a long life for his fiction. . . . There are only a very few serious writers of our times, writing in any language, who have anything to offer, beyond verbal felicity and literary games, to the mature reader. On the strength of [*The Decapitated Chicken, and Other Stories*] it appears that Horacio Quiroga is one of the very few. (pp. 38-40)

> George Garrett, "The Authority of Translation," in
> Review, No. 19, Winter, 1976, pp. 35-40.*

WILLIAM PEDEN   (essay date 1976)

[*Peden is an American critic and educator who has written extensively on the American short story and on American historical figures such as Thomas Jefferson and John Quincy Adams. In the following excerpt, he discusses the principal themes and techniques of Quiroga's short stories.*]

Quiroga's narrative technique is deceptively simple. Structurally, his stories are conventional, adhering for the most part to a narrative mode as old as oral or written tale-telling, a mode later articulated into an esthetic and practiced by Quiroga's self-acknowledged master, Edgar Allan Poe. With few exceptions, Quiroga's stories grow out of a single intense, dramatic, bizarre, or unusual situation. They proceed through a series of incidents that grow out of this basic situation as inevitably as flower develops from seed, as fetus from fertilized egg. They reach a climax that is quickly followed by a shocking, intense, or revelatory ending. In terms of this conventional narrative mode, Quiroga works surely, swiftly, and effectively: scene follows memorable scene with no false notes, little or no wasted effort, few if any wrong moves. And Quiroga's stories achieve what Poe deemed the most important goal of the writer of short fiction—totality of effect. . . . (p. 41)

If his narrative method is conventional, Quiroga's stories are not, nor am I trying to suggest that he is little more than a facile imitator of Poe. Quite the contrary. At their best, Quiroga's stories succeed as entertainment, as art, as commentary on the human situation. And, at his best, his stories are uniquely *Quiroga;* he has his own voice, his own vision. His spectrum is broad, broader than Poe's as the twelve selections in . . . *The Decapitated Chicken* suggest, including as it does children's stories . . . ; realistic fictions like **"A Slap in the Face"** (a story of social protest as didactic as Albert Maltz's Marxist-oriented stories of the American Depression); and tales of horror, terror, madness, violence, and the surreal for which he is best known.

Quiroga—again like Poe—was fascinated by madness, drawn to it like steel to magnet, and was ultimately engulfed in it. **"The Pursued"** is Quiroga's "The Man of the Crowd," and I am sure Quiroga must have had Poe's story in his mind when he wrote what seems to me his most ambitious story. Paradoxical, open-ended, resonant with vibrations of fear, hostility, attraction-repulsion, and ambivalent sexuality, **"The Pursued,"** as far as I am concerned, is Quiroga's masterpiece, a haunting parable of Wandering Jew, Cain-Abel, demented artist, Everyman dehumanized by the tensions of contemporary metropolitan life—whose meanings can perhaps be suggested by La Bruyère's statement that precedes the Poe tale: *Ce grand malheur, de ne pouvoir être seul* ["The great misfortune of not being able to be alone"].

The setting of most of Poe's stories is out of space, out of time, a painted backdrop often more symbolic than literal against which his characters play out their roles. But with Quiroga, setting and place are contemporary realities that can be as deterministic as Zola's Paris or Hardy's Wessex, as spiritually paralyzing as Joyce's Dublin. *Place* with Quiroga is an active agent, a physical and vital force that not only influences but often determines the fate of his characters. It's a harsh world, Quiroga's, dominated by malignant natural forces, parched by the blinding North Argentine sun that destroys Mr. Jones of **"Sunstroke,"** of swollen rivers that threaten the husband and wife of **"In the Middle of the Night,"** of jungles where lurks the deadly *yayaracusu* whose bite kills the protagonist of **"Drifting."** Or it's a world governed by blind chance, by accident, by carelessness, or any combination of the three (as is the case with **"The Son"** or **"The Dead Man"**), or one where his characters are threatened by nameless, unspeakable horrors and/or are physically or psychically maimed by their own individual weaknesses and tensions, as is the case, for example, with the curious and complex relationship between Alicia and Jordan of **"The Feather Pillow,"** a relationship as ominous as the damp and wintry house that serves as setting for the horrors that are to follow.

In effect, Quiroga takes his readers on an existential trip, a "mad pilgrimage" as Tennessee Williams phrases it in an early poem, in which one way or another "the earth destroys her crooked child." A bleak and narrow vision, Quiroga's, but no bleaker than his own life-story, marked as it was by disease, madness, and violent death. Despite this limited vision and to a degree because of it, Quiroga's stories pass what to me is perhaps the ultimate test of a work of fiction, that of memorableness. Quiroga is a master of the stunning effect, the vivid detail, the unforgettable scene that linger painfully in the reader's consciousness, as real as remembrances of past injustices or unhealed wounds. (pp. 41-2)

William Peden, "*Some Notes on Quiroga's Stories,*" in Review, *No. 19, Winter, 1976, pp. 41-3.*

JOHN S. BRUSHWOOD   (essay date 1983)

[*Brushwood is an American educator and critic who has written extensively on Spanish-American literature. In the following excerpt, he discusses Quiroga's literary principles and several of his most significant stories.*]

Quiroga was the first Spanish American writer to pay close attention to how a story is made, and at the same time, dedicate himself almost exclusively to writing short fiction. In a statement of principles for the *cuentista,* he sets forth several ideas that are especially interesting because of his importance as *magister.* Although Quiroga did not consistently assume such a role for himself and was quite aware that some younger writers were not entirely sympathetic to his work, his decalogue for the perfect *cuentista* states his case in no uncertain terms. He first exhorts the writer to have limitless faith in his literary master, and specifically mentions Poe, Maupassant, Kipling, and Chekov. The first two are quite clearly present in Quiroga's work; Kipling is apparent in the stories about anthropomorphized jungle beasts; Chekov's presence is not as easy to specify, but there is certainly no reason to doubt its existence. Beyond this oath of allegiance, Quiroga says that the writer should know before beginning the narration how the story is going to develop. It seems unlikely that he would have much patience with the writer whose characters take charge of the work. He warns against excessive use of adjectives, claiming that if the writer controls language well enough to choose the best substantive, modifiers need be used only sparingly. Writing under the impulse of emotion should be avoided, Quiroga says; once the emotion has cooled, however, the writer does well to re-create it in the experience of his work. Interesting an audience should not be a concern; rather, the *cuentista* should feel certain that what he writes is of interest to the characters about whom he is writing.

In general, these principles suggest a rather comfortable fit into the realist-naturalist tradition. That is indeed where Quiroga is based in literary history, but with modifications caused by the Spanish American literary milieu. He began writing in the early years of the twentieth century, toward the end of *modernismo* and at a time when realism and naturalism were generally recognized, but not always understood. One of his early stories, **"Cuento sin razó, pero cansado"** . . . (**"Story Without Cause, But Weary"**), may be safely thought of as *modernista* because one of its qualities is the sense of ennui associated with the French decadents. There is also in it some of naturalism's inevitability, and this characteristic becomes dominant in many stories, including the well-known **"La gallina degollada"** . . . (**"The Decapitated Chicken"**).

In this story, four idiot brothers commit an act of violence that is suggested to them by their having witnessed an ordinary act that seems analogous—to them—and quite acceptable. Quiroga introduces the brothers in an initial scene, then provides some background followed by emphasis on the parents' marital problems. The conflict that is developed in much of the story is based on the attitude of the parents toward their offspring. When this conflict reaches a climax, it points the reader in a direction different from that actually taken by the story. The narrator—always completely in control of the characters and recounting their actions without detailed characterization—removes the brothers from their regular routine, relates how they witnessed the stimulus action, and returns them to the place in which he first described them. Their subsequent action, wordless and in common accord, is an inevitable result of their mental condition.

The action of **"La gallina degollada"** takes place in the environs of Buenos Aires, but the story is in no way regionalistic. Quiroga often placed his stories in settings that were familiar to him, but his themes are universal. In **"Juan Darién,"** . . . the jungle is a factor, but not in terms of the man-against-nature theme found in many works located in unsettled areas. Rather, **"Juan Darién"** is a story of human injustice in the most general sense, not in terms of an attack on a specific or localized social problem. An animal is transformed into a human being and when his identity is discovered, he suffers the fate of those who threaten society because they are different.

The general structure of **"Juan Darién"** is what one would expect in a realist story: introduction, exposition of conflict, development, climax, and denouement. It is not a realistic story; it is a fantasy, and Quiroga never leaves any room for doubt about what kind of tale we are reading. At the beginning, the narrator states the fact of the animal's marvelous transformation. There is no time to wonder whether or not there may be some natural explanation for this phenomenon. We are dealing with a kind of fairy tale, and the language so indicates when the narrator uses expressions that are similar to English. "Once there was . . ." or "Well, of course . . . ," as introductions to paragraphs. The conflict in **"Juan Darién"** is between animal violence and human violence. Humans are always unjust; their only redeeming trait appears to be in the maternal role—the mother alone knows "the sacred rights of life."

Violence is frequent in Quiroga's work, but its significance varies in important ways. In **"La gallina degollada,"** it creates horror; in **"Juan Darién,"** it is related to justice and injustice. In **"El hombre muerto"** . . . (**"The Dead Man"**), the protagonist comes to a violent end by accident, and one thinks less about the violence itself than about the man's awareness, or lack of awareness, of his condition. The general ambience of "el hombre muerto" tends to make the story appear more regionalistic than is actually the case. The setting is tropical and rural. The man falls on his machete in the course of his work and dies in a period of thirty minutes that are accounted for in the narration. There is no surprise ending, nothing that need be withheld in a discussion of how it works out. It is impossible to summarize the story without duplicating it, however, because the experience of this narrative is the man's growing awareness of his condition. The basic conflict is quite simply between life and death; its development is what the man thinks of his total situation (his immediate condition and its implications). Quiroga uses repetition with good effect as his protagonist becomes increasingly aware of what is happening to him and what it means in terms of the world in which he has lived. The narrator speaks mainly in free, indirect style, so we see what the man sees even though we are being informed by the third-person voice; an occasional comment from this point of view does not alter the basic narration in any significant way. Probably the outstanding device used by Quiroga in this story is a shift of focus in the last paragraph so that we are no longer seeing as the man sees but as he is seen. This change justifies the title; before this conclusion, the man is dying, but has not reached the end. The fact that **"El hombre muerto"** cannot be synopsized satisfactorily characterizes it as a more modern story than the other two by Quiroga. It would be difficult, and pointless, to say that one manner is more typical of the author than the other.

> *John S. Brushwood, "The Spanish American Short Story from Quiroga to Borges," in* The Latin American Short Story: A Critical History, *edited by Margaret Sayers Peden, Twayne Publishers, 1983, pp. 71-96.**

ADDITIONAL BIBLIOGRAPHY

Chapman, Arnold. "Between Fire and Ice: A Theme in Jack London and Horacio Quiroga." *Symposium* XXV, No. 1 (Spring 1970): 17-26.*
Compares action and characterization in "La insolación" and London's "To Build a Fire" and notes similarities between the lives of the authors, concluding that both men "keenly felt themselves participant in the huge American drama, where the sons and grandsons of Europe flung themselves against the last virgin lands . . . with the desperation of men who, alienated from the dying villages and coagulating cities, went alone into the wilderness, to face rejection and death."

De Feo, Ronald. "Review of *The Decapitated Chicken, and Other Stories*." *Commonweal* CIV, No. 19 (19 April 1977): 285-86.
Positive review comparing Quiroga's works with those of other Latin American writers and with those of Edgar Allan Poe.

Englekirk, John E. "Horacio Quiroga." In *An Anthology of Spanish American Literature*, edited by E. Herman Hespelt and others, pp. 680-81. New York: F. S. Crofts and Co., 1946.
Brief biographical and critical essay dividing Quiroga's career into three periods: that of his literary apprenticeship, from 1901 to 1910; that of his mature writing, from 1910 to 1926; and a period of decline until his death in 1937.

Gülmez, Patricia. "Chronology." *Review 76*, No. 19 (Winter 1976): 27-30.
Biographical information.

Imbert, Enrique Anderson. "1895-1910." In his *Spanish-American Literature: A History*, translated by John V. Falconieri, pp. 264-326. Detroit: Wayne State University Press, 1963.*
Discusses the principal themes and techniques of Quiroga's works.

Raymond Roussel

1877-1933

French novelist, dramatist, poet, short story writer, and essayist.

An isolated figure in modern literature, Roussel was a wealthy eccentric whose highly experimental writings reflect his life-long obsession with language and literary invention. His two major works, the novels *Impressions d'Afrique (Impressions of Africa)* and *Locus Solus,* are essentially catalogs of extravagant tales, bizarre creatures and characters, and outlandish machinery. The unusual quality of Roussel's fiction is due in part to the fact that he often wrote using a compositional technique which, as he explained in *Comment j'ai écrit certains de mes livres (How I Wrote Certain of My Books),* inspired the creation of works that are wholly removed from the conventions and concerns of realistic literature and which demonstrate their author's immersion in an unrestricted world of imagination. While the experimental and enigmatic nature of Roussel's writings has discouraged many readers and incurred frequent disapproval from critics, Roussel was hailed as a genius by the Surrealists and traces of his legacy have been found among the authors of the *nouveau roman* ("new novel").

Born to a successful stockbroker and his wife, Roussel had what he described as a "blissful" childhood. At the age of thirteen he left school to study piano at the Paris Conservatory, considering a career as a songwriter. However, he found that lyrics came easily to him but melodies did not, and so he turned instead to poetry. At seventeen he began work on his first long poem, *La doublure,* which recounts the visit of an actor and his mistress to the carnival at Nice, much of the narration being devoted to descriptions of the crowd. Later, while undergoing treatment with the renowned French psychiatrist Pierre Janet, Roussel described this period as one of ecstasy during which he worked feverishly, convinced he was creating a masterpiece. Although *La doublure* was completely ignored when it appeared in 1897, the failure of his first major work did not alter Roussel's belief that he was destined to achieve a literary stature equalled in magnitude only by the historical stature of Napoleon. Roussel spent several reclusive years experimenting with his compositional technique, which is often called the *procédé* ("procedure"), during which time he published only a few short pieces. His enormous wealth allowed him not only to devote as much time as he chose to his writing, but also to pay for the publication of his work.

With the publication of *Impressions of Africa* in 1910, Roussel once again expected tumultuous praise. When none came, he sought a way to make his writing more popular. Thinking the theater would provide a wider audience and a better medium for his highly visual narrative style, Roussel adapted *Impressions of Africa* for the stage and financed the production himself. From the first performance, however, audiences were appalled and outraged. The nearly plotless drama with its unconventional, sometimes shocking assemblage of machinery, beasts, and beings, was incomprehensible even to the sophisticated Parisian audience. On the stage a giant earthworm operated a zither-playing device, an amputee played a flute carved from his own tibia, and African women danced frantically to an accompaniment of their own burps. Roussel was subse-

quently denounced as either a madman or a charlatan. Nevertheless, he wrote a second novel, *Locus Solus,* using the *procédé* and hired a popular novelist, Pierre Frondaie, to write the dramatic adaptation. Although audience reaction to *Locus Solus* was essentially the same as it had been to *Impressions of Africa,* the disastrous performances attracted the notice of the Surrealists, who quickly became champions of Roussel's somewhat indistinct cause. Encouraged by this support, Roussel wrote two plays, *L'étoile au front (The Star on the Forehead)* and *La poussière de soleils.* These too were financed and produced by Roussel, who was once again jeered by public and critics alike. In his final work, *Nouvelles impressions d'Afrique,* Roussel did not use the *procédé.* Some critics believe that, at this point, the author had come to the conclusion that he must abandon that compositional method in order to achieve the popularity he felt he deserved. But *New Impressions of Africa* is, in the opinion of critics, the least comprehensible of all Roussel's works, and it too was ignored. Although the Surrealists were by this time devoted admirers of Roussel, he did not understand them or their work; he was uninterested in the admiration of a small group of literary radicals and remained troubled that he was not universally acknowledged as a genius. It is not clear exactly when Roussel began to abuse alcohol and barbiturates, but near the end of his life he became addicted to both. In 1932, a disappointed Roussel left a final manuscript with his publisher, giving instructions that it be published only after his death. The manuscript, *How I Wrote Certain of My Books,* explains the operation of the *procédé* and reveals Roussel's confidence in the merit of his creations. Soon afterward, Roussel left Paris; in 1933, he died in Italy of a self-administered dose of barbiturates.

Roussel's earliest works are fairly conventional poems which utilize traditional rhymes and meters. It is *La doublure* that critics have seen as the prototype for his later, more experimental fiction. The central, highly descriptive portion of *La doublure,* which concentrates upon the carnival atmosphere at Nice, clearly presages the static quality and preoccupation with the bizarre that would recur throughout Roussel's later work. Lengthy passages lacking in forward action are also present in Roussel's second volume of poetry, titled *La vue,* a collection of three poems which describe in minute detail a label, a carved penholder, and the engraved emblem on a sheet of writing paper. A significant aspect of these early poems is their concern with representations of reality rather than reality itself; in *La doublure* it is masks and costumes, in *La vue* it is depictions of scenery. Critics have called this facet of Roussel's work a manifestation of his need to distance himself as much as possible from the natural world, which he found distasteful, disorderly, and filled with pain.

While Roussel's early writing does exhibit some characteristic features of his later work, it does not make use of his most notable stylistic device: the *procédé*. *Impressions of Africa* was the first novel to use that formula. In its simplest form, the *procédé* began with a pair of nouns, each possessing more than one meaning. Very often, Roussel would link the nouns with the preposition *à,* which itself has a number of meanings, including to, of, and with. A phrase was thus created which could be taken in two entirely different ways: *métier* (occupation or loom) *à aubes* (dawns or blades of a wheel) could mean an occupation which necessitates rising early or a loom which operates using a wheel. The next step of the technique involved the construction of a story or scenario which would begin with one meaning of the phrase and end with the other. Later, the *procédé* evolved to include phrases which were phonetically distorted to form others, by which process *ma chandelle est* (my candle is) could become *marchande zelée* (zealous merchant). Yet the *procédé* was only the formal compositional element of Roussel's work; the phrases chosen and the situations generated by them were all the product of the author's imagination. Critics find in Roussel's fiction, where the elements of fantasy and invention are central, the profound influence of his literary hero, Jules Verne. *Impressions of Africa* is ostensibly the story of a group of shipwrecked actors, their capture by an African chieftain, and their performance of an elaborate pageant in his honor. It is the pageant, however, where strange machines are operated and highly unlikely feats are executed, that takes precedence in the narration. Similarly, in *Locus Solus,* visitors to the estate of a man called Martial Canterel, whom some critics consider a persona of Roussel himself, are shown Canterel's peculiar inventions. The essential element of these novels is the interplay of the *procédé* and the author's imagination, which creates fantastic ideas and images that are loosely linked by the minimal narrative structure. Roussel's final work, *New Impressions of Africa,* is a syntactically complex poem which has been praised for its lyric quality and compared to the work of Stéphane Mallarmé. Yet even Roussel's most enthusiastic admirers have been forced to admit that the stylistic difficulty of *New Impressions of Africa* renders it inaccessible to many readers.

Critical assessment of Roussel's work varies widely. The Surrealists, who sought to free art from the arbitrary constraints of realism and philosophical conservatism, thought Roussel a genius. They praised his work for its liberating inventiveness and its creation of a fantastic yet internally coherent logic which operates completely without reference to any external reality. Modernist poet John Ashbery considers Roussel "one of the greatest and most influential of twentieth-century writers," and Rayner Heppenstall has called *Impressions of Africa* a masterpiece. Most critics, however, have been more reserved in their approach to Roussel's work. While they acknowledge the obvious historical significance of works which break so radically with tradition and admire the creative power of Roussel's mind, they also point out that his enigmatic style suggests deeper meanings which in fact do not exist in these works. Like the majority of Roussel's contemporaries, some modern critics have simply dismissed his work as the product of a mind deranged by obsessions, including an obsession with words; these critics also seriously question the value of fiction which is created by formula. Nevertheless, even his severest detractors admit that the works of a figure as colorful as Roussel, though open to serious reproach, are not devoid of at least psychological interest, and perhaps true literary merit.

PRINCIPAL WORKS

La doublure (poetry) 1897
Chiquenaude (short story) 1900
La vue (poetry) 1904
Impressions d'Afrique (novel) 1910
 [*Impressions of Africa,* 1967]
Impressions d'Afrique (drama) 1911
Locus Solus (novel) 1914
 [*Locus Solus,* 1970]
Locus Solus [adapted by Pierre Frondaie] (drama) 1922
L'étoile au front (drama) 1924
 [*The Star on the Forehead* (partial translation), 1970;
  published in journal *Juillard*]
La poussière de soleils (drama) 1926
Nouvelles impressions d'Afrique (poetry) 1932
 [*The Column Which, When Licked Until the Tongue
  Bleeds, Cures Jaundice* (partial translation), 1964;
  published in journal *Art and Literature*]
Comment j'ai écrit certains de mes livres (poetry, short
  stories, essays, and unfinished novel) 1935
 [*How I Wrote Certain of My Books* (partial translation),
  1977]
Oeuvres complètes. 9 vols. (novels, short stories, poetry,
  dramas, and essay) 1963-72
Correspondence (letters) 1970; published in journal
  Juillard

JEAN COCTEAU (essay date 1930)

[*Cocteau was a French author who has been called a Renaissance man for his varied work in twentieth-century avant garde literature, music, drama, painting, ballet, and film. As a young man Cocteau began experimenting with the infinite possibilities of art once it was freed from rigid restrictions, experiments which often offended contemporary sensibilities and led to his being labeled an enfant terrible. Throughout his life his single goal as an artist was to shock and surprise the complacent. A prominent critic as well as artist, Cocteau's essays in criticism were widely influential. In the following excerpt from* Opium, *a collection of notes on various subjects written while he was being treated for drug addiction, Cocteau comments on Roussel's life and works.*]

Raymond Roussel, or genius in its pure state, inassimilable for the elite. *Locus Solus* questions the whole of literature and advises me once more to beware of admiration and to seek out love, which is mysteriously comprehending. In fact even one of the innumerable admirers of Anatole France or Pierre Loti cannot find one scrap of the genius which atones for their fame if he remains blind in front of *Locus Solus.* He therefore adopts France or Loti for the reason that separates us from them.

This proves, alas, that genius is a question of immediate dosage and slow evaporation.

*   *   *

Ever since 1910 I have heard people laugh about the 'rails of calf's lights' in *Impressions d'Afrique.* Why should you imagine that the fear of being laughed at should affect Roussel? He is alone. If you should find him funny he will prove to you in a few lines (Olga Tcherwonenkoff) his feeling for what is comic set in tactful contrast to his gravely meticulous lyricism.

In a postscript to a recent letter that he wrote to me he quoted this passage from *Les Mariés de la Tour Eiffel:*

> First loudspeaker: But this telegram is dead.

> Second loudspeaker: It's just because it's dead
> that everyone understands it.

This postscript proves that Roussel is not unaware either of what he is or of what is due to him.

Certain words make the public laugh. 'Calf's lights' prevent the delicate statue supported by these rails from being seen. In *Orphée* [a film by Cocteau] the word 'rubber' prevented Heurtebise's phrase 'She has forgotten her rubber gloves' from being heard. When I acted this part I succeeded, through imperceptible preparations, in reducing the laughter and finally in suppressing it. The audience were prepared without knowing it and expected the word 'rubber,' instead of being surprised by hearing it suddenly pronounced. Then they understood the surgical aspect of the term.

*   *   *

Roussel and Proust disprove the legend of the poet's indispensable poverty (his struggle for existence, garrets, and lobbying . . .). Rejection by the various elites and the automatic non-adoption of anything new cannot be explained only by the obstacles that a poor man overcomes gradually. A poor man of genius looks rich.

Thanks to his fortune Proust lived shut in with his world, he could afford the luxury of illness, and he was, in fact, ill because illness was possible; his nervous asthma and his ethic in the shape of fantastic care for his health brought on real illness and death.

Roussel's fortune allows him to live alone and ill without prostituting himself in any way. His riches protect him. He peoples emptiness. There is not the slightest grease-spot on his work. It is a world suspended from elegance, fairyland and fear.

In the end *Impressions d'Afrique* leaves an impression of Africa. The story of the zouave is the only example of writing

comparable to a certain type of painting which is sought by our friend Uhde, and he calls it painting *of the sacred heart.*

Apart from Picasso, in another medium, nobody has made better use of newspaper than Roussel. The judge's cap on Locus Solus's head, the plain round caps worn by Romeo and Juliet and Seil-Kor.

The same applies to the atmospheres in which Roussel's imagination moves. Old Casino decoration, old furniture, old costumes, scenes like those one sees painted on organs, and the fairground booths of prisons, the Decapitator and the Dupuytren Museum. The new is only presented in the shape of the fabulous: the seahorses and the Sauternes, Faustine, Rhedjed's flight, and Fogar's turn.

*   *   *

I have mentioned a similarity between Roussel and Proust. It is a social and physical similarity between silhouettes, voices and nervous habits acquired in the atmospheres where they both passed their youth. But the difference between their work is absolute. Proust saw a great number of people. He lived a most complex night life. He found the material for his great time-pieces outside. Roussel never sees anyone. He finds material only within himself. He even invents historical anecdotes. He operates his automatons without the slightest outside help.

*   *   *

Proust, Swann, Gilberte and Balbec always make me think of Souann in *Impressions d'Afrique,* the ancestor of Talou, and the phrase from *Locus Solus:* 'Gilbert waves over the ruins of Baalbek the famous uneven sistrum of the great poet Missir.'

Roussel's style is a means and not an end. It is a means which has become an end through the power of genius, for the beauty of his style arises from the fact that he applies himself to express difficult things in an accurate way, relying only on his own authority, and leaving no intriguing shadow round him. But since he is an enigma and has nothing round him, this illumination is much more intriguing.

If Giorgio de Chirico took to writing instead of painting I suppose he would create with his pen an atmosphere similar to that of the Place des Trophées.

When we read the description of this square we think of him.

*   *   *

Under the influence of opium one delights in someone like Roussel and does not attempt to share this pleasure. Opium desocialises us and removes us from the community. Further, the community takes its revenge. The persecution of opium addicts is an instinctive defence by society against an antisocial gesture. I regard these notes on Roussel as a proof of gradual return to a certain reduced communal life.

Instead of carrying these books away into my hideout I would like to spread the knowledge of them. I had the opium-addict's laziness. One must beware of the downhill path to the communal grave.

It is to Gide, who generously read *Impressions d'Afrique* to us in the past, that I owe the discovery of *Locus Solus* and the recent reading of the admirable *Poussière de Soleils.* (pp. 107-12)

In Roussel's eyes *the objects that he transfigures remain what they are. It is the least artistic genius. It is the acme of art.* Satie would say it was the triumph of the *amateur.*

Roussel's equilibrium is taken for disequilibrium. He hopes for official praise and he knows his work is misunderstood, thereby proving that official praise is not despicable because it is official but because it operates badly.

*   *   *

Raymond Roussel shows first of all the end without the means and he produces surprises which rest on a feeling of security (*Le Gala des Incomparables*). These means embellish the end of his book. But since they contain the strangeness that they owe to the author's person, they do not weaken the problems that they illuminate and to which they add a new and adventurous lustre.

The divinatory episodes which conclude *Locus Solus* are convincing. Here the author reveals first the experiments and then the devices behind them, but the devices depend on a reality, on Roussel, just as the devices admitted by the conjuror do not make us capable of performing the trick. The illusionist who reveals his device transfers minds from a mystery they reject to a mystery they accept and places to his account approval which formerly enriched the unknown. (pp. 113-14)

> *Jean Cocteau, in his* Opium: The Diary of a Cure, *translated by Margaret Crosland and Sinclair Road, revised edition, Peter Owen Limited, London, 1968, 148 p.*

RAYMOND ROUSSEL   (essay date 1935)

[*In the following excerpt from* How I Wrote Certain of My Books, *Roussel explains the compositional method he employed in his major works.*]

I have always been meaning to explain the way in which I came to write certain of my books (*Impressions d'Afrique, Locus Solus, L'Etoile au Front,* and *La Poussière de Soleils*).

It involved a very special method. And it seems to me that it is my duty to reveal this method, since I have the feeling that future writers may perhaps be able to exploit it fruitfully.

As a young man I had already written stories of some length employing this method.

I chose two almost identical words (reminiscent of metagrams). For example, *billard* [billiard table] and *pillard* [plunderer]. To these I added similar words capable of two different meanings, thus obtaining two almost identical phrases.

In the case of *billard* and *pillard* the two phrases I obtained were:

1. *Les lettres du blanc sur les bandes du vieux billard* . . .
   [The white letters on the cushions of the old billiard table . . .]

2. *Les lettres du blanc sur les bandes du vieux pillard* . . .
   [The white man's letters on the hordes of the old plunderer . . .].

In the first, "lettres" was taken in the sense of lettering, "blanc" in the sense of a cube of chalk, and "bandes" as in cushions.

In the second, "lettres" was taken in the sense of missives, "blanc" as in white man, and "bandes" as in hordes.

The two phrases found, it was a case of writing a story which could begin with the first and end with the second.

Now it was from the resolution of this problem that I derived all my materials.

In the story in question there was a white explorer who, under the title "Among the Blacks" had published a book in the form of missives in which he discussed the hordes of a plunderer (black king).

At the beginning we see someone chalking letters on the cushions of an old billiard table. These letters, in the form of a cryptogram, composed the final sentence: "The white man's letters on the hordes of the old plunderer," and the story as a whole turned on the tale of a rebus based on the explorer's epistolary narratives.

I shall presently show how this story provided the basis for my book *Impressions d'Afrique* written ten years later.

We find three very clear examples of this creative method using two almost identical phrases with different meanings:

1. In **"Chiquenaude,"** a story published by Alphonse Lemerre around 1900.

2. In **"Nanon,"** a story published in *Gaulois du Dimanche* around 1907.

3. In **"Une page du Folklore breton,"** a story published in *Gaulois du Dimanche* around 1908.

As for the origin of *Impressions d'Afrique,* it consisted of reconciling the words *billard* and *pillard.* The "pillard" was Talou; the "bandes" his warlike hordes; the "blanc" Carmichael (the word *lettres* was dropped).

Expanding this method, I began to search for new words relating to *billard,* always giving them a meaning other than that which first came to mind, and each time this provided me with a further creation.

Thus *queue* [billiard cue] supplied me with Talou's gown and train. A billiard cue sometimes carries the "chiffre" (monogram) of its owner; hence the "chiffre" (numeral) stitched on the aforementioned train.

I searched for a word to accompany *bandes* and thought of the *reprises* (darns) in old *bandes* [billiard cushions]. And the word *reprises,* in its musical sense, gave me the Jéroukka, that epic sung by Talou's *bandes* (warlike hordes) whose music consisted of the continual *reprises* [repetitions] of a brief melody.

Searching for a word to go with *blanc* I thought of the *colle* [glue] which sticks the paper to the base of the cube of chalk. And the word *colle,* used in school slang to denote detention or imposition, gave me the three hours confinement imposed on the *blanc* (Carmichael) by Talou.

Abandoning at that point the scope of *billard,* I continued along the same lines. I chose a word and then linked it to another by the preposition *à* [with]; and these two words, each capable of more than one meaning, supplied me with a further creation. (Incidentally, I used this preposition *à* in the above-mentioned groups of words: *queue à chiffre, bandes à reprises, blanc à colle.*) I should point out that the initial stages of this work were difficult and already required a great deal of time.

I would like to cite some examples:

Taking the word *palmier* I decided to consider it in two senses: as a *pastry* and as a *tree.* Considering it as a *pastry,* I searched for another word, itself having two meanings which could be linked to it by the preposition *à;* thus I obtained (and it was,

I repeat, a long and arduous task) *palmier* (a kind of pastry) *à restauration* (restaurant which serves pastries); the other part gave me *palmier* (palmtree) *à restauration* (restoration of a dynasty). Which yielded the palmtree in Trophies Square commemorating the restoration of the Talou dynasty.

Here are some further examples:

1st. *Roue* (wheel) *à caoutchouc* (rubber); 2nd. *roue* (swagger) *à caoutchouc* (rubber tree). Which supplied the rubber tree in Trophies Square where Talou swaggeringly planted his foot on his enemy's corpse.

1st. *Maison* (house) *à espagnolettes* (window fasteners); 2nd. *maison* (royal dynasty) *à espagnolettes* (little Spaniards). Which gave the two young Spanish twins from whom Talou and Yaour were descended. (pp. 3-5)

As the method developed I was led to take a random phrase from which I drew images by distorting it, a little as though it were a case of deriving them from the drawings of a rebus.

I take as an example that of *The Poet and the Moorish Woman*. . . . In this I made use of the song "J'ai du bon tabac." The first line: "J'ai du bon tabac dans ma tabatière" gave me: "jade tube onde aubade en mat (objet mat) a basse tierce" [Jade tube water aubade in mat (mat object) third bass]. We recognize in this latter grouping all the elements from the beginning of the story.

To continue: "Tu n'en auras pas" gave me: "Dune en or a pas (a des pas)" [Golden dune with footstep(s)]. Whence the poet who kissed footprints on a dune.—"J'en ai du frais et du tout râpé" gave me: "Jaude aide orfraie édite oracle paie" [Yellow helper osprey edict oracle pays]. Whence the Chinaman episode.—"Mais ce n'est pas pour ton fichu nez" gave me: "Mets son et bafone, don riche humé" [Ringing and mocking dish, giving rich fumes]. Hence the ringing dish which overcame Schahnidjar.

I continued the story with the song "Au clair de la lune."

1st. "Au clair de la lune mon ami Pierrot"; 2nd. "Eau glaire (cascade d'une couleur de glaire) de là l'anémone à midi négro" [Glairy water (glairy-colored waterfall) from whence the anemone with noon Negro]. Hence the episode set in Eden lit by the midday sun. (pp. 8-9)

This method is, in short, related to rhyme. In both cases there is unforeseen creation due to phonic combinations.

It is essentially a poetic method.

Still, one needs to know how to use it. For just as one can use rhymes to compose good or bad verses, so one can use this method to produce good or bad works.

Locus Solus was written in a like manner. But there I hardly ever used anything but the evolutionary method. That is to say, I drew a series of images from the distortion of some random text, as in the examples from *Impressions d'Afrique* already cited. The method did make a reappearance in its original form with the word *demoiselle* considered in two different senses; furthermore, the second word itself underwent a distortion to link it up with the evolutionary method:

1st. *Demoiselle* (young girl) *à prétendant* [suitor]; 2nd. *demoiselle* (pavior's beetle) *à reître en dents* [soldier of fortune in teeth].

I consequently found myself confronted with the following problem: the execution of a mosaic by a pavior's beetle. Whence

the complicated apparatus described from page 31 onwards. It was moreover a peculiarity of this method to call forth all sorts of *equations of facts* (to quote a phrase that Robert de Montesquiou used in a study of my books) which had to be solved logically. (p. 11)

As I have mentioned previously, I used the same method to write my plays *L'Etoile au Front* and *La Poussière de Soleils*. I remember particularly that in *L'Etoile au Front* the words "singulier" [singular] and "pluriel" [plural] gave me "Saint Julius" and "pelure" [peel] in the Pope St. Julius episode. (One can, furthermore, find among my papers some sheets containing very detailed explanations of how I wrote *L'Etoile au Front* and *La Poussière de Soleils*. One may also discover an episode written immediately after *Locus Solus* and interrupted by mobilisation in 1914 which is mainly concerned with Voltaire and a site filled with glowworms; perhaps this manuscript is worth publishing.)

It goes without saying that this method was nowhere employed in my other works: *La Doublure, La Vue* and *Nouvelles Impressions d'Afrique*.

All the same, it was used to construct the beginning of another book, which has been set in type at the Imprimerie Lemerre, 6, rue des Bergers (an episode set in Cuba).

The poems **"L'Inconsolable"** and **"Têtes de carton du Carnaval de Nice,"** and also the poem **"Mon Ame,"** written when

A letter which Roussel sent along with a duplicate copy of How I Wrote Certain of My Books. *The "confrères" of the greeting were most likely members of the Surrealist group. Collection Bernadette Grimprel.*

I was seventeen and published in the *Gaulois* on July 12th, 1897, have nothing to do with the method.

It is fruitless to search for any links between the book *La Doublure* and the story **"Chiquenaude"**; there are none. (pp. 12-13)

I would also like, in these notes, to pay homage to that man of incommensurable genius, namely Jules Verne.

My admiration for him is boundless.

In certain pages of *Voyage to the Center of the Earth, Five Weeks in a Balloon, Twenty Thousand Leagues under the Sea, From the Earth to the Moon, Trip to the Moon, Mysterious Island* and *Hector Servadec,* he raised himself to the highest peaks that can be attained by human language.

I once had the good fortune to be received by him at Amiens, where I was doing my military service, and there shake the hand which had penned so many immortal works.

O incomparable master, may you be blessed for the sublime hours which I have spent endlessly reading and re-reading your works throughout my life.

It seems apt that I should mention here a rather curious fact. I have traveled a great deal. Notably in 1920-1921 I traveled around the world by way of India, Australia, New Zealand, the Pacific archipeligi, China, Japan and America. (On this voyage I stopped for a while in Tahiti, where I rediscovered several of the original characters used in Pierre Loti's wonderful book.) I already knew the principal countries of Europe, Egypt and all of North Africa, and later I visited Constantinople, Asia Minor and Persia. Now, from all these travels I never took anything for my books. It seems to me that this is worth mentioning, since it clearly shows just how much imagination accounts for everything in my work. (pp. 13-14)

> *Raymond Roussel, "How I Wrote Certain of My Books," translated by Trevor Winkfield, in his* How I Wrote Certain of My Books, *Sun, 1977, pp. 3-20.*

MARCEL DUCHAMP   (interview date 1946)

[*Duchamp was a French artist and critic and a key figure in several major twentieth-century art movements, including Cubism, Dadaism, and Surrealism. His best-known painting,* Nude Descending a Staircase, *is considered a landmark in the development of modern art. In the following excerpt, Duchamp praises Roussel's talent.*]

Brisset and Roussel were the two men in those years whom I most admired for their delirium of imagination. Jean-Pierre Brisset was discovered by Jules Romains through a book he picked up from a stall on the quais. Brisset's work was a philological analysis of language—an analysis worked out by means of an incredible network of puns. He was a sort of Douanier Rousseau of philology. Romains introduced him to his friends. And they, like Apollinaire and his companions, held a formal celebration to honor him in front of Rodin's *Thinker* in front of the Panthéon where he was hailed as Prince of Thinkers.

But Brisset was one of the real people who has lived and will be forgotten. Roussel was another great enthusiasm of mine in the early days. The reason I admired him was because he produced something that I had never seen. That is the only thing that brings admiration from my innermost being—something completely independent—nothing to do with the great

names or influences. Apollinaire first showed Roussel's work to me. It was poetry. Roussel thought he was a philologist, a philosopher and a metaphysician. But he remains a great poet.

It was fundamentally Roussel who was responsible for my glass, *La Mariée mise à nu par ses célibataires, même [The Bride Stripped Bare by her Bachelors, Even].* From his **Impressions d'Afrique** I got the general approach. This play of his which I saw with Apollinaire helped me greatly on one side of my expression. I saw that as a painter it was much better to be influenced by a writer than by another painter. And Roussel showed me the way.

My ideal library would have contained all Roussel's writings—Brisset, perhaps Lautréamont and Mallarmé. Mallarmé was a great figure. This is the direction in which art should turn: to an intellectual expression, rather than to an animal expression. . . . (pp. 413-14)

> *Marcel Duchamp, in an excerpt from an interview with James Johnson Sweeney, in* The Autobiography of Surrealism, *edited by Marcel Jean, The Viking Press, 1980, pp. 412-14.*

MICHEL FOUCAULT   (essay date 1963)

[*A renowned French philosopher and critic, Foucault wrote numerous studies of Western civilization utilizing an eclectic method of analysis which combines elements of psychology, epistemology, and linguistics. His works frequently explore the concept of power and its uses by society. Taking into account theories of cultural relativity, Foucault considers such phenomena as criminality, mental illness, and sexuality not in any moral sense but rather as indicators of what is sanctioned by the dominant or ruling groups of a given society. While Foucault's analyses are considered highly unorthodox and have been disputed, his writings have exerted a marked influence on the development of contemporary thought, and he is regarded as one of France's most important modern thinkers. In the following excerpt, originally published in France in 1963, Foucault portrays Roussel's works as an enigma to which* How I Wrote Certain of My Books *serves as only a partial key.*]

Lyricism is carefully excluded from *How I Wrote Certain of My Books* (the quotations from Dr. Janet that Roussel used to speak about what was undoubtedly the pivotal experience of his life attest to the rigor of this exclusion); there is information in the essay, but no confidences; and yet something definitely is confided through this strange form of the secret that death would preserve and make known. "And I take comfort, for want of anything better, in the hope that perhaps I will have a little posthumous fame with regard to my books." The "how" that Roussel inscribes in the title of his last, revelatory work introduces not only the secret of his language, but also his relationship with such a secret, not to lead us to it, but rather to leave us disarmed and completely confused when it comes to determining the nature of the reticence which held the secret in a reserve suddenly abandoned.

His first sentence, "I have always intended to explain how I wrote certain of my books," clearly shows that his statements were not accidental, nor made at the last minute, but were an essential part of the work and the most constant aspect of his intention. Since his final revelation and original intention now becomes the inevitable and ambiguous threshold through which we are initiated into his work while forming its conclusion, there is no doubt it is deceptive: by giving us a key to explain the work, it poses a second enigma. It dictates an uneasy awareness for the reading of the work: a restless awareness since the secret cannot be found in the riddles and charades that Roussel was so fond of; it is carefully detailed for a reader who willingly lets the cat take his tongue before the end of the game, but it is Roussel who takes the reader's tongue for the cat. He forces the reader to learn a secret that he had not recognized and to feel trapped in an anonymous, amorphous, now-you-see-it-now-you-don't, never really demonstrable type of secret. If Roussel of his own free will said that there *was* a secret, one could suppose that he completely divulged it by admitting it and saying what it was, or else he shifted it, extended and multiplied it, while withholding the principle of the secret and its concealment. Here the impossibility of coming to a decision links all discourse about Roussel with the common risk of being wrong and of being deceived less by a secret than by the awareness that there is secrecy.

In 1932 Roussel sent his printer a portion of the text which would become, after his death, *How I Wrote Certain of My Books*. It was understood that these pages would not be published during his lifetime. The pages were not awaiting his death; rather, this decision was already within them, no doubt because of the immediacy of the revelation they contained. When, on May 30, 1933, he decided what the structure of the book would be, he had long since made plans never to return to Paris. During the month of June he settled in Palermo, where he spent every day drugged and in an intense state of euphoria. He attempted to kill himself, or to have himself killed, as if now he had acquired "the taste for death which hitherto he feared." On the morning he was due to leave his hotel for a drug cure at Kreuzlingen, he was found dead: in spite of his extreme weakness, he had dragged himself and his mattress against the door communicating with the adjoining room of his companion Charlotte Dufrène. This door, which had been open at all times, was locked from the inside. The death, the lock, and this closed door formed, at that moment and for all time, an enigmatic triangle where Roussel's work is both offered to and withdrawn from us. Whatever is understandable in his language speaks to us from a threshold where access is inseparable from what constitutes its barrier—access and barrier in themselves equivocal since in this indecipherable act the question remains, to what end? To release this death so long dreaded and now so suddenly desired? Or perhaps also to discover anew this life from which he had attempted furiously to free himself, but which he had also long dreamed of prolonging into eternity through his work and through the ceaseless, meticulous, fantastic constructions of the works themselves? Is there any other key, apart from the one in this last text, which is there, standing right up against the door? Is it signaling to open—or motioning to close? Is it holding a simple key which is marvelously ambiguous, ready in one turn either to lock in or to open up? Is it carefully shut on an irrevocable death, or is it transmitting beyond that death the exalted state of mind whose memory had stayed with Roussel since he was nineteen and whose illumination he had always sought to recover in vain—except perhaps on this one night?

It is curious that Roussel, whose language is extremely precise, said that *How I Wrote Certain of My Books* was a "secret and posthumous" text. No doubt he meant several things other than the obvious meaning, which is secret until death: that death was a ritual part of the secret, its prepared threshold and its solemn conclusion. Perhaps he meant that the secret would remain secret even in death, giving it an added twist, by which the "posthumous" intensified the "secret" and made it definitive; or even better, death would reveal that there is a secret without showing what it hides, only what makes it opaque and

impenetrable. He would keep the secret by revealing that it is secret, only giving us the epithet but retaining the substance. We are left with nothing, questioning a perplexing indiscretion, a key which is itself locked up, a cipher which deciphers and yet is encoded.

How I Wrote Certain of My Books hides as much, if not more, than it promises to reveal. It only gives us fragments of a breakdown of memory, which makes it necessary, as Roussel said, to use "ellipsis." However general his omissions may be, they are only superficial compared to a more fundamental one, arbitrarily indicated by his simple exclusion, without comment, of a whole series of works. "It goes without saying that my other books, *La Doublure* [The Lining/The Rehearsal/The Understudy], *La Vue* [The View/The Lens/The Vision], and *Nouvelles Impressions d'Afrique*, are absolutely outside of this process." Also outside of the secret are three poetical texts, *L'Inconsolable* (The Inconsolable), *Les Têtes de Carton du Carnaval de Nice* (Cardboard Heads of the Carnival in Nice), and the first poem written by Roussel, "**Mon Ame**" (My Soul). What secret underlies his action of setting them aside, satisfied with a simple reference but without a word of explanation? Do these works hide a key of a different nature, or is it the same, but doubly hidden, to the extent of denying its existence? Could there perhaps be a master key which would reveal a silent law to identify the works coded and decoded by Roussel, and those whose code is not to have any evident code? The idea of a key, as soon as it is formulated, eludes its promise, or rather takes it beyond what it can deliver to a point where all of Roussel's language is placed in question.

There is a strange power in this text whose purpose is to "explain." So doubtful is its status, its point of origin, where it makes its disclosures and defines its boundaries, the space that at the same time it upholds and undermines, that after the initial dazzling there is but one effect: to create doubt, to disseminate it by a concerted omission when there was no reason for it, to insinuate it into what ought to be protected from it, and to plant it even in the solid ground of its own foundation. *How I Wrote Certain of My Books* is, after all, one of *his* books. Doesn't this text of the unveiled secret also hold its own secret, exposed and masked at the same time by the light it sheds on the other works?

From this ambiguous situation one could define certain forms for which Roussel's works would provide the models. (Is it not, after all, the secret's secret?) Perhaps beneath the process revealed in this last text, another set of laws governs even more secretly and in a completely unforeseen way. The structure would be exactly that of *Impressions d'Afrique* or of *Locus Solus*. The scenes performed on stage at the Theater of the Incomparables or the machines in the garden of Martial Canterel have an apparent narrative explanation—an event, a legend, a memory, or a book—which justifies the episodes; but the real key—or in any case, another key at a more profound level—opens the text in all its force and reveals, beneath its marvels, the muffled phonetic explosion of arbitrary sentences. Perhaps in the end, his whole body of work is based on this model: *How I Wrote Certain of My Books* has the same function as the second part of *Impressions d'Afrique* and the explanatory narratives of *Locus Solus,* hiding, beneath the pretext of giving an explanation, the underground force from which his language springs.

It could also be that the revelations made in *How I Wrote Certain of My Books* have only a preparatory value, telling a kind of salutary lie—a partial truth, which signifies that one must look further and in greater depth. Then the work would be constructed on multilevels of secrecy, one ordering the other, but without any one of them having a universal value or being absolutely revelatory. By giving us a key at the last moment, this final text would be like a first retrospective of the works with a dual purpose: it opens the structure of certain texts at the level closest to the surface, but indicates for these and the other works the need for a series of keys, each of which would open its own box, but not the smallest, best protected, most precious one contained inside. This image of enclosure is common with Roussel. It is used with great care in *Documents pour Servir de Canevas* (Documents to Serve as Canvas); *La Poussière de Soleils* aptly uses it as a method for discovering a secret. In *Nouvelles Impressions* it takes the strange form of ever-expanding elucidations always interrupted by the parenthesis of a new light shed on the subject. Each light in turn is broken by a parenthesis of another brightness, originating from the preceding one, which is held suspended and fragmented for a long time. This succession of disruptive and explosive lights forms an enigmatic text, both luminous and shadowy, which these ordered openings transform into an impregnable fortress.

This process can serve as the beginning and the ending of the text, which was the function of the identical ambiguous sentences he used in his youth to frame brief narratives. It can form the necessary perimeter while leaving free the core of language, the field of imagination, without needing any key other than its own game. The process would then function to protect and to release. It would delineate a privileged place, beyond reach, whose rigorous outward form would free it from all external constraints. This self-containment would disconnect the language from all contact, induction, surreptitious communication, and influence, giving it an absolutely neutral space in which to fully develop. The process then would not determine the central configuration of the work, but would only be its threshold, to be crossed the moment it is drawn— more a rite of purification than an architectural structure. Then Roussel would have used it to frame the great ritual of his entire work, repeating it solemnly for everyone once he had completed the cycle for himself. The process would encircle the work, only letting the initiated have access into the void and completely enigmatic space of the ritualized work, which is to say, isolated, but not explained. *How I Wrote Certain of My Books* can be likened to the lens of *La Vue:* a minuscule surface that must be penetrated by looking through it in order to make visible a whole dimension disproportionate to it, and yet which can neither be fixed, nor examined, nor preserved without it. Perhaps the process no more resembles the work itself than the small lens does the seascape of *La Vue* which is brought to light, revealed, and held—on condition that its essential threshold is crossed with a glance.

Roussel's "revelatory" text is so reserved in its description of the action of the process in the work, and in turn the text is so verbose in types of deciphering, rites of threshold and lock, that it is difficult to relate *How I Wrote Certain of My Books* to these particular books and to the others as well. Its positive function of giving an explanation as well as a formula—"It seems to me that it's my duty to reveal it, for I have the impression that writers of the future will perhaps be able to exploit it fruitfully"—quickly becomes a neverending play of indecision, similar to that uncertain gesture on his last night, when Roussel, at the threshold, wanted perhaps to open the door, perhaps to lock it. In a way, Roussel's attitude is the reverse of Kafka's, but as difficult to interpret. Kafka had entrusted

his manuscripts to Max Brod to be destroyed after his death— to Max Brod, who had said he would never destroy them. Around his death Roussel organized a simple explanatory essay which is made suspect by the text, his other books, and even the circumstances of his death.

Only one thing is certain: this "posthumous and secret" book is the final and indispensable element of Roussel's language. By giving a "solution" he turns each word into a possible trap, which is the same as a real trap, since the mere possibility of a false bottom opens, for those who listen, a space of infinite uncertainty. This does not put in question the existence of the key process nor Roussel's meticulous listing of facts, but in retrospect it does give his revelation a disquieting quality.

All these perspectives—it would be comforting to close them off, to suppress all the openings, and to allow Roussel to escape by the one exit that our conscience—seeking respite—will grant him.

André Breton wrote, in *Fronton Virage* (The Wall at the Bend in the Road), "Is it likely that a man outside of all traditions of initiation should consider himself bound to carry to his grave a secret of another order . . . is it not more tempting to assume that Roussel obeyed, in the capacity of an initiate, a word of irrefutable command?" Of course—everything would be strangely simplified then, and the work would close upon a secret whose forbidden nature alone would indicate its existence, essence, content, and necessary ritual. And in relation to this secret all of Roussel's texts would be just so much rhetorical skill, revealing, to whoever knows how to read what they say, the simple, extraordinarily generous fact that they don't say it.

At the absolute limit it could be that the "chain of events" of *La Poussière de Soleils* has something in common—in its form— with the progression in the practice of alchemy, even if there is little chance that the twenty-two changes of scenes dictated by the staging of the play correspond to the twenty-two cards of the Major Arcana in a tarot deck. It is possible that certain outward signs of the esoteric process might have been used as models for the double play on words, coincidence and encounters at the opportune moment, the linking of the twists and turns of the plot, and the didactic voyages through banal objects having marvelous stories which define their true value by describing their origins, revealing in each of them mythical avatars which lead them to the promise of actual freedom.

But if Roussel did use such material, and it is not at all certain that he did, it would have been in the way he used stanzas of *"Au clair de la lune"* and *"J'ai du bon tabac"* in his *Impressions d'Afrique,* not to convey the content through an external and symbolic language in order to disguise it, but to set up an additional barrier within the language, part of a whole system of invisible paths, evasions, and subtle defenses.

Like an arrow, Roussel's language is opposed—by its direction more than by its substance—to an occult language. It is not built on the certainty that there is secrecy, only one secret that is wisely kept silent; on the surface it sparkles with a glaring doubt and hides an internal void: it is impossible to know whether there is a secret or none, or several, and what they are. Any affirmation that a secret exists, any definition of its nature, dries up Roussel's work at its source, preventing it from coming to life out of this void which it animates without ever satisfying our troubled ignorance. In the reading, his works promise nothing. There's only an inner awareness that by reading the words, so smooth and aligned, we are exposed to the unallayed danger of reading other words which are both different and the same. His work as a whole, supported by *How I Wrote Certain of My Books* and all the undermining doubts sown by that text, systematically imposes a formless anxiety, diverging and yet centrifugal, directed not toward the most withheld secrets but toward the imitation and the transmutation of the most visible forms: each word at the same time energized and drained, filled and emptied by the possibility of there being yet another meaning, this one or that one, or neither one nor the other, but a third, or none. (pp. 2-11)

> Michel Foucault, *in his* Death and the Labyrinth: The World of Raymond Roussel, *translated by Charles Ruas, Doubleday & Company, Inc., 1986, 186 p.*

ALAIN ROBBE-GRILLET   (essay date 1963)

[*A French novelist and critic, Robbe-Grillet is perhaps best known as the literary theoretician who proposed the nouveau roman (New Novel), a concept that has gained a wide reference in describing the work of a group of French novelists writing in the 1950s. The New Novelists, including Michel Butor, Marguerite Duras, and Nathalie Sarraute, sought to create narrative forms which could adequately express their existential vision of the world as a place without order or ultimate purpose and which could capture the fragmented, confused nature of subjective experience. Finding the traditional novel forms inadequate, they experimented with new techniques which de-emphasized linear structures such as plot, chronology, and character development and concentrated instead on minute descriptions and sensory impressions. These narrative qualities have made the works of the New Novelists highly controversial, with much of the controversy focusing on Robbe-Grillet's own fiction. As a critic, Robbe-Grillet is generally acknowledged for his insight into the nature of fiction, and his ideas have exerted a marked influence on the development of modern fiction. In the following essay, originally published in 1963 in* Pour un nouveau roman (For a New Novel), *Robbe-Grillet portrays Roussel's works as exercises in pure description devoid of any ulterior significance.*]

Raymond Roussel describes; and beyond what he describes there is nothing, nothing of what can traditionally be called a *message*. To adopt one of the favorite expressions of academic literary criticism, Roussel almost seems to have "nothing to say." No transcendence, no humanist metamorphosis can be applied to the series of objects, gestures, and events which constitute, at first glance, his universe.

On occasion, in order to satisfy the requirements of a very strict descriptive line, he must relate some psychological anecdote, or some imaginary religious custom, an account of primitive mores, a metaphysical allegory.... But these elements never have any "content," any depth; they cannot make in any case the most modest contribution to the study of human character or of the passions, the least contribution to sociology, inspire the slightest philosophical meditation. As a matter of fact, it is always frankly conventional sentiments that are involved (filial love, dedication, self-sacrifice, betrayal—always treated in a copybook manner), or else "gratuitous" rituals, or recognized symbolisms and well-worn philosophies. Between absolute non-sense and an exhausted sense, there remain once again only things themselves, objects, gestures, etc.

On the linguistic level, Roussel answers the requirements of criticism no better. Many have already pointed this out, and of course negatively: Raymond Roussel writes badly. His style is lusterless, neutral. When he abandons the order of observation—that is, of avowed platitude: the realm of "there is" and "is located at a certain distance"—he always employs a banal image, a hackneyed metaphor, itself the stand-by of some arsenal of literary conventions. Lastly the auditory organization of the sentences, the rhythm of the words, their music does not seem to raise any problem for the author's ear. The result is almost continuously without attraction from the point of view of belles-lettres: a prose alternating between simple-minded monotony and laborious cacophonous jumbles, alexandrines that must be counted out on the fingers to reveal their complement of the proper twelve feet.

Thus we are dealing with the exact opposite of what is conventionally called a good writer: Raymond Roussel has nothing to say, and says it badly.... And yet his *oeuvre* is beginning to be acknowledged as one of the most important in French literature in the early part of this century, one which has exercised its spell over several generations of writers and artists, one which we must count among the direct ancestors of the modern novel; whence the continually growing interest that attaches today to his opaque and disappointing works.

Let us consider first the opacity. It is, quite as much, an excessive transparency. Since there is never anything beyond the thing described, that is, since no supernature is hidden in it, no symbolism (or else a symbolism immediately proclaimed, explained, destroyed), the eye is forced to rest on the very surface of things: a machine of ingenious and useless functioning, a post card from a seaside resort, a celebration whose progress is quite mechanical, a demonstration of childish witchcraft, etc. A total transparency, which allows neither shadow nor reflection to subsist, this amounts, as a matter of fact, to a *trompe-l'oeil* painting. The more that scruples, specifications, details of shape and size accumulate, the more the object loses its depth. What we get, then, is an opacity without mystery: as behind a painted back cloth, there is nothing behind these surfaces, no inside, no secret, no hidden motive.

Yet by an impulse of contradiction frequent in modern writing, mystery is one of the formal themes most readily used by Roussel: search for a hidden treasure, problematic origin of some character or object, enigmas of all kinds proposed to the reader as to the heroes in the form of riddles, puns, codes, allusions, apparently absurd series of articles, etc. Concealed exits, underground passageways connecting two apparently unrelated sites, sudden revelations as to the mysteries of a contested consanguinity keep turning up in this rationalistic world in the best tradition of Gothic novels, momentarily transforming the geometric space of the situations and dimensions into a new *Castle of Otranto*.... Actually not, however: the mysteries here are too well controlled. Not only are these enigmas set forth too clearly, analyzed too objectively, and too evidently asserted as enigmas, but even, at the end of a more or less extended discourse, they are actually solved and explained, and this time too with the greatest simplicity considering the extreme complication of the various clues. After having read the description of the disconcerting machinery, we are entitled to the rigorous description of its functioning. After the rebus comes the explanation, and everything is back where it belongs.

It is for this reason that the explanation becomes futile in its turn. It answers the questions asked so well, it so totally exhausts the subject that it seems, ultimately, to be a useless duplication of the machinery itself. And even when we see it functioning and we know to what end, the machinery remains mystifying: for example, the famous pile driver that serves to compose decorative mosaics with human teeth by using the energy of the sun and the wind! The decomposition of the whole into its tiniest parts, the perfect identity of the latter with their function, merely leads to the pure spectacle of a gesture deprived of meaning. Once again, a signification that is too transparent coincides with a total opacity.

Elsewhere, we are initially offered an assemblage of words, as heterogeneous as possible—placed, for example, under a statue, itself possessing many disconcerting features (and described as such)—and we are then at great length told the meaning (always *immediate,* on the verbal level) of the riddle-sentence, and how it is directly related to the statue, whose strange details are then revealed to be entirely necessary, etc. Now these chain elucidations, extraordinarily complex, ingenious, and farfetched as they are, seem so preposterous, so disappointing that it is as if the mystery remained intact. But it is henceforth a mystery that has been filtered, drained, a mystery that has become unnamable. Opacity no longer hides anything. We have the impression of having found a locked drawer, then a key; and this key opens the drawer quite impeccably . . . and the drawer is empty.

Roussel himself seems to have been somewhat mistaken about this aspect of his work, imagining he could lure crowds to the Châtelet theater to attend a cascade of these—as he believed—thrilling enigmas and their successive solution by a patient and subtle hero. Experience, alas, quickly disabused him, as could easily be foreseen. For what he offers is actually riddles *in the void,* concrete but theoretical investigations without event and therefore unable to "catch" anything. Though there are traps on every page, they are merely made to function before our eyes, exhibiting all their secret workings and revealing, in fact, how to avoid becoming their victim. Moreover, even if he has not already been initiated into the Rousselian operations and the necessary disappointment which accompanies their execution, any reader will immediately be struck by the total absence of anecdotal interest—the utter gratuitousness—of the mysteries proposed to his attention. Here again, we have either a complete dramatic blank or else the drama of panoply, with all its conventional accessories. And in this case, whether or not the stories told exceed the limits of the stupefying, the mere way in which they are presented, the naïveté with which the questions are asked (in the genre of "All those present were highly intrigued by . . ." etc.), the style, finally—as remote as possible from the elementary rules of suspense—would be enough to detach the best-disposed reader from these amateur inventors of science fiction and from these folkloric pages controlled like a parade of marionettes.

Then what are these forms which so concern us? And how do they act upon us? What is their meaning? The last two questions it is still, no doubt, too early to answer. The Rousselian forms have not yet become academic; they have not yet been digested by the culture; they have not yet reached the status of values. We can already attempt, however, to name some of them at least. And to begin with, precisely that *investigation* which destroys, in the writing itself, its own object.

This investigation, as we have said, is purely formal. It is above all an itinerary, a logical path which leads from a given condition to another condition—one very similar to the first, though it is achieved by a long detour. We find a new example of this—one which has the additional advantage of being located entirely in the realm of language—in the brief posthumous texts whose architecture has been explained by Roussel himself: two sentences which when spoken sound identical almost to the letter, but whose meanings are totally without connection, on account of the different acceptations in which the similar words are taken. The trajectory here is the story,

the anecdote permitting us to unite the two sentences, which will constitute respectively the first and last sentences of the text. The most absurd episodes will thus be justified by their function as utensils, as vehicles, as intermediaries; the anecdote no longer has any explicit content, but a movement, an order, a composition; it too is no longer anything but a mechanism: simultaneously a reproduction-machine and a modification-machine.

For we must emphasize the importance Roussel attaches to that very slight *modification* in sound separating the two key sentences, not to mention the general modification of the meaning. The narrative has effected, before our eyes, on the one hand a profound change in what the world—and language—means, and on the other a tiny superficial displacement (the altered letter); the text "devours its own tail," but with a slight irregularity, a little wrench—which changes everything.

Frequently, too, we find a simple plastic *reproduction,* like that mosaic produced by the above-mentioned pile driver. Examples abound, whether in the novels, the plays, or the poems, of these images of all kinds: statues, engravings, paintings, or even crude drawings without any artistic character. The best known of these objects is the miniature view set in the shaft of a penholder. Of course, precision of detail is here as great as if the author were showing us a real scene, life-size or even enlarged by some optical device, binoculars, or microscope. An image a few millimeters square thus causes us to see a beach including various persons on the sand, or on the water in boats; there is never anything vague about their gestures, or in the lines of the setting. On the other side of the bay passes a road; and on this road is a car, and in the car is seated a man; this man is holding a cane, whose engraved handle represents . . . , etc.

Sight, the privileged sense in Roussel, rapidly achieves an obsessive acuity, tending to infinity. This characteristic is made doubtless still more provocative by the fact that what is involved is a reproduction. Roussel almost prefers to describe, as we have pointed out, a universe which is not given as real but as already represented. He likes to place an intermediary artist between himself and the world of men. The text we are offered is a relation concerning a double. The excessive enlargement of certain remote or miniature elements here assumes, therefore, a particular value; for the observer has not been able to approach in order to consider at close hand the detail that catches his attention. From all appearances, he too invents, after the fashion of these numerous creators—of machines or methods—who people the entire work. Sight here is an *imaginary* sense.

Another striking characteristic of these images is what we might call their *instantaneity.* The wave about to break, the child rolling a hoop on the beach, elsewhere the statue of a person making an eloquent gesture (even if its meaning is initially missing, a riddle), or an object represented halfway between the ground and the hand which has just dropped it—everything is given as in movement, but frozen in the middle of that movement, immobilized by the representation which leaves in suspense all gestures, falls, conclusions, etc., eternalizing them in the imminence of their end and severing them from their meaning.

Empty enigmas, arrested time, signs which refuse to signify, giant enlargement of the tiny detail, narratives which come full circle: We are in a *flat* and *discontinuous* universe where each thing refers only to itself. A universe of fixity, of repetition, of absolute obviousness, which enchants and discourages the explorer. . . .

And thus the trap reappears, but it is of another nature. Obviousness, transparency preclude the existence of *higher worlds,* of any transcendence; yet, from this world before us we discover we can no longer escape. Everything is at a standstill, everything endlessly reproduces itself, the child forever holds his stick above the leaning hoop, and the foam of the motionless wave is about to fall back. . . . (pp. 79-87)

> *Alain Robbe-Grillet, "Enigmas and Transparency in Raymond Roussel," in his* For a New Novel: Essays on Fiction, *translated by Richard Howard, Grove Press, Inc., 1966, pp. 79-87.*

MICHEL LEIRIS   (essay date 1964)

[*Leiris is a French autobiographer, poet, novelist, ethnographer, and critic. Early in his career, he was associated with the Surrealists, but he later evolved an individualized style which allowed him to explore the nature of myth and the ambiguities of language. His four-volume autobiography,* La règle du jeu *(1948-76), has been compared to Marcel Proust's* Remembrance of Things Past *and praised for its sensitivity and verbal experimentalism. Leiris's father was a close friend of Roussel, and the young Leiris was one of the earliest champions of Roussel's work. In the following excerpt, Leiris finds the principal motivation for Roussel's works to be a pursuit of pure literary invention, an aesthetic doctrine exemplified by Roussel's statement that "imagination counts for everything in my work."*]

Roussel banked consistently on the imagination, and. . . for him there was a clear antithesis between the invented world which is that of "conception" and the given world—the human world in which we live our daily lives and which we cover in our travels—which is that of "reality."

As for reality, it is certain that Roussel—conscious nevertheless of having received a lion's share of it in the form of his immense fortune—expected nothing good to come of it. (p. 13)

Literarily, it seems that Roussel proceeds always as though it were necessary for there to be the maximum number of screens between nature and himself, so that one might in this case compare him to great aesthetes like Baudelaire and Wilde, for whom art was categorically opposed to nature; but, with Roussel, everything happens as though beauty as such were devoid of importance and as though one should retain of art only the inventiveness, that is, the share of pure conception by which art distinguishes itself from nature. In all his work, one notes that the plot (the structure of the work or its point of departure) is of an artificial, not a natural, character: as Pierre Schneider has pointed out . . . , the poem **"Mon Ame"** which subsequently became **"L'Ame de Victor Hugo,"** written by Roussel at the age of 17 and published in the *Gaulois* of July 12, 1897, a poem which is constructed on the line: "My soul is a strange factory," is nothing more than the development of a banal metaphor of the type: "My soul is an Infanta in her court-dress . . ." and it has as its subject poetic creation itself likened to the stratagems of a creating god; the novel in verse *La Doublure*—during the writing of which Roussel experienced that sensation of "universal glory" which he described to Pierre Janet—has for its theme the story of an actor and consists primarily of a description of the maskers and floats of the Carnival at Nice; the three poems **"La Vue," "La Source"** and **"Le Concert"** describe, not actual spectacles, but three pictures: a photograph set in a pen holder, the label on a bottle

Roussel in Carlsbad, 1910.

of mineral water, a vignette in the letterhead of a sheet of writing paper; far from referring to the Africa of travelers, **Impressions d'Afrique** hinges on a fête of a theatrical character given on the occasion of a coronation; **Locus Solus** is the account of a walk through a park full of wonderful inventions; in the play **L'Etoile au Front,** a series of curios forms the pretext for a string of anecdotes and, in **La Poussière de Soleils** it is a question of a new chain of enigmas which lead to the discovery of a treasure; **Nouvelles Impressions d'Afrique** is nothing more than meditations on four tourist attractions of modern Egypt; finally, of the texts collected in **Comment j'ai écrit . . .**, some are given as illustrations of the eminently artificial method of creation explained in the prologue, the others refer to the Carnival at Nice, with the exception of the six **Documents pour servir de Canevas,** which are of the story-within-a-story type so abundantly represented in Roussel's work and which—like the composition with more or less indefinitely prolonged parentheses peculiar to **Nouvelles Impressions d'Afrique**—seems to have served in the most literal way his need to multiply the screens.

In the preamble to **Comment j'ai écrit . . .** [see excerpt dated 1935], Roussel sets forth the completely arbitrary process which he used for writing his prose works, including the plays; he tried nothing similar for the writings in verse, perhaps because the separation, the distance, the departure from reality was provided by the very fact of expressing himself in verse, without its thus being necessary to resort to additional artifice.

"This process is in short related to rhyme. In both cases, there is unforeseen creation due to phonic combinations." . . . In reality, it seems that Roussel's assertion is merely a theoretical justification, and that (except perhaps in regard to **"Mon Ame"**, the first and most "inspired" of his poems, and which he regarded as his fundamental work), rhyme never played for him the role of a catalyst the way puns did, for, in examining the texture of his verse works, one does not see how rhyme could have served him as a propelling force; one would say, on the contrary, that he put into verse works which might well have been written in prose.

However that may be, the following is the process, in its various forms, which provided Roussel with the elements he used in his prose tales:

1. First, two phrases, identical except for one word, with a play on the double meanings of other substantives in both phrases. "Once the two phrases had been found," Roussel indicates, "it was a question of writing a story which could begin with the first and end with the second."

Example: *Les vers* (The lines of verse) *de la doublure* (of the understudy) *dans la pièce* (in the play) *du Forban Talon Rouge* (of "Red-Heel the Buccaneer") and *Les vers* (The worms) *de la doublure* (in the lining) *de la pièce* (of the patch) *du fort pantalon rouge* (of the heavy red trousers)—which forms the basis of the story **"Chiquenaude"**, published in 1900, the first work which the author considered satisfactory after the profound nervous depression which followed the failure of the novel *La Doublure.*

2. A word with two meanings joined to another word with two meanings by the preposition *à*—with—(which becomes the instrument of association of two absolutely dissimilar elements, just as the conjunction *as* is used to associate two more or less similar elements in the classical metaphor by analogy.)

Example: *Palmier* (a kind of cake, or a palm-tree) *à restauration* (a restaurant where cakes are served or the restoration of a dynasty on a throne), a pair of words which, in *Impressions d'Afrique,* produces the palm-tree of the Square of Trophies consecrated to the restoration of the Talou dynasty.

3. A random phrase "from which I drew images by distorting it, a little as though it were a case of deriving them from the drawings of a rebus."

Example: *Hellstern, 5 Place Vendôme*, the address of Roussel's shoemaker, deformed into *hélice tourne zinc plat se rend dôme*—"propeller turns zinc flat goes dome"—which furnished the elements of an apparatus manipulated by the emperor Talou's eldest son (*ibid.*).

In the works of Raymond Roussel elaborated according to this method, literary creation thus includes a first stage which consists in establishing a sentence or expression with a double meaning, or else in "dislocating" a phrase which already exists; the elements to be confronted with each other and brought into play are thus engendered by these fortuitous formal aspects. After the intermediate stage which is constituted by a logical plot joining these elements together, no matter how disparate they may be, comes the formulation of these relationships on as realistic a level as possible, in a text written with the utmost rigor, with no other attempt at style than the strictest application of the conventional rules, with concision and the absence of repetitions of terms coming at the head of the list of the objectives pursued. (pp. 16-19)

It should be noted that this abstention from any strictly stylistic effects led Roussel to an extraordinary transparency of style.

In *Nouvelles Impressions d'Afrique,* the detachment from the real which Roussel seems to have aimed at is obtained in quite another way: the dislocation of the phrase by means of parentheses introducing a practically infinite series of "false bottoms," breaking up, parceling out, disarticulating the thread of the meaning until one loses it. In his analysis of the second canto of *Nouvelles Impressions,* a work destined to become a classic among Rousselian studies, Jean Ferry very justly writes that "even more than the famous Japanese box whose cubes fit exactly one into the other down to the tiniest of them all, the composition evokes two or three large concentric spheres, between whose surfaces, unequally distant, might float other spheres themselves having several layers," an image taken up in a recent article by Renato Mucci for whom there is no Rousselian work in which the end and the beginning do not join each other as is the case in these poems whose single sentence is cut up by multiple parentheses to which footnotes have been grafted, each of these works appearing as a differentiated unity which, throughout the series of elements peculiar to it, takes on a value of concrete universality in turning back upon itself.

Not only does the process employed by Roussel for the composition of his prose works have the immense interest of adding up to a deliberate promotion of language to the rank of a creative agent, instead of contenting itself with using it as an instrument of execution, but it seems that the subjugation to a specious and arbitrary law (obliging a concentration on the difficult resolution of a problem whose given facts are as *independent* as possible of each other) has as a consequence a distraction whose liberating power appears much more efficacious than the abandon, pure and simple, implied by the use of a process like automatic writing. Aiming at an almost total detachment from everything that is nature, feeling and humanity, and working laboriously over materials apparently so gratuitous that they were not suspect to him, Roussel arrived by this paradoxical method at the creation of *authentic* myths, in which his affectivity is reflected in a more or less direct or symbolic way, as is shown by the frequency of certain themes which constitute the leitmotivs of his work and of which the omnipotence of science, the close relation between microcosm and macrocosm, ecstasy, Eden, the treasure to be discovered or the riddle to be solved, artificial survival and post mortem states, masks and costumes, as well as many themes which could be interpreted as stemming from fetishism or sado-masochism, constitute examples (here enumerated without any attempt at a methodical inventory). It is not an exaggeration to say that the establishing of a thematic index of Roussel's work might allow one to discover a psychological content equivalent to those of most of the great western mythologies; this, because the products of Roussel's imagination are, in a way, *quintessential commonplaces:* disconcerting and singular as it may be for the public, he drew on the same sources as popular imagination and childish imagination and, in addition, his culture was essentially popular and childish (melodramas, serial stories, operettas, vaudeville, fairy tales, stories in pictures, etc.) as are his processes (stories within stories, set forms of words used as the structure for a tale, and down to his method of creation by dramatized puns—the literary equivalent of the mechanism used in certain social diversions, charades, for example). No doubt the almost unanimous incomprehension which Roussel unfortunately encountered resulted less from an inability to attain universality than from this bizarre combination of the "simple as ABC" with the quintessential.

Using childish and popular forms to express his own profundity, Roussel reaches down into a common storehouse, and it is thus not surprising that the personal myths he elaborated are liable to converge (as Michel Carrouges maintains) on certain great occult sequences in western thought; so that it is, to say the least, superfluous to explain (as does André Breton in his preface to Jean Ferry) why the scenario of *La Poussière de Soleils* can seem to be based on the traditional evolution of the alchemists' search for the Philosopher's Stone by suggesting that Roussel might have been an adept of hermetic philosophy. In view of the rules of secrecy which the initiates observe (a rule to which Roussel as an initiate would have been by definition subjected, confining himself, according to the custom, to revealing it in an occult way), such a hypothesis escapes refutation and one can only argue, in order to reject it, the absence of any profession of faith of this kind, in his conversation as well as in his writings; still, the fact remains that in spite of certain aspects of Roussel's work (the important role played by techniques of divination, the frequent use of legendary and marvelous elements), this work utterly lacking in effects of shading has an essentially positivist coloring and that nothing we know of this writer of genius—not even the phase in which he was illumined by a sensation of "universal glory"— inclines one to attribute him aspirations of a mystical nature. (pp. 19-21)

It seems in short that if Roussel declared that he preferred "the domain of Conception to that of Reality," the world which he thus contrasted to that of everyday life had no belief in the supernatural as its base. In *Comment j'ai écrit . . .* Roussel prides himself on being a logician and one must admit that his essential ambition of a man pursuing "euphoria" in the almost demigod-like exercise of his intellect, was to be a champion of the imagination: a Victor Hugo, a Jules Verne, a phenomenal chess player, an Oedipus solving riddles. . . . His effort tends toward the creation of a fictive world, entirely fabricated, having nothing in common with reality; what he invents is valid only insofar as it is invented, where he succeeds in creating truth by the force of his genius alone, without having recourse to some further reality. (pp. 22-3)

> *Michel Leiris, "Conception and Reality in the Work of Raymond Roussel," translated by John Ashbery, in* Art and Literature, *No. 2, Summer, 1964, pp. 12-26.*

THE TIMES LITERARY SUPPLEMENT (essay date 1965)

[*In the following excerpt, the critic praises Roussel's work for its liberating inventiveness and its independence from extra-literary motives.*]

The theorists of the *nouveau roman* have ransomed Roussel from the literary embalmers because they see him above all as a creator of fiction, a writer who, widely travelled though he was, turned his back on "reality" as a fit source of material. No paths lead out of Canterel's lonely park into any world of common reference; at Locus Solus he alone is king. He is addressed throughout as "maître" ["master"], and once, significantly, as "champion de la parole" ["champion of the word"]. His kingdom is in fact a linguistic one, his subject words. The pattern of *Locus Solus* is the double one of Roussel's most interesting work, the text moving continually between the posing of some linguistic mystery and its ultimate

clarification. But so exhaustive are the solutions that we are likely to feel cheated. As Robbe-Grillet puts it, the secret drawer is finally opened and found to be empty.

Having rejected the real world, with its distracting psychologies and sociologies, as proper matter for a fiction, Roussel was faced, of course, with the difficult decision of which words to make his books with, since they were all now reduced to an equal status as building bricks. His methods of creation, based on elaborate distortions of sound and meaning, are well known, and by no means indigenous—there are some poems of Ogden Nash, for example, which owe their existence to a similar technique. But the important thing in Roussel's case is that by choosing his popular sayings, lines of poetry and so on, he was acknowledging an external necessity, and one which establishes the limits within which our creative freedom may operate. Thus Canterel constructs his famous mosaic out of human teeth by reliance on the elements, his prodigious achievement having been to predict their vagaries with total accuracy. The original choice of words or phrase having been made and the form of the distortion decided on, then the work takes on its own private necessity, since it becomes the record of the passage from point A to point B. But to conclude, as Robbe-Grillet does, that such a procedure makes the fiction perfectly self-contained seems to ignore what Roussel himself said about the difficulty of finding fertile homonyms. A single one might take up to twenty-four hours to hit upon, as it was essential that it should open the way to a fiction, and many proved a dead end.

Some of the phrases round which *Locus Solus* was constructed have been explained in *Comment j'ai écrit quelques-uns de mes livres;* others might be guessed at, certainly in vain. We are in the position of the greedy brothers of the Princess Hello in this book, who need to reconstitute the magic formula if they are to open the iron grille to wealth and power. But they can only guess at its approximate form and it is left to the fool, who has been entrusted with the secret, finally to turn the key in the lock. The episode is characteristic; the search is for the form of words, the correct repetition of a vital phrase which will restore the heir to her throne.

This theme of restoration is the theme of sanity, as another episode in *Locus Solus* shows. Lucius Egroizard goes mad after the unfortunate death of his little daughter and is brought to Canterel for treatment. In his madness he proves to us that the mother of artistic invention is obsession, and that the way to sanity lies through his perpetual attempts to give substance to a dream by the progressive distortion of the elements offered to his senses by the real world. By experimenting endlessly on the sound of a real voice Lucius eventually comes to hear again the voice of the dead child, and this, we are told, is a big step forward in his cure.

The lesson of *Locus Solus* is above all that the exercise of human freedom demands a literature, or some other art form. It is when we reassemble the contents of our minds and create our own patterns with them that we are most free, not when we invest our attention wholly in the world about us. A future sociology may link this apparent abdication from the accepted responsibilities of the novelist with extra-literary pressures on the sensitive conscience. But if the future of the novel lies in the direction in which the *nouveaux romanciers* often say it lies then Roussel will be found to have moved right into the centre of an aesthetic tradition.

> *"Words in Confusion," in* The Times Literary Supplement, *No. 3328, December 9, 1965, p. 1121.*

THE TIMES LITERARY SUPPLEMENT   (essay date 1966)

[*In the following excerpt, the critic examines the significance of the narrative structure Roussel employed in* Impressions of Africa.]

Impressions of Africa is constructed very much like Roussel's other major prose work, *Locus Solus*. It is divided into two halves. The first consists of a long sequence of disconnected scenes or tableaux, which together make up a carnival in honour of an African king's coronation; some involve action, others are static, but all of them present us with a puzzle about what on earth they might signify. The second half, starting at an earlier point in time than the first, introduces all these disconnected representations singly into a coherent narrative, albeit one so full of literary conventions that it lacks all human interest. A weakness of this book, as compared with *Locus Solus,* is that the puzzles are separated from their "solution" by too long a gap. Not only is their succession in the first half overwhelming, but also the revelations, when they come in the second half, fall a bit flat.

But this binary pattern is the key to deciding just what Roussel is getting at, and it also explains why there is now so much more interest in his work than there was. First we are mystified, then enlightened; first we are shown a series of isolated representations and then they are joined together. The technique is very much that of the detective story and of the *nouveaux romanciers*. Roussel's precocious aim in fact was to define beyond argument in what fiction had to consist if it was to be fiction, and it is an aim he pursues ruthlessly. To his representations he gives the status of facts and to the narrative that joins them that of fiction. Fiction is therefore pure imagination, it can exist because the facts that have lodged in our minds are discontinuous and demand to be put in some significant order. It is moreover—a crucial point where Roussel is concerned— an attempt at restoration, because through a fiction we can recover something of the lost unity of our original perceptions, now turned by time into a lumber-room of images.

Thus the frantic carnival that fills the first half of *Impressions of Africa* is a series of mental images that demand to be lent a meaning. And even within the individual scenes themselves, the ones that involve movement at least, there is evidence of Roussel's purpose. Many of the performers come on to the stage with pieces of completely heterogeneous apparatus, and then proceed to establish some productive commerce between them, by mechanisms that ignore the limitations imposed by the laws of nature. What they produce is frequently a work of art that mirrors Roussel's own, a piece of music or a painting.

The same structure also underlies his methods of phonic distortion, very clearly described by Rayner Heppenstall in his short book on Roussel [see excerpt dated 1967], which sets out to inform rather than to analyse. What Roussel did, broadly speaking, was to start from a linguistic fact, a phrase or a sentence from a book or a poem, and transform it into a motive, a source of movement for him alone, by altering one or more of its phonetic units, thus creating the other term of a possible journey. This is simply a parody of the activity of any creative writer, who must start with fact and end in fancy, a parody because in Roussel's books the process is a purely aleatory one.

From this point of view what he wrote were anti-novels, and his own linking narratives indeed depend on the least authentic of literary conventions, like the shipwreck and the tribal warfare of *Impressions of Africa*. Yet the book is far from being

a negative one, because it forms an instructive parable on the proper uses of the human imagination. In the many examples which Mr. Heppenstall gives of Roussel's distortions it is clear that these were often not only phonic but also grammatical, there are nearly always more nouns in the distorted phrase than in its model. Thus Roussel induces an artificial stasis in his original, and mimics the process of time itself, when it turns our dynamic perceptions into static images. When he later sets out to join up his images he is therefore embarking on the task we all embark on whenever we have cause to reflect on our experience, which involves the animation as it were of our motionless memories.

In his brief run-through of what has so far been written about Roussel in France Mr. Heppenstall seems to underestimate [New Novelist] Michel Butor's very intelligent essay on him. Of *Impressions of Africa,* M. Butor writes: "L'ouvrage raconte une fête de délivrance" ["the work tells of a celebration of deliverance"], a judgment that helps enormously to understand what takes place in this book. It contains indeed many examples of deliverance, which is always effected in the same way, by the correct repetition of some established formula, and once, most significantly of all, by the correct activation of repressed memories. The lesson is obvious; the task of fiction is essentially therapeutic, by manipulation of our stock of images we try to restore their lost unity, try in fact to turn back the clock.

A single example from the end of *Impressions of Africa* will perhaps suffice to make this clear. Before the party of shipwrecked Europeans—exiles be it noted from their rightful home, who had set out on their journey with another destination in mind—can return to their homes, one of them, Carmichael, a singer, has to learn by heart and repeat to the King, their captor, a long and incomprehensible poem about the latter's achievements. The first time he makes a single slight slip in the performance and is locked up, the second time he is word-perfect and release follows immediately. The distortion therefore that he has practised on the original text has made him a captive, and is the guarantee that a fiction will be required for him to be set free, so that it is no surprise when the unnamed narrator of *Impressions of Africa* is called on to rehearse Carmichael for his second performance. If there had been no imperfection, no distortion, there would have been no novel, but since, on the existential plane, it is time that practises this distortion on our minds we can say that there will ever be a need for novels. Roussel has simply defined the novel as the free "play" of the mind, and as a form of therapy based on sound mnemotechnic principles.

> *"By Pun and Homophone," in* The Times Literary Supplement, *No. 3378, November 24, 1966, p. 1061.**

GEORGE STEINER   (essay date 1967)

[*Steiner is a French-born American critic, poet, and fiction writer. He has described his approach to literary criticism as "a kind of continuous inquiry into and conjecture about the relations between literature and society, between poetic value and humane conduct." A central concern of his critical thought is whether or not literature can survive the barbarism of the modern world, particularly in view of the Holocaust. Steiner has written, "We now know that a man can read Goethe or Rilke in the evening, that he can play Bach or Schubert and go to his day's work at Auschwitz in the morning." Steiner's work encompasses a wide range of subjects, including social and literary criticism, linguistics, philosophy, and chess. Though some commentators have found fault with his sometimes exuberant prose style, Steiner is generally regarded as a perceptive and extremely erudite critic. In the following excerpt, Steiner dismisses* Impressions of Africa *as the product of an artistically and psychologically immature personality, granting the work only minor interest in the history of modern literature.*]

Impressions d'Afrique . . . purports to tell the adventures of a grotesque assemblage of shipwrecked and captured Europeans in the African town of Ejur (itself a feeble French pun), capital of his black imperial majesty Talu VII. The time sequence of the tale is distorted in a ham-fisted way: it is only at the halfway point that the narrator informs us of the events leading up to the infantile festivities with which the book opens. But even at that stage the narrative breaks off for further elaborate flashbacks and set pieces. The heart of the whole business is a gala mounted by the marooned actors, singers, pyrotechnicians, fencing masters, mustachioed ex-ballerinas, and hypnotists to celebrate Talu's enthronement over newly conquered territories. The closing pages convey the ransomed passengers back to Marseille. As Mr. Heppenstall points out [see excerpt dated 1967], most of the effects in the book derive from word pairings and from sets of interlocking phonetic associations: "Many details of the story . . . were supplied by a verbal procedure which consisted in taking two nouns, each susceptible of more than one meaning, and linking them together by means of the general-purpose preposition *à*. Picked in the first place to make sense together, each of the two nouns is subsequently taken in a remoter meaning, Roussel's imagination then making what it could of the result."

The response to which cheery comment has to be that he didn't make much. There are inventive patches and one or two bursts

Advertisement for the stage production of Impressions d'Afrique *(Impressions of Africa). Collection Mme. Duard.*

of hallucinatory suggestion. Some of the descriptions of the gala and its *tableaux vivants* are reminiscent, in a feeble way, of the mad Oklahoma circus in Kafka's "Amerika" (the two books are almost contemporary). Madame Adinolfa, the diva, discovers the original manuscript of "Romeo and Juliet," and Roussel's account of this imaginary opus has a kind of undergraduate brio. But the bulk of *Impressions of Africa* is labored tinsel, a charade interminably urged on yawning guests. Peppered with vignettes of Victorian-style sadism and with fairly evident hints of Roussel's sexual inclinations, the book is very difficult to wade through.

This does not rob it of a minor historical interest or a certain desperate integrity of its own. Roussel's use of language as a total game has a prophetic edge. His juggling of time and normal logic, though by no means unique by 1910, does have relevance to the collages of modern art and film. Precedents for Pop Art and Camp can be read into Roussel. And for all its seedy pretensions, *Impressions of Africa* does imply the conjecture that the classic novel had little more to say, that fiction might have to be pushed to extremity before literature could be made new. This revolt against the fixity of classic forms is, I assume, symbolized by the mutation of "Romeo and Juliet." Even Shakespeare reënters the realm of total and absurd possibility. This, if he has come across it, is an invention Jorge Luis Borges might admire. Mr. Heppenstall rightly invokes Borges' name in the context of Roussel. But the difference tells more than does any analogy. Borges' "Fictions" are among the wonders of modern literature. But they are very brief, precisely as if Borges meant to teach us that a surrealistic vision can be sustained only over a short span, as if the fantastic, when it is authentic and rooted in a new syntax, had the quality of an electric arc light, transmuting the landscape but blazing only an instant. Secondly, Borges' dissent from ordinary fiction, his search for symbolic modes more "real" than the facsimiles of current realism, are based on a view of the world both responsible and profoundly educated. Borges has previously mastered all that he fantasticates. Roussel's distortions have behind them no adult experience of order. He belongs, primarily, to the pathology of letters.

Impressions of Africa does little to answer the question of whether it is possible to write a serious novel in which the main theme is the nature and possibility of fiction. (pp. 206, 209-10)

George Steiner, "Games People Play," in The New Yorker, *Vol. XLIII, No. 36, October 28, 1967, pp. 206, 209-12.**

JOHN ASHBERY (essay date 1967)

[*Ashbery is an American poet and critic. His works are noted for their radical experimentalism, demonstrating a rejection of conventional syntax, traditional poetic structure, and definable meaning. Of his work, Ashbery has commented: "There are no themes or subjects in the usual sense, except the very broad one of an individual consciousness confronting or confronted by a world of external phenomena. The work is a very complex, but, I hope, clear and concrete transcript of the impressions left by these phenomena on that consciousness. . . . Characteristic devices are ellipses, frequent changes of tone, voice (that is, the narrator's voice), point of view, to give an impression of flux." While some critics contend that this approach results in fragmented, though elegant, nonsense, Ashbery's works are more often included among the most important and challenging in contemporary American poetry. In the following excerpt, originally published in the* New York Times Book Review *on 20 October 1967, Ashbery comments*] *on Roussel's literary reputation and his significance as a modern writer.*]

Now that clandestinity has achieved status, it seems improbable that there can still be forgotten geniuses. . . .

Nevertheless, one of the greatest and most influential of 20th-century writers remains almost unknown. He is Raymond Roussel, whose work, all but forgotten since his death in 1933, has recently been reprinted in France and elsewhere in Europe, and in England. . . . (p. 59)

Yet Roussel will probably remain, after the current fuss dies down, an obscure celebrity, the delight of a handful of enthusiasts. For one thing, there continues to exist what Rayner Heppenstall [see excerpt dated 1967], the British novelist, poet and critic, calls a "critical vacuum" around Roussel (and one of the shortcomings of Mr. Heppenstall's book is that he makes no attempt to fill it). With the possible exception of Butor and of Michel Leiris [see excerpt dated 1964], none of the writers who have dealt intelligently and sympathetically with Roussel have succeeded in making clear just what is so extraordinary about him: it would seem to be something that can be felt but not communicated. In the absence of effective persuasion, it is unlikely that vast numbers of readers will be induced to read him, and even if they did, they would probably miss the point of Roussel, since it is a point that is easy to miss.

It is difficult and tedious even to describe Roussel's work, since the work itself is purely descriptive. It is also highly condensed; he rewrote each sentence as many as 20 times in order to use the fewest possible words, and he said of one of his poems that he "literally bled over each line." Sometimes in the agony of this process he would roll on the floor of his study like a madman. The result in the case of each of his books is a gigantic dose of minutiae: to describe one is like trying to summarize the Manhattan telephone book. Moreover the force of his writing is felt only gradually; it proceeds from the accumulated weight of this mad wealth of particulars. A page or even a chapter of Roussel, fascinating as it may be, gives no idea of the final effect which is a question of destiny: the whole is more than the sum of its parts. It is an experience unique in literature. (pp. 60-1)

It is characteristic of Roussel that his different periods as a writer have almost nothing in common; works from his early, middle and late years could be by different hands. Certainly nothing in his early writing prepares us for *Impressions of Africa,* which is merely a catalogue of descriptions of fantastic objects and events, held together by a thin ribbon of plot, and delivered in a neutral, antiseptic style which Michel Leiris compares to French prose as students are taught to write it in *lycées.* As in *Locus Solus,* description is followed inexorably by explication. We witness the various attractions in an endless "gala" held in an African native capital. Only after the performance has ended do we learn the reason for its existence and the circumstances of each of the different numbers. It seems that a liner transporting a number of diversely talented Europeans to South America was shipwrecked off the coast of Africa; the voyagers were taken prisoner by Talu, the local potentate, and held for ransom. To while away the time they concoct the various tableaux for a performance to be held on the day of their deliverance. One might logically begin the novel in the middle, saving the beginning for the end, and in fact a printed slip inserted in its later editions advised readers to do so.

Mr. Heppenstall suggests that Roussel might in fact have intended to reprint the book with the two halves in their normal chronological sequence. This may have been the case, but one must bear in mind that Roussel believed the book, and his works in general, to contain "messages" whose content we can only guess at; and that the public, given sufficient prompting, would eventually "understand." It was to this end that he transformed *Impressions of Africa* into a play after its failure to attract attention as a novel, and again reprinted about half of it and of *Locus Solus* in a curious volume of *Selected Pages* even though both volumes were still in print. Alexandre Devarennes, an actor in the stage version of *Impressions* who later became a film director of some note, told me that Roussel had approached him about making a movie of the novel. If he did intend to republish the novel in a more conventional form, it could only have been as a final, despairing concession to a public that could not or would not "understand."

What there was to understand is a much-debated point. Was it merely a question of unraveling all the *jeux de mots* ["word-play"] of which Roussel provides some samples in **"How I Wrote Certain of My Books,"** and perhaps using them to decode a hidden "message" (but of what sort?). Or were there, as André Breton has convincingly argued, arcane alchemical references buried in Roussel, leading to the discovery of a kind of philosopher's stone, which is called in French *le Grand Oeuvre* (the Great Work), suggesting in this case a literary form of alchemy?

Whatever it may have been, there is no doubt that the cart-before-the-horse sequence of both novels is part of their amazing effect, which is perhaps to be distinguished from the effect intended by the author. We are constantly confronted with a mystery whose explanation merely substitutes an even graver mystery. The reasons for Jizmé's "voluntary" execution by lightning or for the staging of a fantastic version of the final scene of Shakespeare's "Romeo and Juliet" are stranger than the events themselves because they are supposed to be real. To quote from Cocteau's remarks on Roussel (in *Opium*) [see excerpt dated 1930]: "The author reveals first the experiments and then the devices behind them, but the devices depend on a reality, on Roussel, just as the devices admitted by the conjurer do not make us capable of performing the trick. The illusionist who reveals his device transfers minds from a mystery they reject to a mystery they accept."

While it is possible to enjoy *Impressions of Africa* as a complex, many-colored pageant or, again in Cocteau's phrase, as "a suspended world of elegance, enchantment and fear," the sources of its extraordinary power are buried in its language—in the word-games that Roussel used to fabricate that language and then plowed under, so to speak. It is true that we might never have suspected their existence if Roussel had not obligingly called our attention to them in **"How I Wrote Certain of My Books."** It is nonetheless true that their presence imparts an undefinable, hypnotic quality to the text, and unfortunately it is a kind that no translation, however gifted (and the Foord-Heppenstall translation is, on the whole, both faithful and fluent) can hope to convey.

One example will suffice: the celebrated phrase *"des rails en mou de veau"* ("rails made of calf's lights") which somehow caught the fancy of the public who came to laugh at the play, and made Roussel notorious overnight. For reasons too complicated to summarize here, King Talu orders the sculptor Norbert Montalescot to construct a statue light enough to move along rails made of this substance on a rolling platform. The resourceful prisoner solves the problem by making his statue of whalebone corset-stays, a supply of which providentially figures in the cargo rescued from the shipwrecked vessel. But, disregarding for the moment the meaning of the French words and the pseudo-rational reason for their being there, we can recognize in them a svelte, secret resonance that implies hidden chambers and secret meanings. The phrase is like a Chinese box that one turns over and over, certain that there is a concealed spring somewhere, that in a moment the lid will fly open, revealing possibly nothing more than its own emptiness, but proving that reality is only a false bottom.

This is the essence of Roussel's genius, and the reason why in France he has been compared to Joyce and to Mallarmé. The comparison is far-fetched, yet it is true that each of these three writers tried to raise the word to a new power; in Roussel's case one feels that it is about to break open, to yield true meaning at last; that it is the lead which alchemy is on the verge of translating into something far more interesting than gold. The miracle does not take place, the surface of his prose remains as stern and correct as the facade of a French prefecture or the gold-lettered bindings of the Grand Larousse. But the attentive reader will have glimpsed the possibility, and his feelings about language will never be the same again. (pp. 62-4)

John Ashbery, "In Darkest Language," in How I Wrote Certain of My Books *by Raymond Roussel, Sun, 1977, pp. 57-64.*

RAYNER HEPPENSTALL (essay date 1967)

[*Heppenstall was an English novelist, critic, and autobiographer who wrote extensively of his experiences with such literary figures as George Orwell and Dylan Thomas. As a literary theorist, he is closely allied with the philosophy of the nouveau roman (New Novel). Heppenstall's later novels demonstrate his allegiance to this school, and he has written perceptively on New Novelists Alain Robbe-Grillet, Michel Butor, and Nathalie Sarraute. Heppenstall has been widely praised for the philosophical and theoretical complexity of his literary criticism. In the following excerpt Heppenstall, who translated* Impressions of Africa, *discusses Roussel's poetry, fiction, and drama, and presents a synopsis of his reputation among French critics.*]

As we are most likely to meet it now, *Mon Âme* occurs as a kind of appendix to the volume *Nouvelles Impressions d'Afrique,* the first and last works in verse first appearing together in volume form, in 1932, thirty-five years after the first appearance of *Mon Âme* in a periodical, the Sunday *Gaulois,* and about thirty-eight after its composition. It is a not-unimpressive work, and Raymond Roussel continued to think highly of it all his life.

When it appeared in a book with the *Nouvelles Impressions,* its title had been altered. It had become *L'Âme de Victor Hugo.* The original poem had been newly prefaced with the brief explanation that, one night, the poet had dreamt that he saw Victor Hugo writing at his work table and that the poem which follows was what he read when he looked over Victor Hugo's shoulder. The penultimate stanza reads:

> À cette explosion voisine
> De mon génie universel,
> Je vois le monde qui s'incline
> Devant ce nom: *Victor Hugo.*

> [At this proximate explosion
> Of my universal genius,
> I see the world which bows
> Before this name: Victor Hugo.]

From the rhyme-pattern, it is clear that the name of Raymond Roussel stood in the first place where that of Victor Hugo now stands and that it was to *his* universal genius the world bowed. Perhaps one day it will transpire when the alteration was made, whether when, in 1897, it first became clear that Roussel's '*génie universel*' was not to be acknowledged straightaway or when, thirty-five years later, still disappointed of his expectations, he arranged the volume, *Nouvelles Impressions d'Afrique,* for publication. In any case, the self-identification with Victor Hugo was not casually improvised at that moment, whatever the moment was. (pp. 20-1)

With all the reservations one has to make, I find *La Doublure* a deeply moving work. Roussel was never again to be straightforwardly moving in that way, essentially the way of 'realistically' putting us in possession of the facts of a simple human story, that of a happy but temporary love in the life of a bad but uncomplaining actor, which may be presumed to have moved the author himself, precisely, it may be, at the fair in Neuilly, where he lived. It is strange that a work composed in the mood of exaltation [psychologist Pierre] Janet depicts should be sensitively concerned with failure. It is perhaps also strange that the first full-scale work of a rich young man should be centred upon a man, apparently no longer young, whose life is so markedly affected by economic pressures. In no general way was Raymond Roussel ever to show himself interested in social problems or preoccupied with the alleviation of modern distress.

A minor point we may note is that the narration in *La Doublure* is conducted wholly in the present tense, as it is also in *L'Inconsolable* and *Têtes de Carton.* It is perhaps a point of more importance that, in so far as a foreigner can judge, Roussel was, from the outset, extraordinarily well-equipped, technically, as a poet. He did not, it is true, attempt any great variety of forms, but what seem to be exemplary alexandrines are added to each other without apparent effort, always lucid, uncontorted, not much padded with the usual *chevilles,* the prose sense carried forward with what, I dare say, might be considered too much *enjambement,* all, in its own odd way, very modern and simple on the surface. But, on the surface, Roussel is rarely obscure.

The title-piece in the volume *La Vue* is a poem of some two thousand lines. The volume contains two further poems, *Le Concert* and *La Source,* of about half that length. Each describes, in far more detail than it is possible to imagine being physically visible, a miniature view. In *La Vue,* it is a sea-side prospect engraved on a lens set into a penholder. In *Le Concert,* it is the heading of a sheet of hotel writing paper, showing the hotel itself, an omnibus standing before it, the lake beyond and public gardens with a bandstand. In *La Source,* the label on a bottle of mineral water shows the spring itself and a girl in peasant costume serving customers with the wholesome draught. (pp. 23-4)

The game is not unamusing, and these are shapely poems. At one time, it may be remembered, M. Robbe-Grillet and his contemporaries were known as the *école du regard* ["school of sight"]. Insofar as mere looking and closely describing is a principal characteristic of their works, *La Vue* may well have been the volume of Roussel's which most affected them. (p. 25)

In the posthumous volume, *Comment J'Ai Écrit Certains de mes Livres,* the seventeen earliest stories are grouped together as *Textes de Grande Jeunesse ou Textes-Genèse* ['Texts from Early Youth, or Genesis-Texts']. The collocation of the two near-homophones '*jeunesse*' and '*genèse*' is no mere example of the punning word-play which was to underpin most of Roussel's work in prose. In the order in which these seventeen stories are printed, the first three are truly *textes-genèse* in a sense which I hope will presently appear, and the suggestion perhaps is that, primitive as they must be considered, they were written a little later than the others, *i.e.*, not in what Roussel regarded as his extreme youth.

All seventeen of them and a number of somewhat later pieces display a strict and invariable formula. The opening phrase of each story is repeated at the end of it, with the change (or omission or addition) of only one letter or (in a single case) one consonantal sound which requires the addition of two letters. The rest of the phrase remains identical to eye and ear. There are, that is to say, no differently spelt homophones or differently pronounced homographs, though other nouns in the phrase may be taken in different senses. (pp. 25-6)

All the stories are told in the first person, and in most of them it is the narrator who, at the end, triumphantly produces the altered phrase, though in no case can his auditors know in what the triumph consists, since they are unaware of what the phrase originally was. A number of characters recur, the rich Goulots, the elderly mathematics teacher Volcan, the painter Dabussol, but this recurrence tells us little about the order in which the stories were written or about any significance in the order in which they are printed. The three printed first are three that were to be rehandled, are in that sense *textes-genèse*, the start of something. The quality of the other tales varies considerably. An element of monotony in the group as a whole is provided by the fact that in no fewer than ten of the stories we are concerned with some painting or drawing, a wrong detail in which generally provides the pay-off lines themselves. Certain words recur ('*sonnettes*', '*raie*', '*bouton*', '*boucle*'). In two stories, there is what appears to be unintended confusion, as though Roussel had simply forgotten what he had told us earlier. Games and practical jokes abound. They are rarely amusing in themselves.

We must remember, however, that Roussel himself did not think well of any of these seventeen early stories and made no attempt to print any of them when they were first written. His reason for including them in the posthumous *Comment J'Ai* was purely to document the earliest, simplest and most open of his verbal procedures. Yet several of the stories are fine or contain fine things. The seventh, for instance, gives us a balloon ascent in which the receding landscape is beautifully rendered. No doubt there is some debt here to Jules Verne, but it is likely enough that the rich and leisured Raymond Roussel occasionally chartered a balloon. (p. 27)

It may be worth insisting at this point that in none of the many early stories can the anguish of a neurotic personality be readily perceived. But, indeed, nowhere in his work does Raymond Roussel strike one as a writer driven to seek expression for deeply buried impulses. All persistent writers and creative artists are perhaps acting under some form of compulsion, and, in one sense of the word, Raymond Roussel was a 'compulsive' writer. I take it, however, that in the main he was simply compelled to pursue an activity he enjoyed and one in which he felt at home, as he rarely did in the world outside. He was driven to create a world, recognisedly unreal but full of order, a world governed by arbitrary and controllable rules, a world of play, a world in large measure innocent. It seems to me particularly true of the early stories. In them, we are recurrently aware of a tenderness felt especially towards little girls. If we

except the melodramatic and theatrical poisoning of the '*brune un peu mûre*' ['dark Spanish beauty, no longer young'], the worst that happens is that one or two practical jokes begin to look as if they might get out of hand.

But nowhere in Raymond Roussel is the human climate oppressive. In *Impressions d'Afrique,* we . . . find that crimes are committed and that discovered criminals are subjected to torture. But the point of the tortures is their ingenuity and appropriateness. Pain, bloodshed and convulsive reactions are nowhere paraded for our delectation. We may wonder at the severity with which the black lovers, Naïr and Jizme, are punished, since they had principally offended Mossem, himself condemned, but in all other cases the sentence is just and may be avoided if the victim repents. The crimes themselves were, for the most part, acts of oppression and treachery committed for greed against the inoffensive and helpless, who also frequently are young. (p. 31)

M. Foucault rightly stresses a tendency in Roussel first to mystify, then to explain, a tendency not only in particular works but throughout the general course of his life and work, ending posthumously with the key provided by *Comment J'Ai Écrit Certains de mes Livres*. There are signs, nevertheless, of Roussel possibly wondering later whether, in *Impressions d'Afrique,* he might not have overdone it, as he was certainly not to do in the succeeding *Locus Solus* or the two plays.

In the dramatic version of 1911-12, all is presented in chronological order, as we may see from the one actor's part salvaged by John Ashbery and printed, in 1964, in the special Roussel number of *Bizarre*. In the *Pages Choisies* of 1918, what we are offered from *Impressions d'Afrique* is simply its second half, with the chapters, originally X to XXVI, renumbered I to XVII and the sentence, on the original page 212, with which the protracted flashback opens, altered to begin, '*Le 15 mars 19 . . .*', not, as it had formerly begun, '*Le 15 mars précédent*'. In a fourth impression of the full text, dated 1932, a slip has been pasted, on which those unfamiliar with the art of Raymond Roussel are recommended to read pages 212-455 first and pages 1-211 subsequently. (pp. 32-3)

The printed slip may have been something of a despairing gesture. It would, in any case, have been more reasonable to recommend first reading pages 212-452, then 1-211, then the final chapter. For the benefit of a few strong-minded readers, it may here be said that, in the English translation, this would mean first reading pages 152-315, then 5-151, then 316-7. (pp. 33-4)

[The] early story, *Parmi les Noirs,* provided a framework for *Impressions d'Afrique* and was truly a *texte-genèse* in that sense. This, it may be remembered, is the story which begins with '*les lettres du blanc sur les bandes du vieux billard*' and ends with '*les lettres du blanc sur les bandes du vieux pillard*', almost identical phrases in which every noun has changed its meaning. (p. 34)

Many details of [*Impressions of Africa*] . . . were supplied by a verbal procedure which consisted in taking two nouns, each susceptible of more than one meaning, and linking them together by means of the general-purpose preposition *à*. Picked in the first place to make sense together, each of the two nouns is subsequently taken in a remoter meaning, Roussel's imagination then making what it could of the result. . . . [It] may be worth pointing out here that the procedure allowed an absolute minimum of free association, was positively counter-Freudian. We do not know precisely how Roussel selected his words. We do know that he was addicted to poring over dictionaries. We do not know just how rigorously, once two words had been paired, he felt bound to abide by the result, however unpromising it might seem. On the other hand, certain of the results appear so forced that we may well be inclined to suppose that the rules of the game did not allow any pair of words, once joined, to be rejected or reshuffled. (pp. 36-7)

Between *Impressions d'Afrique* and *Locus Solus* came the stage version of the former. In this, as has been said, all was arranged in chronological order. *Locus Solus* appearing in 1914, the war intervened between its publication and any possible stage adaptation, whether by its author or by another hand. I imagine *Locus Solus* to have been conceived and written with an eventual stage adaptation in mind. Unlike *Impressions d'Afrique,* it has something of the order that would be required for a stage presentation. This tends to make one feel that it is more satisfactory, more beautiful, formally. In what I have said about *Impressions d'Afrique* and Roussel's apparent later feeling that the order of the chapters might have been changed, there is perhaps also a suggestion that, formally, the book is unsatisfactory. But then, if, with Mr. F. R. Leavis, we are in part to admire a book for the complexity of its organisation, it must be said that the complexity of a book's organisation is doubled if it may and should be read two ways round.

I feel no doubt, in fact, that *Impressions d'Afrique* is Roussel's masterpiece or that it is, quite simply, a masterpiece. On the other hand, if my fellow-Rousselians put in a claim for *Locus Solus,* I shall understand perfectly well what they mean. I am for richness, they for lucid form. (p. 48)

Though described as a novel, *Locus Solus* has even less in the way of over-all narrative framework than *Impressions d'Afrique.* The narrative framework simply is that a group of visitors, including an unnamed first-person narrator, are taken round the ingenious marvels visible on the estate, at Montmorency, about twelve miles outside Paris, of Martial Canterel, rich scientist, magician and illusionist.

As in all the later prose works, including the plays, it is the individual stories told or re-enacted which are of interest. The best of these in *Locus Solus* are of a haunting charm and strangeness. The book is more static than *Impressions d'Afrique.* There is less interplay between the various groups of characters and ingenuities. This is, as it were, a gala performance without real occasion. (p. 49)

In the absence of full texts and numerous photographs and drawings, it is difficult to imagine how certain things in *Impressions d'Afrique* and *Locus Solus* were ever presented on a stage. (p. 54)

In *L'Étoile au Front* and *La Poussière de Soleils,* written for theatrical performance in the first place, there is nothing either flatly impossible for the stage or likely to be unintelligible or invisible upon it. Indeed, with the more lightly stylised and fluid methods of presentation used today, it is not inconceivable that *La Poussière de Soleils* should make an agreeable evening's entertainment. No amount of ingenious stagecraft or subtlety of performance could preserve *L'Étoile au Front* from the prompt onset of boredom and irritation in an audience, despite the many incidental splendours. (p. 55)

The framework of [*L'Étoile au Front*] is conventional. There are three acts. The first takes place in a drawing-room in Marly, the second in the grounds of the same house a week or more later and the third in an antique shop in Paris. The time is (or

was) the present. The characters are a rich collector, two young people, betrothed to each other, who are in his tutelage, the antique dealer, his wife and son, a lawyer, a half-Indian female servant, a male Indian in love with her, another servant and two Indian twin girls who have been saved by the collector from a temple sacrifice. In the first act, it appears that there is to be a main plot, concerned with the abduction or murder of the twin girls by the male Indian, recently arrived in France, and at the end of the act some element of real drama appears in his playing on the divided loyalties of the half-Indian servant. We might have been a little worried, during the act, by the marked disposition of the collector and the betrothed couple to tell each other stories about various *objets d'art* in the room and about the authors of books, but we might also have supposed that these would in due course find their place in the action. We should have noticed two oddities about the dialogue, in the first place the extreme *naïveté* of the many lines of the my-father-as-you-know-was-a-butcher type and in the second place the not always ineffective but soon irritating tendency the characters have to prompt each other with their stories, as though some old theatrical hand had told Roussel to break up his dialogue as much as possible and he had taken the advice excessively to heart. (pp. 55-6)

A number of the stories told on-stage concern, as do stories in all Roussel's large prose-works, real-life personages, here Milton, Rameau and Lope de Vega. The story of Lope de Vega is told in Act I, Scene III, by Geneviève to her *fiancé* Claude. This appealing story concerns a former mistress of Lope's who becomes abbess of a convent for penitent young female sinners. The tradition is that, before she takes the veil, a headless plaster cast is made of each nun's body, and the casts are disposed over a large terrace about a statue of Mary Magdalene, in token of all the desirable young flesh she has saved from perdition. In his later years and at the height of his fame, Lope visits the convent in an official capacity. He will see the plaster casts and know that one of them is that of his former mistress's body. She wishes discreetly to inform him which of them it is, so that his eye will not wander. This she achieves by causing the arrangement of flowers in a triumphal arch to cast on the place of her heart a horizontal figure eight, the mathematical sign for infinity, which a gipsy woman had once traced on the ground for them in answer to a question at the time of their love.

I find this haunting. I also believe (not without murmured assent from him) that it haunted M. Robbe-Grillet, who in *Le Voyeur* makes a very different but no less obsessive use of the horizontal figure eight. A further story in Act II of *L'Étoile au Front* is doubly concerned, as between a king and a queen in a play and as between the actor and actress playing them, with images of desirable nudity, in these two cases not retrospectively but prospectively important. *L'Étoile au Front* was the first work written after a presumed crisis which had taken Roussel to Janet and caused the latter to write about his patient. I do not want to make too much of these tenuous indications, but it is almost as though one were witnessing a timid rebirth of something resembling adult sexuality after twenty-five years of repression, for there was an element of sensuality in *La Doublure,* at the time of the first crisis, and there is none in any of the writing which intervenes.

Alas, the play as a play is lamentable. In real life, nothing is more tedious than the capping of one story by another, whether of dirty stories among members of the commercial classes or of intrinsically wittier anecdotes among people of more education and refinement. The play's reception by its first public was no mere exhibition of unreceptive philistinism. Nowhere perhaps does Raymond Roussel show powerful constructional, architectonic gifts, but at best, like Boccaccio, an artful grouping of his miniatures. In no other work, however, does overall imagination seem to have deserted him so completely as in *L'Étoile au Front,* despite an original determination to arrange all within the framework of a conventional three-act play. Faced only with this work, one might, I feel, have concluded that Raymond Roussel was simply mad, with all that the idea implies in the way of mental incapacity, imaginative incoherency. He was forty-seven when the play was put on.

The title . . . connects up with 'the brand on one's brow, the star one bears resplendent', in the Janet account. It is unconnected with anything whatever in the play until, at the last moment, it appears to provide a poetical flourish and a curtain line. We are referred to the work of a learned psychograph in which a spiritual and creative *élite* are described as having been born, though humbly and of obscure life, with a star on the forehead, a star presumably invisible to all but the spiritual eye. A valuable copy of this book is given by the antique dealer to Geneviève, who concludes the play by saying that perhaps her firstborn will have a star on its forehead.

La Poussière de Soleils, two years later, similarly ends on the words of its title, which are equally unrelated to all that has gone before. All the same, it is a better play. Roussel's odd verbal procedures in themselves are not unlike treasure-hunt clues, and the action of *Poussière* is a treasure hunt, the treasure being a real fortune, its bequeather the formulator of clues and the rival teams mortally in earnest. Here, too, stories are told on the stage, but they are told within relevant situations, and a degree of real suspense is maintained. (pp. 56-8)

Those attracted by the writings of Raymond Roussel have from the beginning found it difficult to say with any precision what it was they found there. To the *surréalistes* he early became, with Lautréamont, the greatest '*magnétiseur*' (the expression is that of their spokesman, André Breton) of our time. This need mean nothing more than that Lautréamont and Roussel, among their predecessors, specially attracted the *surréalistes.* To sustain and justify their interest, moreover, M. Breton had to suppose that at the heart of it all lay something which, to my mind, is clearly not there, *viz.,* some form of occult revelation.

Paul Éluard, it is true, was more affected by the verbal magic and its power to create, though presently carried away by his own rhetoric (in, we may feel, his later political direction). In 1925, he wrote of *L'Étoile au Front:*

> There stand the tellers of tales. One begins, the other goes on. They are marked with the same sign, they are a prey to the same imagination which bears the earth and the heavens on its head. All the stories in the world are woven out of their words, all the world's stars are upon their brows, mysterious mirrors of the magic of dreams and of the most curious, marvellous facts. Are they likely to capture the attention of these insects who buzz faintly while eating and thinking, who barely listen to the storytellers and certainly don't perceive the grandeur of their raving?
>
> Prestidigitators, there they are turning pure and simple words into a crowd of personages over-

whelmed by the objects of passion and what they hold in their hands is a golden ray, and what we see unfolding is truth, dignity, liberty, happiness and love.

> Let Raymond Roussel show us all that never was. There are some few of us to whom that is the only reality which counts.

To-day M. Ferry, *ancien surréaliste,* is inclined to see Roussel himself as the hermetic secret. Since nobody has done more to make a public property of Roussel, it seems odd that he should write, in the issue of *Bizarre* prepared under his supervision:

> Let us try to keep ourselves to ourselves. . . .
> Read Roussel, but don't talk about him. . . .
> Let us read Roussel, but not lend him out. We shouldn't get him back in good condition.

The time has come, in M. Ferry's view, to put even stouter bolts on the ivory tower.

The earliest critic to give Roussel his close attention was not a *surréaliste,* however, but that strange man, Count Robert de Montesquiou, commonly understood to be the original of Proust's Baron de Charlus and regarded as a mere freakish monster of vanity. In 1921 already, he devoted a chapter to this '*auteur difficile*' in his *Élus et Appelés.* Montesquiou states that he is acquainted with M. Roussel, but writes only of *Impressions d'Afrique* and *La Vue* and does not think it reasonable that the 'ordered nightmare' of the former should once have been put on the stage (but had not seen it and so must keep an open mind). The art of *La Vue* he describes as '*un art d'infusoire, mais, je m'empresse de l'ajouter, infusoire de génie*' ['an art of infusoria, but, I hasten to add, infusoria of genius'], an odd thing to say, though no doubt he would have conceded that genius was to be attributed rather to the microscope than to the infusoria it studied. Count Robert's essay is by no means contemptible. There was clearly more to this man than he is commonly given credit for. In describing the over-all shape of *Impressions d'Afrique,* with its parade of mysteries that are later explained, he spoke of '*équations de faits*', that is to say equations made up of facts not of figures, which then had to be solved. The expression was taken up by Roussel and is used by him, explaining his procedures, in *Comment J'Ai.* Equations of facts, in this sense, are, of course, what detective stories present us, and the detectives, with. They are also what appear notably in the opening chapters of most of the stories of Jules Verne.

Jean Cocteau's obituary notice in the *Nouvelle Revue Française* for September 1933 remains impressive. The key-words are '*pureté*' ['purity'] and '*simplicité*' ['simplicity']. When Cocteau describes Raymond Roussel as '*le génie à l'état pur*' ['genius in its pure state'], that, of course, is a different sense of the word. There, '*brut*' ['raw'] could be substituted for '*pur*'. It is not quite the same with '*génie d'une pureté parfaite*' ['genius of perfect purity'], and Cocteau further speaks of '*cette pureté merveilleuse*' ['this marvelous purity'], and of '*la véritable pureté*' ['true purity'], and finally of '*l'extrême point de la simplicité*' ['the ultimate simplicity']. It is a quality we must all certainly recognise in Roussel's work. He was at least as much an innocent, a child of nature, as (Cocteau's own comparison) the *douanier* Rousseau in painting. A weakness in Cocteau's approach to Roussel was that it did not allow him to believe the latter when he tried to tell his new friend that he worked according to a *chiffre,* which he proposed to divulge eventually. Cocteau remained convinced that any code used must be purely instinctive, somnambulistic. The appearance of **Comment J'Ai Écrit Certains de mes Livres** two years later must have disconcerted him a little.

The purity was also hygienic, surgical, like that, says Cocteau, of his own *Enfants Terribles,* who could only live shut away in a room, unable to bear the microbes in the world outside. Like Proust, Roussel lived as though in a vacuum flask, his temperature unrelated to that elsewhere. A similar notion was expressed by Pierre Schneider in 1951 (*Cahiers du Sud,* nos. 306-7). Using the English term, he describes Roussel's world as 'dust-free'. It is also, he says, essentially a daylight world, indeed a high-noon world, in which objects cast no shadow (with the exception, we may note, of the bread-crumbs on the tablecloth upon which Spanish dancers dance in **Impressions of Africa**). M. Schneider's substantial essay is strangely headed. It is called '*La Fenêtre ou Piège à Roussel*'. It is concerned with the act of seeing among poets and with windows, optical instruments and the stage.

Both M. Schneider's essay and the Roussel chapters in the book, *Genèse de la Pensée Moderne,* published the previous year by Marcel Jean and Arpad Nezei, are further concerned with the 'abysses' in any picture of reality revealed by the fact that similar words may signify dissimilar things, that indeed identical words may signify things between which there is no element of identity whatever. The idea was made central to his argument by M. Foucault [see excerpt dated 1963]. According to M. Foucault, Roussel's adventuring among those abysses led inevitably to his suicide.

That Roussel's death took place on the actual threshold of a locked door has too much dazzled M. Foucault with its metaphorical and symbolic possibilities. M. Foucault is too fond of labyrinths, keys and thresholds, too anxious to find in Roussel's moment of death a culmination of the pattern of his work, seen too exclusively in terms of the tendency first to mystify, then to explain. All men's preoccupations in some way 'lead to' death, since all men die. Raymond Roussel attained the age of fifty-six, which is a good deal above average for top-flight writers in our time, if we bracket off a few whose longevity was extreme. It is true that, since he was rich, he escaped pressures to which most of us are subject. It may also be true that to be rich precludes the formation of any usual sense of reality, itself at times a protection, but fifty-six is not bad for a man liable to such alternations of mood and so little a member of any community.

Nevertheless, I do not find M. Foucault's argument wholly foolish. The human world is very largely made up of words and their resonances. Most ways of life are framed within a few accepted *clichés,* and to discover that they are meaningless is as quick a road to despair as any other. Roussel's lifelong preoccupation with words that may be taken in two or more senses or which, sounding alike, point in opposed directions can hardly have failed to suggest to him that all words are treacherous and so that there *are* abysses in any picture of reality. There is a further sense in which his pairs of words in two senses may be taken as 'equations of fact', and at that point all sense of reality totters. In their blandly indifferent way, the logical positivists have directed us towards a nominalism of the same kind, but somehow contrive to preserve their own few comforting clichés intact, perhaps by concentrating mainly on the very large abstractions and believing that the concretely denotative words remain solid. (pp. 83-7)

To me, it is part of the charm of Raymond Roussel that his writings are totally devoid of seriousness. They may obscurely search the reader's heart, but they do not set out to reveal the truth about that troublesome and unreliable organ, let alone to explore the position of man in society, any more than do the farces of P. G. Wodehouse or the ingenious contrivances of a writer of good detective stories. These are not, indeed, though structurally identical, regarded as true novels or novels proper. The increasingly irksome characteristic of true novels or novels proper is their seriousness, their *trompe l'oeil* verisimilitude, their apparent preoccupation with human reality and truth, although everyone knows that a novel is in the first place a pack of lies, however much 'imaginative truth' it may be held in the last place to contain. (p. 91)

Rayner Heppenstall, in his Raymond Roussel: A Critical Study, *University of California Press, 1967, 97 p.*

ROSS CHAMBERS (essay date 1970)

[*In the following excerpt, Chambers explores the underlying parenthetical structure of Roussel's works and traces the development of that structure from its rudimentary stages in Roussel's early poems to its final form in* Impressions of Africa *and* Locus Solus.]

Roussel as a writer was . . . the creator of an entirely fictional universe, and few can have carried as far as he the principle of the autonomy of the work of art from what is called the real world. His books, as Robbe-Grillet says [see excerpt dated 1963], have no 'content' and no 'depth'; they make 'not the least contribution to the study of human character or the passions, not the tiniest contribution to sociology, and contain not the slightest philosophical meditation'. They open a parenthesis in the world, fill it as best they may, then close it again. But a moment's reflection shows that a parenthesis has some odd characteristics: it introduces into the sentence a kind of timeless space, after which the sentence begins again as if nothing had happened; and yet the 'nothing' *has* happened and the progress of the sentence is significantly modified by the content of the parenthesis. The closing bracket may therefore be said to be both identical to and different from the opening bracket. Time has both occurred and not occurred. If Roussel's books have a 'meaning', it is the meaning of their parenthetical form.

His earliest image of the literary process is contained in a juvenile poem entitled **Mon Ame ('My Soul')** and later re-titled more modestly **L'Ame de Victor Hugo** (but with a tell-tale rhyme in -el defiantly unchanged). His 'soul' is described as a mine-shaft, in which the feverish work of forging images and verses goes unceasingly on, while the poet leans solicitously over the edge, surveying the work, receiving the poetry as it emerges golden and gleaming from the fiery depths, and basking in the homage paid to him by the crowds from afar. The function of the world is to provide glory, not subject-matter, and creation occurs in a place isolated from it by the whole depth of the shaft, protected from it by an 'edge' beyond which the poet himself cannot penetrate:

> Penché sur le puits, je regarde
> Au fond, et ce regard suffit
> Pour que, dans la flamme hagarde,
> Monte un prodigieux récit.
>
> [Leaning over the pit, I look
> Down, and my glance suffices
> In the wild flames
> A prodigious tale arises.]

But if this image is itself 'parenthetical', so too is the actual structure of the poem, in which a first section tells of the pit by day, of the author leaning over it, and the worshipping crowds, while a middle section (during which the author is asleep) is concerned with the images, situations and people arising mysteriously in the poet's mind while he attempts to shape them into a 'prodigieux récit', until finally he wakes, whereupon a final section returns to the situation of the beginning, with the difference, however, that the admiring crowd is now that of posterity. We have been taken 'inside the brackets', into a strange domain where a difficult creation occurs *ex nihilo,* and restored to a world now oriented towards the future, a world which has been imperceptibly but vitally changed by the parenthetical activity itself.

When a repetition occurs, the magic is that it establishes an identity across the 'distance' of time, and that is why the parenthesis may express the positive idea of 'progress'. But repetition is also a manifestation of the 'distance' itself, and that is doubtless why in *La Doublure* (**'The Understudy'**)—Roussel's next poem, published in 1897—the change which occurs from bracket to bracket is a decline. We know that as he was writing it Roussel enjoyed a particular sense of euphoria, a form of hallucination in which he imagined himself as a sun radiating glory out into the world. 'What I wrote was surrounded with radiating light, I kept the curtains closed for I was afraid of the slightest crack through which the rays of light emanating from my pen might have escaped, I wanted to draw back the screen all at once and illumine the world.' This is, of course, totally consistent with the forge-image in *Mon Ame,* and henceforth literary activity, the activity of Roussel enclosed in his mansion or his mind as his heroes are enclosed in a parenthesis, was to have for him the function of restoring this sense of euphoria, of sending forth the light of genius into the world. But for the hero of *La Doublure* (and this was to be a truer prediction of Roussel's fate in his lifetime) an escapade between the brackets spells not success but failure.

At his profession, this actor is a flop. As an understudy, his task is the one Roussel assigns to the closing bracket of a parentheses: to bring off a miraculous 'identity' (with his rôle, and with the actor he is replacing) which by its 'difference' will nevertheless be 'better' than the original and consequently a source of glory, like 'drawing back the screen all at once and illumining the world'. But the difference, we have said, may equally be a 'flaw', and just as the content of the parenthesis is the flaw in the identity it creates, so Gaspard's woefully inadequate acting dashes all his ambitions to the ground. In his disappointment he flees from Paris with his lover Roberte, and the long and soporific central part of this 194-page poem is devoted to a description of the carnival at Nice, a scene of unreality described with the utmost 'objectivity', with its procession of cardboard figures and masks, its disguised, confetti-flinging crowds, its firework display. But when we meet the hero again in the third and final part, he is alone and gloomy, working as an actor in a fair-ground troupe, his career hopelessly forfeited. After the 'holiday', his return to real life is a desperate disillusionment. In writing of Gaspard's failure while himself enjoying the euphoria of glory, Roussel was doing what Sartre, in *Les Mots,* has described himself as doing while he was writing *La Nausée:* telling the world of the meaninglessness of existence while privately exulting in the meaningfulness he was thereby giving to his own existence. In each case the 'truth' is double; in Roussel's case it is the double truth of the parenthesis.

The book's other main interest is that, after the difficulties described in the central part of *Mon Ame,* it shows Roussel discovering a first solution to the inescapable problem of how to fill the parenthesis that is literature. What lies between the brackets? The answer will be—parentheses. The book is full of figures of an identity which nevertheless reveals a crucial difference. The hero, we have said, is an understudy, a *doublure* (and the word also means a 'lining', a second piece of cloth inseparable but different from the first). The carnival figures are also walking parentheses: the man and the mask are as dependent on each other, as 'identical' and as 'different' as a pair of brackets, and the figures themselves sometimes represent enigmas, the solution to which depends once again on grasping a difference-in-identity. This latter possibility was developed by Roussel in a long verse-fragment, obviously related in inspiration to *La Doublure,* and entitled *L'Inconsolable.* Here he describes a whole series of figures like the clarinetist, displeased with his instrument and asking: 'Pourquoi ai-je perdu mon son?' ['Why have I lost my sound?'], and from whose doll-like posterior, as he passes, one sees a trickle of bran falling to the pavement (*son* = 'sound' and 'bran'). The figure is divided and different, and yet identical (since what is occurring both front and back is a 'perte de son'); it is complete, and the enigma is solved, only when one has seen both sides, entering the parenthesis, as it were, and emerging from it again, experiencing it as the very figure of Kierkegaardian 'repetition'.

If *La Doublure* fills the parenthesis with perambulating parentheses, poems like *La Vue* (**'The View'**), *Le Concert* (**'The Concert'**) and *La Source* (**'The Spring'**) look forward to a more complex technique of Roussel's. These are all vacation-memories, in which the brackets of the parenthesis are represented by a framework technique. In the present the poet studies the label on a bottle of mineral-water, the illustration on a hotel's letter-head, or a tiny souvenir-photograph set in the handle of a pen. His precise and lengthy description of what he sees is in reality a journey into the mind, a reverie about the past, from which he is interrupted by a return to the present. Here the domain of privilege between the brackets is associated, Proust-like, with memory, and the analogy with Combray in a cup of tea is sometimes inescapable:

> car c'est l'exhalaison
> Des sentiments vecus de toute une saison
> Qui pour moi sort avec puissance de la vue,
> Grâce à l'intensité subitement accrue
> Du souvenir vivace et latent d'un été
> Déjà mort, déjà loin de moi, vite emporté.

> [For it is the breath
> Of a whole season's lived sensations
> Which for me arises most powerfully from the view,
> Thanks to the suddenly increased intensity
> Of the still living, latent memory of a summer
> Already dead, already far from me, rapidly borne
>   away.]

The vein of nostalgia was not to be developed by Roussel with the single-mindedness of Proust, but as an example of 'repetition', of identity with a difference, it deserved an important place in his work. From the point of view of later developments, the most striking aspect of these poems (apart from their strong visual quality, the meticulously 'objective' descriptive technique also to be found in *La Doublure*) is their tendency to proliferate by a chain of parentheses within parentheses. The internal parentheses are no longer autonomous and free as in

La Doublure, but tend to open up within each other: the view is enclosed within the pen, it represents a beach, on the beach a woman sits, she holds a sheet of music, on the music is a drawing representing . . . (it is described in minute detail). This technique is not so very distant from the one Roussel was to use in *Nouvelles Impressions d'Afrique* (**'Further Impressions of Africa'**).

Meanwhile he had invented the form of 'verbal parenthesis' which his admirers have come to call, after him, *le procédé.* He experimented with this technique of invention most of his life, and divulged it posthumously in *Comment j'ai écrit certains de mes livres* (**'How I wrote certain of my books'**) [see excerpt dated 1935]. In its earliest and simplest form, it consisted of discovering a phrase which by a slight modification completely changes its sense. Thus *les lettres du blanc sur les bandes du vieux billard* ('the chalk letters on the sides of the old billiard-table') becomes *les lettres du blanc sur les bandes du vieux pillard* ('the white man's letters concerning the old pillager's hordes'). The two phrases, identical except for the tiny 'flaw' which nevertheless makes 'all the difference', then form the brackets of a literary parenthesis, and the author's task is to invent a tale which will join them with the utmost economy. It will be evident that the *procédé* does not replace the work of the imagination so much as it stimulates it in its task of *création à vide*—indeed it is, if anything, a test of the imagination, as anyone can discover by trying it out, even in a language as rich in homonyms and near-homonyms as French.

The first texts in which the *procédé* was used are relatively short. But *Chiquenaude* (c. 1900) was to show how the method could be extended. Between the brackets formed by the phrases *les vers de la doublure dans la pièce du 'Forban talon rouge'* and *les vers de la doublure dans la pièce du fort pantalon rouge* ('the understudy's verse in the play of the *Foppish Corsair*' / 'the worms in the lining of the patch in the strong red trousers'), Roussel inserts a veritable cascade of *doublures,* which Michel Foucault summarizes when he says: 'It is probable that the sense of satisfaction the text gave Roussel derives . . . from its wonderful organisation by echo-effect, whereby the initial *procédé* (the two near-identical phrases which are to be joined) resonates throughout the text and in the figures which inhabit it: there is repetition, lining, the return of the same, the flaw, the imperceptible difference, doubling, and a fatal tearing apart'. The technique of *La Doublure,* where the space between the brackets is filled holus-bolus with 'doublings', has here been grafted onto the *procédé,* so it is not surprising that the actual 'plot' itself depends partly on the pun latent in the term *doublure.* It was by a kind of reversal of the technique of *Chiquenaude* that Roussel was to discover the principle of composition underlying his two most famous prose-works, *Impressions d'Afrique* and *Locus Solus,* as well as his two plays, *L'Etoile au Front* (**'Star on the Brow'**) and *La Poussière de Soleils* (**'The Dust of Suns'**). Here the 'outer' framework is not verbal but is provided by situation and plot, while the episodes that make up the 'internal' substance of the work derive from the application of the *procédé.*

But by this stage the *procédé* had itself developed. Attracted by the considerable ambiguity of the preposition *à* in French, Roussel began to seek pairs of words, linked by *à,* but susceptible of a double meaning (with or without a change in form). Thus *baleine à îlot* (whale associated with island) suggests *baleine à ilote* (whalebone/helot); *duel à accolade* suggests both a duel leading to an embrace and the Greek dual with a typographical 'bracket'; while *mou à raille* (a spineless

person subject to mockery) suggests *mou à rail* ('liver and lights' for making a rail). What resulted from this particular group of associations was the following, perhaps the most famous passage in *Impressions d'Afrique:*

> The first [statue] evoked a man mortally wounded by a weapon thrust through his heart. (. . .) The statue was black and at first glance seemed hewn from a single block; but gradually the eye perceived a host of grooves running in all directions but which generally formed groups of multiple parallels. In fact the work was wholly made up of innumerable pieces of whalebone, which had been cut and curved as required to model the figure. (. . .) The statue's feet were placed on a very simple vehicle, with a low platform and four wheels also made of ingenious combinations of black whalebone. Two narrow rails, made of a raw, reddish, gelatinous substance which was nothing more nor less than veal liver and lights, were laid across a blackened wooden surface and by their shape if not their colour gave the exact illusion of a portion of railway-line: the four unmoving wheels fitted onto them without crushing them. The carriage-platform formed the upper part of a supporting pedestal, which was quite black and across the main face of which a white inscription read: 'Death of the Helot Saridakis'. Below this, still in snow-white characters could be seen this half-Greek, half-French sign, accompanied by a delicate bracket:
>
>

ηστον

DUEL

ηστην

(Saridakis, as we learn much later, was killed by his master *pour encourager les autres* ['in order to encourage the others'] when he displayed his ignorance of Greek verbs, a pedagogical principle many a language teacher dreams of emulating; and the building of a statue light enough to move on rails of liver and light was an ordeal imposed by the merciless African tyrant Talou.)

It will be seen that here Roussel has used only the second term of his initial pairs, much as the priests of ancient Egypt derived their ritual scenarios not from their myths proper so much as from punning versions of them. This in itself makes it extremely difficult to trace the operation of the *procédé* in Roussel's mature work; but when one learns, for example, that at this stage the words of the familiar little song *J'ai du bon tabac* could 'give' for him *jade tube onde aubade en mat à basse tierce* ('Jade tube wave aubade of dull material in low thirds'), all hope of grasping in any detail the verbal material of which the texts are an echo rapidly fades. Roussel has both revealed and concealed the creative principle of his writing, and his art, like Samuel Beckett's, is as elusive as it is allusive. Add to this a permanent tendency to combine chains of episodes by a complicated technique of internal parenthesis, and it is not surprising that the reader of Roussel is left wandering in slightly baffled amazement through a labyrinthine wonderland of marvels.

But if the works based on the *procédé* form a labyrinth of fictions (and the play *La Poussière de Soleils* is quite explicitly given the structure of a quest), the *Nouvelles Impressions d'Afrique,* on which Roussel worked intermittently between 1915 and 1928, form a verbal labyrinth, the principle of which is precisely that of the parenthesis within the parenthesis. Roussel begins a proposition, but opens a parenthesis before it is complete, then another before the first is complete and so on, closing them all finally one after the other like the lids of so many Chinese boxes. The result for the naïve reader is complete bafflement; for the reader who has been forewarned it is a constant effort not to lose the Ariadne's thread he is clinging to. Jean Ferry, whose readings of *Nouvelles Impressions d'Afrique* are models of meticulous and good-humoured exegesis, suggests that the neophyte might cut his Rousselian teeth on this short note to the fourth *Chant:*

¹Nul n'est sans caresser un ambitieux rêve;
²L'ouvrier croit se voir dictant, lors d'une grève
³(Aujourd'hui l'on raisonne et chacun, l'oeil au but
⁴((Tous nous en avons un; tant que son occiput,
⁵Mis nu dans l'intérêt du fer de la machine,
⁶Tient pour plus d'un quart d'heure encore à son
    échine,
⁷Songeant: 'Perdre sa proie arrive—et c'est fréquent—
⁸A qui la tient le mieux' (((au fait, l'inconséquent
⁹S'enfuit du cabanon, le reclus de la geôle,
¹⁰Le fromage du bec du corbeau qu'on enjôle;
¹¹De se taire, parfois, riche est l'occasion;)))
¹²L'assassin a lui-même un but: l'évasion;))
¹³Que son idéal soit: toucher un gros salaire,
¹⁴Enfanter, voir son grain surabonder sur l'aire
¹⁵Ou contraindre son pouls à choir, à s'assagir,
¹⁶Sent que, pour triompher, mieux vaut penser, agir
¹⁷Que faire—tâcheron, épousée inféconde,
¹⁸Moissonneur ou malade—un vœu dans la seconde
¹⁹Où l'étoile filante élonge sa lueur;),
²⁰Las de donner à boire au bourgeois sa sueur
²¹(C'est pour Pierre, souvent, que Paul souffre et
    travaille;
²²Vespuce, de Colomb, exploita la trouvaille;
²³Et c'est pour emperler tel doigt ou tel plastron
²⁴Qu'une huître est tout labeur;), des lois à son patron;
²⁵La garce en son grenier pense à rouler carrosse;
²⁶Se voir pousser aux mains l'améthyste et la crosse
²⁷Est une fiction chère à tout prestolet.

[1. There is none but caresses an ambitious dream; / 2. The worker imagines himself dictating, during a strike / 3. (These days people are thinking, and each with an eye on the goal / 4. ((We all have one; so long as his nape, / 5. Laid bare in the interests of the blade of the machine (*i.e. the guillotine*) / 6. Still remains attached for another quarter of an hour to his spine, / 7. Thinking: 'To lose one's prey happens—frequently— / 8. Even to those who hold it best' (((and indeed, the irresponsible man / 9. Flees the padded cell, the prisoner his gaol, / 10. And cheese from the beak of the flattered crow; / 11. —The chance to be silent is sometimes eminently to be seized;))) / 12. The assassin himself has his goal: escape;)) / 13. Whether one's ideal be to draw a large salary, / 14. To give birth to children, to grow a superabundant crop. / 15. Or to make one's pulse-rate fall, and grow calm, / 16. Feels that, in order to triumph, it is better to think and to act / 17. Than to make—be one a day-labourer, an infecund bride, / 18. A harvester or a patient—a wish in the second / 19. When the shooting star sends its long gleam across the sky), / 20. Tired of giving his sweat for the bourgeois to drink / 21. (It is often for Peter that Paul suffers and works; / 22. Vespuccio exploited Columbus' discovery; /

23. And it is to adorn with a pearl someone's finger or someone's shirt-front / 24. That an oyster is all toil;), laws to his boss; / 25. The trollop in her attic thinks of lording it in a carriage; / 26. To see the amethyst and the crook burgeon in his hands / 27. Is a fiction dear to every priest-let.]

The statement of line 1 is illustrated (lines 2, 20 and 24) by the worker dreaming of dictating laws to his boss, and by lines 25-27. But the worker's dream sets off a reflection: Everyone has a dream these days (line 3), which is not completed until lines 13-19. For the mention of a goal sets off a new parenthesis: We all have a goal, which occupies lines 4-8 but is not completed until line 12, since at line 8 a new idea is developed and is not completed until line 11. (I am leaving out of account, of course, various incidental parentheses.) The reader who works his way through the labyrinth in the hope of discovering some treasure of knowledge is likely to feel cheated: the 'thought', here as elsewhere in Roussel, is at the level of the commonplace (although Michel Foucault discovers high significance in the central message: *De se taire, parfois, riche est l'occasion*). But one would be wrong to complain, for it is the labyrinth itself that counts, not the treasure. We have been introduced, not to the content, but to the structure of a mind. It may, however, be some consolation to reflect, with Jean Ferry, that this same structure is also that of *A la Recherche du Temps perdu*.

That a structure may be significant *as* a structure is no problem in our 'structuralist' day and age. That myths can be understood as models of the structure of the mind is an idea familiar to readers of Claude Lévi-Strauss. That Roussel's work is best conceived as a myth in this sense is an idea at least worth investigating. The key sentence from *Comment j'ai écrit certains de mes livres* has been picked out by Michel Foucault: 'I was led to take any sentence at all and to *derive images from it by dislocating it*' (my italics). The *procédé* is valuable to Roussel not for itself but for the images it brings him. What is curious, however, is that so frequently the images have the same structure as the *procédé* itself, that is the structure of 'repetition', of an identity flawed with difference as an inevitable result of time. This we know to be the structure of the parenthesis, and traditionally the labyrinth has also served as a symbol of the ambiguity of life in time. But time and again the situations and tales Roussel brings up from the depths of 'Victor Hugo's' mine, the fabulous episodes with which he links the brackets and forms the labyrinth, display in their turn a preoccupation with the prestige, and with the flaw, of repetition.

A hasty reader of *Impressions d'Afrique* might be forgiven for concluding that, the external parenthesis establishing the boundaries outside of which time triumphs unambiguously, the feats performed within that framework by the various characters represent the possibility of true freedom within the 'mind', of complete identity outside of the domain of time. A group of European travellers is shipwrecked off the coast of Africa and held for ransom by the tyrant Talou. They occupy their captivity by planning and bringing off a number of wondrous feats, which together form a kind of astonishing music-hall programme. These feats are repetitions in the sense that they are all secretly inspired by the *procédé*, but many of them also actually involve bringing to 'life' scenes of the past, miraculously reproducing reality and such like. The performance celebrates Talou's (self-) coronation as head of an empire once unified, long divided, and now reunified. But it celebrates also the prisoners' liberation: indeed, for some of them, it is the condition of their liberation. Louise Montalescot, for example, has to create a series of perilous works of art (like the whale-bone statue on the rails of *mou de veau*), and herself perfects a miraculous painting-machine which works by a 'photo-mechanical' process and reproduces with scrupulous accuracy a dawn-scene; Talou is so impressed that he grants her her freedom. Meanwhile the male soprano Carmichaël (androgyny is a natural element of such a book) has been commissioned to sing verses in praise of Talou in the incomprehensible native language; a failure of memory means that he is 'kept back' until he is able to reproduce them accurately, whereupon he too is released. When the prisoners return to Europe, it seems that their stay within the parentheses has been a liberating experience, and the future they are 'returning' to has been immeasurably enriched by the discoveries they have made in Talou's domain.

But the feats of reproduction and repetition they have performed are never perfect. They typically substitute some discontinuous, mechanical or serial reality for the unanalysable and unidirectional fluidity of life; at the very best, their Heath Robinson contraptions or their marvellous discoveries in the vegetable and animal kingdoms are capable of reproducing petrified 'scenes', often duly labelled, which are as astonishingly accurate in their representation of reality, but as much divorced from that same reality, as the *tableaux vivants* they perform in the Theatre of the Incomparables. Louise's painting-machine does indeed reproduce with wondrous accuracy a sunrise in the forest; but it converts the nuances of light into tiny brush-strokes and changing reality into an unchanging picture; and although Carmichaël reproduces the words of his song meticulously, they have no meaning for him whatsoever. Many of Roussel's machines depend for their operation on the discovery of unknown metals, chemicals or plants, the source of whose miraculous properties remains a mystery; or else part of their mechanism is enclosed in a little black box and (although the rest of the machine is described meticulously) is never explained. If the machines symbolize the artistic process—the creation of identities in the mind—these obscurities have a double function: firstly to represent, of course, the irreducible mystery of what goes on in the 'mine', between the brackets of the parenthesis; but also to express the 'distance', the 'difference' that intervenes between any event and its reproduction. Within the parenthesis, the conditions of the parenthesis still apply, and the prisoners do not escape them in Talou's kingdom. If repetition contains a principle of life, it also contains a principle of death: the water-loom weaves a coronation-cloak which symbolizes Talou's unified realm and the creation of perfect identity, but it then reproduces a scene of death and division, the Flood. And if Talou's European prisoners are 'liberated', his native prisoners undergo deaths which reproduce their crimes, like Djezmé who, guilty of love, dies literally by a *coup de foudre* ['a bolt of lightning'].

Locus Solus . . . is perhaps the book to recommend to beginners, for it is a veritable microcosm of Roussel's fictional universe. In it a group of guests is shown over the wonders of Canterel's isolated park. As is to be expected in visiting a parenthesis, the things they first see are reminders of the past, while the last people they call upon are fortune-tellers, who predict the future. But the central episodes are concerned even more manifestly with repetition. A flying earth-rammer constructs a mosaic of human teeth: it 'reproduces' a scene from a legend in which a coincidence with another tale proves liberating. A madman reproduces the jig of bandits trampling his

daughter to death, and so strong is his obsession that the hairs of his head perform the same jig; meanwhile he is working on a means of recreating the sound of his daughter's voice. . . . And nearby stand the refrigerated chambers in which, thanks to the combination of *vitalium* and *résurrectine* invented by Canterel, cadavers are restored to a temporary semblance of life. . . . 'The illusion,' says Roussel, 'was perfect.' But an illusion is all it can be: however meticulous the reproduction, this absurd, unending, repetitive series of mechanical gestures is anything but life. The living dead of *Locus Solus* are a reminder that, if repetition is 'more' than life, it is also 'less' than life, that life within the parenthesis can only be marked by the same ambiguity as the life of the parenthesis itself.

In his lifetime Roussel was as much a failure as his hero Gaspard. It is not hard to understand why. He cannot 'write', in the ordinary sense (but his slightly contorted, nominative style, governed primarily by a principle of economy, cries out for study). In the ordinary sense also, he has nothing to 'say'. There are those today who consider his present (circumscribed) success as something between a passing fad and a sick joke. But it is not surprising, in an age when literature is largely engaged in calling itself into question, that he should have seemed to some a guide to follow, and to others a fascinating *cas-limite* ['limit case'] in which the literary act reveals itself for what it really is, stripped of all the usual 'inessentials'. . . . Roussel is not a fad, and an imagination like his deserves the greatest respect, however much his books may be an acquired taste. He belongs as a writer in the great Cartesian tradition of those who seek in literature an expression of the autonomy and power of the mind; but he is, like Samuel Beckett, one of those latter-day Cartesians who deny the creative power of the mind while they illustrate it, and illustrate it in the very denying. (pp. 72-83)

Ross Chambers, "Literature as Parenthesis: Raymond Roussel," in Meanjin, *Vol. 29, No. 1, March, 1970, pp. 72-83.*

LEON S. ROUDIEZ (essay date 1972)

[*Roudiez is an American critic and educator whose special area of study is modern French fiction. In the following excerpt, Roudiez contrasts the alternate reality created by the Surrealists with that created by Roussel.*]

What is so fascinating about Roussel is that nearly everything he wrote either rejects or ignores what most of us, by tacit consent, construe as reality—even when he appears to concentrate on a minute description of it. His was an inner world, conditioned by language just like ours, but where verbal creation feeds upon itself in the manner of a snowball. Replacing the "inner world" metaphor with a different one, the "world of language" for instance, would bring us very close to the concern of writers such as Philippe Sollers. . . . (p. 12)

If Roussel was not led into the realm of surrealism . . . , he occasionally skirted it and came near enough to be recognized and praised. André Breton himself was intrigued, proclaiming, "Roussel is, along with Lautréamont, the greatest magnetizer of modern times." That Roussel had few readers until the 1960s is irrelevant in this context, for the magnetism Breton refers to has to do with the creative process—what he has called the alchemy of words. Roussel, on the other hand, showed little interest in the surrealists. His works are also lacking in two major surrealist preoccupations: the linking of surreality with reality and the desire to change life. Nor is it clear if any portion of his work could truly be interpreted in terms of a quest for the lost paradise of childhood. He remembered his own with great fondness: "I have delightful memories of my childhood. I may say that I then experienced several years of perfect happiness." It was possibly less urgent for him to seek such a paradise again, for, in some ways, he carried it with him. Pierre Schneider has distinguished his attitude from that of the surrealists by saying: "His entire work is a kind of child's play . . . he plays while they pretend to play." Michel Butor was led by what he calls Roussel's "salvaging of childhood" to mention Proust rather than the surrealists.

It is true that surrealists were attracted by his commonplace descriptions of the fantastic. As J. H. Matthews puts it, "Roussel's inventiveness catches the imagination and disturbs most when, entirely without comment or interpretation, his storyteller merely relates without sign of emotion what he says he has witnessed" [see Additional Bibliography]. But this does not so much imply an acceptance of the surrealists' *merveilleux quotidien* as it does an exclusion of reality, a placing it within parentheses. What remains is a self-sustaining verbal universe, which Breton recognized as one of the very few created in his day. It is a complete one, "a world re-created from scratch by a man fully set on following only the bent of his own mind, insofar as such bent might be unique." This led Roussel along a one-way street, beyond mere exclusion of reality, toward total denial. As he shows no interest in transforming reality, it is tempting to call him an escapist. Still, there are virtues in this escape into language, virtues of which he was in all likelihood unaware. His contemporaries were equally blind and their judgment of him was unduly harsh. If the variety of his more recent admirers seems surprising, it could perhaps be explained by one feature of his works: one could almost describe his creation as the establishment of a void. His logical, consequent, and seemingly matter-of-fact universe appears enchanted because of its availability. There is something in it for almost every reader. (pp. 12-14)

> *Leon S. Roudiez, "Raymond Roussel," in his* French Fiction Today: A New Direction, *Rutgers University Press, 1972, pp. 11-27.*

J. H. MATTHEWS (essay date 1976)

[*Matthews is a Welsh critic and educator who has written extensively on the Surrealists. In the following excerpt, he explains how the machines in Roussel's fiction exemplify his nonrealist literary technique.*]

One of the distinctive features of Roussel's novelistic writing . . . is the loving care lavished upon description of machines that strike us as unlikely, wildly improbable, or even ludicrously impossible. In his *Impressions d'Afrique* . . . one memorable construction consists of a statue representing a mortally wounded man, molded from countless corset-bones, resting on a low wheeled platform, fashioned from the same material and running on parallel rails of calves lights. Relatively uncomplicated, by Roussel's standards, this is a machine to which we shall return. Of more concern, initially, is another invention, far more complex, to which Roussel directs our attention in his novel *Locus Solus,* dating from 1914.

The machine in question is presented as the creation of the gifted inventor Canterel. (pp. 85-6)

This strange piece of machinery has but one function. It is used to position and drive into the ground innumerable human

teeth, to which gold and silver fillings, disease, tobacco stains, and blood stains lend a variety of shades. It operates with such accuracy as to create over a substantial area a mosaic of impressive dimensions. (p. 86)

[This invention] baffles our sense of the utilitarian, having been devised with the purpose of fulfilling its function through the creation of the non-utilitarian object *par excellence,* a work of art. (p. 88)

The credibility of an object realistically described does not rest solely upon the accuracy evidenced in the description of its component parts. To be credible, that object must also appear functionally persuasive. In other words, generally speaking responsiveness to the utilitarian is really the mask behind which we conceal our sense of the rationally acceptable. This is why one does not quite dispose of objections to the machines in *Locus Solus* as irrational, absurd, and impractical by Jean Ferry's expedient of making drawings of them and conjuring with the name of Leonardo da Vinci. Like the majority of readers in Roussel's lifetime, some will continue to find the statue of the mortally wounded helot in *Impressions d'Afrique* not so much difficult to visualize as unworthy of the effort to do so. It is not profusion of descriptive detail, here, that impedes the process by which the public arrives at an impression of how the statue looks. It is, more significantly, the fact that Rousselian creations are likely to be denied reality because rational values do not authorize belief that there is any need for them to exist at all.

Our evaluation of Roussel's achievement, it seems, inevitably must lead to negative conclusions so long as we persist in arguing from the standpoint of rational utility. This is because, on the level of reasonable justification, we are confronted time after time with the disproportion observable between, on the one side, the complexity of a Rousselian invention and the ingenuity brought to its creation and, on the other, the use to which that object is put. But when Roussel's work is under discussion, there is no need to regard the conclusion to which we are led as negative in value. Considering how little satisfaction the Rousselian machine offers, by accepted standards of utility, suggests something quite different. The intricacies of the mechanism's operation are so bewildering as to suggest that they are meant to bewilder us. Could not Roussel, we wonder, be taking care to stress that his machines do not belong in the real world, but exist only outside that world? If there is some substance in this hypothesis, then as we look at things from Roussel's perspective, we recognize that our sense of the utilitarian is of doubtful relevance to a display of creative inventiveness that is aimed at undercutting our notion of justifiable effort, as this is measured on the scale of practical utility. In other words, Raymond Roussel challenges our theories about the relationship between effort and reward, as these find their basis in the idea that, in a rational universe, creative activity must solicit reason's approval. He questions the reality principle, then, as he demonstrates his dedication to the pleasure principle.

Seen in this perspective, the weaknesses that offend our sense of the usefulness of mechanical inventions are transformed into signs of inventive strength. Whether Roussel achieves this result by accident or design matters little, at this point. What does matter is that there is a rationally disconcerting discrepancy between *how* his machines work and *why* they do so. True enough, we are told the reason for which Canterel invented his *demoiselle* ["pile driver"]. All the same, its function as proof of the accuracy of its inventor's skill as a meteorologist is never permitted to overshadow its operation as a dazzlingly precise instrument, used not to forecast the weather, we notice, but to create mosaics. The utilitarian principle—a tribute to the reality principle—is undermined. And there is something more to notice, too. Nothing in the description of the mechanism explains how the *hie* ["pile driver"] could possibly work with such accuracy. However realistic they may seem, the details provided do not convince us of the practical efficiency of the machine. In consequence, they do not persuade us that the *demoiselle* has a right to exist in the world we know.

What all this amounts to is that we cannot hope to understand Roussel's ambitions as a descriptive writer unless we invert the normal procedure by which we measure descriptive accomplishment in a novelist. The complexities of the invented machine are not intended to earn approval from spectators (or readers) who acknowledge the usefulness of the services that the various parts of a piece of machinery, working in unison, can accomplish. And we seriously underestimate Roussel if we assume that he was incapable of realizing this. (pp. 88-90)

Roussel's descriptive technique represents less a departure from realistic norms than an act of provocation directed against these. It does not aim to reduce the distance separating creative imagination from reality, as is more familiarly the case with science fiction. Instead, his method of describing in obsessive detail contributes to maintaining that distance, and even to increasing it. Faced with the task of evoking objects and machines that can have no existence outside his fertile imagination, he writes as though he were engaged in a contest and had as his express purpose stretching credibility to breaking point. (p. 90)

This is what rescues Raymond Roussel from the predicament facing all novelists who write in the realist vein, or, rather, saves him from having to face that predicament. His is not a descriptive method which meets reality in unequal combat. It is not, either, a method which must aspire to producing results having to be measured, finally, against reality, and so destined to be found wanting. Indeed, reading his novels, we are permitted to confuse his inventions neither with natural phenomena nor with those objects created for uses in which the everyday world sees meaning. Insistently, he demonstrates that, as he sees it, the world of literary creation is by definition at variance with the world we call reality. . . .

Far from being dependent upon objective reality and indebted to it for the material described in his writings, Roussel found in the celebrated *procédé* discussed at some length in *Comment j'ai écrit certains de mes livres* a means of making himself, so to speak, independent of reality. Thus, if we come to his work as we would to that of the literary realist—asking where he found the elements upon which he exercises his descriptive talents, and assuming that he borrowed them from the world about him—we soon find ourselves in an impasse. We go much farther if, instead, we remember that Roussel's *procédé* is "parent de la rime" ["related to rhyme"]: "Dans les deux cas," we are told in *Comment j'ai écrit,* "il y a création imprévue due à des combinaisons phoniques" ["In both cases there is unforeseen creation due to phonetic combination"]. . . . Hence the *hie* used to create a mosaic out of teeth was modeled after nothing its creator had actually seen. It was inspired, rather, by the phrase "*Demoiselle* (jeune fille) *à prétendant*" ["young lady with a suitor"], rearranged according to Rousselian procedure as "*Demoiselle* (hie) *à reître en dents*" ["pile-driver with soldier of fortune in teeth"]. (p. 91)

It comes as no surprise to those who know the text well that *Comment j'ai écrit certains de mes livres* provides only the beginnings of an answer to our questions about the origins of *Locus Solus.* All the same, incomplete though the information is that Roussel consents to supply, it serves to make one thing very clear. His method of composition entails a descriptive process that eludes the restrictions we are accustomed to see weighing upon writers in the realist tradition.

One senses nowhere in *Locus Solus,* or in any other of Roussel's writings, a feeling of inadequacy before the spectacle of the real, and there is good reason for this. In Roussel's experience, reality could not attain to the pitch of intensity at which he witnessed the manifestation of sights released by his imagination alone. In this connection, a confession he made to his doctor, Pierre Janet, is especially revealing. Speaking of having felt a sensation of glory at the age of nineteen, he recalled, "Ce que j'écrivais était entouré de rayonnements, je fermais les rideaux, car j'avais peur de la moindre fissure qui eût laissé passer au dehors les rayons lumineux qui sortaient de ma plume, je voulais retirer l'écran tout d'un coup et illuminer le monde" ["What I wrote was surrounded by rays of light; I would shut the drapes, as I was afraid the least opening would permit the light that was coming from my pen to escape, and I wanted to pull aside the screen all at once, and light up the world"].

A gesture intended to shut in the luminous rays emitted by his pen was, at the same time, one that shut out reality. Later, indeed, on a voyage through the South Seas, Roussel was to respond to a letter from an acquaintance who had expressed envy at the thought of his having the opportunity to see so many things, especially sunset in the Pacific, telling her that he had seen nothing, having shut himself up for days in his cabin, writing. To Raymond Roussel external reality had been largely irrelevant ever since his youth. On December 16, 1922, he wrote to Michel Leiris that he preferred "le domaine de la Conception à celui de la Réalité" ["the realm of Ideas to that of Reality"]. He must have spoken even more explicitly to Janet, who reports, "Martial a une conception très intéressante de la beauté littéraire, il faut que l'oeuvre ne contienne rien du réel, aucune observation du monde ou des esprits, rien que des combinaisons tout à fait imaginaires: ce sont déjà des idées d'un monde extra-humain" ["Martial (Janet's pseudonym for Roussel) had an interesting conception of literary beauty; a work must contain nothing real, no observation of the world or its spirit, nothing but completely imaginary combinations: these were ideas of an extra-human world"].

Janet's attempt to define the kind of world that attracted Roussel is of less import to us than the fact that his patient had no interest in trying to ensure that the image of that world offered in his writings be a mirror image of objective reality. Returning to those machines that do not measure up to our customary idea of useful mechanism, we can see better, now, that the ingenuity they exemplify does not reside in their being reminiscent of the machinery designed by man to serve practical purposes in the world as we know it. Roussel expends his ingenuity upon a far more original and, to his mind, more profitable undertaking: upon advancing from *Demoiselle à prétendant* to *Demoiselle a reître en dents.* Rousselian machines do not exist, then, to persuade us that they have as much right to our attention, and upon the same level, as if they were borrowed from the real world. Rather, they appear before us to demonstrate that the only way to advance, in the direction taken by Raymond Roussel, is by means of the imagination. "Chez moi," he confided in *Comment j'ai écrit certains de mes livres,* "l'imagination est tout." The imaginative universe of Raymond Roussel was created not to be assimilated by the world of familiar reality, but to remain forever outside it and beyond its range. (pp. 92-3)

J. H. Matthews, "Beyond Realism: Raymond Roussel's Machines," in Fiction, Form, Experience: The French Novel from Naturalism to the Present, *edited by Grant E. Kaiser, Éditions France-Quebec, 1976, pp. 83-93.*

CHARLES JOHNSON   (essay date 1978)

[*In the following excerpt, Johnson contends that Roussel's compositional technique outlined in* How I Wrote Certain of My Books *(see excerpt dated 1935) was a misuse of the nature and possibilities of language for literary creation.*]

Wonderful eccentrics like Raymond Roussel, who preferred "The domain of Conception to that of Reality," teach us a difficult but valuable lesson about the performance of language at its limits. From Roussel's essay on the extravagant logic behind his novels and plays, called **"How I Wrote Certain of My Books,"** we discover both what is possible and devastating, even disastrous, for a writer. So devastating, in fact, that Jean Cocteau confessed in *Opium* [see excerpt dated 1930] that, "In 1916 I rejected Roussel as likely to place me under a spell from which I could see no escape," and John Ashbery, who includes two workmanlike essays in praise of Roussel, fears "There is hidden in Roussel something so strong, so ominous . . . that one feels the need for some sort of protective equipment when one reads him."

Exactly what there is in Roussel that seduces generally sober men like Cocteau, Foucault, Ashbery [see excerpt dated 1967], and Robbe-Grillet [see excerpt dated 1963], I cannot say (in America, as in France, he shall never have a large following); but **"How I Wrote Certain of My Books"** tells a fascinating tale of Roussel's oblique style of cognition, his approach to composition, and—more importantly—reveals something of the demonic side of language.

Words can, and often do, unravel an already weak mind. Explaining the being of language requires a phenomenological analysis that shows how each word, like a palimpsest, is a tissue of experiences and meanings—a communal property like an old Protestant church, scarred, remodeled, reworked by thousands who've built upon it as they called their experience of reality from concealedness to clarity. The "special method" Roussel felt "future writers may perhaps be able to exploit [more] fruitfully," works in an especially parasitic way on this structure.

Poking at, say, the word "red," we find that it can embody passion, heat, blood, Revolution, fire, the eternal feminine, violence, and a score of other meanings simultaneously; its sense is protean, expansive because our predecessors, ancestors, and contemporaries have enshrined their experience—their *sense* of things—in the word. More than anything else, words are an opening onto the other's interpretation of the world. They teach the other. They teach ways of seeing, shared vision.

But if the word is truly a palimpsest, layer upon layer of signification, it must also embody puns, conflicts in ways of seeing, allegories, and contradictions. There is, then a dark side to language. The sound of a word and its multiple senses may break down, or—in combination with other words—create a bizarre mutation that ensorcels us because, as Ashbery says

of Roussel, "one feels it is about to break open, to yield true meaning at last [but] . . . The miracle never takes place."

For a writer who is dishonest, confused, a lunatic, or all three, language is bountiful enough to let him siphon from this originally *intersubjective,* social project of words a merely subjective utterance—a private world—all his own. So it often is. So it is in Roussel's **"How I Wrote Certain of My Books."** . . .

True enough, there is a certain poetic "purity" in this strange process of unlimited couplings and derivations, just as in any given asylum we have "genius in its pure state" (Cocteau on Roussel). . . .

The writer—like the narrator in Roussel's poem **"La Vue,"** who painstakingly describes a tiny picture set in a penholder, or in **"Le Concert"** an engraving of a band concert on the letterhead of hotel stationery—is a voyeur who, removed from experience, can only play enfeebled variations on the thoughts and feelings of other men accumulated, sedimented in language; like a check forger, you might say, drawing on the bank accounts of his father and friends, contributing nothing until the accounts, finally, are exhausted.

What Sartre has brilliantly written of Jean Genet, and Blanchot of Mallarmé, applies handsomely to Roussel's "experiments." One of the most celebrated phrases created by his technique is *"des rails en mou de veau"* ("rails of calf's lights"). In *Impressions d'Afrique,* this gnomic phrase is torturously explained (in fact, that is the crossword puzzle game Roussel plays when he writes), but Ashbery admits, "The phrase is like a Chinese box that one turns over and over, certain that there is a concealed spring somewhere, that in a moment the lid will fly open, revealing possibly nothing more than its own emptiness, but proving that reality is only a false bottom."

In plain talk, this is Roussel's real aim—to trap us in a phrase that has sucked its blood from real discourse, real men, real literature, and which from the outset *meant to say nothing.* Even as he explains in **"How I Wrote Certain of My Books"** how the words tumbled together into a clot of sounds in his novel, we see that Roussel's intention was, not to speak—it had never been to speak to us—but to create from words fantastic contraptions like those found in the sci-fi novels of Jules Verne: *things.* "Rails of calf's lights" is not a sentence, not even a thought. It has thickness, density—like flesh or steel— and, like all things, is ambiguous.

In good faith, his readers play the game of hermeneutics; they try to call a certain sense from the simple fact that this agglutinous monstrosity has, at least, a familiar grammatical structure. "But," laments Ashbery, "if it seems possible that Roussel did bury a secret message in his work, it seems equally likely that no one will ever succeed in finding out what it is. What he leaves us with is a work that is like the perfectly preserved temple of a cult which has disappeared without a trace."

Ten, maybe twelve years ago, one of my teachers joked about a writer's aid marketed in the 1940s. Called a "Plotto," it was constructed something like a Las Vegas slot machine (or so I imagine), with three little windows (the middle window carried the conjunction *and*), bright knobs on either side, and yielded in the two outside windows a list of words when the knobs were turned together. Twisting these, the desperate writer could by chance and accident draw, say, the words *dirigible* on one side, and *football* on the other. With only the slightest wit, he could wrench from these two linguistic atoms a book like *Black Sunday*.

There is much of this mechanical tomfoolery in Roussel; it hamstrings the creative imagination (another name for *reason*) rather than enhances it. Whether Plottos were really manufactured, or only a myth for tired writers, doesn't matter because the point is the same: language is a *lived* phenomenon too rich, too polymorphous to be contained in a technique of arbitrary combinations and reshufflings. . . .

"How I Wrote Certain of My Books" is, for all the shortcomings of Roussel's technique, a small but interesting document for anyone still interested in charting back corridors in the labyrinth of language—not the "prose of the world" by any means, but those dark places where language, like the serpent Ouroboros, seems to devour itself until nothing—absolutely nothing—remains.

Charles Johnson, in a review of "How I Wrote Certain of My Books," in The American Book Review, *Vol. 1, No. 2, April-May, 1978, p. 11.*

LESLIE HILL   (essay date 1979)

[*Hill is an English critic and educator. In the following excerpt, he explores the relationship between Roussel's psychological make-up and the compositional method he employed in his major fiction.*]

The year 1977 was the centenary of Raymond Roussel's birth. It was not, perhaps, a notably auspicious event. The controversy that greeted his work in earlier decades has to a large extent died away in recent years, leaving the author tidily ensconced in a personal niche in literary history, both as a curiosity standing on the fringes of the Surrealist movement and as a precursor announcing the experiments of the post-War *Nouveau Roman*. Yet this double attribution of Roussel's writings to the post-Romantic heritage of André Breton's subliminal message and to the constructivist lineage of modernism in France still leaves room for critical wonderment. The comparative lull in response to Roussel's work as a writer suggests that the time is ripe for a closer consideration and reappraisal of his status and position within what, today, has come to be known as the modern literary text.

The nub of the problem, as with other innovatory writers in modern literature, is less one of *what* Roussel has to say to the reader, more one of the *how* and the *whence* of such an artistic endeavour. It is a question of the place of literature, the place accorded to literature in Roussel's own life as well as that, within a larger context, occupied by the modern text itself within the world of forms and sense inhabited by the reader. Here Roussel's achievement is, at first glance, far from a simple one. His work spans three different genres, poetry, novel, and theatre, and steps gingerly over the fragile boundaries between these forms. It is characterized more by its single-mindedness than by its variety. It constantly blurs its own specific outline both as a fond evocation of the familiar themes of the popular and the exotic and as a construction of new and often bewildering formal structures. It is a life's enterprise that has met with more derision on the part of its audience than it has known unqualified success.

For these reasons it is not an easy task to assign to Roussel's literary work a stable centre from which all else derives. Fortunately, however, for an inquiry into the underlying position of Roussel's work both within literature and within the world,

there is perhaps one constant which determines, according to differing modes of presence and absence, the complexity of his work. This is the 'procédé très spécial' ['very special procedure'] of word-plays which today, in much discussion of the modern novel in France, bears his name as his personal imprint on literary history. This 'procédé', or device, occupies a strategic place in Roussel's own literary self-esteem. He regarded it as his most peculiar invention and one which would guarantee his literary survival. Even though he guarded its existence during his lifetime as a jealous secret, he took care to reveal its operation and detail in what he planned as his own posthumous literary testament: *Comment j'ai écrit certains de mes livres* [see excerpt dated 1935]. The book that may now be read under that title is a singular document, one that acts as a final, Orpheus-like retrospective on its author's previous writings, as his only, and fragmentary, autobiography, and as a celebratory anthology of his early texts and *juvenilia*. Were it not for the note of tragic pathos running through the book, projecting it into an uncertain yet assured literary future, it would serve as Roussel's only, and best, centennial monument. . . . Yet, rather like an Egyptian pyramid, which it resembles in its pious and self-confident recapitulation of the author's life and acts, *Comment j'ai écrit certains de mes livres* is an enigmatic work, casting a new aura of both clarity and mystery over all that preceded it. (pp. 823-24)

The evaluation of [Roussel's 'procédé'], as might be expected, occupies a dominant place in critical discussion of Roussel's work. In the main, Roussel's commentators have put forward two rather differing, if allied, views of its importance. The first tendency, represented by Jean Ferry and François Caradec, and later, though in a much more sophisticated form, by Jean Ricardou, has placed the emphasis upon the constructivist implications of the device. For the first two critics mentioned, the device supplies Roussel with an aleatory chain of bizarre images and inventions which the author would then fit together into as realistic a narrative as possible. For Ricardou, on the other hand, while the device is still at work in the text as a manufacturing principle, the stress falls on the way the device exploits the non-semantic materiality of the linguistic sign, and on the effects of 'auto-représentation' created in the finished text by this self-reflexive exercise of construction. Other critics, however, reacting against the strain of magical confidence in language evinced by Roussel himself and by this more traditional tendency, have maintained that, far from generating a series of non-discursive semantic fragments of language, the device, from its very inception, falls prey to an inescapable process of verisimilar reduction and recuperation. This, the argument runs, derives from the fact that the initial choice of words, particularly in view of the often idiosyncratic manner in which Roussel carries out his transformations, is motivated by forces other than those of pure chance or attention to the material nature of words. For Laurent Jenny, for example, what is determinant in the last resort is the stereotyped character of the stories Roussel elaborates in the final text. In this respect, writes Jenny, 'l'homophonie n'appar[aît] que comme un "déclencheur" très approximatif, le rôle principal étant joué par la logique du cliché' ['the homophone appears only as an approximate link, the principal role being played by the logic of the cliché']; the device, he continues, is best seen as a simple mystification offering only the illusion of 'une production du sens purement livrée au hasard, uniquement mécanique' ['the production of a sense created only by chance, strictly mechanical'].

There is much to be said for each of these varying approaches to Roussel's device, and I shall return to them later. But what is perhaps most remarkable, in the last analysis, is their mutual solidarity. For each of the critical positions I have mentioned the device is essentially a technical gambit, ancillary to what all consider to be the more decisive business of composition. Yet this technical assumption about the device, authorizing as it does both a constructivist and an obscurantist definition of its operation in the text, needs careful scrutiny. What has to be determined more closely is the position, both personal and artistic, from which the device is articulated.

The question at issue is that of the actual status of Roussel's revelations in *Comment j'ai écrit certains de mes livres* with regard to the series of prose and verse works of which it is the final element in the chain. It is true that at first sight the text of Roussel's revelation would seem to be written from a discursive point of view very different, because of its expositional character, from that of the author's other, artistic compositions. It appears to function, with respect to the earlier writings, as a kind of overhanging buttress of technical clarity safe from the experience of linguistic instability that typifies its content. Yet at the same time the tenor of the revelation is noticeably more anecdotal than rigorously theoretical. The irregular shifts within it from technical insight to autobiographical reminiscence, and from testimony to self-dramatization, redistribute the relation between *logos* and *pathos*. Its overall structure points to a more mobile and friable terrain of self-apprehension than is visible if stress is laid unequivocally on the technical moment described by the text. Roussel's revelation offers a whole network of stratified literary co-ordinates that are as much subjective and autobiographical in their import as they are constructivist in their tactic. For this reason Roussel's final yet liminary text functions less as dogma than as symptom, and needs to be considered more for its implications than for the letter of its assertions. It is these I want to examine now.

I have noted the extent to which Roussel's device works as a strategy of contextual transformation. A series of apparently random verisimilar discursive contexts, ranging from verses out of Victor Hugo to the address of the author's bootmaker, are subjected by Roussel to a process of paradigmatic distortion as words are aligned in vertical lists of graphic similarity or phonetic equivalence, cancelling out any metaphorical kernel of permanence or identity. The vertical rows of language, in Roussel's hands, cluster together in incipient phrastic sequences structured according to a principle of spatial contiguity or on the lines of an associative syntax of prepositional bonding. Idiosyncratic rhyme—rhyme for the subjective mind— replaces alphabetical reason as the basic orientation of Roussel's artistic lexicon.

It is arguable that the device has little to recommend it here beyond its ingenuity or its humour. Yet, as I have suggested, there are complex implications latent in it. Roussel provides some notion of these when he alludes to the art of the rebus, with which his device has distinct affinities. For it will be remembered that the idea of the rebus, about the same time as Roussel himself has recourse to it, is one of the crucial analogies explored by Freud in his analysis of the transformative procedures used in the work of the dream. What is at issue here, in the reference to the rebus, in Roussel as in Freud, is the irremediable figurability of human language, the endless availability of the system of language to the irregular permutations of condensation and displacement at work in the unconscious. Opting for *oratio versa* over *oratio recta,* for the figurative over the prosaic, Roussel reasserts against the positivity of communicational discourse the semantic multiplicities

and the material entropy of individual words. Roussel's device, as Ricardou and others have underlined, constitutes in this way a radical affront to the nominalist realism of literary mimesis. Roussel's enterprise, though in a very different perspective, joins forces here with rhetorical tradition in its exploration, beyond the techniques of oratorical persuasion, of what Michel Foucault describes as the 'espace tropologique' ['tropological space'] of language, constituted, as he puts it, by 'la rotation des mots dans le volume du langage' ['the rotation of words in the mass of language'].

There is a sense, of course, in which this shift in emphasis with regard to language is not at all new. For generations poets have yielded the initiative to words, creating in literature a dance of language irreducible to the stability of spoken communication. For Valéry, indeed, poetry was precisely 'une hésitation prolongée entre le son et le sens' ['a prolonged hesitation between sound and sense']. The rhetorical figures of secondary connotation which in former times were no more than a conventionalized embellishment to verse have long become the very stuff of poetic ambiguity and complexity. Yet in Roussel's case this figurative potential in language, while it constitutes for poets like Valéry the source of the seductive indeterminacy of the poetic effect itself, and becomes the substance of the literary artefact as such, is displaced from the surface of the text into a kind of private *hinterland*. Were it otherwise, Roussel would have had no need to chart out the contours of that *hinterland* in the shape of his *Comment j'ai écrit certains de mes livres*. It indicates that the phenomenon of rhetorical and homophonic reduplication in language concerned Roussel less as a possible source of preciosity or intellectual virtuosity than as a menace to his own subjectivity and his identity. Indeed, it was perhaps only when his life was virtually at a close that Roussel felt able to divulge the nature of the cult animating his whole literary existence.

There is an objection here. It concerns those verse writings which are not covered by the revelation of the device, since this affects, as Roussel points out, only those of his works written in prose. For in fact Roussel is the author of a number of verse texts that make more than common use of *rime riche* and the near-homophonic jingling of entire words. In these poetic compositions, it may be argued, the device leaves its domain of secrecy and rises to the very surface of the text. These writings, however—*La Doublure, La Vue,* and the *Nouvelles Impressions d'Afrique*—Roussel declares to be 'absolument étrangers au procédé ['absolute strangers to the procedure']. Although this is, strictly speaking, true, it is not without significance that the denial is a categorical one. It rather suggests that the place of the device has been supplanted, in the verse works, by the phenomenon of rhyme. The conventional aspects of French rhyming verse film over Roussel's fascination with verbal repetition. But this is not the whole story, for the insistent and unwieldy rhymes of these texts disturb the purely pragmatic character of the prosodic conventions. Through and against the doggerel of rhyme and rhythm there may be seen working the effects of a very personal drama which the text both enacts and keeps at a distance. This drama provokes a double tension. The reader witnesses a curious spectacle that consists in the evanescence and dilution of meaning in favour of the gestual automatism of what Roussel styles elsewhere as 'de piètres vers de douze pieds pleins de chevilles et d'hiatus' ['paltry verses of twelve feet full of chevilles and gaps']. But simultaneously this insistent automatism, with its obsessive imprint of rhythmic affect and syntagmatic distortion, does visibly reiterate the elements of what may be termed, after

Freud, Roussel's 'family romance'. Nowhere is this compact antagonism clearer than in the verse-narrative entitled **'Le Serment de John Glover'** included by Roussel in *Comment j'ai écrit certains de mes livres*. Within the scansions of that narrative, exacerbated doggerel and childhood fantasy merge together with the force of some of Roussel's most characteristic and recurrent themes.

At the heart of Roussel's verse-writing, no less than in the *hinterland* world of the device affecting the prose works, there is a crisis, a crisis that it is the function of literature both to underscore and keep at bay, both to analyse for the self and to articulate as sense for the reader. *Comment j'ai écrit certains de mes livres* records the evidence of the crisis as both a literary and a personal event. It corresponds to a moment in Roussel's work that the writer identifies with the neurasthenic crisis in his personal life sustained at the time of writing *La Doublure*. (pp. 825-28)

The crisis sets in motion what in Freudian terms may be considered as a structural retreat from the test of reality to more archaic narcissistic positions in the self, thus provoking a defusion or disintrication of Roussel's affective commitment to the symbolic—and linguistic—bonds of the speech community. The narcissistic wound sustained in Roussel's personality by the failure of *La Doublure*—though there is good reason to believe that it antedates the publication of the book—releases in this way, against his maternal tongue, the form and structure of Roussel's insertion into the world, a destructive impetus that seeks to displace and transform the nature and place of that insertion. The locus of Roussel's text, as he himself obliquely indicates when discussing the title of *Locus Solus,* becomes in this way singularly recalcitrant, shifting through meaning, to use Michel Leiris's punning description, as a 'biffure'—both erasure and deflection—of his position within the community as a speaking self.

It would be a mistake to conclude from this that Roussel's approach to his art was born from defeat and regression. For from this dislocation of his standing in reality there proceeds a far-reaching remodelling of the quotidian relation between self and language. If Roussel is displaced on the one hand from his position in the symbolic order of society, it is only to take up a more marginal and more probing stance on the edge of that order. There is more method than madness in Roussel's apparent retreat from object identifications. It enables him to disinter from beneath the constraints of social bondage a whole new series of literary and artistic coordinates.

From the inner splitting of Roussel's personal world there emerges, then, not a flow of minor and idiosyncratic obsessions, but the scansions of a differentiated and spectral literary universe. It is a creative world that pivots on a fulcrum of primary identifications: of self with other, of language with reality. It portrays how these identifications, necessary steps in the insertion of the individual within the speech community, are irremediably infused with an ungraspable force of alterity. This alterity is none other than the exteriority of the self to its own images of self-apprehension. Just as Roussel's device mocks the systematic fabric of language with its redoubled distortions of sense, so his literary universe repudiates reality with its population of ghostly doubles and *duplicata*. Reality becomes a simulacrum of its own affective investment. The subjectivity of the artist Roussel becomes ever porous and boundlessly all-enveloping, consuming the specular distance between self and other to the point where literature and reality fuse into the exalted disequilibrium of the writing self. The self no longer

knows its own identity, and the verisimilar realism of the referential universe and the oneiric fantasy of the private world merge. Their terms are no longer stable ones, and Roussel, as he tracks down the literary world of Pierre Loti on the real island of Tahiti, calmly concludes, having recounted his travels around the globe, that 'de tous ces voyages, je n'ai jamais rien tiré pour mes livres. Il m'a paru que la chose méritait d'être signalée tant elle montre clairement que chez moi l'imagination est tout' ['from all these travels, I never took anything for my books. It seems to me that this is worth mentioning, since it clearly shows just how much imagination counts for everything in my work']. . . .

The fierce import for the practice of literature of this complex remodelling of the authorial self is to charge writing with a new intensity, to project literature into a space where communication is no longer commanded by a contract of regulated interpersonal exchange, but where, as Georges Bataille, in another context, suggests, 'ce qui est "communiqué" . . . . est une perte fulgurante' ['what is "communicated" is a painful loss']; there is here a new style of communication by excess which, as Bataille adds, 'demande un défaut, une "faille"; elle entre, comme la mort, par un défaut de la cuirasse. Elle demande une coïncidence de deux déchirures, en moi-même, en autrui' ['demands a defect, a "fault"; it enters, like death, through a chink in the armor. It demands a coincidence of two tears, in the self, in others']. The illuminative chasm in Roussel's sense of self invades the terrain of his inscription into society and sense, propelling the negativity of his gestual linguistic rhythms into the symbolic order of the speech community inhabited by the reader. The fixity of Roussel's identity as a speaking member of that community is collapsed in the ecstatic exaltation of intrapersonal excess.

Serious problems accrue here, however, to Roussel's artistic project. For this overwhelming energetic excess has still to pass from the *hinterland* of the author's personal drama to the foreground of the literary text. Roussel still needs to harness his ecstasy to the production of sense. A new syntagmatic moment has to be grafted on to the paradigmatic conversions worked by the device. It will be remembered how, for those of Roussel's critics I have already quoted, this discursive moment, whether it be seen as following principles of realism, stereotyped repetition, or self-reflexive constructivism, is at heart a secondary operation, autonomous with respect to the device itself. This is clearly however not the case. For this syntagmatic consideration is already present in those initial transformations, in the contextual order of the words that Roussel, according to his own term, chooses to marry together. It is represented in the early forms of the device by the preposition *à*. In the final variation on the device, the 'procédé évolué' ['evolved procedure'], it appears in the guise of what may be called the elasticity principle of the phonetic chain. By this I mean the way Roussel interpolates or syncopates phonemes in the initial contextual fragment in order to arrive at a workable final state. Of course, the syntagmatic consideration was probably never far from Roussel's mind in the actual selection of the initial context, which was, as the author insists, a major and lengthy business. (pp. 830-32)

[What] is disturbing about the device is less that discrete verbal signs should be grouped together according to their graphic or phonetic similarity (an experience available to all who open a dictionary or a grammar book) than that this new inventory of words should generate meaning of a complex literary kind. It is for this reason that the impact of Roussel's device is more imaginatively auto-analytical than solely technical. For by the lesson provided by the device Roussel is able to interpret in his writing the oblique and transversal paths by which, as an artist and as a subject, he is astonished by his language, both struck and stunned by the manner in which his life is written in and against the fabric of his maternal tongue. As Roussel turns on to that tongue the disruptive force of aggressivity released by the shift in his symbolic status within language, the evidence of language returns into his life and his fiction not as a transcendental bond but as an enigmatic object possessing the sought-after mystery of his own birth into meaning. Roussel's work unfolds in this way as an artistic autobiography, confronting language not as a vehicle of finite self-definition but as an undecidable cleavage in the self, as a conflictual simultaneity of both familiarity and strangeness within which selfhood and alterity merge in the form of a literary text possessing no fixed term of stasis.

In this way the narcissistic position of self taken up by Roussel reveals itself to be already and irremediably assailed by the alterity of the self's fall into language. It is an abrupt and critical fall, the laying-bare of which has considerable impact on Roussel's whole artistic endeavour. The writing self may no longer be explored as a closed autarchic world of self-contemplation, but as a fissured space of non-coincidence. No more a stance of mastery, the writing self is henceforth a *casus* [event] and an 'échéance' ['falling due'], a pronominal accident, a singular visceral cry, and a collective script traced upon the nascent and chaotic body of existence. 'What's in a name?', is the question that, together with Joyce's Stephen Dedalus, Roussel's text seems to ask, only to receive as an answer the same question returning as an inverted echo from the world. For indeed, as Stephen adds: 'That is what we ask ourselves in childhood when we write the name we are told is ours'.

Here lies the horizon of Roussel's trajectory through the oddities and loops of human language. The issue at stake is that of the relation between language and self in the modern literary text. Roussel's work, as it is deployed through the incidences of his device, presents a whole programme for the endeavours of literary modernity. In Roussel's experimentation with words there is not the technical exploitation of the constitutional curiosities of human language, nor indeed a naive obsession with the twisted yarn of jokes and puns, but a more critical imbrication of language with subjectivity, of autobiography with fiction, of negativity with sense, a singular fusion of necessary blindness to the enigma of meaning and of piercing insight into the place and position of literary creation in the modern world. Roussel confronts the language of identity—both the identity of language with itself and the language of subjective self-identification—with its margins and contours, perfusing the space of self with the febrile alterity of a system of sense that is, at root, always other than what it is. Here is not the work

of a self-indulgent egotist but of a committed literary artist confronting the world as synonymous with its own saturation as a symbolic fabric of words, clichés, and stereotypes. His personal adventure as a writer is synchronic with a questioning of the statutory fictions of social bondage. Engaging the reader in a parallel scrutiny of his place as a self within sense, this challenging of language as both the pivot and limit of intelligibility in the world makes of Roussel's life's work an artistic endeavour of an exemplary kind. It is only with difficulty that the *pathos* of such an enterprise may be reduced to that of a curiosity in literary history. It offers rather a paradigm of concerted energy outlining the aims and possibilities—indeed the place itself—of modern literature. It is for this reason that, after all, Roussel's centenary was perhaps a significant event. (pp. 834-35)

> *Leslie Hill, ''Raymond Roussel and the Place of Literature,'' in* The Modern Language Review, *Vol. 74, Part 4, October, 1979, pp. 823-35.*

ADDITIONAL BIBLIOGRAPHY

Cherniack-Tzuriel, Abba. ''Roussel's *Impressions of Africa*.'' *The Drama Review* 20, No. 2 (June 1976): 108-23.
 Account of the production of the dramatic adaptation of *Impressions of Africa* and a detailed description of the major scenes of the play.

Cowley, Malcolm. ''*Locus Solus*.'' *Broom* 4, No. 4 (March 1923): 281-83.
 Describes the performance of and audience reaction to Roussel's dramatic adaptation of *Locus Solus*.

Lewis, Roger. ''Enclosed Worlds.'' *New Statesman* 106, No. 2754 (30 December 1983): 19-20.
 Review of *Locus Solus*, which the critic describes as a catalog of ''divine uselessness'' whose author he judges to be ''lunatic.''

Lovitt, Carl. ''Locus Solus: Literary Solitaire.'' *Sub-stance*, No. 10 (1974): 95-109.
 Argues that ''the absence of a specific narrator appears to be the fictional expression of a corresponding absence at the level of the written text. The text seems intent on conveying that—just as the fiction does not emerge from one man's consciousness—it too is not the expression of one man's will.''

Matthews, J. H. ''Raymond Roussel.'' In his *Surrealism and the Novel*, pp. 41-55. Ann Arbor: University of Michigan Press, 1966.
 Discusses those elements of Roussel's work which most interested the Surrealists.

Vitrac, Roger. ''Raymond Roussel.'' *Transition*, No. 12 (March 1928): 148-62.
 Consideration of the ''Roussel enigma,'' with a descriptive overview of his works and critical reputation.

John Ruskin

1819-1900

English critic, essayist, historian, nonfiction writer, poet, novella writer, autobiographer, and diarist.

Endowed with a passion for reforming what he considered his "blind and wandering fellow-men" and convinced that he had "perfect judgment" in aesthetic matters, Ruskin was the author of over forty books and several hundred essays and lectures that expounded his theories of aesthetics, morality, history, economics, and social reform. Although his views were often controversial and critical reception of his works was frequently hostile, Ruskin became one of the Victorian era's most prominent and influential critics of art and society, and his admirers have included such figures as Leo Tolstoy and Mohandas K. Gandhi. Ruskin is also considered one of the greatest prose stylists in the English language and is perhaps as well known today for the eloquence of his prose as for its substance.

Ruskin was the only child of a wealthy London wine merchant and his wife. From an early age he was dominated by his mother, a devout Puritan and strict disciplinarian who was responsible for much of his early education. Her emphasis on Bible study played a prominent role in the formation of Ruskin's prose style as well as his moral thought. A precocious child, Ruskin began studying Latin at the age of seven and Greek shortly thereafter in preparation for what his parents hoped would be a career in the ministry. The elder Ruskins were excessively protective of their son's moral and physical well-being and demanded much of him. In a letter to Ruskin, who was then ten years old, his father wrote: "You are blessed with a fine Capacity & even Genius & you owe it as a Duty to the author of your Being & the giver of your Talents to cultivate your powers & to use them in his Service & for the benefit of your fellow Creatures. You may be doomed to enlighten a People by your Wisdom & to adorn an age by your learning." This parental admonition was to dominate Ruskin's career. According to biographers, Ruskin's interest in art dates from his thirteenth birthday, when he was given a copy of Samuel Rogers's poem "Italy," with illustrations by J. M. W. Turner. Captivated by Turner's depictions of nature, Ruskin conceived what became a lifelong fascination for both landscape painting and Turner's art. Four years later, in 1836, a vicious review of Turner's latest works prompted Ruskin to write an eloquent defense of the artist, but at Turner's request the manuscript was not submitted for publication.

In the fall of 1836 Ruskin left home and entered Oxford University. He was accompanied by his mother, who took rooms nearby and continued to supervise her son's education and activities. During college he published essays on aesthetic subjects and composed a great deal of poetry, much of which concerned nature and all of which is dismissed by critics as uninspired. Ruskin graduated in 1842, and in that same year a further attack on Turner's work prompted Ruskin to compose a second defense of the artist. Although he envisioned the work as a brief pamphlet similar to the essay of 1836, Ruskin found himself unable to limit his argument and the pamphlet gradually developed into a lengthy treatise on art and taste. Published in 1843 as *Modern Painters: Their Superiority in the Art of Landscape Painting to the Ancient Masters,* the work sold slowly

but received praise from such prominent literary figures as Elizabeth Browning, Charlotte Brontë, Walt Whitman, and William Wordsworth, and launched Ruskin's career as an art critic. In order to elaborate the argument begun in *Modern Painters,* he published *Modern Painters II* in 1846, followed in rapid succession by five volumes of architectural studies, two more volumes of *Modern Painters,* and numerous minor works. According to R. H. Wilenski, Ruskin's works of the 1840s and 1850s were generally disparaged by leading artists and architects, who considered Ruskin a pretentious dilettante whose enthusiasm and eloquence were insufficient to offset the amateurish quality of his aesthetic judgments. Undaunted by their criticism, however, Ruskin continued to write prolifically on aesthetic subjects, and his works gained a small following among the cultured public.

During the late 1850s the focus of Ruskin's works gradually shifted from aesthetics to social problems. According to biographers, the sense of mission instilled in Ruskin as a child endowed even his aesthetic studies with an overriding moral purpose, and led him to question the justifiability of the study of art "while the earth is failing under our feet, and our fellows are departing every instant into eternal pain." Commentators note that Ruskin felt additional guilt over his privileged economic position; John D. Rosenberg maintains that "Ruskin's social criticism is in part atonement for pleasures which his large means and exquisitely refined senses enabled him to afford, but which his conscience never allowed him wholly to enjoy." His writings of the late 1850s and the 1860s are dominated by the problems of the underprivileged, the elderly, and the working class, and by proposals for the amelioration of social and economic inequities. Ruskin did not, however, limit his activities exclusively to writing social commentary. During this period he also taught at Frederick D. Maurice's Working Men's College, became a popular public lecturer, and wrote prolifically on numerous subjects, including art, mythology, education, war, law, geology, botany, and ornithology. In addition, he composed a series of opinionated and dogmatic pamphlets, entitled "Notes on the Royal Academy and Other Exhibitions," which further antagonized the art world and received sufficient attention to establish Ruskin as a public figure.

Commentators have observed in Ruskin's writings of the 1860s an increasing diffuseness, which they attribute to emotional distress resulting from failures and frustrations in his personal life. Although married in 1848, Ruskin remained under the domination of his parents, and his inability to assert his independence from them contributed to the discord that beset his marriage. At his wife's request the marriage was annulled in 1854 on the grounds of Ruskin's impotence, causing a minor public scandal. Five years later Ruskin fell in love with eleven-year-old Rose La Touche, a physically weak, mentally unstable, and fanatically devout child who repeatedly rejected Ruskin as a suitor over the course of the next sixteen years, but for whom Ruskin harbored an obsessive passion long after her death at the age of twenty-seven. As Ruskin's emotional distress intensified, his writings and lectures became more personal, fragmented, and at times nearly incoherent, and by the end of the 1860s he had begun to fear insanity.

In 1870, through the intervention of friends, Ruskin was elected Slade Professor of Fine Art at Oxford University. Although pleased with the position, which he felt elevated him from amateur to official status in the art world, Ruskin continued to question the social and moral value of the study of art. In what he considered atonement for his continued work in aesthetics, Ruskin began *Fors Clavigera: Letters to the Workmen and Labourers of Great Britain*, a series of monthly "letters" through which he sought to instigate social action and which he used to publicize his Guild of St. George, a utopian organization devoted to "the health, wealth, and long life of the British nation." Although few reforms were effected by the group, both the Guild and *Fors Clavigera* attracted a great deal of attention, and the increasing eccentricity of Ruskin's behavior established an image in the public mind of a mad prophet and literary genius. Numerous new editions of his previously published works were released, and during the last decades of his life Ruskin acquired a large following. In 1878 he suffered a severe mental breakdown, followed by a series of delusions and obsessions that plagued him until his death. According to biographers his remaining years constituted a struggle to write during periods of lucidity, which alternated with bouts of madness. After spending the last decade of his life in seclusion, Ruskin died in 1900.

The dominant tone of Ruskin's writings on art and architecture was established in *The Poetry of Architecture,* a series of articles published while he was a student at Oxford, in which he wrote: "Our object, let it always be remembered, is not the attainment of architectural data, but the formation of taste." *The Poetry of Architecture* also introduced Ruskin's concept

of an intrinsic relationship between art and morality, which formed the basis of the doctrines developed in his most important study of aesthetics, *Modern Painters*. In Ruskin's view, moral virtue and beauty were inseparable, and the success of a work of art was at least partially a reflection of the integrity of the artist. In accordance with this view, he sought in *Modern Painters* to demonstrate that the superiority of Turner's work to that of his predecessors was the result of his unsurpassed fidelity to nature, arguing that "though the fine arts are *not* necessarily imitative or representative, . . . still the highest of them are appointed also to relate to us the utmost ascertainable truth respecting visible things and moral feelings." Ruskin developed his thesis through minute examinations of both Turner's works and natural phenomena, and by broadening the argument to include discussions of such topics as the purpose of art, the nature of truth and beauty, means of perception, and various social, religious, and philosophical questions. Critics often note that the chaotic nature of *Modern Painters* results both from Ruskin's intentional digressions and from the internal contradictions arising from the evolution of the author's thought during the work's eighteen-year composition. Francis G. Townsend has remarked that "it is not surprising that *Modern Painters* is one of the worst organized books ever to earn the name of literature, nor that a careful reading of it by an intelligent reader leads to confusion rather than enlightenment as to the author's opinions." Critics also object to contradictions in the work resulting from Ruskin's apparent compulsion to legitimize his personal aesthetic prejudices through elaborate theoretical justifications. For example, Vernon Lee writes that "having conceived a perhaps exaggerated aversion" to the manner in which Dutch painters of the seventeenth century represented nature, "Ruskin immediately formulated a theory that minute imitation of nature was base and sinful; and when he conceived a perhaps equally exaggerated admiration for the works of certain extremely careful and even servile English painters of our own times, he was forced to formulate an explanatory theory that minuteness of work was conscientious, appreciative, and distinctly holy." At the same time, at least one critic attributes the strength of Ruskin's works to the apparent chaos other critics find so repellent in *Modern Painters*. Robert Hewisohn asserts that "it is precisely his refusal to distinguish between the normally accepted divisions of thought—aesthetic, ethical, social, economic, philosophical and personal—that is the source of his most important insights."

Like *Modern Painters,* Ruskin's architectural writings are primarily moralistic in nature, arguing that architecture is not only a reflection of the architect's moral state but also of the morality of the era in which it was built. In *The Seven Lamps of Architecture* Ruskin propounded his theories in a series of meditations on what he considered the principal qualities informing architecture: sacrifice, truth, power, memory, beauty, obedience, and life. His most famous study of architecture, *The Stones of Venice,* traces the history of the city in order to demonstrate the effect of national morality on the evolution of art. According to Ruskin, the book had "no other aim than to show that the Gothic architecture of Venice had arisen out of . . . a state of pure national faith, and of domestic virtue, and that its Renaissance architecture had arisen out of . . . a state of concealed national infidelity, and of domestic corruption." Commentators observe that Ruskin's architectural writings are almost exclusively concerned with areas of his particular interest or expertise. As a result, some scholars criticize these works for their excessive preoccupation with such architectural styles as Venetian Gothic and such elements as ornamentation. Others, however, applaud Ruskin's attempt to relate a society's art to its beliefs and values, and consider *The Stones of Venice* both Ruskin's greatest work and one of the most significant studies of architecture written during the Victorian era.

Ruskin's writings on economics are similarly valued for their moral force, rather than for their importance to the study of political economy. Unschooled in economics (he maintained in 1857 that he had "never read any author on political economy, except Adam Smith, twenty years ago"), Ruskin based his economic theories on the same moral principles as those on which he based his aesthetic theories. His most important economic works, including *Unto This Last* and *Munera Pulveris,* are dominated by such ethical concerns as honor and justice, and often combine liberal ideas of social reform with conservative concepts of authoritarian rule. Maintaining that "all prosperity begins in obedience," Ruskin proposed an ideal state that Frederick Kirchhoff has described as "a social system characterized by the filial cooperation of its citizens under the guidance of a paternal ruler." Ruskin's economic works are often criticized for their basis in untenable analogies between the economics of an estate and those of a nation, as well as for the same disorder and illogic that mar his aesthetic writings. Critical reception of these works at the time of their publication was universally hostile and initial sales were poor; however, Ruskin's writings on economics gradually gained popularity and eventually came to exert a strong influence on public thought. Today critics credit these works with helping to raise the social consciousness of Victorian readers and economists. According to Alan Lee, "Misconceived, ill-informed, and often unfair as his onslaught on political economy was, weak as his understanding of it, confused as his own arguments often were, he did manage to confront the science with a stiff moral challenge."

Although his social, aesthetic, and economic theories were often criticized by experts in those fields, Ruskin was the most widely read art and social critic of the Victorian era. His ideas influenced some of the most prominent figures of his time, including Bernard Shaw, William Morris, and Gandhi, who asserted that *Unto This Last* "brought about an instantaneous and practical transformation in my life." Critics today consider Ruskin one of the most perceptive social and cultural observers of his era, and praise his organic vision of art and life. According to Kirchhoff, Ruskin "teaches a way of thinking that not only bridges intellectual disciplines, but fuses intellect with perception and feeling." The conflicting characteristics of Ruskin's works—which have been lauded and disparaged with equal enthusiasm by critics for over a century—have been accurately summarized by Marcel Proust, who wrote that although Ruskin's writings are "often stupid, fanatical, exasperating, false, and irritating," they are also "always praiseworthy and always great."

(See also *Contemporary Authors,* Vol. 114, and *Something About the Author,* Vol. 24.)

PRINCIPAL WORKS

Modern Painters: Their Superiority in the Art of Landscape Painting to the Ancient Masters (criticism) 1843
Modern Painters II (criticism) 1846
The Seven Lamps of Architecture (criticism) 1849
Poems (poetry) 1850
The King of the Golden River (novella) 1851
Pre-Raphaelitism (essay) 1851

The Stones of Venice I (criticism) 1851
The Stones of Venice II (criticism) 1853
The Stones of Venice III (criticism) 1853
Lectures on Architecture and Painting (lectures) 1854
Modern Painters III (criticism) 1856
Modern Painters IV (criticism) 1856
The Political Economy of Art (essays) 1857; also published as *A Joy For Ever* [revised and enlarged edition], 1880
The Two Paths (lectures) 1859
Modern Painters V (criticism) 1860
Unto This Last (essays) 1862
Sesame and Lilies (lectures) 1865
The Crown of Wild Olive (lectures) 1866
The Ethics of the Dust (dialogues) 1866
Time and Tide (essays) 1868
The Queen of the Air (criticism) 1869
Lectures on Art (lectures) 1870
*Fors Clavigera: Letters to the Workmen and Labourers of Great Britain (letters) 1871-84
The Eagle's Nest (lectures) 1872
Munera Pulveris (essays) 1872
Val d'Arno (lectures) 1874
*Proserpina (nonfiction) 1875-86
*St. Mark's Rest (history) 1877-84
The Art of England (lectures) 1883
*Praeterita (unfinished autobiography) 1885-89
**The Poetry of Architecture (criticism) 1893
The Works of John Ruskin. 39 vols. (criticism, lectures, essays, history, poetry, novella, dialogues, textbooks, catalogs, letters, and diaries) 1903-1912
Ruskin's Letters from Venice (letters) 1955
The Diaries of John Ruskin. 3 vols. (diaries) 1956-59

*These works were issued in periodical installments.

**The essays in this collection were originally published in the *Magazine of Architecture* in 1837 and 1838.

[WALT WHITMAN] (essay date 1847)

[*Considered one of America's greatest poets, Whitman was a literary innovator whose poetry decisively influenced the development of modern free verse. His masterpiece, the poetry collection* Leaves of Grass *(1855), was controversial during the author's lifetime for its lack of such conventional poetic devices as rhyme, regular meter, and uniform length of line and stanza, as well as for its frank treatment of sexuality. The collection also addresses the themes of death, immortality, and democracy, and Whitman actively promoted an image of himself as the definitive poet of American democracy and the unsung individual. In the following excerpt, he praises* Modern Painters I.]

The first dip one takes in [*Modern Painters*] will, in all probability, make him pleased with the dashy, manly, clear-hearted style of its author. [The author] tells us in the preface that he began his writing from a feeling of indignation at the shallow and false criticism of the periodicals of the day, on the works of a certain artist. That his writing is entirely devoid of selfish or partial motives we feel confident; no other than a sincere man could make such eloquence as fills these pages. The widest expanse of the ideal, and the most rigid application of mechanical rules, in art, appear to have been mastered by the author of *Modern Painters*. As for artists, we should suppose such a work would be invaluable; and to the general reader it will present many fresh ideas, and afford a fund of intellectual pleasure. Indeed it is worthy of the reading of every lover of what we must call intellectual chivalry, enthusiasm, and a high-toned sincerity, disdainful of the flippant tricks and petty arts of small writers.

[Walt Whitman], in a review of "Modern Painters," in The Brooklyn Daily Eagle, *July 22, 1847, p. 2.*

BLACKWOOD'S EDINBURGH MAGAZINE (essay date 1851)

[*In the following excerpt, the critic discusses what he considers the mixture of shrewd insight and "utter nonsense" in Ruskin's early writings on art and architecture.*]

[We] do not hold Mr Ruskin to be a safe guide in matters of art, and [**Modern Painters II**] demonstrates that he is no safe guide in matters of philosophy. He is a man of undoubted power and vigour of mind; he feels strongly, and he thinks independently: but he is hasty and impetuous; can very rarely, on any subject, deliver a calm and temperate judgment; and, when he enters on the discussion of general principles, shows an utter inability to seize on, or to appreciate, the wide generalisations of philosophy. He is not, therefore, one of those men who can ever become an authority to be appealed to by the less instructed in any of the fine arts, or on any topic whatever; and this we say with the utmost confidence, because, although we may be unable in many cases to dispute his judgment—as where he speaks of paintings we have not seen, or technicalities of art we do not affect to understand—yet he so frequently stands forth on the broad arena where general and familiar principles are discussed, that it is utterly impossible *to be mistaken in the man.* On all these occasions he displays a very marked and rather peculiar combination of power and weakness—of power, the result of natural strength of mind; of weakness, the inevitable consequence of a passionate haste, and an overweening confidence. When we hear a person of this intellectual character throwing all but unmitigated abuse upon works which men have long consented to admire, and lavishing upon some other works encomiums which no conceivable perfection of human art could justify, it is utterly impossible to attach any weight to his opinion, on the ground that he has made an especial study of any one branch of art. Such a man we cannot trust out of our sight a momemt; we cannot give him one inch of ground more than his reasoning covers, or our own experience would grant to him. (p. 326)

In all Mr Ruskin's works, and in almost every page of them, whether on painting, or architecture, or philosophy, or ecclesiastical controversy, two characteristics invariably prevail: an extreme dogmatism, and a passion for singularity. Every man who thinks earnestly would convert all the world to his own opinions; but while Mr Ruskin would convert all the world to his own tastes as well as opinions, he manifests the greatest repugnance to think for a moment like any one else. He has a mortal aversion to mingle with a crowd. It is quite enough for an opinion to be commonplace to insure it his contempt: if it has passed out of fashion, he may revive it; but to think with the existing multitude would be impossible. Yet that multitude are to think with him. He is as bent on unity in matters of taste as others are on unity in matters of religion; and he sets the example by diverging, wherever he can, from the tastes of others.

Between these two characteristics there is no real contradiction; or rather the contradiction is quite familiar. The man who most affects singularity is generally the most dogmatic: he is the very man who expresses most surprise that others should differ from him. No one is so impatient of contradiction as he who is perpetually contradicting others; and on the gravest matters of religion those are often found to be most zealous for unity of belief who have some pet heresy of their own, for which they are battling all their lives. The same overweening confidence lies, in fact, at the basis of both these characteristics. In Mr Ruskin they are both seen in great force. No matter what the subject he discusses,—taste or ecclesiastical government— we always find the same combination of singularity, with a dogmatism approaching to intolerance. (pp. 326-27)

One word on the style of Mr Ruskin. . . . It is very unequal. In both his architectural works he writes generally with great ease, spirit, and clearness. There is a racy vigour in the page. But when he would be very eloquent, as he is disposed to be in the **Modern Painters,** he becomes very verbose, tedious, obscure, extravagant. There is no discipline in his style, no moderation, no respose. Those qualities which he has known how to praise in art he has not aimed at in his own writing. A rank luxuriance of a semi-poetical diction lies about, perfectly unrestrained; metaphorical language comes before us in every species of disorder; and hyperbolical expressions are used till they become commonplace. Verbal criticism he would probably look upon as a very puerile business: he need fear nothing of the kind from us; we should as soon think of criticising or pruning a jungle. To add to the confusion, he appears at times to have proposed to himself the imitation of some of our older writers: pages are written in the rhythm of Jeremy Taylor; sometimes it is the venerable Hooker who seems to be his type; and he has even succeeded in combining whatever is most tedious and prolix in both these great writers. If the reader wishes a specimen of this sort of *modern antique,* he may turn to the fifteenth chapter of the second volume of the **Modern Painters.**

Coupled with this matter of style, and almost inseparable from it, is the violence of his manner on subjects which cannot possibly justify so vehement a zeal. We like a generous enthusiasm on any art—we delight in it; but who can travel in sympathy with a writer who exhausts on so much paint and canvass every term of rapture that the Alps themselves could have called forth? One need not be a utilitarian philosopher— or what Mr Ruskin describes as such—to smile at the lofty position on which he puts the landscape-painter, and the egregious and impossible demands he makes upon the art itself. And the condemnation and opprobrium with which he overwhelms the luckless artist who has offended him is quite as violent. The bough of a tree, "in the left hand upper corner" of a landscape of Poussin's, calls forth this terrible denunciation:—

> This latter is a representation of an ornamental group of elephants' tusks, with feathers tied to the ends of them. Not the wildest imagination could ever conjure up in it the remotest resemblance to the bough of a tree. It might be the claws of a witch—the talons of an eagle—the horns of a fiend; but it is a full assemblage of every conceivable falsehood which can be told respecting foliage—a piece of work so barbarous in every way *that one glance at it ought to prove the complete charlatanism and trickery of the whole system of the old landscape-painters.* . . . I will say here at once, that such draw-

ing as this is as ugly as it is childish, and as painful as it is false; and that the man who could tolerate, much more, who could deliberately set down such a thing on his canvass, *had neither eye nor feeling for one single attribute or excellence of God's works*. He might have drawn *the other stem* in excusable ignorance, or under some false impression of being able to improve upon nature, but this is conclusive and unpardonable. . . .

(pp. 328-29)

The great redeeming quality of Mr Ruskin—and we wish to give it conspicuous and honourable mention—is his love of nature. Here lies the charm of his works; to this may be traced whatever virtue is in them, or whatever utility they may possess. They will send the painter more than ever to the study of nature, and perhaps they will have a still more beneficial effect on the art, by sending the critic of painting to the same school. It would be almost an insult to the landscape-painter to suppose that he needed this lesson; the very love of his art must lead him perpetually, one would think, to his great and delightful study amongst the fields, under the open skies, before the rivers and the hills. But the critic of the picture-gallery is often one who goes from picture to picture, and very little from nature to the painting. Consequently, where an artist succeeds in imitating some effect in nature which had not been before represented on the canvass, such a critic is more likely to be displeased than gratified; and the artist, having to paint for a conventional taste, is in danger of sacrificing to it his own higher aspirations. Now it is most true that no man should pretend to be a critic upon pictures unless he understands the art itself of painting; he ought, we suspect, to have handled the pencil or the brush himself; at all events, he ought in some way to have been initiated into the mysteries of the pallet and the easel. Otherwise, not knowing the difficulties to be overcome, nor the means at hand for encountering them, he cannot possibly estimate the degree of merit due to the artist for the production of this or that effect. He may be loud in applause where nothing has been displayed but the old traditions of the art. But still this is only one-half the knowledge he ought to possess. He ought to have studied nature, and to have loved the study, or he can never estimate, and never feel, that *truth* of effect which is the great aim of the artist. Mr Ruskin's works will help to shame out of the field all such half-informed and conventional criticism, the mere connoisseurship of the picture gallery. On the other hand, they will train men who have always been delighted spectators of nature to be also attentive observers. Our critics will learn how to admire, and mere admirers will learn how to criticise. Thus a public will be educated; and here, if anywhere, we may confidently assert that the art will prosper in proportion as there is an intelligent public to reward it.

We like that bold enterprise of Mr Ruskin's which distinguishes the first volume, that daring enumeration of the great palpable facts of nature—the sky, the sea, the earth, the foliage—which the painter has to represent. His descriptions are often made indistinct by a multitude of words; but there is light in the haze—there is a genuine love of nature felt through them. This is almost the only point of sympathy we feel with Mr Ruskin; it is the only hold his volumes have had over us whilst perusing them. . . . (pp. 329-30)

Surveying Mr Ruskin's works on art, . . . we are at no loss to comprehend that mixture of shrewd and penetrating remark,

of bold and well-placed censure, and of utter nonsense in the shape of general principles, with which they abound. In his *Seven Lamps of Architecture,* which is a very entertaining book, and in his *Stones of Venice,* the reader will find many single observations which will delight him, as well by their justice, as by the zeal and vigour with which they are expressed. But from neither work will he derive any satisfaction if he wishes to carry away with him broad general views on architecture.

There is no subject Mr Ruskin has treated more largely than that of architectural ornament; there is none on which he has said more good things, or delivered juster criticisms; and there is none on which he has uttered more indisputable nonsense. Every reader of taste will be grateful to Mr Ruskin if he can pull down from St Paul's Cathedral, or wherever else they are to be found, those wreaths or festoons of carved flowers—"that mass of all manner of fruit and flowers tied heavily into a long bunch, thickest in the middle, and pinned up by both ends against a dead wall." Urns with pocket-handkerchiefs upon them, or a sturdy thick flame for ever issuing from the top, he will receive our thanks for utterly demolishing. But when Mr Ruskin expounds his principles—and he always has principles to expound—when he lays down rules for the government of our taste in this matter, he soon involves us in hopeless bewilderment. Our ornaments, he tells us, are to be taken from the works of nature, not of man; and, from some passages of his writings, we should infer that Mr Ruskin would cover the walls of our public buildings with representations botanical and geological. But in this we must be mistaken. At all events, nothing is to be admitted that is taken from the works of man.

> I conclude, then, with the reader's leave, that all ornament is base which takes for its subject human work; that it is utterly base—painful to every rightly toned mind, without, perhaps, immediate sense of the reason, but for a reason palpable enough when we do think of it. For to carve our own work, and set it up for admiration, is a miserable self-complacency, a contentment in our wretched doings, when we might have been looking at God's doings.

After this, can we venture to admire the building itself, which is, of necessity, man's own "wretched doing?"

Perplexed by his own rules, he will sometimes break loose from the entanglement in some such strange manner as this:—"I believe the right question to ask, with respect to all ornament, is simply this: Was it done with enjoyment—*was the carver happy while he was about it?*" Happy art! where the workman is sure to give happiness if he is but happy at his work. Would that the same could be said of literature!

How far *colour* should be introduced into architecture is a question with men of taste, and a question which of late has been more than usually discussed. Mr Ruskin leans to the introduction of colour. His taste may be correct; but the fanciful reasoning which he brings to bear upon the subject will assist no one else in forming his own taste. Because there is no connection "between the spots of an animal's skin and its anatomical system," he lays it down as the first great principle which is to guide us in the use of colour in architecture—

> That it be *visibly independent of form*. Never paint a column with vertical lines, but always cross it. Never give separate mouldings separate colours," &c. "In certain places," he con-

tinues, "you may run your two systems closer, and here and there let them be parallel for a note or two, but see that the colours and the forms coincide only as two orders of mouldings do; the same for an instant, but each holding its own course. So single members may sometimes have single colours; *as a bird's head is sometimes of one colour, and its shoulders another, you may make your capital one colour, and your shaft another;* but, in general, the best place for colour is on broad surfaces, not on the points of interest in form. *An animal is mottled on its breast and back, and rarely on its paws and about its eyes;* so put your variegation boldly on the flat wall and broad shaft, but be shy of it on the capital and moulding. . . .

(pp. 347-48)

We do not quite see what we have to do at all with the "anatomical system" of the animal, which is kept out of sight; but, in general, we apprehend there is, both in the animal and vegetable kingdom, considerable harmony betwixt colour and external form. Such fantastic reasoning as this, it is evident, will do little towards establishing that one standard of taste, or that "one school of architecture," which Mr Ruskin so strenuously insists upon. All architects are to resign their individual tastes and predilections, and enrol themselves in one school, which shall adopt one style. We need not say that the very first question—what that style should be, Greek or Gothic—would never be decided. Mr Ruskin decides it in favour of the "earliest English decorated Gothic;" but seems, in this case, to suspect that his decision will not carry us far towards unanimity. The scheme is utterly impossible; but he does his duty, he tells us, by proposing the impossibility.

As a climax to his inconsistency and his abnormal ways of thinking, he concludes his *Seven Lamps of Architecture* with a most ominous paragraph, implying that the time is at hand when no architecture of any kind will be wanted: man and his works will be both swept away from the face of the earth. How, with this impression on his mind, could he have the heart to tell us to build for posterity? Will it be a commentary on the Apocalypse that we shall next receive from the pen of Mr Ruskin? (p. 348)

> *"Mr. Ruskin's Works," in* Blackwood's Edinburgh Magazine, *Vol. LXX, No. CCCXXXI, September, 1851, pp. 326-48.*

[GEORGE ELIOT] (essay date 1856)

[*An English novelist, essayist, poet, editor, short story writer, and translator, Eliot was one of the greatest novelists of the nineteenth century. Her work, including the novels* The Mill on the Floss *(1860) and* Middlemarch: A Study of Provincial Life *(1871-72), is informed by penetrating psychological analysis and profound insight into human character. Played against the backdrop of English rural life, Eliot's novels explore moral and philosophical issues and employ a realistic approach to character and plot development. In the following excerpt, she favorably reviews* Modern Painters III.]

Our table this time does not, according to the favourite metaphor, "groan" under the light literature of the quarter, for the quarter has not been very productive; but, in compensation, we ourselves groan under it rather more than usual, for the harvest is principally of straw, and few grains of precious corn remain after the winnowing. We except one book, however, which is a rich sheaf in itself, and will serve as bread, and seed-corn too, for many days. We mean the [third] volume of Mr. Ruskin's ***Modern Painters,*** to which he appropriately gives the subordinate title, "Of Many Things." It may be taken up with equal pleasure whether the reader be acquainted or not with the previous volumes, and no special artistic culture is necessary in order to enjoy its excellences or profit by its suggestions. Every one who cares about nature, or poetry, or the story of human development—every one who has a tinge of literature, or philosophy, will find something that is for him and that will "gravitate to him" in this volume. Since its predecessors appeared, Mr. Ruskin has devoted ten years to the loving study of his great subject—the principles of art; which, like all other great subjects, carries the student into many fields. The critic of art, as he tells us, "has to take *some* note of optics, geometry, geology, botany, and anatomy; he must acquaint himself with the works of all great artists, and with the temper and history of the times in which they lived; he must be a fair metaphysician, and a careful observer of the phenomena of natural scenery." And when a writer like Mr. Ruskin brings these varied studies to bear on one great purpose, when he has to trace their common relation to a grand phase of human activity, it is obvious that he will have a great deal to say which is of interest and importance to others besides painters. The fundamental principles of all just thought and beautiful action or creation are the same, and in making clear to ourselves what is best and noblest in art, we are making clear to ourselves what is best and noblest in morals; in learning how to estimate the artistic products of a particular age according to the mental attitude and external life of that age, we are widening our sympathy and deepening the basis of our tolerance and charity.

Of course, this treatise "Of many things" presents certain old characteristics and new paradoxes which will furnish a fresh text to antagonistic critics; but, happily for us, and happily for our readers, who probably care more to know what Mr. Ruskin says than what other people think he *ought* to say, we are not among those who are more irritated by his faults than charmed and subdued by his merits. When he announces to the world in his Preface, that he is incapable of falling into an illogical deduction—that, whatever other mistakes he may commit, he cannot possibly draw an inconsequent conclusion, we are not indignant, but amused, and do not in the least feel ourselves under the necessity of picking holes in his arguments in order to prove that he is not a logical Pope. We value a writer not in proportion to his freedom from faults, but in proportion to his positive excellences—to the variety of thought he contributes and suggests, to the amount of gladdening and energizing emotions he excites. Of what comparative importance is it that Mr. Ruskin undervalues this painter, or overvalues the other, that he sometimes glides from a just argument into a fallacious one, that he is a little absurd here, and not a little arrogant there, if, with all these collateral mistakes, he teaches truth of infinite value, and *so* teaches it that men will listen? The truth of infinite value that he teaches is *realism*—the doctrine that all truth and beauty are to be attained by a humble and faithful study of nature, and not by substituting vague forms, bred by imagination on the mists of feeling, in place of definite, substantial reality. The thorough acceptance of this doctrine would remould our life; and he who teaches its application to any one department of human activity with such power as Mr. Ruskin's, is a prophet for his generation. It is not enough simply to teach truth; that may be done, as we all know, to empty walls, and within the covers of unsaleable books; we want it to be so taught as to compel men's attention and sympathy. Very correct singing of very fine music will avail little without a *voice* that can thrill the audience and take possession of their souls. Now, Mr. Ruskin has a voice, and one of such power, that whatever error he may mix with his truth, he will make more converts to that truth than less erring advocates who are hoarse and feeble. Considered merely as a writer, he is in the very highest rank of English stylists. The vigour and splendour of his eloquence are not more remarkable than its precision, and the delicate truthfulness of his epithets. The fine *largo* of his sentences reminds us more of De Quincy than of any other writer, and his tendency to digressiveness is another and less admirable point of resemblance to the English Opium-eater. Yet we are not surprised to find that he does not mention De Quincy among the favourite writers who have influenced him, for Mr. Ruskin's style is evidently due far more to innate faculty than to modifying influences; and though he himself thinks that his constant study of Carlyle must have impressed itself on his language as well as his thought, we rarely detect this. In the point of view from which he looks at a subject, in the correctness of his descriptions, and in a certain rough flavour of humour, he constantly reminds us of Carlyle, but in the mere tissue of his style, scarcely ever. But while we are dilating on Mr. Ruskin's general characteristics, we are robbing ourselves of the room we want for what is just now more important—namely, telling the reader something about the contents of the particular volume before us.

It opens with a discussion of the "Grand Style," which, after an analysis and dismissal of Sir Joshua Reynolds's opinion, that it consists in attending to what is invariable, "the great and general ideas only inherent in universal nature," Mr. Ruskin concludes to be "the suggestion by the imagination of noble grounds for noble emotions." The conditions on which this result depends are, first, *the choice of noble subjects,* i.e., subjects which involve wide interests and profound passions, as opposed to those which involve narrow interests and slight passions. And the choice which characterizes the school of high art, is seen as much in the treatment of the subject as the selection. "For the artist who sincerely chooses the noblest subject, will also choose chiefly to represent what makes that subject noble, namely, the various heroism or other noble emotions of the persons represented." But here two dangers present themselves: that of superseding expression by technical excellence, as when Paul Veronese makes the Supper at Emmaus a background to the portraits of two children playing with a dog; and that of superseding technical excellence by expression. (pp. 625-27)

The second condition of greatness of style is *love of beauty*—the tendency to introduce into the conception of the subject as much beauty as is possible, consistently with truth. (p. 628)

The third characteristic of great art is *sincerity.* The artist should include the largest possible quantity of truth in the most perfect possible harmony. *All* the truths of nature cannot be given; hence a choice must be made of some facts which can be represented from amongst others which must be passed by in silence. "The inferior artist chooses unimportant and scattered truths; the great artist chooses the most necessary first, and afterwards the most consistent with these, so as to obtain the greatest possible and most harmonious scene." Thus, Rembrandt sacrifices all other effects to the representation of the exact force with which the light on the most illumined part of an object is opposed to its obscurer portions. Paul Veronese, on the contrary, endeavours to embrace all the great relations

of visible objects; and this difference between him and Rembrandt as to light and shade is typical of the difference between great and inferior artists throughout the entire field of art. He is the greatest who conveys the largest sum of truth. (pp. 628-29)

The last characteristic of great art is *invention.* It must not only present grounds for noble emotion, but must furnish these grounds by imaginative power, *i.e.,* by an inventive combination of distinctly known objects. Thus imaginative art includes the historical faculties, which simply represent observed facts, but renders these faculties subservient to a poetic purpose. . . .

We have next a discussion of the False Ideal, and first of all, in Religious Art. The want of realization in the early religious painters prevented their pictures from being more than suggestions to the feelings. They attempted to express, not the actual fact, but their own enthusiasm about the fact; they covered the Virgin's dress with gold, not with any idea of representing her as she ever was or will be seen, but with a burning desire to show their love for her. As art advanced in technical power and became more realistic, there arose a more pernicious falsity in the treatment of religious subjects; more pernicious, because it was more likely to be accepted as a representation of fact. (p. 629)

Mr. Ruskin glances rapidly at the False Ideal in profane art—the pursuit of mere physical beauty as a gratification to the idle senses; and then enters into an extended consideration of the True Ideal, distinguished by him into three branches. 1. Purist Idealism, which results from the unwillingness of pure and tender minds to contemplate evil, of which Angelico is the great example, among the early painters; and among the moderns, Stothard exhibits the same tendency in the treatment of worldly subjects. 2. Naturalist Idealism, which accepts the weaknesses, faults, and wrongnesses in all things that it sees, but so places them that they form a noble whole, in which the imperfection of each several part is not only harmless, but absolutely essential, and yet in which whatever is good in each several part shall be completely displayed. 3. The Grotesque Ideal, which is either playful, terrible, or symbolical. The essence of an admirable chapter on "Finish" is, that all real finish is not mere polish, but *added truth.* Great artists finish not to show their skill, nor to produce a smooth piece of work, but to *render clearer the expression of knowledge.*

We resist the temptation to quote any of the very fine things Mr. Ruskin says about the "Use of Pictures," and pass on to the succeeding chapter, in which he enters on his special subject, namely, landscape painting. With that intense interest in landscape which is a peculiar characteristic of modern times, is associated the "Pathetic Fallacy"—the transference to external objects of the spectator's own emotions, as when Kingsley says of the drowned maiden,—

> "They rowed her in across the rolling foam—
> The *cruel, crawling foam.*"

The pleasure we derive from this fallacy is legitimate when the passion in which it originates is strong, and has an adequate cause. But the mental condition which admits of this fallacy is of a lower order than that in which, while the emotions are strong, the intellect is yet strong enough to assert its rule against them; and "the whole man stands in an iron glow, white hot, perhaps, but still strong, and in nowise evaporating; even if he melts, losing none of his weight." Thus the poets who delight in this fallacy are chiefly of the second order—the reflective and perceptive—such as Wordsworth, Keats, and

Tennyson; while the creative poets, for example, Shakspeare, Homer, and Dante, use it sparingly.

Next follows one of the most delightful and suggestive chapters in the volume, on "Classical Landscape," or the way in which the Greeks looked at external nature. (pp. 630-31)

The mediaeval feeling for landscape is less utilitarian than the Greek. Everything is pleasurable and horticultural—the knights and ladies sing and make love in pleasaunces and rose-gardens. There is a more sentimental enjoyment in external nature; but, added to this, there is a new respect for mountains, as places where a solemn presence is to be felt, and spiritual good obtained. As Homer is the grand authority for Greek landscape, so is Dante for the mediaeval; and Mr. Ruskin gives an elaborate study of the landscape in the "Divina Commedia." To the love of brilliancy shown in mediaeval landscape, is contrasted the love of clouds in the modern, "so that if a general and characteristic name were needed for modern landscape art, none better could be found than "the service of clouds." But here again Mr. Ruskin seeks for the spirit of landscape first of all in literature; and he expects to surprise his readers by selecting Scott as the typical poet, and greatest literary man of his age. He, very justly, we think, places Creative literature such as Scott's, above Sentimental literature, even when this is of as high a character as in some passages of Byron or Tennyson.

> To invent a story, or admirably and thoroughly tell any part of a story, it is necessary to grasp the entire mind of every personage concerned in it, and know precisely how they would be affected by what happens; which to do requires a colossal intellect; but to describe a separate emotion delicately, it is only needed that one should feel it oneself; and thousands of people are capable of feeling this or that noble emotion for one who is able to enter into all the feelings of somebody sitting on the other side of the table.... I unhesitatingly receive as a greater manifestation of power the right invention of a few sentences spoken by Pleydell and Mannering across their supper-table, than the most tender and passionate melodies of the self-examining verse.

This appreciation of Scott's power puts us in such excellent humour, that we are not inclined to quarrel with Mr. Ruskin about another judgment of his, to which we cannot see our way, in spite of the arguments he adduces. According to him Scott was eminently *sad*, sadder than Byron. On the other hand, he shows that this sadness did not lead Scott into the pathetic fallacy: the bird, the brook, the flower, and the cornfield, kept their gladsomeness for him, notwithstanding his own melancholy. (pp. 632-33)

> [George Eliot], *in a review of "Modern Painters, Vol. 3,"* in The Westminster Review, *Vol. LXV, No. CXVIII, April 1, 1856, pp. 625-33.*

ANTHONY TROLLOPE (essay date 1865)

[*Trollope was a prolific and popular Victorian novelist whose works are praised for their perceptive, vital characterizations. His most important works include two series of novels, the first portraying London political life and the second middle-class life in an English cathedral town. In the following excerpt, he criti-*

cizes Sesame and Lilies *for its didacticism on subjects he considers outside the purview of Ruskin's authority.*]

[*Sesame and Lilies*] is the publication in a little volume of two lectures by Mr. Ruskin, the first treating "Of Kings' Treasuries," and the second of "Queens' Gardens." To those who are conversant with Mr. Ruskin's writings, it need hardly be told that no national exchequer holds the kings' treasures of which speech is here made, and that the queens' gardens in question lie round neither Buckingham Palace nor Windsor Castle. The kings' treasures are those treasuries of knowledge which are found stored in well-chosen libraries for the edification of men; and the first lecture, applying to them, is called "**Sesame**," because Mr. Ruskin would wish to see the doors of such libraries thrown open somewhat wider than they at present stand. His second lecture, of queens' gardens, is called "**Lilies**," and in that it is his purpose to instruct women generally as to their early preparation for life, and subsequent duties while living.

Mr. Ruskin is well known to us as an art critic, and as one who has written to us on Art in language so beautiful, and with words so powerful, that he has carried men and women away with him in crowds, even before he has convinced their judgments or made intelligible to them the laws which he has inculcated. He has been as the fiddler in the tale, who, when he fiddled, made all men and women dance, even though they were men and women by nature very little given to such exercise. But the fiddler was thus powerful because he understood the art of fiddling. Had he dropped his bow, and got into a pulpit that he might preach, we may doubt whether by his preaching he would have held the crowds whom his music had collected. To a fiddler so foolishly ambitious, *Ne sutor ultra crepidam* [i.e., let the shoemaker stick to his own trade] would have been the advice given by all his friends. It seems that the same advice is needed in this case. Mr. Ruskin had become a musician very potent,—powerful to charm as well as to teach. We danced, and were delighted that we could dance to such music. But now he has become ashamed of his violin, and tells us that his old skill was a thing of nought. He will leave talking to us of the beauties of art and nature, of the stones of Venice, and the wild flowers of Switzerland, and will preach to us out of a high pulpit on political economy and the degradation of men and the duties of women! He goes out of his way in his lecture on "Kings' Treasuries" to read a passage from a work of his own, in which he tells the world how unjust wars are maintained and how just wars should be maintained. That, he says, is the only book worthy of the name of a book which he has written. But the world of English readers, whose approbation of Mr. Ruskin as an art-critic has alone made it possible for him to obtain a hearing as a political economist, will not agree with him. They will still recognise him as a great musician, but they will not accord to him the praise of a great preacher.

Mr. Ruskin, in these preachings of his, has become essentially Carlylesque. He tells us that that which we have taken for our own "judgment" is "mere sham prejudice, and drifted, helpless, entangled weed of castaway thought;" that "most men's minds are indeed little better than rough heath wilderness, neglected and stubborn, partly barren, partly overgrown with pestilent brakes and venomous wind-sown herbage of evil surmise;" and then, further on, in the same lecture, that "what we call our British Constitution has fallen dropsical of late." And in the second lecture, that "this is to me quite the most amazing among the phenomena of humanity." Now it is, I think, felt by most English readers that teaching such as this comes well from Mr. Carlyle, although it sometimes comes in language overstrained and with deeper denunciation of existing Englishmen than existing Englishmen altogether deserve. Mr. Carlyle has for many years been denouncing sham workmen and sham heroes, and using all the powers of his eloquence to produce true work, and, if such may be forthcoming, true heroism also. He has been recognised by us as a preacher, and almost as a prophet, and if in the enthusiasm of his wrath he has allowed himself to be carried away by the ever-increasing strength of his own convictions, we are ready to pardon the abuse he showers upon us, on account of the good that we know that he has done to us. We have sat at his feet and have been instructed. We have listened to his words, and, as we have heard them, have made some inward resolution that they should guide us. But I doubt whether many men will receive Carlylesque denunciations from Mr. Ruskin with any good to their souls. He produces them, indeed, with the grace of poetic expression and the strength of well-arranged, vigorous words; but they do not contain that innate, conspicuous wisdom which alone can make such preachings efficacious.

He first advises men to read, and tells them that they should read attentively. This in itself is very well, and an excellent treatise on reading might probably be given by a man so well instructed as Mr. Ruskin. But when he attempts to define the way in which the general reader should read, he mounts so high into the clouds, that what he says,—if it were not altogether so cloudy as to be meaningless and inoperative,—would quench all reading rather than encourage it. Young or old, boys or girls, we should have our Greek alphabets, and get good dictionaries in Saxon, German, French, Latin, and Greek, in order that we may trace out the real meaning of the words which we read! After this, he is carried away by his wrath against the nation, and tells us that, after all, we are not good enough to read. "My friend, I do not know why any of us should talk about reading. We want some sharper discipline!" "We have despised literature," Mr. Ruskin says, and this he proves by asserting that men will give more for a large turbot than for a book:—but cheap literature he does not like; and he tells us that we are "filthy," because we all thumb the same books from circulating libraries! He says that we have despised Science, and this he proves by showing that the Government has haggled at buying a collection of fossils for £700, as though the science of a nation depended on the propensities or means of the existing Chancellor of the Exchequer! He says that we have despised Art, and proves it by asserting that if all the Titians in Europe were to be made into sandbags to-morrow at the Austrian forts, it would not trouble us as much as the chance of a brace or two of game the less in our game bags! This assertion, which is simply an assertion, I may leave to the judgment of those who know aught of the market value of a Titian in England at the present day. He says that we have despised Nature, and proves it by showing that we,—(not we English, but we mankind, I presume,)—have put a railroad bridge over the fall of Schaffhausen, and by asserting that there is not a quiet valley in England which we have not filled with bellowing fire! He tells us also of the consuming white leprosy of new hotels! That such a man should write on Art may be well, but that he should preach to us either on morals or political economy is hardly to be borne. We have despised compassion, he tells us, and this he proves by a story from the *Daily Telegraph* of lamentable destitution in London, corrected by another story from the *Morning Post*, of equally lamentable Parisian luxury;—as though want and debauchery were evils of which large cities could rid themselves by efforts of compas-

sion! If men were not sinful, if we were gods on the earth, then, indeed—! But we hardly want a lecture from Mr. Ruskin to tell us this.

Throughout his second lecture, which is of "Queens' Gardens," the spirit and the tone are much the same. The words are often arranged with surpassing beauty, with such a charm of exquisite verbal music that the reader,—as was no doubt the hearer also,—is often tempted to forget that they have no definite tendency, and that nothing is to be learned from them by any woman living or about to live. Again, he rebukes his hearers for the coal-furnaces of their country. He is speaking of England, and says,—"The whole country is but a little garden, not more than enough for your children to run on the lawns of, if you would let them *all* run there. And this little garden you will turn into furnace-grounds, and fill with heaps of cinders, if you can!" Then, with less of absurdity, but hardly with more of reason, he speaks of the natural beauties of Snowdon and Holyhead, telling us that such hills, such bays, and blue inlets would have been always loved among the Greeks. "That Snowdon is your Parnassus; but where are its Muses? That Holyhead Mountain is your island of Aegina; but where is its temple to Minerva?" And this he says because a statement as to a Welsh school gives a very deplorable account of its scholars! Then he goes on:—"Oh ye women of England! from the Princess of that Wales to the simplest of you, do not think your own children can be brought into their true fold of rest while these are scattered on the hills as sheep having no shepherd. And do not think your daughters can be trained to the truth of their own human beauty, while the pleasant places which God made at once for their school-room and their playground, lie desolate and defiled. You cannot baptize them rightly in those inch-deep fonts of yours, unless you baptize them also in the sweet waters which the Great Lawgiver strikes forth for ever from the rocks of your native land,—waters which a Pagan would have worshipped in their purity, and you worship only with pollution." Now the meaning of this, if you bolt the bran from the discourse, is simply nothing;—there will be found no flour left good for making bread for any woman. It is to be lamented that Welsh children should be uneducated, and we all hope that our revised system of national instruction will effectually cure such gross ignorance as Mr. Ruskin describes. But English women are not polluted by this ignorance. The causes and excuses for this ignorance are far to seek and difficult to handle, and cannot be now discussed here; but the manner and style and language, by means of which Mr. Ruskin mingles the subject with Snowdon and Parnassus, with Holyhead and Aegina, and with the general duties of women in England, are simply rodomontade.

The line in literature which seems to belong to Mr. Ruskin, partly from the nature of the man, and partly from the special training which he has undergone, is very high, and has become perhaps higher in his hands than it ever was in the hands of any of his predecessors. He has given to us wonderful words on Art, which have had all the exactness of prose and almost all the grace of poetry. He has numbered his readers by tens of thousands, all of whom have seen with clearer eyes, and judged of Art with a truer judgment, because of his teaching. Had it not been so, this change of his, this desire to preach sermons instead of making music with his bow, would be matter of small moment to us. As it is, it is much to be hoped that he will return to that work which he can do better than any of his compeers. (pp. 633-35)

Anthony Trollope, in a review of "Sesame and Lilies," in The Fortnightly Review, *Vol. I, No. 5, July 15, 1865, pp. 633-35.*

T[HOMAS] CARLYLE (letter date 1872)

[A central figure of the Victorian era in England and Scotland, Carlyle was a Scots essayist, historian, critic, and social commentator. In his writings he advocated a Christian work ethic and stressed the importance of order, piety, and spiritual fulfillment. Known to his contemporaries as the "Sage of Chelsea," Carlyle exerted a powerful moral influence on an era of rapidly changing values. His writing strongly influenced Ruskin, who eventually became his close personal friend. In the following excerpt from a letter to Ralph Waldo Emerson, Carlyle recommends Ruskin's works and praises his iconoclasm.]

Do you read Ruskin's **Fors Clavigera,** which he cheerily tells me gets itself reprinted in America? If you don't, *do,* I advise you. Also his **Munera Pulveris,** Oxford-**Lectures on Art,** and whatever else he is now writing,—if you can manage to get them (which is difficult here, owing to the ways he has towards the bibliopolic world!). There is nothing going on among us as notable to me as those fierce lightning-bolts Ruskin is copiously and desperately pouring into the black world of Anarchy all around him. No other man in England that I meet has in him the divine rage against iniquity, falsity, and baseness that Ruskin has, and that every man ought to have. Unhappily he is not a strong man; one might say a weak man rather; and has not the least prudence of management; though if he can hold out for another fifteen years or so, he may produce, even in this way, a great effect. God grant it, say I. (pp. 352-53)

> T[homas] Carlyle, in an extract from a letter to Ralph Waldo Emerson on April 2, 1872, in The Correspondence of Thomas Carlyle and Ralph Waldo Emerson, 1834-1872, Vol. II, edited by C. E. Norton, James R. Osgood and Company, 1883, pp. 350-53.

GEORGE SAINTSBURY (essay date 1876)

[Saintsbury has been called the most influential English literary historian and critic of the late nineteenth and early twentieth centuries. His studies of French literature, particularly A History of the French Novel (1917-19), have established him as a leading authority on such writers as Guy de Maupassant and Honoré de Balzac. Saintsbury adhered to two distinct sets of critical standards: one for the novel and the other for poetry and drama. As a critic of novels, he maintained that "the novel has nothing to do with any beliefs, with any convictions, with any thoughts in the strict sense, except as mere garnishings. Its substance must always be life not thought, conduct not belief, the passions not the intellect, manners and morals not creeds and theories. . . . The novel is . . . mainly and firstly a criticism of life." As a critic of poetry and drama, Saintsbury was a radical formalist who frequently asserted that subject is of little importance, and that "the so-called 'formal' part is of the essence." René Wellek has praised Saintsbury's critical qualities: his "enormous reading, the almost universal scope of his subject matter, the zest and zeal of his exposition," and "the audacity with which he handles the most ambitious and unattempted arguments." In the following excerpt, Saintsbury criticizes the inconsistency of Ruskin's prose style.]

[Audacious] or paradoxical as the assertion may seem, it is at least doubtful whether in strictness we can assign to Mr. Ruskin a position in the very highest rank of writers if we are to adopt style as a criterion. The objection to his manner of writing is an obvious one, and one which he might very likely take as a compliment: it is too spontaneous in the first place, and too entirely subordinate to the subject in the second. I hope that it may be very clearly understood that I can see passages in **Modern Painters** and in the **Stones of Venice** (for I must be permitted to neglect the legions of little books with parody-provoking titles which have appeared in the last three lustres) which, for splendour of imaginative effect, for appropriateness of diction, for novelty and grandeur of conception, stand beyond all chance of successful rivalry, almost beyond all hope of decent parallel among the writings of ancient and modern masters. But in every case this marvellous effect will, when carefully examined, be found to depend on something wholly or partially extrinsic to the style. Mr. Ruskin writes beautifully because he thinks beautifully, because his thoughts spring, like Pallas, ready armed, and the fashion of the armour costs him nothing. Everybody has heard of the unlucky critic whose comment on Scott's fertility was that "the invention was not to be counted for that came to him of its own accord." So it is with Mr. Ruskin. His beauties of style "come to him of their own accord," and then he writes as the very gods might dream of writing. But in the moments when he is off the tripod, or is upon some casual and un-Delphic tripod of his own construction or selection, how is his style altered! The strange touches of unforeseen colour become splashed and gaudy, the sonorous roll of the prophetic sentence-paragraphs drags and wriggles like a wounded snake, the cunning interweaving of scriptural or poetic phrase is patched and seamy. A Balaam on the Lord's side, he cannot curse or bless but as it is revealed to him, whereas the possessor of a great style can use it at will. He can shine on the just and on the unjust; can clothe his argument for tyranny or for liberty, for virtue or for vice, with the same splendour of diction, and the same unperturbed perfection of manner; can convince us, carry us with him, or leave us unconvinced but admiring, with the same unquestioned supremacy and the same unruffled calm. Swift can write a *jeu d'esprit* and a libel on the human race, a political pamphlet and a personal lampoon, with the same felicity and the same vigour. Berkeley can present tar-water and the Trinity, the theory of vision and the follies of contemporary free-thinking, with the same perfect lucidity and the same colourless fairness. But with Mr. Ruskin all depends on the subject, and the manner in which the subject is to be treated. He cannot even blame as he can praise; and there must be many who are ready to accept everything he can say of Tintoret or of Turner, and who feel no call to object to any of his strictures on Canaletto or on Claude, who yet perceive painfully the difference of style in the panegyrist and the detractor, and who would demand the stricter if less obvious justice, and the more artistic if apparently perverted sensitiveness, of the thorough master of style. (pp. 252-53)

> George Saintsbury, "Modern English Prose," in The Fortnightly Review, Vol. XXV, No. 110, February 1, 1876, pp. 243-59.

VERNON LEE (essay date 1881)

[An English novelist, travel writer, and critic who spent most of her life in Italy, Lee wrote widely on art and aesthetics, earning particular praise for her Studies of the Eighteenth Century in Italy (1880). Her philosophy of art held that music and the visual arts should be appreciated for their form alone and not be made to serve any intellectual or didactic function, a role she reserved for literature. In the following excerpt, Lee acknowledges Ruskin as a great thinker but refutes the premise underlying his art criticism that artistic excellence is a reflection of morality.]

John Ruskin stands quite isolated among writers on art. His truths and his errors are alike of a far higher sort than the truths and errors of his fellow-workers: they are truths and errors not

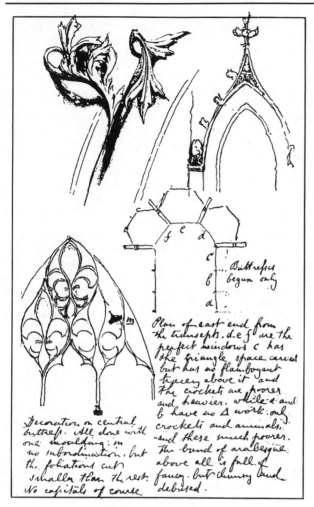

A page from one of the notebooks Ruskin kept while writing The Stones of Venice.

of mere fact, nor of mere reasoning, but of tendency, of moral attitude; and his philosophy is of far greater importance than any other system of aesthetics, because it is not the philosophy of the genius, evolution or meaning of any art or of all art, but the philosophy of the legitimacy or illegitimacy of all and every art.... [The] theories of all other writers on art deal only with the meaning and value of one work or school of art compared with another work or school; they deal only with the question how much of our liking or disliking should we give to this art or to that; they are all true or false within the region allotted to art. But the theories of Ruskin deal with the comparative importance of artistic concerns and the other concerns of our lives: they deal with the problem, how much of our thoughts and our energies we have a right to give to art, and for what reasons we may give any portion of them: it deals with the question of the legitimacy not of one kind of artistic enjoyment more than another, but of the enjoyment of art at all. (pp. 197-99)

John Ruskin has been endowed as have been very few men as an artist, a critic, and a moralist; in the immense chaotic mass, the constantly altered and constantly propped up ruins of an impossible system, which constitute the bulk of his writings, he has taught us more of the subtle reasons of art, he has reproduced with his pen more of the beauty of physical nature, and he has made us feel more profoundly the beauty of moral nature, than has, perhaps, been done separately by any critic, or artist, or moralist of his day. He has possessed within himself two very perfect characters, has been fitted out for two very noble missions:—the creation of beauty and the destruction of evil; and of these two halves each has been warped; of these two missions each has been hampered; warped and hampered by the very nobility of the man's nature: by his obstinate refusal to compromise with the reality of things, by his perpetual resistance to the evidence of his reason, by his heroic and lamentable clinging to his own belief in harmony where there is discord, in perfection where there is imperfection. There are natures which cannot be coldly or resignedly reasonable, which, despite all possible demonstration, cannot accept evil as a necessity and injustice as a fact; which must believe their own heart rather than their own reason; and when we meet such natures, we in our cold wisdom must look upon them with pity, perhaps, and regret, but with admiration and awe and envy. Such a nature is that of John Ruskin. He belongs, it is true, to a generation which is rapidly passing away; he is the almost isolated champion of creeds and ideas which have ceased even to be discussed among the thinking part of our nation; he is a believer not only in Good and in God, but in Christianity, in the Bible, in Protestantism; he is, in many respects, a man left far behind by the current of modern thought; but he is, nevertheless, and unconsciously, perhaps, to himself, the greatest representative of the highly developed and conflicting ethical and aesthetical nature which is becoming more common in proportion as men are taking to think and feel for themselves; his is the greatest example of the strange battles and compromises which are daily taking place between our moral and our artistic halves; and the history of his aspirations and his errors is the type of the inner history of many a humbler thinker and humbler artist around us.

When, nearly forty years ago, Ruskin first came before the world with the wonderful book—wonderful in sustained argument and description, and in obscure, half crazy, half prophetic utterances—called **Modern Painters,** it was felt that a totally new power had entered the region of artistic analysis.... He came into it as an apostle and a reformer, but as an apostle and a reformer strangely different from Winckelmann and Schlegel, from Lessing and Goethe. For, while attacking the architecture of Palladio and the painting of Salvator Rosa; while expounding the landscapes of Turner and the churches of Verona, he was not merely demolishing false classicism and false realism, not merely vindicating a neglected artist or a wronged school: he was come to sweep usurping evil out of the kingdom of art, and to reinstate as its sole sovereign no human craftsman, but God himself.

God or Good: for to Ruskin the two words have but one meaning. God and Good must receive the whole domain of art; it must become the holy of holies, the temple and citadel of righteousness. To do this was the avowed mission of this strange successor, haughty and humble, and tender and wrathful, of the pagan Winckelmann, of the coldly serene Goethe. How came John Ruskin by this mission, or why should his mission differ so completely from that of all his fellows? Why should he insist upon the necessity of morally sanctifying art, instead of merely aesthetically reforming it? Why was it not enough for him that artistic pleasure should be innocent, without trying to make it holy? Because, for Ruskin's nature, compounded of artist and moralist, artistic engagement was a moral danger, a distraction from his duty—for Ruskin was not the mere artist, who, powerless outside his art, may, because he can only, give his whole energies to it; he was not the mere moralist who, indifferent to art, can give it a passing glance without interrupting for a moment his work of good; he felt himself endowed to struggle for righteousness and bound to do so, and he felt himself also irresistibly attracted by mere beauty. To the moral nature of the man this mere beauty, which threatened to absorb his existence, became positively sinful; while he knew that evil was raging without requiring all his energies to quell it, every minute, every thought diverted from the cause of good was so much gain for the cause of evil; innocence, mere negative good, there could not be, as long as there remained positive evil. Thus it appeared to Ruskin. This strange knight-errant of righteousness, conscious of his heaven endowed strength, felt that during every half-hour of delay in the Armida's garden of art, new rootlets were being put forth, new leaves were being unfolded by the enchanted forest of error which overshadowed and poisoned the earth, and which it was his work to hew and burn down; that every moment of reluctant farewell from the weird witch of beauty meant a fresh outrage, an additional defiling of the holy of holies to rescue which he had received his strong muscle and his sharp weapons. Thus, refusing to divide his time and thoughts between his moral work and his artistic, Ruskin must absolutely and completely abandon the latter; if art seemed to him not merely a waste of power, but an absolute danger for his nobler side, there evidently was no alternative but to abjure it for ever. But a man cannot thus abandon his own field, abjure the work for which he is specially fitted; he may mortify, and mutilate and imprison his body, but he cannot mortify or mutilate his mind, he cannot imprison his thoughts. John Ruskin was drawn irresistibly towards art because he was specially organised for it. The impossible cannot be done: nature must find a vent, and the artistic half of Ruskin's mind found its way of eluding the apparently insoluble difficulty: his desire reasoned, and his desire was persuaded. A revelation came to him: he was neither to compromise with sin nor to renounce his own nature. For it struck him suddenly that this irresistible craving for the beautiful, which he would have silenced as a temptation of evil, was in reality the call to his mission; that this domain of art, which he had felt bound to abandon, was in reality the destined field for his moral combats, the realm which he must reconquer for God and for Good. Ruskin had considered art as sinful as long as it was only negatively innocent: by the strange logic of desire he made it positively righteous, actively holy; what he had been afraid to touch, he suddenly perceived that he was commanded to handle. He had sought for a solution of his own doubts, and the solution was the very gospel which he was to preach to others; the truth which had saved him was the truth which he must proclaim. And that truth, which had ended Ruskin's own scruples, was that the basis of art is moral; that art cannot be merely pleasant or unpleasant, but must be lawful or unlawful, that every legitimate artistic enjoyment is due to the perception of moral propriety, that every artistic excellence is a moral virtue, every artistic fault is a moral vice; that noble art can spring only from noble feeling, that the whole system of the beautiful is a system of moral emotions, moral selections, and moral appreciation; and that the aim and end of art is the expression of man's obedience to God's will, and of his recognition of God's goodness.

Such was the solution of Ruskin's scruples respecting his right of giving to art the time and energies he might have given to moral improvement; and such the aesthetical creed which he felt bound, by conviction and by the necessity of self-justification, to develop into a system and to apply to every single case. The notion of making beauty not merely a vague emanation from the divinity, as in the old platonic philosophies,

but a direct result, an infallible concomitant of moral excellence; of making the physical the mere reflexion of the moral, is indeed a very beautiful and noble idea; but it is a false idea. For—and this is one of the points which Ruskin will not admit—the true state of things is by no means always the noblest or the most beautiful; our longing for ineffable harmony is no proof that such harmony exists: the phantom of perfection which hovers before us is often not the mirage of some distant reality, but a mere vain shadow projected by our own desires, which we must follow, but may never obtain. . . . It is . . . one of the wicked anomalies of this world that the true, the existing, is at variance with that which we should wish to exist: we cannot replace with impunity the ugly, the cruel, the mean truth by the charming, the generous fancy; if we do so, we must be prepared to break with all truth, or to compromise with all falsehood: we shall create an evil a hundredfold worse than the one we wished to avoid. We are afraid of a truth which jars upon our sense of the morally desirable: we invent and accept a lie, plausible and noble; and behold! in a moment we are surrounded by a logical work of falsehood, which must be for ever torn and for ever patched up if any portion of truth is to enter.

Such has been the case with John Ruskin; he shrank from owning to himself what we have just recognized, with reluctance, indeed, and sorrow, that the beautiful to whose study and creation he was so irresistibly drawn, had no moral value; that in the great battle between good and evil, beauty remained neutral, passive, serenely egotistic. It was necessary for him that beauty should be more than passively innocent: he must make it actively holy. Only a moral meaning could make art noble; and as, in the deep-rooted convictions of Ruskin, art was noble, a moral meaning must be found. The whole of the philosophy of art must be remodelled upon an ethical basis; a moral value must everywhere sanction the artistic attraction. And thus Ruskin came to construct a strange system of falsehood, in which moral motives applied to purely physical actions, moral meanings given to the merely aesthetically significant, moral consequences drawn from absolutely unethical decisions; even the merest coincidences in historical and artistic phenomena, nay, even in the mere growth of various sorts of plants, nay, even the most ludicrously applied biblical texts, were all dragged forward and combined into a wondrous legal summing-up for the beatification of art; the sense of the impossibility of rationally referring certain aesthetical phenomena to ethical causes producing in this lucid and noble thinker a sort of frenzy, a wild impulse to solve irrational questions by direct appeals for an oracular judgment of God, to be sought for in the most trumpery coincidences of accidents; so that the man who has understood most of the subtle reasons of artistic beauty, who has grasped most completely the psychological causes of great art and poor art, is often reduced to answer his perplexities by a sort of aesthetico-moral key and bible divination, or heads-win tails-lose, toss-up decision. The main pivots of Ruskin's system are, however, but few: first, the assertion that all legitimate artistic action is governed by moral considerations, is the direct putting in practise of the commandments of God; and secondly, that all pleasure in the beautiful is the act of appreciating the goodness and wisdom of God. These two main theories completely balance one another; between them, and with the occasional addition of mystic symbolism, they must explain the whole question of artistic right and wrong. Now for Ruskin artistic right and wrong is not only a very complex, but, in many respects, a very fluctuating question; in order to see how complex and how fluctuating, we must remember what Ruskin is, and what are his aims. Ruskin is no ordinary aesthetician, interested in art only inasmuch as it is a subject for thought, untroubled in the framing of histories, psychological systems of art philosophy by any personal likings and dislikings; Ruskin is essentially an artist, he thinks about art because he feels about art, and his sole object is morally to justify his artistic sympathies and aversions, morally to justify his caring about art at all. With him the instinctive likings and dislikings are the original motor, the system is there only for their sake. He cannot, therefore, like Lessing, or Hegel, or Taine, quietly shove aside any phenomenon of artistic preference which does not happen to fit into his system; he could, like Hegel, assign an inferior rank to painting, because painting has to fall into the category assigned to romantic, that is to say, imperfect art; he could not, like Taine, deliberately stigmatise music as a morbid art because it had arisen, according to his theory, in a morbid state of society; with Ruskin everything must finally yield to the testimony of his artistic sense: everything which he likes must be legitimated, everything which he dislikes must be condemned; and for this purpose the system of artistic morality must for ever be altered, annotated, provided with endless saving-clauses, and special cases. And all this the more especially as, in the course of his studies, Ruskin frequently perceives that things which on superficial acquaintance displeased him, are in reality delightful, in consequence of which discovery a new legislation is required to annul their previous condemnation and provide for their due honour. Thus, having conceived a perhaps exaggerated aversion (due, in great part, to the injustice of his adversaries) to the manner of representing the nature of certain Dutch painters of the 17th century, Ruskin immediately formulated a theory that minute imitation of nature was base and sinful; and when he conceived a perhaps equally exaggerated admiration for the works of certain extremely careful and even servile English painters of our own times, he was forced to formulate an explanatory theory that minuteness of work was conscientious, appreciative, and distinctly holy. Had he been satisfied with mere artistic value, he need only have said that the Dutch pictures were ugly, and the English pictures beautiful; but having once established all artistic judgment upon an ethical basis, it became urgent that he should invent a more or less casuistic reason, something not unlike the *distinguo* by means of which the Jesuit moralists rendered innocent in their powerful penitents what they had declared sinful in less privileged people, to explain that, under certain circumstances, minute imitation was the result of insolence and apathy, and in other cases the sign of humility and appreciation. . . . In this way Ruskin has constructed a whole system of artistic ethics, extremely contradictory and, as we have remarked, bearing as great a resemblance to the text book, full of *distinguos* and *directions of the intention* of one of Pascal's Jesuits as a very morally pure and noble work can bear to a very base and depraved one. And throughout this system scattered fragmentarily throughout his various books, every artistic merit or demerit is disposed of as a virtuous action or a crime; the moral principle established for the explanation of one case naturally involving the prejudgment of another case; and the whole system explaining by moral delinquencies the artistic inferiority of a given time or people, and, on the other hand, attributing the moral and social ruin of a century or a nation to the artistic abominations it had perpetrated. The arrangements of lintels and columns, the amount of incrustation of coloured marble on to brick, the degree to which window traceries may be legitimately attenuated and curled, the value of Greek honeysuckle patterns as compared with Gothic hedge-rose ornaments, all these and a thousand other questions of mere excellence of artistic effect, are dis-

cussed on the score of their morality or baseness, of their truthfulness, or justice, or humility; and Ruskin's madness against any kind of cheating or deception goes to the length, in one memorable passage in the *Seven Lamps of Architecture,* of condemning Correggio's ceiling of St. Paolo at Parma because, as real children might be climbing in a real vine trellise above our heads, there is possibility of deception and of sin; whereas, as none of us expect to see the heavens open above us, there is no possibility of deception, and consequently no sin in Correggio's glory of angels in the Parma Cathedral; thus absolving on the score of morality a rather confused and sprawling composition, and condemning as immoral one of the most graceful and childlike works of the Renaissance. The result of this system of explaining all artistic phenomena by ethical causes is, as we have remarked, that the real cause of any phenomenon, the explanation afforded us by history, is entirely overlooked or even ignominiously rejected. Thus Ruskin attributes the decay of Gothic architecture to "one endeavour to assume, in excessive flimsiness of tracery, the semblance of what it was not"—to its having "sacrificed a single truth." Now the violation of the nature and possibilities of the material, what Ruskin in ethical language calls the endeavour to trick, was not the cause but the effect of a gradual decline in the art. . . . Art, if it lives, must grow, and if it grows it must grow old and die. And this fact gradually, though instinctively, beginning to be felt by all thinkers on art, Ruskin, with his theory of moral aesthetics, could never recognize. For him the corruption of the art is due to the moral corruption of the artist: if the artist remained truthfully modest, the perfection of the art would continue indefinitely.

Again, the necessity of referring all good art to morality and all bad art to immorality, obliges Ruskin to postulate that every period which has produced bad art has been a period of moral decay. The artistic habits which displease him must be a direct result of a vicious way of feeling and acting in all things: the decay of Venetian architecture and sculpture must be distinctly referable to the decay of Venetian morality in the 15th century; and the final corruption and ruin of the state must be traced to the moral obliquity which caused Venetians to adopt pseudo-classic forms in the Riva façade of the Ducal palace; moral degradation and artistic degradation, acting and re-acting on each other, bring about, according to Ruskin, political ruin; the iniquities of the men who became apostates to Gothic architecture are visited upon their distant descendants, upon the Venetians of the days of Campo Formio. Now here again the ethical basis induces a complete historical misconception, a misconception not only in the history of art, but also in the history of civilization. For, just as his system of moral sin and artistic punishment blinds Ruskin to the necessities of change and decay in art, so, also, it prevents his seeing the inevitable necessity of political growth and decline. . . . That immorality is not the cause but the effect of political decline is as little conceived by Ruskin as that neither the one nor the other can be produced by artistic degradation; in his system which makes artistic inferiority the visible expression of moral corruption, and national misfortune its direct punishment, there can be no room for any of the great laws of development and decay which historical science is now beginning to perceive. All things must be carried on upon the miraculous system of Sunday school books, where planks of bridges give way from the cogent mechanical reason that the little boys passing over them have just been telling lies or stealing apples; God is for ever busy unbolting trapdoors beneath the feet of the iniquitous and rolling stones down on the heads of blasphemers. And this same necessity of condemning morally a period whose artistic work in any particular line is aesthetically worthless in Ruskin's judgment, not only leads him into the most absurd misappreciation of the moral value of a time, but entirely forbids his recognizing the fact that the decay of one art is frequently coincident with, and in some measure due to, the efflorescence of another. The independent development of painting required the decay of the architecture of the middle ages, whose symbolical, purely decorative tendency condemned painting to be a sort of allegorical or narrative Arabesque; whose well defined arches might not be broken through by daring perspective, whose delicate cornices might not enclose more than a mere rigid and simply tinted mosaic, or mosaic-like fresco. When, therefore, painting arose mature in the 16th century, architecture was necessarily crumbling. But to Ruskin the 16th century, being the century of bad architecture, is hopelessly immoral, and being immoral, its painting, Raphael, Michel Angelo, Correggio, all except a few privileged Venetians, must needs be swept away as so much rubbish; while the very imperfect painting of the Giottesques, because it belongs to a time whose morality must be high since its architecture is good, is considered as the ideal of pictorial art. Again, Ruskin perceives that the whole plastic art of the 18th century, architecture, sculpture, and painting, are as bad as bad can be; the cause must necessarily be found not in the inevitable decline of all plastic art since the Renaissance, but in the fiendish wickedness of the 18th century, that abominable age which first taught men the meaning of justice as distinguished from mercy, of humanity as distinguished from charity: which first taught us not to shrink from evil but to combat it. And thus, because the 18th century is proved by its smirking furbelowed goddesses and handkerchief-cravatted urns to be utterly, morally, abominable, the one great art which flourished in this period, the glorious music of Bach, and Gluck, and Marcello, and Mozart, must necessarily be silently carted off to the dust heap of artistic baseness.

Thus the radical falsehood of the ethical system of aesthetics warps the whole of Ruskin's view of the genius and evolution of art, of its relations with national morality and political supremacy. But it does more than this. It warps also Ruskin's view of art itself; its sophisms force him to contradict, to stifle his own artistic instincts. For if, as Ruskin has established, we are not permitted to love the beautiful for its own sake, but only because it is supposed to represent a certain moral excellence, that moral excellence must be the sole valuable portion, and equally artistically valuable when separated from the beautiful; while the beautiful must in itself be worthless, and consequently dangerous. The absolutely ugly must, if it awaken virtuous emotion, have a greater artistic value than the beautiful if it awaken none; the macerated hermits, the lepers and cripples of the middle ages must be artistically preferable to the healthy and beautiful athletes of antiquity; compassion for the physically horrible is more virtuous than the desire for the physically beautiful, therefore Ruskin would replace the one by the other; forgetting, even as the middle ages forgot, that the beautiful, the healthy, are the best and happiest for all of us; that we are given sympathy with the physically evil only that we may endure its contact long enough to transform it into the physically good: that we compassionate disease only that we may cure it. (pp. 200-22)

Ruskin, one of the greatest thinkers on art and on ethics, made morality sterile and art base in his desire to sanctify the one by the other. Sterile and base, indeed, only theoretically: for the instinct of the artist and of the moralist has ever broken out in noble self-contradiction, in beautiful irrelevancies; in

those wonderful, almost prophetic passages which seem to make our souls more keen towards beauty and more hardy for good. But all this is incidental, this which is in reality Ruskin's great and useful work. He has made art more beautiful and men better without knowing it—accidentally, without premeditation, in words which are like the eternal truths, grand and exquisite, which lie fragmentary and embedded in every system of theology; the complete and systematic is worthless and even dangerous, for it is false; the irrelevant, the contradictory, is precious, because it is true to our better part. Ruskin has loved art instinctively, fervently, for its own sake; but he has constantly feared lest this love should be sinful or at least base. Like Augustine, he dreads that the Devil may be lurking in the beautiful sunshine; lest evil be hidden in those beautiful shapes which distract his thoughts from higher subjects of good and God; he trembles lest the beautiful should trouble his senses and his fancy, and make him forget his promises to the Almighty. He perceives that pleasure in art is more or less sensuous and selfish; he is afraid lest some day he be called upon to account for the moments he has not given to others, and be chastised for having permitted his mind to follow the guidance of his senses; he trembles and repeats the praise of God, the anathema of pride, he mumbles confused words about "corrupt earth"—and "sinful man,"—even while looking at his works of art, as some anchorite of old may instinctively have passed his fingers across his beads and stammered out an *Ave* when some sight of beauty crossed his path and made his heart leap with unwonted pleasure. Ruskin must tranquillize his conscience about art; he must persuade himself that he is justified in employing his thoughts about it; and lest it be a snare of the demon, he must make it a service of God. He must persuade himself that all the pleasure he derives from art is the pleasure in obeying God, in perceiving his goodness: that the pleasure he derives from a flower is pleasure not in its curves and colours and scent, but in its adaptation to its work, in its enjoyment of existence; that the enjoyment he derives from a grand view is enjoyment of the kindness of God, and the enjoyment in the sight of a noble face is enjoyment of the expression of harmony with God's will; in short, all artistic pleasure must become an act of adoration, otherwise, a jealous God, or a jealous conscience, will smite him for abandoning the true altar for some golden calf fashioned by man and inhabited by Satan. And to this constant moralising, hallowing, nay, purifying of art, are due, as we have seen, the greater number of Ruskin's errors; his system is false, and only evil can spring from it; it is a pretence at a perfection which does not exist, and which, like the pretence at the superhuman virtue of the anchorite and mystic, must end in lamentable folly: in making men lie to their own heart because they have sought to clothe all that is really pure in a false garb of sanctity and have blushed at its naked reality; because it makes a return to nature a return to sin, since what is natural has been forbidden and what is innocent has been crookedly obtained; because it tries to make us think we are nothing but soul, and therefore turns us to brutes when we remember that we are also body, and devils when we perceive that we are also reason. Because, in short, it is a lie, and only falsehood can be born of it. For, in his constant reference to a spiritual meaning, Ruskin has not only wasted and sterilised our moral impulses, but has reduced art to mere foulness; in his constant sanctifying of beauty he makes it appear impure. Above all, in his unceasing attempt to attach a moral meaning to physical beauty, he has lost sight of, he has denied, the great truth that all that which is innocent is moral; that the morality of art is an independent quality equivalent to, but separate from, the morality of action; that beauty is the morality of the physical, as morality is the beauty of the spiritual; that as the moral sense hallows the otherwise egotistic relations of man to man, so also the aesthetic sense hallows the otherwise brutish relations of man to matter; that separately but in harmony, equally but differently, these two faculties make our lives pure and noble. All this Ruskin has forgotten: he has made the enjoyment of mere beauty a base pleasure, requiring a moral object to purify it, and in so doing he has destroyed its own purifying power; he has sanctified the already holy, and defiled with holy water, which implies foulness, the dwelling of holiness. (pp. 225-27)

> *Vernon Lee, "Ruskinism," in her* Belcaro: Being Essays on Sundry Aesthetical Questions, *W. Satchell & Co., 1881, pp. 197-229.*

RICHARD HOLT HUTTON   (essay date 1891)

[*Hutton was an English theologian, critic, and editor of several prominent nineteenth-century magazines. These included the influential Unitarian journal* National Review, *whose editorship he shared with Walter Bagehot from 1855 to 1862, and the* Spectator, *a liberal weekly news magazine where Hutton served as joint-proprietor and editor for the next thirty-five years. Under the editorship of Hutton and his partner Meredith Townsend, the* Spectator *continued its traditional advocacy of human freedom and support for such unpopular causes as workers' rights, colonial independence, and the emancipation of West Indian slaves. In contrast to its liberal political stance, the magazine espoused conservative views on art and literature, generally reflecting the opinions of its upper-middle-class Victorian readership. Hutton's own literary perspective was strongly influenced by his religious beliefs, and his critiques often emphasize the moral value of a work of art. At the same time, Hutton is praised by commentators as a sympathetic and fairminded critic whose aesthetic judgments remained distinct from his moral views. In the following excerpt, which originally appeared in the* Spectator *in 1891, he praises Ruskin's prose style but denounces his poetry.*]

Miss Thackeray gave one of her very charming books the very unpromising title of *Miss Williams' Divagations.* No better general reason why Mr. Ruskin failed as a poet can be assigned than by saying that the two heavy volumes of his poetry . . . might properly be entitled "Mr. Ruskin's Divagations." There is really no wholeness in any one of these pieces of verse, no sign, that I have seen, in any one of them of having proceeded out of a vivid imaginative conception which filled his mind and heart, and which he was eagerly struggling to embody in words. And yet Mr. Ruskin, as we all know, is a great artist in speech. Any number of passages could be extracted from his prose writings in which speech is used with the most consummate art, generally to call up some beautiful scene before the eye, sometimes to impress a true criticism on the mind, not unfrequently to satirise playfully or scornfully some weakness or worldliness of modern society. Open, for instance, his *Seven Lamps of Architecture,* and we find this passage in the chapter on "The Lamp of Memory"—analysing the effect of the memory of the past on the impressions produced by a scene in the Jura—a passage in which the splendour of the description almost rivals the magnificent vision which it seeks to realise for us:—"I came out presently on the edge of the ravine: the solemn murmur of its waters rose suddenly from beneath, mixed with the singing of the thrushes among the pine boughs; and, on the opposite side of the valley, walled all along as it was by grey cliffs of limestone, there was a hawk sailing slowly off their brow, touching them nearly with his wings, and with the shadows of the pines flickering upon his plumage from

Vercelli, *painted by Ruskin in 1846.*

above; but with the fall of a hundred fathoms under his breast, and the curling pools of the green river gliding and glittering dizzily beneath him, their foam globes moving with him as he flew. It would be difficult to conceive a scene less dependent upon any other interest than that of its own secluded and serious beauty; but the writer well remembers the sudden blankness and chill which were cast upon it when he endeavoured, in order more strictly to arrive at the sources of its impressiveness, to imagine it, for a moment, a scene in some aboriginal forest of the New Continent. The flowers in an instant lost their light, the river its music; the hills became oppressively desolate; a heaviness in the boughs of the darkened forest showed how much of their former power had been dependent upon a life which was not theirs, how much of the glory of the imperishable, or continually renewed, creation is reflected from things more precious in their memories than it, in its renewing. Those ever-springing flowers and ever-flowing streams had been dyed by the deep colours of human endurance, valour, and virtue; and the crests of the sable hills that rose against the evening sky received a deeper worship, because their far shadows fell eastward over the iron wall of Joux and the four-square keep of Granson." . . . Or, again, take this scornful description of the English worship of cruel energy and degraded toil contained in the criticism on Turner's picture of "The Garden of the Hesperides":—"The greatest man on our England in the first half of the nineteenth century, in the strength and hope of his faith, perceives this to be the thing he has to tell us of utmost moment, connected with the spiritual world. In each city and country of past time, the master-minds had to declare the chief worship which lay at the nation's heart; to define it; adorn it; show the range and authority of it. Thus in Athens we have 'The Temple of Pallas'; and in Venice 'The Assumption of the Virgin'; here in England is our great spiritual fact for ever interpreted to us,—'The Assumption of the Dragon.' No St. George any more to be heard of; no more dragon-slaying possible; this child, born on St. George's day, can only make manifest the dragon, not slay him, sea-serpent as he is, whom the English Andromeda, not fearing, takes for her lord.''

Now, in passages like these there is evidently the richest affluence of artistic speech, but it is not a kind of affluence that is at all disposed to keep within the strict laws of rhyme and rhythm, or to promote that distinct unity of effect which a poem requires. When one turns to Mr. Ruskin's poems they are almost all divagations. They meander, and they meander with much less significance and continuity of purpose than his prose disquisitions, which, with all their wide offings, and their varied points of departure, and their splendid digressions, do generally converge to a definite point at last, and serve to impress some lessons or to proclaim some gospel. In his poetry it is not so; there you see a good deal of Mr. Ruskin's gentle playfulness and of his mild caprice; much more than of his evangelical zeal. His fairies and gnomes are the most arbitrary of beings; his fancies have no real life in them; his stories have no real passion; his musings no heart; and even his descriptions no fire. For example, take this bit of vituperation against the sensuality and slothfulness of a mountain population in which Mr. Ruskin appears to be quite in earnest, and yet expresses himself in language much more marked by caprice than by force:—

> Have you in heaven no hope—on earth no care—
>   No foe in hell—ye things of stye and stall,
> That congregate like flies, and make the air
>   Rank with your fevered sloth—that hourly call
> The sun, which should your servant be, to bear
>   Dread witness on you, with uncounted wane
> And unregarded rays, from peak to peak
>   Of piny-gnomoned mountain moved in vain?
> Behold, the very shadows that ye seek
>   For slumber, write along the wasted wall
> Your condemnation. They forgot not, they,
>   Their ordered function, and determined fall,
> Nor useless perish. But *you* count your day
>   By sins, and write your difference from clay
> In bonds you break, and laws you disobey.
> God! who hast given the rocks their fortitude,
>   The sap unto the forests, and their food
> And vigour to the busy tenantry
> Of happy, soulless things that wait on Thee,
> Hast Thou no blessing where Thou gav'st Thy blood?
>   Wilt Thou not make Thy fair creation whole?
> Behold and visit this Thy vine for good—
>   Breathe in this human dust its living soul.

''Piny-gnomoned'' is an affected phrase which, I suppose, tries to convey the idea that the shadows of the pine-trees on the mountain-side tell the height of the sun, much in the same way in which the shadows of the gnomon on a sun-dial tell the hour of the day. But that just shows how the fetters of verse appear to constrain Mr. Ruskin into attempting to express what he utterly fails to express. In the comparative freedom of his poetic prose he would probably have given us a telling picture of the impressive effect of these natural sun-dials. . . . (pp. 347-52)

The truth seems to be that, instead of feeling the rhythm of metre and rhyme a stimulus to his imagination, Mr. Ruskin found it a heavy fetter upon his imagination. His poetical prose delights in its rhetorical freedom. He loves to pile up touches, each of which adds to the total effect; and, as a rule, the methods of rhetoric are not only not the methods of poetry, but are essentially different in kind from the methods of poetry. Rhetoric climbs, where poetry soars. Rhetoric takes long sweeps, where poetry concentrates its meaning in a single word. Rhetoric loves to use a little exaggeration, where poetry has a passion for the simplicity of absolute truth. Verse cramps the rhetorician and fires the poet. Mr. Ruskin's prose is, I admit, the very poetry of rhetoric, but his verse is very far from being the rhetoric of poetry. The fixed laws and restrained passion of verse do not suit his genius. He loves a freer hand, and less urgent need to strive for unity of effect. When he writes in verse he becomes either trivial or unnatural, because he cannot well take those wide sweeps and cumulate so freely those minute effects which are the very materials of his art. He can chat in verse with a certain grace and playfulness. One of the best bits I have found in his verse is the description of the shattering and morally confounding effect of a sneeze. But when he addresses himself to any task of higher passion, he needs plenty of elbowroom, for he cannot make up by intensity and concentration for the want of space wherein to wheel and charge, as it were, against the idols which he wishes to reprobate and denounce. Judged by his verse, Mr. Ruskin would seem to be a man without passion, and full of whimsical caprice. Judged by his prose, there is in him a higher and richer rhetoric than any English writer, since Jeremy Taylor, has held at his command. (pp. 353-54)

> *Richard Holt Hutton, ''Why Mr. Ruskin Failed as a Poet,'' in his* Brief Literary Criticisms, *edited by Elizabeth M. Roscoe, The Macmillan Company, 1906, pp. 347-54.*

FRANCIS THOMPSON   (essay date 1898)

[*Thompson was one of the most important poets of the Catholic Revival in nineteenth-century English literature. Often compared to the seventeenth-century metaphysical poets, especially Richard Crashaw, he is best known for his poem ''The Hound of Heaven'' (1893), which displays Thompson's characteristic themes of spiritual struggle, redemption, and transcendent love. Like other writers of the fin de siècle period, Thompson wrote poetry and prose noted for rich verbal effects and a devotion to the values of aestheticism. In the following excerpt from an essay originally published in* Academy *in 1898, he discusses the change in Ruskin's prose style from the ornate elegance of his early works to the relative simplicity and directness of his later works.*]

As a publicly acknowledged teacher, Mr. Ruskin was, and is not, and apparently shall be again. For it is said that among the rising generation of art students his name is great. The sale of his books has never ceased, and with the continually extending circle of his readers his time is bound to come again. Ruskin, for most people, means *Modern Painters*. When Ruskin is praised, or Ruskin's style, it is the Ruskin of those first volumes to whom men turn as typical. Yet if there be but one Ruskin, he has more than one style, and more than one style which is worth considering. We say advisedly ''worth considering.'' For while it is understood that there is a later Ruskin with a different style, it is usually supposed that the later deteriorated from the earlier, partly in substance, but still more in style. Against this idea it is full time to enter a protest.

There are, it may almost be said, three styles in Ruskin. The first and most popular is that of *Modern Painters*. There is his later and mature style; and Mr. Ruskin himself would distinguish a third, which he calls his last manner, and which consists in writing just as the fit comes to him. It may be admitted, in effect, that there is the hasty Ruskin of *Fors Clavigera* and the letters to newspapers, as distinguished from the Ruskin of the lectures; but for our purpose the division we have made is sufficient.

Everyone knows the Ruskin of the early volumes: it is the Ruskin that men love—and women; the style which secured him celebrity, and still makes *Modern Painters* the best read of his books. It is a style of full and copious eloquence, based on the great seventeenth century writers, the masters of rhythmic prose. The sentences are stately and involved, holding in suspension a multitude of clauses, and are sometimes of a length at which Mr. Ruskin himself, in later days, held up hands of playful protest. What he had to say was said with abounding words, with small attempt at succinctness. But what doubtless contributed, and contributes, to secure its paramount popularity was the numerous descriptions of nature in which it abounds, offering full scope for his fancy, his imagination, and his brilliant redundance of diction. These were things which could be followed and enjoyed by any fairly cultivated reader. They appealed also, and still appeal, to women—no bad barometer of popular taste. In the *Frondes Agrestes* (a collection made by a woman) passages of sentiment and natural description largely predominate—as Mr. Ruskin himself gently deprecates in the preface to that selection from *Modern Painters*. This, we suspect, rather than any abstract preferences as to style, or for his earlier art-views rather than his later, explains the greater vogue of the early book. It seems useless to quote specimens from a work so well known. All have seen, for example, at least in quotation, the splendid passage on cloud. But we have the sweep, exuberance, and splendour in this example:

> Green field, and glowing rock, and glancing streamlet, all slope together in the sunshine towards the brows of ravines, where the pines take up their own dominion of saddened shade; and with everlasting roar in the twilight the stronger currents thunder down, pale from the glaciers, filling all their chasms with enchanted cold, beating themselves to pieces against the great rocks that they have themselves cast down, and forcing fierce way beneath their ghastly poise.

As the power of this is obvious—its command of pictorial phrase, such as the lovely "enchanted cold," its ardour and swell of sound—so also are the defects to which it is exposed, and which Mr. Ruskin does not always escape. Sometimes he is betrayed into a touch of slightly obvious sentiment, of somewhat weak fancy—as when he speaks of foam "like the veil of some sea spirit." It is the defect and the strength of youth.

Mr. Ruskin's less regarded later style, if without the redundant splendour, is to our thinking more exquisite, as it is certainly more mature. It appeals, one can understand, less to the many. The flash and spray of many-tinted language he forsakes. But there is a quieter, closer, more intimate beauty of diction, a research of simplicity and directness. Not that he confines himself to Anglo-Saxon; he will use such a word as "accipi-

trine" unhesitatingly, when it is in the right place. The simplicity is in the fewness of words, as compared with the early copiousness, the endeavour after conciseness and pregnancy, the closeness between word and idea. The sentence-structure correspondingly alters; the torrentuous sentence disappears, with its multitudinous members, and instead we have sentences mostly short, direct, of limpid flow. Yet when he uses a longer sentence, nothing can exceed its skill; the charm of the diction, the sweet grace of movement, the lovely shepherding of ordered clauses. Take this quite average example—there are many much finer:

> As this ghastly phantasy of death is to the mighty clouds of which it is written, "The chariots of God are twenty thousand, even thousands of angels," are the fates to which your passion may condemn you—or your resolution raise. You may drift with the phrenzy of the whirlwind—or be fastened for your part in the pacified effulgence of the sky. Will you not let your lives be lifted up, in fruitful rain for the earth, in scatheless snow to the sunshine—so blessing the years to come, when the surest knowledge of England shall be of the will of her Heavenly Father, and the purest heart of England be the inheritance of her simplest children?

The difference between the tranquil, pellucid beauty of this and the tumult of our previously quoted passage must be evident at once. But another charm in the later Ruskin is the greater variety of range and mood. There are passages in which he displays a delightful playfulness; others, again, of an exquisite Socratic irony. Indeed, Plato seems to us largely to have influenced the style of his lectures. A quite Greek mingling of elegance, simplicity, austerity and winning grace, presides over many a page of these Oxford or other addresses. Often they give the best English idea we know of a page from Plato.

When all these qualities are made the medium of high thinking, fine and saddened feeling, noble exhortation, rare, if rather capricious taste, and wide knowledge, the result is work captivating and authoritative for all time. Wise, inconsistent, polished, spontaneous, freakish, exasperating, irresistible, Ruskin is a treasure for the man of understanding—and perdition for the fool. He should be in all hands, except those that would burn their fingers with him. For Ruskin is decidedly of private interpretation, and they who follow him blindly will fall into the pit. (pp. 218-21)

> *Francis Thompson, "Ruskin," in his* Literary Criticisms, Newly Discovered and Collected, *edited by Rev. Terence L. Connolly, S. J., E. P. Dutton and Company Inc., 1948, pp. 218-21.*

BRANDER MATTHEWS   (essay date 1910)

[*An American critic, playwright, and novelist, Matthews wrote extensively on world drama and served for twenty-five years at Columbia as professor of dramatic literature, the first to hold such a position in an American university. Matthews was also a founding member and president of the National Institute of Arts and Letters. Matthews, whose criticism is both witty and informative, has been called "perhaps the last of the gentlemanly school of critics and essayists" in America. In the following excerpt, he discusses what he considers to be negative characteristics of Ruskin's personality and writing.*]

Two things must be admitted in advance by all who adventure themselves in literary criticism. The first of these is that a work of art which has been praised by experts, and which has pleased long and pleased many, in all probability possesses qualities which justify its success,—or which at least explain this. And the second is that the most stimulating criticism is likely to spring from sympathetic appreciation, and that the criticism which has its root in antipathy is likely to be sterile. But even if both these things must be granted, it does not follow that adverse criticism, even of those whose fame may seem to be most solidly founded, is any the less useful. In every generation we have to revise the verdicts rendered by the generations that went before; and this is possible only when we are willing to reopen the case and to listen to fresh argument. (p. 93)

Certainly the Devil's Advocate will have his work laid out for him when he undertakes to dispute Ruskin's right to the reputation that is now allotted to him. That Ruskin was a great writer, in the narrower meaning of the word, is indisputable. He was a master-rhetorician. We may relish his style or we may detest it; but there is no denying that he had a style. He possest what Shakspere called "an exchequer of words." Stevenson credited him with a "large declamatory and controversial eloquence." But John La Farge pointed out that his "use of phraseology that continually recalls to us the forms of the Bible or of the sermon-writer" gradually hypnotizes us until "we begin to believe that beneath such words there must be some graver message than could be contained in forms of ordinary speech: indeed, the use of clear, ordinary speech would have made many of his appeals collapse in ridicule." Mr. Henry James has made it plain that Ruskin's abundant writing about art fails totally to bring out the fact that "Art, after all, is made for us, and not we for art"; and the same writer goes on to say that as to Ruskin's world of art "being a place where we may take life easily, wo to the luckless mortal who enters it with any such disposition; instead of a garden of delight, he finds a sort of assize-court in perpetual session."

It may be claimed that even if Ruskin's theories of pictorial art are now as discredited as Pope's theories of poetry, he is still an inspiring critic in the supreme art of the conduct of life, since he contributed powerfully to the solution of the pressing problems of society. But here the Devil's Advocate would summon other witnesses, as competent in this field as La Farge and Mr. James in the field of pictorial art. Lord Avebury, for one, has asserted that while Ruskin's writings on these subjects "are admirable as guides to conduct and thoroly Christian in spirit," to treat them "as principles of political economy is to confuse two totally different things," since "tables of weights and measures are not condemned as cold and heartless because some people have not enough to eat; and to alter the size of the bushel will not increase the supply of food." And it is a fact, whatever its significance, that Ruskin's contributions to economic theory have been brusht aside by nearly all serious students of social conditions with the same contempt displayed by painters and architects toward his contributions to the theory of the fine arts. It is perhaps not too much to say that those who are most intimately acquainted with these subjects hold that altho Ruskin could talk beautifully, he did not know what he was talking about.

Lord Avebury, it will be noted, declared that Ruskin's writings were thoroly Christian in spirit. And here is where the last stand is likely to be made by the ardent admirers of Ruskin. For example, Charles Eliot Norton asserted his conviction that "no other master of literature in our time endeavored more

earnestly and steadily to set forth, for the help of those he addrest, whatsoever things are true, honest, just, pure, lovely, and of good report." When we read praise like this we can hardly believe our eyes, since Ruskin, in a very large part of his writings, was notoriously querulous and scornful. It is difficult to discover the Christian virtue of humility in a writer who degenerated into little better than a common scold. The Devil's Advocate will have no difficulty in showing that arrogance was as characteristic of Ruskin's attitude as shrieking was characteristic of his utterance. With all his devotion to truth (as his own narrow vision revealed this to him), Ruskin was wholly devoid of tolerance; and, as Lord Morley has told us, "tolerance means reverence for all the possibilities of Truth; it means acknowledgment that she dwells in divers mansions and wears vesture of many colors, and speaks strange tongues . . . it means the charity that is greater even than faith and hope." Can even the most devoted admirer of Ruskin claim that he was dowered with the essential Christian virtues of faith and hope and charity?

After all, it is not too much to insist that a good Christian ought to have good manners. He ought to possess his soul in patience; to control his temper; and to show at least a little loving-kindness. He ought to be a gentleman, in the best meaning of that abused word,—a word frequent in Ruskin's mouth, altho the qualities it denotes were as frequently absent from his works. And the Devil's Advocate could read to the court many a passage from Ruskin's writings which would prove that he had very bad manners, and that they were rooted in a belligerent self-esteem and in an offensive disregard for the feelings of others. No doubt, the Devil's Advocate might feel it to be his duty also to offer in evidence those other pages in which Ruskin reveled in violent eccentricities of thought, and in which he complacently displayed his assumption of special knowledge in departments of learning wherein he was profoundly ignorant. Of course, the counsel for the defense would then read to the court extracts in which the nobler side of Ruskin's nature revealed itself, and in which the exuberant rhetoric was sustained by clear thinking and by kindly feeling. (pp. 101-05)

>   Brander Matthews, "The Devil's Advocate," in his
>   Gateways to Literature and Other Essays, *Charles*
>   *Scribner's Sons, 1912, pp. 93-112.*

R. G. COLLINGWOOD   (lecture date 1919)

[*Collingwood was a highly-respected English archaeologist and philosopher whose writings often center on the relationship between philosophy and history. His father, William Gurshom Collingwood, was Ruskin's secretary, friend, and biographer (see Additional Bibliography). In the following excerpt from a lecture delivered at the Ruskin Centenary Conference in Coniston, England, in 1919, Collingwood examines Ruskin's philosophical principles.*]

To many of you, and those not the least acquainted with the works of Ruskin, the title of my address ["Ruskin's Philosophy"] must seem a paradox. These works, taken as a whole, form an encyclopaedia in which painting, architecture and poetry stand side by side with history, geography and geology, politics and economics, studies in bird-flight and flower-growth, in perspective and prosody. Each of these subjects in turn, and many others, Ruskin made his own and seldom failed to illuminate with fresh observation. The time is long past when he could be regarded as an art-critic who strayed beyond his province to dabble in political economy; and past no less, I hope and believe, is the time when he could be regarded as a social reformer who wasted his youth in art-criticism. To-day we must look at Ruskin as a whole or not at all.

But, looking at him as a whole, and considering what I have called the encyclopaedia of his works, we find that it is an encyclopaedia with a gap. All the arts and almost all the sciences are passed in review; but there is no treatise, however small, on philosophy. (p. 1)

Further, you doubtless recall passages in which he refers to philosophy and philosophers; and, if so, you will remember that the tone of these references is almost always hostile and contemptuous. (p. 3)

When I speak of a man's philosophy, I mean something of this sort. I see a man living a long and busy life; I see him doing a large number of different things, or writing a large number of different books. And I ask myself, do these actions, or these books, hang together? Is there any central thread on which they are all strung? Is there any reason why the man who wrote this book should have gone on to write that one, or is it pure chance? Is there anything like a constant purpose, or a consistent point of view, running through all the man's work?

Now if you ask these questions about a particular man, you will generally find that there are certain central principles which the man takes as fundamental and incontrovertible, which he assumes as true in all his thinking and acting. These principles form, as it were, the nucleus of his whole mental life: they are the centre from which all his activities radiate. You may think of them as a kind of ring of solid thought—something infinitely tough and hard and resistent—to which everything the man does is attached. The ring is formed of a number of different ideas or principles, welded together by some force of mutual cohesion.

This ring of thought—this nucleus of the individual mind—is what I mean by a man's philosophy. Everyone has it, whether he is a philosopher or not: and a man is a great man or a little, a valuable man or a worthless, largely according as this ring is strong or weak in structure, good or bad in material. The acts and decisions which shape a man's life are suspended from this ring of principles; and if the ring is weak a heavy load will snap it; the man's character, as we say, fails to stand the strain and we brand him henceforward as untrustworthy. Or again, if the principles of which the ring is composed are unsound and untrue, then the judgments and actions which issue from them are wrong and mistaken, and we call the man a bad or foolish man. (pp. 6-7)

A great man like Ruskin, then, necessarily has not only a philosophy but an important and interesting philosophy; but, not being a philosopher, Ruskin did not dissect his own mind to find out what his philosophy was. This can only be done by examining his works and finding what general philosophical principles underlie them; and for this purpose it is necessary to be guided not by the language of this or that isolated passage, but by the attitude, the frame of mind, the intellectual merits and defects, exemplified in his work as a whole. Some such analysis as this I shall try to lay before you; but by way of preface I must begin by reminding you of the chief philosophical ideas that were in the air during the period—say 1820 to 1850—when Ruskin's mind was reaching maturity. (p. 8)

One of the most remarkable facts about the history of thought in the middle nineteenth century is the conflict between two methods of thinking which I shall call the Logical and the Historical. The logical method of thinking proceeds on the assumption that every individual fact is an instance of some eternal and unchanging principle, some law to which time makes no difference; and that the general law is more important, more valuable to know, more real, than the particular fact which is a mere instance of it—no better and no worse than countless other instances. The aim of knowledge, therefore, must always be the discovery of these general laws; and the same laws, when discovered, serve as the foundation for further knowledge and for practical activities. The task of the scientist is to explain facts, and to explain a fact is to show what law it exemplifies. The task of the statesman is so to govern his country that its national life shall as far as possible obey and exemplify the eternal principles of justice and the natural rights of man. (p. 9)

The historical habit of mind is in every way a complete contrast. Where the logical mind looks for general laws, the historical mind looks for individual facts, and it explains these facts by appealing not to laws but to other facts. When challenged for an explanation, it asks, not "what general law does this fact illustrate?" but, "in what particular circumstances did it arise?" Employed in the pursuit of art, it asks, not "what are the rules for composing a picture?" but, "what is the most effective way of composing this particular picture?" Faced with the problems of political life, it tries not so much to determine the natural rights of man as to get at the rights and wrongs of this particular war, controversy or proposal. (p. 11)

The conflict between these two types of thought was by no means evenly matched. By the time Ruskin began to write, a consistent logicism no longer existed; it had everywhere been modified by the encroachments of a growing interest in the past; and the change had even begun to affect the philosophers. Thus the Kantian, Sir William Hamilton, was chiefly celebrated for his researches into the history of philosophy.

Historicism was already beginning to show itself as the philosophy of the future. The teaching in which it was systematically expressed, that of Hegel, superseded all previous philosophies when once it was understood; and even while Hegel was still regarded as unintelligible, the movement of thought which he represented was showing its power and gathering weight at the expense of its rival. Of this historical movement Ruskin was a whole-hearted adherent, and every detail of his work is coloured and influenced by the fact. In a quite real sense he was a Hegelian; not that he ever read Hegel, or knew anything about him, but that he had the same outlook on the world, the same instinctive attitude towards reality, which made Hegel rewrite logic in terms of history. (pp. 14-15)

This historicism or Hegelism of Ruskin has a whole cycle of unmistakable consequences. The first which I will ask you to consider, because I believe it to be in his case the most important, is the belief in the unity or solidarity of the human spirit. Every reader must have noticed as characteristic of Ruskin that he never deals with the art of a particular person or nation without dragging in questions of morality, religion, politics, and so on. If he is asked what kind of training will produce good artists in this country, he will reply, "first of all you must remedy your social abuses: then you must set up a general high moral standard, and see that it is followed: and then, you will find, art will come of itself."

He deals with the past in exactly the same spirit. If there is something visibly good or bad in the art of a certain people at a certain date, he always assumes that there must have been

exactly corresponding virtues and vices in their moral and political life. Now this kind of assumption betrays the presence
of a definite theory of the human mind: the belief, namely,
that each form of human activity springs not from a special
faculty—an organ of the mind, so to speak—but from the whole
nature of the person concerned: so that art is not the product
of a special part of the mind called the "aesthetic faculty,"
nor morality the product of a special "moral faculty," but each
alike is an expression of the whole self. Thus, if the ancient
Greek was a man of a definite type and character, his art
exhibited this character in one way, while his political systems
and his religious beliefs exhibited the same character in another
way, translated, as it were, into another language, but otherwise identical.

This principle—the unity and indivisibility of the spirit—Ruskin never questioned and never attempted to prove. He believed
it instinctively; and it can be shown to proceed from the historical trend of his philosophy. The logical habit of mind finds
ultimate reality in the shape of abstract general principles; it
takes the historical fact of, say, ancient Greece, and analyses
this fact into abstract conceptions such as art, religion, political
institutions and so on: and in so doing it feels that it is nearer
to reality than it was before. The historical habit of mind, on
the contrary, takes the historical fact of ancient Greece as a
whole, and regards this fact as ultimately real, or at least, as
real as anything short of the whole universe can be—much
more real than any abstraction such as "art" or "religion."
Thus, for the historical mind, Plato was a Greek who happened
to work at philosophy, and Phidias a Greek who happened to
work at sculpture. The important thing about them is not the
medium in which they worked but the fact that they both expressed the Greek spirit: and therefore you get deeper into the
mind of Phidias by comparing him with Plato than by placing
him side by side with Rodin or Canova or Epstein. For the
logical mind, it is a mere accident that Plato and Phidias were
contemporaries. One belongs to the eternal company of philosophers, the other to the equally eternal and equally exclusive
army of artists.

I shall illustrate later the way in which this principle—the unity
of the spirit—affects Ruskin's practical thinking; for the present
I shall only ask you to observe that it constitutes a breach with
the whole trend of eighteenth-century philosophy and a point
of contact with Hegel, in whose philosophy it was a cardinal
axiom.

The second point in which Ruskin's thought shows a historical
tendency is the emphasis which he lays upon historical causes.
In the hands of a logically-minded person, history becomes a
mere succession of events, fact following fact with little or no
internal cohesion. To a historically-minded person, on the contrary, history is a drama, the unfolding of a plot in which each
situation leads necessarily to the next. Now nothing is more
characteristic of Ruskin than his interest in the causes which
underlie history. Even in his earliest works, he is always pondering on the forces which cause national prosperity and decay;
and it is a habit which remained with him throughout his life.
Indeed, it became progressively stronger; and it was this interest which forced him to devote so much of his life to political
and economic speculation. Here again he was definitely in
agreement with Hegel, for whom every historical period carries
within it the seeds of the next.

The third characteristic to which I want to call your attention
is Ruskin's extreme tolerance. He was not tolerant in the sense
of pretending to approve things which he felt to be wrong; but

he was conspicuously tolerant in the sense of feeling the rightness and value of things which lay outside his own personal
system of ideals.

As an example of this quality, consider his attitude towards
the Middle Ages. He passionately admired and defended many
things both in mediaeval life and in mediaeval art; but he had
no intention of living like a baron or a monk, and painting
pictures like the illuminations in a missal. He never for a
moment wished to reinstate the Middle Ages, or to copy their
characteristic features; and if he had written a *News from Nowhere,* the London of his dreams would not have been built
in the fashion of the fourteenth century. He felt—and this is
a matter on which his language is quite clear and definite—
that the mediaeval ideals of art and life could never satisfy
either him or his contemporaries; that they were wholly un-
suitable for solving the problems of modern life; but that in
spite of all this they contained much that was fine and noble
and sincere, that they were deserving of admiration for what
they accomplished in their day, and that the nineteenth century
could learn much from their study. (pp. 16-20)

This tolerance is the surest mark of the historical as opposed
to the logical mind; and here, in this imaginative sympathy
with the past, as opposed to idolatrous worship of one phase
of the past, Ruskin's kinship with Hegel strikingly appears.
For the Hegelian treatment of history depends on the principle
that every historical phase has its own individual character,
ideals and virtues, and that every phase alike should be an
object of admiration, none of imitation.

I cannot refrain from citing a fourth characteristic of Ruskin's
mind which even more strikingly, perhaps, shows his kinship
with Hegel: I mean his attitude towards the logical problem of
contradiction. Broadly speaking, there are two ways of looking
at this problem. The old logic lays it down that of two contradictory propositions one must be false and the other true.
To contradict yourself, on this view, is a sign of mental confusion: the wise man never contradicts himself. The alternative
view starts from the axiom that there are two sides to every
question, and that there is right on both sides; from this, the
inference is drawn that truth is many-sided and that self-contradiction may easily be a mark not of weakness but of strength—
not of confusion, but of a wide and comprehensive view which
embraces much more truth than the one-sided consistency of
the logicians.

Ruskin adopted the second of these views, and defended it
explicitly in more than one well-known passage. You remember his discussion of the subject in the Cambridge Inaugural
Lecture.

"Perhaps some of my hearers this evening," he says, "may
occasionally have heard it stated of me that I am rather apt to
contradict myself. I hope I am exceedingly apt to do so. I never
met with a question yet, of any importance, which did not
need, for the right solution of it, at least one positive and one
negative answer, like an equation of the second degree. Mostly,
matters of any consequence are three-sided, or four-sided, or
polygonal; and the trotting round a polygon is severe work for
people any way stiff in their opinions. For myself, I am never
satisfied that I have handled a subject properly till I have contradicted myself at least three times."

This in no isolated statement of opinion. Though he chose on
this occasion to pass it off in a half-jocular form, he was
perfectly serious about the principle. It was a firm and habitual
belief with him—an instinctive belief, if you will—that by

contradicting himself he got nearer the truth. It was an idea which he certainly did not get from Hegel; but I need hardly remind you that it is the very centre and core of Hegel's whole philosophy; which may indeed be described as a sustained attempt to live up to the maxim that in every conflict or dispute there is right on both sides. Both in Hegel's case and in Ruskin's, the recognition of this principle is associated with a sympathetic understanding of history; and, as we have already seen, the one is hardly possible without the other. The history of a struggle—and all history is the history of struggles—cannot be written by a man who believes that one party must have been simply right and the other simply wrong.

It is not my intention to defend in detail the use which Ruskin made of this idea. He often contradicted himself in mere petulance or carelessness; often he was driven to it by the excessive one-sidedness of something he had already said. His appeal to the polygonal character of truth covers a multitude of sins that ought never to have been committed; and if he had been less hasty in expression, less summary in thought, I doubt whether he need have appealed to it at all. But my task is to analyse his philosophical principles, not to decide whether he always made the best possible use of them; and this very hastiness of expression is instructive so far as it throws into relief the principle by which he attempted, however unsuccessfully, to justify it. (pp. 20-3)

These observations must suffice for the present as an outline of Ruskin's philosophy. The important point about the various principles which I have enumerated is their close interconnexion; they form a philosophical "ring" of exceedingly solid texture, capable of supporting great strains without damage. I have said that hastiness of expression was a besetting sin of Ruskin's; but it was a defect only rendered possible by the solidity and compactness of his philosophy, which enabled him to think and act quickly where a man with a less homogeneous mind would have stumbled and groped.

But this whole-hearted historicism only accentuated his opposition to the philosophers of his day. (p. 24)

[A] combination of intellectual scepticism with moral dogmatism is so characteristic of the Victorian age that I think you will find it to be the leading feature of the philosophy of that period, taken as a whole. Its effect on the general temper of the age was nothing short of disastrous. It inculcated moral narrowness combined with intellectual apathy, and made the Victorian Englishman appear in the eyes of the world as a prig and a Philistine, religious in it, proud of his ignorance, confident in his monopoly of a sense of justice and "fair play," and boasting of an educational system which did not stuff a boy's head with facts, still less with ideas, but taught him to behave like a gentleman. It was the same fallacy that underlay the typically Victorian suggestion that the doctrines of Christian belief should be given up as being incapable of proof, while the Christian ethics should be preserved, as the best ethical system in existence.

From this specifically Victorian heresy, this intellectual disease which ate like a canker into the whole life of the nineteenth century, Ruskin was entirely and astonishingly free. Most of his contemporaries were tainted with it. Browning himself, to mention one only, in the last resort despaired of the intellect with which he was so generously endowed, and fell back almost with relief on a blind and irrational faith. But there is not the smallest trace of it in the whole works of Ruskin. If he was ever tempted to suggest that the human intellect was by its

inherent limitations debarred from solving certain problems—and he does so speak, in later life, of theological difficulties—he at least never gives back with one hand what he has taken away with the other, or supposes that "conscience" or "faith" may guide us where "intellect" breaks down.

The current of philosophical thought in England was thus absolutely alien to Ruskin's mind. It was not till the seventies, when a few enterprising young men in Oxford began to expound Hegel to their pupils, that ideas akin to those which formed Ruskin's philosophy became part of the main stream of academic thought in this country. Ruskin had been applying in practice since 1840 the philosophical system of which the theory was first published in English in 1865 by James Hutchison Stirling in that queer, incoherent, isolated book *The Secret of Hegel,* and was taken up in the following decade by Wallace and Bradley and others, and in a modified form by T. H. Green, at Oxford.

This, surely, explains Ruskin's attitude to the philosophers of his own day. They were occupied exclusively with the logic of the eighteenth century; abstract, formalistic, unhistorical; largely concerned with imaginary anatomies of the human mind. He was proceeding on the basis of a totally different philosophy, the nineteenth-century historical idealism; supple where the other was rigid, sympathetic where it was hostile; interested in facts where the other cared only for generalities; seizing the character of individual minds as a whole where the other saw only disjointed psychological states; a rich soil for poetry and art while the other starved and stunted the imagination. Little wonder that Ruskin was no friend to philosophers, when he compared their philosophies with the philosophy of his own inmost consciousness.

But it was not only the academic philosophers who were affected by the logicism and Kantianism against which Ruskin rebelled. The old logic and psychology, which the new Kantianism had done little to modify, were deeply rooted in the English popular consciousness, and affected every kind of activity and every branch of thought. Ruskin's intellectual loneliness has often been noticed, but its cause has never been fully understood. He was at cross-purposes with his age: all the fundamental assumptions which underlay his thought contradicted those which underlay that of his contemporaries. Unless he is an egotist, a man is not unhappy when people disagree with his expressed opinions. He merely falls to arguing with them. But you cannot argue with people who dissent from your unexpressed convictions. You have no common ground on which to argue. The only cure is to turn philosopher and drag your convictions and theirs into the daylight. Ruskin was not an egotist: he was lonely and dissatisfied not because people rejected his opinions but because they rejected his philosophy. In face of this attitude he was powerless; for, being no philosopher, he could not analyse the real nature of the conflict between himself and his age, and so could not get the conflict fought out to an issue. It was always a fight in the dark. (pp. 27-30)

I promised to give you a few illustrations of the way in which Ruskin's historical tendencies, and especially his belief in the unity of the mind, influenced his practical thinking. I am the more anxious to do this, because nothing in all Ruskin's work is more striking than the way in which he uses this conviction as a philosophical weapon.

It is a conviction which necessarily issues in a synthetic habit of mind—a habit, I mean, of laying stress on the resemblances and connexions between problems, instead of regarding every problem as intrinsically different from every other. And it is natural that this, again, should result in a frequent appeal to the argument by analogy. Especially is this the case when the analogy is between various activities or functions of the mind. If you believe that these various activities proceed from different "faculties," then clearly you do not hold yourself justified in transferring to one of these faculties a statement which has been proved to hold good of another. But if you believe that there is no such thing as the distinction between faculties, then whatever holds good of one human activity necessarily holds good of all. Strictly speaking therefore this argument is not analogical: for the relation between two instances of a universal law is not one of analogy.

Thus, in the third volume of **Modern Painters** Ruskin answers certain critics who had accused him of dogmatism because he had ventured to lay down in a positive and confident manner principles of right and wrong with regard to painting. Here is the passage:—

"There are laws of truth and right in painting, just as fixed as those of harmony in music or of affinity in chemistry. Those laws are perfectly ascertainable by labour, and ascertainable no otherwise. It is as ridiculous for any one to speak positively about painting who has not given a great part of his life to its study, as it would be for a person who had never studied chemistry to give a lecture on affinities of elements; but it is also as ridiculous for a person to speak hesitatingly about laws of painting who has conscientiously given time to their ascertainment, as it would be for Mr. Faraday to announce in a dubious manner that iron had an affinity for oxygen, and to put it to the vote of his audience whether it had or not."

You observe here the confidence with which he appeals to the philosophy of chemistry in order to settle a disputed point in the philosophy of art. He assumes that chemistry and painting, being each alike an example of the free activity of the human spirit, are governed by the same principles and possess the same kind of validity. A person with less confidence in the unity of the spirit would have declined to assume an analogy between chemistry and painting; and might have gone on to argue that whereas science discovers laws whose truth is the same for everyone, art only reveals beauty, which is a matter of personal taste and knows no law. Ruskin simply sweeps aside all such arguments, unheard, by an appeal to his immutable conviction of the unity of the spirit. What is true of chemistry must on this principle be true of art, and any attempt to prove the contrary is condemned in advance as sophistical.

This analogical method of reasoning is no doubt a dangerous weapon to use; it often misleads, and in unskilled hands may fatally injure the user. But in skilled hands it is a weapon of immense power, clearing the ground of unnecessary argument and accomplishing a vast amount of varied work with the least possible waste of energy; while the alternative method, with all its virtues, is always immensely slow in action and immensely wasteful of power.

Secondly, his conviction of the unity of the mind provides, I believe, the explanation of perhaps the greatest difficulty in all Ruskin's works—his doctrine as to the relation between art and nature. His insistence upon the accurate literal portrayal of nature as the essence of good art—his frequent assertion that the only value a work of art possesses is that it should be an accurate record of a worthy subject—his lack of interest in works of art which did not represent a subject that pleased

him—these facts are, from the point of view of most modern artists and critics, grave defects in his art-criticism. Taken literally, as Ruskin himself generally took them, they are at any rate questionable; and they caused him not a little trouble when he came, for instance, to defend the topographical licence of Turner, or to expound the function of imagination in art. But it seems to me that all this side of his art-criticism—the anti-imaginative, anti-artistic side, if you like—is a symptom of his belief in the unity and solidarity of the human spirit. He is out to deny that art is a thing by itself, which can thrive in a vacuum, cut off from the general interests of humanity. The soil in which art grows is not art but life. Art is expression, and it cannot arise until men have something to express. When you feel so strongly about something—the joys or sorrows of your domestic or national life: the things you see round you: your religious beliefs, and so on—that you must at all costs express your feelings, then art is born. And so you cannot encourage art by teaching people the manual knack of drawing, and hoping that the feeling will come of itself. If you could only teach people to feel, they would teach themselves to draw, fast enough. The problem is not, in Ruskin's own words, how to give gentlemen an artist's education; it is how to give artists a gentleman's education.

The cry of Art for Art's sake, issuing as it did from the analytic or separative tendency in the Victorian mind, expresses everything against which Ruskin was here in revolt. It assumed that Art—with a capital A—was the product of a quite special and unique faculty, and that this faculty had nothing to gain and everything to lose by being worried with irrelevant issues like morality and religion and everyday life. Art could only flourish in properly heated and hermetically sealed rooms, whose heavy curtains kept out every trace of sunshine and all the noises of the world's business. Such a conception of art as this was, I believe, the enemy at which Ruskin was tilting when he laid stress on the importance of the subject in art. He was trying to express the idea that art, to be healthy, must strike its roots deep into the common earth of life, with all its interests and passions and prejudices. He may have mis-stated and at times even misunderstood this idea; but I am convinced that this was the idea which his doctrine of the relation between art and nature aimed at expressing.

Thirdly: the same synthetic view of the human mind has important results in his treatment of history. He notices, and often recurs to it as a mysterious fact, that the attainment of perfection in art seems to herald the downfall of a civilisation, while a high state of moral nobility may coexist with a complete absence of art. Now why is this fact, if it is a fact, so striking to Ruskin? Only because of his profound belief in the unity of the spirit. Without that belief, he would have replied, when the question was raised, "Why shouldn't a man be a good artist and a bad man? Why shouldn't a virtuous man be artistically incompetent? What reason on earth is there to suppose that excellence in morals and in art need ever go together, and why should we be surprised if they don't."

But Ruskin believed that morality issues, not from a moral faculty, but from the nature of the whole man, and so with art; and if the self which you reveal in morality is bad, how can the same self, when you reveal it in terms of art, be good? (pp. 31-5)

[He] never suggests a complete solution. It remains for him a dark and terrible mystery that perfection and death should thus walk hand in hand. (p. 38)

Bearing all this in mind, I think it is not too much to say that Ruskin was in philosophy the best-equipped mind of his generation. The philosophical weapons with which he was provided could smash their way through Coleridge's vague distinctions or Mill's pettifogging logic as easily as Hegel's dialectic could batter Kant or Hume out of recognition at ten miles' range. He did not always handle his guns as well as they deserved, and he sometimes fell back on a secondary armament of obsolete weapons: but when he did get the sights on and began making good practice he annihilated.

The overwhelming superiority of Ruskin's intellectual armament consisted in this fact: that, in an age which was turning from the ideal of abstract, logical, doctrinaire thinking to an ideal of concrete, historical, imaginative thinking, Ruskin alone of Englishmen refrained from putting his new wine into the old bottles of eighteenth-century philosophy. Coleridge, Mill and the rest tried to combine nineteenth-century practice with eighteenth-century principles; and their out-of-date philosophy hampered them at every turn. Ruskin, more independent and original than they, flung his whole mind into the new movement of thought: and that is why, when everyone else was moving stiffly, their feet clogged with the mud of ancient theories, Ruskin alone seems perfectly at his ease, never worried by the care of making ends meet, flying through the air of thought with the freedom and security of a Tintoret angel.

I say he was philosophically the best-equipped mind of his generation. Book-learned in philosophy he was not; but he was no great believer in book-learning. He once laughed at "foolish readers" who doubted the truth of his economic views because he said he had never read books on political economy. "Did they suppose," he asks, "I had got my knowledge of art by reading books?" His philosophical ideas cannot be directly traced to the influence of authors whom he had read, any more than his views on painting or economics. And so I am not concerned to ask what were the sources of his philosophy. It is the character of that philosophy that I wish to make clear to you: its historical and dialectical, as opposed to a mathematical and logical, character; its scorn of scholastic distinctions; its breadth and imaginativeness; above all, its intensely synthetic nature—its refusal to separate any one aspect of life from any other, and its resolute envisagement of the spirit as a single and indivisible whole. Mazzini expressed his opinion of Ruskin's intellect by describing it as the most analytic mind in Europe. This may have been true; but it was the least important part of the truth. Ruskin's greatness lay not in his analytic but in his synthetic power. There were then, and always are, plenty of analytic minds. It is the synthetic mind—the mind that sees the unity of things—that is rare; and it is to this class that Ruskin pre-eminently belongs. (pp. 42-3)

R. G. Collingwood, in his Ruskin's Philosophy, *1922. Reprint by Quentin Nelson, 1971, 43 p.*

BERNARD SHAW (lecture date 1919)

[*Shaw is generally considered the greatest and best-known dramatist to write in the English language since Shakespeare. Following the example of Henrik Ibsen, Shaw succeeded in revolutionizing the English stage, disposing of the romantic conventions and devices of the "well-made play," and instituting the theater of ideas, grounded in realism. During the late nineteenth century, Shaw was also a prominent literary, art, and music critic. In 1895 he became the drama critic for* The Saturday Review, *and his reviews therein became known for their biting wit and brilliance. During his three years at* The Saturday Review, *Shaw determined*

that the theater was meant to be a "moral institution" and "elucidator of social conduct." The standards he applied to drama were quite simple: Is the play like real life? Does it convey sensible, socially progressive ideas? Because most of the drama produced during the 1890s failed to approach these ideals, Shaw usually assumed a severely critical and satirical attitude toward his subjects. As Samuel Hynes has noted, Shaw was driven by a rage to better the world. A Fabian socialist, he wrote criticism that was often concerned with the humanitarian and political intent of the work under discussion. In the following excerpt from a lecture delivered at the 1919 Ruskin Centenary Exhibition at the Royal Academy of Arts, London, Shaw discusses Ruskin's political convictions.]

I think Ruskin was more misunderstood as a politician than in any other department of his activity. People complained that he was unintelligible. I do not think he was unintelligible. If you read his political utterances, the one thing that you cannot say of them is that they were unintelligible. You would imagine that no human being could ever have been under the slightest delusion as to what Ruskin meant and was driving at. But what really puzzled his readers—and incidentally saved his life, because he certainly would have been hanged if they had grasped what he was driving at, and believed that he believed it—was that he was incredible. You see, he appealed to the educated, cultivated, and discontented. It is true that he addressed himself to the working classes generally; and you can find among the working classes, just as Mr Charles Rowley has found in the Ancoats quarter of Manchester, a certain proportion of workingmen who have intellectual tastes and artistic interests. But in all classes his disciples were the few who were at war with commercial civilization. I have met in my lifetime some extremely revolutionary characters; and quite a large number of them, when I have asked, "Who put you on to this revolutionary line? Was it Karl Marx?" have answered, "No, it was Ruskin." Generally the Ruskinite is the most thoroughgoing of the opponents of our existing state of society.

Now, the reason why the educated and cultured classes in this country found Ruskin incredible was that they could not bring themselves to believe that he meant what he was saying, and indeed shouting. He was even shouting in such terms that if I were to describe it merely as abusive I should underdo the description. Think of the way in which his readers were brought up! They were educated at our public schools and universities; they moved in a society which fitted in with those public schools and universities; they had been brought up from their earliest childhood as, above everything, respectable people; taught that what respectable people did was the right and proper thing to do, was good form and also high culture; that such people were the salt of the earth; that everything that existed in the way of artistic culture depended on their cultured and leisured existence. When you have people saturated from their childhood with views of that kind, and they are suddenly confronted with a violently contrary view, they are unable to take it in. For instance, to put it quite simply, they knew that there were the Ten Commandments, and that the Ten Commandments were all right; and they argued from this that as respectable people were all right in everything they did they must be living according to the Ten Commandments. Therefore, their consciences were entirely untroubled.

I have here a volume of Ruskin which I took up this morning, intending to read it, but had not time. I opened it at random, and happened on a page on which Ruskin gave the Ten Commandments according to which in his conception our polite and cultured society really lives. This is the only passage I shall read today, though I feel, of course, the temptation that every lecturer on Ruskin feels to get out of his job by reading, because anything he reads is likely to be better than anything he can say of his own. Ruskin says:

> Generally the ten commandments are now: Thou shalt have any other god but me. Thou shalt worship every bestial imagination on earth and under it. Thou shalt take the name of the Lord in vain and to mock the poor; for the Lord will hold him guiltless who rebukes and gives not; thou shalt remember the sabbath day to keep it profane; thou shalt dishonor thy father and thy mother; thou shalt kill, and kill by the million, with all thy might and mind and wealth spent in machinery for multifold killing; thou shalt look on every woman to lust after her; thou shalt steal, and steal from morning till evening; the evil from the good, and the rich from the poor; thou shalt live by continual lying in millionfold sheets of lies; and covet thy neighbor's house, and country, and wealth and fame, and everything that is his. And finally, by word of the Devil, in short summary, through Adam Smith, a new commandment give I unto you: that ye hate oneanother.

If anybody is going to tell me, here or elsewhere, that this is unintelligible, I do not know what to think of that person's brains. Nothing could well be clearer. But, as I have said, and repeat, it was profoundly incredible to those to whom it was addressed.

Ruskin's political message to the cultured society of his day, the class to which he himself belonged, began and ended in this simple judgment: "You are a parcel of thieves." That is what it came to. He never went away from that, and he enforced it with a very extraordinary power of invective. Ruskin was a master of invective. Compare him, for instance, with Cobbett. Cobbett had immense literary style, and when he hated a thing, he hated it very thoroughly indeed. Think of Cobbett's writing about the funding system—think of his writing about the spoliation of the Church by Henry VIII—think of his writing about the barrenness of Surrey, which cultured society likes so much and which Cobbett loathed as a barren place—think of what he said about "barbarous, bestial Malthus"—think of Cobbett at the height of his vituperation. Then go on to Karl Marx. Karl Marx was a Jew who had, like Jeremiah, a great power of invective. . . . Yet when you read these invectives of Marx and Cobbett, and read Ruskin's invectives afterwards, somehow or other you feel that Ruskin beats them hollow. Perhaps the reason was that they hated their enemy so thoroughly. Ruskin does it without hatred, and therefore he does it with a magnificent thoroughness. You may say that his strength in invective is as the strength of ten because his heart is pure. And the only consequence of his denunciation of society was that people said, "Well, he can't possibly be talking about us, the respectable people"; and so they did not take any notice of it.

I must now go on to Ruskin's specific contribution to economics and sociology, because that, as you know, today means a contribution to politics. In Ruskin's own time this was not so clear. People did not understand then that your base in politics must be an economic base and a sociological base. We all know it today, and know it to our cost; and will know it to our still greater cost unless we find a way out, which, it seems, lies not very far from Ruskin's way. Ruskin took up the trea-tises of our classic political economy, the books by which our Manchester Capitalism sought to justify its existence. In this he did what Karl Marx had done before; and, like Marx, he did it in a way which I do not like exactly to describe as a corrupt way, because you cannot think of corruption in connection with Ruskin: nevertheless, he did not take it up as a man with a disinterested academic enthusiasm for abstract political economy. I think we must admit that, like Marx, he took it up because he was clever enough to see that it was a very good stick to beat the Capitalist dog with.

Marx took up the theory of value which had been begun by Adam Smith, and developed by Malthus, and, seeing that he could turn it against Capitalism, tried to re-establish it on a basis of his own. Thus we got his celebrated theory of value, which is now a celebrated blunder. What Ruskin did was this. He held up to us the definition of value given by the economists, and said: "These gentlemen define value as value in exchange. Therefore," he said, "a thing that you cannot exchange has no value: a thing that you can exchange has value. Very well. When on my way to Venice I go through Paris, I can buy there for two francs fifty an obscene lithograph, produced by the French to sell to English tourists. When I reach Venice, I go to the Scuola di San Rocco and look at the ceiling painted there by Tintoretto, because it is one of the treasures of the world. But that ceiling cannot be sold in the market. It has no exchange value. Therefore, according to John Stuart Mill, the obscene lithograph has a higher value than the ceiling, which in fact has no value at all. After that, I have no further use for your political economy. If that is the way you begin, I hesitate to go on to the end; for I know where your journey must land you—in hell. You may be under the impression that after all hell is a thing you can think of later on; but you are mistaken: you are already at your destination: the condition in which you are living is virtually hell." Then he gave his version of your Ten Commandments. If you had said to him, "We may be in hell; but we feel extremely comfortable," Ruskin, being a genuinely religious man, would have replied, "That simply shews that you are damned to the uttermost depths of damnation, because not only are you in hell, but you like being in hell."

Ruskin got no farther than that in political economy. It was really a pregnant contribution, but he did not go on. Having knocked the spurious law of value into a cocked hat, he did not go on to discover a scientific law of value; and he took no interest in and never reached that other very revolutionary law, the law of economic rent. I see no sign in his writings that he ever discovered it.

When Karl Marx (let me make this contrast) demonstrated that, in his phrase, the workingman was being exploited by the Capitalist—and Karl Marx took a great deal of trouble to establish what he called the rate of surplus value: that is to say, the rate at which the Capitalist was robbing the workingman—he made a pretense of doing the thing mathematically. He was not a mathematician, but he had a weakness for posing as a mathematician and using algebraic symbols. He tried to determine the quantitative aspect of exploitation. That sort of thing did not interest Ruskin. Ruskin said to the Capitalist, "You are either a thief or an honest man. I have discovered that you are a thief. It does not matter to me whether you are a fifty per cent. thief or a seventy per cent. thief. That may be interesting to men of business who are interested in figures. I am not. Sufficient to me that you are a thief. Having found out that you are a thief, I can now tell you what your taste in art will be. And as I do not like a thievish taste in art I suggest you should become an honest man.'' And I daresay the Capitalists who read it said: ''Aha! that serves Jones right!'' I doubt if they ever applied it to themselves.

Though Ruskin was certainly not a completely equipped economist, I put him, nevertheless, with Jevons as one of the great economists, because he knocked the first great hole in classic economics by shewing that its value basis was an inhuman and unreal basis, and could not without ruin to civilization be accepted as a basis for society at all. Then Jevons came along and exploded the classic value theory from the abstract scientific side. Marx also never grasped the law of rent, never understood one bit of it any more than Ruskin did. Nevertheless, Marx did establish Marxism, a thing of which you hear a good deal, and which is therefore worth defining. Marxism does not mean this or that particular theory: it does mean that the economic question is fundamental in politics and sociology. No doubt some of Marx's disciples—after the way of disciples—have pushed that view a little hard. (pp. 132-37)

Marx said, in effect, ''If you will bring me the tool or machine with which a man worked, I will deduce from it with infallible certainty his politics, his religion, his philosophy, and his view of history and morals.'' That, of course, . . . was a great swank. Nevertheless, it epitomizes an important truth, and makes you feel the dramatic power with which Marx brought into economics and politics his view of the fundamental importance of economics. Our own historian, Buckle, had taken very much the same line; but I think I can give you a simpler illustration of the importance of the economic basis, and why it was that Ruskin, beginning as an artist with an interest in art—exactly as I did myself, by the way—was inevitably driven back to economics, and to the conviction that your art would never come right whilst your economics were wrong.

The illustration I will give you is this. Here am I addressing you, a cultivated audience. I wish to keep before you the most elevated view of all the questions Ruskin dealt with. I am straining all my mental faculties and drawing on all my knowledge. Now suppose you were to chain me to this table and invite me to go on and on. What would happen? Well, after some hours a change would take place in the relative importance of the things presenting themselves to my mind. At first, I should be thinking of Ruskin, and attending to my business here as a lecturer on Ruskin. But at last my attention would shift from the audience in front of me to that corner of the room behind me, because that is where the refreshment room is. I should, in fact, be thinking of nothing but my next meal. I should finally reach a point at which, though I am a vegetarian, I should be looking at the chubbiest person in the audience, and wishing I could eat that chubby person.

That is the real soundness of Marxism and of Ruskin's change of ground from art to economics. You may aim at making a man cultured and religious, but you must feed him first; and you must feed him to the point at which he is reasonably happy, because if you feed him only to the point at which you can make a bare drudge of him and not make him happy, then in his need for a certain degree of happiness he will go and buy artificial happiness at the public-house and other places. Workingmen do that at the present day: indeed we all do it to a certain extent, because all our lives are made more or less unhappy by our economic slavery, whether we are slaves or masters. Economics are fundamental in politics: you must begin with the feeding of the individual. Unless you build on that, all your superstructure will be rotten.

There you have the condition postulated by Marx and every sensible man. That is why Ruskin, when he was twenty, gave you **Modern Painters,** and at thirty, **The Stones of Venice,** also about art, but very largely about the happiness of workingmen who made the art; for the beauty of Venice is a reflection of the happiness of the men who made Venice. When he was forty he wrote **Unto this Last,** and there took you very far away from art and very close to politics. At fifty he gave us the **Inaugural Lectures,** and, finally, **Fors Clavigera,** in which you find his most tremendous invectives against modern society.

Now, since Ruskin's contemporaries neglected him politically because they found the plain meaning of his words incredible, I put the question whether in the course of time there has developed any living political activity on behalf of which you might enlist Ruskin if he were living at the present time. It goes without saying, of course, that he was a Communist. He was quite clear as to that. But now comes the question, What was his attitude towards Democracy? Well, it was another example of the law that no really great man is ever a democrat in the vulgar sense, by which I mean that sense in which Democracy is identified with our modern electoral system and our system of voting. Ruskin never gave one moment's quarter to all that. He set no store by it whatever, any more than his famous contemporary, Charles Dickens—in his own particular department the most gifted English writer since Shakespear, and resembling Ruskin in being dominated by a social conscience. (pp. 137-39)

Ruskin, like Dickens, understood that the reconstruction of society must be the work of an energetic and conscientious minority. Both of them knew that the government of a country

Rose La Touche, from a drawing by Ruskin.

is always the work of a minority, energetic, possibly conscientious, possibly the reverse, too often a merely predatory minority which produces an illusion of conscientiousness by setting up a convention that what they want for their own advantage is for the good of society. They pay very clever people to prove it, and the clever people argue themselves into believing it. The Manchester or anti-Ruskin school had plenty of sincere and able apologists. If you read Austin's lectures on jurisprudence, for instance, you will find a more complete acknowledgment of the horrors inevitable under Capitalism than in most Socialist writers, because Austin had convinced himself that they are the price of liberty and of progress. But then nobody in his day conceived Socialism as a practical alternative: indeed, it was not then practicable. Austin's argument, or rather his choice of evils, is no longer forced on us, so we need not concern ourselves about it except as a demonstration that Ruskin's skepticism as to government by the people as distinguished from government of the people for the people is shared by his most extreme and logical opponents as well as by his kindred spirits. (pp. 140-41)

> Bernard Shaw, "Ruskin's Politics," in his Platform
> and Pulpit, edited by Dan H. Laurence, Hill and
> Wang, 1961, pp. 130-44.

VIRGINIA WOOLF (essay date 1927)

[*Woolf is one of the most prominent figures of twentieth-century English literature. Like her contemporary James Joyce, with whom she is often compared, Woolf is remembered as one of the most innovative of the stream-of-consciousness novelists. Concerned primarily with depicting the life of the mind, she revolted against traditional narrative techniques and developed a highly individualized style. Woolf's works, noted for their subjective explorations of characters' inner lives and their delicate poetic quality, have had a lasting effect on the art of the novel. A discerning and influential critic and essayist as well as a novelist, Woolf began writing reviews for the* Times Literary Supplement *at an early age. Her critical essays, which cover almost the entire range of English literature, contain some of her finest prose and are praised for their insight. Along with Lytton Strachey, Roger Fry, Clive Bell, and several others, Woolf and her husband Leonard formed the literary coterie known as the "Bloomsbury Group." In the following excerpt, Woolf discusses* Praeterita.]

That an abridgement of *Modern Painters* should lately have been published may be held to prove that while people still want to read Ruskin, they have no longer the leisure to read him in the mass. Happily, for it would be hard to let so great a writer recede from us, there is another and much slighter book of Ruskin's, which contains as in a teaspoon the essence of those waters from which the many-colored fountains of eloquence and exhortation sprang. *Praeterita*—"outlines of scenes and thoughts perhaps worthy of memory in my past life" as he called it—is a fragmentary book, written in a season of great stress toward the end of his life, and left unfinished. It is, for these reasons perhaps, less known than it should be; yet if anybody should wish to understand what sort of man Ruskin was, how he was brought up, how he came to hold the views he did, he will find it all indicated here; and if he wishes to feel for himself the true temper of his genius, these pages, though much less eloquent and elaborate than many others, preserve it with exquisite simplicity and spirit.

Ruskin's father was "an entirely honest" wine merchant, and his mother was the daughter of the landlady of the Old King's Head at Croydon. The obscurity of his birth is worth notice because he paid some attention to it himself, and it influenced

him much. His natural inclination was to love the splendor of noble birth and the glamor of great possessions. Sitting between his father and mother when they drove about England in their chariot taking orders for sherry, he loved best to explore the parks and castles of the aristocracy. But he owned manfully, if with a tinge of regret, that his uncle was a tanner and his aunt a baker's wife. Indeed, if he reverenced aristocracy and what it stood, or should stand for, he reverenced still more the labors and virtues of the poor. To work hard and honestly, to be truthful in speech and thought, to make one's watch or one's table as well as tables and watches can be made, to keep one's house clean and pay one's bills punctually were qualities that won his enthusiastic respect. The two strains are to be found conflicting in his life and produce much contradiction and violence in his work. His passion for the great French cathedrals conflicted with his respect for the suburban chapel. The color and warmth of Italy fought with his English puritanical love of order, method and cleanliness. Though to travel abroad was a necessity to him, he was always delighted to return to Herne Hill and home. Again, the contrast finds expression in the marked varieties of his style. He is opulent in his eloquence, and at the same time meticulous in his accuracy. He revels in the description of changing clouds and falling waters, and yet fastens his eye to the petals of a daisy with the minute tenacity of a microscope. He combined, or at least there fought in him, the austerity of the puritan and the sensuous susceptibility of the artist. Unluckily for his own peace of mind, if nature gave him more than the usual measure of gifts and mixed them with more than her usual perversity, his parents brought him up to have far less than the usual power of self-control. Mr. and Mrs. Ruskin were both convinced that their son John was to become a great man, and in order to insure it they kept him like any other precious object, in a cardboard box wrapped in cotton wool. Shut up in a large house with very few friends and very few toys, perfectly clothed, wholesomely nourished and sedulously looked after, he learned, he said, "Peace, obedience, faith," but on the other hand, "I had nothing to love . . . I had nothing to endure . . . I was taught no precision nor etiquette of manners. . . . Lastly and chief of evils, my judgment of right and wrong, and power of independent action, were entirely undeveloped; because the bridle and blinkers were never taken off me." He was not taught to swim, that is to say, but only to keep away from the water.

He grew up, therefore, a shy, awkward boy, who was intellectually so highly precocious that he could write the first volume of *Modern Painters* before he was twenty-four, but was emotionally so stunted that, desperately susceptible as he was, he did not know how to amuse a lady for an evening. His efforts to ingratiate himself with the first of those enchanting girls who made havoc of his life reminded him, he said, of the efforts of a skate in an aquarium to get up the glass. Adèle was Spanish-born, Paris-bred and Catholic-hearted, he notes, yet he talked to her of the Spanish Armada, the Battle of Waterloo and the doctrine of Transubstantiation. Some such pane of glass or other impediment was always to lie between him and the freedom of ordinary intercourse. Partly the boyish days of anxious supervision were to blame. He had much rather go away alone and look at things, he said, than stay at home and be looked at. He did not want friends; he marvelled that anyone should be fond of a creature as impersonal and self-contained as a *camera lucida* or an ivory foot-rule. And then he was still further withdrawn from the ordinary traffic of life by Nature who, to most people only the background, lovely or sympathetic to their own activities, was to him a presence mystic, formidable, sublime, dominating the little human figures in the foreground. But though she thus rapt him from his fellows, Nature did not console him. The cataract and the mountain did not take the place of the hearth and lamplight and children playing on the rug; the beauty of the landscape only made more terrible to him the wickedness of man. The rant and fury and bitterness of his books seem to spring, not merely from the prophetic vision, but from a sense of his own frustration. More eloquent they could hardly be; but we cannot help guessing that had little John cut his knees and run wild like the rest of us, not only would he have been a happier man, but instead of the arrogant scolding and preaching of the big books, we should have had more of the clarity and simplicity of *Praeterita.*

For in *Praeterita,* happily, there is little left of these old rancors. At last Ruskin was at peace; his pain was no longer his own, but everybody's pain; and when Ruskin is at peace with the world, it is surprising how humorously, kindly, and observantly he writes of it. Never were portraits more vividly drawn than those of his father and mother; the father, upright, able, sensitive, yet vain, too, and glad that his clerk's incompetence should prove his own capacity; the mother, austere and indomitably correct, but with a dash of "the Smollettesque" in her, so that when a maid toppled backward over a railing in full view of a monastery, she laughed for a full quarter of an hour. Never was there a clearer picture of English middle-class life when merchants were still princes and suburbs still sanctuaries. Never did any autobiographer admit us more hospitably and generously into the privacy of his own experience. That he should go on for ever talking, and that we should still listen, is all we ask, but in vain. Before the book is finished the beautiful stream wanders out of his control and loses itself in the sands. Limpid as it looks, that pure water was distilled from turmoil; and serenely as the pages run, they resound with the echoes of thunder and are lit with the reflections of lightning. For the old man who sits now babbling of his past was a prophet once and had suffered greatly. (pp. 165-66)

Virginia Woolf, in a review of "Praeterita," in The New Republic, *Vol. LIII, No. 682, December 28, 1927, pp. 165-66.*

R. H. WILENSKI   (essay date 1933)

[*Wilenski was an English artist, art historian, and critic, and the author of the highly-regarded* John Ruskin: An Introduction to Further Study of His Life and Works. *In the following excerpt from that work, Wilenski discusses central characteristics of Ruskin's writings.*]

Ruskin's writings fill thirty-three volumes in the Library, Edition. Of these the major portion consist of lectures essays, pamphlets, notes and journalism. The 'books' properly so called are *Modern Painters, I, Modern Painters, II, The Seven Lamps of Architecture, The Stones of Venice, Unto This Last* (with *Munera Pulveris*), *Ethics of the Dust,* and the long autobiographical fragment, *Praeterita.* Most of these books are to some extent constructed. The other writings are all irregular, if not chaotic, in form.

Laurence Binyon has said that Ruskin was 'driving all one way'. This is true of his central contributions in all fields. But much reconstruction and pruning are necessary before we can discover what those central contributions are. Ruskin built up polygons of doctrine for the study of Art, Social and Political Economy, and the problem of War, which were valuable in his own day, and, as I see things, are still valuable to-day.

But his polygons are not in constructed formation; they exist only as isolated blocks scattered over the thirty-three volumes; and they are obscured and overlaid by incidentals. Before we can arrive at the real character of these valuable polygons we have first to distinguish the main theories from the incidentals—a task that can only perfectly be accomplished by complete knowledge of the circumstances of his life and the workings of his mind—and we have then to set aside the incidentals and collect the scattered parts of the main figures and assemble them in the forms that were always in Ruskin's mind, though he himself could never assemble them. Or, to put it differently—before we can understand what he wanted us most to understand in his writings we have to rearrange them all and rewrite most of them.

To separate the essential from the incidental in a book or a page by Ruskin is often very difficult. In his writings the confusing irrelevancies and discursions are as *real* and *organic* as the essentials. The incidentals are branches from the main trunk of his personal psychosis—they are not pseudo-branches tied on with string. Ruskin's writing was always genuinely personal. He never decked himself with other people's ideas. When we examine most people's writings—as when we examine most people's pictures or sculpture—we find that 80 or 90 or 100 per cent of the content is derived from other people. I find a large proportion of derivative content in Ruskin's drawings—and I regard most of them as negligible for that reason. But I do not find it in his writings at any period of his life.

After 1852 he learned a lot from Carlyle. But learning from a man is one thing, and stealing his ideas is another. Ruskin was susceptible to a powerful influence like Carlyle's; he called him 'my Master' and it was many years before he ceased to write to him as 'Dear Mr. Carlyle'. But Carlyle never referred to Ruskin as 'my imitator' or 'my follower' or 'my pupil'; he referred to his 'flightiness' (meaning the flittering of his thoughts caused by his mental weakness), but he recognised his originality and accepted him as a brother, saying: 'We stand in a minority of two.'

Ruskin was influenced by other people as well as by Carlyle—by Plato, Xenophon, Dante, Turner. But he always set their ideas to the service of his own. At all periods he used data provided by scholars. In his later years he would send his assistants to collect such data saying, 'What else are the professors there for?' In the 'forties and the early 'fifties he read some art history and did some research work himself; and he liked to make a parade of scholarly erudition. But he was never a scholar. He always looked on scholarship in itself as a playlike activity. Driven by the mobility of his interest he indulged in the pastime when the spirit moved him; but he never used any data in his writings except such as could be made to serve his personal ideas. Every word that he wrote had become *his own word* before it appears as an extract from archives or as a paraphrase from some ancient dictionary of heraldry, or as a quotation from Dante or Blake or Anatole France.

The digressions, discursions, and irrelevancies that abound in his writings are never 'padding'. They have a life of their own which often conflicts with or obscures or partially destroys the central theme. Even his lightest and most bantering and journalistic passages have this quality. They are never trivial. And this applies not only to his public writings, but also to his letters. As a rule when we read a man's letters in order to get at his mind and heart we can 'skip' a great proportion which is conventional nothingness or light gossip. But, except in his early years and during his married life in Venice, Ruskin never wrote gossip in his letters, and even at that early period he never wrote a conventional line. If we skip three lines of any of the thousands of his published letters we miss three lines of the real man. He says somewhere that he could never indulge in the pleasure of saying 'nothing worth'. It is true. It was one of the pleasures to which he was not drawn and in which, therefore, he never indulged.

Even in the lighter incidental passages in Ruskin's books, sentence after sentence is a book in itself—with a life of its own independent of the sentence before and the sentence following. Again and again we meet pages where each sentence reveals that curious intensity of idea *at the moment* which seems to go with morbid mobility of interest and must be parallel to that morbid visual hyper-reaction to detail to which Ruskin confessed as early as 1854 in his comments on Hunt's *The Awakening Conscience,* and which he tells us was a characteristic of his vision during his attacks of madness. Anyone can quote Ruskin in any sense on any topic he has touched upon. Ruskin calendars can be compiled by Tories, Fascists, and Communists, by photographic painters and Cubist artists, by Chauvinists and Pacifists, by parsons and agnostics. All can claim him as their man. And yet Binyon is right—he was really driving all one way. The incidentals always bear relation to the man's attitudes even though they may bear little or no relation to their immediate context. In the lecture on serpents, *A Caution to Snakes,* for example, which he wrote in 1880, we read:

> A serpent is a honeysuckle with a head put on. . . . Nothing is more mysterious in the compass of creation than the relation of flowers to the serpent tribe [especially] in carnivorous, insect-eating and monstrous insect-begotten structures. . . . In the most accurate sense, the honeysuckle is an ''anguis''—a strangling thing.

This is an incidental remark in his discussion of the movement of serpents (Living Waves), but it is closely related to the doctrine of Typical and Vital Beauty—the doctrine of the Universal Analogy—which he had put forward thirty-five years earlier, in his Theory of Art. . . .

Then again in the same lecture we get this:

> I endeavoured to find out some particulars . . . in my scientific books; but though I found pages upon pages of description of the scales and wrinkles about snakes' eyes, I could come at no account whatever of the probable range or distinctness in the sight of them; and though extreme pains had been taken to exhibit, in sundry delicate engravings, their lachrymatory glands and ducts, I could neither discover the occasions on which rattle-snakes wept, nor under what consolations they dried their eyes.

This from another speaker would be merely wit. From Ruskin it symbolised a lifelong attitude to scholarship and science, allied to the attitude which led him in Social Economics to differentiate Wealth and Illth, and to set aside the postulate of the Economic Man as useless and absurd.

Or consider this—from a paper which he read to the Metaphysical Society in 1871:

> A painter . . . may, I think, be looked upon as only representing a high order of sensational creatures, incapable of any but physical ideas and impressions; and . . . we should be much more docile than we are if we were never occupied in efforts to conceive things above our natures. To take an instance, in a creature somewhat lower than myself. I came by surprise the other day on a cuttle-fish in a pool at low tide. On being touched with the point of my umbrella, he first filled the pool with ink, and then finding himself still touched in the darkness, lost his temper, and attacked the umbrella with much psyche or anima, hugging it tightly with all his eight arms, and making efforts, like an impetuous baby with a coral, to get it into his mouth. On my offering him a finger instead, he sucked that with two or three of his arms with an apparently malignant satisfaction and, on being shaken off, retired with an air of frantic misanthropy into the cloud of his ink. . . . It seems to me not a little instructive to reflect how entirely useless such a manifestation of a superior being was to his cuttle-fish mind, and how fortunate it was for his fellow-octopods that he had no command of pens as well as ink, nor any disposition to write on the nature of umbrellas or of men.

From an Oxford don this would be just academic banter. From Ruskin, in April, 1871, it was related to his concept of that 'incredulity . . . of help given by any Divine power to the thoughts of men' of which he had written:

> This form of infidelity merely indicates a natural incapacity for receiving certain emotions; though many honest and good men belong to this insentient class, they are not to be thought of except as more or less mechanical or animal forces, which must be dealt with by similar forces, not by reasoning.

Then again the compelling power of the incidentals often derives from the aspect of his mental illness which drove him to use his pen as a means of rationalising his self-indulgence or of relieving his obsessions. Such passages are real and organic because they are autobiography disguised. And it is such passages which give quality to a poor book like *Mornings in Florence,* and even sometimes to the fragments in books of *Selections.*

Nevertheless before we can arrive at Ruskin's main contributions to the study of Art, Social and Political Economy, and War, we have to disengage the digressions and the discursions from the main theories. And when we have done that we find autobiography also in the formulation of the main ideas.

Ruskin . . . was a genius in the sense that he had a great imaginative grasp of first principles and refused to assume that a pretty blossom means a wholesome fruit. But even for his central contributions the jumping-off point was frequently a rationalisation of his self-indulgence, when its character was not determined either by his social conscience working in conjunction with or in conflict with his manic hyperconfidence or in conjunction with or in conflict with his sick mind's need to persuade itself of health. The factors . . . in his action—the drive of his social conscience, the manic impulse to preach, the rationalisations of his self-indulgence, the obsessions—all appear not only in the confusing digressions and excursions but also in his central work.

He was always learning—or rather he was always learning by fits and starts. He learned as the imaginative genius learns, by suddenly piercing to the heart of a thing and understanding it. In his manic moods he boasted of this power. Even in his depressed moods he very seldom doubted it. And he really had it.

But because of his manic hyper-confidence he always assumed that no further leap was necessary or possible until he was ready to leap again. In the field of Art he knew all that he ever was to know by the time he was forty. Thereafter he merely restated and reillustrated fragments of his earlier theories, corrected some minor errors, and used the contemplation of works of art as a means of satisfying his morbid impulse to perseverate and of relieving his obsessions. As far as art was concerned his receptivity closed down in 1859. But he had already begun to leap from point to point in another field. He began to know something of Social and Political Economy at the age of thirty, and he knew all he was to know by the age of forty-two. But again he had already started on another exploration—the exploration of the problem of War. In that field he had realised nothing at all till he was forty; but from 1859 onwards he leapt from comprehension to comprehension. And the points at which he arrived—at forty, forty-two and sixty—in these three fields, are points beyond which, as my knowledge goes, few men, if any, have far advanced to-day. (pp. 185-91)

R. H. Wilenski, in his John Ruskin: An Introduction to Further Study of His Life and Work, *Faber & Faber Limited, 1933, 406 p.*

SIR KENNETH CLARK   (lecture date 1946)

[*Clark is an English scholar, lecturer, museum director, poet, and preeminent historian of art and culture. He has produced a wide variety of both scholarly and popular works noted for their erudition, breadth of knowledge, and precise prose. In the following excerpt from his inaugural lecture as Slade Professor of Fine Arts at Oxford University, a chair first held by Ruskin, Clark examines Ruskin's view of the relationship of art to nature and to morality.*]

[Although] Ruskin often announced his beliefs in a forceful and memorable style, his dicta are both self-contradictory and imprecise. The first charge he would have welcomed, for he said that he never felt he was approaching the truth until he had contradicted himself at least three times. The second charge would, I fear, have annoyed him greatly, for he took pains to be a precise writer, and was slightly ashamed of his birthright of eloquence. But rhetoric is a habit of mind which nothing can restrain; once Ruskin was under way not even his scrupulous conscience could prevent him from putting things in the most telling fashion. This is particularly distracting when we come to look closely at the two ideas on which he felt most strongly, and about which recent critics believe him to have been most extravagantly mistaken: the relation of art to nature and the relation of art to morals.

It would be easy to find in Ruskin's works a number of sentences which, read in isolation, suggest a belief that all art depends on copying appearances with the closest possible fidelity; that, to quote one of the earliest of such statements, 'every alteration in the features of nature has its origin either in powerless indolence or blind audacity'. Even this sentence, read in its context, turns out to be no more than a refutation of the deadly doctrine of ideal form, a refutation which practically every great artist of the time, Ingres as well as Courbet,

would have supported in similar words. If there is one point on which Ruskin was consistent throughout his life, it is that art is never mere imitation. Take, for example, his definition of sculpture in the second series of Oxford lectures known as *Aratra Pentelici*. 'Sculpture is essentially the production of a pleasant bossiness or roundness of surface; and the pleasantness of that bossy condition to the eye is irrespective of imitation on one side and of structure on the other.' The admirer of Mr. Henry Moore's sculpture could not ask for more unequivocal support. Ruskin perceived very vividly what he called 'These abstract relations and inherent pleasantness, whether in space, number or time, and whether of colours or sounds', but believed that they should be 'the subject of a special branch of art philosophy', and to this alone he confined the word aesthetics. He also recognized and accurately described the two elements which transform a visual impression into a work of art, the quality of love which the artist feels for his object, and the quality of order which he is able to impose on it. Nevertheless, the popular notion of Ruskin as the prophet of unquestioning devotion to nature represents an aspect of the truth. The position is well put in his second Oxford lecture (in other respects the weakest of the series) on the relation between art and religion:

> Every art is properly called fine which demands the exercise of the full faculties of heart and intellect. For though the fine arts are *not* necessarily imitative or representative, for their essence is in being occupied in the actual production of beautiful form or colour, still the highest of them are appointed also to relate to us the utmost ascertainable truth respecting visible things and moral feelings.

To this may be added a passage from the preface to the *Two Paths* in which Ruskin says: 'The law which it has been my effort chiefly to illustrate is the dependence of all noble design, in any kind, on the sculpture or painting of Organic Form.' Here no doubt, we touch on a peculiarity of temperament. Ruskin's intense preference for organic as opposed to abstract or geometric forms was part of the same limitation which led him to misjudge Renaissance architecture, to ignore Piero della Francesca, and, when all is said, to overrate Turner. It was indeed a symptom of the lack of a sense of order and proportion which confused his encyclopaedic philosophy. Yet as a basis of aesthetic theory these two quotations have the support of art history. Ruskin himself put his belief historically when he contrasted two artifacts of the early middle ages, a drawing of an angel from a Celtic psalter and a carved relief of the temptation of Eve from Modena cathedral. The first sets out to decorate a space with certain accepted symbols and achieves its end completely. It is consistent in style, skilfully executed, and perfectly fulfils as Ruskin pointed out, with pleasant malice, the Aristotelian principles of the Beautiful—Order, Symmetry, and the Definite. The second, which sets out to convey a moral truth by means of a story, is uncouth to the point of absurdity and far from its maker's intentions. Yet Ruskin was right in saying that the style of the Celtic angel is wholly sterile, whereas the twelfth-century carving, in spite of its crudity, is the direct ancestor of Jacopo della Querica and Michelangelo.

Ruskin never gave very satisfactory reasons why art for art's sake is a blind-alley occupation, and, although I share his belief, its justification would take me too far from the subject of this lecture. But I would emphasize how far this sense of the fullness of life and of human purpose removes Ruskin's theories not only from aestheticism, but also from the mere craftsmanship which some of his followers, or at least the followers of William Morris, mistook for a chief part of his doctrines. Craftsmanship may have its place in education as an exponent of the balance between mental and physical control. But Ruskin's theory of nature as the message and life-spirit of art affects education far more deeply than that.

In case any one imagines that this part of Ruskin's teaching has been put out of date by later critics, may I point out how very similar are the beliefs of the most influential critic of our own time, Roger Fry? In his first lecture as Slade professor at Cambridge he described, under the titles of sensibility and vitality, exactly those qualities which Ruskin found that the artist drew from his absorption in nature. The application of this principle by these two great critics, who apparently differ so widely from one another, leads to the same conclusion: that the most fatal defect in a work of art is for the artist to be more interested in displaying his own skill than in conveying the idea. As a result, both placed a high value on what used to be called primitive art; and for luxury art, art designed for the gratification of rich people, they reserved their most severe condemnations. A continental critic might point out that this attitude is peculiarly English, and reflects the fact that both Ruskin and Fry came of Puritan stock.

This leads me to the second and more difficult of Ruskin's critical ideas, the relation of art to morals. This is certainly not the occasion on which to attack a problem which has occupied students of philosophy for centuries. But we cannot talk sense about Ruskin without remembering that he was above all a moralist. His first words as a child were 'people, be good!', and one of the last works he wrote with full possession of his faculties ends with the words: 'Human nature, in its fullness is necessarily moral.' His belief in goodness was so entwined with his belief in art that he never took sufficient care in describing their relationship. In his inaugural there are two statements of his position. Here is the first: 'The art of any country is the exponent of its social and political virtues': and here is the second: 'The art, or general productive and formative energy of any country, is the exponent of its ethical life.' As you see, these are two very different propositions. The first is historically untenable. We have only to think of the artistic epoch which Ruskin most admired, the Italian *quattrocento,* to see that great art is not always accompanied by social and political virtue. But the second statement must, on the whole, be true; and was important to Ruskin in relation to his own times. For, in developing the contrast between the nineteenth and the thirteenth centuries, with which Carlyle had astonished the world some forty years earlier, he was able to show how the degraded artifacts of his time revealed a materialism, a contempt for real values and an obstinate blindness to economic misery, which the outward forms of social life disguised. Logically the danger of this attitude, a danger of which Ruskin was unaware, is that the argument turns back on itself. We find ourselves saying that an epoch which produces great works of art must be fundamentally good. We adapt our conception of virtue to harmonize with our conception of art, just as Ruskin occasionally suspended his own exquisite aesthetic responses in the interests of his over-simplified notion of morality.

Over-simplified: there, perhaps, is one key to the problem. In relating a work of art to the spirit of an age it is tempting to take the most convenient evidence, to accept society at its face value and shirk the real effort of imagination, to say nothing of the learning which any true assessment of national feeling involves. Yet, the court of Charles II and the intrigues of the Cabal had little to do with the England of Milton, Vaughan, and Wren. And in relating works of art to the character of an individual artist, the problem is even more delicate, for, with a genuine artist, the self projected in his work may be the only real indication of his moral stature. Ruskin, like most moralists, would not make allowances for the many-sidedness of an epoch or a personality. Just as his magnificent prose is sometimes falsified by a too-frequent use of antithesis, so his judgements fail from his fondness for sharp and categorical contrasts; and we grow impatient of a system by which the greatest spirits of the past are made the subject of Sunday-school rebukes. But we must not let Ruskin's failure to apply a moral theory or art drive us into an aesthetic of mere sensation. Of all that we owe him, no debt, I believe, is heavier than this: that he delivered us from the mechanical precepts of picture-making which dominated the early nineteenth century, and showed us that a work of art is great in proportion as it expresses some important element of human life. (pp. 15-19)

Sir Kenneth Clark, in his Ruskin at Oxford, *Oxford at the Clarendon Press, Oxford, 1947, 24 p.*

JOHN D. ROSENBERG   (essay date 1961)

[*An American educator and critic, Rosenberg is the author of the highly-regarded study* The Darkening Glass: A Portrait of Ruskin's Genius. *In the following excerpt from that work, he discusses* Fors Clavigera.]

Of all that Ruskin wrote in the last two decades of his career, nothing is stranger, more chaotic, yet more essentially the expression of his genius than *Fors Clavigera.* It is like no other book in our literature, and perhaps should not be called a book at all, but the diary of a nobly gifted mind, disturbed but not deceived by its sickness.

Written in the form of *Letters to the Workmen and Labourers of Great Britain, Fors* was published monthly from 1871 until Ruskin's breakdown in 1878; thereafter publication was intermittent, the series ending with the Christmas letter of 1884. The dates are revealing, for they almost exactly parallel the years of Ruskin's activity at Oxford and suggest that *Fors* was written in part as a guilty reaction to his work as Professor of Fine Art. Within a year of his inaugural lecture, he published the first issue of *Fors;* the last appeared on the eve of his final resignation from Oxford. Only then, it seems, did he feel free to give himself to the pleasing labor of *Praeterita.*

Ruskin's old, anxious conflict between the study of art and the reformation of society, between self-indulgence and self-sacrifice, persisted throughout his Oxford years: "I began the writing of *Fors,*" he explained in one of the letters, "as a bywork to quiet *my* conscience, that I might be happy in . . . my own proper life of Art-teaching, at Oxford and elsewhere; and, through my own happiness, rightly help others." But his conscience would not be stilled; for fourteen years the bywork was the central achievement of his life.

Fors is first and most simply an anatomy of the folly, ugliness, and brutality of the age. Its 600,000 words record Ruskin's lonely pilgrimage through Europe and his cry of *nausée* at the desolation and horror of the entire earthly city. *Fors* is also the diary of an inner despair, a private wasteland of the spirit. There are letters which, in the magnitude of their isolation, open out upon a terrifying night of the soul. Reading them, as

Cardinal Manning phrased it, is like listening to the beating of one's heart in a nightmare.

The image is perfect, for it conveys not only the peculiar loneliness of *Fors* but its almost frightening immediacy. Ruskin is at once closer to his reader in *Fors,* yet more alienated from the world he describes, than in any other of his books. As his hold on reality became more tenuous, his style became more intimate, until on the pages of *Fors* one seems to touch the lineaments of thought itself without the intervening medium of words. Rich in all the intonations of the spoken voice, capable almost of physical gesture, the letters are even more immediate than speech; one is less aware of the rhythms of the voice than of the pulse of thought—that scarcely audible and most complex of all musics, the music of consciousness itself.

Ruskin's thought is so rapid, so various, yet so intense that each sentence is charged with a vitality of its own. The cry of a fig-vendor outside Ruskin's rooms in Venice, faces in a railway carriage, a little girl spinning a top on a street in Oxford, an infant left to freeze in the snow, newspaper accounts of weddings, murders, banquets, wars—these make up the tableaux of topical trivia and monstrousness which give *Fors* its insistent actuality. Yet if *Fors* is the most topical of Ruskin's books, it is also the most timeless. Its surface reality, always shifting yet startlingly clear, is absorbed into the larger, fixed reality of Ruskin's isolation. And, like Ruskin, we are the observers of a spectacle which is utterly engrossing but from which we are utterly apart. This being entrapped in a world which we can see and touch but not enter gives the book its obsessive quality, its peculiar suspension of time and absence of motion. The external world is less real than the mind which describes it, and which lies open and animate before us.

Because the letters were written in the haste of the moment's mood, they are devoid of all formal decorum and are as varied in tone as they are in subject. Trivial or violent, fantastic or momentous, they are in the strictest sense letters and, like all good letters, are profoundly personal. Yet the reader is never quite certain to whom they are addressed. Several appeal directly to the "Workmen and Labourers" of Great Britain to join Ruskin's Guild of St. George. The affairs of the Guild, the plans and perplexities of its "Master," form a kind of leitmotif loosely connecting the letters. Others, with their exegeses of the Bible, Dante, and *Dame Wiggins of Lee,* their digressions on Ruskin's childhood and the growth of snails, have as little to do with Ruskin's workmen or their Guild as do the habits of the humblebee, which he charmingly describes in the fifty-first letter.

Certain letters seem to arise from nowhere and lead nowhere, but capture with a fixed intensity some isolated moment of feeling or vision. *Fors* was written as much to arrest these moments, to transmit them whole from Ruskin's to the reader's mind, as to propound a scheme of social reform. "The solitude at last became too great to be endured," he wrote in *Fors* of the cause of his madness. Much earlier in the letters he had abandoned his customary salutation—"My friends"—and had ceased to sign his name at their close. Yet, he told his readers, "you will probably know whom they come from, and I don't in the least care whom they go to." He did not care because self-expression for its own sake had become a vital condition of his being, and it was far more imperative for him that the letters be written than that they be read. His anonymity was the sign of his own estrangement; yet he could no more cease writing the letters than refrain from noting in his diary the blank or hostile faces which passed him in the streets. *Fors*

was his last link with a communicable world before the solitude became too great to be endured.

Ruskin's fear of that final solitude is the subject of the great Christmas letter of 1874. It opens with a quietly ironic account of the progress of St. George's Guild. The few subscriptions he received during the years of his mendicancy, Ruskin writes, might have disappointed him if he had anticipated a sudden acceptance of his scheme for achieving national felicity. But he is content to amuse himself with his stones and pictures, and can ignore for a time the distress and disease all around him. Such even-tempered obliviousness is, after all, what most people call "rational," and he must fight steadily to keep himself out of Hanwell or Bedlam.

He is not surprised at his readers' shyness in joining the Guild, for he himself has had little success in charitably administering his funds. He tried to purify one of the polluted springs of the River Wandel, but instead of taking care of itself when once clean, the spring required "continual looking after, like a child getting into a mess." Similarly, he was forced to abandon his efforts to keep a street ideally clean in the heart of the St. Giles slums, for he could not attend to all the sweeping himself, and the crew of crossing-sweeps he employed was headed, alas, by a rogue. He next set up a tea shop in Paddington Street to supply the poor with an unadulterated product at reasonable prices. But since he would not compete with the neighboring tradesmen in false advertising and for months could not decide upon the proper coloring for his sign, "Mr. Ruskin's tea-shop" languished, along with the two old servants of his mother who sold the tea in his employ.

Ruskin's tone of self-mockery, his deliberate affectation or helpless display of folly, leave the reader at a loss whether to admire his eccentric benevolences or pity their absurdity. We wish that he were more clearly sane—or insane—and are forced to wonder if his folly might not be wisdom and our own sanity a species of madness. He raises the question himself by pointing to the delicacy of the distinction implied by those on either side of "that long wall at Hanwell," and asking, "Does it never occur to me . . . that I may be mad myself?"

"I am so alone now in my thoughts and ways," he answers, "that if I am not mad, I should soon become so, from mere solitude, but for *my* work." It is a hard time for all men's wits, for those who know the truth "are like to go mad from isolation; and the fools are all going mad in 'Schwärmerei' [Rosenberg explains in a footnote that "Ruskin uses the word in Carlyle's sense of fanatical enthusiasms blindly shared by the masses."]—only that is much the pleasanter way." It is pleasant madness for Lord Macaulay, for instance, in whose eyes we are giants of intellect "compared to the pigmies of Bacon's time, and the minor pigmies of Christ's time . . . the microscopic pigmies of Solomon's time, and, finally, the vermicular and infusorial pigmies—twenty-three millions to the cube inch—of Mr. Darwin's time!"

The tone of the letter has shifted from the muted ironies Ruskin had directed against himself at its opening to the sharper thrusts which he directs at the fools surrounding him. Then, in one of the climactic paragraphs of *Fors,* he drops the mask of the ironist and writes as a voice in the wilderness, crying out in the agony of his isolation and raging at the horror of an alien world:

> But for us of the old race—few of us now
> left,—children who reverence our fathers, and
> are ashamed of ourselves; comfortless enough

in that shame, and yearning for one word or glance from the graves of old, yet knowing ourselves to be of the same blood, and recognizing in our hearts the same passions, with the ancient masters of humanity;—we, who feel as men, and not as carnivorous worms; we, who are every day recognizing some inaccessible height of thought and power, and are miserable in our shortcomings,—the few of us now standing here and there, alone, in the midst of this yelping, carnivorous crowd, mad for money and lust, tearing each other to pieces, and starving each other to death, and leaving heaps of their dung and ponds of their spittle on every palace floor and altar stone,—it is impossible for us, except in the labour of our hands, not to go mad.

Throughout *Fors* there is something diseased in the very vigor and incontinence of the invective. Ruskin repeatedly fails in his resolve to keep from mounting the "Cathedra Pestilentiae," the seat of the scornful, from which, as Carlyle phrased it, he poured "fierce lightning-bolts . . . into the black world of Anarchy all around him." The British are a nation of "thieves and murderers . . . a mere heap of agonizing human maggots, scrambling and sprawling over each other for any manner of rotten eatable thing they can get a bite of." Their Parliament is a place of "havoc and loosed dogs of war," their press so many square leagues of "dirtily printed falsehood," their politics "a mad-dog's creed," their populace a "rotten mob of money-begotten traitors," their clergy sellers "of a false gospel for hire." Britannia herself, Empress of the Seas, is a "slimy polype, multiplying by involuntary vivisection, and dropping half putrid pieces of itself wherever it crawls or contracts."

Despite their ferocity, passages like these reflect the delight Ruskin took in the sheer exuberance and virtuosity of his invective. To be sure, it was a perilous pleasure which exacerbated the very irritability he fought to control. "Sun set clear," he wrote in his diary: "I knelt down to pray that it might not go down on my wrath." The "wild and whirling words" of *Fors* bear witness to his lost battles and are signs of the same pathological fury which disfigures *Mornings in Florence* and *St. Mark's Rest*. But if they are the symptoms of Ruskin's imbalance, they are as well a sort of self-administered therapy. "I don't *anger* my soul," he told a reader of *Fors,* "I relieve it, by all violent language. . . . I *live* in chronic fury . . . only to be at all relieved in its bad fits by studied expression."

The relief Ruskin derived from violent language he also found in the wild inconsequence of wit. He affected the very madness which he feared, assuming an antic disposition in order to say in seeming jest what no man could say in earnest and still be thought sane. "If I took off the Harlequin's mask for a moment," he tells his readers, "you would say I was simply mad." Ruskin's stratagem is Hamlet's stratagem, born of the same fear and cloaking the same inner bafflement. Indeed, the mind which animates *Fors* is as swift and subtle as Hamlet's, yet as tempestuous as Lear's and as wayward as the Fool's. Ruskin is never more himself in *Fors* than when he seems to speak through the mouth of the Fool, whose wisdom and charity underscore our own brute folly. Such is the method behind his madness when, after some seventy letters indicting the inhumanity of man, he tells his working-class readers that if they wish to become true gentlemen, they must first be the kindly servants of beasts:

To all good and sane men and beasts, be true brother; and as it is best, perhaps, to begin with all things in the lowest place, begin with true brotherhood to the beast: in pure simplicity of practical help, I should like a squad of you to stand always harnessed, at the bottom of any hills you know of in Sheffield,—where the horses strain;—ready there at given hours; carts ordered not to pass at any others: at the low level, hook yourselves on before the horses; pull them up too, if need be; and dismiss them at the top with a pat and a mouthful of hay. Here's a beginning of chivalry, and gentlemanly life for you, my masters.

A pat and a mouthful of hay, my masters. . . . The tone is perfect; again one hears echoes of the Fool, alone with his abused master and the pilloried Kent, diverting them with the tale of the fellow who out of pure kindness buttered his horse's hay.

Both the outrage and the anguish of *Fors* would have been too oppressive were it not for such sudden, startling shifts of tone. Ruskin's account of himself standing alone amidst a carnivorous crowd is immediately followed by his description of a dimpled, contented pig, feeding on a mess of ambrosial rottenness, with whom he would fain change places. The letter which contains his portrait of Britannia as a putrid polyp begins with an elaborate recipe for Yorkshire Goose Pie. The vegetable soup on which Theseus feasted upon his return to Athens figures in half a dozen letters and, along with like trivia, serves as a bizarre leitmotif relieving the tension of the letters and grounding them in an antic yet earthy actuality.

Sometimes Ruskin's effect defies analysis, for it lies on that border between oppositely charged emotions where laughter is indistinguishable from tears. This is the note he strikes in one of his letters from Venice, written on his balcony at the Ca' Ferro overlooking the Grand Canal. Between the shafts of the palace window

the morning sky is seen pure and pale, relieving the grey dome of the church of the Salute; but beside that vault, and like it, vast thunderclouds heap themselves above the horizon . . . all so massive, that half-an-hour ago, in the dawn, I scarcely knew the Salute dome and towers from theirs; while the sea-gulls, rising and falling hither and thither in clusters above the green water beyond my balcony, tell me that the south wind is wild on Adria.

He has beside him a little cockle-shell, which he would like to draw and describe in peace. This is his proper business, his good friends tell him, yet he cannot mind it and be happy. It would please his friends and himself if he went on living in his Venetian palace, "luxurious, scrutinant of dome, cloud, and cockle-shell." He could do so by selling his books for large sums, if he chose to bribe the reviewers, stick bills on lampposts, and say nothing displeasing to the bishops of England:

But alas! my prudent friends, little enough of all that I have a mind to may be permitted me. For this green tide that eddies by my threshold is full of floating corpses, and I must leave my dinner to bury them, since I cannot save; and

put my cockle-shell in cap, and take my staff
in hand, to seek an unencumbered shore.

The tide of floating corpses would strike us as merely mad, as
some grotesque apparition, were it not for the banter about
cockle-shells and bill-stickings which immediately precedes it.
Instead the green tide emerges as the perfect symbol of Ruskin's
guilt over the wretchedness of the world beyond the purview
of his palace. Even so, the image retains an almost hallucinatory power, at once muted and enriched with echoes from
the mad Ophelia's song:

> . . . By his cockle hat and staff
> And his sandal shoon.

With touches as deft as this Ruskin sustains his antic progress
through *Fors,* bearing the cockle cap and staff of the solitary
pilgrim, and not unwilling to exchange the pilgrim's cap for
that of the fool.

One mark of Ruskin's folly throughout *Fors* is his reckless and
absolute candor. Perhaps because he cared so deeply for his
ideas, he cared not at all for the figure he cut while advocating
them. "I neither wish to please, nor displease you; but to
provoke you to think," he told those readers who complained
that he wrote of things which little concerned them in words
they could not easily understand. Remarkably personal, the
letters are no less remarkably disinterested. They express the
idiosyncrasies, obsessions, tastes, and distastes of a man who
is simply and guilelessly the center of his own universe; yet
they are so unremittingly sincere, so devoid of posturing or
illusion, that the term subjective simply does not apply. Perhaps
because we habitually associate the objective with the impersonal, we cannot comprehend a mind which is at once so
passionately disinterested, yet so passionately itself. Certain
passages in *Fors* are almost frightening in their illusionlessness,
in that quality of detachment we associate with the Olympians
or the dead. Such, for instance, is the letter which opens with
a note from a young lady who had written to Ruskin of the
"wicked things" people were saying about him:

> They say you are "unreasoning," "intolerably
> conceited," "self-asserting"; that you write
> about what you have no knowledge of (Politic.
> Econ.); and two or three have positively as-
> serted, and tried to persuade me, that you are
> mad—really mad!! They make me so angry, I
> don't know what to do with myself.

To which he could in truth reply:

> Indeed, my dear, it is precisely because . . .
> the message that I have brought is not mine,
> that they are thus malignant against me for
> bringing it. "For this is the message that ye
> have heard from the beginning, that we should
> love one another."

In defiance of this message, modern society had become in
Ruskin's eyes a monstrous contrivance for defrauding one's
neighbor and turning the fruitful garden of earth into a wasteland. His road mendings and street sweepings, his lectures and
books had not perceptibly altered the face of England or the
hearts of its inhabitants. And so, using *Fors* as his sounding
board, he set out singlehandedly to rebuild Jerusalem in England's once green and pleasant land. Would any of his readers
join him in giving a tenth of their wealth for the purchase of
land which would be cultivated by hand, aided only by the
force of wind or wave? The fund would not be an investment

but a "frank and simple gift to the British people . . . to be
spent in dressing the earth and keeping it,—in feeding human
lips,—in clothing human bodies,—in kindling human souls."
Its work would begin modestly enough, perhaps in a few poor
men's gardens:

> We will try to take some small piece of English
> ground, beautiful, peaceful, and fruitful. We
> will have no steam-engines upon it, and no
> railroads; we will have no untended or un-
> thought-of creatures on it; none wretched, but
> the sick; none idle but the dead. We will have
> no liberty upon it; but instant obedience to known
> law, and appointed persons: no equality upon
> it; but recognition of every betterness that we
> can find, and reprobation of every worse-
> ness. . . . We will have plenty . . . of corn and
> grass in our fields,—and few bricks. We will
> have some music and poetry; the children shall
> learn to dance to it and sing it. . . . We will
> have some art, moreover; we will at least try
> if, like the Greeks, we can't make some pots
> [with pictures of] butterflies, and frogs, if noth-
> ing better. . . . Little by little, some higher art
> and imagination may manifest themselves among
> us; and feeble rays of science may dawn for
> us. . . . nay—even perhaps an uncalculating and
> uncovetous wisdom, as of rude Magi, present-
> ing, at such nativity, gifts of gold and frankin-
> cense.

(pp. 186-96)

A quarter of a century earlier Ruskin had tried to reform England by replacing the coiling smoke of her cities with the
spires of Gothic cathedrals. He had no illusions about his failure. But he never abandoned his vision of a pre-industrial
England purged of smoke, *laissez faire,* and the New Poor
Houses. The St. George's Guild was his final, futile attempt
to realize this vision, to revive not a medieval style but a
medieval society, with a feudal peasantry as loyal as the servants in his father's household, and lords as filled with *noblesse
oblige* as Ruskin himself. Victorian England could no more
have fed and clothed itself according to his principles than the
inhabitants of William Morris's pastoral utopia could have
subsisted in their machineless paradise. *Fors Clavigera,* and
not St. George's Guild, is the only worthy monument to his
broken and fantastic labors of the 1870s. (pp. 198-99)

> *John D. Rosenberg, in his* The Darkening Glass: A
> Portrait of Ruskin's Genius, *Columbia University
> Press, 1961, 274 p.*

HAROLD BLOOM   (essay date 1965)

[*Bloom is one of the most prominent contemporary American
critics and literary theorists. In* The Anxiety of Influence *(1973),
Bloom formulated a controversial theory of literary creation called
revisionism. Influenced strongly by Freudian theory, which states
that "all men unconsciously wish to beget themselves, to be their
own fathers," Bloom believes that all poets are subject to the
influence of earlier poets and that, to develop their own voice,
they attempt to overcome this influence through a process of
misreading. By misreading, Bloom means a deliberate, personal
revision of what has been said by another so that it conforms to
one's own vision: "Poetic influence—when it involves two strong,
authentic poets—always proceeds by a misreading of the prior
poet, an act of creative correction that is actually and necessarily
a misrepresentation. The history of poetic influence . . . is a his-*

John Ruskin of Glenfinlas *by John Everett Millais, 1853.*

tory of anxiety and self-serving caricature, of distortion, of perverse, wilful revisionism." In this way the poet creates a singular voice, overcoming the fear of being inferior to poetic predecessors. Bloom's later books are applications of this theory, extended in Kabbalah and Criticism *(1974) to include the critic or reader as another deliberate misreader. Thus, there is no single reading of any text, but multiple readings by strong poets or critics who understand a work only in ways that allow them to assert their own individuality or vision. In addition to his theoretical work, Bloom is one of the foremost authorities on English Romantic poetry and has written widely on the influence of Romanticism upon contemporary literature. In the following excerpt, originally published in 1965 as an introduction to* The Literary Criticism of John Ruskin, *he discusses Ruskin's literary criticism.*]

There are three major areas of Ruskin's achievement: art, social, and literary criticism, and this essay is wholly devoted to only one of the three. I have allowed myself a broad interpretation of "literary criticism," since Ruskin is very much an anticipatory critic in regard to some schools of literary criticism in our own time. Ruskin is one of the first, if not indeed the first, "myth" or "archetypal" critic, or more properly he is the linking and transitional figure between allegorical critics of the elder, Renaissance kind, and those of the newer variety, like Northrop Frye, or like W. B. Yeats in his criticism. Even if he did not have this unique historical position, Ruskin would stand as one of the handful of major literary critics in nineteenth-century England, though his importance has been obscured by misapprehensions about his work. Most histories of literary criticism tag Ruskin as a "moral" critic which is true only in Ruskin's own terms, but not at all in conventional ones. An Oxford lecture delivered by him in 1870 makes clear the special sense in which Ruskin insists upon the morality of art:

> You must first have the right moral state, or you cannot have art. But when the art is once obtained, its reflected action enhances and completes the moral state out of which it arose, and, above all, communicates the exultation to other minds which are already morally capable of the like. For instance take the art of singing, and the simplest perfect master of it—the skylark. From him you may learn what it is to sing for joy. You must get the moral state first, the pure gladness, then give it finished expression, and it is perfected in itself, and made communicable to others capable of such joy. Accuracy in proportion to the rightness of the cause, and purity of the emotion, is the possibility of fine art. You cannot paint or sing yourself into being good men; you must be good men before you can either paint or sing, and then the colour and sound will complete in you all that is best . . .

In this passage the "right moral state" and "being good men" are phrases that suggest conventional moral attitudes, yet the only moral state mentioned is that of the skylark, "the pure gladness." Behind Ruskin's passage are Wordsworth and Shelley, both in their skylark poems, and in their insistence upon the poet's joy and on poems as necessarily recording the best and happiest moments of the happiest and best minds. Ruskin's literary theory is primarily a Wordsworthian one, and as such it shows a family resemblance to all such theories down to Wallace Stevens, with his eloquent, Paterian insistence that "the morality of the poet's radiant and productive atmosphere is the morality of the right sensation." Ruskin's morality, as a critical theorist, is a morality of aesthetic contemplation, like the morality of *Tintern Abbey*. It is not, in content, an Evangelical morality, though its fervor stamps it as a displaced version of Evangelicism. Ruskin's literary criticism has an explicit moral purpose, as Wordsworth's poetry does also, yet the purpose no more disfigures the criticism than it does the poetry. To understand Ruskin's criticism we need to study not only the pattern of Ruskin's life and career, but also the radical version of Romanticism his entire sensibility incarnated. Literary criticism rarely communicates the critic's own *experience* of literature, but in Ruskin's hands it very nearly always does, and in doing so touches upon the incommunicable. Ruskin did not believe that the imagination could create truth, but he did believe that it was the crucial faculty for the communication and interpretation of truth. Though Ruskin's judgment as a critic was fairly unsteady (he once declared Mrs. Browning's *Aurora Leigh* to be the greatest poem in the language), his central aesthetic experience was so powerful as to make him an almost miraculous medium for the truth of imagination to work through in order to reach sensibilities less uniquely organized than his own. In this respect, as in so many others, he resembles Wordsworth. Thus, speaking of Gothic as being representative of our universal childhood, Ruskin observes that all men:

> look back to the days of childhood as of greatest happiness, because those were the days of greatest wonder, greatest simplicity, and most vigorous imagination. And the whole difference between a man of genius and other men . . . is that the first remains in great part a child, seeing with the large eyes of children, in perpetual wonder, not conscious of much knowledge,—conscious, rather, of infinite ignorance,

and yet infinite power; a fountain of eternal admiration, delight, and creative force within him, meeting the ocean of visible and governable things around him.

If this is the source of creative imagination, it follows tragically but pragmatically that the workings of the mature imagination must be compensatory, for the story of art must be one in which gain can come only through loss, and the subsequent memory of the glorious time preceding loss. This pattern is familiar to every reader of Wordsworth, and is nowhere more eloquently expressed than it is by Ruskin. In a letter (28 September 1847) written to Walter Brown, once his tutor at Christ Church, Ruskin states the central experience of his life in phrases directly borrowed from the *Intimations* Ode:

> . . . there was a time when the sight of a steep hill covered with pines cutting against blue sky, would have touched me with an emotion inexpressible, which, in the endeavour to communicate in its truth and intensity, I must have sought for all kinds of far-off, wild, and dreamy images. Now I can look at such a slope with coolness, and observation of *fact*. I see that it slopes at twenty or twenty-five degrees; I know the pines are spruce fir—"Pinus nigra"—of such and such a formation; the soil, thus, and thus; the day fine and the sky blue. All this I can at once communicate in so many words, and this is all which is necessarily seen. But it is not all the truth: there is something else to be seen there, which I cannot see but in a certain condition of mind, nor can I make anyone else see it, but by putting him into that condition, and my endeavour in description would be, not to detail the facts of the scene, but by any means whatsoever to put my hearer's mind into the same ferment as my mind . . .

Ruskin's activity as a critic of all the arts, of society, and of nature, is a quest to fulfill that "endeavour in description." What makes him a tragic critic (if so odd a phrase may be allowed) is his post-Wordsworthian and post-Turnerian sense of reality. In reply to Walter Brown's Wordsworthian statement of recompense for a loss of primal delight in nature, Ruskin wrote a letter (27 November 1847) which is an epilogue to the *Intimations* Ode:

> . . . You say, in losing the delight I once had in nature I am coming down more to fellowship with others. Yes, but I feel it a fellowship of blindness. I may be able to get hold of people's hands better in the dark, but of what use is that, when I have no where to lead them but into the ditch? Surely, devoid of these imaginations and impressions, the world becomes a mere board-and-lodging house. The sea by whose side I am writing was once to me a friend, companion, master, teacher; now it is *salt water,* and salt water only. Is this an increase or a withdrawal of *truth*? I did not before lose hold or sight of the fact of its being salt water; I could consider it so, if I chose; my perceiving and feeling it to be more than this was a possession of higher *truth,* which did not interfere with my hold of the physical one.

This sense of loss haunts Ruskin's criticism, until at last it becomes the apocalyptic desire of his later works, from *Modern Painters V* . . . on to *Praeterita.* . . . Kenneth Clark has said, very accurately, that Ruskin was by nature an impressionist, to which one can add that an apocalyptic impressionist is a very strange being; it is difficult to conceive of Revelation as Proust would have written it, yet that is what the prophetic Ruskin gives us. Ruskin remained true to Wordsworth and Turner in being interested primarily in *appearances,* and in taking those appearances as final realities. Yet Wordsworth learned how to evade the apocalyptic element even in the sublime modes of poetry, and Turner, like Keats, thought the earth and the sun to be enough. If there is a central meaning to Ruskin's great change about 1860, it is that his movement from description to prophecy refused to abandon the external world or the arts that he had learned to scrutinize so accurately. Instead Ruskin demanded more from both nature and art than even he had asked earlier, and so made more terrible the process of loss his sensibility had made inevitable. The Ruskin of the Storm Cloud [the later years of mental illness] is what Wordsworth would have been, had he allowed his characteristic dialectic of love between man and nature to survive, unchanged, the crisis of 1805, out of which *Peele Castle* was written as palinode.

This is the terrible pathos of Ruskin's art as a critic, that no one else has had so intense an intimation of loss within the imaginative experience itself. Remembering the vision that was his as a child, Ruskin could say that "for me, the Alps and their people were alike beautiful in their snow, and their humanity; and I wanted, neither for them nor myself, sight of any thrones in heaven but the rocks, or of any spirits in heaven but the clouds." This primary humanism never left Ruskin, as it did finally leave the older Wordsworth. What preserved it in Ruskin was the greater purity of his own Wordsworthianism; like the poet John Clare, he excelled Wordsworth as a visionary, and *saw* constantly what the greater poet could see only by glimpses:

> . . . My entire delight was in observing without being myself noticed,—if I could have been invisible, all the better. I was absolutely interested in men and their ways, as I was interested in marmots and chamois, in tomtits and trout. If only they would stay still and let me look at them, and not get into their holes and up their heights! The living inhabitation of the world—the grazing and nesting in it,—the spiritual power of the air, the rocks, the waters, to be in the midst of it, and rejoice and wonder at it, and help it if I could,—happier if it needed no help of mine,—this was the essential love of *Nature* in me, this the root of all that I have usefully become, and the light of all that I have rightly learned.

If we call Ruskin's view of nature or of the self a mythical one, we need to qualify the classification, as Ruskin scarcely believed his view of either to be the product of his own creative powers. Wordsworth, and most of the Romantics after him, sought continuity between the earlier and the future self even at the expense of present time; Wordsworth indeed is mute in the face of nature at the living moment. Ruskin, like Blake, celebrated the pulsation of an artery, the flash of apprehension in which the poet's work is done. And, again like Blake, Ruskin placed his emphasis on *seeing* as the special mark of imagination. For Ruskin, unlike Wordsworth, the deepest imaginative effects are connected with the finite phenomena of nature, and the minute particulars of artistic detail. Wordsworth valued most highly in poetry "those passages where things are lost in each other, and limits vanish," but Ruskin, regarding art or nature, never ceased to see firm, determinate outlines, and every subtlety of detail. Ruskin, unlike Wordsworth, would not sacrifice either the landscape or the moment to the quest for continuity. Wordsworth's rewards for such sacrifices were immense, as Ruskin well knew, for no other writer has felt or made others feel so great a sense of the renewal of the past in the present, through the renovating influence of nature. Ruskin was an extraordinary psychologist, though a largely involuntary one, and did not believe that the therapy for an individual consciousness could come largely through a pursuit of after-images. Yet he wished to believe this, frequently wrote in the Wordsworthian mode, and achieved his final, autobiographical vision and last broken intervals of lucidity primarily through following Wordsworth's example, by tracing the growth of his own imagination. If Ruskin became one of the ruins of Romanticism, and even one of its victims, he became also one of its unique masters, who could justify asserting that "the greatest thing a human soul ever does in this world is to see something, and tell what it saw in a plain way. Hundreds of people can talk for one who can think, but thousands can think for one who can see. To see clearly is poetry, prophecy and religion all in one." Yet to see clearly was finally no salvation for Ruskin, but only gave him a maddening sense of loss, in the self and in nature alike.

Ruskin never gave up insisting that all art, literature included, was worship, but this insistence does not make him either a "religious" or a "moral" critic of literature. Though he moved in outward religion from Evangelical Protestantism to agnostic naturalism and on finally to a private version of primitive Catholicism, Ruskin's pragmatic religion always remained a Wordsworthian "natural piety," in which aesthetic and spiritual experience were not to be distinguished from one another. Ruskin's literary taste was formed by the King James Bible, more than any other reading, and therefore from the start he associated expressive and devotional values. In this also he stands with the great Romantics, whose theories of the Imagination are all displaced, radical Protestant accounts of the nakedness of the soul before God.

Ruskin's own theory of the Imagination is clearly derived from Coleridge's, and it has been argued that all Ruskin adds to his master's account is a multiplication of unnecessary entities. Yet Ruskin does add to Coleridge's theory a confidence in the autonomy of the imagination that Coleridge himself never possessed. Indeed it is Coleridge whose criticism is distorted by the claims of conventional morality and institutional religion, and not Ruskin. Ruskin could not have written "that it has pleased Providence, that the divine truths of religion should have been revealed to us *in the form of* poetry" (italics mine) or that "an undevout poet is mad: in the strict sense of the word, an undevout poet is an impossibility." Because he lacked Coleridge's doubts, Ruskin allowed himself to elaborate upon Coleridge's categories, there being no point at which he felt the imagination had to yield to a higher or more assured faculty. If these elaborations have failed to be influential, they yet remain interesting in themselves and indicate where a less inhibited Romantic theory of Imagination may still quarry for its materials.

Fundamentally Ruskin favored two groups of poets, those like Dante, Spenser, Milton, and Wordsworth who dealt in detail with the whole destiny of man, from creation to apocalypse, and those he had loved in his own youth, like Scott and Byron. It is in the first that Ruskin's great strength as a critic lies, since he is given to special pleading for his childhood favorites. But there is an honorable place for special pleading in criticism, if it is done with the eloquent passion and exquisite discrimination of a Ruskin.

It is in his examination of the larger outlines of the structure of literature that Ruskin appears today to have been a major critical innovator. Because of his intimate knowledge of biblical and classical iconology, and of Dante, Spenser, and Milton as the heirs of such iconology, Ruskin arrived at a comprehensive theory of literature, which he never made fully explicit but which is evident throughout his criticism. One major assumption of this theory is that all great poetry whatsoever is allegorical; and that what it allegorizes is a fundamental myth of universal man, his fall from Paradise and his quest for a revelation that would restore him to Paradise. This myth is clearest in the Ruskin of the 1860s, of *The Queen of the Air,* and of *Sesame and Lilies.*

Though it is an obsession in the later Ruskin, a consciousness of this myth was always present in his criticism, since he relied from the start on a Wordsworthian experience of paradisal intimations within a wholly natural context. The Wordsworthian principle of continuity and dialectic of love between man and nature were generalized by the older Ruskin into the universal figures he had encountered in his early journeys from Genesis to Revelation. The symbols of *Modern Painters V, Munera Pulveris, Sesame and Lilies,* and *The Queen of the Air* are primarily biblical ones, even when Ruskin investigates the many guises of Athena in the elaborate mythologizings of *The Queen of the Air.* The Garden of Eden, the Serpent or Dragon, the unfallen maiden who replaces Mother Eve and becomes the prime hope of salvation; these are for Ruskin the principal figures in a mythopoeic fantasia of his own, which is almost too available for psychoanalytical reduction, of the kind to which Ruskin is generally subjected in our time. When, in *The Queen of the Air,* this fantasia is mixed with extraordinary excursions into botany, political economy, and primordial folklore, the result demands a reader more exuberant than most Ruskin scholars have been.

The Queen of the Air, in one of its aspects, resembles some works of Elizabethan mythography like Henry Reynolds' *Mythomystes,* but an even closer parallel can be found in Blake's poetry and prose. Like Ruskin, Blake counterpoints both classical and biblical myth against an imaginative story of his own, which in itself is a deliberate modification of Milton's accounts of Fall and Redemption. Ruskin does not seem to invent "Giant Forms" or titanic personages, as Blake does, but he invents and explores states-of-being in a manner very similar to Blake's, though he does not give them Blake's kind of categorical names. Ruskin's Athena is finally a goddess of his own creation, and as such she is one of the major myth-makings of the Victorian age.

Ruskin's earlier, and more Wordsworthian literary criticism, is dominated by the problem of landscape, in the same way that his later criticism centers on typological figures of redemption. *Modern Painters III* . . . contains Ruskin's principal achievement as a literary critic before he entered upon his own mythical phase, but it is an achievement that has been misunderstood, partly because Ruskin's famous formulation of the Pathetic Fallacy has been misinterpreted. The theory of the Pathetic Fallacy is a searching criticism of Romanticism from within, for the sake of saving the Romantic program of humanizing nature from extinction through excessive self-indulgence. Ruskin is the first writer within the Romantic tradition to have realized the high spiritual price that had to be paid for Wordsworthianism, the human loss that accompanied the "abundant recompense" celebrated in *Tintern Abbey.*

Ruskin was, more so even than most artists and critics, a kind of natural phenomenologist, to use a term now in fashion, or simply, a man to whom things spoke, and who spent his life describing "the ordinary, proper, and true appearances of things to us." Ruskin knew that, as man and artist, his debts and affinities were to what he called the second order of poets, the "Reflective or Perceptive" group (Wordsworth, Keats, Tennyson) and not to the first order, the "Creative" group (Shakespeare, Homer, Dante). Ruskin's purpose in expounding the Pathetic Fallacy, which characterizes the second order, is not to discredit the Wordsworthian kind of poetry, but to indicate its crucial limitation, which he knew himself to share.

Wordsworth and his followers present states of mind that "produce in us a falseness in all our impressions of external things." A. H. R. Ball, the most sympathetic student of Ruskin's literary criticism, was convinced that the theory of the Pathetic Fallacy contradicted Ruskin's own imaginative theory, which may be true, but the contradiction, if it exists, is only a seeming one. Ruskin understood that Romantic poetry, and its imaginative theory, were grounded upon the Pathetic Fallacy, the imputation of life to the object-world. To believe that there is the one life only, within us and abroad, was to heal the Enlightenment's split in consciousness between adverting mind and the universe of things, but at the price that the intuitive phenomenologist in Ruskin understood and resented. The myth of continuity, in Wordsworth and in his followers, Ruskin included, is the result of a homogeneity of sense-experience, which can result only from reduction. The psychiatrist J. H. Van den Berg, in his fascinating study, *Metabletica,* traces this reduction to Descartes, who saw objects as localized space, extensiveness. Wordsworth's quest was to find a way out of all dualisms, Cartesian included, but ironically Wordsworth and his school followed Descartes, unknowingly, in reducing the present to an elaborated past, and making the future also only a consequence of the past. Ruskin's formulation of the Pathetic Fallacy is a profound protest against nineteenh-century homogeneities, particularly landscape homogeneities. It is perhaps sour wit, but it seems true to remark that Wordsworth could see only landscapes that he had seen before, and that no landscape became visible to him that he had not first estranged from himself.

Ruskin's protest is against this estrangement of things, and against the Romantic delight in seeing a reduction, and then elevating that reduction to the ecstasy of enforced humanization. Van den Berg remarks somberly that the Romantic inner self became necessary when contacts between man and the external world became less valued. Ruskin's rejection of Romantic mythopoeia as the Pathetic Fallacy shows a similar distrust of Wordsworthian self-consciousness, but the later Ruskin put such distrust aside, and became the major Romantic mythmaker of the Victorian era. The aesthetic tragedy of Ruskin is that works like *Sesame and Lilies* and *The Queen of the Air* are giant Pathetic Fallacies, but the mingled grandeur and ruin of those books only make them still more representative of post-Romantic art, and its central dilemma. Ruskin may yet seem the major and most original critic that Romanticism has produced, as well as one of its most celebrated avatars. (pp. 174-83)

Harold Bloom, "Ruskin as Literary Critic," in his The Ringers in the Tower: Studies in Romantic Tradition, *The University of Chicago Press, 1971, pp. 169-83.*

RICHARD ELLMANN (essay date 1968)

[*Ellmann is the author of the definitive biography of James Joyce. He has also written widely on early twentieth-century Irish literature, most notably on William Butler Yeats and Oscar Wilde. In the following excerpt, Ellmann discusses autobiographical elements in* The Stones of Venice.]

The Stones of Venice will always stand primarily as a work of art criticism. But criticism, as Wilde said, is the only civilized form of autobiography, and it is as a fragment—a large fragment—of Ruskin's autobiography that the book claims an added interest. In novels and poems we take for granted that some personal elements will be reflected, but in works of nonfiction we are more reluctant, and prefer to postulate an upper air of abstraction in which the dispassionate mind contemplates and orders materials that already have form and substance. Yet even the most impersonal of writers, Thucydides, writing about the fortunes of another city, shaped his events, as Cornford suggests, by preconceptions absorbed from Greek tragedy. Ruskin made no pretence of Thucydidean impersonality, and the influence of his reading of the Bible is manifest rather than latent. But some problems of his own life also were projected on to the Venetian scene. Rather than diminishing the book's value, they merge with its talent and add to its intensity.

It may be easier to be convinced that *The Stones of Venice* is in part autobiographical if we remember Ruskin's candid admission that *Sesame and Lilies,* a book he wrote a few years later, was a reflection of one particular experience. His preface expressly states that the section in it called 'Lilies' was generated by his love for Rose La Touche. This love impelled him to idealize women, he says, even though 'the chances of later life gave me opportunities of watching women in states of degradation and vindictiveness which opened to me the gloomiest secrets of Greek and Syrian tragedy. I have seen them betray their household charities to lust, their pledged love to devotion; I have seen mothers dutiful to their children, as Medea; and children dutiful to their parents, as the daughter of Herodias. . . .' His love for Rose La Touche also covertly leads him to quarrel in the book with pietism because Rose was that way inclined. *The Stones of Venice* dwells less obviously, but with the same insistence, on the virtues and defects of the feminine character. As Ruskin remarks in *Sesame and Lilies,* 'it has chanced to me, untowardly in some respects, fortunately in others (*because it enables me to read history more clearly*), to see the utmost evil that is in women. . . .' To Ruskin Venice is always *she* (to Mary McCarthy, invariably *it*), and the gender is not merely a form of speech but an image to be enforced in detail.

Accordingly Ruskin distinguishes two stages, with medieval Venice as virgin and Renaissance Venice as whore. The moment of transition is, apparently, the moment of copulation, and the moment of copulation is therefore (as in a familiar view of the Garden of Eden) the fall. When Ruskin describes the fallen state, he attributes to the city the very taste for masqued balls and merriment which he had ostentatiously tolerated in his wife. 'She became in after times', he declares, 'the revel of the earth, the masque of Italy: and *therefore* is she now desolate, but her glorious robe of gold and purple was given her when first she rose a vestal from the sea, not when she became drunk with the wine of her fornication.' At the end of the first volume he again asserts, 'It was when she wore the ephod of the priest, not the motley of the masquer, that the fire fell upon her from heaven. . . .' After that fire came another which changed the virgin city to its contrary:

> Now Venice, as she was once the most religious, was in her fall the most corrupt, of European states; and as she was in her strength the centre of the pure currents of Christian architecture, so she is in her decline the source of the Renaissance. It was the originality and splendour of the Palaces of Vicenza and Venice which gave this school its eminence in the eyes of Europe; and the dying city, magnificent in her dissipation, and graceful in her follies, obtained wider worship in her decrepitude than in her youth, and sank from the midst of her admirers into her grave.

Ruskin cannot bring himself to sketch out 'the steps of her final ruin. That ancient curse was upon her, the curse of the cities of the plain, "pride, fulness of bread, and abundance of idleness." By the inner burning of her own passions, as fatal as the fiery reign of Gomorrah, she was consumed from her place among the nations, and her ashes are choking the channels of the dead salt sea.' Just how passions should burn except inwardly may not be clear, especially since we can't suppose that Ruskin favoured the translation of sensual thought into sensual action, but pride, gluttony, and sloth secure a more sinister confederate in the unnameable sin of lust, whose self-generated fire is contrasted with that fire which had earlier fallen on the city from heaven.

Ruskin's stridency shows how much he had this problem at heart. In fact, consummation and defilement were irrevocably united for him, in his life as in his criticism. The Renaissance (a new term then but already favourable in its connotations) was for him not a rebirth but a relapse. (In *De Profundis* Wilde accepted this view.) Ruskin's revulsion extended from coupling to begetting to having been begot. He had more trouble than most people in allowing that he was himself the product of his parents' intercourse. A small indication is to be found in an epitaph which he wrote for his mother (who already had an epitaph) long after her death, consecrating a memorial well, as he writes, 'in memory of a maid's life as pure, and a mother's love as ceaseless. . . .' In Ruskin's mind his mother had immaculately passed from maid to mother without ever becoming a wife.

This singular epitaph may illuminate a point never adequately explained, why Ruskin dated the fall of Venice not only to an exact year, but to a specific day, 8 May 1418. His own explanation is that this was the death day of the aged Venetian military leader Carlo Zeno, and he makes his usual citation of Pierre Daru's *Histoire de la République de Venise* as his authority. But Daru doesn't give Zeno's death such consequence. Ruskin might more easily, and more consistently with his own views, have taken the year 1423, when the old Doge Tommaso Mocenigo died and the new Doge, Foscari, began his less glorious rule. He is alone among writers on Venice in attaching this significance to Zeno's death day, and in view of his known penchant for numerology the date invites attention. If Ruskin had been born exactly four hundred years after this date, in 1818, rather than in 1819, the choice might seem related to his theatrical self-laceration, as if to regret he had ever been born. But his terrors were for intercourse and conception rather

than for birth. I venture to propose that the date so carefully selected was, putatively, four hundred years to the day before his own conception—that act so impossible for him to meditate on with equanimity. That the moment of Venice's fall should be reiterated in the moment of his own begetting and be followed by his birth into an England only too ready (as he announces on the first page of his book) to fall—like a semi-detached Venice—anchored firmly the relationships Ruskin wished to dwell upon. In his parents' fall, as in that of our first parents, he saw the determination of an age's character and of his own.

Margaret Ruskin's marriage had made her a mother, while Effie Ruskin's 'dissolute' behaviour in Venice had made her—in fancy if not in fact—an adultress. Moral blame, from which his mother was freed, was shunted to his wife. Ruskin's own later summary of *The Stones of Venice* confirms that he had this theme in mind. In *The Crown of Wild Olive* . . . he wrote, '*The Stones of Venice* had, from beginning to end, no other aim than to show that the Renaissance architecture of Venice had arisen out of, and in all its features indicated, a state of concealed national infidelity, and of domestic corruption.' The trip to Scotland which Ruskin, his wife, and Millais took in 1853 strengthened the metaphors, and in later life he accused Millais of infidelity—artistic infidelity he called it—to the Pre-Raphaelite principles as Ruskin had earlier enunciated them. Venice, his wife, and his friend were all guilty of the same crime.

Necessary as Ruskin found it to think of himself as wronged, there were moments when he recognized his own culpability. After the annulment of his marriage he came, by a series of mental leaps, to try a revision of his character. In 1858, while looking at Veronese's *Solomon and Sheba* in Turin, he suddenly felt a wave of sympathy for the 'strong and frank animality' of the greatest artists. He disavowed his earlier religious zeal, and became (though at the urging of his father and of Rose La Touche's mother he didn't publicly say so) quite sceptical. Then, as Wilenski points out, he began to acknowledge that his theory of history in *The Stones of Venice* was mistaken. Writing to Froude in 1864, he stated firmly, 'There is no law of history any more than of a kaleidoscope. With certain bits of glass—shaken so, and so—you will get pretty figures, but what figures, Heaven only knows. . . . The wards of a Chubb's lock are infinite in their chances. Is the Key of Destiny made on a less complex principle?' This renunciation of historical law was intellectually daring, and emotionally as well, for it meant that he was trying to alter those 'pretty figures' which earlier had enabled him to lock his own conception and marriage into the history of Venice. (pp. 45-50)

*Richard Ellmann, "Overtures to Wilde's 'Salome',"
in* Yearbook of Comparative and General Literature,
No. 17, 1968, pp. 17-28.

JAMES CLARK SHERBURNE   (essay date 1972)

[In the following excerpt, Sherburne explores Ruskin's view of the organicism of art, nature, and society.]

The thirty-nine volumes of Ruskin's work seem, at first sight, a chaotic assemblage in which chronology alone supplies the unifying element. After further study, the impression of chaos remains, but it is a chaos of vitality, not of disintegration, or rather of the struggle between the two. Whether Ruskin writes on art, nature, or economics, there are the inevitable digressions and irrelevancies. These are never mere padding. They are alive and often the start of another unfinished book. Their vitality stems not from their immediate context but from their relation to a more general theory or point of view. This holds true also for the larger division between Ruskin's art and social criticism. The former carries within it the seeds of its own demise. The shift from art to society involves no new approach but an extension of the same approach to a new field and the use of many of the same arguments.

This quality of "wholeness" is a remarkable feature of Ruskin's work. Every thinker, after scholarly tailoring, comes to be cut of whole cloth. With Ruskin, the interwoven temper of his mind immediately strikes one. More remarkable is the fact that the formal wholeness of Ruskin's thought finds a reflection in the specific content of his theories on nature, art, architecture, and society. It is as though his elaboration of theory and the much less conscious pattern of his intellectual processes are singularly fused. In the shaping of doctrines for public consumption, Ruskin does not take the usual steps of detachment from the inner workings of his mind. The pulse of his thought is there on the page, to be felt. For whatever reason, he seems inspired to rationalize or idealize an instinctively adopted mode of thought—his sense of the whole as a living unity. (p. 1)

Ruskin's general approach, as "realized" in his specific theories, stresses interdependence, continuity, and unity. Whether deliberately or not, he follows Coleridge's dictum that the mind employs method when it studies "the relation of things." Such a search for wholeness characterized most of the great minds of the Romantic movement. Schelling, Hegel, and Coleridge himself, for example, attempt to find a deeper coherence beneath the contrasting forms of human knowledge and criticize the Enlightenment for achieving a superficial harmony. Ruskin would have sympathized with Coleridge when he declared, "The universe itself! What but an immense heap of little things? . . . My mind feels as if it ached to . . . know something *great,* something *one* and *indivisible.*" Although Ruskin's search for wholeness fails in the end, it gives to the chaotic surface of his thought a deeper unity which justifies his efforts.

The tendency to see each thing as "itself a living part of a live whole," or, to use William Blake's phrase, "to see a World in a Grain of Sand," leads Ruskin into a dimension where phenomena refuse to stand as impenetrable, self-contained entities. Each subject that he studies appears now as the integral part of a larger whole and now as a whole composed of lesser parts. In each case, the relationship of part to whole is one of vital interdependence: the part cannot exist in isolation from the whole, nor can the whole survive without its sustaining part. "It is all a Tree: circulation of sap and influences, mutual communication of every minutest leaf . . . with every other greatest and minutest portion of the whole." Carlyle's metaphor captures the essence of Ruskin's attempt to relate the chief counters of his discussion—nature, art, society, man—and his sometimes exaggerated identification of art and morality or art and life. The term organicism best describes this method of seeing all things in relation. Although a difficult word, its choice is sanctioned by Ruskin's use of the adjective "organic," his preference for natural metaphors, and his participation in the Romantic tradition of organicism. By "organic," Ruskin never means a purely physical relation. For him, as for his Oxford friend, the naturalist William Buckland (1784-1856), nature reflects or is penetrated by a realm of spiritual significance. Art, society, and man follow nature in this respect.

Ruskin's organicism appears early in the discussion of "Typical Beauty" in volume two of **Modern Painters**. . . . He defines "Typical Beauty" as "that external quality of bodies . . . which may be shown to be in some sort typical of the Divine attributes." Two of the attributes or ideas suggested by the material qualities of things are "unity" and "purity." Although Ruskin's terminology is a confusing blend of the Platonic and the Christian, his description of unity and purity reveals his insistence on seeing things as wholes composed of living, interdependent parts. Ruskin's second classification of beauty, "Vital Beauty," reinforces the concepts of unity and purity from a different angle.

The importance of "unity" for Ruskin is evident in the tendency of his discussion to veer from beauty to "general perfection." Paraphrasing the theologian Richard Hooker (1554-1600), he writes:

> Hence the appearance of separation or isolation in anything, and of self-dependence, is an appearance of imperfection; but all appearances of connection and brotherhood are pleasant and right, both as significative of perfection in the things united, and as typical of that Unity which we attribute to God . . . that Unity which consists . . . in the necessity of His inherence in all things that be. . . .

After noting various superficial or mechanical forms of unity, Ruskin turns to "Essential Unity" or "unity of membership." This is the "unity of things separately imperfect into a perfect whole . . . the great unity of which other unities are but parts and means." Since "unity of membership" demands an integral fusion of parts, it is impossible without a "difference and opposition" in the members. The work of art should possess this unity. Ruskin compares the harmony of an artistic whole to that of a tree painted by Turner. If we break off "the merest stem or twig of it, it all goes to pieces. . . . There is not so much as a seed of it but it lies on the tree's life. . . ."

Ruskin's description of unity echoes Aristotle's view that, "if the presence or absence of a thing makes no visible difference, it is not an integral part of the whole." Although Ruskin had read Aristotle carefully, he does not refer to him here but turns to the Romantics. Coleridge defines beauty as "Multeity in Unity" or "that in which the many, still seen as many, becomes one." A true poem possesses a living unity which can only result from the fusion or interpenetration of its parts. For Wordsworth, the excellence of Shakespeare's dramas lies in the fact that "his materials, . . . heterogeneous as they often are, constitute a unity of their own. . . ." In order to distinguish "organic" unity from the mechanical organization or "uniformity in variety" valued by eighteenth-century literary criticism, Coleridge, Carlyle, and Hazlitt anticipate Ruskin in stressing the "contraries," the "difference and opposition," of the members of the whole. Coleridge defines unity as "the reconciliation of opposite and discordant qualities" and makes this the first principle of his literary criticism. Ruskin traces his own view of the reconciliation of opposites to Plato's *Timaeus* as well as to the Romantics.

As the adjective "organic" implies, the Romantic concept of artistic unity has its source in a vision of nature and life. The similarity of the terms used by Romantics to describe art and nature appears clearly in Coleridge's fragment on *The Theory of Life*. He defines life as "the principle of unity in multeity" or "the power which unites a given *all* into a whole." The key to the ''process and mystery of production and life'' is the reconciliation of opposites. A similar view of nature and art forms the basis of Carlyle's use of the organic metaphor. The work of art is not a ''divisible Aggregate'' but a ''living indivisible whole'' bound together by ''organic filaments,'' an aesthetic conviction to which the structure of *Sartor Resartus* (1833) gives ample testimony. Ruskin's emphasis on ''unity of membership'' is not original. Behind it, there lies a tradition of Romantic theorizing which views organic unity as the characteristic of living things and the key to the transference of metaphors from the realm of nature to that of art. In Ruskin, this tradition is reinforced by a much older tradition of Platonists, Aristotelians, and Christian philosophers like Richard Hooker and Jeremy Taylor who view oneness or unity as the attribute of ultimate reality. Ruskin inherits these traditions in a haphazard fashion, selects what he finds useful, and creates his own vocabulary of organicism.

The most important word in this vocabulary is ''purity,'' the key to organic unity and a crucial element in typical beauty. In his discussion of purity, the ''type of Divine energy,'' Ruskin is pointing to the unifying ground which makes possible the fusing of apparent contraries in nature and art. Romantics describe this ground or energy in terms which blend the spiritual and the physical. The word most often chosen is ''life.'' Coleridge speaks of the ''one life within us and abroad,'' and Wordsworth of the ''one interior life that lives in all things.'' For both poets, this life is transcendental. In the tradition of Plotinus, Bishop Berkeley, and the German Romantics, they describe it as a ''spiritual underpresence,'' the ''Soul of all the Worlds,'' and identify it with mind, spirit, or God. To avoid the extremes of pantheism and traditional religion, the Romantics often write vaguely of ''the sentiment of Being,'' an ''active Principle'' at work in all things, ''something far more deeply interfused,'' or, in the case of Carlyle, simply of ''force'' and ''power.'' Of the terms used to describe the unifying ground in nature and art, ''energy'' is the one Ruskin prefers. He speaks of the quality which distinguishes ''nature and Turner from all their imitators'' as ''this fulness of character absorbed in universal energy.'' In his choice of words, he resembles Blake, who identifies ''energy'' with life and makes it the chief counter in his battle with mechanism. Blake, in fact, is the only writer before Ruskin to relate energy and purity. Elsewhere in Romantic thought and poetry and the tradition of Platonic and Christian philosophy, purity leads a tenuous existence as one of many qualities of the ground of Being.

Ruskin's discussion of purity in volume two of **Modern Painters** owes its vagueness and brevity to the fact that here he is touching on the living root of his organic approach. Here he is reaching an awareness of the materialistic basis of the organic metaphor. While other elements of typical beauty—infinity, moderation, symmetry, repose, unity—are desired because they express divine attributes, purity is desired for its material condition. Purity is not essentially a moral or spiritual term: ''the original notion of this quality is altogether material,'' and ''the use of the terms purity, spotlessness, etc., in moral subjects, is merely metaphorical.'' Ruskin demonstrates the material origin of the concept by studying ideas of impurity. These ideas refer to

> conditions of matter in which . . . the negation of vital or energetic action is most evident; as in corruption and decay of all kinds, wherein particles which once, by their operation on each other, produced a living and energetic whole,

are reduced to a condition of perfect passiveness, in which they are seized upon and appropriated, one by one, piecemeal, by whatever has need of them, without any power of resistance or energy of their own. . . .

Ruskin's description of impurity reminds one of Blake's fear of ''Ulro,'' the Newtonian universe of dead matter, and Wordsworth's fear of a world where everything is ''in disconnection, dead and spiritless,'' where everything ''meets foes irreconcilable and at best doth live but by variety of disease.'' For Ruskin, purity is the opposite of death, disconnection, and isolation. It is an ''active condition of substance'' and depends on a ''vital and energetic connection among particles.'' ''Thus the purity of the rock, contrasted with the foulness of dust or mould, is expressed by the epithet 'living,' very singularly given to rock, in almost all language (singularly, because life is almost the last attribute one would ascribe to stone, but for this visible energy and connection of its particles). . . .'' Similarly, the purity of color is dependent on ''the full energizing of the rays that compose it.''

Light itself is Ruskin's preferred analogue for the purity or energy which pervades living wholes. In this, he is heir to a long line of thinkers, including the Cambridge Platonists, Berkeley, and Carlyle, who conceive of the principle of ''life'' or the divine ''underpresence'' in terms of light or ''Living Fire.'' Earlier thinkers, however, make no attempt to suggest a material origin for the energy pervading the universe. Light, for them as for Coleridge, is the ''material symbol of an Idea'' and is chosen because it is the least earthbound of possible symbols. Ruskin confronts directly, if only momentarily, the possibility that energy or purity is essentially a material condition—that it is *really* light and that the spiritual terms used to describe it are metaphors for a physical reality.

Ruskin cannot rest in this interpretation. With the transcendental urge of a Schelling or a Coleridge, he escapes to higher realms. ''And so in all cases,'' he writes, ''I suppose that pureness is made to us desirable, because expressive of that constant presence and energizing of the Deity by which all things live and move, and have their being; and that foulness is painful as the accompaniment of disorder and decay, and always indicative of withdrawal of Divine support.'' At the end of his discussion, Ruskin identifies purity and spirituality by declaring the essential characteristic of matter to be inertia and by placing the energy or purity which overcomes this on the side of spirit.

The materialistic root of Ruskin's concept of purity distorts his theoretical divisions and causes purity to overlap with ''Vital Beauty.'' ''Vital Beauty'' characterizes only living phenomena. Ruskin defines it as the ''appearance of felicitous fulfilment of function in living things''—the appearance of ''happiness.'' It results from the complete unfolding of an inner principle of life which adapts the functions of parts to the purpose of the whole. In a beautiful plant, ''every leaf and stalk is seen to have a function, to be constantly exercising that function, and as it *seems, solely* for the good and the enjoyment of the plant.'' Man's inherent vitality leads to the conscious development of his intellectual and spiritual life as well as the natural development of his physical propensities. Although vital beauty resembles Aristotle's notion of form as the ''actuality of the thing,'' Ruskin could have derived the idea from many sources. Coleridge asks: ''May not the sense of Beauty originate in our perception of the fitness of the means to the end in and for the animal itself?'' With its suggestion of healthy energy and proper functioning of parts, Ruskin's concept of vital beauty has important social implications.

The inner vitality which generates vital beauty is identical with the energy of "purity." It has a positively physical basis. Again, Ruskin resists a materialistic interpretation and points to the moral or spiritual significance of the degrees of vitality found in organisms. The poet George Herbert (1593-1633) praises the "orange tree, that busy plant." So Ruskin can declare that "there is not any organic creature but, in its history and habits, will exemplify to us some moral excellence or deficiency." "Of the outward seemings and expressions of plants, there are few but are in some way good and therefore beautiful, as of humility, and modesty, and love of places and things. . . ." In a similar vein, he speaks of the "earnest ant" and "unwearied bee," the "foulness of the sloth," or the "sweetness and gentleness" of the gazelle and ox. The shift from a material to a spiritual level of interpretation here and in the chapter on "purity" is significant. Ruskin's descriptions of plants and animals suggest that this fault or seam in his organic approach permits the incursion of traditional Victorian morality.

Though unstable, the organic basis of Ruskin's view of unity and purity cannot be doubted. It appears again in volume five of **Modern Painters,** where he makes "The Law of Help" the most important principle of artistic composition. In the following passage, one can see the organic metaphor at work and the interesting use of the word "pure." One can also see, in Ruskin's choice of the words "clean" and "holy," his tendency to shift from the material to the moral or spiritual plane:

> Composition may be best defined as the help of everything in the picture by everything else. . . .
>
> In substance which we call "inanimate," as of clouds, or stones, their atoms may cohere to each other, or consist with each other, but they do not help each other. The removal of one part does not injure the rest.
>
> But in a plant, the taking away of any one part does injure the rest. . . . If any part enters into a state in which it no more assists the rest, and has thus become "helpless," we call it also "dead."
>
> The power which causes the several portions of the plant to help each other, we call life. Much more is this so in an animal. We may take away the branch of a tree without much harm to it; but not the animal's limb. Thus, intensity of life is also intensity of helpfulness—completeness of depending of each part on all the rest. The ceasing of this help is what we call corruption; and in proportion to the perfectness of the help, is the dreadfulness of the loss. . . .
>
> The decomposition of a crystal is not necessarily impure at all. The fermentation of a wholesome liquid begins to admit the idea slightly; the decay of leaves yet more; of flowers, more; of animals, with greater painfulness and terribleness in exact proportion to their original vitality; and the foulest of all corruption is that of the body of man. . . .

> When matter is either consistent, or living, we call it pure, or clean; when inconsistent or corrupting (unhealthful), we call it impure, or unclean. The greatest uncleanliness being that which is essentially most opposite to life.
>
> Life and consistency, then, both expressing one character (namely, helpfulness of a higher or lower order), the Maker of all creatures and things, "by whom all creatures live, and all things consist," is essentially and for ever the Helpful One, or in softer Saxon, the "Holy" One. . . .
>
> A pure or holy state of anything, therefore, is that in which all its parts are helpful or consistent. . . . The highest or organic purities are composed of many elements in an entirely helpful state. The highest and first law of the universe—and the other name of life is, therefore, "help." The other name of death is "separation." Government and co-operation are in all things and eternally the laws of life. Anarchy and competition, eternally, and in all things, the laws of death. . . .

The word "energy" occurs later in the passage: "Also in true composition, everything not only helps everything else a *little,* but helps with its utmost power. Every atom is in full energy; *all* that energy is kind."

This passage is very important. It places Ruskin in the tradition of Romantic organicism and reveals his application of the organic metaphor to painting. Ruskin's hierarchy of organic entities—crystals, plants, and animals—echoes Coleridge's criteria of organic evaluation: "extension," that is, the number and variety of the component parts, and "intensity," the degree of their interdependence. His comparison of organic unity with various states of corruption, disorganization, or impurity also strikes a familiar note. Behind this comparison lies the Romantic distinction between "organic" and "mechanical" form, or, to use Blake's terms, between "Living Form" and "Mathematical Form." As Coleridge explains it, mechanical form is fabricated or imposed *ab extra,* while organic form is generated or evolved *ab intra.* In mechanical form, the component elements are juxtaposed externally, not fused internally. They fall easy prey to corruption or disorganization. Coleridge's distinction leads in turn to the crucial one between "mechanical" and "vital" philosophy. The former knows only of "the relations of unproductive particles to each other." It can hold good only for a "dead nature." In an organic or vital philosophy, elements "actually interpenetrate" one another to form a living whole. Early in his career, but late in the Romantic movement, Ruskin enters the lists on the side of Blake, Coleridge, and Carlyle against a "Mechanico-corpuscular Philosophy" of death.

Ruskin's participation in the battle is important, for he applies the organic approach not only to art and nature but also to man, society, and economics. One might recall his preference for the word "help" in the long passage on composition. It is not the only time that a playful etymological speculation is the bearer of a real advance in Ruskin's argument. As Francis Townsend remarks, one could substitute "society" for "nature" and "men" for "parts" and have the essence of Ruskin's social criticism. His ideal state resembles nature and art in that it joins its members, each fully developed yet each individually imperfect, into a vital unity—"fulness of character absorbed in universal energy." In volume two of *Modern Painters,* Ruskin points the way to his social ideal by suggesting that every individual is born defective in some respects so that mankind as a whole can cultivate the virtues of fellowship and love. This is the source of his vision of Gothic architecture and his critique of economic competition.

Ruskin is not the first Romantic to perceive the social implications of organicism. Coleridge and Carlyle precede him in applying the organic approach to society. Wordsworth moves in a similar direction although without the philosophical preoccupations of Coleridge. After declaring that a true poem, like nature,

> reconciles
> Discordant elements and makes them move
> In one society,

he turns his attention to national societies in *The Convention of Cintra* (1809). Edmund Burke (1729-1797) in England and Johann Gottfried von Herder (1744-1803) in Germany pioneer in the social application of the organic metaphor. Burke describes society as a delicate organism and speaks of the "great contexture of the mysterious whole." He is intensely aware of the interdependence of elements in the Empire, in the constitution, and in the "commonwealth" of Europe. With more radical intent, Blake also grasps the social relevance of the distinction between organism and machine. If Ruskin is not the first to see the broader ramifications of the organic approach, he is the most thorough in applying his perception to social and economic phenomena. His statement, "Government and co-operation are in all things and eternally the laws of life. Anarchy and competition, eternally, and in all things, the laws of death," forms a constant refrain in his social criticism. (pp. 1-10)

> *James Clark Sherburne, in his* John Ruskin; or, The Ambiguities of Abundance: A Study in Social and Economic Criticism, *Cambridge, Mass.: Harvard University Press, 1972, 366 p.*

KRISTINE OTTESEN GARRIGAN (essay date 1973)

[*Garrigan is an American educator and critic. In the following excerpt, she discusses the critical emphases in Ruskin's writings on architecture.*]

Ruskin's ideas on architecture did not change substantially over time; rather, they grew by accretion. He himself frequently asserted that age had only confirmed his basic impressions; . . . his 1880 notes to *The Seven Lamps* and those of 1879-81 to *The Stones of Venice* are filled with affecting instances of wry self-congratulation. A particularly telling one: "A great deal of this talk is flighty, and some of it fallacious . . . but the sentiment and essential truth of general principle in the chapter induce me to reprint . . . it in this edition." (p. 33)

From the first, . . . Ruskin was never very deeply distressed by the unexpectedly narrow limits of his experience; in *Modern Painters I* . . . , though he claims familiar acquaintance with every important work of art from Antwerp to Naples, he draws his examples of "the ancients" largely from the Dulwich and National Galleries—but not merely because they were accessible to his readers, which he cites as his reason. Rather, they were the galleries he *knew* extremely well. Yet both collections at the time consisted primarily of seventeenth- and eighteenth-century paintings; the National Gallery had been open to the

A letter from Ruskin to M. H. Spielmann.

public for just five years and had fewer than two hundred pictures. Similarly, Turner had shown 555 paintings and watercolors by the end of 1843, but Ruskin mentions only 45 in *Modern Painters I*. The resultant distortions may be excused as a matter of innocent, youthful self-confidence, and indeed before writing *Modern Painters II* Ruskin worked at expanding his background. His later writings, however, still tend to be equally limited; greater knowledge usually led simply to one small range of examples being superseded by another. Extensiveness of experience mattered little compared to intensiveness of experience.

Moreover, Ruskin never questioned the universal validity of his own preferences, of "my affections, as well as my experience." If Ruskin thought the Doge's Palace and Giotto's Tower were the most beautiful buildings in the world, then obviously they were, and everyone else should think so too. But everyone else would have to be persuaded on more objective grounds than the mere fact of Ruskin's delight, and it was the casuistic lengths to which he was forced in providing ex post facto "logical" justifications for his highly idiosyncratic prejudices that led to some of his most celebrated contradictions. Ruskin could never simply prefer anything: he was driven to exalt it, to establish its absolute superiority by denigrating the alternatives.

Hence, although Ruskin is renowned as an interpreter of Gothic, what he most frequently writes about is Gothic at its least typical, the Italian species, because that was the Gothic he knew and loved best. It is worth briefly reviewing the unique qualities of Italian Gothic, then, because they help to explain both the nature of Ruskin's emphases and the incompleteness of his view of the Gothic style.

The most basic point to be made regarding Italian Gothic, the one which explains many of its singular characteristics, is that Italy, unlike the transalpine countries, had a strong, persistent classical heritage. The soaring verticality and complicated diagonal divisions and interpenetrations of space that mark the Gothic style were alien to the classical tradition of volumetric clarity and serene resolution of horizontal and vertical elements. Thus Italian Gothic is quite simple structurally—transparently logical and balanced rather than spectacularly intricate. (pp. 35-6)

Perhaps the most important Italian Gothic quality . . . , however, one that assumes a variety of significant manifestations, is its distinctness of parts. In Northern Gothic, buildings have a pervasive organic quality—spaces interpenetrate, constructive elements fuse into a total architectural fabric, so that interior and exterior echo and explain each other. The Southern monument, on the other hand, reflecting Italy's classical and Romanesque achievements, is built on a principle of addition rather than fusion. The disparate parts of the building coordinate, but each also preserves and declares its own identity. These qualities are especially clear on the exterior; the typical facade is a flat, massive screen, often taller and wider than the building back of it—a false front; in some instances, the windows punched out of it may even be dummy. (p. 37)

Italian Gothic is, on the one hand, in its characteristics of space and mass, more classical than Gothic, and, on the other hand, in the independent prominence allowed to highly finished sculpture and painting, even anti-Gothic. Gothic in Italy was an engrafted style (the Italian Renaissance architects actually labeled it *"maniera tadesca,"* the German style) modified by previous long tradition into an original, often impressive, but fundamentally bastardized mode. Ironically, its most pronounced qualities, its serenely elegant volumes and simple rectilinear modules, anticipate the Renaissance forms by which Italian Gothic was so early and readily superseded.

It is apparent, therefore, that for a variety of unique reasons, Italian Gothic was a style quite different from the Gothic north of the Alps, a distinction Ruskin was perfectly able to recognize. But he was unable to view the two kinds dispassionately; despite his early affection for Norman Gothic, his interest in Italian Gothic implies a rejection of Northern forms. It was at Lucca, not at Winchester or Rouen or Cologne, that he felt he had truly discovered medieval architecture and committed himself to the serious study of it. Furthermore, as he was to admit rather offhandedly in *Stones of Venice I,* his new awareness of Italian architecture interfered with his continued appreciation of its Northern counterpart. . . . (p. 38)

His Italian preferences become the more apparent—and the more final—when we consider the extensive use he makes of North/South contrasts throughout his work. Fittingly, his earliest effort, *The Poetry of Architecture,* "rose immediately out of my sense of the contrast between the cottages of Westmoreland and those of Italy." Even the basic first volume of *Stones* is permeated with these contrasts. . . . Ruskin found establishing polarities essential to his arguments; indeed, his use of contrasts was one of the bases for the accusations of plagiarism that he endured. And . . . his alternatives are couched in terms that by their very nature force a moral judgment. Ruskin's contrasts almost never consist of equal pairs; both quantities are frequently stated extremely, and one side is clearly meant to be unattractive or untenable. It is indicative that the contrast at the very heart of his social criticism is Life/Death. Therefore, even the North/South contrasts intended as neutral illustrations usually have a prejudicial edge.

The quintessential North/South contrast in Ruskin is, of course, the magnificent Salisbury/St. Mark's passage in *Stones of Venice II.* The Northern building is a great bleak pile of "mouldering wall of rugged sculpture and confused arcades, shattered, and grey, and grisly with heads of dragons and mocking fiends, worn by the rain and swirling winds into yet unseemlier shape, and coloured on their stony scales by the deep russet-orange lichen, melancholy gold," surrounded by a lawn on which we must take care not to step, in turn bordered by "somewhat diminutive and excessively trim houses" with "little shaven grass-plots," the sole signs of well-regulated life being the tradesmen's delivery carts and the canons' children walking with their nursemaids; this static scene is punctuated only by the cacophony of rooks circling like predators amid the towers, "a drift of eddying black points." Then we are presented with the glorious Venetian spectacle of bustling St. Mark's Place, the church itself an Arabian Nights phantasm come to pulsating life, glistening with rich color, even to the irridescence of the gentle doves placidly nestling among the marble foliage:

> . . . a multitude of pillars and white domes, clustered into a long low pyramid of coloured light; a treasure-heap, it seems, partly of gold, and partly of opal and mother-of-pearl, hollowed beneath into five great vaulted porches, ceiled with fair mosaic, and beset with sculpture of alabaster, clear as amber and delicate as ivory,—sculpture fantastic and involved, of palm leaves and lilies, and grapes and pomegranates, and birds clinging and fluttering among the branches. . . . And round the walls of the porches there are set pillars of variegated stones, jasper and porphyry, and deep-green serpentine spotted with flakes of snow, and marbles, that half refuse and half yield to the sunshine, Cleopatra-like, "their bluest veins to kiss" . . . and above them, in the broad archivolts, a continuous chain of language and of life—angels, and the signs of heaven, and the labours of men, each in its appointed season upon the earth; and above these, another range of glittering pinnacles, mixed with white arches edged with scarlet flowers,—a confusion of delight . . . until at last, as if in ecstasy, the crests of the arches break into a marble foam, and toss themselves far into the blue sky in flashes and wreaths of sculptured spray, as if the breakers on the Lido shore had been frost-bound before they fell, and the sea-nymphs had inlaid them with coral and amethyst.

"Between that grim cathedral of England and this," exclaims Ruskin, "what an interval!" Indeed. Seen as Ruskin so memorably describes them, it is small wonder that he should side with the medieval South and declare:

> . . . those who study the Northern Gothic remain in a narrowed field—one of small pinnacles, and dots, and crockets, and twitched

faces—and cannot comprehend the meaning of a broad surface or a grand line. . . . The Gothic of the Ducal Palace of Venice is in harmony with all that is grand in all the world: that of the North is in harmony with the grotesque Northern spirit only.

It is logical, then, that the characteristics of architecture that attracted Ruskin and which thus came to constitute his emphases in his architectural writings should be those of medieval Italy. (This is only the most obvious explanation—although one generally overlooked by Ruskin critics . . .). The first of these emphases is his preoccupation with architectural *surfaces;* Ruskin conceives of a building as a series of *planes.* These planes may be undecorated, beautiful in themselves because of the lovely patterns inherent in their materials, especially the different kinds of marble—many available only in the South. Perhaps partly as a reflection of his keen early interest in geology, Ruskin was always fascinated by rich building materials; often in his writings, as in the St. Mark's passage above, he revels in exhausting their varieties by reciting them in splendid Miltonic catalogues. "For again and again I must repeat it," he tells us in *Praeterita,* "my nature is a worker's and a miser's; and I rejoiced, and rejoice still, in the mere quantity of chiselling in marble, and stitches in embroidery; and was never tired of numbering sacks of gold and caskets of jewels in the Arabian Nights. . . ." (pp. 40-3)

Clearly Ruskin's love of opulent materials is related to his still greater love of color, and in architecture, especially of color worked into elegant incrusted patterns; the tinted plates of the first edition of *Stones,* for instance, are filled with samples of flat, multi-hued inlaid marble decorations from the facades of Venetian palaces and churches. "I cannot . . . consider architecture as in anywise perfect without colour," he asserts in *The Seven Lamps,* and "the colours of architecture should be those of natural stones." The magnificence of St. Mark's resides almost wholly in its color; "it is on its value as a piece of perfect and unchangeable colouring, that the claims of this edifice to our respect are finally rested."

Furthermore, throughout Ruskin's works, whether on nature or the arts, color is regarded as "of all God's gifts to the sight of man, . . . the holiest, the most divine, the most solemn." Color is always associated by Ruskin with moral and spiritual integrity ("the purest and most thoughtful minds are those which love colour the most"), even with intellectual and physical health. Conversely, he labels the loss or lack of color as symptomatic of spiritual decline and artistic enervation; his most persistent argument for rejecting Renaissance architecture is the "numbness" of its "barren stone." Yet at least in part this same standard must be applied to Northern Gothic as well; the Salisbury/St. Mark's passage is, at bottom, entirely a contrast of coloration. The Northern builders lacked the broad range of delicately shaded veneering materials available in the South; the dull greys and buffs of their freestone could only be masked by paint, Ruskin explains, the colors being applied quite literally rather than subtly: "Flames were painted red, trees green, . . . the result . . . being often far more entertaining than beautiful." Moreover, the depth of the carving—again a function of the difference in materials—compelled the Northern architect "to use violent colours in the recesses, . . . and thus injured his perception of more delicate colour harmonies. . . ." (pp. 43-4)

At any rate, if the proper colors of architecture are those of natural stones, it follows that Northern Gothic must, by an unkind quirk of geological fate, be inferior to that of the medieval South. But color itself is finally an abstract quality, basically independent of form, which Ruskin himself consistently notes, especially in *Modern Painters;* as an architectural characteristic, it is two-dimensional, a *surface stain.*

Yet when Ruskin goes beyond color and its patterns to talk about more complicated embellishments of the planes of a building, his emphasis is likewise two-dimensional. Again, this emphasis derives partly from his love of marble and his preoccupation with it as the supreme architectural material. . . . [Ruskin explains] how marble permits broad, undecorated areas in a building because of its inherent beauty. Even the decorated surfaces, however, will receive only shallow carving, particularly when they are veneers. This is especially the case in Venetian architecture because of its strong Byzantine heritage, as Ruskin repeatedly explains in *Stones of Venice.* Nonetheless, he emphasizes shallow relief throughout his writings on architecture, and in his later Oxford lectures on sculpture as well. In *Stones of Venice I* he argues: "It is to be remembered that, by a deep and narrow incision, an architect has the power, at least in sunshine, of drawing a black line on stone just as vigorously as it can be drawn with chalk on grey paper; and that he may thus, wherever and in the degree that he chooses, substitute *chalk sketching* for sculpture." But in *Lectures on Art* (1870) he drops the distinction between sculpture and "sketching" altogether, maintaining that "sculpture is indeed only light and shade drawing in stone." In *Aratra Pentelici* (1872) he states, "A great sculptor uses his tool exactly as a painter his pencil," and it is there also that he defines sculpture as "essentially the production of a pleasant bossiness or roundness of surface." In a London lecture from the same period, **"The Flamboyant Architecture of the Valley of the Somme"** (1869), he declares: "there is not a greater distinction between vital sculpture for building, and dead sculpture, than that a true workman paints with his chisel,—does not carve the form of a thing, but cuts the effect of its form."

These more direct later pronouncements on the superiority of low relief are quite consistent, however, with his implied earlier positions, especially that expressed in the **"Review of Lord Lindsay"** (1847), where he faults the author for not having sufficiently insisted "on what will be found to be a characteristic of all the truly Christian or spiritual, as opposed to classical, schools of sculpture—the scenic or painter-like management of effect. The marble is not cut into the actual form of the thing imaged, but oftener into a perspective suggestion of it. . . ." It is significant that in *Stones of Venice* one of the most damning points he believes he can make about the decadence of the Renaissance is that tomb figures are no longer supine, but rise up, as if in death trying to assert continued bodily existence. Despite his love of sculpture, Ruskin almost never examines the free-standing variety; rather he devotes himself to sculpture intimately associated with architecture: "Sculpture, separated from architecture, always degenerates into effeminacies and conceits; architecture, stripped of sculpture, is at best a convenient arrangement of dead walls; associated, they not only adorn, but reciprocally exalt each other." They not only exalt, however, but *affirm* each other; for "all good wall ornament . . . retains the expression of firm and massive substance, and of broad surface," from "mere inlaid geometrical figures up to incrustations of elaborate bas-relief." Thus even in praising sculptured detail so lavishly as he does throughout his works, Ruskin still conceives it more in two dimensions than three, in keeping with the planar emphasis of Italian Gothic. (pp. 44-6)

The second of Ruskin's major architectural emphases, and one that has underlain much of the preceding analysis, is his stress on ornamental elements, especially sculptural detail. Sculpture was by far the most important architectural component for Ruskin; in *Aratra Pentelici* he asserts that some of the best buildings he knows are simply "minute jewel cases for sweet sculpture." This emphasis is clearest in the addenda he provides to Lectures 1 and 2 of *Lectures on Architecture and Painting* (1854), in which he purports to distill for his readers the gist of the propositions he desires to maintain about architecture. Of the six basic propositions enunciated, five deal exclusively with ornamentation. For Ruskin, ornament is *"the principal part of architecture.* That is to say, the highest nobility of a building does not consist in its being well built, but in its being nobly sculptured or painted"; therefore, "no person who is not a great sculptor or painter *can* be an architect. If he is not a sculptor or painter, he can only be a *builder*." In his 1855 preface to the second edition of *Seven Lamps* Ruskin even asserts that "there are only two fine arts possible to the human race, sculpture and painting. What we call architecture is only the association of these in noble masses, or the placing them in fit places," and it is their combination that becomes the entire basis for "artistical and rational admiration" of architecture.... Thus it was obvious that he would constantly emphasize in his own writing the statuary, the floral mouldings, the mosaics. What is less obvious is the extent to which they constituted virtually his *entire* emphasis in architecture.

Ruskin's preoccupation with detail is especially evident in the illustrative plates he chose for his architectural works. Rarely are we given a view of anything larger than a window, door, or balcony; rarely are we permitted any perspective on how this window or door or balcony forms part of an architectural whole, although the opposite may obtain and additional plates be offered of still smaller details from those features. (pp. 48-9)

His preoccupation with detail was one of the main points on which he was attacked by contemporaries; as might be expected, Ruskin justified his emphasis on a variety of grounds, all having moral bearings. "It is often said, with some appearance of plausibility, that I dwell in all my writings on little things and contemptible details; and not on essential and large things," he remarks in the addenda to *Lectures on Architecture and Painting,* but he goes on to contend that an understanding of minuteness precedes an understanding of size. Modern architects, he asserts, cannot master detail; they are merely builders, copyists: "Let them first learn to invent as much as will fill a quatrefoil, or point a pinnacle, and then it will be time to reason with them on the principles of the sublime." He also argues, however, that the same creative skills are involved in each instance: whoever can design small things perfectly, can design whatever he chooses, because "to arrange (by invention) the folds of a piece of drapery, or dispose the locks of hair on the head of a statue, requires as much sense and knowledge of the laws of proportion, as to dispose the masses of a cathedral."

The analogy between great and small also forms the basis of another of his justifications, that small and large are all part of a unifying continuum: the pebble is a mountain in miniature, the humblest detail is full of meaning and necessary to a just appreciation of the whole. For "greatness can only be rightly estimated when minuteness is justly reverenced. Greatness is the aggregation of minuteness...." This argument pervades the volumes of *Modern Painters* and forms the basis for the series of chapters "The Law of Help," "The Task of the

Least," and "The Rule of the Greatest" in the fifth volume. In "The Task of the Least," on one of the surprisingly rare occasions in his major books when he analyzes the total composition of a work of art, Ruskin takes a plate from Turner's *Rivers of France* series and impressively demonstrates how the most seemingly insignificant bits are crucial to the effect of the whole, concluding, "It is the necessary connection of all the forms and colours, down to the last touch, which constitutes great or inventive work, separated from all common work by an impassable gulf." Ruskin regularly applies the same standard to architecture, as in *Lectures on Architecture and Painting,* when, after minutely analyzing a less-than-two-feet-square portion of Lyons facade and showing how its tiniest rosebud cannot be obliterated without artistic injury, he exclaims, "Yet just observe how much design, how much wonderful composition, there is in this building of the great times . . . and having examined this well, consider what a treasure of thought there is in a cathedral front...." In *Stones of Venice I* he states as a general principle: "a noble building never has any extraneous or superfluous ornament; . . . all its parts are necessary to its loveliness, and . . . no single atom of them could be removed without harm to its life."

Moreover, the artist's treatment of detail is an index of his moral worth—always an important concern for Ruskin; truly noble men show respect for all forms of being, and therefore express themselves with as much care in tiny ways as in great: "Greatness of mind is not shown by admitting small things, but by making small things great under its influence. He who can take no interest in what is small, will take false interest in what is great...." Thus, he explains, "in the little bits which I fix upon for animadversion, I am not pointing out solitary faults, but only the most characteristic examples of the falsehood which is everywhere...." And again, though in this instance Ruskin is specifically discussing painting, he habitually judged architecture in a similar manner, the more so because of his perennial insistence that no one who is not a great sculptor or painter *can* be an architect.

Finally, Ruskin impliedly offers a metaphysical vindication for his emphasis. Life is a series of divine fragments glimpsed through a glass darkly: "the work of the Great Spirit of nature is as deep and unapproachable in the lowest as in the noblest objects"; "the least thing is as the greatest and one day as a thousand years in the eyes of the Maker of great and small things."

> Our whole happiness and power of energetic action depend upon our being able to breathe and live in a cloud; content to see it opening here and closing there; rejoicing to catch, through the thinnest films of it, glimpses of stable and substantial things; but yet perceiving a nobleness even in the concealment, and rejoicing that the kindly veil is spread where the untempered light might have scorched us, or the infinite clearness wearied.

Yet despite his repeated declarations that details are to be seen as part of a magnificently unified whole, when Ruskin discusses them he tends to analyze them in isolation—just as his architectural plates so beautifully but incompletely depict them. The whole is simply not there as a constant reference point. This emphasis too is partly traceable to his overriding interest in Italian Gothic; we have noted how its sculpture is sparsely distributed compared to that of the Northern style, how its finish is more smoothly sophisticated and will, therefore, yield to more concentrated aesthetic analysis. Besides, the best examples of medieval Italian sculpture—those found in the pulpits, tombs, or low-relief plaques which Ruskin considers basically architectural—are scarcely creations of the anonymous, imperfect workman described in "The Nature of Gothic," but are the masterpieces of identifiable proud personalities like Niccola and Giovanni Pisano and Jacopo della Quercia. In other words, they virtually ask to be viewed in isolation. (pp. 51-4)

But Ruskin not only focuses on small bits at the expense of the larger view, he actually exalts their independent value: "beauty cannot be parasitical. There is nothing so small or so contemptible, but it may be beautiful in its own right. The cottage may be beautiful, and the smallest moss that grows on its roof, and the minutest fibre of that moss which the microscope can raise into visible form, and all of them in their own right, not less than the mountains and the sky. . . ." Moreover, discussing the bas-reliefs at the base of Giotto's Tower in *Mornings in Florence,* he clearly suggests that seeing details in isolation is necessary to their full appreciation:

> At first you may be surprised at the smallness of their scale in proportion to their masonry; but this smallness of scale enabled the master workmen of the tower to execute them with their own hands. . . . It is in general not possible for a great workman to carve, himself, a greatly conspicuous series of ornament; nay, even his energy fails him in design, when the bas-relief extends itself into incrustation, or involves the treatment of great masses of stone. If his own does not, the spectator's will.

Certainly this is the assumption underlying his contention in *Lectures on Architecture and Painting* that the principal part of a building is that "in which its mind is contained, . . . its sculpture and painting. I do with a building as I do with a man, watch the eye and the lips: when they are bright and eloquent, the form of the body is of little consequence."

This viewpoint also helps explain Ruskin's frequent assertion that architectural ornament bears no necessary relation to a building's structure. . . . [According to A. W. N. Pugin's second "True Principle"] all ornament should consist of enrichment of the essential construction of the building. By the time of Ruskin's major writing on architecture, the notion that ornament, not only of buildings but of carpets and teapots, must be secondary and appropriate to the form of the object being adorned, had achieved fairly wide currency among better design theorists. Ruskin, however, steadfastly denied this position. He maintains first of all that ornament is beautiful for its own sake; its only "function . . . is to make you happy." "It is the expression of man's delight in God's work," and is thus separated from any considerations of mere utility: "I have said . . . repeatedly . . . that the most beautiful things are the most useless; I never said superfluous. I said useless in the well-understood and usual sense, as meaning, inapplicable to the service of the body." It follows, therefore, that ornament cannot be subordinated to or dictated by structural considerations but should only be measured by its aesthetic contribution to the building. (pp. 54-5)

Furthermore, the emotional and mental responses evoked by ornament and by structure are totally different, even inimical; this is one of the first points enunciated in *The Stones of Venice:* "And, above all, do not try . . . to connect the delight which you take in ornament with that which you take in construction or usefulness. They have no connection; and every effort that you make to reason from one to the other will blunt your sense of beauty, or confuse it with sensations altogether inferior to it." (p. 56)

From the foregoing evidence it becomes clear why Ruskin ignores architectural contexts, focusing instead on isolated decorations: structure is an entirely different subject from ornamentation, requiring a distinct and lower species of emotional and intellectual response; indeed, a response that even diminishes one's ability to perceive beauty, and which is scarcely worth analysis or depiction, therefore, in books aimed at inculcating appreciation for the highest forms of architectural splendor.

One important point, however, remains to be made about Ruskin's criteria for fine ornamental detail: it should be visually, and preferably even physically, accessible. "Another character of my perceptions I find curiously steady," he tells us in *Praeterita,* "—that I was only interested by things near me, or at least clearly and visibly present. . . . [I]t remained—and remains—a part of my grown-up temper." Ruskin repeatedly praises buildings that are comparatively small and delicate, ones of which he can *see* all the parts. This preference for the modestly proportioned structure derives logically out of his fascination with beautiful surfaces and delicate details that we have already examined, and leads in turn to his regular assertion of the superiority of the South:

> Neither delicacy of surface sculpture, nor subtle gradations of colour, can be appreciated by the eye at a distance; and since we have seen that our sculpture is generally to be only an inch or two in depth, and that our colouring is in great part to be produced with the soft tints and veins of natural stones, it will follow necessarily that none of the parts of the building can be removed far from the eye, and therefore that the whole mass of it cannot be large. . . . And therefore we must not be disappointed, but grateful, when we find all the best work of the building concentrated within a space comparatively small; and that, for the great cliff-like buttresses and mighty piers of the North, shooting up into indiscernible height, we have here low walls spread before us like the pages of a book, and shafts whose capitals we may touch with our hand.
>
> (pp. 56-7)

It was noted previously that Ruskin was driven to exhaust particular works of art, that he returned to them again and again, looking at them more and more microscopically. . . . It was this constantly moving closer and closer to a beautiful object, pursuing its mystery into more and more restricted compass, that was the essence of his desire to take St. Mark's or Verona up into his mind, touch by touch. Moreover, as Ruskin himself inadvertently confesses in *The Two Paths* . . . , the high state of imaginative excitement reached in such a process causes a disproportionate emphasis on smallness:

> Remember that when the imagination and feelings are strongly excited, they will not only bear with strange things, but they will *look* into *minute* things with a delight unknown in hours of tranquility. . . . Things trivial at other times assume a dignity or significance which we can-

not explain; but which is only the more attractive because inexplicable: and the powers of attention, quickened by the feverish excitement, fasten and feed upon the minutest circumstances of detail, and remotest traces of intention.

And this same disproportion carries over into the architectural writings that his almost erotic love of Venice and Verona inspired.

This desire to see, to feel every stone of a building is at the root of what might be called Ruskin's "visual functionalism," that is, his insistence that all ornament should be treated and placed with reference to the physical circumstances of the spectator. Significantly, a main criterion for judging good Gothic, he says, is whether "the sculpture is *always* so set, and on such a scale, that at the ordinary distance from which the edifice is seen, the sculpture shall be thoroughly intelligible and interesting." Indicative, too, is his casual comment in *The Seven Lamps* that "it was a wise feeling which made the streets of Venice so rich in external ornament, for there is no couch of rest like the gondola." The best architectural detail is that which can be comfortably contemplated at close range, like pictures in a gallery. Finally, this emphasis on visual accessibility has, of course, important implications for Ruskin's dislike of those architectural qualities deriving from magnitude.... (pp. 58-9)

[There] is a distinct, if perverse, logic to Ruskin's system of argument. For Ruskin, details are not merely the basis for the entire appreciation of the building, but they finally constitute the very definition of architecture, and its claim to be a Fine Art. Indeed, the necessarily utilitarian character of architecture must condemn it to a lesser place in the ranking of the arts. In a note to *Modern Painters II*, Ruskin makes this point quite explicit:

> I do not assert that the accidental quality of a theoretic pursuit, as of botany for instance, in any way degrades it, though it cannot be considered as elevating it. But essential utility, a purpose to which the pursuit is in some measure referred, as in architecture, invariably degrades, because then the theoretic part of the art is comparatively lost sight of; and thus architecture takes a level below that of sculpture or painting, even when the powers of mind developed in it are of the same high order.

In an emendation to the 1883 "Re-arranged Edition" of this volume, he declares approvingly: "This old note already anticipates the subjection of the constructive to the decorative science of architecture which gave so much offence, to architects capable only of construction, in the *Seven Lamps,* written two years later, and *Stones of Venice.*" According to Ruskin, it is the decorative science that constitutes architectural nobility, and decoration can only be rightly judged in isolation— whether as two-dimensional sheaths of richly patterned geological "painting" or as delicately carved low-relief sculpture—because ornament requires a totally different emotional response and intellectual analysis from that elicited by constructive science. Effects proceeding from the management of larger architectural elements—effects deriving from the dispositions of masses and volumes, spacious bays and soaring vaults and ranges of galleries and chapels—are, in the end, "mere building," a completely separate subject.

Thus Ruskin's critical emphases are both extremely specific and surprisingly limited, rooted in his love for a singular species of medieval architecture. Unwittingly but felicitously, the novelist Henry James, describing the beauties of St. Mark's in a fine 1882 appreciation of Venice, aptly explains why that monument held the lifelong enchantment for Ruskin that it did— because the very qualities that James notes are precisely those which we have discussed here; they constitute the *sum* of architecture for Ruskin:

> ... it is almost a spiritual function,—or, at the worst, an amorous one,—to feed one's eyes on the mighty color that drops from the hollow vaults and thickens the air with its richness.... The strange figures in the mosaic pictures, bending with the curve of niche and vault, stare down through the glowing dimness; and the burnished gold that stands behind them catches the light on its little, uneven cubes. St. Mark's owes nothing of its character to the beauty of proportion or perspective; there is nothing grandly balanced or far-arching; there are no long lines nor triumphs of the perpendicular.... Beauty of surface, of tone, of detail, of things near enough to touch and kneel upon and lean against,—it is from this the effect proceeds. In this sort of beauty the place is incredibly rich, and you may go there every day and find afresh some lurking pictorial nook. It is a treasury of bits....
>
> (pp. 59-61)

Kristine Ottesen Garrigan, in her Ruskin on Architecture: His Thought and Influence, *The University of Wisconsin Press, 1973, 220 p.*

RICHARD L. STEIN   (essay date 1975)

[*In the following excerpt, Stein explores Ruskin's attitude toward the interpretation of a work of art by comparing his writings on art with those of Dante Gabriel Rossetti and Walter Pater, and by analyzing his critique of Turner's painting* The Slave Ship.]

The problem of objectivity reappears in various guises throughout the writing of Ruskin, Rossetti, and Pater. The Preface to Pater's *Renaissance* examines the relation of the feeling of beauty to its source in a specific object or experience; the introductory sonnet in Rossetti's *The House of Life* describes an ideal poem in which the description of a specific moment is balanced against the poet's evocation of his own soul; and Ruskin begins the chapter on "pathetic fallacy" in *Modern Painters III* by complaining about the artificial distinction implied in the very terms "objective" and "subjective." All three writers introduce nonliterary arts into their work to avoid such false dichotomies, to permit the merger of relatively "objective" and "subjective" modes into one allusive, complex form of discourse. The balanced concerns of the literature of art culminate the exploration, observable throughout Romantic writing, of the relation of the artist's consciousness to the external, phenomenal world. Similarly, the simultaneous focus on objective and subjective elements, a work of art and feelings inspired by it, helps to clarify the problematic relation of artist and audience which haunts Romantic and post-Romantic writers. The external artifact mediates between the writer interpreting it and his audience, creating a middle ground on which the most elusive personal vision can become accessible and convincing.

Perhaps the very presence of a second work of art encourages the writer to experiment more freely with his own creation, as both a stimulus and a control for certain literary energies. [G. Robert] Stange has credited the art criticism of Ruskin and Pater with opening the way for some of the prose techniques of modern fiction, and the claim of modernism can be extended to Rossetti as well. But it is not simply that a new literary genre elicited new styles. Experimentation is fostered by the inevitable reference within it to another, actual work of art, which keeps the literature of art at arm's length from solipsism. The writer gains freedom to innovate in his poetry or prose by virtue of the presence of that second artifact, which implicitly asserts that his feelings have meaning beyond what Pater calls "the narrow chamber of the individual mind." . . . (pp. 10-11)

[Certain] isolated passages reveal each writer's most characteristic and distinctive modes of treating art. At various points in their writing, the discussion of art acquires a new intensity, and the interpretation of a specific work of art takes on a quality of ritual. Invariably the writings about art of all three authors move toward central, self-contained rituals of interpretation, in which the contemplation of art under the guidance of literature is endowed with an almost magical power to transform the being of the spectator. The simultaneous acts of reading and viewing are meant to involve a totality of response that in turn can produce a harmony of perception, all the faculties of the reader becoming attuned, if momentarily, under the joint influence of art and literature. The ritual quality of the styles of all three writers forces the reader to experience the contemplation of art as an all-consuming act, one that can involve a fundamental reorientation of the self.

English readers might have been expected to be familiar with "The Slave Ship" . . . , which had been exhibited at the Royal Academy in 1840, three years before the first volume of ***Modern Painters*** was published. Ruskin discusses it there . . . , in a section titled "The Truth of Water," as an example of Turner's fidelity to nature. Yet it also contains proof of the painter's imaginative power—"the noblest sea that Turner has ever painted, and if so, the noblest certainly ever painted by man." Ruskin demonstrates the interdependence of these virtues: Turner's "nobility" depends on his mastery of natural phenomena; his art translates physical "facts" into harmonious expressions of his imagination.

Ruskin's description begins with the "facts," the weather conditions and topography of the scene: "It is a sunset on the Atlantic, after prolonged storm; but the storm is partially lulled, and the torn and streaming rain-clouds are moving in scarlet lines to lose themselves in the hollow of the night. The whole surface of sea included in the picture is divided into two ridges of enormous swell, not high, nor local, but a low broad heaving of the whole ocean, like the lifting of its bosom by deep-drawn breath after the torture of the storm." Ruskin is careful to allude to the spiritual qualities of the scene only after noting its specific naturalistic reference. It is as if his own response to the power of the painting follows from his understanding of Turner's command of time, place, and weather conditions. Earlier in the chapter he had discussed the importance of representing the massiveness of the ocean as a sign of its physical power and sublimity. Turner's ability to reproduce that "enormous swell . . . a low broad heaving of the whole ocean" represents his simultaneous insight into the facts and

moral of the sea; and Ruskin's prose begins to be more emotive with the description of this double insight.

The passage underscores Turner's control of natural phenomena in its reference to his division of the sea—and the entire canvas—by a brilliant shaft of light from the sunset, cutting across the sky and the swells. A comparison of Ruskin's subsequent language with the painting itself shows that this center-line organizes not only the images in the painting but his own responses to "The Slave Ship." His eyes seem to move back toward and away from the center of the picture as he tries to describe Turner's visual effects and their relation to moral insights:

> Between these two ridges the fire of the sunset falls along the trough of the sea, dyeing it with an awful but glorious light, the intense and lurid splendour which burns like gold, and bathes like blood. Along this fiery path and valley, the tossing waves by which the swell of the sea is restlessly divided lift themselves in dark, indefinite, fantastic forms, each casting a faint and ghastly shadow behind it along the illumined foam. They do not rise everywhere, but three or four together in wild groups, fitfully and furiously, as the under strength of the swell compels or permits them; leaving between them treacherous spaces of level and whirling water, now lighted with green and lamp-like fire, now flashing back the gold of the declining sun, now fearfully dyed from above with the indistinguishable images of the burning clouds, which fall upon them in flakes of crimson and scarlet, and give to the reckless waves the added motion of their own fiery flying.

The necessary motion of our eyes following Ruskin's description of the painting has become part of the natural energy of the scene. Within the canvas itself, for example, the clouds are not "flying," although they may be represented as in a state of motion. But as we glance from point to point in the sky and in the sea, we begin to experience the different quantities of light as changes in light, and the picture gains energy and life. Different points in space are translated by Ruskin's prose into different points in time: "Now flashing back the gold of the declining sun, now fearfully dyed from above with the indistinguishable images of the burning clouds." Similarly, he interprets the alterations in tone within the painting—becoming darker toward the left—as alterations over time. Ruskin's verbal adjectives transform Turner's picture of sunset into a narrative of the sun setting:

> Purple and blue, the lurid shadows of the hollow breakers are cast upon the mist of night, which gathers cold and low, advancing like the shadow of death upon the guilty ship as it labours amidst the lightning of the sea, its thin masts written upon the sky in lines of blood, girded with condemnation in that fearful hue which signs the sky with horror, and mixes its flaming flood with the sunlight, and, cast far along the desolate heave of the sepulchral waves, incarnadines the multitudinous sea.

By the end of this passage, the clouds no longer seem to be "moving in scarlet lines to lose themselves in the hollow of the night." Rather, the night-mist "gathers cold and low, advancing like the shadow of death upon the guilty ship.'' From our reference point at the center of the picture, the storm seems to move toward us, making the moral connotations of the subject active and even more threatening. It is, then, primarily the narrative element in Ruskin's prose that enables him to ''read'' ''The Slave Ship'' for its moral meaning. There are, in fact, two narratives—the account of a changing natural scene and the story of a divine judgment passed against a ''guilty'' ship—and the passage dramatizes their interdependence. Neither Ruskin nor Turner would ascribe a moral value to such scenes without first understanding them in phenomenological terms: in nature and in art, a physical ''reading'' precedes a moral one; we must understand facts before we can interpret their meaning.

Consider the way in which Ruskin introduces the most explicit moral judgment in his prose. Throughout the passage we have been directed to the power and sublimity of Turner's scene, often manifested only in ''indistinguishable images.'' But by the end, natural fury finds a specific object: ''the mist of night'' is ''advancing like the shadow of death upon the guilty* ship.'' The asterisk is Ruskin's. His footnote elucidates the nature of the ship's guilt: ''She is a slaver, throwing her slaves overboard. The near sea is encumbered with corpses.'' Just as our eyes have moved to the bottom of Ruskin's page, so has his prose shifted our attention in a long diagonal line from the upper-left to the lower-right corner of the picture, where Turner includes what seem to be vague outlines of manacled limbs and other floating animal or human forms. Returning again to the writing, we find our focus diverted upward again, to the ship's masts and the sky behind them; but it is difficult not to glance down once more to the grotesque seaborn figures in the foreground. The layout, as well as the content of the prose, dramatize the visual balance Turner creates between these portions of his painting. As our eyes move between them, we see the slave ship itself, integrated into this visual relationship by its size, shape, and color.

Ruskin's prose, then, shows how Turner gives aesthetic substance to his moral vision. The footnote provides another demonstration that moral generalizations must have a source in facts. But the primary facts of ''The Slave Ship'' are its formal components, and Ruskin calls attention to the way these contribute to the primary meaning of the picture. Turner organizes ''The Slave Ship'' around the relationship of storm-cloud, corpses and flotsam, and the slaver itself. Ruskin's prose makes us feel that the clouds advance on the ship *because of* those abandoned corpses. As his note indicates, a slave ship is an appropriate victim of such natural wrath. Certainly as we follow the progress of Ruskin's writing and return from the foreground in the lower-right canvas to the relation between cloud and ship, we feel more intensely the threatening, overhanging power of the sky in the picture.

In the description of ''The Slave Ship'' Ruskin is ''reading'' moral messages in both nature and art. Throughout *Modern Painters,* he refers to nature as an artist, and he clearly believes that the most powerful natural forms, colors, and ''effects'' are divinely intended as lessons for man. God might well summon up the elements to pass final judgment on a slave ship in just the way Turner has described; and it is of no small importance to Ruskin's treatment that the picture is based on the artist's reading about the shipwreck of an actual slaver. But Ruskin is also insisting that such a scene could be represented only by an artist of Turner's imaginative power. Indeed, at some points in the passage it is difficult to separate Turner's

role as the painter of an actual storm and God's role as its controller. By whose art are the ship's ''thin masts written upon the sky in lines of blood''? The force of the entire passage is to assert that without the intervention of a great artist a scene of this sort would be beyond our ability of comprehension. Just as Ruskin guides the reader in understanding Turner, so the painter (with Ruskin's aid) instructs us in the art of seeing nature and ''reading'' her moral narratives.

In this sense, the passage on ''The Slave Ship'' is not merely a moral narrative but an artistic one as well. Its energy defines not simply the moral ideas in nature, but the process that gives them power, substance, and order in art. Ruskin's subject is the act of creation itself—and the analogy of Turner's creation and God's is implicit here and throughout *Modern Painters*. The drama of the prose recreates the imaginative insight from which Turner painted ''the most sublime of subjects and impressions . . . the power, majesty, and deathfulness of the open, deep, illimitable sea.'' A central goal—if not the central goal—of the passage is to create the illusion that we have shared this vision with its creator. The language of interpretation generates a ritual which endows the reader and spectator with an intensity of consciousness approaching that of Turner or Ruskin himself. And in the sense that Ruskin invites us to repeat the process, his account of the painting provides an almost magical formula for experiencing this heightened state of being.

I am labeling this formula ''ritual,'' not so much to suggest the sanctity of art in Ruskin's aesthetics (although that element is clearly present), as to indicate the almost religious value he assigns to the act of interpretation itself. Both Pater and, to a slightly less extent, Rossetti share this conviction of the necessity of interpretation for producing an ultimate aesthetic response, greater than either art or literature alone could supply. In the description of ''The Slave Ship,'' the act of apprehension supplies the reader, when in the presence of the artifact, with a method for repeatedly experiencing a condition of imaginative grace, a Romantic fullness and intensity of vision that Ruskin finds distant from the imaginative capacities of his own age. (pp. 11-17)

> *Richard L. Stein, in an introduction to his* The Ritual of Interpretation: The Fine Arts as Literature in Ruskin, Rossetti, and Pater, *Cambridge, Mass: Harvard University Press, 1975, pp. 1-33.*

ALAN LEE   (essay date 1981)

[*Lee was an American educator and historian. In the following excerpt, he discusses Ruskin's theories of political economy.*]

No one now reads Ruskin for his economics. He has had virtually no place in the recent renaissance in the study of the history of economic thought, and there has been no suggestion that the omission is a grave one. Yet he spent a good half of his life writing about political economy, directly or tangentially. Although the customary view that he experienced something like a change of life in the late 1850s, moving from art to social criticism, has been replaced by a more plausible and accurate one in which the transition was nothing like so sudden or unpresaged, it must be admitted that there was a marked change of emphasis which centred upon the two semi-serialized works *Unto this last* . . . and *Munera Pulveris*. . . . The former was the first and most memorable of Ruskin's attempts to grapple with orthodox political economy, and arguably it was the storm of hostile criticism which greeted it that led him to devote so much of the remainder of his life to social criticism and theory, and which in turn brought him the fame attaching to a Victorian sage.

Such fame, however, was not necessarily conducive to the understanding of his meaning and significance. The numerous studies of Ruskin's social thought, which began to flow well before his death, have each tended to present the reader with a different Ruskin: Ruskin the Socialist, the Social Reformer, the New Liberal, the Medievalist and later the Technocrat and Institutionalist. Whilst not wishing to dismiss these versions out of hand, it may be suggested that there is another, less commonly found, but more authentic Ruskin, Ruskin the Tory, which fits the development and nature of his thought rather better than any of these, though it may diminish his relevance for later generations and sever the cord between Ruskin and, at its most absurd, Harold Wilson. . . .

People drank Ruskin in increasingly large draughts from the 1880s on, yet it is not entirely clear what they were drinking, or what they thought Ruskin was giving them. If, as is so often claimed, it made them into socialists and revolutionaries, it is legitimate to ask what sort of socialists and revolutionaries it could have made them into. As *Unto this last* was the chief vehicle of his social and economic thought any analysis of it must be made with this in mind.

If, however, we try immediately to look at Ruskin's political economy as set out in that book, we encounter the major difficulty that Ruskin was not a systematic thinker. His mind worked primarily in terms of visual perception, not verbal analysis, and he deliberately eschewed logic, hypothesis and system. . . . His writing was aphoristic, thickly larded with allusions to the Bible and, increasingly as he grew older and less mentally stable, with usually dubious etymological digressions. His role tended to be, as one of his most astute contemporary critics put it, 'a brilliant partisan in a random guerilla warfare'. So the concepts he used were rarely those of political economy: honour, justice, honesty and above all life and death. When he came to discuss wealth, value, utility, demand or labour it was only in terms of his own list of fundamentals. Nowhere do we find the painstaking logical analysis which characterized the economics of his day, and, indeed, of ours. He had received no training in the subject and his reading in it was not wide. Moreover, after the hostile reception of *Unto this last* he seems to have read less modern work than before, to have preferred Fawcett's popularization of Mill to the original, and to have been content in the main with second-hand accounts and reviews. (pp. 68-9)

Given this paucity of economic study, orthodox or otherwise, it is scarcely surprising that Ruskin's own political economy differed radically from the mainstream teaching of his day. Much of it sprang from his own fertile mind, but there were two major sources essential to its understanding, the Bible and Carlyle.

Knowing much of the Bible by heart, Ruskin naturally drew freely upon it whatever his subject. Much of his criticism of the objects and methodology of political economy, as he understood it, was based, even in his 'unconverted' period, on the teaching of the good Book. (p. 74)

But it was to Carlyle that he turned most often after the Bible. He kneeled at the feet of his 'master' . . . both intellectually and literally, 'the greatest of our English thinkers', 'our one quite clear-sighted teacher'. . . . Carlyle it was who damned political economy as 'the dismal science', had attacked 'the cash-payment as the sole nexus', had sacramentalized work,

had spoken of the true mastership of governing and of the chivalry of work, had, in fact, made virtually all the bricks with which Ruskin was to construct his own economic edifice. Ruskin had *Past and Present* off by heart . . . , and advised his readers to do likewise, later claiming that 'all has been said' in *Sartor, Past and Present* and the *Latter-Day Pamphlets* 'that needs to be said'. . . . It is only in the shadow of this debt that the peculiar language and concerns of Ruskin's economics can be understood, and that debt itself must be set in the context of Ruskin's own Toryism.

There are ample indications that Ruskin was, as he claimed, 'by nature and instinct Conservative'. 'I am,' he confessed in *Fors*, 'and my father was before me, a violent Tory of the old school'. . . . It was from his father in Edinburgh that he first learnt his Toryism, which consisted in part of a distrust of 'liberty', still associated with the terrors of the French Revolution. But it consisted of more than this. The parallel between fifteenth-century Venice and nineteenth-century England was only too obvious in the first volume of *Stones,* and the moral interpretation of history there provided was also the interpretation he gave to contemporary society. In place of 'Liberty' and 'anarchy' was set order, hierarchy, obedience and place. 'All anarchy is the forerunner of poverty, and all prosperity begins in obedience'. . . . He shared the medievalist fashion of the times in locating these virtues in pre-Renaissance Europe, but more importantly the concept of an organic, status-based society, founded on legitimate authority, gave him a platform from which he could launch into contemporary liberalism, the chief ideological prop of which was, as he rightly perceived, political economy. Not least of the errors of Adam Smith, in Ruskin's eyes, was his delineation of 'a system of natural liberty'.

As he wrote to the Social Democrat Sidney Cockerell in 1886, 'of course I am a Socialist—of the most stern sort—but I am also a Tory of the sternest sort'. Discipline, not liberty, still less equality, was the common factor here. Bernard Shaw, so often an idiosyncratic and unreliable source, was surely right in this instance in linking Ruskin, Toryism and Bolshevism: 'The Tory is a man who believes that those who are qualified by nature and training for public work, and who are naturally a minority, have to govern a mass of the people', and what consciousness would do for the Bolsheviks, education would do for Ruskin. 'Educate, or govern, they are one and the same word'. . . . His confessions to socialism or communism were, though widely quoted, few in number, and it was only if one defined socialism in some such terms as his disciple J. A. Hobson did, namely the belief 'that industry should be directed by the motive of social good, not individual gain', could Ruskin easily be shepherded into the Socialist fold. That he figured so prominently in the culture of the English labour movement is something we must return to later. For now it is sufficient to note that his claim to be 'a Communist of the old school' . . . rested on a decidedly paternalistic version of 'old communism', not inaccurate in itself, but likely, even in his own time, to mislead. What he certainly did not mean was the abolition of private property, which was the commonly understood characteristic of communist ideas. 'Men, and their property, must both be produced together—not one to the loss of the other'. . . . The division of property would mean its destruction . . . , and he claimed that without the protection of private property the worker would effectively forfeit his right to the produce of his labour. . . . Whatever similarities his later bureaucratic versions of Utopia might have had with later 'socialisms', Ruskin eschewed both the name and the thing as soulless and futile. . . .

It was a moral change that was called for, and he thought socialism did not provide that. . . . The socialist would disable the rich in the name of justice, Ruskin would educate them. . . .

For Ruskin 'the impossibility of Equality' . . . was the premise upon which his paternalistic society was to be built. In his early examination of political economy, *A Joy For Ever* . . . , he claimed that poverty was the result of 'wilfulness, when there should have been subordination', and he consequently urged the necessity of 'paternity, or fatherhood' in the nation. . . . In *The Stones of Venice* Volume 1 he emphasized that architecture was the expression *'of the mind of manhood by the hands of childhood'* . . . ; in the 'Nature of Gothic' the supposed *locus classicus* of his 'socialism', he looked forward to the time 'when men will see that to obey another man, to labour for him, yield reverence to him or to his place, is not slavery. It is often the best kind of liberty—liberty from care'. . . . All this appears again in *Unto this last* where he urged 'the advisability of appointing such [eternally superior] person or persons to guide, to lead, or on occasion even to compel and subdue, their inferiors according to their own better knowledge or wiser will' . . . , perhaps one of his most Rousseavian passages.

He saw no injustice in a society ordered on such principles, the basis of what he termed 'mastership', and his theory of work is central here. He thought it essential to avoid reducing men to the numerical equivalents of each other (which was the way which political economy would shortly turn). He noted, in relation to Sismondi, '(as if any man consenting to obey another had not a nobler will in obeying than in rebelling)', and in *Unto this last* the logical conclusion is drawn that death is the only real freedom possible to us.

Neither liberty nor equality was Ruskin's goal, but Justice, which required the care, not the exploitation, of fools, honesty, honour and work, and all this would result in wealth. . . . These were the central concerns of *Unto this last*. It was not so much the internal weaknesses of orthodox economy with which Ruskin was concerned, as its ideological and moral associations with liberalism and industrialism, and in this sense his was a real 'Tory' view.

Unto this last was, however, rather untypical of Ruskin's economic writings, in that whilst all that had gone before had focused upon 'work' and 'art' there is practically no discussion of these subjects in the book, an indication, perhaps, of how deliberately he had set out to deal directly with 'the bastard science'. The book was, of course, no finished treatise, having been cut short in the *Cornhill*, and it must remain doubtful whether Ruskin was capable of such a work in any case, but it was intended to be a serious and rigorous piece of criticism.

The first essay, **'The Roots of Honour',** derived its force of argument from its attack on the methodology of political economy, especially the practice of looking merely to individual self-interest, and the model of the 'economic man'. Ruskin insisted that this was misconceived, for 'the disturbing elements in the social problem . . . alter the essence of the creature under examination'. . . . To imagine otherwise was as if to try to understand man by examining his skeleton alone, 'the ossifant theory of progress'. . . . Whilst this was to exaggerate the classical position, it did serve Ruskin's purpose of arguing that political economy was thus made impotent to deal with 'the first vital problem which [it] has to deal with (the relation between employer and employed)'. . . . Labour relations could not be deduced from the mere play of interests; God had made

life too complex for strategies of that sort to work. Instead, the only publicly discernible criterion was Justice, wherein lay 'the roots of honour'. . . . Affection had to replace self-interest, and co-operation competition. . . .

He was, however, under no delusion that the affective motives would triumph on their own; they were all too easily smothered by competition. Therefore, wages had to be fixed justly, as he thought those in the professions were so fixed. It is important not to misconstrue this as a plea for a 'living wage', or a fixed remuneration for all, even in the same job; rather it was to call for a fixed payment for work of a certain grade. The bad workman would not be able to undercut the good one; he would not be able to work at that job at all. . . . This assumed a high degree of fluidity in the supply of labour, and seemed to imply that the aggregate demand for labour was fixed. It is difficult to see here, as some have done, the glimmer of a dynamic analysis.

Indeed, it was not part of Ruskin's purpose to provide such an analysis. When he spoke of the professions he touched the heart of the matter. It was important, for example, to exclude the merchant from the professions, because there self-interest had replaced self-sacrifice, the true mark of the profession. If gentlemen were to take again to trade, or, in somewhat more alarming fashion, if the merchant were to learn to die in providing his service, and become a father to his employees, or the captain of his ship, things might improve. . . . What promised to be a new analysis of economic behaviour, then, turns out to be a homily for merchants, a tribute to the professions.

The second essay, however, returned to the more usual ground of political economy, the subject of 'wealth'. Ruskin was unhappy about the way in which orthodox economics treated wealth as a given, rather than a subject for further study. He, therefore, distinguished between political economy proper and 'mercantile economy', the science of 'getting rich'. . . . If such claims were tendentious, and many of his jibes, particularly against Smith, were unfair, Ruskin can be said to have made a valuable point, namely that 'Riches are a power', and entail, so he said, an equivalent poverty on the part of those over whom they exercise power. . . . Such an argument had a long and distinguished lineage, including at the time Ruskin was writing, Marx, but it was obviously an unwelcome message to the readers of the *Cornhill*, who liked to think that wealth remedied, but did not entail poverty. . . .

Ruskin, however, was no egalitarian, and he accepted that inequalities properly directed, and the accumulation of riches properly spent, would benefit society, as long as it did not lead to a permanent rift between rich and poor, workers and idlers. . . . Contemporaries accused him, rightly, of confusing national and individual wealth, but this was a necessary consequence of his 'moral' approach. He may have had an organic view of society, but he rejected the heart of the classical conception, namely a self-righting and self-sustaining *system,* in which individual self-interest would ensure harmony. Thus, he could never accept the primacy of exchange in the classical theory, for that was not real wealth. The activities of the middle-man were barren. . . . There was no virtue in the cheapness of exchange. What was the *cost* of buying cheap, of selling dear? It could only be resolved by each man's innate knowledge of what was just. . . . The failure of modern wealth to command the authority due to it indicated that modern society had not elevated but diminished those over whom it had power, and, thereby, diminished wealth itself. . . .

The third essay continued this moral critique, and the issue of 'robbing the poor because he is poor' . . . , for all riches sprang firstly from the labour of the poor. Certain conflicts of interest, Ruskin agreed, were inevitable, but they had no need to be as destructive as they were, the laws of political economy could be managed so as to accord more closely with justice. . . . While he did spend some time on the concept of 'utility', there can be no doubt that at the heart of his economics there was a labour theory of value: 'the just price is the [price] of the productive labour of mankind'. . . . He was critical of the Ricardian labour embodied theory . . . , but he rejected the view that it was merely value in exchange that had to be measured. Money, he argued, was the payment in general for specific labour services, and the value of these would vary with the variability of labour, an admission, of course, which was to prove fatal to the Ricardian theory. Ruskin did not see this (and Ricardo had chosen to ignore it). He persisted in arguing that underlying all such exchanges of labour were units of work which had 'a worth, just as fixed and real as the specific gravity of a substance' . . . , what he elsewhere referred to as 'intrinsic value'. . . . While he clearly thought that there was positive worth attaching to labour, and justice was the equitable exchange of such worths, he never managed to show how it was possible to know, and to compare, these worths. Later he grappled with the problem in another way, but it is reasonably clear what the implication here was, namely, that it was inconceivable that men did not in fact know the difference between push-pin and poetry, and that Bentham's suggestion that they did not, or that it did not matter, was self-evidently rubbish; justice, like taste in art, was held to be self-evident for those who would see.

The pricing of labour also entailed the distribution of power. Cheap labour concentrated employment and, therefore, power, in few hands and hindered social mobility; justly rewarded labour, on the other hand, would encourage employees to employ others, spread wealth more evenly and multiply it at the same time. . . . The germ of a dynamic model of production and distribution may be detected here, but there is no real indication as to what the relationship between them is, not enough even to put him amongst the ranks of the underconsumptionists, of whom he disapproved anyway. One of the most striking lacunae in Ruskin's economic writings, in fact, is the lack of coherent discussion of capital.

The fourth essay had perforce to be something of a portmanteau, but dealt in the main with value, price and wealth. . . . Here we come to a central piece of his political economy, the notion of 'unproductive labour', that is labour (or capital, for Ruskin seems to have treated capital as stored-up labour) spent on things which themselves did not aid future production, one of Mill's 'fundamental propositions on capital'. Ruskin rejected it, but not on the grounds that velvet and iron were equally items of consumption—he adopted his own distinction between goods and what he once termed 'bads'. . . . In *A Joy For Ever* he had strenuously denied the proposition that *any* and *all* expenditure could produce employment and wealth, and in *The Two Paths* he took the socialist view that the rich actually robbed the poor by their expenditure, by using their labour on luxuries instead of necessities. . . . What concerned Ruskin was not the aggregate of demand but the worth of what was produced, or the use to which it was put, and, whereas he later admitted that all consumption contributed to demand, he insisted on distinguishing between the consumption of the labourer and that of the warmonger, blackmailer or thief. . . . His attack on Mill's admittedly untenable version of the 'wages-

fund' doctrine, that 'a demand for commodities is not a demand for labour', was vitiated by his insistence that the demand for some commodities was not, indeed, a demand for labour. . . .

He did, however, try to sort out the problem of value and price, unresolved at the time, and in doing so some have argued that he presaged future marginalist theories. Yet this must be based on the view that he rejected the labour theory of value, conceiving of all value as the relation between demand (or use) and supply. However, he was prevented from adopting such a position because his initial premise was that all value in exchange was founded upon real, 'intrinsic' worth. . . . He was thus left in the realm of metaphysics . . . , in which, some would say necessarily, the theory of value had consistently dwelt. For Ruskin 'value' was a matter of the giving of life. . . . Mill had said that wealth was a matter of possession and use, but Ruskin countered by arguing that with the former had to go the power to use, and that the latter depended on the capacity of the user; so not 'everything to every man, but . . . the right thing to the right man'. . . .

Ruskin thought exchange irrelevant to this. Like the eighteenth-century Physiocrats he denied that there could be gain in exchange *per se* . . . , but as he also held that individuals were qualitatively different, and not equal, he could not logically dismiss the possibility of any net advantages from exchange. For the economists the market would decide, but Ruskin had little faith in that. . . . Instead he turned again to 'labour'; exchange which resulted in a net addition to 'good' or 'vital' labour was an addition to wealth. . . . The distinction hinged on consumption, 'the end, crown, and perfection of production'. . . . Understandably this has attracted much praise from later critics who rightly point to a neglect of the subject in classical theory, but again one must not assume that Ruskin was defending consumption as the motor of a dynamic economy. Like Marx and some contemporary German historicists he questioned the desirability of accumulation without end, and in the distinction he made between 'Production for the Ground, and for the Mouth' . . . was not only a moral critique of capitalism, but the hint that capitalism might undermine itself. Typically, however, it remained a hint, and we are led away again to the realm of moral evaluation and the famous phrase summarizing all of Ruskin's economics, 'THERE IS NO WEALTH BUT LIFE'. . . .

After this climax there followed a handful of notes on various subjects, most importantly on population, which, although without direct reference to Malthus, adhered in some respects quite closely to his views. Rejecting colonization as a temporary palliative, he advocated restraint in reproduction and in consumption. . . . Luxury now could intensify misery, though in a future society he allowed that might be avoided. . . . He, therefore, called for individual moral regeneration, not social revolution; 'true felicity of the human race must be by individual, not public effort'. . . .

The practical sections of the book, on trade unions and wages, Ruskin dismissed as its least important parts . . . , and although there is a plea for 'forethought' and a sketch of what might be termed a mixed economy . . . *Unto this last* did not discuss the role of the State. It had been prominent in *A Joy For Ever* and the more totalitarian aspects of Ruskin's vision came out in *Time and Tide,* but it is clear that such policy conclusions were implied by the book, based as it was on a concept of commutative justice. (pp. 75-83)

It has not been possible to do justice to the whole of Ruskin's 'economics', but it is not unfair to conclude that Ruskin was no political economist, and that he will not be read as one. Misconceived, ill-informed and often unfair as his onslaught on political economy was, weak as his understanding of it, confused as his own arguments often were, he did manage to confront the science with a stiff moral challenge. In scope and methodology particularly he found weak spots, and in his insistence upon the social relations which were consequent upon the distribution of wealth, he sought to make more concrete an abstract logical discipline; but it was his call to justice not his claim to have set the science of political economy on a new footing that appealed to his readers, at a time when 'social justice' was becoming the common change of political debate. (p. 85)

                    Alan Lee, "Ruskin and Political Economy: 'Unto This Last'," in New Approaches to Ruskin: Thirteen Essays, *edited by Robert Hewison, Routledge & Kegan Paul, 1981, pp. 68-88.*

ELIZABETH K. HELSINGER (essay date 1982)

[*Helsinger is an American educator and critic who has written extensively on Ruskin. In the following excerpt, she examines Ruskin's combination of history, travel writing, and social criticism in* The Stones of Venice.]

Historical consciousness plays a larger role in Ruskin's criticism than is usually acknowledged. Ruskin called *The Stones of Venice* a history, but as history it has had few defenders. The account of Venetian architecture in *Stones* is shaped throughout by an extrahistorical intention: to celebrate medieval art and values and to condemn, on moral as well as aesthetic grounds, Renaissance Italy and nineteenth-century England. Ruskin's history, even more than Carlyle's, seems to have few connections with nineteenth-century historicism, hence with the history of history. But this judgment is not itself sufficiently historical. Looking back at contemporary models and sources for *The Stones of Venice,* I find that Ruskin's term "history" had meanings for early Victorian readers with which his own work is in complete accord. In *Stones* and the large body of contemporary literature to which it is most closely related, history is approached through travel, and travel experienced as history. Ruskin's book, shaped to meet a traveler-reader's practical needs and formal expectations, belongs to a loose genre of travel histories that reflected and shaped the historical attitudes of a good many English readers in the first part of the nineteenth century. Common to all these works is an implicit identification between the activity of the reader exploring history and that of the tourist exploring landscapes: the facts of the history book are the artifacts encountered by the traveler. Ruskin calls the stones of Venice his archives; the metaphor reflects the experience of the traveler-reader for whom *Stones* and many popular history and travel books were intended.

But *Stones* is of course more than history presented as travel. Ruskin's readers, tourists in search of the picturesque, become his subjects no less than Gothic workmen. His central chapter, "The Nature of Gothic," begins with an attack on contemporary modes of producing and consuming art. One can read this shift from past to present as a shift from history to criticism, a shift that thereby distorts the historical accuracy of the book. But in many respects this chapter is the book's greatest historical achievement. Ruskin's sharply critical attitude toward the Victorian manufacturer-consumer results in an idealization of the middle ages, but it also permits the historicization of

contemporary attitudes toward history and art. The confrontation between a contemporary traveler and a foreign past becomes a means for presenting an historicized view of the present and, particularly, of the traveler's habits of perception. Ruskin was not the first Englishman to use the travel-as-history trope to explore the perceptual limitations of the traveler-reader; he recognized Byron, Turner, Prout, and Carlyle as his predecessors. But *Stones* is at once closer to the popular literature it resembles and more consistently critical of the perceptual habits of the traveler-reader it addresses.

"The Nature of Gothic" has traditionally been cited as the beginning of Ruskin's social criticism, and so it is. It is the historical self-consciousness cultivated in that chapter as much as the economic and social analysis, however, which seems to mark the transformation of the amateur writer on art into the cultural critic. Ruskin's writing before *Stones* is remarkably ahistorical. The stones of Venice and the English travelers who see them are historical entities as the subjects of Ruskin's earlier books—the truths of nature and art or the lamps of architecture—are not. The full title of the first volume of *Modern Painters (Their Superiority in the Art of Landscape Painting to the Ancient Masters)* points to the discontinuity between Claude and Turner which Ruskin repeatedly asserts there. In the three volumes of *Modern Painters* that follow *Stones,* however, Ruskin takes a very different approach, tracing changes in perception, taste, and belief. Claude appears as one of Turner's teachers, not simply as the negative pole of a comparison between false and true landscape painting. *Stones* gave Ruskin experience with modes of historical thought prevalent in the early nineteenth century, and these continued to shape his work, even though he wrote no more histories. The book seems to have showed Ruskin that his proper work, though not history, was criticism based on historical self-consciousness. I take it that this view of the place of *Stones* in his work became clear to Ruskin as he wrote. Volumes two and three, increasingly critical of the cultural attitudes of Victorian readers, explicitly point to a critical, historical treatment of the present as the proper approach to the subject of Turner and landscape art— a program carried out in Ruskin's next major books, *Modern Painters III-V.* The shift of focus from Gothic workman to Victorian reader is an exercise in historical perception as well as an act of criticism. With this shift in focus, Ruskin extends his historical perspective from art to contemporary attitudes to art; at that point, history becomes a necessary part of Ruskin's efforts to reform the perceptual habits and cultural attitudes of his readers. To understand this development in Ruskin we need to look more closely at the way in which *Stones* combines tourism with historical narrative and puts these to critical use.

But are either popular travel histories or critical juxtapositions of past and present very significant in the history of history? Neither of these Victorian versions of history makes historical explanation and reconstruction a primary goal. Although they may lead to a more historical consciousness of the present, they do not assume that all truths are historical and relative. They accept the possibility of absolute and ahistorical judgment that may transcend the limitations of the moment, and then proceed to make such judgments—like Ruskin's violent condemnation of the Renaissance—an integral part of their historical accounts. These procedures have long been regarded as completely opposed to the objectivizing tendency of nineteenth-century historicism. Recent critics, however, have suggested that the objectivity pursued by the historicists was born of the same assumptions as the nostalgia and the sweeping judgments expressed by romantic—and many Victorian—writers. The historicist's search for an objective, scientific method might be regarded as an impossible attempt to cancel the historicity of interpretation no less than the romantic's assumption of absolute moral or religious values as criteria for judgment. Such criticism calls into question the common distinction by which romantic history, like Carlyle's and Ruskin's, is seen as less central to the development of modern historical methods than scientific historicism. If one accepts this criticism as a (negative) correction to the current view, then the travel histories and cultural criticism of the English Victorians acquire a greater interest for the history of history. Though these Victorians, like the scientific historicists, were unwilling to historicize all truth, they were often more concerned to explore the historical dimensions of contemporary perception and judgment. In this history of history, Ruskin's *Stones* occupies a modest but highly interesting position. (pp. 140-43)

> *Elizabeth K. Helsinger, in her* Ruskin and the Art of the Beholder, *Cambridge, Mass.: Harvard University Press, 1982, 342 p.*

DAVID SONSTROEM (essay date 1982)

[*Sonstroem is an American educator and critic who has written numerous essays on Victorian authors. In the following excerpt, he examines imagery common to* Modern Painters III *and* Modern Painters IV *and discusses Ruskin's exploration of reverie and focused thought as means of perception.*]

At the outset of *Modern Painters III*—subtitled "Of Many Things"—Ruskin declares that he intends to pursue his considerations "just as they occur to us, without too great scrupulousness in marking connections, or insisting on sequences." He insouciantly defends his procedure with this disarming simile: "I suspect that system-makers, in general, are not of much more use . . . than . . . the old women [of Pomona] who tie cherries upon sticks, for the more convenient portableness of the same. . . . but if they can be had in their own wild way of clustering about their crabbed stalk, it is a better connection for them than any other." A consequence of Ruskin's proceeding in his "own wild way" is that, although *Modern Painters III* and *IV* (both published in 1856) bristle with a host of stimulating observations and conceptions, the volumes give a misleading sense of incoherence. The common critical view is that they "form together a splendid if exasperating medley which defies any brief description." Therefore, despite Ruskin's low view of system makers, I propose to string some of his leading ideas on a stick, to show at least one implicit, coherent, sustained purpose in the two volumes.

Modern Painters III and *IV* are unified, first, by a common area of exploration—perception—and, second, by a common complex of imagery. With respect to the first, the end for which Ruskin writes is, as in his earlier works, finally religious vision—discerning God. His immediate subject matter, painting, can be regarded as his contemplative raw material. Art is chiefly useful to him for furnishing accounts of right and wrong perception, to be used as steppingstones on the way to attaining that vantage point from which man is able to behold God; "To see clearly is poetry, prophecy, and religion,—all in one." . . .

The goal is exactly that of Volume I, but attaining it is now found to be much more difficult. Gone is the excited, spontaneous, easy assumption of a divine Creator behind the vibrant natural prospects. Ruskin's task has been made more difficult by the dimming of his sense of nature as figuring forth God. Nature is no longer seen as God's uniformly harmonious mas-

terpiece, for now Ruskin recognizes "a dark and plague-like stain in the midst of the gentle landscape" . . . , "a leprosy of decay through every breeze, and every stone." . . . For the first time we even find speculations that the universe is godless, dead at the core. Volumes III and IV are shot through with the imagery of decay and detritus, as in this apocalyptic passage: "The earth, as a tormented and trembling ball, may have rolled in space for myriads of ages before humanity was formed from its dust; and as a devastated ruin it may continue to roll, when all that human dust shall again have been mingled with ashes that never were warmed by life, or polluted by sin." . . . Discussing Wordsworth's "Intimations" ode, he recollects his own earlier excitement in the presence of nature, finding that the "religious feeling mingled with it" . . . was an indefinite, unreflective one. Although he then experienced "a continual perception of Sanctity in the whole of nature, from the slightest thing to the vastest;—an instinctive awe . . . such as we sometimes imagine to indicate the presence of a disembodied spirit" . . . , the feeling faded. Even though Ruskin can "in great part still restore the old childish feeling" . . . , he is now somewhat suspicious of its significance because he holds it partly due to mere novelty rather than to the soul's prenatal memories as Wordsworth had conjectured. As, then, Ruskin proceeds to build forthrightly upon the glittering foundation of Volume I, he also finds himself in the very Keatsian position of asking of that earlier, jubilant work, "Was it a vision, or a waking dream?"

Modern Painters III and *IV* are unified not only by this common area of exploration but also by a common complex of imagery. The Turner of Volume I was the "master" who "strode farther and deeper, and more daringly into dominions before unsearched or unknown; . . . impatient in his step . . . impetuous in his success . . . exalted in his research." . . . Ruskin's personification, in Volume II, of the rightly directed imagination "goes straight forward up the hill; no voices nor mutterings can turn it back, nor petrify it from its purpose." . . . But the following passages are typical of Volumes III and IV:

> Now we have some hard hill-climbing to do; and the remainder of our investigation must be carried on, for the most part, on hands and knees. . . .
>
> Some men . . . however slipping or stumbling at the wayside, have yet their eyes fixed on the true gate and goal (stumbling, perhaps, even the more because they have), and will not fail of reaching them. . . .
>
> The difficulty is, that out of these facts, right and left, the different forms of misapprehension branch into grievous complexity, and branch so far and wide, that if once we try to follow them, they will lead us quite from our mark into other separate . . . discussions. . . .
>
> Our whole happiness and power of energetic action depend upon our being able to breathe and live in the cloud; content to see it opening here and closing there; rejoicing to catch, through the thinnest films of it, glimpses of stable and substantial things; but yet perceiving a nobleness even in the concealment. . . .

The hills prove to be precipitous mountains, so the gait is reduced from an impetuous stride to stumbling and crawling. "Grievous complexity" transforms straightforward progress into confused choosing among the many treacherous "by-ways that may open, on right hand or left." . . . Eyes cannot, in fact, be always "fixed on the true gate and goal" but must settle for catching mere misty "glimpses of stable and substantial things." In short, the clouds and mountains extensively described in Volume IV are employed as symbols in both of these volumes for Ruskin's own tortuous processes of thought and for the ambiance of modern man generally in his arduous and bewildering journey through life.

The symbols furnish Ruskin with a mode of exploration as well as a mode of description. His way of working through the problems confronted in these volumes includes, besides observation and ratiocination, an extensive, tentative play with the host of associations that can be attached to journeys, clouds, and mountains. He proceeds in large part through his images. (pp. 85-8)

In *Modern Painters III* and *IV* the locus of significance has shifted for Ruskin from the external world to what we might call the landscape within. He can justly maintain that the shift is accounted for by the programmatic movement of his discourse upon landscape painting from the examination of Truth to that of Beauty and Relation. But the shift can also be seen as the consequence of his no longer viewing nature as God's masterpiece: "Half the world will not see the terrible and sad truths which the universe is full of." . . . External nature now being seen as diseased and dilapidated, the artist must use it as his raw material in creating a masterpiece of landscape through the exercise of his imagination. The artist of these volumes transforms his materials rather than merely replicates them, for he creates or discovers within himself that comprehensive order which the artist of Volume I discovered without.

The importance of the imagination is revealed in Ruskin's now seeing the apprehension of a landscape as usually involving reverie, whether someone is viewing a natural scene, delineating it, or viewing a delineation. Ruskin goes as far as to say that great art may properly be defined as "the Art of *Dreaming*" . . . and to proclaim, "A universe of noble dream-land lies before us, yet to be conquered." . . . The nature of true reverie is set forth in a passage given here at length:

> Suppose that three or four persons come in sight of a group of pine-trees. . . . One, perhaps an engineer, is struck by the manner in which their roots hold the ground, and sets himself to examine their fibres, in a few minutes retaining little more consciousness of the beauty of the trees than if he were a rope-maker untwisting the strands of a cable: to another, the sight of the trees calls up some happy association, and presently he forgets them, and pursues the memories they summoned: a third is struck by certain groupings of their colours, useful to him as an artist, which he proceeds immediately to note mechanically for future use, with as little feeling as a cook setting down the constituents of a newly discovered dish; and a fourth, impressed by the wild coiling of boughs and roots, will begin to change them in his fancy into dragons and monsters, and lose his grasp of the scene in fantastic metamorphosis: while, in the mind of the man who has most the power of contemplating the thing itself, all these perceptions and trains of idea are partially present, not distinctly, but in a mingled and perfect har-

mony. . . . Fancy, and feeling, and perception, and imagination, will all obscurely meet and balance themselves in him. . . .

A common external stimulus evokes mental activity in all five persons, but it can be said of only the first four that the trees evoke a *train* of thought, directed or meandering. The "mingled" mental activity of the fifth is better seen as a cumulation—what Ruskin subsequently calls a "garland of thoughts," grouped and fastened about one's perception of the natural object as a center—a disposition reminiscent of those cherries "clustering about their crabbed stalk." The most notable quality of the "garland" is its "perfect harmony," quite other from any that the trees may or may not possess of themselves. Though derived from nature, the harmonious masterpiece is man's creation, the work of his reverie. But such dreaming is not a denial of the natural world—far from it. For, Ruskin argues, it is just such a dreamer who "has most the power of contemplating the thing itself"; his poised being permits a more comprehensive original impression than that of the first four viewers, who notice only a single aspect of the tree. Furthermore, the clinging imagination of the dreamer does not stray very far from the directly perceived object, whereas the centrifugal imaginations of the first four quickly distort or abandon it. But the dreamer's vision is achieved at the cost of sharpness of focus; his many perceptions present themselves "obscurely," "not distinctly." The "garland of thoughts" about an object is frequently likened to a cloud gathered about a mountain peak. Clouds, then, represent the blurred focus of a reverie as well as the profound mysteriousness of nature.

Two general benefits result from the rightly functioning reverie. The basal benefit is "exalting any visible object, by gathering round it, in farther vision, all the facts properly connected with it; this being, as it were, a spiritual or second sight, multiplying the power of enjoyment according to the fulness of the vision." . . . The second benefit has to do with far more than enjoyment, but it is reserved for only the noblest instances, where reverie becomes nothing less than divine inspiration: "I . . . have used . . . the word Inspiration, not carelessly nor lightly, but in all logical calmness and perfect reverence." . . . The possibility of the influence of inspiration on the production of artistic, literary, or architectural works is a fresh consideration for Ruskin. He has glanced at it a few times in previous works but without giving full attention to its possibilities or even expressing full conviction as he does, for example, when he refers in *Modern Painters II* to the power of the imagination as inexplicable—"inexplicable because proceeding from an imaginative perception *almost* superhuman" (. . . emphasis added). Most of his earlier pertinent remarks have attributed imaginative insights to "intuition and intensity of gaze" . . .—to human faculties alone. But here in Volume III, in the midst of his chapter "Of the Naturalist Ideal," the possibility that God may be painting the interior landscape and directing the dream suddenly strikes home.

> All the great men *see* what they paint before they paint it,—see it in a perfectly passive manner,—cannot help seeing it if they would; whether in their mind's eye, or in bodily fact, does not matter; very often the mental vision is, I believe, in men of imagination, clearer than the bodily one; but vision it is . . . the whole scene, character, or incident passing before them as in second sight, whether they will or no, and requiring them to paint it as they

see it . . . it being to them . . . always a true vision or Apocalypse, and invariably accompanied in their hearts by a feeling correspondent to the words,—"Write the things *which thou hast seen,* and the things which *are*." . . .

Here is something quite other than the teasing suggestion of divinity in external nature. The God who obscures himself behind the clouds of the natural world may yet speak plainly to the imaginations of a certain "dream-gifted" few. It may be better to follow, not Nature, but the Gleam. Enlivened to the possibility, Ruskin seems willing to sacrifice man's autonomy of imagination in exchange for a greater assurance of God's presence.

Ruskin's imagery expands to include the new possibility. The clouds of reverie may be clouds of confusion, but now they may also be the atmosphere of the oracular, "God's dwelling-place." For

> we find God going before the Israelites in a pillar of cloud; revealing Himself in a cloud on Sinai; appearing in a cloud on the mercy seat; filling the Temple of Solomon with the cloud when its dedication is accepted; appearing in a great cloud to Ezekiel; ascending into a cloud before the eyes of the disciples on Mount Olivet; and in like manner returning to judgment. "Behold, He cometh with clouds, and every eye shall see Him." . . .

In like wise, the mountains can become a "Sinai" . . . , where God speaks to his Moses.

But is a given reverie a true vision or an insubstantial dream? Much of the two volumes is taken up with Ruskin's frequent and sometimes prolonged judgment of the reverie as he sifts it for trustworthiness. Ultimately its origin is more crucial than its validity, because the demonstration of genuine inspiration would be a kind of proof of God's existence. (pp. 88-92)

Ruskin is also alive to its misuses and inherent weaknesses. For example, he anticipates modern psychology in recognizing "a strange connection between the reinless play of the imagination, and a sense of the presence of evil" . . . ; "the imagination, when at play, is curiously like bad children, and likes to play with fire." . . . Of course he differs from the orthodoxy of our own day in seeking to prevent or repress fetid exhalations of the subterranean self. In addition, he sees the imagination misemployed in "creating, for mere pleasure, false images, where it is its *duty* to create true ones; or in turning what was intended for the mere refreshment of the heart into its daily food, and changing the innocent pastime of an hour into the guilty occupation of a life." . . . And another example of misuse is the production of Pathetic Fallacies—perceptual falsifications arising from strong feeling. Ruskin sees this use of the imagination as unavoidable by practically everyone at some time or other, and as the expression or result of a morbid state rather than the cause of one. Or, rather, it is the cause of one only insofar as it leads people to cultivate it as "poetic," thereby inclining themselves to abjure their responsibility to see rightly as best they can. If one thus seeks to distort his vision, he feeds the modern penchant for cloudy vagueness. Carried to the extreme, it produces disbelief in the accuracy, the truth, of *any* perception—a disbelief implied in an "infinitely sad" saying of a contemporary painter, "If you look for curves, you will see curves; if you look for angles, you will see angles." . . .

Even more serious than the misuses of the imagination are its inherent weaknesses, which pertain even when it is properly directed. Ruskin probes these limitations with a vigor remarkable in one whose hopes for the reverie are so evident. The main such weakness is that it hinders the dreamer from action, from social usefulness in particular. The components of the reverie are not "purposeful" . . . because in a "curiously languid and neutralized . . . condition," "The thoughts are beaten to a powder so small that . . . they are not good for much." . . . The dream's inherent "obscurity," "indistinctness," "indeterminateness," "dimness" (Ruskin runs the gamut of synonyms) prevent focused action. Ruskin holds that

> among men of average intellect the most useful members of society are the dissectors, not the dreamers. It is not that they love nature or beauty less, but that they love result, effect, and progress more; and when we glance broadly along the starry crowd of benefactors to the human race, and guides of human thought, we shall find that this dreaming love of natural beauty— or at least its expression—has been more or less checked by them all, and subordinated either to hard work or watching of *human* nature. . . .

Referring to his own youthful pleasure in mountain scenery, he finds that it led him "to ramble over hills when I should have been learning lessons, and lose days in reveries which I might have spent in doing kindnesses." . . . The dreamer overlooks the substantial wrongs before his eyes while "rambling" alone over the misty hills of his mind.

The dream's incompatibility with the material present and with focused action can be reduced to its incompatibility with linear thought. Dreams "cannot be caught in any other shape than that they come in" . . . , and the "shape" of a dream is, as we have seen, the indeterminate one of a garland or cloud. The dreamer's "ignorance of all rules" may be "glorious" if it betokens true inspiration; but "men who have this habit of clustering and harmonizing their thoughts are a little too apt to look scornfully upon the harder workers who tear the bouquet to pieces to examine the stems. . . . to dissect a flower may sometimes be as proper as to dream over it." . . . Ruskin's imagery proclaims the seeming irreconcilability between the two modes of thought.

Ruskin's attitude toward regular, directed thought is as divided as that toward the dream. I have already noted his disparagement of thoughts in sequence, like cherries tied to a stick. Elsewhere he seizes upon the especial weakness of such thinking.

> So long as our idea of the multitudes who inhabit the ravines . . . remains indistinct, that idea comes to the aid of all the other associations which increase our delight. But let it once arrest us, and entice us to follow out some clear course of thought respecting the causes of the prosperity or misfortune of the Alpine villagers, and the snowy peak again ceases to be visible, or holds its place only as a white spot upon the retina, while we pursue our meditations upon the religion or the political economy of the mountaineers. . . . let the reasoning powers be shrewd in excess . . . and it will go hard but that the visible object will suggest so much that

it shall be soon itself forgotten, or become, at the utmost, merely a kind of keynote to the course of purposeful thought. . . .

Directed thinking involves the loss not only of a vivid sense of the "keynote" object itself but also of any sense of sanctity pertaining to the object. Ruskin recalls that his own sense of a sacred aura surrounding natural things was gradually dissipated just when his "practical power increased." . . . Nevertheless, "some clear course of thought respecting the causes of the prosperity or misfortune of the Alpine villagers" is decidedly needed by the world at large. Although "Newton, probably, did not perceive whether the apple which suggested his meditations on gravity was withered or rosy," he did right to wander "away in thought from the thing seen to the business of life." . . .

We see that one of the cloudy steeps that modern man must scale is the reconciliation of antithetical mental activities. Should he cultivate his imagination, thereby courting inspiration as a warrant of divine presence and, in the process, reconstructing a restored version of the broken world on the canvas of his imagination? Or should he quit dreaming in order to sharpen his thoughts, especially with respect to relieving the human suffering that cowers amidst those crumbled stones? Ruskin's implicit conclusion is to alternate the two mental modes. He implies as much by remarking that the "Dimness and Untraceableness" of the thoughts of a reverie "is not a *fault* in the thoughts, *at such a time*" (. . . second emphasis added). Again, one can sense nature as animated by a divine presence, first in childhood, and then later, and more satisfactorily, after "the active life is nobly fulfilled." . . . Ruskin's practice of arranging mankind into orders of being also shows his desire to harmonize the two ways of thinking—"the lowest, sordid and selfish, which neither sees nor feels; the second, noble and sympathetic, but which sees and feels without concluding or acting; and the third and highest, which loses sight in resolution, and feeling in work." . . . It would seem that a linear, active existence has carried the day against a dreaming existence. But Ruskin soon posits three new stages, which show man raised above even this last order of being: "It is in raising us from the first state of inactive reverie to the second of useful thought, that scientific pursuits are to be chiefly praised. But in restraining us at this second stage, and checking the impulses towards higher contemplation, they are to be feared or blamed." . . . In short, a stage composed of clear thought and practical action may be useful in elevating man from his unsatisfactory modern state of suggestive but lonely and indefinite dozing to a "higher contemplation," both authentic and clear. Although the cloudless dream of the inspired soul remains the objective, the times call for directed thought and action and no further dreaming along the way. (pp. 95-8)

> *David Sonstroem, "Prophet and Peripatetic in 'Modern Painters' III and IV," in* Studies in Ruskin: Essays in Honor of Van Akin Burd, *edited by Robert Rhodes and Del Ivan Janik, Ohio University Press, 1982, pp. 85-114.*

BEVERLY SEATON (essay date 1985)

[In the following excerpt, Seaton discusses Ruskin's botanical study Proserpina.*]*

Ruskin's editor E. T. Cook first placed *Proserpina* in the genre of flower books: "There are many books of 'floral fancies,' and as a rule they are among the most vapid forms of litera-ture." According to Cook, Ruskin's purpose was "to associate the study of flowers—their modes of growth, their specialities of form and colour—with the place they have held in the thoughts and fancies, the mythologies and the literature, the art and the religion of the civilized world." . . . Such an enterprise was hardly original, of course, but Ruskin's efforts to so study flowers illuminate several aspects of his thinking.

Ruskin was interested in botany throughout his life, often writing about flowers in his major works, but his flower references are not systematic. Fragmentary and incoherent as it is, *Proserpina,* however, begins to look more coherent and systematic when viewed in the context of other Victorian flower books. I am not claiming that Ruskin was influenced by writers like Hibberd and Kitto, but only that he participated in the same kind of thinking about flowers that they did. He shared with them an Evangelical background, and his familiarity with gift annuals, albums, and similar publications brings him close to the world of popular publishing which produced flower books for mass consumption.

In *The Poison Sky,* Raymond Fitch notes that all of Ruskin's works from the period when *Proserpina* was written (1875-1886) "strove toward a general system for the interpretation of the sacred everywhere." Thus, Fitch thinks, Ruskin became increasingly anti-science. In his insightful reading of *Proserpina,* Frederick Kirchhoff has also pointed out that Ruskin was developing "a science against science." Certainly, *Proserpina* expresses distrust of science; Ruskin often breaks out into peevish invective, as when he calls scientists "human bats; men of semi-faculty and semi-education." . . . Conventional flower writers, on the other hand, either ignored science altogether or were scientists—botanists, horticulturists, sometimes physicians—who interpreted nature through religious inclination as much as through observation shaped by scientific training. Most agreed that scientific knowledge was not the main purpose of studying flowers, but rather spiritual enlightenment. In *Proserpina,* Ruskin was trying to reorganize botany along lines acceptable to him, revising the classificatory and analytical systems of the science in accord with aesthetic and moral considerations, purging the flowers of unwholesome names and sexual connotations. Ruskin was looking at the process from the other end, one might say; he was trying to remake science according to morality instead of trying to find moral meaning in the nature revealed by science. Just listing the titles of Charles Darwin's botanical works published in the years when Ruskin was writing *Proserpina*—*Insectivorous Plants* (1875), *The Effects of Cross- and Self-Fertilization* (1876), *The Different Forms of Flowers on Plants of the Same Species* (1877), *The Power of Movement in Plants* (1880), and *The Formation of Vegetable Mould, Through the Action of Worms* (1881)—suggests the view of plants that Ruskin was trying to combat. In *Proserpina,* Ruskin turned to some of the same topics which interested Darwin, such as plant motion, with quite different results. While Darwin through careful study established some of the principles of plant mobility, Ruskin made comments on "caprice." . . . Most conventional flower writers, while not all "Darwinians," of course, found no fault with the sort of botanical work Darwin was doing, but Ruskin was fully aware of the materialistic implications of science. One passage will illustrate Ruskin's posture as what might be called a moral scientist—his definition of the "perfect or pure flower."

> A perfect or pure flower, as a rose, oxalis, or campanula, is always composed of an unbroken whorl, or corolla, in the form of a disk, cup,

bell, or, if it draw together again at the lips, a narrow-necked vase. This cup, bell, or vase, is divided into similar petals (or segments, which are petals carefully joined), varying in number from three to eight, and enclosed by a calyx whose sepals are symmetrical also.

An imperfect, or, as I am inclined rather to call it, an "injured" flower, is one in which some of the petals have inferior office and position, and are either degraded, for the benefit of others, or expanded and honoured at the cost of others. . . .

We especially notice Ruskin's personification of plants through the value words he attaches to them—"perfect," "pure," "imperfect," "injured," "inferior," "degraded"—and also the moral point he makes about the inferior flowers. Not only are they inferior according to design considerations, but morally—they have irregular arrangements of petals which either degrade some petals for the benefit of others or put some forward at the expense of others. These remarks, and hundreds of others like them, Ruskin apparently intended to serve as the basis of a new scientific classification. To show his difference from the conventional flower book writers, here is a passage on a similar theme, the perfect flower, from a piece which explains all the different parts of the flower in J. L. K.'s *The Voice of Flowers:*

> That on the left hand with figures is a fuchsia. It represents what botanists call a *perfect* flower; that is, one which possesses all the various parts described below, which is not the case with all flowers. The perfect flower has four circles, one within the other. The calyx . . . represents the first or outer circle. The calyx is the cup which contains and surrounds the blossoms. In some flowers the calyx is all one piece, in others it is divided into several pieces, which are then called *sepals*. In the picture the calyx is really one piece, though, as you see, deeply divided,—a little figure which may remind us of something far more important than the flower, namely, the Church of Christ, which is ever *one,* though so deeply divided in the sight of men. . . .

Both Ruskin and J. L. K. sought spiritual meaning in the study of plants. The deep, and important, difference is that Ruskin wanted to establish a consistency in the way we look at both the natural and the spiritual world. He did not see any reason to approach the process of understanding with complete knowledge of the facts, as he makes clear in a passage about Roman history (he is discussing the names of kinds of stems). He does not know much Roman history at all, he confides, but he does know "the significance of what I find, better than perhaps even Mr. Smith [the historian] himself." . . . He felt the same way about nature. One is reminded here of Johann Wolfgang von Goethe's work on plant morphology, which exhibits some of the same motivations as *Proserpina*. Goethe was disappointed that his efforts were not taken seriously by scientists.

While Ruskin was trying to remake botany as well as to find spiritual significance in its study, he found himself involved in typological thought in a curious manner. For he looked at nature, and found revealed there not God, but Man, and not generalized Man, but a construct one might name Moral Man,

an ideal to set over against "fallen" human nature. A passage in the work of Leo Grindon comes to mind: "For the true analogist, wherever he may be, however he may shift his standing ground, always finds himself in the *middle* of nature, his particular subject for the time being the clue and textbook to the whole." . . . Kirchhoff explains that Ruskin's quest for a new understanding of myth and "natural religion" in the classical sense, while meant as a corrective to science, in fact led to a better understanding of mankind rather than to a new appreciation of religion. . . . Sometimes it seems that, as Ruskin reorders the families of plants, he is also remaking human nature; thus he articulates a science which does not contain Man but is somehow an extension of universal values which apply alike to people and flowers. Ruskin saw that modern science, as epitomized by "Mr. Darwin, and his school" . . . , was incompatible with religious and moral values in a way unsuspected by a devout botanist like Balfour or a science-minded clergyman like Hugh Macmillan. He did not focus on evolution and natural selection alone, but these of course concerned him, especially in connection with such "nasty" issues as reproduction. It is interesting to contrast Ruskin's method of dealing with the threat posed by science with that of Alfred, Lord Tennyson in *In Memoriam*. Tennyson makes metaphorical use of evolution, creating a new version of the ending of the traditional elegy, locating Arthur Henry Hallam not in Heaven with Christ, but ahead of us on the evolutionary scale, a "noble type." Ruskin's vision of the "noble type" seems to be drawn forth by his study of nature and myth (in both *Proserpina* and *The Queen of the Air*), which he saw as the "science" of earlier men, their understanding of nature. But both Ruskin and Tennyson, sensing the incompatibility of science and religion, found in a higher form of mankind the synthesis of value.

In typological terms, we can say that Ruskin found Moral Man to be the antitype rather than God; in some passages, he even suggests that the reader is the measure and source of values. For instance, in this passage the reader is asked to see him or herself as the heir of the harvest: "the eternal Demeter,—Mother, and Judge,—brings forth, as the herb yielding seed, so also the thorn and the thistle, not to herself, but *to thee*." . . . The reader is also the standard of aesthetic proportion; in explaining the superiority of the laurel leaf, Ruskin writes, "That you *can* so hold it, or make a crown of it, if you choose, is the first thing I want you to note of it;—the proportion of size, namely, between the leaf and *you*. Great part of your life and character, as a human creature, has depended on that." . . . This direct appeal to the reader has the tone of an Evangelical preacher like J. L. K.; we are also reminded that Ruskin defined the audience for *Proserpina* as young people.

Basing his system on idealized human values, Ruskin proceeds to set forth the lessons of the plants. Writing of the mosses, for instance, he says that no plants "teach so well the Humility of Death." He is speaking of the death of the mind: "If we think honestly, our thoughts will not only live usefully, but even perish usefully—like the moss—and become dark, not without due service. But if we think dishonestly, or malignantly, our thoughts will die like evil fungi,—dripping corrupt dew." . . . The methodology of this passage is exactly what is found in many of the conventional flower writers, but without a directly religious implication. Similarly, in a passage sounding like it might have come from any of Macmillan's flower sermons, he compares the method of dying of the ling with that of other plants: "The utter loss and far-scattered ruin of the cistus and wild rose,—the dishonoured and dark contortion of the convolvulus,—the pale wasting of the crimson heath of

Appenine, are strangely opposed by the quiet closing of the brown bells of the ling, each making of themselves a little cross as they die; and so enduring into the days of winter.'' . . . The deathbed of the Christian, Evangelical icon of supreme importance, is obviously "prophesied" here, both in the description of the death scene and the finding of the cross on the flower. This passage on the ling is perhaps the only place in which Ruskin is thinking in specifically Christian terms, but his moral typology is basically Evangelical.

Representative of Ruskin's botanical moralizing is his passage on the nature of weeds. He amends Margaret Gatty's famous definition of a weed as "a vegetable out of its place" to "a vegetable which has an innate disposition to *get* into the wrong place." He theorizes that Mrs. Gatty probably would not have so defined the weed because "she perhaps would have felt herself to be uncharitably dividing with vegetables her own little evangelical property of original sin." Despite the mocking tone of this remark, Ruskin goes on to develop just exactly this line of thought, that weeds are plants which seem to have an innate capacity for "sin" (which, for plants, he defines as hindering "other people's business"). . . . He led into the discussion of weeds by associating the poppy as a weed in wheat fields with its depiction in decorative work of "classic schools," in a confused and confusing passage . . . which seems to imply that artists once associated grain and weeds together in a way symbolic of "the feudal, artistic, and moral power of the northern nations." That his consideration of the poppy should lead to weeds in general is understandable, for the poppy as a weed in the wheat field is a traditional symbol. J. L. K., for example, writes: "As it flaunts its gaudy corolla among the russet corn what a striking symbol it seems to be of fashionable religiousness and voluntary humility." He goes on to point out that "the poppy has a 'voice' as sombre as the black tint of its own corolla. It seems to say to the vain professor, 'beware, therefore, lest that come upon you which is spoken of in the prophets!' ''. . .

Ruskin finds many correspondences between plants and human beings. In a long passage on the thistle, he explains the suitability of the thistle to represent Scottish character, epitomized in "the greatest of these ground-growing Scotchmen, Adam Smith." . . . In another place, he compares the joints of seaweeds and some cacti to "the minds of so many people whom one knows" characterized by "a knobby, knotty, prickly, malignant stubbornness, and incoherent opinionativeness." . . . But, of course, the most pervasive correspondence, if the most traditional, is his connection of flowers with women.

In his chapter called "Genealogy," Ruskin is at his most explicit in linking flowers to females when he explains the "conditions" attached to the use of Latin endings for plant names. The *us* endings are to be used for plants which have masculine qualities; *um* endings will "always indicate some power either of active or suggestive evil." The best flower names, of course, will have feminine *a* endings, and "if they are real names of girls, will always mean flowers that are perfectly pretty and perfectly good." But, he says, in a marvelous example of that sort of Victorian little-girl sentiment so well illustrated in some of the drawings of his protegé Kate Greenaway, "no name terminating in 'a' will be attached to a plant that is neither good nor pretty." . . . Most of the associations Ruskin makes between flowers and females refer to little girls rather than to women. As one would expect, Ruskin's association of flowers with females avoids all mention of reproduction. While he was as aware as the other writers that the Linnaean sexual system

of classification had been superseded, he was still not satisfied, for botanists still spoke of floral beauty as an aspect of reproduction. He called botanical studies of flower reproduction "obscene processes and prurient apparitions," and he was especially revolted at the "nasty" alliance between flowers and insects. Conventional flower writers were not of one mind about the loves of the flowers. Floral beauty, Grindon explained, was analogous to the maiden in her bridal finery. But, like Ruskin, Macmillan claimed that flowers exist to please human beings with their beauty, and he even went so far as to write a sermon called "Neuter Flowers" which makes it clear that God loves beauty for its own sake. Or, in Ruskin's words, "It is because of its [the flower's] beauty that its continuance is worth Heaven's while." . . .

Ruskin also found that flowers, like people, can and should be ranked socially. The top flower in a family, provided that it is a family of beautiful and good flowers, is called the queen (*regina*) of that family. Flowers not close in shape to the rose are "rightly thought of as reduced to a lower rank in creation," with the suggestion that these "inferior forms of flower" are produced by "blight, bite, or ill-breeding." . . . Leaves of certain shapes are inferior to those of other shapes, that is, are "of inferior power and honour." . . . One hallmark of weeds is that they are plants which will grow anywhere; they have "no choice of home, no love of native land," and thus are "ungentle." . . .

A considerable strain of national pride runs through *Proserpina,* perhaps signalled by the words of the subtitle, "The Scotland and England Which My Father Knew." In a chapter on the leaf, in the midst of many quotations from the Bible, comes this passage: "So that you see, whenever a nation rises into consistent, vital, and, through many generations, enduring power, *there* is still the Garden of God; still it is the water of life which feeds the roots of it; and still the succession of its people is imaged by the perennial leafage of trees of Paradise. Could this be said of Assyria, and shall it not be said of England?" . . . But, of course, he is speaking of a moral England, an idealized England, fulfilling the conditions set down in Psalm 1. Ruskin's connections between plants and human governments are not very specific, however, and are not always expressed in conventionally symbolic ways:

> All the most perfect fruits are developed *from exquisite forms either of foliage or flower*. The vine leaf, in its generally decorative power, is the most important, both in life and in art, of all that shade the habitations of men. The olive leaf is, without any rival, the most beautiful of the leaves of timber trees; and its blossom, though minute, of extreme beauty. The apple is essentially the flower of the rose, and the peach of her only rival in her own colour. The cherry and orange blossoms are the two types of floral snow.
>
> And lastly, let my readers be assured, the economy of blossom and fruit, with the distribution of water, will be found hereafter the most accurate test of wise national government. . . .

Ruskin wants to bring together art, flowers, morality, fruitfulness, economy, and "wise national government" by some method stronger than mere association, relating them systematically to botanical forms, but he does not succeed on any but a metaphoric level.

Ruskin's vision of the union of science and morality, of the useful and beautiful, is a vision of nature purged of evil. As he puts it, in a splendidly hyperbolic passage:

> For all this, the real reasons will be known only when human beings become reasonable. For, except a curious naturalist or wistful mission-ary, no Christian has trodden the labyrinths of delight and decay among these garlands, but men who had no other thought than how to cheat their savage people out of their gold, and give them gin and smallpox in exchange. But, so soon as true servants of Heaven shall enter these Edens, and the Spirit of God enter with them, another spirit will also be breathed into the physical air; and the stinging insect, and venomous snake, and poisonous tree, pass away before the power of the regenerate human soul. . . .

The Reverend Hugh Macmillan could have put it no better. Ruskin is writing about the exploration of tropical jungles, but his subject gets away from him in his excitement. The flowers and vines of the jungle become important moral and intellectual and aesthetic questions awaiting the "true servant of Heaven."

Thus **Proserpina**, though it is in many ways similar to the many popular "floral fancies," differs from them significantly in the direction and complexity of Ruskin's thought. While writing in a form so typically Victorian as the flower books, he moved beyond the standard typological equation to a new synthesis, or what he hoped would be a new synthesis, of nature, science, and morality. One reason that **Proserpina** is such a difficult text is that this synthesis, motivated by Ruskin's profoundly utopian hopes and fears, was logically impossible. (pp. 272-80)

> Beverly Seaton, "Considering the Lilies: Ruskin's 'Proserpina' and Other Victorian Flower Books," in Victorian Studies, Vol. XXVIII, No. 2, Winter, 1985, pp. 255-82.*

ADDITIONAL BIBLIOGRAPHY

Alexander, Edward. *Matthew Arnold, John Ruskin, and the Modern Temper.* Columbus: Ohio State University Press, 1973, 310 p.*
Comparative study of the lives and works of Ruskin and his contemporary Arnold.

————. "*Praeterita:* Ruskin's Remembrance of Things Past." *Journal of English and Germanic Philology* LXXIII, No. 3 (July 1974): 351-62.
Discusses the composition, publication, and principal themes of the book, as well as its impact on Marcel Proust.

Ball, Patricia M. *The Science of Aspects: The Changing Role of Fact in the Work of Coleridge, Ruskin, and Hopkins.* London: Athlone Press, 1971, 163 p.*
Examines "alliances and sympathies of vision" between the works of Ruskin, Samuel Taylor Coleridge, and Gerard Manley Hopkins, attempting to discover a pattern in "the imaginative features uniting and at the same time diversifying nineteenth-century writing."

Beard, Charles A. "Ruskin and the Babble of Tongues." *New Republic* LXXXVII, No. 1131 (5 August 1936): 370-72.
Argues that England's twentieth-century economic policy more clearly reflects Ruskin's theory of an intrinsic relationship between economics and morals—a theory criticized during his lifetime as sentimental nonsense—than it does prevailing Victorian economic doctrines.

Bell, Quentin. *Ruskin.* London: Hogarth Press, 1978, 164 p.
Critical survey.

Benson, Arthur Christopher. *Ruskin: A Study in Personality.* New York: G. P. Putnam's Sons, 1911, 323 p.
Seven lectures written "with the hope of provoking a discrimi-nating interest in the man's life and work, and with the wish to present a picture of one of the most suggestive thinkers, the most beautiful writers, and the most vivid personalities of the last gen-eration."

"Modern Light Literature—Art." *Blackwood's Edinburgh Magazine* LXXVIII, No. CCCCLXXXII (December 1855): 702-17.*
Negative evaluation of Ruskin's early art criticism, observing that "Mr. Ruskin utters his censures with a shrewish pertinacity in which there is no enjoyment."

Bradley, John L. *An Introduction to Ruskin.* Boston: Houghton Mifflin, 1971, 137 p.
Short biography with informative critical commentary, considered one of the best brief introductions to Ruskin.

Brand, Dana. "A Womb with a View: The 'Reading' Consciousness in Ruskin and Proust." *Comparative Literature Studies* XVIII, No. 4 (December 1981): 487-502.*
Assesses the extent of Ruskin's influence on the works of Marcel Proust.

Brownell, W. C. "Ruskin." In his *Victorian Prose Masters,* pp. 205-30. New York: Charles Scribner's Sons, 1901.
Cites a tendency in Ruskin's writings toward emotion rather than intellectual analysis and criticizes what Brownell considers the resulting formlessness and superficiality of Ruskin's works.

Casillo, Robert. "Olaf Stapledon and John Ruskin." *Science Fiction Studies* 9, No. 3 (November 1982): 306-21.*
Examines the influence of Ruskin's social criticism on Stapledon's works.

Chesterton, G. K. "John Ruskin." In his *A Handful of Authors: Essays on Books and Writers,* pp. 147-56. New York: Sheed and Ward, 1953.
Discusses the reflection of Ruskin's egotism in his works.

Collingwood, W. G. *The Life and Work of John Ruskin.* 2 vols. Boston: Houghton, Mifflin, 1893, 565 p.
Biography and critical study by Ruskin's personal secretary.

Columbus, Claudette Kemper. "Ruskin's *Praeterita* as Thanatogra-phy." In *Approaches to Victorian Autobiography,* edited by George P. Landow, pp. 109-27. Athens: Ohio University Press, 1979.
Examines how "the compulsions of negation override the record of [Ruskin's] achievements" in *Praeterita.* Columbus maintains that "however influential and recognized he became, his feeling that he had initiated nothing vital brought him not to the invention of reality, the art of autobiography, but to thanatography, the re-expression of repressions of original and static death."

Conner, Patrick. *Savage Ruskin.* Detroit: Wayne State University Press, 1979, 189 p.
Examines Ruskin's career as an art critic.

Dearden, James S. *Facets of Ruskin.* London: Charles Skilton, 1970, 164 p.
Nineteen essays detailing various aspects of Ruskin's life, in-cluding "John Ruskin—Oil Painter," "John Ruskin's Tour of the Lake District in 1837," and "Ruskin and Cork High School."

Fitch, Raymond E. *The Poison Sky: Myth and Apocalypse in Ruskin.* Athens: Ohio University Press, 1982, 722 p.
Examines mythic and apocalyptic themes, symbols, and imagery in Ruskin's writings.

Hewison, Robert. *John Ruskin: The Argument of the Eye.* Princeton, N.J.: Princeton University Press, 1976, 228 p.

Discusses the development throughout Ruskin's career of the visual element in his writings.

Hilton, Tim. *John Ruskin: The Early Years, 1819-1859*. New Haven: Yale University Press, 1985, 301 p.
Biography.

Holroyd, Michael. Review of *The Brantwood Diary of John Ruskin*, by John Ruskin. *Spectator* 227, No. 7465 (24 July 1971): 137-38.
Negative review calling the diary "accurate, meticulous, unforgettably dull," and "without any literary value whatever."

Hunt, John Dixon, and Holland, Faith M., eds. *The Ruskin Polygon: Essays on the Imagination of John Ruskin*. Manchester, England: Manchester University Press, 1982, 284 p.
Contains essays by ten critics, including John Dixon Hunt ("*Oeuvre* and Footnote"), Jeffrey L. Spear ("'*These* Are the Furies of Phlegethon': Ruskin's Set of Mind and the Creation of *Fors Clavigera*"), and Richard A. Macksey ("Proust on the Margins of Ruskin").

James, Henry. "Contemporary Notes on Whistler vs. Ruskin." In his *Views and Reviews*, pp. 207-14. 1908. Reprint. Freeport, N.Y.: Books for Libraries Press, 1968.*
Reprints two articles originally published in 1878 and 1879 concerning a libel suit brought against Ruskin by James Whistler for a review in which Ruskin wrote of one of Whistler's paintings: "I have seen and heard much of cockney impudence before now, but never expected to hear a coxcomb ask 200 guineas for flinging a pot of paint in the public's face." The jury ruled in favor of Whistler, awarding him one farthing in damages.

Leonard, Diane R. "Proust and Virginia Woolf, Ruskin and Roger Fry: Modernist Visual Dynamics." *Comparative Literature Studies* XVIII, No. 3 (September 1981): 333-43.*
Considers Ruskin one of the founders of "a modernist tradition which took as its aim the creation of a new optics," examining the influence of his works on visual representation in the writings of Marcel Proust, Roger Fry, and Virginia Woolf.

MacCarthy, Desmond. "Ruskin." In his *Portraits*, pp. 234-41. 1931. Reprint. London: Douglas Saunders, 1955.
Biographical and critical essay.

Maslenikov, Oleg A. "Ruskin, Bely, and the Solovyovs." *Slavonic and East European Review* XXXV, No. 84 (December 1956): 15-23.*
Speculates that Ruskin's works may have helped to inspire Andrei Bely's *Third Symphony*, presenting evidence that the symphony's characters are based largely on symbols found in Ruskin's writings.

McLaughlin, Elizabeth T. *Ruskin and Gandhi*. Lewisburg, Pa.: Bucknell University Press, 1974, 202 p.*
Examines the influence of Ruskin's works on the philosophical and economic ideas of Mohandas K. Gandhi.

Quennell, Peter. *John Ruskin: The Portrait of a Prophet*. London: Collins, 1949, 149 p.
Biography whose stated objective "is to portray John Ruskin both as a writer and as a personality: to show the close connection between his personal growth and his literary development: and to suggest how the frustration of his private hopes finally brought an end to his career of public usefulness."

Rossetti, William Michael. *Ruskin, Rossetti, Pre-Raphaelitism: Papers 1854 to 1862*. London: George Allen, 1899, 327 p.*
Contains numerous letters from Ruskin to Dante Gabriel Rossetti.

Saintsbury, George. "Mr. Ruskin." In his *Corrected Impressions: Essays on Victorian Writers*, pp. 198-218. London: William Heinemann, 1895.
Notes weaknesses and contradictions in Ruskin's works, while praising his prose as "the very finest . . . (without exception and

beyond comparison) which has been written in English during the last half of the nineteenth century."

Salomon, Louis B. "The Pound-Ruskin Axis." *College English* 16, No. 5 (February 1955): 270-76.*
Notes similarities in the personalities, interests, and convictions of Ruskin and Ezra Pound.

San Juan, E., Jr. "Ruskin and Exuberance/Control in Literature." *Orbis Litterarum* XXIII (1968): 257-64.
Analyzes the "pathetic fallacy," a term Ruskin used to describe the attribution of human characteristics and emotions to nature.

Sanders, Charles Richard. "Carlyle's Letters to Ruskin." *Bulletin of the John Rylands Library Manchester* 41, No. 1 (September 1958): 208-38.*
Reprints thirty-six letters from Thomas Carlyle to Ruskin, with commentary by Sanders.

Spear, Jeffrey L., and Hunt, John Dixon. "An Unused Preface by John Ruskin for *St. Mark's Rest*." *Princeton University Library Chronicle* XLIV, No. 2 (Winter 1983): 115-25.
Examines the importance of Venice to Ruskin's imagination and writings and reprints the discarded preface.

Stein, Roger B. *John Ruskin and Aesthetic Thought in America, 1840-1900*. Cambridge, Mass.: Harvard University Press, 1967, 321 p.
Discusses the influence of Ruskin's works upon American thought, maintaining that "Ruskin's ideas helped to change the intellectual landscape, but both the unresolved issues in his theories of art and the cultural needs of the American people helped to transform Ruskin's ideas, to harness them to native purposes."

Stephen, Leslie. "John Ruskin." In his *Studies of a Biographer*, Vol. III, pp. 78-110. New York: G. P. Putnam's Sons, 1907.
General discussion of Ruskin's aesthetic and economic theories, critical judgments, and prose style.

Townsend, Francis G. *Ruskin and the Landscape Feeling: A Critical Analysis of His Thought during the Crucial Years of His Life, 1843-56*. Illinois Studies in Language and Literature, vol. XXXV, no. 3. Urbana: University of Illinois Press, 1951, 94 p.
Examines a central theme of Ruskin's early writings, the study of nature as a means of moral improvement.

Trollope, Anthony. Review of *The Crown of Wild Olive*, by John Ruskin. *Fortnightly Review* 5, No. XXVII (15 June 1866): 381-84.
Unfavorable review maintaining that "Mr. Ruskin allows himself to be so carried away by his own eloquence that he will state and prove anything."

Unrau, John. *Looking at Architecture with Ruskin*. London: Thames and Hudson, 1978, 180 p.
Analysis of Ruskin's architectural writings. Although predominantly concerned with Ruskin's approach to ornamentation, Unrau also draws attention to rarely-cited passages in Ruskin's works in order to discredit the charge that Ruskin was exclusively interested in detail and ornamentation and neglected the structural aspects of architecture in his criticism.

Whitehouse, J. Howard, ed. *Ruskin the Prophet, and Other Centenary Studies*. New York: E. P. Dutton, 1920, 157 p.
Contains essays by eight critics, including John Masefield ("Ruskin"), W. R. Inge ("Ruskin and Plato"), and J. A. Hobson ("Ruskin as Political Economist").

Woolf, Virginia. "Ruskin." In her *The Captain's Death Bed, and Other Essays*, pp. 48-52. New York: Harcourt, Brace, 1950.
Maintains that Ruskin was forced into the role of a preacher and reformer—for which he was temperamentally ill-suited—by his Victorian contemporaries, who tended to deify individuals of genius.

(Mayer André) Marcel Schwob

1867-1905

(Also wrote under pseudonym of Loyson-Bridet) French short story writer, biographer, essayist, historian, critic, and translator.

Schwob was a highly respected scholar and man of letters in late nineteenth-century French literature. An authority on medieval and classic literature, he wrote short stories and biographies that evoke the distant past while portraying episodes of human tragedy and perversity. Schwob was also influential in the French Symbolist movement, and in the prefaces to such works as *Coeur double* and *Le roi au masque d'or et autres nouvelles (The King in the Golden Mask, and Other Writings)* he articulated his conception of the Symbolist aesthetic as experimentation with form, precise selection of details, and a concern with the nature of art as opposed to the realistic representation of human life.

Schwob was born in Chaville, near Paris, into a prominent and highly educated family. His father, a government functionary and newspaper publisher, came from a lineage of rabbis and physicians, and his mother could trace her Jewish ancestry to the second crusade of the twelfth century. When Schwob was a young boy his family moved to Nantes, where he was a brilliant student and mastered English and German at an early age, gaining the background for his later work in translating foreign literatures. Sent to continue his education at Lycée Sainte-Barbe in Paris, he lived with an uncle, a librarian and an expert in ancient languages and history who taught him the importance of high standards in making translations and encouraged his appreciation of legends and of children's and adventure stories. Schwob's own interest in classic and medieval studies—particularly the fifteenth-century milieu of French poet François Villon—influenced the Villonesque poetry and morbidly Poesque short stories of his early teens. In 1885 he left school to serve a mandatory two-year period in the military and upon discharge applied for admission to the Ecole Normale Supérieure, which was denied. However, he was accepted at the Sorbonne, where he met Léon Daudet, Paul Claudel, and other writers with whom he formed lasting associations, and he graduated in 1888 at the top of his class.

Schwob's *Etude de l'argot français*, a paper on French slang written in collaboration with Georges Guieysse, was published in 1889 and received high praise from the French academic community. Even more successful was *Le jargon des coquillards*, published the following year and including newly discovered material about Villon. At about this time Schwob began attending the Tuesday literary gatherings at the home of Stéphane Mallarmé, and became one of the early contributors to the Symbolist journal *Mercure de France*. These activities led to professional friendships with André Gide, Rémy de Gourmont, Maurice Maeterlinck, and others. A regular contributor to the journals *L'événement* and *L'écho de Paris*, Schwob later collected many of the short stories and sketches which originally appeared in these magazines in *Coeur double, The King in the Golden Mask, Mimes*, and *La lampe de psyché*. The death of his young mistress inspired him to write the biographical tribute *Le livre de Monelle (The Book of Monelle)*, a work published in 1894 to the immediate praise of contem-

poraries, who hailed it as a representative masterpiece of their time. Schwob also translated the works of others, most notably Daniel Defoe's *Moll Flanders* and Shakespeare's *Hamlet*, the latter done especially for the celebrated French actress Sarah Bernhardt. He wrote introductions to the works of French and English contemporaries at their requests and was honored with book dedications that include Alfred Jarry's *Ubu Roi* and Paul Valéry's *Monsieur Teste*. For many years he carried on mutually adulatory correspondences with Robert Louis Stevenson and George Meredith, both of whom are portrayed in sketches in *Spicilège*.

During the last decade of his life Schwob's health declined, and a serious stomach ailment requiring a series of five operations left him a near invalid dependent upon morphine as a painkiller. He travelled to Samoa, Spain, Italy, and Portugal—often in the company of the American writer F. Marion Crawford—trying in vain to find a congenial climate and environment in which to recuperate. After his marriage to actress Marguerite Moréno in 1900, he spent most of his time at home doing research and receiving the many French and English writers who sought him out. He began a lecture series on Villon at the Ecole des Hautes Etudes Sociales in Paris in 1904, but discontinued the course because of poor health. He died of pneumonia in 1905.

Schwob's conceptions of the function and form of literature closely parallel those of other French Symbolist writers. The characteristics of Symbolism are perhaps best understood when contrasted with those of Naturalism, another literary movement of the late nineteenth century. Naturalism was allied with the rise of scientism and thus held that the truest manner of presenting human life was in terms of physical and biological forces, which the Naturalists considered the determining factors in shaping individuals and groups. To an extent, Symbolism was a reaction against the aims of Naturalism. The Symbolists' primary concern was with the expression of their own inward sensations and experiences. The highly individualized nature of the Symbolists' material often resulted in works that were harshly criticized as obscure or incomprehensible. Reflecting Symbolist theories, Schwob placed the responsibility of discerning the underlying meaning of a work on the reader, whom he regarded as a collaborator in the interpretive process. In his preface to *Coeur double* Schwob also proffered the idea that true art is a spontaneous recreation of unique crises that arise from the conflict between the external forces of life and the inner forces of individual personalities, and that these crises, when judiciously chosen and presented without psychological analysis of their motivating causes, reveal the secret of an individual existence. A guiding concept of Schwob's works, particularly his biographical writings, is the opposition between the scientific practice of seeking what is common among individuals with the artistic practice of seeking what is unique.

The stories and sketches collected in *Coeur double, The King in the Golden Mask, Mimes,* and *La lampe de psyché* render the lives of ordinary people unique by depicting their specific emotions, idiosyncracies, and states of mind. These skillfully crafted tales display a predilection for the portrayal of death, illness, insanity, and criminal life, as well as what Anatole France has termed Schwob's natural aptitude for vividly depicting all periods of history, "from the age of the polished stone implement down to our own," in forms that imitate the literary style of each period. Critics such as Henry Copley Greene consider these historical sketches unoriginal, though effective in their evocation of terror and of the past; however, France has argued that Schwob's dependence on literary models does not diminish his distinctive qualities, but rather results in a "composite manner which is peculiar to himself." Schwob's most distinctive collection, *The King in the Golden Mask,* is characterized by Alex Szogyi as prose poems that thrust the reader into "bleak, antique, occult landscapes, a surreal world invariably leading to bloodletting, humiliation, and death."

In addition to short stories, Schwob wrote other works that are less easily classified into genres: *The Book of Monelle* is a biographical tribute which Greene considers "a thing of half lights and whispered phrases"; *La croisade des enfants (The Children's Crusade)* and *Vies imaginaires (Imaginary Lives)* recreate individualized portraits based on familiar historical and legendary information; and *Spicilège* contains essays on such writers as Stevenson, Meredith, and Villon, monologues about art, love, perversity, and laughter, and dialogues between fictional personalities. In *The Book of Monelle,* which many critics regard as Schwob's masterpiece, the moods and personal characteristics of the subject are revealed through the author's evocation of her kindness, compassion, and gentleness. The work's three sections of dream-like prose poetry present insights into Monelle's philosophy of life, allegories based on her companions which illustrate the varieties of human nature, and a record of the lovers' time together. William Brown Meloney notes the ambiguity which leads to a variety of inter-

pretations of *The Book of Monelle* but, like Schwob himself, places the responsibility on readers to draw upon their own experiences to arrive at an understanding of the work. John Erskine agrees that the specific meaning of the work is difficult to discern because of the author's fanciful sublimation of true experience; despite this difficulty, he has stated that "I feel in every word of those pages a touching regret for the frailty and inadequacy of the human spirit, and a continued yearning for that wisdom of which Monelle was a passing glimpse."

The nature of Schwob's writings, particularly his scholarly contributions to medieval and classical studies, restricted interest in his work to a small and specialized circle, thus placing it, for the most part, outside the concerns of the general reader. Modern critics consider his fictional works more important for the influence they had on younger writers than for their intrinsic appeal. However, Schwob continues to be admired for his literary artistry. René Lalou has stated that "even if the subject chosen leaves us indifferent, the minute execution forces our admiration. . . . All—even the most insignificant in subject— will be preserved from oblivion by the perfection of a style at once simple and full, mellow and rich, without useless ornaments."

PRINCIPAL WORKS

Etude de l'argot français [with Georges Guieysse]
  (treatise) 1889
Le jargon des coquillards (treatise) 1890
Coeur double (short stories and sketches) 1891
  [*Coeur double* published in *The King in the Golden Mask, and Other Writings* (partial translation), 1982]
Le roi au masque d'or et autres nouvelles (short stories) 1892
  [*The King in the Golden Mask, and Other Writings* (partial translation), 1982]
Le livre de Monelle (biography) 1894
  [*The Book of Monelle,* 1929]
Mimes (prose poems) 1894
  [*Mimes,* 1901]
La croisade des enfants (sketches) 1896
  [*The Children's Crusade,* 1898]
Spicilège (essays, monologues, conversations, and sketches) 1896
Vies imaginaires (fictional biography) 1896
  [*Imaginary Lives,* 1924]
La lampe de psyché (short stories) 1903
Moeurs des diurnales [as Loyson-Bridet] (satire) 1903
François Villon: Redactions et notes (criticism) 1912
Oeuvres complètes. 10 vols. (short stories, biography, essays, history, and nonfiction) (1927)
Chroniques (essays and short stories) 1981

ANATOLE FRANCE (essay date 1892)

[*France is one of the most conspicuous examples of an author who epitomized every facet of literary greatness in his own time but who lost much of his eminence to the shifting values of posterity. He embodied what are traditionally regarded as the intellectual and artistic virtues of French writing: clarity, control, perceptive judgment of worldly matters, and the Enlightenment virtues of tolerance and justice. His novels gained an intensely devoted following for their lucid appreciation of the pleasures*] *and pains of human existence and for the tenderly ironic vantage from which it was viewed. A persistent tone of irony, varying in degrees of subtlety, is often considered the dominant trait of France's writing. In his critical works this device of ironic expression becomes an effective tool of literary analysis. In the following excerpt from a review originally published in 1892, France gives a favorable assessment of the stories in the collection* Coeur double.]

I marvel that intelligent men of good judgment who are not unread should find pleasure in manufacturing for the public every year a volume of fiction, and that they should cheerfully devote themselves to this sort of work without reflecting that our century, supposing it to be in this respect more fortunate than those preceding it, will leave behind it at most a score of readable novels. It is, however, if we come to think of it, an excessive pretension to seek to impose three hundred and fifty pages of imaginary incidents on the public once a year! In how much better taste is the tale or the short story! How much more delicate a medium! Discreeter, and better calculated to please the intelligent reader, whose life is full, and who knows the value of time. Is not brevity the supreme mark of good breeding in the writer? The short story is sufficient for all purposes; in this form of fiction a great deal of meaning can be contained in a few words. A well-constructed short story is the delight of the connoisseur, and the exacting reader finds contentment therein. It is an elixir, a quintessence, a precious ointment. . . . Accordingly I intend no faint praise of M. Schwob when I say that he has published an excellent collection of short stories. M. Schwob has entitled his book *Coeur double*; his reasons for doing so I do not very clearly understand, even though he has explained them at length in his preface. This preface pleases me, because it speaks of Euripides and Shakespeare and breathes a fervent love of letters. But I dare not flatter myself that I clearly understand it. M. Schwob, like a new Apuleius, is fond of affecting the accent of a literary mystic. It does not displease him that the torches should smoke at the Muses' banquet. I believe he would even be rather annoyed if I had too easily penetrated the mysteries of his ethic and the silent orgies of his æsthetic. He is greatly occupied with Aristotle, who considered that the tragic poet should correct terror by pity, and he flatters himself that in his *Coeur double* he has observed this precept of the Stagyrite. He may be right, but I am not impressed by his argument, and I am quite unable to discover the mysterious tie which in his opinion unites his tales and makes them an indivisible whole. I am not acquainted with M. Schwob. I am told that he is very young, and that being so, his preface may be regarded as one of the delightful follies of youth. (pp. 302-03)

But I know of no one but M. Schwob who, while still quite young, could have written such narratives, so vigorous in style, so sure in their development and so powerful in feeling. He promises us Terror and Pity. I have seen but little of Pity, but I have felt the Terror. M. Schwob is henceforth revealed as a master of the art of evoking all the phantoms of fear and communicating a new shudder to his hearers. Although occasionally he derives from Edgar Allan Poe and Charles Dickens (the influence of Dickens is perceptible in **"Le Squelette"**), although he displays a natural and methodical aptitude for imitating the most varied forms of art, although one of his tales is most excellent Petronius, while another recalls the Oriental apologues of the Abbé Blanchet, and another might have been borrowed from some Buddhist volume, he is none the less original; he has a composite manner which is peculiar to himself, and he has invented a mode of the fantastic which is sincere and individual. It would be rather difficult to define

this fantastic quality or to reveal its sources. M. Schwob does not appear to be particularly credulous; he has no partiality for the miraculous; he refuses to have anything to say to the spiritualists, and, far from investing the performances of the spirits with poetry and passion, as M. Gilbert-Augustin Thierry has done in his *Rediviva*, he derides Monsieur Medium with a ponderous, terrible gaiety slightly flavored with ale and gin. . . . M. Schwob is not tempted by novel theories of "the beyond." The old theories leave him equally incredulous. In his hands the fantastic is wholly internal; it results from the peculiar structure of the minds which he examines, or the picturesqueness of the superstitions that haunt his characters, or merely from a wild idea entertained by very simple persons. He shows us neither spectres nor phantoms; he shows us the victims of hallucination. And their hallucinations are quite enough to terrify us. Nothing could be more terrifying than the rich Roman freedman, another Trimalcio, who saw vampires devouring a corpse:

> Suddenly the crowing of the cock startled me and an icy breath of the morning breeze rustled the tops of the poplars. I was leaning against the wall; through the window I saw the sky, now of a lighter grey, and to eastward a streak of white and rosy pink. I rubbed my eyes, and when I looked at my mistress I saw—may the gods help me!—that her body was covered with black bruises, dark blue spots, large as the ace on a card—yes, as large as an ace—scattered all over her skin. Then I shouted and ran toward the bed; the face was a waxen mask, beneath which one saw the flesh hideously gnawed; no nose was left, no lips, no cheeks, no eyes; the birds of the night had pierced them with their sharp beaks, like plums. And each blue patch was a funnel-shaped hole, at the bottom of which gleamed a clot of blood; and there was no heart, no lungs, no viscera whatever; for the chest and abdomen were stuffed with wisps of straw.

See also the tale of the three Breton *gabelous* who pursue the galleon of Captain Jean Florin on the seas. This galleon, loaded with the treasure of Montezuma, never came to land. Here again, in this story of the phantom vessel, the terror is produced by a gross and poetical superstition which the narrator compels us to share with the three sailors.

One may say of M. Schwob, as of Ulysses, that he is subtle and acquainted with the various ways of men. In his tales are pictures of all periods, from the age of the polished stone implement down to our own. But M. Schwob has a special liking, a predilection for those very simple beings, heroes or criminals, in whom ideas are revealed in crude, unmitigated, violent colours.

I do not know whether he is a Breton; his name does not seem to point to it; but his most skilfully drawn characters, those depicted with the most picturesque and sympathetic touch, are Bretons, soldiers or sailors (see **"Poder," "Les Noces d'Ary," "Pour Milo"** and **"Les Trois Gabelous"**).

In any case, this Breton can at need speak the purest Parisian argot. He talks slang, as far as I can judge, with an elegance that even M. Victor Measy might envy.

He loves crime for its picturesqueness. Of the last night of Cartouche in the Courtille he has given us a picture in the manner of Jeaurat, the painter in ordinary of Mam'selle Javotte and Mam'selle Masson, with a certain exquisite quality which Jeaurat has not. And in his studies of the outer boulevards M. Schwob recalls the pencil of Raffaelli, whom he surpasses in perverse and melancholy poetry.

What shall I say in conclusion? There are nearly forty tales in **Coeur double.** These tales are all curious or unusual, full of strange emotion, with a sort of magic in their art and their style. Five or six of them—**"Les Stryges," "Le Dom," "La Vendeuse d'ambre," "La Dernière Nuit," "Poder"** and **"Fleur de cinq pierres"**—are, of their kind, actual masterpieces. (pp. 304-07)

> *Anatole France, "M. Marcel Schwob," in his* On Life & Letters, *fourth series, edited by J. Lewis May and Bernard Miall, translated by Bernard Miall, Dodd, Mead and Company, Inc., 1924, pp. 301-07.*

ROBERT LOUIS STEVENSON (letter date 1894)

[*Stevenson was a Scottish novelist and poet. His novels* Treasure Island *(1883),* Kidnapped *(1886), and* Dr. Jekyll and Mr. Hyde *(1886) were considered popular literary classics upon publication and firmly established his reputation as an inventive stylist and riveting storyteller. Stevenson is also noted for his understanding of youth, which is evident both in his early "boy's novels," as they were known, and in his much-loved* A Child's Garden of Verses *(1885). Although Stevenson and Schwob never met, they began a friendship based on mutual admiration of each other's works and sustained the friendship through correspondence until Stevenson's death. In the following excerpt, Stevenson discusses the merits of* Mimes *as well as Schwob's potential as a writer.*]

I have read **Mimes** twice as a whole; and now, as I write, I am reading it again as it were by accident, and a piece at a time, my eye catching a word and travelling obediently on through the whole number. It is a graceful book, essentially graceful, with its haunting agreeable melancholy, its pleasing savoury of antiquity. At the same time, by its merits, it shows itself rather as the promise of something else to come than a thing final in itself. You have yet to give us—and I am expecting it with impatience—something of a larger gait; something daylit, not twilit; something with the colours of life, not the flat tints of a temple illumination; something that shall be *said* with all the clearnesses and the trivialities of speech, not *sung* like a semi-articulate lullaby. It will not please yourself as well, when you come to give it us, but it will please others better. It will be more of a whole, more worldly, more nourished, more commonplace—and not so pretty, perhaps not even so beautiful. No man knows better than I that, as we go on in life, we must part from prettiness and the graces. We but attain qualities to lose them; life is a series of farewells, even in art; even our proficiencies are deciduous and evanescent. So here with these exquisite pieces the XVIIth, XVIIIth, and IVth of the present collection. You will perhaps never excel them; I should think the **'Hermes,'** never. Well, you will do something else, and of that I am in expectation. (pp. 321-22)

> *Robert Louis Stevenson, in a letter to Marcel Schwob on July 7, 1894, in his* The Letters of Robert Louis Stevenson, *edited by Sidney Colvin, Charles Scribner's Sons, 1911, pp. 321-22.*

VANCE THOMPSON (essay date 1900)

[*Thompson was an American biographer, essayist, poet, and dramatist. Along with James Huneker, he started the journal* M'lle New York, *which was instrumental in introducing contemporary European authors to American readers. In the following excerpt, Thompson examines what he regards as the "Erasmian quality" of Schwob's works.*]

It is difficult to think of Marcel Schwob without applying to him the epithet Ἐρασμιος and all its amiable derivatives. He has the wit and tenderness and learning—a touch, too, of the pedantry—of that sixteenth century Dutchman who sank his own name in a Greek word. In a word, he is yeasted with the Erasmian principle. There is the widest possible divulsion between his calm, far-seeing philosophy and the angry and vehement speculations of the fashionable scientists. His definition of art is a masterpiece of clear-thinking: "Art is opposed to general ideas; it describes only the individual; it desires only the unique. It does not class; it declasses." And in all his work he has practised this neglected art of "differentiating existences"—if I may use a comprehensive phrase of M. Rémy de Gourmont. It is his purpose to create or re-create individual life. Let me take a definite illustration.

In all history there is nothing as inexplicable as the Children's Crusade—nothing more strangely pathetic. To the historian it has always been a stumbling-block. Even to Pope Innocent III, it was a divine mystery. And to-day the faith that led these dead innocents to death and slavery is as dark a riddle as it was eight centuries ago. Something called to them like the voice of a bird. From Germany and Flanders and France they set out on their pilgrimage to the Saviour's tomb in Jerusalem. Tiny pilgrims were they, with birchen staves and crosses of woven flowers. There were more than seven thousand children in white garments. They filled the road like a swarm of white bees. And as they marched toward the sea—to death and captivity—they sang the songs of Him whose tomb they sought in far-off Judea.

You will seek in vain through the great histories for any vital picture of this strange adventure of the Lord's children. The perfume and tenderness—even the meaning—is crushed out in the rough grip of historical synthesis. Marcel Schwob has told the story in his own way [in **La croisade des enfants**]—he has re-created for you the individual. (pp. 184-85)

This book is a perfect illustration of Marcel Schwob's system. It differentiates existences. It re-creates the individual life. Across the waste of years it summons those little martyrs, full of blind, victorious faith, who sought the Saviour's tomb and were destroyed. It makes them live again. Garlanded with flowers, they walk the white roads, singing the songs of the cross. And as you read there comes to you something of their tragic and miraculous faith. You see with their eyes and with the eyes of the leper and the white pope.

In the **Mimes** it was his purpose to re-create Greek life. He painted twenty little pictures. In one you see the old cook, in one hand his kitchen-knife, in the other a conger eel, and the old man chatters of the life of the house; again a sycophant passes; or perhaps the children play with wooden swallows, or the poet fares ill in his inn; a disguised slave sets out on his adventures, or a shepherd pipes in the rich Sicilian meadows; here a sailorman comes boasting from the perils of the sea, and there Kinné wanders with her lover. Each figure is as distinct as the men and women you see from your window. It is as though you had made a little journey into Greece and tarried at an inn and foregathered with a few simple folk. Your stay was short and so you came away without meeting Socrates, but you say: "At all events, I know Greece—the next time I go there I shall take letters of introduction to some of the famous men of the hour.'' In re-creating individuals M. Schwob has created Greek life—as no one else has done it. (pp. 188-89)

The Erasmian quality of Marcel Schwob's work is more conspicuous of course in his colloquies. As Erasmus summed up the thought of his age in those conversations which are now too much neglected—given over indeed to lads to whet their Latinity on—M. Schwob has in his dialogues netted the more lawless thought of our own day. Until he brought it back to modishness the colloquy had vanished from modern literature. Like the fashion of linking a series of letters into a novel, it is a not wholly unartificial form. Indeed, even Erasmus felt the need of apologizing for it. ''In these troubled and violent times,'' he said, ''it would not be prudent to send this book out without furnishing it with an escort.'' His plea for the utility of colloquies may stand for M. Schwob's *apologia*. How efficient an art-form the colloquy is in the hands of a master, you may learn from **''L'Amour.''** The conversation is carried on by Hylas, the actor, Rodion Raskolnikoff (Dostoiewsky's hero), Herr Baccalaureus, and Sir Willoughby Patterne (of *The Egoist*). Can you imagine a more delightful conversation? And it is carried on lightly, with faint touches of irony and joyous mystifying excursions into erudition, quite in the best Erasmian manner. In fact, to one who wishes to make the acquaintance of Marcel Schwob, I would recommend *Spicilège*, wherein may be found not only the dialogues, but the best study of François Villon ever made. (pp. 192-93)

> *Vance Thompson, ''The New Erasmus: Marcel Schwob,'' in his* French Portraits: Being Appreciations of the Writers of Young France, *Richard G. Badger & Co., 1900, pp. 184-93.*

HENRY COPLEY GREENE (essay date 1905)

[*In the following excerpt from his preface to his translation of* The Children's Crusade, *Greene discusses Schwob's life and works.*]

Only a seer would have taken Marcel Schwob, the outer man, for the delicate and dreamy author of the **Children's Crusade**. . . . [For] only insight into his dreams and deeds, and the generosities and subtleties of his endlessly acquisitive, endlessly shaping brain, could have found the tenderness with which Schwob was to breathe into this series of tales the spirit of those wistful, wild bands of children who, seven centuries ago, surged towards the sepulchre of Christ. (pp. vii-viii)

[The] mind with which he created works of such rare imagination, of criticism, too, and of scholarship, lives not only in written words but in a compelling personal influence which still broadens and enriches the furrows of French literature. (p. viii)

At twenty-one his power of study had brought him recognition as an expert on the dialects of Villon's time; and his mental adventurousness had grown into so strange a zest that he enjoyed no imaginary companionship more than that of Villon's familiars, a society of ''haggard poets, vagabond clerks, beggars and criminals whose names, whose vocabulary, whose very gestures'' Schwob intimately knew. (pp. ix-x)

[Like] the men in his story, **''Les Portes de l'Opium,''** he was possessed by such a passion for new sensations that he seems to have found, both in literature and in the stranger regions of life, terrors almost more haunting than those depicted by Poe.

Astray as Schwob probably was, we must not suppose him self-centered. In the enervated reaction from his strains, he grew very acutely sensitive to the plight of all sufferers, whether near or far, real or imaginary, present or past or future. Their pain filled him with a pity which, following Schwob's ingenious interpretation of Aristotle's formulation of tragedy purged away terror and brought a purifying peace. But this peace was incomplete. ''To live,'' Ibsen has said, ''is to join combat with fantastic beings born in the secret chambers of our hearts and brains.'' And however false or forced this may be of the average man's life, it was solidly true of Schwob's. For the man that he was in his early twenties, life almost consisted in battling with his imagination. After having ''enough pity on its creatures to submit himself to them and suffer that they might live,'' it was essential for him to master them, and in his own striking phrase, ''project them'' into the forms of art.

The first product of this process was a series of stories first printed in the *Écho de Paris*, and published, when Schwob was twenty-four, in a volume called **Coeur Double**. This collection proved him a clever craftsman. In a wide range of analytic reading and in critical studies printed in the *Événement*, Schwob had sought out and formulated much of the method of literature. What he discovered, moreover, was less a theory than an instrument whose stops he governed, in **Coeur Double**, with a skill that gave evidence of the keenest practice. But if the technique of short story writing was at his fingers' ends, his stories themselves showed little originality. Imitated to be sure from valid masters, they generally made their effect: though **''La Squelette,''** with its would-be American humour, seemed to Mark Twain ''a peculiarly unpleasant little production,'' the ghostliness of **''Le Train Numero 081''** and the murderous and supernatural horror of **''L'Homme Voilé''** might well have won praise from Poe. And one story, **''Les Sans-Gueule,''** rose out of imitation into personal originality. In its vividness and the strange calm of its style, in the tenderness and pathos which transfused its grotesqueness, it was essentially and individually Schwob's.

When Schwob, two years later, published his next volume of stories, he was absorbed in a new atmosphere of ideas. A student not merely of Aristotle but of modern philosophers, and a sounder of mysteries both human and divine, he had come to feel that the whole universe had its existence in the mind of a God whose reason weaves together, by their unseen resemblances, things to us the most diverse, and whose imagination creates in their divine diversity, things to us the most flatly alike. Thus while nothing could lack some sacred relation to the rest, the differences which, for our imagination, mark things off in individual uniqueness, gained such a transcendental value that noting them became, for Schwob, the spiritual function of art.

Now how far such a sanction may have stimulated and balanced his imagination, or how far literary practice and human experience may have developed his artistic power, is a problem which eludes analysis. But the fact remains that *Le Roi au Masque d'Or*, published when these thoughts were uppermost in his mind, shows an imaginative grasp and mastery new in Schwob's life. His subjects, to be sure, still reveal his old craving for the strange. As he himself wrote, ''I have made a book full of masks and hidden faces; a king masked with gold, a savage with a muzzle of fur, Italian highwaymen with pestiferous faces and French highwaymen with false heads, galley slaves helmed with red, young girls suddenly aged in a mirror, and a singular crowd of lepers, embalmers, eunuchs, assassins, madmen and pirates.'' Yet Schwob's treatment of all these is anything but the imitative riot which one might expect. Through the whole book the current of his style flows with a still surface in which the hues of gold, of ice, and of storm clouds glow through reflected visions. These visions, moreover, are definite; each figure in them is different from all others under heaven; and many, in their uniqueness, are more than individual. Many a vision, many a figure in this book involves a large, a deeply felt meaning, and a meaning intimately characteristic of Schwob himself. The golden mask of the title story, seen in an almost hallucinatory dream, hides and reveals a woe whose pathos is poignantly tragic in this, that masks and blindness prevail too long for sympathy to bring it succour. The visionary ice and blood and the wolves of **"La Mort d'Odjigh"** embody the pensive, the pitying triumph of self sacrifice rewarded with unconscious ferocity. Finally, out of the storm of **"La Flute,"** and out of the calm of its tropical sea, an old man's breathing transformed, in a primitive and miraculous instrument, by the fluttering of his fingers, stirs in the soul cries of dying men and dream-children's wailing which, but for the crimes of the world, would surely have been shouts of life, and sweet laughter in the sunlight.

But Schwob was by no means wholly absorbed in such visions. Still the student, still the eager craftsman, he was nourishing his artistic power on the arts of Greece. Definite and delicate as he had already made it, he enhanced it further by a *tour de force,* imitating from Herondas, in a volume called **Mimes,** a series of melancholy and graceful monologues whose slightest word carries harmonious suggestions of classic character and classic scene. Still as Stevenson wrote from Apia, in a comradely letter to Schwob, "By its merits this book shows itself rather a promise of something else to come than a thing final in itself. You have yet to give us—and I am expecting it with impatience—something of a larger gait; something daylit, not twilit; something with the colours of life, not the flat tints of a temple illumination; something that shall be said with all the clearness and the trivialities of speech, not sung like a semi-articulate lullaby. It will not please yourself as well when you come to give it to us, but it will please others better. It will be more of a whole, more worldly, more nourished, more commonplace, and not so pretty, perhaps not even so beautiful. . . . Well, you will do something else, and of that I am in expectation" [see excerpt dated 1894].

Schwob did indeed do something else: before three years had passed he had written **The Children's Crusade** which, while more of a whole, was neither worldly nor commonplace; and while no less beautiful, pleased the world more. But as Stevenson would have seen, had he known the inner man, Schwob's life and temperament made this little masterpiece inevitably something twilit, not daylit, something with the flat tints of a temple illumination, not with the colours of life. And even these mystical tones, as he would surely have seen, had to be underlaid with deep studies and with dreams.

The first and artistically the most original of these is a thing of half lights and whispered phrases, **Le Livre de Monelle,** in which Schwob carved on smooth ivory, pale perfect figures "tormented with egotism and voluptuousness and cruelty and haughtiness and patience and compassion", and in which he depicted at the end a coloured and primitive vision of his own past and future. (pp. xi-xix)

With the same erudition, human interest, and zest for artistic method with which he had studied Villon, the Greeks and Poe, he ransacked English literature from the Elizabethans, Tourneur and Ford, to Defoe, to De Quincy, to George Meredith and to Stevenson; wrote an essay on Ford's *'Tis Pity She is a*
Whore, translated Defoe's *Moll Flanders,* and wrote studies of George Meredith and Stevenson which throw vivid sidelights on the ceaseless mental activity of the one and the romantic visualizing faculty of the other. With the same tireless brilliancy he analyzed his contemporaries and predecessors at home; applied what he learned from all this study in **Vies Imaginaires,** a series of keenly individualized lives of typical gods and men; and formulated his discoveries in these conclusions as to the nature of art: that originality in literature is a question of form, not of substance; that great creative force may be found in the obscure imagination of the people; and finally, that masterpieces may be "born from the collaboration of a genius with the offspring of unknown fathers."

True or false of others, all this became true of Schwob himself. His imagination weary of gold and of red spices, his mind satiated with learning, he found a new creative power in the obscure and ignorant but imaginative faith of the child crusaders of long ago; and impregnating the chronicles of nameless thirteenth century scribes with the pity which had grown within him into actual genius for compassion, he created a work of art, not new in substance, but wholly original in form. In a series of delicately individual monologues he made this new Ring and the Book, a prose poem in which now a wandering brother, now a leper, now two children, now a scribe, now a Mahomedan, now a Pope recounts his own slight part in the Children's Crusade. And in the cycle of their tales Schwob told the whole sweet story. Thus he gave life anew to the child crusaders; thus recreated their tragic and miraculous spirit, and like Gregory the Pope, built for them as a memorial, this Church of the New Innocents, where godly pilgrims may worship the faith of little children, that "faith which does not know." (pp. xxi-xxiii)

It is . . . as a man of research and a critic that Schwob will be most solidly known when his personal influence on French letters has become too diffused for recognition. Yet even then, the colour, the style, the tragic pathos of some three or four of his short stories and the perfection of one or two of his **Mimes** will be remembered by the French; and in America, too, men may remember, and remembering love, the genius for compassion with which he transfigured the "temple illumination" of his Children's Crusade. (pp. xxv-xxvi)

> *Henry Copley Greene, in a preface to* The Children's Crusade *by Marcel Schwob, translated by Henry Copley Greene, Thomas B. Mosher, 1905, pp. vii-xxvi.*

RENÉ LALOU   (essay date 1922)

[*Lalou was a prominent French essayist and critic and the author of a comprehensive history of modern French literature entitled* La littérature française contemporaine *(Contemporary French Literature, 1922; revised edition 1941). As a critic Lalou was noted for his impartiality and frankness (he had no strong ties to any literary movements), for his historical discrimination and perspective, and for the balance and clarity of his critical judgments. Lalou's works include studies of such modern authors as André Gide, Paul Valéry, and Roger Martin du Gard, as well as essays on such classic literary figures as C. A. Sainte-Beuve, Charles Baudelaire, and Gérard de Nerval. In English translation, Lalou's critical works have been credited with introducing the works of leading modern French writers to the English-speaking world. Lalou also helped to make the works of numerous English authors accessible to the French through his translations of the works of Shakespeare, Edgar Allan Poe, and George Meredith, and through critical studies of modern English authors, the best known of which is his* Panorama de la litterature anglaise contemporaine*

(1927). In the following excerpt from Contemporary French Literature, *Lalou gives a positive appraisal of the collection* Spicilège.]

It is by *Spicilège* that Marcel Schwob should be approached to grasp the diversity and the strength of his mind. One will admire the fineness of his psychological essays on Laughter or Perversity. One will appreciate the ease of his erudition in the studies on Greek courtesans (**"Plangôn et Bacchis"**) or the Christian legends (**"Saint Julien l'Hospitalier"**). One will see him sympathetically hospitable to every greatness, revealing to the French the great Meredith "giving the spectacle of the most prodigious intellectual function of this century." One will feel what pleasure this historian-artist had in studying, apropos of François Villon, the "jargon of the *coquillards*" and resurrecting that confused life. One will recognize the perfection attained by this universal curiosity in the dialogues on love, art and anarchy. Nothing is more finished than the first of these conversations where, in an atmosphere of Platonic poetry and of Socratic irony, a host, momentarily transformed into an actor of the Middle Ages, examines with his guests (who incarnate, under the names of Hylas, Herr Baccalaureus, Rodion Raskolnikoff and Sir Willoughby, lessons of antique materialism, Mephistophelian logic, Dostoïevsky and Meredith) the question whether women can be called the puppets or shadows of love.

In the study on Robert Louis Stevenson, Schwob indicates the predecessors who have most struck his imagination: Villon with his gallows-birds, Shakespeare whose Falstaff "gives up the ghost like an old pirate," Poe and the skull nailed to a tree in "The Gold Bug," the narratives of filibusters. He unites in the same respect Odysseus, Robinson Crusoe, Arthur Gordon Pym and Captain Kidd; and if he praises Stevenson, it is to praise above all the "romanticism of his realism."

Indefatigable reader, relentless worker, passionately fond of history, languages, chemistry and astrology, master of several ancient and modern languages, translator of Shakespeare and Defoe, Schwob put this formidable erudition at the service of his imagination as a storyteller. We have seen to whom his preferences were given. They were not exclusive. If he announced that the novel should become "a novel of adventure," the volume entitled *La Lampe de Psyché* shows that this saying should be taken "in the largest sense." *La Croisade des enfants* and *L'Etoile de bois* tell two simple legends with sober precision. *Mimes* revives in a series of exquisite genre pictures an antique life idealized with refinement. *Le Livre de Monelle* finally remains a breviary of all the influences which acted upon Symbolist sensibility. In each of these varied evocations his talent unites the same descriptive firmness with the same pensive grace.

His most precious originality is, however, revealed in the numerous stories of *Coeur double*, of *Le Roi au masque d'or* and of the *Vies imaginaires*. (pp. 151-52)

Each volume of stories contains the same wealth of human history from the most remote times to the present. His gifts as an animator never fail. In them reigns, declares Léon Daudet, "a perfect taste, never a false step, or a surcharge." Even if the subject chosen leaves us indifferent, the minute execution forces our admiration. In the mediaeval narratives, particularly, the reader will sometimes incline to Paul Valéry's attitude: "Marcel Schwob's astonishing conversation won me to his own charm more than to its sources. I drank as long as it lasted . . . I did not feel for the erudition all the fervour due it." There is erudition, above all, in **"Blanche la sanglante"** or **"Les Faux Saulniers"**; but even there, where the care for

historic reconstitution a little overweighs the human interest, the touch keeps a rare distinctness, equally happy whether Schwob faithfully follows the tradition (**"Clodia"**) or amuses himself in opposing it (**"Pétrone"**). His art is equal to any mystery, whether in **"La Cité dormante," "Les Embaumeuses"** or **"Les Faulx Visaiger."** He plays upon the sombrest sentiments of the soul, the terror of **"La Peste"** and of **"La Charrette,"** the gruesome humour of **"Un Squelette"** (very superior to the imitations of Mark Twain in **"Sur les dents"** and **"L'Homme gras"**), the awakening of instinct in criminals (**"Cruchette," "Crève-Coeur,"**) which conduct the reader to evocations of the guillotine (**"Fleur de cinq pierres," "Instantanées"**) and to presentiments of **"La Terre future"**; the fantastically tragic (**"Le train 081"**) ending in the most lyrical lunacy (**"Arachné," "Béatrice"**). He excels equally in vast syntheses where the portrait of a man of thought sums up the picture of a whole epoch (**"Empédocle," "Lucrèce"**) and in stories of piracy told with a dry irony of which **"MM. Burke et Hare, assassins,"** offers the most successful example. Like Villiers, he levies upon the latest discoveries of science (**"La Machine à parler"**) and of applied psychology (**"L'Homme double," "L'Homme voilé"**). He utilizes so-called subversive doctrines in that **"Ile de la liberté"** where Gourmont saw the witty statement of "fakerism-anarchy"; but perhaps his most admirable stories are those he situates outside of historic times, the powerful visions of **"L'Incendie terrestre"** and **"La Vendeuse d'ambre,"** the grandiose **"Roi au masque d'or"** which his symbolism dates without weakening it, and that dense masterpiece, **"La Mort d'Odjigh."** All—even the most insignificant as to subject—will be preserved from oblivion by the perfection of a style at once simple and full, mellow and rich, without useless ornaments. If allegorical figures were still the fashion, one would like to imagine, on the threshold of his work, as his worthiest Muse, the woman he has described in two fragrant sentences: "Her breasts were supported by a red strophe and the soles of her sandals were perfumed. For the rest, she was beautiful and long of body, and very desirable in colour." (pp. 152-53)

René Lalou, "Symbolism," in his Contemporary French Literature, *translated by William Aspenwall Bradley, Alfred A. Knopf, 1924, pp. 94-158.**

JOHN ERSKINE (essay date 1929)

[*Erskine was an American novelist, autobiographer, and critic who specialized in Elizabethan poetry. His satiric novels, most notably* The Private Life of Helen of Troy *(1925), demythicize legendary and historical figures. In the following excerpt from his preface to* The Book of Monelle, *Erskine examines the work as an "allegorical fantasy."*]

The Book of Monelle is one of those rare works which one hesitates to call a masterpiece, and yet it holds in the interest of discriminating readers a place usually accorded only to perfect things. It would be easy to say that it is a failure—that Marcel Schwob did not express in it what he had in his heart, yet the impression it continues to make, even on readers who demand of their books absolute form and clarity, is so poignant and haunting that one is at a loss to know what greater success a book could have.

The episode out of which it grew, the episode described by Mr. Meloney in his introduction [see excerpt dated 1929], meant more to Marcel Schwob apparently than it would to most men. It is easy to see that he was primarily a bookish person, a scholar, a grammarian, an antiquarian. His familiarity with life was great, but it was of an indirect kind. His fate was to think much about experience before he had it, and to approach it with heavy prepossessions built up from his reading. Monelle was to him a reincarnation of De Quincey's Anne, or of the street girl legend connects with Napoleon. Probably he never saw her as she was. After their too brief happiness, her death left him with memories which he could state only as poetic interpretations and sublimations. When he tried to write the record of his most real experience, the result was the allegorical fantasy which is here translated.

Reality is of many kinds. To Marcel Schwob it is intellectual and spiritual. His memory of Monelle makes upon us its poignant and haunting effect chiefly because of the pathetic desire to understand love which we feel in every sentence. Mr. Meloney finds in the book a parallel to the *Vita Nuova*. I myself am more struck by the difference between the two books. In the *Vita Nuova* Dante's search for peace is by way of immense love, completely stated. In *The Book of Monelle* the love is assumed, but it seems to me not stated at all. I find in it rather an impassioned desire, as I said, to transpose experience into some form in which it will be understandable. The book is less a record of passion and grief than a meditation on the sort of wisdom which is charity. The charity, I take it, is less for Monelle than for the writer himself—for all of us.

We are told that Monelle appealed to this bookish scholar through a certain childlike simplicity and sincerity. How much he idealized her we can only guess, but in his record of her he tries to describe mature experience in terms of childlike innocence. If in the first section of the book, which to many readers is the most memorable, he sets down the wise sayings of this girl, it is as though he were remembering the precocious things that come from the mouths of babes. If you remind yourself that she was not altogether an innocent child I suppose the intention of Schwob's book is to challenge you with a sharp question, whether even out of a sad fate one might not emerge with a child's heart untouched. The knowledge of Monelle's way of life makes a necessary contrast to her words. If the book is not explicit in its philosophy, it is rich in philosophic questions, and in implied pleadings for all human nature. Whatever Monelle suffered or committed of shabbiness and degradation, differs only in degree with the conduct of any of us, though we may prefer to say our human weakness is different in kind. Not all of us, however, share the profound perceptions which Schwob puts into her lips.

Monelle says in one or two places that she is many things to many people. Well, that is only as we are all many-sided and full of illusions. The respectable person may be generous, selfish, courageous or mean, and still in any case respectable. Such a girl as Monelle, given to a wretched mode of living, may also be courageous or mean, spiritual or voluptuous, generous or selfish, or she might be all of these things at once. In the second section of the book, "The Sisters of Monelle," Schwob writes a series of child allegories in which he attempts to illustrate this many-sidedness of human nature. In this part of the book, perhaps, he is the most difficult to follow. He has sublimated experience to such a degree of fancy that for the specific meaning of his fable we need a key. Yet I doubt if any one would find essential difficulty in recognizing the mood or the characteristic which each fable would record.

The third section of the book is as biographical as Schwob would permit himself, on this subject at least, to be. The coming of the girl into his life, her power over his soul, her affinity with innocence and beautiful things, the inspiration and peace she gave him, and her death at last, are portrayed still in an allegory somewhat over-subtle, but in an allegory which ought not to be difficult for the sensitive. One wonders at the end of the "Flight of Monelle," for example, whether it is his own love which ascribes to her such a questing heart, or whether she had passed through human misery urged on by wisdom so essentially spiritual. She tells him to forget her in order not to lose her; in other words, not to dwell upon the unhappiness of her loss, lest the blessed memory of their love should be spoiled. She tells him that she has found a white kingdom—that having lived through passion in this world she found misery, but having lived through misery she has found peace. And she dies with a vision half expressed that in this white kingdom of peace something still finer might be discovered. (pp. 11-15)

I said that the book did not seem to me a parallel to *Vita Nuova*. All possible difference between the great medieval poet and this modern man is in the last chapter of the book, which you may call cynical, if you choose, or, in another mood, profoundly beautiful and tragic. "The Resurrection of Monelle" is in the attachment the writer forms for some one else. Perhaps Monelle, then, is only his love, not the object of it, only the perpetual illusion he sets up—perhaps it is the illusion that all of us create.

And yet Mr. Meloney may be right—there may be a parallel after all to the *Vita Nuova*, for even there, as we remember, Dante found himself falling in love with another woman after Beatrice had been dead a year. And long before, Virgil, the poet whom Dante loved, told us of what terror Dido suffered when she recognized once more in her heart the vestiges of the ancient flame. Dido hated herself for this discovery, and Dante was profoundly penitent. One must be eager to find cynicism, if one insists on finding it in the last pages of Monelle's book. I feel in every word of those pages a touching regret for the frailty and inadequacy of the human spirit, and a continued yearning for that wisdom of which Monelle was a passing glimpse. (pp. 15-16)

> *John Erskine, in a preface to* The Book of Monelle *by Marcel Schwob, translated by William Brown Meloney V, The Bobbs-Merrill Company, 1929, pp. 11-16.*

WILLIAM BROWN MELONEY V (essay date 1929)

[*Meloney was an American novelist and literary critic. In the following excerpt from his introduction to* The Book of Monelle, *he discusses the background to Schwob's composition of this work.*]

One rainy evening in the fall of 1891 Marcel Schwob, who was destined to become one of the foremost scholarly and literary figures of his times, met a frail young creature who will go down in the literature of the world as the girl Monelle. . . . Reared in the stern Jewish tradition which presupposed for him a career in either science or religion, he had lived solely in a realm of ideas and abstractions. His life had known neither gentleness nor affection; what emotions he possessed were concerned with the things of the mind. Women had played no part in his scheme of things. . . . (p. 19)

Monelle was not interested in the scholar or the artist, she was concerned with the man, Marcel Schwob. She knew that he was lonely, as she was lonely. In a simple childlike way she sensed his passionate need for affection and so she went to him.

There is very little known of the story of Monelle's life or of the story of their life together. One may conjecture that she was a shop girl of very modest origin, but all that is known is that they lived together for two years, that her name was Louise and that Marcel Schwob called her Monelle. When she died, out of the grief and the pain of his loss he wrote of her *Le Livre de Monelle* which was immediately acclaimed by many of the critics of that day as one of the literary treasures of the world. Anatole France wrote to him:

> I do not know of anything more beautiful than Monelle. With the deep understanding and anything more beautiful than Monelle. With the deep understanding and the exact precision of the artist you have expressed in this book sadness and sweetness and the infinite of profound thought. I admire you and I love you.
>
> (pp. 20-1)

[No] two readers of this book have agreed in their interpretations of its meaning. Like the Saint Gaudens' Memorial for Mrs. Adams this book expresses the varying experiences and emotions of those who come to it. Some French puritans, while admitting its rare beauty, are mystified by certain aspects of Schwob's philosophy, while others protest that despite the intrinsic merits of *The Book of Monelle* it is not typical of the French tradition in literature. Nor are their protests unfounded. This book is unique, it is timeless, and in common with a small body of fine literature it represents no nation's literary tradition. (p. 21)

The details of Marcel Schwob's life with Monelle are shrouded in mystery. We know more of her death than of her life. The miserable conditions in which she had lived and the cheap clothing which could not protect her against the damp cold of Paris winters sapped her strength. She suffered a prolonged cold and then came the doctor of Jules Renard and spoke the word *tuberculosis*. On the seventh of December of 1893 Jules Renard writes that he had purchased a box of grapes and oranges to take to the sick girl. In the intimacy of his diary he notes: "What joy she will have! Coming from me, his dearest friend, they will be golden fruit to her." He mounted the stairway and softly opened the door. Marcel Schwob came to him in the agony of grief; Monelle, his love, had that moment died. His loss devastated him. It was less the departure of a lover; it was as if he had lost an only child.

For months he was as a man lost in life. He could think only, speak only of Monelle. Anatole France, Byvanck and the Daudets tried to console him and help him. Slowly he withdrew himself from even the society of those dearest to his heart. He destroyed everything which might remind him of Monelle, the letters they had written, such of her intimate possessions as remained to him, then he commenced to write *Le Livre de Monelle,* that, by giving expression to his sorrow, he might destroy not only sorrow but his memory as well. (pp. 45-6)

He wrote of Monelle as the very consummation of love; out of the pain of his loss he fashioned from their life together a poem in prose. Marcel Schwob never wrote a *Divine Comedy* but he equals, if indeed he does not exceed, the sublime majesty of a *Vita Nuova* for *Le Livre de Monelle* was the *Vita Nuova* of his life.

He had been deeply touched by the story De Quincey tells in the *English Opium Eater* of the gentle Anne, and the legend of the little girl Napoleon met one evening under the iron gates of the *Palais Royale;* through his life with Monelle these stories assumed a new and deeper meaning for him. These women were prostitutes but for at least one moment in their lives they showed themselves capable of deep compassion, of great gentleness and transcendent purity. When he comes to write *Le Livre de Monelle* he speaks in parable; he says that Monelle is the essence of goodness in all woman, that she is this woman and that woman and last of all that she is none other than one of *these litle women of pleasure*. She was all that is good, compassionate, gentle and kind. She is one of those who have

> come through the cold and the rain to kiss your brow, to brush their lips across your eyes, to drive from you the terror and the sadness that you know. . . . When they have done perhaps they must go to others who have need of them.
>
> You only know them while they are compassionate. You must not think of those other hours, you must not think of what they do in the shadows. . . . Anne bringing the empty glass back to the wine dealer, were they not perhaps coarse and obscene? These are but creatures of the body. They have come out of some somber impasse to give a kiss of pity under the glaring light of some full-thronged thoroughfare. In that moment they were divine.
>
> You must forget all the rest.

Le Livre de Monelle appeared in 1894. In the journals Maeterlinck, Mallarmé, Coppée and Rodenbach acclaimed it as the masterpiece of their years.

Once *Le Livre de Monelle* appeared, Marcel Schwob never again mentioned Monelle or the part she played in his life. Theirs was a variation of the story of Pygmalion and Galatea for he had loved Monelle in the flesh. When she died he fashioned of her a work of art. To the world he ever held this cold front, and any discussion of Monelle with his friends was simply as a piece of writing. In his heart? It is simple to formulate a philosophy of nihilism but difficult to execute it. "Do not look too long into black amber," he wrote. Yet it would seem that from the time of Monelle's death until his own, Marcel Schwob peered long into the black amber of his dreams. (pp. 46-8)

With the death of Monelle he blossomed into true greatness. Monelle had brought him from within himself into new and strange realms of thought and life, she humanized him. To him she was both child and lover, and the love they shared together was beyond that love which man usually finds with woman. With her, life assumed new and undreamed-of values: values which were to make him more important in the world of letters, a man of new and greater depths to his friends. Later he was to love, to worship and to marry a woman, but it was not the same relationship he had known with Monelle. No thing, no person in his later life came as close to him as his memories of her; could touch the inner part of him that came to be in that short adventure in the art of living. (p. 49)

> *William Brown Meloney V, in an introduction to* The Book of Monelle *by Marcel Schwob, translated by William Brown Meloney V, The Bobbs-Merrill Company, 1929, pp. 19-66.*

S. A. RHODES (essay date 1934)

[*Rhodes was an American poet and critic who specialized in French literature. In the following excerpt, he discusses Schwob's conceptions of the function and form of literary art.*]

In the preface to *Cœur Double,* Marcel Schwob states the argument against the naturalistic novel in the 19th century most succinctly, if perhaps somewhat obviously. He decries its pedantic aping of the ways of science, its uninspired proneness to render life in art static, to make all the multifarious aspects of seeming reality converge toward a few unphilosophical, ill-digested, synthetic half-truths. He diagnoses the case as a frustration of the æsthetic principle in many of these novels; as a misapplication, or distortion by their authors, of the legitimate secrets of the craft of novel-writing. For the true scientific processes are inductive, whereas the technique resorted to in the naturalistic novel, especially by Zola, is deductive. This is to make the elaboration of a synthetic phenomenon equivalent to the mere enumeration of its constituents. A generalization drawn from the superficial observation of similarities between the diverse elements of a series does not interpret, or truly recreate that series. It forms only a banal abstraction, or insignificant speculation, which leaves the mainsprings of reality undivulged. And that holds true whether the series in the case deals with love or with the belly of Paris. "Life dwells in what is individual and intimate, and not in what is general and impersonal; the aim of art is to give to what is subjective and particular the illusion of what is universal." This is worth retaining. The monotonous, or even picturesque, detailing of anthropological and biological incidents cannot lead automatically to a deduction of the truths of a soul. Hence for the novelist to attempt to convert natural and mathematical laws into literary formulas, to observe like the biologist, to experiment like the chemist, and to make deductions like the mathematician, is to frustrate the very purposes of art. For that is giving to literature deterministic tendencies, purposes and aims which do not properly fall within its provinces. Schwob is specific in this respect. "Science," he says, "seeks to attain to the universal through what is inevitable, or permanent; art must seek to reach it through what is contingent; for science, life is circumscribed and fixed; for art, it is intermittent and free; science discovers generalities of an extensive nature; art must render sensible those of an intensive nature; if the realm of science is deterministic, that of art is subjective and free."

The sequence of Schwob's logic in this seems flawless. What art is interested in is what it can conceivably recreate—that is, the spontaneous, unshackled aspects of life it finds in nature, free from any self-opinionated psychological or physiological motives. He illustrates his point startlingly by quoting the stanza from Hamlet referring to the passage of Fortinbras' troops through Denmark.

> How stand I then,
> That have a father kill'd, a mother stain'd,
> Excitements of my reason and my blood,
> And let all sleep, while to my shame I see
> The imminent death of twenty thousand men,
> That for a fantasy and trick of fame
> Go to their graves. . . .

The passage of the troops is a dramatic incident external to Hamlet. His reaction to it forms his inner drama, finding expression in the words at the end of the speech:

> O, from this time forth,
> My thoughts be bloody, or be nothing worth!

And Schwob remarks: "Thus, a spiritual reality is created, and Hamlet has assimilated into his inner life an event of the external world."

In this instance it is a fortuitous, unforeseen incident that sheds a transparent light on the quality of a soul. Life is filled with such unpremeditated, unique "adventures" or "crises", however, which are the result of conflicts between the external forces of life and the inner forces in man. Art lies in the rendition, or recreation, of these "crises", and not in the analysis and synthesis of their motivating causes, apriorily determined by the application of scientific formulas. Omitting all pseudo-scientific descriptions, all the mock insight into life of a syllabus-psychology, and all untutored biological searchings, "the novel of the future," Schwob predicted, "will doubtless be a novel of *adventures* in the broadest sense of the word, a romance of the crises in the conflicts between the inner world and the outer."

This is already the substance of his conception of the biographical art. In *Le Roi au Masque d'Or,* his ideas show a further progression, however. He regards human beings as differentiated into a series of very relative, but, nevertheless, intrinsic entities. The differences between them may be so small as to be undistinguishable by the layman. It is only, what he terms, "un souci d'artiste" which can give one a sense of the subtle disparities that exist. The parallelism between things, he says, "is a philosophical expression of their unlikenesses"; and this in turn "is an aesthetic expression of the ultimate harmony between them." This may sound paradoxical, but Marcel Schwob was mercilessly logical. He thinks of the differences between things in terms of secrets never revealed. Just as masks are the visible symbols of concealed faces, so words are the evident symbols of concrete realities. These realities are but the outward manifestations of the mystery of life. Our sharpened senses give us a keen insight into them, and our intelligence classifies them into a synthetic whole. When the artist, or the biographer, conceives his creatures intellectually, or scientifically "he conceives them through their resemblances; when he conceives them with his creative imagination, he recreates them in their diversity."

His premise is thus based on the search for the moments of crisis in a life, for only they reveal the secret meaning of an existence, even when they do so thanks to trifling details alone, if they are judiciously chosen. And that leads to the quest of the particular; of what is most different from the general; of what is most original, relatively.

This is almost at the opposite pole of the scientific method, so-called, for instead of searching for that which is common to all, Schwob looks for what is most unlike all. The common run of biographies, up to his time, consisted of "those two fat volumes, with which it is our custom to commemorate the dead", of which Strachey speaks, and which left the reader in the dark regarding the inner individuality of historical figures. They revealed only those of their salient characteristics which affected the general course of events. But art, Schwob remarked, shuns abstract generalizations. "It describes what is exceptional; it seeks only what is unique. It does not pigeon-hole, and level reality; it distinguishes and sets it off." The ideas of great men, those that can be traced back and forth through the stages of history, are the common property of mankind. What is uniquely theirs, what reveals them intimately, that alone is what can give them individuality and reality. So, when a biography relates the life of a great man only as he looked upon the public platform, it deceives us and falsifies the image of reality. Contrarily, the book that portrays a man in all his idiosyncrasies reveals him in all his unspoilt genuineness, and comes closest to being a work of art. Casting about in history for illustrations of this latter type of biography, Schwob stops, naturally, at John Aubrey (1626-1697) and Boswell. In Aubrey's *Brief Lives,* he found the first illustration of what he was after. "What uncertainty doe we find in printed histories," declared Aubrey in his letter to Anthony Wood on transmitting his manuscript to him, "they either treading too near on the heeles of trueth that they dare not speake, or els for want of intelligence (things being antiquated) become too obscure and darke?" And farther in the letter he adds: "I remember one saying of general Lambert's, that 'the best of men are but men at the best': of this, you will meet with divers examples in this rude and hastie collection." The emphasis in this saying is on *men,* of course. Aubrey was not interested in the professional poses of his subjects, but in their secret individualities. He did not seek to establish a connection between individual details and general ideas. He sought, on the contrary, to draw from each individual "his unique trait which differentiates him forever from other men."

Ideally then, the task of the biographer, Marcel Schwob declared, consists "in individualizing the personalities of two philosophers who have invented the same metaphysical system." Or, as the Japanese painter Hokusai (1760-1849) would have it, the problem resides in detecting the disparity that exists between two seemingly similar lines, which is all the art of drawing, whether with a pencil or a pen. Schwob studies the *Lives* of Aubrey; and what attracts him are the little incidents, the peculiar traits, the singular habits that give color and character to those "lives", and about which Aubrey apologized, "for though to soome at present it might appeare too triviall, yet hereafter 'twould not be scorned but passe for antiquity." And Schwob remarks: "It is evident that Aubrey had a perfect comprehension of his art. We must not presume that he underestimated the importance of the philosophic ideas of Descartes or of Hobbes. But he had no special interest in them. He tells us very appropriately that Descartes himself has explained his method to the world.... He thinks he has thrown sufficient light on Francis Bacon when he discloses that he had bright and gentle eyes, light reddish-brown in color, and not unlike the eyes of an adder. But he is not as great an artist as Holbein. He does not know how to trace an immortal portrait by traits that are distinctive, and yet bearing a degree of resemblance to an absolute ideal. He gives life to an eye, a nose, a leg, a grimace of any of his models; he is incapable of giving life to an entire figure. Old Hokusai saw justly that the aim consisted in giving to an individual the illusion of universality. Aubrey lacked this penetrating insight." And he lacked besides what is essential to all art: form. "How unfortunate it is that the style of this excellent biographer should fail to rise to the level of the high conception he had of his art. His book would have been then the eternal source of relaxation of cultivated minds."

But Schwob had a more modern illustration at hand. Boswell had what Aubrey lacked: form. But unfortunately he fell short in something Aubrey possessed to an eminent degree: conciseness. If Schwob could have condensed Boswell's book into ten pages, he would have considered it the long-awaited work of art. The genius of Dr. Johnson was the epitome of good sense. Expressed with the exceptional intensity of Boswell's style, it acquires a quality that is unique in literature. Only it seemed to Schwob a cumbersome inventory that resembled the dictionaries of the Doctor himself. "One might draw from it a *Scientia Johnsoniana,* with an index. Boswell lacked the artistic courage to choose."

In Aubrey and in Boswell Schwob saw the precursors of the modern biographer. But he bemoaned, in the first, his lack of

style, and, in the second, his lack of discriminatory taste, or selection, both essentials of art. "The secret of the biographer lies precisely in his ability to choose. He is not concerned with the external truth of things; he must create within a chaos of human factors.... The biographer, like an inferior deity, must know how to select from among an infinity of possible incidents what is unique." This faculty will distinguish the artist as biographer from the mere erudite or historical biographer. "Patient scholars have collected for the biographer ideas, physical traits, and events. Their labors are gathered in chronicles, memoirs, correspondence, *scholia.* From all this paraphernalia the biographer extracts the fine substance of something that bears resemblance to no other creation." (pp. 112-16)

How much Schwob was justified in his critique is evident now that the art of biography has adopted his point of view. We have swerved in modern times from the Greek concept of tragedy flaring up as a denouement of the conflict between the passions. We are less interested now in the ultimate result of the crises that constitute the ascending or descending evolutions in a life, than in the manifestations and dramatic possibilities of these crises themselves. We prefer to be lost in the inner labyrinth of an obscure and tortuous, but intriguing soul, than to bask in the limelight of one who is well-known, though worthy and lofty.... "If one were to seek to excel in the art rendered illustrious by Aubrey and Boswell," says Schwob, "he would have to describe faithfully not the life of the greatest man of his time, nor that of the most famous in the past, but the existences of men of all times and conditions, irrespective of their divine, mediocre, or criminal natures, providing they were unique." And that is what Schwob himself did. (pp. 116-17)

S. A. Rhodes, "Marcel Schwob and the Art of Biography," in The Romanic Review, *Vol. XXV, No. 2 (April-June 1934), pp. 112-17.*

GLORIA L. HOBBS (essay date 1966)

[In the following excerpt, Hobbs examines Schwob's portrayal of prostitutes in his works.]

The genius of Schwob lies in his ability to penetrate a culture or an era and to capture even the atmosphere of these lands and times with his words. This technique is basic to his art of composition, for in the three initial lines of the preface to his first publication, he states:

> La vie humaine est d'abord intéressante pour elle-même; mais, si l'artiste ne veut pas représenter une abstraction, il faut qu'il la place dans son milieu.

> [Human life is at first interesting in itself; but, if the artist does not want to portray an abstraction, it is necessary to place this life in its milieu.]

In "Eschyle et Aristophane" Schwob admonishes the reader to consider tragedy only from the viewpoint of an ancient Greek in order to appreciate the difference in the dramatic art of Eschylus, Sophocles and Euripides. With the echoes of Taine in the background, he recommends the rejection of the present and the donning of the mental garb of the *milieu* and *moment* under consideration. According to Schwob, the writer creates an animated, convincing work if he is totally transported into the environment and time of his subject and participates therein. But the erudite young author knew that his talent was not that of the creative artist and laid no claims to originality. His works, the result of information derived from long hours of research and investigation, are mostly a medley of truth and fantasy, a photographic reproduction of worlds distant in time and space from his own.

To most prose writers of the 1890's, including Schwob, themes of sadistic pleasures, sexual abnormalities, and sterility in aesthetic tastes were the vehicles for their artistic creativity. Yet, amid all this examination of the decadent and the depraved in humanity, Schwob's works reflected an unusual degree of concern and compassion for the child-prostitute and the courtesan. In his mind, these were the innocents of this earth with their credulous, unpretentious attitude towards life. Moving in their own spheres as if unaware of man's institutions, they become the preferred of God or the gods. And whereas innocence is compatible with childhood, its identification with prostitution, although seemingly unique, is not uncommon in literary circles.

Schwob admires the courtesan of ancient times, for she performed her tasks as the representative of Aphrodite. In the dialogue **"L'Amour"** he discusses the situations of the *hétaire,* his favorite word for the courtesan of the Hellenic world, and evidently one of the names for the goddess of love. Quoting mostly from Plato's *Republic,* he makes a marked distinction between the *hétaires,* "les véritables poupées de l'Aphrodite populaire" ["veritable puppets of the popular Aphrodite"]. and other women, actresses who wear the mask of love and really experience nothing. It was not difficult for Schwob to accept the demarcation of Plato because of his intimate relationship with the world of make-believe through his talented actress-wife, Mme Moréno, and because of his own skill in presenting fiction as convincingly as truth. He approves of the wisdom of the ancients who made their prostitutes sacred because the latter were, in truth, manifestations of a divinity. . . . These ideas of the godly nature of the concubine are also to be found in the *Memorabilia* and the *Banquet* of Xenophon. And Socrates even went so far as to elevate the role of the *entremetteur* in his explanation of the beauty of this profession. . . . In spite of the fact that Socrates saw in this occupation something divine, Dante later put the procurer in the first ditch of Malebolge in Hell along with the seducer. Dante attempted to bridge the gap between two great Italian cultures, but Schwob was only influenced by the values of Antiquity in his presentation of its mores. Schwob develops his appraisal of the status of the courtesan on the writings of some of ancient Greece's greatest minds.

Théodota is Schwob's ideal Greek *hétaire,* for she unselfishly shared her love for Alcibiades with Timandra. Even at the death of Alcibiades, the two women together washed and buried him in spite of the danger of political repercussions. Théodota is the simple, good woman, and in her naive, selfless, considerate actions, Schwob saw the divinity of the gods and the innocence of mankind. He becomes obsessed with this vision of the prostitute, repeating its theme and modeling all other *hétaires* and *filles amoureuses* according to her temperament. . . . Schwob, like the Ionian people, held these women in high esteem for their qualities of self-sacrifice and compassion and their monolithic desire to serve and please the beloved. . . . In essence Schwob sees the characteristics of Théodota as obligatory for those who follow the profession of Aphrodite.

The lives and conditions of the *hétaires* are quite different from those of the *filles amoureuses.* With the Greek courtesan, there was a feeling of continuity and permanency, since the profes-

sion was taught in schools and was passed on from mother to daughter and from their slaves to their slaves' daughters. Theirs is an art, accepted by society and dignified by divine protection. But in the lives of the numerous little prostitutes that trudge through Schwob's collections, there is a sense of hopelessness and morbidity. His child-like women, about ten or twelve years of age, are usually found outside of cemeteries or at city gates. The reader never has the feeling that Schwob's modern little *prostituées* will have a future or know great joy, so surrounded are they by destruction, poverty and deception. Very rarely is any of them redeemed by a legitimate love and marriage as in the case of the heroine of *Moll Flanders,* a novel admired and translated by Schwob. There is a maturity about his courtesans of olden times that his more recent ones do not possess. The latter, rejected by society, are called "la pauvre fille divine" ["poor divine girl"], "la petite" ["little one"], "la fille amoureuse" ["amorous girl"], "l'enfant" ["child"], "la fillette" ["little girl"], "ma petite sœur" ["my little sister"], "la fillette commune" ["communal girl"], etc. . . .

In **"L'Amour,"** Schwob establishes the divinity of these young creatures also. Whereas the Greek courtesans are called the dolls of Aphrodite, these unfortunate little girls are the toys of Eros, who casts them aside mercilessly when he tires of them. As playthings of the child-god of love, they are an unhappy lot without control over their actions. (pp. 341-44)

As a result of his research, Schwob was able to establish a relationship between his child-prostitutes and a Greek god. However, he was also able to call on his own experiences in composing his brief accounts about them, for, in his youth, he had befriended Louise, an immature young *fille amoureuse,* referred to as "la petite Vise." It is difficult to determine if this association actually contributed to the formation of his theories, or if he had possessed many of his ideas concerning these nameless creatures before his acquaintance with her. In the case of the impressionable young Schwob, much of what he states symbolically about these credulous beings could have been the preconceived notions of his imagination about existences such as hers. In addition, Schwob tried to destroy all there was of "la petite Vise" after her death on December 7, 1893. At any rate, the result of their relationship was the collection of stories entitled the **Livre de Monelle,** one of the few examples of Schwob's intermingling of life and literature. Monelle and her sisters represent the *petites prostituées* of all times who come out of the night and show pity for their fellowman—the unknown little girl "simple et bonne" for Napoleon at eighteen; Anne for De Quincey, the opium eater; "la petite Nelly" for Dostoievsky; the fictional Sonia ("elle a existé comme les autres," a dit Schwob) ["she lived like the others," said Schwob] for Rodion.

Throughout his literary career, Schwob, like Maurice Maeterlinck, Henri Bataille, and Francis Jammes, pursued his portrayals of the world of children. (p. 345)

Marcel Schwob was obsessed with the courtesan and the child-prostitute even though he lived in an age whose authors preferred the beautiful but terrifying Cleopatra about whom he did not write, and the treacherous Salomé whom he seems to suggest. Yet, his portrayal of the innocence and godliness of the prostitutes of this world was not his invention. The less the reader knew about a subject or an idea, the greater was Schwob's success at merging fact and fancy into a seemingly original creation. Admittedly the basis for virtue in his heroines was novel, and his overpowering need to justify their way of life extended far beyond that of his contemporaries. It might have been that his homosexual tendencies caused him to identify himself with their plight, or that "la petite Vise" haunted his mind and manuscripts, or that he felt compelled to share his knowledge and appreciation of their roles in other ages and other times. More than likely, Schwob's persistence with this theme is a combination of all three elements plus the appraisal of his wife who said years after his death: "Son âme tendre connaissait toutes les nuances de la pitié" ["Her tender soul knew all the nuances of pity"]. (p. 346)

> *Gloria L. Hobbs, "The Divinity and Innocence of Schwob's Courtesans," in* The French Review, *Vol. XL, No. 3, December, 1966, pp. 341-46.*

JAMES P. GILROY   (essay date 1982-83)

[*In the following excerpt from his review of* Chroniques, *previously uncollected short stories, editorials, and articles written by Schwob between 1891 and 1894, Gilroy discusses Schwob's importance in the evolution of modern fiction.*]

The introduction [to *Chroniques*] rightly emphasizes Schwob's pivotal role in the development of a new kind of novel, one conceived in reaction against the "realist" tradition of the earlier nineteenth century. Schwob himself described this new style of writing fiction as "impressionistic" and considered it a new classicism. . . . He rejected the "scientific realism" of Balzac and Zola as well as the minute analysis of psychological causality practiced by Flaubert. He felt that the novel of the future should be an "artificial reproduction" by the literary artist of the structures of nature, a "synthesis," a "symmetrical construction." . . . His ideal was a novel wherein plot and character development are not important. Instead, the work of fiction becomes a series of fragments united by a common underlying idea, emotion or state of mind. The latter gives meaning to the work's constituent parts and is itself made manifest through a reciprocal illumination of each part by the others, in the context of the whole. Like Greek tragedy, to which he compares it, the novel will become "une composition dont le total explique chacune des parties" ["a composition in which the whole explains each of the parts"]. . . . The principle of esthetic form will once again govern the literary presentation of amorphous reality:

> Nous touchons aujourd'hui, après le romantisme et le naturalisme, à une nouvelle période de symétrie. L'Idée qui est fixe et immobile semble devoir se substituer de nouveau aux Formes Matérielles qui sont changeantes et flexibles.

> [We are approaching today, after Romanticism and Naturalism, a new period of symmetry. The Idea that is fixed and immovable seems bound once more to replace Material Forms which are changing and flexible. . . .]

Schwob's own fictional works, like *Coeur double* . . . and *Le Livre de Monelle* . . . are illustrations of these theories and anticipate the more celebrated realization of Schwob's ideal in Proust and the *nouveau roman*. Moreover, like many practitioners of recent French fiction, Schwob emphasized the need for the reader's active collaboration in the understanding and liberation of the novel's hidden subject. The final synthesis is the reader's responsibility. (p. 177)

> *James P. Gilroy, in a review of "Chroniques," in* Nineteenth-Century French Studies, *Vol. 11, Nos. 1 & 2, Fall, 1982 & Winter, 1983, pp. 177-78.*

ALEX SZOGYI   (essay date 1985)

[*Szogyi is an American critic, editor, and translator. In the following excerpt, he discusses the merits and shortcomings of the translation* The King in the Golden Mask, and Other Writings.]

Marcel Schwob was much esteemed during his relatively short life. . . . Alfred Jarry's *Ubu Roi* and Paul Valéry's *Monsieur Teste* were dedicated to him. With Pierre Louÿs, he corrected the final draft of Oscar Wilde's *Salomé*, (Wilde wrote the play in French) and his translation of *Hamlet* was a starring vehicle for Sarah Bernhardt. It was Edmond de Goncourt who called Schwob a "hallucinatory resurrector of the past." In *The King in the Golden Mask*, the only translation of his writings now in print, we are thrust into bleak, antique, occult landscapes, a surreal world invariably leading to bloodletting, humiliation and death. Each of the minuscule prose poems seems to be a bridge between Poe, whose work haunted Schwob, and Jorge Luis Borges. These translations are awkward and arid, but some pieces manage to be memorable. **"The Fat Man"** evokes a diabolical fear of sweetness and diabetes. The high point of the collection is Schwob's introduction to *Les Vies Imaginaires* . . . , his book of portraits which attempt to revamp the art of historical biography. He suggests, "Louis XIV's shifts of policy may have been caused by his fistula." Schwob wished to evoke the uniqueness of men, be they divinities, mediocrities or criminals. Pity he did not live long enough to perfect a style that might have catapulted him into the realm of a Genet or a Borges.

> *Alex Szogyi, in a review of "The King in the Golden Mask, and Other Writings," in* The New York Times Book Review, *April 21, 1985, p. 24.*

ADDITIONAL BIBLIOGRAPHY

Cambiaire, Celestin Pierre. "Poe and Marcel Schwob." In his *The Influence of Edgar Allan Poe*, pp. 204-11. New York: G. E. Stechert, 1927.*
> Discussion of similarities of theme and subject in the works of Schwob and Edgar Allan Poe. Cambiaire notes that both writers wrote about the sickly, the dying, the insane, and the criminal, and that many sections in Schwob's stories can be directly traced to similar passages in Poe's work.

Green, John A. "Marcel Schwob: 1867-1967." In *The French Review* XL, No. 4 (February 1967): 522-32.
> Examines Schwob's effect on and importance to the avant-garde literary movements of the late nineteenth century. Green contends that despite Schwob's inferiority as a writer when compared to such contemporaries as Paul Claudel, André Gide, and Stéphane Mallarmé, these greater writers admired Schwob's works because they embodied many of the main traits—such as anarchy, intellectualism, and esoteric taste—that marked the breakdown of traditional forms in literature, music, and the visual arts in the 1890s.

——. "Marcel Schwob and Paul Leautaud, 1903-1905." In *Modern Language Quarterly* XXIX (1968): 415-22.*
> Traces Schwob's influence and encouragement during Paul Leautaud's early career through letters written by Schwob and entries in Leautaud's journal.

"Marcel Schwob's *Le livre de Monelle.*" *The New York Times Book Review* (26 May 1929): 2.

Positive review in which the work is called "one of the minor masterpieces of French letters."

O'Sullivan, Vincent. "Two Lives." *Dublin Magazine* 3 (January 1928): 33-44.*

Discussion of Schwob's reputation and influences. O'Sullivan argues that while Schwob's writing is consistently admirable, the actual substance of such works as *Le livre de Monelle* and *Moeurs des diurnales* is derived from the works of Friedrich Nietzsche, Fedor Dostoevsky, and various English writers, particularly Robert Louis Stevenson. He considers only *La lampe de psyché* an original and lasting accomplishment that "nobody else in France, or in England either, could have written."

Rhodes, S. A. "Marcel Schwob and André Gide." *The Romanic Review* XXII, No. 1 (January-March 1931): 28-37.*

Examination of the similarities between Schwob's *Le livre de Monelle* and Gide's *Les nourritures terrestres*. Rhodes argues that Gide's personal relationship with Schwob, and perhaps Schwob's work, was influential in shaping the diction, moral and esthetic viewpoints, and other aspects of the work that marked Gide's break from the Symbolist influence of his early mentor Stéphane Mallarmé.

Whibley, Charles. "Marcel Schwob." *The Academy* 68, No. 1715 (18 March 1905): 276-77.

Analyzes Schwob's works in various genres as reflections of his personality and temperament.

White, Iain. Introduction to *The King in the Golden Mask, and Other Writings,* by Marcel Schwob, translated by Iain White, pp. 1-13. Manchester, England: Carcanet New Press, 1982.

Discussion of Schwob's life and career, his influence on other writers, and the milieu in which his talent developed.

(Joseph) Lincoln Steffens

1866-1936

American journalist, autobiographer, essayist, and short story writer.

Steffens was perhaps the most prominent figure of what came to be called the "muckraking" movement, Theodore Roosevelt's term for a type of American journalism that flourished between 1901 and approximately 1914. During this period, reporters worked to uncover dishonest methods and unscrupulous motives in business and government. Steffens became widely known for his exposures of governmental corruption and his disclosures that the worst abuses of power and influence in the United States were not carried out covertly but were widely known and generally accepted as the way the system operated. His eventual disillusionment with a public indifferent to institutionalized dishonesty led Steffens, like many intellectuals of his generation, to embrace communism as the solution to the problems that he perceived in American society. His *Autobiography,* written near the end of a long and productive life, is regarded not only as the testimonial to that life but as a clear account of the path taken by Steffens and many others of his time who became disenchanted with the American system and turned to the Soviet Union as a model for change.

Steffens was born in San Francisco to a wealthy family of pioneer stock. As the oldest child and only son, he was indulged and somewhat spoiled by his parents and sisters, recalling in his *Autobiography* that his youth was an idyllic time devoted to horses, dogs, and guns, with little parental pressure to excel at school, where he was usually at the bottom of his class. After graduating from the University of California at Berkeley with an undistinguished scholastic record, Steffens decided to study philosophy and psychology at the great universities of Europe, and pursued an eclectic education in Berlin, Heidelberg, Munich, Leipzig, and Paris. While abroad, Steffens secretly married Josephine Bontecou, another American student. Upon Steffens's return to the United States in 1892, his father suggested that it was time he stop investigating the theoretical side of life and earn a living, though his family later stressed that they would not thus have thrown Steffens upon his own resources had they known he had a wife to support. The sudden necessity to provide for himself and his family led Steffens into the profession of journalism, and from there to national and eventually international prominence.

The 1880s and 1890s were decades of great advances in the printing and periodical publishing industries. Recent inventions included cheaper papermaking processes, the high-speed press, and the half-tone process, which made it possible for the first time to print photographs in newspapers. These technological advances, coupled with a rise in national literacy, encouraged the development of national consumer marketing in periodical publications. Newspaper and magazine publishers, accruing extra revenue from advertisers, were able to reduce significantly the single-copy price of their publications. Concurrent with these developments, the United States Congress lowered postal rates for printed matter, and an unprecedentedly wide and constantly growing new market of newspaper and magazine readers was created.

Steffens first found work as a reporter for the noted conservative paper the *New York Evening Post.* He became adept at the human-interest story, which he typically wrote as a first-person, present-tense narrative, making no pretense to strict objectivity but openly incorporating his own opinions and reactions. Adopting the persona of the uninformed innocent in order to draw out his subjects, Steffens quickly made a name for himself as a skilled interviewer. He later alternately presented himself in his writings as a wide-eyed naïf gradually learning (and often being shocked by) the ways of the world, and as a wise and wily interrogator whose skillful questioning could inveigle the truth from the most slippery characters. It is now generally accepted by critics that Steffens's ingenuousness was no more than a pose, and that he had always possessed a greater level of sophistication than he was willing to acknowledge. For several years Steffens paid particular attention to the lives of poor immigrants in slum sections of New York. He became fascinated with documenting the chasm between American-born children of immigrants, who invariably turned away from their parents' cultural traditions, and their elders, who attempted to preserve old ways in the new world.

In 1901 Steffens left the *Evening Post* to work for *McClure's Magazine.* The step from newspaper to magazine writing was an important one for Steffens, who was anxious to escape the tyranny of hourly deadlines and reach a wider and more cultured readership. *McClure's,* with a growing circulation of three hundred and sixty thousand readers, was one of the primary forums for muckraking journalism at the turn of the century, and Steffens was one of the earliest practitioners of the style. In fact, in his *Autobiography* he claimed the distinction of having been the first muckraker. Many historians of the period similarly assign him primacy in the movement; however, it has also been noted that many other writers were doing this kind of reporting at the same time as Steffens. For example, Ida Tarbell had been researching her *History of the Standard Oil Company* for several years, and installments of this lengthy work appeared in *McClure's* concurrently with many of Steffens's first muckraking articles. Initially hired as a managing editor, Steffens spent only a few months behind a desk before magazine owner S. S. McClure sent him to St. Louis to investigate rumors of corruption in the city government. Steffens's subsequent investigations in that city, and of the city governments of Chicago, Minneapolis, Pittsburgh, Philadelphia, and New York, resulted in the series of articles later published as *The Shame of the Cities.* Further investigative articles probing corruption at the state and federal levels of government were later gathered and published as *The Struggle for Self-Government* and *Upbuilders.*

Steffens approached his material differently from those muckrakers who attempted to startle readers with sensationalistic exposés of hitherto unknown evils in high places. His emphasis was not on uncovering little-known abuses of power, but on stressing the fact that most corruption in government was widely known and tolerated by a constituency whose compliance with a corrupt system permitted and even encouraged it to flourish. "Isn't our corrupt government, after all, representative?" Steffens asked in his introduction to *The Shame of the Cities.* Although many reforms were enacted during the era of the muckrakers, Steffens believed that such measures inspired only increasingly more sophisticated and elusive forms of corruption. Disillusioned with the inability of his muckraking efforts to effect fundamental changes in American society, Steffens lost interest in the movement at about the same time that the movement itself was losing momentum due to decreased public interest and increasingly sensational and irresponsible articles by unscrupulous journalists.

During his years as a muckraking journalist, Steffens had earned a reputation for not merely identifying instances of wrongdoing, but for suggesting and even instituting reform measures. After abandoning the muckraking movement he became a popular lecturer on such topics and increasingly sought ways to involve himself in major political and historical events more directly than by merely reporting on them. Early in 1911, after the death of his first wife, Steffens entered an active phase of public life that led him to travel widely for the next fourteen years. He offered to mediate and advise in the celebrated McNamara bombing case in San Francisco, suggesting to defense attorney Clarence Darrow that his clients plead guilty to a bombing that had caused twenty deaths; this bold plea-bargaining attempt was intended to give Darrow the chance to demonstrate the collective "social guilt" of the anti-labor-union faction that had been the bomb target. The plan failed and the McNamaras were sentenced to life in prison. The outcome did not daunt Steffens, who maintained that his plan had been a sound one, and for many years he worked without success to effect the McNamaras' release.

Steffens gradually began to see communism as the answer to the social problems that had been impervious to muckraking.

Believing in the inevitability and desirability of revolution as a means of effecting social change, he closely followed the events of the Mexican and the Russian revolutions, making extended trips to both countries and interviewing many of the principals involved. In his *Autobiography,* Steffens claimed that during the course of the Mexican Revolution his personal intervention with a badly misinformed President Wilson prevented a second Spanish-American war. Critics have noted that such grandiose statements occur frequently in the *Autobiography.* Although he wrote little about his three trips to the Soviet Union in 1917, 1919, and 1923, his impressions formed the basis of public lectures in which he spoke glowingly of life in post-Revolutionary Russia. His growing enthusiasm for the Soviet system alienated his largely middle-class American readership, and he entered a period of popular and critical disregard. Steffens later maintained that he was the victim of an organized effort to censor or silence his reports on Russia; nevertheless, he was selected to be part of a secret fact-finding mission sent by the American government to the Kremlin. An account of this journey, "Report on the Bullitt Mission to Russia," appeared in the *Nation* in 1919. He also attended the Paris Peace Conference as a reporter. In London following the conference, he met Ella Winter, a student of political science and economics more than thirty years his junior. They began living together and married in 1924 upon learning that Winter was pregnant. Although the couple subsequently divorced, saying that their union was more meaningful with no legal ties, they remained together, first in London, later in Italy and then Carmel, California, until Steffens's death.

The birth of Steffens's son inspired him to begin writing essays on the experience of new fatherhood at an age when many men were becoming grandfathers. While Winter worked outside of their home, Steffens delighted in providing most of their child's primary care. The realization that he would probably not live to see his son grow to adulthood led him to begin writing his *Autobiography,* a massive undertaking that occupied him for six years. Upon its appearance in 1931 it was acclaimed a classic of American autobiography, restoring Steffens to a prominent place in American letters as well as elevating him to the status of a major twentieth-century "personality." Steffens presented his life as a long process of "unlearning" all of the commonly accepted truths that had been presented to him through many years of formal schooling, and of learning "how things really work" and "how easy it is to play and win at the game."

Steffens's *Autobiography* was a bestseller upon publication and remained extremely influential throughout the 1930s due to its inclusion in the political science curricula of many universities. However, Steffens's reputation suffered a severe setback during the Cold War atmosphere of the 1950s, when many commentators ignored all other aspects of his work to attack his celebration of communism and the Soviet Union. As fear of communism subsided, critics began to take a more expansive view of Steffens's career. He is now viewed as a representative figure demonstrating the alternating extremes of idealism and disillusionment experienced by many American intellectuals during the first decades of the twentieth century. Critics have noted that unlike many other socially concerned intellectuals of his era, such as H. L. Mencken, Steffens never succumbed to unrelenting cynicism. Late in his life, despite his perception of a deep-rooted corruption in American society, he still hoped that a later generation could salvage crumbling American ideals. His *Autobiography,* in particular, was written to satisfy his desire to pass on to a new generation what he believed to be hard-found truths. For this reason, although some critics call such a vision naive, his journalism and autobiography remain important commentaries on early twentieth-century America.

PRINCIPAL WORKS

The Shame of the Cities (journalism) 1904
The Struggle for Self-Government (journalism) 1906
Upbuilders (journalism) 1909
"Report on the Bullitt Mission to Russia" (journalism) 1919; published in journal *The Nation*
Moses in Red: The Revolt of Israel as a Typical Revolution (fable) 1926
The Autobiography of Lincoln Steffens (autobiography) 1931
The Letters of Lincoln Steffens. 2 vols. (letters) 1936
Lincoln Steffens Speaking (essays and short stories) 1936
The World of Lincoln Steffens (journalism, essays, and fables) 1962

LINCOLN STEFFENS (essay date 1904)

[*In the following excerpt, Steffens prefaces* The Shame of the Cities *with a discussion of the types of corruption he found in major American cities and his prescription for improving the performance of elected officials.*]

[*The Shame of the Cities*] is not a book. It is a collection of articles reprinted from *McClure's Magazine*. Done as journalism, they are journalism still, and no further pretensions are set up for them in their new dress. This classification may seem pretentious enough; certainly it would if I should confess what claims I make for my profession. But no matter about that; I insist upon the journalism. And there is my justification for separating from the bound volumes of the magazine and republishing, practically without re-editing, my accounts as a reporter of the shame of American cities. They were written with a purpose, they were published serially with a purpose, and they are reprinted now together to further that same purpose, which was and is—to sound for the civic pride of an apparently shameless citizenship.

There must be such a thing, we reasoned. All our big boasting could not be empty vanity, nor our pious pretensions hollow sham. American achievements in science, art, and business mean sound abilities at bottom, and our hypocrisy a race sense of fundamental ethics. Even in government we have given proofs of potential greatness, and our political failures are not complete; they are simply ridiculous. But they are ours. Not alone the triumphs and the statesmen, the defeats and the grafters also represent us, and just as truly. Why not see it so and say it?

Because, I heard, the American people won't "stand for" it. You may blame the politicians, or, indeed, any one class, but not all classes, not the people. Or you may put it on the ignorant foreign immigrant, or any one nationality, but not on all nationalities, not on the American people. But no one class is at fault, nor any one breed, nor any particular interest or group of interests. The misgovernment of the American people is misgovernment by the American people.

When I set out on my travels, an honest New Yorker told me honestly that I would find that the Irish, the Catholic Irish, were at the bottom of it all everywhere. The first city I went to was St. Louis, a German city. The next was Minneapolis, a Scandinavian city, with a leadership of New Englanders. Then came Pittsburg, Scotch Presbyterian, and that was what my New York friend was. "Ah, but they are all foreign populations," I heard. The next city was Philadelphia, the purest American community of all, and the most hopeless. And after that came Chicago and New York, both mongrel-bred, but the one a triumph of reform, the other the best example of good government that I had seen. The "foreign element" excuse is one of the hypocritical lies that save us from the clear sight of ourselves.

Another such conceit of our egotism is that which deplores our politics and lauds our business. This is the wail of the typical American citizen. Now, the typical American citizen is the business man. The typical business man is a bad citizen; he is busy. If he is a "big business man" and very busy, he does not neglect, he is busy with politics, oh, very busy and very businesslike. I found him buying boodlers in St. Louis, defending grafters in Minneapolis, originating corruption in Pittsburg, sharing with bosses in Philadelphia, deploring reform in Chicago, and beating good government with corruption funds in New York. He is a self-righteous fraud, this big business man. He is the chief source of corruption, and it were a boon if he would neglect politics. But he is not the business man that neglects politics; that worthy is the good citizen, the typical business man. He too is busy, he is the one that has no use and therefore no time for politics. When his neglect has permitted bad government to go so far that he can be stirred to action, he is unhappy, and he looks around for a cure that shall be quick, so that he may hurry back to the shop. Naturally, too, when he talks politics, he talks shop. His patent remedy is quack; it is business.

"Give us a business man," he says ("like me," he means). "Let him introduce business methods into politics and government; then I shall be left alone to attend to my business."

There is hardly an office from United States Senator down to Alderman in any part of the country to which the business man has not been elected; yet politics remains corrupt, government pretty bad. . . . The business man has failed in politics as he has in citizenship. Why?

Because politics is business. That's what's the matter with it. That's what's the matter with everything,—art, literature, religion, journalism, law, medicine,—they're all business, and all—as you see them. Make politics a sport, as they do in England, or a profession, as they do in Germany, and we'll have—well, something else than we have now,—if we want it, which is another question. But don't try to reform politics with the banker, the lawyer, and the dry-goods merchant, for these are business men and there are two great hindrances to their achievement of reform: one is that they are different from, but no better than, the politicians; the other is that politics is not "their line." There are exceptions both ways. Many politicians have gone out into business and done well. . . , and business men have gone into politics and done well. . . . They haven't reformed their adopted trades, however, though they have sometimes sharpened them most pointedly. The politician is a business man with a specialty. When a business man of some other line learns the business of politics, he is a politician, and there is not much reform left in him. Consider the United States Senate, and believe me.

The commercial spirit is the spirit of profit, not patriotism; of credit, not honor; of individual gain, not national prosperity; of trade and dickering, not principle. "My business is sacred," says the business man in his heart. "Whatever prospers my business, is good; it must be. Whatever hinders it, is wrong; it must be. A bribe is bad, that is, it is a bad thing to take; but it is not so bad to give one, not if it is necessary to my business." "Business is business" is not a political sentiment, but our politician has caught it. He takes essentially the same view of the bribe, only he saves his self-respect by piling all his contempt upon the bribe-giver, and he has the great advantage of candor. "It is wrong, maybe," he says, "but if a rich merchant can afford to do business with me for the sake of a convenience or to increase his already great wealth, I can afford, for the sake of a living, to meet him half way. I make no pretensions to virtue, not even on Sunday." And as for giving bad government or good, how about the merchant who gives bad goods or good goods, according to the demand?

But there is hope, not alone despair, in the commercialism of our politics. If our political leaders are to be always a lot of political merchants, they will supply any demand we may create. All we have to do is to establish a steady demand for good government. The bosses have us split up into parties. To him parties are nothing but means to his corrupt ends. He "bolts" his party, but we must not; the bribe-giver changes his party, from one election to another, from one county to another, from one city to another, but the honest voter must not. Why? Because if the honest voter cared no more for his party than the politician and the grafter, then the honest vote would govern, and that would be bad—for graft. It is idiotic, this devotion to a machine that is used to take our sovereignty from us. If we would leave parties to the politicians, and would vote not for the party, not even for men, but for the city, and the State, and the nation, we should rule parties, and cities, and States, and nation. If we would vote in mass on the more promising ticket, or, if the two are equally bad, would throw out the party that is in, and wait till the next election and then throw out the other party that is in—then, I say, the commercial politician would feel a demand for good government and he would supply it. That process would take a generation or more to complete, for the politicians now really do not know what good government is. But it has taken as long to develop bad government, and the politicians know what that is. If it would not "go," they would offer something else, and, if the demand were steady, they, being so commercial, would "deliver the goods."

But do the people want good government? . . . Isn't our corrupt government, after all, representative? (pp. 1-6)

No, the contemned methods of our despised politics are the master methods of our braggart business, and the corruption that shocks us in public affairs we practice ourselves in our private concerns. There is no essential difference between the pull that gets your wife into society or for your book a favorable review, and that which gets a heeler into office, a thief out of jail, and a rich man's son on the board of directors of a corporation; none between the corruption of a labor union, a bank, and a political machine; none between a dummy director of a trust and the caucus-bound member of a legislature; none between a labor boss like Sam Parks, a boss of banks like John D. Rockefeller, a boss of railroads like J. P. Morgan, and a political boss like Matthew S. Quay. The boss is not a political, he is an American institution, the product of a freed people that have not the spirit to be free.

And it's all a moral weakness; a weakness right where we think we are strongest. Oh, we are good—on Sunday, and we are "fearfully patriotic" on the Fourth of July. But the bribe we pay to the janitor to prefer our interests to the landlord's, is the little brother of the bribe passed to the alderman to sell a city street, and the father of the air-brake stock assigned to the president of a railroad to have this life-saving invention adopted on his road. . . . We are pathetically proud of our democratic institutions and our republican form of government, of our grand Constitution and our just laws. We are a free and sovereign people, we govern ourselves and the government is ours. But that is the point. We are responsible, not our leaders, since we follow them. We *let* them divert our loyalty from the United States to some "party"; we *let* them boss the party and turn our municipal democracies into autocracies and our republican nation into a plutocracy. We cheat our government and we let our leaders loot it, and we let them wheedle and bribe our sovereignty from us. True, they pass for us strict laws, but we are content to let them pass also bad laws, giving away public property in exchange; and our good, and often impossible, laws we allow to be used for oppression and blackmail. And what can we say? We break our own laws and rob our own government, the lady at the customhouse, the lyncher with his rope, and the captain of industry with his bribe and his rebate. The spirit of graft and of lawlessness is the American spirit. (pp. 6-8)

"Blame us, blame anybody, but praise the people," this, the politician's advice, is not the counsel of respect for the people, but of contempt. By just such palavering as courtiers play upon the degenerate intellects of weak kings, the bosses, political, financial, and industrial, are befuddling and befooling our sovereign American citizenship; and—likewise—they are corrupting it.

And it is corruptible, this citizenship. "I know what Parks is doing," said a New York union workman, "but what do I care. He has raised my wages. Let him have his graft!". . .

The people are not innocent. That is the only "news" in all the journalism of these articles, and no doubt that was not new to many observers. It was to me. When I set out to describe the corrupt systems of certain typical cities, I meant to show simply how the people were deceived and betrayed. But in the very first study—St. Louis—the startling truth lay bare that corruption was not merely political; it was financial, commercial, social; the ramifications of boodle were so complex, various, and far-reaching, that one mind could hardly grasp them. (p. 9)

It was impossible in the space of a magazine article to cover in any one city all the phases of municipal government, so I chose cities that typified most strikingly some particular phase or phases. Thus as St. Louis exemplified boodle; Minneapolis, police graft; Pittsburg, a political and industrial machine; and Philadelphia, general civic corruption; so Chicago was an illustration of reform, and New York of good government. All these things occur in most of these places. There are, and long have been, reformers in St. Louis, and there is today police graft there. Minneapolis has had boodling and council reform, and boodling is breaking out there again. Pittsburg has general corruption, and Philadelphia a very perfect political machine. Chicago has police graft and a low order of administrative and general corruption which permeates business, labor, and society generally. As for New York, the metropolis might exemplify almost anything that occurs anywhere in American cities, but no city has had for many years such a good administration as was that of Mayor Seth Low.

That which I have made each city stand for, is that which it had most highly developed. It would be absurd to seek for organized reform in St. Louis, for example, with Chicago next door; or for graft in Chicago with Minneapolis so near. After Minneapolis, a description of administrative corruption in Chicago would have seemed like a repetition. Perhaps it was not just to treat only the conspicuous element in each situation. But why should I be just? I was not judging; I arrogated to myself no such function. I was not writing about Chicago for Chicago, but for the other cities, so I picked out what light each had for the instruction of the others. But, if I was never complete, I never exaggerated. Every one of those articles was an understatement, especially where the conditions were bad, and the proof thereof is that while each article seemed to astonish other cities, it disappointed the city which was its subject. Thus my friends in Philadelphia, who knew what there was to know, and those especially who knew what I knew, expressed surprise that I reported so little. . . . I cut twenty thousand words out of the Philadelphia article and then had not written half my facts. I know a man who is making a history of the corrupt construction of the Philadelphia City Hall, in three volumes, and he grieves because he lacks space. You can't put all the known incidents of the corruption of an American city into a book.

This is all very unscientific, but then, I am not a scientist. I am a journalist. I did not gather with indifference all the facts and arrange them patiently for permanent preservation and laboratory analysis. I did not want to preserve, I wanted to destroy the facts. My purpose was no more scientific than the spirit of my investigation and reports; it was, as I said above, to see if the shameful facts, spread out in all their shame, would not burn through our civic shamelessness and set fire to American pride. That was the journalism of it. I wanted to move and to convince. That is why I was not interested in all the facts, sought none that was new, and rejected half those that were old. I often was asked to expose something suspected. I couldn't; and why should I? Exposure of the unknown was not my purpose. The people: what they will put up with, how they are fooled, how cheaply they are bought, how dearly sold, how easily intimidated, and how led, for good or for evil—that was the inquiry, and so the significant facts were those only which everybody in every other town would recognize, from their common knowledge of such things, to be probable. But these, understated, were charged always to the guilty persons when individuals were to blame, and finally brought home to the people themselves, who, having the power, have also the responsibility, they and those they respect, and those that guide them. (pp. 10-13)

I think I prize more highly than any other of my experiences the half-dozen times when grafting politicians I had "roasted," as they put it, called on me afterwards to say, in the words of one who spoke with a wonderful solemnity:

"You are right. I never thought of it that way, but it's right. I don't know whether you can do anything, but you're right, dead right. And I'm all wrong. We're all, all wrong. I don't see how we can stop it now; I don't see how I can change. I can't, I guess. No, I can't, not now. But, say, I may be able to help you, and I will if I can. You can have anything I've got."

So you see, they are not such bad fellows, these practical politicians. I wish I could tell more about them: how they have helped me; how candidly and unselfishly they have assisted me to facts and an understanding of the facts, which, as I warned them, as they knew well, were to be used against them. If I could—and I will some day—I should show that one of the surest hopes we have is the politician himself. Ask him for good politics; punish him when he gives bad, and reward him when he gives good; make politics pay. Now, he says, you don't know and you don't care, and that you must be flattered and fooled—and there, I say, he is wrong. I did not flatter anybody; I told the truth as near as I could get it, and instead of resentment there was encouragement. After **"The Shame of Minneapolis,"** and **"The Shamelessness of St. Louis,"** not only did citizens of these cities approve, but citizens of other cities, individuals, groups, and organizations, sent in invitations, hundreds of them, "to come and show us up; we're worse than they are."

We Americans may have failed. We may be mercenary and selfish. Democracy with us may be impossible and corruption inevitable, but these articles, if they have proved nothing else, have demonstrated beyond doubt that we can stand the truth; that there is pride in the character of American citizenship; and that this pride may be a power in the land. So this little volume, a record of shame and yet of self-respect, a disgraceful confession, yet a declaration of honor, is dedicated, in all good faith, to the accused—to all the citizens of all the cities in the United States. (pp. 17-18)

> *Lincoln Steffens, "Introduction: And Some Conclusions," in his* The Shame of the Cities, *1904. Reprint by Hill and Wang, 1957, pp. 1-18.*

THE NATION   (essay date 1906)

[*The following excerpt is taken from an anonymous review of* The Struggle for Self-Government.]

[**The Struggle for Self-Government**] is a reprint of the author's magazine work of the past two years, with little alteration saving the addition of a footnote here and there. The title hardly represents the contents, which deal more with corrupt conditions than with efforts for improvement. Mr. Steffens objects to having his work classified with the "literature of exposure," since he maintains that he writes only what everybody knows. In the various chapters, dealing with six different States, there is constant insistence on a fundamental identity of origin for all the corruption encountered, and that origin is the use of the machinery of government by unscrupulous business interests for private ends. . . . Self-government, Mr. Steffens holds, and not "good government," should be the first demand. The worst buccaneers who ever got possession of a city or State may consent to give "good government," clean streets, effective police administration, etc., merely as a blind to cover immensely more profitable channels of corruption. Once establish a genuinely representative government of the people, and good government will be a comparatively simple problem.

If there is any serious fault to be found with this book it is a fault of style rather than of substance. A reader whose imagination is not already unduly heated on the subject, by the constant perusal of the more sensational dailies, can hardly fail to get an impression of exaggeration, and still a careful examination gives one no basis upon which to accuse Mr. Steffens of exaggerations of fact. . . . The trouble, apparently, lies in too continual effort for emphatic form of statement. One's ear grows tired of such persistent hammering, and a temptation to drop the book as the mere ranting of an insincere "yellow journalist'' is the price which the author pays for conceding too much to the latter's habits of speech. We fear that the dedication [to the czar of Russia] runs more chance of passing as a bit of up-to-date journalism than as the effective political satire evidently intended. Mr. Steffens has qualifications for very useful work as a reformer if he will but avoid a pit or two upon the brink of which he seems inclined to play.

A review of "The Struggle for Self-Government," in
The Nation, *Vol. LXXXIII, July 5, 1906, p. 19.*

H. L. MENCKEN   (essay date 1931)

[*From the era of World War I until the early years of the Great Depression, Mencken was one of the most influential figures in American letters. His strongly individualistic, irreverent outlook on life and his vigorous, invective-charged writing style helped establish the iconoclastic spirit of the Jazz Age and significantly shaped the direction of American literature. As a social and literary critic—the roles for which he is best known—Mencken was the scourge of evangelical Christianity, public service organizations, literary censorship, boosterism, provincialism, democracy, all advocates of personal or social improvement, and every other facet of American life that he perceived as humbug. In his literary criticism, Mencken encouraged American writers to shun the anglophilic, moralistic bent of the nineteenth century and to practice realism, an artistic call-to-arms that is most fully developed in his essay "Puritanism as a Literary Force," one of the seminal essays in modern literary criticism. A man who was widely renowned or feared during his lifetime as a would-be destroyer of established American values, Mencken once wrote: "All of my work, barring a few obvious burlesques, is based upon three fundamental ideas; 1. That knowledge is better than ignorance; 2. That it is better to tell the truth than to lie; and 3. That it is better to be free than to be a slave." In the following excerpt, Mencken discusses Steffens's role as a reporter and the conclusions that he reached about American government.*]

Mr. Steffens, ever since the close of his student years in Germany, France and England, has been in practice as a journalist, and in his day he performed some journalism of a very high order, but the thumping error on page 318 of his autobiography, whereby he shows that he is not clear about the difference between a composing-room and a press-room, is not needed to show that the whole bent of his mind is essentially unjournalistic. As an actual newspaper reporter, I suspect, he must have been something of a duffer, and as a city editor he was plainly far more interested in literature than in news. Even as a muck-raker, though his reporting, by that time, had become, within its limits, magnificent, he functioned mainly, not as a recorder of events, but as a shaper of them. The true journalist lets the other fellow scheme and sweat; his business is simply to record the ensuing failure. But Steffens always thrust his oar in, and so played the victim in a long series of wrecks, beginning with that of Dr. Parkhurst's effort to evangelize New York, culminating in that of the defense in the Mooney-Billings case, and ending dismally with the débâcle of the Liberals at Versailles.

Well, if he has been unjournalistic, in his career, he is also unjournalistic in the conclusions he draws from it. Reform, he believes, is a dead goose; the American people have definitely decided that they prefer corruption. They have not yet become quite as complacent as the people of France, but they have already got beyond the self-deception of the people of England, and are no longer either blind to the nature of the government they live under, or hopeful that it can be improved. But if Mr. Steffens thus seems to put up his shutters to the tune of a cynical whistle, it is surely not the shrill falsetto of the city-room. Facing the irremediable, he is disposed to believe that, after all it is quite tolerable. "Isn't a strong man, however bad, socially better than a weak man, however good?" So he has pleasant things to say, not only of Mooney and Billings, the dynamiters, but also of their enemies, the Babbitti of Los Angeles; not only of Roosevelt the police commissioner but also of Bill Devery; not only of the idealists who died so horribly at Versailles but also of Clemenceau and even Wilson. All of them, he seems to think, were simply poor fish, swept along by incomprehensible currents. The bad were sometimes charming fellows and the good had more in them than goodness. It is a good-humored commentary upon our day and nation. Moreover, it is competently written. (pp. 382-83)

H. L. Mencken "Footprints on the Sands of Time,"
in American Mercury, *Vol. XXIII, No. 91, July, 1931,*
pp. 382-83.

C. C. REGIER   (essay date 1932)

[*Regier's* The Era of the Muckrakers *examines the course of the muckraking movement in American journalism. In the following excerpt from that work, Regier places Steffens at the forefront of all phases of muckraking, at both local and federal levels.*]

The years 1900, 1901, and 1902 witnessed the real beginnings of the muckraking movement. (p. 49)

[In 1902] the October number of *McClure's* . . . printed an article by Claude H. Wetmore and Lincoln Steffens on **"Tweed Days in St. Louis,"** and announced that in the next issue it would begin the serial publication of Ida M. Tarbell's "History of the Standard Oil Company."

With the Steffens and the Tarbell articles *McClure's* inaugurated the policy which it followed with great success for a period of years, and the era of the muckrakers had begun. In January, 1903, Mr. McClure wrote:

> We did not plan it so; it is a coincidence that this number contains three arraignments of American character such as should make every one of us stop and think. **"The Shame of Minneapolis,"** the current chapter of the Standard Oil, Mr. Ray Stannard Baker's "The Right to Work," it might all have been called "The American Contempt of Law." Capitalists, workingmen, politicians, citizens—all breaking the law or letting it be broken. Who is there left to uphold it? . . . There is no one left— none but all of us.

McClure's had stumbled on muckraking without premeditation. For years S. S. McClure had been winning a reputation as one of the shrewdest, most ingenious editors in the country. Eccentric, imaginative, enthusiastic, he was constantly seeing opportunities for brilliant articles. He had secured such fiction writers as Rudyard Kipling and O. Henry when almost no one else knew their names; he had obtained exclusive stories about such inventions as the wireless telegraph and the Roentgen ray before the scientific world had heard of them; he had cultivated the popular interest in biography by securing entertaining writers and by introducing plenty of illustrations. (pp. 55-6)

Slowly McClure built up a staff that would round out his own qualities. In John S. Phillips he had early found an associate who combined calmness, good judgment, and tact with no slight editorial gifts. Miss Ida M. Tarbell he had employed to do biographies for him, and he came to appreciate her abilities as an investigator as well as a writer. Ray Stannard Baker had come to the staff as a young journalist with an interest in writing short stories. And Lincoln Steffens had brought to the magazine a mind trained both in the universities and in the offices of leading New York newspapers.

When these people gathered together to discuss policies, the electricity of brilliant ideas was in the air. (p. 56)

At some such meeting as this, Miss Tarbell, more than three years before the articles appeared, proposed that, in view of the importance of an interest in the trust problem, it might be well to tell the story of a representative monopoly. McClure was sceptical of the value of the historical approach, but he allowed himself to be convinced, and Miss Tarbell began the laborious task of consulting all the Congressional investigations, court records, and other documents which threw light on the growth of the Standard Oil Company. It was merely coincidence that the first of her articles was ready at just about the time when Steffens, who had long been considering a series of stories on subjects of current news value, received Claude Wetmore's account of happenings in St. Louis. And it was also a coincidence that Baker, whose interest in labor problems began while he was still in college, began at this particular time to write about these problems in *McClure's*. (pp. 56-7)

Once muckraking was fairly started, it covered practically every aspect of American life. . . . "Tweed Days in St. Louis" (by Claude H. Wetmore and Lincoln Steffens in *McClure's*, October, 1902), has already been referred to as marking the opening of a new epoch, and . . . Lincoln Steffens may be regarded as in some respects the real founder of the muckraking movement. . . . (p. 59)

Lincoln Steffens, who was born in San Francisco and educated in the schools of that city, at the University of California, and at the universities of Berlin, Heidelburg, Leipzig, and the Sorbonne, began his journalistic career as a reporter for the New York *Evening Post*. Allan Nevins, in his history of that newspaper, states that Steffens was one of the best journalists New York ever had, and he rose rapidly in the profession. He was a police reporter when Roosevelt was a police commissioner, and the friendship between the two began at that time. Later he was city editor of the *Commercial Advertiser*.

Steffens, then, had had an unusual academic training and a notable career in journalism when, at the invitation of John S. Phillips, he became managing editor of *McClure's* in 1901. S. S. McClure, however, on his return from Europe, informed Steffens that he did not know how to edit a magazine, and told him to get out of the office and start reporting. Steffens went to Chicago, looking for copy, and there received the tip to go to St. Louis. It was his idea that the public never received an accurate impression of what was happening from the newspapers, simply because it was impossible to understand a story that was spread out over weeks and even months. He believed that magazines could bring all the facts together, make a unified and comprehensible story, and interest and help the public. He had no idea of muckraking; he was interested in a journalistic experiment.

In St. Louis he found the kind of material he had been looking for, and he secured Claude Wetmore to write the story. He was not, however, satisfied with what Wetmore did. Wetmore was too close to the events he described, saw them as too extraordinary, left out too much that was important. Steffens

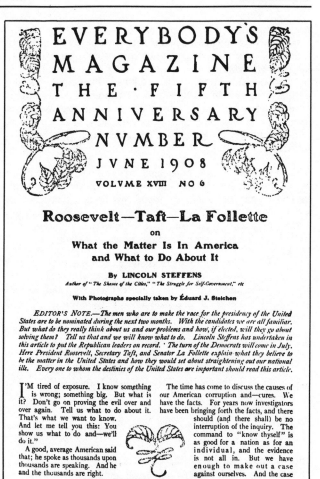

An early muckraking article given the front page of Everybody's Magazine.

rewrote the story, and, to satisfy Wetmore, both names were signed to it. That decided Steffens that he must write his own stories, and he went to Minneapolis for material. It was **"The Shame of Minneapolis"** (*McClure's*, January, 1903), that put the series on the map.

In Minneapolis a politician named Ames had been twice elected mayor by the Republicans and twice by the Democrats. Immediately after his fourth election (1901), Steffens asserted, Ames began to gather about him a group of plunderers and opened the city to all kinds of criminals. He made his brother, Colonel Fred W. Ames, chief-of-police, and he appointed an ex-gambler, Norman W. King, as chief of detectives. (pp. 59-60).

Steffens also told how Minneapolis had been saved from the Ames gang, largely through the efforts of one Hovey C. Clarke. Clarke was foreman of the grand jury that met in April, 1902, and he collected evidence at his own expense, rejecting bribes and defying threats against his life. One member of the gang after another was indicted and convicted, and Mayor Ames fled to Indiana after having been indicted for extortion, conspiracy, and bribe-offering. On November 4, 1902, a new administration was elected. (p. 61)

Steffens depended largely . . . on materials that had been brought out in the courts. As he saw the same phenomena recurring in. . . . various cities, he became more and more convinced that there were underlying causes. He began to believe in the possibility of a science of politics. In time he found he could predict, once he knew the state of corruption a particular city had reached, what stage it would next develop. As he realized that the politicians were not themselves to blame but were the victims of a system, he commenced blaming business men. He made the revolutionary discovery that whenever a bribe is taken, a bribe must have been given. But as he studied further, he decided that the business men were as much victims as the politicians.

What he wanted to do more than anything else was to make people see that corruption could not be laid at the door of any particular party or group. He found that he had succeeded in waking people up, but he discovered that they were looking to him to provide them with simple remedies. When he was asked how to deal with corruption, he replied flatly:

> As if I knew; as if we knew; as if there were any one way to deal with this problem in all places under any circumstances. There isn't and if I had gone around with a ready made reform scheme in the back of my head, it would have served only to keep me from seeing straight the facts that would not support my theory. The only editorial scheme we had was to study a few choice examples of bad government, and tell how the bad was accomplished, then seek out, here and abroad, some typical good governments and explain how the good was done;— not how to do it, mind you, but how it was done.

After he had written on the cities, Steffens wrote on state governments. He left *McClure's* with the group that founded the *American*, and wrote on various political topics. On leaving the *American*, he was associated for a time with *Everybody's*, and for a few weeks represented a newspaper syndicate in Washington. When the war broke out in 1914, Steffens was in Europe, studying municipal conditions there and finding the same cycles he had observed in America. Forced to abandon this work, he decided to make a study of revolutions and went to Mexico to watch developments. Then, when the Russian revolution came, he hastened to Russia to see if revolutions followed any definite laws. Since the war he has spent much of his time in San Remo, Italy, but recently he has returned to this country, and in 1931 published his charming and stimulating *Autobiography*. (pp. 70-1).

As in municipal exposure so in state exposure Steffens easily ranks first among the muckrakers. In 1904 he wrote about Missouri, Illinois, and Wisconsin; and in the following year about Rhode Island, New Jersey, and Ohio.

In opening this series—**"Enemies of the Republic"**—he stated that every time he attempted to trace to its source the political corruption of a city ring, the stream of pollution branched off in the most unexpected directions and spread out in a network of veins and arteries so complex that hardly any part of the body politic seemed clear of it. Corruption was not confined to politics, but extended into finance and industry. Miss Tarbell had shown it in the trust, Mr. Baker in the labor union, and his investigations of municipal government had always drawn him out of politics into business and out into the state and the nation. The source of sustenance of our bad government was not politicians, the bribe-takers, but the bribe-givers, the cap-

tains of industry. The highway of corruption, he wrote, is the "road to success."

In his article on Missouri he explained what he meant by the "System." It was corruption settled into a "custom of the country"; the betrayal of trust established as the form of government. A few bribes, or even a hundred bribes, might not be so bad, but in Missouri—as elsewhere—there was a System of bribery—"corruption installed as the motive, the purpose, the spirit of a state government." The "combine" was composed of dishonest legislators of both parties who were usually in the pay of big business interests, and were controlled by the lobby. The lobby also controlled the honest legislators, for they represented the corporations and big businesses which contributed to the campaign funds. Such contributions were everywhere the first step toward corruption. It was wholesale bribery which bought also the honest legislator. The lobby served both the party and business.

When [St. Louis prosecuting attorney Joseph W.] Folk and Attorney-General Crow exposed Missouri it was found that it was not only state interests that were corrupting politics, but that national concerns which operated all over the United States were also involved. Among these were the American Sugar Refining Company, the American Book Company, and the Royal Baking Powder Company. Steffens had much to say about the last named concern, to show that "good" business makes for bad politics. (pp. 83-5)

The federal government was attacked less frequently, but it did not escape untouched. After having muckraked the cities and the states Steffens went to Washington. In his articles on the states he had repeatedly alluded to the national government as a part of the "system," and at last he was ready to subject it to the same sort of investigation. The city of Washington, he soon learned, was governed much in the same fashion that other cities were governed, in spite of the fact that the citizens were disfranchised and that the city was directly under the control of Congress. Public service corporations and banks controlled, and congressmen sold out to high finance.

Fortunately for Steffens, President Roosevelt was not only a liberal himself but he was a personal friend. (p. 108)

When Steffens first came to the national capital with the intention of exposing the federal government, Roosevelt was unwilling to tell of his experiences with the Senate and House machines, with the federal courts, and with the forces in the government of the District of Columbia. The reason for this was that Roosevelt was trying to work and deal with them. "He was not a reformer in the White House; he was a careerist on the people's side." He was trying to wrangle some concessions from the powers that be and make them do some things for the country at large. In return for the congressmen's votes for his favorite measures he would appoint their candidates to office. Once Steffens wanted to know which had been the President's "most outrageous appointment." The answer was that he had appointed the brother of a senator's mistress to the attorneyship of a certain city. Up to that time the senator mentioned had consistently voted against Roosevelt, but since then he sometimes voted his way. Another reason for Roosevelt's reluctance to collaborate with the muckraker was his realization that he was no hero fighting for a representative democracy. "He had no economics, he never understood the political issue between the common and the special interests; neither as a police commissioner nor as a president did he grasp the difference between morality and representation."

Early in 1906, however, he gave Steffens *carte blanche*, directing all officials and employees of the government to tell him anything he might wish to know about the running of the government—not incompatible with the public interests; and he promised that the officials should not be hurt. The subject on which Steffens was especially anxious to throw light was the question as to what our federal government represented. He showed that neither house of Congress nor the executive departments were representative. In one article he stated that the President had to ''bribe'' congressmen—by appointments—to vote for the people's measures.

He wrote about ten weekly articles for a newspaper syndicate of about one hundred members in which he exposed his findings in Washington. The editors did not find this material sensational enough; so Steffens quit. He was through with muckraking in the old form. (pp. 108-09)

Steffens, after a long stay in Europe, is back in this country and, as mentioned above, has just published his *Autobiography*. He has come to the conclusion that the movement toward union of big business with politics is inevitable. Like an old contented lover he accepts conditions as they are. ''I have been contending,'' he writes, ''with all my kind, always against God. . . . The world which I tried so hard, so honestly, so dumbly, to change has changed me. . . . And as for the world in general, all that was or is or ever will be wrong with that is my—our thinking about it.'' (p. 214)

> *C. C. Regier, in his* The Era of the Muckrakers, *1932. Reprint by Peter Smith, 1957, 254 p.**

CARL SANDBURG (essay date 1938)

[*Sandburg was a poet, biographer, and folklorist who is often said to have captured the essence of America in his works. He recorded and celebrated the history of the American people in such free-verse poems as* ''Chicago'' *and* ''The People, Yes,'' *works which reflect his respect and hopes for the common man. Sandburg's massive six-volume biography of Abraham Lincoln won the Pulitzer Prize in biography in 1939 and he was awarded a second Pulitzer for his* Collected Poems *in 1951. In the following excerpt, Sandburg notes that Steffens's published* Letters *provide insight into his character not found in the* Autobiography.]

Some of us began reading Lincoln Steffens at the time when he first reached an immense American public with his series of magazine articles on *The Shame of the Cities*. We began to read him then, some of us, and we followed him on through the *Autobiography* and its postscript volume, *Lincoln Steffens Speaking*. He never once lost us as readers. Whether we said yes or no or maybe to what he was writing, we went on reading him these thirty years and more. Always he had something on the ball. You could never be sure what he was going to throw till it came. He carried an assortment of curves and a wicked straight ball. His style most often was so distinctly his own that what he put forth didn't need his signature.

The same style that was there in his public writings is found often in his private letters. Furthermore, many will agree that in this collection of letters [*The Letters of Lincoln Steffens, Volumes I and II*] there are moments when he surpasses in sheer writing, in vivid human utterance, the best spots in the books hitherto published. ''I would like,'' he set forth dreamily in 1920 out of the chaotic world war aftermath, ''to spend the evening of my life watching the morning of a new world.'' Not in any piece written for public consumption could he have been quite so frank and abrupt about his stormy discontent with

higher education as when in 1923 he wrote to a sister: ''Damn these universities, all of them. They have made my life one of *unlearning* literally, and all my discoveries are of well-known, well-kept secrets.'' Such sentences are not for one smooth easy reading and letting it go at that. You may find yourself going back to them for what you didn't get the first time which might connect with how to win friends inside of yourself and how better to find people you know to be living under your own hat.

About a million miles from being a Narcissus was Steffens. Yet how he did study himself, how he did try to fathom mankind by searching and cross-examining and spying on and carrying out counter-espionage on the single specimen piece of humanity nearest and most available, the solitary and brooding Lincoln Steffens himself. Somberly, after disentangling himself from the scenes of the Versailles peace conference, after travel and sojourn in the far-flung U.S.S.R. adventure, did he write to a sister of how he was baffling himself in thought and speech and was not sure what to do about it. ''I have some perceptions that are clear, but I notice contradictions in my conversations. Others don't; I can put my ideas over on men, but myself I can't fool.'' He was frankly asking himself at one point whether he was through as a writer, freely confessing, ''My stuff does not of itself take form and so help write itself. This scares me. Form is the essence of the creative faculty, and I may have lost that.'' And a little later this was not terrorizing to him at all. What of it? ''My writing is not important, and finding out things is very important.''

He never let up on these fishing expeditions into the deep sea currents, the sun spots and the ice floes, of his swarmingly alive mind. . . . The debauchery of the human mind accomplished by learning too much that must be later unlearned—this so often weighed heavily on him, haunted him, one letter to a sister having the confession, ''You have no idea how much my thinking centers around your children: the lies they are learning and how to save them from the errors I have made; and am still making. I could write my book to them . . . a warning to Youth.'' (pp. vii-viii)

Seldom has a lover and rebuker of humanity had so good a time in his earth travel. He might have founded a cult or movement had he been utterly solemn. He might have been a prophet, acclaimed and wearing garments intended to impress disciples and populace, if he had worn a straight face and had no knack of laughter. Prophets must beware of the horselaugh.

With this animated bundle of letters, the shelf of his writings comes to an end. Of his outgivings of counsel and companionship, there is no more. Now he may be studied as one of the classics. He had enough doubts and faiths to make a classic. (pp. viii-ix)

> *Carl Sandburg, in a memorandum to* The Letters of Lincoln Steffens: 1889-1919, Vol. I *by Lincoln Steffens, edited by Ella Winter and Granville Hicks, Harcourt Brace Jovanovich, 1938, pp. vii-ix.*

FLOYD DELL (essay date 1938)

[*An American novelist and dramatist, Dell is best known today as the author of* Moon-Calf (1920), *a novel which captures the disillusioned spirit of the Jazz Age. For several years he was a member, along with Carl Sandburg, Ben Hecht, Theodore Dreiser, and others, of the Chicago Renaissance, a group of writers who legitimized the American Midwest as a source of artistic material and achievement. A Marxist during his early career, Dell moved from Chicago to New York in 1914, and served as editor of the socialist periodical the* Masses *and its successor, the* Liberator, *for ten years. During the 1920s, Dell was associated with the bohemia of Greenwich Village and, with a series of novels and one-act plays, became known as a spokesman for society's rebels and nonconformists. His socialist sympathies softened over the years, although he remained an outspoken leftist throughout his career. In the following excerpt, Dell, in reviewing Steffens's* Letters, *summarizes Steffens's life and career.*]

Time has an irony of its own. Ten years ago, Lincoln Steffens was an aging and almost forgotten American journalist—so unremembered that the American editors of the new Encyclopedia Britannica did not give him even a passing mention in those thoughtful pages—an omission that may now seem quite incredible. One of the old crowd of "muckrakers," a friend of the reformers of a bygone era, and more recently an obscure dabbler in international affairs, he had been wandering about Europe since the World War, writing his reminiscences. It was a book that he got very "tired of writing and expected very little of." Even those who loved him well and wished him luck could not have imagined that this long-labored manuscript of their old friend "Stef" was going to be recognized at once as one of the world's great autobiographies.

The Autobiography of Lincoln Steffens was the kind of masterpiece which could not very well be neglected by the public. It had too much charm, humor, wisdom and power. It painted too well for a younger generation the picture of what was already for them a historic past—the times of Theodore Roosevelt and Woodrow Wilson. It told not only dramatically but critically the story of a gallant pre-war idealism that struggled and failed. Above all, it was not an old man's book. It had in it none of the wistful pathos of the backward glance at brighter days. It was the creation of an eager mind that looked forward with youthful curiosity into the future.

One of the reasons why it became the kind of book it was is revealed incidentally in these *Letters of Lincoln Steffens*. He wrote it that way for his little boy, Pete. Steffens had at the age of fifty-eight taken a new young wife, a third of a century younger than himself (twenty-five years old, that is to say), and had become for the first time the father of a child. Through this child's eyes he was imaginatively seeing himself and all the momentous affairs in which he had been involved. Thinking of his son as a future reader of his book, he wanted to write "of big things merrily."

Packed as the *Autobiography* is with the rich materials of his life experiences, it nevertheless leaves out much of Lincoln Steffens. Fortunately he was fond of his family and friends, and wrote them long and frequent letters, from which about a thousand have been very expertly selected by Ella Winter and Granville Hicks. The letters are interesting for many reasons—partly because of the persons and personages to whom they are written; partly because of their subjects, which are sometimes of public importance; but chiefly because of their intimacy, humor, charm and self-revelation. Steffens was a born letter-writer, and the world would be poorer without this collection.

Even more than the *Autobiography*, these letters present to us the extraordinary personality that was Lincoln Steffens. He seemed to all who knew him or about him a paradoxical and baffling character. . . .

The philosophical young idealist from California, studying abroad and writing home, gives no hint of the cauldron of political energy that seethes and bubbles somewhere within him. Thrown abruptly on his own resources, and getting a reporter's job in New York, he becomes before our eyes a young go-getter, clearly destined for success. Within a short time he knows all the big politicians and financiers and is trusted by them. He is making good and there is a touch of arrogance in his pride—this game is easy to beat, after all! Then circumstances fling him into the middle of a municipal reform crusade. He becomes a "reformer," but with this remarkable difference—he is a friend of all the crooks; and they trust him; he asks them for advice on how to beat their game; and they give him what he asks for.

A funny kind of reformer! The fact is that he likes "bad" people—if they are big and bold bad people. He despises weaknesss, adores power and is fascinated by those people (chiefly bad) who hold the secret of power. They in turn are flattered and fascinated by their pupil. They explain their crooked games to him. He comes back and explains the whole crooked mechanism more deeply to them. They are caught in a net, a web—a shimmering Anarcho-Christian spider web such as we shall see Steffens spinning everywhere he goes, with the most extraordinary flies caught, or half caught, in it.

This reporter had a genius for a kind of politics that was, then, comparatively new to America—the politics of peacemaking. Wherever the battle lines were drawn and all hell about to break loose, he could walk in and talk to the leaders and stop—or almost stop—the war. He added to the warm passion of the peacemaker the cold, relentless logic of a Machiavelli. He knew expertly every detail of the quarrel, and could defend each side to the other like a lawyer. To some people he would seem Christlike, to others Satanic. His gifts were wonderful, possibly dangerous, certainly queer. And if he failed—so did everybody else. His are among the most interesting failures of a society racked by internal hostilities that seemed destined to destroy it. He went out into no-man's-land to preach peace.

In the mean time, as a professional "muck raker," he made friends with the leading reformers all over the country, and those friendships stayed firm till death. . . .

He was a profound teacher in his public speeches, and a terrible tease. Half of what he said always contradicted the other half, and left earnest souls bewildered. He dropped, with the utmost sincerity, into humor that left an impression of insincerity. He distrusted "straight thinking," being convinced, as he said, that "the world of thought is round."

His private world of thought was a complicated pagoda in which there was floor beneath floor of belief and disbelief—under every faith a deeper cynicism, and under every cynicism a naïve hope, with winding stairs where his mind went up and down between one thought and the next—and beneath all, what?

How could any one trust him? But everybody did, if they got near enough to hear him talk. He had the McNamara dynamiting case all fixed up—everything was to be forgiven and forgotten all around. It didn't work out that way, but to the end of his days Steffens was convinced that it was the "good people"—set on by the preachers—who spoiled everything. He trusted the big bad men on both sides.

That fiasco cast a cloud over his whole life. It seemed at one time to be the end of his career as a Machiavellian peace maker. But a few years later, when there might be war in earnest between the United States and Mexico, Steffens spun his shimmering web across the Gulf—successfully, this time. He won the complete confidence both of Carranza and his leaders and of Wilson and his Cabinet; he advised both where to yield, and they took his advice. "You're working us for the Mexicans," said an American. "And I'm working the Mexicans for you," he replied.

It was just natural for him to be on both sides of all controversies. . . .

The depression disillusioned him about America's ability to work out its own kind of destiny. There was nothing left, then, but Communism. In speaking to some Harvard students he had commended the open mind, but "suddenly turned and bade them close their minds, to act when the time came." The time had come for him—it was a choice now between the futile barbarities of Fascism and the hard world-reconstruction of Communism, and he closed his mind absolutely to any criticism of Soviet Russia or the Communist ideal.

At peace, lit with an inward joy, the frail old Sage and Saint of Carmel lay in bed and received the young visitors who made pilgrimages to what was already a shrine. He died in 1936, aged seventy, loved and mourned by young people all over the country to whom he had come to stand in some way as a kind of grand symbolic father and friend.

> *Floyd Dell, "Lincoln Steffens, Peace-Making Reporter," in* New York Herald Tribune Books, *October 23, 1938, p. 3.*

OSCAR CARGILL (essay date 1951)

[*An American educator, historian, and literary critic, Cargill edited critical editions of the works of such major American authors as Henry James, Walt Whitman, Frank Norris, and Thomas Wolfe. In the following excerpt, Cargill summarizes Steffens's career and attacks the superficiality of his understanding of the Russian Revolution.*]

He wore an artist's tie; his hair was chewed off in bangs across his forehead, which was deeply seamed; wrinkles swept up from the corner of the eye into the knotted veins on the temple and sprayed down thickly to serrate the warm cheek. When he engaged you, it was with a speculative glance from behind smudged glasses that had slipped on the nose; when he talked, he deferred to you and there was humor in the way his moustache complemented his lips and the dab of hair on his chin bobbed at you. You knew already that he was the best interviewer in the world; what you did not know was that he was the most able insinuator also of his own opinions. Others, however, had found that out—Professor Arthur Holcombe, for example, who required his students in government to read Steffens' *Autobiography,* introducing the famous muckraker to a packed meeting at Harvard, warned the boys that Steffens was "the best, most dangerous high-power salesman in America." And Holcombe added, of course humorously, "Look out, or you'll get some new ideas."

"High-power salesman . . . of new ideas"—it sounded like an honorable title and the man to whom it was applied was sufficiently pleased with it to repeat innumerable times the anecdote conferring it. But despite a long-cultivated habit of self-deprecation, the title-bearer was not a severe self-critic; had he been, there might have been humiliation in the thought that the youth who had gone to Germany in 1889 to study philosophy had become a mere peddler of the world's most dangerous commodity. But no more than that other famous dilettante, Henry Adams, did Lincoln Steffens carry away very much from

the German universities. His *Letters* do not support the recollection of *The Autobiography* that he "worked hard, . . . read everything, heard everybody." They complain of difficulties with the language if the subject was at all abstruse; they raise objections if what was received conflicted with a deep-seated urgency to justify a will-to-do-good. He enjoyed, however, German music and beer as Adams enjoyed Gothic architecture and stained glass; unlike Adams, who found "German manners, even at Court, . . . sometimes brutal," Steffens discovered in the Germans much to admire and to copy: "A government meant to govern. . . . I envy them their official life, their city organization, their *aristocracy*. This may shock your American sensibilities enough, so I will go no further and say what more un-American I admire in this Empire."

Steffens' youthful admiration for German municipal government aided him a dozen years later to achieve national fame as a critic of American cities. . . . [In 1892] he got a reporter's job with the New York *Evening Post*. Personal charm and a will to succeed carried Steffens rapidly upward as a reporter. Under E. L. Godkin, the youth developed a simple but supple style—the hallmark of those who in his time had had to please Godkin. That merciless editor and cold reformer suppressed without killing his tyro's penchant to editorialize, but the tyro was never to appreciate his discipline. "As a writer, I was permanently hurt by my years on the *Post*," he recollected in his *Autobiography;* if one reads between the lines one senses the resentment of checked ardour in a youth who wished to castigate the iniquities that Jacob Riis, the Reverend Charles Parkhurst, Theodore Roosevelt, and Godkin himself had won the right to castigate. It hurt almost intolerably to possess an unventable righteousness in an environment of do-gooders under a reforming editor who wished, however, to set his own policy.

To cease to be a pair of legs for his editor's mind became Steffens' mastering ambition. He does not tell directly how long he was frustrate at this, but it was approximately a dozen years—until the articles comprising *The Shame of the Cities* were published. From the *Post* he went in 1897 to the city department of the *Commercial Advertiser;* here he was defeated by the nature of his task, that of giving their daily assignments to his reporters. Yet he achieved a vicarious release by building up a staff of "amateur" writers whom he let "color" the news; he would not hire "professional" newspaper men and actually fired those already on the staff. Success with his unusual news staff gave Steffens a reputation in the trade and led the ebullient Sam McClure to offer him the post of managing editor for *McClure's Magazine*. In the interview prior to accepting this offer, when asked what his policy might be, Steffens indicated that he would "put news into the magazine," meaning thereby that he would fill it with the "colored" factual articles which represented to him the quintessence of good journalism. Because McClure delegated no real authority, Steffens was unhappy and unproductive in the office of the magazine. Taking to the road in search of new writers and new materials, he picked up a "lead" in Chicago which brought him in contact with Joseph W. Folk, a conscientious prosecutor who was trying to clean up St. Louis. Steffens gave Folk's campaign national publicity in an article called **"Tweed Days in St. Louis,"** written by Claude H. Wetmore and corrected by Steffens in his editorial capacity before it appeared in the magazine in October, 1902.

"I started our political muckraking."—How this simple statement in *The Autobiography,* where "our" refers to *McClure's*

Magazine, got translated into "I started muckraking," which Louis Filler, Lisle Rose, and others have gone to some pains to refute, remains something of a mystery; but it is a fair conjecture that the immense vogue which Steffens was to have later led to assigning him a primary role at a time when the contribution of others was forgotten. **"Tweed Days in St. Louis"** did start political muckraking in *McClure's* and Steffens did give the assignment and map and correct the article; hence his more limited statement is correct and not the general inference that has been drawn from it. Though muckraking as a fact-assembling, libel-proof technique of exposure can be traced back to Henry D. Lloyd's "The Story of the Great Monopoly" in the *Atlantic* in 1881, the *concerted* effort that best deserves that name began with the simultaneous publication in *McClure's* in January, 1903, of Steffens' independent article, **"The Shame of Minneapolis,"** another chapter of Ida Tarbell's *The History of the Standard Oil Company* (serialization of which had begun two months previously), and Ray Stannard Baker's "The Right to Work." This conjunction, which was fortuitous, was turned into a "movement" by Sam McClure who saw and called attention to the fact editorially that all three articles demonstrated American contempt for law. The demand for *McClure's* cleaned the newsstands; other publishers and editors took the hint and soon American magazines were filled with exposures of the nation's general wickedness and especially (since this made a more general appeal to popular indignation) of the machinations of "malefactors of great wealth."

To Steffens personally the exposures of municipal corruption on which he had embarked with the encouragement of McClure in **"The Shame of Minneapolis"** meant more than the correction of American city government: they meant finding his own voice. He inserted his opinions into his leading paragraph and arranged his testimony and evidence to support those opinions, while at the same time totaling the facts in the specific municipal situation. But his editorializing did not please his publisher. "Mr. McClure was interested in facts, startling facts, not in philosophical generalizations." McClure, it would seem, was willing to admit the general turpitude, but he did not take Steffens' sensational view of it. "He hated, he feared, my dawning theory," says Steffens. And what was that theory? That American democracy fails at the municipal level, that the people will not rule, that "boss rule" is more efficient than intermittent reform by amateurs. When the articles were gathered in the book **The Shame of the Cities,** the "dawning theory" fully emerged, strident and positive, as a conclusive condemnation of reform and a defense of efficient bossism. (pp. 430-33)

The public reaction to his thesis was as to hyperbole, though he followed up his series on the cities with one on the states, reiterating his ideas. But Steffens himself emerged, curiously enough, as an authority on methods of government reform. New importance, perhaps as well as new opportunity, made Sam McClure's loosely exercised restrictions more intolerable and an offer to go in with some of his colleagues in founding a new periodical, the *American Magazine,* more appealing. Steffens resigned from *McClure's* to discover that his associates expected only expert reporting from him. "The editing of the *American Magazine* . . . was more cautious and interfering than S. S. McClure's dictatorship. . . . I wanted to do Washington, D.C., and the Federal government. And most of all I wanted to stop muckraking." Steffens gives different reasons in different places why he wished to abandon muckraking: first, it seemed "useless"; and second, he had made the discovery that "I was preferring the conscious crooks, and yet I was one of the righteous." However futile it appeared to muckrake and

however much it bothered him to do so, he continued the practice as a free-lance after quitting the *American* and selling his stock in it. (pp. 433-34)

He was in Europe when the war began in August; he headed for Mexico, he tells us, on "the theory . . . that the inevitable war would bring the inevitable revolution." But his motivation was probably simpler, even, than that. In 1914 Americans were not as yet interested in Europe; they were interested in Mexico where we had landed, and lately withdrawn, marines at Vera Cruz in the course of a revolution which was of great inconvenience to American tourists and business men. It would appear that Steffens made a purely journalistic choice between competing with the Associated Press coverage of European statesmen and the more open conditions of reporting in Mexico. He was not averse to adding to his income; his wife had died and he was playing with the idea of remarrying. In Mexico he managed to ingratiate himself with Carranza, conversed easily with him about his aims, joined his *entourage,* and wrote home sympathetic "inside" stories about him. . . . After the death of his wife, Steffens had first gone, at the invitation of John Reed, to live in Greenwich Village. . . . He went to Mabel Dodge Luhan's with Reed, where he seems to have been more impressed with [radical labor leader Bill] Haywood than with the Bohemian artists, yet thereafter he wore an artist's tie. Was it steeping in this atmosphere that made Steffens a revolutionist? Or was it only his yen for publicity? (pp. 438-39)

Invited to accompany Charles R. Crane and his party to Russia after the February revolution Steffens made his first visit to that country; back by June, he became the first American to develop a brief, tourist's glance into an authoritative lecture on Russia, emphasizing especially his conviction that the Russians would not make a separate peace. His remarks so closely bordered on the treasonable that Steffens expected arrest and was warned by the police at one lecture.

After the Bolshevik revolution in October Steffens publicly espoused the aims of the Russian communists without affiliating himself with any of the groups that were to coalesce into the Communist Party. . . . At the end of April, 1918, . . . police of San Diego halted him while he was lecturing, and other lectures which had been arranged for were cancelled. Steffens had the audacity to write Colonel House that he had been choked off for discussing Woodrow Wilson's peace terms, and in his *Autobiography* he calls his lecturing an "experiment" on behalf of peace, leading to martyrdom. "It has not been forgotten that I spoke for peace when there was war; many communities will not read, hear, or heed me." Yet Steffens was permitted to go to the Peace Conference as a reporter.

The Russians had not been invited to the Paris conference because of the uncertainty of whom to address as in authority in that country, and a proposal to bring representatives of all Russian groups together failed. At the suggestion of President Wilson an "unofficial" commission, headed by William C. Bullitt, was sent to interview Lenin and discuss peace terms. Bullitt was permitted to choose his companions and, among others, selected Lincoln Steffens. In all, Steffens was in Russia only two weeks, but had the satisfaction of an interview with Lenin, whom he found "a liberal by instinct." . . . Steffens had picked up enough material on this mission to be ready for a new series of lectures in the fall of 1920, when he returned to the United States. His trip was under the management of the "Red Star League" and for the first time he found a really sympathetic audience of "intellectuals"—"upper class and labor, university men (professors and students), and Socialists, with blocks of Communist-Bolsheviki.'' As for the lecture, it ''grows clearer, firmer, *redder*, as I repeat it, adding more and more facts and thoughts and recollections. . . .''

Steffens made a third brief trip to Russia in 1923. As on previous trips he saw little of the life of the people (''we went to the theatre, operas, ballets. We met our friends, American, English, German, and Russian. I soon got what I wanted to know. . . .''), but relied on what others told him. He was an interviewer, which he held a cut above a reporter. But this time he postponed returning to America to lecture. Two women held him in Europe, one of whom eventually became his second wife. He began work on two books—*Moses in Red* and his *Autobiography*. The first was frankly propaganda and ineffective; the second was ostensibly something else, but in point of fact, the most effective piece of pro-communist literature issued in the United States since the Bolshevik triumph.

Moses in Red: The Revolt of Israel as a Typical Revolution . . . holds that the books of Moses are ''a revolutionary classic'' and that the revolt and exodus of Israel is ''the history of a revolution.'' The plagues sent on Egypt, in this analogy-finding book, are examples of ''the Divine Sabotage''; they were followed by ''the Red Terror of God.'' Moses, like Carranza, Mussolini, and Lenin, was an absolute dictator during the exodus. ''In revolutions, in wars, and in all such disorganizing, fear-spreading crises in human affairs, nations tend to return to the first, the simplest, and perhaps the best form of government: a dictatorship.'' In the main, an apologetic for the terror in Russia, *Moses in Red* does not follow the orthodox communist line wholly, for Steffens maintains that ''the righteous people [his name for the bourgeoisie] can be saved, . . . they do not have to be killed.'' It is all a matter of apprising them of the historical certainties, so that they will submit. That perhaps is the ill-begotten aim of the book. If the ''righteous'' prize ''liberty'' they should know that ''freedom will be the last achievement of man.'' How lightly the author took his freedom to publish his book!

What *Moses in Red* lacked, *The Autobiography* possessed—the ingeniously insinuating personality of the man. It tells the story of the ''liberal failure'' as the ''confession'' of a great-hearted, simple-minded, ingenuous man, himself the very personification of liberalism. Steffens ''muckraked'' himself: he ''admitted'' professional jealousy so far as other journalists were concerned; he ''admitted'' a demonstrable sappy credence in the avowals of those in power; he ''admitted'' a stupid reliance on the intentions of ''the good, church-going Christians.'' Yet while proving himself a tremendously deceived ''man of good-will,'' he built himself up by enlarging the part he played in the events he was witness to and by telling off a long bead roll of celebrities whom he had known ''intimately'' (for a matter of minutes): Theodore Roosevelt, Woodrow Wilson, Colonel House, Mussolini, Lenin, Trotsky, Judge Gary, President Eliot, and others. In his representation of his exchanges with these, it is Steffens who asks the probing and unanswerable questions or makes the illuminating deduction. . . . How often the curtain rings down on an episode with Steffens in sole possession of the stage! Unless it be *The Education of Henry Adams* no other book of our time chronicles so much disbelief and cynicism, yet unlike *The Education* Steffens' book matches every disbelief with naive hope and every cynicism with childlike faith, until in this mounting and dramatic alternation (note the sequence involves disillusionment with all forms of Western government from local to international) reform is finally rejected for revolution. Climactic, on page 799 of the one-volume edi-

tion, is the retort to Bernard Baruch's question, ''So you've been over into Russia?'': ''I answered very literally, *'I have been over into the future, and it works.'*'' This became the most-repeated single utterance of the decade among left-wingers and fellow-travelers. Floyd Dell, reviewing Steffens' *Letters,* where there is much less sense of progression but more of the cancellation of hope by doubt, asks the question, ''How could anyone trust him?'' and answers by observing, ''But everyone did if they got near enough to hear him talk'' [see excerpt dated 1938]. The success of *The Autobiography* is the sense it imparts of proximity—you are in a close circle, you are alone with Steffens—and hear him talk. *The Autobiography* is conversational, intimate; you think the conversation is between Steffens and someone else, but it is between Steffens and you. During it, you surrender everything you have.

The Autobiography was one of the best-selling books of the depression years. . . . At one time or another some class in government, economics, or English in practically every college in the land used the book as ''required'' reading; an abridged edition found wide adoption in the public schools. Steffens' own explanation of why it ''kept going like a novel'' is that the young people read it. In all truth, *The Autobiography* swept a generation of young people off its feet. . . . There was a spate of books by young writers, like George Soule's *The Coming American Revolution* and John Chamberlain's *Farewell to Reform,* that accepted Steffens' thesis that reforms ''must'' fail and only revolution can succeed. Though they were immediately refuted by the New Deal, many of the bright young men who even assisted in that enterprise had no conviction of the value of what they were doing. They were the *deracinés*—the Hisses and the Remingtons of the New Deal.

Though he preached revolution and converted more young intellectuals to revolution than any other propagandist of his times, Steffens probably never became a member of the Communist Party. He declined to be a candidate of that party for U.S. Senator from California after returning to his native state, and he declined to be a columnist for *New Masses.* He explained that it would be ''no fun'' to have a column in *New Masses.* . . . Indeed, Steffens was more valuable to Communism outside the Party than in it—he made converts wherever he spoke or was read. . . . He generally followed the Party line, he endorsed Party candidates, and he acted as treasurer to undertakings surreptitiously sponsored by the Party but appearing as something else.

Handwritten note from President Theodore Roosevelt authorizing Steffens's investigations of the federal government.

Steffens' untrammeled success was someone's fault. The English clearly discerned him for what he was and forbade him the Empire as early as 1922. Should he have been restricted and his book suppressed in this country? It could not have been done without really bringing him martyrdom and increasing his power and prestige; it could not have been done without jeopardizing the rights of freedom of press and speech. What was needed was an informed and vigorous critical challenge to all that Steffens stood for. Today it is shocking to read the uncritical reviews that hailed *The Autobiography.* . . . [Whereas] *The Autobiography* is categorical and specific about the failures alleged in the American system, the Russian system was embraced without any demonstration of its merits. The *Letters* show that Steffens knew nothing about Russia specifically. Just as his own converts accepted what he stood for at the emotional level, so his own acceptance of "the future" was emotional. . . . Challenged at the end of his life by Sidney Hook to explain rationally his defense of the Soviet dictatorship, Steffens replies imperturbably that he has given up the effort to think things out; he "feels" the communists are right. The soft ground of sentiment on which his propaganda was based could have been exposed very readily when *The Autobiography* was published; by 1938 we should not have had to entertain this sort of eulogistic, but nevertheless accurate, picture of his end [see excerpt by Floyd Dell]:

> At peace, lit with an inward joy, the frail old Sage and Saint of Carmel lay in bed and received young visitors who made pilgrimages to what was already a shrine. He died in 1936, aged seventy, loved and mourned by young people all over the country to whom he had come to stand in some way as a kind of symbolic father and friend.

(pp. 439-44)

Oscar Cargill, "Lincoln Steffens: Pied Piper of the Kremlin," in The Georgia Review, *Vol. V, No. 4, Winter, 1951, pp. 430-44.*

GRANVILLE HICKS (essay date 1952)

[*Hicks was an American critic whose famous study* The Great Tradition: An Interpretation of American Literature since the Civil War *(1933) established him as the foremost advocate of Marxist critical thought in Depression-era America. Throughout the 1930s, he argued for a more socially engaged brand of literature and severely criticized such writers as Henry James, Mark Twain, and Edith Wharton, for he believed they failed to confront the realities of their society and, instead, took refuge in their own work. Hicks was shocked by the effects of the Great Depression and believed that events demanded a new commitment on the part of writers to clearly understand and express their times. In Marxist terms this meant that all American artists should comprehend the growth of capitalism and its negative side effects, such as war, periodic depressions, and the exploitation and alienation of the working class. Thus the question Hicks posed was always the same: to what degree did an artist come to terms with the economic condition of the time and the social consequences of those conditions? What he sought from American literature was an extremely critical examination of the capitalist system itself and what he considered its inherently repressive nature. After 1939, Hicks sharply denounced communist ideology, which he called a "hopelessly narrow way of judging literature," and in his later years adopted a less ideological posture in critical matters. In the following excerpt, Hicks traces the course of Steffens's gradual acceptance of Soviet communism as the alternative to the problems*

of the American "system" about which he had been writing for nearly forty years.]

In the spring of 1931, just as it was becoming apparent to all but a few diehards that prosperity was not around the corner, there appeared *The Autobiography of Lincoln Steffens,* possibly the most influential book of the 1930's. Persons my age or a little older—I was in my thirtieth year when the *Autobiography* was published—found in the book a recapitulation of much that we had seen or at any rate known about, and it strengthened convictions we had already formed or were forming. The book's effect on us, however, considerable as it was, was as nothing compared with its effect on younger persons, those in college or just out of it, who had experienced only the expansiveness and extravagance of the 20's. Where we had felt more or less disillusionment with the war and the peace and the fruitlessness of reformist hopes, Versailles and Woodrow Wilson's New Freedom were for them merely words in the history books. The overwhelming fact of their lives was the depression, which compelled them to ask: "How did we get this way? How did we come to such a pass?" Steffens's answer in the *Autobiography* had the force of revelation.

For nearly forty years he had been a reporter, a muckraker, a student of politics, and as he set forth his experiences in the *Autobiography,* the lesson they taught became obvious: every type of corruption led him straight to big business, to special privilege; what was wrong was "the system." To change the system was the only conceivable cure for our evils.

Actually, Steffens did not in the *Autobiography* preach Communism or any other dogma. To some of us, indeed, his broad-mindedness was annoying. The system must be changed, our ideas and moral standards must be changed, but perhaps, he told us, various kinds of change were possible. Lenin had made one kind of change in Russia, Mussolini had made another in Italy. Perhaps the United States was working out a third way of change in the "new capitalism." We read and we smiled: Steffens himself had made it clear that Mussolini's fascism solved no fundamental problems, and as for the "new capitalism," it had died while the *Autobiography* was on the presses. We knew that Russian Communism was the only practical alternative; and soon after the book was published, Steffens showed that he agreed.

For those of us who were well on our way to Communism when the *Autobiography* appeared, the book had one special importance: it showed that there was a strictly American path to Communist conclusions, and even in our alienation from the American social order, this mattered more than perhaps we were ready to admit. Steffens's life was full of traditional American motifs: he had led a Tom Sawyer boyhood; he had gone abroad to study, like Henry Adams and so many of Adams's New England predecessors; he had been a struggling journalist, and a success. And yet out of all this he came to Communism.

For most people today, when Communism seems so utterly "foreign," Steffens's Americanism presents a problem, indeed the central problem. (pp. 147-48)

In Steffens's lively and charming account of his boyhood and youth, there is not much that we can seize upon as explaining the later course of his life. Somehow, however, as we know from the *Letters,* he became an earnest seeker after wisdom and truth.

He was . . . a young man in quest of the absolute, and his disillusionment was by no means so amusing as he makes it sound in the *Autobiography*. He traveled from university to university, and only gradually gave up his confidence in Hegelian metaphysics to become, as he thought, an empiricist—but it is significant that when he turned from philosophy to science, it was in the hope of finding a "scientific" basis for ethics.

Forced to give up his researches into scientific ethics in order to earn a living, he became a journalist, and a very good one. But ethical problems remained uppermost in his thinking, and he became obsessed as a journalist with the inadequacy of accepted morality to cope with American politics, where lying, bribery, and other immoral acts, as he discovered, were matters of course. It was a discovery that other journalists had made before him, but Steffens refused to take refuge in the easy cynicism of the average newspaper man—which is, of course, no different from the cynicism of most people who are in the know. He wanted to find ways of eliminating political corruption, and he also wanted to understand it. As his understanding grew, he developed one of his characteristic devices, the use of paradox, and in his writings of the 90's we first find those speculations on the goodness of bad men and the badness of good men that are so frequent in the *Autobiography*. The trick was excellent journalism, but for Steffens it was more than a trick: it was a way of holding irreconcilable facts in suspension.

Steffens became a muckraker by accident; or perhaps it would be more accurate to say that the muckraking movement itself was an accident, one for which he was partly responsible. There was nothing novel about the exposing of evils; as one of Steffens's colleagues, Ray Stannard Baker, was fond of pointing out, the muckrakers could find plenty of precedents in both the Old Testament and the New. In the United States after the Civil War, however, the literature of exposure took on a peculiar tone of urgency, because it was concerned not only with the denunciation of evils but also with the exploration of mysteries. (pp. 148-49)

The muckraking movement . . . was made possible by the rise of the cheap magazine in the 1890's. Having had a spectacular success on the New York *Evening Post* and the *Commercial Advertiser,* Steffens was invited in 1901 to become managing editor of one of the most popular of these new magazines, *McClure's*. His first job was an exposure of corruption in St. Louis; in the issue of *McClure's* that carried his second article, **"The Shame of Minneapolis,"** appeared an installment of Ida Tarbell's *History of the Standard Oil Company* and Ray Stannard Baker's "The Right to Work." The muckraking movement had begun, though it was not to find its name until Theodore Roosevelt supplied it, derisively, in 1906.

It was a triumph of popular journalism, spreading from *McClure's* into rival magazines, such as *Cosmopolitan, Everybody's, Collier's,* and, after Steffens and some of his associates on *McClure's* had taken it over, the *American*. Many other magazines took up the idea before the vogue began to decline in 1911 or 1912. Upton Sinclair charged in *The Brass Check* that muckraking was deliberately suppressed, and there is something in this charge, but it must also be said that muckraking simply wore itself out as journalistic fashions will. The early muckrakers documented their exposures with considerable care, but sensationalists moved into the field, and the public got tired. Furthermore, some of the muckrakers themselves, including Steffens, began to question the value of what they were doing.

Steffens eventually was to become convinced that it had accomplished nothing. (p. 149)

In the beginning, however, Steffens had no doubts about the effectiveness of what he was doing. He worked hard to get the facts, he wrote clearly and persuasively, and he believed that his readers would respond to his challenge. In his introduction to the first collection of his articles, *The Shame of the Cities* . . . , he wrote: "The real triumph of the year's work was the complete demonstration it has given, in a thousand little ways, that our shamelessness is superficial, that beneath it lies a pride which, being real, may save us yet. . . . We Americans may have failed. We may be mercenary and selfish. Democracy with us may be impossible and corruption inevitable, but these articles, if they have proved nothing else, have demonstrated beyond doubt that we can stand the truth; that there is pride in the character of American citizenship; and that this pride may be a power in the land." His second book, *The Struggle for Self-Government* . . . , he introduced with an ironic dedication to the Czar of Russia, informing him that he need not fear to grant his subjects representative government, free speech, a free press, education, and the suffrage. "For have I not shown, Sire, that we, the great American people, have all that we want of all these things, and that, nevertheless, our government differs from yours—in essentials—not so much as you thought, not so much as your people think, and not nearly so much as my people think?" This, of course, was principally a way of pricking that American pride to which the earlier introduction had alluded. In *Upbuilders* . . . Steffens employed direct exhortation: "Wherever the people have found a leader who was loyal to them; brave; and not too far ahead, there they have followed him, and there has begun the solution of our common problem; the problem of the cities, states, and nations—the problem of civilized living in human communities."

These three introductions are the closest thing we have to a formal statement of Steffens's political views in his muckraking period. They all express a belief that the majority of the people will exercise their political rights honestly and intelligently if they are given the truth and if they have the proper kind of leadership. Actually, however, his views were undergoing a change during these years. In the *Autobiography* he says that as early as 1904 he had reached these conclusions: "Political corruption is not a matter of men or classes or education or character of any sort; it is a matter of pressure. Wherever the pressure is brought to bear, society and government cave in. The problem, then, is one of dealing with the pressure, of discovering and dealing with the cause or the source of the pressure to buy and corrupt." "But," he continues, "I did not, I could not, write that yet. I still believed, and my readers still believed, that there were some kinds of men that would neither buy nor sell and that the job was to get such men into power."

Obviously Steffens was coming close to socialism, and he was not unaware of that fact. In 1908 he laid some of his ideas before Theodore Roosevelt in a letter, and Roosevelt replied that what he was advocating amounted to socialism, adding, "What is needed is the *fundamental fight for morality*." Steffens answered: "You point ahead to Socialism, and it may well be that we shall have to go that far. If we do, to get things right, then I, for one, should be willing to go there."

That same year Steffens did an article on Eugene Debs, the Socialist candidate for President, and Debs commented: "You have written from and have been inspired by a social brain, a social heart and a social conscience and if you are not a Socialist I do not know one.'' Steffens summed it all up in a letter to his sister: ''As for Socialism, I certainly am socialistic, but I'm not yet a Socialist.''

When he had finished with muckraking, Steffens tried his hand as a practical reformer in Boston, with the idea of combining the resources of the good bad men and the bad good men. One is surprised, not that the idea failed but that its failure surprised Steffens. (pp. 149-50)

Steffens hesitated to declare himself a revolutionary. He was out of favor now. . . . Personally as well he was at loose ends, for his wife had died early in 1911. But instead of becoming an active radical, he was content to sit back and ''watch and report developments.''

In the summer of 1914 Steffens went to Europe with a group of millionaires. It was not an important trip for him, but it provides the occasion for one of the crucial chapters of the *Autobiography*. In the long section on muckraking, Steffens has already demonstrated that reform won't work in America. . . . Now, in reporting on this brief expedition shortened by the onset of war, he can say that all European countries are in the same situation as the United States, only at more advanced stages of decay. (p. 151)

What the reader of the *Autobiography* in 1931 was not likely to notice was that Steffens arrived at this generalization on the basis of very little evidence. When he was muckraking the American cities, he had come to believe that he would find the same forces at work in each, and his investigation seemed to prove him right. I have an idea now that there was less uniformity than he thought there was, but the fact remains that he did a careful study of each place he discussed, and even if his generalizations were extravagant, his factual account of what was going on was largely dependable. In Europe, on the other hand, he did not have to look, for he knew exactly what he would see.

This is important, for it reveals the pattern of Steffens's reporting from this time on. When the war broke out, he tells us, he was interested only in revolution, and so he went to Mexico to see how a revolution worked. He knew exactly what was going to happen, and of course it did: Carranza failed to ''abolish privileges and close up the sources of corruption,'' and so the revolution failed. When he went to Kerensky's Russia in the spring of 1917, he again knew what he was going to see, and he saw it.

And it was just so when he visited Lenin's Russia two years later. Steffens talked with the Communist leaders, especially Lenin, and they said the things he had hoped they would say. (p. 152)

Once more, however, Steffens refused to become an active revolutionary. . . . He spent the 20's in France and Italy, thinking, watching, and enjoying life. His only important publication in those years was *Moses in Red*, a parable of the revolution defending dictatorship and the terror.

But during those years, when his name had almost been forgotten in America, Steffens was first meditating upon and then writing the book that was to make him as famous and as influential in the 30's as he had been in the muckraking decade. The chief purpose of the *Autobiography* was to report his two great discoveries: first, that corruption was inherent in the ''system'' and that reform was therefore impossible; second, that the Russian Revolution showed us our way of salvation.

This second point he stated explicitly, but he confused the issue, for many readers, by saying not only that he had seen the Future in Russia and that it worked but also that he had seen Mussolini and Mussolini worked, and furthermore that he had seen the new capitalism—and *it* worked.

How much he meant by all these qualifications is not easy to determine. Most of the *Autobiography* was written while America was prospering—it was finished in the summer of 1930—and even if he had not had the failure of *Moses in Red* to remind him, Steffens would have known that this was no time to preach Communist revolution. Moreover, his own role, as he portrayed it in the book, was that of the skeptic, the hard-headed searcher for truth, and he could not afford to expose himself as a dogmatist. Besides, he still thought of himself as a man who was open to new ideas.

If one reads carefully, however, one realizes that Steffens was making only minor concessions. What the case of Mussolini proved was that the Bolshevik technique of revolution could be employed by the right as well as the left; but, Steffens was careful to point out, Mussolini had borrowed Lenin's methods without borrowing his aims; his revolution was a challenge to liberalism, but it was doomed to failure.

His attitude toward the new capitalism offers a more difficult problem. His letters show that he was honestly impressed by the achievements of mass production when he returned to the United States in 1927. He saw not only new methods of production but also the progress of scientific research in industry, and a shift of control into the hands of the young managers rather than the old financiers. . . . Steffens makes it clear that what he saw in the new capitalism was a process by which business was taking over government, whereas in a ''real'' revolution government took over business. Government by business might work for a time, but in the long run Steffens expected it to be superseded by ''the'' revolution.

In other words, what he wrote in the *Autobiography* about the new capitalism was a mere pretense of open-mindedness. When he began his muckraking, Steffens believed that it was his mission to give the people the truth. But increasingly, as he so frankly admits, he came to feel that the people could not take the whole truth, and by the time he wrote the *Autobiography* he had fully formed the habit of telling his readers only so much of the truth as he thought it was good for them to know. He was, in effect, anticipating the ''Popular Front'' of the 30's, whose ''leaders'' pretended to beliefs they did not really hold in order to bring the ''masses'' closer to their real goals. And like the men of the ''Popular Front,'' Steffens did not necessarily understand the implications of what he was doing.

In any case, once the *Autobiography* was published, Steffens felt ready to throw off the guise of ironic detachment, and began openly to preach Russian Communism. Nothing shook his faith. When the executions began after the assassination of Kirov, he wrote calmly that Russia had become liberal too fast and that the reinstitution of the Terror was absolutely necessary. And in a letter that he sent to be read at a Communist party rally in San Francisco in 1934, he said: ''Communism can solve our problem. Communism does solve our problem—in Soviet Russia. That's my muckraker's proclamation; that the American Communist Party program meets our American capitalist situation precisely, and it is the only American party that meets it—head on: all of it: the political corruption, the poverty and plenty, the periodic depressions of business—all our troubles; and proposes to solve them at any cost. . . .''

It should not be hard to imagine what such a statement meant to persons like myself, who were not, as is usually supposed, miraculously certain about the Communism to which they had committed themselves but, on the contrary, were constantly carrying on a rearguard action against a swarm of doubts. Steffens's assurance cleared away the doubts like a blast of machine gun fire, for he was our wise man and he had seen the Future with his own eyes. And the younger people, for whom the *Autobiography* was the one true map of the American economic wilderness, regarded his words as marching orders—and they marched, a lot of them, straight into the party. (pp. 152-54)

Steffens . . . meant by the system just one thing: the private ownership of the means of production. It was responsible, he believed, for all our economic, political, and social evils, and these evils could be cured only if the system was changed. To desire to change the system, therefore, was not only compatible with love of country; it was the highest patriotism.

Actually, it was not patriotism that should have inoculated Steffens—and all of us—against Communism in the 30's, but liberalism. And many liberals, to be sure, did remain firm; but many others went over to Communism, and their conversion can only be regarded as a failure of liberalism or what currently passed by that name. The failure may become more comprehensible if we understand what happened to Lincoln Steffens.

If there is one clear pattern in Steffens's thinking, it is his search for *a* solution. Although he soon lost the faith in absolute truth that he held when he began his studies in Germany, he never lost a kind of absolutist impatience. It never seems to have occurred to him that the struggle for good government might be unending. Like the good journalist who finishes one story and goes on to the next, or like the scientist who clears away numerous false hypotheses before he comes to the right solution, Steffens ''eliminated'' one social solution after another—muckraking, municipal reform, Christianity. But there had to be *a* solution.

Of course he was right in rejecting the conventional notion that the evils of politics can be explained simply in terms of bad men, but he was betrayed by his desire to solve the problem once and for all. In the story of Adam and Eve, which he often used in lectures and repeated in the *Autobiography,* he put the blame for original sin not on Adam, not on Eve, not on Satan, but on the apple. The trouble, he insisted, was ''it''—the system. That Adam, Eve, Satan, and the apple might all be guilty, in various ways and perhaps in different degrees, was an idea he never entertained. By blaming the apple alone, he left no ground for moral judgment or even for moral speculation, and the result of that was, not that he got away from the making of moral judgments—he was always making such judgments, just as Marx and Lenin were—but that his bases of judgment were exempted from that process of constant examination and reexamination which alone can keep morality sweet.

By 1908 Steffens was convinced that all political evils could be traced to the system; by 1913 or 1914 he had accepted the Marxist idea of revolution; in 1919 he saw ''the Future.'' His constant use of that phrase is terribly revealing: he believed that the shape of the future was already determined, that he knew what it was going to be, that he could recognize it when he saw it. Liberty, Lenin said, will come in two or three generations, and Steffens believed him. Other men, such as

Bertrand Russell, went to Russia and guessed that the future would be something like what now exists, a constantly worsening tyranny. But Steffens brushed Russell off: ''Russell is the most amazing failure to get it.''

In the writings of some of Steffens's contemporaries—such as Russell, Morris Cohen, John Dewey—one finds a liberalism that is genuinely pluralistic and experimental. (It is well not to forget this; those whose ''reexamination'' of liberalism has led them only to other orthodoxies, other ''solutions,'' are closer to Lincoln Steffens than they think.) However, the ordinary liberalism of the market place and the forum had a simple faith in the powers of reason, and tended to believe that social problems could be ''solved.'' The liberal of the 20's was proud of his willingness to listen to other people's solutions, though as a rule he had solutions of his own; but it was in terms of solutions that he customarily thought, not in terms of a never-ending, many-sided struggle with a multiform and constantly changing reality.

It would be easy to say that much of what was called liberalism in the 20's and earlier did not deserve the name, that it was near-socialism or some other kind of quasi-radicalism, but I doubt that such an excursion into semantics would be profitable. It is better to take liberalism as we find it, recognizing that there are many varieties, and then say that by and large the liberalism that prevailed in the United States from 1900 to 1930 was too uncritical, too inflexible, and too unimaginative to cope with the complex realities of contemporary society. Hence many liberals, when confronted with a major economic and political crisis, had nothing with which to resist the appeal of a system of absolutes such as Communism.

The observation is pointed up by the case of Lincoln Steffens, who was in many ways so much more critical, flexible, and imaginative than most of his contemporaries. The case is the more significant because it is impossible to explain Steffens away in terms of personal interests or psychological compulsions. You cannot even say that he was panicked into Communism, for he was a Communist long before the depression. You have to grant that he came to Communism by using his mind, and that fact, from our present position and with our present perspective, serves to remind us how fallible an instrument the human mind can be.

The case of Lincoln Steffens is worth reviewing today, not as a warning against Communism—nothing could be less necessary than that—but as a warning against a type of mind that did not die in 1936, or 1939, or 1945. The quest for certainty is being carried on today with acute, and understandable, eagerness. Its more obvious forms are on the conservative side: the return to religious dogma, the recrudescence of laissez-faire, hysterical ''Americanism.'' But there are also panaceas with liberal labels, and although most of the rank-and-file liberals, after burning their fingers in Stalin's fire, have learned to be skeptical, it is not so certain that they have learned to be critical in any bold, imaginative way. We are not likely to make Steffens's particular mistake, but who will say that we are safe from his kind of mistake? (pp. 154-55)

> *Granville Hicks, ''Lincoln Steffens: He Covered the Future,'' in* Commentary, *Vol. 13, No. 2, February, 1952, pp. 147-55.*

BARROWS DUNHAM (essay date 1961)

[*Dunham is an American educator and critic. In the following excerpt, he examines Steffens's view of politics, history, and human nature.*]

Lincoln Steffens was, what you wouldn't expect to find, a newsman among moralists, and therefore a moralist among newsmen. This double function, which he quite consciously assumed, gave delicious play to his native perspicacity and tolerance. For, although his sharpness had in it some of the steel of distaste, he pretty much liked everyone he met. In fact, you can estimate your own breadth of tolerance by measuring it against his. If you will make a list of, say, twenty celebrities to whom, or of whom, he wrote approvingly, you will surely find there some people about whom you yourself could not write approvingly at all.

Thus a busy life and a vast acquaintance confirmed in Steffens the habit of liking well-established *bêtes noires*. It was not because he wished to avoid conformity; it was because he repeatedly found that the *bêtes noires*, taken separately and in sequence, would, as one came to know them, disclose virtues and even a certain valor behind the obliquity of their public acts. Grafters, corrupt in taking graft, would be honest in sharing it: for example, Schmittberger, the New York police captain, "a good man doing bad things" [as Steffens characterized Schmittberger in his *Autobiography*]. (p. xi)

Even with the bleak or comic villains of the thirties, like Hitler and Mussolini, Steffens' condemnation fell upon policies rather than persons. And whenever a policy was recognizably attached both to an end and to existing circumstances, he could see that the policy "made sense," even though he might not like the sense that it made. In short, in Steffens' view, the trouble with politics does not arise from some incurable vice in human motives but from certain highly curable defects in the organization of society. These defects are most apparent when a society, like ours, rewards antisocial behavior with wealth, prestige, and power. The trouble, he told an audience on a famous occasion, was not Adam, who had in any case blamed Eve, who had in turn blamed the serpent. The source of evil was quite different: "it was, it is, the apple."

Steffens, that is to say, took the view of history which history takes of itself. On the whole, in history, the villains disappear, and that is their just and proper punishment. They could not live on in their villainies as benefactors do in benefactions; on the contrary, men have had to remove such tracks and vestiges with all possible speed. And so the villains survive as names, proper names made common, to serve for warnings. Such personages being subtracted, there remains in history the shock of multitudes upon other multitudes, the "play of forces," in which public dislocations are more fatal than private faults, and social discord than any mere greed.

As Steffens took history's view of history, so he took Shakespeare's view of man—which is, alas, not usually the view men take of one another. Shakespeare knew how to feel for villains without approving villainy and without any elevation of self-esteem. Steffens could do this too. He was at peace with his own motives, and he had no need to draw satisfaction from the sight of other people's vices. Throughout the history of thought, I believe it will be found that those who take a low view of human nature began with a low view of their own, whereas those who never doubted their own decency look for human salvation in the great remedies of social change. The rest of us, who don't know quite what to make of ourselves, waver between a dread of natural depravity and a dream of utopian bliss.

For us in this last and largest category Steffens is excellent medicine. We need his confidence in man, which was the

projection of his serenity in himself. Throughout his writings there is description of events around him, and commentary upon those events; but, so far as I know, there is not the smallest anxiety about his own motives and feelings, nor indeed much attention to them. His autobiographical manner is as different as can be from Augustine's or Rousseau's. Yet the motives are perfectly clear—the wit, the love, the enchantment with all things human. It is, I suppose, not the only good way to live a life, but it must surely be one of the best ways.

There are, however, perils even here. It is all very well to take history's view of history and Shakespeare's of human nature, but what does one do about organized activity for social reform? (pp. xi-xiii)

[Steffens became] a sort of public moralist, who described the facts and let the facts suggest their own remedies. If, as he discovered, the trail of corruption ran through various visible malefactors and disappeared among the most respected citizens, then it was clear that not much would be gained by punishing the visible malefactors. What was needed was a reconstitution of the whole economy so that respected men would not, by virtue of their social role, have to be the hidden sources of corruption.

Thus Steffens' career as a muckraker led him well to the left of center. His first-hand acquaintance with the Mexican rev-

Everybody's Magazine

VOL. XXIII   SEPTEMBER 1910   NO. 3

IT

An Exposition

of the Sovereign Political Power

of Organized Business

By

LINCOLN STEFFENS

AUTHOR OF "THE STRUGGLE FOR SELF-GOVERNMENT," "THE SHAME OF THE CITIES," "UPBUILDERS."

Editors' Note: This is the first of a series of articles in which Mr. Steffens is to do to business what he did to politics. He reported so that everybody saw it, the business in American government: city, state, national. He proposes now to describe, so that we can all comprehend it, the politics in business; all business, but especially big, corporate business.

As to Mr. Steffens' qualifications for this large task, all we need add here to what is known of him, is that his turn from machine politics to the mechanism of business is a return to his first love. Mr. Steffens began his career as a reporter in Wall Street

The BOSS of All The Bosses

IT is said in Wall Street that one man is supreme down there now. If that is so, it is time to talk business. We have been neglecting business; we have been paying too much attention to politics; all of us have; the American people. And the cost of living is but a part of the price we shall have to pay for our absorption in our public affairs. It is true we have something to show for it; there's a balance to our

credit: We are beginning to understand politics. Even our politicians are beginning to understand politics a little. And their lessons should not be interrupted. But our public business isn't our only business. We all have our private business also to attend to, and if one man dominates that, it means that the boss has developed in business as well as in politics. And if that is so, it is high time to understand business; it is time even for business men to understand business.

For if Mr. J. P. Morgan is the boss of

Steffens's initial article muckraking big business.

olution and the Russian confirmed that place. Accordingly, when the Great Depression arrived, when idle men could not find work in idle factories because both the men and the factories had already produced "too much," when the labor movement moved again and society began to wear the look of youth, Steffens was prepared to follow the Communist Party as he saw it at work in California. (p. xiii)

Steffens was the most American of all the Americans who in those days, in fact or in imagination, went over into the future and perceived that the future would work. For myself, I well remember his distant pull upon the mind. Later in those years I was myself caught up in the general striving towards Paradise—a place it then seemed we could reach with no more severity of struggle than would make us worthy to get there. It was a kind of enlightenment—rational, not mystical—and its first effect was to make me eager to know my own people more warmly and intimately than before. In this mood I read for the first time Steffens' *Autobiography,* and I was at once at home in my country. The book does the same thing for me now, as freshly as ever: so do all his writings. I do believe that a study of the Steffens canon is essential to patriotism.

At first sight, he appears to be producing this effect, very oddly, by cataloguing vices, cheats, deceptions. But these mischiefs turn out to be masks, which, when removed, disclose pathetically "good men doing bad things." So then it is possible after all to love—or at least to like—those who govern us? Well, if that is possible, we can love nearly anybody. We can think of our fellow citizens as striving for the best, even though they get horribly tangled in the process.

But neither this amenity nor Steffens' movement to the Left is what stays with me and sustains me most. What Steffens gives is a hard ground lit by a cool, clear light: the seeing of things as things in fact *are*. This seeing is always hard to come by. It is dimmed by the fear that things are too dreadful to be seen. But when you have got it—and to the extent that you have got it—then for the first time you are truly secure. The seen reality may indeed be dangerous, as in our time a great many realities are. But all the comforts of illusion are as nothing compared to the solace of apprehended fact.

Many men, from many epochs, have taught me this; but Steffens' voice is the one I have oftenest in my ear. He is saying, perhaps, "I don't mean to keep the boys from succeeding in their professions. All I want to do is to make it impossible for them to be crooks and not know it. Intelligence is what I am aiming at, not honesty. We have, we Americans, quite enough honesty now. What we need is integrity, intellectual honesty." These words were in fact addressed to President Eliot of Harvard, who thereupon bowed politely and walked away.

A paradox as thorny as true, with a sting in every truth and thorn. But then this really *is* our condition, is it not? What we need *is* integrity, intellectual honesty, the clear seeing of the real world.

The thing about Steffens is, he shows us how. (pp. xiii-xiv)

> *Barrows Dunham, in an introduction to* The World of Lincoln Steffens *by Lincoln Steffens, edited by Ella Winter and Herbert Shapiro, Hill and Wang, 1962, pp. xi-xiv.*

ELLA WINTER (essay date 1962)

[*In the following excerpt Steffens's second wife explains why, in addition to his journalism, Steffens wrote fables, parables, and essays in the form of imaginary conversations.*]

As long as I knew him, Lincoln Steffens wanted his Fables collected and published in book form. He had been dogged by what he felt to be his inability to find a form to sum up, to express, all he had thought and felt as a result of his newspaper work and his many experiences. He came back to this plaint over and over in letters and in conversation. He knew you could not "tell it straight": either it would not be accepted or it would not be published. . . .

Steffens chose the fable form to try and solve some of the contradictions of "the typical problems that fretted all my life"; in this form he could be teaching, and teaching by implication, allegory, paradox, with humor and irony. He turned to Bible stories for the same reason and had planned both a life of Jesus and a story of Satan. What he actually did write—not as a scholar elucidating texts—was a long fable; the story of Moses as a revolutionary leader and of "Israel as a typical Revolution." Steffens had studied at first hand both the Mexican and Russian revolutions and wanted to tell what he saw in them that could be applied to his own country and its problems.

He took nine years to write *Moses in Red,* and when it was finished it happened that a Philadelphia publisher wrote and asked if he had anything "ready for publication." He had *Moses* and sent it to them, and they published it (in 1926) when we were still living in Europe; but unfortunately a fire burnt their warehouse to the ground, and only four hundred copies of the *Moses* were salvaged, so that virtually—except for libraries—it went unread and one can say is now being published for the first time.

Another form in which Steffens chose to say the unusual and irregular things he had to say was imaginary conversations with or articles addressed to the small son he had at the age of fifty-seven. He had never had a child before, and the experience was so overwhelming that he wanted to concentrate on sharing with him. . . . (p. vii)

And in the Carmel years, from 1927 to 1936, Steffens wrote comments and paragraphs, book reviews and editorials, short or longer articles, for little local papers or for national magazines, that again tried to cover all his thinking about people, societies, politics. In the last two years, spent in bed after a coronary thrombosis, he read a good deal, and in reviews of biographies or autobiographies, usually about some well-known or well-loved friend—Darrow, John Reed, Fremont Older— he used the opportunity to consider the answers to his own quest for truth. Occasionally an introduction to a book or official report served the same purpose. . . .

What fascinated me was that Steffens was not only observer and reporter but always and very deeply teacher and friend. He wanted to know about motives: not only how men behaved but why they did what they did as individuals and members of society. He was intrigued and puzzled by the conflicts between individual and social man. Why, for instance, did bankers and businessmen seem to have "a whole system of morals" which they could "express almost too definitely in the concrete," while they could not get at "the general unconscious principles and unrecognized motives"? And why did he love the "big bad bosses" while disapproving and condemning what they did?

I think it might truly be said that Lincoln Steffens was a humanist who loved—humorously and with considerable understanding—"good" and "bad" men, thieves and artists, crooks and politicians, and all the perplexed and confused people he came to know in a long life. He particularly loved students and young people, to whom he wanted to explain what he thought caused the "evils" he had found, what made men act as they did, and how things might be better. He often explained to the many young people who visited us, particularly in the last years of his life, why he did not think "mere" reforms would reform—why exposure alone would not bring about a better society, and how one possible solution he thought he had found might abolish the causes of the corruption he had seen. (p. viii)

> *Ella Winter, in a preface to* The World of Lincoln
> Steffens *by Lincoln Steffens, edited by Ella Winter*
> *and Herbert Shapiro, Hill and Wang, 1962, pp. vii-ix.*

CHRISTOPHER LASCH (essay date 1965)

[*An American historian and educator, Lasch has united political radicalism and cultural conservatism in his analyses of American society. One of his major concerns is to examine how capitalism and its progressive allies have dismantled traditional institutions and values in service to the creation of a bureaucratic, consumption-oriented society. Lasch's much-discussed* The Culture of Narcissism *(1978) traces the social and psychological effects of the shift from entrepreneurial to bureaucratic capitalism. Although some critics have questioned Lasch's use of Marxist analytical concepts and have criticized his neglect of empirical evidence, many agree that he sheds new light on the crises of American society. In the following excerpt, Lasch discusses Steffens's disillusioning experiences with radicalism and reform movements, tracing his developing desires for a new American culture based on scientific thought and his belief that such a culture would be developed by subsequent generations.*]

The 1920's, it is said, were a time of "disillusionment." Progressivism had failed. The war for democracy had ended in the debacle of Versailles; idealism gave way to "normalcy." Defeated, intellectuals turned away from reform. Following H. L. Mencken, they now ridiculed "the people," whom they had once idolized. Many of them fled to Europe. Others cultivated the personal life, transferring their search for salvation from society to the individual. Still others turned to Communism. In the general confusion, only one thing was certain: the old ideals, the old standards, were dead, and liberal democracy was part of the wreckage.

Such is the standard picture of the twenties; but it is a gross distortion, a caricature, of the period. It has the unfortunate effect, moreover, of isolating the twenties from the rest of American history, of making them seem a mere interval between two periods of reform, and thus of obscuring the continuity between the twenties and the "progressive era" on the one hand and the period of the New Deal on the other. (p. 251)

The picture of the twenties as "disillusioned" derives from such books as Frederick Lewis Allen's *Only Yesterday,* a popular account written in 1931 under the misapprehension that the "twenties" had ended decisively in the year 1929, the year of the great depression. Books like Allen's, which did so much to influence subsequent interpretation of the twenties, derived in turn from the writings of "disillusioned" contemporaries. The image of the twenties as a period of "tired radicalism" finds its justification, it would seem, in the works of the tired radicals themselves and in the larger literature of disenchantment of which they were a part. Fitzgerald's men and women mourned the loss of innocence; Hemingway's could no longer bear to hear such words as "sacred, glorious, and sacrifice and the expression in vain." ... Other liberals agreed ... [that] prewar progressivism had been superficial, timid, and moral-

istic, bent on reforming men rather than conditions. John Chamberlain spoke for a whole generation, it seemed, in making his *Farewell to Reform.* But the most sustained and thoroughgoing indictment of progressivism was to be found in *The Autobiography of Lincoln Steffens,* which traced in great detail, step by step, Steffens's progress—typical, it seemed, of his time—from reform to revolution; and it was this famous book, hailed from the moment of its publication as a minor classic of American letters, which more than any other set the style for writing about the decline of the progressive movement in the aftermath of the "great crusade." When historians attribute the decline of progressivism to its own shortcomings, to its naïve belief in the power of moral exhortation and to its confidence that special interests could be expected to act in the general interest, they are echoing the argument that Steffens advanced so persuasively in 1931, in explanation of his own conversion from liberalism to Communism. (pp. 252-53)

The radicals and bohemians of the twenties claimed to have lost their illusions about the world, but if their own earlier testimony is to be believed, they had never had any illusions to begin with—not, at any rate, the particular illusions they later claimed to have lost. (p. 253)

[One must remember] the extent to which disillusion, for many American intellectuals, had early become an end in itself. One of the dogmas of the new radicalism was that appearances were illusory. Behind the political façade was the "invisible government." Beneath the smiling surface of American life was the "submerged tenth." Beneath the moral man was the inner, uncivilized man. Muckraking, history, social work, psychological theory, all seemed to lead to the same conclusion: that reality was precisely what cultured people, respectable people, sought to keep hidden. Disillusionment, therefore—the loss of the illusion that the world actually worked as the official guardians of the social order, parents, preachers, and teachers, pretended it worked—was the necessary beginning of wisdom.

It also tended to become ... a style or attitude, deliberately adopted, in which a certain type of rebellion expressed itself as a matter of convention. One reason why the twenties seem particularly disillusioned is that the convention had become by that time so general that it was taken up by people whose rebellion went no further than an impatience with parental restraint. But if that was so, it was precisely because older men had already established the pattern, long before the war, the peace, and the excitements of the 1920's. The muckrakers, among others, had already made it clear that a hard-boiled skepticism about the canting morality of the middle class was indispensable equipment for aspiring young rebels; and none of the muckrakers had taken more delight in turning official morality upside down than Lincoln Steffens.... Yet so pervasive was the myth of disillusionment in the twenties that Steffens himself succumbed to it; he spoke of himself, at times, as a man whose illusions had survived intact right down to the end of the war. That he knew better, the *Autobiography* itself makes clear in many places; in spite of which, however, historians persist in reading it as a study of disenchantment and, beyond that, of the way in which a burning sense of injustice drove so many liberals in the postwar years into the regrettable but essentially humanitarian heresy of Communism. (pp. 254-55)

In his *Autobiography* and in a number of letters written while he was working on it, Steffens accused the muckrakers of substituting mere exposure for analysis, and he accused himself of having shared their illusion that the people would elect good men to office once the bad men were exposed. It was only after the experience of the war and two revolutions, the Mexican and the Russian, that he had been able to see, he said, that muckraking had been a "great mistake," that it had only "improved the graft system" and "protracted the age of folly."

Yet *The Shame of the Cities,* published in 1904—the book which won Steffens a reputation as a muckraker—was actually one of the first attacks on muckraking. It contained passages of earnest moralizing, of the kind which Steffens later came to associate with progressivism in general, but it also contained attacks on progressivism which showed that Steffens was already "disillusioned" with reform. . . . Nor was it enough simply to expose evils. Steffens insisted several times in *The Shame of the Cities* that he was exposing nothing that was not already common knowledge. The people knew all about Minneapolis, St. Louis, Pittsburgh, and the rest. The people were "not innocent." That was "the only 'news' in all the journalism of these articles," and even that, Steffens added, was probably news only to himself. He had set out initially, he said, to show how the people were "deceived and betrayed" but had found instead that they willingly tolerated the corruption that openly flourished all about them. Already Steffens was using to good effect the autobiographical device around which, twenty-five years later, he built the account of his "life of unlearning." Already he was exaggerating his innocence for literary effect.

But not only for literary effect; he wanted to show also that he had arrived at his mature ideas by a process of scientific experimentation. The pose of disillusionment was essential to the pose of detachment. If it could be shown that he had clung to his preconceived assumptions about the world until the facts of the matter left him no choice but to give them up, he could not be accused of having bent the facts to suit his wishes. Like all the new radicals, Steffens was fascinated by science, but the degree of his fascination was unusual, as was the thoroughness with which he tried to reduce historical phenomena to natural laws. He seems . . . to have had a horror of the subjective and the delusional, for he went to great lengths, returning to the subject again and again, to prove that his own wishes ran counter to his political and social discoveries. (pp. 256-58)

Steffens's early career, if one disregards the pattern he himself wished to impose on it, reveals the elements one finds in the careers of so many intellectuals of his time—not only the cult of science but the whole pattern of rebellion associated with the rise of the new radicalism. His letters, together with what information one can reliably gather from the early portions of the *Autobiography,* tell a familiar story: the restlessness and uncertainty born of having actively to choose a career, instead of accepting it as given; the mounting disgust with cultural "advantages" one nevertheless continued dutifully to pursue; the sense of unworthiness; the longing for experience. Steffens inherited opportunities that his parents had not enjoyed. His father had worked by day and sent himself through commercial college by night; migrated from Illinois to California, traveling by horseback through a West that was still wild; and beginning as a bookkeeper in Sacramento, had risen to affluence as a merchant. In this way he accumulated the fortune that sent his son to Berkeley and then to the universities of Europe, where he dabbled in philosophy and aesthetics, traveled, acquired a taste for expensive clothes, and met a well-to-do young woman named Josephine Bontecou whom he secretly married. Here was the painful contrast, felt by so many of Steffens's con-

temporaries, between the pioneer generation and their over-educated children, the latter blessed with advantages which only delayed their entrance into "life." (pp. 259-60)

[Steffens] had pursued culture with the same dutiful and over-earnest zeal which drove Jane Addams, in these same years, from one cathedral to another; only to find that there was nothing in it which held his interest. "Classical music is a bore," he wrote to his sister; eventually he came to enjoy it, but only after a struggle. He approached art, moreover, with an inhibiting uncertainty about the reliability of his own opinions, afraid, as always, of giving himself away as a "sucker." (Without Ruskin, he wrote home, "I don't know what I should do, for I was without any sound taste and must have been led by popular verdict or, worse still, by my natural and unsound taste." It is hardly any wonder that he came home at last, vaguely intending to go into business or teach, with a heavy sense of failure. . . . (p. 261)

Stranded in New York with a wife and no money except what he could bring himself to take from her mother, Steffens found a job on the New York *Evening Post* and plunged into the teeming life of the city with the same exhilaration with which Jane Addams had discovered the west side of Chicago. He reveled in "this American living," "the complex, crude, significant but mixed facts of hard, practical life." Eagerly he sought "the striving, struggling, battling, of the practical world, which far outranks the philosophic heaven." (pp. 261-62)

The way in which these early experiences influenced his emerging social philosophy is clear. Reality was action, the turmoil and strife of "life as it is lived." There were "strong" men who accepted the hard facts of life as they found them and "weak" men who idealized existence by theorizing about it. The strong men were "insiders," the weak men "suckers." News was inside dope: "what reporters know and don't report." Politics likewise lay mostly hidden behind a polite façade; the real government was an "invisible government." History was not what was taught in books but what strong men were doing behind the scenes. Reality, in short, was in every instance precisely the opposite of what people were taught to believe. "Good people" were really bad people, because their illusions did more harm than the intelligent crimes of the "big bad men."

Steffens claimed that it took him years to learn these things and that he learned them only as a result of his investigations first into the corruption of American cities and then into the Mexican and Russian revolutions. In fact, it seems to have been the other way around: his preconceptions about the nature of politics and society antedated the investigations and to a large extent predetermined their outcome. Thus he made it his practice, in any inquiry, to go directly to the "big men" who ran things.

> Calling with my card at the editorial office, I would ask the office boy: "Say, kid, who is 'it' here?"
>
> "Why," he would answer, "Mr. So-and-so is the editor."
>
> "No, no," I protested, "I don't mean the front, I mean—really."
>
> "Oh, you mean the owner. That's Mr. Blank."
>
> Feigning disgust and disappointment, I would say, "The owner, he's only the rear as the

editor is the front. What I mean is, who's running the shebang? Who knows what's what and—who decides?''

(pp. 262-63)

Given these techniques as a reporter, given also his instinctive admiration for the big men behind the scenes, it is not surprising that Steffens came to the conclusion that it was not the bosses who were to blame for corruption but the people themselves, who put the bosses in power and kept them there because they were too lazy to govern themselves. Steffens's contempt for democratic processes, although not formally admitted into his political thought until later, was firmly rooted in experiences that antedated his activities as a muckraker. ''The bosses especially attract me,'' he wrote to his father at the outset of his first trip for *McClure's*. Even earlier, according to the *Autobiography*, he had discovered that he liked the crooks better than the reformers. '''He's a crook,' I would tell a reporter, 'but he's a great crook,' and I think now that I meant he was a New York crook and therefore a character for us and all other New Yorkers to know intimately and be proud of.'' Steffens was neither the first nor the last young man from the provinces to celebrate crooks as ''characters,'' in deliberate defiance of the conventional view of things. The gesture was bound up with his plunge, after years of formal schooling, into the turmoil of urban life. ''I take it all,'' he wrote self-consciously to a college friend, ''and let the brutal facts resolve themselves into as much truth as my mental digestion is able to find.'' The more brutal the facts and the more unpalatable, from the point of view of conventional morality, the truths to which they led, the greater the young rebel's delight in discovering them.

Steffens was prepared in advance, in short, to find what he found as a muckraker and published in *The Shame of the Cities* and *The Struggle for Self-Government:* that American politics were ruled by strong ''bad'' men who remained ''invisible'' only because ''good'' people, too weak to govern themselves, preferred not to recognize their existence. That Steffens found what he was looking for does not mean that what he found was untrue. On the contrary, his explanation of political corruption, so far as it went, conformed more closely to the facts than the popular theories which his articles helped to explode— in particular, the theory that corruption flourished only where large numbers of immigrants sustained the political machine in power. (Philadelphia, Steffens pointed out, had few immigrants but was the worst-governed city in the country.) It is not the accuracy of his account of political corruption that is at issue but the accuracy of his account of his own career. According to Steffens, his career proceeded from one disillusionment to another, experience compelling him constantly to revise his ideas about it. According to contemporary evidence, most of the assumptions at which he claimed to have arrived only after a life of ''unlearning'' were present almost from the beginning—byproducts, it would seem, of his early discovery that the world of intellect and ''culture'' paled into nothingness when compared with the world of action.

In his very first report for *McClure's*, the famous exposé of the ''shamelessness of St. Louis,'' Steffens had discovered that ''corruption was not merely political,'' as many reformers had assumed, but ''financial, commercial, social'' as well. It was not enough, therefore, for reformers to turn out the politicians and put a ''businessman's administration'' in their place. The businessmen themselves were corrupt. (pp. 263-65)

In *The Shame of the Cities* the implications of these findings were only partially explored, but *The Struggle for Self-Government,* which appeared only two years later, left no doubt about their broader meaning. By 1906 Steffens had already come to realize that political corruption was a *system:* ''a regularly established custom of the country, by which our political leaders are hired, by bribery, by the license to loot, and by quiet moral support, to conduct the government of city, State and Nation, not for the common good, but for the special interests of private business.'' In short, ''the highway of corruption is the road to success.'' Or, as Steffens wrote to his sister a few years later: ''Society is made up of legitimate grafters.'' But when he began to write about national politics in these terms, Steffens found that editors were no longer interested in him. They complained ''that I showed up no graft, wrote nothing sensational. That was their criterion: dishonesty, stealing, graft. If an honest senator honestly served a trust that was no disservice to the people; that was not wrong.'' Everywhere he encountered this ''failure of imagination,'' this inability to see that graft was not so much a crime as a social ''process'' whereby democracy was transformed into plutocracy, thereby eliminating the need for graft.

Steffens came to the conclusion, therefore, that what was needed, if American society was to be made over, was not a moral awakening but a better appreciation of the nature of American society—not morality but ''intelligence.'' What was needed, as he loved to put it, was ''honest crooks''; for an intelligent crook was an ''unhappy crook.'' This paradox, so maddening to orthodox progressives, was another way of saying that society was made up of legitimate grafters. It was another way of saying that capitalist society was made up of perfectly respectable people engaged in giving and seeking special favors, not illegally but under the approved rules of the system, without the least suspicion that they were doing anything reprehensible. Not the grafters but the system itself was corrupt, in short; but until people realized that the system was corrupt, they would have neither the inclination nor the ability to change it. Hence Steffens's plea for intelligence and his impatience with the reforms which by focusing attention on the crimes of the ''big bad men'' merely reinforced the self-righteousness of the ordinary citizen.

Once the problem was stated in this way, Steffens's temperamental preference for bad men over good men could be stated more precisely than before. . . . The bad men were admirable above all because they knew what they were doing. The good people, on the other hand, did the same things, or at least condoned them, under the impression that they were doing good. Thus Steffens's indictment of capitalism was also an indictment of the hypocrisy of middle-class morality, and he turned to the bad men for the same reason other intellectuals turned to the working class, because they were outcasts from respectable society. The more he became convinced that there was no virtue in the virtuous, the more Steffens tended to identify himself with the crooks. (pp. 265-67)

[The] radical impulse was [closely] allied with the effort of introspection. It was for that reason that the new radicals wrote most freely and convincingly in the autobiographical vein: what they had to say about American society was inseparable from the record of their own re-education or ''disillusionment.'' The problem of society was a problem preeminently of consciousness or, in Steffens's phrase, intelligence—a problem, at bottom, not of politics or economics but of psychology and culture. Stated in psychological terms, the problem, as Steffens had come to see it, was that good people could not admit to themselves that they were doing bad things. The very violence with which they reacted to Steffens's ideas showed at once how great was their need to deceive themselves and how disastrous were the psychological consequences of the deception. When Steffens tried to convince Theodore Roosevelt that the patronage system was a form of "legitimate" bribery and that Roosevelt, under the rules of the system, "had to" give bribes, Roosevelt "was appalled, almost speechless; his balled fists and wrenching arms wanted to express him." Roosevelt's fury was the rage of the righteous man, and it could only confirm Steffens in his thesis that American society suffered from an excess of "unconscious guilt."

If the problem was psychological, it was also cultural, since the source of guilt, Steffens thought, was the disparity between middle-class ideals and the political and economic demands of an industrial society. The reason good people could not admit to themselves that they were doing bad things was that their political ideas did not know the distinction between the goodness of the actor or agent and the evil of the system which *compelled* him to do wrong. Having "tried out on a few individuals the healing effect of the sight of themselves as honest men doing dishonest things, as law-abiding citizens breaking the law," Steffens was convinced of the efficacy of this kind of therapy; but he was also convinced that a thoroughgoing social reformation would have to wait upon the overthrow of the whole system of ideas which enabled an entire people systematically to delude themselves about their way of life.... Later he formulated the matter more broadly: if society was ever to be reformed, the old culture, the culture of the middle class, would have to give way completely. The "intellectual culture" would have to give way to the "scientific culture," as he came to call it. The "historical, experimental method of 'seeing'" would have to take the place of the "logical" method. Intelligence, in short, would have to replace virtue as the acknowledged aim of social life. (pp. 271-72)

[Although] Steffens several times changed his mind about the means of bringing about the social transformation he hoped to see, he never changed his mind about the nature of the transformation itself. When he welcomed the Russian revolution, it was because he saw the revolution as the "experimental" method in action. When he acclaimed the "new capitalism" of the 1920's, it was for the same reason: the managers, he thought—practical men interested not in profits but in the most efficient method of organizing production—had expropriated the capitalists, and "either way," the Russian or the American, "the race is saved." (p. 273)

The depression eventually killed Steffens's enthusiasm for the new capitalism, but not for technocracy, which still seemed to him a harbinger of the new approach to social problems. Meanwhile he continued to argue for the Russian revolution, long after most of his friends had deserted it, because he assumed that Communists and technocrats (in spite of their noisy disagreements) were working for the same thing. "Doing the job," he thought, "is the Communist virtue." Beyond that, there was the prospect that mass employment, in America as in Russia, would bring mass leisure and thereby "free taste and beauty." Just as he himself had begun life "looking for the good and found nothing but the beautiful," so the new society, having got rid of the impulse to judge, would liberate the impulse to enjoy. The "scientific culture" presented itself to Steffens not as a drab and regimented anti-utopia but as a realm of unexpected beauty. (pp. 273-74)

At the same time, Steffens had to concede that the new society was "hard, dull, level, moral," as he put it after coming out of Soviet Russia in 1919. Revolutionaries were "righteous." "I admire them tremendously, but I don't like to be with them." He had seen the future and it "worked"; but he preferred to live in the present. "We are not going to like the Rule of Labor," he predicted. After the "hard morality of Moscow," Paris, even the Paris of the peace conference, struck him like a fresh breeze of spring. (p. 274)

From [1924] until his death in 1936, Steffens grew progressively more enthusiastic about the Soviet Union—partly, it may be, as a result of his new wife's influence—at a time when other liberals and socialists were coming back from Russia with reports of misery and repression on a vast scale. He accepted the reports as true; he had no wish to minimize the cost of revolution; but he insisted that the cost had to be paid and that the reign of terror and violence was a phase through which all revolutions necessarily passed. It was pointless to deplore it; the terror was historically inevitable. The trouble with liberal critics of the revolution was that they expected the revolution to conform to their own wishes, their own preconceived theories of "right and wrong." (p. 276)

Toward the end of his life, however, he became increasingly uncritical of the Soviet Union.... In February, 1936, he wrote to his friend Sam Darcy, district organizer of the Communist Party in California, that he and his family intended to apply for a passport to Russia—which shows that he contemplated at least another visit—but his health gave way and he was unable to leave his bed. Letters from Russia urged him to come, but his condition was such that he could not proceed. A few weeks later he died.

The proposed trip to the Soviet Union, together with Steffens's general leftward swing, have to be considered ... against the general crisis of Western life in the mid-thirties. The depression seemed to have paralyzed the democracies of Western Europe and North America, thereby bearing out the contention, long maintained by people such as Steffens, that liberal democracy could not survive the rigors of the twentieth century. Only the Fascists and the Communists seemed to be getting things done. The United States itself, under Franklin Roosevelt, seemed to be moving, if not toward outright Fascism, toward a modified state capitalism. That did not necessarily mean that one had a moral obligation to choose between Communism and an American variety of statism. One could have rejected all such alternatives. But given the feeling that one had to choose, Steffens's choice of Communism in the thirties was no more reprehensible or misguided than the anti-Communist liberals' choice of the "free world" in the forties and fifties.

If anything, Steffens's choice—or more accurately, the manner in which he made it—was morally more attractive than the choice made by the anti-Communist liberals in the aftermath of the Second World War. They announced their decision with loud protestations of self-righteousness, coupled with strident attacks on younger liberals who did not share their all-encompassing hatred of the Soviet Union; Steffens based his turn to the Left on a strong sense of his own fallibility. In the generational struggle that developed within the liberal community as a result of the cold war, the older generation insisted again and again, in a manner that struck younger liberals as completely arbitrary, on its own superior wisdom and experience; in its eyes, those who could not bring themselves to see the cold war as a clear-cut struggle between Truth and Error were simply repeating the mistakes of the thirties (in spite of the fact that the international situation had appreciably altered in the meantime). Steffens, on the other hand, believed that the younger generation could see things that eluded his own. This confidence in youth became the dominant note of his later writings. However sentimental, however misplaced his confidence, it accounted for much of the serenity and charm of the last phase of his life. It rescued Steffens from the bitterness that afflicted so many of the disappointed liberals of his time. Above all, it saved him from intolerance and dogmatism, to which so many of them eventually succumbed. Even in the act of embracing a dogmatic and intolerant ideology—if he can be said to have "embraced" it—he himself came more and more to embody the liberal virtues of tolerance and intellectual modesty which some of the later defenders of liberalism so conspicuously lacked.

Having discovered that he himself had no desire to live in the Soviet Union—and as late as 1930 he was repeating his wish not to go back—Steffens did not reconsider the revolution, he reconsidered himself. He wrote first *Moses in Red* . . . and then the *Autobiography* . . . , to show that "all that was or is or ever will be wrong with [the world] is my—our thinking about it." The Book of Moses, he thought, furnished a parallel not merely with the Russian revolution but with his own inability wholly to accept it. Moses, having led his people out of Egypt, was struck down by God as he was about to enter the Promised

Editorial cartoon of Steffens that appeared in the New York Tribune *after the McNamara trial.* © I.H.T. Corporation. *Reprinted by permission.*

Land. Why? Because Moses was not fit to live in the new society. . . . The future, then as now, belonged to the young; the older generation had lived too long in Egypt to adapt themselves to the austere virtue of the Promised Land. (pp. 278-81)

The *Autobiography,* following close after *Moses in Red,* was among other things a celebration of youth. Its composition coincided with the birth and infancy of Steffens's son Pete, whom Steffens doted on and avidly studied. His observations convinced him that children, uncorrupted by the wisdom of the grown-up world, were the true revolutionaries and the true scientists. "Why do grown-ups grow up?" asks "Pete" in one of the letters Steffens wrote, in his son's voice, to his mother-in-law. "And why, with all my clear perception of their bunk, why do I aspire to grow up?" The same question echoes through the *Autobiography,* in which learning is seen as a process of getting back to the intuitive understanding of childhood. Children knew, or quickly learned, that "nothing was what it was supposed to be." . . .

Watching his son, together with his own "experience in unlearning" (capped by the six years' labor on the *Autobiography*), left Steffens with "a deep faith in the (intellectual) courtesy and a high hope in the inborn capability of our successors—youth." It is not surprising therefore to find him identifying himself, in 1934, with the young Communists "out in the field." (p. 282)

It cannot be too strongly insisted upon . . . that Steffens grasped something which eluded the liberal anti-Communists: that the real mission of the Russian revolution, and of the Mexican revolution too, was the modernization of backward countries. He saw that the underlying issue of the First World War was the question of which of the European countries was to "bring the backward countries into our system." He saw too that the Bolsheviks "had respect for our efficiency" and "envied and planned to imitate our mass production . . . our big business production, our chain stores and other beginnings of mass distribution." He saw, in short, what others have discovered only in the 1950's or have yet to discover at all, that Communism represented a stage in the struggle of backward countries for economic development and national self-sufficiency. He saw these things with particular clarity in the case of Mexico; and if his observations on Mexico remain today the most vivid and convincing of his writings, it is because the Mexican rather than the Russian revolution has proved (contrary to early expectations, contrary to the expectations of Steffens himself) to be the prototype of the twentieth-century revolution. But he also saw these things, though less clearly, in the case of Soviet Russia, at a time when other liberals could see in the revolution no more than a struggle for democracy betrayed.

Unfortunately, Steffens was not content to rest the case for the revolution on economic grounds alone; he was not content to argue that the revolution, insofar as it provided a means of modernization and national independence, was both necessary and desirable. He insisted that it was also *inevitable,* ordained by the inscrutable laws of history. He insisted, moreover, that it would lead not only to a new form of economic organization but to a new and better culture. Communism, for Steffens, represented above all a great advance of the human spirit. In seeing it so, he was influenced in part by Ella Winter; but the idea of the "scientific culture" was his own, and he had been talking about it long before her visit to Russia confirmed what he had already decided in his own mind. He had long ago decided that the trouble with American society was not so much political or economic as cultural—the gap between middle-class ethics and the realities of industrialism. It followed that nothing short of a cultural revolution—a new way of thinking—would save what was worth saving of civilization. It was inevitable, if anything in history can ever be said to be inevitable, that Steffens should have identified the revolution in Russia with his own private ambition, conceived while he was still a student in Europe, at a time when only a handful of dedicated zealots dreamed of a Communist revolution, to find and formulate a scientific basis for ethics. (pp. 284-85)

> Christopher Lasch, *"The Education of Lincoln Steffens," in his* The New Radicalism in America, 1889-1963: The Intellectual as a Social Type, *Alfred A. Knopf, 1965, pp. 251-85.*

PATRICK F. PALERMO (essay date 1978)

[*Palermo is an American educator and critic who has written extensively on politics and history. In the following excerpt from his survey of Steffens's life and career, Palermo discusses the revolutionary fable* Moses in Red *and the* Autobiography.]

In 1917, Steffens witnessed two events that irrevocably changed both his life and the course of modern history. During the first months of that year, the Russian autocracy tottered and then fell under the weight of carrying on a costly, deadly modern war with a primitive economy and an equally backward governmental bureaucracy. One month later, President Woodrow Wilson led the United States into World War I for the announced purpose of ending the necessity of war by making "the world safe for democracy." For the next two years, Lincoln Steffens tried to join these two "young" people together in the pursuit of a better world. First with hope and then with desperation, Steffens attempted to make himself and his writing a positive link between the United States and Russia, liberalism and revolution, and between Wilson and Lenin. As long as his expectations for cooperation or reconciliation remained high, Steffens found no contradictions between the methods and goals of the Russian Revolution and the principles of American liberalism. It was the failure of Wilson at the Paris Peace Conference and Steffens' second visit to Russia that left Steffens a "broken liberal" and an avid apologist for the Bolshevik-led revolution.

American liberals greeted the first news of the Russian Revolution with enthusiasm, and Steffens was, of course, no exception. What distinguished Steffens from other liberals was his opportunity to observe the revolution first hand. In March 1917, Charles Crane, Chicago millionaire and Russian expert, was asked by the Wilson administration to examine the new liberal-revolutionary regime in Russia. By a stroke of good fortune, Steffens ran across his old friend Crane in Washington, and the millionaire asked Steffens to join his small delegation. Without hesitation, Steffens seized this once in a lifetime opportunity to see a revolution in its formative stage. Steffens spent the next six weeks in Russia observing the people, their leaders, and the revolution. Not surprisingly, Steffens returned to the United States with a glowing description of the character and promise of the Russian Revolution. (pp. 100-01)

During this period, Steffens was sure that both liberal America and revolutionary Russia wanted to end the pernicious war with a just peace. For Steffens, World War I was nothing more than a destructive, monstrous act perpetrated by selfish governments. . . . (p. 101)

In many respects, Steffens found the Russian Revolution to be an extension of the American dream. In **"Midnight In Russia,"** published in *McClure's* in May 1918, Steffens used a Jewish-American officer in the Red Army to teach his American audience "'to know and to love Russia.'" In Steffens' account, this young officer visits Steffens one cold, snowy night in Moscow to tell him why he had become a revolutionary. The son of a Russian Jew, the soldier had fled czarist Russia as a boy with his father to "'our vision of the land of promise: America.'" Instead of finding a utopia, the father and child "'were misled, misdirected—robbed, till we had nothing. Nothing. It was an awakening—from the dream.'" At the outbreak of World War I, the young man had returned to Russia to defend his motherland and had stayed to join the revolution. As he told Steffens, he was now a revolutionary, confidently struggling to realize "'that vision of the United States'" in Russia.

This story must have both reassured and disturbed its readers. On the one hand, Steffens was placing the Russian Revolution squarely within the scope of the American political tradition. The revolution was following the path of the American experiment. According to Steffens, the Russian revolutionaries were only sharing the dream of "'our fathers, the Puritan fathers who found and founded the American colonies.'" As Steffens explained it to the Jewish-American soldier and his American audience, the American vision had become the "'dream of all mankind.'" Put this way, the Russian Revolution was certainly no threat to the United States. Still, this story contained a very definite tension. The Jewish-American soldier had been unable to realize the American dream in the United States. To find his "'dream,'" he had been forced to return to Russia. This could not have been very comforting to American readers, who remained convinced that the United States was the center of democracy and progress. Yet Steffens' interest was only to take a gentle swipe at America's self-image. In the end, Steffens portrayed the revolution as little more than progressive liberalism in Russian clothing. (p. 102)

For Steffens, it was the willingness of the Russian people to use radical methods to gain their goals that marked the difference between the Russian Revolution and American progressivism. (p. 106)

Despite his protestations to the contrary, Steffens was not, during this period, interested in the Russian Revolution as a historic prototype. Although he insisted that he was observing the revolution with the detachment of a social scientist, Steffens was actually basing his description and analysis on long-held liberal assumptions. Neither his belief in the goodness and innocence of human nature nor his faith in the social solidarity of the pastoral, semiprimitive community took into account the fact of social change. These liberal ideals were static—timeless in their validity and their application to social reality. In traditional American liberal ideology, these concepts of human nature and community often served as part of the fixed foundation for American democracy. Like so many other liberals, Steffens used such ideals to judge the nature and character of social change. At this point, Steffens was not concerned with processes of history. For liberals, including Steffens, the inevitability of progress took care of that question.

By the end of World War I, the faith in progress was the last, strong underpinning of the whole liberal-progressive ideology. With other reformers, Steffens did not recognize that the liberal concept of progress had a basic flaw. Although he was not aware of it, Steffens was always confusing history with progress. Essentially, Steffens believed in progress—that being the continual advancement of mankind toward the realization of fixed and unchanging social ideals. For Steffens, history was the description of past progress and not the maker of the future. As a consequence, Steffens' entire early analysis of the Russian Revolution had nothing to do with the course of Russian history. When Steffens claimed that the triumph of the revolution was the victory of "human nature in the raw," he was denying that history shaped the character of the revolution. When he placed the origins of the social-political ideals of the revolution within a primitive communalism, he was making the future the product of a mythical past. In his ahistorical analysis, Steffens was dismissing the Industrial Revolution, urbanization, and the rise of the modern state as causal factors in the revolution. As a liberal, Steffens was confusing static ideals with dynamic social change, progress with history. (pp. 107-08)

[Steffens] confined himself to the task of explaining and supporting the revolution. Shortly after his second visit to Russia, he conceived the idea of writing a parable to explain the inexorable pattern of revolutions. Long fascinated with the figure of Moses, Steffens chose the exodus of the Jews from Egypt to serve as his story line. It took him approximately six years to turn this idea into a polished manuscript. In good part, this long delay was caused by his lingering doubts about the Russian experiment. It was only after Steffens made his third and final visit to the Soviet Union in 1923 that he was able to dispel these reservations. Finally published in 1926, *Moses In Red* is Steffens' most complete defense of the Russian revolution.

Steffens insisted that *Moses In Red* was not just about the Bolshevik revolution. His parable about the flight of the children of Israel under the leadership of Moses was, as far as Steffens was concerned, the story of all revolutions. He believed that revolutions were inevitable consequences of human interference in social evolution. In his introduction to the book, he defined revolution as a "natural phenomenon, as natural and as understandable as a flood, a fire, or a war . . . an epidemic of disease, or a pimple on the nose. It has its causes and its natural history." This made it possible for Steffens, the self-proclaimed scientific observer, to discover and analyze the natural laws that governed each and every revolution. He even held out some hope that this knowledge might make revolutions "preventable" by eliminating the impediments to "evolution" that caused them. This proved to be no easy out for those trying to avoid the consequences of a revolution. Steffens simply meant that the alternative to revolution was full and immediate support of the goals of the revolution.

This was clear from his carefully calculated choice of a story from the Old Testament. In the first chapter of *Moses In Red,* "The Point of View," Steffens established how the Bible offered him a unique social perspective. He had first discovered this during his investigations of American corruption and reform. Quite by accident, Steffens had found a striking similarity between the life of Jesus as it was told in the New Testament and the careers of such reformers as Judge Ben Lindsey and Tom Johnson. Like Jesus, these progressive leaders offered reform based on "love and understanding," but were rejected by the "righteous" citizens of society. This led Steffens to reject reform and the New Testament and to embrace the need for revolution and the lessons of the Old Testament. Obviously, Steffens was using the Bible to show how he had changed his own social perspective—his point of view. As a reformer, he had asked all citizens, including the righteous, to accept the gentle, loving Christ. As a student of revolution,

he was making these same righteous people face the implacable Jehovah of history.

Surely, Steffens realized that there was little difference between the point of view of the righteous and that of the revolutionary. Both judged men and events with their own kind of uncompromising certitude. For Steffens, the historical determinist, there was no appeal against the necessity of the natural laws that shaped human conduct. Using this as the basis for his criticisms, Steffens turned *Moses In Red* into a harsh, almost unrelenting attack on liberalism. He began by dismissing the liberal's faith in democratic government. In its place, he offered the "general law" that the dictatorship was the *"first, the simplest and perhaps the best form of government."* From his supposedly dispassionate observations, Steffens had learned that dictators were the only ones who could bring order and direction to societies caught in crisis. Accordingly, he reasoned that the belief that men valued liberty first and foremost was only the product of *"man-made laws and soul-felt idealism."* In fact, history showed that the "natural law" contradicted the ideals of democracy. Men sought security and then, having secured it, granted freedom.

For all the boldness of his attack on liberal values, Steffens could not bring himself to denounce overtly his own long-held liberal faith in the wisdom of the people. He left the repudiation of this belief in the virtuous, collective citizenry to the parable itself. This indirect approach was markedly different from the usual format Steffens used to reject liberal values in *Moses In Red*. In other cases, he refuted a liberal principle with the general laws of nature and then made the parable support his point. With the ideal of the people, he forced the symbolism of the Old Testament story to carry the whole burden of his criticism. In Steffens' scheme, the exodus from Egypt represents the "typical revolution," and the children of Israel personify "the people—any people." The Jews do not resemble, in any manner or form, the "wise . . . mass of man" of *Upbuilders* or even the "gentle beast" of his early essays about the Russian Revolution.

In the parable, the people are not the strength of the revolution, but rather the "chief difficulty" blocking its success. The children of Israel, the people, are incapable of seizing their freedom, but have it pushed upon them by the pharaoh. As the symbol of the old order, the pharaoh is the "indispensible force" that makes the timid Israelites give up their bonds. This was not a new argument on the part of Steffens. He had long contended that a reactionary government inevitably caused its own overthrow with its repressive measures. Steffens used this story to make a significantly different point. He was not only maintaining that the Egyptian ruler caused the people to revolt, a truism in Marxist doctrine, but that he was responsible for their success. In Steffens' revolutionary parable, the children of Israel never lose their "disposition to return to . . . their chains." At no point do the people develop a class consciousness. Instead, it is only the retributive efforts of the pharaoh that prevent the people from embracing their old bondage. Even after they are free of the old regime, the Israelites are not ready for the promised land—Steffens' symbol for a revolutionary society. Again and again, the people falter, and Moses, the revolutionary dictator, is forced to implement the bloodiest kind of terror to keep them on the correct path toward the promised land. By the end of the story, it is obvious that even this is fruitless and that the future is reserved for the "unspoiled, the untaught, the unformed" next generation.

The overall tone of *Moses In Red* is one of dark pessimism. The book is strewn with the wreckage of liberal principles and ideals, with little mention or praise of positive aspects of the revolution. In fact, Steffens wrote *Moses In Red* more as a disillusioned liberal than as a devoted revolutionary. This was in keeping with Steffens' own accurate image of himself as a "broken liberal" who wholeheartedly supported the Russian Revolution. He never claimed to be a Marxist ideologue. Consequently, his defense of the Bolshevik Revolution had a negative quality. In *Moses In Red,* Steffens did not entreat his readers to support or join the Communists. Readily admitting the "tragedy" and "horror" of a revolution, he only asked that they understand the inevitability of the revolutionary process. Regrettably, the terror, both red and white, was a natural phenomenon that "always" accompanied a revolution. For Steffens, the only hope for man was to learn the "divine truth as God reveals it to us in nature." With such knowledge, there was at least the possibility that the people might bloodlessly and peacefully reach their historic, shared destiny.

However, *Moses In Red* does not support even this dim hope. As created by Steffens, Moses himself, the revolutionary leader, is little more than a passive tragic figure. The dominant character in the parable is Jehovah, who represents nature. Jehovah is the master of the revolutionary process, and Moses is his servant. Steffens appeared to be taking his revenge on Lenin for reducing him to being a spectator of history. He made Moses—Lenin—follow the plan of nature and did not give him either the satisfaction of saving his people or of entering the promised land. In *Moses In Red,* Steffens reduced the revolutionary leader to being as unworthy of the future as any unredeemable liberal. In fact, the dictator's vision of the promised land proved to be no more possible than Steffens' old liberal dream. . . . Ironically, Steffens' model revolutionary leader had no more ability to see, much less shape, the future than the most unscientific of liberals.

This, of course, was in sharp contrast to much of what he wrote concerning revolutionary leaders. He was ambiguous about the role of strong men in the revolutionary process from his essays on Mexico until his death. In his study of the Mexican revolution, Steffens consistently described leaders such as Carranza as servants of events. This was easy to do with Mexico, which had no dynamic figure dominating its revolution. The emphasis was different with Lenin and Mussolini. In their cases, Steffens often blurred the relationship between their decisive leadership and the direction of history. Steffens felt more comfortable giving men credit for change, and these leaders provided him with the opportunity to put men back at the center of the action. When, on the other hand, the movement of history became the focus of his writing, Steffens lost his enthusiasm. His vision of the future became darker, and there was less place for the willful man of action.

Until *Moses In Red,* Steffens had always insisted that the scientific study of human activity was the essential basis for progress. Social advancement was no more than a combination of such knowledge with motivation and correct purpose. This was premised on his belief that all men had a "common, controllable fate"—the basis for much of his exuberance for life. As a public man, Steffens wanted to take part in the planning, announcing, and managing of a bright future. In *Moses In Red,* he denied that this was possible even for the Bolsheviks. He now felt that science could not serve as a guide to help man shape malleable nature. Such information was only a map that helpless man might use to plot the inevitable course of history.

Moses In Red is Steffens' cheerless acceptance of this fate for both himself and mankind. Fortunately, Steffens was finding solace and joy not in his public career, but in his private life.

At the very time Steffens' career was going into steep, apparently irreversible, decline, his private life was taking a definite turn for the better. In April 1919, Steffens met Ella Winter, a student at the London School of Economics who was serving as an aid to Felix Frankfurter at the Paris Peace Conference. Bright, articulate, energetic, and idealistic, she was everything that Steffens admired in youth. The worldly wise journalist was soon guiding his young friend around Paris and through the maze of intrigue and politics that was the peace conference. Despite numerous obstacles, not the least of which was the great difference in their ages, they quickly developed a deep affection for each other. After several attempts by Steffens to end their relationship, they finally decided to marry in 1924. To his great surprise (Steffens was in his fifties and his first marriage had been barren) and joy, he quickly became a father. Peter Stanley Steffens was born in November of 1924. After some fleeting misgivings, Steffens settled into his position as father and responsible family man. At an age when most men look forward to retirement, Steffens was beginning a whole new life.

Fatherhood immediately and deeply affected Steffens' art as well as his life. From the birth of Peter to his own death a dozen years later, Steffens wrote numerous articles and essays describing and philosophizing about the experience of being a parent. In **"Radiant Fatherhood,"** written within a year of his son's birth, Steffens recalled the emotions and feelings of becoming a parent for the first and, in his case, only time. (pp. 113-18)

Although written during the same period, the tone of these essays is markedly different from that of his political tracts. The latter are cold, often harsh attacks on Steffens' political foes. They contain none of the warm, generous optimism expressed in his discussions of his private life. These differences are more than a matter of style and subject matter. Essentially, Steffens was separating his public from his private perspective. As a defender of the Russian Revolution, Steffens accepted the inevitability of the historical process. There was no room for flexibility or sympathy in this political philosophy; one either supported the immutable laws of social change or became their victim. In his personal life, Steffens wanted the opposite to be true. (p. 119)

Steffens hoped to guarantee his son a bright or, at least, financially secure future with the royalties from his *Autobiography*. Since Peter was instrumental in the writing of the book, it was altogether fitting that he reap the economic benefit of its sale. Even as he began the *Autobiography,* Steffens admitted that Peter was making "my book possible and purposeful." As he watched his son grow and change, Steffens remembered his own childhood, his parents, and his home in California. Steffens, with his son to inspire him, wrote quickly without revisions. . . . Things went smoothly until he reached the section about his first wife, Josephine. Then for long, frustrating periods of time, there was nothing "but rejected shreds of paper."

The fun had gone out of it. For the next four years, Steffens plodded along in fits and starts, writing his story, one that was often painful to recreate on paper. As he struggled to recapture his past, he tired of Europe and longed for home. In 1928 after almost a decade of living in France and Italy, he returned to the United States and settled in Carmel, California, the site of a new artist colony on the Pacific coast. There, with the encouragement of his wife, his friends, and especially his publisher, Alfred Harcourt, he managed to complete the lengthy manuscript. Finally done with what had become a tedious project, Steffens relaxed and decided upon such minor details as the title. Although the author favored his original choice, "'My Life of Unlearning,'" he settled for the more standard title, *The Autobiography of Lincoln Steffens.* The two volume work was published in April 1931 and was greeted, as Steffens boasted, with a "shout of acclamation" from the critics. He proudly announced to his mother-in-law that "the publisher says the book will go on selling for a generation; as a sort of classic of our day." This is an accurate but too modest estimation of *The Autobiography.*

As an essay about his life and times, *The Autobiography* continues to make fascinating reading. Here was a man who grew up in the America of the Golden West and genuine cowboys and Indians. Steffens recaptured his childhood so well that the first section of *The Autobiography*, entitled **"A Boy on Horseback,"** was later published as a separate volume. Steffens wrote these chapters with a simple directness that reflected the uncomplicated life of growing up in Sacramento, California, in the late nineteenth century. With few exceptions, **"A Boy on Horseback"** has none of the moral asides and judgments that characterize the rest of the volumes. On the contrary, Steffens filled this section with the "sweetness" and "beauty" with which he recalled his happy, adventuresome childhood. Steffens had decided not to interpret the "wondering mentality of that age" but to save that kind of analysis for his later, more complicated years.

The first section is in sharp contrast to the remainder of *The Autobiography.* While Steffens grew up in the comforting simplicity of nineteenth century rural, Protestant America, he made his fame and fortune in the bustling, complex, industrial, urban nation of this century. This was a disturbing but familiar change to millions of Americans, and Steffens managed to capture the ambiguity of their feelings in his *Autobiography.* On the one hand, they shared the author's sense of loss and **"A Boy on Horseback"** typified their common, often nostalgic memory of the past. At the same time, they recognized that modern society offered untold opportunity to those who would seize it. Faced with a choice between two kinds of America, they, like Steffens, stayed in the city and hustled. In *The Autobiography,* Steffens' childhood becomes an idyllic vision of that older, purer American that could be used by Steffens and his audience to measure, silently, the cost of that decision.

In this rapidly changing world, Steffens seemed to have known everyone and have done everything. In brilliant vignettes, almost short stories, Steffens introduced his readers to many of the important, often legendary, figures of his generation.... Certainly, his fame as a journalist and muckraker gave Steffens such opportunities. Just as importantly, he lived in New York for much of his career. During his lifetime, that city was the undisputed American center for the arts, finance, culture, publishing, and the entry point for European ideas and politics into the United States. The second section of *The Autobiography,* "Seeing New York First," reveals why this city proved irresistible to the young, the talented, and the bold. It was where men like Steffens started for the top and where they stayed once they got there.

Still, New York alone could not explain the stunning diversity of Steffens' friendships. Ironically, this was made possible by the very moralistic, liberal culture that Steffens was supposedly trying to bury with his life story. Americans born and raised in this nineteenth century milieu shared the feeling that all men wanted, or should want, essentially the same things for themselves and their society. In politics as well as in the arts, there was a common belief that each individual sought the best. This expressed itself as a sense of responsibility for the general improvement of one's craft or profession and for the progress of the nation. It gave American society its unity and basis for communication. No matter how men differed in profession, philosophy, and even politics, they remained in agreement about the nature of their social responsibility. Consequently, they met, exchanged views, disagreed, and established friendships in full appreciation of this commonality of purpose.

The Autobiography is a fitting testimonial to the unity and generosity of this liberal culture. By Steffens' own admission, his always changing and increasingly radical views and activities seldom, if ever, cost him a friend or kept him from making new and interesting acquaintances. Steffens himself was ready to think the best of people no matter how much he disagreed with them. He was sure that, given knowledge and opportunity, criminals, urban bosses, and even big businessmen would willingly serve the public good. Although *The Autobiography* is a vigorous repudiation of liberalism, it is not a vitriolic personal attack on its standardbearers. The "Life" treats Woodrow Wilson as a tragic figure rather than as a villain. What Steffens wrote about muckrakers and muckraking epitomized his attitude. "Those were innocent days; we were all innocent folk; but no doubt all movements, whether for good or evil, are as innocent of intentions as ours." He tempered his criticism with warmth and condemned no one for the failures of reform. Thus, in the very act of denunciation, Steffens expressed and reaffirmed, perhaps unwittingly, what many think to be the saving grace of American liberalism.

However, *The Autobiography* is more than a chronicle of the author's experiences in that fascinating and rapidly changing world. It is his very personal effort to make sense of his life in those hectic times. Yet the book is less than a confession. Steffens considered that kind of public self-examination distasteful. While writing the first chapters of his own story, he had read Frederic Howe's autobiography, *The Confessions of a Reformer,* which he found much to his liking. As Steffens told its author, who was his longtime friend, "it's an honest man's story, honestly told, and I think that they have had enough of personal (psychological, sex) confessions and are relieved to find an autobiography which reveals the world; not the author, except as a hero." This was the very perspective Steffens wanted in his own book. He was interested in "showing up the world and not me."

Nevertheless, Steffens did not reach this decision easily. In debates with friends about the format of the book, he wavered back and forth about the merits of including his personal or "inside" story. First of all, he argued that no one even expected him to have worthwhile observations or opinions about the intimate aspects of life. Anyway, Steffens doubted that he had either the insight or the talent to write about such matters. His own judgment that he lacked facility at this sort of writing was correct. In the few chapters of *The Autobiography* where Steffens discussed what he called the "natural life," his style is awkward and his presentation clumsy. His description of his first encounter with sex reflects the discomfort of the author with such topics. Steffens hurried through the episode without pausing to examine its importance or meaning; indeed, it is impossible for the reader to tell what actually occurred. It is little wonder that Steffens felt safer talking about his public self.

Even his wives receive an ''outside'' treatment in *The Autobiography.* At first, Steffens planned to exclude them completely from the story.... In the end, Steffens found it impossible to eliminate them, but he did severely limit their presence. Inevitably, they appear as aspects of his relationship with society. (pp. 122-26)

Steffens recognized that this intense focus on what he called his ''outside'' life could be regarded as a substantial weakness by the critics. Without an extensive discussion of his private self, Steffens feared that his ''life'' would lack both balance and drama. His concern about this emphasis on his exterior life at the expense of his interior feelings was, in many respects, a modern contrivance. In the nineteenth century, an individual's exterior life was thought to reflect his or her interior state. An alteration in a person's relationship with the world evidenced a change in psychological condition and vice versa. An autobiography, more often than not, was a description of the author's social consciousness or recognition of a moral imperative. Public testimonials, especially political and religious ones, were expressions of the person's innermost feelings. After World War I, such essentially nineteenth century figures as Henry Adams and William Allen White continued this literary tradition with their autobiographical works. This is the format of *The Autobiography,* that appeared in print midway between Adams' *The Education of Henry Adams* and White's *The Autobiography of William Allen White.* Although Steffens understood the demands of modern literature, he could not bring himself to write a probing self-examination of his psyche. Instead, he wrote an autobiography that used his public life to reveal the social side of the private man.

Steffens' life story is a classic tale of American innocence and optimism. As usual, Steffens chose to develop his ideas in a paradoxical fashion. For many readers, *The Autobiography* seems to have quite the opposite theme; it appears to be a touching story of lost innocence and subsequent disillusionment. Steffens supplied plenty of evidence to support this contention. As the author described his life, it was a series of lost hopes and unfulfilled dreams. In the course of his career, he embraced and abandoned genteel Republican reform, muckraking, progressivism, and Christian anarchism. Finally, Steffens lost all faith in American liberalism, which had once formed the very core of his social-political perspective. By the conclusion of *The Autobiography,* Steffens had apparently given up the moral idealism of discredited liberalism for the inevitability of historical materialism. Although correct in every detail, this synopsis misses the real point of the book.

The Autobiography is far from being a chronicle of disillusionment. Admittedly, it is the tale of lost illusions, but that is not the same thing. According to Steffens, he spent much of his life ''unlearning'' what he thought was certain and right. These discoveries did not leave him bitter and cynical. Quite the contrary was true. Early in his career, Steffens realized that ''it was as pleasant to change one's mind as it was to change one's clothes. The practice led one to other, more fascinating— theories.'' In essence, he was never disillusioned; he simply lost his illusions over and over again. For this reason, Steffens had little patience with those liberals who let Wilson's failure at Versailles drive them to political despair. Instead of developing a new revolutionary social vision to take the place of liberalism, these disillusioned radicals satisfied themselves with

''bitterness, cynicism, drink, sex—aplenty.'' Steffens saw no need to follow this ''subjective'' course. For him, the repudiation of once held principles cleared the way for new ideals and led to a reaffirmation of his social optimism.

No doubt, this attitude is not the product of naivete. Certainly, Steffens willingly accepted, even romanticized, this kind of innocence. He devoted a good portion of *The Autobiography* to his unsophisticated, protected childhood in semifrontier California and his discovery of the worldly wisdom of Europe and the raw excitement of New York. In this Jamesian sense of American innocence, such a life should have led to disillusionment. American writers have often used this concept of innocence either to accept or reject what has been essentially a European claim to superiority. Although Steffens believed in the special virtues of this kind of pristine innocence, he was unwilling to identify experience with disillusionment. As much as anyone of his generation, Steffens knew the world, its people, and its leaders. While he admitted that these experiences opened his simple, Western eyes, he never conceded that they caused him to lose hope for himself and society. Throughout his life, he approached each new adventure with the same fresh anticipation of his boyhood days in California.

In *The Autobiography,* innocence is, in its fullest sense, the disposition to combine experience with fresh hope. It is more than a willingness to confront men, institutions, and ideas without the prejudice of previous disappointments. Innocence is the psychological capacity to make new experiences the efficacious basis for an ever-changing but always optimistic system of beliefs. This is not the innocence of true believers who let the righteousness of their faith cut them off from the reality of the world. Such innocence had led to the failure of liberalism. To the readers of *The Autobiography,* Steffens ''offered the old rule of my experience; to look at facts, let them destroy an illusion, and not to be cast down, but go on studying the facts, sure that in those very same facts would be found constructive material with which to build up another—illusion, no better, perhaps, but other than the old one.'' Thus, experience never ended with cynicism, but always became the foundation for new beliefs.

According to Steffens, it was his application of the objective methods of science that made possible this continued renewal of confidence that man could solve his problems. Yet, Steffens used science in an unusual way. Despite his claims to the contrary, he employed science not so much to create new theories as to destroy old ones. In *The Autobiography,* the examination of facts and experience inevitably led to the loss of belief. Steffens used the detached methodology of science to clear away principles, assumptions, ideas, and moral standards. In this way, he lost his faith in good men, good government, reform, progressivism, formal Christianity, and, of course, liberalism. From his boyhood to the moment he completed *The Autobiography,* Steffens saw the same pattern to his life. Discarded principles were quickly, almost effortlessly, replaced by other theories and ideals. For this reason, he thought the best title for his life story would be ''My Life of Unlearning.''

The Autobiography proves Steffens to be anything but a social scientist. He showed none of the respect for facts so essential to the methods of science.... He was not interested in arranging the events of his life in such an objective manner that the disinterested reader might judge him and his activities. For Steffens, as always, the facts were of no consequence in and by themselves. He included only those events and occurrences in *The Autobiography* that served to shape and illuminate his social-political consciousness. He began the last chapter with the observation that "seeing is one motion; believing is another." His ability to combine the two without sacrificing the virtues of either was central to his special kind of innocence.

In this respect, *The Autobiography* is less Steffens' life story than it is a reaffirmation of his faith in the world. In fact, he used the book to support his latest cause. He reiterated his by then well-known belief that the Russian experiment was the wave of the future. Still, *The Autobiography* is dominated by the "boy on horseback" and not by the hardened, unforgiving defender of the revolution. For Steffens, the young were the best hope of social redemption. They, unfettered by false knowledge and values, saw the open-ended possibilities of life. The youth of the United States, Russia, Mexico, and even Italy were making their systems work. Finally, to his surprise, he found cause for optimism in his native land. The managers had replaced the owners as the decisionmakers in society. He viewed these technocrats as planning the economy efficiently for the maximum good of all, not as manipulating the market for the outdated motive of profit. For all his apparent certainty, Steffens appreciated the irony of his latest convictions. Beliefs, by their very nature, were necessary but fleeting things, and this willing believer was sure that he would again change his mind. He finished *The Autobiography* with this thought. "My life was worth my living. And as for the world in general, all that was or is or ever will be wrong with that is my—our thinking about it."

Steffens continued to think and write about himself and the world until his death in August 1936. Despite the success of *The Autobiography* and the clamor for a sequel, Steffens never again undertook a major piece of writing. In one way or another, *The Autobiography* contained all the books, either fact or fiction, that he had ever considered writing. In any case, the aging journalist was tired and wanted to relax and enjoy his new eminence in both American letters and radical politics. He went on the lecture circuit and was a great success until failing health forced him to return home to California. Even then, Steffens managed to keep his name in print. He wrote a few articles for such major national magazines as *Cosmopolitan*, but mostly he contributed to leftist periodicals and local California newspapers. Shortly before his death, Steffens gathered much of this material into one last volume, *Lincoln Steffens Speaking*.

More often than not, these articles, essays, fables, and vignettes concerned American capitalism and politics, their failure in the Great Depression, and the alternative offered by communism. Steffens' faith in the "new" capitalism did not last beyond the initial stages of the Depression. When the American economy collapsed suddenly in late 1929, Steffens expected the managers of industry to bring back prosperity by maintaining high wages and full employment. When businessmen began firing workers and cutting production to save expenditures and create scarcities, Steffens lost all confidence in the ability of capitalism to reform itself. From the start, he was sure that the reform program of the New Deal was doomed to failure. For him, "President Roosevelt's policy of proceeding by evolution to adjust the institutions and machinery of the United States to change will not be possible." This meant, Steffens concluded, that America must look to Russia and communism for the answers.

During the final years of his life, Steffens became an ever more vocal defender of the Soviet Union and outspoken advocate of communism at home. He lost all tolerance for criticism of Soviet policy. Steffens insisted that the Russian ruler had no choice but to suppress the privileged classes with the terror in the early 1930s. While, admittedly, this was done at "great cost," it was the only way to end internal opposition to the Russian "social experiment." In fact, Steffens claimed that the Communists, especially Stalin, had become so generous—liberal—with their enemies as to encourage resistance to their programs. This forced Stalin to reinstitute the terror to protect the revolution. This was an imaginative, if inaccurate, explanation of the first phase of the Russian dictator's massive purges of the peasants, the party, and finally, the army. At home, Steffens encouraged all radical and dissident elements to unify under the Communist party. Only with the leadership of the Communists could Americans understand their economic problems and proceed to their permanent solution.

Yet for someone who had seen the future, he remained unsure of its shape. If life had taught him anything, Steffens told his youthful readers, it was *"that nothing is known positively and completely."* This is the message that he has passed on through his writing to every generation of Americans in this century. It was the way that he lived his life with expectations that made him a great journalist. His continual need to see and believe in the world made it obligatory that he be involved in the world. He was always ready to share each experience and every discovery with his audience. Consequently, he never tired of the ever-changing world; his outlook remained optimistic, and his prose crisp and fresh. In this sense, his writing was indistinguishable from his life, and both exemplified the kind of American innocence that saw the frontier as a metaphor for a willingness to confront new experiences with the optimism of a believer.

In a word, Steffens was a great journalist. He was not a great writer or thinker. He influenced the attitude of those who knew him and not their style or thought. His two most famous proteges, Walter Lippman and John Reed, ended having little in common with their mentor except that they, too, became great journalists. Today, Steffens remains a model for investigative reporting. He was the first to understand and master this peculiarly American art. Steffens realized that the exposure of misdeeds was not enough for Americans. Like Steffens, they wanted the "shameful" facts destroyed. When Steffens equated the knowledge of wrongdoing with a demand for reform, he was speaking the language of his audience. Modern investigative reporting is founded on the special American virtue of seeing public wrong as the opportunity for the general good. In this century, it is a story as old as *The Shame of the Cities* and as new as Watergate. (pp. 126-31)

> *Patrick F. Palermo, in his* Lincoln Steffens, *Twayne Publishers, 1978, 148 p.*

ROBERT STINSON (essay date 1979)

[*Stinson is an American educator and critic who has written extensively on the history of the United States since 1865 and on the history of journalism and historical writing. In the following excerpt he discusses the early years of Steffens's journalistic and literary career, including Steffens's first three muckraking books,* The Shame of the Cities, The Struggle for Self-Government, *and* Upbuilders.]

The decade that began with Steffens's move to *McClure's Magazine* was a period of considerable growth for him personally and professionally. Latent talents flowered and he became famous. In the [1890s] he had published skillful vignettes

Steffens and his son Pete at their Italian home, 1925. From The Letters of Lincoln Steffens, *edited by Ella Winter and Granville Hicks. Harcourt Brace Jovanovich, 1938. Copyright 1938 by Harcourt Brace Jovanovich, Inc. Reproduced by permission of the publisher.*

less as a newspaper reporter and more as a muckraker. To be sure, the magazine articles which made up *Shame of the Cities* and the other books rested on his new sensitivity to human interest. But Steffens's muckraking pieces were more purposive than descriptive, and he composed them more with the reformer's sense of argument than the feature writer's more neutral aim of evoking a slice of life. (pp. 45-6)

Steffens became disillusioned with muckraking before the movement lost its general vogue, but while he was part of it the sense of creating and belonging to something larger than himself was exhilarating and contributed to his growing self-confidence. (p. 48)

Self-confidence showed in his writing, too. Each of his major works requires detailed, individual analysis, but some general points can be made here. For one thing, each successive collection of articles from *Shame of the Cities* through *Struggle for Self-Government* and *Upbuilders* revealed an increase in militancy and personal engagement. The early essays on St. Louis and Minneapolis in *Shame of the Cities* are largely free of sweeping generalizations about all political society, but the book's later essays, though they also concern specific cities, are more broadly interpretive. Steffens's next two books are filled with a new self-assurance and, often, cocky moral pronouncement.

Yet sometimes the tone of street-wise authority masked a layer of uncertainty. He was not as naive during these years as the *Autobiography* makes him out, but his muckraking was nonetheless often a mixture of penetrating realism, unschooled idealism, and embarrassing sentimentalism. He was realistic, for example, in pointing out the difference between the constitutional description of government and public office, on one hand, and the actual, less visible operation of government on the other. His insistence that official rhetoric and private behavior were not the same thing was a simple but important concept.

Then, in other parts of his writing, Steffens seemed to forget this lesson himself and slip into naive, uncritical expectations. He imagined that "the people," abused by corrupt governments, existed apart from economic, religious, and geographical interest groups, and he was often puzzled by their disinclination to rise as a body to throw off their oppressors once they were taught who the oppressors were. He seemed in such moods to think that reform was only a matter of substituting patriotic officeholders for special interest men and "general legislation" for laws benefitting railroad magnates, steel monopolists and other businessmen. . . .

Steffens would later organize his autobiography around his passage from ignorance to understanding. But evidence from the muckraking pieces themselves suggests that such a view was no mere hindsight. For all his strident posturing, Steffens seemed to know he did not understand everything yet. His tales of city politics were often cast in polarities, with reformers and bosses representing ignorance and knowledge respectively. Steffens seemed to admire the bosses—men like Cincinnati's George Cox, for example—because, despite their uncouth brutality, they possessed what he wanted: knowledge. They had knowledge of their cities but also of human nature itself. He could like the reformers, too, but only at the point when, as citizens, they cast off their innocence and began to acquire a tough-mindedness equal to that of their corrupt adversaries. Otherwise he had no use for them. (pp. 48-9)

of city life which were buried in the back pages of newspapers or obscure magazines. But in the next ten years Steffens published long, well-considered articles in national monthlies and saw them collected in three successive books [*The Shame of the Cities, The Struggle for Self-Government,* and *Upbuilders*]. (p. 45)

His own self-confidence grew in these years, and he began to follow impulses to independence. Shortly after the turn of the century, for example, he started signing his work Lincoln Steffens, instead of Joseph or J. Lincoln Steffens, his father's name. He was to work on salary—a hundred dollars a week—for S. S. McClure, but after five years he joined the 1906 "palace revolt" at *McClure's* and withdrew, along with John S. Phillips, Ida M. Tarbell, Ray Stannard Baker and other staff members to buy and write for the *American Magazine.* Then, two years later, angry with the way his colleagues handled his copy, Steffens sold his *American* interests and became a freelance writer with only occasional fixed responsibilities to the magazines for which he wrote. By that time, 1908, his name was well-known wherever it appeared.

It was well-known, and it was synonymous with "muckraking." And, no matter how interesting or worth recovering Steffens's 1890s newspaper writing is, he is remembered now

[In May 1902 Steffens] learned of the fight Joseph W. Folk, prosecuting attorney for St. Louis, was waging against bribery and corruption in that municipal government. [S. S. McClure] had apparently suggested that city and state governments might be ripe for dramatic treatment, and the prospect of an article on St. Louis rekindled Steffens's own interest in urban government. He visited Folk in St. Louis and then wrote back to New York that if the magazine took up state governments, the magazine should ask William Allen White, the emerging reform journalist from Kansas, to do it, but if *McClure's* was to have a series on cities, he wanted to handle it himself. "If I should be trusted with the work," he said, "I think I could make my name." (p. 51)

At first, McClure envisioned the series of articles which became *Shame of the Cities* as an international study to include Birmingham, England and Naples, Italy, but Steffens finally limited it to six American cities: St. Louis (two articles), Minneapolis, Pittsburgh, Philadelphia, Chicago and New York. . . .

Considering its reputation as an original and influential book, it may be wise to begin an evaluation of *Shame of the Cities* by making clear what it was not. For one thing, it was not a series of stunning new facts pulled out of reluctant sources and never revealed before. Steffens, of course, never claimed that it was, and, in fact, one of his stated reasons for writing was to publicize not only the things people did not know about corruption in their cities but also the *fact* that they knew things and allowed them to continue anyway. This complacent knowledge was itself the "shame" of Minneapolis or any other city. Much of Steffens's information came from open court testimony and public reports of local citizens' reform groups, while considerably less of his reporting came from personal contacts with the bribers and boodlers themselves. And, though he and the other muckrakers became famous for naming names and fixing places in articles that were supposed to have been as thorough as grand jury indictments, Steffens's names and places came from public documents with established legal pedigrees. Not infrequently when he did have private information, he omitted the principals' names with conspicuous blank spaces or replaced them with general terms like "Mr. Councilman."

If the result often made Steffens a mere summarizer of known graft prosecutions, his very summarizing became a revelation in the broader sense that readers in one city may have realized for the first time that corruption was everywhere. The articles had a powerful cumulative effect, and Steffens could ask, given so many incidents of corruption, whether vice and bribery were not really a problem of the total American culture. The asking of such a question . . . revealed at least a new category of thinking about old, known problems.

Further, *The Shame of the Cities* was not a systematic treatise on urban government cast in a well-articulated theoretical framework. Above all it was a popular magazine series, largely descriptive and often dramatic with the clashing of personalities in brilliantly highlighted bits of dialogue. Later, when Steffens relived the writing of the articles in his autobiography, he stressed his development of a "theory of graft" which soon bulked so large that McClure and the rest of the staff began to resist it. Yet a reading of the pieces themselves reveals that Steffens hinted at and implied more about corruption as a function of American culture than he fully argued.

Nonetheless, whatever they lacked in careful exposition, Steffens's ideas were there, and three of them may be singled out as themes in *The Shame of the Cities*. The first, that business-

men's private needs always took precedence over the public good, was prefigured in a bitter essay Steffens published in October 1901, many months before he first visited Joseph Folk in St. Louis but after a varied observation of the New York political scene. In **"Great Types of Modern Business—Politics"** he attacked the notion that reform could best be achieved by electing businessmen to office since business was the very corruptor of social and political life in the first place. "Politics is a business," he said.

> That's what's the matter with it! That's what is the matter with everything—art, literature, religion, journalism, law, medicine—they're all business and all—as you see them. Make politics a sport, as they do in England, or a profession, as they do in Germany, and we'll have—well, something else than we have now, if we want it, which is another question. But don't try to reform politics with the banker, the lawyer and the drygoods merchant, for these are businessmen [see excerpt dated 1904]. . . .

When Steffens wrote a preface to bring the articles together as *The Shame of the Cities* in 1904, he simply inserted this paragraph and others from the earlier essay and then went on to elaborate the point. Businessmen were guilty on two counts: once because the biggest among them offered bribes to politicians in order to secure lucrative franchises and city contract business, and again because the smaller "average" businessmen were careless and neglectful of government—the good of the community—as they followed the narrow line of private money-making. (pp. 52-4)

Related to the problem presented by businessmen was a second theme: that the chief blame for corruption in government rested not with the grafters and boodlers but with their victims, "the people," for they were the ones who knew it was happening and did not rise to stop it. Steffens claimed this idea came to him gradually as he travelled from one city to the next, but later he said in his autobiography that he first saw the principle when he went to the race track as a boy and learned from the jockeys how horse races were fixed so that the favorite who, by all the visible standards of judgment—pedigree, jockey, previous record—ought to win was held back to lose. But the people in the stands ("suckers" Steffens learned to call them, including one day his father) did not want to hear about the fix and bet money on horses whose chances they judged by the usual standards. It was they, the boy decided, who made the fix possible. And it was millions more of them in American society who made municipal corruption possible. "The people are not innocent," he wrote after the last article was published. "That is the only 'news' in all the journalism of these articles. . . ."

Whatever its origin, the idea was rooted in Steffens's assumption that men could be moved by one of two conflicting interests, the public and the private, and his assumption, too, that citizens were aware of the difference and were therefore responsible for the choice they made one way or the other. They could vote for the boodlers or they could vote for "St. Louis," but they had no right to expect anything more than what they chose. Steffens's categories tended to be starkly drawn and allowed for little qualification. Citizens confronted with this simple choice were generally just "the people," or "the Pittsburghers." In Minneapolis they were stereotyped to fit the region as "Miles, Hans and Ole," but Steffens did not recognize differentiation among them according to where they lived, how much they earned, or where they went to church. One gets the impression, reading the essays today, that Steffens did not know his cities as well as his reputation for thoroughness suggested.

The people seldom chose the public interest because they were gullible and easily taken in by politics organized around parties. No one questioned the need for party organization and no one asked whether or not there was another choice beyond Republicans and Democrats even when it was clear that neither party represented anything above the interests of the few. Steffens hoped to shame urban citizens into rising against parties and reaching consciousness as an independent third force which would have only the public good in mind when it went to the polls.

At times Steffens seemed to reject political organization altogether, and his argument was then reminiscent of the fears manifested by George Washington, James Madison, and others among the founding fathers who cautioned against the rise of political parties on the grounds that parties embodied only factional interests and would create permanent and threatening divisiveness. But elsewhere he argued more realistically that good government was possible if the people could find and follow leaders who had the community in mind and would use a *political* methodology borrowed from the very politicians they wanted to beat. America was a country in which demand called forth supply, he argued, and if bosses and their machines thrived on supplying what a few private interests demanded, the people need only create a demand for government in the public interest and give their votes to new political organizations that would supply it.

How could this be done? Steffens insisted that *The Shame of the Cities* was not a manual of reform, but he did demonstrate the possibilities for success or failure by reviewing the cases of St. Louis, in all its "shamelessness," and Chicago, **"Half Free and Fighting On."** Steffens wrote two articles on St. Louis and together they are a detailed chronicle of bribery and election fraud well-known, he claimed, to the people of St. Louis and presided over by Colonel Ed Butler, boss of the city's Democratic machine. (pp. 55-7)

But Chicago was a different story. For years "everybody was for himself, and no one for Chicago" until in 1895 civic-minded men formed the Municipal Voters' League—"the Nine," as they came to be called—headed by George E. Cole. Cole's virtue was that he was a businessman who had sense enough to know that he needed a *political* solution to Chicago's problems. Suggestions that there be more newspaper exposures and more graft prosecutions were set aside in favor of direct political intervention in the municipal elections of 1895. First the Nine published the records of corrupt Aldermen running for re-election and then, by threatening to publish more sensitive information, they blackmailed many of them into retirement. Next, Cole's group worked at the ward level to influence the make-up of party tickets. They did not insist upon total honesty, just more honesty—"a likely rascal to beat the rascal that was in and known"—among the candidates the Nine supported. They offered decisive League support to the minority party's candidate in exchange for a say in who the candidate would be. Steffens summed up their accomplishments: "I should say that the basic unstated principle of this reform movement, struck out early in the practice of the Nine, was to let the politicians rule, but through better and better men whom the Nine forced upon them with public opinion." What made it all work, of course, was the crystallization of that public opinion. Steffens

did not go into why the "Chicagoans" rose to the occasion when the "St. Louisans" could not; it was enough for him to know that they did.

The question was, of course, which case was typical, St. Louis or Chicago? Steffens hoped it was Chicago but seemed to suspect that it was St. Louis, and his suspicion was related to the third theme in *Shame of the Cities:* that corruption was the necessary product of American culture. The repeated incidence of corruption from one city to the next was enough to suggest a cultural interpretation. "Evidently," he once told S. S. McClure, "you could shoot me out of a gun fired at random and, wherever I lighted, there would be a story, the same way." But did the scope of it mean it was peculiarly American? A standard explanation assured that it was not, that corruption was carried like a disease to America with the current waves of foreign immigrants; wherever they went it would flourish. But Steffens visited Philadelphia, "the most American of our greater cities" with 47 per cent of its population native born of native parents, and found it "corrupt and contented," the worst-governed city in the country. Nor, as others suggested, was bad government a function of youth, for he found it in the oldest cities as well as the newest.

Still the closest Steffens came to a theory of his own, apart from noting the neglect of the people and the powerful private drives unleashed by the commercial spirit, was a vague suggestion in the Philadelphia article that cities must pass through "typical stages of corruption," from a period of "miscellaneous loot with a boss for chief thief" at one end to "absolutism" at the other. New York in the 1860s under Tweed was an example of the first stage, and St. Louis was at present just emerging from that stage. Evolution through the middle stages was not spelled out, but Philadelphia represented something dangerously close to the last stage. This was so not just because Philadelphians were largely disenfranchised ("The honest citizens of Philadelphia have no more rights at the polls than the negroes down South"), but because it was run by a city Republican machine which was controlled by a state Republican machine which was itself tied to the national Republican organization. "This is the ideal of party organization," he wrote, "and, possibly, is the end toward which our democratic republic is tending. If it is, the end is absolutism. Nothing but a revolution could overthrow this oligarchy, and there is its danger."

On the whole, however, Steffens's theories, even when connected to such stark warnings, were probably of more interest to himself than they were to his readers. What attracted them more was the impression he gave of the scope of corrupt politics and, beyond that, his extraordinary skill at sheer characterization, a literary rather than a scientific approach. What distinguished Steffens from other journalists was his keen sense of how things *looked:* a careful eye for appearances and the symbolic value thrown up by objective data. (pp. 58-60)

The real attraction of Steffens's work was his skill at weaving tales of corruption around personalities. Whatever his theories, no impersonal forces of economics or demography really shaped Steffens's cities; they were in the grip of bosses and reformers with sharply defined personal histories and characters. Almost every city had a boss like St. Louis's Ed Butler or Minneapolis's "Doc" Ames, and when there were two bosses in one city, they worked as one. Thus Steffens described Chris Magee and William Flinn of Pittsburgh as two parts of a split personality. . . . And the bosses were brazen, cocky men, all seeming to mouth Boss William Marcy Tweed's earlier famous taunt, "What are you going to do about it?" When they talked to Steffens they seemed willing to spill all with a smiling assurance that no one could touch them. Steffens made as much of this as he could because he, too, wanted to taunt his readers, to repeat and amplify the insult with the intention of goading them into action.

Steffens described the reformers, too, so that his articles emphasized characteristics which tended to "type" them. They all seemed to resemble St. Louis's Joseph W. Folk, "a thin-lipped, firm-mouthed, dark little man, who never raises his voice." Quiet-spoken, ordinary citizens—perhaps the way Steffens imagined his own readers—the reformers were at first reluctant to leave private life and start fights with the bosses, but once involved, they fought tenaciously, uncompromisingly in ways that must command the respect of the bosses themselves. (pp. 61-2)

Writing in terms of personalities had been standard policy at *McClure's* for a decade, well before the magazine's muckrake phase, but it was especially useful in Steffens's work. Another tested device was to write part or all of an article as the story of the reporter's own visit to the people involved. Steffens was just learning to use this device to give a sense of the urgent present to articles which otherwise often dealt with the history of one or another city's corruption. He reported conversations with citizens about local politics and gave his readers tours of cities' decaying streets in an effort to bring home the very present physical consequences of bad government.

The Shame of the Cities made Steffens famous for his detailed exposition of corruption in high places. Yet he also knew when to avoid masses of detail in favor of a more careful and sparse selection of symbolic events—things which would stay in a reader's mind the longer because they stood alone and uncluttered on the page. (p. 62)

Both Steffens's critique of urban America and the manner in which he expressed it had one thing in common: they were both models of a new kind of journalism aimed at specific social change. "I wanted to move and to convince," he said when the last article was published. Such a concept of journalism was not new in itself, of course, for others had understood the power of the press before him. Joseph Pulitzer's New York *World* had been using sensationalism as a tool for social awareness and change since the 1880s, and some of Steffens's own newspaper work during the 1890s had leaned in that direction. But these had been local efforts aimed at local problems. *The Shame of the Cities* united substance with style in an attempt to create a national reform consciousness, and the popularity of his work was some measure of his success. (pp. 62-3)

> *Robert Stinson, in his* Lincoln Steffens, *Frederick Ungar Publishing Co., 1979, 168 p.*

CHRISTOPHER P. WILSON (essay date 1981)

[*In the following excerpt, Wilson provides background on the development of newspaper reporting as a profession during the 1890s and discusses Steffens's career as a reporter.*]

By most historians' accounts, the decade of the 1890s was the culmination of the "age of the reporter." As the contemporary enthusiasts of the new journalism put it, the style of Pulitzer had "liberated" the reporter from the strictures of personal opinion and mere partisanship and placed him as the primary agent of a system of "powerful impersonality," facts and "or-

ganized intelligence." Observers like Allan Forman, editor of the trade magazine *The Journalist,* hailed the departure of modern newspapermen from an earlier image as unkempt, besotten "bohemians" and their arrival as true professionals. At the pinnacle of their craft, successful reporters like Julian Ralph, Richard Harding Davis and Julius Chambers recounted the reporter's exploits on landscapes both urban and international; several of these writers easily made the transition to literary fame. In the dawn of the Progressive era, the reporter was adopted not only as an aesthetic pathfinder, but also as a social and political hero—the public's agent of "exposure."

Against this continuing din the dissenting voice of Lincoln Steffens' *Autobiography* . . . seems lonely indeed. In the sections recounting brief years at E. L. Godkin's *Evening Post,* Steffens' memoir presents its reporter-protagonist against an ironic backdrop of how news is "made": produced, distributed and even fabricated. The *Autobiography* treats news as an illusory thing, and consequently portrays the reporter not so much as a heroic investigator as a man ambiguously involved in a "system" of newsmaking. Of course, this ironic revision was partly attributable to the more radical ideas of an older man; Steffens' recollection of his muckraking career was equally unflattering. Yet there is much to suggest that Steffens' dissenting vision—the style of thought which led him not just to see things, but see *through* them—was equally a product of a reaction against his daily experience as a reporter.

The reporter's increasingly pivotal role in the late nineteenth century was an outgrowth of the now-familiar transformation of metropolitan journalism from "personal" or partisan affiliations, emphasizing editorial opinion, to a professionalized occupation centering around its "independent" function of news gathering and distribution. This institutional transformation, aided by technological innovations, enabled the expansions in production, circulation and personnel which are now commonplace items in textbook histories. (pp. 41-2)

These developments hinted that the same forces that had catapulted the reporter to his *public* prominence were internally limiting his power and compromising his autonomy. In fact, the inner world of the reporter was often one of bureaucratic instability and intense pressure. The narrowing gap between the news and its deadline intensified the pace of modern journalism; news, perhaps more than any other commodity, had to be "fresh," and it lost its value if not harvested, packaged and delivered in a few hours. Thus the quiet, cultured "club" atmosphere of papers like Charles A. Dana's *New York Sun,* carefully avoiding "undue splutter" and needless "hurry," was gradually being displaced by the boiler shop environment favored by men like Hearst, Pulitzer and Chicago editor Melville Stone. The reporter was both the instrument and object of this new emphasis on activity: some editors even resorted to the ruse of putting two men on the same assignment. Other modern circumstances—the bureaucratic pressures of "office politics," absentee ownership and fluctuating staff sizes—gave rise to repeated complaints by even successful reporters. Seasoned professionals like Chambers, Ralph, Franklin Matthews, Will Irwin, Jacob Riis, Edward T. Townsend—and even, after all, Richard Harding Davis—all at one time or another acknowledged the decidedly un-romantic aspects of modern reporting. (pp. 42-3)

For the most part, the activity of the reporter was insured by a modern method of office organization: the assignment system. This procedure, as John Given of the *Sun* put it [in his *Making a Newspaper* (1907)], had taken the element of chance out of reporting, eliminating men who strolled "haphazard about the streets" or who stood "idle at a street corner waiting for something to happen."... Whereas older offices like the *Sun* had a "laissez-faire" attitude toward reporters' work, the new journals applied the assignment system as a form of office discipline and planning which clearly cut back on the autonomy the reporter had once enjoyed. (p. 43)

Unsure about his future prospects, Steffens had at first envisioned the newspaper profession as a temporary occupation, even though he applied himself industriously. Initially, there seemed to be no "market" for his "brand of goods," but then his "literary sponsor," Robert Underwood Johnson of the *Century,* placed him at the *Post* among "cultured and refined men." Even in the 1930s, Steffens recalled fondly the style of the "gentleman reporter" which the generation of Dana and Godkin had made famous. But the *Autobiography* also recalled the "office politics" which divided Godkin and the *Post*'s conservative owners from those who wanted deeper involvement with the growing commerce of crime news. Steffens served his apprenticeship, in other words, on a kind of historical dividing line.

Experiencing many of the vicissitudes common to young reporters—entranced by his city, yet feeling the pressures of long hours, low pay on the "space system," and little time for outside work—Steffens nonetheless advanced quickly, and landed his first major assignment: to cover Wall Street. The *Autobiography* recalls ironically how the "original American boob"... who had rebelled against business culture now attempted to compile a list of leading financiers who might help "their" paper, the *Post,* ride through a panic. But Steffens soon discovered that bankers used his confidence to release stories when they wanted to, particularly to "break a bad piece of news, like a big failure, in the cool, dull, matter-of-fact terms of the *Evening Post.*"... Steffens, in other words, converted the *Post*'s dislike of sensationalism into a positive asset during the panic. With the financiers' help, the young reporter began to plan canned stories well in advance....

Steffens the reporter was further educated by James B. Dill, the financier credited with the U.S. Steel merger. At the time, Steffens was investigating the allegations that Dill had orchestrated the New Jersey legislation which allowed for "plain financial crimes."... But Dill confessed these crimes—and others—with such complete candor that Steffens was totally disarmed; then Dill revealed that he himself had helped the "exposure" stories along for their "advertising"... benefits. The *Autobiography* then adds a remarkable confession:

> I did not write all that Dill told me; not then;
> I never have. I could not at the time, because,
> as I have said, I was too imbued with the Wall
> Street spirit and view of things to speak as this
> lawyer [Dill] did of the holies of the holy....
> I was a Wall Street man myself, unconsciously,
> but literally. That's how I came finally to understand
> what corruption is and how it gets a
> man, not as the Reds and the writers think, but
> as the Whites and the Righteous are: rogues
> outside, but inside honest men.

In short, Steffens had discovered his own "corruption"—his implicit acceptance of a system of newsgathering that controlled what he saw and wrote.

Steffens' next assignment was police headquarters, relatively new territory for the conservative *Post.* (p. 45)

Once again, the young reporter began by courting familiarity with his sources: with Parkhurst, then with policemen. But now he found an environment hardly as congenial toward the *Post* as Wall Street had been. The *Post*'s prior aloofness—and perhaps Steffens' own gentlemanly manner—seemed to put his sources on guard.... This time, however, Steffens made a different decision from what he had at Wall Street: rather than play the "insider" Steffens said he resolved to "be a free lance at police headquarters."...

To his surprise, Steffens discovered that the groundwork for his freelance strategy had been laid by Jacob Riis of the *Evening Sun.* Steffens followed Riis' example by avoiding the "combine" strategy of the reporters' rooms, in which reporters divided news events among themselves only to return and copy from one another.... (p. 46)

Steffens' attempt to remodel the journalist role into a form of detached social criticism gave him an implicitly radical vision of "news." The reporter was not simply, in most cases, an uninvolved observer; Steffens' awareness of this allowed him, for a time, to step outside the standard categories of political Mugwumpery. Riis showed Steffens how the "clubbing" of strikers by policemen could never be "news;"... Steffens himself discoverd how he could create a "crime wave" simply by reporting more crime...; he learned how the police system of cooperation with criminals was often disguised by an exciting "cover-up" scenario of heroic detective work.... The *Autobiography* portrays an urban universe where distinctions like "good men" and "bad," or "corruption" and "reform," are not all what they seem. Instead of an objective social laboratory, Steffens discovered a universe where "exposure" only led to the perfection of corruption, reform only to the persistence of crime.

Steffens' awareness of the reporter's ambiguous role in this urban "system" was an essential source of a vision both ironic and realistic. As he moved on to become editor of his own *Commercial Advertiser,* his antipathies to modern journalism became apparent. Speaking to lost literary ambitions of his own, Steffens created an office for "cultured" Ivy Leaguers who were willing to "talk art"..., an environment which flaunted modern principles of discipline, aggressiveness and specialization. His main criterion for staff was that "they did not intend to be journalists."... Steffens' tenure at the *Commercial Advertiser*—which ended when he collapsed with "symptoms of nervous prostration"—closed his newspaper chapter. But his brief apprenticeship as a reporter surely provided ample training for his muckraking career, particularly for *The Shame of the Cities.* Even as he moved on to *McClure's,* however, his involvement with the ambiguities of "selling" news was far from over.

Not willing to forsake his achievements entirely, Steffens in truth had only modified the heroism of the reporter in his description of the *Post* years. But if his portrait of the news gatherer was only more ironic than the standard accounts, it was perhaps also more candid. Most important, his account may have a particularly contemporary relevance. Steffens' memoir suggests that the highly publicized battles of Progressive reform were, in reality, a form of "media politics" in perhaps its embryo form. Dazzled by more modern media (F.D.R. and the radio, J.F.K. and television) we often neglect the historical coincidence of, for example, T.R. and the expanded power of the printed word—an expansion that extended to magazines and books as well. What Steffens discovered was that the writer was often called upon to play a pivotal role in this process of news management. His dissent reflected his ability to "muckrake" himself—and come to terms with the ambiguities of the "era of the reporter." (pp. 46-7)

> *Christopher P. Wilson, "The Era of the Reporter Reconsidered: The Case of Lincoln Steffens," in* Journal of Popular Culture, *Vol. 15, No. 2, Fall, 1981, pp. 41-9.*

ADDITIONAL BIBLIOGRAPHY

Aaron, Daniel. *Writers on the Left: Episodes in American Literary Communism.* New York: Harcourt, Brace & World, 1961, 460 p.*
 Contains scattered references to Steffens's conversion to and public espousal of Soviet communism.

Cochran, Bud T. "Lincoln Steffens and the Art of Autobiography." *College Composition and Communication* XVI, No. 2 (May 1965): 102-05.
 Finds the *Autobiography* deficient as such because it reveals so little about Steffens's day-to-day life.

Filler, Louis. *Crusaders for American Liberalism,* pp. 55ff. Yellow Springs, Ohio: The Antioch Press, 1939.*
 Calling Steffens "the first muckraker," Filler outlines his journalistic career and his involvement in the McNamara bombing case.

Hofstadter, Richard. "Muckraking: The Revolution in Journalism." In his *The Age of Reform: From Bryan to F. D. R.,* pp. 185-96. New York: Alfred A. Knopf, 1965.*
 Overview of the importance of muckraking journalism to the Progressive era, with frequent mention of Steffens.

Horton, Russell M. *Lincoln Steffens.* New York: Twayne Publishers, Inc., 1974, 169 p.
 Survey of Steffens's life and career.

Joughin, Louis. Introduction to *The Shame of the Cities,* by Lincoln Steffens, pp. v-ix. New York: Hill and Wang, 1957.
 Assesses the strengths and weaknesses of Steffens's first collection of muckraking articles.

Kaplan, Justin. *Lincoln Steffens: A Biography.* New York: Simon and Schuster, 1974, 380 p.
 Definitive biography examining Steffens's life in great detail.

Kazin, Alfred. "Progressivism: The Superman and the Muckrake." In his *On Native Grounds,* pp. 91-126. New York: Harcourt, Brace and Co., 1942.*
 Surveys the development of "the modern spirit in American literature" during the Progressive period—the years 1904 through 1917—a time marked by the influence of Darwinism, imperialism, Nietzschean thought, socialism, and literary and artistic Naturalism. Steffens is mentioned throughout.

———. "A Biography of a Famous Autobiographer." *The New York Times Book Review* (31 March 1974): 3.
 Enthusiastic tribute to the "charming, fascinatingly episodic" life that Steffens portrayed in his *Autobiography* and that Justin Kaplan further explored in his biography.

Luhan, Mabel Dodge. *Movers and Shakers: Volume 3 of Intimate Memories.* New York: Harcourt, Brace and Co., 1936, 542 p.
 Contains scattered references to Steffens, whom Luhan credits with suggesting her famous "Evenings"—gatherings of prominent radicals, intellectuals, and artistic and literary figures.

Lydenberg, John. "Henry Adams and Lincoln Steffens." *The South Atlantic Quarterly* XLVIII, No. 1 (January 1949): 42-64.*
 Extensive comparison of the literary developments of Adams and Steffens within the traditions of American Naturalism.

Madison, Charles A. "Lincoln Steffens: Muckraker's Progress." In his *Critics and Crusaders: A Century of American Protest,* pp. 395-418. New York: Henry Holt & Co., 1947.
 Chronological examination of Steffens's career, emphasizing his desire not merely to uncover but to eradicate the corruption he encountered, and his later conviction that the Mexican and Russian revolutions presaged a bright future for humankind.

Pomeroy, Earl. Introduction to *Upbuilders,* by Lincoln Steffens, pp. xix-xxxvii. 1909. Reprint. Seattle: University of Washington Press, 1968.
 Calls the essays collected in *Upbuilders* a reliable indication of significant stages in Steffens's intellectual development.

Sampson, R.V. "Lincoln Steffens: An Interpretation." *The Western Political Quarterly* VIII, No. 1 (March 1955): 58-67.
 Account of Steffens's gradual development of his theories of corruption, business, politics, and government that adheres closely to Steffens's own explications of his ideological growth.

Shapiro, Herbert. "Lincoln Steffens: Light and Shadow on His Historical Image." *The American Journal of Economics and Sociology* 31, No. 3 (June 1972): 320-26.
 Survey of the major critical and biographical studies of Steffens's life and thought.

———. "Lincoln Steffens: The Muckraker Reconsidered." *The American Journal of Economics and Sociology* 31, No. 4 (October 1972): 427-38.
 Retrospective discussion of Steffens's impact on his times and his continued relevance as a thinker.

Sinclair, Upton. "Steffens: The Man and the Muckraker." *Institute of Social Studies Bulletin* I, No. 6 (Summer 1952): 62, 71-2.
 Briefly outlines Steffens's communist activities, with some personal reminiscence and comment.

Stein, Harry. "Lincoln Steffens: Interviewer." *Journalism Quarterly* 46 (Winter 1969): 727-36.
 Approbatory assessment of Steffens's persuasive and successful techniques as an interviewer.

Tarbell, Ida. *All in the Day's Work.* New York: Macmillan Co., 1939, 412 p.*
 Autobiography by a contemporary and coworker of Steffens, with frequent scattered references to Steffens.

Weinberg, Arthur, and Weinberg, Lila. *The Muckrakers: The Era in Journalism that Moved America to Reform.* New York: Capricorn Books, 1964, 449 p.*
 Collection of excerpts from the most significant muckraking articles to appear in American journals between 1902 and 1912, with prefatory comments by the editors. Several articles by Steffens are excerpted, and his career is summarized in the epilogue.

Whitfield, Stephen J. "Muckraking Lincoln Steffens." *The Virginia Quarterly Review* 54, No. 1 (Winter 1978): 87-101.
 Biographical study that explores many of the contradictions in Steffens's character and professed beliefs.

Wilson, Harold S. *McClure's Magazine and the Muckrakers.* Princeton: Princeton University Press, 1970, 347 p.*
 History of the well-known pioneer muckraking journal that includes a discussion of Steffens's contributions.

Winter, Ella. *And Not to Yield.* New York: Harcourt, Brace & World, 1963, 308 p.
 Anecdotal biography by Steffens's second wife.

Ziff, Larzer. "The School in the Cemetery: Newspapers." In his *The American 1890s: Life and Times of a Lost Generation,* pp. 146-65. New York: The Viking Press, 1966.*
 Examination of the early muckraking efforts of newspaper reporters, with numerous references to Steffens.

George Sterling

1869-1926

American poet, essayist, and playwright.

Both celebrated and condemned for his poetry, which is archaic in style yet modern in the nihilistic sensibility it expresses, Sterling was one of the major figures in the bohemian society of writers and artists who congregated around Carmel, California, in the early decades of the twentieth century. His use of traditional verse forms and classical diction links him with the poets of the nineteenth century rather than with those of the twentieth, who were at that time beginning to experiment freely with form in their work. While some critics have called Sterling's poetic style outdated, others, including such major figures as Ambrose Bierce and Theodore Dreiser, have praised the rich imagination and technical skill demonstrated in his work.

Born in Sag Harbor, New York, Sterling was the eldest son of a prosperous physician and his wife. The Sterlings were one of the most highly respected families in the area, being descendants of the first Puritan settlers, and Sterling's father was a deeply religious man who hoped that all his sons would enter the clergy. Sterling was accordingly enrolled in an appropriate course of study at St. Charles College. He was, however, a high-spirited, rebellious youth, and poorly suited for such a profession. After his third year at St. Charles, he informed his father that he did not wish to return for a fourth. At the age of twenty, having failed to select for himself a respectable vocation, Sterling was sent to Oakland, California, to work in his uncle's real estate office.

Arriving in the San Francisco Bay area in 1890, Sterling found a lusty atmosphere highly congenial to his temperament. He spent his days working in his uncle's office and his evenings socializing with bohemian artists. He soon became acquainted with one of San Francisco's most colorful figures, the flamboyant poet Joaquin Miller, whose secluded estate was a gathering place for local artists and whose homemade liquor was generously dispensed to all visitors. Stimulated by this environment, Sterling began to write poetry, often during the ferry ride from his home to his job. In 1892 he met noted author and journalist Ambrose Bierce, an event which Sterling himself considered the most important in his life. Bierce enjoyed the young poet's adulation, and when Sterling sought his counsel in the matter of poetry, he gladly assumed the role of mentor. Aided and encouraged by Bierce, Sterling began to submit his work to various publications, and in 1903 his first volume of poetry, *The Testimony of the Suns, and Other Poems,* was issued. Although Sterling's subsequent work appeared in many local publications, he did not become nationally known until 1907, when Bierce presented Sterling's poem "A Wine of Wizardry" in *Cosmopolitan* magazine. In his prefatory remarks, Bierce compared the poem to Milton's *Comus* and called Sterling the greatest poet "this side of the Atlantic." Critics were quick to refute such obviously exaggerated claims, and Bierce, notorious for his caustic wit, was equally quick to respond to their comments, insulting several critics in the process. This incident, while not entirely fortuitous, did in fact draw attention to Sterling's work, and his poetry soon began

Photograph by Ida Krajewski

to appear in such prestigious publications as the *Smart Set* and *Poetry*.

By the time "A Wine of Wizardry" appeared, Sterling was already a major Bay area celebrity, not only because his poems were locally popular, but also because his congeniality had earned for him a large coterie of distinguished friends and the unofficial title "King of Bohemia." He moved to Carmel, hoping to find both leisure and inspiration, but the solitude of his cabin was only temporary, as the bohemians soon followed their "king." Carmel thus became a thriving artists' colony, with Sterling's home serving as the center of conviviality and the site of bacchanalia, often including such literary personages as Jack London and Sinclair Lewis. Despite the constant revelry at the Carmel cabin, Sterling continued to write, if irregularly, and some of his best work was produced there. The beauty of the rugged California coastline inspired his most famous sonnets, including "The Black Vulture." Eventually, however, Sterling's excesses became a problem; after a series of tragic personal losses, including the death of his friend Jack London, he began to drink more heavily and to suffer acute gastric pain as a result. In 1926, during one such attack, he ended his life with a dose of cyanide.

Critics view Sterling's work as a continuation of several developments in nineteenth-century literature. Like the English Romantics, whom he admired greatly, Sterling used an artificial "poetic" diction and dealt with such issues as the nature of truth and beauty. His use of bizarre and grotesque imagery, his disregard for conventional morality, and his preoccupation with escape and transcendence have led several critics to connect him with the nineteenth-century school of Decadent poetry and with its progenitors Edgar Allan Poe and Charles Baudelaire. Bierce, too, was an admirer of the Romantics and the Decadents, and he strongly urged Sterling to follow their example. These influences are clearly manifested in "A Wine of Wizardry," a poem in which Sterling envisions the journey of an anthropomorphized Fancy through a fantasy world which is filled with macabre and often gruesome phenomena. While much of Sterling's work is imitative, certain aspects of it are considered highly original. An avid devotee of the science of astronomy, Sterling found the cosmos exciting and the names of celestial bodies lyrical, using them often in his poetry. His interest in the discoveries then being made in the other sciences and their philosophical implications led him to question the nature and meaning of existence, as in "The Testimony of the Suns," and to reject traditional concepts of the importance of the human race. Many critics believe that Sterling's sonnets are his best work, the strict demands of that form serving to restrain the excesses of diction and imagery that mar some of his longer pieces.

Critics generally agree that Sterling's decision to utilize traditional poetic forms and diction, whether conscious or not, was an unfortunate one, and that Bierce's counsel in this matter was detrimental to Sterling's career. Although he was highly praised by the West Coast critics of his time, he was largely ignored by the major East Coast critics, who were more impressed with radical new poets, such as Ezra Pound and HD (Hilda Doolittle), whose writings were just then beginning to appear and whose ideas were to become dominant in twentieth-century poetry. While Sterling is better known today for his colorful life and many renowned acquaintances than for his poetry, his work is generally considered to be the product of a talented and imaginative mind.

PRINCIPAL WORKS

The Testimony of the Suns, and Other Poems (poetry)
  1903
The Triumph of Bohemia (drama) [first publication] 1907
A Wine of Wizardry, and Other Poems (poetry) 1909
The House of Orchids, and Other Poems (poetry) 1911
Beyond the Breakers, and Other Poems (poetry) 1914
*Ode on the Opening of the Panama and Pacific
  International Exposition* (poetry) 1915
The Caged Eagle, and Other Poems (poetry) 1916
The Binding of the Beast, and Other War Verse (poetry)
  1917
Lilith (drama) [first publication] 1919
Rosamund (drama) [first publication] 1920
Sails and Mirage (poetry) 1921
Selected Poems (poetry) 1923
Truth (drama) [first publication] 1923
Robinson Jeffers: The Man and the Artist (criticism) 1926
Sonnets to Craig (poetry) 1928
After Sunset (poetry) 1939
"Some Letters of George Sterling" (letters) 1961;
    published in journal *California Historical Society
    Quarterly*
"Seventeen George Sterling Letters" (letters) 1968;
    published in journal *Jack London Newsletter*

"Letters of George Sterling to James Branch Cabell"
    (letters) 1972; published in journal *American
    Literature*
"George Sterling's Letters to the Upton Sinclairs: A
    Selection" (letters) 1973; published in journal
    American Book Collector
"Pleasure and Pain" (essay) 1973; published in journal
    Resources for American Literary Studies

THE NEW YORK TIMES (essay date 1904)

[*In the following excerpt, the critic reviews* The Testimony of the Suns, and Other Poems.]

In *The Testimony of the Suns and Other Poems,* by George Sterling, there is no effort toward originality in either subject or phraseology, but there is a nice sense of personal vision and thoughtful contemplation, and also there is a touch of intellectual passion that gives to the author's mental attitude toward common things the delicate dignity and reserve in utterance most grateful to the mind weary of an overflow of sentiment....

In his dedicatory poem Mr. Sterling questions the right of art to exist for its own sake independent of moral and utilitarian ends:

> Shall Art annul and Song disclaim
>   The laws that guard their deeper good?
>   Or hold so little understood
> The larger issues of their fame?
>
> Can Song accord the light she brings
>   In crypts where beauty never woke!
>   Share with Utility his yoke,
> Yet roam her sky on lucent wings?

The question is one that must sooner or later present itself to every serious mind by which art is seriously regarded, and Mr. Sterling is not, of course, asking an answer from any but his own spirit. The doubt so sincerely and gravely expressed in his poem suggests, however, what Henry James wrote long ago in discussing the ethical equipment of Charles Baudelaire. "To deny the relevancy of subject matter and the importance of the moral quality of a work of art strikes us as, in two words, very childish ... to count out the moral element in one's appreciation of an artistic total is exactly as sane as it would be (if the total were a poem) to eliminate all the words in three syllables, or to consider only such portions of it as had been written by candle light. It is simply a part of the essential richness of inspiration, it has nothing to do with the artistic effect. The more a work of art feels it at its source, the richer it is: the less it feels it the poorer it is." This is the clearest possible expression of the standard accepted by all great artists, and the presence of the moral quality at the source of Mr. Sterling's poetry is what gives it the note of character that promises permanence. And he has been able to deliver his message without contortions of style. In his management of his simple metres and in his discriminating use of words fitted to his thought he gives the pleasure that can be gained only from such respectful use of the intellectual instrument.

> "The Versifiers," in The New York Times, *March
> 12, 1904, p. 172.**

AMBROSE BIERCE   (essay date 1907)

[*Bierce was an American short story writer, journalist, essayist, and critic whose literary reputation is based on his short stories of the Civil War and of the supernatural; the latter are often compared to the works of Edgar Allan Poe. Like Poe, Bierce professed to be primarily concerned with the artistry of his fiction, yet critics find him more intent on conveying his personal misanthropy and pessimism. Bierce is also noted for his journalistic work, which manifests the author's personality in its sardonic wit and acerbic tone. In the following excerpt from his comments prefacing the first appearance of* "A Wine of Wizardry" *in the September, 1907, issue of* Cosmopolitan *magazine, Bierce praises Sterling's poem.*]

In this remarkable poem ["**A Wine of Wizardry**"] the author proves his allegiance to the fundamental faith of the greatest of those "who claim the holy Muse as mate"—a faith which he has himself "confessed" thus:

> Remiss the ministry they bear
>   Who serve her with divided heart;
>   She stands reluctant to impart
> Her strength to purpose, end, or care.

Here, as in all his work, we shall look in vain for the "practical," the "helpful." The verses serve no cause, tell no story, point no moral. Their author has no "purpose, end, or care" other than the writing of poetry. His work is as devoid of motive as is the song of a skylark—it is merely poetry. No one knows what poetry is, but to the enlightened few who know what is poetry it is a rare and deep delight to find it in the form of virgin gold. "Gold," says the miner "vext with odious subtlety" of the mineralogist with his theories of deposit—"gold is where you find it." It is no less precious whether you have crushed it from the rock, or washed it from the gravel, but some of us care to be spared the labor of reduction, or sluicing. Mr. Sterling's reader needs no outfit of mill and pan.

I am not of those who deem it a service to letters to "encourage" mediocrity—that is one of the many ways to starve genius. From the amiable judgment of the "friendly critic" with his heart in his head, otherwise unoccupied, and the *laudator literarum* who finds every month, or every week—according to his employment by magazine or newspaper—more great books than I have had the luck to find in a half-century, I dissent. My notion is that an age which produces a half-dozen good writers and twenty books worth reading is a memorable age. I think, too, that contemporary criticism is of small service, and popular acclaim of none at all, in enabling us to know who are the good authors and which the good books. Naturally, then, I am not overtrustful of my own judgment, nor hot in hope of its acceptance. Yet I steadfastly believe and hardily affirm that George Sterling is a very great poet—incomparably the greatest that we have on this side of the Atlantic. And of this particular poem I hold that not in a lifetime has our literature had any new thing of equal length containing so much poetry and so little else. It is as full of light and color and fire as any of the "ardent gems" that burn and sparkle in its lines. It has all the imagination of *Comus* and all the fancy of *The Faerie Queene*. If Leigh Hunt should return to earth to part and catalogue these two precious qualities he would find them in so confusing abundance and so inextricably interlaced that he would fly in despair from the impossible task.

Great lines are not all that go to the making of great poetry, but a poem with many great lines is a great poem, even if it have—as usually it has, and as "**A Wine of Wizardry**" has not—prosaic lines as well. (pp. 179-82)

One of a poet's most authenticating credentials may be found in his epithets. In them is the supreme ordeal to which he must come and from which is no appeal. The epithets of the versifier, the mere metrician, are either contained in their substantives or add nothing that is worth while to the meaning; those of the true poet are instinct with novel and felicitous significances. They personify, ennoble, exalt, spiritualize, endow with thought and feeling, touch to action like the spear of Ithuriel. The prosaic mind can no more evolve such than ditch-water in a champagne-glass can sparkle and effervesce, or cold iron give off coruscations when hammered. Have the patience to consider a few of Mr. Sterling's epithets, besides those in the lines already quoted:

"Purpled" realm; "striving" billows; "wattled" monsters; "timid" sapphires of the snow; "lit" wastes; a "stainèd" twilight of the South; "tiny" twilight in the jacinth, and "wintry" orb of the moonstone; "winy" agate and "banded" onyx; "lustrous" rivers; "glowering" pyres of the burning-ghaut, and so forth.

Do such words come by taking thought? Do they come ever to the made poet?—to the "poet of the day"—poet by resolution of a "committee on literary exercises"? Fancy the poor pretender, conscious of his pretense and sternly determined to conceal it, laboring with a brave confusion of legs and a copious excretion of honest sweat to evolve felicities like these! (pp. 185-86)

> Ambrose Bierce, "A Poet and His Poem," in his
> The Collected Works of Ambrose Bierce: The Opinionator, Vol. X, *Gordian Press, Inc., 1966, pp.
> 177-86.*

AMBROSE BIERCE   (essay date 1907)

[*In the following excerpt from the December, 1907, issue of* Cosmopolitan *magazine, Bierce responds to the criticism provoked by his introduction to the first publication of* "A Wine of Wizardry."]

When a man of genius who is not famous writes a notable poem he must expect one or two of three things: indifference, indignation, ridicule. In commending Mr. George Sterling's "**A Wine of Wizardry**" . . . , I had this reception of his work in confident expectation and should have mistrusted my judgment if it had not followed. The promptitude of the chorus of denunciation and scorn has attested the superb character of the poet's work and is most gratifying.

The reason for the inevitable note of dissent is not far to seek; it inheres in the constitution of the human mind, which is instinctively hostile to what is "out of the common"—and a work of genius is pretty sure to be that. It is by utterance of uncommon thoughts, opinions, sentiments and fancies that genius is known. All distinction is difference, unconformity. He who is as others are—whose mental processes and manner of expression follow the familiar order—is readily acceptable because easily intelligible to those whose narrow intelligence, barren imagination, and meager vocabulary he shares. "Why, that is great!" says that complacent dullard, "the average man," smiling approval. "I have thought that a hundred times myself!"—thereby providing abundant evidence that it is not great, nor of any value whatever. To "the average man" what is new is inconceivable, and what he does not understand affronts him. And he is the first arbiter in letters and art. In this "fierce democracie" he dominates literature with a fat and heavy hand—

a hand that is not always unfamiliar with the critic's pen. (pp. 189-90)

Naturally, not all protagonists of the commonplace who have uttered their minds about this matter are entitled to notice. The Baseball Reporter who, says Mr. Brisbane, "like Mr. Sterling, is a poet," the Sweet Singer of Slang, the Simian Lexicographer of Misinformation, and the Queen of Platitudinaria who has renounced the sin-and-sugar of youth for the milk-and-morality of age must try to forgive me if I leave them grinning through their respective horse-collars to a not unkind inattention.

But Deacon Harvey is a person of note and consequence. On a question of poetry, I am told, he controls nearly the entire Methodist vote. Moreover, he has a notable knack at mastery of the English language, which he handles with no small part of the ease and grace that may have distinguished the impenitent thief carrying his cross up the slope of Calvary. Let the following noble sentences attest the quality of his performance when he is at his best:

> A natural hesitation to undertake analysis of the unanalyzable, criticism of the uncriticizable, or, if we may go so far, mention of the unmentionable, yields to your own shrewd forging of the links of circumstance into a chain of duty. That the greatest poem ever written on this hemisphere, having forced its way out of a comfortable lodgment in the brain of an unknown author, should be discovered and heralded by a connoisseur whose pre-eminence is yet to be established, is perhaps in itself not surprising, and yet we must admit that the mere rarity of such a happening would ordinarily preclude the necessity, which otherwise might exist, of searching inquiry as to the attributed transcendentalism of merit.

Surely a man who habitually writes such prose as that must be a good judge of poetry or he would not be a good judge of anything in literature. And what does this Prince Paramount of grace and clarity find to condemn in poor Mr. Sterling's poem? Listen with at least one ear each:

> We are willing to admit at the outset that in the whole range of American, or, for that matter, English, poetry there is no example of a poem crowded with such startling imagery, ambitiously marshaled in lines of such lurid impressiveness, all of which at once arrest attention and would bewilder the esthetic sensibility of a Titan. The poem is made up of an unbroken series of sententious and striking passages, any one of which would have distinguished a whole canto of Dante or Keats, neither of whom would have ventured within that limit to use more than one—such was their niggardly economy.

Here is something "rich and strange" in criticism. Heretofore it has been thought that "wealth of imagery" was about the highest quality that poetry could have, but it seems not; that somewhat tiresome phrase is to be used henceforth to signify condemnation. Of the poem that we wish to commend we must say that it has an admirable poverty of imagination. Deacon Harvey's notion that poets like Dante and Keats deliberately refrained from using more than one "sententious and striking passage" to the canto "goes near to be fonny." They used as many as occurred to them; no poet uses fewer than he can. If he has only one to a canto, that is not economy; it is indigence.

I observe that even so good a poet and so appreciative a reader of Mr. Sterling as Miss Ina Coolbrith has fallen into the same error as Deacon Harvey. Of "the many pictures presented in that wondrous **'Wine of Wizardry,'**" this accomplished woman says: "I think it is a 'poem'—a great poem—but one which, in my humble estimate, might have been made even greater could its creator have permitted himself to drop a little of what some may deem a weakening superfluity of imagery and word-painting."

If one is to make "pictures" in poetry one must do so by word-painting. (I admit the hatefulness of the term "word-painting," through overuse of the name in praise of the prose that the thing defaces, but it seems that we must use it here.) Only in narrative and didactic poetry, and these are the lowest forms, can there be too much of imagery and word-painting; in a poem essentially graphic, like the one under consideration, they are the strength and soul of the work. **"A Wine of Wizardry"** is, and was intended to be, a series, a succession, of unrelated pictures, colored (mostly red, naturally) by what gave them birth and being—the reflection of a sunset in a cup of ruddy wine. To talk of too much imagery in a work of that kind is to be like Deacon Harvey.

Imagery, that is to say, imagination, is not only the life and soul of poetry; it is the poetry. That is what Poe had in mind doubtless, when he contended that there could be no such thing as a long poem. He had observed that what are called long poems consist of brief poetical passages connected by long passages of metrical prose—*recitativo*—of oases of green in deserts of gray. The highest flights of imagination have always been observed to be the briefest. George Sterling has created a new standard, another criterion. In **"A Wine of Wizardry,"** as in his longer and greater poem, **"The Testimony of the Suns,"** there is no *recitativo*. His imagination flies with a tireless wing. It never comes to earth for a new spring into the sky, but like the eagle and the albatross, sustains itself as long as he chooses that it shall. His passages of poetry are connected by passages of poetry. In all his work you will find no line of prose. Poets of the present and the future may well "view with alarm" as Statesman Harvey would say—the work that Sterling has cut out for them, the pace that he has set. Poetry must henceforth be not only qualitative but quantitative: it must be *all* poetry. If wise, the critic will note the new criterion that this bold challenge to the centuries has made mandatory. The "long poem" has been shown to be possible; let us see if it become customary.

In affirming Mr. Sterling's primacy among living American poets I have no apology to offer to the many unfortunates who have written to me in the spirit of the man who once said of another: "What! that fellow a great man? Why, he was born right in my town!" It is humbly submitted, however, that unless the supply of great men is exhausted they must be born somewhere, and the fact that they are seen "close to" by their neighbors does not supply a reasonable presumption against their greatness. Shakspeare himself was once a local and contemporary poet, and even Homer is known to have been born in "seven Grecian cities" through which he "begged his bread." Is Deacon Harvey altogether sure that he is immune to the popular inability to understand that the time and place of a poet's nativity are not decisive as to his rating? He may find a difficulty in believing that a singer of supreme excellence was born right in *his* country and period, but in the words that I have quoted from him he has himself testified to the fact. To be able to write ''an unbroken series of sententious and striking passages''; to crowd a poem, as no other in the whole range of our literature has done, with ''startling imagery'' ''in lines of impressiveness,'' lurid or not; to ''arrest attention''; to ''bewilder the Titans,'' Deacon Harvey at their head—that is about as much as the most ambitious poet could wish to accomplish at one sitting. The ordinary harpist harping on his Harpers' would be a long time in doing so much. How any commentator, having in those words conceded my entire claim, could afterward have the hardihood to say, ''The poem has no merit,'' transcends the limits of human comprehension and passes into the dark domain of literary criticism.

Nine in ten of the poem's critics complain of the fantastic, grotesque, or ghastly nature of its fancies. What would these good persons have on the subject of wizardry?—sweet and sunny pictures of rural life?—love scenes in urban drawing-rooms?—beautiful sentiments appropriate to young ladies' albums?—high moral philosophy with an ''appeal'' to what is ''likest God within the soul''? Deacon Harvey (O, I cannot get away from Deacon Harvey: he fascinates me!) would have ''an interpretation of vital truth.'' I do not know what that is, but we have his word for it that nothing else is poetry. And no less a personage than Mrs. Gertrude Atherton demands, instead of wizardry, an epic of prehistoric California, or an account of the great fire, preferably in prose, for, ''this is not an age of poetry, anyway.'' Alas, poor Sterling!—damned alike for what he wrote and what he didn't write. Truly, there are persons whom one may not hope to please.

It should in fairness be said that Mrs. Atherton confesses herself no critic of poetry—the only person, apparently, who is not—but pronounces Mr. Sterling a ''recluse'' who ''needs to see more and read less.'' From a pretty long acquaintance with him I should say that this middle-aged man o' the world is as little ''reclusive'' as any one that I know, and has seen rather more of life than is good for him. And I doubt if he would greatly gain in mental stature by unreading Mrs. Atherton's excellent novels.

Sterling's critics are not the only persons who seem a bit blinded by the light of his genius: Mr. Joaquin Miller, a born poet and as great-hearted a man as ever lived, is not quite able to ''place'' him. He says that this ''titanic, magnificent'' poem is ''classic'' ''in the Homeric, the Miltonic sense.'' **''A Wine of Wizardry''** is not ''classic'' in the sense in which scholars use that word. It is all color and fire and movement, with nothing of the cold simplicity and repose of the Grecian ideal. Nor is it Homeric, nor in the Miltonic vein. It is in no vein but the author's own; in the entire work is only one line suggesting the manner of another poet—the last in this passage:

> Who leads from hell his whitest queens, arrayed
> In chains so heated at their master's fire
> That one new-damned had thought their bright attire
> Indeed were coral, till the dazzling dance
> So terribly that brilliance shall enhance.

That line, the least admirable in the poem, is purely Byronic. Possibly Mr. Miller meant that Sterling's work is like Homer's and Milton's, not in manner, but in excellence; and it is. (pp. 192-201)

Ambrose Bierce, ''An Insurrection of the Peasantry,'' in his The Collected Works of Ambrose Bierce:

The Opinionator, Vol. X, *Gordian Press, Inc., 1966, pp. 189-208.*

BRIAN HOOKER   (essay date 1909)

[In the following excerpt, Hooker praises Sterling's facility as a poet but criticizes the absence in his work of ideas or a philosophy.]

Stevenson once said that a young man had better begin the profession of letters by learning to string words together beautifully; then, if he should later have great things to say, he would have the means of saying them. Mr. Sterling has naturally an ear and a gift of striking phrase; and he has developed these into some power of verse and the foundations of a style. He feels life vividly, though with a certain carelessness of simple and common things which may be a sign of aspiration; for while a man is still Endymion to each new moon, he is not yet ready to appreciate a blade of grass. Mr. Sterling is thus by way of being able to express whatever may be given to him. As yet, his work has embodied no very important ideas, and his style, therefore, as a powerful creature unyoked, shows a tendency to prance wantonly, rising at times into a plangent fanfare of declamation or lapsing into languorous dalliance of delicious words. . . . **''A Wine of Wizardry,''** which has already been unreasonably praised, sins notably in both respects, and illustrates, moreover, another of his faults, the tendency to loose incoherence of structure in his longer poems. It is probably the worst thing in [*A Wine of Wizardry, and Other Poems*]. Among the best is the sonnet to Romance:

> Thou passest, and we know thee not, Romance!
>   Thy gaze is backward, and thy heart is fed
>   With murmurs and with music of the dead.
> Alas, out battle! for the rays that glance
> On thy dethroning sword and haughty lance
>   Are of forgotten suns and stars long fled;
>   Thou weavest phantom roses for thy head,
> And ghostly queens in thy dominion dance.
>
> Would we might follow thy returning wings,
>   And in thy farthest haven beach our prow—
>   Thy dragons conquered and thine oceans crossed—
> And find thee standing on the dust of kings,
>   A lion at thy side, and on thy brow
>   The light of sunsets wonderful and lost!

Rhetoric, perhaps; but how many living Americans can be so successfully rhetorical? And **''Tasso to Leonora''** shows a power of lyric monologue still more potential.

> Never had lover's dusk such moon as thou!
> Never had moon adoring such as mine!
> For at thy spirit in her majesty
> Mine own is greatly humbled, and forgets
> Its haughtiness, forsaking at thy feet
> Song's archangelic panoply of light,
> And sits a child before thee, and is glad.
> Yea, though I deem the silences of love
> More beautiful than music, or the hush
> Of ocean twilights, yet my soul to thine
> Swoons deaf and blind, with living lips that ache
> And cry to thee its joy and wonderment.

The man who can write like this may go far, if his nature grows into a message to humanity; or, if he purveys the blossom for the fruit, or has already reached his uttermost, may degenerate into a mere maker of pleasant noises. It is too soon to be sure of a new poet; time will show. (pp. 371-72)

Brian Hooker, "*Some Springtime Verse,*" *in* The Bookman, *New York, Vol. XXIX, No. 4, June, 1909, pp. 365-72.**

THE NEW YORK TIMES   (essay date 1911)

[*In the following excerpt, the critic reviews* The House of Orchids, and Other Poems.]

The saying goes that poets are born, not made, but the fact is, there is a superfluity of both kinds. It is a pity that the two so seldom exist in combination. If Mr. George Sterling had died immediately after the publication of **"The Testimony of the Suns"** and **"A Wine of Wizardry"** he might have been considered a very perfect example of the "born" poet. They were noteworthy, not so much as poetry—though that was not lacking—as a stage in fermentation. **"A Wine of Wizardry,"** in particular, was a wild welter of adjectives rising from working genius. In [*The House of Orchids*], however, . . . Mr. Sterling has added to his earlier unusual qualities of imagination and of expression the restraint needed to make them truly effective. It contains no verse descriptive of "the bleeding sun's phantasmagoric gules," nor of "the blue-eyed vampire" smiling against a "leprous moon," but one could quote from it an hundred lines of exceptional beauty. . . .

Next to restraint, the most marked gain that Mr. Sterling shows in this volume over those that have preceded it, is in a sense of proportion. Here and there, however, we still feel a slight lack of it. It intrudes a comic line (to our gasoline-steeped sense) in a charming poem, **"The Faun":**

> At noon great Caesar's chariot past,
> A poison on the air—

It hails that diligent harrower of the literary field, Mr. Ambrose Bierce, as "Thou eagle who hast gazed upon the sun." But that is a small tribute, considering that Mr. Bierce has been hailing Mr. Sterling for some years past as the greatest poet on this side of the Atlantic. And since Mr. Bierce's hail seems likely to be justified, now that Mr. Sterling has found himself, there is a possibility that Mr. Bierce, in his turn, may yet qualify for eaglehood. So, on second thought, it may be wise to suspend judgment even on a point which at first seemed a fair mark for criticism!

"The House of Orchids," which gives its exotic and suggestive name to the book—Mr. Sterling has a genius for titles—is often exquisite, but, like the flower itself, carries no universal appeal. **"An Altar of the West,"** on the other hand, is just as finely wrought and voices to a degree that inarticulate emotion, the ache of beauty, which every man, in his own way, has at one time or another felt.

> Beauty, what dost thou here?
> Why hauntest thou the House where
>   Death is lord
>   And o'er thy crown appear
> The inexorable shadow and the sword?
> Art not a mad mirage above a grave?

> The foam foredriven of a perished
>   wave?
>   A clarion afar?
> A lily on the waters of despond?
> A ray that leaping from our whitest
>   star
> Shows but the night beyond?
> And yet thou seemest more than all
>   the rest
>   That eye and ear attest—
> A watch-tower on the mountains
>   whence we see
>   On future skies
>   The rose of dawn to be;
> The altar of an undiscovered shore;
> A dim assurance and a proud surmise;
>   A gleam
>   Upon the bubble, Time;
> The vision fleet, sublime,
> Of sorrowed man, the brute that dared
>   to dream.

"*A Poet Who Finds Himself,*" *in* The New York Times, *June 25, 1911, p. 400.*

EDWIN MARKHAM   (essay date 1914)

[*Markham was an American poet, critic, and protégé of Ambrose Bierce. His best-known poem, "The Man with the Hoe," is typical of his work, exhibiting strong rhythms, a declamatory style, and an element of socialist political philosophy. In the following excerpt, Markham praises the lyric beauty of Sterling's work.*]

George Sterling has four books of poems to prove him a poet of fine imaginative powers. His poems carry a certain relish of eternity in their themes and their implications. They sing of stars and seas and the soul's high dreams. Even the flower, in its frail duration of an hour, he looks at from God's side, trying to find its larger meaning in the plan of infinity. The orchid brings him intimations of eternity, of mystery, of some marvelous beauty-loving power at the soul of things.

The sea speaks for him a various language, hinting unfathomable desire for vision or announcement, sounding the antiphone of the might-have-been and the nevermore-to-be:

> The echo of man's travail on the wind,
> A sigh of great departures, and the breath
> Of pinions incontestable by death.

The night also brings to this poet secrets and sorceries:

> Where seas of dream break on a phantom shore
> To mysteries of music evermore.

Although Mr. Sterling's verse has not the local color that Wordsworth and Burns afford the tourist, still his landscapes have the large freedom of his own Pacific. His poem, **"An Altar of the West,"** is full of the magic and the majesty of the cypressed cliffs that hold back his western seas:

> Past Carmel lies a headland that the deep—
>   A Titan at his toil—
> Has graven with the measured surge and sweep
> Of waves that broke ten thousand years ago.

Thus he opens an ode of lofty music and meanings. His nature poems are not finished with the jeweled work of Madison Cawein. Yet in **"A Wine of Wizardry,"** which took our hearts with its strange beauty, Mr. Sterling shows his feeling for color and luster of phrase and line, as he does also in his dim-gleaming **"Gardens of the Sea."**

Mr. Sterling's **"Wine of Wizardry"** raised in the literary world the question, "Is it a great poem?" The chief difficulty in answering this question lies in the fact that **"A Wine of Wizardry"** can scarcely be called a poem. It does not seem to me to have the organic unity essential to every work of art. Mr. Sterling gives us the words, the images and the fine lines; but they are not fused into a living whole.

In every literary creation there must be a central figure with something that corresponds to a woven plot followed by a consistent crisis. There must be dramatic movement. The central figure in a poem is often only a unifying Idea; yet this must be there to serve as the pivot for the wheel of the action.

In brief, every work of art must be organic. It must come forth like a living thing; so unified that no part can be torn away without destroying the beauty and symmetry of the whole. If any part can be taken away without offense, then that part is surplus and renders the work inartistic.

Now, in **"A Wine of Wizardry"** the parts have no vital union. You can omit a passage, and yet the rest will not be affected: you will feel no sense of deficiency. The passages can even be shifted about without disturbing our sense of harmony.

It may be that Mr. Sterling intended to give us only a series of weird pictures. If so, he has made a remarkable success. As you read his wizard pages, you feel as though you were voyaging up some tropic stream darkened with excess of foliage and bloom, where through the rifts in the leafy roofs you get glimpses of a blazing sky, or catch at times the iris flash of giant flowers or brilliant birds, the gleam of jeweled lizards or the coil of coruscating serpents. Considered as a series of gorgeous dissolving views, **"A Wine of Wizardry"** is unequaled by anything else in our literature: it stands alone, a marvel of color and verbal beauty.

In his sonnets, George Sterling holds a high place—perhaps the highest in our American achievement in this field. Longfellow's exquisite sonnets have less imaginative sweep. Mr. Sterling works out his sonnets under the strict laws of the art. They are not merely fourteen chance lines: they have an organic unity. The octet contains the swell of the billow, and the sextet contains its harmonious subsidence. More than this, the rhymes are arranged according to the hard terms of the Petrarchian model. Mr. Sterling's most striking sonnet sequence is his daring trio on **"Oblivion."** (pp. 356-59)

> *Edwin Markham, "Intellectual California: A Few of Her Story-Writers, Poets, Painters, Scientists, Historians," in his* California the Wonderful, *Hearst's International Library Co., 1914, pp. 328-77.**

H. M. [HARRIET MONROE] (essay date 1916)

[*As the founder and editor of* Poetry, *Monroe was a key figure in the American "poetry renaissance" that took place in the early twentieth century.* Poetry *was the first periodical devoted primarily to the works of new poets and to poetry criticism, and from 1912 until her death in 1936 Monroe maintained an editorial policy of printing "the best English verse which is being written today, regardless of where, by whom, or under what theory of art it is written." In the following excerpt, Monroe comments on Sterling's unrealized poetic potential.*]

The Pacific states are loyal to their own artists to a degree which other sections of this vast nation might well emulate. Because, in spite of the manifest danger of provincialism, art, like charity, should begin at home; indeed, must begin at home if it is not to be a wanderer on the face of the earth, seeking forlornly an alien audience.

So it was a satisfaction to discover, everywhere along "The Coast," a devotion to Mr. George Sterling which was not alone enthusiasm for his poetry, but also pride in him as a personality and a possession. As California loves Keith and certain later painters because they were—and are—faithful interpreters of her beauty, so she rewards this poet for his love of her.

One can forgive her if she seems to overrate him. I own to my surprise on hearing one enthusiast call him "the greatest poet since Dante," and on finding him the only living poet whose words were inscribed—along with Confucius and Firdausi, with Shakespeare and Goethe, on the triumphal arches of the Panama-Pacific Exposition. I rubbed my eyes—had I been blind and deaf? In 1909 and 1911 I had read *A Wine of Wizardry* and *The House of Orchids* without discovering a poet of the first order. Manifestly, I must re-read these books, and add the poet's first volume, *The Testimony of the Suns,* and his latest, *Beyond the Breakers*. All of which I have done.

Now, if I can not quite rise to the Californian estimate, at least I find in Mr. Sterling a gift, a poetic impulse, which might have carried him much further than it has as yet. His first long poem, **"The Testimony of the Suns,"** does indeed make one feel the sidereal march, make one shiver before the immensity and shining glory of the universe—this in spite of shameless rhetoric which often threatens to engulf the theme beyond redemption, and in spite of the whole second part, an unhappy afterthought. Already the young poet's brilliant but too facile craftsmanship was tempted by the worst excesses of the Tennysonian tradition: he never *thinks*—he *deems*; he does not *ask*, but *crave*; he is *fain* for this and that; he deals in *emperies* and *auguries* and *antiphons*, in *causal throes* and *lethal voids*—in many other things of tinsel and fustian, the frippery of a bygone fashion. He can smother his idea in such pompous phrasing as this:

> Shall yet your feet essay, unharmed,
> 　The glare of cosmic leaguers met
> 　Round stellar strongholds gulfward set,
> With night and fire supremely armed?

And yet this is the poet, and this the poem, capable at times of lyric rapture:

> O Deep whose very silence stuns!
> 　Where Light is powerless to illume,
> 　Lost in immensities of gloom
> That dwarf to motes the flaring suns. . . .
> 　　　　　　　　　　　　　(pp. 307-08)

If I dwell upon this early poem, it is because the best and worst qualities of the poet are in it. His later work never gives us such a hint of grandeur, or falls into deeper abysses of rhetoric. *A Wine of Wizardry* leaves me cold. I don't care whether

> So Fancy's carvel seeks an isle afar
> Led by the Scorpion's rubescent star,

or whether

> She wanders to an iceberg oriflammed
> With rayed auroral guidons of the North.

In fact, I cannot follow the poor lady's meanderings through a maze of words. And although the next book, *The House of Orchids,* contains a good poem in simpler diction, **"The Faun,"** and two or three fine sonnets, especially **"Aldebaran at Dusk,"** it does not fulfil the promise of the first volume. Nor does the latest book.

Beyond the Breakers begins thus:

> The world was full of the sound of a great wind
>   out of the West,
> And the tracks of its feet were white on the trampled
>   ocean's breast.
> And I said, "With the sea and wind I will mix my
>   body and soul,
> Where the breath of the planet drives and the
>   herded billows roll."

>   (pp. 310-11)

The truth is, this sort of pomposity has died the death. If the imagists have done nothing else, they have punctured the gas bag—English poetry will be henceforth more compact and stern— "as simple as prose," perhaps. . . .

When Mr. Sterling learns to avoid the "luscious tongue" and the "honeyed wine," he may become the poet he was meant to be. (p. 311)

> *H. M.* [*Harriet Monroe*], *"The Poetry of George Sterling,"* in Poetry, *Vol. VII, No. VI, March, 1916, pp. 307-13.*

JOHN GOULD FLETCHER   (essay date 1923)

[*Fletcher was an American critic and poet. Initially associated with Ezra Pound and the Imagists, he later became linked to the Southern Agrarians, a group which sought to preserve the traditional values and rural character of the American South through both literature and political activism. His poetry often incorporates elements drawn from other art forms, such as music and painting, and is considered innovative and influential. In the following excerpt, Fletcher attacks the philosophical nihilism that he perceives in Sterling's poetry.*]

It is obvious that [George Sterling] is no victim of a craze for self-advertisement, that he has not been turned away from his early vocation by too immediate a success. Rather is his the case of an arrested mental development. His first book, *The Testimony of the Suns,* contains in essence all that he has ever said since. He is one of those unfortunate beings who early become aware of the thought that man is quite probably an insignificant and contemptible accident in the cosmic process of the universe. He has never been able to comfort himself with the thought that even if human life matters nothing whatever to the indifferent and changeless gods, it is for us to make it matter a good deal to ourselves. He has become the victim of his own corroding scepticism, a scepticism common enough in our modern industrial and competitive democracies—a scepticism which is in itself a symptom of that disease which has been eating at the vitals of the world since the beginning of the nineteenth century. *The Testimony of the Suns,* which still remains after twenty years his chief contribution to American poetry, is, despite its too-pompous verbalism, a noble and inspiring achievement, utterly defeating its own ends. It sets out to preach negation, the vanity of human effort, the uselessness of human life. But it convinces us exactly of the contrary. If life is the vain illusion that Mr. Sterling would persuade us it is, then we have only to struggle a little harder,

that is all. We have but one task before us, to make our illusions divinely perfect by sacrificing mind, heart and soul to the cause, not of the gods, but of mankind. This, which Keats saw, Mr. Sterling can not see, and therefore he has remained purblind— a versifier lavishing his craft on subjects beneath the dignity of a true poet. (pp. 548-49)

> *John Gould Fletcher, "Out Where the West Begins," in* The Freeman, *Vol. VII, No. 179, August 15, 1923, pp. 548-49.*

LOUIS UNTERMEYER   (essay date 1923)

[*A poet during his early career, Untermeyer is better known as an anthologist of poetry and short fiction, an editor, and a master parodist. Horace Gregory and Marya Zaturenska have noted that Untermeyer was "the first to recognize the importance of the anthology in voicing a critical survey of his chosen field." Notable among his anthologies are* Modern American Poetry *(1919),* The Book of Living Verse *(1931),* A Treasury of Laughter *(1946), and* New Modern American and British Poetry *(1950). Untermeyer was a contributing editor to the* Liberator *and the* Seven Arts, *and served as poetry editor of the* American Mercury *from 1934 to 1937. In the following excerpt, he discusses some strengths and weaknesses of Sterling's poetry.*]

Sterling's rhetoric is high-pitched, strepitant, unrestrained; a flamboyance that finds expression in the very titles of his volumes: [*The Testimony of the Suns, A Wine of Wizardry, The House of Orchids, The Binding of the Beast*]. . . . The long poems are full of oratorical trumpets; they move to such brassy declamations as:

> Shall augury his goal impart,
>   Or mind his hidden steps retrace
> To mausolean pits of space
> Where throbs the Hydra's crimson heart?
>
> Ephemeral, may Life declare
>   What quarry from the Lion runs,
>   And sways the inexorable suns
> Where gape the abysses of his lair?

It is a glittering and archaic vocabulary on which Sterling depends; too often his theatrical effects are conjured up by clouds of polysyllabic adjectives and the repetition of such epithets as "abysmal flame," "firmamental gloom," "darkened vastitude," "warring voids," "long passion-swoons," "leprous moon," "Night's primordial realm." In one quatrain (the last of **"The Swimmers"**), he can employ three such rumbling classicisms as "evanescent," "immeasured," "immaculate." (pp. 290-91)

But Sterling is not always so prodigal with his pomposities. In his *Selected Poems* . . . , many of the shorter poems are more controlled if not quieter. Of its *genre,* the last of the three sonnets on Oblivion is characteristic.

"THE DUST DETHRONED"

> Sargon is dust, Semiramis a clod!
>   In crypts profaned the moon at midnight peers;
>   The owl upon the Sphinx hoots in her ears,
> And scant and sere the desert grasses nod
> Where once the armies of Assyria trod,
>   With younger sunlight splendid on the spears;
>   The lichens cling the closer with the years,
> And seal the eyelids of the weary god.

Where high the tombs of royal Egypt heave,
The vulture shadows with arrested wings
The indecipherable boasts of kings,
    As Arab children hear their mother's cry
And leave in mockery their toy . . . they leave
    The skull of Pharaoh staring at the sky.

Occasionally Sterling speaks in a less vociferous pitch; there are times when he allows a mood to sing itself without forcing his note or intensifying the *timbre*. **"The Last Days"** is one of the most successful of these simpler moments; a calm rhythm that flows gravely to its calmer conclusion.

    Days departing linger and sigh:
    Stars come soon to the quiet sky;
    Buried voices, intimate, strange,
    Cry to body and soul of change;
    Beauty, eternal, fugitive,
    Seeks the home that we cannot give.

Such couplets, less dazzling than the gaudy imagery of the more orotund stanzas, have more chance of surviving. It is when his ornate tropes cease trying to impress us, that Sterling is most impressive. **"The Black Vulture,"** his best as well as his best-known sonnet, emphasizes his ability to be forceful without the strained extravagance. (pp. 291-92)

> Louis Untermeyer, *"The Traditionalists," in his* American Poetry since 1900, *Holt, Rinehart & Winston, Publishers, 1923, pp. 286-304.**

THEODORE DREISER   (essay date 1926)

[*Considered among America's foremost novelists, Dreiser was one of the principal American exponents of literary Naturalism. He is known primarily for his novels* Sister Carrie *(1901),* An American Tragedy *(1926), and the Frank Cowperwood trilogy (1912-47); in each the author combined his vision of life as a meaningless series of animal impulses with a sense of sentimentality and pity for humanity's lot. Deeply concerned with the human condition but contemptuous of traditional social, political, and religious remedies, Dreiser associated for many years with the American socialist and communist movements, an interest reflected in much of his writing after 1925. In the following excerpt from his introduction to* Lilith, *Dreiser praises the beauty of Sterling's dramatic poem.*]

The deepest impression I take after several readings of this exalted lyric drama is one of noble and even ecstatic lines and thoughts,—a theme and form as severe and as beautiful as the draperies of Phidias, yet suffused with a sensitive and sensuous mood conveying beauty and passion as rich and moving as light in jewels or wine, and thoughts as flashing and irradiating as light gleaming through crystals or rubies.

    Black, inexorable reefs,
    Whereon the freezing billows mount and
      mourn.

    There is no wind along the summer grass—
    Day runs upon unshaken dews.

    With bellies like Hell's roof, and eyes of
      ice.

    The moon, a silver bowl,
    Pours witch-wine on the world.

    A music from a silence past the world.

Sterling as a young man.

But I might quote a hundred instead of a paltry quintet of lines. More interesting, to me, is the truth that the poetic and philosophic sources of such a poem-play as this are inherent and implicit in the very fabric of life—not borrowed from dubious philosophic and historic sources which in this instance contribute nothing. Not Euripides nor Aeschylus nor Shakespeare nor Shelley would more deftly or artfully extract from the very evidence of our few limited senses a clearer or more moving, and, by the same token, more intriguing, indictment of this sorry scheme of things than is here.

For more definitely here than in any play or poem I have ever read is presented the ensorcelling power of sex or passion which so persistently betrays men and women to their ruin. In the instance of Urlan, the father, and Tancred, the son, in this play, wife, mother, father, son, are all involved in a brutal and destroying tangle by the sex lure. The father, for sake of Lilith, is not only willing to desecrate the memory and tomb of his wife, but also to slay his son. The son is not only willing to desecrate the memory and tomb of his mother, but does slay his father. Passion, or the sex lure as embodied in Lilith, is the brutal and indifferent thing so constantly encountered in life itself. It sears and slays with the utmost callousness, and yet so high and terrible is the power of it (as in life itself) that it stands forth in the lines and thoughts of Sterling with a color and a grandeur that are classic.

On the other hand it is quite obvious that indicted and flayed as is life by this lyric tragedy, still, so exquisite is the form and the thought of this precious flower of consciousness, to say nothing of the delights of the argument of the play, that set over against the pain it decries, there is a subtle element of failure in the indictment. If life can produce a thought form such as this (Lilith) or the delights promised or evoked by Lilith—the absolute of love and beauty—then it is not so unendurable, be its darker phases what they may.

But of this the author is himself quite well aware. For in discussing the philosophy of the poem—which more truly than anything else it really is—he insisted that it was purely an "allegory of temptation," without any profound philosophic determination to consign life irrevocably to the roll of either good or evil.

"I've let reason and idealism fight it out," he once said to me. "I've made the poem moon-haunted, as a symbol of the illusory quality of love and idealism generally. And I've ended it with a contrast between pleasure and pain as indicative of that strangest and most awful of our human faculties—our ability to be happy when we know others are in agony. I can never forgive myself and humanity for that."

In this poem, it is true, Lilith (the absolute of beauty, love and desire) is pictured as extracting joy from the suffering of another. On the other hand, she is the cause of an intense joy that sets itself over against pain as its equivalent, its fair exchange and reward.

And Tancred (the unquenchable optimism or deluded faith of the world), so accepts it—or her. And while in this poem Lilith has unquestionably the better of the argument, Tancred as definitely accepts life and endures for his illusions with a sublimity of faith and courage which make pain seem ineffectual, if not all but trivial. And in real life (whatever may be said for the Tancred of this play—his tortured, seeking mood or philosophy) the contemplative phase of life that broods over the mysteries, leads to no such spiritual hell as that which is here pictured as finally overwhelming Tancred. We live and suffer, true enough. There are sufficient mental as well as physical tortures to make "dumb with awful news" the contemplative and brooding among the sensitive and the wise. But are *all* sensitive—or *all* wise? Are not most men comfortably and even joyously deluded? Read the words of the fool and the cook in this play.

I think myself that the worst that is shown here—as anywhere in life, really—is the eternal balance between good and evil, pleasure and pain. And I think Sterling thinks so too. Under the reigning conditions, whatever they are, plainly humanity muddles along, and not too horribly, either.

But the beauty of this poem! The arch deftness and clarity of the argument and its presentation! The loveliness of the scenes and the world that it presents! Its architectonic as well as its lyric wholesomeness! It is compact of a noble and haunting sense of beauty. At the same time, because of its modernity as to astronomical truth, as well as its conception of pleasure and pain as the two realities, it rings richer in thought than any American dramatic poem with which I am familiar. More, it poses the problem of good and evil in life in so intriguing and delectable a form that even he who is content with the non-argumentative contemplation of beauty must still pause to question of himself or life whether either pleasure or pain are desirable realities. And if so, to realize then that beauty itself is the same, desirable or undesirable, since with these others it is most inexorably entwined, and may not be separated from them. (pp. vii-xii)

> *Theodore Dreiser, in an introduction to* Lilith: A
> Dramatic Poem *by George Sterling, The Macmillan
> Company, 1926, pp. vii-xii.*

GEORGE STERLING   (letter date 1926)

[*In the following letter to Theodore Dreiser, Sterling explains his dramatic poem* Lilith, *for which Dreiser wrote an introduction (see excerpt dated 1926).*]

I've no critical reviews of **Lilith.** for I brought it out myself, only 300 copies, and those to give to friends. . . .

As for "poetic and philosophic sources and theory for the same," I must admit I'm in a quandry for a reply. I have followed the main poetic (dramatic) tradition as to the *form* of the poem, but have put more sheer *beauty* (I hope) into it than has gone into other American dramatic poems, for the reason that I was after more than drama. I made the poem moon-haunted, as a symbol of the illusory quality of pleasure and pain as indicative of that strangest and most awful of human faculties, our ability to be happy when we know others are in agony. I can never forgive myself nor humanity for that.

As to the philosophy of the poem, which is purely an allegory of temptation, I've let reason and idealism fight it out, and though so keen a mind as yours can discern that Lilith has utterly the better of the argument (which is the crux of the poem), yet I have put into the mouth of Tancred the best that can be said for the optimist, and many readers will believe that he is right. I think that is the better way, as denoting the eternal balance between good and evil (pleasure and pain).

I think that the poem, in its modernity as to astronomical truth, and its conception of pleasure and pain as the two realities goes deeper in thought than other American dramatic poems, for it does not take life as a bad joke, for pain demands more pity than that. I know that there are folk who deny the reality of pain and pleasure, and of course certain yogis and other enthusiasts are able to escape, apparently, the effects of pain. But for the vast bulk of humanity, as it now stands, pain is indeed a reality that admits of no mystical quibbling, and the hypnotized person, told that he is in pain, *feels* it, regardless of its illusory cause. We can be sure only of our own sensations. All the rest is debatable, aside from, perhaps, mathematics.

Schopenhauer claims that *pain* is the only reality, and it is indeed the greatest one. Nevertheless, pleasure is more than the absence of pain, as witness the violence and individuality of the sex-ecstasy, for instance. I should say that absence of pain was contentment, rather than actual pleasure. The pendulum is then at the bottom of its arc, though on its way toward either pain or pleasure.

Of course the modern school of verse-writers will kick about my traditional form and spirit, my archaisms like thee and thou, but Robinson [Jeffers] himself is nearly as old-fashioned in his last Guinevere drama, without the cosmic importance of a portion of my theme. (pp. 16-17)

> *George Sterling, in a letter to Theodore Dreiser on
> February 13, 1926, in* The Dreiser Newsletter, *Vol.
> 4, No. 1, Spring, 1973, pp. 16-17.*

LÉONIE ADAMS   (essay date 1926)

[*Adams was an American poet and critic. In the following excerpt, she reviews* Lilith.]

Mr. Dreiser in a prefatory note commends **Lilith** for unique richness of thought, "because of its modernity as to astronomical truth as well as its conception of pleasure and pain as the two realities" [see excerpt dated 1926]. The astronomical bearing, which, if it exists at all, is secondary, may be disregarded. The major thesis would appear to resolve itself to this: man is subject to an overriding passion (that is the passion of sex), which is sinful and moreover a cheat, debasing without recompense his nobler part. Even if, being purged by age or what not, he is able to resist this passion, it is in face of a presumption that there is no morality anyway, that the race is doomed to extinction, and that the senses are the only certain indices of anything.

The importance of this as a contribution to thought is not even dubious. Some such insidious medley of rational idea and conventional emotion has staggered most reflective adolescents. Yet worse themes have been the subject of good verse. Unfortunately, and notwithstanding Mr. Dreiser's raptures over its æsthetics, this poem is nondescript.

The structure is limp, and except for a slight variation in the last act, of an appalling symmetry. Exactly when Tancred by a show of speechifying and occasional songs has proved himself most the devoted son, the true friend, the husband of a pure girl, the temptress appears as by evocation and makes short work of the nicer affections. The personages are traditional, the basic invention is as simple as that of a morality play; but the telling naïveté of the morality is lacking. There is a superstructure of claptrap: mediæval sets, paladins and jesting servitors, a fool, a magician who exclaims, "Bubbles on poison!" Furthermore, whatever has been her moral standing to date, here Lilith is much degraded æsthetically. She becomes a cinema sin, an abominable apparition in diaphanous robes, who is saluted by a burst of expletives (typically "O God! O Christ!") and herself makes very free with feeble voluptuous metaphor.

Mr. Sterling is a veteran poet, the author of numerous lyrics and dramatic poems. Naturally his professional facility asserts itself in some good lines; but this grandiose effort betrays him to his worst side, to an almost wholly derivative verse, to all manner of rhetoric, the tawdrily pretty, the grotesque, the pompous. (pp. 99-100)

> *Léonie Adams, "Poetic Drama," in* The New Republic, *Vol. XLVIII, No. 615, September 15, 1926, pp. 99-100.**

ROBINSON JEFFERS   (essay date 1926)

[*Jeffers was an American poet, playwright, and critic. His works reflect a personal philosophy synthesized from his knowledge of classical thought, his interest in modern philosophy, and his great reverence for nature. Jeffers believed that an anthropocentric attitude was dangerous and foolish, and that humans, created and then abandoned by an uncaring God, were essentially doomed, like Oedipus, to live out horrific and inevitable destinies. As a result, much of his poetry deals with the tragedy he considered inherent in human existence. Jeffers preferred to use traditional verse forms, and while his long narrative poems have been criticized for their didacticism, his shorter lyric pieces, especially those which describe the beauty of the California coastal regions, have been highly praised. Jeffers was a reclusive man, and Sterling was one of his few close friends. In the following excerpt, originally published as an obituary tribute in the* Carmel Cymbal *for November, 1926, Jeffers praises Sterling's poetry.*]

George Sterling was the one poet I know of who made poetry purely because he loved it, as one loves and writes in early youth. With most writers the devotion soon becomes impure; there is an attitude to present or a story to tell, perhaps a reputation to make, even a cause to vindicate; some effect or other is aimed at; Sterling loved poetry for its own beauty, by lifelong unfaltering instinct. Disinterestedly; his own or another's; provided only that it had some elements of goodness.

He valued poetry as the organ of its appropriate beauty rather than as a means of expression. His life was troubled and his philosophy involved hopelessness; his face, during the two or three years since I met him, had in repose even a look of torture; he would not let his work be troubled; neither grief nor desire nor despair might enter his poems except restrained and sublimated. Accordingly his work has no ugliness and only distant passion; it is all lyrical; his dramatic and narrative poems are not great as play or story but for the lyric loveliness that fills them; for the detachable songs; and for the splendor of great lines, like these about the coming of night:

> Till that great wave whose foam is dawn and sunset
> Ebbed slowly, leaving them the stranded stars.

Such lines as these, and their quality is constant in all his work from earliest to latest, are reserved above the reach or need of praise. (pp. 135-36)

> *Robinson Jeffers, "'A Great Poet on Sterling'," in his* A Bibliography of the Works of Robinson Jeffers, *edited by S. S. Alberts, 1933. Reprint by Cultural History Research, Inc., 1966, pp. 135-36.*

CLARK ASHTON SMITH   (essay date 1927)

[*Smith was an American author of horror and fantastic fiction noted for its lush and intricate prose style (reflecting his work as a poet influenced by the nineteenth-century Decadents), and for its narrative perspectives that both reject and transcend the normal course of human affairs. His expertise was in the interplanetary or fantastic tale which allowed for the unrestrained, and invariably nightmarish, use of his artistic imagination. In the following excerpt, Smith discusses some characteristics of Sterling's best work.*]

Turning today the pages of [George Sterling's] many volumes, I, like others who knew him, find it difficult to read them in a mood of dispassionate or abstract criticism. But I am not sure that poetry should ever be read or criticized in a perfectly dispassionate mood. A poem is not a philosophic or scientific thesis, or a problem in Euclid, and the essential "magic" is more than likely to elude one who approaches it, as too many do, in a spirit of cold-blooded logic. After all, poetry is properly understood only by those who love it.

Sterling, I remember, considered **"The Testimony of the Suns"** his greatest poem. Bierce said of it, that, "written in French and published in Paris, it would have stirred the very stones of the street." In this poem, there are lines that evoke the silence of infinitude, verses in which one hears the crash of gliding planets, verses that are clarion calls in the immemorial war of suns and systems, and others that are like the cadences of some sidereal requiem, chanted by the seraphim over a world that is "stone and night." (pp. 79-80)

I feel a peculiar partiality for **"A Wine of Wizardry,"** the most colorful, exotic, and, in places, macabre, of Sterling's poems. (This, however, is not tantamount to saying that I consider it necessarily his most important achievement.) Few things in literature are more serviceable as a test for determining whether people feel the verbal magic of poetry—or whether they merely comprehend and admire the thought, or philosophic content. It is not a poem for the literal-minded, for those lovers of the essential prose of existence who edit and read our "Saturday

Reviews'' and ''Literary Digests.'' In one of the very last letters that he wrote me, Sterling said that no one took the poem seriously any more, ''excepting cranks and mental hermits.'' It is not ''vital'' poetry, he said, as the word ''vital'' is used by our self-elected high-brows (which probably, means, that it is lacking in ''sex-kick,'' or throws no light on the labor problem and the increase of moronism). I was unable to agree with him. Personally, I find it impossible to take the ''vital'' school with any degree of seriousness, and see it only as a phase of materialism and didacticism. The proponents of the utile and the informative should stick to prose—which, to be frank, is all that they achieve, as a rule. Before leaving **''A Wine of Wizardry,''** I wish, for my own pleasure, to quote a favorite passage:

> Within, lurk orbs that graven monsters
> clasp;
> Red-embered rubies smoulder in the
> gloom,
> Betrayed by lamps that nurse a sullen
> flame,
> And livid roots writhe in the marble's
> grasp,
> As moaning airs invoke the conquered
> rust
> Of lordly helms made equal in the dust.
> Without, where baleful cypresses make
> rich
> The bleeding sun's phantasmagoric
> gules,
> Are fungus-tapers of the twilight witch,
> Seen by the bat above unfathomed pools,
> And tiger-lilies known to silent ghouls,
> Whose king hath digged a sombre car-
> canet
> And necklaces with fevered opals set.

No, **''A Wine of Wizardry''** is not ''vital verse.'' Thank God for *that*, as Benjamin de Casseres would say.

Notable, also, in Sterling's second volume, is the lovely **''Tasso to Leonora''** and **''A Dream of Fear.''** His third volume, *A House of Orchids,* is compact of poetry; and, if I were to name my favorites, it would be equivalent to quoting almost the entire index. However, the dramatic poem, *Lilith* is, I believe, the production by which he will be most widely known. One must go back to Swinburne and Shelley to find its equal as a lyric drama. The tragedy and poetry of life are in this strange allegory, and the hero, Tancred, is the mystic analogue of all men. Here, in the conception of Lilith, the eternal and ineluctable Temptress, Sterling verges upon that incommensurable poet, Charles Baudelaire. In scene after scene, one hears the fugue of good and evil, of pleasure and pain, set to chords that are almost Wagnerian. Upon the sordid reality of our fate there falls, time after time, a light that seems to pass through lucent and iridescent gems; and vibrant echoes and reverberant voices cry in smitten music from the profound of environing mystery.

One might go on, to praise and quote indefinitely; but, in a sense, all that I can write or could write seems futile, now that Sterling is ''one with that multitude to whom the eternal Night hath said, I am.'' Anyway, his was not, as Flecker's,

> The song of a man who was dead
> Ere any had heard of his song.

From the beginning, he had the appreciation and worship of poetry lovers, if not of the crowd or of the critical moguls and pontiffs. (p. 80)

Clark Ashton Smith, ''George Sterling—An Appreciation,'' in Overland Monthly and Out West Magazine, *Vol. LXXXV, No. 3, March, 1927, pp. 79-80.*

HENRY LOUIS MENCKEN   (essay date 1927)

[*From the era of World War I until the early years of the Great Depression, Mencken was one of the most influential figures in American letters. His strongly individualistic, irreverent outlook on life and his vigorous, invective-charged writing style helped establish the iconoclastic spirit of the Jazz Age and significantly shaped the direction of American literature. In the following excerpt, Mencken, who was a close friend of Sterling, assesses the poet's accomplishments in an obituary tribute.*]

Let us not mourn for George. He had a happy life and the end of it was a swift and happy death. He was almost ideally the free artist of Beethoven's famous saying. He practiced an art that he loved; he lived out his days among pleasant friends; he was not harassed by sordid cares; he had enough of fame for any rational man. What endless joy he got out of his work! Every new poem was to him an exhilarating emotional experience. He was a sound workman, and he knew it. What more could any man ask of the implacable fates?

Much that he wrote, I believe, will live. There will be no American anthology for a century to come without his name in it. For the rare quality of timelessness was in nearly all his work. He wrote, not to meet a passing fashion, but to measure up to an immemorial ideal. The thing he sought was beauty, and from that high quest nothing ever dissuaded him. The winds of doctrine roared about him without shaking him. What was transiently cried up did not escape him: he was, in fact, intensely interested in everything new and strange. But his own course was along older paths, and he kept to it resolutely to the end.

It has been my destiny to know many artists, great and small. Of them all, George was easily the most charming. There was a divine rakishness about him that never staled. He enjoyed living as he enjoyed working. Who will ever forget his kindness, his delight in companionship, his unflagging gusto? Dying at fifty-seven, he was still a boy. That imperishable boyishness, perhaps, was the greatest of all his gifts.

Henry Louis Mencken, ''Sterling,'' in Overland Monthly and Out West Magazine, *Vol. LXXXV, No. 12, December, 1927, p. 363.*

LIONEL STEVENSON   (essay date 1929)

[*A respected Canadian literary critic, Stevenson was also the author of several biographies, each highly acclaimed for the author's scholarship, wit, and clarity. In the following excerpt, Stevenson explains why Sterling's work has been undervalued.*]

Sterling wove for himself a lovely and many-colored garment from the most magnificent textiles which he could discover, and by perpetually wearing it he gave an impression of dignity and aloofness which is decidedly his own. His inmost self being never allowed explicit utterance, the reader has the interest of seeking to discern it beneath the convolutions of the robe. Such indirection may prevent Sterling from achieving the transcendent power of the greatest poetry, but it offers the double pleasure of its external richness of beauty and its tantalizing hints of the strange and tragic identity within.

He embodied his poems in the traditional forms—ode, sonnet, blank verse, allegorical drama, and the various stanza patterns perfected by Keats, Shelley, and Tennyson. His imagery was ornate, expressing itself with many adjectives and indulging in the sensuous delight of sumptuous colors, haunting music, luxurious fabrics. It is easy to see in his choice of imagery the traits of the Roman Catholic ritual which became familiar to him at an impressionable period of his boyhood. His diction was admirable alike for its appreciation of the connotative value of words and for its harmonizing of their sound-values. Like Tennyson, he could condense into a single appropriate word a whole thought or image for the well-informed reader to expand. His love of romantic strangeness led him to use many archaic or otherwise unfamiliar words, effective both by their beauty of sound and by their glamorous suggestions of the unknown. He had Milton's partiality for impressive proper names. On the other hand, along with these good traits he had inherited from his antecedents a less defensible habit—trivial enough, it is true, but superficially visible and tending to annoy the reader out of all proportion to its unimportance. This was the special "poetic diction" of "thee" and "thou," of "mid" and "'neath," of "lo," and "'tis," and "ne'er." The manifest artificiality of such locutions has been very unfortunate in provoking condemnations which pay no heed to the profounder qualities of the poems.

It is probably the foregoing traits which prevent Sterling from being a great sonneteer, in spite of his addiction to the sonnet form. Being so strictly conditioned in dimensions and pattern, the sonnet must give particularly strong indications of emotion and honesty on the part of the poet, to avoid being entirely artificial. It is for this reason that Spenser's sonnet-sequence falls so far below that of Sidney, although the latter would have been incapable of the sustained magnificence of the *Faerie Queene*; and George Sterling's **Sonnets to Craig** resemble the *Amoretti* in failing to stir the reader with lines of memorable power. The best of Sterling's sonnets are those which are pictorial and impersonal.

Although the first impression made by his poetry is concerned with his technical skill and his wealth of imagery, further reading proves that he is not devoid of an underlying philosophy. The most frequent of his ideas, and the one which applies directly to his concern with technique, is his concept of beauty. He was obsessed with an ideal of beauty as something remote and elusive, only to be perceived in dreams and flashes of insight, faintly reflected in music and poetry. The function of the poet, therefore, was to use every possible means of capturing the fleeting spirit. Since music simulates it most successfully, poetry must use the metrical and phonetic devices which approximate musical effects. Poetry must abjure every literal and familiar element, accumulate as many images of strange loveliness as it can discover, and cherish all the past embodiments of visionary beauty, such as the beings of classic mythology. In the attempt to suggest this supernal and inhuman beauty, he uses certain recurrent themes, such as gems, moonlight and sea-foam; his repetition of them does not betray poverty of invention, but signifies the fact that out of an unusually extensive treasury he consciously selects these again and again as the clearest symbols of what he wishes to convey. (pp. 407-09)

It is natural, therefore, that he should seek to preserve the devices by which earlier poets had contributed to the recording of beauty's rare apparitions. A very interesting summary of his favorite poets, in phrases which reveal genuine critical acumen, occurs in the poem entitled **"Music"**. . . . It is significant that the only American name included is Poe's. Sterling followed the Poe model in those of his poems which express the morbid side of his imagination, and he pays generous tribute to Poe again in one of his best sonnets. (pp. 410-11)

Anyone with serious pretensions to the title of poet must have formulated some theory of existence, no matter how chary of didacticism he may be; and Sterling could not dwell always in a realm of pure fantasy. Such a poem as **"A Wine of Wizardry,"** extending to over two hundred lines of sheer imagery, piling up weird Poe-like scenes, all flushed with the unearthly glare of sunset reflected in wine, was a *tour de force* which he could not often repeat. Most of his poems betray an excogitated view of existence.

The most frequent theme is the melancholy fact of man's futility. Our perception of beauty being always so brief and imperfect, our puny efforts are ephemeral in contrast with the eternity of beauty's spirit. Each being is inevitably isolated, helplessly striving to communicate with a fellow-soul. Typical of scores of his reflective poems is the sonnet **"Illusion"**:

> I am alone in this grey shadowland,—
>> This world of phantoms I can never know,—
>> This throng of seekers wandering to and fro,
> Moved by a hidden god's unheard command;
> And tho' we knew the clasp of eye and hand,
>> We watchers of the planet's passing show,
>> Yet soon the "now" shall be the "long ago,"
> And soon the prow shall grate on Lethe's strand.
>
> Bring on the lights, the music and the wine,
>> Ere the long silence give our feast to scorn!
>>> Let us forget all that we dread we are,
> And let the mind's unknown horizon shine,
>> As the heart graces with mirage of morn
>>> The light about its lost and lonely star.

A closely related idea is that of the transience of all ambition and fame, as expressed in the **"Three Sonnets on Oblivion,"** of which the first may be quoted:

> Her eyes have seen the monoliths of kings
>> Upcast like foam of the effacing tide:
>> She hath beheld the desert stars deride
> The monuments of Power's imaginings—
> About their base the wind Assyrian flings
>> The dust that throned the satrap in his pride:
>> Cambyses and the Memphian pomps abide
> As in the flame the moth's presumptuous wings.
>
> There gleams no glory that her hand shall spare,
>> Nor any sun whose rays shall cross her night,
>>> Whose realm enfolds man's empire and its end.
> No armor of renown her sword shall dare,
>> No council of the gods withstand her might:
>>> Stricken at last Time's lonely Titans bend.

The underlying thought of these poems is not particularly modern. Of the two sonnets just quoted, the first recalls the Greek hedonists and the second recalls the Hebrew prophets. The thoughts have been revitalized, however, by recent scientific revelations of aeonic time and interstellar space. Sterling could never lose sight of the new perspective, in which the solar system becomes unutterably insignificant. This terrible fascination showed itself in his first and most ambitious long poem,

"**The Testimony of the Suns.**" The poem excels the efforts of other writers to depict the astronomical vastitudes of the universe, because they were usually actuated by pre-conceived theories, betraying them into abstraction and exposition, whereas Sterling, with his dread of being didactic, strove only to present the imaginative aspect of the theme. Considering the stupendous scope of the poem, it is a great achievement. Even though the necessity of maintaining an exalted mood of grandeur infects some of the stanzas with rhetoric, the majority of them are magnificently vivid and profound, and the general effect of the poem is to make the reader's imagination actively aware of those splendors which the calculations of astronomy imply but fail to display. Sterling discovered the astonishing beauty and dignity of the names of constellations, and made gorgeous use of "Fomalhaut," "Alderbaran," "Procyon," "Betelgeuse," "Antares," and "Altair." Throughout his later poems he returned to those enchanted words when he wished to induce the highest moods of exaltation.

With such a theme, however, he could not utterly ignore philosophic implications. Avoiding the dullness of rational argumentation, he nevertheless conveys what seem to him the indubitable inferences. He declares nothing with certitude, but his questions point toward only one sort of answer—the impotence and eternal loneliness of human beings, involved in some vast and incomprehensible law of cyclic recurrence. (pp. 416-18)

His view on the subject of the soul's immortality is strictly agnostic. Consistent with all his poems is the one called "**Mystery**":

> Men say that sundered by enormous nights
>   Burn star and nearest star.
> That where companioned seem the sister lights
>   The great abysses are.
>
> So held by Life's unsympathetic dark,
>   We press to hidden goals.
> From gulfs unshared the friending fires we mark,
>   And we are lonely souls—
>
> Your hearts, O friends! beyond their veiling bars,
>   Are hidden deep away.
> Your faces gleam familiar as the stars,
>   And as unknown as they.

His creed, therefore, is one of resignation and fatalism. Neither affirming nor denying, he counsels passivity as the sole means of enduring life, with escape into the frankly unreal realm of fantasy as the only anodyne. None of the poems concludes on a note of hope; "**The Testimony of the Suns,**" after speaking of man's ambition "to know what Permanence abides beyond the veil the senses draw," ends with an apostrophe to Life:

> So shall thy seed on worlds to be,
>   At altars built to suns afar,
>   Crave from the silence of the star
> Solution of thy mystery;
>
> And crave unanswered, till, denied
>   By cosmic gloom and stellar glare,
>   The brains are dust that bore the pray'r,
> And dust the yearning lips that cried.

Similarly in **Lilith**, lest the idealism expressed by Tancred in the last act should imply optimism in the author, the effect is invalidated by closing on a note of human selfishness and cruelty, leaving a hint of cynicism just as Eugene O'Neill does by a similar device at the end of *Lazarus Laughed.*

We are in a position now to understand why Sterling was not accorded a preeminent place in the poetry of his era. On the one hand, the intellectuals were hatching their revolt from orthodox forms, and contemned his traditional technique and archaic diction; on the other hand, the general reading public had several reasons for shunning him. First of all, he was erudite, requiring in his reader an eclectic literary background and a keen perception of symbolism. His wide vocabulary, his frequent classical and other learned allusions, his condensation of imagery, were barriers for those who would run as they read. Secondly, the imaginative excursions which he provided were either gruesome or despondent. He could rival the most horrific tales of Poe in such poems as "**A Wine of Wizardry**" and "**The Hidden Pool**"; and when his mood was less nightmarish he still distressed his compatriots by despising their practical and self-satisfied world and seeking mischievously to stir in them improvident longings for the unattainable. To placid and prosperous people, the romantic escape is an insidious menace. Finally, his philosophic outlook was depressing; for those who look for a "message" in poetry, Sterling's bleak questionings and profound disillusionment were repellant. The elaborate beauty with which he invested his despair made it only the more bitter. The average happiness-seeking mortal recoils from such uncompromising unfaith as this:

> The stranger in my gates—lo! that am I,
>   And what my land of birth I do not know,
>   Nor yet the hidden land to which I go.
> One may be lord of many ere he die,
> And tell of many sorrows in one sigh,
>   But know himself he shall not, nor his woe,
>   Nor to what sea the tears of wisdom flow,
> Nor why one star is taken from the sky.
>
> An urging is upon him evermore,
>   And tho' he bide, his soul is wanderer,
>   Scanning the shadows with a sense of haste
> Where fade the tracks of all who went before—
>   A dim and solitary traveller
>   On ways that end in evening and the waste.

There is not the passion of a temporary mood in such a poem; it has the calmness and discipline of permanent conviction; and all the armor of self-righteousness cannot shield the reader from unwilling response.

Thus alienated from the conventional *bourgeoisie* of his time by his outlook, and from the radical *intelligentsia* by his technique, Sterling was appreciated only by the few who could place his poetry against an assimilated background of European culture. To them it was clear that he was alone among American poets of the twentieth century in attaching himself to the great tradition of English literature, not as an imitator but in the true apostolic succession. Those who found pleasure in the sensuous luxury of Keats, the empyrean vision of Shelley and Blake, the fantastic glooms of Poe, the metrical subtleties of Tennyson, could enjoy similar traits in Sterling. And yet he was not an anachronism in his century. Recent scientific and philosophic concepts were the roots of his tree of knowledge; the melancholy and agnostic fatalism which he derived from them was entirely consistent with the views of the only English poets who were maintaining the discussion of such themes, Thomas Hardy, for example, and A. E. Housman, and John Masefield. It is difficult to believe that future historians of American literature will fail to recognize that by taking the full poetic vow and devoting himself to the arduous service of "pure poetry" he saved an era of his nation's literature from entire provincialism. He is a citizen of the world of poetry, and as long as that world survives his claim will be acknowledged. (pp. 418-21)

Lionel Stevenson, "George Sterling's Place in Modern Poetry," in The University of California Chronicle, *Vol. XXXI, No. 4, October, 1929, pp. 404-21.*

KEVIN STARR (essay date 1973)

[*In the following excerpt, Starr examines Sterling's work in the context of the arts in California.*]

[Nothing] in life or art seemed to work out for George Sterling. The laureate of California, the friend of the great, the admired of all, he destroyed himself in self-rejection and bitterness. Because his failures as man and poet were so inextricably bound up with California, because he willingly undertook a symbolic role, the tragedy of George Sterling—those things which failed him—had a pronounced regional significance.

First of all, Sterling inherited a restricted muse. If a tradition existed in California poetry, or at least if a trend was apparent, it was that of a defensive aestheticism which confined itself to highly formal verse patterns and minor ranges of thought and emotion. Throughout the nineteenth century, poetry in California tended to be escapist and amateur. No one talent capable of reversing its wistful, plaintive direction appeared, although the effort of Joaquin Miller to introduce historical themes and an epic sense, however much it resulted in more posturing declamation than solid verse, deserves credit as a sustained attempt to make the poet in California serve larger ends, to rise above the compulsive minor key. For all the bohemians' talk of California as a nursery of the arts, the local poet tended in the early years to define himself against circumstances. Amidst the undeveloped and the matter-of-fact, they wished to be genteel. Taken as a whole, and with the exclusion of isolated poems by the most competent practitioners (Charles Augustus Stoddard, Ina Coolbrith, John Rollin Ridge, Joaquin Miller, and Edward Rowland Sill), poetry in California had few high moments, few times when it engaged in any significant way the abundant nature which so manifestly challenged it or the ranges of thought and feeling which it had to attempt if it were to move beyond plaintive prettification. As he began to write verse in the early 1890's, George Sterling fell prey to this restriction of intent. A trivial time for American poetry in general, Sterling's weaknesses were not totally the fault of California, whose poetic narrowness only intensified the parochial spirit of the age. Sterling sought emotional solace in poetry, the magic of word-music and the elusive quest for Beauty, capitalized and Neoplatonic. As far as possible, he banished intellection and human reference, preferring to pursue—polysyllabically and in archaic verse forms—the cosmic, the exotic, the remote. Working as the private secretary to his uncle, an East Bay real estate mogul, and finding the routines of business very tedious, Sterling's need for personal escape dovetailed with the larger escape of the California poetic tradition. Accustomed to the sort of poetry he wrote, Californians rewarded Sterling for authenticating the enduring value of what they liked best. (pp. 270-71)

Sterling often regretted that he had not drawn more upon his New England background as a way of countering a totally Californian involvement. Born in 1869 in the former Yankee whaling town of Sag Harbor, Long Island, Sterling prided himself upon a distinguished New England heritage which went back to the seventeenth century. Coming to California when just out of his teens, he kept throughout his life a highly nasal Yankee way of speaking. The problem was, however, that Sterling, the uprooted, could never decide what was important about his New England heritage, beyond its snob appeal. With the exception of his maternal grandfather, Wickham Sayre Havens, a retired whaling captain who became the subject of one of Sterling's best poems, he seems to have made no deep connection with the New England past, although, as Mary Austin pointed out, some of his best work had a Sag Harbor setting. Sterling returned to the East at times of adult crisis, revisiting the scenes of his boyhood, browsing through the gravestones of his ancestors buried in Connecticut across the choppy waters of Long Island Sound. New England remained a haunting, ill-defined memory, confused by his family's alienating conversion to Roman Catholicism, unstructured by systematic education. Its best ideas and impulses, the cumulative drama of the New England conscience, had taken no deep roots in his soul. Once in a while a feeling surfaced in him that he should be doing better, that he should be carrying on some great New England labor in California through poetry as had been carried on in the past through religion; but he never knew what to do in response to these promptings and was left with only an aftertaste of discontent. Part of Sterling's attraction to Bierce arose out of the fact that he confused Bierce's purism and snobbery with high purpose in the New England manner. Sterling never managed to become the bringer of New England's gifts. Neither expatriate nor missionary, he fell victim to the sufferings of both conditions. (p. 275)

[For] a generation of Californians, George Sterling embodied life lived for art. He was not a major figure in terms of local achievement if compared to, say, John Muir, Mary Austin, Frank Norris, and Jack London in literature; Arthur Putnam and Douglas Tilden in sculpture; Xavier Martinez, Charles Rollo Peters, Percy Gray, Francis McComas, and William Keith in painting; or the architects of the Bay Region style, Willis Polk and Bernard Maybeck especially. A case can be made that David Starr Jordan, who turned to verse only as recreation from his duties as president of Stanford, was in fact a better poet. Yet Sterling served as the archpriest of the whole revival. No gathering of Bay Area talent seemed complete without him. In the long run his poetry would turn out to be tragically passé, and in provincial gratitude Californians overrated it scandalously; but for a brief moment, in his own time, before the verdict of history was in, George Sterling held his own. Singlehandedly, he revived poetry in California, opening it up to new ranges of consideration. In terms of its plaintive aestheticism, its lack of symbolic intensity or engagement with reality, Sterling's verse belonged to the old provincial poetry. On the other hand it occasionally possessed a sub-philosophical relationship to local materials and a passion for transcendence which forecast the achievement of Robinson Jeffers. Sterling's sonnet **"The Black Vulture"** suggested a mode which one wishes had been more characteristic:

> Aloof within the day's enormous dome,
>   He holds unshared the silence of the sky.
>   Far down his bleak, relentless eyes descry
> The eagle's empire and the falcon's home—
> Far down, the galleons of sunset roam;
>   His hazards on the sea of morning lie;
>   Serene, he hears the broken tempest sigh
> Where cold sierras gleam like scattered foam.

And least of all he holds the human swarm—
Unwitting now that envious men prepare
To make their dream and its fulfilment one,
When, poised above the caldrons of the storm,
Their hearts, contemptuous of death, shall dare
His roads between the thunder and the sun.

A very old-fashioned exercise, **"The Black Vulture"** has all of Sterling's faults of archaic diction and poetic self-consciousness. In its attention and balance, however, in its ambitious use of Californian material, it was perhaps his best poem. (pp. 277-79)

So many of Sterling's fellow bohemians, lost in a dark night, had wandered over a precipice that California stood mocked in general unhappiness. Philosophical pessimism compounded neuroses and they succumbed because everything failed them. In a way, their uncritical pessimism, so bewildering to Saxon in *The Valley of the Moon,* was a sign of provincialism and lack of major talent. They suffered, many of them, from bad ideas. At a time when avant-garde America, in Chicago, in New York, in European exile, was renewing itself through connection with the forward thrust of Continental aesthetics, Sterling was feeling the full weight of a played-out European despair, which allowed his personal disorders the dangerous justification of theory. Inflamed by philosophy, the flirtation with self-destruction which arose out of psychic distress became fixed in formula—and then irresistible. (pp. 285-86)

Kevin Starr, "Bohemian Shores," in his Americans and the California Dream: 1850-1915, Oxford University Press, 1973, pp. 239-87.*

THOMAS E. BENEDIKTSSON (essay date 1980)

[*Benediktsson is an American critic and educator. In the following excerpt he surveys Sterling's major and minor poems and collections, beginning with the title poem of the poet's first collection,* The Testimony of the Suns.]

Sterling's "star poem" was composed over a period spanning several months. After Sterling submitted to Bierce the draft of the first part of the poem in March 1902, the two exchanged letters and drafts with revisions suggested by Bierce or volunteered by Sterling. From the first, Bierce was dazzled by the new poem: "It is a new field, the broadest yet discovered. To paraphrase Coleridge, 'you are the first that ever burst / Into that silent (unknown) sea'—A silent sea *because* no one else has burst into it in full song. True, there have been short incursions across the 'border,' but only by way of episode. The tremendous phenomena of Astronomy have never had adequate poetic treatment, their meaning adequate expression. You must make it your own domain. You shall be the poet of the skies, the prophet of the suns."

Lately Sterling had been reviving his boyhood interest in astronomy, and he had decided to treat galactic phenomena in a long poem, at the same time dealing with some philosophical and moral problems posed by science. In this respect he was of course following a Victorian poetic tradition, but in the poem he would assault Victorian morality and spiritual doubt from a consistent perspective of cosmic determinism.

Two contemporary writers, Ernst Haeckel and H. G. Wells, were direct influences on Sterling's [**"The Testimony of the Suns"**]. Haeckel, the German biologist who was one of the chief survivors among the early Darwinians, had published in 1899 a work of popular philosophy entitled *Die Welträtsen.*

Translated into English in 1900 as *The Riddle of the Universe,* the book was enormously popular in the United States among the intellectual avant-garde. Haeckel repudiated traditional concepts of a personal God, an immortal soul, and a free human will; consequently, his work was a strong influence on naturalists like Dreiser.

In his "law of substance," Haeckel combines the laws of conservation and energy into a single principle, which in turn implies an infinitely extended universe of eternal duration and transformation: " . . . in the collision of two heavenly bodies which rush towards each other at inconceivable speed, enormous quantities of heat are liberated, while the pulverized masses are hurled and scattered about space. The eternal drama begins afresh—the rotating mass, the condensation of its parts, the formation of new meteorites, their combination into larger bodies and so on."

If Haeckel had introduced to Sterling the conception of a cosmic storm far beyond human perceptions, it was H. G. Wells who first showed him some of the imaginative possibilities of the theme. In 1904 he wrote to Wells that **"The Testimony of the Suns"** had been partly inspired by the short story "Under the Knife." In this tale, the narrator is undergoing an operation and is near death when he has a vision of his soul spinning through space and time: "Stars glowing brighter and brighter with their circling planets catching the light in a ghostly fashion as I neared them, shone out and vanished again into inexistence; faint comets, clusters of meteorites, winking specks of matter, eddying light-points, whizzed past, some perhaps a hundred millions of a mile or so from me at most, few nearer, travelling with unimaginable rapidity, shooting constellations, momentary darts of fire, through that black, enormous night." Wells's story showed Sterling the way in which a sublime poetry could be written about the stars—poetry that would both fit the Bierce formula and as well convey Sterling's own naturalism, influenced by Haeckel.

In its final version, **"The Testimony of the Suns"** has two parts, containing in all 162 four-line stanzas. . . . Part I describes the "war" of the stars in the cosmos, and Part II attempts to relate human life to that universal war. The poem opens with a contrast between the perspective of "Time," or the temporal vision of man, and "Eternity," or the absolute vision of universal law. "In the eyes of time," then, the evening skies seem peaceful, intransigent, and beyond all human conflict. But to the eyes of Eternity, the skies are a vast battleground: the stars are at war; their movements are such that one will inevitably collide with another, causing it to disintegrate into a nebula or dead star. In the eternal flux of the cosmos, however, nebulae eventually evolve into new stars. Thus, there is an external process of creation and destruction in the heavens, quite remote from human concerns, and so alien to human time that it takes a supreme intellectual effort even to conceptualize it.

In describing these wars in the heavens, Sterling uses two primary types of imagery. One, naturally enough, is martial:

O armies of eternal night,
How flame your guidons on the dark!
Silent we turn from Time to hark
What final Orders sway your might. . . .

Another common source of imagery is the sea:

The war whose waves of onslaught, met
Where night's abysses storm afar,

> Break on the high, tremendous bar
> Athwart that central ocean set—. . . .

In many stanzas of the poem, Sterling exploits the rhetorical effects which Bierce taught him to regard as "sublime." For example, several of them employ apostrophes to various stars; each of these is a slight variation on the same expression of wonder at the immense scope and mystery of the conflict. . . . Dying and newly engendered stars are part of the spectacle of the night skies; "smit. suns . . . startle back the gloom" . . . , and the new light of the nova makes its way to the uncomprehending eyes of humanity. Do we believe that this maelstrom has a beginning and an ending? If we do, we are fools.

The mist of a nebula marks the collision of stars in some cosmic past; but the nebula will evolve to new suns, which will foster a reawakening life, the birth of reason, and the emergence of a civilization, until once again, there will be seen "The nearing sun's enormous disc, / Blood-red at dusk of sullen noon". . . . Again, the collision of stars will create a new nebula, witnessed, perhaps, by the "barbaric eyes" . . . of denizens of the worlds of Betelgeuse and Altair.

Sterling goes on at length to discuss the folly and vanity of those men who try to question the laws of the universe as science has revealed them. The delusions that men fall prey to can be grouped into two categories: the speculations that mankind is eternal, and the "dream of Faith" that there is a life beyond death. These are never to be fulfilled, because law is unalterable; and man is subject to the same law of destruction that controls the destinies of stars. Even if there is an apocalypse for man, it will certainly not bring the universe to an end:

> Shall Godhead dream a transient thing?
> Strives He for that which now he lacks?
> Shall Law's dominion melt as wax
> At touch of Hope's irradiant wing? . . .

Would the Almighty be subject to whim? This is what men are asserting if they believe in any kind of human redemption. The first part of the poem ends on a note of "unfathomed mystery," . . . preparing the reader for Part Two, in which Sterling intended to develop further the pathos of human attempts to anthropomorphize the universe.

It should be clear by now that **"The Testimony of the Suns"** has little attraction for the modern reader. It is filled with archaisms and overly "sublime" rhetorical effects, and it lacks precise statement of its ideas. It is difficult to elucidate such lines as these:

> Charged, the immeasured gulfs transmit
> Her [Law's] mandate to the fonts of life,
> Inciting to the governed strife
> Whereby the lethal voids are lit,
>
> With augment of imperious tides
> On vague, illimitable coasts,
> And battle-haze of merging hosts
> To which the flare of Vega rides. . . .

The second part of the poem especially falls prey to these excesses. In the effort to sustain the grandeur, Sterling allows his stanzas to become strident and nearly hysterical at times, and at other times deadly monotonous. . . . (pp. 73-7)

A major reason for the poem's failure to sustain interest is the counsel of Bierce. Afraid that Sterling would descend to the level of mere humanity in the second part of the poem, Bierce had written, "If you descend from Arcturus to Earth, from your nebulae to your neighbors, from life to lives, from the measureless immensities of space to the petty passions of poor insects, won't you incur the peril of anti-climax? I doubt if you can touch the 'human interest' after those high themes without an awful tumble. I should be sorry to see the poem 'Peter out' or 'soak in.' It would be as if Goethe had let his 'Prologue in Heaven' expire in a coon-song." Accordingly, Sterling abandoned any plan he might have had to vary the perspective of his poem. Instead he wrote dozens of stanzas with the same basic ideas and rhetorical effects. Bierce approved entirely, and remarked in his marginal notes to the completed manuscript, "This grows better the more frequently it is read. It is as high a note as was ever struck—and held." His failure to encourage Sterling to develop a sense of restraint might have been the worst effect of his influence.

Behind the excesses of the rhetoric, however, is the revelation of a cosmic abyss, reinforced by the astronomical theme and leading only to despair:

> O Space and Time and stars at strife,
> How dreadful your infinity!
> Shrined by your termless trinity
> How strange, how terrible, is life! . . .

Humanity will always seek "to know what permanence abides / Beyond the veil the senses draw". . . . But there will be no revelations: men are trapped in time, and they will

> . . . crave unanswered, till, denied
> By cosmic gloom and stellar glare,
> The brains are dust that bore the pray'r
> And dust the yearning lips that cried. . . .

The poem's final statement, then, is of "the impotence and eternal loneliness of human beings, involved in some vast and incomprehensible law of cyclic recurrence." And thus, despite its flaws, **"The Testimony of the Suns"** is historically significant. Along with the then-forgotten poems of Stephen Crane and the still unknown poems of Robinson, it is one of the earliest naturalist poems in America. Almost Schopenhauerian in its emphasis upon the primacy of pain, it is in its way a remarkable poem for the "twilight interval" in which it was written. Bierce had helped make Sterling into a significant transitional figure—a poet whose nineteenth-century rhetoric and traditional stock of images contrast sharply with a very modern sense of despair.

Yet in **"The Testimony of the Suns"** the despair seems submerged in an exultant, almost joyous chanting—the catalogue of stars, the repeated questions—that remind us of Margaret Marshall's comment about Fitzgerald: "The gusto with which *This Side of Paradise* and *The Beautiful and the Damned* were written was clearly affirmative, though the theme was disintegration." Like the young Fitzgerald, Sterling was reveling in his success. Bierce had called him "the prophet of the suns," and with this accolade he felt that he had found his voice and his theme. (pp. 78-9)

Aside from the title poem, the most ambitious lyrics in *The Testimony of the Suns and Other Poems* deal with Romantic, neo-Platonic themes of beauty and inspiration. In all of these, the emphasis is on the impossible, inexpressible beauty of which we catch glimpses, but which truly belongs to a shadowy, far-off realm beyond death; several of these poems, including **"To Imagination," "Poesy,"** and **"The Ideal,"** stress the poet's calling to capture as much of beauty's essence as possible, and to offer its poor reflection to the world. One of the more extended of these is **"The Spirit of Beauty,"** a blank-verse lyric of forty-eight lines. In a vision, Beauty appears to the dreaming poet:

> As a mist she fled
> Before mine eyes enchanted; and her face
> Was like a lily hidden in holy dusks—
> Even such as gaze, in vision far from Time,
> From out the skies of dream land, being moons
> In slumber's realm of shadow. And her eyes
> Were great with griefs unsearchable, and gleamed
> Sorrow beyond them, like the larger dew
> Of Aidenn, having each Love's perfect star
> Mirrored therein. And with her came the hush
> That follows music dying, or its peace
> About all dead things beautiful. . . .

She speaks to him in words that he cannot understand, and her voice is followed by the silence that

> Lay sweeter than all harmony: therein
> Slept Music and her dreams, and there was set
> The silence that enfolds the ineffable. . . .

The poem contains a common paradox in all of Sterling's poems that evoke an ideal. Perfection—here Beauty—is always seen as the absence of its opposite, and as such is always a negative attribute; the perfect language lacks words, the perfect beauty lacks substance, the perfect music is silence. Not only does the paradox convey a stock theme of Decadent poetry— that we only can catch a fleeting glimpse of Beauty, which is beyond perception and beyond the language to express it—it also betrays a risk that Sterling as lyricist was always taking: in his quest for language and imagery that could convey the essence of Beauty without its substance, he could very easily end up with nothing at all. (pp. 82-3)

If Sterling's early verses, published in *The Testimony of the Suns and Other Poems,* show affinities with the themes of the European Decadence, then his poems of the Carmel years display a very conscious exploitation of those themes. In fact, in the poems we will examine here, nearly every characteristic of Decadence can be found: the search for novelty, the interest in the exotic and unnatural, the aesthetic assumption that poetry is a means of enchantment, with a concurrent emphasis on language as an evocative and connotative instrument, the rhetorical ornamentation (resulting at times in a disintegration of artistic unity), the scorn of contemporary society, and the many allusions to an exotic past. . . .

As these qualities tend to pervade Sterling's work, others diminish. Certain forms disappear. Gone is the *In Memoriam* stanza as a vehicle for extended discourse on a serious theme (later in his career Sterling employs the ode and then the blank-verse drama for this purpose); also gone is the blank-verse meditation. But more important, gone forever are verses of metaphysical speculation which assume the existence of a spiritual realm. In *Testimony* . . . , several lyrics—"A White Rose," "Reincarnation," and "The Soul's Exile," for example—display neo-Platonic themes of a preexistent harmony of the soul with the eternal spirit. Other lyrics—"**Music,**" "**The Spirit of Beauty**"—present poetry and its sister art, music, as pathways to the divine realm. In Sterling's second book, *A Wine of Wizardry and Other Poems* . . . , these neo-Platonic lyrics are replaced by poems which reveal a deepening sense of loss and abandonment (present in *Testimony* but not nearly as pervasive) and a desperate, often self-destructive sort of hedonism.

Sterling's shift to Decadence is very evident in the playful perversity of **"A Wine of Wizardry,"** the poem which made him famous. In this long lyric, the dominant aesthetic principle seems to be that poetry is an exquisitely useless activity whose main function is to invoke extremes of sensation. The odd detachment of the poem would suggest that this is a rather effete sort of experimentation; yet the highly mannered language seems like a fabric stretched over an abyss of despair, hidden from the reader's view only by the gaudiness of that fabric.

As the poem begins, the speaker is drinking from a crystal goblet of red wine and musing into its depths. While he meditates, Fancy, a personification so abstract that she seems completely separate from his consciousness, "awakes with brow caressed by poppy-bloom," and wings her way to numerous bizarre and sinister scenes. Throughout the poem she remains unrealized except as a winged female figure, alternately fascinated, repelled, or disappointed by the various stages of her journey. As a dramatization of the visionary possibilities of the poetic sensibility heightened by wine, Fancy's very abstractness is a *fin-de siècle* version of transcendence, an attempt to explore imaginatively the possibilities of rapture-in-horror. Yet there is a sort of self-directed irony in the poem which generates not horror but humor. The imaginative journey is not so serious an attempt to explore sensation as it is an occasion for effects of imagery and color, and an opportunity for *épater le bourgeois* by being simply outrageous.

In the imagery of **"A Wine of Wizardry,"** the visual element is predominant; and as in most of Sterling's descriptive poems, scenes are cast from a distance. Fancy's visits are made from afar, as befits such places as a grotto with "wattled monsters" and a "cowled magician," a polar iceberg with hidden sapphires, a battle of Titans against Olympians, a revel of Celtic elves, a Syrian treasure-house, and a multitude of other exotic and grotesque scenes. Through all of these visions with their varied splendors and horrors shines the ruddy glare of the red wine, until the entire poem seems suffused in a baleful, bloody light. . . . (pp. 87-8)

"A Wine of Wizardry" seems to spring from a typically Decadent impulse to break free from the self into a fantasy world, vaguely mystical but admittedly illusory: an impulse reminiscent of Baudelaire but lacking Baudelaire's sense of self-immolation. In a sense, the poem is incantatory, attempting through language and imagery to create extremes of sensation, and thus to release the imprisoned self from ordinary experience. The dominant tone is of horror tinged with morbid fascination and, occasionally, with macabre humor. But at the same time there is a strange detachment throughout the poem, and its final impression is jaded, disappointed, and *ennuyé*.

Like **"The Testimony of the Suns,"** then, **"A Wine of Wizardry"** is about the failure of transcendence and the need to escape from the here and now. In **"Testimony,"** the infinite abysses of space provide a direction for imaginative escape, whereas in **"Wine"** to escape is to retreat into fantasy. Both poems imply the futility of human aspirations, and in both there is an undertone of hysteria which suggests the urgency of the problem that ordinary reality will not solve. The poet's attempt to break through the prison of self will always fail, and he will either be left to ponder on oblivion—"dust the yearning lips that cried"—or to simulate pleasure—"smile as one content". (pp. 90-1)

Within a two- or three-year span following the appearance of the notorious **"A Wine of Wizardry"** in Bierce's *Cosmopol-*

itan, Sterling began to find an increasingly favorable reception in the national literary magazines, and significantly, it was with the sonnet form that he found his most appreciative public. At this time the sonnet was very popular both with critics and general readers of poetry, and Sterling's excursions into the form began to be highly regarded. (p. 98)

Looking at the sonnets that appeared in *The House of Orchids and Other Poems,* one can see that certain essential characteristics of Sterling's lyrics were unchanged by his growing inclination for the sonnet form. The nebular theme of **"The Testimony of the Suns,"** the pervasive agnosticism, the persistent striving after the ineffable, the love of cold images of Beauty, and the lyric raptures remain. But the sonnet offers Sterling some control over his most distressing tendencies: diffuseness of thought and excesses of imagery, allusion, and rhetoric. In poems like **"Aldebaran at Dusk,"** the sonnet form permits him to exploit his most promising lyric asset: a careful attention to verbal effects, generating a mood of quiet beauty tinged with a strain of melancholy.

By and large, Sterling was quite comfortable with the sonnet form, and it was as a sonneteer that he began to develop his widest reputation. (pp. 101-02)

The House of Orchids and Other Poems . . . , Sterling's third volume, represents a milestone in his career for two reasons. First, it is with this collection that he became completely established with the American public as a significant poetic voice; no longer was he a poet of regional fame, but a promising younger poet. Second, and paradoxically, *House of Orchids* was the *last* volume of poems that Sterling could produce with such assurance. Ever after . . . , he would have to cope with the awareness that his Decadent manner was out of fashion and that the wave of the future would be a *vers libre* which he could not hope to and would not wish to imitate. How these two perceptions can be simultaneously true is a peculiar irony of Sterling's career, and is also the key to his importance as a transitional figure in the history of American poetry. (p. 103)

Despite the continuous emphasis on universalism in the familiar cosmic themes, the nature poems in *House of Orchids* are distinctly regional. When, for instance, in a sonnet he employs the motif of sunset over the ocean—a favorite symbol for passing time, oblivion, or the inevitability of death—he is also reminding the reader that he is a West Coast poet. Biographical evidence indicates that Sterling was an excellent observer of the physical world. From his childhood on, as his friends have testified, he possessed a keen awareness of birds, wildflowers, and the beautiful minutiae of nature that the less observant would pass over. The five Carmel diaries, with their frequent descriptions of changing seasons, attest to his perceptive eye. Yet the poems in *House of Orchids* which are inspired by the northern California coast seldom portray nature accurately or objectively. Instead, like the earlier nature poems we have already examined, the observed setting serves as a point of departure into the subjective and visionary.

In **"An Altar of the West,"** for example, an irregular ode of some 220 lines, the specific locale is Point Lobos, the southern boundary of Carmel Bay. But there is no sense of particularity in Sterling's portrayal of this spot; it could be any awesome headland or, for that matter, nearly any natural object which gives the observer an impression of great beauty. In fact, the first sixty lines are an extended apostrophe to Beauty, who animates the "dryad-haunted" hills, and who inspires the "ghostly rains" of the "wine-souled" autumn season. When at last Point Lobos itself is mentioned, it is described in a rather subjective and rhetorical manner:

> Past Carmel lies a headland that the deep—
>   A Titan at his toil—
> Has graven with the measured surge and sweep
> Of waves that broke ten thousand years ago.
>   Here winds assail
>   That blow
>   From unfamiliar skies
> And isolating waters of the West. . . .

Point Lobos is a "vast, Tree-shaggy land," a "granite bulwark," a "mount of granite, steep and harsh, where cling / Along its rugged length / The cypress legions". . . . The poem makes that familiar tentative movement from the real to the imagined:

> See how the wave in sudden anger flings
> White arms about a rock to drag it down!
>   No siren sings,
> But in that pool of crystal gleams her crown,
>   Flung on a rocky shelf—
> Grey jewels cold and agates of the elf
> That in yon scarlet cavern still is hid,
>   'Mid shells that mock the dawn. . . .

This ostentatious diction carries the poem through a long afternoon, evening, and night at Point Lobos. Sterling's real subjects, however, are the relation of human life to the universe and the transitory nature of beauty. It is nature poetry like this that prompted the Imagist critics to dub Sterling and Edward Rowland Sill, an earlier poet, "The cosmic California school."

Following the starry night to the moment when the abysmal "writhing fog" comes to obliterate all the beauty of the shoreline, **"An Altar of the West"** comments that Beauty has no business haunting the House of Death. Though beauty seems a portent of eternity, it may well be the "ray that leaping from our whitest star / Shows but the night beyond." Yet, in a now typical equivocation, Sterling speculates that beauty may be "The altar of an undiscovered shore," or the mad, sublime vision of "sorrowed man, the brute that dared to dream." . . . (pp. 105-07)

Often in Sterling's poems the ending softens the dominant cynicism of the rest of the work. There is evidence that he deliberately tried to spare his readers from the more despairing side of his vision, by tacking on endings that he did not really endorse; the practice might also have been an attempt to meet the overgenteel requirements of his magazine publishers, requirements which, despite himself, influenced him. But in the final analysis this sort of equivocation must be seen as a reluctance to confront the implications of his own pessimism, which threatened the foundation on which his lyrical impulse was so precariously poised. (pp. 110-11)

Despite the critical success of *The House of Orchids and Other Poems,* and despite his now-secure reputation as a sonneteer of great skill, by 1913 it had become clear to Sterling that the magazines were not altogether receptive to his best work. They wanted "human interest" rather than chill aestheticism, direct expression of sentiment rather than recondite astronomical allusions or densely textured imagery. He was able to rationalize their criticism as the pedestrianism of the cultural Philistine, but when younger poets whom he respected concurred, he was forced to reevaluate his position. (p. 116)

Opinions like this held some sway over Sterling, and when in 1913 he began consciously to try to make a living through his poetry he began to write lighter verse, more "human" in sentiment, and far less esoteric in diction or allusion. To some degree he was successful, but to the detriment of his own aesthetic views: art was anathema to the publishing world, and if he had to adapt himself to its standards, then he would have to get "the disease of art" out of his system.

The fourth collected volume, *Beyond the Breakers and Other Poems* . . . , attests to Sterling's resolve to write poetry that would please his critics—and to the difficulty he had in doing so. There are several set-pieces in Sterling's usual vein; for example, the sonnet **"The Muse of the Incommunicable"** presents a typical theme of the intransigence of beauty:

> The wind of lonely places is her wine.
>   Still she eludes us, hidden, husht and fleet,
>   A star withdrawn, a music in the gloom.
>
> Beauty and death her speechless lips assign,
>   Where silence is, and where the surf-loud feet
>   Of armies wander on the sands of doom.

Other poems reflect customary concerns, and emphasize the deepening cynicism we have noticed in the previous volumes. **"The Last Monster"** describes man as the bestial product of centuries of bestial evolution. **"War"** and **"Christmas Under Arms"** portray the folly and brutality of war. (pp. 116-17)

But many of the poems in *Beyond the Breakers* depart from the usual themes. The title poem, for instance, is a tribute to the manly sport of swimming. **"Ballad of Two Seas"** and **"Ballad of St. John of Nepomuk"** are excursions into light narrative verse. **"Past the Panes"** ends in a genteel cliché, "O strange! that humble things should be / Of stature more than mountains are . . ." . . . . There are even conventionally pious lyrics with sentiments completely at odds with Sterling's own views. (p. 117)

If anything, *The Caged Eagle and Other Poems* . . . reinforces the impression that Sterling's muse, beset by the double nemesis of genteel editors and Imagist critics, was in eclipse. Many of the poems betray their popular magazine destinations: **"A Dog Waits His Dead Mistress," "An Autumn Thrush," "Time and Tear," "To an Old Nurse."** Hackneyed and sentimental, these do not meet Sterling's own standards for serious work, but they had proven to be salesworthy. (p. 122)

The publication of [*The Binding of the Beast and Other War Verse*] was, aesthetically speaking, probably the low point of Sterling's career, and it is notable that after the war his confidence in his work seems to have returned. He found a steady market for his poems among more conservative literary journals; his poems appeared regularly in *Nation, Bookman, Harper's Monthly, Literary Digest,* and *Overland Monthly*. With this exposure he was rather widely known, but primarily as a regional poet and a traditionalist. (p. 130)

Sails and Mirage . . . , the last collected volume of new verse of Sterling's lifetime, is a testament to his acceptance of his own limitations, and his desire to make the best of them. Returning to the aestheticism of his earlier volumes, but dropping some of the archaisms and stilted diction which had weakened his style, Sterling produced his most consistently effective volume. Though essentially nostalgic in its adherence to the nineteenth-century tradition, *Sails and Mirage* contains some of Sterling's best poetry.

Aside from the disappearance of archaisms and poetic expletives ("Lo!" "Alas!") from this volume, several other characteristics of Sterling's work seem to have changed. Gone is the grandiose tone of voice which dominated **"The Testimony of the Suns," the "Sonnets of Oblivion,"** and **"The Binding of the Beast."** For the most part, the bewildering phantasmagoria of imagery, as in **"A Wine of Wizardry,"** is gone also. The tone is more restrained, less forced or strident. Devotion to beauty is still an important motif, but the vague Platonism and mystical speculation are completely absent, and in their place are poems which define Beauty as a life-sustaining illusion, and several poems which express longing for death. Thus the strain of pessimism, which we noted was growing in the first three volumes, dominates the last one.

Many poems are variations of earlier models. **"The Setting of Antares,"** for example, is an impressionistic mood-piece quite like **"Aldebaran at Dusk."** In the octave of this poem, possibly Sterling's best sonnet, there is a collection of images with complex tones. It is clear, and "the summer night is old"; there is a calmly moving sea, "with troubled moonlight on its tranquil breast." The wind and water have held a "truce of silence," and the stars are setting, "silvery and cold." Even with these conflicting connotations of age, grief, respite from strife, and beautiful, inhuman coldness, there is a feeling of unity in the scene, created by the tranquil cadences of the language, and by the resolution of the contraries, when the sestet shows us that the entire poem is about death:

> Antares, heart of blood, how stir your wings,
> Above the sea's mysterious murmurings!
>   The road of death leads outward to thy light,
>   And thou art symbol for a time of him
>   Whose fated star, companionless and dim,
> Sinks to the wide horizon of the Night.

Sterling also returns to earlier forms with three groups of ocean sonnets, two of which, **"Sonnets by the Night Sea"** and **"Sonnets on the Sea's Voice,"** are continuations of sonnet sequences published in *The House of Orchids*. **"Ocean Sunsets,"** a group of three linked sonnets, uses a unifying metaphor of sunset's journey around the world as a vast, endless billow of light which sweeps the oceans of the earth:

> Along the mighty rondure of the world
>   Forever and forever sweeps that wave,
>   From Arctic mountains to the southern floe,
> In soundlessness on purple islands hurled,
>   With opalescent wash of hues that lave
>   Old summits, sacred in that afterglow. . . .

These sonnets, like many other poems in the volume, are pure mood-pieces—excursions into literary Impressionism, in which the emotional effect of the language is more important than its denotative content. An especially effective touch in the quotation above is the combination of "soundlessness," referring to the movement of light across the world, with the onomatopoeia of "opalescent wash," in which there is an impression of the sound of this "surf" of light. Thus Sterling plays delicately with the synaesthesia implied by his metaphor.

In the third **"Ocean Sunsets"** sonnet, Sterling abandons pure Impressionism to make a thematic statement which differs widely from similar earlier statements. Not only is Beauty—here, the beauty of sunsets—the fair ideal that we seek endlessly and fruitlessly, but it is our creation entirely. As long as there is a perceiving eye or a conceiving imagination, Beauty will exist. But when man is no more, Beauty will cease to be also:

> Thy marvel is of man and not of thee,
> And he being not, no longer shalt thou be.
>   Parent and worshipper of loveliness,
>   He walks a realm forbidden to the brute.
>   An alchemist whose spirit can transmute
>   Color and form to beauty's pure excess. . . .

The solipsism of this statement represents Sterling's resolution of a long-term contradiction, which in fact is a central dilemma in all Decadent poetry. As a materialist he denied the existence of spirit, but as a poet the quest for spiritual beauty had been his primary inspiration. But here Beauty is understood as an act of the transforming imagination of man, not a vaguely Platonic ideal or a fleeting but transcendent Presence. Thus, in a way, Sterling is undercutting the principle by which he always has written poetry, exposing the false premises of his own notion of poetic inspiration, inherited from the Romantics but incompatible with materialism. (pp. 131-33)

[In] **"The Wine of Illusion"** the lie of transcendence is what sustains the spirit. A personified figure in "opalescent grey"— a color of illusions—stands surrounded by dead stars. She offers the speaker a crystal cup:

> Drink this or perish. There is naught beside.
>   This is the draft that fashions men from swine,
>   And tho thy heart deny me in its pride,
> Yet of my cup of dreams its blood is red
> And thy lips wet with my creative wine! . . .

The dead stars, of course, are symbols of man's transitory nature, and the wine, of the false ideals of beauty and immortality which have sustained him.

Testaments to the power of illusion, which supports life, and tributes to reason, which denies the value of life, these divergent expressions of Sterling's pessimism are the culmination of tendencies in his poems from the first. (p. 135)

Stevenson is right in asserting that Sterling was noteworthy in his effort to perpetuate the English Romantic tradition [see excerpt dated 1929], but more importantly, he was one of the first American poets to base an artistic vision on the failure of human progress and the need to confront radical despair. Though Sterling may remain best known for his remarkable personal relationships with other writers and for his role in the history of American Bohemianism, he should also be known as an important transitional poet, who, attempting to reconcile nineteenth-century poetic theory with a distinctly twentieth-century sense of alienation, helped prepare the way for the emergence of Modernism in America. (p. 161)

> *Thomas E. Benediktsson, in his* George Sterling, *Twayne Publishers, 1980, 183 p.*

TONY J. STAFFORD   (essay date 1982)

[*In the following excerpt, Stafford analyzes the structure of* "A Wine of Wizardry."]

Contrary to contemporary opinion, including Bierce's, ["**A Wine of Wizardry**"] is not a mere verbal and imagistic orgy, but a carefully controlled work of art. Its subject is the imagination, its purpose to define its power, but the definition process is subtle and complex. The poem is basically a vision of flight, induced by a sunset and a glass of wine into which the sun shines. The agent of the vision is the imagination, and the quality of the vision bespeaks imagination's power. This purpose also determines the nature of the parts, the structure, the imagery, the sound, and the atmosphere, and by their characteristics contribute to the definition. This unity of purpose, content, and technique gives the poem an integrated wholeness seemingly unnoticed by its early critics.

The structure helps to define the imagination in several ways. The poem seems disjointed by its swift movement from place to place and by the vastness of the space covered, for it roams over heaven, earth, and hell. It does not move in any geographical order, but soars over vast abysses of space and time from one sentence to the next. This feeling of rapidity of movement, of ubiquity, and of freedom suggests the illimitable power of Fancy. But the structure does even more. Each section contains a visit to both a place of innocence and of evil. In section one, it travels from a beach where maidens play to an underworld cavern of a cowled magician's; in II, it goes from a quiet garden of the East to an eastern tomb filled with incantations to Satan; in III, it leaves a cathedral-like grove to learn of Circe's art; in IV, after again seeing Satan's cavern, it seeks the silence of night; and in section V, after a visit to Merlin's tomb, it flies to "a star above the sunset lees." Innocence is associated with places and objects of nature (beaches, silent gardens, quiet groves, and lights of the sky), while evil connects with Satan, the netherworld, tombs, and occult activity. This embracing of both innocence and evil in each section suggests that Fancy is important in determining these states and has the potential for either but is in itself neither. Each section also contains other kinds of opposition. The places visited are of contrasting kinds, hot and cold, quiet and noisy, holy and evil, dead and alive, and destructive and creative. This juxtapositioning communicates the diversity and completeness of Fancy, while at the same time creates tensions which generate the poem's power.

Bierce and others made much of the poem's rich imagery, but failed to realize that the images are vital to the poem's purpose. Although there are many kinds, the main groups of images seem to relate to empires, the occult, the Satanic, the charnelhouse, jewelry, religion, and nature. Each type suggests certain characteristics of the imagination while at the same time connects with the sunset-wine motif and with the others in a way as to give the poem a complex unity. A sampling of each gives an impression of its quality and its relation to the poem's purpose. The empire imagery centers around kings, queens, palaces, and kingdoms and seems to have Medieval overtones.

> She goes to watch, beside a lurid moat,
> The kingdoms of the afterglow suffuse
> A sentinel mountain stationed toward the night.

Lines such as "Far on shadowy tow'rs Droop blazoned banners" and "as moaning airs invoke the conquered rust Of lordly helms made equal in the dust" relate to this group and phrases like "empress of a purpled realm," "palaces of silence," "wicked queen," and even the "battlements of sunset" in the very first line belong to it. Associated with the imagination in this way, they suggest its royalty and its rulership over man. Another large and highly suggestive family of images is the occult. There are references to a "cowled magician," "infernal rubrics," "the tawny flutes of sorcery," "gyving spells," the "mystic word," "dim augury," "powers of wizardry," and "a sick enchantress," all dominated of course by the title itself. The occult motif seems to work in several different directions, for it bespeaks the magical lure of the imagination, the power of Fancy to explore the mysterious, as well as the unknown's appeal to the imagination. Still another important group is that of the Satanic and netherworld. Visits to caverns where Satan controls and incantations to "Satan's might" stand out, but the most vivid passage is when Fancy

> turns
> To caverns where a demon altar burns,
> And Satan, yawning on his brazen seat,
> Fondles a screaming thing his fiends have flayed,
> Ere Lilith come his indolence to greet,
> Who leads from hell his whitest queens.

In the context of the poem, Fancy's power to lead man into the caverns of hell infers her diabolical control over man as well as her pagan response to beauty which is worshipped in itself as the supreme spirit. The Satanic images help capture this atmosphere. . . . Jewelry images so predominate that the effect is a general feeling of richness, and their association with Fancy suggests the imagination's value. Religious images also appear, for Fancy is capable of worshipping,

> in the hushed cathedral's jeweled gloom,
> Ere Faith return, and azure censers fume,
> She kneels, in solemn quietude, to mark
> The suppliant day from gorgeous oriels float
> And altar-lamps immure the deathless spark;

and worthy of being worshipped, for the poet says, "I . . . Drink at her font, and smile as one content." The religious motif connects with the wine which is part of the original impetus in the experience. Such overtones suggest the sacredness of the fancy and the poet's veneration of the imagination. Nature of course is basic in the poem, for the poem describes Fancy's response to nature, to a sunset. In addition to frequent mentionings of the sea, beach, sky, moon, and stars, there are also flowers, "woodland shade," mountains, mornings, autumn, and other aspects of nature. They all suggest that the imagination responds to and belongs to nature.

The division of the images into groups is in one way misleading, for an interrelationship exists among them. Many images belong to more than one group. For example, castles and moats are empire images, but they also relate to the religious motif by their Medieval association as well as with Merlin, who also connects with the occult. This interparticipation is repeated with many references and achieves a unity and compression, paganness. A baffling group of images concerns the charnel-house, tombs, blood, and vampires. Fancy visits "a porphyry crypt," "a wicked queen's unhallowed tomb," tombs which "betray their ghastly trust," "glowering pyres" and a "burning-ghaut," and hears "tomb-thrown echoings." She is fascinated by "vipers' blood," "silent ghouls," "crimson bubbles [which] rise from battle-wrecks," and "a caldron vext with harlots' blood." This imagistic motif is climaxed and explained by the lines near the end:

> The blue-eyed vampire, sated at her feast,
> Smiles bloodily against the leprous moon.

It becomes clear that Fancy herself is the vampire, an insatiable feeder on red, but, in her case, on the red objects of nature. It is the central metaphor for the imagination in the poem, it relates to the vision of flight, and it implies the imagination's tendency to roam the universe, thirsting for red beauty.

Three other groups of images include jewelry, religion, and nature. Jewelry references abound in the poem. At one point the poet merely catalogues the jewels which Fancy sees beneath the ocean: "jacinth," "the moonstone-crystal," "coral twigs," "winy agates," "translucencies of jasper," "folds of banded onyx, and vermilion breast Of cinnabar." But jewels are used mostly as adjectives to enrich the descriptions: "onyx waters," "opals of the shattered light," "sapphires of the snow," "ruby-sanded beach," "garnet-crusted lamps," and stars, "red-embered rubies smolder[ing] but at the same time tension is created by much imagistic juxtaposition. For example, the holiness of religious references opposes the evil of the Satanic, the empire overtones, which echo of power and permanence, contrast with the death in the tombs and charnel-house motif, and the concreteness and orderliness of nature counteracts the indefiniteness of the occult. This opposition, however, is countered by a unification based on their appeal to Fancy, their contribution to the definition of the imagination, and, most importantly, by the fact that they all relate in some way to the color red, the fires of the underworld where dwells Satan, the blood of the charnel-house, the rubrics of the occult, the lights and jewels of nature, and the wine of religion. Through this preponderance of red in the imagery, the poem takes on the red glow of the wine and sunset which moved the poet originally. Finally, the images are the fabric of the poem, and their profusion creates a feeling of inexhaustibility, power, and richness, and this effect too is a statement about the imagination.

Like Gerard Manly Hopkins before him and Dylan Thomas after him, Sterling was very much aware of the importance of sound in poetry, as demonstrated here where he creates a richness of sound appropriate to the atmosphere and subject matter. He uses a variety of techniques, one of the most common being alliteration. In one line he can alliterate three times, "Fondles a thing his fiends have flayed"; or four, "For this the fays will dance, for elfin cheer" and "In turbid dyes that tinge her torture-dome." But he surpasses all effort in one instance where he works three of one kind and six of another in three lines:

> Behold a beacon burn on evening skies,
> As fed with sanguine oils at touch of night.
> Forth from the pharos-flame a radiance flies.

He is quite adept with onomatopoeia, using it with restraint and skill. He talks about the "moaning airs," "mid hiss of oils," "a screaming thing," seas "where waters mutter," and "whispers from the night." He also has a sure sense of assonance and uses it regularly to enrich the sound. He brings words together like "droop" and "woodland," "dyes" and "twilight," "each" and "sea"; sometimes he packs lines with assonance as in

> Ere Faith return, and azure censers fume,
> She kneels in solemn quietude.

These lines incidentally exemplify another habit of Sterling's. He laces the sound together by first establishing the "tur" in "return" and then echoes part of it in the "ur" of "azure" and the other part in the "tu" of "quietude." Occasionally he even teases the ear with homonyms as in "by tales the wind of ocean tell." Finally, Sterling is aware of the power of sound for reinforcing meaning. For example, in the lines "sips Her darkest wine, and smiles with wicked lips," the sibilants suggest the action of sipping and the unrounded vowels (the "i's") catch the muscular feel of the smile. Again, toward the end of the poem, tensions are released as Fancy becomes satiated, and just at this point the sound communicates the cessation of flight: "But evening now is come, and Fancy folds Her splendid plumes." The quietness of the lines contrast with the roar of words to this point and prepare the reader for relaxation from the vision. Throughout the poem there is an hypnotic effect to the rush of words, and the general feeling is one of headlong flight, which communicates the soaring of the imagination, and the feeling that once started there is no stop until complete satisfaction is attained.

The organic wholeness of **"A Wine of Wizardry"** is achieved in one final way. As a definition of the power of the imagination, the poem itself is a demonstration and demands simultaneously of the reader the active involvement of his own imagination. Its final unity is realized by embracing the reader's imagination, and the statements it makes about Fancy must be proved by the reader's utilization of these qualities. If the reader faults in engaging his own imagination, the truth of the poem is destroyed, its final unity remains unachieved, and the poem fails. Thus the cause of the poem's failure in its own day becomes clear; it was not Sterling's fancy which failed, but his readers'. In measuring the imagination, Sterling was accurate in judging its potential, as demonstrated by his poem; he was wrong in assuming the same degree in all poetry readers, as shown by the poem's initial reception. (pp. 35-7)

> *Tony J. Stafford, "George Sterling and the Wine of Fancy," in* The Romantist, *Nos. 4-5, 1982, pp. 33-8.*

ADDITIONAL BIBLIOGRAPHY

Angoff, Charles. Foreword to *George Sterling: A Centenary Memoir-Anthology*, pp. 5-16. South Brunswick, N. J.: Poetry Society of America, 1969.
　　Brief discussion of Sterling's life and work.

Austin, Mary. "The Land of Little Rain." In her *Earth Horizon*, pp. 296-304. New York: Houghton Mifflin, 1932.*
　　Biographical notes written by a close friend.

Bennet, Raine Edward. "Don Passé." *The Literary Review* 15, No. 2 (Winter 1971-72): 133-47.
　　Personal reminiscences about Sterling's life.

Berkelman, Robert G. "George Sterling on 'The Black Vulture'." *American Literature* 10, No. 2 (May 1938): 223-24.
　　Reprint of a letter written by Sterling explaining his poem.

Bland, Henry Meade. "Sterling, the Poet of Seas and Stars." *Overland Monthly* LXVI, No. 6 (December 1915): 474-78.
　　Discussion of some thematic and stylistic characteristics of "The Testimony of the Suns."

Brazil, John. "George Sterling: Art, Politics, the Retreat to Carmel." *The Markham Review* 8 (Winter 1979): 27-33.
　　Discussion of Sterling's attitudes and lifestyle.

Dunbar, John. "Letters of George Sterling to Carey McWilliams." *The California Historical Society Quarterly* XLVI, No. 3 (September 1967): 235-52.
　　Letters written to Ambrose Bierce's biographer.

Everson, William. Chapter Ten. In his *Archetype West: The Pacific Coast as a Literary Region*, pp. 49-65. Berkeley: Oyez, 1976.*
　　Consideration of the relationship between Sterling and Robinson Jeffers.

Gregory, Horace, and Zaturenska, Marya. "Three Poets of the Sierras." In their *A History of American Poetry 1900-1940*, pp. 44-58. New York: Harcourt, Brace and Company, 1942.*
　　Biographical and critical sketch.

Gross, Dalton. "George Sterling's Letters to William Stanley Braithwaite: The Poet Versus the Editor." *American Book Collector* 24, No. 2 (November-December 1973): 18-20.*
　　Sterling's letters to the editor of the Boston *Transcript*.

Longtin, Ray C. "George Sterling." In his *Three Writers of the Far West*, pp. 185-249. Boston: G. K. Hall, 1980.
　　Annotated bibliography of writings about Sterling and his work.

"A Poet Who Finds Himself." *The New York Times Book Review* XVI, No. 25 (25 June 1911): 400.
　　Review of "The House of Orchids."

Noel, Joseph. *Footloose in Arcadia: A Personal Record of Jack London, George Sterling, and Ambrose Bierce.* New York: Carrick and Evans, 1940, 330 p.*
　　Much little-known biographical information.

Payne, William Morton. "Recent Poetry." *The Dial* 51 (16 August 1911): 103-07.*
　　Favorable review of *The House of Orchids, and Other Poems.*

Sinclair, Upton. "Adonais." In his *Money Writes!*, pp. 159-66. New York: Albert and Charles Boni, 1927.
　　Biographical comments written by a close friend.

Slade, Joseph W. "George Sterling, 'Prophet of the Suns'." *The Markham Review*, No. 2 (May 1968): 4-10.
　　Examines the major influences in Sterling's life.

Sydney-Fryer, Donald. "Hesperian Laureate." *The Romantist*, No. 1 (1977): 13-42.
　　Biographical overview.

Walker, Dale L. "Poet of the Mist: George Sterling." *The Romantist*, No. 3 (1979): 39-42.
　　Discussion of Sterling's life and work.

(Adeline) Virginia Woolf

1882-1941

English novelist, critic, essayist, short story writer, diarist, and biographer.

The following entry presents criticism of Woolf's novel *Mrs. Dalloway* (1925). For a complete discussion of Woolf's career, see *TCLC*, Volumes 1 and 5.

Mrs. Dalloway represents Woolf's first successful attempt to produce a novel in her own distinctive narrative style, rejecting the boundaries of traditional European narrative form, which she believed had become too artificial and restrictive for increasingly poetic, impressionistic renderings of life. The novel marks the emergence of Woolf's mature narrative voice, as well as the perfection of the experimental narrative technique employed tentatively in her preceding novel, *Jacob's Room,* in which she illuminated aspects of characters' personalities through series of individual impressions revealed to the reader by interior monologue. Encompassing one day in the life of an introspective, upper-class, Westminster woman, *Mrs. Dalloway* is often discussed in terms of its affinities with James Joyce's similarly constructed *Ulysses* (1922). However, though both novels are written in stream of consciousness style, scholars stress that Woolf's novel greatly differs from Joyce's not only in length, setting, and characterization, but, perhaps most importantly, in its development of Woolf's lifelong aesthetic concern: the interrelationship of time, existence, and the human psyche. It is believed that by her treatment of these subjects in her strikingly individual prose style, Woolf composed one of the most subtly powerful and memorable English novels of the post-World War I era.

Deriving its title from the protagonist of the novel, Clarissa Dalloway, *Mrs. Dalloway* is first of all a study of character. Woolf's approach to characterization greatly diverged from that of her Victorian and Edwardian predecessors. In 1924, the year preceding the novel's publication, she issued an apologia for modern fiction entitled *Mr. Bennett and Mrs. Brown*. Written while the composition of *Mrs. Dalloway* was still under way, this work was a harbinger of Woolf's subsequent artistic direction. In this essay she attacked such writers as Arnold Bennett, John Galsworthy, and H. G. Wells for their technique of representing characters by means of extended passages describing their backgrounds and personality traits. By contrast, Woolf believed it a considerable refinement of the novel form to present seemingly disconnected, though significantly revealing, glimpses of characters. Woolf contended that such glimpses, when viewed together, would satisfy the reader's curiosity while remaining compatible with her belief that one's individuality could never be conveyed in words alone. Encouraged by the success of *Jacob's Room*, in which she used recurrent imagery to partially overcome the difficulty of maintaining a unified narrative while employing such nontraditional techniques, she planned to further her experimentation, hoping to arrive at a literary form that more accurately represented life's complexities. Given her growing artistic confidence, *Mrs. Dalloway* took on colossal proportions in her mind. As she records in a diary entry written during the first stages of the novel: "In this book I have almost too many ideas. I want to give life and death, sanity and insanity; I want to criticise the

social system, and to show it at work, at its most intense." Fusing these aims with her avowed intent not to bend to the formulaic dictates of past writers, Woolf portrayed her protagonist as the embodiment of nearly all the dominant themes of the novel.

Symbolically, according to critics, Clarissa Dalloway represents clarity, purity, and sensitivity to the moment. Her marriage to Richard Dalloway, a member of Parliament, is one not of passion but of convenience and respectability. Several modern critics contend that the chief conflict of the novel concerns Clarissa Dalloway's sexual identity. Through Woolf's process of character development, in which characters recall and reflect upon pivotal points in their pasts, we learn of an epiphanic moment which occurred some time before the Dalloways' marriage when Clarissa was kissed by a close female friend, Sally Seton. This, according to some critics, represents the only moment in her life in which her actions conformed with her true sexual nature. The moment, however, is interrupted by the appearance of Peter Walsh, a vibrant young man who wants to marry Clarissa. Ultimately, Clarissa rejects both Walsh and Seton in favor of a man she concludes will be the least demanding and most socially respectable marital partner: the established, romantically undemanding Dalloway. Critic Emily Jensen terms this decision Clarissa's "respectable suicide''—a living death in which she sacrifices personal integrity for social standing and security.

Woolf declared the character of the mentally stricken war veteran Septimus Warren Smith to be Clarissa Dalloway's ''double.'' Like Sally Seton, he also profoundly affects Clarissa's understanding of herself and her relationship to the world. Although the two never meet they are closely linked thematically. Near the beginning of the novel, Clarissa, while gazing into a bookstore window, reads the dirge from Shakespeare's *Cymbeline* that begins: ''Fear no more the heat o' the sun / Nor the furious winter's rages.'' She repeats the phrase throughout the day, as does Septimus, who, near the end of the novel, commits suicide after realizing that his psychiatrist, like society in general, wishes him to conform to a life incompatible with his nature and atemporal, romantic view of life. In addition to heightening the affinities between Septimus and Clarissa, the passage from Shakespeare suggests to some critics Woolf's acceptance of suicide as a viable means of obtaining personal freedom by defying constrictive British mores, manifestations of which Woolf, as a member of the progressive-minded Bloomsbury Group, continually challenged.

Biographers stress the importance of the suicide theme in *Mrs. Dalloway*, noting Woolf's own recurring bouts with mental illness which, following several attempts to take her own life, culminated in her suicide in 1941. Her exploration of the darker recesses of the human mind in *Mrs. Dalloway* has been cited by numerous critics and attributed not only to her personal experience but to her encounter with the studies of psychoanalyst Sigmund Freud, which Virginia and Leonard Woolf's Hogarth Press published in English translation before Freud was widely known in England. Through continual exploration of the thoughts and beliefs of her characters, particularly Clarissa and Septimus, Woolf is credited with greatly advancing the scope of the psychological novel.

Yet, some scholars argue that psychologically based criticisms of Woolf's novel pay too little attention to the work's overall significance. As James Hafley has stated: ''*Mrs. Dalloway* is not primarily about Clarissa, or about any of its other characters. Rather, it is about life and reality or time; both character and circumstance are means to the end of expressing a unified vision of experience.'' Several critics concur with this thesis, noting Woolf's subordination of plot and characterization to an integral structure in which the inexorable chiming of London's Big Ben, and the interweaving of characters' thoughts and of past and present time, are enforced by several antipodal motifs signifying social unity and individuality, oppression and freedom—opposites which radiate throughout the novels of Woolf and indicate her aesthetic search for the ideals of social and personal harmony within the real, discordant world. In summary, Reuben Arthur Brower has submitted that ''the central metaphor of Clarissa's narrative (and of the novel) is . . . two-fold: the exhilarated sense of being a part of the forward moving process and the recurrent fear of some break in this absorbing activity. . . .'' It is this characteristic which most scholars believe affords *Mrs. Dalloway* its remarkable power and poignancy.

Often termed a difficult book due to its atemporal, seemingly plotless structure and disjointed character development, *Mrs. Dalloway* has drawn adverse criticism since its publication. One major objection to the work, levied by Wyndham Lewis, is that however fine the prose may be, the novel as a whole represents a weak and narrow documentation of English life. Another complaint, made by D. S. Savage, is that *Mrs. Dal-*loway fails to affirm the value of human life, though other critics contend that this theme is repeatedly broached in the novel. It remains the opinion of most Woolf critics that *Mrs. Dalloway* is a high fictional achievement, and though perhaps not her greatest work, it is one of her most studied. Its telling examination of the human persona and its relationship to the outer world, expertly wrought in a then relatively unexplored form, justifies its standing as a significant novel of the twentieth century.

(See also *Contemporary Authors*, Vol. 104 and *Dictionary of Literary Biography*, Vol. 36: *British Novelists, 1890-1929—Modernists*.)

JOSEPH WOOD KRUTCH   (essay date 1925)

[*Krutch is widely regarded as one of America's most respected literary and drama critics. Noteworthy among his works are* The American Drama since 1918 *(1939), in which he analyzed the most important dramas of the 1920s and 1930s, and* ''Modernism'' in Modern Drama *(1953), in which he stressed the need for twentieth-century playwrights to infuse their works with traditional humanistic values. A conservative and idealistic thinker, he was a consistent proponent of human dignity and the preeminence of literary art. In the following excerpt, Krutch favorably reviews* Mrs. Dalloway.]

Mrs. Woolf is a sort of decorous James Joyce. Her method, which consists in recording the stream of consciousness as it flows through the minds of her characters, is essentially the same as his, and her new novel [*Mrs. Dalloway*], dealing like *Ulysses* with the events of a single day, tells such story as it has to tell through the medium of the recollections which stir vaguely in the memories of her people. Mrs. Woolf prefers to choose her characters from among those who, owning an allegiance to good society, have had both their manners and their thoughts disciplined by its conventions, and she discovers none of those grotesque monsters whom Mr. Joyce finds inhabiting the jungles of the mind; but this difference, which is merely a difference in temperament and experience, has nothing to do with the method, which is the same in both cases and consists essentially in the attempt to catch life upon the wing, to discard the conventional patterns of story-telling, and to deal with the ultimate stuff of consciousness.

Acts have thoughts behind them, even spoken words have been selected and arranged, so that to describe either is to describe something at least one step removed from the soul; but those unuttered monologues which constitute the bulk of both *Ulysses* and *Mrs. Dalloway* are intended to represent consciousness as it first comes into being, bubbling up from the brain which generates it and constituting the stuff of which character is made. One may go, if one likes, a little deeper and discuss, by the psychoanalytic method, the origin of moods and desires; but to do that is to pass beyond consciousness, for consciousness begins at the point at which Mr. Joyce and Mrs. Woolf describe it. Miscellaneous, vague, and chaotic, composed of memories, moods, sensations, and desires mingled helter-skelter with things tragic and comic, trivial and important treading upon the heels of one another, the stream goes continuously on from the moment we wake until it trails off, fainter and fainter, into slumber or death. From this fast-moving current we snatch bits here and there to fashion into words or to clutch at as resolutions, and by these we are judged; but the real ''I'' is the ever-flowing stream known only to ourselves, and it is with this ''I'' that Mrs. Woolf deals. (pp. 631-32)

It is the distinction of Mrs. Woolf that, unlike most of those who employ her method, she applies it to the presentation of persons who are leading orderly lives, and that she makes it serve the purpose of realizing more intimately the charm of quiet people. The day which she has chosen to present is the day upon which her central character meets after many years the old lover whom she did not marry, and in the course of the three hundred pages which record this day nothing happens except that the reader is brought into intimate contact with a group of people and made to participate in their consciousness. Mrs. Dalloway is not, by ordinary standards, a remarkable person. She has played no important role in life and she is not consciously a philosopher, but it is obvious that as she has moved through the world she has achieved a certain serenity in the midst of the eternal flux; and this, so I think, Mrs. Woolf means us to guess to be the secret of her charm. A little withdrawn, a little lacking, perhaps, in passion, she nevertheless manages to maintain a poise as the stream flows by and to create by her decorum and *savoir faire* a semblance of orderliness in a disordered world. As she watches the changing spectacle of the London streets, talks with her former lover, or greets with formal ease the arrival of her guests, she seems to assure those who come near her that life, even though it have neither harmony nor meaning, may yet be lived with a certain comeliness if one does not ask too much of it; and thus Mrs. Woolf reinvestigates a very old sort of loveliness. The method which she uses is the newest and most radical, but the charm which she exploits—the charm of decorum and resignation—is the most conservative thing in the world. (p. 632)

Joseph Wood Krutch, ''The Stream of Consciousness,'' in The Nation, *Vol. CXX, No. 3126, June 3, 1925, pp. 631-32.*

VIRGINIA WOOLF   (diary date 1925)

[*In the following excerpt from a diary entry, Woolf reflects on criticism of* Mrs. Dalloway *given by her longtime friend Lytton Strachey.*]

No, Lytton does not like **Mrs. Dalloway**, &, what is odd, I like him all the better for saying so, & don't much mind. What he says is that there is a discordancy between the ornament (extremely beautiful) & what happens (rather ordinary—or unimportant). This is caused he thinks by some discrepancy in Clarissa herself; he thinks she is disagreeable & limited, but that I alternately laugh at her, & cover her, very remarkably, with myself. So that I think as a whole, the book does not ring solid; yet, he says, it is a whole; & he says sometimes the writing is of extreme beauty. What can one call it but genius? he said! Coming when, one never can tell. Fuller of genius, he said than anything I had done. Perhaps, he said, you have not yet mastered your method. You should take something wilder & more fantastic, a frame work that admits of anything, like *Tristram Shandy*. But then I should lose touch with emotions, I said. Yes, he agreed, there must be reality for you to start from. Heaven knows how you're to do it. But he thought me at the beginning, not at the end. And he said the C.R. [*The Common Reader*] was divine, a classic; Mrs. D. [*Mrs. Dalloway*] being, I fear, a flawed stone. This is very personal, he said & old fashioned perhaps; yet I think there is some truth in it. For I remember the night at Rodmell when I decided to

give it up, because I found Clarissa in some way tinselly. Then I invented her memories. But I think some distaste for her persisted. Yet, again, that was true to my feeling for Kitty, & one must dislike people in art without its mattering, unless indeed it is true that certain characters detract from the importance of what happens to them. None of this hurts me, or depresses me. Its odd that when Clive [Bell] & others (several of them) say it is a masterpiece, I am not much exalted; when Lytton picks holes, I get back into my working fighting mood, which is natural to me. I don't see myself a success. I like the sense of effort better.

Virginia Woolf, in a diary entry on June 18, 1925, in her The Diary of Virginia Woolf: 1925-1930, *Vol. 3, edited by Anne Olivier Bell, Harcourt Brace Jovanovich, 1980, p. 32.*

VIRGINIA WOOLF   (essay date 1928)

[*In the following introduction to the Modern Library edition of* Mrs. Dalloway, *Woolf capsulizes her thoughts on that novel and fiction writing in general.*]

It is difficult—perhaps impossible—for a writer to say anything about his own work. All he has to say has been said as fully and as well as he can in the body of the book itself. If he has failed to make his meaning clear there it is scarcely likely that he will succeed in some few pages of preface or postscript. And the author's mind has another peculiarity which is also hostile to introductions. It is as inhospitable to its offspring as the hen sparrow is to hers. Once the young birds can fly, fly they must; and by the time they have fluttered out of the nest the mother bird has begun to think perhaps of another brood. In the same way once a book is printed and published it ceases to be the property of the author; he commits it to the care of other people; all his attention is claimed by some new book which not only thrusts its predecessor from the nest but has a way of subtly blackening its character in comparison with its own.

It is true that the author can if he wishes tell us something about himself and his life which is not in the novel; and to this effort we should do all that we can to encourage him. For nothing is more fascinating than to be shown the truth which lies behind those immense façades of fiction—if life is indeed true, and if fiction is indeed fictitious. And probably the connection between the two is highly complicated. Books are the flowers or fruit stuck here and there on a tree which has its roots deep down in the earth of our earliest life, of our first experiences. But here again to tell the reader anything that his own imagination and insight have not already discovered would need not a page or two of preface but a volume or two of autobiography. Slowly and cautiously one would have to go to work, uncovering, laying bare, and even so when everything had been brought to the surface, it would still be for the reader to decide what was relevant and what not. Of **Mrs. Dalloway** then one can only bring to light at the moment a few scraps, of little importance or none perhaps; as that in the first version Septimus, who later is intended to be her double, had no existence; and that Mrs. Dalloway was originally to kill herself, or perhaps merely to die at the end of the party. Such scraps are offered humbly to the reader in the hope that like other odds and ends they may come in useful.

But if one has too much respect for the reader pure and simple to point out to him what he has missed, or to suggest to him what he should seek, one may speak more explicitly to the reader who has put off his innocence and become a critic. For though criticism, whether praise or blame, should be accepted in silence as the legitimate comment which the act of publication invites, now and again a statement is made without bearing on the book's merits or demerits which the writer happens to know to be mistaken. One such statement has been made sufficiently often about **Mrs. Dalloway** to be worth perhaps a word of contradiction. The book, it was said, was the deliberate offspring of a method. The author, it was said, dissatisfied with the form of fiction then in vogue, was determined to beg, borrow, steal or even create another of her own. But, as far as it is possible to be honest about the mysterious process of the mind, the facts are otherwise. Dissatisfied the writer may have been; but her dissatisfaction was primarily with nature for giving an idea, without providing a house for it to live in. The novelists of the preceding generation had done little—after all why should they?—to help. The novel was the obvious lodging, but the novel it seemed was built on the wrong plan. Thus rebuked the idea started as the oyster starts or the snail to secrete a house for itself. And this it did without any conscious direction. The little note book in which an attempt was made to forecast a plan was soon abandoned, and the book grew day by day, week by week, without any plan at all, except that which was dictated each morning in the act of writing. The other way, to make a house and then inhabit it, to develop a theory and then apply it, as Wordsworth did and Coleridge, is, it need not be said, equally good and much more philosophic. But in the present case it was necessary to write the book first and to invent a theory afterwards.

If, however, one singles out the particular point of the book's methods for discussion it is for the reason given—that it has been made the subject of comment by critics, not that in itself it deserves notice. On the contrary, the more successful the method, the less it attracts attention. The reader it is to be hoped will not give a thought to the book's method or to the book's lack of method. He is concerned only with the effect of the book as a whole on his mind. Of that most important question he is a far better judge than the writer. Indeed, given time and liberty to frame his own opinion he is eventually an infallible judge. To him then the writer commends **Mrs. Dalloway** and leaves the court confident that the verdict whether for instant death or for some years more of life and liberty will in either case be just. (pp. v-ix)

> *Virginia Woolf, in an introduction to her* Mrs. Dalloway, The Modern Library, *1928, pp. v-ix.*

WYNDHAM LEWIS (essay date 1934)

[*Lewis was an English novelist who, with T. S. Eliot, Ezra Pound, and T. E. Hulme, was instrumental in establishing the anti-Romantic movement in literature during the first decades of the twentieth century. He also emerged as a leader of the Vorticist movement founded by Pound. Although its principles are vague, critical consensus holds that Vorticism is related to Imagism in poetry and to Cubism in painting, and that one of its primary characteristics is a belief in the total impersonality of art, achieved by fragmenting and reordering the elements of experience into a new and more meaningful synthesis. Pound and Lewis established the short-lived but now-famous periodical* Blast *to give the movement a voice and a rallying point. Lewis's savage, satiric fiction has been compared to the work of Jonathan Swift and Alexander Pope. His best-known novel,* The Apes of God *(1930), is a long and aggressive satire on the cultural life of England in the 1920s. Some critics believe he will eventually be ranked with Eliot, Pound, and James Joyce as one of the most fascinating, controversial,*

and influential writers of the early twentieth century. In the following excerpt, Lewis censures what he perceives as a narrow and timid representation of life in Woolf's works, utilizing Mrs. Dalloway *to illustrate his point.*]

In the present chapter I am compelled . . . to traverse the thorny region of feminism, or of militant feminine feeling. I have chosen the back of Mrs. Woolf—if I can put it in this inelegant way—to transport me across it. I am sure that certain critics will instantly object that Mrs. Woolf is extremely insignificant—that she is a purely feminist phenomenon—that she is taken seriously by no one any longer today, except perhaps by Mr. and Mrs. Leavis—and that, anyway, feminism is a dead issue. But that will not deter me, any more than the other thorny obstacles, from my purpose: for while I am ready to agree that the intrinsic literary importance of Mrs. Woolf may be exaggerated by her friends, I cannot agree that as a symbolic landmark—a sort of party-lighthouse—she has not a very real significance. And she has crystallized for us, in her critical essays, what is in fact *the feminine*—as distinguished from the feminist—standpoint. She is especially valuable in her 'clash' with what is today, in fact and indeed, a dead issue, namely nineteenth-century scientific 'realism,' which is the exact counterpart, of course, in letters, of French Impressionism in art (Degas, Manet, Monet).

But the photographic Degas, he is literally the end of the world, luckily—he is more than off the map; and following forty years behind the French mid-nineteenth century realists, the late Mr. Bennett was such a dead horse (dragging such a dead issue) that Mrs. Woolf was merely engaged in an undergraduate exercise in her pamphlet about him, it might be asserted. In spite of that, so long as prose-fiction continues to be written, the school of 'realism' will always have its followers, in one degree or another. Mr. Hemingway is a case in point, and so is Mr. Faulkner. But in any work at all of prose-fiction, however *disembodied* in theory, there is, as an important, and indeed essential component, a great deal of the technique of 'realism': further than that, it could quite well be contended that most of its technique was the realistic technique, put into the service of the depicting of the 'disembodied.' (pp. 159-60)

[When] Mrs. Woolf, the orthodox 'idealist,' tremulously squares up to the big beefy brute, Bennett [in her **Mr. Bennett and Mrs. Brown**], plainly the very embodiment of commonplace *matter*—it is, in fact, a rather childish, that is to say an oversimple, encounter. It is a cat and dog match, right enough: but such 'spiritual' values as those invoked upon Mrs. Woolf's side of the argument, are of a spiritualism which only exists upon that popular plane, as the complement of hard-and-fast matter. The one value is as tangible, popular and readily understood by the 'plain reader' as the other. I doubt if, at bottom, it is very much more than a boy and girl quarrel (to change the metaphor from dog-and-cat). I believe it is just the old incompatibility of the eternal feminine, on the one hand, and the rough footballing 'he' principle—the eternal masculine—on the other. There is nothing more metaphysical about it than that. (p. 161)

I must assume that you do not know, or I must recall to your mind, the parable of Mrs. Brown and Mr. Bennett. Mrs. Woolf tells us, in a skilful little sketch, how she enters the carriage of a suburban train, and in so doing intrudes unwittingly upon the rather passionate conversation of two people—one, *very large,* a blustering, thick-set, middle-aged bully of a *man:* the other, *very small,* a very pathetic, poor little old lady (not *quite* a lady—''I should doubt if she was an educated woman,'' says

Mrs. Woolf—but none the less to be pitied for *that*!). The big bully had obviously been bullying the weaker vessel: and Mrs. Woolf calls the former Mr. Smith, the latter Mrs. Brown. As to make conversation before the inquisitive stranger in the other corner, or else dreaming aloud, the little old woman asks her *vis-à-vis* if he could tell her whether, after being the host for two years running of caterpillars, an oak-tree dies. And while Mr. Smith (who is a shamefaced coward, as are all big bullies come to that) is eagerly replying to this impersonal question, glad to be able to mask beneath an irrelevant stream of words his blackguardly designs upon the defenceless old lady, Mrs. Brown begins, without moving, to let fall tear after tear into her lap. Enraged at this exhibition of weakness on the part of Mrs. Brown (which he probably would refer to as 'waterworks' or something brutal of that sort) the big bully, ignoring the presence of a third party, leans forward and asks Mrs. Brown point blank if she will do, yes or no, what he asked her to do just now, and poor Mrs. Brown says yes, she will. At that moment Clapham Junction presents itself, the train stops, and the big bully (probably jolly glad to escape from the eye of public opinion, as represented by Mrs. Woolf we are told—for he had little streaks of decency left perhaps) hurriedly leaves the train.

Now the point of this story is, we are told, that Mrs. Woolf, being born a novelist of course, and this episode occurring apparently before she had written any novels (1910 is the date implied) is in a quandary as to what to do. She would have *liked* to write a novel about Mrs. Brown, she tells us. But how was she to do it? For after all Wells, Galsworthy and Bennett (the only novelists apparently that, true child of her time, she knew about) had not taught her how to do it: the only tools (she apologises for this professional word) available were those out of the tool-box of this trio. And alas! they were not suitable for the portrayal of Mrs. Brown. So what was poor little she to do?

She then enlarges upon her dilemma—which she tells us was also the dilemma of D. H. Lawrence, of E. M. Forster and the rest of the people she recognizes as the makers and shakers of the new-age (*all*, to a man, ruined by the wicked, inappropriate trio—I need not repeat the names).

Finding himself in the same compartment with Mrs. Brown, Wells would have looked out of the window, with a blissful faraway Utopian smile on his face. He would have taken no interest in Mrs. Brown. Galsworthy would have written a tract round her: and Bennett would have neglected her 'soul' for her patched gloves and stockings.

This was really a terrible situation for a novelist to be in, in 1910: and everything that has happened since, or to be more accurate, that has *not* happened since, is due to the shortcomings of this diabolical trio (but especially, we are led to understand, to the defective pen of the eminent Fivetowner).

And what this has meant for the novelist, it has meant also for the poet, essayist, historian and playwright. *The sins of the fathers shall be visited*—it is the old old story: it is the instinctive outcry of the war-time Sitwells and Sassoons, that it was their fathers and grandfathers who had caused the war—which, as I have been at pains to point out elsewhere (*The Great Blank of the Missing Generation*) is very much neglecting the fact that there were many other and more formidable persons in the world at the same time as the amiable and probably inoffensive old gentlemen who were responsible for this recriminating offspring: and that probably those progenitors of a 'sacrificed'

generation were just as powerless as their sons, or fathers, to cope with the forces, visible and invisible, which precipitated the World-War—although they no doubt deserve a curse or two, just as we do ourselves, for being so short-sighted, and so ill-equipped for defence, against all the dangers that beset a modern democracy.

What Mrs. Woolf says about the three villains of this highly artificial little piece is perfectly true, as far as it goes: "the difference perhaps is," she writes, "that both Sterne and Jane Austen were interested in things in themselves; in character in itself: in the book in itself." Of course, of course! who would not exclaim: it is not 'perhaps' the difference—is as plain as the nose was on Hodge's face. Of course Sterne and Jane Austen were a different kettle of fish, both to Mrs. Woolf's three sparring partners or Aunt Sallies, and to Mrs. Woolf herself.

And then Mrs. Woolf goes on to tell us that we must not expect too much of Messrs. Eliot, Joyce, Lawrence, Forster, or Strachey either. For they all, in their way, were in the same unenviable position. All were boxed up with some Mrs. Brown or other, longing to 'bag' the old girl, and yet completely impotent to do so, because no one was there on the spot to show them how, and they could not, poor dears, be expected to do it themselves! Do not complain of *us*, then, she implores her public. Show some pity for such a set of people, born to such a forlorn destiny! You will never get anything out of us except a little good stuff by fits and starts, a sketch or a fragment. Mr. Eliot, for instance, gives you a pretty line—a solitary line. But you have to hold your breath and wait a long time for the next. There are no "Passion flowers at the gate dropping a splendid tear" (cf *A Room of One's Own*)—not in *our* time. There are just disjointed odds and ends!

"We must reconcile ourselves to a season of failures and fragments. We must reflect that where so much strength is spent on finding a way of telling the truth, the truth itself is bound to reach us in rather an exhausted and chaotic condition. Ulysses, Queen Victoria, Mr. Prufrock—to give Mrs. Brown some of the names she has made famous lately—is a little pale and dishevelled by the time her rescuers reach her."

There you have a typical contemporary statement of the position of letters today. Its artificiality is self-evident, if you do no more than consider the words: for *Ulysses* however else it may have arrived at its destination, was at least not *pale*. But here, doubtless, Mrs. Woolf is merely confusing the becoming pallor, and certain untidiness of some of her own pretty salon pieces with that of Joyce's masterpiece (indeed that masterpiece is implicated and confused with her own pieces in more ways than one, and more palpable than this, but into that it is not necessary to enter here). As to the "strength spent in finding a way," that takes us back to the fable of Mrs. Brown, and the fearful disadvantage under which Mrs. Woolf laboured. Anyone would suppose from what she says that at the time in question Trollope, Jane Austen, Flaubert, Maupassant, Dostoievsky, Turgenev, Tolstoy, etc., etc., etc., etc., were entirely inaccessible to this poor lost 'Georgian' would-be novelist: it is as though she, Bennett, Wells and Galsworthy had been the only people in the world at the time, and as if there had been no books but their books, and no land but England.

The further assumption is that, prior to *Prufrock, Ulysses* and Mr. Lytton Strachey's biographies, there had been either (1) no rendering of anything so exclusive and remote as the 'soul' of a person: or else (2) that the fact that there was not much 'soul' in the work of Mr. Bennett made it very very difficult for Mr. Joyce to write *Ulysses:* and that by the time he had succeeded in some way in banishing Mr. Bennett, he had only strength enough left to concoct a 'pale' little 'fragment,' namely *Ulysses.*

But, again, it is obviously the personal problems of Mrs. Woolf getting mixed up with the problems of Mr. Joyce above all people! For it is quite credible that Clayhanger, astride the island scene—along with his gigantic colleagues, Forsyte and Britling—was a very real problem for the ambitious budding pre-war novelist (especially as she was a little woman, and they were great big burly men—great 'bullies' all three, like all the men, confound them!).

But let us at once repudiate, as false and artificial, this account of the contemporary situation in the 'Mrs. Brown' fable. Joyce's *Ulysses* may be 'a disaster'—a failure—as Mrs. Woolf calls it in her Plain Reader. But it is not a fragment. It is, of its kind, somewhat more robustly 'complete' than most of the classical examples of the novel, in our tongue certainly. It is not the half-work in short, 'pale' and 'dishevelled,' of a crippled interregnum. Nor is there anything *half-there* about D. H. Lawrence's books. Far from being 'pale,' they are much too much the reverse.

If you ask: Do you mean then that there is nothing in this view at all, of ours being a period of *Sturm und Drang,* in which new methods are being tried out, and in which the artistic production is in consequence tentative? I reply: There is nothing new in the idea at all, if you mean that the present time differs from any other in being experimental and in seeking new forms: or if you seek to use that argument to account for mediocrity, or smallness of output, or any of the other individual 'failures' that occur as a result of the natural inequality of men, and the certain precariousness of the creative instinct—subject, in the case of those over-susceptible to nervous shock, to intermittency of output, and, in extreme cases, to extinction.

Then why, you may enquire, is it an opinion that is so widely held?—Because—I again make answer—the people who have been most influential in literary criticism, for a number of years now, have been interested in the propagation of this account of things—just as the orthodox economists have, consciously or not, from interested motives, maintained in its place the traditional picture—that of superhuman *difficulty*—of some *absolute* obstructing the free circulation of the good things of life.

Those most influential in the literary world, as far as the 'highbrow' side of the racket was concerned, have mostly been minor personalities, who were impelled to arrange a sort of bogus 'time' to take the place of the real 'time'—to bring into being an imaginary 'time,' small enough and 'pale' enough to accommodate their not very robust talents. That has, consistently, been the so-called 'Bloomsbury' technique, both in the field of writing and of painting, as I think is now becoming generally recognized. And, needless to say, it has been very much to the disadvantage of any vigorous manifestation in the arts; for anything above the *salon* scale is what this sort of person most dislikes and is at some pains to stifle. And also, necessarily, it brings into being a quite false picture of the true aspect of our scene.

So we have been invited, all of us, to install ourselves in a very dim Venusberg indeed: but Venus has become an introverted matriarch, brooding over a subterranean "stream of consciousness"—a feminine phenomenon after all—and we

are a pretty sorry set of knights too, it must be confessed,—at least in Mrs. Woolf's particular version of the affair.

> I saw pale kings, and princes too,
> Pale warriors, death-pale were they all. . . .

It is a myopic humanity, that threads its way in and out of this 'unreal city,' whose objective obstacles are in theory unsubstantial, but in practice require a delicate negotiation. In our local exponents of this method there is none of the realistic vigour of Mr. Joyce, though often the incidents in the local 'masterpieces' are exact and puerile copies of the scenes in his Dublin drama (cf. the Viceroy's progress through Dublin in *Ulysses* with the Queen's progress through London in **Mrs. Dalloway**—the latter is a sort of undergraduate imitation of the former, winding up with a smoke-writing in the sky, a pathetic 'crib' of the firework display and the rocket that is the culmination of Mr. Bloom's beach-ecstasy). But to appreciate the sort of fashionable dimness to which I am referring, let us turn for a moment to Mrs. Woolf, where she is apeeping in the half-light:

"She reached the park gates. She stood for a moment, looking at the omnibuses in Piccadilly." She should really have written *peeping* at the omnibuses in Piccadilly!—for "she would not say of anyone in the world now that they were this or were that. She felt very young: at the same time unspeakably aged. She sliced like a knife through everything: and at the same time was outside, looking on. She had a perpetual sense as she watched the taxicabs, of being out, out, far out to sea and alone: she always had the feeling that it was very, very dangerous to live even one day." To live *outside,* of course that means. Outside it is terribly *dangerous*—in that great and coarse Without, where all the he-men and he-girls 'live-dangerously' with a brutal insensibility to all the *risks* that they run, forever in the public places. But this *dangerousness* does, after all, make it all very *thrilling,* when peeped-out at, from the security of the private mind: "and yet to her it was absolutely absorbing: all this, the cabs passing."

Those are the half-lighted places of the mind—in which, quivering with a timid excitement, this sort of intelligence shrinks, thrilled to the marrow, at all the wild goings-on! A little old-maidish, are the Prousts and sub-Prousts I think. And when two old maids—or a company of old maids—shrink and cluster together, they titter in each other's ears and delicately tee-hee, pointing out to each other the red-blood antics of this or that upstanding figure, treading the perilous Without. That was the manner in which the late Lytton Strachey lived—peeping more into the past than into the present, it is true, and it is that of most of those associated with him. And—minus the shrinking and tittering, and with a commendable habit of standing, half-concealed, but alone—it was the way of life of Marcel Proust. (pp. 163-69)

> *Wyndham Lewis, "Virginia Woolf ('Mind' and 'Matter' on the Plane of a Literary Controversy)," in his* Men without Art, *1934. Reprint by Russell & Russell, Inc., 1964, pp. 158-71.*

BERNARD BLACKSTONE   (essay date 1949)

[*Blackstone was an English scholar and multilinguist best remembered for his studies of George Gordon, Lord Byron and of Eastern Mediterranean culture. In the following excerpt, Blackstone discusses characterization and the importance of time in* Mrs. Dalloway, *comparing the novel to Woolf's other fiction.*]

Mrs Dalloway is a much bigger job than any of the novels that go before it. There is a double plot. There is a greater variety of well-realised characters. There is a subtler manipulation of time—the action exists in the past as much as in the present. And there is a *leit-motiv*—the song from *Cymbeline*—running through and occurring to both Mrs Dalloway and Septimus Warren Smith at critical moments. The personality of Clarissa Dalloway is presented to us with a fullness and intricacy which we rarely get in a character in fiction. She dominates the book— she passes, as she herself feels, into other people's lives and environments, so that we see Peter Walsh and Doris Kilman as moths circling round her flame; and even Septimus Warren Smith, whom she never sees, finds his life illuminated by the thought which passes from her brain to his: 'Fear no more the heat o' the sun.' Then, in return, we know Mrs Dalloway through the minds of other people as much as through her own thoughts. The final clear picture is gained from the integration of a series of distortions, ranging from the subtle distortion of egotism in her own thinking about herself, to the gross distortion of hatred in Doris Kilman's mental picture. Richard, Peter Walsh, Lady Bruton, Sally Seton, all have their separate pictures, which are laid before us in turn; but we are not invited to choose. For each of these persons wishes to impose his own picture as the correct one; and what the story is about, we soon learn, is the crime of making or accepting any imposition. Mrs Dalloway is herself, above the power of any alien vision to change her into its likeness; but she is only secure because of her money and social position. If she were as defenceless as Septimus Warren Smith there would be many Sir William Bradshaws eager to teach her a sense of proportion, to drag her out of her attic room.

What then are we to think of Mrs Dalloway at the end? Not wholly admirable, certainly, this woman who preferred the 'safe' Richard to the unsteady Peter; who loves parties and Duchesses; who is annoyed at criticism. She does not try to penetrate deeply below the surface of society; Richard's Armenians (or is it Albanians?) mean nothing to her. Her life is intuitive, not ratiocinative. But where her instincts are concerned—how magnificently right! She sees through Sir William Bradshaw, she understands Richard and Peter, she pities and admires (while she detests) Miss Kilman. If only she could have met Rezia and Septimus in the Park, we tell ourselves regretfully, she would certainly have spoken to them (as Peter realised), she would have protected them and Sir William would not have got near them. And it is this instinctive rightness which attracted all hearts to her, which enslaved Peter in spite of himself, and sent Richard home with flowers and the words he could not bring himself to say. She does not pretend, she is herself, and she wants everybody else to be themselves. She is in love with life, with its diversity and colour; and if there is something she has missed, she doesn't moan about it, she sits down and mends her green dress. Yet this consciousness of having missed something (something she might have had with the failure Peter) brings a sadness into her eyes, a certain hardness into her manner, a little artificiality into her voice when she is caught off her guard. In Virginia Woolf's next novel, *To the Lighthouse,* we shall meet another character very like Clarissa Dalloway; but Mrs Ramsay hasn't missed what Clarissa has missed; the hardness isn't there, and there is a new depth.

It isn't only a question of marriage, but of love too. Clarissa comes to think love as detestable as religion; and the book gives us many aspects of this passion. Her own love for Sally, the protecting love of a woman for a woman; her love for Peter and Richard, each different; Peter's love for her and his foolish loves for the wrong women; Miss Kilman's love for Elizabeth: what complications all these introduce into life! Is it possible to have the clear vision of reality when such disturbing colours flash in front of the eyes? Is to love always to go up into the tower alone and leave the others blackberrying in the sun?

The sense of loneliness in marriage fills *Mrs Dalloway*. Has she any friends—real friends? We certainly do not hear of them. Peter leaves her, she has no time to visit Sally Seton, Lady Bruton criticises her and asks Richard to lunch without her. She has only acquaintances, people she asks to parties for her husband's sake. Even Elizabeth is taken from her by Miss Kilman. The novel is the portrait of a lonely woman, who is yet indomitable, kindly, full of life. (pp. 93-5)

The novel has a quality of pity and a dramatic intensity which Virginia Woolf has not given us since *The Voyage Out.* It is an extraordinary art which develops the abnormal episode of Septimus Warren Smith and keeps it going against the other strand of the Dalloways without its leaping out of the frame. It is analogous to the technique of musical counterpoint, even, perhaps, of writing music in two keys at once; but there is no suggestion of a *tour de force*. While the story of Mrs Dalloway mounts up slowly and unemphatically to its climax which is the party, the story of Septimus and Rezia proceeds with horrible and growing intensity to the suicide. This presentation is extremely moving, with something of the atmosphere of Greek drama. Holmes and Bradshaw are the Furies, Septimus has the rôle of Orestes. But the two doctors are unworthy of their parts, Mrs Woolf hates them with a kind of personal hatred; and sometimes the feeling of evil, of suffocation, becomes too poignant. The scenes of Septimus's hallucinations are beautifully done; it is the madness of a poet which is being portrayed, which only a little understanding, a little peace would be enough to bring back to sanity. And Rezia is one of the most moving characters in modern fiction. She is loyal without needing to understand; and that is the greatest kind of loyalty, for it depends on a right relation between persons and not on a community of ideas.

The idea of Time dominates *Mrs Dalloway*. A single day, Wednesday, unfolds the action of the story, and there are no artificial chapter divisions. The stages of the day itself are, however, clearly indicated. The early morning, when Clarissa steps out of her house in Westminster; eleven o'clock when Peter bursts in; half-past eleven when Peter, in Trafalgar Square, receives a strange illumination; a quarter to twelve when Septimus smiles at the man in the grey suit who is dead; precisely twelve o'clock when Septimus and Rezia enter Sir William Bradshaw's house and Clarissa Dalloway lays her green dress on the bed; half-past one when Hugh Whitbread and Richard Dalloway meet for luncheon at Lady Bruton's in Brook Street; three o'clock when Richard comes home with his flowers; half-past three when Clarissa sees the old lady move away from the window; six when Septimus kills himself and Peter thinks with admiration of civilisation. Time is an inexorable stream knitting together the incongruous, separating friends, and making nonsense of emotions. In a single day, a lifetime may be lived through. Virginia Woolf is to take up this treatment of time again, and develop it along still more complex lines, in *To the Lighthouse*.

With its time-limit, and its sense of destiny, the insistent hours pressing on, the texture of *Mrs Dalloway* is closer-knit than that of the preceding novels. There is a sense of pressure, strain and (with London's buses and ambulances and the royal car and the aeroplane) of business, which never becomes confusion because Mrs Woolf holds all the strings perfectly distinguished. The moments of alleviation and escape are briefer and tinged with haste. Clarissa experiences one, Peter experiences one and so does Septimus; but they do not hold the place in *Mrs Dalloway* that they have in some of the other novels. They do not blossom, as it were; they die in the bud. They do not give even the sensation of meaning, though it is 'almost expressed' in Clarissa's attic room. These moments are smothered in the vast official life of London. Then, too, the narrative technique has become more *serré*. The gain in intensity is balanced by a corresponding loss in expansiveness and allusion. There is no time to pause and enjoy the sights. There are no fine imaginative descriptions as of the British Museum in *Jacob's Room*. Clarissa's house is dismissed in a paragraph. We spend quite a long time in Regent's Park, but we have no leisure to look about us. Septimus's delusions, Peter's memories, it is on these that we must fix our attention. There are boys playing cricket, there is little Elise Mitchell who runs full tilt into Rezia, there are trees, swallows, flies; but it is a poor collection when we think of *Kew Gardens* and *Jacob's Room,* with their brilliant evocation of the life of things. Things, in *Mrs Dalloway,* are swamped by the tangled lives of men.

The style, light and easy, an eminently civilised prose, lacks the overtones of *Jacob's Room.* It is as though the light of imagination had been stuffed altogether into poor Septimus's head, leaving the rest of the book a little pallid, as freckles draw colouring matter from the rest of the body. In *Jacob's Room* one feels Mrs Woolf is playing delightedly with a new instrument, weaving melody-patterns for the sheer beauty of them. Serious and indeed tragic as the theme of the book is, it does not hold the writer from feats of virtuosity. *Jacob's Room* is Mrs Woolf's *Songs of Innocence,* *Mrs Dalloway* her *Songs of Experience.* It is not the war that has intervened— *Jacob's Room* is post-war too, and is almost a sigh of relief that it is all over; it is the experience of the years following the war. Deferred shell-shock is Sir William Bradshaw's diagnosis of Septimus's malady; deferred war-shock might, perhaps, be our account of the total motii of *Mrs Dalloway.* The full weight of such a tremendous catastrophe cannot be felt all at once. Only in *To the Lighthouse* do we find her climbing again out of the trough and regaining the brilliance of *Jacob's Room.* (pp. 96-8)

> *Bernard Blackstone, in his* Virginia Woolf: A Commentary, *The Hogarth Press, 1949, 255 p.*

D. S. SAVAGE   (essay date 1950)

[*Savage is an English poet, literary scholar, and social reformer devoted to pacifist and human rights causes. In the following excerpt, Savage charges that* Mrs. Dalloway, *like all Woolf's works, is ultimately unsatisfying, as it depicts a world in which disparate events are given no real differentiation and human life is accorded no special value.*]

Among the women writers of our time there is none whose *prestige* stands higher than that of Virginia Woolf. It is because I believe this prestige to be unfounded that I am here proposing a drastic revaluation of her work.

The legend of Virginia Woolf as an 'artist' pure and simple, projecting, in an experiential vacuum, sensitive and delicate word-patterns devoid of all but the most essentially aesthetic content, is one which can have taken root only in a society in which there exists the most lamentable indifference both to life

and art. The following passage from a review of a typically adulatory book about Virginia Woolf's novels is representative of the prevalent inert and thoughtless acceptance of this legend:

> Of Mrs. Woolf's style this book does not directly treat, yet . . . here, if anywhere, the style *is* the writer . . . her best work is a sequence of illuminating moments woven into a complete design; and for that design her imagination used its own language—an impressionistic, highly charged, emotive prose that differs at times little, if at all, from poetry; its texture shot with grace, sensitivity, and subtle awareness. Over a human landscape of deliberately limited dimensions her delicate rhythms drift and play like soft clouds through which gleams the dappled sunlight of her pity and her humour, her sympathy for the sorrows and frustrations of her fellow men and women, and her ironic smile at their weaknesses and foibles. . . .

To the question, 'Yes—but what are Virginia Woolf's novels *about*? What view of life do they reflect? What particular insights do they display?' one receives no satisfactory answer.

That Virginia Woolf's novels are tenuous, amorphous and vague, that her prose expresses a state of sensitized generality, is true. Nevertheless, this condition has definite psychic roots, and in itself raises the question of value. . . . [Beneath] the imprecisions, vaguenesses and generalities of the particular work there is an underlying, basic preoccupation which gives rise to those qualities: that the merely aesthetic approach to her work begs the question, and that beneath the aesthetic surface there runs a theme of a totally non-aesthetic character. In bringing this theme to light, in revealing the unconscious psychological process which determines the aesthetic form of the work, my aim is to explode the theory of aestheticism, and to show that no artistic work can exist in independence of its maker's human preoccupations and beliefs. (pp. 70-1)

Virginia Woolf's work as a novelist falls roughly into three periods. There is the early period of conventional fictionalizing represented by her two first novels, *The Voyage Out* and *Night and Day.* There is the period of experiment marked by the discarding of those fictional properties which she was unable to utilize, and issuing in *Jacob's Room*—the first novel in what was to be recognized as her characteristic manner—and later, in an ascending scale, in *Mrs. Dalloway* and *To the Lighthouse.* And lastly, there is the descent into an increasingly despairing vacuousness and dissipation of perception through *The Waves, The Years,* and finally *Between the Acts,* marked by a disintegration of form expressing a surrender of all significance to the accidental process of time. (p. 71)

It is not until *Mrs. Dalloway* . . . that we reach a work in which it is possible to trace the drawing together in Virginia Woolf's mind of the impulsion towards belief [in the totality of life] on the one hand and on the other the inability to make any decisive movement of belief and thus to discriminate which led to the narrowing of vision to the elementary conditions of momentary experience. *Mrs. Dalloway* is curiously compounded of this dual movement of belief and unbelief.

In the early essay on **'Modern Fiction',** Virginia Woolf charges the 'conventional' novelists whose manner she had attempted to follow, with writing of unimportant things, with spending their skill and industry on 'making the trivial and the transitory appear the true and the enduring'. 'For us at this moment,' she wrote, 'the form of fiction most in vogue more often misses than secures the thing we seek. Whether we call it life or spirit, truth or reality, this, the essential thing, has moved off.' What, then, is the enduring, the true, which it is the novelist's task to capture? She does not know; but she ventures to suppose that it may be found by a form of passive receptiveness to experience. 'Let us not take it for granted,' she wrote in that early essay, 'that life exists more fully in what is commonly thought big than in what is commonly thought small.' Unable to distinguish between this value and that she takes the barest unit of disparate experience and concentrates upon it, in the supposition or the hope that within that, if anywhere, must lie the secret of life's *indigenous* significance.

The inability to discriminate between levels of life, to make choices between 'good' and 'bad', 'right' and 'wrong', or 'desirable' and 'undesirable', besides thrusting the individual so affected back upon the naked and isolated moment of perception, places him furthermore in a position where, if any kind of positive 'significance' is to be attempted (and life can be endowed with significance only by an interior act of affirmation—of *belief*), then, inevitably, undifferentiated, elementary life has to be accepted unreservedly and in its totality. In *Mrs. Dalloway* we see not only the results of the period of experimental, impressionistic, *momentary* writing applied to the novel; we also see the attainment of a sustained, though of course ultimately spurious, 'significance' through the continuous act of complete and undiscriminating acceptance of every moment of undifferentiated existence, each separate atom of which is presumed to contain an equal fragment of *indigenous* meaning.

In *Mrs. Dalloway,* in fact, the specific absence of belief which is shown in the earlier novels is revealed in its reverse aspect. It takes on the appearance of belief—a positive acceptance and affirmation, not of any particular level of reality, but of *everything,* without discrimination: except, significantly enough, of that which would imply the possibility, or the need, of discrimination. 'One can only hope that they will have the same vision and the same power to believe, without which life would be so meaningless,' writes old Mrs. Hilbery, of Katharine and her fiancé in *Night and Day:* to believe, that is, not in any specific reality or value, but simply to believe, in everything, perhaps; in 'life'. And one can only take Clarissa Dalloway as exemplifying this 'belief'—a belief so total that it engulfs the whole of experience, and which on examination turns out to be a positive inversion of unbelief. Besides representing the combination of *happiness* and *belief,* Clarissa Dalloway is an incarnation of life itself, the stream and efflorescence of natural, material, feminine existence. A sentimental, worldly sort of average sensual woman, she is presented lyrically and quite uncritically through a rose-tinted haze, the trivialities of her pointless, sensational life inflated to universal proportions. (pp. 80-2)

The vague, fluid characters in this book—Clarissa herself, her whimsical, Puckish lover, Peter Walsh, and Septimus Warren Smith—are bathed in the tender warmth of their author's undiscriminating sympathy. It is interesting, that being so, to find that there are also portrayed two characters who are given at least potential definition by the decisiveness of their attitude to life, in which they stand in polar opposition to the indecisive fluidity of the other chief characters. And it is intriguing to watch the manner in which these two characters are pursued by their creator with a gratuitous vindictiveness which seems at first sight unaccountable.

To Clarissa Dalloway is opposed the maliciously-drawn minor figure of Miss Kilman, her daughter's teacher, who, she fears, is alienating the girl's affection from her. Between Mrs. Dalloway and Miss Kilman there is an unspoken but vibrant antagonism, which flashes out as Miss Kilman, leaving Mrs. Dalloway's house with the girl, encounters her employer on the landing. . . . Subsequently Miss Kilman is made to disgrace herself before Mrs. Dalloway's daughter, and is left, a pathetic figure, covered with humiliation.

Humiliation is the portion also of the other character who is so unsympathetic as to possess a definite, formulated attitude to life. Sir William Bradshaw, the nerve specialist who is called in to deal with the neurasthenic Septimus, is presented as a thick-skinned, domineering egotist, who applies to human beings a sovereign test of normality and sense of proportion. (pp. 84-5)

It would seem that just as Clarissa Dalloway and Septimus Warren Smith are linked in an unconscious psychic sympathy, representing as they do the human mind's state of fluid and unprincipled openness to the undifferentiated phenomena of elementary existence, so the decisive attitudes of Miss Kilman and Sir William Bradshaw converge—and converge upon that threatening imperative towards *conversion*, the imposition of a definite view of life upon the fluid, the indefinite, which is felt as inexpressibly menacing to everything that Clarissa Dalloway herself values and represents. Pondering on Miss Kilman, and the challenge she is seen to present to her own undiscriminating acceptance, Mrs. Dalloway asks herself:

> Why creeds and prayers and mackintoshes? when . . . that's the miracle, that's the mystery: that old lady, she meant, whom she could see going from chest of drawers to dressing-table. She could still see her. And the supreme mystery which Kilman might say she had solved, or Peter might say he had solved, but Clarissa didn't believe either of them had the ghost of an idea of solving, was simply this: here was one room; there another. Did religion solve that, or love?

Sir William Bradshaw, like Miss Kilman, is disgraced. When Septimus Warren Smith is in a condition of intense neurotic excitement, he insists upon entering his room, with the result that Septimus flings himself out of the window and is killed. Towards the end of the story, at Mrs. Dalloway's party, the climax of her day, she learns from Sir William Bradshaw, who is one of the guests, of the young man's death. . . .

> . . . But this young man who had killed himself—had he plunged his treasure? 'If it were now to die, 'twere now to be most happy,' she had said to herself once, coming down, in white. Or there were the poets and thinkers. Suppose he had had that passion, and had gone to Sir William Bradshaw, a great doctor, yet to her obscurely evil, without sex or lust, extremely polite to women, but capable of some indescribable outrage—forcing your soul, that was it—if this young man had gone to him, and Sir William had impressed him, like that, with his power, might he not then have said (indeed she felt it now), Life is made intolerable; they make life intolerable, men like that?

Then (she had felt it only this morning) there was the terror; the overwhelming incapacity, one's parents giving it into one's hands, this life, to be lived to the end, to be walked with serenely; there was in the depths of her heart an awful fear. Even now, quite often if Richard had not been there reading the *Times,* so that she could crouch like a bird and gradually revive, send roaring up that immeasurable delight, rubbing stick to stick, one thing with another, she must have perished. She had escaped. But that young man had killed himself.

Such then is the psychological structure of *Mrs. Dalloway.* Although, as a novel, it represents the peak of Virginia Woolf's achievement, just as it marks the highest, most buoyant point on the graph of her emotional progression, it shows no authentic advance over her earlier works: no movement of the mind, that is, into new territory. Apparently, affirmative in mood, its innocency is in fact, retrogressive and corrupt. And its apparent affirmation of life is merely the reverse aspect of its rejection of that which alone could give life meaning and value: i.e., a positive, spiritual affirmation which, facilitating the introduction of a principle of choice, of discrimination, would make life subject to differentiation and thus to the realization of meaning.

And yet, despite its at times cloying sentimentality, *Mrs. Dalloway* is perhaps Virginia Woolf's most satisfactory novel, for it has an organic structure which derives from the successful dramatic presentation of a view of life. It is in fact the only novel of Virginia Woolf's in which tension is achieved through the opposition of characters embodying contrary principles of conduct. The lack of such tension in the rest of her work results from the monistic conception of existence which sets all characters alike within the same undifferentiated flow of life, and makes inward and outward conflict alike inconceivable. (pp. 85-7)

> *D. S. Savage, "Virginia Woolf," in his* The Withered Branch: Six Studies in the Modern Novel, *Eyre & Spottiswoode, 1950, pp. 70-105.*

REUBEN ARTHUR BROWER　(essay date 1951)

[*Brower was a distinguished American scholar who wrote widely on English literature. In the following excerpt, he discusses the importance of recurrent metaphors to an understanding of* Mrs. Dalloway.]

The best preparation for understanding *Mrs. Dalloway* is to read *The Tempest,* or *Cymbeline,* or, better still, *A Winter's Tale.* One might go further and say that in her singleness of vision and in her handling of words, Virginia Woolf has a Shakespearean imagination. If that sounds like nonsense—and it may— perhaps by the end of this chapter the reader will agree that it sounds 'so like sense, that it will do as well.'

Mrs. Dalloway has a story and some characters—by conventional standards, a fragmentary dramatic design—but the fragments of which the novel is composed would not seem related or particularly significant without another sort of connection. The dramatic sequences are connected through a single metaphorical nucleus, and the key metaphors are projected and sustained by a continuous web of subtly related minor metaphors and harmonizing imagery.

Once we have seen this design and the vision of experience it implies, we shall understand why *Mrs. Dalloway* takes the form it does, why as a story it has properly no beginning or ending. It opens one morning with Clarissa Dalloway in the midst of preparing for a party; it closes in the early hours of the next morning with Clarissa very much involved in giving the party. The major event of her day is the return of Peter Walsh, the man she had almost married instead of Richard Dalloway, a successful M.P. Clarissa and Richard have a daughter, Elizabeth, who is temporarily attached to a religious fanatic, a woman with the Dickensian name of Miss Kilman. There is also in the novel another set of characters who at first seem to have no connection with Clarissa and her world: Septimus Smith, a veteran of the First World War, and his Italian wife, Rezia, a hatmaker by trade. Septimus, who is suffering from shell shock, is being treated—somewhat brutally—by a hearty M.D., Dr. Holmes. During the day of Clarissa's preparations, Septimus visits Sir William Bradshaw, an eminent psychiatrist, who recommends rather too firmly that Septimus should be taken to a sanatorium. In the late afternoon, as Dr. Holmes comes to take him away, Septimus jumps from the balcony of his room and kills himself. That evening, Sir William Bradshaw reports the story of his death at Clarissa's party.

Readers of the novel will recognize this outline as more or less accurate, but they will want to add that the impression it gives is very remote from their remembered experience of *Mrs. Dalloway.* For the peculiar texture of Virginia Woolf's fiction has been lost. The ebb and flow of her phrasing and the frequent repetition of the same or similar expressions, through which her characteristic rhythmic and metaphorical designs are built up, have completely disappeared.

No one needs to be shown that the novel is full of odd echoes. The Shakespearean tag, 'Fear no more,' occurs some six or seven times; certain words turn up with surprising frequency in the various interior monologues: 'life,' 'feel,' 'suffer,' 'solemn,' 'moment,' and 'enjoy.' Less obvious, and more peculiar to Virginia Woolf is the recurrence in the individual monologues of expressions for similar visual or aural images. Some of these images—the aeroplane and the stopped motorcar are examples—connect separate dramatic sequences in a rather artificial way; but others, such as Big Ben's striking and the marine images, often connect similar qualities of experience and so function as symbolic metaphors. There are many repeated words, phrases, and sentences in the novel, besides those already quoted, which gradually become metaphorical: 'party,' 'Holmes and Bradshaw,' 'there she was,' 'plunge,' 'wave' and 'sea,' 'sewing,' 'building' and 'making it up,' 'Bourton,' et cetera. Almost innumerable continuities, major and minor, may be traced through the various recurrent expressions; but as compared with Shakespeare's practice in *The Tempest,* the continuities are less often built up through the use of explicit metaphors. The repeated word does not occur in a conventional metaphorical expression, and its metaphorical value is felt only after it has been met in a number of contexts. Virginia Woolf's most characteristic metaphors are purely symbolic.

I can indicate from the adjective 'solemn' how a recurrent expression acquires its special weight of meaning. By seeing how metaphor links with metaphor, the reader will also get a notion of the interconnectedness of the entire novel. The word appears on the first page of *Mrs. Dalloway:*

> How fresh, how calm, stiller than this of course,
> the air was in the early morning; like the flap

of a wave; the kiss of a wave; chill and sharp and yet (for a girl of eighteen as she then was) solemn, feeling as she did, standing there at the open window, that something awful was about to happen. . . .

It is echoed at once, on the next page, in the first account of Big Ben's striking (an important passage in relation to the whole novel):

> For having lived in Westminster—how many years now? over twenty,—one feels even in the midst of the traffic, or waking at night, Clarissa was positive, a particular hush, or solemnity; an indescribable pause; a suspense (but that might be her heart, affected, they said, by influenza) before Big Ben strikes. There! Out it boomed. First a warning, musical; then the hour, irrevocable. The leaden circles dissolved in the air.

'Solemn,' which on our first reading of the opening page had only a vague local meaning of 'something awful about to happen,' is now connected with a more particularized terror, the fear of a suspense, of a pause in experience. Each time that 'solemn' is repeated in subsequent descriptions of Big Ben, it carries this additional meaning. The word recurs three times in the afternoon scene in which Clarissa looks across at an old woman in the next house:

> How extraordinary it was, strange, yes, touching, to see the old lady (they had been neighbours ever so many years) move away from the window, as if she were attached to that sound, that string. Gigantic as it was, it had something to do with her. Down, down, into the midst of ordinary things the finger fell making the moment solemn.

And a little further on:

> . . . Big Ben . . . laying down the law, so solemn, so just . . . on the wake of that solemn stroke which lay flat like a bar of gold on the sea.

In the early morning scene near the end of the book, Clarissa goes to the window, again sees the old lady, and thinks, 'It will be a solemn sky . . . it will be a dusky sky, turning away its cheek in beauty.' In all but the last passage there is some suggestion in the imagery of Big Ben's stroke coming down and marking an interruption in the process of life. By the end of the book we see the significance in the use of 'solemn' on the first page in a passage conveying a sharp sense of freshness and youth. The terror symbolized by Big Ben's 'pause' has a connection with early life, '. . . one's parents giving it into one's hands, this life, to be lived to the end.' The 'something awful . . . about to happen' was associated with 'the flap of a wave, the kiss of a wave'; the 'solemnity' of life is a kind of 'sea-terror' (so Shakespeare might express it in *The Tempest*). Wave and water images recur in other 'solemn' passages: 'the wave,' 'the wake,' 'the leaden circles dissolved in the air.' So, through various associations, 'solemn' acquires symbolic values for the reader: some terror of entering the sea of experience and of living life and an inexplicable fear of a 'suspense' or interruption.

While following a single symbolic adjective in *Mrs. Dalloway*, we have seen that it was impossible to interpret one continuity apart from several others. Various expressions—'solemn,' 'wave,' 'Big Ben,' 'fear,' and 'pause'—kept leading us toward the key metaphor of the book. The metaphor that links the continuities and gives unity to the dramatic design of *Mrs. Dalloway* is not a single, easily describable analogy, but two complementary and extremely complex analogies which are gradually expressed through recurrent words and phrases and through the dramatic pattern of the various sequences. Though they are salient in the sequences of nearly all the main characters, they are best interpreted from Clarissa's, since her experience forms the center of attention for the reader.

One of the two metaphorical poles of the novel emerges in a passage that comes just after the first account of Big Ben's striking:

> Such fools we are, she thought, crossing Victoria Street. For Heaven only knows why one loves it so, how one sees it so, making it up, building it round one, tumbling it, creating it every moment afresh; but the veriest frumps, the most dejected of miseries sitting on doorsteps (drink their downfall) do the same; can't be dealt with, she felt positive, by Acts of Parliament for that very reason: they love life. In people's eyes, in the swing, tramp, and trudge; in the bellow and the uproar; the carriages, motor cars, omnibuses, vans, sandwich men shuffling and swinging; brass bands; barrel or-

Portrait of Woolf by her sister Vanessa Bell. From Virginia Woolf: A Biography, *by Quentin Bell. The Hogarth Press, 1972. Copyright © 1972 by Quentin Bell. Reproduced by permission of The Hogarth Press and the author.*

gans; in the triumph and the jingle and the strange high singing of some aeroplane overhead was what she loved; life; London; this moment of June.

The key phrase here is 'they love life,' and what is meant by 'life' and 'loving it' is indicated by the surrounding metaphors—'building it,' 'creating it every moment,' 'the swing, tramp, and trudge'—and also by the various images of sights, sounds, and actions.

'Life' as expressed in Mrs. Dalloway's morning walk (and in the walks of Peter and of her daughter Elizabeth) consists first in the doings of people and things and in the active perception of them. To meet Clarissa's approval, people 'must do something,' as she did in 'making a world' in her drawing room, in 'assembling' and 'knowing' all sorts of individuals, in running her house, and in giving 'her parties,' which were for her 'life.' But the perception, the savoring of these doings of oneself and of others is itself a creation. For Mrs. Dalloway, 'enjoying' and 'loving' is 'creating' and 'building up,' not passive enjoyment. Life is experienced in successively created 'moments'; the sense of succession, of process, is inseparable from Clarissa's feeling about life; it is implicit in her movement along the streets, 'this astonishing and rather solemn progress with the rest of them, up Bond Street.' She thinks of 'all this' as '*going on* without her.' ('This' and 'all this' also become metaphors for life.) Later, in Elizabeth's experience of going up Fleet Street, all these metaphors are explicitly combined: 'this van; this life; this procession.' To live, then, is to enter into the process of action and active perception, to be absorbed in the successive moments: '. . . yet to her it was absolutely absorbing; all this.'

But the sense of being absorbed in the process is inseparable from a fear of being excluded, from the dread that the process may be interrupted. The progress is a 'solemn' one, the adjective suggesting (as elsewhere) the terror of 'plunging' into experience. The sense of being *in* experience is inseparable from the sense of being *outside* of it:

> She sliced like a knife through everything; at the same time was outside, looking on. She had a perpetual sense, as she watched the taxi cabs, of being out, out, far out to sea and alone; she always had the feeling that it was very, very dangerous to live even one day.

Though the terror lies in having to go through with life, paradoxically the escape from terror lies in building up delight and sharing in the process:

> Even now, quite often if Richard had not been there reading the *Times,* so that she could crouch like a bird and gradually revive, send roaring up that immeasurable delight, rubbing stick to stick, one thing with another, she must have perished.

The central metaphor of Clarissa's narrative (and of the novel) is thus twofold: the exhilarated sense of being a part of the forward moving process and the recurrent fear of some break in this absorbing activity, which was symbolized by the 'suspense' before Big Ben strikes. We are to feel all sorts of experiences qualified as at once 'an absorbing progression' and 'a progression about to be interrupted.' Such in crudely schematic terms are the two analogies which make up the metaphorical nucleus of the novel. As my analysis has indicated, this complex metaphor is expressed through countless variant minor metaphors and images.

Both of the major aspects of the metaphor are intricately linked in the wonderful sewing scene in which Clarissa's old lover, Peter Walsh, returns to announce his plans for a second marriage:

> Quiet descended on her, calm, content, as her needle, drawing the silk smoothly to its gentle pause, collected the green folds together and attached them, very lightly, to the belt. So on a summer's day waves collect, overbalance, and fall; collect and fall; and the whole world seems to be saying 'That is all' more and more ponderously, until even the heart in the body which lies in the sun on the beach says too, That is all. Fear no more, says the heart. Fear no more, says the heart, committing its burden to some sea, which sighs collectively for all sorrows, and renews, begins, collects, lets fall. And the body alone listens to the passing bee; the wave breaking; the dog barking, far away barking and barking.

Through the wave simile the opening statement expands in a metaphorical bloom which expresses in little the essence of the novel. The quiet, calm, and content (Clarissa's absorption in what she is doing) and the rhythmic movement of the needle are the points in the immediate situation from which the two main meanings of the key metaphor grow. The comparison between sewing and wave movements draws in these further levels of meaning, thanks to the nice preparation of earlier scenes and the delicate adjustment of those that follow. There are the wave and sea images which have been appearing when Clarissa recalls the terror of early life or when she hears Big Ben's solemn stroke. Much later in the novel, there is Clarissa at her party in her 'silver-green mermaid's dress . . . lolloping on the waves.' Here, in the scene with Peter, as in the final party scene, the waves mainly symbolize Clarissa's complete absorption in her life: 'That is all'—the phrase she had used twice while shopping and which had come back in her musings on 'the solemn progress up Bond Steet.' There is for the heart at this moment nothing but the process, and the individual becomes a mere percipient body, intensely aware of the immediate sensation. But the moment has a dual value, as has been suggested by the oblique allusions to solemnity and terror ('waves,' 'ponderously,' 'That is all'). So the reader is perfectly prepared for the return of 'Fear no more,' which it is now clear suggests both freedom from fear and the fear of interruption. . . . (pp. 124-29)

[To] a remarkable extent the central metaphor penetrates and organizes the novel. The dramatic sequences of the principal characters are all linked with Clarissa's through a shuttling pattern of verbal reminiscences. (Curious readers may amuse themselves by finding dozens more than can be cited here.) Although 'life' is peculiarly the key figure in Clarissa's experience, it is important in that of other characters, including Septimus and Miss Kilman, who are unable to 'live' as Clarissa does.

We may begin with Peter Walsh, who as a lover has the role of one of the 'interrupters' and 'destroyers.' But in the two accounts of his walks through London, he shows much of Clarissa's eager experience of life. He sets off on his morning walk, speaking rhythmically her parting words, 'Remember my party, remember my party.' He then 'marches up White-hall' as she has gone 'up Bond Street,' and he too 'makes up' life (his mild 'escapade with the girl'). During his evening walk, he expresses Clarissa's sense of enjoyment:

> Really it took one's breath away, these mo-ments . . . absorbing, mysterious, of infinite richness, this life.

Elizabeth also shares her mother's perceptiveness, and in her bus ride has an experience closely paralleling Clarissa's morn-ing walk. As all three characters pass through the 'procession' of experience, they savor life as a series of exquisite moments, a sensation summed up by the motif of the scene in which Richard brings Clarissa the roses: 'Happiness is this.'

The crude parallel between the roles of Mrs. Dalloway and Septimus is obvious; the finer relations and how they are ex-pressed may be best seen by tracing the links made through the 'life' metaphor. While Clarissa usually feels her inclusion *in* everything and only occasionally feels *outside,* Septimus is almost always 'alone' and unable to connect with the world about him. (pp. 130-31)

All of the related analogies that make up the key metaphor are combined near the end of the novel, at the point when Bradshaw tells Clarissa of Septimus' death and when Clarissa, reflecting on its meaning, looks out of the window at the old lady going to bed. Bradshaw, a man 'capable of some indescribable crime—forcing your soul, that was it—,' momentarily ruins her party ('in the middle of my party, here's death, she thought . . .'). But Clarissa immediately recognizes that Septimus' death has a further meaning in relation to his life and hers. By killing himself Septimus had defied the men who make life intolerable, and though he had 'thrown it away,' he had not lost his in-dependence of soul. This (in so far as we can define it) is 'the thing' he had preserved. By contrast Clarissa had sacrificed some of this purity. She had made compromises for the sake of social success, 'She had schemed; she had pilfered.' But she had not given in to Peter, and by marrying Richard she had been able to make a life of her own. The delight, though impure, remained. The old lady, in her second appearance as in her first, symbolizes the quiet maintenance of one's own life, which is the only counterbalance to the fear of 'interrup-tion' whether by death or compulsion.

This scene shows in the highest degree the concentration of various dramatic relationships through a central metaphor. What we would emphasize here is Virginia Woolf's literary feat in achieving this result—literary in the primitive sense of Frost's pun, 'feat of words.' The unity of [Woolf's] design depends on the building up of symbolic metaphors through an exquisite management of verbal devices: through exact repetitions, rem-iniscent variations, the use of related eye and ear imagery, and the recurrence of similar phrase and sentence rhythms. The novel has as a result a unique closeness of structure which is only slightly dependent on story, though also supported by the time patterns which David Daiches has chosen to emphasize [see excerpt dated 1960]. What is most remarkable is the way in which so many different experiences have been perceived through a single metaphorical vision: the lives of Clarissa, Peter, Richard, Septimus, and Rezia as glimpsed at various periods, and of Elizabeth at the moment of growing up. Most of the characters are seen, too, in some relation to the persons who 'make life intolerable': Miss Kilman, Holmes, Bradshaw, and Peter in his role as lover. Experience, rich and various in its range, has struck the mind of the novelist at a single angle

and been refracted with perfect consistency. This singleness in reception and expression, as evidenced in the metaphorical design, is what we mean by integrity of imagination in Virginia Woolf.

But there are certainly points in the novel at which this sin-gleness of vision shows signs of strain. Philistine readers have observed that the men of the novel are not full-blooded or are barely 'men' at all—a type of criticism that could be applied with disastrous results to *Tom Jones,* or *Emma,* or *The Portrait of a Lady.* But the strain that is truly a sign of weakness appears in the relating of dramatic elements through the central met-aphorical nucleus. That Peter is no man—whether we mean not lifelike or not masculine—is a relevant comment only be-cause of the symbolic role in which he is sometimes cast. As a lover he stands in Clarissa's thoughts for one of the dark 'forcers of the soul'; but in much of his behavior he is described as a womanish sort of person who has little power to manage himself or to move others. In one rather embarrassing episode, Peter's half-imaginary pursuit of a young girl, Virginia Woolf is apparently attempting to present his passionate side. The lack of lively sensuous detail in this narrative contrasts very badly with the glowing particularity of Mrs. Dalloway's walk through Bond Street or with the vividness of Peter's impres-sions of a London evening, while by way of a poor compen-sation there is a good deal of generalized emotional language: 'vast philanthropy,' 'exquisite delight,' 'mournful tenderness,' 'laughing and delightful,' et cetera. Peter calls this 'making up' an 'exquisite amusement,' which is in this instance a pain-fully accurate label. The metaphor ceases to be an instrument through which experience is connected for us in a new relation and remains a simple declaration of a connection never made.

On occasion Virginia Woolf becomes so fascinated with this instrument that she elaborates the metaphor out of all proportion to its expressive value. (pp. 133-35)

Perhaps the most obvious examples of metaphorical elaboration for its own sake are the super-literary, pseudo-Homeric similes which adorn various pages of *Mrs. Dalloway.* Whether they are in origin Proustian or eighteenth-century Bloomsbury, we could wish that they might be dropped. Here is a relatively short example from the scene following the sewing passage:

> 'Well, and what's happened to you?' she said. So before a battle begins, the horses paw the ground; toss their heads; the light shines on their flanks; their necks curve. So Peter Walsh and Clarissa, sitting side by side on the blue sofa, challenged each other. His powers chafed and tossed in him. He assembled from different quarters all sorts of things; praise; his career at Oxford; his marriage, which she knew nothing whatever about; how he had loved; and alto-gether done his job.

The contrast between such a literary pastiche and the wave-sewing simile shows us in part what is wrong. The particular sense images, 'paw,' 'toss,' 'light shines,' are not grounded on the dramatic and narrative level, since there is no preparation for this Homeric horse-play in the account of Clarissa's and Peter's talk and gestures. (By contrast the wave motion was anticipated through describing Clarissa's movements as she sewed.) So the reader is unprepared to take the further jump to the psychological levels of the metaphor. The efforts to show any similarity in Peter's internal 'chafings' and 'tossings' come too late. The metaphor is crudely explained; but it doesn't work. Such simulations—like Peter's escapade and the solitary traveler's vision—are verbally inert matter, sending no radiations through the reader's experience of the novel.

But what is vital in the writing of *Mrs. Dalloway* is both more nearly omnipresent and more unobtrusive. To say, as I did at the beginning of this chapter, that Virginia Woolf creates a Shakespearean pattern of metaphor tells us something, of course; but to see how she connects diverse moments of experience by playing on a single analogy, or on a single word, tells us much more. As Clarissa is thinking of the death of Septimus Smith, she says to herself: 'But this young man who had killed himself—had he plunged holding his treasure?' She has just recalled that he had 'plunged' by 'throwing himself from a window,' which in turn echoes his earlier agonies ('falling through the sea, down, down') and his actual death ('flung himself vigorously, violently down'). But Septimus' 'plunge' recalls experiences of a very different sort in Clarissa' social life:

> . . . as she stood hesitating one moment on the threshold of her drawing-room, an exquisite suspense, such as might stay a diver before plunging while the sea darkens and brightens beneath him. . . .

'Darkens' suggests that 'plunge' has also a more fearful significance, as we saw on the first page of the novel:

> What a lark! What a plunge! For so it had always seemed to her, when, with a little squeak of the hinges, which she could hear now, she had burst open the French windows and plunged at Bourton into the open air. How fresh, how calm, stiller than this of course, the air was in the early morning; like the flap of a wave; the kiss of a wave; chill and sharp and yet (for a girl of eighteen as she then was) solemn, feeling as she did, standing there at the open window, that something awful was about to happen . . .

Septimus' plunge from the window is linked with those earlier windows and 'the triumphs of youth' and thereby with the exhilarating and 'solemn' sense of delight in life's process (the 'treasure'). This twofold sense of life is constantly being expressed through the central metaphor of *Mrs. Dalloway*. The recurrence of a single word is a quiet indication of the subtlety and closeness of the structure which Virginia Woolf was 'building up' as she wrote this novel. (pp. 135-37)

> Reuben Arthur Brower, "Something Central which Permeated: Virginia Woolf and 'Mrs. Dalloway'," in his The Fields of Light: An Experiment in Critical Reading, Oxford University Press, 1951, pp. 123-37.

JAMES HAFLEY (essay date 1954)

[*In the following excerpt, Hafley contends that Woolf did not utilize stream of consciousness technique in her fiction. In contrast to most critics, he examines Woolf's evocation of life in* Mrs. Dalloway *while according specific attention to what little real impact writings by Henri Bergson, Marcel Proust, and James Joyce had on the special narrative properties of the novel.*]

Mrs. Dalloway is not primarily about Clarissa, or about any of its other characters. Rather, it is about life and reality or time; both character and circumstance are means to the end of expressing a unified vision of experience. Just as, in **"Mr. Ben-**nett and Mrs. Brown,"** Virginia Woolf had defined Mrs. Brown as "the spirit we live by, life itself," so in *Mrs. Dalloway* emphasis is placed not so much upon Mrs. Dalloway the individual person as upon Mrs. Dalloway's ability to mirror "life itself": she is what might be called a carrier of life. This life or "spirit" is communicated, not by means of Mrs. Dalloway's "room," but by her consciousness.

Bergson had defined life as "consciousness launched into matter." *Mrs. Dalloway* represents the conflict, not between person and person, but between duration and false time. On twenty occasions during the course of the novel, clocks strike—"shredding and slicing, dividing and subdividing, the clocks . . . nibbled at the June day, counselled submission, upheld authority, and pointed out in chorus the advantages of a sense of proportion"—and against the materiality of this spatialized day in London is placed the spirituality, the true duration, of Mrs. Dalloway's consciousness, the continuity of which denies that "dividing and subdividing." Mrs. Dalloway refuses to separate herself as an individual from the rest of the world. "She felt herself everywhere; not 'here, here, here'; and she tapped the back of the seat; but everywhere. She waved her hand, going up Shaftesbury Avenue. She was all that." "She would not say of any one in the world now that they were this or were that . . . to her it was absolutely absorbing; all this; the cabs passing; and she would not say of Peter, she would not say of herself, I am this, I am that." Clarissa will not circumscribe herself, separate herself from anyone or anything else.

There are two villains in this novel: the goddesses of proportion and conversion. In the distinguished psychiatrist Sir William Bradshaw is enshrined "proportion, divine proportion, Sir William's goddess." Sir William is also a worshipper at the shrine of conversion, but it is the pathetic Doris Kilman in whom conversion lives most obviously. The crime these goddesses commit is destruction of freedom by enforcement of obedience to an artificial society. Sir William sets himself up as judge of what is madness, what sense; Miss Kilman of what is evil, what good. Having decided, they proceed to correct whatever wanders from their personal conception of normality: it is conversion who "feasts on the wills of the weakly, loving to impress, to impose, adoring her own features stamped on the face of the populace"; who "bestows her blessing on those who, looking upward, catch submissively from her eyes the light of their own."

Just as this greatest crime is an imposition of the self and its standards upon others, so the greatest virtue is surrender of the self, not to its own or another's arbitrary rule, but to what Bergson would call the spirit or supraconsciousness—memory: pure-time existence or duration. It is this surrender that Clarissa and Septimus, each on a different level, are finally able to accomplish—this that constitutes the real movement of the novel. For the morning-to-evening movement is set up as a false, a spatial movement; opposed to it is the true movement of reality.

This becomes perfectly clear when the relationship between Clarissa and Septimus is considered. Virginia Woolf says: "In the first version Septimus, who later is intended to be [Mrs. Dalloway's] double, had no existence . . . Mrs. Dalloway was originally to kill herself, or perhaps merely to die at the end of the party." In either event there would have been the breaking down of the wall between self and not-self that is the novel's affirmation; but the novel as it stands is much more satisfying than it would have been if this had occurred only on the physical level. Both Septimus and Mrs. Dalloway are insane—he actually, she in a metaphorical sense—for neither will accept the "sanity" around them as real. Both Septimus and Mrs. Dalloway have therefore to find a way of escaping from the false life to what they believe true reality. Septimus, a victim of shock in the war, does this by defying his doctors and leaping from a window to his death, and Clarissa by annihilating her individuality (and thus killing her self—gaining true individuality).

Septimus does not wish to die when he commits suicide; he dies, not to escape life, but to escape death in life. In his insanity, like one of Shakespeare's "wise fools," he speaks truth. He thinks: "Leaves were alive; trees were alive. And the leaves being connected by millions of fibres with his own body, there on the seat, fanned it up and down; when the branch stretched he, too, made that statement''; and he moans that he suffers from "eternal loneliness," and mutters that "communication is health; communication is happiness." He is thus echoing Clarissa's belief that "she was all that." It is his love of life, his belief in unity, then, that Septimus affirms by casting away his physical individuality.

Throughout the novel, Clarissa has been moving toward the same self-effacement. When, at her party, she hears of the young man's suicide, she retires to a little room and empathetically experiences Septimus' death. Then suddenly she realizes their affinity. "A thing there was that mattered; a thing, wreathed about with chatter, defaced, obscured in her own life, let drop every day in corruption, lies, chatter. This he had preserved. Death was defiance. Death was an attempt to communicate; people feeling the impossibility of reaching the centre which, mystically, evaded them; closeness drew apart; rapture faded, one was alone. There was an embrace in death." She thinks, as she has thought before: "If it were now to die, 'twere now to be most happy." In the light of her whole past life, which has been recaptured by her during the day, she goes on, having criticized herself, to realize that "no pleasure could equal . . . this having done with the triumphs of youth, lost herself in the process of living."

> The clock began striking. The young man had killed himself; but she did not pity him; with the clock striking the hour, one two, three, she did not pity him, with all this going on . . . the words came to her, Fear no more the heat of the sun. . . . She felt somehow very like him— the young man who had killed himself. She felt glad that he had done it; thrown it away. The clock was striking. The leaden circles dissolved in the air. He made her feel the beauty; made her feel the fun. . . . And she came in from the little room.

John Graham, in a distinguished essay, writes that when Clarissa "leaves the little room she returns to the larger room of human relations" and symbolizes time's transfiguration by eternity. Thus far he seems to have the correct interpretation. But when he adds that "we must retain the limiting, protecting identity which is ours in time if we are to triumph over time," it becomes probable that his interpretation is not a description of what really happens in the novel. Clarissa has come in from the little room of her own identity to the large room of reality itself. It is made explicit that her party is much more than a social gathering—and so her entrance more than the assumption of a social identity: her parties are an "offering." Nor, as the little-room scene makes just as explicit, does Clarissa retain her individual identity; rather it is a case of "not I, but Time

in me." Clarissa has in a strict sense found her life by losing it.

Clarissa is constantly afraid of losing her life. She is not yet completely recovered from a recent illness; she is more than a little jealous when her husband goes by himself to lunch with Lady Bruton; above all, she is aware of growing old, of being old. "She feared time itself, and read on Lady Bruton's face, as if it had been a dial cut in impassive stone, the dwindling of life; how year by year her share was sliced; how little the margin that remained was capable any longer of stretching, of absorbing, as in the youthful years, the colours, salts, tones of existence, so that she filled the room she entered, and felt often . . . an exquisite suspense, such as might stay a diver before plunging." This fear of time—of false time—runs through the book. Beginning the day, Clarissa glances into Hatchards' window and sees a book lying open there. "Fear no more the heat o' the sun / Nor the furious winter's rages," she reads. The phrase "Fear no more" recurs four times in the novel, three times to Clarissa and once in Septimus' thought; although its first appearance is ironic—Clarissa *does* fear—the phrase gathers new and increased meaning with each use, and comes finally to have its literal meaning for her.

This is not to say that Clarissa comes unaware to her final affirmation; even at the beginning of the novel, she has within her all the potentialities that are to become actualities. (pp. 61-6)

That Virginia Woolf had read and learned from Proust is evident not only in the characterization of **Mrs. Dalloway,** but also in a Proustian use of metaphor that does much to give this novel its total effect. In her series of articles on "Phases of Fiction" in the *Bookman*, Virginia Woolf said that, through his use of metaphor, Proust had been able to achieve poetic effects in his novel: he was able to rise above the specific details to a generalization about all of experience, and at the same time to give the details themselves symbolic value. She herself put this device to use again and again in **Mrs. Dalloway**. . . . (p. 69)

A . . . complex and extensive use of such metaphor occurs toward the end of the novel; the entire party sequence is given meaning, and the meaning itself made dynamic, through the implications of the figure here. Clarissa is leading the prime minister through the room. "She wore ear-rings, and a silver-green mermaid's dress. Lolloping on the waves and braiding her tresses she seemed, having that gift still; to be; to exist; to sum it all up in the moment as she paused; turned . . . laughed, all with the most perfect ease and air of a creature floating in its element. But age had brushed her; even as a mermaid might behold in her glass the setting sun on some very clear evening over the waves." The water image has appeared throughout the novel to symbolize unity; Bergson said: "The unity of the impulse which, passing through generations, links individuals with individuals, species with species, and makes of the whole series of the living one single immense wave flowing over matter." Clarissa is above the waves, but Peter thinks that she "must now, being on the very verge and rim of things, take her leave." And she does. Going off into the little room, she thinks of Septimus' leap from the window. "Had he plunged holding his treasure?" His act, then, was a plunge, the same kind of plunge with which the novel began—"What a lark! What a plunge! For so it had always seemed to her, when . . . she had burst open the French windows and plunged at Bourton into the open air . . . the air was . . . like the flap of a wave; the kiss of a wave." Again throughout the novel the appearance, the matter, of clock time has been denied by true time in an air-water metaphor often repeated: Big Ben strikes, and "the leaden circles dissolved in the air." There follows, in the little room, Clarissa's rich identification with Septimus and her own plunge, dissolution, annihilation.

The certainty with which Virginia Woolf used metaphor in *Mrs. Dalloway* should be sufficient indication that she "imitated" Proust only in the best sense of the word. Her early novels show that what she found in Proust was largely a confirmation of ideas she had already begun to work out for herself, and—more important—proof that such ideas could be rendered into great art. It is natural that Proust appealed to Virginia Woolf; her own concerns, her own terms—impressions, facts, reality, time—were his. (pp. 70-1)

Many critics have, although for the most part ignoring the relation of Proust's art to *Mrs. Dalloway,* declared that the book was profoundly influenced by James Joyce, especially by *Ulysses.* For example, J. Isaacs calls it an "inspired imitation of *Ulysses,*" and A. R. Reade thinks it possibly a criticism of *Ulysses.* The two reasons why most critics see such an influence are that both *Mrs. Dalloway* and *Ulysses* take place on one day, and that both, supposedly, employ the "stream of consciousness" method.

Just as Virginia Woolf explicitly admired *À la Recherche du temps perdu,* she explicitly disliked *Ulysses.* . . . [She] described *Ulysses* as "a memorable catastrophe—immense in daring, terrific in disaster." It is doubtful that she would have wished to imitate a novel about which she had such an opinion. Certainly she admired Joyce's attempt; certainly she approved his experimentation; just as certainly she considered *Ulysses* a failure.

If *Mrs. Dalloway* is not an imitation of Joyce's novel, neither does it seem a criticism, inspired or otherwise, except insofar as any novel written by an author aware of his contemporaries and not completely satisfied with their achievements is, by its very difference, a criticism; and in this sense *Mrs. Dalloway* cannot be called a criticism of any other novel in particular.

Both *Ulysses* and *Mrs. Dalloway* take place on one day. Virginia Woolf knew Greek and read the Greek tragedians in the original; *Oedipus Rex* also takes place on one day. In other words, this fact in itself is superficial: what is important is *why* these novels take place on one day, and Joyce's reasons for the unity of time seem very different from Virginia Woolf's. If Joyce used the single day as a unity, Virginia Woolf used it as a diversity. Joyce attempted to show all that a single day can hold; Virginia Woolf, to show that there is no such thing as a single day. Joyce exhausted a day; Virginia Woolf destroyed a day. This is not to say that one was right and one wrong, but only that each was doing a different thing and so employing unity of time for a different reason.

Although *Mrs. Dalloway* does take place on a single day, it does not employ the stream-of-consciousness technique. Virginia Woolf "is generally mentioned as the most refined and lucid exponent of the stream of consciousness method"; actually, she never did use it—here or elsewhere—mainly because it was completely out of accord with her "vision."

A stream-of-consciousness passage is a transcription of verbal thought so direct that it seems to bare a human mind. The reader has the illusion of receiving everything; the author creates the illusion of having selected nothing, rejected nothing, corrected nothing. All is given directly from the point of view of the character involved. The famous concluding section of *Ulysses* is a perfect example: it is a singularly interesting record of a singularly uninteresting mind. Joyce's only comment is that there can be no comment; never before was a writer so completely impersonal, and so very much in the way by reason of his utter absence. In *Pilgrimage* Dorothy M. Richardson resorts to dots, either for the sake of clarity; or—what seems more probable—because she conceives the consciousness as blinking, so to speak; or because she is allowing for nonverbal awareness. But Molly Bloom never blinks, and neither does Joyce.

Virginia Woolf, on the other hand, is always present in her novels. The style of her novels coincides perfectly with the vision of life that she saw and that the novels communicate. Beneath the diverse points of view presented to the reader, there is the impersonal narrator—the central intelligence—of which, in and after *Mrs. Dalloway,* the reader is never allowed to become immediately aware, but which extends the idea of a common impulse beneath diversity. The narrator speaks directly, but never in the first person; so that although the reader has often a momentary illusion of entering a character's consciousness, he never "actually does so"—he does not share the characters' thoughts or watch them, but is only told about them. (pp. 72-4)

Virginia Woolf did not, in *Mrs. Dalloway* or elsewhere, use the stream-of-consciousness technique in any exact sense of the term; and it is improbable that Joyce had a direct effect upon either *Mrs. Dalloway* or any other of Virginia Woolf's novels. The two authors saw life from entirely different points of view, despite the fact that both worked in part with Bergsonistic concepts.

Mrs. Dalloway itself, according to one of its critics, is told with "a technical mastery unparalleled in English fiction." If this praise seems excessive, even in the light of Virginia Woolf's own later work, it is true that in *Mrs. Dalloway* Virginia Woolf was able to regulate her perspective and adequately to formalize a consistent interpretation of experience. She herself was not completely satisfied with this novel: her diary shows that she did not especially like Clarissa Dalloway. Even before the novel was published, she was thinking of a new one that she felt to be more subtle, more human, more interesting.

This reaction—this absorption in "some new book which not only thrusts its predecessor from the nest but has a way of subtly blackening its character in comparison with its own" [see Woolf excerpt dated 1928]—is the artist's, but not at all necessarily the critic's. It did lead to what can be called Virginia Woolf's creative modulation of the perspective she had now mastered, for *To the Lighthouse* is at once an end in itself and an important step toward something as different from *Mrs. Dalloway* as *Mrs. Dalloway* is different from *The Voyage Out.* (pp. 75-6)

> *James Hafley, in his* The Glass Roof: Virginia Woolf as Novelist, *University of California Press, 1954, 195 p.*

IRENE SIMON (lecture date 1958)

[*In the following excerpt from a lecture delivered May 8, 1958, at the University of London, Simon demonstrates the significance of several images to structural and thematic coherency in* Mrs. Dalloway.]

Virginia Woolf's dissatisfaction with the Edwardian novel because it failed to express 'reality', led her to create a new form of fiction which could convey her own sense of life, or, as she called it, '(the) luminous halo, (the) semi-transparent envelope surrounding us from the beginning of consciousness to the end' (*The Common Reader,* I . . .). What in fact she wishes to express is an apprehension of the essence of reality. The sentient mind, on which emotions, perceptions, thoughts, impinge thus becomes in her novels the channel through which reality is viewed; we are immersed in the flux or stream of consciousness, which both reflects and colours the world outside. This is a purely subjective method, since the world outside has no reality except as perceived by a sensibility, since the meaning of life consists in the quality that this sensibility perceives or creates.

Such a method clearly derives from a fundamental scepticism as to the nature of reality, a scepticism which can only be overcome by raising personal intuitions of values to the level of intimations of truth. The author's and the characters' immersion in their sensibility is an indication of their lack of 'belief' and of their search for meaning; it also reveals the essential solitude of the individual. Virginia Woolf's characters are all confronted with the same problem: what is the meaning of life? But the answer vouchsafed to those who 'have their vision', is expressed in terms of harmony created, of meaningful relations between elements: it is the answer of the aesthetic sensibility to the apparent confusion of life, an answer that cannot be translated into conceptual terms. The characters are also obsessed by their separateness: it is at once their most precious treasure and the source of their isolation; they try to overthrow the barriers between selves and to reach out to each other, but they also resent any intrusion into the privacy of their souls. Finally, being immersed in the subjective world of perceptual experience, the characters cannot but see everything—themselves, others, and the world around—as dominated by change; and they try to find permanence or stability, something that endures in the midst of the flow. Hence the main themes of Virginia Woolf's whole work: life and death, time and the absolute, singleness and oneness, confusion and order. Hence also the main problem for the novelist: to render the flux and yet let a pattern emerge.

Given such a view of life, it is not surprising that Virginia Woolf should have rejected the conventions of plot and character as used traditionally to bring order and significance into the raw material, and should have resorted to means which properly belong to poetry in order to convey the significance perceived or the value felt in experience. It is a commonplace to say that she composes her novels as lyric poems, and that images are an essential element of her style and composition. My purpose is to try and discover what function the images serve in her novels, and whether she can use them as structural elements on which to base her narrative. (pp. 180-81)

The effect of most images in *Mrs. Dalloway* is to blur the hard outline of objects and to translate them into a world where fancy endows them with a new face and gives them a significance which facts cannot convey. Thus, a newspaper placard going up in the air is seen as a kite, and its playfulness at once makes light of the business on which people are intent. Rumours move about the streets of London 'like a cloud, swift, veil-like upon hills', thus endowing people and things with a dream-like quality. . . . The point of such comparisons is to make us wonder whether what we have accepted as everyday world is really so. The effect is exhilarating, because the world suddenly appears strange and new to our eyes.

The impression of strangeness is even stronger when, for instance, an eye becomes 'a cup that overflowed and let the rest run down its china walls unrecorded' . . . , where the strangeness is enhanced by the literal application of the image eye / cup; but the implied comparison does not add anything to the experience, it presents it in a startling way, and therefore draws attention to itself. There are a good many images of this kind in *Mrs. Dalloway,* which critics have occasionally praised as 'metaphysical' or as truly of the imagination. (p. 181)

Sometimes, the fantasy which creates the images is that which spins fairy tales, and all the characters in *Mrs. Dalloway* weave stories around the people they encounter. It is not surprising therefore to come across images that distinctly call up a fairytale atmosphere. Thus Clarissa, remembering Peter's criticism of her, takes up her needle and 'like a queen whose guards have fallen asleep and left her unprotected . . . so that one can stroll in and have a look at where she lies with the brambles curving over her summoned to her help the things she did, the things she liked'. . . . For a moment she becomes the Sleeping Beauty, and Peter half prince, half enemy, threatens her privacy. But at once the vision vanishes, and they are seen as knights challenging each other in the lists. These impressions only flash through the mind; we are not given time to look at the image too closely, because all that it implies need not, and in fact should not, be brought into play. The charm of such images lies in their vagueness, so that for a moment we half descry worlds in which one is not tied to facts and figures. But the setting of this novel does not allow for a full acknowledgement of such worlds and they are felt as fantasies.

Sometimes the meaning of the image cannot be grasped until a scene from the past is evoked, a scene which the present emotion recalls. Thus Peter, remembering that he had wanted to marry Clarissa 'was overcome by his own grief, which rose like a moon looked at from a terrace, ghastly beautiful with light from the sunken day'. . . . The scene in the moonlight at Bourton is then recalled, and we understand that for Peter the moon is inseparable from the pain he then felt and has become a symbol of his grief. It is almost as though the image could not speak for itself, and the following reminiscence was necessary to make its burden clear. Similarly, when we read that the evening light 'paled and faded above the battlements and prominences', and began to disappear, but 'London would have none of it, and rushed her bayonet into the sky, pinioned her, constrained her to partnership in revelry . . .' . . . , we are baffled by the unaccountable feeling that turns buildings into bayonets *and* leads on to a partnership in revelry. The image makes us pause; then we remember a similar image earlier on in the novel. As Clarissa muses over death, wondering whether it matters that she must cease completely, she feels that she will survive on the ebb and flow of things 'being laid out like a mist between the people she knew best, who lifted her on their branches as she had seen the trees lift the mist'. . . . Somehow the later image is a reflection of the former, and therefore suggests the relation between life and death, between individual existence and survival in others, between singleness and merging.

These and other images suggest the relation in a painting between verticals and horizontals, or rather horizontally undulating lines, a relation which is somehow significant of two attitudes at once opposed and interdependent. If that is so, then the apparently baffling image of the bayonets pinioning the sky may have a thematic significance, as have several other images in the novel. (pp. 181-82)

I will consider three [such images]: the shilling thrown into the Serpentine, the old lady seen in her room, and Clarissa holding the hot-water can.

As Clarissa is walking in the morning, her thoughts turn now to the people around, now to scenes from her youth. 'She remembered Sylvia, Fred, Sally Seton—such hosts of people; and dancing all night; and the waggons plodding past to market; and driving home across the Park. She remembered once throwing a shilling into the Serpentine. But every one remembered.' . . . As we read, this strikes us as one of the many things she remembers, like the waggons plodding to market, a trivial incident which for some reason happens to be stored in her memory. For Virginia Woolf does leave room in her novel for trivial incidents, e.g. seeing Jorrocks' *Jaunts and Jollities* in the shop-window, for the odds and ends of things, because the hints and guesses one is to follow to get at the meaning of life must emerge from the apparent confusion of things. Though the reminiscences of Clarissa are followed by a meditation on death, though flinging the coin into the Serpentine *may* suggest destruction, it is only at the end of the novel . . . that the meaning appears, when the sentence is repeated: Clarissa remembers 'throwing a shilling into the Serpentine, *never anything more*'. The additional words relate her gesture to Septimus' death, of which she has just heard, since he has flung *his life* away.

It is fashionable nowadays when discussing imagery to assume that images, in poetic drama for instance, can affect the reader or spectator, even though he remains unaware of them at the moment; and that there happens a kind of recognition when the same, or a similar, image is used later on, so that some link is established, however unconsciously. I cannot but wonder, however, whether such effects can be relied upon in a context that is not a closely organised poem. In this particular case, it seems to me that few readers are likely to remember that a hint has been given at the beginning of the novel. Virginia Woolf's use of a device primarily poetic takes no account of certain conditions of fiction.

I would say that her use of the other two motifs is more successful. In the morning Clarissa remembers her love for Sally Seton; she remembers 'standing in her bed-room at the top of the house holding the hot-water can in her hands and saying aloud, ''She is beneath this roof''' . . . . The ecstasy, which had then made her feel 'if it were now to die, 'twere now to be most happy', had brought her a kind of revelation. At the end of her party, she suddenly sees Sally and feels that 'one might put down the hot-water can quite composedly'. . . . Though the motifs are as far apart as in the first example, here the relation appears at once, simply because on the first occasion the motif was part of a significant moment, which remains embedded in our minds. Othello's words are repeated a little later too, when Clarissa hears of Septimus' suicide. The two scenes are linked easily: when Clarissa paused to hold the moment in her hands, and when the moment has lost its significance.

A similar pattern is established by the motif of the old lady moving about her room. Clarissa sees her just after her encounter with Miss Kilman and in the evening after hearing of Septimus' suicide. In both cases, the old lady going about her own business, undisturbed, answers Clarissa's wish to let 'everybody merely be themselves'. . . . Her sense that there is something solemn about the privacy of the soul . . . is gratified by the sight of the old lady 'quietly going to bed alone'. Both Miss Kilman, from whom Clarissa has just escaped, and Sir William Bradshaw, from whom Septimus has escaped, try to intrude into other people's souls. In both cases, the significance remains implicit, and the reader is likely to remember the former occasion only because it follows on the expression of violent feelings. On the other hand, the incident does not call attention to itself as does Clarissa's remark about the hot-water can at the party. The motif works less obtrusively, but is sufficiently clear to suggest a pattern of emotions.

The images I have discussed so far suggest a variety of impressions and qualities; they weave around people and things a luminous halo that endows them with value. Other images, however, are capable of suggesting the significance of life as felt by a character. Such is the image of the nun, as applied to Clarissa. The main quality of the image is its ambivalence; as such it can convey Clarissa's attitude to life, her love and her fear of it, her longing for privacy and her wish to merge; it can also express the twofold movement of withdrawal and gift, and imply the relation of self to other selves.

After her walk through London, Clarissa comes home and enters the hall 'as cool as a vault'; she feels 'like a nun who has left the world and feels fold round her the familiar veils and the response to old devotions'. . . . The image implies the religious feeling, the sense of offering and thankfulness; it implies a serenity and acceptance of life which gives value to the world she has just left. This is a moment of peace at the centre of the whirling world. But the peace is soon shattered by 'the shock of Lady Bruton asking Richard to lunch without her'. . . . The cool vault becomes a tower, the nun withdraws from the world into the emptiness at the heart of life . . . , solitude becomes isolation, and virginity is no longer equated with purity but with coldness, with the fear of giving oneself away. Yet devotion and isolation, purity and coldness must be taken together to arrive at the meaning of life as Clarissa sees it. The bed with the sheets stretched tight across it becomes a symbol for the separation of the individual as opposed to the moments of sudden revelation, when the world comes closer. The moment of revelation is presented in such terms as to suggest a kind of mystical experience. It therefore seems as if the nun's seclusion and her coldness, the attic room and the narrow bed were conditions of the momentary illuminations, as if withdrawing 'into the world of perpetual solitude' were the necessary preparation for the final coming together.

Later in the day, remembering that Peter criticises her for her parties, that Richard thinks it foolish of her to get excited over them, she realises that they are wrong, and, 'lying on the sofa, cloistered' she says that her parties are an offering, though she wonders: an offering to whom? . . . Thus, more than a hundred pages later, here is the image of the nun and her devotion, even with the same scepticism that had made her exclaim in the morning that 'not for a moment did she believe in God'. . . . It is probably because of this scepticism that Virginia Woolf can use this image only sparingly, and turns to the waves and the sea to suggest the twofold movement.

The image appears already in the opening sentences. When Clarissa leaves her house, the early morning air is fresh 'as if issued to children on a beach', and she *plunges* into it as when she stepped out into the garden at Bourton. The solemnity of the morning at Bourton is later transferred to the pause in the traffic and to the hush before Big Ben strikes. The flow of people and of carriages through Westminster brings to Clarissa the same excitement and awe as diving into a strange element, so that the love and fear of the everflowing life around her, the wish to be taken into it and the fear of being swallowed by it, are suggested at this early stage in the novel. Yet there is also the suggestion that this exciting pageant is a vain show, that Clarissa's absorption in the life around her, as later on her love of parties and of assembling, leaves unsatisfied a deeper desire in her. Even while immersed in the flow, she seems to be groping for the 'still point of the turning world'. Just as the moment of June is an intersection of past and present, so time and timelessness intersect, and even Big Ben's 'leaden circles dissolve in the air.'

Clarissa loves the divine vitality that makes people move about and lifts the leaves in the Park on its *waves,* as she had loved dancing and riding. The image of the waves first brought in to express the freshness of the morning air, expands to contain the 'waves of divine vitality'; being firmly established, it can endow a mere statement with a weight of significance far beyond the actual words: 'To dance, to ride, she had adored all that'. . . . Properly speaking, this is no image, but who shall say now where image and statement of fact can be divided from each other? It is just the purpose of Virginia Woolf to abolish the distinction between dream and reality; she effects this by mixing images with gestures, thoughts with impressions, visions with pure sensations, and by presenting them as mirrored on a consciousness. As a consequence, almost everything becomes an image projected on a screen.

By the time Clarissa reaches the Park Gates, the memory of Peter Walsh impinges more and more on her thoughts, and this brings to the fore the other theme, her sense of loneliness and of being an outsider. Peter had often scolded her for her coldness; now as she watches the taxicabs, she has a sense of 'being far out at sea, alone'. The image derives from the actual situation, but renders more than a sensation. Its connection with the plunge into the morning air and the fear of being lost in the waves relates it to the basic image developed from the start, and leads on to the incident she remembers: of once throwing a shilling into the Serpentine.

As incidents and persons float up in her memory, so she may now imagine surviving on the ebb and flow of things, here in the streets of London. . . . There comes the consoling thought that we are part of everything and live in each other. By now, the image of the sea, the waves, the flux, has developed into a symbol of life; the fear of loneliness and the fear of being lost in the flux, the love of the flux and the love of independent existence, the twofold movement of merging and separating, of existing individually and being annihilated, are subsumed in the image, which, thanks to its ambivalence, can be used to express both aspects of the theme.

Whenever things come together and harmonise, Clarissa feels secure as if borne up on a wave, lifted on its crest, submerged by it; when the wave falls, leaving the body on the beach, the heart is at peace. (pp. 183-86)

Sometimes the sea appears as a dangerous element and the individual as lost in the midst of it, fearing to be carried away by it. This happens in moments of separation, when the self seems to be threatened. These moments come and go, as the waves collect and fall, for there are 'tides in the body' . . . , and memories float up or sink. Like the traffic, the mind ebbs and flows, the train of thoughts or impressions moves rhythmically from past to present, from joy to sorrow, and man is borne by the waves or left on the beach. The image of the sea and the waves is fundamental to this kind of composition, and very often, as in the passage quoted, the very sentences mould themselves on the movement of the waves.

Clarissa's 'double', the shell-shocked Septimus, is haunted by the same fear and love; he is at once relieved and appalled by his loneliness; he, too, has his revelations and tries to communicate. He is repeatedly presented as a drowned sailor on a rock, far out at sea; he has gone under the sea and has been dead, and yet is now alive, and he feels himself drawing to the shore of life. . . . He sees the trees of the Park rising and falling like waves, and to him the sun is now terrifying now gentle. All these link the two characters and their search for meaning. The same peace descends on him when he lies on the sofa as when Clarissa sews quietly in her room. His thoughts at this moment are a variation on Clarissa's dream of waves collecting and falling; they embrace the same elements, and end on the same comforting note: 'Fear no more, says the heart in the body; fear no more'. . . . As Clarissa muses on his suicide, the words she had read that morning in the shop-window once more recur to her: 'Fear no more the heat of the sun'. . . .

The phrase recurs to link the parts, and implies that the sun is the enemy. Yet again the image is ambivalent, for sometimes the heat of the sun is kind and gentle, whether to Peter in the park, or to Septimus at peace on the shore of the world, or about to kill himself. But everyone is suffering from the heat, and Septimus is terrified of the world bursting into flames, of falling through the sea into the flames . . . ; when Clarissa hears of his suicide, 'her dress flames, her body burns' . . . with the pain of the rusty spikes going through his body.

From these few examples, we may conclude that in **Mrs. Dalloway** many images are used to release objects and people from their matter-of-fact ordinariness and to reveal some essence perceived by fancy or imagination. By such means, Virginia Woolf achieves what David Daiches has called 'the dissolution of experience into tenuous insights'. A more important purpose is served by ambivalent images which can suggest a complex relation of people to life, because they can expand so as to include contraries and imply a rhythm or tension between these contraries. This latter kind of images contributes to the inner organisation of impressions and thoughts, and the movement of the novel is partly at least determined by them.

But only partly. For it is true that **Mrs. Dalloway,** as a critic has said, is 'rigidly structured and mechanically fitted together'. The mechanical devices which Virginia Woolf uses to give the novel a 'skeletal structure' are too well-known for me to dwell on this point. Her use of them suggests that she could not rely entirely on her imagery to provide the organisation from within. Perhaps the central 'incident' in the novel cannot bear the weight of meaning that it is intended to carry: Clarissa's party is her solution to the mystery of isolated selves, an instance of communication, her offering. But assembling people in a drawing-room does sound a little trivial as an answer to the problem of life. Because the objective correlative is hardly adequate, the images which express some aspects of the theme fail to fuse, and the need is felt to establish the relations by means of other devices. (pp. 186-88)

Irene Simon, "Some Aspects of Virginia Woolf's Imagery," in English Studies, Vol. 41, No. 3, June, 1960, pp. 180-96.

DAVID DAICHES (essay date 1960)

[*Daiches is a prominent English scholar and critic who has written extensively on English and American literature. He is especially renowned for his in-depth studies of such writers as Robert Burns, Robert Louis Stevenson, and Virginia Woolf. His criticism in*

general is best characterized as appreciative in content and attached to no single methodology. Summarizing his conception of
the critic's role in the essay "The 'New Criticism': Some Qualifications" (1950), Daiches wrote: "In the last analysis, the test
of [a work's] value can be judged only by the receiver, and judged
by him on some kind of 'affective' theory. . . . Literature exists
to be read and enjoyed, and criticism, at least in its pedagogical
aspect, exists in order to increase awareness and so to increase
enjoyment. The purely philosophical critic may entertain himself
by trying to isolate the quiddity of poetry . . . but the 'appreciative'
critic will use any means at his disposal—analytic, descriptive,
histrionic, yes, even historical—to arouse alert interest, to produce that communicative impact without which all further critical
discussion is useless." In the following excerpt, Daiches examines
the structure of Mrs. Dalloway, commenting on themes, organization, and Woolf's development of the stream of consciousness
method.]

In Virginia Woolf more than in any other English novelist the
writer of fiction faces squarely the problem of the breakdown
of a public sense of significance and its consequences for the
novel. A novelist who could ask, "What is meant by reality?"
and reply, "It would seem to be something very erratic, very
undependable—now to be found in a dusty road, now in a
scrap of newspaper in the street, now in a daffodil in the sun";
who specifically points out "the power of their belief" and
the security of public conviction about fundamentals which
distinguish Scott and Jane Austen from her own contemporaries—such a novelist does not have to wait for the critic to come
along and explain what she is doing and why she is doing it.
She saw one aspect of the modern problem with remarkable
clarity, and consciously developed a view of fictional art which
would enable her to deal with it. Of course she saw this not
only as a modern problem but as a deep personal need—the
need to develop a kind of fiction which would render persuasively the quality of her own personal insights into experience.
"Quality" is the word to use here, for Mrs. Woolf was concerned less with projecting any given view of what is significant
in experience than with the sort of thing, the moods, intuitions,
blending of memories, sudden awarenesses of the symbolic in
the real, that suggests how the inner life is really lived. The
material environment, which she criticized Bennett and Wells
and Galsworthy for concentrating on, was for her at most only
a background, and even changes in status and fortune (where
they occur in her novels, which is rarely) are shown as less
interesting than the states of consciousness associated with
them. Even the change from life to death can be less significant
for her than the mutations of one person's consciousness into
the differing recollections of that person, and the differing
responses to the meaning of his or her personality, left in the
consciousnesses of others after he or she has died. Mrs. Dalloway, reflecting on what death might mean, speculates that
perhaps in death she would become "part of people she had
never met; being laid out like a mist between the people she
knew best, who lifted her on their branches as she had seen
the trees lift the mist, but it spread ever so far, her life, herself."
And in the last part of *To the Lighthouse* the dead Mrs. Ramsay
is an important part of the texture of other consciousnesses.

It is true that in the rhythms of her prose, in the muted lilt of
her sentences with their repetitions and qualifications and subtle
fading from direct speech to brooding description and back
again, Virginia Woolf sometimes provokes the reaction that it
is all mere self-indulgent musing, an irresponsible playing about
with life. But this is unjust. The novels are most carefully
organized to present real patterns of meaning, and both characters and events are—by virtue of the way they are presented

and of the part they play in the total pattern—endowed with
symbolic significance that is much more than a mere sense of
mood. Yet sense of mood is her starting point. The credibility
of her best novels is established by the almost hypnotic force
with which the author compels the reader to accept the mood
she sets, with all its variations, as the novel flows on to its
conclusion. Nothing could be further removed from Victorian
fiction, in which the interest was maintained by public symbols,
gain or loss of money, sudden fortune or sudden disgrace, or
obvious emotional changes concerned with love or hate or hope
or disappointment. The charge that Virginia Woolf's is an art
of leisure, of unconcern with the practical affairs of daily life,
is true but absurdly irrelevant. It might equally be made against
the music of Mozart or the poems of Henry Vaughan. The
important thing is that this delicate rendering of the different
shades of experience, this subtle presentation of the texture of
consciousness as it is woven by the individual's response to
life, is made real and moving in Virginia Woolf's art. (pp.
187-89)

Mrs. Woolf's particular kind of refinement of life led eventually to the emergence of one theme which dominates all her
fiction, from *Mrs. Dalloway* to *The Years*. This is a theme
characteristically abstract, characteristically philosophical, to
which action, character, and commentary are alike subordinated; the theme of time, death, and personality and the relations of these three to each other and to some ultimate which
includes them all. Significance in events is increasingly judged
in terms of these three factors. It is not so much the quality of
the observation of life (as it is in Katherine Mansfield) which
makes her points, but reflection after observation. A twofold
process of rarification goes on. First, life is refined before it
is observed with the artist's eye; second, the results of observation are meditatively chewed on as they are being presented
to the reader. A certain lack of body in her work is the result.
(pp. 194-95)

The aeration of her style which was one of the many ways in
which Mrs. Woolf tried to free herself from the inhibiting
features of the traditional novel—an aeration which *Night and
Day* showed her to be much in need of, and which is shown
in process in *Monday or Tuesday*—was perhaps carried a little
too far in *Jacob's Room*, and in her following novel, *Mrs.
Dalloway* . . . , there is a successful attempt to redress the balance. By this time the "stream of consciousness" technique
had become almost a commonplace in fiction, and the problem
was not so much to win freedom to employ it as to find a way
of disciplining it. It is one thing to have the relation between
your characters' impressions clear in your own mind and quite
another to have them objectively clear in the form of the work
itself. Virginia Woolf seems to have grappled carefully with
the latter problem in *Mrs. Dalloway:* she limits its scope in
time and place; her characters are few and their relations to
each other clear-cut; impressions and thought processes are
assigned clearly to those to whom they belong, even at the risk
of losing some immediacy of effect; the time scheme is patterned with extraordinary care; and altogether the novel represents as neat a piece of construction as she has ever achieved.
It is therefore an excellent example to take for a more detailed
technical analysis.

Just as Joyce in *Ulysses* takes one day in the life of Leopold
Bloom and enlarges its implications by patterning its events
with sufficient care, so Virginia Woolf takes from morning to
evening in the life of Mrs. Dalloway and builds her story
through the events of this short time. (Events, of course, in-

clude psychological as well as physical happenings.) Being a far shorter and less ambitious work than *Ulysses, Mrs. Dalloway* employs a simpler and more easily analyzable technique. The whole novel is constructed in terms of the two dimensions of space and time. We either stand still in time and are led to contemplate diverse but contemporaneous events in space or we stand still in space and are allowed to move up and down temporally in the consciousness of one individual. If it would not be extravagant to consider personality rather than space as one dimension, with time as the other, we might divide the book quite easily into those sections where time is fluid and personality stable or where personality is fluid and time is stable, and regard this as a careful alternation of the dimensions. So that at one point we are halted at a London street to take a peep into the consciousness of a variety of people who are all on the spot at the same moment in the same place, and at another we are halted within the consciousness of one individual moving up and down in time within the limits of one individual's memory. (pp. 202-03)

It would be simple to go through *Mrs. Dalloway* to show how first we get the "stream of consciousness" of a particular character; then we pause to look over the character's environment and take a glance inside the minds of other characters who are in or relevant to that environment; then we come to rest within the mind of one of those other characters and investigate his consciousness for a while; and then again we emerge to contemplate the environment, etc. And each time we pause to investigate the mind of any one character in some detail, that mind takes us into the past, and we escape altogether from the chronological time sequence of the story. As in *Ulysses,* though on a much smaller scale, the past figures more than the present, even though the action covers one single day.

Mrs. Woolf, although her scope is much more limited than Joyce's, takes much more care than Joyce does to put up signposts. When we are staying still in time and moving rapidly through the minds of various characters, Mrs. Woolf is very careful to mark those points of time, to see to it that the unifying factor which is holding these quite disparate consciousnesses together is made clear to the reader. That is why the clocks of London chime right through the book, from start to finish. When we wander through different personalities, we are kept from straying by the time indications, and, conversely, when we go up and down in time through the memory of one of the characters, we are kept from straying by the constant reminder of the speaker's identity. There is nothing haphazard about the striking of the clocks:

> "The time, Septimus," Rezia repeated. "What is the time?"
>
> He was talking, he was starting, this man must notice him. He was looking at them.
>
> "I will tell you the time," said Septimus, very slowly, very drowsily, smiling mysteriously. As he sat smiling at the dead man in the grey suit the quarter struck—the quarter to twelve.
>
> And that is being young, Peter Walsh thought as he passed them.

We pass from Septimus Smith to Peter Walsh, and the striking of the hour marks the transition. If we are not to lose our way among the various consciousnesses, we must understand why we are taken from one to another: because they impinge in time, and that impingement is symbolized by the striking of

the clock. Almost every fifteen minutes is indicated by a clock chiming, or in some other way, throughout the book. We can always find out, at most by looking a page ahead or consulting the previous page, just what time of day it is. And these indications of time are most clearly given when we are about to go from personality to personality. . . . (pp. 206-07)

Similarly, when we pause within the consciousness of one character only to move up and down in time within that consciousness, the identity of the thinker, which this time is the unifying factor, is stressed. The opening paragraphs provide a characteristic example:

> Mrs. Dalloway said she would buy the flowers herself.
>
> For Lucy had her work cut out for her. The doors would be taken off their hinges; Rumpelmayer's men were coming. And then, thought Clarissa Dalloway, what a morning—fresh as if issued to children on a beach.
>
> What a lark! What a plunge! For so it had always seemed to her, when, with a little squeak of the hinges, which she could hear now, she had burst open the French windows and plunged at Bourton into the open air. How fresh, how calm, stiller than this of course, the air was in the early morning; like the flap of a wave; the kiss of a wave; chill and sharp and yet (for a girl of eighteen as she then was) solemn, feeling as she did, standing there at the open window, that something awful was about to happen. . . .

The compromise between reported and direct thought here seems to be due to Mrs. Woolf's desire to keep the unifying factor always present to the reader's mind, but it has some interesting results. The "I" of the reverie becomes an indeterminate kind of pronoun midway between "she" (which it would have been had Mrs. Woolf used the straight objective reporting of the traditional novel) and the first personal pronoun employed naturally by the real "stream of consciousness" writer. It is not surprising to find Mrs. Woolf frequently taking refuge in "one," as in the following very characteristic sentence: "For having lived in Westminster—how many years now? over twenty— one feels even in the midst of the traffic, or waking at night, Clarissa was positive, a particular hush, or solemnity. . . ."

Here the movement is from a suppressed "I" (in the parenthetical clause) to a "one" and then, on account of the necessity of stressing the unifying factor, namely the identity of Clarissa Dalloway, to a straight third-person use of "Clarissa." We might note, too, the frequent use of the present participle (". . . she cried to herself, pushing through the swing doors"; "she thought, waiting to cross," ". . . she asked herself, walking towards Bond Street"), which enables her to identify the thinker and carry her into a new action without interrupting the even flow of the thought stream; and the frequent commencement of a paragraph with "for," the author's conjunction (not the thinker's), whose purpose is to indicate the vague, pseudological connection between the different sections of a reverie.

The plot in *Mrs. Dalloway* is made to act out the meaning of the reverie in a most interesting manner. As the heroine reflects on the nature of the self and its relation to other people, on the importance of contact and at the same time the necessity of keeping the self inviolable, of the extremes of isolation and domination, other characters in London at the same time—

some encountered by and known to Mrs. Dalloway, and others quite unknown to her—illustrate in their behavior, thoughts, relations to each other, and so on, different aspects of these problems. Hugh Whitbread, whom she meets early in her morning shopping, is the perfect social man, handsome, well-bred, "with his little job at Court," who has almost lost his real personality in fulfilling his social function; though, Mrs. Dalloway reflects, he is "not a positive imbecile as Peter made out; not a mere barber's block," there is an element of glossy unreality about him. It is significant that at this stage Peter Walsh should come into Mrs. Dalloway's mind, for Peter (the man she had loved and who had loved her but whom she had refused to marry because he made too many claims on her individuality and wished to dominate her personality with his own) is at the other extreme, the individual who never really adjusts to society; he stands in some ways for the independent and assertive self, all the more vulnerable for its independence. Later on in the novel he turns up at Mrs. Dalloway's (having conveniently just returned from India) and is invited to her party that evening, where he takes his place both as part of the pattern of Mrs. Dalloway's past and as a particular kind of sensibility recording appropriate impressions. The delicate working-out of differing degrees of selfhood and social adjustment can be compared and contrasted with the same sort of thing as it is done by a great novelist working in an assured social world through public symbols. In Jane Austen's *Pride and Prejudice* we are also shown differing degrees of selfhood and of adjustment, but the degrees have moral implications and there is an ideal adjustment in which morality as well as happiness resides. Elizabeth Bennet, who at first depends too impulsively on personal impressions and personal desires, learns to modify her individualism in response to the demands of the social world of other people, while Darcy, who at first leans too much on his place in society, learns to modify his social pride and to trust also the claims of individuality: flanking each of them at the extremes of immoral absurdity is the self-indulgent individualism of Lydia and the preposterous snobbery of Lady Catherine de Bourgh. Such a moral pattern, depending on the belief (shared with her readers) that an ideal adjustment between self and society was both desirable and possible, was unavailable to Virginia Woolf, who sees the problem as psychological rather than as moral.

Nevertheless there are moral implications, of a much more personal kind, in *Mrs. Dalloway.* Septimus Warren Smith, whose experience in the war has led him to a state of mind in which he cannot respond at all to the reality of the existence of other people, is driven mad by this meaningless isolation of the self, and his madness is exacerbated into suicide by the hearty doctors who insist that all he has to do is to imitate the public gestures of society (eat porridge for breakfast and play golf) and he will become an integrated character again. That this ideal of integration is mechanical and false is made clear by the picture of Lady Bradshaw (the wife of the specialist whose visit drives Septimus to his death) as a creature bullied into nothingness by the public face of her husband. And, even more significantly, Virginia Woolf brings the Bradshaws to Mrs. Dalloway's party that evening, and when Sir William Bradshaw tells her of the young man who had committed suicide that afternoon, Mrs. Dalloway feels a pang of sympathy and understanding for the victim and a revulsion against Sir William. She sees Sir William as "obscurely evil," "extremely polite to women, but capable of some indescribable outrage—forcing your soul, that was it"; and she sees herself for a moment as the doomed young man, associating his death with themes in her own meditations that have already been traced throughout

the novel. At the same time as this kind of plot-weaving is going on, we are also shown characters and actions who weave a pattern of the moment and the flux, the self standing like an upright sword amid the waters of the time and the flow of consciousness and the world of other selves. Mrs. Dalloway watches through her window an old lady in the house opposite getting ready for bed, and as she looks at her through glass this becomes a symbol of how we are related to others—through an invisible glass wall (a device used more conspicuously in *To the Lighthouse*). The old lady puts her light out and goes to bed, and contact is lost. Mrs. Dalloway returns to the party, and as she reappears Peter Walsh is seized by "extraordinary excitement." The reality of Mrs. Dalloway's personality, her actual presence at that time and place, suddenly overwhelms him:

> It is Clarissa, he said.
>
> For there she was.

That is how the novel ends, with the emphasis on identity. But this is not a solution, or a resolution; it is simply a phase of an endless pattern of which the elements are personality, consciousness, time, relationship, and the basic theme, the relation of loneliness to love.

The above remarks are not meant to constitute an analysis of *Mrs. Dalloway,* which would require a long chapter to itself, but only an indication of how Virginia Woolf builds up her characteristic kind of novel. It should be added that in spite of the meditative refinement that goes on throughout the book we are also given a vivid sense of London in the early 1920's: the social scene—although its relevance for the individual remains problematical—is set with greater concreteness and brilliance than it is in any other of her more successful novels. We may feel that the refining intellect is mocked by the sheer actuality of the city bustle which is presented so effectively, but that feeling is at times shared by the heroine herself. The flux and the moment, the individual and his social environment, were constantly challenging each other. "In people's eyes, in the swing, tramp, and trudge; in the bellow and the uproar; the carriages, motor cars, omnibuses, vans, sandwich men shuffling and swinging; brass bands; barrel organs; in the triumph and the jingle and the strange high singing of some aeroplane overhead was what she loved; life; London; this moment of June." (pp. 207-12)

David Daiches, "Virginia Woolf," in his The Novel and the Modern World, *revised edition, The University of Chicago Press, 1960, pp. 187-218.*

ALEX PAGE   (essay date 1961)

[In the following excerpt, Page examines the parallel characterization of Clarissa Dalloway and Septimus Warren Smith.]

Virginia Woolf's novel *Mrs. Dalloway* has that rare virtue of defying all interpretations that would set a final seal upon its meaning. For every reader it presents a journey of discovery, levying upon him a direct and individual contribution. Perhaps this is the best that can be said of any work of art. The intricate structure, the richness of metaphorical description, the quick succession of shadowy states of paradise and purgatory, all of which we find in *Mrs. Dalloway,* and, even more remarkably, the mad "double" haunting the protagonist, challenge the reader again and again. One feels that the novel can never be pinned down, but that one ought never to stop trying. My object here is to take Virginia Woolf's expressed intent seriously and look

View from Woolf's study in Monk House. Photograph by Gisele Freund. Reproduced by permission of The John Hillelson Agency Limited, as agents for the photographer.

in detail at the nature of Septimus Smith's "doubleness" to Clarissa Dalloway. While a number of important parallels have been pointed out by distinguished commentators, I should like to limit myself specifically to the way the two principals react to their environment and how they see themselves, to the conclusions we can draw therefrom about their character, and to the sense in which we can see them merge into one personality in the famous concluding scene of the novel. My feeling is that the extraordinary interlocking quality of Virginia Woolf's devices exacts a fairly specific contribution from the reader—a contribution that turns a seeming reverie of several people into a story.

The struggles that the author had with the material of the novel are vividly recorded in *A Writer's Diary.* Her problem was precisely that of creating plot for a person like Clarissa Dalloway, whose life is essentially ordinary and uneventful but who is endowed with an exquisite sensibility, and of preventing that plot from reverting into a compendium of metaphors and descriptive passages. Virginia Woolf asks herself again and again if she is being merely "clever" or "glittery" or "tinselly," if the novel will drown in ornament, if she is skirting "central things" by relying too heavily on "beautification of language." Myself, I see her creation of Septimus as a bid for more than "mere accomplishment," for more than being "tin-

selly." By presenting us with an ingeniously wrought parallel, in which what is viably human and attractive about Clarissa Dalloway becomes overwrought, inflammatory and destructive in Septimus, she reaches "central things." She wrote: "I dig out beautiful caves behind my characters: I think that gives exactly what I want; humanity, humour, depth. The idea is that the caves shall connect and each come to daylight at the present moment." . . . The way the caves connect is, I think, important and gives us ultimately a possible meaning of the novel. To look ahead for a moment, the reader is put in a position from which he is to mediate, as it were, between Clarissa Dalloway and Septimus Smith, for not only do those caves connect, but they front a labyrinth in which lurk terror and destruction. In short, the reader is notified—and with growing urgency—of the danger that besets Clarissa.

We first meet Mrs. Dalloway and Septimus Warren Smith rambling through London, killing time before an important later appointment—Clarissa's party and Septimus' consultation with a specialist. Both events will seal their respective fates. Clarissa is alone and yet in the presence of the myriad facets she encounters in objects, people, the life around her, London. All her senses partake to a high degree, including her sense, if it can be called that, of "making up things," projecting the future, reconstructing the past. But it is not a wholly sensuous experience, for there is a vague foreboding, an undefined threat: things are "too good to last," "something awful was about to happen," and "She always had the feeling that it was very, very dangerous to live even one day." I think it can be noted early that she has both a yearning to yield herself to a pure state of sensuous gratification and, at the same time, obeys a pull back into awareness of who she is and the role she must play in life. One feels she enjoys a high level of integration; she is a person who can look without because she dare look within. She has the resources to tell herself to "fear no more." In contrast, there is a "look of apprehension" on Septimus Warren Smith's face when we first meet him, and the terror takes this form: "The world has raised its whip; where will it descend?" His response is a sullen, unfocused anger. He is not the sensitive observer and partaker of the world around him—Clarissa's dominant states—but an obstacle: "It is I who am blocking the way." Moreover, he is not on his own, but "assisted" by his wife Rezia, who is more a nursemaid than a wife. She mirrors his doubtful condition as she veers from loyalty to an uncomprehending bewilderment as to who this man is. But he remains alone: when she takes his arm she notices that it is without feeling, "a piece of bone." The contrast is set: Clarissa, rich in material things and rich in the vitally human powers to see, to react, to feel, to sense the waves of life in their presentness; Septimus, buffeted and drowning by that same presentness. For both the "world wavered and quivered," but only for Smith did it threaten "to burst into flames."

The most striking connection between the two principals is the way they receive impressions and the way these are turned into metaphor. This is Septimus:

> And there the motor car stood with drawn blinds and upon them a curious pattern like a tree, Septimus thought, and this gradual drawing together of everything to one centre before his eyes, as if some horror had come almost to the surface and was about to burst into flames, terrified him. . . .

And now Clarissa:

Clarissa guessed; Clarissa knew of course; she had seen something white, magical, circular, in the footman's hand, a disc inscribed with a name,—the Queen's, the Prince of Wales's, the Prime Minister's?—which, by force of its own lustre, burnt its way through . . . to blaze among candelabras, glittering stars, breasts stiff with oak leaves, Hugh Whitbread and all his colleagues, the gentlemen of England, that night in Buckingham Palace. And Clarissa, too, gave a party. She stiffened a little; so she would stand at the top of her stairs. . . .

One can best describe Septimus' metaphors by saying that they seem to have no bottom; they spread out into infinity, as it were. He starts from himself, his terror takes over, he loses focus, he raises anchor from the here and now, and he finds himself, in response to nearly every stimulus, beyond space and time. In contrast, Clarissa, in a swift, sure line of associations, builds on what she sees, builds a world all her own—a modest one though it be of royalty itself. The detail remains in focus, for it returns again to herself, her immediate concern and pleasure, her party.

If we call Septimus' hypersensitivity one of raw, bare nerve-endings suppurating in the void, hers is directed, fructified, and infused by this sense of self. While he is at the mercy of his environment, of every chance stimulation, she has, we feel, some measure of control over it. In that sense he can be regarded as "unhinged," as incapable, essentially, of determining what to admit and what to shut out. Clarissa's day began with the domestic detail that in preparation for her party "doors would be taken off their hinges"—an opening up for a very specific purpose. But nearly total license reigns in Septimus' imaginings.

The point may be made in another way. We are in his febrile consciousness as he sits later in Regent's Park and hears a nurse's voice, which is

> like a mellow organ, but with a roughness in her voice, like a grasshopper's, which rasped his spine deliciously and sent running up into his brain waves of sound which, concussing, broke. . . . He lay very high, on the back of the world. The earth thrilled beneath him. Red flowers grew through his flesh; their stiff leaves rustled by his head. Music began clanging against the rocks up here. . . .

All the senses are jumbled together in one such overpowering emotion that he can never tell where he ends and where this pulsating, vibrating world begins—"His body was macerated until only the nerve fibres were left. It was spread like a veil upon a rock." This spontaneous loss of self is one source of his fear. Curiously, we have a glimpse of Clarissa in earlier days, manifesting a wish (more: asserting a creed) to merge herself with the world around her. Peter Walsh recalls: "Sitting on the bus going up Shaftesbury Avenue, she felt herself everywhere; not 'here, here, here'; and she tapped the back of the seat; but everywhere. She waved her hand, going up Shaftesbury Avenue. She was all that." . . . But the stress is on "she." What in her is velleity, perhaps even a bit of attitudinizing, becomes fearful, accomplished reality in Septimus. It is a sign to the reader of the danger in which we are to see Mrs. Dalloway as she moves along on this most beautiful of London days.

There are indeed many things that strike the reader as beautiful in this novel, but none I think so much as the several descriptions of trees. The readiness and intensity with which both Clarissa and Septimus react to the look of trees draw upon Virginia Woolf's most magical metaphors. First, it should be noted that Clarissa's love for the world she so sensuously apprehends is continually reawakened by trees: she is aware of "odd affinities she had with people . . . even trees." She speaks of the "leaf-encumbered forest, the soul"; trees have a kind of "divine vitality" as "things that survive." The best she can say of a happy moment is that it is a "bud on the tree of life." One realizes that trees stand for more than one item in the scores of beautiful objects she encounters on her ramble. Biblical allusions aside, they seem to signify to Clarissa a wished-for permanence that prefigures and postdates man's life, while they are at the same time the most seductive, ardent beckonings to aliveness *now*. One is tempted to call them symbols of the mystique of nature—all the more, since there is in Septimus a curiously congruous manner of seeing trees. Here are three instances among many in which trees urge a grandiose leap upon him:

> Men must not cut down trees. There is a God. . . .

> Trees are alive . . . there is no crime. . . .

> Do not cut down trees: tell the Prime Minister. . . .

We find that the violence with which trees register on his senses fires his delusions, as there is a concurrent (and rather pathetic) reach for a dignified rally. Trees take Clarissa away from herself into quasi-theological reveries *and* into a deeply felt presentness; they draw Septimus into impossible summonings for supra-national action—but also action here and now.

The neatness of such a parallel, however, must be questioned when we come across a wonderful metaphor like this: "The trees dragged their leaves like nets through the depths of the air"; or to a response such as this: "To watch a leaf quivering in the rush of air was an exquisite joy." Both of these occur in the mind of Septimus, but they could as easily have been Clarissa's. This raises a delicate question. Does Virginia Woolf attempt to tighten the relationship between the two; that is, does she make the double resemble the original in *some* aspects to a point at which they become indistinguishable in order to remind the reader that they are really one? Or did she indeed, as she feared in her *Diary* . . . , merely write essays about herself, and distinguish insufficiently between her two protagonists? To me, these two possibilities struggle one against the other. One cannot fail to detect the ubiquitous author in all her characters by her rhythms, cadences, and metaphors—they often sound alike, whether we are inside their minds or are told something about them. Still, I find a deliberate differentiation among them, especially her two main characters, the eminently sane Clarissa and the pathetically insane Septimus. But they are both antipodal and can be seen converging—and thereby, I think, the plot moves. (pp. 115-19)

[If] we look upon feelings as an accumulation of knowledge, Clarissa's experiences, the felt truths of her past, are accessible to her; she can utilize that stock for present purposes: she has "the power of taking hold of experience, of turning it round, slowly, in the light." To Septimus such an overview is not at hand. The past to him is whatever the moment evokes, with the unhappy result that each reminiscence casts him only more adrift. In a strange flashback we see him as a neurasthenic Keats, a footloose refugee in London:

[He could be found] writing; found tearing up his writing; found finishing a masterpiece at three o'clock in the morning and running out to pace the streets, and visiting churches, and fasting one day, drinking another, devouring Shakespeare, Darwin, *The History of Civilization,* and Bernard Shaw. . . .

If one compares this to Clarissa's past, one detects too much indulgence in sensations and feelings for their own sake—something Clarissa longs to do but refrains from doing. How much of his past is reclaimable? If he overreacted then to all he touched, it is not so astonishing to find a sudden paralysis of feeling when faced with the death of his friend Evans, which really mattered. Indiscriminateness in gauging one's feelings results in a journey from tumult to chaos. The difference between the two characters is crucial and deserves emphasis: to control feelings may provide for a *modus vivendi;* to shut them out, to extirpate them, means death. To my mind there is no doubt that Virginia Woolf meant us to be clear about that. (pp. 121-22)

A counter to the failure of [Septimus'] feeling, perhaps, is his assuming the role of Messiah. "Change the world," he shouts (to himself). "Make it known." "No crime, universal love." He composes one manifesto after another. I see in this a kind of impotent reaching for potency and very much related to an earlier point about his metaphors having no bottom, losing sight of the self, radiating outward from no center. Clarissa, too, arrives with a message, in one sense: her party is constructed meticulously like a baroque edifice. More particularly, her sensibility strikes us as a great creative force. Peter Walsh knows "she had the gift of making a world of her own wherever she went." It is a gift in which she herself luxuriates: "Heaven only knows why one loves it so, how one sees it so, making it up, building it round one, tumbling it, creating it every moment afresh." We are shown two modes of creativity, one that constructs a habitable world, the other nullified by extravagant ambitiousness. Again we are made to ponder how closely Clarissa's chief virtue borders on the destructive.

The last point that I wish to make in exploring the nature of Septimus' "doubleness" to Clarissa is the surprising manner in which both communicate with the rest of the world. Clarissa is not dependent on words; in fact, her vital relationships with her husband, with Peter, and with her daughter disdain them. She understands fully what Richard does say and also what he finds unable to say when he presents her with a large bouquet of roses. She is intuitively aware of the criticisms Peter has of her, as well as of his stifled cry for succor. And yet she suspects that she has failed to pass on to her daughter her own special gifts, and at the end of the party, after she has lived through her crisis, she knows she will never be able to share her insights with her husband. We have a sense of her being irrevocably separate, sealed off, from the rest. In Septimus the power to communicate has nearly wholly crumbled. He is aware of "people" and "faces" hovering near him; he tries to make out their language but he cannot. Again he dimly knows, for he writes: "Communication is health—communication is happiness." Weak puns are left to him, for instance, "he's in Hull," but flames and tortures immediately appear and the bottom falls out. In the lyrical scene preceding his death (also reminiscent of *King Lear*), he does somehow manage to communicate with Rezia, and she with him, by means of the hat he helps her fashion—"he had become himself then." Never so much as in these, his last moments, does he remind us of Clarissa, for she too can really only talk to others by the objects of the felt reality that embed her.

What I have tried to show is that Septimus' character is in all essentials Clarissa's, but taken to a deadly extreme. Both spend the day wandering, but he to his death; both react vigorously to the world around them, but he in dire anguish; both mean to shape their lives, and they succeed—she with a workable compromise, he by defying his compellers; both live on a kind of border, but his is by far the more exposed; both can "feel," but his feelings become a torture chamber; both are creators, she of the possible, he of the extravagantly far-fetched; failure of communication throttles him, whereas it frustrates her. One way of looking at him, then, is as a warning, the warning that beneath Clarissa's regulated, shiny life lies an abyss, that her extraordinary gifts contain the seeds of poison. At the end of the novel Clarissa's reaction to the disclosure of his suicide gives us a new view of him—and we have learned to trust Clarissa's reactions. What she perceives with shattering clarity is his courage, his defiance, the utter integrity of his commitment against human agencies that would "force the soul," and that have, in part, forced hers. It is the purity and strength of his act that move her so.

A more clinical way of putting it is this: she recognizes that he is the id to her ego. In that sense I take him as her double and see them "merge" at the end. I would not push the psychological analogy beyond her recognition in him of qualities that (she intuitively apprehends) parallel hers; they are chiefly the qualities of pure emotion and energy which, in contradistinction to her, brook no compromise. In a recent essay Keith Hollingsworth has made a persuasive case for Septimus Smith's being "the incarnation of the death-instincts, [and] Clarissa Dalloway of the instincts of life" in fairly literal Freudian terms. My enlargement of this view consists in claiming that Septimus can also be taken as the forces, the vitality, and the perils of the id. Freud in his *New Introductory Lectures in Psycho-Analysis* called the id "a chaos, a cauldron of seething excitement" and went on to say that

> instincts fill it with energy, but it has no organisation and no unified will, only an impulsion to obtain satisfaction for the instinctual needs, in accordance with the pleasure-principle. . . . Contradictory impulses exist side by side without neutralising each other. . . .

Furthermore, the id cannot escape annihilation by external forces without the "cortical layer" of the ego. Clarissa, seen as the highly conscious ego of a double personality, reveres Septimus' (or the id's) act for what it is—an act of impulsive generosity ("he flung it away," he "plunged holding his treasure"), a gesture so magnanimous that it disdains pity, so honest that it is its own reward. But in paying it obeisance, she is recalled to her own insufficiencies and her own half-way measures. For once the comparison between the two tends to her own disadvantage: "She had schemed, she had pilfered. She was never wholly admirable." Before she can fall prey to self-accusations and self-hatred—and perhaps at this moment she is most exposed to the danger that has dogged her all day—she catches sight of the elderly lady next door, who, in her calm preparations for bed, carries out her appointed, age-old tasks. Clarissa accepts that calm, that regularity of life as a model for her own, for she knows she cannot will a pure act such as that of Septimus—that strength she lacks. This is her "sense of proportion," this enables her to "assemble."

The compromise is between knowing what there is and what one can do, between the integrity of the impulses and the exigencies of the world. This compromise is a function of the ego. It entails an eternal falling-short, but it also enables Clarissa "to feel the beauty . . . feel the fun." Her return to her party, so dramatically seen through the sudden onrush of excitement in Peter Walsh, means to us, the readers, who have accompanied her on this fateful day, that she has been saved from the danger to which her wonderful sensibility has exposed her (and to which, in his own way, Septimus succumbed), but that the payment exacted is the crystalline knowledge of that danger. (pp. 122-24)

> *Alex Page, "A Dangerous Day: Mrs. Dalloway Discovers Her Double," in* Modern Fiction Studies, *Vol. VII, No. 2, Summer, 1961, pp. 115-24.*

RENÉ E. FORTIN   (essay date 1965)

[*In the following excerpt, Fortin explains that a clearer understanding of Virginia Woolf's thought may be aided by an examination of religious symbols and values in* Mrs. Dalloway.]

The real question confronting the literary critic, despite Edward Albee, is not who is afraid of Virginia Woolf, but who understands Virginia Woolf. There is general agreement about her formal contributions to the modern novel, but the ultimate significance of her art is a matter of dispute. Walter Allen, for example, in *The Modern Novel . . .* , finds her ultimate significance quite limited; granting her some moments of revelation and illumination, he warns, however, that these "sometimes don't amount to much more than a series of short, sharp, feminine gasps of ecstasy." Other critics are more generous, conceding that some substance is to be found in her novels, though they cannot quite agree as to precisely where this substance lies: the novels, accordingly, have been read in the light of Bergson, Freud, Plato, British empiricism, and even Chinese quietism. (p. 23)

This diversity of critical opinion is little less than startling; one might well agree with Shakespeare's Cicero that

> Indeed, it is a strange-disposed time:
> But men may construe things after their fashion,
> Clean from the purpose of the things themselves.

I am convinced that **Mrs. Dalloway** is very much at the center of the Woolf problem and that grasping the meaning of this novel would contribute greatly to a clearer assessment of Virginia Woolf's thought. I am convinced, moreover, that this novel can be made accessible to the reader, not by imposing a philosophical system upon it, but by carefully examining the traditional religious symbols and values which the novel explores. The fundamental problem of **Mrs. Dalloway** is the fragmentation of the modern world, the loss of unity within society and within the individual himself. And though the novel implies that Christianity has been a monumental failure in its attempt to safeguard the unity of man, it nevertheless engages in a careful re-assessment of traditional Christian values. The imagery of this novel, in fact, suggests that the central action of the heroine is to find an adequate substitute for Christianity and, specifically, for the sacramental sense of reality which is fostered. Only by a restoration of this sacramental sense of reality, Virginia Woolf argues, can man regain his integrity, his wholeness.

The precision with which the problem is stated is remarkable, for the spiritual vacuum of modern society is initially drama-tized by an extremely suggestive parody of sacramental imagery. From Mrs. Dalloway's encounter with a government vehicle in the early part of the novel emerges one of the central metaphors. The vehicle is described with religious imagery: "But now mystery had touched them with her ring; they had heard the voice of authority: the spirit of religion was abroad with her eyes bandaged tight and her lips gaping wide." After the car is stopped by a policeman and then allowed to proceed when identification is shown, the religious imagery becomes even more specific:

> Clarissa guessed; Clarissa knew of course; she had seen something white, magical, circular, in the footman's hand, a disc inscribed with a name—the Queen's, the Prince of Wales's, the Prime Minister's?—which, by force of its own luster, burnt its way through . . . to blaze among candelabras, glittering stars, breasts stiff with oak leaves, Hugh Whitbread and all his colleagues. . . .

The white, magical, circular disc possessed of religious significance hardly needs the additional notion of "Whitbread" to be identified with the Host of the Eucharist, or at least the ironic modern equivalent of it. The function of Christianity in this secular age, the passage hints, has been assumed by the government; it is the government which is invested with authority and mystery, which provides a sense of community to the populace. The ironic tone leaves no doubt that the government is considered unworthy to take on the functions abdicated by Christianity.

Immediately after the car vanishes, an airplane appears, writing an indecipherable message across the sky, "as if destined to cross from West to East on a mission of the greatest importance which would never be revealed. . . ." The airplane (which, in its West to East flight, significantly reverses the historic course of Christianity) is interpreted as a religious phenomenon by various people. To Septimus Smith, the airplane heralds the "birth of a new religion," inspiring in him an ecstatic perception of the unity of being:

> . . . leaves were alive; trees were alive. And the leaves being connected by millions of fibres with his own body, there on the seat, fanned it up and down; when the branch stretched he, too, made that statement. The sparrows, fluttering, rising, and falling in jagged fountains were part of the pattern. . . .

To another observer, the airplane was a "symbol . . . of man's soul; of his determination to get outside his body, beyond his house, by means of thought, Einstein, speculation, mathematics, the Mendelian theory. . . ." . . . And to yet another observer, the airplane is related to that symbol which it supersedes, the cathedral with its altar and cross "the symbol of something which has soared beyond seeking and questioning and knocking of words together and has become all spirit, disembodied, ghostly. . . ."

But the new religion symbolized by the airplane is also fraudulent: its "marvelous revelation" is first mysterious, then insignificant when it is finally decipherable. The message which the airplane is communicating is the word "toffee"; the airplane, identified with the strange gods of science and technology, with the kind of speculation that has replaced traditional thought, offers no solace to man: its "mission of the greatest importance" is to serve commerce.

Other and more obvious perversions of the religious instinct are the cults of the Goddess Proportion and the Goddess Conversion. The Goddess Proportion, around which has grown the cult of respectability, conformity, and efficiency, has as her high-priest Sir William Bradshaw, the psychiatrist, who "not only prospered himself, but made England prosper, secluded her lunatics, forbade childbirth, penalized despair, made it impossible for the unfit to propagate their views until they too shared his sense of proportion." Sir William, in his complacency and shallowness, feels that there is nothing wrong with the modern psyche that common sense cannot overcome.

But the Goddess Conversion, a sister Goddess of whom he is also a dedicated worshipper, is more insidious, for she "feasts on the wills of the weakly, loving to impress, to impose, adoring her own features stamped on the face of the populace." This goddess, that is, represents the will for power, the tyranny of a strong personality over a weaker one. Miss Kilman, the zealous Christian who would bludgeon others into her convictions, is another devotee of the Goddess Conversion, whose tyranny extends into all human relationships, even that of love: "love and religion [muses Mrs. Dalloway] would destroy the privacy of the soul."

Much of the religious imagery, therefore, is charged with a powerful irony extended to expose the fraudulence and oppressiveness of the modern versions of religion. Mrs. Dalloway, in fact, twice professes herself to be an atheist . . . , and she is even bitter in her denunciation of religion:

> Love and religion! How detestable they are! . . .
> The cruelest things in the world, she thought,
> seeing them clumsy, hot, domineering, hypo-
> critical, eavesdropping, jealous, infinitely cruel
> and scrupulous, dressed in a mackintosh coat,
> on the landing; love and religion.

But the religious imagery is much more subtle than it would seem to be, for despite the bitter antagonism against religion expressed through Mrs. Dalloway, the novel moves through its religious imagery into an admittedly tentative and partial but nonetheless significant affirmation. The complexity of meaning inherent in the religious imagery emerges above all in the characterization of Septimus Smith, who lurks enigmatically on the periphery of Clarissa Dalloway's life. Septimus Smith is initially perplexing: what are we to make of a Christ figure in an atheistic, anti-religious novel? The insanity of Septimus, suggesting a continuation of the ironic view of religion, is certainly to be taken into account. But the unmistakable sympathy with which he is treated by the author as well as the eventual identification of Septimus and Mrs. Dalloway compel us to find at least some residual significance in the Christ analogue. Septimus and the traditional Christian values which cling to him cannot be entirely dissolved by irony.

In my opinion, he can best be understood as a device of intensification (reminiscent of the Gloucester sub-plot in *King Lear*). His function is apparently to provide a heightened version of Mrs. Dalloway, with whom his spiritual kinship is later asserted. Where Clarissa is hedged in by her domestic environment, Septimus, his perceptions intensified by his insanity, penetrates the boredom of life to reveal at once its horror and its glory. He is ecstatic in his visions of beauty: "The trees waved, brandished. We welcome, the world seemed to say; we accept; we create. Beauty, the world seemed to say . . . all of this, calm and reasonable as it was, made out of ordinary

things as it was, was the truth now: beauty, that was the truth now. Beauty was everywhere."

But he is flagellated as well by the sordidness of existence:

> This was now revealed to Septimus; the mes-
> sage hidden in the beauty of words. The secret
> signal which one generation passes, under dis-
> guise, to the next is loathing, hatred, despair.
> For the truth is . . . that human beings have
> neither kindness nor faith, nor charity beyond
> what serves to increase the pleasure of the mo-
> ment.

The agony of Septimus is precisely that of Mrs. Dalloway, but raised to a higher power; isolated like her, he yearns for the unity and integrity of existence which would give significance to his life. What is at stake in this novel is the very worth of life itself, and the struggle is waged especially in the tortured mind of Septimus, "the Lord who had come to renew society . . . the scapegoat, the eternal sufferer. . . ." Whether or not Septimus consummates his symbolic redemptive role is kept in suspense throughout; even at the very moment before his suicide, Septimus is ambivalent about life: "But he would wait [to commit suicide] till the very last moment. He did not want to die. Life was good. The sun hot. Only human beings— what did *they* want?"

The suicide of Septimus is crucial to the meaning of the novel; but significantly, its implications are cloaked in ambiguity. For Mrs. Dalloway, who is expectedly very much moved by his death, is nonetheless inconsistent in her appraisal, viewing it alternately as a triumph and a disaster. Her first reaction borders on jubilation:

> Death was defiance. Death was an attempt to
> communicate; people feeling the impossibility
> of reaching the centre which, mystically, evaded
> them; closeness drew apart; rapture faded, one
> was alone. There was an embrace in death.

But she then re-assesses the situation:

> Somehow it was her disaster—her disgrace. It
> was her punishment to see sink and disappear
> here a man, there a woman, in this profound
> darkness, and she forced to stand here in her
> evening dress.

Neither is this, however, the final statement of her attitude. After a further consideration of the death, she concludes that "she felt somehow very like him—the young man who had killed himself. She felt glad that he had done it; thrown it away. . . . He made her feel the beauty; made her feel the fun." Her final estimate is vaguely affirmative, and the precise meaning of Septimus' death remains a matter of conjecture. Despite this ambiguity, however, Septimus Smith has fulfilled his strategic function: to focus our attention upon the religious dimensions of the novel.

It is against this background of religious imagery, transvaluated or often ironic in effect, that Mrs. Dalloway's actions take on a precise meaning. This precise meaning begins to unfold when she is described as a nun: ". . . she felt like a nun who has left the world and feels fold around her the familiar veils and the response to old devotions. . . . It was her life, and, bending her head over the hall table, she bowed beneath the influence, felt blessed and purified. . . ." The image of the nun is appropriate in many ways; above all, it immediately points to the isolation of Mrs. Dalloway, who even in her marriage cannot effectively communicate with another person. She has renounced conjugal life, unable "to dispel a virginity preserved through childbirth which clung to her like a sheet."

But the nun image expands in significance as the novel develops; in this early description of Mrs. Dalloway there is already implicit the sacredness with which Mrs. Dalloway feels life is—or should be—permeated. She seeks to penetrate through the veil of ordinary human experience to the mystical center. These moments of illumination (attained, according to her testimony, only in encounters with other women) bridge the gap between persons to provide moments of communion: "Only for a moment, but it was enough. It was a sudden revelation. . . . Then, for that moment, she had seen an illumination, a match burning in a crocus; an inner meaning almost expressed. But the close withdrew; the hard softened."

The great affirmation of which she is capable is that the human personality is sacred; she looks upon the mystery of the human soul with reverence and almost religious awe. It is important, therefore, to detect the tension in her yearning for unity, for communion. Human beings, she feels, must attain unity, but they must attain it without losing individual integrity; a soul must make contact with, but must neither dominate nor submit to another. This is for Mrs. Dalloway the "supreme mystery," the delicate balance between isolation and involvement: "Here was one room; there another. Did religion solve that, or love?" She continues elsewhere:

> And there is a dignity in people; a solitude; even between husband and wife a gulf; and that one must respect, thought Clarissa, watching him open the door; for one would not part with it oneself, or take it against his will, from one's husband, without losing one's independence, one's self-respect—something, after all, priceless.

To establish the kind of communication which would not violate the mystery of the soul is the self-appointed mission of Clarissa Dalloway. And her parties, for which she is the object of polite scorn or, at best, condescension, are her means of establishing this delicate relationship. She is the "perfect hostess" . . . whose special gift is to unite, to be "composed so for the world only into one centre, one diamond, one woman who sat in her drawing-room and made a meeting-point, a radiancy no doubt in some dull lives, a refuge for the lonely to come to, perhaps."

But the parties are more than social gatherings; it is crucial to note that they are described quite precisely as "offerings":

> But suppose Peter says to her, 'yes, yes, but your parties—what's the sense of your parties?' all she could say was (and nobody could be expected to understand): They're an offering; which sounded horribly vague . . . she felt if only they could be brought together; so she did it. And it was an offering; to combine, to create; but to whom? An offering for the sake of offering, perhaps. Anyhow, it was her gift.

The precise sense in which her parties are offerings is revealed by her relationship with Septimus; just as Septimus, if he were to consummate his archetypal redemptive mission, would offer himself to save mankind, so does Mrs. Dalloway, through her parties, offer herself as sacrifice; she is "the woman who was

that very night to give a party; of Clarissa Dalloway; of herself."

Furthermore, the virtual identification of Septimus and Mrs. Dalloway reveals the extent of her offering: the death of Septimus in the course of her party is, symbolically, the death of Clarissa herself. It was, in fact, Virginia Woolf's original intention to climax the party with the death of the heroine. . . . (pp. 23-9)

The conclusion is, I think, inescapable: a party which involves an offering, a sacrifice in the form of a symbolic death, and a sense of communion in the participants obviously invites identification with the Mass. Mrs. Dalloway, in her parodic Mass, is indeed the "perfect hostess," offering herself, like Christ, as priest and victim to restore the integrity of man.

It would certainly seem, therefore, that the inseparable Christian mysteries of the Holy Eucharist and the Mystical Body are directly and profoundly involved in the meaning of *Mrs. Dalloway.* Virginia Woolf sees disunity everywhere in human experience: man is isolated from man, lacking the "something central" around which a corporate society could form. He is, moreover, split in his own experience, tortured above all by irreconcilability of matter and spirit. Mrs. Dalloway's genuine love for her husband, as we have seen, cannot express itself physically, while Septimus is himself disgusted by "the getting of children, the sordidity of mouth and belly!" . . . It is significantly these Christian mysteries of the Eucharist and the Mystical Body which fit the Christian to his world and his world to him. . . . (p. 29)

The parody of the Eucharist at the beginning of the novel—the white, magical, circular disc—has, in effect, revealed the central action of the novel: a search for a renewed sacramental sense of reality which would re-establish the integrity and significance of human experience. In a very precise sense, Mrs. Dalloway does not *find* this sacramental sense, she *becomes* herself the sacrament which will make man whole.

To point out Mrs. Woolf's careful parody of the Christian mysteries and her indebtedness to Christian sacramental doctrine serves to define the issues which the novel probes. But we must remember, in pursuing her meaning, that the symbols are transvaluated, that, in other words, their dogmatic content is radically altered. The author evidently had little sympathy for Christianity, and she is most decidedly not urging a wholesale return to the Christian communion. Her exact meaning, in fact, is blurred by a gentle and all-pervasive irony from which even Septimus and Mrs. Dalloway cannot entirely escape. However, we may conjecture with some certitude that the novel is a statement of secular humanism: the vague hope that man will have a renewed harmony in his life lies in the possibility of self-redemption. Mrs. Dalloway's appraisal of her action reveals the central tragedy of her life, that there is no God to whom (and in the more accurate Christian sense, with whom) the Sacrifice can be offered. ". . . it was an offering; to combine, to create; but to whom? An offering for the sake of offering, perhaps. Anyhow, it was her gift." . . . In the absence of anything else, man must become his own sacrament.

This much is, I think, quite clear. But a radical uncertainty lingers in other areas. Throughout the novel, horror of the flesh has been symptomatic of psychic maladjustment (in a much more than merely Freudian sense—though I am not discounting Freudian interpretations, I feel that Mrs. Dalloway's psychological problem is symptom rather than cause for her anguish, the issues in the novel far transcending psychology). The tone of the novel conveys what clearly seems to be a criticism of the angelism of Mrs. Dalloway, Septimus, and Miss Kilman. The virginity which Mrs. Dalloway has been unable to dispel in her marriage is but another example of the time that is out of joint; in symbolic terms, the bells of Big Ben—symbolizing the masculine and physical nature of love—continue to ring two minutes before the bells of St. Margaret's, symbolizing the feminine and spiritual nature of love.... This inability to reconcile sex and soul, the novel implies, is the peculiar spiritual sickness of modern man. And yet, the "sacrifice" of Mrs. Dalloway apparently does nothing to reconcile sex and soul. Despite the relative success of the party, there is no indication that the transformed and almost transfigured Mrs. Dalloway has come to terms with her fleshliness. Her affirmation of life in this novel is at best tentative, since the "sacrament" of Mrs. Dalloway has brought about a limited communion between people but has apparently not redeemed the world of matter. (pp. 30-1)

> René E. Fortin, "Sacramental Imagery in 'Mrs. Dalloway'," in Renascence, Vol. XVIII, No. 1, Autumn, 1965, pp. 23-31.

JEREMY HAWTHORN (essay date 1975)

[*Hawthorn is an English literary scholar whose criticism is informed by Marxist thought. In the following excerpt, Hawthorn traces the development of themes of social and psychological alienation in* Mrs. Dalloway.]

> Mrs Dalloway said she would buy the flowers herself.
>
> 'I will come,' said Peter, but he sat on for a moment. What is this terror? what is this ecstasy? he thought to himself. What is it that fills me with extraordinary excitement?
>
> It is Clarissa, he said.
>
> For there she was....

In between the 'Mrs Dalloway' of the first line of Virginia Woolf's novel [*Mrs. Dalloway*] and the 'Clarissa' of the concluding lines of its last page, the reader is led to an awareness of the enormous complexity of the character in question. On a simple level we can say that we move from a view of 'Mrs Dalloway'—the married woman bearing her husband's name and thus seen in terms of her relationship with other people—to 'Clarissa', a person in her own right. But this ignores the fact that the final, extraordinarily striking, view of Clarissa's 'full selfhood' is achieved through the eyes of another person, Peter Walsh. It is also worth noting that although this powerful perception of Clarissa's human distinctness is presented in terms of an epiphany, a sudden illumination, the progression through the tenses (I will come, It is Clarissa, For there she was), suggests that this view of her full selfhood that Peter Walsh obtains is dependent upon a knowledge of Clarissa's existence over time, from the days of his acquaintance with her at Bourton to the contact with her which he knows is to come after her party.

Mrs. Dalloway, I would argue, is an extended investigation of the paradoxes contained implicitly in the opening and closing lines of the novel. Clarissa Dalloway is seen as an individual whose identity varies according to the situation in which she finds herself; at different times, and with different people, she

appears to be a different person. And yet 'there she was'. Along with Peter Walsh, the reader feels that in spite of the multiple, even contradictory, aspects of her personality which are revealed to him, Clarissa Dalloway is *there,* distinct, unique. (p. 9)

Virginia Woolf seems to be fascinated by the fact that a human being's distinctness only reveals itself through contact with other people, and can only be fully perceived by another person. We exist simultaneously in terms of but distinct from other people—together with and apart from them. Thus on the one hand Clarissa can feel that Peter Walsh 'made her see herself'.... But on the other hand the novel suggests, paradoxically, that human beings are possessed of a central irreducible core of identity, which exists independently of other people. Throughout the novel the words 'self' and 'soul' are used to suggest this irreducible centre.

In her diary Virginia Woolf commented on the 'peculiar repulsiveness of those who dabble their fingers self approvingly in the stuff of others' souls', and in spite of the expressed belief of Clarissa's that to know her one must search out the people who completed her, *Mrs. Dalloway* also insists on the importance of a respect for the privacy of the soul. Sir William Bradshaw wants to dabble his fingers in Septimus's soul: he is introduced, ironically we feel, as one who has 'understanding of the human soul', but Clarissa feels that he is capable of 'forcing your soul'. Miss Kilman's desire to subdue Clarissa's soul and its mockery is likewise seen as an inexcusable desire to intrude into the privacy of another person's inner-self.

Again, we come face to face with a paradox. The soul is private, and must not be 'forced', but it can be destroyed by being made *too* private, by too much protection. We know that Peter Walsh talked to Clarissa about the defects of her soul at Bourton, and he associates the death of her soul with her symbolic rejection of sexuality when she left the table in confusion in response to Sally Seton's 'daring' remark. Sally, on the other hand, feared that the Hughs and the Dalloways and all the other perfect gentlemen would stifle Clarissa's soul. When Dr Holmes bursts into Septimus's room he is involved in a symbolic action similar to Peter Walsh's bursting in on Clarissa; both are guilty, in different ways, of wanting to force the soul of another person. Septimus kills himself rather than surrender the privacy of his soul, and Clarissa rejects Peter Walsh, for:

> ... with Peter everything had to be shared; everything gone into. And it was intolerable....

Yet in attempting to preserve that necessary privacy Clarissa may, the reader suspects, have stifled her own soul. Unlike Peter, who at one point in the novel comes to the conclusion that he no longer needs people, Clarissa needs her privacy to be tempered with human contact:

> She had a sense of comedy that was really exquisite, but she needed people, always people, to bring it out....
>
> (pp. 12-13)

In cutting herself off from Peter, we feel that she may have cut herself off from a necessary contact with others.... Both [Clarissa and Septimus]—although on different levels—need other people whilst fearing the threat to their privacy that contact with others involves.

How is such a paradoxical combination of needs to be reconciled? One way of reconciling two contradictory or apparently irreconcilable pressures is to alternate between them. It would appear that in a number of different areas this alternation between irreconcilables presented itself to Virginia Woolf as the most effective solution to various problems. In her essay **'Life and the Novelist',** she writes that:

> [The novelist] must expose himself to life. . . .
> But at a certain moment he must leave the company and withdraw, alone. . . .

Clarissa, like the novelist, feels the need both to expose herself to life, and to withdraw, alone. Her party is, for her, an exposure, but in the middle of it she feels the need to withdraw alone to the privacy of her room. (pp. 13-14)

Mrs. Dalloway, unlike the 'classical novel' of the nineteenth century, presents the reader with no moral or other overview within which all contradictions can be subsumed, or by reference to which all conflicts can be resolved.

Clarissa leads a life that is full of contradictions, and so her self too is lacking in consistency. Now it is arguable that in *any* social situation men and women will have both public and private lives. What needs to be added to this assertion is that the extent of the privacy that men and women need will vary from situation to situation, and that the existence of contradictions between these different aspects of a single life is by no means universal. To put the argument the other way round, it seems hard to deny that one of the characteristics of capitalist society is that the distinction between public and private lives is magnified, and that there is a qualitative change from a *distinction* to a *contradiction* between the two. Clarissa is forced to be one person in one situation, and another person in a different situation, because there are fundamental contradictions in the society of which she is a part and in the human relationships which constitute it. Any search for the 'real' Clarissa on the part of either the reader, or of a character such as Peter Walsh, is thus doomed to failure. Peter Walsh's Clarissa is different from Richard Dalloway's Clarissa. Clarissa herself would like to 'compose' a unified and consistent self. The question that she has to answer before she does this, however, is the question that is posed explicitly in the novel on a number of occasions: 'to whom?'. (pp. 15-16)

We cannot work out what [Clarissa Dalloway] is like, what she *is,* merely by studying what she thinks of herself, or what Peter Walsh, or Richard Dalloway, or Doris Kilman think of her. She *is* all these things, and only her whole life, including all her thoughts about herself and her relationships with other people, exhausts the possible information about her.

Clarissa's great moral strength comes from her attempt—in her party—to draw people out of their isolation in much the same way as she draws the folds of her dress together with her needle. In her famous essay **'Modern Fiction',** Virginia Woolf wrote that the novelist was able to put himself at any point of view, or even, to some extent, to combine different views. Her early manuscript notes for *Mrs. Dalloway* include the aim of giving two points of view at once (an aim that many different artists, working in different art forms, seem to have shared in the early part of the present century). Certainly the whole novel seems to be trying to connect and combine (but not necessarily to reconcile) different and contradictory views of Clarissa, which seem to be related to contradictions in Clarissa herself which are, in part at least, the product of a divided society. (pp. 16-17)

The reason why Clarissa *appears* to be a different person to different people is that she lives in a society in which it is essential for the successful individual to *be* a different person in different circumstances and with different people. As a result, Clarissa can never satisfactorily answer the worrying question, 'Who am I?'. (pp. 22-3)

Mrs. Dalloway is saturated with the problems of a society which embodies—and in that sense causes—alienation. Not only are the characters in the novel alienated from one another, but the book itself is an attempt to overcome artistically the novelist's alienation from her reading public. The 'oyster' of *Mrs. Dalloway* needs a shell in which to secrete itself much as characters in the novel do—both as a way of protecting an essential identity and also as a means of communication. What is more, *Mrs. Dalloway* needs a very new sort of novelistic shell. The more the important life experienced by men and women in a particular society is a public one, then the more the novelist or artist can communicate this central importance through public, observable characteristics. The more that the important life experienced by men and women in a particular society is at least partially private, however, then the more the novelist is obliged to *create* public conventions to convey that for which none exist outside art.

The words 'to whom?' recur a number of times in *Mrs. Dalloway,* (and in *The Waves*), and are associated with most of the major characters in the novel [Rezia, Peter Walsh, Septimus and Clarissa herself]. . . . All of these characters feel that they have something to do, give or say—but to whom they do not know. It seems possible that Virginia Woolf's offering—her novel—is made with as little confidence about the identity of the recipient. . . . The truth is that the [novel's narrative] style allows the privacy of Clarissa's thoughts to be carried almost parasitically on the wings of the narrator-reader address. To this extent the very style of *Mrs. Dalloway* is totally appropriate to what is to be conveyed, as whilst actually communicating the inner 'oyster' of Clarissa and other characters to the reader it also conveys their lack of anyone with whom they can really communicate. (pp. 23-5)

There seems little doubt that Virginia Woolf's experience of what she called 'madness' contributed to her sense of the dissolution of human identity. Yet it would be a mistake to see the whole question of self-dissolution or division in *Mrs. Dalloway* as a clinical matter. Certain social forces which had been developing in British society for some time were making a sharp division between the public and the private necessary for more and more people. It is worth remarking on the fact that in one sense Septimus Smith, the 'mad' character in *Mrs. Dalloway,* is *not* 'divided' in the way that other characters are, and it is arguable that it is his attempt to synthesise the public and the private that results in his inability to conform to the requirements of his society. (p. 28)

When we turn to *Mrs. Dalloway* . . . and consider the relationship between the divided selves of a single character, we need to bear in mind that we are dealing not with an eccentric offshoot of Virginia Woolf's madness, but with a specific example of a phenomenon which appears so insistently in the literature of this period that it suggests some common, fundamental reality underlying it. In her 1928 *Introduction* to the novel, Virginia Woolf claimed that a first version of the novel was written in which Septimus Smith did not appear, and that he was introduced later as Clarissa Dalloway's 'double' [see excerpt dated 1928]. It is as if the novelist has taken the divided selves of one character, and has turned them into two people.

In this same *Introduction,* Virginia Woolf also informed the reader that in this first version of the novel, Clarissa was, '. . . originally to kill herself, or perhaps merely to die at the end of the party'. (p. 29)

We do not need the evidence of her *Introduction* to see that there are close affinities and relationships between Septimus and Clarissa, even though they never meet. Virginia Woolf's fear that the reviewers would say that the mad scenes did not connect with the Dalloway scenes seems to have been unwarranted. Poetic techniques are used to relate Septimus and Clarissa with each other in the novel; both are beak-nosed, bird-like, associated with similar patterns of imagery and literary echoes such as the refrain from *Cymbeline* (which is sung in the play to Imogen, in the mistaken belief that she is dead). Septimus thinks that 'something tremendous [is] about to happen', Clarissa that 'something awful was about to happen'. Such parallels and contrasts can be added to. Clarissa 'feels' the death of Septimus whereas he had been unable to feel the death of Evans. . . . (pp. 29-30)

It is certainly important to be constantly aware that Septimus is a victim of the war, whilst the Dalloways are representative of politics and government. Years before the writing of **Three Guineas** Virginia Woolf had a very clear idea of the connection between the brutality of war and the 'screen-making habits' of English males of the governing classes. I want it to be clear that I am not arguing for an interpretation of *Mrs. Dalloway* in terms of an overt, consistent political message. What I am saying is that Virginia Woolf saw important connections between social institutions and individual characteristics, and that the relationship between Clarissa and Septimus in the novel is not just metaphysical and psychological, but has an important *social* dimension too.

I would suggest, therefore, that Septimus's madness plays a complex and multiple role in the novel. On one level it is an extreme *symbol* of that alienation from human contact that all of the characters suffer from to a greater or a lesser extent. On another level, as a result of the specifically social links which are drawn between Septimus (who lost the ability to feel through the war), and characters such as Sir William Bradshaw (who is a servant and eager supporter of that 'civilisation' which is associated with the war), Septimus's madness is seen as the *result* of particular pressures engendered by an alienating society.

Certainly, the introduction of a mad character into the novel allows the presentation of an extreme form of alienation. Madness is the supreme isolator, and the more a man needs other men, the more madness is feared. (pp. 31-2)

Madness cuts off Septimus from nearly all real human contact:

> But Rezia could not understand him. Dr. Holmes was such a kind man. He was so interested in Septimus. He only wanted to help them, he said. He had four little children and he had asked her to tea, she told Septimus.
>
> So he was deserted. . . .

Dr Holmes's invitation to his wife makes Septimus feel deserted in just the same way that Lady Bruton's invitation to her husband makes Clarissa feel that she is alone. Both need people and are terrified of solitude, but Clarissa, although often apparently teetering on the edge of the horror that encompasses Septimus, has certain lifelines which preserve her. Both Septimus and Clarissa make gifts. But Septimus's gift of his life

only completes his isolation in death, symbolised by the enclosing ambulance representative, as Peter Walsh feels, of 'civilisation'. Clarissa's gift of her party, on the other hand, really does succeed in bringing people together for a short time. . . . The embrace that Septimus finds in death is sought because he cannot find it in that human contact achieved momentarily at her party that recharges Clarissa's spiritual reserves. The traditional association of sex and death surely stems from a recognition that sex involves some extinction of privacy, some breaking down of the walls of the self, that prefigures the complete extinction of the self in death.

Septimus's dying words—'I'll give it you!'—are thus extremely significant, as they point to the thing that both he and Clarissa most want to do—to *give.* The final extinction of self that Septimus throws himself to in his suicide jump is described in terms that have been used to describe heterosexual passion earlier on, because Virginia Woolf sees close and significant parallels between the act of giving a life and giving in sex. It is Clarissa's fear of 'losing herself' as Septimus loses himself that accounts for her lack of 'something central that permeated', for her inability to give herself—as we say, 'body and soul'— to a sexual relationship. It is thus revealing that there is a distinctly sexual element in Clarissa's imagination of Septimus's death-scene:

> He had thrown himself from a window. Up had flashed the ground; through him, blundering, bruising, went the rusty spikes. There he lay with a thud, thud, thud in his brain, and then a suffocation of blackness. . . .

Clarissa concludes that there is an embrace in death, but in the descriptions of her inability to give herself to either Peter Walsh or, sexually, to Richard, we can see her fear that there is death in an embrace, that abandonment to passion is beyond her because she fears the loss of self—seen symbolically magnified in Septimus's death—that it threatens.

I have said that in *Mrs. Dalloway* madness is seen both as a symbol and a result of alienation. Because madness does cut the individual off from other people, it is to be expected that many of the characteristics resulting from mental disorder may resemble those which result from a society which denies its members full human contact. Furthermore, such a society would be likely to exacerbate any predisposition towards mental disorder in an individual who had difficulty in making contact with other people. (pp. 32-4)

Septimus is irredeemably alone because, unlike Clarissa, he has completely shut himself off from feeling rather than taking risks and exposing his vulnerability—although to this it must be added that his experience of the war placed a greater pressure on him than did Clarissa's more restricted social experience. Clarissa's parties . . . involve vulnerability and risk as well as being an offering; they enable her to regenerate her sense of identity through the development of relationships based on openness and honesty. (p. 37)

In the party with which *Mrs. Dalloway* culminates . . . it is Clarissa's ability to *give,* to be more interested in other people than in herself, that is exaggerated, brought to the surface, and revealed as her 'offering'. Unable to give herself to Peter Walsh or, fully, to Richard, she is still able to expose herself to the vulnerability of the party and thus, in some measure, to save herself from the fate of Septimus, a fate that her other retreats from commitment threaten her with. (p. 84)

The short stories of *Mrs. Dalloway's Party* stress the atomism and fragmentation of parties, whereas the party with which *Mrs. Dalloway* ends succeeds in breaking down this initial fragmentation and achieving a 'moment' of communion.

Virginia Woolf was certainly clear that the party was to be a crucial culminating episode in the novel.... The party 'expresses life in every variety and full of anticipation', it is used as a heightened example of the problems with which the whole novel has been concerned, as well as offering a temporary escape from these problems. People at the party maintain a hold on their sense of identity and humanity but at the same time move out into genuine contact with other people; their separate selves are brought together through the action of Clarissa, whose 'threads' hold all of them together, albeit temporarily. By the end of the party, after it has passed its awkward stage when failure is still a possibility, no one asks, 'Who am I?'; instead characters perceive both their own and other people's identities in an unusually clear and uncomplicated way:

> It is Clarissa, he said.
>
> For there she was.

The party is not just Clarissa's gift, it is the occasion for communal giving, for that 'conspiracy' which will recharge the participants' social sense and will allow them temporarily to escape from their alienated selves. (pp. 84-5)

At the very start of the novel Clarissa sees her party as a means to 'kindle and illuminate', and her rôle as hostess is presented as a specifically feminine rôle. Just as Clarissa cannot understand the nature of masculine passion, of Peter Walsh's love for her, so too she knows that her parties do not have the importance to Peter Walsh or to Richard that they have to her. Clarissa's rôle as hostess is aptly symbolised in her sewing—drawing together the folds of her dress with her needle—drawing people together at her party. Peter thinks of her as the perfect hostess, and there is a strong element of disparagement in his judgement. The basis for this negative attitude can perhaps be found in Peter's thoughts early on in the novel about the bell of St Margaret's, which is compared to the voice of a hostess:

> Yet, though she is perfectly right, her voice,
> being the voice of the hostess, is reluctant to
> inflict its individuality....

It is this submerging of the hostess's individuality that must precede the communion of the party that annoys Peter's masculine desire to assert individuality, to encourage the 'screen-making habit'. (p. 86)

Being the perfect hostess is a gift for Clarissa in both senses of the word; it is a facility she possesses, but it is also a contribution, an offering, whereby she suppresses her egocentricity, her personal and private life, to contribute to something wider. Thus she speaks, as hostess, to Peter Walsh 'as if they had never met before', but this suppression of purely personal relationships allows a more general, non-exclusive and non-excluding contact to materialise—a feminine sense of communion which goes beyond the hard lines of the passionate, masculine relationship desired by Peter Walsh. To go to a party, people have to leave their rooms, and to make the party work they must forsake the separate rooms of their alienated identities and come together in a new, different, collective identity.... It is worth noting that the last eight pages of *Mrs. Dalloway* are concerned with Clarissa only from the point of view of other people's awareness of her; the last time we are

'inside' her consciousness is when she is alone, looking out of her window at the old lady. It is as if the movement of point of view in the novel reflects her loss of consciousness of self at the moment of success for the party. (pp. 87-8)

We are meant, then, to take the party in *Mrs. Dalloway* seriously. All must 'finally bear upon' it; it must express 'life in every variety and full of anticipation'—a symbol of that feminine gift for bringing people together, for reducing the 'screen-making habit', which will bring people into unalienated relationships and states of being. But is the party adequate to the symbolic weight put upon it in the novel? Irene Simon has suggested that it is not:

> ... Clarissa's party is her solution to the mystery of isolated selves, an instance of communication, her offering. But assembling people in a drawing-room does sound a little trivial as an answer to the problem of life. Because the objective correlative is hardly adequate, the images which express some aspects of the theme fail to fuse, and the need is felt to establish the relations by means of other devices [see excerpt dated 1960].

There is obviously a sense in which any symbol can be made to appear inadequate by being considered in too literal a manner, and there is a hint of unfairness here in the slighting reference to 'assembling people in a drawing-room'. But this apart, the objection raises some central questions about the adequacy or inadequacy of Virginia Woolf's suggested solution to the problem of human isolation and alienation. My own feeling is that although *Mrs. Dalloway* presents and defines the problem in a strikingly impressive way, the reader is left with the feeling that the implied solutions are less than adequate. (p. 89)

Georg Lukács has argued that in all great writing it is essential that characters be depicted in all-sided interdependence with each other and with their social existence, and he criticises 'Modernist' writing because in it the interaction of social forces remains unseen and characters 'act past one another'. Now he is referring primarily to Joyce in this argument, but his objection has some bearing on *Mrs. Dalloway*. Certainly, one of the problems that many of the characters in the novel face is that they *do* seem to 'act past one another', and as Clarissa herself says,

> ... how could they know each other? You met
> every day; then not for six months, or years.
> It was unsatisfactory, they agreed, how little
> one knew people....

If this 'acting past one another' is to be criticised, surely it is not a question of criticising the novelist's portrayal of it so much as of criticising the causes which lie behind it in life itself. *Mrs. Dalloway* can present the unsatisfactoriness of the situation, but includes no real solution to it. The critic William Troy, in a pioneer essay on Virginia Woolf's work [see *TCLC*, Vol. 1], has argued that her writing was concerned mainly with one class of people whose experience was largely vicarious, whose contacts with actuality were incomplete, unsatisfactory or inhibited, and who rarely allowed themselves even the possibility of action. The result, he suggests, is that 'experience' for her characters is an unsatisfactory thing because it involves no active impact of character upon reality. Clarissa does not know who her offering is for; she is, ultimately, without an aim other than that of finding an aim.

It seems to me that these reservations about the strength of Virginia Woolf's art are serious ones, and perhaps explain why it is that our admiration for **Mrs. Dalloway** is one that is hedged around with a number of reservations. We are led in this novel into the heart of the experience of human alienation, but we are not shown the way out, the way forward. By this I do not mean that Virginia Woolf fails to provide an adequate social or political analysis of the situation of her characters, but that potential sources of strength *in the novel* very often fail to be developed. The lack of the sort of alternative vantage point that the work of Peter Walsh—or Richard—or Lucy—might have provided, is not one that can be easily ignored in any final evaluation of the novel. As Dr Leavis put it, the envelope surrounding her dramatized sensibilities may have been 'semi-transparent', '. . . but it seems to shut out all the ranges of experience accompanying those kinds of preoccupation, volitional and moral, with an external world which are not felt primarily as preoccupation with one's consciousness of it'. The party is obviously intended to be an occasion where such kinds of non-self-regarding preoccupation with things outside oneself take place, but the reader may feel that the 'objective correlative' of the party is just not adequate to the task that the novel sets it to perform.

There is one lonely but important exception to the general criticisms of the lack of a satisfactory positive element in the novel that I have been making. Just before his suicide, Septimus is drawn out of his madness and makes real contact with Rezia in the process of their joint attempt to make a hat for Mrs Peters. For once, in this scene, characters in the novel are more interested in something outside themselves than in their consciousness of something outside themselves, and they make contact with each other by *working* together to achieve something outside themselves. The activity involves Rezia's job as a hat-maker, and we can note that activity with a needle is about the only practical work that Virginia Woolf consistently allows to her characters. The limitations of her social experience and vision are as apparent in this exception as they are in the absence of other productive work of an isolated or collective kind in her writing. But in this scene Rezia draws Septimus out of his madness and alienation through involving him in her work with a needle and thread just as, earlier, Clarissa had symbolically drawn the folds of her dress together with her needle. It is, initially, almost as if Rezia's ignoring of him to concentrate on her work allows Septimus to regain contact with her:

> 'Just now!' She said that with her Italian accent.
> She·said that herself. He shaded his eyes so
> that he might see only a little of her face at a
> time, first the chin, then the nose, then the
> forehead, in case it were deformed, or had some
> terrible mark on it. But no, there she was, per-
> fectly natural, sewing, with the pursed lips that
> women have, the set, the melancholy expres-
> sion, when sewing. . . .

'There she was.' As with Peter Walsh's perception of Clarissa's 'equivalent centre of self', as George Eliot expresses it in *Middlemarch,* Septimus's perception of Rezia 'there', saying things 'herself', comes when the person whose identity is fully perceived is occupied in something *outside herself*. Just as Peter Walsh's admiration of Clarissa is at its highest extent when she is 'outside herself', being the 'perfect hostess' and making her gift, so Septimus can make contact with Rezia without fear when she too is 'perfectly natural', concentrating on sewing.

It seems to me that there is a rather simple point to make about these two instances, which is that for people of the social class to which most of Virginia Woolf's characters belong, the opportunity to be taken outside of oneself by work is not common. Is it not rather revealing that Virginia Woolf, in the passage quoted above, refers to, '. . . the pursed lips that women have, the melancholy expression, when sewing'? Surely that look that she describes is the look that any face, male or female, wears when its owner is concentrating on some task which involves undivided attention, and it is a measure of the limitations of Virginia Woolf's social experience that she should associate it particularly and (by implication) exclusively with women sewing.

Once Septimus has made this human contact, he can talk to Rezia. He talks to her not about himself, or herself, or their relationship, but about the hat, which he takes out of her hands and calls an 'organ grinder's monkey's hat'. The contact rejoices Rezia's heart, it is the closest they have been for weeks, and their closeness, paradoxically, involves both being taken out of themselves in the act of concern with something apart from them. They find each other and their relationship by forgetting both. It is because characters in **Mrs. Dalloway** are, too often, concerned with themselves, with their relationships, rather than with something outside themselves that demands their active, collaborative transformation, that the very thing they seek forever eludes them. It is noteworthy that Septimus and Rezia are not 'conscious of being conscious' of the hat; Septimus is just involved in the perceived separateness of Rezia's identity as revealed through her sewing, and Rezia moves from absorption in that sewing to rejoicing at the contact Septimus makes with her. Marx suggests that alienation is overcome when

> The *senses* . . . become directly in their practice
> *theoreticians*. They relate themselves to the *thing*
> for the sake of the thing, but the thing itself is
> an *objective human* relation to itself and to man,
> and vice versa. Need or enjoyment have con-
> sequently lost their *egotistical* nature. . . .

Now Marx here is describing a hypothetical state of affairs following the social transcendence of private property, but we can, in the contact that Rezia and Septimus make, see this sort of transcendence in embryo. Both lose their egocentricity in the *joint* activity of making the hat:

> What had she got in her work-box? She had
> ribbons and beads, tassels, artificial flowers.
> She tumbled them out on the table. He began
> putting odd colours together—for though he
> had no fingers, could not even do up a parcel,
> he had a wonderful eye, and often he was right,
> sometimes absurd, of course, but sometimes
> wonderfully right.

> 'She shall have a beautiful hat!' he murmured,
> taking up this and that, Rezia kneeling by his
> side, looking over his shoulder. Now it was
> finished—that is to say the design; she must
> stitch it together. But she must be very, very
> careful, he said, to keep it just as he had made
> it.

(pp. 93-7)

The passage is so straightforward that it is easy to miss the fact that, in the context of **Mrs. Dalloway,** it is unique, for here thought and action, character and contemplation, are brought together. We are told, it is true, that in the midst of the party it made no difference to Mrs Walker whether there was one Prime Minister more or less among the guests, but we are not shown in any detail what *did* make a difference to her, are not shown her actively grappling with her duties as we are shown Rezia and Septimus thinking and doing the same thing. Clarissa is always *doing* something—going somewhere, buying something, sewing, crossing a street—yet whenever her thoughts are revealed to us they seem to be unconnected with whatever it is she is engaged in. As David Lodge puts it, 'We do not always think of eternity while serving potatoes; sometimes we just think of serving potatoes'. Virginia Woolf's characters never do'. That 'never' is perhaps, in view of our consideration of the hat-making scene in *Mrs. Dalloway,* somewhat of an exaggeration, but not much of one. Of course, particular styles have the effect, sometimes, of developing a momentum which moulds the material they present; thus it is difficult for a character in one of Browning's dramatic monologues to seem other than talkative. But the disjunction between thought and action in Virginia Woolf's fiction is no mere stylistic matter—if there is such a thing as a 'mere' stylistic matter.

When the hat is finally completed, something qualitatively unique in the whole novel has been portrayed, and, as a result, a qualitatively unique form of human communion emerges from it:

Leonard and Virginia Woolf, 1939. Photograph by Gisele Freund. Reproduced by permission of The John Hillelson Agency Limited, as agents for the photographer.

It was wonderful. Never had he done anything which made him feel so proud. It was so real, it was so substantial, Mrs Peters' hat.

'Just look at it,' he said.

Yes, it would always make her happy to see that hat. He had become himself then, he had laughed then. They had been alone together. Always she would like that hat.

(pp. 97-8)

In her essay **'The New Biography',** published in 1927, Virginia Woolf writes that

Truth of fact and truth of fiction are incompatible; yet he [the biographer] is now more than ever urged to combine them. For it would seem that the life which is increasingly real to us is the fictitious life; it dwells in the personality rather than in the act. . . .

It is this separation of personality from act that characterises most effectively the alienated state of those who people Virginia Woolf's fiction in general, and *Mrs. Dalloway* in particular. Like Mr Ramsay in *To the Lighthouse,* Virginia Woolf's fundamental concern is really with, 'Subject and object and the nature of reality,' and it is her inability to synthesise personality and act that prevents her exploring it beyond a certain point, the inability of a social class that sees its personalities to be separate from the acts of those who produce the wealth they live on. We can apply to Virginia Woolf the criticism that Marx, in his first thesis on Feuerbach, makes of 'all hitherto existing materialism', that it conceives of the 'thing'

. . . only in the form of the *object* or of *contemplation,* but not as *human sensuous activity, practice* . . .

It is only for this brief moment during the hat-making scene that we are involved in 'human sensuous activity', in *practice* rather than disembodied contemplation, and for this brief moment the characters involved rise above their alienated condition. (pp. 98-9)

We are given in the novel an extraordinarily powerful picture of men and women fighting a central inadequacy in their lives—the inadequacy of alienation—but we are shown no real way of escape from it. Thus, in the last resort life, alas, escapes.

In *Night and Day* Katharine Hilbery asks why there should be

this perpetual disparity between the thought and the action, between the life of solitude and the life of society, this astonishing precipice on one side of which the soul was active and in broad daylight, on the other side of which it was contemplative and dark as night? . . .

In *Mrs. Dalloway,* as much as in *Night and Day,* we must give Virginia Woolf the credit for having asked the question and for having exposed one of the central issues of our time. That she was unable to answer the question she posed is no ground for belittling her achievement. (p. 105)

Jeremy Hawthorn, in his Virginia Woolf's "Mrs. Dalloway": A Study in Alienation, *Sussex University Press,* 1975, 111 p.

T. E. APTER   (essay date 1979)

[*In the following excerpt, Apter discusses Woolf's approach to human perception and imagination in* Mrs. Dalloway.]

The eye is not a simple recording machine; the relation between eye and object is not like that of a seal upon wax. Karl Popper began a lecture with the following instructions: 'Take a pencil and paper; carefully observe, and write down what you have observed.' The students naturally asked what he wanted them to observe. Popper explained that this apparently straightforward instruction 'Observe!' is meaningless: 'Observation is always selective. It needs a chosen object, a definite task, an interest, a point of view, a problem. And its description presupposes a descriptive language, with property words; it presupposes similarity and classification, which in turn presupposes interests, points of views and problems.' Virginia Woolf, throughout her mature fiction, is interested in exploring this selective aspect of observation. She is interested in the way one uses perception as a springboard for thoughts and memories, so that perception becomes laden with symbols. She is interested in the pace with which one passes from one point of focus to another, and in the way that pace measures individual, mental time outside the force of public time. She is interested in the different stories that can be told about what is seen, and she shows that these differences are not merely tales tagged on to the thing seen, but part and parcel of what a character observes.

In *Mrs Dalloway* everyone in the West End sees the same large car with the blind drawn, but each character makes a different inference about the person inside the car, according to his respective notion of greatness, just as each character offers a different reading of the aeroplane's sky-writing. There are cases in which it makes sense to say that the character's theory of what it is he perceives (behind the drawn blind, or in the sky) is either correct or mistaken. More commonly, however, individual interpretations cannot be either corrected or confirmed by further observation. Peter Walsh sees, in the woman singing outside the tube station in Regent's Park, the passing ages: he does not infer that she—or someone like her—has been standing there for centuries; he sees in her song something enduring and triumphant. The essential vitality of his vision of the woman is not denied by the essential pathos of Lucrezia's vision of her: Lucrezia hears the woman's song as an ancient song of love and, feeling the impotence of her own love for Septimus, she reveals her own state through her pity for that useless upsurge of love.

Just as the old woman and her song *are* these different things, the sounds of the bells, either to different people or to the same person at different times, reveal different aspects of the people who hear them. Outside the offices of Sir William Bradshaw the chimes of the clock shred and slice, divide and subdivide, nibble away at the June day to uphold authority and the advantages of a sense of proportion. As the young, shy Elizabeth Dalloway is presented to Peter, the chimes of Big Ben sound with extraordinary vigour, as if an inconsiderate young man were swinging dumb-bells: the image is shared by all of them, for to Clarissa and Peter, Elizabeth's youth represents the relentless vigour of time, while Elizabeth feels the chimes as a bullying force of the public, objective world. As Peter leaves Clarissa, he hears the chimes first, as he thinks about the woman's interminable parties, as leaden circles dissolving in the air; then, thinking of her as hostess, he hears church bells not as cold and dissolving, but as something which buries itself in the heart, 'something alive which wants to confide it-

self'. . . . A moment later, through thoughts of Clarissa's illness and of the time that has passed since their youth and intimacy, the church bells become a tolling for death, so insistent that he has to protest that they are both still alive. The different things he hears cannot be accounted for by any difference of auditory sensation; yet he is not simply imagining what he hears. The sounds of the chimes and bells are open to many possible responses; these different responses are determined by the individual character's imagination, yet these different responses reveal not mere individual fantasies but different aspects of reality. Even Septimus Warren Smith's apparently mad visions have this kind of truth; the world makes sense that way, one can respond to it that way, one's response reveals new aspects of the world.

The perceiver who notes new possibilities, who vitalises new aspects of reality, is the creative perceiver, and this creativeness is Virginia Woolf's measure of truth. The perceiver who sees only what is publicly known and publicly accepted, kills the world as he observes it. Clarissa knows that through her observation of the world, she has given something of herself to the world, and that this extends beyond and will survive her individual life. . . . (pp. 50-2)

'What a morning—fresh as if issued to children on a beach,' thinks Mrs Dalloway . . . , and the language in which her movements are described—she 'had burst open the French windows', and she had 'plunged at Bourton into the open air' . . .—displays the eagerness of her vision. She recognises that part of her love for the world around her is the love for the creative act of perception itself:

> For Heaven only knows why one loves it so, how one sees it so, making it up, building it round one, tumbling it, creating it every moment afresh . . . . In people's eyes, in the swing, tramp and trudge . . . in the triumph and the jingle and the strange high singing of some aeroplane overhead was what she loved; life; London; this moment of June.
>
> (pp. 54-5)

The importance of imagination in this novel lies to a great extent in its capacity to make the present moment vivid, to endow the present with one's mood and memories, to draw the things one sees into one's own world and, at the same time, to discover the special vital qualities of the external objects. Repeatedly the characters focus on their immediate impressions: 'what she loved was this, here, now, in front of her.' . . . The attributes upon which she focuses become substantives; in the florist's 'this beauty, this scent, this colour' appeal to her. . . . Septimus, too, admires 'this exquisite beauty' . . . , but the vividness of objects also terrorises him: for, always in Virginia Woolf's writings, where there is the possibility of joy, there is the possibility of terror. The creativeness of perception can get out of hand; the vitality seen in the world can become aggressive; the part of one's self one gives to the world one sees can make one feel robbed of one's self.

Alongside their vivid immediacy, objects contain within them the sense of time. In her bedroom Mrs Dalloway sees 'the glass, the dressing-table, and all the bottles afresh' . . . and the sight makes her feel the pressure of all other mornings. The capacity of the present to contain the past naturally makes the past appear as immediate. Memories become entangled in present thoughts and perceptions. There is a warmth, somewhat comical, in the way memories appear as present thoughts, and help one with one's present arguments; as a result, the mind, despite its sharp focus on the present, is seen as far-ranging and swift. Clarissa's meeting Hugh Whitbread in the West End leads her to reflect upon her reaction to him—and then to consider the reactions of people who matter to her. Clarissa's husband is driven mad by Hugh, and not only had Peter Walsh never a good word to say for Hugh, but he had never forgiven Clarissa for liking him. Thus Clarissa must defend her liking of Hugh; she begins to criticise Peter; she feels the tension of their past friendship and she tries to defend herself against his attack. Then she decides that this Peter who criticises her is Peter at his worst, and that, after all, he would be 'adorable to walk with on a morning like this'. . . . She returns to her appreciation of the morning, and this appreciation makes the best in her past spring up before her: 'some days, some sights bringing him back to her calmly, without the old bitterness; which perhaps was the reward of having cared for people; they came back in the middle of St James's Park on a fine morning—indeed they did.' . . . Peter's company—conjured through memory, sharing the vividness of the lovely day—is so real that the pleasant aspects of his company cannot remain—as they would in mere fantasy—unadulterated by the tension in their relationship, and by her own ambivalent feelings: 'So she would still find herself arguing in St James's Park, still making out that she had been right—and she had too—not to marry him.' . . . However, if Peter were with her now, he would be looking at her, and she is afraid he would think her aged. In imagining Peter's company, she must imagine his independent vision. She tries to protect herself against it by clinging to this precious moment in June: to remind herself of her power to make the present real, and to make it hers, is to deny the reality of ordinary time.

Sensitivity to the present moment, to the vitality in the immediate surroundings, actually destroys the bounds of the present and the immediate. Following a description of Mrs Dalloway's delight and interest in Bond Street and the June morning is a paragraph describing all London—including what the King and Queen are doing and what people in shops are doing. Mrs Dalloway herself is not said to imagine these scenes, though this must be taken as an exaggerated statement of the way imagination can appear as actual vision. Her immediate, vivid perception opens the whole city to her; the imagination, stimulated by creative perception, becomes far-sighted, integrating perception.

This vision of London as a whole, with all its people connected, is linked to Clarissa's desire to give a party. The party is an expression of her vision; it is her means of realising and sharing it: 'she, too, was going that very night to kindle and illuminate; to give her party'. . . . Her excitement is due to her sense that, in giving this party, 'she is part of it all'. (pp. 55-6)

The act of giving a party is not simply an offering of a completed, finished vision. . . . Her fear of a profound exploration of her self, which is a fear of profound communication, makes the party suitable as a realisation of her sense of what it is to draw people together.

The images in *Mrs Dalloway* have neither the poetic independence (independence from any character's perception) nor the sardonic sharpness familiar in *Jacob's Room*. The responses of various characters are inter-linked; the response of one develops the response of another; the image used by one character is extended or modified by an image used by another character. The psychological truth underlying this technique is that however individual one's impressions, they are influenced—and in turn influence—the impressions of others. For, as Clarissa understands: 'she felt herself everywhere; not "here, here, here"'; and she tapped on the back of the seat; but everywhere . . . so that to know her, or anyone, one must seek out the people who completed them . . .'. (p. 57)

This novel is a brighter, more positive novel than *Jacob's Room*. Self-expression, self-realisation, emerge as real possibilities. Nonetheless, the deepest, the most real part of the self is hidden, and wants to keep itself hidden. Repeatedly the self is described as an underwater creature and, accordingly, it is seen to have a continuous motion, a peculiar freedom and isolation, a capacity to plunge deeper and deeper, a tendency to see objects as luminous and distorted. The mobility and freedom associated with an underwater creature are complemented by the similarity so many of the characters are said to have to birds: Scope Purvis, seeing Mrs Dalloway in the West End, thinks that she is perched on the curb like a bird, whereas she feels herself to be far out at sea . . .; Septimus Warren Smith is 'beak-nosed' and Lucrezia is like a bird in her vulnerability and timidity, surrounded by enormous trees . . ., and Sally Seton, with her brazen independence, reminds Clarissa of a cockatoo. The shared qualities of an underwater creature and a flying creature make these images virtually interchangeable. The birds indicate movement towards life, and the underwater creatures indicate movements towards death, but these two apparently opposing movements are closely related; they are different aspects of the same movement. (pp. 57-8)

The participation of the self in perception indicates a continuing death: if what one perceives is part of the self, then changing, vanishing perceptions reveal a changing, vanishing self—yet only by so participating in perception does the world come alive. All the characters who are capable of bringing their world to life share an awareness of the passing of life; but each responds differently. Peter Walsh feels that his susceptibility to the moment when life and death come together has been his undoing; it has made it impossible for him to plan or to be practical. One impression after another falls upon him until it reaches the deep, dark cellar where he stands . . .; the deep, dark place of the self, the negative possessions of the self, are the result of the extent to which the self belongs to the external world. As Peter reflects, to know Clarissa is to know the things she loved, the things she observed and brought to life by her creative vision; and if, as Clarissa supposes, she will live on in those things after her death, she must also live on in them while she lives; it is not only in death that the world is haunted by fragmented, un-owned parts of the self.

Just as Clarissa believes, joyfully, that she will live on in the world she sees, that she gives her self to the world she sees, Septimus is robbed of his self by the external world. He endows objects with so much of himself that he has nothing left; he has nothing of the private, secluded self which both Peter and Clarissa relish. Septimus lacks the capacity to save anything of himself. Whereas Clarissa enjoys a sense of floating away on the colours in the florist's shop, Septimus will be carried irretrievably away by them. Whereas Clarissa feels the objects in the bedroom giving her back something of her past self, objects threaten Septimus either by penetrating him (as the flowers do when they grow through his hands) or by refusing to soften their distinction from him. Lucrezia leaves him to open the door to Dr Holmes, and Septimus is terrified of being alone forever among the sideboard and the bananas. The absurdity of his fear is eclipsed by the pathos of his terror. Alone, he can find no private flow of thought in which his perceptions become his own and which heals the fragmentation and alien-ation of interruption. A few minutes before, sitting with his wife, watching her sew and sharing her laughter, he had almost found it, but the entry of Dr Holmes is the entry of the com-placent public who will rob him of this small chance of privacy and who will deny the reality of his own vision.

Even in his frantic throwing away of his own life, there is a sanity—that is, a legitimate response to reality—which Clarissa endorses as she retreats to the small room adjoining that in which her party is being held. She can understand why a young man would relinquish his own life to preserve that integrity which the party tends to destroy. The old woman Clarissa sees through the window, the complement of the old man Septimus sees across the street as he hurls himself from the window, represents the purely personal, private life which Clarissa has pilfered in her desire for social success, and she is ashamed to be forced to watch this woman—who is lost in the process of living—in her evening dress. . . . Clarissa's gladness at the young man's suicide, while she and her friends go on living and throwing parties, is the relief of having part of her needs expressed by someone else. With this need fulfilled, she can 'assemble' and return to her task as hostess. In such a state she can deny the definitions her friends try to force upon her; she can communicate the individual and unbounded reality of her self. (pp. 71-2)

> *T. E. Apter, in his* Virginia Woolf: A Study of Her Novels, *New York University Press, 1979, 167 p.*

EMILY JENSEN (essay date 1983)

[*In the following excerpt, Jensen contends that Clarissa Dallo-way's decision to adhere to a conventional, heterosexual lifestyle is, in effect, a suicide of her essentially homosexual self.*]

Virginia Woolf's **Mrs. Dalloway** presents one day in the life of Clarissa Dalloway, a day that begins with her going to pick up the flowers for a party she is giving that evening and ends about 3:00 A.M., while the party is still going on. Not much to hang a novel on, but with the memories and associations that lace the narrative, we acquire an intricately woven image of the woman who figures at the center. As others have ob-served, she is a woman who is both enthusiastically involved in the process of living and simultaneously terrified of some interruption to that involvement.

It is my thesis that Clarissa Dalloway's fear of interruption is the most important feature of her personality and, concomi-tantly, that the event that is the source of that fear is the most important fact of her life. In that historic interruption of ''the most exquisite moment of her whole life,'' . . . Clarissa agrees to deny her love for Sally Seton, decides marriage to Peter Walsh is impossible, and chooses instead to marry Richard Dalloway and become respectable. No simple girlhood crush, Clarissa's love for Sally Seton is a profound reality that per-meates her adult life. Through its metaphoric structure, the novel reveals that Clarissa felt her only real love for Sally Seton, denied that and married Richard, not Peter Walsh, be-cause Richard would demand less of her emotionally . . . and would provide the means for a respectable life. Crippled by heterosexual convention, her life thereafter, her ''process of living,'' is her ''punishment'' for having denied herself that love. She identifies with Septimus Smith as one who committed suicide to preserve the ''treasure'' of his homosexual feelings, and whose madness is the overt expression of her more guarded emotional life, a life in which she balances contempt for herself

as the perfect hostess and praise for her ability to be the perfect hostess. Both Peter Walsh, who sees through her . . . , and Miss Kilman, through whom she sees herself, help expose the delicacy of that balance. While Clarissa's choice in itself—to deny her love for Sally, break off with Peter, and marry Rich-ard—is not by definition self-destructive, the way it is pre-sented in **Mrs. Dalloway** suggests that it is destructive for Clar-issa Dalloway. It is, in fact, on a par with Septimus Smith's more obvious suicide, as stated by Clarissa's specific identi-fication with him at the end of the novel: ''she felt somehow very like him—the young man who had killed himself.'' . . . (pp. 162-63)

It is neither insignificant nor unrelated (as very little is in this novel of delicate weavings, tiny stitches overlaying other stitches to form a textured pattern) that Septimus Smith survives the war and the loss of his friend Evans to discover that he has lost the ability to feel; in his case, as in Clarissa's, the feeling that is lost is for a person of his own sex. Nor is it unrelated that both of them call upon Shakespeare: while Clarissa iden-tifies with Othello's passion for Desdemona, Septimus focuses on the meaning behind Shakespeare's words, that ''love be-tween man and woman was repulsive.'' . . . Taken together, these allusions give us the quality of the feeling subsequently lost and the homosexual nature of it.

For both Clarissa and Septimus, the feeling is lost by an in-terruption: war cuts short Septimus's feeling for Evans, and, because he does not understand the meaning of that relation-ship, he participates in what becomes a frustration of his ability to feel at all, aided certainly by the advice of Dr. Holmes that he owed a duty to his wife. . . . Thus two bastions of masculine power and authority—the military and the medical profes-sion—converge to inhibit Septimus's feeling. Peter Walsh, a man whose ''good opinion'' . . . Clarissa wanted, interrupts Clarissa's feeling for Sally Seton. They were all walking on the terrace at Bourton when

> she and Sally fell a little behind. Then came the most exquisite moment of her whole life passing a stone urn with flowers in it. Sally stopped; picked a flower; kissed her on the lips. . . . There she was alone with Sally. . . .
>
> ''Star-gazing?'' said Peter.
>
> It was like running one's face against a granite wall in the darkness! It was shocking; it was horrible!
>
> Not for herself. She felt only how Sally was being mauled already, maltreated; she felt his hostility; his jealousy; his determination to break into their companionship. . . .
>
> ''Oh this horror!'' she said to herself, as if she had known all along that something would in-terrupt, would embitter her moment of happi-ness. . . .

''She had burst open the French windows and plunged at Bour-ton into the open air'' . . . and smashed headfirst ''against a granite wall in the darkness.'' The clash of imagery from the open air and flapping waves of the first scene to the granite wall of this scene is tactile in its intensity and telling in its effects on Clarissa. Why, then, does she say the horror is ''not for herself'' but only for Sally, who indeed had managed to upset most of the residents at Bourton by her unconventional behavior. Yet Clarissa understands their relationship as having sprung "from a sense of being in league together, a presentiment of something that was bound to part them (they spoke of marriage always as a catastrophe),'' . . . and certainly that is what lies on the other side of the granite wall for both of them. One reason Clarissa might see Peter's interruption as more horrible for Sally than for herself is that in this lovers' triangle, it is Sally with whom Peter is competing for Clarissa's love. This is clear both from Clarissa's father's equal dislike of Peter and Sally . . . and from Peter and Sally's memory of their intimacy when Peter was courting Clarissa. . . . More important, however, is that Clarissa had been expecting some such cessation of her moment with Sally: the horror for her, in fact, is the recognition that what she had feared all along does happen. Even in Clarissa's tryst with Sally where they both talked of marriage as the catastrophe that would separate them, the protectiveness "was much more on her side than Sally's.'' . . . This is so largely, no doubt, because of Clarissa's view of Sally as a woman who dared "say anything, do anything,'' . . . rather than as a woman who cared enough about social convention to know that any passion she felt for another woman would not be allowed, "not in this world. No,'' . . . as Clarissa says in another context about loving Miss Kilman.

But Clarissa does care enough about convention to know "that something would interrupt, would embitter her moment of happiness.'' Sally's perception of this quality in Clarissa is particularly acute: in the final scene of the novel she tells Peter that "Clarissa was at heart a snob. . . . And it was that that was between them, she was convinced.'' . . . Because Clarissa does care about convention and respectability, she is relieved on one level when Peter interrupts her moment with Sally:

> Yet, after all, how much she owed him later. . . .
> She owed him words: "sentimental,'' "civilized''; they started up every day of her life as if he guarded her. . . . "Sentimental,'' perhaps she was to be thinking of the past. . . .

Thus ends Clarissa's impassioned memory of her past with Sally, "the most exquisite moment of her whole life'' carefully packed away and—thanks to Peter—labeled "sentimental'' and presumably also not "civilized.'' Or, what is more likely, because loving Sally is not accepted as "civilized,'' it is best for Clarissa to see it as "sentimental.'' And the words that condemn Clarissa's love for Sally to a memory of exquisite moments lost are not far removed from those words that Sir William Bradshaw worships in Septimus Smith's case: the twin goddesses, Proportion and Conversion. Proportion is his term for conventional heterosexual life (men should be like him, women like Lady Bradshaw), and Conversion is the means by which it is maintained: "she feasts on the wills of the weakly, loving to impress, to impose, adoring her own features stamped on the face of the populace.'' . . . It is not at all surprising that Septimus jumps out a window to avoid Bradshaw, and Clarissa reckons "one wouldn't like Sir William to see one unhappy. No; not that man.'' . . . The authoritarian words that condemn both of them are parallel in that "sentimental'' is the other side of "civilized'' in the same way that Conversion is the other side of Proportion: for the socially elite, the educated and refined Clarissa, labeling behavior "sentimental'' is just as condemning, hence as effective in changing it, as the more direct method of conversion is for the masses. While Septimus must be institutionalized to acquire Bradshaw's "sense of proportion,'' . . . Clarissa has Peter's words to "guard'' her every day so that instead of plunging "at Bourton into the open air'' and risking the threat of a granite wall to impede her, she

"plunged into the very heart of the moment . . . of this June morning'' . . . ; that is, she gave up Sally, broke off with Peter, married Richard, and became the respectable M.P.'s wife who gives parties to enhance Richard's position . . . , all the while trying to convince herself that "this'' is the life she wants.

That this respectable life represents a choice with suicidal implications becomes clear in Clarissa's final scene in the novel, the scene that brings together all the verbal strains begun earlier. She is alone in a room away from the party, and she is thinking of Septimus Smith's suicide and its relevance to her own life.

> A thing there was that mattered; a thing wreathed about with chatter, defaced, obscured in her own life, let drop every day in corruption, lies, chatter. This he had preserved. . . .

> But this young man who had killed himself— had he plunged holding his treasure? "If it were now to die, 'twere now to be most happy,'' she had said to herself once, coming down in white. . . .

While the literal context makes it clear that Clarissa's "thing that mattered'' and Septimus's "treasure'' are synonymous, the verbal associations clarify that both refer to the integrity of homosexual love and of the selves involved in that love. Thinking of his treasure immediately calls up Clarissa's moment with Sally, inherent both in the line from Shakespeare and in the partial repetition of that intense moment, "coming down to dinner in a white frock to meet Sally Seton!'' . . . Clarissa's assessment of her denial of that moment and therefore denial of her love for Sally Seton is bitter in its self-revelation: to admit that that love was "defaced, obscured in her own life, let drop every day in corruption, lies, chatter'' is devastating, given that the life Clarissa chose to live out, to make up, to build up, was that of a hostess creating the perfect environment for her invited guests; with the blinders off she sees it for what it is: banal chatter, a life of corruption and lies. Further, using "plunge'' to describe Septimus's suicidal leap recalls the other times Clarissa uses the word, always to describe an enthusiastic leap into life, whether life at Bourton, this moment, or the drawing room. As used here, the word implies that there is no difference between his leap into death and hers into the life she has chosen; both are suicidal.

It is not surprising that the question Clarissa had asked herself earlier in the day—What had she done with her life? . . .— here enters her consciousness with an increased sense of terror to it. . . . Nor is it surprising that she consoles herself by being thankful to Richard, who, by providing her with the context for a respectable life, makes it possible for her to ignore the question generally. (pp. 164-68)

The question we must ask is the same one Clarissa asks herself in response to Septimus Smith's suicide: at what cost to herself does she maintain her respectable life? Certainly there is the guilt for a wasted life, as imaged through Kilman and as called up by the solemn pause before Big Ben strikes each hour, by the old woman who lives opposite, and finally by Septimus Smith's suicide. These offer a fairly constant reminder of the self she has denied in choosing respectability. Yet she manages to counter these generally with the consolation that she does well what she has chosen to do: she gives smashing parties, she makes it possible for others to enjoy themselves, and she accepts her vicarious pleasure as what is possible for her, even to the extent of feeling thankful to Richard for providing the context in which her self-sacrifice is seen as respectable. (pp. 175-76)

It seems to me that Clarissa's question whether Septimus preserved the "treasure" by killing himself comes out of her full awareness that, in her life of respectability, she has not. Certainly she has preserved her sexual integrity: it is significant that she retains a "virginity" in an attic bedroom, an image that recalls the "bedroom at the top of the house" . . . in Bourton where she first experienced her passion for Sally. And it is equally significant that she married Richard, not Peter, for Richard allows her her virginal attic bedroom, whereas with Peter "everything had to be shared." . . . But this kind of self-denying virginity is no more effective in sustaining her love for Sally than are Septimus Smith's visions and voices of the dead Evans; Evans is in fact dead and, for Clarissa, Sally might as well be: at best Sally is a ghost out of the past whom Clarissa has avoided over the years and whose married name she cannot even remember. Clarissa's approval of Septimus's literal suicide reveals the extent to which she understands the self-destruction involved in her own life. She recognizes that she has committed her own kind of suicide: she has in fact committed one of the most common of suicides for women, that respectable destruction of the self in the interest of the other, firmly convinced that in this world where the dice fall with the white on top, "that is all" that is possible. (p. 178)

Emily Jensen, "Clarissa Dalloway's Respectable Suicide," in Virginia Woolf: A Feminist Slant, edited by Jane Marcus, University of Nebraska Press, 1983, pp. 162-79.

LYNDALL GORDON (essay date 1984)

[*In the following excerpt, Gordon discusses* Mrs. Dalloway *in relation to Woolf's personal and professional life, her view of fiction, and the artistic intentions that lay behind her work.*]

Between the low-point of what looked like incurable madness in 1915 and the triumphant publication of *To the Lighthouse* in 1927, Virginia Woolf remade herself as a modern artist. E. M. Forster, in an essay on the anonymity of great art, said that artists have two personalities, one public, one private, and that art comes from the obscure depths. Virginia Woolf developed a mercurial public manner—she called it 'doing my tricks'—at Bloomsbury parties. With a little encouragement she threw off words like a musician improvising. Her voice seemed to preen itself with self-confidence in its verbal facility as she leant sideways, a little stiffly in her chair, to address her visitor in a bantering manner. She confounded strangers with wildly fictitious accounts of their lives or shot malicious darts at friends who, the night before, she might have flattered outrageously. Good readers often say that they cannot bear Virginia Woolf. Some mean, I think, that her public manner affected her work. I see it in her unresolved attitude to the gushy side of the London socialite, Mrs Dalloway, and, later, throughout the frothy *Orlando,* a fictional biography of her aristocratic new friend, Victoria Sackville-West.

But to go back to Forster's two personalities, what is important about Virginia Woolf is her serious core. At a certain moment, she admitted, 'I see through what I'm saying and detest myself; & wish for the other side of the moon . . .'. This dark side, the subject of this biography, is hardest at this stage of her career to discern. The public personality outstares her. But the core is always there, in her marriage and in her best work which is never gushy, mercurial, malicious but poetic and

searching, and protected, in a sense, by the glittering carapace of the public act.

In short, there is a gap between the sociable Virginia Woolf of Bloomsbury and even the businesslike Virginia of the diary and the experimental novelist. She put all the private force of feeling into the novels; the diary and letters, on the other hand, were tossed off with effervescent nonchalance. (pp. 176-77)

A Man Ray photograph of Virginia Woolf with jutting profile, red lipstick, and shorn hair projected an image of bold modernity, as did the jaunty 'affair' with Vita. In *Mrs. Dalloway,* Peter Walsh, who has been in India from 1918 to 1923, returns to find that 'every woman, even the most respectable, had . . . lips cut with a knife . . . there was design, art, everywhere'. Publicly explicitness, flamboyance replaced shadow but, in Virginia Woolf's novels, attention to shadow deepened. *Mrs. Dalloway* and *To the Lighthouse* explore madness, memory, people such as Septimus Warren Smith and Lily Briscoe who are haunted by the past. To give this shadow-life the defining shape of art, she followed characters' minds as, repeatedly, they came to rest at a certain point in their past.

Composing *Mrs. Dalloway,* Virginia Woolf resolved on a process of 'tunnelling'. She wanted to dig 'caves' behind her characters, to enter that silent life that the first three novels simply circle as unknown—unknown, that is, to Rachel, Katharine, and Jacob. With Mrs Dalloway and Septimus, she chose maturer people, burdened by memories and themselves able to explore the connecting caves behind the public images of hostess and war veteran, setting off the sane restricted exercise from the insane reckless one.

Virginia Woolf thought the most cogent criticism came from Lytton Strachey, who found Mrs Dalloway disagreeable and limited and complained that, as the writer set it down in her diary, 'I alternately laugh at her, & cover her, very remarkably, with myself.' The portrait may not entirely cohere but, as Virginia Woolf moved from a detached, mocking view of Mrs Dalloway into the shadows of her past, she brought herself closer to artistic maturity. If she were to become a great novelist, she had to learn, as Katherine Mansfield had advised, to 'merge' with someone alien to herself (or her sister or brother, the family sources of the first three novels). And if she were to transcend the modish disillusion of the post-war period she had, as Forster had urged, to create a lovable character.

The initial problem was how to express through a lovable figure her disgust with the literary society of the early 1920s with its 'hidden satire, gorging of pate de foie gras in public, improprieties, & incessant celebrities'. She admitted a certain fascination for the 'slippery mud' of Garsington, the Oxfordshire home of Lady Ottoline Morrell, in which soil were planted young men 'no bigger than asparagus'. 'A loathing overcomes me of human beings', she went on, '—their insincerity, their vanity—A . . . rather defiling talk with Ott[oline] last night . . . & then the blend in one's own mind of suavity & sweetness with contempt & bitterness. . . . I want to give the slipperiness of the soul. I have been too tolerant often. The truth is people scarcely care for each other.'

She speaks here in exactly the terms of Septimus Smith who thinks that people 'have neither kindness, nor faith, nor charity beyond what serves to increase the pleasure of the moment'. The madman does not appear in Virginia Woolf's first plan for the novel, in her manuscript of *Jacob's Room,* on 6 October 1922. Her first idea was a short book of six or seven scenes grouped around Mrs Dalloway but done separately, beginning with 'Mrs. Dalloway in Bond Street' and ending with 'The Party'. On 6 October she was still preoccupied with the 'party consciousness'. Then, she revised the idea drastically in her diary on 14 October to bring in the madman and, with him, her own loathing. Suddenly, she had the idea of a novel that could balance contradictory attitudes to society: 'I adumbrate here a study of insanity & suicide: the world seen by the sane & the insane side by side.'

With Septimus to carry the whole burden of estrangement, the author was now free to indulge the party consciousness of Mrs Dalloway. In fact, the Dalloway scenes are overblown with her slightly dubious lovability, an over-compensation for the slight sneer that occasionally may be detected. Mrs Dalloway is said to be not an exact portrait of Kitty Maxse, but fictional licence cannot cover an uncertain conception. As Quentin Bell observes, Virginia Woolf came closest to exact portraiture when she loved her subject. She did not love Kitty who, as her mother's protegée, had appeared 'the paragon for wit, grace, charm and distinction'. The earliest sketch, 'Mrs. Dalloway in Bond Street', gives a satiric edge to Clarissa Dalloway's fashionable snobbery. Clarissa thinks: 'It would be intolerable if dowdy women came to her party! Would one have liked Keats if he had worn red socks?' But then the author's own snobbery consorts with Clarissa's when an explosion in Bond Street makes shop-women cower while two upper-middle-class customers, buying long white gloves, sit bravely upright. And then, with another shift in *Mrs. Dalloway,* the author covers the hostess with her own dream: 'She had a perpetual sense, as she watched the taxi cabs, of being out, out, far out to sea and alone.'

This flighty treatment of Mrs Dalloway is passed off as 'the power of taking hold of experience, of turning it round, slowly, in the light'. Theoretically, this is a rational exercise in justice as proposed by Sir James Stephen: 'To be conscious of the force of prejudice in ourselves . . . , to know how to change places internally with our antagonists . . . and still to be unshaken, still to adhere with fidelity to the standard we have chosen—this is a triumph.' His granddaughter wanted to do justice to the world governed by Big Ben as it chimes the hours, to the regimen of politicians, their hostesses, and Harley Street. She intended to salute and, with Mrs Dalloway's final alignment with the estranged Septimus, to undercut. And, through this exercise, she would balance her own mind. 'Positiveness, dogmatism', said Sir James, 'may accompany the firmest convictions, but not the convictions of the firmest minds. The freedom with which the vessel swings at anchor, ascertains the soundness of her anchorage.' This judicious swing, Virginia Woolf did achieve briefly in the novel's climactic scene.

There is only the faintest connection between the fashionable Clarissa and the broken Smith. When Sir William Bradshaw excuses his lateness at Clarissa's party on account of Smith's suicide, she withdraws to take in the fact of death. Mrs Dalloway's awakening to fellow-feeling with a madman is no more than a moment hidden in darkness, but it transforms her. She is no longer the bright hostess in a filmy green frock, leading in the Prime Minister, for alone in that dark room she meets a self never fully acknowledged, capable of an unprecedented imaginative reach.

The first draft swings Mrs Dalloway more explicitly into Smith's camp. Watching an old woman across the way prepare for bed, she is shamed for her oblivion to the lives of the obscure. Smith presents the 'unknown' face of those who go down in 'pitiable yet heroic dumbness'.

As Big Ben strikes twelve her joy in this insight mounts to a crescendo. Then, as the outer life surges back with the sound of motor-horns and the chatter from her drawing-room, she goes back determined, as the draft puts it, 'to breast her enemy', specified here as the enforcer of normality, Sir William. It is this subversive glow that makes Clarissa so exciting to Peter Walsh when she returns.

The novel's concluding sentences ask the reader to compose Clarissa Dalloway out of the shifting scenes that reflect her existence, past and present, deep and shallow. Peter, who has always loved her, demonstrates the requisite act of composition as she comes back, through the door, to her party:

> It is Clarissa, he said.
>
> For there she was.

Virginia Woolf tries to sweep us via the lover's rapture into an imaginative response. But can we be sure who is there?

In the next novel [*To the Lighthouse*], the rapture Mrs Ramsay provokes is plausible, but here, as later in *Orlando,* there is a scented adoration which is not easy to share. By contrast, the prose has a terse vigour when Virginia Woolf turns to the indomitable Victorian relics, Lady Bruton, a robust battleaxe with an inherited sense of duty, and Miss Parry, a born explorer. These eccentrics are unquestionably lovable and Virginia Woolf describes them with indulgent humour. She indulges Mrs Dalloway in a more extravagant and potentially more mocking way, the gush edged with faint satire. . . . (pp. 188-91)

Clarissa has the familiar pathos of a woman whose face (as Mrs Richard Dalloway) is unreal. She thinks back repeatedly to her life's turning-point when, as a young girl at Bourton, she had chosen the soothing, worldly Dalloway rather than the demanding, passionate Peter Walsh, a man rather like Leonard Woolf, who values independence of mind and personal freedom above social or monetary success. Peter has never quite recovered from Clarissa's refusal: from that moment his life has been unsettled, makeshift, flirtatious, though never self-deceiving. He sees clearly that as a girl Clarissa had the kind of timidity that would harden in middle age into a prudish conservatism. This Peter defines as 'the death of the soul'.

In one of her letters Virginia Woolf said, rather enigmatically, that she had to complete the character of Clarissa with the character of Septimus. Clarissa's half-conscious withering is parodied by the madman's spiritual sickness. His attitude is fatal in that it refuses, together with society's norms, the comforting illusions and accommodations which keep us sane. We practise sanity as a matter of course; Virginia Woolf did so deliberately, and wrote *Mrs. Dalloway* from 1923 all through 1924, for the first time without interruption from illness. Through her sympathies with Mrs Dalloway she accommodated society; through Smith she demonstrated the cost of insanity—but never forgetting what sanity costs us in oblivion.

Discarding both the chapter format of the novel of event and the extreme fragmentation of *Jacob's Room,* Virginia Woolf devised here and again in *To the Lighthouse* a divided form which could define, almost diagrammatically, the antitheses of sanity and insanity, public and private, day and night, present and past. *Mrs. Dalloway* is a balancing act, borne out of the balanced life that Virginia achieved by the mid-1920s. This delicate balance is sustained, in the novel, within the strict structure of the hours of one day, from 11 a.m. to 12 p.m. The hours, designed to measure out the day of doctors and politicians, hold also more elusive interior dramas in their 'leaden rings'.

The fixity of this outer casing was emphasized in the first draft, called 'The Hours', by more attention to the six chimes that follow Smith's suicide and the twelve chimes that follow Clarissa's awakening. Virginia Woolf was transforming the novel in accordance with the aim of the Post-Impressionists, as she understood it from Roger Fry, that modern art should not seek to imitate form but to create form. The artist, in other words, invents a form to express a certain experience as Clarissa's moment of awakening finds its perfect expressive form in her midnight perspective on the fading daylight of an obscure suicide.

The revised novel plays down the hours as well as the critical perspectives of the frustrated lovers, Peter and Rezia. The effect is to draw Clarissa and Septimus forward, embedding us directly in their minds. They are united formally by the hours, more subtly by the rhythmic movement of their minds and their common preoccupation with death.

The rhythmic waves of consciousness flow through the hours as through a channel. The chimes have a deceptive finality like the full stop at the end of a sentence which is part of the rise and fall of rhythmic prose. In 1919 Lytton Strachey praised Virginia Woolf as the creator of a new version of the sentence. Her sentence is like the deep wave of the mind in repose, first recorded on the electroencephalogram in 1924. The physiologist, Colin Blakemore, calls this the mind in its natural state, when it is receptive to impressions but unwilling to place them on preordained maps of consciousness. (pp. 192-93)

Mrs Dalloway is thus at rest as she sews her party dress:

> Quiet descended on her, calm, content, as her needle, drawing the silk smoothly to its gentle pause, collected the green folds together and attached them very lightly, to the belt. So on a summer's day waves collect, overbalance, and fall; collect and fall; and the whole world seems to be saying 'that is all' more and more ponderously.

Sewing, Mrs Dalloway reposes in the involuntary rhythm of nature, most often symbolized in Virginia Woolf by the waves.

In the same way, Smith's agitated consciousness comes to rest as he trims a hat for his wife, at which point he returns to sanity (ironically, just before the doctor arrives to cart him off to a Home, which precipitates his quite rational suicide).

These parallel waves of consciousness fulfil the plan, proposed in 1917, to 'slip easily from one thing to another, without any sense of . . . obstacle. I want to sink deeper and deeper, away from the surface, with its hard separate facts.'

Virginia Woolf's sense of fact, like her sentence, transforms the traditional novel. How wonderful, she says, to discover that Sunday luncheons, Archbishops, table-cloths, and the Lord High Chancellor 'were not entirely real'. Like scientists we must redefine fact as mystery, 'crack' through the paving stone, and be enveloped in the mist. *Mrs. Dalloway* ignores the blatant fact of suicide, scorns the obtruding force of Dr Holmes, and dwells instead on the mind of a man as he trims a hat. The moment of importance, she says in **'Modern Fiction'**, falls not here but there. To become a work of art, she dictates in **'The Art of Fiction',** the novel must 'cut adrift from the tea-table', that is, from the laborious reproduction of external detail, in

order to explore hidden facts in the caves of consciousness. (pp. 193-94)

It occurred to Virginia Woolf that it might be possible to give aesthetic definition to a woman's voice. It has, she said on the opening page of the first draft of *Mrs. Dalloway*, 'a vibration in the core of the sound so that each word, or note, comes fluttering, alive, yet with some reluctance to inflict its vitality, some grief for the past which holds it back, some impulse nevertheless to glide into the recesses of the heart'. (pp. 194-95)

'I am a woman . . . when I write', Virginia Woolf concluded in 1929. In the 1920s she had developed a recognizable authorial voice, punctuated by silence or comic deflation, but always rising again like a wave surging forward. The sentence pulsates beyond the period with continued suggestion. Dorothy Richardson's 'feminine' sentence, Proust's sensibility, and Fry's claim for expressive art may have bolstered Virginia Woolf, but her experiments, if traced to their source, arose too early to be other than her own.

She may have copied minor effects from T. S. Eliot and Joyce: the modern city scene and the hours that propel the narrative. Eliot's 'Unreal City', though, has the single-mindedness of a vision, a projection of the poet's inner world of nightmare. Virginia Woolf's London, in contrast, has the multiplicity of a real city observed by a native: the dun zoo animals overlooking Regent's Park, the discreet gloss of Harley Street, the bus ride along the Strand, the lingerie department in the Army and Navy Stores, the isolated kneelers in Westminster Abbey.

The moderns never wrote anything one wants to read about death, thinks Mrs Dalloway in Bond Street. Murmuring old, comforting lines, 'From the contagion of the world's slow stain / He is secure . . .' and 'Fear no more the heat o' the sun / Nor the furious winter's rages', Mrs Dalloway, like Septimus, has a sense of posthumous existence. Mrs Dalloway can reasonably state her belief that some residue of herself will linger on in the lives of others she has known and in the scenes of her past (much as Jacob survives his death). Septimus's own sense of the dead is so obsessive that it obliterates his very existence. The dead literally visit him and he has auditory hallucinations similar to Virginia Woolf's, of birds singing in Greek 'of life beyond a river where the dead walk'. Five years after the end of the war he is still locked mentally to the fate of his dead comrades, especially to his commanding officer, Evans. He goes through the motions of living—he weds, returns for a while to the office—but cannot compose, as the writer did, a marriage, a new life.

Another subtle link between the two halves of *Mrs. Dalloway* is Smith's portentous message of altruism. Having witnessed war he wants no less than to change the world. The supreme secret, to be revealed at once to the Cabinet, is 'universal love'. Again, Clarissa in her modest way brings out the sane script. Without much fuss, she brings people together and sets youths going. This is her gift.

'The merit of this book', Virginia Woolf wrote in a notebook, 'lies in its design, which is original—very difficult.' The two halves of this design did not naturally converge. That they cohere at all was a feat of ingenuity. In her next novel, she chose to emphasize rather than minimize the divided design, in this case a more natural, chronological break between two ages, Victorian and Modern. An early notion was to put into words the pure flight of time, like a vacant corridor leading through the war into the post-war period. She called it simply 'Time Passes'.

Virginia Woolf drew an initial diagram for *To the Lighthouse* as two blocks connected by the corridor of time. In the first block Lily Briscoe begins a painting; in the last block she completes it. Why must ten years pass before that painting can be completed? Virginia Woolf combined a sense of mystery with the exactness of a curious scientist. Her sense of mystery was searching, directed, not a floating vagueness. The clear-cut, almost diagrammatic design of her greater novels frames, in each case, an experiment that leads to a resounding conclusion. (pp. 195-96)

Lyndall Gordon, in her Virginia Woolf: A Writer's Life, *W. W. Norton & Company, 1984, 341 p.*

ADDITIONAL BIBLIOGRAPHY

Ames, Kenneth J. "Elements of Mock-heroic in Virginia Woolf's *Mrs. Dalloway.*" *Modern Fiction Studies* 18, No. 3 (Autumn 1972): 363-74.
   Documents in *Mrs. Dalloway* elements of the neoclassical mock-heroic, as typified by Alexander Pope's *The Rape of the Lock.*

Baldanza, Frank. "Clarissa Dalloway's 'Party Consciousness'." *Modern Fiction Studies* II, No. 1 (February 1956): 24-30.
   Examines the importance of the social party to Clarissa Dalloway's conception of life.

Bazin, Nancy Topping. "*Jacob's Room* and *Mrs. Dalloway.*" In her *Virginia Woolf and the Androgynous Vision,* pp. 89-123. New Brunswick, N.J.: Rutgers University Press, 1973.
   Two-part chapter, of which the latter section explores character and action in *Mrs. Dalloway.*

Benjamin, Anna S. "Towards an Understanding of the Meaning of Virginia Woolf's *Mrs. Dalloway.*" *Wisconsin Studies in Contemporary Literature* 6, No. 2 (Summer 1965): 214-27.
   Studies the relationship between Woolf's circular time structure and the question of life's meaning in *Mrs. Dalloway.*

Blunt, Katherine K. "Jay and Hawk: Their Song, and Echoes in *Mrs. Dalloway.*" *Virginia Woolf Quarterly* II, No. 364 (Summer & Fall 1976): 313-37.
   Analyzes the characters of Clarissa Dalloway and Septimus Warren Smith, their common traits as well as their literary antecedents.

DiBattista, Maria. "*Mrs. Dalloway:* Virginia Woolf's Memento Mori." In her *Virginia Woolf's Major Novels: The Fables of Anon,* pp. 22-63. New Haven, Conn.: Yale University Press, 1980.
   Reading of *Mrs. Dalloway* as a work in which Woolf emerged as a distinctive literary personality and began "to formulate and implement her philosophy of anonymity in which the creative mind consciously absents itself from the work it creates."

Edwards, Lee R. "War and Roses: The Politics of *Mrs. Dalloway.*" In *The Authority of Experience: Essays in Feminist Criticism,* edited by Arlyn Diamond and Lee R. Edwards, pp. 160-77. Amherst: University of Massachusetts Press, 1977.
   Discusses Clarissa Dalloway and Septimus Warren Smith in relation to their participation in a world where social roles are imposed on individuals.

Fleishman, Avrom. "*Mrs. Dalloway.*" In his *Virginia Woolf: A Critical Reading,* pp. 69-95. Baltimore: Johns Hopkins University Press, 1975.
   Study of several themes in *Mrs. Dalloway* prefaced by the assertion that "as a series of experiments with the emergent techniques of perspectival narration, temporal discontinuity, and rhythmic juxtaposition of elements, *Mrs. Dalloway* may be considered the first important work of the literary period initiated by *Ulysses*—although hardly an advance upon it."

Gamble, Isabel. "The Secret Sharer in *Mrs. Dalloway.*" *Accent* XVI, No. 4 (Autumn 1956): 235-51.*
   Studies the theme of self-recognition in *Mrs. Dalloway* and Joseph Conrad's "The Secret Sharer."

Gelfant, Blanche H. "Love and Conversion in *Mrs. Dalloway.*" *Criticism* VIII, No. 3 (Summer 1966): 229-45.
   Investigates the struggle between forces of love and conversion in *Mrs. Dalloway.*

Henke, Suzette A. "*Mrs. Dalloway:* The Communion of Saints." In *New Feminist Essays on Virginia Woolf,* edited by Jane Marcus, pp. 125-47. Lincoln: University of Nebraska Press, 1981.
   Contends that "narrative action in *Mrs. Dalloway* is set in a . . . symbolic context of ritual sacrifice and eucharistic communion."

Hoffmann, Charles G. "From Short Story to Novel: The Manuscript Revisions of Virginia Woolf's *Mrs. Dalloway.*" *Modern Fiction Studies* XIV, No. 2 (Summer 1968): 171-86.
   Traces the development and revision of *Mrs. Dalloway* through an examination of Woolf's manuscript notebooks for the novel.

Kelley, Alice van Buren. "*Mrs. Dalloway.*" In her *The Novels of Virginia Woolf: Fact and Vision,* pp. 88-113. Chicago: University of Chicago Press, 1971.
   Study of the physical and spiritual worlds in *Mrs. Dalloway.*

Love, Jean O. "Preexistent Unity: *Mrs. Dalloway.*" In her *Worlds in Consciousness: Mythopoetic Thought in the Novels of Virginia Woolf,* pp. 145-60. Berkeley and Los Angeles: University of California Press, 1970.
   Examines *Mrs. Dalloway* as "the myth of preexistent and transcendent unity and consciousness Brahma-like or Mana-like, in which all men take part and are at one, even while they experience illusions of separateness."

Marcus, Jane, ed. *Virginia Woolf: A Feminist Slant.* Lincoln: University of Nebraska Press, 1983, 281 p.
   Compendium of biographical and critical studies of Woolf and her work by feminist writers. A 1983 essay by Emily Jensen from this collection is excerpted in the entry.

Miller, J. Hillis. "Virginia Woolf's All Souls' Day: The Omniscient Narrator in *Mrs. Dalloway.*" In *The Shaken Realist: Essays in Modern Literature in Honor of Frederick J. Hoffman,* edited by Melvin J. Friedman and John B. Vickery, pp. 100-27. Baton Rouge: Louisiana State University Press, 1970.
   Examines the narrative techniques Woolf used in *Mrs. Dalloway* and how they contribute to the development of the novel's themes. Miller also discusses writing as an ordering process in Woolf's life.

Moon, Kenneth. "Where is Clarissa? Doris Kilman and Recoil from the Flesh in Virginia Woolf's *Mrs. Dalloway.*" *CLA Journal* XXIII, No. 3 (March 1980): 273-86.
   Contends that insights into the character of Clarissa Dalloway are offered through that character's contact with Doris Kilman.

Oltean, Stefan. "Textual Functions of Free Indirect Discourse in the Novel *Mrs. Dalloway* by Virginia Woolf." *Revue Roumaine de Linguistique* XXVI, No. 6 (November-December 1981): 533-47.
   Examination of narrative techniques in *Mrs. Dalloway.*

Poresky, Louise A. "*Mrs. Dalloway:* The Privacy of the Soul." In her *The Elusive Self: Psyche and Spirit in Virginia Woolf's Novels,* pp. 98-125. Newark: University of Delaware Press, 1981.
   Discusses thematic similarities in the novels *Mrs. Dalloway* and *Jacob's Room,* noting the refined stylistic technique of *Mrs. Dalloway.*

Rice, Thomas Jackson. *Virginia Woolf: A Guide to Research.* New York: Garland Publishing, 1984, 258 p.
   Annotated bibliography of studies of Woolf's writings.

Richter, Harvena. "The Canonical Hours in *Mrs. Dalloway.*" *Modern Fiction Studies* 28, No. 2 (Summer 1982): 236-40.
   Correlates time referents in *Mrs. Dalloway* with those of monastic canonical hours.

Rosenberg, Stuart. "The Match in the Crocus: Obtrusive Art in Virginia Woolf's *Mrs. Dalloway*." *Modern Fiction Studies* XIII, No. 2 (Summer 1967): 211-20.
    Studies authorial intrusions into the narration of *Mrs. Dalloway*.

Ruotolo, Lucio. "*Mrs. Dalloway:* The Unguarded Moment." In *Virginia Woolf: Revaluation and Continuity,* edited by Ralph Freedman, pp. 141-60. Berkeley and Los Angeles: University of California Press, 1980.
    Detailed character study of Clarissa Dalloway.

Schaefer, Josephine O'Brien. "*Mrs. Dalloway:* 1925." In her *The Three-Fold Nature of Reality in the Novels of Virginia Woolf,* pp. 85-109. The Hague: Mouton, 1965.
    Finds *Mrs. Dalloway* to be a perfectly structured novel, comparable to those of Gustave Flaubert.

Schlack, Beverly Ann. "A Freudian Look at *Mrs. Dalloway*." *Literature and Psychology* XXIII, No. 2 (1973): 49-58.
    Freudian psychoanalytic study of character, imagery, and motivation in *Mrs. Dalloway*.

Thakur, N. C. "*Mrs. Dalloway*." In *The Symbolism of Virginia Woolf,* pp. 55-71. London: Oxford University Press, 1965.
    Examination of symbolism in *Mrs. Dalloway*.

Wright, Nathalia. "*Mrs. Dalloway:* A Study in Composition." *College English* 5, No. 7 (April 1944): 351-58.
    Technical study of character, temporal, and thematic patterns found in *Mrs. Dalloway*.

Wyatt, Jean M. "*Mrs. Dalloway:* Literary Allusion as Structural Metaphor." *PMLA* 88, No. 3 (May 1973): 440-51.
    Stresses the importance of literary allusion in *Mrs. Dalloway* to the novel's overall structure.

Appendix

The following is a listing of all sources used in Volume 20 of *Twentieth-Century Literary Criticism*. Included in this list are all copyright and reprint rights and acknowledgments for those essays for which permission was obtained. Every effort has been made to trace copyright, but if omissions have been made, please let us know.

THE EXCERPTS IN TCLC, VOLUME 20, WERE REPRINTED FROM THE FOLLOWING PERIODICALS:

The Academy, v. LIV, October 8, 1898.

The Adelphi, v. III, January, 1926.

The American Book Review, v. 1, April-May, 1978. © 1978 by *The American Book Review.* Reprinted by permission.

American Mercury, v. XXIII, July, 1931. Copyright 1931, renewed 1959, by American Mercury Magazine, Inc. Used by permission of The Enoch Pratt Free Library of Baltimore in accordance with the terms of the will of H. L. Mecken.

Art and Literature, n. 2, Summer, 1964 for "Conception and Reality in the Work of Raymond Roussel" by Michel Leiris, translated by John Ashbery. © 1967 by Art and Literature, SELA (Société Anonyme d'Editions Littéraires et Artistiques), 1000, Lausanne, Switzerland. Reprinted by permission of John Ashbery.

The Athenaeum, n. 4225, October 17, 1908; n. 4663, September 12, 1919.

Blackwood's Edinburgh Magazine, v. LXX, September, 1851.

The Bookman, New York, v. XXIX, June 1909; v. LXXV, November, 1932.

The Brooklyn Daily Eagle, July 22, 1847.

Bulletin of The Museum of Modern Art, v. XIII, September, 1946.

The University of California Chronicle, v. XXXI, October, 1929.

The Carmel Cymbal, November 24, 1926.

Commentary, v. 13, February, 1952 for "Lincoln Steffens: He Covered the Future" by Granville Hicks. Copyright © 1952, renewed 1980 by Granville Hicks. All rights reserved. Reprinted by permission of the publisher and Russell & Volkening, Inc. as agents for the author.

Adams, Robert Martin. From *After Joyce: Studies in Fiction After "Ulysses."* Oxford University Press, 1977. Copyright © 1977 by Robert Martin Adams. Reprinted by permission of Oxford University Press, Inc.

Adcock, A. St. John. From *Gods of Modern Grub Street: Impressions of Contemporary Authors.* Frederick A. Stokes Company, 1923. Copyright 1923 by Harper & Row, Publishers, Inc. Renewed 1950 by Mrs. St. John Adcock. Reprinted by permission of Harper & Row, Publishers, Inc.

Alexander, Calvert, S.J. From *The Catholic Literary Revival: Three Phases in Its Development from 1845 to the Present.* The Bruce Publishing Company, 1935.

Alter, Robert. From *Defenses of the Imagination: Jewish Writers and Modern Historical Crisis.* Jewish Publication Society of America, 1977. Copyright © 1977 by The Jewish Publication Society. All rights reserved. Used through the courtesy of The Jewish Publication Society and the author.

Anderson, Rachel. From an introduction to *Joanna Godden.* By Sheila Kaye-Smith. Virago Press Limited, 1983. Introduction copyright © Rachel Anderson 1983. All rights reserved. Reprinted by permission.

Apter, T. E. From *Virginia Woolf: A Study of Her Novels.* New York University Press, 1979. Copyright © 1979 by T. E. Apter. All rights reserved. Reprinted by permission of New York University Press.

Barooshian, Vahan D. From *Russian Cubo-Futurism, 1910-1930: A Study in Avant-Gardism.* Mouton, 1974. © copyright 1974 Mouton & Co., Publishers. Reprinted by permission of Mouton Publishers, a Division of Walter de Gruyter & Co.

Behrman, S. N. From *The Suspended Drawing Room.* Stein and Day, 1965. Copyright 1965 by S. N. Behrman. All rights reserved. Reprinted with permission of Stein and Day Publishers.

Benediktsson, Thomas E. From *George Sterling.* Twayne, 1980. Copyright 1980 by Twayne Publishers. All rights reserved. Reprinted with the permission of Twayne Publishers, a division of G. K. Hall & Co., Boston.

Blackstone, Bernard. From *Virginia Woolf: A Commentary.* The Hogarth Press, 1949.

Bloom, Harold. From an introduction to *The Literary Criticism of John Ruskin.* By John Ruskin, edited by Harold Bloom. Anchor Books, 1965. Copyright © 1965 by Harold Bloom. All rights reserved. Reprinted by permission of Doubleday & Company, Inc.

Braybrooke, Patrick. From *Some Goddesses of the Pen.* The C. W. Daniel Company, 1927.

Breton, André. From "'Anthology of Black Humour'," translated by Stephen Schwartz, in *What Is Surrealism? Selected Writings.* Edited by Franklin Rosemont. Monda, 1978. Copyright © 1978 by Franklin Rosemont. All rights reserved. Reprinted by permission.

Brower, Reuben Arthur. From *The Fields of Light: An Experiment in Critical Reading.* Oxford University Press, 1951. Copyright 1951 by Oxford University Press, Inc. Renewed 1979 by Helen P. Brower. Reprinted by permission of the publisher.

Brown, Edward J. From an introduction to *Snake Train: Poetry and Prose.* By Velimir Khlebnikov, edited by Gary Kern, translated by Gary Kern & others. Ardis, 1976. © 1976 by Ardis Publishers. Reprinted by permission.

Brushwood, John S. From "The Spanish American Short Story from Quiroga to Borges," in *The Latin American Short Story: A Critical History.* Edited by Margaret Sayers Peden. Twayne, 1983. Copyright 1983 by Twayne Publishers. All rights reserved. Reprinted with the permission of Twayne Publishers, a division of G. K. Hall & Co., Boston.

Burlyuk, David, Alexey Kruchonykh, Vladimir Mayakovsky, and Velimir Khlebnikov. From "A Slap in the Face of Public Taste," translated by Alexander Kaun, in *Soviet Poets and Poetry.* By Alexander Kaun. University of California Press, 1943.

Campana, Dino. From a letter to Giuseppe Prezzolini on January 6, 1914, in *Orphic Songs.* By Dino Campana, translated by I. L. Salomon. October House Inc., 1968. Copyright © 1968 by I. L. Salomon. Reprinted by permission.

Carlyle, Thomas. From an extract from a letter to Ralph Waldo Emerson on April 2, 1872, in *The Correspondence of Thomas Carlyle and Ralph Waldo Emerson, 1834-1872, Vol. II.* Edited by C. E. Norton. James R. Osgood and Company, 1883.

Cavaliero, Glen. From *The Rural Tradition in the English Novel, 1900-1939.* Rowman and Littlefield, 1977. © Glen Cavaliero 1977. All rights reserved. Reprinted by permission.

Chandler, Frank W. From *Modern Continental Playwrights*. Harper & Brothers, 1931. Copyright, 1931, by Harper & Row, Publishers, Inc. Renewed 1958 by Adele Chandler. Reprinted by permission of Harper & Row, Publishers, Inc.

Clark, Sir Kenneth. From *Ruskin at Oxford*. Oxford at the Clarendon Press, Oxford, 1947.

Cocteau, Jean. From *Opium: The Diary of a Cure*. Translated by Margaret Crosland and Sinclair Road. Revised edition. Peter Owen Limited, London, 1968. Translation © Margaret Crosland and Sinclair Road 1957, 1968. Reprinted by permission.

Collingwood, R. G. From *Ruskin's Philosophy*. Titus Wilson & Son, Publishers, 1922.

Costich, Julia Field. From *The Poetry of Change: A Study of Surrealist Works of Benjamin Péret*. North Carolina Studies in the Romance Languages and Literatures, 1979. Reprinted by permission of The University of North Carolina Press.

Daiches, David. From *The Novel and the Modern World*. Revised edition. University of Chicago Press, 1960. © 1960 by The University of Chicago. Reprinted by permission of The University of Chicago Press and the author.

Dreiser, Theodore. From an introduction to *Lilth: A Dramatic Poem*. By George Sterling. The Macmillan Company, 1926.

Drew, Elizabeth A. From *The Modern Novel: Some Aspects of Contemporary Fiction*. Harcourt Brace Jovanovich, 1926. Copyright, 1926, by Harcourt Brace Jovanovich, Inc. Renewed 1953 by Elizabeth A. Drew. Reprinted by permission of the publisher.

Dunham, Barrows. From an introduction to *The World of Lincoln Steffens*. By Lincoln Steffens, edited by Ella Winter and Herbert Shapiro. Hill and Wang, 1962. Copyright © 1962 by Hill and Wang, Inc. All rights reserved. Reprinted by permission of Hill and Wang, a division of Farrar, Straus and Giroux, Inc.

Englekirk, John Eugene. From *Edgar Allen Poe in Hispanic Literature*. Instituto de las Españas, 1934.

Erskine, John. From a preface to *The Book of Monelle*. By Marcel Schwob, translated by William Brown Meloney, V. The Bobbs-Merrill Company, 1929. Copyright, 1929, renewed 1956, by William Brown Meloney, V. Reprinted with permission of Macmillan Publishing Company.

Foucault, Michel. From *Death and the Labyrinth: The World of Raymond Roussel*. Translated by Charles Ruas. Doubleday, 1986. English translation copyright © 1986 by Doubleday & Company, Inc. All rights reserved. Reprinted by permission of the publisher.

France, Anatole. From *On Life & Letters, fourth series*. Edited by J. Lewis May and Bernard Miall, translated by Bernard Miall. Dodd, Mead and Company, Inc., 1924.

Franco, Jean. From *An Introduction to Spanish-American Literature*. Cambridge at the University Press, 1969. © Cambridge University Press 1969. Reprinted by permission.

Garrigan, Kristine Ottesen. From *Ruskin on Architecture: His Thought and Influence*. The University of Wisconsin Press, 1973. Copyright © 1973 The Regents of the University of Wisconsin System. All rights reserved. Reprinted by permission.

George, W. L. From *Literary Chapters*. Little, Brown, 1918. Copyright, 1918, by W. L. George. Renewed 1946 by the Literary Estate of W. L. George. All rights reserved. Reprinted by permission of Little, Brown and Company.

Gergley, Emro Joseph. From *Hungarian Drama in New York: American Adaptations, 1908-1940*. University of Pennsylvania Press, 1947. Copyright 1947, renewed 1974, by Emro Joseph Gergely. Reprinted by permission of the author.

Gershman, Herbert S. From *The Surrealist Revolution in France*. The University of Michigan Press, 1969. Copyright © by Herbert S. Gershman 1969. All rights reserved. Reprinted by permission.

Golino, Carlo L. From a preface to *Contemporary Italian Poetry: An Anthology*. Edited by Carlo L. Golino. University of California Press, 1962. Copyright © 1962 by The Regents of the University of California. Reprinted by permission of the University of California Press.

Gordon, Lyndall. From *Virginia Woolf: A Writer's Life*. Norton, 1984. Copyright © 1984 by Lyndall Gordon. All rights reserved. Reprinted by permission of W. W. Norton & Company, Inc.

Greene, Henry Copley. From a preface to *The Children's Crusade*. By Marcel Schwob, translated by Henry Copley Greene. Thomas B. Mosher, 1905.

Györgyey, Clara. From *Ferenc Molnár*. Twayne, 1980. Copyright 1980 by Twayne Publishers. All rights reserved. Reprinted with the permission of Twayne Publishers, a division of G. K. Hall & Co., Boston.

Hafley, James. From *The Glass Roof: Virginia Woolf as Novelist*. University of California Press, 1954.

Meloney, William Brown, V. From an introduction to *The Book of Monelle*. By Marcel Schwob, translated by William Brown Meloney, V. The Bobbs-Merrill Company, 1929. Copyright, 1929, renewed 1956, by William Brown Meloney, V. Reprinted with permission of Macmillan Publishing Company.

Mencken, H. L. From *Prejudices, first series*. Knopf, 1919. Copyright 1919 by Alfred A. Knopf, Inc. Renewed 1947 by H. L. Mencken. Reprinted by permission of the publisher.

Montale, Eugenio. From *The Second Life of Art: Selected Essays of Eugenio Montale*. Edited and translated by Jonathan Galassi. The Ecco Press, 1982. Translations copyright © 1977, 1978, 1979, 1980, 1981, 1982 by Jonathan Galassi. All rights reserved. Reprinted by permission.

Montefiore, Janet. From an introduction to *The History of Susan Spray: The Female Preacher*. By Sheila Kaye-Smith. Virago Press Limited, 1983. Introduction copyright © Janet Montefiore 1983. All rights reserved. Reprinted by permission.

Nims, John Frederick. From "Dino Campana (1885-1932)," in *The Poem Itself*. Edited by Stanley Burnshaw & others. Holt, Rinehart and Winston, 1960. Copyright © 1960 by Stanley Burnshaw. All rights reserved. Reprinted by permission of Henry Holt and Company, Inc.

Palermo, Patrick F. From *Lincoln Steffens*. Twayne, 1978. Copyright 1978 by Twayne Publishers. All rights reserved. Reprinted with the permission of Twayne Publishers, a division of G. K. Hall & Co., Boston.

Pendry, E. D. From *The New Feminism of English Fiction: A Study in Contemporary Women-Novelists*. Kenkyusha Ltd., 1956.

Poggioli, Renato. From *The Poets of Russia: 1890-1930*. Cambridge, Mass.: Harvard University Press, 1960. Copyright © 1960 by the President and Fellows of Harvard College. Excerpted by permission.

Regier, C. C. From *The Era of the Muckrakers*. The University of North Carolina Press, 1932.

Robbe-Grillet, Alain. From *For a New Novel: Essays on Fiction*. Translated by Richard Howard. Grove Press, 1966. Copyright © 1965 by Grove Press, Inc. All rights reserved. Reprinted by permission of Grove Press, Inc.

Roby, Kinley E. From *A Writer at War: Arnold Bennett 1914-1918*. Louisiana State University Press, 1972. Copyright © 1972 by Louisiana State University Press. All rights reserved. Reprinted by permission of Louisiana State University Press.

Rosenberg, John D. From *The Darkening Glass: A Portrait of Ruskin's Genius*. Columbia University Press, 1961. Copyright © 1961 Columbia University Press. Reprinted by permission of the publisher.

Roudiez, Leon S. From *French Fiction Today: A New Direction*. Rutgers University Press, 1972. Copyright © 1972 by Rutgers University, The State University of New Jersey. Reprinted by permission of Rutgers University Press.

Roussel, Raymond. From "How I Wrote Certain of My Books," translated by Trevor Winkfield, in *How I Wrote Certain of My Books*. By Raymond Roussel. Sun, 1977. © 1977 Sun. Reprinted by permission.

Salomon, I. L. From an introduction to *Orphic Songs*. By Dino Campana, translated by I. L. Salomon. October House Inc., 1968. Copyright © 1968 by I. L. Salomon. Reprinted by permission.

Sandburg, Carl. From a memorandum to *The Letters of Lincoln Steffens: 1889-1919, Vol. I*. By Lincoln Steffens, edited by Ella Winter and Granville Hicks. Harcourt Brace Jovanovich, 1938. Copyright, 1938, by Harcourt Brace Jovanovich, Inc. Renewed 1966 by Ella Winter, Granville Hicks, and Carl Sandburg. Reprinted by permission of the publisher.

Savage, D. S. From *The Withered Branch: Six Studies in the Modern Novel*. Eyre & Spottiswoode, 1950.

Schade, George D. From an introduction to *The Decapitated Chicken and Other Stories*. By Horacio Quiroga, edited and translated by Margaret Sayers Peden. University of Texas Press, 1976. Copyright © 1976 by the University of Texas Press. All rights reserved. Reprinted by permission of the publisher and George D. Schade.

Schlant, Ernestine. From *Hermann Broch*. Twayne, 1978. Copyright 1978 by Twayne Publishers. All rights reserved. Reprinted with the permission of Twayne Publishers, a division of G. K. Hall & Co., Boston.

Schmidt, Paul. From editorial comments in *The King of Time: Selected Writings of the Russian Futurian*. By Velimar Khlebnikov, edited by Charlotte Douglas, translated by Paul Schmidt. Cambridge, Mass.: Harvard University Press, 1985. Copyright © 1985 by the Dia Art Foundation. All rights reserved. Excerpted by permission of the publishers.

Shaw, Bernard. From *Ruskin's Politics*. Christophers, 1921.

Sherburne, James Clark. From *John Ruskin, or the Ambiguities of Abundance: A Study in Social and Economic Criticism*. Cambridge, Mass.: Harvard University Press, 1972. Copyright © 1972 by the President and Fellows of Harvard College. All rights reserved. Excerpted by permission.

Sonstroem, David. From ''Prophet and Peripatetic in 'Modern Painters' III and IV,'' in *Studies in Ruskin: Essays in Honor of Van Akin Burd*. Edited by Robert Rhodes and Del Ivan Janik. Ohio University Press, 1982. © copyright 1982 by Ohio University Press. All rights reserved. Reprinted by permission of David Sonstroem.

Spell, Jefferson Rea. From *Contemporary Spanish-American Fiction*. University of North Carolina Press, 1944. Copyright, 1944, The University of North Carolina Press. Renewed 1972 by Lota Rea Wilkinson. Reprinted by permission.

Starr, Kevin. From *Americans and the California Dream: 1850-1915*. Oxford University Press, 1973. Copyright © 1973 by Oxford University Press, Inc. Reprinted by permission.

Steffens, Lincoln. From ''Introduction: And Some Conclusions,'' in *The Shame of the Cities*. By Lincoln Steffens. McClure, Phillips & Co., 1904.

Stein, Richard L. From an introduction to *The Ritual of Interpretation: The Fine Arts as Literature in Ruskin, Rossetti, and Pater*. By Richard L. Stein. Cambridge, Mass.: Harvard University Press, 1975. Copyright © 1975 by the President and Fellows of Harvard College. All rights reserved. Excerpted by permission.

Stevenson, Robert Louis. From a letter to Marcel Schwob on July 7, 1894, in *The Letters to Robert Louis Stevenson to His Family and Friends, Vol. II*. Charles Scribner's Sons, 1899.

Stinson, Robert. From *Lincoln Steffens*. Ungar, 1979. Copyright © 1979 by Frederick Ungar Publishing Co., Inc. Reprinted by permission.

Stone, Donald D. From ''The Art of Arnold Bennett: Transmutation and Empathy in 'Anna of the Five Towns' and 'Riceyman Steps','' in *Modernism Reconsidered*. Harvard English Studies 11. Edited by Robert Kiely with John Hildebidle. Cambridge, Mass.: Harvard University Press, 1983. Copyright 1983 by the President and Fellows of Harvard College. All rights reserved. Excerpted by permission.

Thompson, Vance. From *French Portraits: Being Appreciations of the Writers of Young France*. Richard G. Badger & Co., 1900.

Thomson, Boris. From *Lot's Wife and the Venus of Milo: Conflicting Attitudes to the Cultural Heritage in Modern Russia*. Cambridge University Press, 1978. © Cambridge University Press 1978. Reprinted by permission of Cambridge University Press.

Tynyanov, Yury. From ''On Khlebnikov,'' translated by Charlotte Rosenthal, in *Major Soviet Writers: Essays in Criticism*. Edited by Edward J. Brown. Oxford University Press, 1973. Copyright © 1973 by Oxford University Press, Inc. Reprinted by permission.

Untermeyer, Louis. From *American Poetry Since 1900*. Holt, Rinehart & Winston, 1923. Copyright 1923 by Holt, Rinehart & Winston. Renewed 1951 by Louis Untermeyer. Reprinted by permission of Holt, Rinehart & Winston, Publishers.

Vroon, Ronald. From *Velimir Xlebnikov's Shorter Poems: A Key to the Coinages*. Department of Slavic Languages and Literatures, The University of Michigan, 1983. © 1983 by University of Michigan. Reprinted by permission.

Walker, Dorothea. From *Sheila Kaye-Smith*. Twayne, 1980. Copyright 1980 by Twayne Publishers. All rights reserved. Reprinted with the permission of Twayne Publishers, a division of G. K. Hall & Co., Boston.

West, Rebecca. From *Arnold Bennett Himself*. The John Day Company, 1931.

Wilenski, R. H. From *John Ruskin: An Introduction to Further Study of His Life and Work*. Faber and Faber Ltd., 1933.

Winter, Ella. From a preface to *The World of Lincoln Steffens*. By Lincoln Steffens, edited by Ella Winter and Herbert Shapiro. Hill and Wang, 1962. Copyright © 1962 by Hill and Wang, Inc. All rights reserved. Reprinted by permission of Hill and Wang, a division of Farrar, Straus and Giroux, Inc.

Woolf, Virginia. From *The Common Reader*. Harcourt Brace Jovanovich, 1925, L & V. Woolf, 1925. Copyright 1925 by Harcourt Brace Jovanovich, Inc. Renewed 1953 by Leonard Woolf. Reprinted by permission of Harcourt Brace Jovanovich, Inc. In Canada by the author's Literary Estate and The Hogarth Press.

Woolf, Virginia. From a diary entry of June 18, 1925, in *The Diary of Virginia Woolf: 1925-1930, Vol. 3*. By Virginia Woolf, edited by Anne Olivier Bell. Harcourt Brace Jovanovich, 1980, Hogarth Press, 1980. Diary and appendix II copyright © 1980 by Quentin Bell and Angelica Garnett. Reprinted by permission of Harcourt Brace Jovanovich, Inc. In Canada by the Literary Estate of Virginia Woolf and The Hogarth Press.

Woolf, Virginia. From an introduction to *Mrs. Dalloway*. By Virginia Woolf. The Modern Library, 1928.

Cumulative Index to Authors

This index lists all author entries in the Gale Literary Criticism Series and includes cross-references to other Gale sources. References in the index are identified as follows:

AITN: *Authors in the News*, Volumes 1-2

CAAS: *Contemporary Authors Autobiography Series*, Volumes 1-3

CA: *Contemporary Authors* (original series), Volumes 1-117

CANR: *Contemporary Authors New Revision Series*, Volumes 1-17

CAP: *Contemporary Authors Permanent Series*, Volumes 1-2

CA-R: *Contemporary Authors* (revised editions), Volumes 1-44

CLC: *Contemporary Literary Criticism*, Volumes 1-37

CLR: *Children's Literature Review*, Volumes 1-10

DLB: *Dictionary of Literary Biography*, Volumes 1-47

DLB-DS: *Dictionary of Literary Biography Documentary Series*, Volumes 1-4

DLB-Y: *Dictionary of Literary Biography Yearbook*, Volumes 1980-1984

LC: *Literature Criticism from 1400 to 1800*, Volumes 1-3

NCLC: *Nineteenth-Century Literature Criticism*, Volumes 1-12

SAAS: *Something about the Author Autobiography Series*, Volume 1

SATA: *Something about the Author*, Volumes 1-43

TCLC: *Twentieth-Century Literary Criticism*, Volumes 1-20

YABC: *Yesterday's Authors of Books for Children*, Volumes 1-2

A. E. 1867-1935 . . . . TCLC **3, 10**
See also Russell, George William
See also DLB 19

Abbey, Edward 1927- . . . . CLC **36**
See also CANR 2
See also CA 45-48

Abé, Kōbō 1924- . . . . CLC **8, 22**
See also CA 65-68

Abell, Kjeld 1901-1961 . . . . CLC **15**
See also obituary CA 111

Abish, Walter 1931- . . . . CLC **22**
See also CA 101

Abrahams, Peter (Henry) 1919- . . . . . CLC **4**
See also CA 57-60

Abrams, M(eyer) H(oward)
1912- . . . . CLC **24**
See also CANR 13
See also CA 57-60

Abse, Dannie 1923- . . . . CLC **7, 29**
See also CAAS 1
See also CANR 4
See also CA 53-56
See also DLB 27

Achebe, Chinua
1930- . . . . CLC **1, 3, 5, 7, 11, 26**
See also CANR 6
See also CA 1-4R
See also SATA 38, 40

Ackroyd, Peter 1917- . . . . CLC **34**
See also CA 25-28R

Acorn, Milton 1923- . . . . CLC **15**
See also CA 103
See also AITN 2

Adamov, Arthur 1908-1970 . . . . . CLC **4, 25**
See also CAP 2
See also CA 17-18
See also obituary CA 25-28R

Adams, Alice (Boyd) 1926- . . . . . . CLC **6, 13**
See also CA 81-84

Adams, Douglas (Noel) 1952- . . . . CLC **27**
See also CA 106
See also DLB-Y 83

Adams, Henry (Brooks)
1838-1918 . . . . TCLC **4**
See also CA 104
See also DLB 12, 47

Adams, Richard (George)
1920- . . . . CLC **4, 5, 18**
See also CANR 3
See also CA 49-52
See also SATA 7
See also AITN 1, 2

Adamson, Joy(-Friederike Victoria)
1910-1980 . . . . CLC **17**
See also CA 69-72
See also obituary CA 93-96
See also SATA 11
See also obituary SATA 22

Addams, Charles (Samuel)
1912- . . . . CLC **30**
See also CANR 12
See also CA 61-64

Adler, C(arole) S(chwerdtfeger)
1932- . . . . CLC **35**
See also CA 89-92
See also SATA 26

Adler, Renata 1938- . . . . CLC **8, 31**
See also CANR 5
See also CA 49-52

Ady, Endre 1877-1919 . . . . TCLC **11**
See also CA 107

Agee, James 1909-1955 . . . . TCLC **1, 19**
See also CA 108
See also DLB 2, 26
See also AITN 1

Agnon, S(hmuel) Y(osef Halevi)
1888-1970 . . . . CLC **4, 8, 14**
See also CAP 2
See also CA 17-18
See also obituary CA 25-28R

Ai 1947- . . . . CLC **4, 14**
See also CA 85-88

Aiken, Conrad (Potter)
1889-1973 . . . . CLC **1, 3, 5, 10**
See also CANR 4
See also CA 5-8R
See also obituary CA 45-48
See also SATA 3, 30
See also DLB 9, 45

Aiken, Joan (Delano) 1924- . . . . CLC **35**
See also CLR 1
See also CANR 4
See also CA 9-12R
See also SAAS 1
See also SATA 2, 30

Ajar, Emile 1914-1980
See Gary, Romain

Akhmatova, Anna
   1888-1966. . . . . CLC 11, 25
   See also CAP 1
   See also CA 19-20
   See also obituary CA 25-28R

Aksakov, Sergei Timofeyvich
   1791-1859. . . . . NCLC 2

Aksenov, Vassily (Pavlovich) 1932-
   See Aksyonor, Vasily (Pavlovich)

Aksyonov, Vasily (Pavlovich)
   1932-. . . . . CLC 22, 37
   See also CANR 12
   See also CA 53-56

Akutagawa Ryūnosuke
   1892-1927. . . . . TCLC 16

Alain-Fournier 1886-1914 . . . . TCLC 6
   See also Fournier, Henri Alban

Alarcón, Pedro Antonio de
   1833-1891. . . . . NCLC 1

Albee, Edward (Franklin III)
   1928-. . . . . CLC 1, 2, 3, 5, 9, 11, 13, 25
   See also CANR 8
   See also CA 5-8R
   See also DLB 7
   See also AITN 1

Alberti, Rafael 1902-. . . . . CLC 7
   See also CA 85-88

Alcott, Amos Bronson
   1799-1888. . . . . NCLC 1
   See also DLB 1

Alcott, Louisa May 1832-1888. . . . . NCLC 6
   See also CLR 1
   See also YABC 1
   See also DLB 1, 42

Aldiss, Brian (Wilson) 1925- . . . . CLC 5, 14
   See also CAAS 2
   See also CANR 5
   See also CA 5-8R
   See also SATA 34
   See also DLB 14

Aleichem, Sholom 1859-1916. . . . . . TCLC 1
   See also Rabinovitch, Sholem

Aleixandre, Vicente
   1898-1984. . . . . CLC 9, 36
   See also CA 85-88
   See also obituary CA 114

Alepoudelis, Odysseus 1911-
   See Elytis, Odysseus

Alexander, Lloyd (Chudley)
   1924-. . . . . CLC 35
   See also CLR 1, 5
   See also CANR 1
   See also CA 1-4R
   See also SATA 3

Alger, Horatio, Jr. 1832-1899. . . . . NCLC 8
   See also SATA 16
   See also DLB 42

Algren, Nelson
   1909-1981. . . . . CLC 4, 10, 33
   See also CA 13-16R
   See also obituary CA 103
   See also DLB 9
   See also DLB-Y 81, 82

Allen, Heywood 1935-
   See Allen, Woody
   See also CA 33-36R

Allen, Roland 1939-
   See Ayckbourn, Alan

Allen, Woody 1935-. . . . . .CLC 16
   See also Allen, Heywood
   See also DLB 44

Allingham, Margery (Louise)
   1904-1966. . . . . .CLC 19
   See also CANR 4
   See also CA 5-8R
   See also obituary CA 25-28R

Allston, Washington
   1779-1843. . . . . NCLC 2
   See also DLB 1

Almedingen, E. M. 1898-1971. . . . . .CLC 12
   See also Almedingen, Martha Edith von
   See also SATA 3

Almedingen, Martha Edith von 1898-1971
   See Almedingen, E. M.
   See also CANR 1
   See also CA 1-4R

Alonso, Dámaso 1898-. . . . . .CLC 14
   See also CA 110

Alta 1942-. . . . . .CLC 19
   See also CA 57-60

Alter, Robert 1935-. . . . . .CLC 34
   See also CANR 1
   See also CA 49-52

Alther, Lisa 1944- . . . . .CLC 7
   See also CANR 12
   See also CA 65-68

Altman, Robert 1925-. . . . . .CLC 16
   See also CA 73-76

Alvarez, A(lfred) 1929-. . . . . CLC 5, 13
   See also CANR 3
   See also CA 1-4R
   See also DLB 14, 40

Amado, Jorge 1912- . . . . .CLC 13
   See also CA 77-80

Ambler, Eric 1909- . . . . CLC 4, 6, 9
   See also CANR 7
   See also CA 9-12R

Amichai, Yehuda 1924- . . . . CLC 9, 22
   See also CA 85-88

Amiel, Henri Frédéric
   1821-1881. . . . . NCLC 4

Amis, Kingsley (William)
   1922-. . . . . CLC 1, 2, 3, 5, 8, 13
   See also CANR 8
   See also CA 9-12R
   See also DLB 15, 27
   See also AITN 2

Amis, Martin 1949-. . . . . CLC 4, 9
   See also CANR 8
   See also CA 65-68
   See also DLB 14

Ammons, A(rchie) R(andolph)
   1926-. . . . . CLC 2, 3, 5, 8, 9, 25
   See also CANR 6
   See also CA 9-12R
   See also DLB 5
   See also AITN 1

Anand, Mulk Raj 1905- . . . . .CLC 23
   See also CA 65-68

Anaya, Rudolfo A(lfonso)
   1937-. .CLC 23
   See also CANR 1
   See also CA 45-48

Andersen, Hans Christian
   1805-1875. . . . . NCLC 7
   See also CLR 6
   See also YABC 1

Anderson, Jessica (Margaret Queale)
   19??-. . . . . .CLC 37
   See also CANR 4
   See also CA 9-12R

Anderson, Jon (Victor) 1940- . . . . . .CLC 9
   See also CA 25-28R

Anderson, Lindsay 1923- . . . . .CLC 20

Anderson, Maxwell 1888-1959 . . . . TCLC 2
   See also CA 105
   See also DLB 7

Anderson, Poul (William)
   1926-. .CLC 15
   See also CAAS 2
   See also CANR 2, 15
   See also CA 1-4R
   See also SATA 39
   See also DLB 8

Anderson, Robert (Woodruff)
   1917-. . . . . .CLC 23
   See also CA 21-24R
   See also DLB 7
   See also AITN 1

Anderson, Roberta Joan 1943-
   See Mitchell, Joni

Anderson, Sherwood
   1876-1941. . . . . TCLC 1, 10
   See also CA 104
   See also DLB 4, 9
   See also DLB-DS 1

Andrade, Carlos Drummond de
   1902-. . . . . .CLC 18

Andrews, Cicily Fairfield 1892-1983
   See West, Rebecca

Andreyev, Leonid (Nikolaevich)
   1871-1919. . . . . TCLC 3
   See also CA 104

Andrézel, Pierre 1885-1962
   See Dinesen, Isak
   See also Blixen, Karen (Christentze
   Dinesen)

Andrić, Ivo 1892-1975 . . . . .CLC 8
   See also CA 81-84
   See also obituary CA 57-60

Angelique, Pierre 1897-1962
   See Bataille, Georges

Angell, Roger 1920-. . . . . .CLC 26
   See also CANR 13
   See also CA 57-60

Angelou, Maya 1928- . . . . CLC 12, 35
   See also CA 65-68
   See also DLB 38

Annensky, Innokenty
   1856-1909. . . . . TCLC 14
   See also CA 110

Anouilh, Jean (Marie Lucien Pierre)
   1910-. . . . . .CLC 1, 3, 8, 13
   See also CA 17-20R

Anthony, Florence 1947-
   See Ai

Anthony (Jacob), Piers 1934-. . . . . . .CLC 35
   See also Jacob, Piers A(nthony)
   D(illingham)
   See also DLB 8

Antoninus, Brother 1912-
  See Everson, William (Oliver)

Antonioni, Michelangelo 1912- . . . . .CLC **20**
  See also CA 73-76

Antschel, Paul 1920-1970
  See Celan, Paul
  See also CA 85-88

Apollinaire, Guillaume
  1880-1918. . . . . .TCLC **3, 8**
  See also Kostrowitzki, Wilhelm Apollinaris
  de

Appelfeld, Aharon 1932- . . . . .CLC **23**
  See also CA 112

Apple, Max (Isaac) 1941- . . . . CLC **9, 33**
  See also CA 81-84

Aquin, Hubert 1929-1977. . . . . .CLC **15**
  See also CA 105

Aragon, Louis 1897-1982. . . . . . . CLC **3, 22**
  See also CA 69-72
  See also obituary CA 108

Arbuthnot, John 1667-1735. . . . . .LC **1**

Archer, Jeffrey (Howard)
  1940- . . . . .CLC **28**
  See also CA 77-80

Archer, Jules 1915- . . . . .CLC **12**
  See also CANR 6
  See also CA 9-12R
  See also SATA 4

Arden, John 1930- . . . . CLC **6, 13, 15**
  See also CA 13-16R
  See also DLB 13

Arguedas, José María
  1911-1969. . . . . CLC **10, 18**
  See also CA 89-92

Argueta, Manlio 1936- . . . . .CLC **31**

Armah, Ayi Kwei 1939- . . . . CLC **5, 33**
  See also CA 61-64

Armatrading, Joan 1950- . . . . .CLC **17**
  See also CA 114

Arnim, Achim von 1781-1831 . . . . . NCLC **5**

Arnold, Matthew 1822-1888 . . . . . . NCLC **6**
  See also DLB 32

Arnow, Harriette (Louisa Simpson)
  1908- . . . . CLC **2, 7, 18**
  See also CANR 14
  See also CA 9-12R
  See also DLB 6
  See also SATA 42

Arp, Jean 1887-1966. . . . . .CLC **5**
  See also CA 81-84
  See also obituary CA 25-28R

Arquette, Lois S(teinmetz)
  See Duncan (Steinmetz Arquette), Lois
  See also SATA 1

Arrabal, Fernando 1932- . . . . . CLC **2, 9, 18**
  See also CANR 15
  See also CA 9-12R

Arrick, Fran . . . . .CLC **30**

Artaud, Antonin 1896-1948 . . . . TCLC **3**
  See also CA 104

Arthur, Ruth M(abel)
  1905-1979. .CLC **12**
  See also CANR 4
  See also CA 9-12R
  See also obituary CA 85-88
  See also SATA 7
  See also obituary SATA 26

Arundel, Honor (Morfydd)
  1919-1973. . . . . .CLC **17**
  See also CAP 2
  See also CA 21-22
  See also obituary CA 41-44R
  See also SATA 4
  See also obituary SATA 24

Asch, Sholem 1880-1957. . . . . TCLC **3**
  See also CA 105

Ashbery, John (Lawrence)
  1927- . . . . . CLC **2, 3, 4, 6, 9, 13, 15, 25**
  See also CANR 9
  See also CA 5-8R
  See also DLB 5
  See also DLB-Y 81

Ashton-Warner, Sylvia (Constance)
  1908-1984. . . . . .CLC **19**
  See also CA 69-72
  See also obituary CA 112

Asimov, Isaac
  1920- . . . . CLC **1, 3, 9, 19, 26**
  See also CANR 2
  See also CA 1-4R
  See also SATA 1, 26
  See also DLB 8

Aston, James 1906-1964
  See White, T(erence) H(anbury)

Asturias, Miguel Ángel
  1899-1974. . . . . CLC **3, 8, 13**
  See also CAP 2
  See also CA 25-28
  See also obituary CA 49-52

Atheling, William, Jr. 1921-1975
  See Blish, James (Benjamin)

Atherton, Gertrude (Franklin Horn)
  1857-1948. . . . . .TCLC **2**
  See also CA 104
  See also DLB 9

Atwood, Margaret (Eleanor)
  1939- . . . . .CLC **2, 3, 4, 8, 13, 15, 25**
  See also CANR 3
  See also CA 49-52

Auchincloss, Louis (Stanton)
  1917- . . . . .CLC **4, 6, 9, 18**
  See also CANR 6
  See also CA 1-4R
  See also DLB 2
  See also DLB-Y 80

Auden, W(ystan) H(ugh)
  1907-1973. . . . . CLC **1, 2, 3, 4, 6, 9,
                                            11, 14**
  See also CANR 5
  See also CA 9-12R
  See also obituary CA 45-48
  See also DLB 10, 20

Auel, Jean M(arie) 1936- . . . . .CLC **31**
  See also CA 103

Austen, Jane 1775-1817 . . . . NCLC **1**

Avison, Margaret 1918- . . . . CLC **2, 4**
  See also CA 17-20R

Ayckbourn, Alan
  1939- . . . . .CLC **5, 8, 18, 33**
  See also CA 21-24R
  See also DLB 13

Aymé, Marcel (Andre)
  1902-1967. .CLC **11**
  See also CA 89-92

Ayrton, Michael 1921-1975 . . . . .CLC **7**
  See also CANR 9
  See also CA 5-8R
  See also obituary CA 61-64

Azorín 1874-1967. . . . . .CLC **11**
  See also Martínez Ruiz, José

Azuela, Mariano 1873-1952. . . . . . . TCLC **3**
  See also CA 104

"Bab" 1836-1911
  See Gilbert, (Sir) W(illiam) S(chwenck)

Babel, Isaak (Emmanuilovich)
  1894-1941. . . . . .TCLC **2, 13**
  See also CA 104

Babits, Mihály 1883-1941. . . . . . . TCLC **14**
  See also CA 114

Bacchelli, Riccardo 1891- . . . . .CLC **19**
  See also CA 29-32R

Bach, Richard (David) 1936- . . . . . . .CLC **14**
  See also CA 9-12R
  See also SATA 13
  See also AITN 1

Bachman, Richard 1947-
  See King, Stephen (Edwin)

Bagehot, Walter 1826-1877 . . . . . . NCLC **10**

Bagnold, Enid 1889-1981 . . . . .CLC **25**
  See also CANR 5
  See also CA 5-8R
  See also obituary CA 103
  See also SATA 1, 25
  See also DLB 13

Bagryana, Elisaveta 1893- . . . . .CLC **10**

Baillie, Joanna 1762-1851 . . . . NCLC **2**

Bainbridge, Beryl
  1933- . . . . . . .CLC **4, 5, 8, 10, 14, 18, 22**
  See also CA 21-24R
  See also DLB 14

Baker, Elliott 1922- . . . . .CLC **8**
  See also CANR 2
  See also CA 45-48

Baker, Russell (Wayne) 1925- . . . . . .CLC **31**
  See also CANR 11
  See also CA 57-60

Bakshi, Ralph 1938- . . . . .CLC **26**
  See also CA 112

Baldwin, James (Arthur)
  1924- . . . . . .CLC **1, 2, 3, 4, 5, 8, 13, 15,
                                             17**
  See also CANR 3
  See also CA 1-4R
  See also SATA 9
  See also DLB 2, 7, 33

Ballard, J(ames) G(raham)
  1930- . . . . .CLC **3, 6, 14, 36**
  See also CANR 15
  See also CA 5-8R
  See also DLB 14

Balmont, Konstantin Dmitriyevich
  1867-1943. . . . . .TCLC **11**
  See also CA 109

Balzac, Honoré de 1799-1850 . . . . . NCLC **5**

Bambara, Toni Cade 1939- . . . . .CLC **19**
  See also CA 29-32R
  See also DLB 38

Banks, Iain 1954- . . . . .CLC **34**

Banks, Lynne Reid 1929- . . . . .CLC **23**
  See also Reid Banks, Lynne

Author Index

Banks, Russell 1940-............CLC 37
See also CA 65-68

Banville, Théodore (Faullain) de
1832-1891.................. NCLC 9

Baraka, Amiri
1934-.......CLC 1, 2, 3, 5, 10, 14, 33
See also Baraka, Imamu Amiri
See also Jones, (Everett) LeRoi
See also DLB 5, 7, 16, 38

Baraka, Imamu Amiri
1934-.......CLC 1, 2, 3, 5, 10, 14, 33
See also Baraka, Amiri
See also Jones, (Everett) LeRoi
See also DLB 5, 7, 16, 38

Barbey d'Aurevilly, Jules Amédée
1808-1889.................. NCLC 1

Barbusse, Henri 1873-1935 .... TCLC 5
See also CA 105

Barea, Arturo 1897-1957 .... TCLC 14
See also CA 111

Barfoot, Joan 1946-..............CLC 18
See also CA 105

Baring, Maurice 1874-1945 ...... TCLC 8
See also CA 105
See also DLB 34

Barker, George (Granville)
1913-.....................CLC 8
See also CANR 7
See also CA 9-12R
See also DLB 20

Barker, Howard 1946- ....CLC 37
See also CA 102
See also DLB 13

Barker, Pat 19??-................CLC 32

Barnes, Djuna
1892-1982........ CLC 3, 4, 8, 11, 29
See also CANR 16
See also CA 9-12R
See also obituary CA 107
See also DLB 4, 9, 45

Barnes, Peter 1931-...............CLC 5
See also CA 65-68
See also DLB 13

Baroja (y Nessi), Pío
1872-1956.................. TCLC 8
See also CA 104

Barondess, Sue K(aufman) 1926-1977
See Kaufman, Sue
See also CANR 1
See also CA 1-4R
See also obituary CA 69-72

Barrett, (Roger) Syd 1946-
See Pink Floyd

Barrett, William (Christopher)
1913-.....................CLC 27
See also CANR 11
See also CA 13-16R

Barrie, (Sir) J(ames) M(atthew)
1860-1937................... TCLC 2
See also CA 104
See also YABC 1
See also DLB 10

Barrol, Grady 1953-
See Bograd, Larry

Barry, Philip (James Quinn)
1896-1949................. TCLC 11
See also CA 109
See also DLB 7

Barth, John (Simmons)
1930-.....CLC 1, 2, 3, 5, 7, 9, 10, 14,
                                    27
See also CANR 5
See also CA 1-4R
See also DLB 2
See also AITN 1, 2

Barthelme, Donald
1931-...... CLC 1, 2, 3, 5, 6, 8, 13, 23
See also CA 21-24R
See also SATA 7
See also DLB 2
See also DLB-Y 80

Barthelme, Frederick 1943-........CLC 36
See also CA 114

Barthes, Roland 1915-1980 ....CLC 24
See also obituary CA 97-100

Bassani, Giorgio 1916- ....CLC 9
See also CA 65-68

Bataille, Georges 1897-1962.......CLC 29
See also CA 101
See also obituary CA 89-92

Baudelaire, Charles
1821-1867.................. NCLC 6

Baum, L(yman) Frank
1856-1919.................. TCLC 7
See also CA 108
See also SATA 18
See also DLB 22

Baumbach, Jonathan 1933- ..... CLC 6, 23
See also CANR 12
See also CA 13-16R
See also DLB-Y 80

Baxter, James K(eir)
1926-1972....................CLC 14
See also CA 77-80

Bayer, Sylvia 1909-1981
See Glassco, John

Beagle, Peter S(oyer) 1939- ....CLC 7
See also CANR 4
See also CA 9-12R
See also DLB-Y 80

Beard, Charles A(ustin)
1874-1948.................. TCLC 15
See also CA 115
See also SATA 18
See also DLB 17

Beardsley, Aubrey 1872-1898 ..... NCLC 6

Beattie, Ann 1947-.........CLC 8, 13, 18
See also CA 81-84
See also DLB-Y 82

Beauvoir, Simone de
1908-........... CLC 1, 2, 4, 8, 14, 31
See also CA 9-12R

Becker, Jurek 1937- .... CLC 7, 19
See also CA 85-88

Becker, Walter 1950-
See Becker, Walter and Fagen, Donald

Becker, Walter 1950- and
        Fagen, Donald 1948- ....CLC 26

Beckett, Samuel (Barclay)
1906-......CLC 1, 2, 3, 4, 6, 9, 10, 11,
                                14, 18, 29
See also CA 5-8R
See also DLB 13, 15

Beckman, Gunnel 1910-...........CLC 26
See also CANR 15
See also CA 33-36R
See also SATA 6

Becque, Henri 1837-1899......... NCLC 3

Beddoes, Thomas Lovell
1803-1849.................. NCLC 3

Beecher, John 1904-1980..........CLC 6
See also CANR 8
See also CA 5-8R
See also obituary CA 105
See also AITN 1

Beerbohm, (Sir Henry) Max(imilian)
1872-1956................... TCLC 1
See also CA 104
See also DLB 34

Behan, Brendan
1923-1964...........CLC 1, 8, 11, 15
See also CA 73-76
See also DLB 13

Behn, Aphra 1640?-1689 .... LC 1
See also DLB 39

Belasco, David 1853-1931........ TCLC 3
See also CA 104
See also DLB 7

Belcheva, Elisaveta 1893-
See Bagryana, Elisaveta

Belinski, Vissarion Grigoryevich
1811-1848.................. NCLC 5

Belitt, Ben 1911- ....CLC 22
See also CANR 7
See also CA 13-16R
See also DLB 5

Bell, Acton 1820-1849
See Brontë, Anne

Bell, Currer 1816-1855
See Brontë, Charlotte

Bell, Marvin 1937-............. CLC 8, 31
See also CA 21-24R
See also DLB 5

Bellamy, Edward 1850-1898 ...... NCLC 4
See also DLB 12

**Belloc, (Joseph) Hilaire (Pierre Sébastien
        René Swanton)**
1870-1953............... TCLC 7, 18
See also CA 106
See also YABC 1
See also DLB 19

Bellow, Saul
1915-.....CLC 1, 2, 3, 6, 8, 10, 13, 15,
                                25, 33, 34
See also CA 5-8R
See also DLB 2, 28
See also DLB-Y 82
See also DLB-DS 3
See also AITN 2

Belser, Reimond Karel Maria de 1929-
See Ruyslinck, Ward

Bely, Andrey 1880-1934.......... TCLC 7
See also CA 104

Benary-Isbert, Margot
1889-1979....................CLC 12
See also CANR 4
See also CA 5-8R
See also obituary CA 89-92
See also SATA 2
See also obituary SATA 21

Benavente (y Martinez), Jacinto
1866-1954...................TCLC 3
See also CA 106

Benchley, Peter (Bradford)
1940-......................CLC 4, 8
See also CANR 12
See also CA 17-20R
See also SATA 3
See also AITN 2

Benchley, Robert 1889-1945 ...... TCLC 1
See also CA 105
See also DLB 11

Benedikt, Michael 1935-........ CLC 4, 14
See also CANR 7
See also CA 13-16R
See also DLB 5

Benet, Juan 1927- ....CLC 28

Benét, Stephen Vincent
1898-1943.................. TCLC 7
See also CA 104
See also YABC 1
See also DLB 4

Benn, Gottfried 1886-1956....... TCLC 3
See also CA 106

Bennett, (Enoch) Arnold
1867-1931................TCLC 5, 20
See also CA 106
See also DLB 10, 34

Bennett, George Harold 1930-
See Bennett, Hal
See also CA 97-100

Bennett, Hal 1930-................CLC 5
See also Bennett, George Harold
See also DLB 33

Bennett, Jay 1912-................CLC 35
See also CANR 11
See also CA 69-72
See also SATA 27

Bennett, Louise (Simone)
1919-.......................CLC 28
See also Bennett-Coverly, Louise Simone

Bennett-Coverly, Louise Simone 1919-
See Bennett, Louise (Simone)
See also CA 97-100

Benson, Jackson J. 1930-.........CLC 34
See also CA 25-28R

Benson, Sally 1900-1972..........CLC 17
See also CAP 1
See also CA 19-20
See also obituary CA 37-40R
See also SATA 1, 35
See also obituary SATA 27

Benson, Stella 1892-1933 .... TCLC 17
See also DLB 36

Bentley, E(dmund) C(lerihew)
1875-1956................. TCLC 12
See also CA 108

Bentley, Eric (Russell) 1916- ....CLC 24
See also CANR 6
See also CA 5-8R

Berger, John (Peter) 1926-...... CLC 2, 19
See also CA 81-84
See also DLB 14

Berger, Melvin (H.) 1927- ....CLC 12
See also CANR 4
See also CA 5-8R
See also SATA 5

Berger, Thomas (Louis)
1924-............. CLC 3, 5, 8, 11, 18
See also CANR 5
See also CA 1-4R
See also DLB 2
See also DLB-Y 80

Bergman, (Ernst) Ingmar
1918-.......................CLC 16
See also CA 81-84

Bergstein, Eleanor 1938- ....CLC 4
See also CANR 5
See also CA 53-56

Bernanos, (Paul Louis) Georges
1888-1948.................. TCLC 3
See also CA 104

Bernhard, Thomas 1931- .... CLC 3, 32
See also CA 85-88

Berrigan, Daniel J. 1921-...........CLC 4
See also CAAS 1
See also CANR 11
See also CA 33-36R
See also DLB 5

Berrigan, Edmund Joseph Michael, Jr.
1934-1983
See Berrigan, Ted
See also CANR 14
See also CA 61-64
See also obituary CA 110

Berrigan, Ted 1934-1983 ....CLC 37
See also Berrigan, Edmund Joseph
   Michael, Jr.
See also DLB 5

Berry, Chuck 1926-...............CLC 17

Berry, Wendell (Erdman)
1934-.................CLC 4, 6, 8, 27
See also CA 73-76
See also DLB 5, 6
See also AITN 1

Berryman, John
1914-1972..... CLC 1, 2, 3, 4, 6, 8, 10,
                                    13, 25
See also CAP 1
See also CA 15-16
See also obituary CA 33-36R

Bertolucci, Bernardo 1940- ....CLC 16
See also CA 106

Besant, Annie (Wood)
1847-1933.................. TCLC 9
See also CA 105

Bessie, Alvah 1904-1985..........CLC 23
See also CANR 2
See also CA 5-8R
See also obituary CA 116
See also DLB 26

Beti, Mongo 1932-................CLC 27

Betjeman, John
1906-1984...........CLC 2, 6, 10, 34
See also CA 9-12R
See also obituary CA 112
See also DLB 20
See also DLB-Y 84

Betti, Ugo 1892-1953............. TCLC 5
See also CA 104

Betts, Doris (Waugh)
1932-...................CLC 3, 6, 28
See also CANR 9
See also CA 13-16R
See also DLB-Y 82

Bidart, Frank 19??-................CLC 33

Bienek, Horst 1930-............ CLC 7, 11
See also CA 73-76

Bierce, Ambrose (Gwinett)
1842-1914?...............TCLC 1, 7
See also CA 104
See also DLB 11, 12, 23

Binyon, T(imothy) J(ohn)
1936-.......................CLC 34
See also CA 111

Bioy Casares, Adolfo
1914-..................CLC 4, 8, 13
See also CA 29-32R

Bird, Robert Montgomery
1806-1854.................. NCLC 1

Birdwell, Cleo 1936-
See DeLillo, Don

Birney (Alfred) Earle
1904-.................CLC 1, 4, 6, 11
See also CANR 5
See also CA 1-4R

Bishop, Elizabeth
1911-1979...... CLC 1, 4, 9, 13, 15, 32
See also CA 5-8R
See also obituary CA 89-92
See also obituary SATA 24
See also DLB 5

Bishop, John 1935- ....CLC 10
See also CA 105

Bissett, Bill 1939-................CLC 18
See also CANR 15
See also CA 69-72

Biyidi, Alexandre 1932-
See Beti, Mongo
See also CA 114

Bjørnson, Bjørnstjerne (Martinius)
1832-1910.................. TCLC 7
See also CA 104

Blackburn, Paul 1926-1971 ....CLC 9
See also CA 81-84
See also obituary CA 33-36R
See also DLB 16
See also DLB-Y 81

Blackmur, R(ichard) P(almer)
1904-1965................. CLC 2, 24
See also CAP 1
See also CA 11-12
See also obituary CA 25-28R

Blackwood, Algernon (Henry)
1869-1951.................. TCLC 5
See also CA 105

Blackwood, Caroline 1931- ...... CLC 6, 9
See also CA 85-88
See also DLB 14

Blair, Eric Arthur 1903-1950
See Orwell, George
See also CA 104
See also SATA 29

Blais, Marie-Claire
1939-............. CLC 2, 4, 6, 13, 22
See also CA 21-24R

Blaise, Clark 1940-............... CLC 29
See also CAAS 3
See also CANR 5
See also CA 53-56R
See also AITN 2

Blake, Nicholas 1904-1972
See Day Lewis, C(ecil)

Blasco Ibáñez, Vicente
1867-1928................. TCLC 12
See also CA 110

Blatty, William Peter 1928-........ CLC 2
See also CANR 9
See also CA 5-8R

Blish, James (Benjamin)
1921-1975................... CLC 14
See also CANR 3
See also CA 1-4R
See also obituary CA 57-60
See also DLB 8

Blixen, Karen (Christentze Dinesen)
1885-1962
See Dinesen, Isak
See also CAP 2
See also CA 25-28

Bloch, Robert (Albert) 1917-....... CLC 33
See also CANR 5
See also CA 5-8R
See also DLB 44
See also SATA 12

Blok, Aleksandr (Aleksandrovich)
1880-1921................. TCLC 5
See also CA 104

Bloom, Harold 1930-............. CLC 24
See also CA 13-16R

Blume, Judy (Sussman Kitchens)
1938-................... CLC 12, 30
See also CLR 2
See also CANR 13
See also CA 29-32R
See also SATA 2, 31

Blunden, Edmund (Charles)
1896-1974.................... CLC 2
See also CAP 2
See also CA 17-18
See also obituary CA 45-48
See also DLB 20

Bly, Robert 1926- ..... CLC 1, 2, 5, 10, 15
See also CA 5-8R
See also DLB 5

Bochco, Steven 1944?-
See Bochco, Steven and Kozoll, Michael

Bochco, Steven 1944?- and
Kozoll, Michael 1940?- .... CLC 35

Bødker, Cecil 1927-............... CLC 21
See also CANR 13
See also CA 73-76
See also SATA 14

Boell, Heinrich (Theodor) 1917-1985
See Böll, Heinrich
See also CA 21-24R
See also obituary CA 116

Bogan, Louise 1897-1970.......... CLC 4
See also CA 73-76
See also obituary CA 25-28R
See also DLB 45

Bogarde, Dirk 1921-.............. CLC 19
See also Van Den Bogarde, Derek (Jules
Gaspard Ulric) Niven
See also DLB 14

Bograd, Larry 1953-.............. CLC 35
See also CA 93-96
See also SATA 33

Böhl de Faber, Cecilia 1796-1877
See Caballero, Fernán

Boileau-Despréaux, Nicolas
1636-1711................. LC 3

Böll, Heinrich (Theodor)
1917-1985...... CLC 2, 3, 6, 9, 11, 15,
27

See also Boell, Heinrich (Theodor)

Bolt, Robert (Oxton) 1924- .... CLC 14
See also CA 17-20R
See also DLB 13

Bond, Edward 1934-...... CLC 4, 6, 13, 23
See also CA 25-28R
See also DLB 13

Bonham, Frank 1914-.............. CLC 12
See also CANR 4
See also CA 9-12R
See also SATA 1

Bonnefoy, Yves 1923- .... CLC 9, 15
See also CA 85-88

Bontemps, Arna (Wendell)
1902-1973................. CLC 1, 18
See also CLR 6
See also CANR 4
See also CA 1-4R
See also obituary CA 41-44R
See also SATA 2
See also obituary SATA 24

Booth, Martin 1944-.............. CLC 13
See also CAAS 2
See also CA 93-96

Booth, Philip 1925-.............. CLC 23
See also CANR 5
See also CA 5-8R
See also DLB-Y 82

Booth, Wayne C(layson) 1921- ..... CLC 24
See also CANR 3
See also CA 1-4R

Borchert, Wolfgang 1921-1947 .... TCLC 5
See also CA 104

Borges, Jorge Luis
1899-.......CLC 1, 2, 3, 4, 6, 8, 9, 10,
13, 19
See also CA 21-24R

Borowski, Tadeusz 1922-1951 ..... TCLC 9
See also CA 106

Borrow, George (Henry)
1803-1881.................. NCLC 9
See also DLB 21

Bosschère, Jean de
1878-1953.................. TCLC 19

Bourget, Paul (Charles Joseph)
1852-1935.................. TCLC 12
See also CA 107

Bourjaily, Vance (Nye) 1922-........ CLC 8
See also CAAS 1
See also CANR 2
See also CA 1-4R
See also DLB 2

Bourne, Randolph S(illiman)
1886-1918................. TCLC 16

Bowen, Elizabeth (Dorothea Cole)
1899-1973...... CLC 1, 3, 6, 11, 15, 22
See also CAP 2
See also CA 17-18
See also obituary CA 41-44R
See also DLB 15

Bowering, George 1935-.......... CLC 15
See also CANR 10
See also CA 21-24R

Bowering, Marilyn R(uthe)
1949-.....................CLC 32
See also CA 101

Bowers, Edgar 1924-.............. CLC 9
See also CA 5-8R
See also DLB 5

Bowie, David 1947-.............. CLC 17
See also Jones, David Robert

Bowles, Jane (Sydney)
1917-1973.................... CLC 3
See also CAP 2
See also CA 19-20
See also obituary CA 41-44R

Bowles, Paul (Frederick)
1910-................... CLC 1, 2, 19
See also CAAS 1
See also CANR 1
See also CA 1-4R
See also DLB 5, 6

Box, Edgar 1925-
See Vidal, Gore

Boyd, William 1952-.............. CLC 28
See also CA 114

Boyle, Kay 1903-........... CLC 1, 5, 19
See also CAAS 1
See also CA 13-16R
See also DLB 4, 9

Boyle, Patrick ....CLC 19

Boyle, T. Coraghessan 1948-....... CLC 36

Brackenridge, Hugh Henry
1748-1816.................. NCLC 7
See also DLB 11, 37

Bradbury, Edward P. 1939-
See Moorcock, Michael

Bradbury, Malcolm (Stanley)
1932-.....................CLC 32
See also CANR 1
See also CA 1-4R
See also DLB 14

Bradbury, Ray (Douglas)
1920-................CLC 1, 3, 10, 15
See also CANR 2
See also CA 1-4R
See also SATA 11
See also DLB 2, 8
See also AITN 1, 2

Bradley, David (Henry), Jr.
1950-.....................CLC 23
See also CA 104
See also DLB 33

Bradley, Marion Zimmer
1930-.....................CLC 30
See also CANR 7
See also CA 57-60
See also DLB 8

Bragg, Melvyn 1939-.............CLC **10**
See also CANR 10
See also CA 57-60
See also DLB 14

Braine, John (Gerard) 1922-..... CLC **1, 3**
See also CANR 1
See also CA 1-4R
See also DLB 15

Brammer, Billy Lee 1930?-1978
See Brammer, William

Brammer, William 1930?-1978.....CLC **31**
See also obituary CA 77-80

Brancati, Vitaliano
1907-1954................ TCLC **12**
See also CA 109

Brancato, Robin F(idler) 1936-.....CLC **35**
See also CANR 11
See also CA 69-72
See also SATA 23

Brand, Millen 1906-1980...........CLC **7**
See also CA 21-24R
See also obituary CA 97-100

Brandes, Georg (Morris Cohen)
1842-1927................. TCLC **10**
See also CA 105

Branley, Franklyn M(ansfield)
1915-......................CLC **21**
See also CANR 14
See also CA 33-36R
See also SATA 4

Brathwaite, Edward 1930-.........CLC **11**
See also CANR 11
See also CA 25-28R

Brautigan, Richard
1935-1984....... CLC **1, 3, 5, 9, 12, 34**
See also CA 53-56
See also obituary CA 113
See also DLB 2, 5
See also DLB-Y 80, 84

Brecht, (Eugen) Bertolt (Friedrich)
1898-1956.............TCLC **1, 6, 13**
See also CA 104

Bremer, Fredrika 1801-1865..... NCLC **11**

Brennan, Christopher John
1870-1932.................. TCLC **17**

Brennan, Maeve 1917-.............CLC **5**
See also CA 81-84

Brentano, Clemens (Maria)
1778-1842.................. NCLC **1**

Brenton, Howard 1942-...........CLC **31**
See also CA 69-72
See also DLB 13

Breslin, James (E.) 1930-
See Breslin, Jimmy
See also CA 73-76

Breslin, Jimmy 1930-..............CLC **4**
See also Breslin, James (E.)
See also AITN 1

Bresson, Robert 1907-.............CLC **16**
See also CA 110

Breton, André 1896-1966..... CLC **2, 9, 15**
See also CAP 2
See also CA 19-20
See also obituary CA 25-28R

Breytenbach, Breyten
1939-.................... CLC **23, 37**
See also CA 113

Bridgers, Sue Ellen 1942-..........CLC **26**
See also CANR 11
See also CA 65-68
See also SAAS 1
See also SATA 22

Bridges, Robert 1844-1930....... TCLC **1**
See also CA 104
See also DLB 19

Bridie, James 1888-1951 .... TCLC **3**
See also Mavor, Osborne Henry
See also DLB 10

Brin, David 1950-................CLC **34**
See also CA 102

Brink, André (Philippus)
1935-.................. CLC **18, 36**
See also CA 104

Brinsmead, H(esba) F(ay)
1922-......................CLC **21**
See also CANR 10
See also CA 21-24R
See also SATA 18

Brittain, Vera (Mary)
1893?-1970.................. CLC **23**
See also CAP 1
See also CA 15-16
See also obituary CA 25-28R

Broch, Hermann 1886-1951...... TCLC **20**
See also CA 117

Brodsky, Iosif Alexandrovich 1940-
See Brodsky, Joseph
See also CA 41-44R
See also AITN 1

Brodsky, Joseph
1940-................CLC **4, 6, 13, 36**
See also Brodsky, Iosif Alexandrovich

Brodsky, Michael (Mark)
1948-......................CLC **19**
See also CA 102

Bromell, Henry 1947-.............CLC **5**
See also CANR 9
See also CA 53-56

Bromfield, Louis (Brucker)
1896-1956................ TCLC **11**
See also CA 107
See also DLB 4, 9

Broner, E(sther) M(asserman)
1930-......................CLC **19**
See also CANR 8
See also CA 17-20R
See also DLB 28

Bronk, William 1918-.............CLC **10**
See also CA 89-92

Brontë, Anne 1820-1849......... NCLC **4**
See also DLB 21

Brontë, Charlotte
1816-1855................NCLC **3, 8**
See also DLB 21
See also DLB 39

Brooke, Henry 1703?-1783 .... LC **1**
See also DLB 39

Brooke, Rupert (Chawner)
1887-1915................ TCLC **2, 7**
See also CA 104
See also DLB 19

Brookner, Anita 1938- .... CLC **32, 34**
See also CA 114

Brooks, Cleanth 1906-............CLC **24**
See also CA 17-20R

Brooks, Gwendolyn
1917-............. CLC **1, 2, 4, 5, 15**
See also CANR 1
See also CA 1-4R
See also SATA 6
See also DLB 5
See also AITN 1

Brooks, Mel 1926-................CLC **12**
See also Kaminsky, Melvin
See also CA 65-68
See also DLB 26

Brooks, Peter 1938-................CLC **34**
See also CANR 1
See also CA 45-48

Brooks, Van Wyck 1886-1963......CLC **29**
See also CANR 6
See also CA 1-4R
See also DLB 45

Brophy, Brigid (Antonia)
1929-.............. CLC **6, 11, 29**
See also CA 5-8R
See also DLB 14

Brosman, Catharine Savage
1934-......................CLC **9**
See also CA 61-64

Broughton, T(homas) Alan
1936-......................CLC **19**
See also CANR 2
See also CA 45-48

Broumas, Olga 1949-.............CLC **10**
See also CA 85-88

Brown, Claude 1937-.............CLC **30**
See also CA 73-76

Brown, Dee (Alexander) 1908- .....CLC **18**
See also CANR 11
See also CA 13-16R
See also SATA 5
See also DLB-Y 80

Brown, George Mackay 1921-.......CLC **5**
See also CANR 12
See also CA 21-24R
See also SATA 35
See also DLB 14, 27

Brown, Rita Mae 1944- ....CLC **18**
See also CANR 2, 11
See also CA 45-48

Brown, Rosellen 1939-............CLC **32**
See also CANR 14
See also CA 77-80

Brown, Sterling A(llen)
1901-................... CLC **1, 23**
See also CA 85-88

Brown, William Wells
1816?-1884................. NCLC **2**
See also DLB 3

Browne, Jackson 1950-...........CLC **21**

Browning, Elizabeth Barrett
1806-1861.................. NCLC **1**
See also DLB 32

Browning, Tod 1882-1962........CLC **16**

Bruccoli, Matthew J(oseph)
1931-........................CLC 34
See also CANR 7
See also CA 9-12R

Bruce, Lenny 1925-1966..........CLC 21
See also Schneider, Leonard Alfred

Brunner, John (Kilian Houston)
1934-.......................CLC 8, 10
See also CANR 2
See also CA 1-4R

Bryan, C(ourtlandt) D(ixon) B(arnes)
1936-........................CLC 29
See also CANR 13
See also CA 73-76

Bryant, William Cullen
1794-1878...................NCLC 6
See also DLB 3, 43

Bryusov, Valery (Yakovlevich)
1873-1924..................TCLC 10
See also CA 107

Buchheim, Lothar-Günther
1918-........................CLC 6
See also CA 85-88

Buchwald, Art(hur) 1925-.........CLC 33
See also CA 5-8R
See also SATA 10
See also AITN 1

Buck, Pearl S(ydenstricker)
1892-1973..............CLC 7, 11, 18
See also CANR 1
See also CA 1-4R
See also obituary CA 41-44R
See also SATA 1, 25
See also DLB 9
See also AITN 1

Buckler, Ernest 1908-1984........CLC 13
See also CAP 1
See also CA 11-12
See also obituary CA 114

Buckley, William F(rank), Jr.
1925-..................CLC 7, 18, 37
See also CANR 1
See also CA 1-4R
See also DLB-Y 80
See also AITN 1

Buechner, (Carl) Frederick
1926-.....................CLC 2, 4, 6, 9
See also CANR 11
See also CA 13-16R
See also DLB-Y 80

Buell, John (Edward) 1927-.......CLC 10
See also CA 1-4R

Buero Vallejo, Antonio 1916-.....CLC 15
See also CA 106

Bukowski, Charles 1920-......CLC 2, 5, 9
See also CA 17-20R
See also DLB 5

Bulgakov, Mikhail (Afanas'evich)
1891-1940...............TCLC 2, 16
See also CA 105

Bullins, Ed 1935-.............CLC 1, 5, 7
See also CA 49-52
See also DLB 7, 38

Bulwer-Lytton, (Lord) Edward (George Earle Lytton) 1803-1873 ....NCLC 1
See also Lytton, Edward Bulwer
See also DLB 21

Bunin, Ivan (Alexeyevich)
1870-1953...................TCLC 6
See also CA 104

Bunting, Basil 1900-1985.........CLC 10
See also CANR 7
See also CA 53-56
See also obituary CA 115
See also DLB 20

Buñuel, Luis 1900-1983..........CLC 16
See also CA 101
See also obituary CA 110

Burgess, Anthony
1917-.....CLC 1, 2, 4, 5, 8, 10, 13, 15, 22
See also Wilson, John (Anthony) Burgess
See also DLB 14
See also DLB-Y 84
See also AITN 1

Burke, Kenneth (Duva)
1897-.....................CLC 2, 24
See also CA 5-8R
See also DLB 45

Burney, Fanny 1752-1840 ....NCLC 12
See also DLB 39

Burns, Robert 1759-1796............LC 3

Burns, Tex 1908?-
See L'Amour, Louis (Dearborn)

Burnshaw, Stanley 1906- ....CLC 3, 13
See also CA 9-12R

Burr, Anne 1937-.................CLC 6
See also CA 25-28R

Burroughs, Edgar Rice
1875-1950...................TCLC 2
See also CA 104
See also DLB 8
See also SATA 41

Burroughs, William S(eward)
1914-............. CLC 1, 2, 5, 15, 22
See also CA 9-12R
See also DLB 2, 8, 16
See also DLB-Y 81
See also AITN 2

Busch, Frederick 1941-......CLC 7, 10, 18
See also CAAS 1
See also CA 33-36R
See also DLB 6

Bush, Ronald 19??-..............CLC 34

Butler, Samuel 1835-1902 ....TCLC 1
See also CA 104
See also DLB 18

Butor, Michel (Marie François)
1926-............. CLC 1, 3, 8, 11, 15
See also CA 9-12R

Buzzati, Dino 1906-1972..........CLC 36
See also obituary CA 33-36R

Byars, Betsy 1928-...............CLC 35
See also CLR 1
See also CA 33-36R
See also SAAS 1
See also SATA 4

Byatt, A(ntonia) S(usan Drabble)
1936-.......................CLC 19
See also CANR 13
See also CA 13-16R
See also DLB 14

Byrne, David 1953?- ....CLC 26

Byrne, John Keyes 1926-
See Leonard, Hugh
See also CA 102

Byron, George Gordon (Noel), Lord Byron
1788-1824...............NCLC 2, 12

Caballero, Fernán 1796-1877 .... NCLC 10

Cabell, James Branch
1879-1958...................TCLC 6
See also CA 105
See also DLB 9

Cable, George Washington
1844-1925...................TCLC 4
See also CA 104
See also DLB 12

Cabrera Infante, G(uillermo)
1929-.....................CLC 5, 25
See also CA 85-88

Cain, G. 1929-
See Cabrera Infante, G(uillermo)

Cain, James M(allahan)
1892-1977..............CLC 3, 11, 28
See also CANR 8
See also CA 17-20R
See also obituary CA 73-76
See also AITN 1

Caldwell, Erskine 1903- ......CLC 1, 8, 14
See also CAAS 1
See also CANR 2
See also CA 1-4R
See also DLB 9
See also AITN 1

Caldwell, (Janet Miriam) Taylor (Holland)
1900-1985.................CLC 2, 28
See also CANR 5
See also CA 5-8R
See also obituary CA 116

Calisher, Hortense 1911- ......CLC 2, 4, 8
See also CANR 1
See also CA 1-4R
See also DLB 2

Callaghan, Morley (Edward)
1903-.....................CLC 3, 14
See also CA 9-12R

Calvino, Italo
1923-1985........ CLC 5, 8, 11, 22, 33
See also CA 85-88
See also obituary CA 116

Campana, Dino 1885-1932.......TCLC 20
See also CA 117

Campbell, John W(ood), Jr.
1910-1971....................CLC 32
See also CAP 2
See also CA 21-22
See also obituary CA 29-32R
See also DLB 8

Campbell, (Ignatius) Roy (Dunnachie)
1901-1957...................TCLC 5
See also CA 104
See also DLB 20

Campbell, (William) Wilfred
1861-1918...................TCLC 9
See also CA 106

Camus, Albert
1913-1960...... CLC 1, 2, 4, 9, 11, 14, 32
See also CA 89-92

Canby, Vincent 1924- . . . . .CLC 13
  See also CA 81-84

Canetti, Elias 1905- . . . . CLC 3, 14, 25
  See also CA 21-24R

Cape, Judith 1916-
  See Page, P(atricia) K(athleen)

Čapek, Karel 1890-1938. . . . . TCLC 6
  See also CA 104

Capote, Truman
  1924-1984. . . . . . CLC 1, 3, 8, 13, 19, 34
  See also CA 5-8R
  See also obituary CA 113
  See also DLB 2
  See also DLB-Y 80, 84

Capra, Frank 1897- . . . . .CLC 16
  See also CA 61-64

Caputo, Philip 1941- . . . . .CLC 32
  See also CA 73-76

Cardenal, Ernesto 1925- . . . . .CLC 31
  See also CANR 2
  See also CA 49-52

Carey, Ernestine Gilbreth 1908-
  See Gilbreth, Frank B(unker), Jr. and
    Carey, Ernestine Gilbreth
  See also CA 5-8R
  See also SATA 2

Carleton, William 1794-1869. . . . . .NCLC 3

Carlisle, Henry (Coffin) 1926- . . . . . .CLC 33
  See also CANR 15
  See also CA 13-16R

Carman, (William) Bliss
  1861-1929. . . . . TCLC 7
  See also CA 104

Carpentier (y Valmont), Alejo
  1904-1980. . . . . CLC 8, 11
  See also CANR 11
  See also CA 65-68
  See also obituary CA 97-100

Carr, John Dickson 1906-1977 . . . . . .CLC 3
  See also CANR 3
  See also CA 49-52
  See also obituary CA 69-72

Carr, Virginia Spencer 1929- . . . . . .CLC 34
  See also CA 61-64

Carrier, Roch 1937- . . . . .CLC 13

Carroll, Jim 1951- . . . . .CLC 35
  See also CA 45-48

Carroll, Lewis 1832-1898. . . . . NCLC 2
  See also Dodgson, Charles Lutwidge
  See also CLR 2
  See also DLB 18

Carroll, Paul Vincent
  1900-1968. . . . . .CLC 10
  See also CA 9-12R
  See also obituary CA 25-28R
  See also DLB 10

Carruth, Hayden
  1921- . . . . CLC 4, 7, 10, 18
  See also CANR 4
  See also CA 9-12R
  See also DLB 5

Carter, Angela 1940- . . . . .CLC 5
  See also CANR 12
  See also CA 53-56
  See also DLB 14

Carver, Raymond 1938- . . . . CLC 22, 36
  See also CANR 17
  See also CA 33-36R
  See also DLB-Y 84

Cary, (Arthur) Joyce
  1888-1957. . . . . TCLC 1
  See also CA 104
  See also DLB 15

Casares, Adolfo Bioy 1914-
  See Bioy Casares, Adolfo

Casey, John 1880-1964
  See O'Casey, Sean

Casey, Michael 1947- . . . . .CLC 2
  See also CA 65-68
  See also DLB 5

Casey, Warren 1935-
  See Jacobs, Jim and Casey, Warren
  See also CA 101

Cassavetes, John 1929- . . . . .CLC 20
  See also CA 85-88

Cassill, R(onald) V(erlin)
  1919- . . . . CLC 4, 23
  See also CAAS 1
  See also CANR 7
  See also CA 9-12R
  See also DLB 6

Cassity, (Allen) Turner 1929- . . . . . . .CLC 6
  See also CANR 11
  See also CA 17-20R

Castaneda, Carlos 1935?- . . . . .CLC 12
  See also CA 25-28R

Castro, Rosalía de 1837-1885 . . . . . NCLC 3

Cather, Willa (Sibert)
  1873-1947. . . . . TCLC 1, 11
  See also CA 104
  See also SATA 30
  See also DLB 9
  See also DLB-DS 1

Catton, (Charles) Bruce
  1899-1978. . . . . .CLC 35
  See also CANR 7
  See also CA 5-8R
  See also obituary CA 81-84
  See also SATA 2
  See also obituary SATA 24
  See also DLB 17
  See also AITN 1

Caunitz, William 1935- . . . . .CLC 34

Causley, Charles (Stanley)
  1917- . . . . .CLC 7
  See also CANR 5
  See also CA 9-12R
  See also SATA 3
  See also DLB 27

Caute, (John) David 1936- . . . . .CLC 29
  See also CANR 1
  See also CA 1-4R
  See also DLB 14

Cavafy, C(onstantine) P(eter)
  1863-1933. . . . . TCLC 2, 7
  See also CA 104

Cavanna, Betty 1909- . . . . .CLC 12
  See also CANR 6
  See also CA 9-12R
  See also SATA 1, 30

Cayrol, Jean 1911- . . . . .CLC 11
  See also CA 89-92

Cela, Camilo José 1916- . . . . CLC 4, 13
  See also CA 21-24R

Celan, Paul 1920-1970 . . . . CLC 10, 19
  See also Antschel, Paul

Céline, Louis-Ferdinand
  1894-1961. . . . . . . CLC 1, 3, 4, 7, 9, 15
  See also Destouches, Louis Ferdinand

Cendrars, Blaise 1887-1961 . . . . . . .CLC 18
  See also Sauser-Hall, Frédéric

Césaire, Aimé (Fernand)
  1913- . . . . CLC 19, 32
  See also CA 65-68

Chabrol, Claude 1930- . . . . .CLC 16
  See also CA 110

Challans, Mary 1905-1983
  See Renault, Mary
  See also CA 81-84
  See also obituary CA 111
  See also SATA 23
  See also obituary SATA 36

Chambers, Aidan 1934- . . . . .CLC 35
  See also CANR 12
  See also CA 25-28R
  See also SATA 1

Chambers, James 1948-
  See Cliff, Jimmy

Chandler, Raymond
  1888-1959. . . . . TCLC 1, 7
  See also CA 104

Chaplin, Charles (Spencer)
  1889-1977. . . . . .CLC 16
  See also CA 81-84
  See also obituary CA 73-76
  See also DLB 44

Chapman, Graham 1941?-
  See Monty Python
  See also CA 116

Chapman, John Jay
  1862-1933. . . . . TCLC 7
  See also CA 104

Char, René (Emile)
  1907- . . . . CLC 9, 11, 14
  See also CA 13-16R

Charyn, Jerome 1937- . . . . CLC 5, 8, 18
  See also CAAS 1
  See also CANR 7
  See also CA 5-8R
  See also DLB-Y 83

Chase, Mary Ellen 1887-1973 . . . . . . .CLC 2
  See also CAP 1
  See also CA 15-16
  See also obituary CA 41-44R
  See also SATA 10

Chateaubriand, François René de
  1768-1848. . . . . NCLC 3

Chatterji, Saratchandra
  1876-1938. . . . . TCLC 13
  See also CA 109

Chatterton, Thomas 1752-1770 . . . . . . LC 3

Chatwin, (Charles) Bruce
  1940- . . . . .CLC 28
  See also CA 85-88

Chayefsky, Paddy 1923-1981 . . . . . . .CLC 23
  See also CA 9-12R
  See also obituary CA 104
  See also DLB 7, 44
  See also DLB-Y 81

Chayefsky, Sidney 1923-1981
    See Chayefsky, Paddy

Cheever, John
        1912-1982...... CLC 3, 7, 8, 11, 15, 25
    See also CANR 5
    See also CA 5-8R
    See also obituary CA 106
    See also DLB 2
    See also DLB-Y 80, 82

Cheever, Susan 1943-............CLC 18
    See also CA 103
    See also DLB-Y 82

Chekhov, Anton (Pavlovich)
        1860-1904................ TCLC 3, 10
    See also CA 104

Chernyshevsky, Nikolay Gavrilovich
        1828-1889.................. NCLC 1

Cherry, Caroline Janice 1942-
    See Cherryh, C. J.

Cherryh, C. J. 1942-.............CLC 35
    See also DLB-Y 80

Chesnutt, Charles Waddell
        1858-1932.................. TCLC 5
    See also CA 106
    See also DLB 12

Chesterton, G(ilbert) K(eith)
        1874-1936................ TCLC 1, 6
    See also CA 104
    See also SATA 27
    See also DLB 10, 19, 34

Ch'ien Chung-shu 1910-..........CLC 22

Child, Lydia Maria 1802-1880 .... NCLC 6
    See also DLB 1

Child, Philip 1898-1978 ....CLC 19
    See also CAP 1
    See also CA 13-14

Childress, Alice 1920-......... CLC 12, 15
    See also CANR 3
    See also CA 45-48
    See also SATA 7
    See also DLB 7, 38

Chislett, (Margaret) Anne
        1943?-......................CLC 34

Chitty, (Sir) Thomas Willes 1926-
    See Hinde, Thomas
    See also CA 5-8R

Chomette, René 1898-1981
    See Clair, René
    See also obituary CA 103

Chopin, Kate (O'Flaherty)
        1851-1904............... TCLC 5, 14
    See also CA 104
    See also DLB 12

Christie, Agatha (Mary Clarissa)
        1890-1976............CLC 1, 6, 8, 12
    See also CANR 10
    See also CA 17-20R
    See also obituary CA 61-64
    See also SATA 36
    See also DLB 13
    See also AITN 1, 2

Christie, (Ann) Philippa 1920-
    See Pearce, (Ann) Philippa
    See also CANR 4

Chulkov, Mikhail Dmitrievich
        1743-1792.....................LC 2

Churchill, Caryl 1938- ....CLC 31
    See also CA 102
    See also DLB 13

Churchill, Charles 1731?-1764 ...... LC 3

Ciardi, John (Anthony) 1916- ......CLC 10
    See also CAAS 2
    See also CANR 5
    See also CA 5-8R
    See also SATA 1
    See also DLB 5

Cimino, Michael 1943?- ....CLC 16
    See also CA 105

Clair, René 1898-1981 ....CLC 20
    See also Chomette, René

Clampitt, Amy 19??-...............CLC 32
    See also CA 110

Clare, John 1793-1864 .... NCLC 9

Clark, (Robert) Brian 1932- ......CLC 29
    See also CA 41-44R

Clark, Eleanor 1913-........... CLC 5, 19
    See also CA 9-12R
    See also DLB 6

Clark, Mavis Thorpe 1912?- ....CLC 12
    See also CANR 8
    See also CA 57-60
    See also SATA 8

Clark, Walter Van Tilburg
        1909-1971....................CLC 28
    See also CA 9-12R
    See also obituary CA 33-36R
    See also SATA 8
    See also DLB 9

Clarke, Arthur C(harles)
        1917-........... CLC 1, 4, 13, 18, 35
    See also CANR 2
    See also CA 1-4R
    See also SATA 13

Clarke, Austin 1896-1974........ CLC 6, 9
    See also CAP 2
    See also CA 29-32
    See also obituary CA 49-52
    See also DLB 10, 20

Clarke, Austin C(hesterfield)
        1934-........................CLC 8
    See also CA 25-28R

Clarke, Shirley 1925- ....CLC 16

Clash, The.......................CLC 30

Claudel, Paul (Louis Charles Marie)
        1868-1955............... TCLC 2, 10
    See also CA 104

Clavell, James (duMaresq)
        1924-..................... CLC 6, 25
    See also CA 25-28R

Cleaver, (Leroy) Eldridge
        1935-........................CLC 30
    See also CANR 16
    See also CA 21-24R

Cleese, John 1939-
    See Monty Python
    See also CA 112, 116

Cleland, John 1709-1789 .... LC 2
    See also DLB 39

Clemens, Samuel Langhorne 1835-1910
    See Twain, Mark
    See also CA 104
    See also YABC 2
    See also DLB 11, 12, 23

Cliff, Jimmy 1948-...............CLC 21

Clifton, Lucille 1936- ....CLC 19
    See also CLR 5
    See also CANR 2
    See also CA 49-52
    See also SATA 20
    See also DLB 5, 41

Clutha, Janet Paterson Frame 1924-
    See Frame (Clutha), Janet (Paterson)
    See also CANR 2
    See also CA 1-4R

Coburn, D(onald) L(ee) 1938-......CLC 10
    See also CA 89-92

Cocteau, Jean (Maurice Eugene Clement)
        1889-1963............CLC 1, 8, 15, 16
    See also CAP 2
    See also CA 25-28

Coetzee, J(ohn) M. 1940-...... CLC 23, 33
    See also CA 77-80

Cohen, Arthur A(llen) 1928- .... CLC 7, 31
    See also CANR 1, 17
    See also CA 1-4R
    See also DLB 28

Cohen, Leonard (Norman)
        1934-........................CLC 3
    See also CANR 14
    See also CA 21-24R

Cohen, Matt 1942-...............CLC 19
    See also CA 61-64

Colegate, Isabel 1931-.............CLC 36
    See also CANR 8
    See also CA 17-20R
    See also DLB 14

Coleridge, Samuel Taylor
        1772-1834.................. NCLC 9

Colette (Sidonie-Gabrielle)
        1873-1954..............TCLC 1, 5, 16
    See also CA 104

Collier, Christopher 1930-
    See Collier, Christopher and Collier, James
        L(incoln)
    See also CANR 13
    See also CA 33-36R
    See also SATA 16

Collier, Christopher 1930- and
    Collier, James L(incoln)
        1928-.......................CLC 30

Collier, James L(incoln) 1928-
    See Collier, Christopher and Collier, James
        L(incoln)
    See also CLR 3
    See also CANR 4
    See also CA 9-12R
    See also SATA 8

Collier, James L(incoln) 1928- and
    Collier, Christopher 1930-
    See Collier, Christopher and Collier, James
        L(incoln)

Collins, Hunt 1926-
    See Hunter, Evan

Collins, (William) Wilkie
        1824-1889.................. NCLC 1
    See also DLB 18

Colman, George 1909-1981
    See Glassco, John

Colum, Padraic 1881-1972........CLC 28
    See also CA 73-76
    See also obituary CA 33-36R
    See also SATA 15
    See also DLB 19

Colvin, James 1939-
    See Moorcock, Michael

Colwin, Laurie 1945- .... **CLC 5, 13, 23**
    See also CA 89-92
    See also DLB-Y 80

Comfort, Alex(ander) 1920-........CLC 7
    See also CANR 1
    See also CA 1-4R

Compton-Burnett, Ivy
    1892-1969....... **CLC 1, 3, 10, 15, 34**
    See also CANR 4
    See also CA 1-4R
    See also obituary CA 25-28R
    See also DLB 36

Comstock, Anthony
    1844-1915................. **TCLC 13**
    See also CA 110

Condon, Richard (Thomas)
    1915-................CLC 4, 6, 8, 10
    See also CAAS 1
    See also CANR 2
    See also CA 1-4R

Connell, Evan S(helby), Jr.
    1924- .... **CLC 4, 6**
    See also CAAS 2
    See also CANR 2
    See also CA 1-4R
    See also DLB 2
    See also DLB-Y 81

Connelly, Marc(us Cook)
    1890-1980....................CLC 7
    See also CA 85-88
    See also obituary CA 102
    See also obituary SATA 25
    See also DLB 7
    See also DLB-Y 80

Conrad, Joseph
    1857-1924..............TCLC 1, 6, 13
    See also CA 104
    See also SATA 27
    See also DLB 10, 34

Conroy, Pat 1945- ....CLC 30
    See also CA 85-88
    See also DLB 6
    See also AITN 1

Constant (de Rebecque), (Henri) Benjamin
    1767-1830................. **NCLC 6**

Cook, Robin 1940-................CLC 14
    See also CA 108, 111

Cooke, John Esten 1830-1886 ..... **NCLC 5**
    See also DLB 3

Cooper, James Fenimore
    1789-1851................. **NCLC 1**
    See also SATA 19
    See also DLB 3

Coover, Robert (Lowell)
    1932-................CLC 3, 7, 15, 32
    See also CANR 3
    See also CA 45-48
    See also DLB 2
    See also DLB-Y 81

Copeland, Stewart (Armstrong) 1952-
    See The Police

Coppard, A(lfred) E(dgar)
    1878-1957................... **TCLC 5**
    See also CA 114
    See also YABC 1

Coppola, Francis Ford 1939-.......CLC 16
    See also CA 77-80
    See also DLB 44

Corcoran, Barbara 1911-............CLC 17
    See also CAAS 2
    See also CANR 11
    See also CA 21-24R
    See also SATA 3

Corman, Cid 1924-................CLC 9
    See also Corman, Sidney
    See also CAAS 2
    See also DLB 5

Corman, Sidney 1924-
    See Corman, Cid
    See also CA 85-88

Cormier, Robert (Edmund)
    1925-.................... **CLC 12, 30**
    See also CANR 5
    See also CA 1-4R
    See also SATA 10

Corn, Alfred (Dewitt III)
    1943-....................CLC 33
    See also CA 104
    See also DLB-Y 80

Cornwell, David (John Moore) 1931-
    See le Carré, John
    See also CANR 13
    See also CA 5-8R

Corso, (Nunzio) Gregory
    1930-.................... **CLC 1, 11**
    See also CA 5-8R
    See also DLB 5, 16

Cortázar, Julio
    1914-1984..... **CLC 2, 3, 5, 10, 13, 15,
                                    33, 34**
    See also CANR 12
    See also CA 21-24R

Corvo, Baron 1860-1913
    See Rolfe, Frederick (William Serafino
        Austin Lewis Mary)

Ćosić, Dobrica 1921-..............CLC 14

Costain, Thomas B(ertram)
    1885-1965....................CLC 30
    See also CA 5-8R
    See also obituary CA 25-28R
    See also DLB 9

Costello, Elvis 1955- ....CLC 21

Couperus, Louis (Marie Anne)
    1863-1923................. **TCLC 15**
    See also CA 115

Cousteau, Jacques-Yves 1910-......CLC 30
    See also CANR 15
    See also CA 65-68
    See also SATA 38

Coward, Nöel (Pierce)
    1899-1973.............. **CLC 1, 9, 29**
    See also CAP 2
    See also CA 17-18
    See also obituary CA 41-44R
    See also DLB 10
    See also AITN 1

Cowper, William 1731-1800 ...... **NCLC 8**

Cox, William Trevor 1928-
    See Trevor, William
    See also CANR 4
    See also CA 9-12R

Cozzens, James Gould
    1903-1978............... **CLC 1, 4, 11**
    See also CA 9-12R
    See also obituary CA 81-84
    See also DLB 9
    See also DLB-Y 84
    See also DLB-DS 2

Crane, (Harold) Hart
    1899-1932................. **TCLC 2, 5**
    See also CA 104
    See also DLB 4

Crane, R(onald) S(almon)
    1886-1967....................CLC 27
    See also CA 85-88

Crane, Stephen
    1871-1900.............. **TCLC 11, 17**
    See also CA 109
    See also DLB 12
    See also YABC 2

Craven, Margaret 1901-1980.......CLC 17
    See also CA 103

Crawford, F(rancis) Marion
    1854-1909................. **TCLC 10**
    See also CA 107

Crawford, Isabella Valancy
    1850-1887................. **NCLC 12**

Crayencour, Marguerite de 1913-
    See Yourcenar, Marguerite

Creasey, John 1908-1973 ....CLC 11
    See also CANR 8
    See also CA 5-8R
    See also obituary CA 41-44R

Crébillon, Claude Prosper Jolyot de (fils)
    1707-1777.................... **LC 1**

Creeley, Robert (White)
    1926-........CLC 1, 2, 4, 8, 11, 15, 36
    See also CA 1-4R
    See also DLB 5, 16

Crews, Harry 1935-............. **CLC 6, 23**
    See also CA 25-28R
    See also DLB 6
    See also AITN 1

Crichton, (John) Michael
    1942-...................... **CLC 2, 6**
    See also CANR 13
    See also CA 25-28R
    See also SATA 9
    See also DLB-Y 81
    See also AITN 2

Crispin, Edmund 1921-1978 ....CLC 22
    See also Montgomery, Robert Bruce

Cristofer, Michael 1946-..........CLC 28
    See also CA 110
    See also DLB 7

Crockett, David (Davy)
    1786-1836................. **NCLC 8**
    See also DLB 3, 11

Croker, John Wilson
    1780-1857................. **NCLC 10**

Cronin, A(rchibald) J(oseph)
1896-1981....................CLC 32
See also CANR 5
See also CA 1-4R
See also obituary CA 102
See also obituary SATA 25

Cross, Amanda 1926-
See Heilbrun, Carolyn G(old)

Crothers, Rachel 1878-1953...... TCLC 19
See also CA 113
See also DLB 7

Crowley, Aleister 1875-1947 ...... TCLC 7
See also CA 104

Crumb, Robert 1943-.............CLC 17
See also CA 106

Cryer, Gretchen 1936?- ....CLC 21
See also CA 114

Csáth, Géza 1887-1919......... TCLC 13
See also CA 111

Cudlip, David 1933- ....CLC 34

Cullen, Countee 1903-1946 .... TCLC 4
See also CA 108
See also SATA 18
See also DLB 4

Cummings, E(dward) E(stlin)
1894-1962........ CLC 1, 3, 8, 12, 15
See also CA 73-76
See also DLB 4

Cunningham, J(ames) V(incent)
1911-1985................ CLC 3, 31
See also CANR 1
See also CA 1-4R
See also obituary CA 115
See also DLB 5

Cunningham, Julia (Woolfolk)
1916-........................CLC 12
See also CANR 4
See also CA 9-12R
See also SATA 1, 26

Cunningham, Michael 1952- ......CLC 34

Dąbrowska, Maria (Szumska)
1889-1965...................CLC 15
See also CA 106

Dabydeen, David 1956?-..........CLC 34

Dagerman, Stig (Halvard)
1923-1954................. TCLC 17

Dahl, Roald 1916- .... CLC 1, 6, 18
See also CLR 1, 7
See also CANR 6
See also CA 1-4R
See also SATA 1, 26

Dahlberg, Edward
1900-1977.............. CLC 1, 7, 14
See also CA 9-12R
See also obituary CA 69-72

Daly, Maureen 1921-.............CLC 17
See also McGivern, Maureen Daly
See also SAAS 1
See also SATA 2

Däniken, Erich von 1935-
See Von Däniken, Erich

Dannay, Frederic 1905-1982
See Queen, Ellery
See also CANR 1
See also CA 1-4R
See also obituary CA 107

D'Annunzio, Gabriele
1863-1938.................. TCLC 6
See also CA 104

Danziger, Paula 1944-............CLC 21
See also CA 112, 115
See also SATA 30, 36

Darío, Rubén 1867-1916......... TCLC 4
See also Sarmiento, Felix Ruben Garcia
See also CA 104

Darley, George 1795-1846 .... NCLC 2

Daryush, Elizabeth
1887-1977................ CLC 6, 19
See also CANR 3
See also CA 49-52
See also DLB 20

Daudet, (Louis Marie) Alphonse
1840-1897................... NCLC 1

Daumal, René 1908-1944 .... TCLC 14
See also CA 114

Davenport, Guy (Mattison), Jr.
1927-................... CLC 6, 14
See also CA 33-36R

Davidson, Donald (Grady)
1893-1968............. CLC 2, 13, 19
See also CANR 4
See also CA 5-8R
See also obituary CA 25-28R
See also DLB 45

Davidson, Sara 1943- ....CLC 9
See also CA 81-84

Davie, Donald (Alfred)
1922-................CLC 5, 8, 10, 31
See also CAAS 3
See also CANR 1
See also CA 1-4R
See also DLB 27

Davies, Ray(mond Douglas)
1944-.....................CLC 21
See also CA 116

Davies, Rhys 1903-1978 ....CLC 23
See also CANR 4
See also CA 9-12R
See also obituary CA 81-84

Davies, (William) Robertson
1913-...............CLC 2, 7, 13, 25
See also CANR 17
See also CA 33-36R

Davies, W(illiam) H(enry)
1871-1940.................. TCLC 5
See also CA 104
See also DLB 19

Davis, Rebecca (Blaine) Harding
1831-1910.................. TCLC 6
See also CA 104

Davison, Frank Dalby
1893-1970.................CLC 15
See also obituary CA 116

Davison, Peter 1928-.............CLC 28
See also CANR 3
See also CA 9-12R
See also DLB 5

Davys, Mary 1674-1732 .... LC 1
See also DLB 39

Dawson, Fielding 1930-............CLC 6
See also CA 85-88

Day, Thomas 1748-1789.............LC 1
See also YABC 1
See also DLB 39

Day Lewis, C(ecil)
1904-1972............... CLC 1, 6, 10
See also CAP 1
See also CA 15-16
See also obituary CA 33-36R
See also DLB 15, 20

Dazai Osamu 1909-1948........ TCLC 11
See also Tsushima Shūji

Defoe, Daniel 1660?-1731............LC 1
See also SATA 22
See also DLB 39

De Hartog, Jan 1914- ....CLC 19
See also CANR 1
See also CA 1-4R

Deighton, Len 1929- .... CLC 4, 7, 22
See also CA 9-12R

De la Mare, Walter (John)
1873-1956.................. TCLC 4
See also CA 110
See also SATA 16
See also DLB 19

Delaney, Shelagh 1939-............CLC 29
See also CA 17-20R
See also DLB 13

Delany, Samuel R(ay, Jr.)
1942-...................... CLC 8, 14
See also CA 81-84
See also DLB 8, 33

De la Roche, Mazo 1885-1961......CLC 14
See also CA 85-88

Delbanco, Nicholas (Franklin)
1942-..................... CLC 6, 13
See also CAAS 2
See also CA 17-20R
See also DLB 6

Delibes (Setien), Miguel
1920-................... CLC 8, 18
See also CANR 1
See also CA 45-48

DeLillo, Don 1936- ......CLC 8, 10, 13, 27
See also CA 81-84
See also DLB 6

De Lisser, H(erbert) G(eorge)
1878-1944................. TCLC 12
See also CA 109

Deloria, Vine (Victor), Jr.
1933-.....................CLC 21
See also CANR 5
See also CA 53-56
See also SATA 21

Del Vecchio, John M(ichael)
1947-.....................CLC 29
See also CA 110

Dennis, Nigel (Forbes) 1912- ....CLC 8
See also CA 25-28R
See also DLB 13, 15

De Palma, Brian 1940-.............CLC 20
See also CA 109

De Quincey, Thomas
1785-1859.................. NCLC 4

Deren, Eleanora 1908-1961
See Deren, Maya
See also obituary CA 111

Deren, Maya 1908-1961 . . . . .CLC 16
  See also Deren, Eleanora

Derleth, August William
      1909-1971. . . . . .CLC 31
  See also CANR 4
  See also CA 1-4R
  See also obituary CA 29-32R
  See also SATA 5
  See also DLB 9

Derrida, Jacques 1930-. . . . . .CLC 24

Desai, Anita 1937-. . . . . CLC 19, 37
  See also CA 81-84

De Saint-Luc, Jean 1909-1981
  See Glassco, John

De Sica, Vittorio 1902-1974 . . . . . . .CLC 20

Destouches, Louis Ferdinand 1894-1961
  See Céline, Louis-Ferdinand
  See also CA 85-88

Deutsch, Babette 1895-1982 . . . . . . .CLC 18
  See also CANR 4
  See also CA 1-4R
  See also obituary CA 108
  See also DLB 45
  See also SATA 1
  See also obituary SATA 33

De Vries, Peter
      1910-. . . . . CLC 1, 2, 3, 7, 10, 28
  See also CA 17-20R
  See also DLB 6
  See also DLB-Y 82

Dexter, Pete 1943-. . . . . .CLC 34

Diamond, Neil (Leslie) 1941-. . . . . . .CLC 30
  See also CA 108

Dick, Philip K(indred)
      1928-1982. . . . . CLC 10, 30
  See also CANR 2, 16
  See also CA 49-52
  See also obituary CA 106
  See also DLB 8

Dickens, Charles 1812-1870 . . . . .NCLC 3, 8
  See also SATA 15
  See also DLB 21

Dickey, James (Lafayette)
      1923-. . . . . CLC 1, 2, 4, 7, 10, 15
  See also CANR 10
  See also CA 9-12R
  See also DLB 5
  See also DLB-Y 82
  See also AITN 1, 2

Dickey, William 1928-. . . . . CLC 3, 28
  See also CA 9-12R
  See also DLB 5

Dickinson, Peter (Malcolm de Brissac)
      1927-. . . . . CLC 12, 35
  See also CA 41-44R
  See also SATA 5

Didion, Joan 1934- . . . . CLC 1, 3, 8, 14, 32
  See also CANR 14
  See also CA 5-8R
  See also DLB 2
  See also DLB-Y 81
  See also AITN 1

Dillard, Annie 1945-. . . . . .CLC 9
  See also CANR 3
  See also CA 49-52
  See also SATA 10
  See also DLB-Y 80

Dillard, R(ichard) H(enry) W(ilde)
      1937-. . . . . .CLC 5
  See also CANR 10
  See also CA 21-24R
  See also DLB 5

Dillon, Eilis 1920- . . . . .CLC 17
  See also CAAS 3
  See also CANR 4
  See also CA 9-12R
  See also SATA 2

Dinesen, Isak 1885-1962 . . . . . . CLC 10, 29
  See also Blixen, Karen (Christentze Dinesen)

Disch, Thomas M(ichael)
      1940-. . . . . CLC 7, 36
  See also CANR 17
  See also CA 21-24R
  See also DLB 8

Disraeli, Benjamin 1804-1881 . . . . .NCLC 2
  See also DLB 21

Dixon, Paige 1911-
  See Corcoran, Barbara

Döblin, Alfred 1878-1957 . . . . . . .TCLC 13
  See also Doeblin, Alfred

Dobrolyubov, Nikolai Alexandrovich
      1836-1861. . . . . .NCLC 5

Dobyns, Stephen 1941-. . . . . .CLC 37
  See also CANR 2
  See also CA 45-48

Doctorow, E(dgar) L(aurence)
      1931-. . . . . CLC 6, 11, 15, 18, 37
  See also CANR 2
  See also CA 45-48
  See also DLB 2, 28
  See also DLB-Y 80
  See also AITN 2

Dodgson, Charles Lutwidge 1832-1898
  See Carroll, Lewis
  See also YABC 2

Doeblin, Alfred 1878-1957
  See also CA 110

Doerr, Harriet 1914?-. . . . . .CLC 34

Donleavy, J(ames) P(atrick)
      1926-. . . . . .CLC 1, 4, 6, 10
  See also CA 9-12R
  See also DLB 6
  See also AITN 2

Donnell, David 1939?-. . . . . .CLC 34

Donoso, José 1924- . . . . . . .CLC 4, 8, 11, 32
  See also CA 81-84

Donovan, John 1928- . . . . .CLC 35
  See also CLR 3
  See also CA 97-100
  See also SATA 29

Doolittle, Hilda 1886-1961
  See H(ilda) D(oolittle)
  See also CA 97-100
  See also DLB 4, 45

Dorn, Ed(ward Merton)
      1929-. . . . . CLC 10, 18
  See also CA 93-96
  See also DLB 5

Dos Passos, John (Roderigo)
      1896-1970. . . . . CLC 1, 4, 8, 11, 15, 25, 34
  See also CANR 3
  See also CA 1-4R
  See also obituary CA 29-32R
  See also DLB 4, 9
  See also DLB-DS 1

Dostoevski, Fedor Mikhailovich
      1821-1881. . . . . .NCLC 2, 7

Douglass, Frederick
      1817-1895. . . . . .NCLC 7
  See also SATA 29
  See also DLB 1, 43

Dourado, (Waldomiro Freitas) Autran
      1926-. .CLC 23
  See also CA 25-28R

Dowson, Ernest (Christopher)
      1867-1900. . . . . TCLC 4
  See also CA 105
  See also DLB 19

Doyle, (Sir) Arthur Conan
      1859-1930. . . . . TCLC 7
  See also CA 104
  See also SATA 24
  See also DLB 18

Dr. A 1933-
  See Silverstein, Alvin and Virginia
  B(arbara Opshelor) Silverstein

Drabble, Margaret
      1939-. . . . . . . .CLC 2, 3, 5, 8, 10, 22
  See also CA 13-16R
  See also DLB 14

Dreiser, Theodore (Herman Albert)
      1871-1945. . . . . .TCLC 10, 18
  See also CA 106
  See also DLB 9, 12
  See also DLB-DS 1

Drexler, Rosalyn 1926-. . . . . .CLC 2, 6
  See also CA 81-84

Dreyer, Carl Theodor
      1889-1968. . . . . .CLC 16
  See also obituary CA 116

Droste-Hülshoff, Annette Freiin von
      1797-1848. . . . . NCLC 3

Drummond de Andrade, Carlos 1902-
  See Andrade, Carlos Drummond de

Drury, Allen (Stuart) 1918-. . . . . . . .CLC 37
  See also CA 57-60

Dryden, John 1631-1700 . . . . .LC 3

Duberman, Martin 1930-. . . . . .CLC 8
  See also CANR 2
  See also CA 1-4R

Dubie, Norman (Evans, Jr.)
      1945-. . . . . .CLC 36
  See also CANR 12
  See also CA 69-72

Du Bois, W(illiam) E(dward) B(urghardt)
      1868-1963. . . . . .CLC 1, 2, 13
  See also CA 85-88
  See also SATA 42
  See also DLB 47

Dubus, Andre 1936- . . . . .CLC 13, 36
  See also CANR 17
  See also CA 21-24R

Duclos, Charles Pinot 1704-1772 . . . . .LC 1

Dudek, Louis   1918-. . . . . CLC 11, 19
See also CANR 1
See also CA 45-48

Dudevant, Amandine Aurore Lucile Dupin
1804-1876
See Sand, George

Duerrenmatt, Friedrich   1921-
See also CA 17-20R

Duffy, Maureen   1933-. . . . . .CLC 37
See also CA 25-28R
See also DLB 14

Dugan, Alan   1923-. . . . . CLC 2, 6
See also CA 81-84
See also DLB 5

Duhamel, Georges   1884-1966 . . . . . . .CLC 8
See also CA 81-84
See also obituary CA 25-28R

Dujardin, Édouard (Émile Louis)
1861-1949. . . . . TCLC 13
See also CA 109

Duke, Raoul   1939-
See Thompson, Hunter S(tockton)

Dumas, Alexandre (*père*)
1802-1870. . . . . NCLC 11
See also SATA 18

Dumas, Alexandre (*fils*)
1824-1895. . . . . NCLC 9

Dumas, Henry (L.)   1934-1968. . . . . .CLC 6
See also CA 85-88
See also DLB 41

Du Maurier, Daphne   1907- . . . . . CLC 6, 11
See also CANR 6
See also CA 5-8R
See also SATA 27

Dunbar, Paul Laurence
1872-1906. . . . . TCLC 2, 12
See also CA 104
See also SATA 34

Duncan (Steinmetz Arquette), Lois
1934-. . . . . .CLC 26
See also Arquette, Lois S(teinmetz)
See also CANR 2
See also CA 1-4R
See also SATA 1, 36

Duncan, Robert
1919-. . . . . CLC 1, 2, 4, 7, 15
See also CA 9-12R
See also DLB 5, 16, 37

Dunlap, William   1766-1839 . . . . . . NCLC 2
See also DLB 30, 37

Dunn, Douglas (Eaglesham)
1942-. CLC 6
See also CANR 2
See also CA 45-48
See also DLB 40

Dunn, Stephen   1939-. . . . . .CLC 36
See also CANR 12
See also CA 33-36R

Dunne, John Gregory   1932-. . . . . . . .CLC 28
See also CANR 14
See also CA 25-28R
See also DLB-Y 80

Dunsany, Lord (Edward John Moreton Drax Plunkett)   1878-1957. . . . . TCLC 2
See also CA 104
See also DLB 10

Durang, Christopher (Ferdinand)
1949-. . . . . .CLC 27
See also CA 105

Duras, Marguerite
1914-. . . . . CLC 3, 6, 11, 20, 34
See also CA 25-28R

Durrell, Lawrence (George)
1912-. . . . . CLC 1, 4, 6, 8, 13, 27
See also CA 9-12R
See also DLB 15, 27

Dürrenmatt, Friedrich
1921-. . . . . CLC 1, 4, 8, 11, 15
See also Duerrenmatt, Friedrich

Dylan, Bob   1941-. . . . . .CLC 3, 4, 6, 12
See also CA 41-44R
See also DLB 16

East, Michael   1916-
See West, Morris L.

Eastlake, William (Derry)   1917-. . . . .CLC 8
See also CAAS 1
See also CANR 5
See also CA 5-8R
See also DLB 6

Eberhart, Richard   1904- . . . . CLC 3, 11, 19
See also CANR 2
See also CA 1-4R

Echegaray (y Eizaguirre), José (María Waldo)   1832-1916. . . . . TCLC 4
See also CA 104

Eckert, Allan W.   1931-. . . . . .CLC 17
See also CANR 14
See also CA 13-16R
See also SATA 27, 29

Eco, Umberto   1932- . . . . .CLC 28
See also CANR 12
See also CA 77-80

Eddison, E(ric) R(ucker)
1882-1945. . . . . TCLC 15
See also CA 109

Edel, (Joseph) Leon   1907- . . . . . CLC 29, 34
See also CANR 1
See also CA 1-4R

Eden, Emily   1797-1869. . . . . NCLC 10

Edgeworth, Maria   1767-1849 . . . . . NCLC 1
See also SATA 21

Edmonds, Helen (Woods)   1904-1968
See Kavan, Anna
See also CA 5-8R
See also obituary CA 25-28R

Edmonds, Walter D(umaux)
1903-. .CLC 35
See also CANR 2
See also CA 5-8R
See also SATA 1, 27
See also DLB 9

Edson, Russell   1905-. . . . . .CLC 13
See also CA 33-36R

Edwards, G(erald) B(asil)
1899-1976. . . . . .CLC 25
See also obituary CA 110

Ehle, John (Marsden, Jr.)
1925-. . . . . .CLC 27
See also CA 9-12R

Ehrenbourg, Ilya (Grigoryevich)   1891-1967
See Ehrenburg, Ilya (Grigoryevich)

Ehrenburg, Ilya (Grigoryevich)
1891-1967. . . . . CLC 18, 34
See also CA 102
See also obituary CA 25-28R

Eich, Guenter   1907-1971
See also CA 111
See also obituary CA 93-96

Eich, Günter   1907-1971. . . . . .CLC 15
See also Eich, Guenter

Eichendorff, Joseph Freiherr von
1788-1857. . . . . .NCLC 8

Eigner, Larry   1927- . . . . .CLC 9
See also Eigner, Laurence (Joel)
See also DLB 5

Eigner, Laurence (Joel)   1927-
See Eigner, Larry
See also CANR 6
See also CA 9-12R

Eiseley, Loren (Corey)
1907-1977. . . . . .CLC 7
See also CANR 6
See also CA 1-4R
See also obituary CA 73-76

Ekeloef, Gunnar (Bengt)   1907-1968
See Ekelöf, Gunnar (Bengt)
See also obituary CA 25-28R

Ekelöf, Gunnar (Bengt)
1907-1968. . . . . .CLC 27
See also Ekeloef, Gunnar (Bengt)

Ekwensi, Cyprian (Odiatu Duaka)
1921-. . . . . .CLC 4
See also CA 29-32R

Eliade, Mircea   1907-. . . . . .CLC 19
See also CA 65-68

Eliot, George   1819-1880. . . . . NCLC 4
See also DLB 21, 35

Eliot, T(homas) S(tearns)
1888-1965. . . . . . . CLC 1, 2, 3, 6, 9, 10,
                                  13, 15, 24, 34
See also CA 5-8R
See also obituary CA 25-28R
See also DLB 7, 10, 45

Elkin, Stanley L(awrence)
1930-. . . . . CLC 4, 6, 9, 14, 27
See also CANR 8
See also CA 9-12R
See also DLB 2, 28
See also DLB-Y 80

Elledge, Scott   19??-. . . . . .CLC 34

Elliott, George P(aul)
1918-1980. . . . . .CLC 2
See also CANR 2
See also CA 1-4R
See also obituary CA 97-100

Ellis, A. E. . . . . .CLC 7

Ellis, (Henry) Havelock
1859-1939. . . . . TCLC 14
See also CA 109

Ellison, Harlan   1934- . . . . CLC 1, 13
See also CANR 5
See also CA 5-8R
See also DLB 8

Ellison, Ralph (Waldo)
1914-. . . . . CLC 1, 3, 11
See also CA 9-12R
See also DLB 2

Elman, Richard 1934-............CLC 19
See also CAAS 3
See also CA 17-20R

Éluard, Paul 1895-1952 ....TCLC 7
See also Grindel, Eugene

Elvin, Anne Katharine Stevenson 1933-
See Stevenson, Anne (Katharine)
See also CA 17-20R

Elytis, Odysseus 1911- ....CLC 15
See also CA 102

Emecheta, (Florence Onye) Buchi
1944-........................CLC 14
See also CA 81-84

Emerson, Ralph Waldo
1803-1882...................NCLC 1
See also DLB 1

Empson, William
1906-1984........ CLC 3, 8, 19, 33, 34
See also CA 17-20R
See also obituary CA 112
See also DLB 20

Enchi, Fumiko 1905-.............CLC 31

Ende, Michael 1930-..............CLC 31
See also SATA 42

Endo, Shusaku 1923- .... CLC 7, 14, 19
See also CA 29-32R

Engel, Marian 1933-1985.........CLC 36
See also CANR 12
See also CA 25-28R

Enright, D(ennis) J(oseph)
1920-.................. CLC 4, 8, 31
See also CANR 1
See also CA 1-4R
See also SATA 25
See also DLB 27

Ephron, Nora 1941- .... CLC 17, 31
See also CANR 12
See also CA 65-68
See also AITN 2

Epstein, Daniel Mark 1948-........CLC 7
See also CANR 2
See also CA 49-52

Epstein, Jacob 1956-..............CLC 19
See also CA 114

Epstein, Leslie 1938-..............CLC 27
See also CA 73-76

Erdman, Paul E(mil) 1932- ....CLC 25
See also CANR 13
See also CA 61-64
See also AITN 1

Erenburg, Ilya (Grigoryevich) 1891-1967
See Ehrenburg, Ilya (Grigoryevich)

Eseki, Bruno 1919-
See Mphahlele, Ezekiel

Esenin, Sergei (Aleksandrovich)
1895-1925 .... TCLC 4
See also CA 104

Eshleman, Clayton 1935-...........CLC 7
See also CA 33-36R
See also DLB 5

Espriu, Salvador 1913-1985........CLC 9
See also obituary CA 115

Evans, Marian 1819-1880
See Eliot, George

Evans, Mary Ann 1819-1880
See Eliot, George

Evarts, Esther 1900-1972
See Benson, Sally

Everson, R(onald) G(ilmour)
1903-.......................CLC 27
See also CA 17-20R

Everson, William (Oliver)
1912- .... CLC 1, 5, 14
See also CA 9-12R
See also DLB 5, 16

Evtushenko, Evgenii (Aleksandrovich) 1933-
See Yevtushenko, Yevgeny

Ewart, Gavin (Buchanan)
1916-.......................CLC 13
See also CANR 17
See also CA 89-92
See also DLB 40

Ewers, Hanns Heinz
1871-1943.................. TCLC 12
See also CA 109

Ewing, Frederick R. 1918-
See Sturgeon, Theodore (Hamilton)

Exley, Frederick (Earl)
1929-...................... CLC 6, 11
See also CA 81-84
See also DLB-Y 81
See also AITN 2

Ezekiel, Tish O'Dowd 1943- ....CLC 34

Fagen, Donald 1948-
See Becker, Walter and Fagen, Donald

Fagen, Donald 1948- and
Becker, Walter 1950-
See Becker, Walter and Fagen, Donald

Fair, Ronald L. 1932-.............CLC 18
See also CA 69-72
See also DLB 33

Fairbairns, Zoë (Ann) 1948- ....CLC 32
See also CA 103

Fairfield, Cicily Isabel 1892-1983
See West, Rebecca

Fallaci, Oriana 1930- ....CLC 11
See also CANR 15
See also CA 77-80

Fargue, Léon-Paul 1876-1947 .... TCLC 11
See also CA 109

Farigoule, Louis 1885-1972
See Romains, Jules

Fariña, Richard 1937?-1966 ....CLC 9
See also CA 81-84
See also obituary CA 25-28R

Farley, Walter 1920-..............CLC 17
See also CANR 8
See also CA 17-20R
See also SATA 2, 43
See also DLB 22

Farmer, Philip José 1918- ...... CLC 1, 19
See also CANR 4
See also CA 1-4R
See also DLB 8

Farrell, J(ames) G(ordon)
1935-1979.....................CLC 6
See also CA 73-76
See also obituary CA 89-92
See also DLB 14

Farrell, James T(homas)
1904-1979...........CLC 1, 4, 8, 11
See also CANR 9
See also CA 5-8R
See also obituary CA 89-92
See also DLB 4, 9
See also DLB-DS 2

Farrell, M. J. 1904-
See Keane, Molly

Fassbinder, Rainer Werner
1946-1982....................CLC 20
See also CA 93-96
See also obituary CA 106

Fast, Howard (Melvin) 1914-.......CLC 23
See also CANR 1
See also CA 1-4R
See also SATA 7
See also DLB 9

Faulkner, William (Cuthbert)
1897-1962....... CLC 1, 3, 6, 8, 9, 11,
14, 18, 28
See also CA 81-84
See also DLB 9, 11, 44
See also DLB-DS 2
See also AJTN 1

Fauset, Jessie Redmon
1884?-1961...................CLC 19
See also CA 109

Faust, Irvin 1924- ....CLC 8
See also CA 33-36R
See also DLB 2, 28
See also DLB-Y 80

Federman, Raymond 1928- ....CLC 6
See also CANR 10
See also CA 17-20R
See also DLB-Y 80

Feiffer, Jules 1929- .... CLC 2, 8
See also CA 17-20R
See also SATA 8
See also DLB 7, 44

Feinstein, Elaine 1930-............CLC 36
See also CA 69-72
See also CAAS 1
See also DLB 14, 40

Feldman, Irving (Mordecai)
1928-.......................CLC 7
See also CANR 1
See also CA 1-4R

Fellini, Federico 1920- ....CLC 16
See also CA 65-68

Felsen, Gregor 1916-
See Felsen, Henry Gregor

Felsen, Henry Gregor 1916-........CLC 17
See also CANR 1
See also CA 1-4R
See also SATA 1

Fenton, James (Martin) 1949-......CLC 32
See also CA 102
See also DLB 40

Ferber, Edna 1887-1968..........CLC 18
See also CA 5-8R
See also obituary CA 25-28R
See also SATA 7
See also DLB 9, 28
See also AITN 1

Ferlinghetti, Lawrence (Monsanto)
1919?-...............CLC 2, 6, 10, 27
See also CANR 3
See also CA 5-8R
See also DLB 5, 16

Ferrier, Susan (Edmonstone)
1782-1854...................NCLC 8

Feuchtwanger, Lion
1884-1958..................TCLC 3
See also CA 104

Fiedler, Leslie A(aron)
1917-..................CLC 4, 13, 24
See also CANR 7
See also CA 9-12R
See also DLB 28

Field, Eugene 1850-1895 .... NCLC 3
See also SATA 16
See also DLB 21, 23, 42

Fielding, Henry 1707-1754.......... LC 1
See also DLB 39

Fielding, Sarah 1710-1768 .... LC 1
See also DLB 39

Fierstein, Harvey 1954- ....CLC 33

Figes, Eva 1932-..................CLC 31
See also CANR 4
See also CA 53-56
See also DLB 14

Finch, Robert (Duer Claydon)
1900-......................CLC 18
See also CANR 9
See also CA 57-60

Findley, Timothy 1930-...........CLC 27
See also CANR 12
See also CA 25-28R

Fink, Janis 1951-
See Ian, Janis

Firbank, (Arthur Annesley) Ronald
1886-1926..................TCLC 1
See also CA 104
See also DLB 36

Firbank, Louis 1944-
See Reed, Lou

Fisher, Roy 1930- ....CLC 25
See also CANR 16
See also CA 81-84
See also DLB 40

Fisher, Rudolph 1897-1934 ...... TCLC 11
See also CA 107

Fisher, Vardis (Alvero)
1895-1968....................CLC 7
See also CA 5-8R
See also obituary CA 25-28R
See also DLB 9

FitzGerald, Edward
1809-1883..................NCLC 9
See also DLB 32

Fitzgerald, F(rancis) Scott (Key)
1896-1940.............TCLC 1, 6, 14
See also CA 110
See also DLB 4, 9
See also DLB-Y 81
See also DLB-DS 1
See also AITN 1

Fitzgerald, Penelope 1916-........CLC 19
See also CA 85-88
See also DLB 14

FitzGerald, Robert D(avid)
1902-......................CLC 19
See also CA 17-20R

Flanagan, Thomas (James Bonner)
1923-......................CLC 25
See also CA 108
See also DLB-Y 80

Flaubert, Gustave
1821-1880...............NCLC 2, 10

Fleming, Ian (Lancaster)
1908-1964.................CLC 3, 30
See also CA 5-8R
See also SATA 9

Fleming, Thomas J(ames)
1927-......................CLC 37
See also CANR 10
See also CA 5-8R
See also SATA 8

Fo, Dario 1929-..................CLC 32
See also CA 116

Follett, Ken(neth Martin)
1949-......................CLC 18
See also CANR 13
See also CA 81-84
See also DLB-Y 81

Forbes, Esther 1891-1967.........CLC 12
See also CAP 1
See also CA 13-14
See also obituary CA 25-28R
See also DLB 22
See also SATA 2

Forché, Carolyn 1950- ....CLC 25
See also CA 109
See also DLB 5

Ford, Ford Madox
1873-1939...............TCLC 1, 15
See also CA 104
See also DLB 34

Ford, John 1895-1973............CLC 16
See also obituary CA 45-48

Forester, C(ecil) S(cott)
1899-1966...................CLC 35
See also CA 73-76
See also obituary CA 25-28R
See also SATA 13

Forman, James D(ouglas)
1932-......................CLC 21
See also CANR 4
See also CA 9-12R
See also SATA 8, 21

Forrest, Leon 1937-...............CLC 4
See also CA 89-92
See also DLB 33

Forster, E(dward) M(organ)
1879-1970...... CLC 1, 2, 3, 4, 9, 10,
13, 15, 22
See also CAP 1
See also CA 13-14
See also obituary CA 25-28R
See also DLB 34

Forster, John 1812-1876........ NCLC 11

Forsyth, Frederick 1938- ..... CLC 2, 5, 36
See also CA 85-88

Forten (Grimk), Charlotte L(ottie)
1837-1914..................TCLC 16

Foscolo, Ugo 1778-1827 .... NCLC 8

Fosse, Bob 1925- ....CLC 20
See also Fosse, Robert Louis

Fosse, Robert Louis 1925-
See Bob Fosse
See also CA 110

Foucault, Michel
1926-1984................ CLC 31, 34
See also CA 105
See also obituary CA 113

**Fouqué, Friedrich (Heinrich Karl) de La
Motte** 1777-1843............ NCLC 2

Fournier, Henri Alban 1886-1914
See Alain-Fournier
See also CA 104

Fournier, Pierre 1916- ....CLC 11
See also CANR 16
See also CA 89-92

Fowles, John (Robert)
1926-......CLC 1, 2, 3, 4, 6, 9, 10, 15,
33
See also CA 5-8R
See also DLB 14
See also SATA 22

Fox, Paula 1923- .... CLC 2, 8
See also CLR 1
See also CA 73-76
See also SATA 17

Fox, William Price (Jr.) 1926-......CLC 22
See also CANR 11
See also CA 17-20R
See also DLB 2
See also DLB-Y 81

Frame (Clutha), Janet (Paterson)
1924-................CLC 2, 3, 6, 22
See also Clutha, Janet Paterson Frame

France, Anatole 1844-1924 ...... TCLC 9
See also Thibault, Jacques Anatole
Francois

Francis, Dick 1920-............ CLC 2, 22
See also CANR 9
See also CA 5-8R

Francis, Robert (Churchill)
1901-......................CLC 15
See also CANR 1
See also CA 1-4R

Frank, Anne 1929-1945 .... TCLC 17
See also CA 113
See also SATA 42

Franklin, (Stella Maria Sarah) Miles
1879-1954.................. TCLC 7
See also CA 104

Fraser, Antonia (Pakenham)
1932-......................CLC 32
See also CA 85-88
See also SATA 32

Fraser, George MacDonald
1925-......................CLC 7
See also CANR 2
See also CA 45-48

Frayn, Michael 1933- .... CLC 3, 7, 31
See also CA 5-8R
See also DLB 13, 14

Frederic, Harold 1856-1898...... NCLC 10
See also DLB 12, 23

Fredro, Aleksander 1793-1876 .... NCLC 8

Freeman, Douglas Southall
1886-1953 . . . . **TCLC 11**
See also CA 109
See also DLB 17

Freeman, Mary (Eleanor) Wilkins
1852-1930 . . . . **TCLC 9**
See also CA 106
See also DLB 12

French, Marilyn 1929- . . . . **CLC 10, 18**
See also CANR 3
See also CA 69-72

Freneau, Philip Morin
1752-1832 . . . . **NCLC 1**
See also DLB 37, 43

Friedman, B(ernard) H(arper)
1926- . . . . **CLC 7**
See also CANR 3
See also CA 1-4R

Friedman, Bruce Jay 1930- . . . . . . **CLC 3, 5**
See also CA 9-12R
See also DLB 2, 28

Friel, Brian 1929- . . . . **CLC 5**
See also CA 21-24R
See also DLB 13

Friis-Baastad, Babbis (Ellinor)
1921-1970 . . . . **CLC 12**
See also CA 17-20R
See also SATA 7

Frisch, Max (Rudolf)
1911- . . . . **CLC 3, 9, 14, 18, 32**
See also CA 85-88

Fromentin, Eugène (Samuel Auguste)
1820-1876 . . . . **NCLC 10**

Frost, Robert (Lee)
1874-1963 . . . . . . **CLC 1, 3, 4, 9, 10, 13,
15, 26, 34**
See also CA 89-92
See also SATA 14

Fry, Christopher 1907- . . . . . . **CLC 2, 10, 14**
See also CANR 9
See also CA 17-20R
See also DLB 13

Frye, (Herman) Northrop
1912- . . . . **CLC 24**
See also CANR 8
See also CA 5-8R

Fuchs, Daniel 1909- . . . . **CLC 8, 22**
See also CA 81-84
See also DLB 9, 26, 28

Fuchs, Daniel 1934- . . . . **CLC 34**
See also CANR 14
See also CA 37-40R

Fuentes, Carlos
1928- . . . . **CLC 3, 8, 10, 13, 22**
See also CANR 10
See also CA 69-72
See also AITN 2

Fugard, Athol 1932- . . . . . . **CLC 5, 9, 14, 25**
See also CA 85-88

Fuller, Charles (H., Jr.) 1939- . . . . . **CLC 25**
See also CA 108, 112
See also DLB 38

Fuller, (Sarah) Margaret
1810-1850 . . . . **NCLC 5**
See also Ossoli, Sarah Margaret (Fuller
marchesa d')
See also DLB 1

Fuller, Roy (Broadbent)
1912- . . . . **CLC 4, 28**
See also CA 5-8R
See also DLB 15, 20

Futrelle, Jacques 1875-1912 . . . . . **TCLC 19**
See also CA 113

Gadda, Carlo Emilio
1893-1973 . . . . **CLC 11**
See also CA 89-92

Gaddis, William
1922- . . . . **CLC 1, 3, 6, 8, 10, 19**
See also CA 17-20R
See also DLB 2

Gaines, Ernest J. 1933- . . . . . **CLC 3, 11, 18**
See also CANR 6
See also CA 9-12R
See also DLB 2, 33
See also DLB-Y 80
See also AITN 1

Gale, Zona 1874-1938 . . . . **TCLC 7**
See also CA 105
See also DLB 9

Gallagher, Tess 1943- . . . . **CLC 18**
See also CA 106

Gallant, Mavis 1922- . . . . **CLC 7, 18**
See also CA 69-72

Gallant, Roy A(rthur) 1924- . . . . **CLC 17**
See also CANR 4
See also CA 5-8R
See also SATA 4

Gallico, Paul (William)
1897-1976 . . . . **CLC 2**
See also CA 5-8R
See also obituary CA 69-72
See also SATA 13
See also DLB 9
See also AITN 1

Galsworthy, John 1867-1933 . . . . . . **TCLC 1**
See also CA 104
See also DLB 10, 34

Galt, John 1779-1839 . . . . **NCLC 1**

Gann, Ernest K(ellogg) 1910- . . . . . . **CLC 23**
See also CANR 1
See also CA 1-4R
See also AITN 1

García Lorca, Federico
1899-1936 . . . . **TCLC 1, 7**
See also CA 104

García Márquez, Gabriel
1928- . . . . **CLC 2, 3, 8, 10, 15, 27**
See also CANR 10
See also CA 33-36R

Gardner, John (Champlin, Jr.)
1933-1982 . . . . . . **CLC 2, 3, 5, 7, 8, 10,
18, 28, 34**
See also CA 65-68
See also obituary CA 107
See also obituary SATA 31, 40
See also DLB 2
See also DLB-Y 82
See also AITN 1

Gardner, John (Edmund)
1926- . . . . **CLC 30**
See also CANR 15
See also CA 103
See also AITN 1

Garfield, Leon 1921- . . . . **CLC 12**
See also CA 17-20R
See also SATA 1, 32

Garland, (Hannibal) Hamlin
1860-1940 . . . . **TCLC 3**
See also CA 104
See also DLB 12

Garneau, Hector (de) Saint Denys
1912-1943 . . . . **TCLC 13**
See also CA 111

Garner, Alan 1935- . . . . **CLC 17**
See also CANR 15
See also CA 73-76
See also SATA 18

Garner, Hugh 1913-1979 . . . . **CLC 13**
See also CA 69-72

Garnett, David 1892-1981 . . . . **CLC 3**
See also CA 5-8R
See also obituary CA 103
See also DLB 34

Garrett, George (Palmer)
1929- . . . . **CLC 3, 11**
See also CANR 1
See also CA 1-4R
See also DLB 2, 5
See also DLB-Y 83

Garrigue, Jean 1914-1972 . . . . **CLC 2, 8**
See also CA 5-8R
See also obituary CA 37-40R

Gary, Romain 1914-1980 . . . . **CLC 25**
See also Kacew, Romain

Gascar, Pierre 1916-
See Fournier, Pierre

Gaskell, Elizabeth Cleghorn
1810-1865 . . . . **NCLC 5**
See also DLB 21

Gass, William H(oward)
1924- . . . . **CLC 1, 2, 8, 11, 15**
See also CA 17-20R
See also DLB 2

Gautier, Théophile 1811-1872 . . . . . **NCLC 1**

Gaye, Marvin (Pentz)
1939-1984 . . . . **CLC 26**
See also obituary CA 112

Gee, Maurice (Gough) 1931- . . . . **CLC 29**
See also CA 97-100

Gelbart, Larry (Simon) 1923- . . . . . . **CLC 21**
See also CA 73-76

Gelber, Jack 1932- . . . . **CLC 1, 6, 14**
See also CANR 2
See also CA 1-4R
See also DLB 7

Gellhorn, Martha (Ellis) 1908- . . . . . **CLC 14**
See also CA 77-80
See also DLB-Y 82

Genet, Jean 1910- . . . . . **CLC 1, 2, 5, 10, 14**
See also CA 13-16R

Gent, Peter 1942- . . . . **CLC 29**
See also CA 89-92
See also DLB-Y 82
See also AITN 1

George, Jean Craighead 1919- . . . . . **CLC 35**
See also CLR 1
See also CA 5-8R
See also SATA 2

Author Index

George, Stefan (Anton)
   1868-1933............... TCLC 2, 14
   See also CA 104

Gerhardi, William (Alexander) 1895-1977
   See Gerhardie, William (Alexander)

Gerhardie, William (Alexander)
   1895-1977.................... CLC 5
   See also CA 25-28R
   See also obituary CA 73-76
   See also DLB 36

Gertler, T(rudy) 1946?- .... CLC 34
   See also CA 116

Gessner, Friedrike Victoria 1910-1980
   See Adamson, Joy(-Friederike Victoria)

Ghelderode, Michel de
   1898-1962................ CLC 6, 11
   See also CA 85-88

Ghiselin, Brewster 1903- .... CLC 23
   See also CANR 13
   See also CA 13-16R

Giacosa, Giuseppe 1847-1906 ..... TCLC 7
   See also CA 104

Gibbon, Lewis Grassic
   1901-1935................. TCLC 4
   See also Mitchell, James Leslie

Gibran, (Gibran) Kahlil
   1883-1931................ TCLC 1, 9
   See also CA 104

Gibson, William 1914- .... CLC 23
   See also CANR 9
   See also CA 9-12R
   See also DLB 7

Gide, André (Paul Guillaume)
   1869-1951................ TCLC 5, 12
   See also CA 104

Gifford, Barry (Colby) 1946-...... CLC 34
   See also CANR 9
   See also CA 65-68

Gilbert, (Sir) W(illiam) S(chwenck)
   1836-1911.................. TCLC 3
   See also CA 104
   See also SATA 36

Gilbreth, Ernestine 1908-
   See Carey, Ernestine Gilbreth

Gilbreth, Frank B(unker), Jr. 1911-
   See Gilbreth, Frank B(unker), Jr. and
      Carey, Ernestine Gilbreth
   See also CA 9-12R
   See also SATA 2

Gilbreth, Frank B(unker), Jr. 1911- and
   Carey, Ernestine Gilbreth
   1908-....................... CLC 17

Gilchrist, Ellen 1939- .... CLC 34
   See also CA 113, 116

Gilliam, Terry (Vance) 1940-
   See Monty Python
   See also CA 108, 113

Gilliatt, Penelope (Ann Douglass)
   1932-.................. CLC 2, 10, 13
   See also CA 13-16R
   See also DLB 14
   See also AITN 2

Gilman, Charlotte (Anna) Perkins (Stetson)
   1860-1935.................. TCLC 9
   See also CA 106

Gilmour, David 1944-
   See Pink Floyd

Gilroy, Frank D(aniel) 1925-........ CLC 2
   See also CA 81-84
   See also DLB 7

Ginsberg, Allen
   1926-........ CLC 1, 2, 3, 4, 6, 13, 36
   See also CANR 2
   See also CA 1-4R
   See also DLB 5, 16
   See also AITN 1

Ginzburg, Natalia 1916-........ CLC 5, 11
   See also CA 85-88

Giono, Jean 1895-1970........ CLC 4, 11
   See also CANR 2
   See also CA 45-48
   See also obituary CA 29-32R

Giovanni, Nikki 1943-........ CLC 2, 4, 19
   See also CLR 6
   See also CA 29-32R
   See also SATA 24
   See also DLB 5
   See also AITN 1

Giovene, Andrea 1904-............. CLC 7
   See also CA 85-88

Gippius, Zinaida (Nikolayevna) 1869-1945
   See also Hippius, Zinaida
   See also CA 106

Giraudoux, (Hippolyte) Jean
   1882-1944................ TCLC 2, 7
   See also CA 104

Gironella, José María 1917-........ CLC 11
   See also CA 101

Gissing, George (Robert)
   1857-1903.................. TCLC 3
   See also CA 105
   See also DLB 18

Glanville, Brian (Lester) 1931- ...... CLC 6
   See also CANR 3
   See also CA 5-8R
   See also DLB 15
   See also SATA 42

Glasgow, Ellen (Anderson Gholson)
   1873?-1945................ TCLC 2, 7
   See also CA 104
   See also DLB 9, 12

Glassco, John 1909-1981 .... CLC 9
   See also CANR 15
   See also CA 13-16R
   See also obituary CA 102

Glasser, Ronald J. 1940?- .... CLC 37

Glissant, Edouard 1928-........... CLC 10

Glück, Louise 1943- .... CLC 7, 22
   See also CA 33-36R
   See also DLB 5

Godard, Jean-Luc 1930-........... CLC 20
   See also CA 93-96

Godwin, Gail 1937-...... CLC 5, 8, 22, 31
   See also CANR 15
   See also CA 29-32R
   See also DLB 6

Goethe, Johann Wolfgang von
   1749-1832.................. NCLC 4

Gogarty, Oliver St. John
   1878-1957................. TCLC 15
   See also CA 109
   See also DLB 15, 19

Gogol, Nikolai (Vasilyevich)
   1809-1852.................. NCLC 5

Gökçeli, Yasar Kemal 1923-
   See Kemal, Yashar

Gold, Herbert 1924- .... CLC 4, 7, 14
   See also CANR 17
   See also CA 9-12R
   See also DLB 2
   See also DLB-Y 81

Goldbarth, Albert 1948-........... CLC 5
   See also CANR 6
   See also CA 53-56

Goldberg, Anatol 19??-........... CLC 34

Golding, William (Gerald)
   1911-........ CLC 1, 2, 3, 8, 10, 17, 27
   See also CANR 13
   See also CA 5-8R
   See also DLB 15

Goldman, Emma 1869-1940 ..... TCLC 13
   See also CA 110

Goldman, William (W.) 1931-....... CLC 1
   See also CA 9-12R
   See also DLB 44

Goldmann, Lucien 1913-1970 ......CLC 24
   See also CAP 2
   See also CA 25-28

Goldsberry, Steven 1949-.........CLC 34

Goldsmith, Oliver 1728?-1774....... LC 2
   See also SATA 26
   See also DLB 39

Gombrowicz, Witold
   1904-1969............... CLC 4, 7, 11
   See also CAP 2
   See also CA 19-20
   See also obituary CA 25-28R

Gómez de la Serna, Ramón
   1888-1963....................CLC 9
   See also obituary CA 116

Goncharov, Ivan Alexandrovich
   1812-1891................... NCLC 1

Goncourt, Edmond (Louis Antoine Huot) de
   1822-1896
   See Goncourt, Edmond (Louis Antoine
      Huot) de and Goncourt, Jules (Alfred
      Huot) de

Goncourt, Edmond (Louis Antoine Huot) de
   1822-1896 and Goncourt, Jules (Alfred
   Huot) de 1830-1870 .... NCLC 7

Goncourt, Jules (Alfred Huot) de 1830-1870
   See Goncourt, Edmond (Louis Antoine
      Huot) de and Goncourt, Jules (Alfred
      Huot) de

Goncourt, Jules (Alfred Huot) de 1830-1870
   and Goncourt, Edmond (Louis Antoine
   Huot) de 1822-1896
   See Goncourt, Edmond (Louis Antoine
      Huot) de and Goncourt, Jules (Alfred
      Huot) de

Goodman, Paul
   1911-1972.............. CLC 1, 2, 4, 7
   See also CAP 2
   See also CA 19-20
   See also obituary CA 37-40R

Gordimer, Nadine
   1923-......... CLC 3, 5, 7, 10, 18, 33
   See also CANR 3
   See also CA 5-8R

Gordon, Caroline
    1895-1981..............CLC 6, 13, 29
    See also CAP 1
    See also CA 11-12
    See also obituary CA 103
    See also DLB 4, 9
    See also DLB-Y 81

Gordon, Mary (Catherine)
    1949-.................CLC 13, 22
    See also CA 102
    See also DLB 6
    See also DLB-Y 81

Gordon, Sol 1923-................CLC 26
    See also CANR 4
    See also CA 53-56
    See also SATA 11

Gordone, Charles 1925-.........CLC 1, 4
    See also CA 93-96
    See also DLB 7

Gorenko, Anna Andreyevna 1889?-1966
    See Akhmatova, Anna

Gorky, Maxim 1868-1936 .... TCLC 8
    See also Peshkov, Alexei Maximovich

Goryan, Sirak 1908-1981
    See Saroyan, William

Gotlieb, Phyllis (Fay Bloom)
    1926-........................CLC 18
    See also CANR 7
    See also CA 13-16R

Gould, Lois 1938?- .... CLC 4, 10
    See also CA 77-80

Gourmont, Rémy de
    1858-1915..................TCLC 17
    See also CA 109

Goyen, (Charles) William
    1915-1983...............CLC 5, 8, 14
    See also CANR 6
    See also CA 5-8R
    See also obituary CA 110
    See also DLB 2
    See also DLB-Y 83
    See also AITN 2

Goytisolo, Juan 1931-........CLC 5, 10, 23
    See also CA 85-88

Grabbe, Christian Dietrich
    1801-1836..................NCLC 2

Gracq, Julien 1910-...............CLC 11

Grade, Chaim 1910-1982.........CLC 10
    See also CA 93-96
    See also obituary CA 107

Graham, R(obert) B(ontine) Cunninghame
    1852-1936..................TCLC 19

Graham, W(illiam) S(ydney)
    1918-........................CLC 29
    See also CA 73-76
    See also DLB 20

Graham, Winston (Mawdsley)
    1910-........................CLC 23
    See also CANR 2
    See also CA 49-52

Granville-Barker, Harley
    1877-1946..................TCLC 2
    See also CA 104

Grass, Günter (Wilhelm)
    1927-.......CLC 1, 2, 4, 6, 11, 15, 22,
                                        32
    See also CA 13-16R

Grau, Shirley Ann 1929- .... CLC 4, 9
    See also CA 89-92
    See also DLB 2
    See also AITN 2

Graves, Robert 1895- ......CLC 1, 2, 6, 11
    See also CANR 5
    See also CA 5-8R
    See also DLB 20

Gray, Amlin 1946-...............CLC 29

Gray, Francine du Plessix
    1930-........................CLC 22
    See also CAAS 2
    See also CANR 11
    See also CA 61-64

Gray, John (Henry)
    1866-1934.................. TCLC 19

Gray, Simon (James Holliday)
    1936-................CLC 9, 14, 36
    See also CAAS 3
    See also CA 21-24R
    See also DLB 13
    See also AITN 1

Greeley, Andrew M(oran)
    1928-........................CLC 28
    See also CANR 7
    See also CA 5-8R

Green, Hannah 1932-........CLC 3, 7, 30
    See also Greenberg, Joanne
    See also CA 73-76

Green, Henry 1905-1974 .... CLC 2, 13
    See also Yorke, Henry Vincent
    See also DLB 15

Green, Julien (Hartridge)
    1900-..................... CLC 3, 11
    See also CA 21-24R
    See also DLB 4

Greenberg, Ivan 1908-1973
    See Rahv, Philip
    See also CA 85-88

Greenberg, Joanne (Goldenberg)
    1932-..................CLC 3, 7, 30
    See also Green, Hannah
    See also CANR 14
    See also CA 5-8R
    See also SATA 25

Greene, Bette 1934-...............CLC 30
    See also CLR 2
    See also CANR 4
    See also CA 53-56
    See also SATA 8

Greene, Gael......................CLC 8
    See also CANR 10
    See also CA 13-16R

Greene, Graham
    1904-.......CLC 1, 3, 6, 9, 14, 18, 27,
                                        37
    See also CA 13-16R
    See also SATA 20
    See also DLB 13, 15
    See also AITN 2

Gregor, Arthur 1923-..............CLC 9
    See also CANR 11
    See also CA 25-28R
    See also SATA 36

Gregory, Lady (Isabella Augusta Persse)
    1852-1932.................. TCLC 1
    See also CA 104
    See also DLB 10

Grendon, Stephen 1909-1971
    See Derleth, August (William)

Greve, Felix Paul Berthold Friedrich
    1879-1948
    See Grove, Frederick Philip
    See also CA 104

Grey, (Pearl) Zane
    1872?-1939.................. TCLC 6
    See also CA 104
    See also DLB 9

Grieg, (Johan) Nordahl (Brun)
    1902-1943.................. TCLC 10
    See also CA 107

Grieve, C(hristopher) M(urray) 1892-1978
    See MacDiarmid, Hugh
    See also CA 5-8R
    See also obituary CA 85-88

Griffin, Gerald 1803-1840 .... NCLC 7

Griffiths, Trevor 1935-............CLC 13
    See also CA 97-100
    See also DLB 13

Grigson, Geoffrey (Edward Harvey)
    1905-........................CLC 7
    See also CA 25-28R
    See also DLB 27

Grillparzer, Franz 1791-1872 ..... NCLC 1

Grimm, Jakob (Ludwig) Karl 1785-1863
    See Grimm, Jakob (Ludwig) Karl and
        Grimm, Wilhelm Karl

Grimm, Jakob (Ludwig) Karl 1785-1863
    and **Grimm, Wilhelm Karl**
    1786-1859.................. NCLC 3
    See also SATA 22

Grimm, Wilhelm Karl 1786-1859
    See Grimm, Jakob (Ludwig) Karl and
        Grimm, Wilhelm Karl

Grimm, Wilhelm Karl 1786-1859 and
    Grimm, Jakob (Ludwig) Karl
    1785-1863
    See Grimm, Jakob (Ludwig) Karl and
        Grimm, Wilhelm Karl

Grindel, Eugene 1895-1952
    See also CA 104

Grove, Frederick Philip
    1879-1948.................. TCLC 4
    See also Greve, Felix Paul Berthold
        Friedrich

Grumbach, Doris (Isaac)
    1918-................... CLC 13, 22
    See also CAAS 2
    See also CANR 9
    See also CA 5-8R

Grundtvig, Nicolai Frederik Severin
    1783-1872.................. NCLC 1

Guare, John 1938-.........CLC 8, 14, 29
    See also CA 73-76
    See also DLB 7

Gudjonsson, Halldór Kiljan 1902-
    See Laxness, Halldór (Kiljan)
    See also CA 103

Guest, Barbara 1920- ....CLC 34
    See also CANR 11
    See also CA 25-28R
    See also DLB 5

Guest, Judith (Ann) 1936-...... CLC 8, 30
    See also CANR 15
    See also CA 77-80

Author Index

Guild, Nicholas M. 1944- . . . . .CLC 33
See also CA 93-96

Guillén, Jorge 1893-1984 . . . . .CLC 11
See also CA 89-92
See also obituary CA 112

Guillevic, (Eugène) 1907- . . . . .CLC 33
See also CA 93-96

Gunn, Bill 1934- . . . . .CLC 5
See also Gunn, William Harrison
See also DLB 38

Gunn, Thom(son William)
1929- . . . . .CLC 3, 6, 18, 32
See also CANR 9
See also CA 17-20R
See also DLB 27

Gunn, William Harrison 1934-
See Gunn, Bill
See also CANR 12
See also CA 13-16R
See also AITN 1

Gurney, A(lbert) R(amsdell), Jr.
1930- . . . . .CLC 32
See also CA 77-80

Gustafson, Ralph (Barker)
1909- .CLC 36
See also CANR 8
See also CA 21-24R

Guthrie, A(lfred) B(ertram), Jr.
1901- .CLC 23
See also CA 57-60
See also DLB 6

Guthrie, Woodrow Wilson 1912-1967
See Guthrie, Woody
See also CA 113
See also obituary CA 93-96

Guthrie, Woody 1912-1967 . . . . . . .CLC 35
See also Guthrie, Woodrow Wilson

Guy, Rosa (Cuthbert) 1928- . . . . .CLC 26
See also CANR 14
See also CA 17-20R
See also SATA 14
See also DLB 33

Haavikko, Paavo (Juhani)
1931- . . . . CLC 18, 34
See also CA 106

Hacker, Marilyn 1942- . . . . . . .CLC 5, 9, 23
See also CA 77-80

Haggard, (Sir) H(enry) Rider
1856-1925 . . . . .TCLC 11
See also CA 108
See also SATA 16

Haig-Brown, Roderick L(angmere)
1908-1976 . . . . .CLC 21
See also CANR 4
See also CA 5-8R
See also obituary CA 69-72
See also SATA 12

Hailey, Arthur 1920- . . . . .CLC 5
See also CANR 2
See also CA 1-4R
See also DLB-Y 82
See also AITN 2

Haley, Alex (Palmer) 1921- . . . . . CLC 8, 12
See also CA 77-80
See also DLB 38

Hall, Donald (Andrew, Jr.)
1928- . . . . .CLC 1, 13, 37
See also CANR 2
See also CA 5-8R
See also SATA 23
See also DLB 5

Hall, (Marguerite) Radclyffe
1886-1943 . . . . .TCLC 12
See also CA 110

Halpern, Daniel 1945- . . . . .CLC 14
See also CA 33-36R

Hamburger, Michael (Peter Leopold)
1924- . . . . CLC 5, 14
See also CANR 2
See also CA 5-8R
See also DLB 27

Hamill, Pete 1935- . . . . .CLC 10
See also CA 25-28R

Hamilton, Edmond 1904-1977 . . . . . . .CLC 1
See also CANR 3
See also CA 1-4R
See also DLB 8

Hamilton, Gail 1911-
See Corcoran, Barbara

Hamilton, Mollie 1909?-
See Kaye, M(ary) M(argaret)

Hamilton, Virginia (Edith)
1936- . . . . .CLC 26
See also CLR 1
See also CA 25-28R
See also SATA 4
See also DLB 33

Hammett, (Samuel) Dashiell
1894-1961 . . . . .CLC 3, 5, 10, 19
See also CA 81-84
See also AITN 1

Hammon, Jupiter
1711?-1800? . . . . .NCLC 5
See also DLB 31

Hamner, Earl (Henry), Jr.
1923- . . . . .CLC 12
See also CA 73-76
See also DLB 6
See also AITN 2

Hampton, Christopher (James)
1946- . . . . .CLC 4
See also CA 25-28R
See also DLB 13

Hamsun, Knut 1859-1952 . . . . . TCLC 2, 14
See also Pedersen, Knut

Handke, Peter 1942- . . . . . .CLC 5, 8, 10, 15
See also CA 77-80

Hanley, James 1901- . . . . . . .CLC 3, 5, 8, 13
See also CA 73-76

Hannah, Barry 1942- . . . . .CLC 23
See also CA 108, 110
See also DLB 6

Hansberry, Lorraine
1930-1965 . . . . .CLC 17
See also CA 109
See also obituary CA 25-28R
See also DLB 7, 38
See also AITN 2

Hanson, Kenneth O(stlin)
1922- . . . . .CLC 13
See also CANR 7
See also CA 53-56

Hardwick, Elizabeth 1916- . . . . .CLC 13
See also CANR 3
See also CA 5-8R
See also DLB 6

Hardy, Thomas
1840-1928 . . . . .TCLC 4, 10, 18
See also CA 104
See also SATA 25
See also DLB 18, 19

Hare, David 1947- . . . . .CLC 29
See also CA 97-100
See also DLB 13

Harlan, Louis R(udolph) 1922- . . . . .CLC 34
See also CA 21-24R

Harper, Frances Ellen Watkins
1825-1911 . . . . .TCLC 14
See also CA 111

Harper, Michael S(teven)
1938- . . . . CLC 7, 22
See also CA 33-36R
See also DLB 41

Harris, Christie (Lucy Irwin)
1907- . . . . .CLC 12
See also CANR 6
See also CA 5-8R
See also SATA 6

Harris, Joel Chandler
1848-1908 . . . . .TCLC 2
See also CA 104
See also YABC 1
See also DLB 11, 23, 42

**Harris, John (Wyndham Parkes Lucas)
Beynon** 1903-1969
See Wyndham, John
See also CA 102
See also obituary CA 89-92

Harris, MacDonald 1921- . . . . .CLC 9
See also Heiney, Donald (William)

Harris, Mark 1922- . . . . .CLC 19
See also CAAS 3
See also CANR 2
See also CA 5-8R
See also DLB 2
See also DLB-Y 80

Harris, (Theodore) Wilson
1921- . . . . .CLC 25
See also CANR 11
See also CA 65-68

Harrison, James (Thomas) 1937-
See Harrison, Jim
See also CANR 8
See also CA 13-16R

Harrison, Jim 1937- . . . . .CLC 6, 14, 33
See also Harrison, James (Thomas)
See also DLB-Y 82

Harriss, Will(ard Irvin) 1922- . . . . . .CLC 34
See also CA 111

Harte, (Francis) Bret(t)
1836?-1902 . . . . .TCLC 1
See also CA 104
See also SATA 26
See also DLB 12

Hartley, L(eslie) P(oles)
1895-1972 . . . . CLC 2, 22
See also CA 45-48
See also obituary CA 37-40R
See also DLB 15

Hartman, Geoffrey H. 1929-.......CLC 27

Haruf, Kent 19??-.................CLC 34

Harwood, Ronald 1934-...........CLC 32
See also CANR 4
See also CA 1-4R
See also DLB 13

Hašek, Jaroslav (Matej Frantisek)
1883-1923..................TCLC 4
See also CA 104

Hass, Robert 1941-..............CLC 18
See also CA 111

Hauptmann, Gerhart (Johann Robert)
1862-1946..................TCLC 4
See also CA 104

Havel, Václav 1936-............CLC 25
See also CA 104

Haviaras, Stratis 1935-............CLC 33
See also CA 105

Hawkes, John (Clendennin Burne, Jr.)
1925-......CLC 1, 2, 3, 4, 7, 9, 14, 15, 27

See also CANR 2
See also CA 1-4R
See also DLB 2, 7
See also DLB-Y 80

Hawthorne, Nathaniel
1804-1864...............NCLC 2, 10
See also YABC 2
See also DLB 1

Hayden, Robert (Earl)
1913-1980...........CLC 5, 9, 14, 37
See also CA 69-72
See also obituary CA 97-100
See also SATA 19
See also obituary SATA 26
See also DLB 5

Haywood, Eliza (Fowler)
1693?-1756....................LC 1
See also DLB 39

Hazzard, Shirley 1931-............CLC 18
See also CANR 4
See also CA 9-12R
See also DLB-Y 82

H(ilda) D(oolittle)
1886-1961........ CLC 3, 8, 14, 31, 34
See also Doolittle, Hilda

Head, Bessie 1937-................CLC 25
See also CA 29-32R

Headon, (Nicky) Topper 1956?-
See The Clash

Heaney, Seamus (Justin)
1939-........... CLC 5, 7, 14, 25, 37
See also CA 85-88
See also DLB 40

Hearn, (Patricio) Lafcadio (Tessima Carlos)
1850-1904................ TCLC 9
See also CA 105
See also DLB 12

Heat Moon, William Least
1939-.........................CLC 29

Hébert, Anne 1916-........ CLC 4, 13, 29
See also CA 85-88

Hecht, Anthony (Evan)
1923-..................CLC 8, 13, 19
See also CANR 6
See also CA 9-12R
See also DLB 5

Hecht, Ben 1894-1964..............CLC 8
See also CA 85-88
See also DLB 7, 9, 25, 26, 28

Heidegger, Martin 1889-1976 .....CLC 24
See also CA 81-84
See also obituary CA 65-68

Heidenstam, (Karl Gustaf) Verner von
1859-1940............... TCLC 5
See also CA 104

Heifner, Jack 1946-...............CLC 11
See also CA 105

Heilbrun, Carolyn G(old)
1926-.........................CLC 25
See also CANR 1
See also CA 45-48

Heine, Harry 1797-1856
See Heine, Heinrich

Heine, Heinrich 1797-1856........ NCLC 4

Heiney, Donald (William) 1921-
See Harris, MacDonald
See also CANR 3
See also CA 1-4R

Heinlein, Robert A(nson)
1907-............ CLC 1, 3, 8, 14, 26
See also CANR 1
See also CA 1-4R
See also SATA 9
See also DLB 8

Heller, Joseph
1923-........... CLC 1, 3, 5, 8, 11, 36
See also CANR 8
See also CA 5-8R
See also DLB 2, 28
See also DLB-Y 80
See also AITN 1

Hellman, Lillian (Florence)
1905?-1984..... CLC 2, 4, 8, 14, 18, 34
See also CA 13-16R
See also obituary CA 112
See also DLB 7
See also DLB-Y 84
See also AITN 1, 2

Helprin, Mark 1947-.....CLC 7, 10, 22, 32
See also CA 81-84

Hemingway, Ernest (Miller)
1899-1961...... CLC 1, 3, 6, 8, 10, 13, 19, 30, 34
See also CA 77-80
See also DLB 4, 9
See also DLB-Y 81
See also DLB-DS 1
See also AITN 2

Henley, Beth 1952- ....CLC 23
See also Henley, Elizabeth Becker

Henley, Elizabeth Becker 1952-
See Henley, Beth
See also CA 107

Henley, William Ernest
1849-1903................... TCLC 8
See also CA 105
See also DLB 19

Hennissart, Martha
See Lathen, Emma
See also CA 85-88

Henry, O. 1862-1910 .... TCLC 1, 19
See also Porter, William Sydney

Hentoff, Nat(han Irving) 1925-.....CLC 26
See also CLR 1
See also CANR 5
See also CA 1-4R
See also SATA 27, 42

Heppenstall, (John) Rayner
1911-1981..................CLC 10
See also CA 1-4R
See also obituary CA 103

Herbert, Frank (Patrick)
1920-.............. CLC 12, 23, 35
See also CANR 5
See also CA 53-56
See also SATA 9, 37
See also DLB 8

Herbert, Zbigniew 1924-...........CLC 9
See also CA 89-92

Herbst, Josephine 1897-1969......CLC 34
See also CA 5-8R
See also obituary CA 25-28R
See also DLB 9

Herder, Johann Gottfried von
1744-1803..................NCLC 8

Hergesheimer, Joseph
1880-1954.................. TCLC 11
See also CA 109
See also DLB 9

Herlagñez, Pablo de 1844-1896
See Verlaine, Paul (Marie)

Herlihy, James Leo 1927-..........CLC 6
See also CANR 2
See also CA 1-4R

Herriot, James 1916-..............CLC 12
See also Wight, James Alfred

Hersey, John (Richard)
1914-................CLC 1, 2, 7, 9
See also CA 17-20R
See also SATA 25
See also DLB 6

Herzen, Aleksandr Ivanovich
1812-1870..................NCLC 10

Herzog, Werner 1942-.............CLC 16
See also CA 89-92

Hesse, Hermann
1877-1962...... CLC 1, 2, 3, 6, 11, 17, 25
See also CAP 2
See also CA 17-18

Heyen, William 1940-......... CLC 13, 18
See also CA 33-36R
See also DLB 5

Heyerdahl, Thor 1914-............CLC 26
See also CANR 5
See also CA 5-8R
See also SATA 2

Heym, Georg (Theodor Franz Arthur)
1887-1912................. TCLC 9
See also CA 106

Heyse, Paul (Johann Ludwig von)
1830-1914................. TCLC 8
See also CA 104

Hibbert, Eleanor (Burford)
1906-.........................CLC 7
See also CANR 9
See also CA 17-20R
See also SATA 2

Higgins, George V(incent)
1939-................CLC 4, 7, 10, 18
See also CA 77-80
See also DLB 2
See also DLB-Y 81

Highsmith, (Mary) Patricia
1921-...................CLC 2, 4, 14
See also CANR 1
See also CA 1-4R

Highwater, Jamake 1942-..........CLC 12
See also CANR 10
See also CA 65-68
See also SATA 30, 32

Hill, Geoffrey 1932-..........CLC 5, 8, 18
See also CA 81-84
See also DLB 40

Hill, George Roy 1922-............CLC 26
See also CA 110

Hill, Susan B. 1942- ....CLC 4
See also CA 33-36R
See also DLB 14

Hilliard, Noel (Harvey) 1929- ......CLC 15
See also CANR 7
See also CA 9-12R

Himes, Chester (Bomar)
1909-1984.............CLC 2, 4, 7, 18
See also CA 25-28R
See also obituary CA 114
See also DLB 2

Hinde, Thomas 1926- ....CLC 6, 11
See also Chitty, (Sir) Thomas Willes

Hine, (William) Daryl 1936- ....CLC 15
See also CANR 1
See also CA 1-4R

Hinton, S(usan) E(loise) 1950-......CLC 30
See also CLR 3
See also CA 81-84
See also SATA 19

**Hippius (Merezhkovsky), Zinaida
(Nikolayevna)** 1869-1945 ..... TCLC 9
See also Gippius, Zinaida (Nikolayevna)

Hiraoka, Kimitake 1925-1970
See Mishima, Yukio
See also CA 97-100
See also obituary CA 29-32R

Hirsch, Edward 1950-.............CLC 31
See also CA 104

Hitchcock, (Sir) Alfred (Joseph)
1899-1980...................CLC 16
See also obituary CA 97-100
See also SATA 27
See also obituary SATA 24

Hoagland, Edward 1932-..........CLC 28
See also CANR 2
See also CA 1-4R
See also DLB 6

Hoban, Russell C(onwell)
1925-..................... CLC 7, 25
See also CLR 3
See also CA 5-8R
See also SATA 1, 40

Hobson, Laura Z(ametkin)
1900-................... CLC 7, 25
See also CA 17-20R
See also DLB 28

Hochhuth, Rolf 1931- .... CLC 4, 11, 18
See also CA 5-8R

Hochman, Sandra 1936-........ CLC 3, 8
See also CA 5-8R
See also DLB 5

Hochwälder, Fritz 1911-...........CLC 36
See also CA 29-32R

Hocking, Mary (Eunice) 1921- .....CLC 13
See also CA 101

Hodgins, Jack 1938-..............CLC 23
See also CA 93-96

Hodgson, William Hope
1877-1918.................. TCLC 13
See also CA 111

Hoffman, Daniel (Gerard)
1923-...............CLC 6, 13, 23
See also CANR 4
See also CA 1-4R
See also DLB 5

Hoffman, Stanley 1944- ....CLC 5
See also CA 77-80

Hoffmann, Ernst Theodor Amadeus
1776-1822................... NCLC 2
See also SATA 27

**Hofmannsthal, Hugo (Laurenz August
Hofmann Edler) von**
1874-1929.................. TCLC 11
See also CA 106

Hogg, James 1770-1835 .... NCLC 4

Holden, Ursula 1921- ....CLC 18
See also CA 101

Holland, Isabelle 1920-............CLC 21
See also CANR 10
See also CA 21-24R
See also SATA 8

Holland, Marcus 1900-1985
See Caldwell, (Janet Miriam) Taylor
(Holland)

Hollander, John 1929- .....CLC 2, 5, 8, 14
See also CANR 1
See also CA 1-4R
See also SATA 13
See also DLB 5

Hollis, Jim 1916-
See Summers, Hollis (Spurgeon, Jr.)

Holt, Victoria 1906-
See Hibbert, Eleanor (Burford)

Holub, Miroslav 1923- ....CLC 4
See also CANR 10
See also CA 21-24R

Honig, Edwin 1919-...............CLC 33
See also CANR 4
See also CA 5-8R
See also DLB 5

Hood, Hugh (John Blagdon)
1928-.................... CLC 15, 28
See also CANR 1
See also CA 49-52

Hope, A(lec) D(erwent) 1907- ....CLC 3
See also CA 21-24R

Hopkins, John (Richard) 1931-......CLC 4
See also CA 85-88

Horgan, Paul 1903-................CLC 9
See also CANR 9
See also CA 13-16R
See also SATA 13

Horwitz, Julius 1920- ....CLC 14
See also CANR 12
See also CA 9-12R

Hougan, Carolyn 19??-............CLC 34

Household, Geoffrey (Edward West)
1900-.......................CLC 11
See also CA 77-80
See also SATA 14

Housman, A(lfred) E(dward)
1859-1936................TCLC 1, 10
See also CA 104
See also DLB 19

Housman, Laurence
1865-1959................... TCLC 7
See also CA 106
See also SATA 25
See also DLB 10

Howard, Elizabeth Jane
1923-.................... CLC 7, 29
See also CANR 8
See also CA 5-8R

Howard, Maureen 1930-........ CLC 5, 14
See also CA 53-56
See also DLB-Y 83

Howard, Richard 1929- .... CLC 7, 10
See also CA 85-88
See also DLB 5
See also AITN 1

Howard, Robert E(rvin)
1906-1936................... TCLC 8
See also CA 105

Howells, William Dean
1837-1920................TCLC 7, 17
See also CA 104
See also DLB 12

Howes, Barbara 1914- ....CLC 15
See also CAAS 3
See also CA 9-12R
See also SATA 5

Hrabal, Bohumil 1914-............CLC 13
See also CA 106

Huch, Ricarda (Octavia)
1864-1947................. TCLC 13
See also CA 111

Hueffer, Ford Madox 1873-1939
See Ford, Ford Madox

Hughes, Edward James 1930-
See Hughes, Ted

Hughes, (James) Langston
1902-1967...... CLC 1, 5, 10, 15, 35
See also CANR 1
See also CA 1-4R
See also obituary CA 25-28R
See also SATA 4, 33
See also DLB 4, 7

Hughes, Richard (Arthur Warren)
1900-1976................. CLC 1, 11
See also CANR 4
See also CA 5-8R
See also obituary CA 65-68
See also SATA 8
See also obituary SATA 25
See also DLB 15

Hughes, Ted 1930-..... CLC 2, 4, 9, 14, 37
See also CLR 3
See also CANR 1
See also CA 1-4R
See also SATA 27
See also DLB 40

Hugo, Richard F(ranklin)
　1923-1982.............CLC **6, 18, 32**
　See also CANR 3
　See also CA 49-52
　See also obituary CA 108
　See also DLB 5

Hugo, Victor Marie
　1802-1885...............NCLC **3, 10**

Humphreys, Josephine 1945-.......CLC **34**

Hunt, E(verette) Howard (Jr.)
　1918-........................CLC **3**
　See also CANR 2
　See also CA 45-48
　See also AITN 1

Hunt, (James Henry) Leigh
　1784-1859..................NCLC **1**

Hunter, Evan 1926-........CLC **1, 11, 31**
　See also CANR 5
　See also CA 5-8R
　See also SATA 25
　See also DLB-Y 82

Hunter, Kristin (Eggleston)
　1931-.......................CLC **35**
　See also CLR 3
　See also CANR 13
　See also CA 13-16R
　See also SATA 12
　See also DLB 33
　See also AITN 1

Hunter, Mollie (Maureen McIlwraith)
　1922-.......................CLC **21**
　See also McIlwraith, Maureen Mollie
　　Hunter

Hurston, Zora Neale
　1901?-1960...............CLC **7, 30**
　See also CA 85-88

Huston, John (Marcellus)
　1906-.......................CLC **20**
　See also CA 73-76
　See also DLB 26

Huxley, Aldous (Leonard)
　1894-1963......CLC **1, 3, 4, 5, 8, 11,**
　　　　　　　　　　　　18, 35
　See also CA 85-88
　See also DLB 36

Huysmans, Charles Marie Georges
　1848-1907
　See also Huysmans, Joris-Karl
　See also CA 104

Huysmans, Joris-Karl
　1848-1907..................TCLC **7**
　See also Huysmans, Charles Marie Georges

Hyde, Margaret O(ldroyd)
　1917-.......................CLC **21**
　See also CANR 1
　See also CA 1-4R
　See also SATA 1, 42

Ian, Janis 1951-..................CLC **21**
　See also CA 105

Ibargüengoitia, Jorge
　1928-1983..................CLC **37**
　See also obituary CA 113

Ibsen, Henrik (Johan)
　1828-1906.............TCLC **2, 8, 16**
　See also CA 104

Ibuse, Masuji 1898-...............CLC **22**

Ichikawa, Kon 1915-..............CLC **20**

Idle, Eric 1943-
　See Monty Python
　See also CA 116

Ignatow, David 1914-........CLC **4, 7, 14**
　See also CAAS 3
　See also CA 9-12R
　See also DLB 5

Immermann, Karl (Lebrecht)
　1796-1840..................NCLC **4**

Inge, William (Motter)
　1913-1973...............CLC **1, 8, 19**
　See also CA 9-12R
　See also DLB 7

Innaurato, Albert 1948-..........CLC **21**
　See also CA 115

Innes, Michael 1906-
　See Stewart, J(ohn) I(nnes) M(ackintosh)

Ionesco, Eugène
　1912-..........CLC **1, 4, 6, 9, 11, 15**
　See also CA 9-12R
　See also SATA 7

Irving, John (Winslow)
　1942-..................CLC **13, 23**
　See also CA 25-28R
　See also DLB 6
　See also DLB-Y 82

Irving, Washington 1783-1859 .... NCLC **2**
　See also YABC 2
　See also DLB 3, 11, 30

Isaacs, Susan 1943-...............CLC **32**
　See also CA 89-92

Isherwood, Christopher (William Bradshaw)
　1904-..................CLC **1, 9, 11, 14**
　See also CA 13-16R
　See also DLB 15

Ishiguro, Kazuo 1954?-...........CLC **27**

Ishikawa Takuboku
　1885-1912..................TCLC **15**

Ivask, Ivar (Vidrik) 1927- ....CLC **14**
　See also CA 37-40R

Jackson, Jesse 1908-1983.........CLC **12**
　See also CA 25-28R
　See also obituary CA 109
　See also SATA 2, 29

Jackson, Laura (Riding) 1901-
　See Riding, Laura
　See also CA 65-68

Jackson, Shirley 1919-1965.......CLC **11**
　See also CANR 4
　See also CA 1-4R
　See also obituary CA 25-28R
　See also SATA 2
　See also DLB 6

Jacob, (Cyprien) Max
　1876-1944..................TCLC **6**
　See also CA 104

Jacob, Piers A(nthony) D(illingham) 1934-
　See Anthony (Jacob), Piers
　See also CA 21-24R

Jacobs, Jim 1942-
　See Jacobs, Jim and Casey, Warren
　See also CA 97-100

Jacobs, Jim 1942- and
　　Casey, Warren 1935-........CLC **12**

Jacobson, Dan 1929-..........CLC **4, 14**
　See also CANR 2
　See also CA 1-4R
　See also DLB 14

Jagger, Mick 1944-
　See Jagger, Mick and Richard, Keith

Jagger, Mick 1944- and
　　Richard, Keith 1943-.........CLC **17**

Jakes, John (William) 1932- ....CLC **29**
　See also CANR 10
　See also CA 57-60
　See also DLB-Y 83

James, C(yril) L(ionel) R(obert)
　1901-.......................CLC **33**

James, Daniel 1911-
　See Santiago, Danny

James, Henry (Jr.)
　1843-1916..................TCLC **2, 11**
　See also CA 104
　See also DLB 12

James, M(ontague) R(hodes)
　1862-1936..................TCLC **6**
　See also CA 104

James, P(hyllis) D(orothy)
　1920-.......................CLC **18**
　See also CA 21-24R

James, William 1842-1910......TCLC **15**
　See also CA 109

Jandl, Ernst 1925-................CLC **34**

Jarrell, Randall
　1914-1965.........CLC **1, 2, 6, 9, 13**
　See also CLR 6
　See also CANR 6
　See also CA 5-8R
　See also obituary CA 25-28R
　See also SATA 7

Jarry, Alfred 1873-1907......TCLC **2, 14**
　See also CA 104

Jean Paul 1763-1825.............NCLC **7**

Jeffers, (John) Robinson
　1887-1962.........CLC **2, 3, 11, 15**
　See also CA 85-88
　See also DLB 45

Jefferson, Thomas 1743-1826 .... NCLC **11**
　See also DLB 31

Jellicoe, (Patricia) Ann 1927-.......CLC **27**
　See also CA 85-88
　See also DLB 13

Jennings, Elizabeth (Joan)
　1926-.......................CLC **5, 14**
　See also CANR 8
　See also CA 61-64
　See also DLB 27

Jennings, Waylon 1937-..........CLC **21**

Jensen, Laura (Linnea) 1948- ......CLC **37**
　See also CA 103

Jerrold, Douglas 1803-1857.......NCLC **2**

Jewett, Sarah Orne 1849-1909 .... TCLC **1**
　See also CA 108
　See also SATA 15
　See also DLB 12

Jhabvala, Ruth Prawer
　1927-..................CLC **4, 8, 29**
　See also CANR 2
　See also CA 1-4R

Jiles, Paulette 1943-..............CLC 13
See also CA 101

Jiménez (Mantecón), Juan Ramón
1881-1958..................TCLC 4
See also CA 104

Joel, Billy 1949-..................CLC 26
See also Joel, William Martin

Joel, William Martin 1949-
See Joel, Billy
See also CA 108

Johnson, B(ryan) S(tanley William)
1933-1973..................CLC 6, 9
See also CANR 9
See also CA 9-12R
See also obituary CA 53-56
See also DLB 14, 40

Johnson, Charles 1948-............CLC 7
See also CA 116
See also DLB 33

Johnson, Diane 1934- ....CLC 5, 13
See also CANR 17
See also CA 41-44R
See also DLB-Y 80

Johnson, Eyvind (Olof Verner)
1900-1976....................CLC 14
See also CA 73-76
See also obituary CA 69-72

Johnson, James Weldon
1871-1938................TCLC 3, 19
See also Johnson, James William
See also CA 104

Johnson, James William 1871-1938
See Johnson, James Weldon
See also SATA 31

Johnson, Lionel Pigot
1867-1902..................TCLC 19
See also DLB 19

Johnson, Marguerita 1928-
See Angelou, Maya

Johnson, Pamela Hansford
1912-1981...............CLC 1, 7, 27
See also CANR 2
See also CA 1-4R
See also obituary CA 104
See also DLB 15

Johnson, Uwe
1934-1984..............CLC 5, 10, 15
See also CANR 1
See also CA 1-4R
See also obituary CA 112

Johnston, Jennifer 1930- ....CLC 7
See also CA 85-88
See also DLB 14

Jones, D(ouglas) G(ordon)
1929-......................CLC 10
See also CANR 13
See also CA 29-32R
See also CA 113

Jones, David
1895-1974............CLC 2, 4, 7, 13
See also CA 9-12R
See also obituary CA 53-56
See also DLB 20

Jones, David Robert 1947-
See Bowie, David
See also CA 103

Jones, Diana Wynne 1934-........CLC 26
See also CANR 4
See also CA 49-52
See also SATA 9

Jones, Gayl 1949- .... CLC 6, 9
See also CA 77-80
See also DLB 33

Jones, James 1921-1977......CLC 1, 3, 10
See also CANR 6
See also CA 1-4R
See also obituary CA 69-72
See also DLB 2
See also AITN 1, 2

Jones, (Everett) LeRoi
1934-........CLC 1, 2, 3, 5, 10, 14, 33
See also Baraka, Amiri
See also Baraka, Imamu Amiri
See also CA 21-24R

Jones, Madison (Percy, Jr.)
1925-........................CLC 4
See also CANR 7
See also CA 13-16R

Jones, Mervyn 1922-..............CLC 10
See also CANR 1
See also CA 45-48

Jones, Mick 1956?-
See The Clash

Jones, Nettie 19??-................CLC 34

Jones, Preston 1936-1979.........CLC 10
See also CA 73-76
See also obituary CA 89-92
See also DLB 7

Jones, Robert F(rancis) 1934- ....CLC 7
See also CANR 2
See also CA 49-52

Jones, Terry 1942?-
See Monty Python
See also CA 112, 116

Jong, Erica 1942-.........CLC 4, 6, 8, 18
See also CA 73-76
See also DLB 2, 5, 28
See also AITN 1

Jordan, June 1936- ....CLC 5, 11, 23
See also CLR 10
See also CA 33-36R
See also SATA 4
See also DLB 38

Jordan, Pat(rick M.) 1941- ....CLC 37
See also CA 33-36R

Josipovici, G(abriel) 1940-..........CLC 6
See also CA 37-40R
See also DLB 14

Joubert, Joseph 1754-1824........NCLC 9

Joyce, James (Augustine Aloysius)
1882-1941..............TCLC 3, 8, 16
See also CA 104
See also DLB 10, 19, 36

Just, Ward S(wift) 1935- .... CLC 4, 27
See also CA 25-28R

Justice, Donald (Rodney)
1925-....................CLC 6, 19
See also CA 5-8R
See also DLB-Y 33

Kacew, Romain 1914-1980
See Gary, Romain
See also CA 108
See also obituary CA 102

Kacewgary, Romain 1914-1980
See Gary, Romain

Kafka, Franz
1883-1924..............TCLC 2, 6, 13
See also CA 105

Kahn, Roger 1927- ....CLC 30
See also CA 25-28R

Kaiser, (Friedrich Karl) Georg
1878-1945.................. TCLC 9
See also CA 106

Kallman, Chester (Simon)
1921-1975....................CLC 2
See also CANR 3
See also CA 45-48
See also obituary CA 53-56

Kaminsky, Melvin 1926-
See Brooks, Mel
See also CANR 16

Kane, Paul 1941-
See Simon, Paul

Kanin, Garson 1912-..............CLC 22
See also CANR 7
See also CA 5-8R
See also DLB 7
See also AITN 1

Kaniuk, Yoram 1930-.............CLC 19

Kantor, MacKinlay 1904-1977......CLC 7
See also CA 61-64
See also obituary CA 73-76
See also DLB 9

Karamzin, Nikolai Mikhailovich
1766-1826.................. NCLC 3

Karapánou, Margaríta 1946-.......CLC 13
See also CA 101

Karl, Frederick R(obert) 1927-.....CLC 34
See also CANR 3
See also CA 5-8R

Kassef, Romain 1914-1980
See Gary, Romain

Kaufman, Sue 1926-1977........ CLC 3, 8
See also Barondess, Sue K(aufman)

Kavan, Anna 1904-1968........ CLC 5, 13
See also Edmonds, Helen (Woods)
See also CANR 6

Kavanagh, Patrick (Joseph Gregory)
1905-1967....................CLC 22
See also CA 25-28R
See also DLB 15, 20

Kawabata, Yasunari
1899-1972.........CLC 2, 5, 9, 18
See also CA 93-96
See also obituary CA 33-36R

Kaye, M(ary) M(argaret)
1909?-....................CLC 28
See also CA 89-92

Kaye, Mollie 1909?-
See Kaye, M(ary) M(argaret)

Kaye-Smith, Sheila
1887-1956.................. TCLC 20
See also DLB 36

Kazan, Elia 1909- .... CLC 6, 16
See also CA 21-24R

Kazantzakis, Nikos
1885?-1957................TCLC 2, 5
See also CA 105

Kazin, Alfred 1915-..............CLC 34
  See also CANR 1
  See also CA 1-4R

Keane, Mary Nesta (Skrine) 1904-
  See Keane, Molly
  See also CA 108, 114

Keane, Molly 1904-..............CLC 31
  See also Keane, Mary Nesta (Skrine)

Keates, Jonathan 19??-..............CLC 34

Keaton, Buster 1895-1966 ....CLC 20

Keaton, Joseph Francis 1895-1966
  See Keaton, Buster

Keats, John 1795-1821 .... NCLC 8

Keene, Donald 1922-..............CLC 34
  See also CANR 5
  See also CA 1-4R

Keller, Gottfried 1819-1890...... NCLC 2

Kelley, William Melvin 1937- ......CLC 22
  See also CA 77-80
  See also DLB 33

Kellogg, Marjorie 1922-............CLC 2
  See also CA 81-84

Kemal, Yashar 1922- .... CLC 14, 29
  See also CA 89-92

Kemelman, Harry 1908-............CLC 2
  See also CANR 6
  See also CA 9-12R
  See also DLB 28
  See also AITN 1

Kendall, Henry 1839-1882....... NCLC 12

Keneally, Thomas (Michael)
      1935-......... CLC 5, 8, 10, 14, 19, 27
  See also CANR 10
  See also CA 85-88

Kennedy, John Pendleton
      1795-1870.................. NCLC 2
  See also DLB 3

Kennedy, Joseph Charles 1929-
  See Kennedy, X. J.
  See also CANR 4
  See also CA 1-4R
  See also SATA 14

Kennedy, William 1928-..... CLC 6, 28, 34
  See also CANR 14
  See also CA 85-88

Kennedy, X. J. 1929- ....CLC 8
  See also Kennedy, Joseph Charles
  See also DLB 5

Kerouac, Jack
      1922-1969...... CLC 1, 2, 3, 5, 14, 29
  See also Kerouac, Jean-Louis Lebrid de
  See also DLB 2, 16
  See also DLB-DS 3

Kerouac, Jean-Louis Lebrid de 1922-1969
  See Kerouac, Jack
  See also CA 5-8R
  See also obituary CA 25-28R
  See also AITN 1

Kerr, Jean 1923-.................CLC 22
  See also CANR 7
  See also CA 5-8R

Kerr, M. E. 1927-............ CLC 12, 35
  See also Meaker, Marijane
  See also SAAS 1

Kerrigan, (Thomas) Anthony
      1918-..................... CLC 4, 6
  See also CANR 4
  See also CA 49-52

Kesey, Ken (Elton)
      1935-..............CLC 1, 3, 6, 11
  See also CA 1-4R
  See also DLB 2, 16

Kessler, Jascha (Frederick)
      1929-.......................CLC 4
  See also CANR 8
  See also CA 17-20R

Kettelkamp, Larry 1933-..........CLC 12
  See also CANR 16
  See also CA 29-32R
  See also SATA 2

Kherdian, David 1931-.......... CLC 6, 9
  See also CAAS 2
  See also CA 21-24R
  See also SATA 16

Khlebnikov, Velimir (Vladimirovich)
      1885-1922.................. TCLC 20
  See also CA 117

Khodasevich, Vladislav (Felitsianovich)
      1886-1939................. TCLC 15
  See also CA 115

Kielland, Alexander (Lange)
      1849-1906.................. TCLC 5
  See also CA 104

Kiely, Benedict 1919- ....CLC 23
  See also CANR 2
  See also CA 1-4R
  See also DLB 15

Kienzle, William X(avier)
      1928-.......................CLC 25
  See also CAAS 1
  See also CANR 9
  See also CA 93-96

Killens, John Oliver 1916-........CLC 10
  See also CAAS 2
  See also CA 77-80
  See also DLB 33

King, Francis (Henry) 1923- ....CLC 8
  See also CANR 1
  See also CA 1-4R
  See also DLB 15

King, Stephen (Edwin)
      1947-.................. CLC 12, 26, 37
  See also CANR 1
  See also CA 61-64
  See also SATA 9
  See also DLB-Y 80

Kingman, (Mary) Lee 1919- ....CLC 17
  See also Natti, (Mary) Lee
  See also CA 5-8R
  See also SATA 1

Kingston, Maxine Hong
      1940-.................. CLC 12, 19
  See also CANR 13
  See also CA 69-72
  See also DLB-Y 80

Kinnell, Galway
      1927-.......... CLC 1, 2, 3, 5, 13, 29
  See also CANR 10
  See also CA 9-12R
  See also DLB 5

Kinsella, Thomas 1928- ..... CLC 4, 19
  See also CA 17-20R
  See also DLB 27

Kinsella, W(illiam) P(atrick)
      1935-.......................CLC 27
  See also CA 97-100

Kipling, (Joseph) Rudyard
      1865-1936................ TCLC 8, 17
  See also CA 105
  See also YABC 2
  See also DLB 19, 34

Kirkup, James 1927-..............CLC 1
  See also CANR 2
  See also CA 1-4R
  See also SATA 12
  See also DLB 27

Kirkwood, James 1930- ....CLC 9
  See also CANR 6
  See also CA 1-4R
  See also AITN 2

Kizer, Carolyn (Ashley) 1925-......CLC 15
  See also CA 65-68
  See also DLB 5

Klausner, Amos 1939-
  See Oz, Amos

Klein, A(braham) M(oses)
      1909-1972.....................CLC 19
  See also CA 101
  See also obituary CA 37-40R

Klein, Norma 1938-..............CLC 30
  See also CLR 2
  See also CANR 15
  See also CA 41-44R
  See also SAAS 1
  See also SATA 7

Klein, T.E.D. 19??-..............CLC 34

Kleist, Heinrich von
      1777-1811.................. NCLC 2

Klimentev, Andrei Platonovich 1899-1951
  See Platonov, Andrei (Platonovich)
  See also CA 108

Klinger, Friedrich Maximilian von
      1752-1831.................. NCLC 1

Klopstock, Friedrich Gottlieb
      1724-1803.................. NCLC 11

Knebel, Fletcher 1911-............CLC 14
  See also CAAS 3
  See also CANR 1
  See also CA 1-4R
  See also SATA 36
  See also AITN 1

Knowles, John 1926-......CLC 1, 4, 10, 26
  See also CA 17-20R
  See also SATA 8
  See also DLB 6

Koch, Kenneth 1925- .... CLC 5, 8
  See also CANR 6
  See also CA 1-4R
  See also DLB 5

Koestler, Arthur
      1905-1983....... CLC 1, 3, 6, 8, 15, 33
  See also CANR 1
  See also CA 1-4R
  See also obituary CA 109
  See also DLB-Y 83

Kohout, Pavel 1928- ....CLC 13
  See also CANR 3
  See also CA 45-48

Konrád, György 1933- .... CLC **4, 10**
See also CA 85-88

Konwicki, Tadeusz 1926- .... CLC **8, 28**
See also CA 101

Kopit, Arthur (Lee)
1937- .... CLC **1, 18, 33**
See also CA 81-84
See also DLB 7
See also AITN 1

Kops, Bernard 1926- .... CLC **4**
See also CA 5-8R
See also DLB 13

Kornbluth, C(yril) M.
1923-1958 .... TCLC **8**
See also CA 105
See also DLB 8

Kosinski, Jerzy (Nikodem)
1933- .... CLC **1, 2, 3, 6, 10, 15**
See also CANR 9
See also CA 17-20R
See also DLB 2
See also DLB-Y 82

Kostelanetz, Richard (Cory)
1940- .... CLC **28**
See also CA 13-16R

Kostrowitzki, Wilhelm Apollinaris de
1880-1918
See Apollinaire, Guillaume
See also CA 104

Kotlowitz, Robert 1924- .... CLC **4**
See also CA 33-36R

Kotzwinkle, William
1938- .... CLC **5, 14, 35**
See also CLR 6
See also CANR 3
See also CA 45-48
See also SATA 24

Kozol, Jonathan 1936- .... CLC **17**
See also CANR 16
See also CA 61-64

Kozoll, Michael 1940?-
See Bochco, Steven and Kozoll, Michael

Kramer, Kathryn 19??- .... CLC **34**

Krasicki, Ignacy 1735-1801 .... NCLC **8**

Krasiński, Zygmunt
1812-1859 .... NCLC **4**

Kraus, Karl 1874-1936 .... TCLC **5**
See also CA 104

Kristofferson, Kris 1936- .... CLC **26**
See also CA 104

Krleža, Miroslav 1893-1981 .... CLC **8**
See also CA 97-100
See also obituary CA 105

Kroetsch, Robert 1927- .... CLC **5, 23**
See also CANR 8
See also CA 17-20R

Krotkov, Yuri 1917- .... CLC **19**
See also CA 102

Krumgold, Joseph (Quincy)
1908-1980 .... CLC **12**
See also CANR 7
See also CA 9-12R
See also obituary CA 101
See also SATA 1
See also obituary SATA 23

Krutch, Joseph Wood
1893-1970 .... CLC **24**
See also CANR 4
See also CA 1-4R
See also obituary CA 25-28R

Krylov, Ivan Andreevich
1768?-1844 .... NCLC **1**

Kubrick, Stanley 1928- .... CLC **16**
See also CA 81-84
See also DLB 26

Kumin, Maxine (Winokur)
1925- .... CLC **5, 13, 28**
See also CANR 1
See also CA 1-4R
See also SATA 12
See also DLB 5
See also AITN 2

Kundera, Milan
1929- .... CLC **4, 9, 19, 32**
See also CA 85-88

Kunitz, Stanley J(asspon)
1905- .... CLC **6, 11, 14**
See also CA 41-44R

Kunze, Reiner 1933- .... CLC **10**
See also CA 93-96

Kuprin, Aleksandr (Ivanovich)
1870-1938 .... TCLC **5**
See also CA 104

Kurosawa, Akira 1910- .... CLC **16**
See also CA 101

Kuttner, Henry 1915-1958 .... TCLC **10**
See also CA 107
See also DLB 8

Kuzma, Greg 1944- .... CLC **7**
See also CA 33-36R

Labrunie, Gérard 1808-1855
See Nerval, Gérard de

**Laclos, Pierre Ambroise François Choderlos
de** 1741-1803 .... NCLC **4**

**La Fayette, Marie (Madelaine Pioche de la
Vergne, Comtesse) de**
1634-1693 .... LC **2**

Laforgue, Jules 1860-1887 .... NCLC **5**

Lagerkvist, Pär (Fabian)
1891-1974 .... CLC **7, 10, 13**
See also CA 85-88
See also obituary CA 49-52

Lagerlöf, Selma (Ottiliana Lovisa)
1858-1940 .... TCLC **4**
See also CLR 7
See also CA 108
See also SATA 15

La Guma, (Justin) Alex(ander)
1925- .... CLC **19**
See also CA 49-52

Lamartine, Alphonse (Marie Louis Prat) de
1790-1869 .... NCLC **11**

Lamb, Charles 1775-1834 .... NCLC **10**
See also SATA 17

Lamming, George (William)
1927- .... CLC **2, 4**
See also CA 85-88

LaMoore, Louis Dearborn 1908?-
See L'Amour, Louis (Dearborn)

L'Amour, Louis (Dearborn)
1908- .... CLC **25**
See also CANR 3
See also CA 1-4R
See also DLB-Y 80
See also AITN 2

**Lampedusa, (Prince) Giuseppe (Maria
Fabrizio) Tomasi di**
1896-1957 .... TCLC **13**
See also CA 111

Lancaster, Bruce 1896-1963 .... CLC **36**
See also CAP-1
See also CA 9-12R
See also SATA 9

Landis, John (David) 1950- .... CLC **26**
See also CA 112

Landolfi, Tommaso 1908- .... CLC **11**

Landwirth, Heinz 1927-
See Lind, Jakov
See also CANR 7

Lane, Patrick 1939- .... CLC **25**
See also CA 97-100

Lang, Andrew 1844-1912 .... TCLC **16**
See also CA 114
See also SATA 16

Lang, Fritz 1890-1976 .... CLC **20**
See also CA 77-80
See also obituary CA 69-72

Langer, Elinor 1939- .... CLC **34**

Lanier, Sidney 1842-1881 .... NCLC **6**
See also SATA 18

Larbaud, Valéry 1881-1957 ...... TCLC **9**
See also CA 106

Lardner, Ring(gold Wilmer)
1885-1933 .... TCLC **2, 14**
See also CA 104
See also DLB 11, 25

Larkin, Philip (Arthur)
1922- .... CLC **3, 5, 8, 9, 13, 18, 33**
See also CA 5-8R
See also DLB 27

Larsen, Nella 1893-1964 .... CLC **37**

Larson, Charles R(aymond)
1938- .... CLC **31**
See also CANR 4
See also CA 53-56

Latham, Jean Lee 1902- .... CLC **12**
See also CANR 7
See also CA 5-8R
See also SATA 2
See also AITN 1

Lathen, Emma .... CLC **2**
See also Hennissart, Martha
See also Latsis, Mary J(ane)

Latsis, Mary J(ane)
See Lathen, Emma
See also CA 85-88

Lattimore, Richmond (Alexander)
1906-1984 .... CLC **3**
See also CANR 1
See also CA 1-4R
See also obituary CA 112

Laurence, (Jean) Margaret (Wemyss)
1926- .... CLC **3, 6, 13**
See also CA 5-8R

Lautréamont, Comte de
  1846-1870.................. NCLC 12

Lavin, Mary 1912-............ CLC 4, 18
  See also CA 9-12R
  See also DLB 15

Lawrence, D(avid) H(erbert)
  1885-1930............. TCLC 2, 9, 16
  See also CA 104
  See also DLB 10, 19, 36

Lawrence, T(homas) E(dward)
  1888-1935.................. TCLC 18
  See also CA 115

Laxness, Halldór (Kiljan)
  1902-........................CLC 25
  See also Gudjonsson, Halldór Kiljan

Laye, Camara 1928-1980.......... CLC 4
  See also CA 85-88
  See also obituary CA 97-100

Layton, Irving (Peter) 1912- .... CLC 2, 15
  See also CANR 2
  See also CA 1-4R

Lazarus, Emma 1849-1887 .... NCLC 8

Leacock, Stephen (Butler)
  1869-1944.................. TCLC 2
  See also CA 104

Lear, Edward 1812-1888 .... NCLC 3
  See also CLR 1
  See also SATA 18
  See also DLB 32

Lear, Norman (Milton) 1922- ......CLC 12
  See also CA 73-76

Leavis, F(rank) R(aymond)
  1895-1978....................CLC 24
  See also CA 21-24R
  See also obituary CA 77-80

Leavitt, David 1961?- ....CLC 34
  See also CA 116

Lebowitz, Fran(ces Ann)
  1951?-................... CLC 11, 36
  See also CANR 14
  See also CA 81-84

Le Carré, John
  1931-............. CLC 3, 5, 9, 15, 28
  See also Cornwell, David (John Moore)

Le Clézio, J(ean) M(arie) G(ustave)
  1940-........................CLC 31
  See also CA 116

Leduc, Violette 1907-1972 ....CLC 22
  See also CAP 1
  See also CA 13-14
  See also obituary CA 33-36R

Lee, Andrea 1953-................CLC 36

Lee, Don L. 1942-................CLC 2
  See also Madhubuti, Haki R.
  See also CA 73-76

Lee, (Nelle) Harper 1926-..........CLC 12
  See also CA 13-16R
  See also SATA 11
  See also DLB 6

Lee, Lawrence 1903-..............CLC 34
  See also CA 25-28R

Lee, Manfred B(ennington) 1905-1971
  See Queen, Ellery
  See also CANR 2
  See also CA 1-4R
  See also obituary CA 29-32R

Lee, Stan 1922- ....CLC 17
  See also CA 108, 111

Lee, Vernon 1856-1935........ TCLC 5
  See also Paget, Violet

Leet, Judith 1935-................CLC 11

Le Fanu, Joseph Sheridan
  1814-1873.................. NCLC 9
  See also DLB 21

Leffland, Ella 1931-...............CLC 19
  See also CA 29-32R
  See also DLB-Y 84

Léger, (Marie-Rene) Alexis Saint-Léger
  1887-1975
  See Perse, St.-John
  See also CA 13-16R
  See also obituary CA 61-64

Le Guin, Ursula K(roeber)
  1929-.................. CLC 8, 13, 22
  See also CLR 3
  See also CANR 9
  See also CA 21-24R
  See also SATA 4
  See also DLB 8
  See also AITN 1

Lehmann, Rosamond (Nina)
  1901-........................CLC 5
  See also CANR 8
  See also CA 77-80
  See also DLB 15

Leiber, Fritz (Reuter, Jr.)
  1910-........................CLC 25
  See also CANR 2
  See also CA 45-48
  See also DLB 8

Leithauser, Brad 1953-............CLC 27
  See also CA 107

Lelchuk, Alan 1938-...............CLC 5
  See also CANR 1
  See also CA 45-48

Lem, Stanislaw 1921- .... CLC 8, 15
  See also CAAS 1
  See also CA 105

L'Engle, Madeleine 1918-..........CLC 12
  See also CLR 1
  See also CANR 3
  See also CA 1-4R
  See also SATA 1, 27
  See also AITN 2

Lennon, John (Ono)
  1940-1980....................CLC 35
  See also Lennon, John (Ono) and
    McCartney, Paul
  See also CA 102

Lennon, John (Ono) 1940-1980 and
    McCartney, Paul 1942- ....CLC 12

Lennon, John Winston 1940-1980
  See Lennon, John (Ono)

Lentricchia, Frank (Jr.) 1940-......CLC 34
  See also CA 25-28R

Lenz, Siegfried 1926- ....CLC 27
  See also CA 89-92

Leonard, Elmore 1925-........ CLC 28, 34
  See also CANR 12
  See also CA 81-84
  See also AITN 1

Leonard, Hugh 1926-.............CLC 19
  See also Byrne, John Keyes
  See also DLB 13

Lerman, Eleanor 1952-............CLC 9
  See also CA 85-88

Lermontov, Mikhail Yuryevich
  1814-1841.................. NCLC 5

Lesage, Alain-René 1668-1747....... LC 2

Lessing, Doris (May)
  1919-....CLC 1, 2, 3, 6, 10, 15, 22
  See also CA 9-12R
  See also DLB 15

Lester, Richard 1932-.............CLC 20

Leverson, Ada 1865-1936........ TCLC 18

Levertov, Denise
  1923-.........CLC 1, 2, 3, 5, 8, 15, 28
  See also CANR 3
  See also CA 1-4R
  See also DLB 5

Levi, Primo 1919-................CLC 37
  See also CANR 12
  See also CA 13-16R

Levin, Ira 1929-.............. CLC 3, 6
  See also CANR 17
  See also CA 21-24R

Levin, Meyer 1905-1981............CLC 7
  See also CANR 15
  See also CA 9-12R
  See also obituary CA 104
  See also SATA 21
  See also obituary SATA 27
  See also DLB 9, 28
  See also DLB-Y 81
  See also AITN 1

Levine, Philip
  1928-........... CLC 2, 4, 5, 9, 14, 33
  See also CANR 9
  See also CA 9-12R
  See also DLB 5

Levitin, Sonia 1934- ....CLC 17
  See also CA 29-32R
  See also SATA 4

Lewis, Alun 1915-1944........... TCLC 3
  See also CA 104
  See also DLB 20

Lewis, C(ecil) Day 1904-1972
  See Day Lewis, C(ecil)

Lewis, C(live) S(taples)
  1898-1963......... CLC 1, 3, 6, 14, 27
  See also CLR 3
  See also CA 81-84
  See also SATA 13
  See also DLB 15

Lewis, (Harry) Sinclair
  1885-1951.............. TCLC 4, 13
  See also CA 104
  See also DLB 9
  See also DLB-DS 1

Lewis, Matthew Gregory
  1775-1818.................. NCLC 11
  See also DLB 39

Lewis, (Percy) Wyndham
  1882?-1957................. TCLC 2, 9
  See also CA 104
  See also DLB 15

Lewisohn, Ludwig 1883-1955 .... TCLC 19
See also CA 107
See also DLB 4, 9, 28

Lezama Lima, José
1910-1976 .... CLC 4, 10
See also CA 77-80

Li Fei-kan 1904-
See Pa Chin
See also CA 105

Lie, Jonas (Lauritz Idemil)
1833-1908 .... TCLC 5

Lieber, Joel 1936-1971 .... CLC 6
See also CA 73-76
See also obituary CA 29-32R

Lieber, Stanley Martin 1922-
See Lee, Stan

Lieberman, Laurence (James)
1935- .... CLC 4, 36
See also CANR 8
See also CA 17-20R

Lightfoot, Gordon (Meredith)
1938- .... CLC 26
See also CA 109

Liliencron, Detlev von
1844-1909 .... TCLC 18

Lima, José Lezama 1910-1976
See Lezama Lima, José

Lind, Jakov 1927- .... CLC 1, 2, 4, 27
See also Landwirth, Heinz
See also CA 9-12R

Lindsay, David 1876-1945 .... TCLC 15
See also CA 113

Lindsay, (Nicholas) Vachel
1879-1931 .... TCLC 17
See also CA 114
See also SATA 40

Lipsyte, Robert (Michael)
1938- .... CLC 21
See also CANR 8
See also CA 17-20R
See also SATA 5

Liu E 1857-1909 .... TCLC 15
See also CA 115

Lively, Penelope 1933- .... CLC 32
See also CLR 7
See also CA 41-44R
See also SATA 7
See also DLB 14

Livesay, Dorothy 1909- .... CLC 4, 15
See also CA 25-28R
See also AITN 2

Llewellyn, Richard 1906-1983 ...... CLC 7
See also Llewellyn Lloyd, Richard (Dafydd Vyvyan)
See also DLB 15

Llewellyn Lloyd, Richard (Dafydd Vyvyan)
1906-1983
See Llewellyn, Richard
See also CANR 7
See also CA 53-56
See also obituary CA 111
See also SATA 11

Llosa, Mario Vargas 1936-
See Vargas Llosa, Mario

Lloyd, Richard Llewellyn 1906-
See Llewellyn, Richard

Lockhart, John Gibson
1794-1854 .... NCLC 6

Lodge, David (John) 1935- .... CLC 36
See also CA 17-20R
See also DLB 14

Logan, John 1923- .... CLC 5
See also CA 77-80
See also DLB 5

Lombino, S. A. 1926-
See Hunter, Evan

London, Jack 1876-1916 ...... TCLC 9, 15
See also London, John Griffith
See also SATA 18
See also DLB 8, 12
See also AITN 2

London, John Griffith 1876-1916
See London, Jack
See also CA 110

Long, Emmett 1925-
See Leonard, Elmore

Longfellow, Henry Wadsworth
1807-1882 .... NCLC 2
See also SATA 19
See also DLB 1

Longley, Michael 1939- .... CLC 29
See also CA 102
See also DLB 40

Lopate, Phillip 1943- .... CLC 29
See also CA 97-100
See also DLB-Y 80

López y Fuentes, Gregorio
1897-1966 .... CLC 32

Lord, Bette Bao 1938- .... CLC 23
See also CA 107

Lorde, Audre (Geraldine)
1934- .... CLC 18
See also CANR 16
See also CA 25-28R
See also DLB 41

Loti, Pierre 1850-1923 .... TCLC 11
See also Viaud, (Louis Marie) Julien

Lovecraft, H(oward) P(hillips)
1890-1937 .... TCLC 4
See also CA 104

Lowell, Amy 1874-1925 .... TCLC 1, 8
See also CA 104

Lowell, James Russell
1819-1891 .... NCLC 2
See also DLB 1, 11

Lowell, Robert (Traill Spence, Jr.)
1917-1977 ...... CLC 1, 2, 3, 4, 5, 8, 9, 11, 15, 37
See also CA 9-12R
See also obituary CA 73-76
See also DLB 5

Lowndes, Marie (Adelaide Belloc)
1868-1947 .... TCLC 12
See also CA 107

Lowry, (Clarence) Malcolm
1909-1957 .... TCLC 6
See also CA 105
See also DLB 15

Loy, Mina 1882-1966 .... CLC 28
See also CA 113
See also DLB 4

Lucas, George 1944- .... CLC 16
See also CA 77-80

Lucas, Victoria 1932-1963
See Plath, Sylvia

Ludlum, Robert 1927- .... CLC 22
See also CA 33-36R
See also DLB-Y 82

Ludwig, Otto 1813-1865 .... NCLC 4

Lugones, Leopoldo
1874-1938 .... TCLC 15
See also CA 116

Lu Hsün 1881-1936 .... TCLC 3

Lukács, Georg 1885-1971 .... CLC 24
See also Lukács, György

Lukács, György 1885-1971
See Lukács, Georg
See also CA 101
See also obituary CA 29-32R

Lurie, Alison 1926- .... CLC 4, 5, 18
See also CANR 2, 17
See also CA 1-4R
See also DLB 2

Luzi, Mario 1914- .... CLC 13
See also CANR 9
See also CA 61-64

Lytle, Andrew (Nelson) 1902- ...... CLC 22
See also CA 9-12R
See also DLB 6

Lytton, Edward Bulwer 1803-1873
See Bulwer-Lytton, (Lord) Edward (George Earle Lytton)
See also SATA 23

Maas, Peter 1929- .... CLC 29
See also CA 93-96

Macaulay, (Dame Emile) Rose
1881-1958 .... TCLC 7
See also CA 104
See also DLB 36

MacBeth, George (Mann)
1932- .... CLC 2, 5, 9
See also CA 25-28R
See also SATA 4
See also DLB 40

MacCaig, Norman (Alexander)
1910- .... CLC 36
See also CANR 3
See also CA 9-12R
See also DLB 27

MacDiarmid, Hugh
1892-1978 .... CLC 2, 4, 11, 19
See also Grieve, C(hristopher) M(urray)
See also DLB 20

Macdonald, Cynthia 1928- ..... CLC 13, 19
See also CANR 4
See also CA 49-52

MacDonald, George
1824-1905 .... TCLC 9
See also CA 106
See also SATA 33
See also DLB 18

MacDonald, John D(ann)
1916- .... CLC 3, 27
See also CANR 1
See also CA 1-4R
See also DLB 8

Macdonald, (John) Ross
1915-1983........ CLC **1, 2, 3, 14, 34**
See also Millar, Kenneth

MacEwen, Gwendolyn 1941-.......CLC **13**
See also CANR 7
See also CA 9-12R

Machado (y Ruiz), Antonio
1875-1939................. TCLC **3**
See also CA 104

Machado de Assis, (Joaquim Maria)
1839-1908................. TCLC **10**
See also CA 107

Machen, Arthur (Llewellyn Jones)
1863-1947................... TCLC **4**
See also CA 104
See also DLB 36

MacInnes, Colin 1914-1976..... CLC **4, 23**
See also CA 69-72
See also obituary CA 65-68
See also DLB 14

MacInnes, Helen 1907-.............CLC **27**
See also CANR 1
See also CA 1-4R
See also SATA 22

Macintosh, Elizabeth 1897-1952
See Tey, Josephine
See also CA 110

Mackenzie, (Edward Montague) Compton
1883-1972....................CLC **18**
See also CAP 2
See also CA 21-22
See also obituary CA 37-40R
See also DLB 34

Mac Laverty, Bernard 1942-.......CLC **31**
See also CA 116

MacLean, Alistair (Stuart)
1922-..................... CLC **3, 13**
See also CA 57-60
See also SATA 23

MacLeish, Archibald
1892-1982............... CLC **3, 8, 14**
See also CA 9-12R
See also obituary CA 106
See also DLB 4, 7, 45
See also DLB-Y 82

MacLennan, (John) Hugh
1907-..................... CLC **2, 14**
See also CA 5-8R

MacNeice, (Frederick) Louis
1907-1963.............. CLC **1, 4, 10**
See also CA 85-88
See also DLB 10, 20

Macpherson, (Jean) Jay 1931-......CLC **14**
See also CA 5-8R

Macumber, Mari 1896-1966
See Sandoz, Mari (Susette)

Madden, (Jerry) David
1933-..................... CLC **5, 15**
See also CAAS 3
See also CANR 4
See also CA 1-4R
See also DLB 6

Madhubuti, Haki R. 1942-.........CLC **6**
See also Lee, Don L.
See also DLB 5, 41

Maeterlinck, Maurice
1862-1949................. TCLC **3**
See also CA 104

Maginn, William 1794-1842...... NCLC **8**

Mahapatra, Jayanta 1928-.........CLC **33**
See also CANR 15
See also CA 73-76

Mahon, Derek 1941-..............CLC **27**
See also CA 113
See also DLB 40

Mailer, Norman
1923-......CLC **1, 2, 3, 4, 5, 8, 11, 14, 28**
See also CA 9-12R
See also DLB 2, 16, 28
See also DLB-Y 80, 83
See also DLB-DS 3
See also AITN 2

Mais, Roger 1905-1955.......... TCLC **8**
See also CA 105

Major, Clarence 1936-......... CLC **3, 19**
See also CA 21-24R
See also DLB 33

Major, Kevin 1949-..............CLC **26**
See also CA 97-100
See also SATA 32

Malamud, Bernard
1914-......CLC **1, 2, 3, 5, 8, 9, 11, 18, 27**
See also CA 5-8R
See also DLB 2, 28
See also DLB-Y 80

Mallarmé, Stéphane
1842-1898................... NCLC **4**

Mallet-Joris, Françoise 1930-......CLC **11**
See also CANR 17
See also CA 65-68

Maloff, Saul 1922-................CLC **5**
See also CA 33-36R

Malouf, David 1934-..............CLC **28**

Malraux, (Georges-) André
1901-1976........ CLC **1, 4, 9, 13, 15**
See also CAP 2
See also CA 21-24R
See also obituary CA 69-72

Malzberg, Barry N. 1939-.........CLC **7**
See also CANR 16
See also CA 61-64
See also DLB 8

Mamet, David 1947-........ CLC **9, 15, 34**
See also CANR 15
See also CA 81-84
See also DLB 7

Mamoulian, Rouben 1898-.........CLC **16**
See also CA 25-28R

Mandelstam, Osip (Emilievich)
1891?-1938?............... TCLC **2, 6**
See also CA 104

Manley, (Mary) Delariviere
1672?-1724................... LC **1**
See also DLB 39

Mann, (Luiz) Heinrich
1871-1950................. TCLC **9**
See also CA 106

Mann, Thomas
1875-1955............. TCLC **2, 8, 14**
See also CA 104

Manning, Olivia 1915-1980..... CLC **5, 19**
See also CA 5-8R
See also obituary CA 101

Mano, D. Keith 1942-.......... CLC **2, 10**
See also CA 25-28R
See also DLB 6

Mansfield, Katherine
1888-1923................. TCLC **2, 8**
See also CA 104

Marcel, Gabriel (Honore)
1889-1973..................CLC **15**
See also CA 102
See also obituary CA 45-48

Marchbanks, Samuel 1913-
See Davies, (William) Robertson

Marinetti, F(ilippo) T(ommaso)
1876-1944................. TCLC **10**
See also CA 107

Markandaya, Kamala (Purnalya)
1924-........................CLC **8**
See also Taylor, Kamala (Purnalya)

Markfield, Wallace (Arthur)
1926-........................CLC **8**
See also CAAS 3
See also CA 69-72
See also DLB 2, 28

Markham, Robert 1922-
See Amis, Kingsley (William)

Marks, J. 1942-
See Highwater, Jamake

Marley, Bob 1945-1981 ....CLC **17**
See also Marley, Robert Nesta

Marley, Robert Nesta 1945-1981
See Marley, Bob
See also CA 107
See also obituary CA 103

Marmontel, Jean-François
1723-1799..................... LC **2**

Marquand, John P(hillips)
1893-1960................. CLC **2, 10**
See also CA 85-88
See also DLB 9

Márquez, Gabriel García 1928-
See García Márquez, Gabriel

Marquis, Don(ald Robert Perry)
1878-1937................. TCLC **7**
See also CA 104
See also DLB 11, 25

Marryat, Frederick 1792-1848 .... NCLC **3**
See also DLB 21

Marsh, (Edith) Ngaio
1899-1982....................CLC **7**
See also CANR 6
See also CA 9-12R

Marshall, Garry 1935?- ....CLC **17**
See also CA 111

Marshall, Paule 1929-.............CLC **27**
See also CA 77-80
See also DLB 33

Marsten, Richard 1926-
See Hunter, Evan

Martin, Steve 1945?-..............CLC **30**
See also CA 97-100

Martínez Ruiz, José 1874-1967
See Azorín
See also CA 93-96

Martínez Sierra, Gregorio 1881-1947
See Martínez Sierra, Gregorio and Martínez Sierra, María (de la O'LeJárraga)
See also CA 104, 115

Martínez Sierra, Gregorio 1881-1947 and
  Martínez Sierra, María (de la
  O'LeJárraga) 1880?-1974 .... **TCLC 6**

Martínez Sierra, María (de la O'LeJárraga)
  1880?-1974
  See Martínez Sierra, Gregorio and Martínez
  Sierra, María (de la O'LeJárraga)
  See also obituary CA 115

Martínez Sierra, María (de la O'LeJárraga)
  1880?-1974 and **Martínez Sierra,**
  Gregorio 1881-1947
  See Martínez Sierra, Gregorio and Martínez
  Sierra, María (de la O'LeJárraga)

Martinson, Harry (Edmund)
  1904-1978....................**CLC 14**
  See also CA 77-80

Masaoka Shiki 1867-1902....... **TCLC 18**

Masefield, John (Edward)
  1878-1967....................**CLC 11**
  See also CAP 2
  See also CA 19-20
  See also obituary CA 25-28R
  See also SATA 19
  See also DLB 10, 19

Mason, Bobbie Ann 1940-.........**CLC 28**
  See also CANR 11
  See also CA 53-56

Mason, Nick 1945-
  See Pink Floyd

Mason, Tally 1909-1971
  See Derleth, August (William)

Masters, Edgar Lee
  1868?-1950.................. **TCLC 2**
  See also CA 104

Mastrosimone, William 19??- ......**CLC 36**

Matheson, Richard (Burton)
  1926-.......................**CLC 37**
  See also CA 97-100
  See also DLB 8, 44

Mathews, Harry 1930- ....**CLC 6**
  See also CA 21-24R

Matthias, John (Edward) 1941-......**CLC 9**
  See also CA 33-36R

Matthiessen, Peter
  1927-................**CLC 5, 7, 11, 32**
  See also CA 9-12R
  See also SATA 27
  See also DLB 6

Maturin, Charles Robert
  1780?-1824.................. **NCLC 6**

Matute, Ana María 1925-.........**CLC 11**
  See also CA 89-92

Maugham, W(illiam) Somerset
  1874-1965.............**CLC 1, 11, 15**
  See also CA 5-8R
  See also obituary CA 25-28R
  See also DLB 10, 36

Maupassant, (Henri René Albert) Guy de
  1850-1893.................. **NCLC 1**

Mauriac, Claude 1914-.............**CLC 9**
  See also CA 89-92

Mauriac, François (Charles)
  1885-1970................. **CLC 4, 9**
  See also CAP 2
  See also CA 25-28

Mavor, Osborne Henry 1888-1951
  See Bridie, James
  See also CA 104

Maxwell, William (Keepers, Jr.)
  1908-.......................**CLC 19**
  See also CA 93-96
  See also DLB-Y 80

May, Elaine 1932-.................**CLC 16**
  See also DLB 44

Mayakovsky, Vladimir (Vladimirovich)
  1893-1930................ **TCLC 4, 18**
  See also CA 104

Maynard, Joyce 1953-.............**CLC 23**
  See also CA 111

Mayne, William (James Carter)
  1928-.......................**CLC 12**
  See also CA 9-12R
  See also SATA 6

Mayo, Jim 1908?-
  See L'Amour, Louis (Dearborn)

Maysles, Albert 1926-
  See Maysles, Albert and Maysles, David
  See also CA 29-32R

Maysles, Albert 1926- and **Maysles, David**
  1932-.......................**CLC 16**

Maysles, David 1932-
  See Maysles, Albert and Maysles, David

Mazer, Norma Fox 1931-.........**CLC 26**
  See also CANR 12
  See also CA 69-72
  See also SAAS 1
  See also SATA 24

McBain, Ed 1926-
  See Hunter, Evan

McCaffrey, Anne 1926- ....**CLC 17**
  See also CANR 15
  See also CA 25-28R
  See also SATA 8
  See also DLB 8
  See also AITN 2

McCarthy, Cormac 1933-...........**CLC 4**
  See also CANR 10
  See also CA 13-16R
  See also DLB 6

McCarthy, Mary (Therese)
  1912-............. **CLC 1, 3, 5, 14, 24**
  See also CANR 16
  See also CA 5-8R
  See also DLB 2
  See also DLB-Y 81

McCartney, (James) Paul
  1942-.......................**CLC 35**
  See also Lennon, John (Ono) and
  McCartney, Paul

McClure, Michael 1932-........ **CLC 6, 10**
  See also CANR 17
  See also CA 21-24R
  See also DLB 16

McCourt, James 1941-.............**CLC 5**
  See also CA 57-60

McCrae, John 1872-1918....... **TCLC 12**
  See also CA 109

McCullers, (Lula) Carson
  1917-1967.............**CLC 1, 4, 10, 12**
  See also CA 5-8R
  See also obituary CA 25-28R
  See also SATA 27
  See also DLB 2, 7

McCullough, Colleen 1938?- ....**CLC 27**
  See also CANR 17
  See also CA 81-84

McElroy, Joseph 1930-.............**CLC 5**
  See also CA 17-20R

McEwan, Ian 1948-...............**CLC 13**
  See also CA 61-64
  See also DLB 14

McGahern, John 1935-.......... **CLC 5, 9**
  See also CA 17-20R
  See also DLB 14

McGinley, Phyllis 1905-1978.......**CLC 14**
  See also CA 9-12R
  See also obituary CA 77-80
  See also SATA 2
  See also obituary SATA 24
  See also DLB 11

McGinniss, Joe 1942- ....**CLC 32**
  See also CA 25-28R
  See also AITN 2

McGivern, Maureen Daly 1921-
  See Daly, Maureen
  See also CA 9-12R

McGrath, Thomas 1916- ....**CLC 28**
  See also CANR 6
  See also CA 9-12R
  See also SATA 41

McGuane, Thomas (Francis III)
  1939-.................. **CLC 3, 7, 18**
  See also CANR 5
  See also CA 49-52
  See also DLB 2
  See also DLB-Y 80
  See also AITN 2

McHale, Tom 1941-1982 .... **CLC 3, 5**
  See also CA 77-80
  See also obituary CA 106
  See also AITN 1

McIlwraith, Maureen Mollie Hunter 1922-
  See Hunter, Mollie
  See also CA 29-32R
  See also SATA 2

McInerney, Jay 1955-.............**CLC 34**
  See also CA 116

McIntyre, Vonda N(eel) 1948-......**CLC 18**
  See also CA 81-84

McKay, Claude 1890-1948....... **TCLC 7**
  See also CA 104
  See also DLB 4, 45

McKuen, Rod 1933- .... **CLC 1, 3**
  See also CA 41-44R
  See also AITN 1

McLuhan, (Herbert) Marshall
  1911-1980...................**CLC 37**
  See also CANR 12
  See also CA 9-12R
  See also obituary CA 102

McManus, Declan Patrick 1955-
  See Costello, Elvis

McMurtry, Larry (Jeff)
  1936-............. **CLC 2, 3, 7, 11, 27**
  See also CA 5-8R
  See also DLB 2
  See also DLB-Y 80
  See also AITN 2

McNally, Terrence 1939- .... CLC **4, 7**
See also CANR 2
See also CA 45-48
See also DLB 7

McPhee, John 1931- .... CLC **36**
See also CA 65-68

McPherson, James Alan 1943- ..... CLC **19**
See also CA 25-28R
See also DLB 38

McPherson, William 1939- .... CLC **34**
See also CA 57-60

McSweeney, Kerry 19??- .... CLC **34**

Mead, Margaret 1901-1978 .... CLC **37**
See also CANR 4
See also CA 1-4R
See also obituary CA 81-84
See also SATA 20
See also AITN 1

Meaker, M. J. 1927-
See Kerr, M. E.
See Meaker, Marijane

Meaker, Marijane 1927-
See Kerr, M. E.
See also CA 107
See also SATA 20

Medoff, Mark (Howard)
1940- .... CLC **6, 23**
See also CANR 5
See also CA 53-56
See also DLB 7
See also AITN 1

Megged, Aharon 1920- .... CLC **9**
See also CANR 1
See also CA 49-52

Mehta, Ved (Parkash) 1934- .... CLC **37**
See also CANR 2
See also CA 1-4R

Mellor, John 1953?-
See The Clash

Meltzer, Milton 1915- .... CLC **26**
See also CA 13-16R
See also SAAS 1
See also SATA 1

Melville, Herman
1819-1891 .... NCLC **3, 12**
See also DLB 3

Mencken, H(enry) L(ouis)
1880-1956 .... TCLC **13**
See also CA 105
See also DLB 11, 29

Mercer, David 1928-1980 .... CLC **5**
See also CA 9-12R
See also obituary CA 102
See also DLB 13

Meredith, George 1828-1909 ..... TCLC **17**
See also DLB 18, 35

Meredith, William (Morris)
1919- .... CLC **4, 13, 22**
See also CANR 6
See also CA 9-12R
See also DLB 5

Mérimée, Prosper 1803-1870 ..... NCLC **6**

Merrill, James (Ingram)
1926- .... CLC **2, 3, 6, 8, 13, 18, 34**
See also CANR 10
See also CA 13-16R
See also DLB 5

Merton, Thomas (James)
1915-1968 .... CLC **1, 3, 11, 34**
See also CA 5-8R
See also obituary CA 25-28R
See also DLB-Y 81

Merwin, W(illiam) S(tanley)
1927- .... CLC **1, 2, 3, 5, 8, 13, 18**
See also CANR 15
See also CA 13-16R
See also DLB 5

Metcalf, John 1938- .... CLC **37**
See also CA 113

Mew, Charlotte (Mary)
1870-1928 .... TCLC **8**
See also CA 105
See also DLB 19

Mewshaw, Michael 1943- .... CLC **9**
See also CANR 7
See also CA 53-56
See also DLB-Y 80

**Meynell, Alice (Christiana Gertrude
Thompson)** 1847-1922 .... TCLC **6**
See also CA 104
See also DLB 19

Michaels, Leonard 1933- .... CLC **6, 25**
See also CA 61-64

Michaux, Henri 1899-1984 ...... CLC **8, 19**
See also CA 85-88
See also obituary CA 114

Michener, James A(lbert)
1907- .... CLC **1, 5, 11, 29**
See also CA 5-8R
See also DLB 6
See also AITN 1

Mickiewicz, Adam 1798-1855 ..... NCLC **3**

Middleton, Christopher 1926- ..... CLC **13**
See also CA 13-16R
See also DLB 40

Middleton, Stanley 1919- .... CLC **7**
See also CA 25-28R
See also DLB 14

Miguéis, José Rodrigues 1901- ..... CLC **10**

Miles, Josephine
1911-1985 .... CLC **1, 2, 14, 34**
See also CANR 2
See also CA 1-4R
See also obituary CA 116

Mill, John Stuart 1806-1873 ..... NCLC **11**

Millar, Kenneth
1915-1983 .... CLC **1, 2, 3, 14, 34**
See Macdonald, Ross
See also CANR 16
See also CA 9-12R
See also obituary CA 110
See also DLB 2
See also DLB-Y 83

Millay, Edna St. Vincent
1892-1950 .... TCLC **4**
See also CA 104
See also DLB 45

Miller, Arthur
1915- .... CLC **1, 2, 6, 10, 15, 26**
See also CANR 2
See also CA 1-4R
See also DLB 7
See also AITN 1

Miller, Henry (Valentine)
1891-1980 .... CLC **1, 2, 4, 9, 14**
See also CA 9-12R
See also obituary CA 97-100
See also DLB 4, 9
See also DLB-Y 80

Miller, Jason 1939?- .... CLC **2**
See also CA 73-76
See also DLB 7
See also AITN 1

Miller, Walter M(ichael), Jr.
1923- .... CLC **4, 30**
See also CA 85-88
See also DLB 8

Millhauser, Steven 1943- .... CLC **21**
See also CA 108, 110, 111
See also DLB 2

Milne, A(lan) A(lexander)
1882-1956 .... TCLC **6**
See also CLR 1
See also CA 104
See also YABC 1
See also DLB 10

Miłosz, Czesław
1911- .... CLC **5, 11, 22, 31**
See also CA 81-84

Miró (Ferrer), Gabriel (Francisco Víctor)
1879-1930 .... TCLC **5**
See also CA 104

Mishima, Yukio
1925-1970 .... CLC **2, 4, 6, 9, 27**
See also Hiraoka, Kimitake

Mistral, Gabriela 1889-1957 ...... TCLC **2**
See also CA 104

Mitchell, James Leslie 1901-1935
See Gibbon, Lewis Grassic
See also CA 104
See also DLB 15

Mitchell, Joni 1943- .... CLC **12**
See also CA 112

Mitchell (Marsh), Margaret (Munnerlyn)
1900-1949 .... TCLC **11**
See also CA 109
See also DLB 9

Mitchell, W(illiam) O(rmond)
1914- .... CLC **25**
See also CANR 15
See also CA 77-80

Mitford, Mary Russell
1787-1855 .... NCLC **4**

Modiano, Patrick (Jean) 1945- ..... CLC **18**
See also CANR 17
See also CA 85-88

Mohr, Nicholasa 1935- .... CLC **12**
See also CANR 1
See also CA 49-52
See also SATA 8

Mojtabai, A(nn) G(race)
1938- .... CLC **5, 9, 15, 29**
See also CA 85-88

Molnár, Ferenc 1878-1952 .... TCLC **20**
See also CA 109

Momaday, N(avarre) Scott
1934- .... CLC **2, 19**
See also CANR 14
See also CA 25-28R
See also SATA 30

Monroe, Harriet 1860-1936 . . . . . . **TCLC 12**
See also CA 109

Montagu, Elizabeth 1720-1800 . . . . **NCLC 7**

Montague, John (Patrick)
1929- . . . .**CLC 13**
See also CANR 9
See also CA 9-12R
See also DLB 40

Montale, Eugenio
1896-1981 . . . . **CLC 7, 9, 18**
See also CA 17-20R
See also obituary CA 104

Montgomery, Marion (H., Jr.)
1925- . . . .**CLC 7**
See also CANR 3
See also CA 1-4R
See also DLB 6
See also AITN 1

Montgomery, Robert Bruce 1921-1978
See Crispin, Edmund
See also CA 104

Montherlant, Henri (Milon) de
1896-1972 . . . . **CLC 8, 19**
See also CA 85-88
See also obituary CA 37-40R

Monty Python . . . .**CLC 21**
See also Cleese, John

Mooney, Ted 1951- . . . .**CLC 25**

Moorcock, Michael (John)
1939- . . . . **CLC 5, 27**
See also CANR 2, 17
See also CA 45-48
See also DLB 14

Moore, Brian
1921- . . . .**CLC 1, 3, 5, 7, 8, 19, 32**
See also CANR 1
See also CA 1-4R

Moore, George (Augustus)
1852-1933 . . . . **TCLC 7**
See also CA 104
See also DLB 10, 18

Moore, Marianne (Craig)
1887-1972 . . . . . . **CLC 1, 2, 4, 8, 10, 13,**
                                                              19
See also CANR 3
See also CA 1-4R
See also obituary CA 33-36R
See also DLB 45
See also SATA 20

Moore, Thomas 1779-1852 . . . . **NCLC 6**

Morante, Elsa 1918- . . . .**CLC 8**
See also CA 85-88

Moravia, Alberto
1907- . . . . **CLC 2, 7, 11, 18, 27**
See also Pincherle, Alberto

Moréas, Jean 1856-1910 . . . . **TCLC 18**

Morgan, Berry 1919- . . . .**CLC 6**
See also CA 49-52
See also DLB 6

Morgan, Edwin (George)
1920- . . . .**CLC 31**
See also CANR 3
See also CA 7-8R
See also DLB 27

Morgan, Frederick 1922- . . . .**CLC 23**
See also CA 17-20R

Morgan, Robin 1941- . . . .**CLC 2**
See also CA 69-72

Morgenstern, Christian (Otto Josef Wolfgang)
1871-1914 . . . . **TCLC 8**
See also CA 105

Mori Ōgai 1862-1922 . . . . **TCLC 14**
See also Mori Rintaro

Mori Rintaro 1862-1922
See Mori Ōgai
See also CA 110

Mörike, Eduard (Friedrich)
1804-1875 . . . . **NCLC 10**

Moritz, Karl Philipp 1756-1793 . . . . . . **LC 2**

Morris, Julian 1916-
See West, Morris L.

Morris, Steveland Judkins 1950-
See Wonder, Stevie
See also CA 111

Morris, William 1834-1896 . . . . **NCLC 4**
See also DLB 18, 35

Morris, Wright
1910- . . . . **CLC 1, 3, 7, 18, 37**
See also CA 9-12R
See also DLB 2
See also DLB-Y 81

Morrison, James Douglas 1943-1971
See Morrison, Jim
See also CA 73-76

Morrison, Jim 1943-1971 . . . .**CLC 17**
See also Morrison, James Douglas

Morrison, Toni 1931- . . . . **CLC 4, 10, 22**
See also CA 29-32R
See also DLB 6, 33
See also DLB-Y 81

Morrison, Van 1945- . . . .**CLC 21**
See also CA 116

Mortimer, John (Clifford)
1923- . . . .**CLC 28**
See also CA 13-16R
See also DLB 13

Mortimer, Penelope (Ruth)
1918- . . . .**CLC 5**
See also CA 57-60

Moss, Howard 1922- . . . . **CLC 7, 14**
See also CANR 1
See also CA 1-4R
See also DLB 5

Motley, Willard (Francis)
1912-1965 . . . .**CLC 18**
See also obituary CA 106

Mott, Michael (Charles Alston)
1930- . . . . **CLC 15, 34**
See also CANR 7
See also CA 5-8R

Mowat, Farley (McGill) 1921- . . . . . .**CLC 26**
See also CANR 4
See also CA 1-4R
See also SATA 3

Mphahlele, Es'kia 1919-
See Mphahlele, Ezekiel

Mphahlele, Ezekiel 1919- . . . .**CLC 25**
See also CA 81-84

Mrożek, Sławomir 1930- . . . . **CLC 3, 13**
See also CA 13-16R

Mueller, Lisel 1924- . . . .**CLC 13**
See also CA 93-96

Muir, Edwin 1887-1959 . . . . **TCLC 2**
See also CA 104
See also DLB 20

Mujica Láinez, Manuel
1910-1984 . . . .**CLC 31**
See also CA 81-84
See also obituary CA 112

Muldoon, Paul 1951- . . . .**CLC 32**
See also CA 113
See also DLB 40

Mull, Martin 1943- . . . .**CLC 17**
See also CA 105

Munro, Alice 1931- . . . . **CLC 6, 10, 19**
See also CA 33-36R
See also SATA 29
See also AITN 2

Munro, H(ector) H(ugh) 1870-1916
See Saki
See also CA 104
See also DLB 34

Murdoch, (Jean) Iris
1919- . . . . . .**CLC 1, 2, 3, 4, 6, 8, 11, 15,**
                                                         22, 31
See also CANR 8
See also CA 13-16R
See also DLB 14

Murphy, Sylvia 19??- . . . .**CLC 34**

Murry, John Middleton
1889-1957 . . . . **TCLC 16**

Musgrave, Susan 1951- . . . .**CLC 13**
See also CA 69-72

Musil, Robert (Edler von)
1880-1942 . . . . **TCLC 12**
See also CA 109

Musset, (Louis Charles) Alfred de
1810-1857 . . . . **NCLC 7**

Myers, Walter Dean 1937- . . . .**CLC 35**
See also CLR 4
See also CA 33-36R
See also SATA 27, 41
See also DLB 33

Nabokov, Vladimir (Vladimirovich)
1899-1977 . . . . **CLC 1, 2, 3, 6, 8, 11,**
                                                         15, 23
See also CA 5-8R
See also obituary CA 69-72
See also DLB 2
See also DLB-Y 80
See also DLB-DS 3

Nagy, László 1925-1978 . . . .**CLC 7**
See also obituary CA 112

Naipaul, Shiva 1945-1985 . . . .**CLC 32**
See also CA 110, 112
See also obituary CA 116

Naipaul, V(idiadhar) S(urajprasad)
1932- . . . .**CLC 4, 7, 9, 13, 18, 37**
See also CANR 1
See also CA 1-4R

Nakos, Ioulia 1899?-
See Nakos, Lilika

Nakos, Lilika 1899?- . . . .**CLC 29**

Nakou, Lilika 1899?-
See Nakos, Lilika

Narayan, R(asipuram) K(rishnaswami)
1906- . . . . **CLC 7, 28**
See also CA 81-84

Nash, (Frediric) Ogden
    1902-1971....................CLC 23
    See also CAP 1
    See also CA 13-14
    See also obituary CA 29-32R
    See also SATA 2
    See also DLB 11

Nathan, George Jean
    1882-1958.................TCLC 18
    See also CA 114

Natsume, Kinnosuke 1867-1916
    See Natsume, Sōseki
    See also CA 104

Natsume, Sōseki
    1867-1916...............TCLC 2, 10
    See also Natsume, Kinnosuke

Natti, (Mary) Lee 1919-
    See Kingman, (Mary) Lee
    See also CANR 2

Naylor, Gloria 1950-..............CLC 28
    See also CA 107

Neihardt, John G(neisenau)
    1881-1973....................CLC 32
    See also CAP 1
    See also CA 13-14
    See also DLB 9

Nekrasov, Nikolai Alekseevich
    1821-1878..................NCLC 11

Nelligan, Émile 1879-1941.......TCLC 14
    See also CA 114

Nelson, Willie 1933-..............CLC 17
    See also CA 107

Nemerov, Howard
    1920-................CLC 2, 6, 9, 36
    See also CANR 1
    See also CA 1-4R
    See also DLB 5, 6
    See also DLB-Y 83

Neruda, Pablo
    1904-1973........CLC 1, 2, 5, 7, 9, 28
    See also CAP 2
    See also CA 19-20
    See also obituary CA 45-48

Nerval, Gérard de 1808-1855.....NCLC 1

Nervo, (José) Amado (Ruiz de)
    1870-1919.................TCLC 11
    See also CA 109

Neufeld, John (Arthur) 1938-......CLC 17
    See also CANR 11
    See also CA 25-28R
    See also SATA 6

Neville, Emily Cheney 1919-.......CLC 12
    See also CANR 3
    See also CA 5-8R
    See also SATA 1

Newbound, Bernard Slade 1930-
    See Slade, Bernard
    See also CA 81-84

Newby, P(ercy) H(oward)
    1918-....................CLC 2, 13
    See also CA 5-8R
    See also DLB 15

Newlove, Donald 1928-............CLC 6
    See also CA 29-32R

Newlove, John (Herbert) 1938-.....CLC 14
    See also CANR 9
    See also CA 21-24R

Newman, Charles 1938-.........CLC 2, 8
    See also CA 21-24R

Newman, Edwin (Harold)
    1919-......................CLC 14
    See also CANR 5
    See also CA 69-72
    See also AITN 1

Newton, Suzanne 1936-...........CLC 35
    See also CANR 14
    See also CA 41-44R
    See also SATA 5

Ngugi, James (Thiong'o)
    1938-................CLC 3, 7, 13, 36
    See also Ngugi wa Thiong'o
    See also Wa Thiong'o, Ngugi
    See also CA 81-84

Ngugi wa Thiong'o
    1938-................CLC 3, 7, 13, 36
    See also Ngugi, James (Thiong'o)
    See also Wa Thiong'o, Ngugi

Nichol, B(arne) P(hillip) 1944-.....CLC 18
    See also CA 53-56

Nichols, Peter 1927-...........CLC 5, 36
    See also CA 104
    See also DLB 13

Niedecker, Lorine 1903-1970......CLC 10
    See also CAP 2
    See also CA 25-28

Nietzsche, Friedrich (Wilhelm)
    1844-1900...............TCLC 10, 18
    See also CA 107

Nightingale, Anne Redmon 1943-
    See Redmon (Nightingale), Anne
    See also CA 103

Nin, Anaïs
    1903-1977........CLC 1, 4, 8, 11, 14
    See also CA 13-16R
    See also obituary CA 69-72
    See also DLB 2, 4
    See also AITN 2

Nissenson, Hugh 1933-..........CLC 4, 9
    See also CA 17-20R
    See also DLB 28

Niven, Larry 1938-................CLC 8
    See also Niven, Laurence Van Cott
    See also DLB 8

Niven, Laurence Van Cott 1938-
    See Niven, Larry
    See also CANR 14
    See also CA 21-24R

Nixon, Agnes Eckhardt 1927-......CLC 21
    See also CA 110

Norman, Marsha 1947-............CLC 28
    See also CA 105
    See also DLB-Y 84

Norris, Leslie 1921-..............CLC 14
    See also CANR 14
    See also CAP 1
    See also CA 11-12
    See also DLB 27

North, Andrew 1912-
    See Norton, Andre

North, Christopher 1785-1854
    See Wilson, John

Norton, Alice Mary 1912-
    See Norton, Andre
    See also CANR 2
    See also CA 1-4R
    See also SATA 1, 43

Norton, Andre 1912-..............CLC 12
    See also Norton, Mary Alice
    See also DLB 8

Norway, Nevil Shute 1899-1960
    See Shute (Norway), Nevil
    See also CA 102
    See also obituary CA 93-96

Nossack, Hans Erich 1901-1978.....CLC 6
    See also CA 93-96
    See also obituary CA 85-88

Nova, Craig 1945-...........CLC 7, 31
    See also CANR 2
    See also CA 45-48

Nowlan, Alden (Albert) 1933-......CLC 15
    See also CANR 5
    See also CA 9-12R

Noyes, Alfred 1880-1958.........TCLC 7
    See also CA 104
    See also DLB 20

Nunn, Kem 19??-.................CLC 34

Nye, Robert 1939-................CLC 13
    See also CA 33-36R
    See also SATA 6
    See also DLB 14

Nyro, Laura 1947-................CLC 17

Oates, Joyce Carol
    1938-.....CLC 1, 2, 3, 6, 9, 11, 15, 19,
                           33
    See also CA 5-8R
    See also DLB 2, 5
    See also DLB-Y 81
    See also AITN 1

O'Brien, Darcy 1939-..............CLC 11
    See also CANR 8
    See also CA 21-24R

O'Brien, Edna
    1932-............CLC 3, 5, 8, 13, 36
    See also CANR 6
    See also CA 1-4R
    See also DLB 14

O'Brien, Flann
    1911-1966.........CLC 1, 4, 5, 7, 10
    See also O Nuallain, Brian

O'Brien, Richard 19??-............CLC 17

O'Brien, Tim 1946-...........CLC 7, 19
    See also CA 85-88
    See also DLB-Y 80

O'Casey, Sean
    1880-1964.........CLC 1, 5, 9, 11, 15
    See also CA 89-92
    See also DLB 10

Ochs, Phil 1940-1976.............CLC 17
    See also obituary CA 65-68

O'Connor, Edwin (Greene)
    1918-1968...................CLC 14
    See also CA 93-96
    See also obituary CA 25-28R

O'Connor, (Mary) Flannery
    1925-1964......CLC 1, 2, 3, 6, 10, 13,
                          15, 21
    See also CANR 3
    See also CA 1-4R
    See also DLB 2
    See also DLB-Y 80

O'Connor, Frank
    1903-1966................ CLC 14, 23
    See also O'Donovan, Michael (John)

O'Dell, Scott 1903- ....CLC 30
    See also CLR 1
    See also CANR 12
    See also CA 61-64
    See also SATA 12

Odets, Clifford 1906-1963 ...... CLC 2, 28
    See also CA 85-88
    See also DLB 7, 26

O'Donovan, Michael (John) 1903-1966
    See O'Connor, Frank
    See also CA 93-96

Ōe, Kenzaburō 1935- .... CLC 10, 36
    See also CA 97-100

O'Faolain, Julia 1932- .... CLC 6, 19
    See also CAAS 2
    See also CANR 12
    See also CA 81-84
    See also DLB 14

O'Faoláin, Seán
    1900-................CLC 1, 7, 14, 32
    See also CANR 12
    See also CA 61-64
    See also DLB 15

O'Flaherty, Liam
    1896-1984................ CLC 5, 34
    See also CA 101
    See also obituary CA 113
    See also DLB 36
    See also DLB-Y 84

O'Grady, Standish (James)
    1846-1928................... TCLC 5
    See also CA 104

O'Hara, Frank
    1926-1966.............. CLC 2, 5, 13
    See also CA 9-12R
    See also obituary CA 25-28R
    See also DLB 5, 16

O'Hara, John (Henry)
    1905-1970......... CLC 1, 2, 3, 6, 11
    See also CA 5-8R
    See also obituary CA 25-28R
    See also DLB 9
    See also DLB-DS 2

Okigbo, Christopher (Ifenayichukwu)
    1932-1967....................CLC 25
    See also CA 77-80

Olds, Sharon 1942- ....CLC 32
    See also CA 101

Olesha, Yuri (Karlovich)
    1899-1960....................CLC 8
    See also CA 85-88

Oliphant, Margaret (Oliphant Wilson)
    1828-1897................ NCLC 11
    See also DLB 18

Oliver, Mary 1935- .... CLC 19, 34
    See also CANR 9
    See also CA 21-24R
    See also DLB 5

Olivier, (Baron) Laurence (Kerr)
    1907-.......................CLC 20
    See also CA 111

Olsen, Tillie 1913- .... CLC 4, 13
    See also CANR 1
    See also CA 1-4R
    See also DLB 28
    See also DLB-Y 80

Olson, Charles (John)
    1910-1970...... CLC 1, 2, 5, 6, 9, 11,
                                      29
    See also CAP 1
    See also CA 15-16
    See also obituary CA 25-28R
    See also DLB 5, 16

Olson, Theodore 1937-
    See Olson, Toby

Olson, Toby 1937-................CLC 28
    See also CANR 9
    See also CA 65-68

Ondaatje, (Philip) Michael
    1943-.................... CLC 14, 29
    See also CA 77-80

Oneal, Elizabeth 1934-
    See Oneal, Zibby
    See also CA 106
    See also SATA 30

Oneal, Zibby 1934-...............CLC 30
    See also Oneal, Elizabeth

O'Neill, Eugene (Gladstone)
    1888-1953................TCLC 1, 6
    See also CA 110
    See also AITN 1
    See also DLB 7

Onetti, Juan Carlos 1909- ...... CLC 7, 10
    See also CA 85-88

O'Nolan, Brian 1911-1966
    See O'Brien, Flann

O Nuallain, Brian 1911-1966
    See O'Brien, Flann
    See also CAP 2
    See also CA 21-22
    See also obituary CA 25-28R

Oppen, George
    1908-1984.............. CLC 7, 13, 34
    See also CANR 8
    See also CA 13-16R
    See also obituary CA 113
    See also DLB 5

Orlovitz, Gil 1918-1973 ....CLC 22
    See also CA 77-80
    See also obituary CA 45-48
    See also DLB 2, 5

Ortega y Gasset, José
    1883-1955................... TCLC 9
    See also CA 106

Orton, Joe 1933?-1967 .... CLC 4, 13
    See also Orton, John Kingsley
    See also DLB 13

Orton, John Kingsley 1933?-1967
    See Orton, Joe
    See also CA 85-88

Orwell, George
    1903-1950..............TCLC 2, 6, 15
    See also Blair, Eric Arthur
    See also DLB 15

Osborne, John (James)
    1929-.................CLC 1, 2, 5, 11
    See also CA 13-16R
    See also DLB 13

Osceola 1885-1962
    See Dinesen, Isak
    See also Blixen, Karen (Christentze
        Dinesen)

Oshima, Nagisa 1932-.............CLC 20
    See also CA 116

Ossoli, Sarah Margaret (Fuller marchesa d')
    1810-1850
    See Fuller, (Sarah) Margaret
    See also SATA 25

Otero, Blas de 1916-..............CLC 11
    See also CA 89-92

Owen, Wilfred (Edward Salter)
    1893-1918.................. TCLC 5
    See also CA 104
    See also DLB 20

Owens, Rochelle 1936- ....CLC 8
    See also CAAS 2
    See also CA 17-20R

Owl, Sebastian 1939-
    See Thompson, Hunter S(tockton)

Oz, Amos 1939-...... CLC 5, 8, 11, 27, 33
    See also CA 53-56

Ozick, Cynthia 1928- .... CLC 3, 7, 28
    See also CA 17-20R
    See also DLB 28
    See also DLB-Y 82

Ozu, Yasujiro 1903-1963 ....CLC 16
    See also CA 112

Pa Chin 1904-....................CLC 18
    See also Li Fei-kan

Pack, Robert 1929- ....CLC 13
    See also CANR 3
    See also CA 1-4R
    See also DLB 5

Padgett, Lewis 1915-1958
    See Kuttner, Henry

Page, Jimmy 1944-
    See Page, Jimmy and Plant, Robert

Page, Jimmy 1944- and
    Plant, Robert 1948- ....CLC 12

Page, P(atricia) K(athleen)
    1916-...................... CLC 7, 18
    See also CANR 4
    See also CA 53-56

Paget, Violet 1856-1935
    See Lee, Vernon
    See also CA 104

Palamas, Kostes 1859-1943 .... TCLC 5
    See also CA 105

Palazzeschi, Aldo 1885-1974 ....CLC 11
    See also CA 89-92
    See also obituary CA 53-56

Paley, Grace 1922- .... CLC 4, 6, 37
    See also CANR 13
    See also CA 25-28R
    See also DLB 28
    See also AITN 1

Palin, Michael 1943-
    See Monty Python
    See also CA 107

Pancake, Breece Dexter 1952-1979
    See Pancake, Breece D'J

Pancake, Breece D'J
    1952-1979....................CLC 29
    See also obituary CA 109

Parker, Dorothy (Rothschild)
      1893-1967....................CLC 15
   See also CAP 2
   See also CA 19-20
   See also obituary CA 25-28R
   See also DLB 11, 45

Parker, Robert B(rown) 1932-......CLC 27
   See also CANR 1
   See also CA 49-52

Parkman, Francis 1823-1893..... NCLC 12
   See also DLB 1, 30

Parks, Gordon (Alexander Buchanan)
      1912-................... CLC 1, 16
   See also CA 41-44R
   See also SATA 8
   See also DLB 33
   See also AITN 2

Parnell, Thomas 1679-1718.......... LC 3

Parra, Nicanor 1914- ....CLC 2
   See also CA 85-88

Pasolini, Pier Paolo
      1922-1975................ CLC 20, 37
   See also CA 93-96
   See also obituary CA 61-64

Pastan, Linda (Olenik) 1932-......CLC 27
   See also CA 61-64
   See also DLB 5

Pasternak, Boris
      1890-1960.............. CLC 7, 10, 18
   See also obituary CA 116

Patchen, Kenneth
      1911-1972.............. CLC 1, 2, 18
   See also CANR 3
   See also CA 1-4R
   See also obituary CA 33-36R
   See also DLB 16

Pater, Walter (Horatio)
      1839-1894.................... NCLC 7

Paterson, Katherine (Womeldorf)
      1932-.................... CLC 12, 30
   See also CLR 7
   See also CA 21-24R
   See also SATA 13

Patmore, Coventry Kersey Dighton
      1823-1896.................... NCLC 9
   See also DLB 35

Paton, Alan (Stewart)
      1903-.................. CLC 4, 10, 25
   See also CAP 1
   See also CA 15-16
   See also SATA 11

Paulding, James Kirke
      1778-1860................... NCLC 2
   See also DLB 3

Paulin, Tom 1949-.................CLC 37
   See also DLB 40

Pavese, Cesare 1908-1950 .... TCLC 3
   See also CA 104

Payne, Alan 1932-
   See Jakes, John (William)

Paz, Octavio 1914-..... CLC 3, 4, 6, 10, 19
   See also CA 73-76

Peake, Mervyn 1911-1968 ....CLC 7
   See also CANR 3
   See also CA 5-8R
   See also obituary CA 25-28R
   See also SATA 23
   See also DLB 15

Pearce, (Ann) Philippa 1920-.......CLC 21
   See also Christie, (Ann) Philippa
   See also CA 5-8R
   See also SATA 1

Pearl, Eric 1934-
   See Elman, Richard

Peck, John 1941-.................CLC 3
   See also CANR 3
   See also CA 49-52

Peck, Richard 1934- ....CLC 21
   See also CA 85-88
   See also SATA 18

Peck, Robert Newton 1928-........CLC 17
   See also CA 81-84
   See also SAAS 1
   See also SATA 21

Peckinpah, (David) Sam(uel)
      1925-1984....................CLC 20
   See also CA 109
   See also obituary CA 114

Pedersen, Knut 1859-1952
   See Hamsun, Knut
   See also CA 104

Péguy, Charles (Pierre)
      1873-1914................... TCLC 10
   See also CA 107

Percy, Walker
      1916-.......... CLC 2, 3, 6, 8, 14, 18
   See also CANR 1
   See also CA 1-4R
   See also DLB 2
   See also DLB-Y 80

Pereda, José María de
      1833-1906................. TCLC 16

Perelman, S(idney) J(oseph)
      1904-1979........ CLC 3, 5, 9, 15, 23
   See also CA 73-76
   See also obituary CA 89-92
   See also DLB 11, 44
   See also AITN 1, 2

Péret, Benjamin 1899-1959 ...... TCLC 20
   See also CA 117

Peretz, Isaac Leib
      1852?-1915................. TCLC 16
   See also CA 109

Perrault, Charles 1628-1703 .... LC 2
   See also SATA 25

Perse, St.-John 1887-1975 ...... CLC 4, 11
   See also Léger, (Marie-Rene) Alexis Saint-
   Léger

Pesetsky, Bette 1932-..............CLC 28

Peshkov, Alexei Maximovich 1868-1936
   See Gorky, Maxim
   See also CA 105

Peterkin, Julia (Mood)
      1880-1961....................CLC 31
   See also CA 102
   See also DLB 9

Peters, Robert L(ouis) 1924- ....CLC 7
   See also CA 13-16R

Petrakis, Harry Mark 1923- ....CLC 3
   See also CANR 4
   See also CA 9-12R

Petry, Ann (Lane) 1912-......CLC 1, 7, 18
   See also CANR 4
   See also CA 5-8R
   See also SATA 5

Phillips, Jayne Anne 1952-..... CLC 15, 33
   See also CA 101
   See also DLB-Y 80

Phillips, Robert (Schaeffer)
      1938-....................CLC 28
   See also CANR 8
   See also CA 17-20R

Piccolo, Lucio 1901-1969 ....CLC 13
   See also CA 97-100

Piercy, Marge
      1936-............ CLC 3, 6, 14, 18, 27
   See also CAAS 1
   See also CA 21-24R

Pincherle, Alberto 1907-
   See Moravia, Alberto
   See also CA 25-28R

Piñero, Miguel (Gomez) 1947?-......CLC 4
   See also CA 61-64

Pinget, Robert 1919-........ CLC 7, 13, 37
   See also CA 85-88

Pink Floyd.......................CLC 35

Pinkwater, D(aniel) M(anus)
      1941-.......................CLC 35
   See also Pinkwater, Manus
   See also CLR 4
   See also CANR 12
   See also CA 29-32R

Pinkwater, Manus 1941-
   See Pinkwater, D(aniel) M(anus)
   See also SATA 8

Pinsky, Robert 1940-........... CLC 9, 19
   See also CA 29-32R
   See also DLB-Y 82

Pinter, Harold
      1930-........CLC 1, 3, 6, 9, 11, 15, 27
   See also CA 5-8R
   See also DLB 13

Pirandello, Luigi 1867-1936....... TCLC 4
   See also CA 104

Pirsig, Robert M(aynard)
      1928-..................... CLC 4, 6
   See also CA 53-56
   See also SATA 39

Plaidy, Jean 1906-
   See Hibbert, Eleanor (Burford)

Plant, Robert 1948-
   See Page, Jimmy and Plant, Robert

Plante, David 1940-........... CLC 7, 23
   See also CANR 12
   See also CA 37-40R
   See also DLB-Y 83

Plath, Sylvia
      1932-1963....... CLC 1, 2, 3, 5, 9, 11,
                                      14, 17
   See also CAP 2
   See also CA 19-20
   See also DLB 5, 6

Platonov, Andrei (Platonovich)
      1899-1951.................. TCLC 14
   See also Klimentov, Andrei Platonovich

Platt, Kin 1911-....................CLC 26
   See also CANR 11
   See also CA 17-20R
   See also SATA 21

Plimpton, George (Ames)
 1927-........................CLC 36
 See also CA 21-24R
 See also SATA 10
 See also AITN 1

Plomer, William (Charles Franklin)
 1903-1973.................. CLC 4, 8
 See also CAP 2
 See also CA 21-22
 See also SATA 24
 See also DLB 20

Plumly, Stanley (Ross) 1939-......CLC 33
 See also CA 108, 110
 See also DLB 5

Poe, Edgar Allan 1809-1849 ...... NCLC 1
 See also SATA 23
 See also DLB 3

Pohl, Frederik 1919-..............CLC 18
 See also CAAS 1
 See also CANR 11
 See also CA 61-64
 See also SATA 24
 See also DLB 8

Poirier, Louis 1910-
 See Gracq, Julien

Poitier, Sidney 1924?-.............CLC 26

Polanski, Roman 1933-.............CLC 16
 See also CA 77-80

Police, The......................CLC 26

Pollitt, Katha 1949-..............CLC 28

Pomerance, Bernard 1940-........CLC 13
 See also CA 101

Ponge, Francis (Jean Gaston Alfred)
 1899-......................CLC 6, 18
 See also CA 85-88

Poole, Josephine 1933- ....CLC 17
 See also CANR 10
 See also CA 21-24R
 See also SATA 5

Pope, Alexander 1688-1744.........LC 3

Popa, Vasko 1922-.................CLC 19
 See also CA 112

Porter, Katherine Anne
 1890-1980..... CLC 1, 3, 7, 10, 13, 15,
                                        27
 See also CANR 1
 See also CA 1-4R
 See also obituary CA 101
 See also obituary SATA 23, 39
 See also DLB 4, 9
 See also DLB-Y 80
 See also AITN 2

Porter, Peter (Neville Frederick)
 1929-.................. CLC 5, 13, 33
 See also CA 85-88
 See also DLB 40

Porter, William Sydney 1862-1910
 See Henry, O.
 See also CA 104
 See also YABC 2
 See also DLB 12

Potok, Chaim 1929-.......CLC 2, 7, 14, 26
 See also CA 17-20R
 See also SATA 33
 See also DLB 28
 See also AITN 1, 2

Pound, Ezra (Loomis)
 1885-1972..... CLC 1, 2, 3, 4, 5, 7, 10,
                              13, 18, 34
 See also CA 5-8R
 See also obituary CA 37-40R
 See also DLB 4, 45

Powell, Anthony (Dymoke)
 1905-.......... CLC 1, 3, 7, 9, 10, 31
 See also CANR 1
 See also CA 1-4R
 See also DLB 15

Powell, Padgett 1952-..............CLC 34

Powers, J(ames) F(arl)
 1917-....................CLC 1, 4, 8
 See also CANR 2
 See also CA 1-4R

Pownall, David 1938- ....CLC 10
 See also CA 89-92
 See also DLB 14

Powys, John Cowper
 1872-1963.............. CLC 7, 9, 15
 See also CA 85-88
 See also DLB 15

Powys, T(heodore) F(rancis)
 1875-1953...................TCLC 9
 See also CA 106
 See also DLB 36

Pratt, E(dwin) J(ohn)
 1883-1964...................CLC 19
 See also obituary CA 93-96

Preussler, Otfried 1923-..........CLC 17
 See also CA 77-80
 See also SATA 24

Prévert, Jacques (Henri Marie)
 1900-1977...................CLC 15
 See also CA 77-80
 See also obituary CA 69-72
 See also obituary SATA 30

Prévost, Abbé (Antoine Francois)
 1697-1763.....................LC 1

Price, (Edward) Reynolds
 1933-.................... CLC 3, 6, 13
 See also CANR 1
 See also CA 1-4R
 See also DLB 2

Price, Richard 1949-.......... CLC 6, 12
 See also CANR 3
 See also CA 49-52
 See also DLB-Y 81

Priestley, J(ohn) B(oynton)
 1894-1984...............CLC 2, 5, 9, 34
 See also CA 9-12R
 See also obituary CA 113
 See also DLB 10, 34
 See also DLB-Y 84

Prince (Rogers Nelson) 1958?-......CLC 35

Prince, F(rank) T(empleton)
 1912-......................CLC 22
 See also CA 101
 See also DLB 20

Pritchard, William H(arrison)
 1932-......................CLC 34
 See also CA 65-68

Pritchett, V(ictor) S(awdon)
 1900-.................. CLC 5, 13, 15
 See also CA 61-64
 See also DLB 15

Procaccino, Michael 1946-
 See Cristofer, Michael

Prokosch, Frederic 1908-..........CLC 4
 See also CA 73-76

Proust, Marcel 1871-1922 ..... TCLC 7, 13
 See also CA 104

Pryor, Richard 1940- ....CLC 26

P'u Sung-ling 1640-1715............. LC 3

Puig, Manuel 1932-.......CLC 3, 5, 10, 28
 See also CANR 2
 See also CA 45-48

Purdy, A(lfred) W(ellington)
 1918-................... CLC 3, 6, 14
 See also CA 81-84

Purdy, James (Amos)
 1923-.............CLC 2, 4, 10, 28
 See also CAAS 1
 See also CA 33-36R
 See also DLB 2

Pushkin, Alexander (Sergeyevich)
 1799-1837................... NCLC 3

Puzo, Mario 1920-.........CLC 1, 2, 6, 36
 See also CANR 4
 See also CA 65-68
 See also DLB 6

Pym, Barbara (Mary Crampton)
 1913-1980............ CLC 13, 19, 37
 See also CANR 13
 See also CAP 1
 See also CA 13-14
 See also obituary CA 97-100
 See also DLB 14

Pynchon, Thomas (Ruggles, Jr.)
 1937-........CLC 2, 3, 6, 9, 11, 18, 33
 See also CA 17-20R
 See also DLB 2

Quasimodo, Salvatore
 1901-1968...................CLC 10
 See also CAP 1
 See also CA 15-16
 See also obituary CA 25-28R

Queen, Ellery 1905-1982 .... CLC 3, 11
 See also Dannay, Frederic
 See also Lee, Manfred B(ennington)

Queneau, Raymond
 1903-1976...............CLC 2, 5, 10
 See also CA 77-80
 See also obituary CA 69-72

Quin, Ann (Marie) 1936-1973.......CLC 6
 See also CA 9-12R
 See also obituary CA 45-48
 See also DLB 14

Quinn, Simon 1942-
 See Smith, Martin Cruz

Quiroga, Horatio (Sylvestre)
 1878-1937................... TCLC 20
 See also CA 117

Quoirez, Françoise 1935-
 See Sagan, Françoise
 See also CANR 6
 See also CA 49-52

Rabe, David (William)
 1940-..................CLC 4, 8, 33
 See also CA 85-88
 See also DLB 7

Rabinovitch, Sholem 1859-1916
See Aleichem, Sholom
See also CA 104

Radcliffe, Ann (Ward)
1764-1823.................NCLC 6
See also DLB 39

Radnóti, Miklós 1909-1944 ...... TCLC 16

Rado, James 1939-
See Ragni, Gerome and
Rado, James
See also CA 105

Radomski, James 1932-
See Rado, James

Radvanyi, Netty Reiling 1900-1983
See Seghers, Anna
See also CA 85-88
See also obituary CA 110

Raeburn, John 1941-.............CLC 34
See also CA 57-60

Ragni, Gerome 1942-
See Ragni, Gerome and Rado, James
See also CA 105

Ragni, Gerome 1942- and
Rado, James 1939-..........CLC 17

Rahv, Philip 1908-1973 ....CLC 24
See also Greenberg, Ivan

Raine, Craig 1944- ....CLC 32
See also CA 108
See also DLB 40

Raine, Kathleen (Jessie) 1908-......CLC 7
See also CA 85-88
See also DLB 20

Rand, Ayn 1905-1982.........CLC 3, 30
See also CA 13-16R
See also obituary CA 105

Randall, Dudley (Felker) 1914-......CLC 1
See also CA 25-28R
See also DLB 41

Ransom, John Crowe
1888-1974........ CLC 2, 4, 5, 11, 24
See also CANR 6
See also CA 5-8R
See also obituary CA 49-52
See also DLB 45

Rao, Raja 1909-.................CLC 25
See also CA 73-76

Raphael, Frederic (Michael)
1931-................... CLC 2, 14
See also CANR 1
See also CA 1-4R
See also DLB 14

Rattigan, Terence (Mervyn)
1911-1977..................CLC 7
See also CA 85-88
See also obituary CA 73-76
See also DLB 13

Raven, Simon (Arthur Noel)
1927-......................CLC 14
See also CA 81-84

Rawlings, Marjorie Kinnan
1896-1953................. TCLC 4
See also CA 104
See also YABC 1
See also DLB 9, 22

Ray, Satyajit 1921- ....CLC 16

Read, Herbert (Edward)
1893-1968....................CLC 4
See also CA 85-88
See also obituary CA 25-28R
See also DLB 20

Read, Piers Paul 1941-...... CLC 4, 10, 25
See also CA 21-24R
See also SATA 21
See also DLB 14

Reade, Charles 1814-1884 .... NCLC 2
See also DLB 21

Reade, Hamish 1936-
See Gray, Simon (James Holliday)

Reaney, James 1926-.............CLC 13
See also CA 41-44R
See also SATA 43

Rechy, John (Francisco)
1934-................CLC 1, 7, 14, 18
See also CANR 6
See also CA 5-8R
See also DLB-Y 82

Redgrove, Peter (William)
1932-.......................CLC 6
See also CANR 3
See also CA 1-4R
See also DLB 40

Redmon (Nightingale), Anne
1943-......................CLC 22
See also Nightingale, Anne Redmon

Reed, Ishmael
1938-........ CLC 2, 3, 5, 6, 13, 32
See also CA 21-24R
See also DLB 2, 5, 33

Reed, John (Silas) 1887-1920...... TCLC 9
See also CA 106

Reed, Lou 1944-.................CLC 21

Reid, Christopher 1949-...........CLC 33
See also DLB 40

Reid Banks, Lynne 1929-
See Banks, Lynne Reid
See also CANR 6
See also CA 1-4R
See also SATA 22

Reiner, Max 1900-
See Caldwell, (Janet Miriam) Taylor (Holland)

Remark, Erich Paul 1898-1970
See Remarque, Erich Maria

Remarque, Erich Maria
1898-1970....................CLC 21
See also CA 77-80
See also obituary CA 29-32R

Renard, Jules 1864-1910 .... TCLC 17

Renault, Mary
1905-1983.............. CLC 3, 11, 17
See also Challans, Mary
See also DLB-Y 83

Rendell, Ruth 1930- ....CLC 28
See also CA 109

Renoir, Jean 1894-1979 ....CLC 20
See also obituary CA 85-88

Resnais, Alain 1922- ....CLC 16

Rexroth, Kenneth
1905-1982........ CLC 1, 2, 6, 11, 22
See also CA 5-8R
See also obituary CA 107
See also DLB 16
See also DLB-Y 82

Reyes y Basoalto, Ricardo Eliecer Neftali
1904-1973
See Neruda, Pablo

Reymont, Wladyslaw Stanislaw
1867-1925.................. TCLC 5
See also CA 104

Reynolds, Jonathan 1942?- ....CLC 6
See also CA 65-68

Reznikoff, Charles 1894-1976 ....CLC 9
See also CAP 2
See also CA 33-36
See also obituary CA 61-64
See also DLB 28, 45

Rezzori, Gregor von 1914-.........CLC 25

Rhys, Jean
1894-1979........ CLC 2, 4, 6, 14, 19
See also CA 25-28R
See also obituary CA 85-88
See also DLB 36

Ribeiro, Darcy 1922-..............CLC 34
See also CA 33-36R

Ribeiro, João Ubaldo (Osorio Pimentel)
1941-.......................CLC 10
See also CA 81-84

Ribman, Ronald (Burt) 1932- ....CLC 7
See also CA 21-24R

Rice, Elmer 1892-1967 ....CLC 7
See also CAP 2
See also CA 21-22
See also obituary CA 25-28R
See also DLB 4, 7

Rice, Tim 1944-
See Rice, Tim and Webber, Andrew Lloyd
See also CA 103

Rice, Tim 1944- and
Webber, Andrew Lloyd
1948-.......................CLC 21

Rich, Adrienne (Cecile)
1929-.......... CLC 3, 6, 7, 11, 18, 36
See also CA 9-12R
See also DLB 5

Richard, Keith 1943-
See Jagger, Mick and Richard, Keith

Richards, I(vor) A(rmstrong)
1893-1979................ CLC 14, 24
See also CA 41-44R
See also obituary CA 89-92
See also DLB 27

Richards, Keith 1943-
See Richard, Keith
See also CA 107

Richardson, Dorothy (Miller)
1873-1957.................. TCLC 3
See also CA 104
See also DLB 36

Richardson, Ethel 1870-1946
See Richardson, Henry Handel
See also CA 105

Richardson, Henry Handel
1870-1946................. TCLC 4
See also Richardson, Ethel

Richardson, Samuel 1689-1761....... LC 1
See also DLB 39

Richler, Mordecai
    1931-............ **CLC 3, 5, 9, 13, 18**
    See also CA 65-68
    See also SATA 27
    See also AITN 1

Richter, Conrad (Michael)
    1890-1968....................**CLC 30**
    See also CA 5-8R
    See also obituary CA 25-28R
    See also SATA 3
    See also DLB 9

Richter, Johann Paul Friedrich   1763-1825
    See Jean Paul

Riding, Laura   1901- .... **CLC 3, 7**
    See also Jackson, Laura (Riding)

Riefenstahl, Berta Helene Amalia   1902-
    See Riefenstahl, Leni
    See also CA 108

Riefenstahl, Leni   1902-............**CLC 16**
    See also Riefenstahl, Berta Helene Amalia

Rilke, Rainer Maria
    1875-1926.............**TCLC 1, 6, 19**
    See also CA 104

Rimbaud, (Jean Nicolas) Arthur
    1854-1891.................. **NCLC 4**

Ritsos, Yannis   1909-........ **CLC 6, 13, 31**
    See also CA 77-80

Rivers, Conrad Kent   1933-1968 ..... **CLC 1**
    See also CA 85-88
    See also DLB 41

Robbe-Grillet, Alain
    1922-........**CLC 1, 2, 4, 6, 8, 10, 14**
    See also CA 9-12R

Robbins, Harold   1916- ....**CLC 5**
    See also CA 73-76

Robbins, Thomas Eugene   1936-
    See Robbins, Tom
    See also CA 81-84

Robbins, Tom   1936- .... **CLC 9, 32**
    See also Robbins, Thomas Eugene
    See also DLB-Y 80

Robbins, Trina   1938- ....**CLC 21**

Roberts, (Sir) Charles G(eorge) D(ouglas)
    1860-1943................... **TCLC 8**
    See also CA 105
    See also SATA 29

Roberts, Kate   1891-1985 ....**CLC 15**
    See also CA 107
    See also obituary CA 116

Roberts, Keith (John Kingston)
    1935-.....................**CLC 14**
    See also CA 25-28R

Robinson, Edwin Arlington
    1869-1935.................. **TCLC 5**
    See also CA 104

Robinson, Jill   1936-..............**CLC 10**
    See also CA 102

Robinson, Kim Stanley   19??-.......**CLC 34**

Robinson, Marilynne   1944- ....**CLC 25**
    See also CA 116

Robinson, Smokey   1940- ....**CLC 21**

Robinson, William   1940-
    See Robinson, Smokey
    See also CA 116

Roddenberry, Gene   1921- ....**CLC 17**

Rodgers, Mary   1931- ....**CLC 12**
    See also CANR 8
    See also CA 49-52
    See also SATA 8

Rodgers, W(illiam) R(obert)
    1909-1969....................**CLC 7**
    See also CA 85-88
    See also DLB 20

Rodriguez, Claudio   1934-.........**CLC 10**

Roethke, Theodore (Huebner)
    1908-1963........ **CLC 1, 3, 8, 11, 19**
    See also CA 81-84
    See also DLB 5

Rogers, Sam   1943-
    See Shepard, Sam

Rogers, Will(iam Penn Adair)
    1879-1935.................. **TCLC 8**
    See also CA 105
    See also DLB 11

Rogin, Gilbert   1929-.............**CLC 18**
    See also CANR 15
    See also CA 65-68

Rohmer, Eric   1920-.............**CLC 16**
    See also Scherer, Jean-Marie Maurice

Roiphe, Anne (Richardson)
    1935-...................... **CLC 3, 9**
    See also CA 89-92
    See also DLB-Y 80

**Rolfe, Frederick (William Serafino Austin
    Lewis Mary)**   1860-1913..... **TCLC 12**
    See also CA 107
    See also DLB 34

Rölvaag, O(le) E(dvart)
    1876-1931................. **TCLC 17**
    See also DLB 9

Romains, Jules   1885-1972 ....**CLC 7**
    See also CA 85-88

Romero, José Rubén
    1890-1952................. **TCLC 14**
    See also CA 114

Rooke, Leon   1934-.............. **CLC 25, 34**
    See also CA 25-28R

Rosa, João Guimarães
    1908-1967...................**CLC 23**
    See also obituary CA 89-92

Rosenberg, Isaac   1890-1918...... **TCLC 12**
    See also CA 107
    See also DLB 20

Rosenblatt, Joe   1933-.............**CLC 15**
    See also Rosenblatt, Joseph
    See also AITN 2

Rosenblatt, Joseph   1933-
    See Rosenblatt, Joe
    See also CA 89-92

Rosenthal, M(acha) L(ouis)
    1917-......................**CLC 28**
    See also CANR 4
    See also CA 1-4R
    See also DLB 5

Ross, (James) Sinclair   1908- ....**CLC 13**
    See also CA 73-76

Rossetti, Christina Georgina
    1830-1894................. **NCLC 2**
    See also SATA 20
    See also DLB 35

Rossetti, Dante Gabriel
    1828-1882.................. **NCLC 4**
    See also DLB 35

Rossetti, Gabriel Charles Dante   1828-1882
    See Rossetti, Dante Gabriel

Rossner, Judith (Perelman)
    1935-................... **CLC 6, 9, 29**
    See also CA 17-20R
    See also DLB 6
    See also AITN 2

Rostand, Edmond (Eugène Alexis)
    1868-1918................... **TCLC 6**
    See also CA 104

Roth, Henry   1906-...........**CLC 2, 6, 11**
    See also CAP 1
    See also CA 11-12
    See also DLB 28

Roth, Philip (Milton)
    1933-......**CLC 1, 2, 3, 4, 6, 9, 15, 22,
                                          31**
    See also CANR 1
    See also CA 1-4R
    See also DLB 2, 28
    See also DLB-Y 82

Rothenberg, Jerome   1931-..........**CLC 6**
    See also CANR 1
    See also CA 45-48
    See also DLB 5

Roumain, Jacques   1907-1944 .... **TCLC 19**

Rourke, Constance (Mayfield)
    1885-1941................. **TCLC 12**
    See also CA 107
    See also YABC 1

Roussel, Raymond   1877-1933 .... **TCLC 20**
    See also CA 117

Rovit, Earl (Herbert)   1927-.........**CLC 7**
    See also CA 5-8R

Rowson, Susanna Haswell
    1762-1824.................. **NCLC 5**
    See also DLB 37

Roy, Gabrielle   1909-1983...... **CLC 10, 14**
    See also CANR 5
    See also CA 53-56
    See also obituary CA 110

Różewicz, Tadeusz   1921- .... **CLC 9, 23**
    See also CA 108

Ruark, Gibbons   1941-...............**CLC 3**
    See also CANR 14
    See also CA 33-36R

Rubens, Bernice   192?- .... **CLC 19, 31**
    See also CA 25-28R
    See also DLB 14

Rudkin, (James) David   1936- ......**CLC 14**
    See also CA 89-92
    See also DLB 13

Rudnik, Raphael   1933-.............**CLC 7**
    See also CA 29-32R

Ruiz, José Martínez   1874-1967
    See Azorín

Rukeyser, Muriel
    1913-1980..........**CLC 6, 10, 15, 27**
    See also CA 5-8R
    See also obituary CA 93-96
    See also obituary SATA 22

Rule, Jane (Vance)   1931-..........**CLC 27**
    See also CANR 12
    See also CA 25-28R

Rulfo, Juan 1918- ....CLC 8
  See also CA 85-88

Runyon, (Alfred) Damon
  1880-1946...................TCLC 10
  See also CA 107
  See also DLB 11

Rushdie, (Ahmed) Salman
  1947-....................CLC 23, 31
  See also CA 108, 111

Rushforth, Peter (Scott) 1945-......CLC 19
  See also CA 101

Ruskin, John 1819-1900.........TCLC 20
  See also CA 114
  See also SATA 24

Russ, Joanna 1937-..............CLC 15
  See also CANR 11
  See also CA 25-28R
  See also DLB 8

Russell, George William 1867-1935
  See A. E.
  See also CA 104

Russell, (Henry) Ken(neth Alfred)
  1927-.......................CLC 16
  See also CA 105

Ruyslinck, Ward 1929-...........CLC 14

Ryan, Cornelius (John)
  1920-1974...................CLC 7
  See also CA 69-72
  See also obituary CA 53-56

Rybakov, Anatoli 1911?- ....CLC 23

Ryga, George 1932-..............CLC 14
  See also CA 101

Sabato, Ernesto 1911-........ CLC 10, 23
  See also CA 97-100

Sachs, Marilyn (Stickle) 1927-......CLC 35
  See also CLR 2
  See also CANR 13
  See also CA 17-20R
  See also SATA 3

Sachs, Nelly 1891-1970............CLC 14
  See also CAP 2
  See also CA 17-18
  See also obituary CA 25-28R

Sackler, Howard (Oliver)
  1929-1982...................CLC 14
  See also CA 61-64
  See also obituary CA 108
  See also DLB 7

Sade, Donatien Alphonse François, Comte de
  1740-1814...................NCLC 3

Sadoff, Ira 1945-.................CLC 9
  See also CANR 5
  See also CA 53-56

Safire, William 1929- ....CLC 10
  See also CA 17-20R

Sagan, Carl (Edward) 1934- ......CLC 30
  See also CANR 11
  See also CA 25-28R

Sagan, Françoise
  1935-............ CLC 3, 6, 9, 17, 36
  See also Quoirez, Françoise

Sainte-Beuve, Charles Augustin
  1804-1869..................NCLC 5

Sainte-Marie, Beverly 1941-
  See Sainte-Marie, Buffy
  See also CA 107

Sainte-Marie, Buffy 1941- ....CLC 17
  See also Sainte-Marie, Beverly

Saint-Exupéry, Antoine (Jean Baptiste Marie Roger) de 1900-1944 .... TCLC 2
  See also CA 108
  See also SATA 20

Saki 1870-1916..................TCLC 3
  See also Munro, H(ector) H(ugh)

Salama, Hannu 1936-.............CLC 18

Salamanca, J(ack) R(ichard)
  1922-.................... CLC 4, 15
  See also CA 25-28R

Salinas, Pedro 1891-1951........ TCLC 17

Salinger, J(erome) D(avid)
  1919-..................CLC 1, 3, 8, 12
  See also CA 5-8R
  See also DLB 2

Salter, James 1925-.................CLC 7
  See also CA 73-76

Saltus, Edgar (Evertson)
  1855-1921...................TCLC 8
  See also CA 105

Samarakis, Antonis 1919-...........CLC 5
  See also CA 25-28R

Sánchez, Luis Rafael 1936- ....CLC 23

Sanchez, Sonia 1934-...............CLC 5
  See also CA 33-36R
  See also SATA 22
  See also DLB 41

Sand, George 1804-1876......... NCLC 2

Sandburg, Carl (August)
  1878-1967........ CLC 1, 4, 10, 15, 35
  See also CA 5-8R
  See also obituary CA 25-28R
  See also SATA 8
  See also DLB 17

Sandburg, Charles August 1878-1967
  See Sandburg, Carl (August)

Sandoz, Mari (Susette)
  1896-1966...................CLC 28
  See also CANR 17
  See also CA 1-4R
  See also obituary CA 25-28R
  See also SATA 5
  See also DLB 9

Saner, Reg(inald Anthony)
  1931-.......................CLC 9
  See also CA 65-68

Sansom, William 1912-1976...... CLC 2, 6
  See also CA 5-8R
  See also obituary CA 65-68

Santiago, Danny 1911- ....CLC 33

Santmyer, Helen Hoover 1895-.....CLC 33
  See also CANR 15
  See also CA 1-4R
  See also DLB-Y 84

Santos, Bienvenido N(uqui)
  1911-......................CLC 22
  See also CA 101

Sarduy, Severo 1937- ....CLC 6
  See also CA 89-92

Sargeson, Frank 1903-1982 ....CLC 31
  See also CA 25-28R
  See also CA 106

Sarmiento, Felix Ruben Garcia 1867-1916
  See also CA 104

Saroyan, William
  1908-1981........ CLC 1, 8, 10, 29, 34
  See also CA 5-8R
  See also obituary CA 103
  See also SATA 23
  See also obituary SATA 24
  See also DLB 7, 9
  See also DLB-Y 81

Sarraute, Nathalie
  1902-.......... CLC 1, 2, 4, 8, 10, 31
  See also CA 9-12R

Sarton, (Eleanor) May
  1912-.................... CLC 4, 14
  See also CANR 1
  See also CA 1-4R
  See also SATA 36
  See also DLB-Y 81

Sartre, Jean-Paul
  1905-1980...... CLC 1, 4, 7, 9, 13, 18, 24
  See also CA 9-12R
  See also obituary CA 97-100

Sassoon, Siegfried (Lorraine)
  1886-1967...................CLC 36
  See also CA 104
  See also Obituary CA 25-28R
  See also DLB 20

Saura, Carlos 1932-...............CLC 20
  See also CA 114

Sauser-Hall, Frédéric-Louis 1887-1961
  See Cendrars, Blaise
  See also CA 102
  See also obituary CA 93-96

Sayers, Dorothy L(eigh)
  1893-1957...............TCLC 2, 15
  See also CA 104
  See also DLB 10, 36

Sayles, John (Thomas)
  1950-.................. CLC 7, 10, 14
  See also CA 57-60
  See also DLB 44

Scammell, Michael 19??- ....CLC 34

Schaeffer, Susan Fromberg
  1941-.................. CLC 6, 11, 22
  See also CA 49-52
  See also SATA 22
  See also DLB 28

Schell, Jonathan 1943- ....CLC 35
  See also CANR 12
  See also CA 73-76

Scherer, Jean-Marie Maurice 1920-
  See Rohmer, Eric
  See also CA 110

Schevill, James (Erwin) 1920-.......CLC 7
  See also CA 5-8R

Schisgal, Murray (Joseph)
  1926-.......................CLC 6
  See also CA 21-24R

Schlee, Ann 1934- ....CLC 35
  See also CA 101
  See also SATA 36

Schmitz, Ettore 1861-1928
  See Svevo, Italo
  See also CA 104

Schneider, Leonard Alfred 1925-1966
  See Bruce, Lenny
  See also CA 89-92

Author Index

Schnitzler, Arthur 1862-1931 ..... **TCLC 4**
See also CA 104

Schorer, Mark 1908-1977 .... **CLC 9**
See also CANR 7
See also CA 5-8R
See also obituary CA 73-76

Schrader, Paul (Joseph) 1946-...... **CLC 26**
See also CA 37-40R
See also DLB 44

Schreiner (Cronwright), Olive (Emilie
Albertina) 1855-1920 .... **TCLC 9**
See also CA 105
See also DLB 18

Schulberg, Budd (Wilson) 1914-..... **CLC 7**
See also CA 25-28R
See also DLB 6, 26, 28
See also DLB-Y 81

Schulz, Bruno 1892-1942 .... **TCLC 5**
See also CA 115

Schulz, Charles M(onroe)
1922-..................... **CLC 12**
See also CANR 6
See also CA 9-12R
See also SATA 10

Schuyler, James (Marcus)
1923-..................... **CLC 5, 23**
See also CA 101
See also DLB 5

Schwartz, Delmore
1913-1966............... **CLC 2, 4, 10**
See also CAP 2
See also CA 17-18
See also obituary CA 25-28R
See also DLB 28

Schwartz, Lynne Sharon 1939-..... **CLC 31**
See also CA 103

Schwarz-Bart, André 1928-...... **CLC 2, 4**
See also CA 89-92

Schwarz-Bart, Simone 1938-........ **CLC 7**
See also CA 97-100

Schwob, (Mayer Andre) Marcel
1867-1905............... **TCLC 20**
See also CA 117

Sciascia, Leonardo 1921-........ **CLC 8, 9**
See also CA 85-88

Scoppettone, Sandra 1936-......... **CLC 26**
See also CA 5-8R
See also SATA 9

Scorsese, Martin 1942-............. **CLC 20**
See also CA 110, 114

Scotland, Jay 1932-
See Jakes, John (William)

Scott, Duncan Campbell
1862-1947................ **TCLC 6**
See also CA 104

Scott, F(rancis) R(eginald)
1899-1985................... **CLC 22**
See also CA 101
See also obituary CA 114

Scott, Paul (Mark) 1920-1978 .... **CLC 9**
See also CA 81-84
See also obituary CA 77-80
See also DLB 14

Scudéry, Madeleine de 1607-1701..... **LC 2**

Seare, Nicholas 1925-
See Trevanian
See also Whitaker, Rodney

Sebestyen, Igen 1924-
See Sebestyen, Ouida

Sebestyen, Ouida 1924-............. **CLC 30**
See also CA 107
See also SATA 39

Seelye, John 1931-................. **CLC 7**
See also CA 97-100

Seferiades, Giorgos Stylianou 1900-1971
See Seferis, George
See also CANR 5
See also CA 5-8R
See also obituary CA 33-36R

Seferis, George 1900-1971 ...... **CLC 5, 11**
See also Seferiades, Giorgos Stylianou

Segal, Erich (Wolf) 1937-....... **CLC 3, 10**
See also CA 25-28R

Seger, Bob 1945- .... **CLC 35**

Seger, Robert Clark 1945-
See Seger, Bob

Seghers, Anna 1900-............... **CLC 7**
See Radvanyi, Netty

Seidel, Frederick (Lewis) 1936-..... **CLC 18**
See also CANR 8
See also CA 13-16R
See also DLB-Y 84

Seifert, Jaroslav 1901- .... **CLC 34**

Selby, Hubert, Jr.
1928-.................. **CLC 1, 2, 4, 8**
See also CA 13-16R
See also DLB 2

Sender, Ramón (José)
1902-1982..................... **CLC 8**
See also CANR 8
See also CA 5-8R
See also obituary CA 105

Serling, (Edward) Rod(man) 1924-1975
See also CA 65-68
See also obituary CA 57-60
See also DLB 26
See also AITN 1

Serpières 1907-
See Guillevic, (Eugène)

Service, Robert W(illiam)
1874-1958................. **TCLC 15**
See also CA 115
See also SATA 20

Seton, Cynthia Propper
1926-1982..................... **CLC 27**
See also CANR-7
See also CA 5-8R
See also obituary CA 108

Settle, Mary Lee 1918-............. **CLC 19**
See also CAAS 1
See also CA 89-92
See also DLB 6

Sexton, Anne (Harvey)
1928-1974...... **CLC 2, 4, 6, 8, 10, 15**
See also CANR 3
See also CA 1-4R
See also obituary CA 53-56
See also SATA 10
See also DLB 5

Shaara, Michael (Joseph)
1929-......................... **CLC 15**
See also CA 102
See also DLB-Y 83
See also AITN 1

Shaffer, Anthony 1926-............. **CLC 19**
See also CA 110
See also CA 116
See also DLB 13

Shaffer, Peter (Levin)
1926-............... **CLC 5, 14, 18, 37**
See also CA 25-28R
See also DLB 13

Shalamov, Varlam (Tikhonovich)
1907?-1982................... **CLC 18**
See also obituary CA 105

Shamlu, Ahmad 1925- .... **CLC 10**

Shange, Ntozake 1948- .... **CLC 8, 25**
See also CA 85-88
See also DLB 38

Shapiro, Karl (Jay) 1913-..... **CLC 4, 8, 15**
See also CANR 1
See also CA 1-4R

Sharpe, Tom 1928- ..../..... **CLC 36**
See also CA 114
See also DLB 14

Shaw, (George) Bernard
1856-1950................. **TCLC 3, 9**
See also CA 104, 109
See also DLB 10

Shaw, Irwin 1913-1984...... **CLC 7, 23, 34**
See also CA 13-16R
See also obituary CA 112
See also DLB 6
See also DLB-Y 84
See also AITN 1

Shaw, Robert 1927-1978 .... **CLC 5**
See also CANR 4
See also CA 1-4R
See also obituary CA 81-84
See also DLB 13, 14
See also AITN 1

Sheed, Wilfrid (John Joseph)
1930-.................... **CLC 2, 4, 10**
See also CA 65-68
See also DLB 6

Sheffey, Asa 1913-1980
See Hayden, Robert (Earl)

Shepard, Jim 19??- .... **CLC 36**

Shepard, Lucius 19??-............. **CLC 34**

Shepard, Sam 1943- ......**CLC 4, 6, 17, 34**
See also CA 69-72
See also DLB 7

Sherburne, Zoa (Morin) 1912- ..... **CLC 30**
See also CANR 3
See also CA 1-4R
See also SATA 3

Sheridan, Richard Brinsley
1751-1816................... **NCLC 5**

Sherman, Martin .... **CLC 19**
See also CA 116

Sherwin, Judith Johnson
1936-..................... **CLC 7, 15**
See also CA 25-28R

Sherwood, Robert E(mmet)
  1896-1955................... TCLC 3
  See also CA 104
  See also DLB 7, 26

Shiel, M(atthew) P(hipps)
  1865-1947................... TCLC 8
  See also CA 106

Shiga Naoya 1883-1971...........CLC 33
  See also CA 101
  See also obituary CA 33-36R

Shimazaki, Haruki 1872-1943
  See Shimazaki, Tōson
  See also CA 105

Shimazaki, Tōson 1872-1943..... TCLC 5
  See also Shimazaki, Haruki

Sholokhov, Mikhail (Aleksandrovich)
  1905-1984................ CLC 7, 15
  See also CA 101
  See also obituary CA 112
  See also SATA 36

Shreve, Susan Richards 1939-......CLC 23
  See also CANR 5
  See also CA 49-52
  See also SATA 41

Shulman, Alix Kates 1932-...... CLC 2, 10
  See also CA 29-32R
  See also SATA 7

Shuster, Joe 1914-
  See Siegel, Jerome and Shuster, Joe

Shute (Norway), Nevil
  1899-1960...................CLC 30
  See also Norway, Nevil Shute

Shuttle, Penelope (Diane) 1947-......CLC 7
  See also CA 93-96
  See also DLB 14, 40

Siegel, Jerome 1914-
  See Siegel, Jerome and Shuster, Joe
  See also CA 116

Siegel, Jerome 1914- and
  Shuster, Joe 1914- ....CLC 21

Sienkiewicz, Henryk (Adam Aleksander Pius)
  1846-1916................... TCLC 3
  See also CA 104

Sigal, Clancy 1926-................CLC 7
  See also CA 1-4R

Silkin, Jon 1930- .... CLC 2, 6
  See also CA 5-8R
  See also DLB 27

Silko, Leslie Marmon 1948-........CLC 23
  See also CA 115

Sillanpää, Franz Eemil
  1888-1964....................CLC 19
  See also obituary CA 93-96

Sillitoe, Alan 1928- .... CLC 1, 3, 6, 10, 19
  See also CAAS 2
  See also CANR 8
  See also CA 9-12R
  See also DLB 14
  See also AITN 1

Silone, Ignazio 1900-1978..........CLC 4
  See also CAP 2
  See also CA 25-28
  See also obituary CA 81-84

Silver, Joan Micklin 1935-........CLC 20
  See also CA 114

Silverberg, Robert 1935- ....CLC 7
  See also CAAS 3
  See also CANR 1
  See also CA 1-4R
  See also SATA 13
  See also DLB 8

Silverstein, Alvin 1933-
  See Silverstein, Alvin
    and Silverstein, Virginia B(arbara
    Opshelor)
  See also CANR 2
  See also CA 49-52
  See also SATA 8

Silverstein, Alvin 1933- and **Silverstein,
  Virginia B(arbara Opshelor)**
  1937-.......................CLC 17

Silverstein, Virginia B(arbara Opshelor)
  1937-
  See Silverstein, Alvin and Silverstein,
    Virginia B(arbara Opshelor)
  See also CANR 2
  See also CA 49-52
  See also SATA 8

Simak, Clifford D(onald) 1904-......CLC 1
  See also CANR 1
  See also CA 1-4R
  See also DLB 8

Simenon, Georges (Jacques Christian)
  1903-.............. CLC 1, 2, 3, 8, 18
  See also CA 85-88

Simenon, Paul 1956?-
  See The Clash

Simic, Charles 1938-......... CLC 6, 9, 22
  See also CA 29-32R

Simms, William Gilmore
  1806-1870.................. NCLC 3
  See also DLB 3, 30

Simon, Carly 1945-...............CLC 26
  See also CA 105

Simon, Claude 1913-......... CLC 4, 9, 15
  See also CA 89-92

Simon, (Marvin) Neil
  1927-................... CLC 6, 11, 31
  See also CA 21-24R
  See also DLB 7
  See also AITN 1

Simon, Paul 1941-................CLC 17
  See also CA 116

Simonon, Paul 1956?-
  See The Clash

Simpson, Louis (Aston Marantz)
  1923-.................CLC 4, 7, 9, 32
  See also CANR 1
  See also CA 1-4R
  See also DLB 5

Simpson, N(orman) F(rederick)
  1919-.......................CLC 29
  See also CA 11-14R
  See also DLB 13

Sinclair, Andrew (Annandale)
  1935-................... CLC 2, 14
  See also CANR 14
  See also CA 9-12R
  See also DLB 14

Sinclair, Mary Amelia St. Clair 1865?-1946
  See Sinclair, May
  See also CA 104

Sinclair, May 1865?-1946...... TCLC 3, 11
  See also Sinclair, Mary Amelia St. Clair
  See also DLB 36

Sinclair, Upton (Beall)
  1878-1968.............. CLC 1, 11, 15
  See also CANR 7
  See also CA 5-8R
  See also obituary 25-28R
  See also SATA 9
  See also DLB 9

Singer, Isaac Bashevis
  1904-........CLC 1, 3, 6, 9, 11, 15, 23
  See also CLR 1
  See also CANR 1
  See also CA 1-4R
  See also SATA 3, 27
  See also DLB 6, 28
  See also AITN 1, 2

Singh, Khushwant 1915-...........CLC 11
  See also CANR 6
  See also CA 9-12R

Sinyavsky, Andrei (Donatevich)
  1925-.......................CLC 8
  See also CA 85-88

Sissman, L(ouis) E(dward)
  1928-1976............... CLC 9, 18
  See also CA 21-24R
  See also obituary CA 65-68
  See also DLB 5

Sisson, C(harles) H(ubert) 1914-.....CLC 8
  See also CAAS 3
  See also CANR 3
  See also CA 1-4R
  See also DLB 27

Sitwell, (Dame) Edith
  1887-1964.................. CLC 2, 9
  See also CA 9-12R
  See also DLB 20

Sjoewall, Maj 1935-
  See Wahlöö, Per
  See also CA 65-68

Sjöwall, Maj 1935-
  See Wahlöö, Per

Skelton, Robin 1925-..............CLC 13
  See also CA 5-8R
  See also AITN 2
  See also DLB 27

Skolimowski, Jerzy 1938-..........CLC 20

Skolimowski, Yurek 1938-
  See Skolimowski, Jerzy

Skrine, Mary Nesta 1904-
  See Keane, Molly

Škvorecký, Josef (Vaclav)
  1924-.......................CLC 15
  See also CAAS 1
  See also CANR 10
  See also CA 61-64

Slade, Bernard 1930- ....CLC 11
  See also Newbound, Bernard Slade

Slaughter, Frank G(ill) 1908- ......CLC 29
  See also CANR 5
  See also CA 5-8R
  See also AITN 2

Slavitt, David (R.) 1935-........ CLC 5, 14
  See also CAAS 3
  See also CA 21-24R
  See also DLB 5, 6

Author Index

Slesinger, Tess 1905-1945....... **TCLC 10**
See also CA 107

Slessor, Kenneth 1901-1971....... **CLC 14**
See also CA 102
See also obituary CA 89-92

Smart, Christopher 1722-1771 .... **LC 3**

Smith, A(rthur) J(ames) M(arshall)
1902-1980.................**CLC 15**
See also CANR 4
See also CA 1-4R
See also obituary CA 102

Smith, Betty (Wehner)
1896-1972.................**CLC 19**
See also CA 5-8R
See also obituary CA 33-36R
See also SATA 6
See also DLB-Y 82

Smith, Cecil Lewis Troughton 1899-1966
See Forester, C(ecil) S(cott)

Smith, Dave 1942-................**CLC 22**
See also Smith, David (Jeddie)
See also DLB 5

Smith, David (Jeddie) 1942-
See Smith, Dave
See also CANR 1
See also CA 49-52

Smith, Florence Margaret 1902-1971
See Smith, Stevie
See also CAP 2
See also CA 17-18
See also obituary CA 29-32R

Smith, Lee 1944-................**CLC 25**
See also CA 114
See also DLB-Y 83

Smith, Martin Cruz 1942-........**CLC 25**
See also CANR 6
See also CA 85-88

Smith, Martin William 1942-
See Smith, Martin Cruz

Smith, Patti 1946-................**CLC 12**
See also CA 93-96

Smith, Sara Mahala Redway 1900-1972
See Benson, Sally

Smith, Stevie 1902-1971...... **CLC 3, 8, 25**
See also Smith, Florence Margaret
See also DLB 20

Smith, Wilbur (Addison) 1933-.....**CLC 33**
See also CANR 7
See also CA 13-16R

Smith, William Jay 1918-..........**CLC 6**
See also CA 5-8R
See also SATA 2
See also DLB 5

Smollett, Tobias (George)
1721-1771.....................**LC 2**
See also DLB 39

Snodgrass, W(illiam) D(e Witt)
1926-................**CLC 2, 6, 10, 18**
See also CANR 6
See also CA 1-4R
See also DLB 5

Snow, C(harles) P(ercy)
1905-1980....... **CLC 1, 4, 6, 9, 13, 19**
See also CA 5-8R
See also obituary CA 101
See also DLB 15

Snyder, Gary 1930-..... **CLC 1, 2, 5, 9, 32**
See also CA 17-20R
See also DLB 5, 16

Snyder, Zilpha Keatley 1927- ......**CLC 17**
See also CA 9-12R
See also SATA 1, 28

Sokolov, Raymond 1941- ....**CLC 7**
See also CA 85-88

Sologub, Fyodor 1863-1927 .... **TCLC 9**
See also Teternikov, Fyodor Kuzmich

Solwoska, Mara 1929-
See French, Marilyn

Solzhenitsyn, Aleksandr I(sayevich)
1918-.....CLC 1, 2, 4, 7, 9, 10, 18, 26,
                                                    34
See also CA 69-72
See also AITN 1

Sommer, Scott 1951-..............**CLC 25**
See also CA 106

Sondheim, Stephen (Joshua)
1930-........................**CLC 33**
See also CA 103

Sontag, Susan
1933-............ **CLC 1, 2, 10, 13, 31**
See also CA 17-20R
See also DLB 2

Sorrentino, Gilbert
1929-................**CLC 3, 7, 14, 22**
See also CANR 14
See also CA 77-80
See also DLB 5
See also DLB-Y 80

Soto, Gary 1952-.................**CLC 32**

Souster, (Holmes) Raymond
1921-..................... **CLC 5, 14**
See also CANR 13
See also CA 13-16R

Southern, Terry 1926-..............**CLC 7**
See also CANR 1
See also CA 1-4R
See also DLB 2

Southey, Robert 1774-1843 .... **NCLC 8**

Soyinka, Akin-wande Oluwole 1934-
See Soyinka, Wole

Soyinka, Wole 1934-.....**CLC 3, 5, 14, 36**
See also CA 13-16R

Spacks, Barry 1931-..............**CLC 14**
See also CA 29-32R

Spark, Muriel (Sarah)
1918-.......... **CLC 2, 3, 5, 8, 13, 18**
See also CANR 12
See also CA 5-8R
See also DLB 15

Spencer, Elizabeth 1921- ....**CLC 22**
See also CA 13-16R
See also SATA 14
See also DLB 6

Spencer, Scott 1945-..............**CLC 30**
See also CA 113

Spender, Stephen (Harold)
1909-................**CLC 1, 2, 5, 10**
See also CA 9-12R
See also DLB 20

Spicer, Jack 1925-1965........ **CLC 8, 18**
See also CA 85-88
See also DLB 5, 16

Spielberg, Peter 1929-..............**CLC 6**
See also CANR 4
See also CA 5-8R
See also DLB-Y 81

Spielberg, Steven 1947-...........**CLC 20**
See also CA 77-80
See also SATA 32

Spillane, Frank Morrison 1918-
See Spillane, Mickey
See also CA 25-28R

Spillane, Mickey 1918-........ **CLC 3, 13**
See also Spillane, Frank Morrison

Spitteler, Carl (Friedrich Georg)
1845-1924.................. **TCLC 12**
See also CA 109

Spivack, Kathleen (Romola Drucker)
1938-........................**CLC 6**
See also CA 49-52

Springsteen, Bruce 1949-..........**CLC 17**
See also CA 111

Spurling, Hilary 1940- ....**CLC 34**
See also CA 104

Staël-Holstein, Anne Louise Germaine
Necker, Baronne de
1766-1817.................. **NCLC 3**

Stafford, Jean 1915-1979..... **CLC 4, 7, 19**
See also CANR 3
See also CA 1-4R
See also obituary CA 85-88
See also obituary SATA 22
See also DLB 2

Stafford, William (Edgar)
1914-.................... **CLC 4, 7, 29**
See also CAAS 3
See also CANR 5
See also CA 5-8R
See also DLB 5

Stanton, Maura 1946-..............**CLC 9**
See also CANR 15
See also CA 89-92

Stark, Richard 1933-
See Westlake, Donald E(dwin)

Stead, Christina (Ellen)
1902-1983.............**CLC 2, 5, 8, 32**
See also CA 13-16R
See also obituary CA 109

Steffens, (Joseph) Lincoln
1866-1936.................. **TCLC 20**
See also CA 117
See also SAAS 1

Stegner, Wallace (Earle) 1909- ......**CLC 9**
See also CANR 1
See also CA 1-4R
See also DLB 9
See also AITN 1

Stein, Gertrude 1874-1946...... **TCLC 1, 6**
See also CA 104
See also DLB 4

Steinbeck, John (Ernst)
1902-1968...... **CLC 1, 5, 9, 13, 21, 34**
See also CANR 1
See also CA 1-4R
See also obituary CA 25-28R
See also SATA 9
See also DLB 7, 9
See also DLB-DS 2

Steiner, George 1929- . . . . .CLC 24
See also CA 73-76

Steiner, Rudolf(us Josephus Laurentius)
1861-1925 . . . . TCLC 13
See also CA 107

Stephens, James 1882?-1950 . . . . . . TCLC 4
See also CA 104
See also DLB 19

Steptoe, Lydia 1892-1982
See Barnes, Djuna

Sterling, George 1869-1926 . . . . . . TCLC 20
See also CA 117

Stern, Richard G(ustave) 1928- . . . . . .CLC 4
See also CANR 1
See also CA 1-4R

Sternberg, Jonas 1894-1969
See Sternberg, Josef von

Sternberg, Josef von
1894-1969 . . . . .CLC 20
See also CA 81-84

Sterne, Laurence 1713-1768 . . . . LC 2
See also DLB 39

Sternheim, (William Adolf) Carl
1878-1942 . . . . TCLC 8
See also CA 105

Stevens, Mark 19??- . . . . .CLC 34

Stevens, Wallace
1879-1955 . . . . TCLC 3, 12
See also CA 104

Stevenson, Anne (Katharine)
1933- . . . . CLC 7, 33
See also Elvin, Anne Katharine Stevenson
See also CANR 9
See also DLB 40

Stevenson, Robert Louis
1850-1894 . . . . NCLC 5
See also CLR 10
See also YABC 2
See also DLB 18

Stewart, J(ohn) I(nnes) M(ackintosh)
1906- . . . . CLC 7, 14, 32
See also CAAS 3
See also CA 85-88

Stewart, Mary (Florence Elinor)
1916- . . . . CLC 7, 35
See also CANR 1
See also CA 1-4R
See also SATA 12

Stewart, Will 1908-
See Williamson, Jack

Sting 1951-
See The Police

Stitt, Milan 1941- . . . . .CLC 29
See also CA 69-72

Stoker, Bram (Abraham)
1847-1912 . . . . TCLC 8
See also CA 105
See also SATA 29
See also DLB 36

Stolz, Mary (Slattery) 1920- . . . . .CLC 12
See also CANR 13
See also CA 5-8R
See also SATA 10
See also AITN 1

Stone, Irving 1903- . . . . .CLC 7
See also CAAS 3
See also CANR 1
See also CA 1-4R
See also SATA 3
See also AITN 1

Stone, Robert (Anthony)
1937?- . . . . CLC 5, 23
See also CA 85-88

Stoppard, Tom
1937- . . . . . CLC 1, 3, 4, 5, 8, 15, 29, 34
See also CA 81-84
See also DLB 13

Storey, David (Malcolm)
1933- . . . . .CLC 2, 4, 5, 8
See also CA 81-84
See also DLB 13, 14

Storm, Hyemeyohsts 1935- . . . . .CLC 3
See also CA 81-84

Storm, (Hans) Theodor (Woldsen)
1817-1888 . . . . NCLC 1

Storni, Alfonsina 1892-1938 . . . . . . TCLC 5
See also CA 104

Stout, Rex (Todhunter)
1886-1975 . . . . .CLC 3
See also CA 61-64
See also AITN 2

Stow, (Julian) Randolph 1935- . . . . .CLC 23
See also CA 13-16R

Stowe, Harriet (Elizabeth) Beecher
1811-1896 . . . . NCLC 3
See also YABC 1
See also DLB 1, 12, 42

Strachey, (Giles) Lytton
1880-1932 . . . . TCLC 12
See also CA 110

Strand, Mark 1934- . . . . CLC 6, 18
See also CA 21-24R
See also DLB 5
See also SATA 41

Straub, Peter (Francis) 1943- . . . . . .CLC 28
See also CA 85-88
See also DLB-Y 84

Strauss, Botho 1944- . . . . .CLC 22

Straussler, Tomas 1937-
See Stoppard, Tom

Streatfeild, Noel 1897- . . . . .CLC 21
See also CA 81-84
See also SATA 20

Stribling, T(homas) S(igismund)
1881-1965 . . . . .CLC 23
See also obituary CA 107
See also DLB 9

Strindberg, (Johan) August
1849-1912 . . . . TCLC 1, 8
See also CA 104

Strugatskii, Arkadii (Natanovich) 1925-
See Strugatskii, Arkadii (Natanovich) and
Strugatskii, Boris (Natanovich)
See also CA 106

Strugatskii, Arkadii (Natanovich) 1925-
and **Strugatskii, Boris
(Natanovich)** 1933- . . . . .CLC 27

Strugatskii, Boris (Natanovich) 1933-
See Strugatskii, Arkadii (Natanovich) and
Strugatskii, Boris (Natanovich)
See also CA 106

Strugatskii, Boris (Natanovich) 1933- and
Strugatskii, Arkadii (Natanovich) 1925-
See Strugatskii, Arkadii (Natanovich) and
Strugatskii, Boris (Natanovich)

Strummer, Joe 1953?-
See The Clash

Stuart, (Hilton) Jesse
1906-1984 . . . . CLC 1, 8, 11, 14, 34
See also CA 5-8R
See also obituary CA 112
See also SATA 2
See also obituary SATA 36
See also DLB 9
See also DLB-Y 84

Sturgeon, Theodore (Hamilton)
1918-1985 .CLC 22
See also CA 81-84
See also obituary CA 116
See also DLB 8

Styron, William
1925- . . . . CLC 1, 3, 5, 11, 15
See also CANR 6
See also CA 5-8R
See also DLB 2
See also DLB-Y 80

Sudermann, Hermann
1857-1928 . . . . TCLC 15
See also CA 107

Sue, Eugène 1804-1857 . . . . NCLC 1

Sukenick, Ronald 1932- . . . . CLC 3, 4, 6
See also CA 25-28R
See also DLB-Y 81

Suknaski, Andrew 1942- . . . . .CLC 19
See also CA 101

Summers, Andrew James 1942-
See The Police

Summers, Andy 1942-
See The Police

Summers, Hollis (Spurgeon, Jr.)
1916- . . . . .CLC 10
See also CANR 3
See also CA 5-8R
See also DLB 6

**Summers, (Alphonsus Joseph-Mary Augustus)
Montague** 1880-1948 . . . . TCLC 16

Sumner, Gordon Matthew 1951-
See The Police

Susann, Jacqueline 1921-1974 . . . . . . .CLC 3
See also CA 65-68
See also obituary CA 53-56
See also AITN 1

Sutcliff, Rosemary 1920- . . . . .CLC 26
See also CLR 1
See also CA 5-8R
See also SATA 6

Sutro, Alfred 1863-1933 . . . . TCLC 6
See also CA 105
See also DLB 10

Sutton, Henry 1935-
See Slavitt, David (R.)

Svevo, Italo 1861-1928 . . . . TCLC 2
See also Schmitz, Ettore

Swados, Elizabeth 1951- . . . . .CLC 12
See also CA 97-100

Author Index

Swados, Harvey 1920-1972 ....CLC 5
See also CANR 6
See also CA 5-8R
See also obituary CA 37-40R
See also DLB 2

Swarthout, Glendon (Fred)
1918- ....CLC 35
See also CANR 1
See also CA 1-4R
See also SATA 26

Swenson, May 1919- ....CLC 4, 14
See also CA 5-8R
See also SATA 15
See also DLB 5

Swift, Jonathan 1667-1745..........LC 1
See also SATA 19
See also DLB 39

Swinburne, Algernon Charles
1837-1909..................TCLC 8
See also CA 105
See also DLB 35

Swinfen, Ann 19??- ....CLC 34

Swinnerton, Frank (Arthur)
1884-1982....................CLC 31
See also obituary CA 108
See also DLB 34

Symons, Arthur (William)
1865-1945.................TCLC 11
See also CA 107
See also DLB 19

Symons, Julian (Gustave)
1912-.................CLC 2, 14, 32
See also CAAS 3
See also CANR 3
See also CA 49-52

Synge, (Edmund) John Millington
1871-1909..................TCLC 6
See also CA 104
See also DLB 10, 19

Syruc, J. 1911-
See Miłosz, Czesław

Tabori, George 1914- ....CLC 19
See also CANR 4
See also CA 49-52

Tagore, (Sir) Rabindranath
1861-1941...................TCLC 3
See also Thakura, Ravindranatha

Talese, Gaetano 1932-
See Talese, Gay

Talese, Gay 1932- ....CLC 37
See also CANR 9
See also CA 1-4R
See also AITN 1

Tamayo y Baus, Manuel
1829-1898..................NCLC 1

Tanizaki, Jun'ichirō
1886-1965.............CLC 8, 14, 28
See also CA 93-96
See also obituary CA 25-28R

Tarkington, (Newton) Booth
1869-1946..................TCLC 9
See also CA 110
See also SATA 17
See also DLB 9

Tate, (John Orley) Allen
1899-1979...... CLC 2, 4, 6, 9, 11, 14,
                                       24
See also CA 5-8R
See also obituary CA 85-88
See also DLB 4, 45

Tate, James 1943-...........CLC 2, 6, 25
See also CA 21-24R
See also DLB 5

Tavel, Ronald 1940- ....CLC 6
See also CA 21-24R

Taylor, C(ecil) P(hillip)
1929-1981...................CLC 27
See also CA 25-28R
See also obituary CA 105

Taylor, Eleanor Ross 1920- ....CLC 5
See also CA 81-84

Taylor, Elizabeth
1912-1975................CLC 2, 4, 29
See also CANR 9
See also CA 13-16R
See also SATA 13

Taylor, Kamala (Purnaiya) 1924-
See Markandaya, Kamala (Purnaiya)
See also CA 77-80

Taylor, Mildred D(elois) 19??-......CLC 21
See also CA 85-88
See also SATA 15

Taylor, Peter (Hillsman)
1917-...............CLC 1, 4, 18, 37
See also CANR 9
See also CA 13-16R
See also DLB-Y 81

Taylor, Robert Lewis 1912-........CLC 14
See also CANR 3
See also CA 1-4R
See also SATA 10

Teasdale, Sara 1884-1933........ TCLC 4
See also CA 104
See also DLB 45
See also SATA 32

Tegnér, Esaias 1782-1846........NCLC 2

Teilhard de Chardin, (Marie Joseph) Pierre
1881-1955..................TCLC 9
See also CA 105

Tennant, Emma 1937- ....CLC 13
See also CANR 10
See also CA 65-68
See also DLB 14

Teran, Lisa St. Aubin de 19??-.....CLC 36

Terry, Megan 1932- ....CLC 19
See also CA 77-80
See also DLB 7

Tertz, Abram 1925-
See Sinyavsky, Andrei (Donatevich)

Teternikov, Fyodor Kuzmich 1863-1927
See Sologub, Fyodor
See also CA 104

Tey, Josephine 1897-1952 .... TCLC 14
See also Mackintosh, Elizabeth

Thackeray, William Makepeace
1811-1863.................. NCLC 5
See also SATA 23
See also DLB 21

Thakura, Ravindranatha 1861-1941
See Tagore, (Sir) Rabindranath
See also CA 104

Thelwell, Michael (Miles)
1939-........................CLC 22
See also CA 101

Theroux, Alexander (Louis)
1939-.....................CLC 2, 25
See also CA 85-88

Theroux, Paul
1941-........ CLC 5, 8, 11, 15, 28
See also CA 33-36R
See also DLB 2

Thibault, Jacques Anatole Francois
1844-1924
See France, Anatole
See also CA 106

Thiele, Colin (Milton) 1920-........CLC 17
See also CANR 12
See also CA 29-32R
See also SATA 14

Thomas, Audrey (Grace)
1935-...................CLC 7, 13, 37
See also CA 21-24R
See also AITN 2

Thomas, D(onald) M(ichael)
1935-.................CLC 13, 22, 31
See also CANR 17
See also CA 61-64
See also DLB 40

Thomas, Dylan (Marlais)
1914-1953.................TCLC 1, 8
See also CA 104
See also DLB 13, 20

Thomas, Edward (Philip)
1878-1917................ TCLC 10
See also CA 106
See also DLB 19

Thomas, John Peter 1928-
See Thomas, Piri

Thomas, Joyce Carol 1938-....CLC 35
See also CA 113, 116
See also SATA 40
See also DLB 33

Thomas, Lewis 1913- ....CLC 35
See also CA 85-88

Thomas, Piri 1928- ....CLC 17
See also CA 73-76

Thomas, R(onald) S(tuart)
1913-.....................CLC 6, 13
See also CA 89-92
See also DLB 27

Thompson, Francis (Joseph)
1859-1907................. TCLC 4
See also CA 104
See also DLB 19

Thompson, Hunter S(tockton)
1939-.....................CLC 9, 17
See also CA 17-20R

Thoreau, Henry David
1817-1862...................NCLC 7
See also DLB 1

Thurber, James (Grover)
1894-1961..............CLC 5, 11, 25
See also CANR 17
See also CA 73-76
See also SATA 13
See also DLB 4, 11, 22

Thurman, Wallace 1902-1934..... TCLC 6
See also CA 104

Tieck, (Johann) Ludwig
  1773-1853 . . . . NCLC 5

Tillinghast, Richard 1940- . . . . CLC 29
  See also CA 29-32R

Tindall, Gillian 1938- . . . . CLC 7
  See also CANR 11
  See also CA 21-24R

Tocqueville, Alexis de
  1805-1859 . . . . NCLC 7

Tolkien, J(ohn) R(onald) R(euel)
  1892-1973 . . . . CLC 1, 2, 3, 8, 12
  See also CAP 2
  See also CA 17-18
  See also obituary CA 45-48
  See also SATA 2, 32
  See also obituary SATA 24
  See also DLB 15
  See also AITN 1

Toller, Ernst 1893-1939 . . . . TCLC 10
  See also CA 107

Tolson, Melvin B(eaunorus)
  1900?-1966 . . . . CLC 36
  See also Obituary CA 89-92

Tolstoy, (Count) Alexey Nikolayevich
  1883-1945 . . . . TCLC 18
  See also CA 107

Tolstoy, (Count) Leo (Lev Nikolaevich)
  1828-1910 . . . . TCLC 4, 11, 17
  See also CA 104
  See also SATA 26

Tomlin, Lily 1939- . . . . CLC 17

Tomlin, Mary Jean 1939-
  See Tomlin, Lily

Tomlinson, (Alfred) Charles
  1927- . . . . CLC 2, 4, 6, 13
  See also CA 5-8R
  See also DLB 40

Toole, John Kennedy
  1937-1969 . . . . CLC 19
  See also CA 104
  See also DLB-Y 81

Toomer, Jean
  1894-1967 . . . . CLC 1, 4, 13, 22
  See also CA 85-88
  See also DLB 45

Torrey, E. Fuller 19??- . . . . CLC 34

Tournier, Michel 1924- . . . . . . CLC 6, 23, 36
  See also CANR 3
  See also CA 49-52
  See also SATA 23

Townshend, Peter (Dennis Blandford)
  1945- . . . . CLC 17
  See also CA 107

Trakl, Georg 1887-1914 . . . . TCLC 5
  See also CA 104

Traven, B. 1890-1969 . . . . CLC 8, 11
  See also CAP 2
  See also CA 19-20
  See also obituary CA 25-28R
  See also DLB 9

Tremblay, Michel 1942- . . . . CLC 29

Trevanian 1925- . . . . CLC 29
  See also Whitaker, Rodney
  See also CA 108

Trevor, William
  1928- . . . . CLC 7, 9, 14, 25
  See also Cox, William Trevor
  See also DLB 14

Trilling, Lionel
  1905-1975 . . . . CLC 9, 11, 24
  See also CANR 10
  See also CA 9-12R
  See also obituary CA 61-64
  See also DLB 28

Trogdon, William 1939-
  See Heat Moon, William Least
  See also CA 115

Trollope, Anthony 1815-1882 . . . . . NCLC 6
  See also SATA 22
  See also DLB 21

Troyat, Henri 1911- . . . . CLC 23
  See also CANR 2
  See also CA 45-48

Trudeau, G(arretson) B(eekman) 1948-
  See Trudeau, Garry
  See also CA 81-84
  See also SATA 35

Trudeau, Garry 1948- . . . . CLC 12
  See also Trudeau, G(arretson) B(eekman)
  See also AITN 2

Truffaut, François 1932-1984 . . . . . . CLC 20
  See also CA 81-84
  See also obituary CA 113

Trumbo, Dalton 1905-1976 . . . . CLC 19
  See also CANR 10
  See also CA 21-24R
  See also obituary CA 69-72
  See also DLB 26

Tryon, Thomas 1926- . . . . CLC 3, 11
  See also CA 29-32R
  See also AITN 1

Ts'ao Hsüeh-ch'in 1715?-1763 . . . . LC 1

Tsushima Shūji 1909-1948
  See Dazai Osamu
  See also CA 107

Tsvetaeva (Efron), Marina (Ivanovna)
  1892-1941 . . . . TCLC 7
  See also CA 104

Tunis, John R(oberts)
  1889-1975 . . . . CLC 12
  See also CA 61-64
  See also SATA 30, 37
  See also DLB 22

Tuohy, Frank 1925- . . . . CLC 37
  See also DLB 14

Tuohy, John Francis 1925-
  See Tuohy, Frank
  See also CANR 3
  See also CA 5-8R

Turco, Lewis (Putnam) 1934- . . . . . . CLC 11
  See also CA 13-16R
  See also DLB-Y 84

Tutuola, Amos 1920- . . . . CLC 5, 14, 29
  See also CA 9-12R

Twain, Mark
  1835-1910 . . . . TCLC 6, 12, 19
  See also Clemens, Samuel Langhorne
  See also DLB 11

Tyler, Anne 1941- . . . . CLC 7, 11, 18, 28
  See also CANR 11
  See also CA 9-12R
  See also SATA 7
  See also DLB 6
  See also DLB-Y 82

Tyler, Royall 1757-1826 . . . . NCLC 3
  See also DLB 37

Tynan (Hinkson), Katharine
  1861-1931 . . . . TCLC 3
  See also CA 104

Unamuno (y Jugo), Miguel de
  1864-1936 . . . . TCLC 2, 9
  See also CA 104

Underwood, Miles 1909-1981
  See Glassco, John

Undset, Sigrid 1882-1949 . . . . TCLC 3
  See also CA 104

Ungaretti, Giuseppe
  1888-1970 . . . . CLC 7, 11, 15
  See also CAP 2
  See also CA 19-20
  See also obituary CA 25-28R

Unger, Douglas 1952- . . . . CLC 34

Unger, Eva 1932-
  See Figes, Eva

Updike, John (Hoyer)
  1932- . . . . . . CLC 1, 2, 3, 5, 7, 9, 13, 15,
                                    23, 34
  See also CANR 4
  See also CA 1-4R
  See also DLB 2, 5
  See also DLB-Y 80, 82
  See also DLB-DS 3

Uris, Leon (Marcus) 1924- . . . . . . CLC 7, 32
  See also CANR 1
  See also CA 1-4R
  See also AITN 1, 2

Ustinov, Peter (Alexander)
  1921- . . . . CLC 1
  See also CA 13-16R
  See also DLB 13
  See also AITN 1

Vaculík, Ludvík 1926- . . . . CLC 7
  See also CA 53-56

Valenzuela, Luisa 1938- . . . . CLC 31
  See also CA 101

Valera (y Acalá-Galiano), Juan
  1824-1905 . . . . TCLC 10
  See also CA 106

Valéry, Paul (Ambroise Toussaint Jules)
  1871-1945 . . . . TCLC 4, 15
  See also CA 104

Valle-Inclán (y Montenegro), Ramón (María)
  del 1866-1936 . . . . TCLC 5
  See also CA 106

Vallejo, César (Abraham)
  1892-1938 . . . . TCLC 3
  See also CA 105

Van Ash, Cay 1918- . . . . CLC 34

Vance, Jack 1916?- . . . . CLC 35
  See also DLB 8

Vance, John Holbrook 1916?-
  See Vance, Jack
  See also CANR 17
  See also CA 29-32R

Van Den Bogarde, Derek (Jules Gaspard Ulric) Niven 1921-
See Bogarde, Dirk
See also CA 77-80

Van der Post, Laurens (Jan)
1906-....................CLC 5
See also CA 5-8R

Van Doren, Carl (Clinton)
1885-1950.................. TCLC 18
See also CA 111

Van Doren, Mark
1894-1972................. CLC 6, 10
See also CANR 3
See also CA 1-4R
See also obituary CA 37-40R
See also DLB 45

Van Druten, John (William)
1901-1957.................. TCLC 2
See also CA 104
See also DLB 10

Van Duyn, Mona 1921- .... CLC 3, 7
See also CANR 7
See also CA 9-12R
See also DLB 5

Van Itallie, Jean-Claude 1936- ......CLC 3
See also CAAS 2
See also CANR 1
See also CA 45-48
See also DLB 7

Van Peebles, Melvin 1932-...... CLC 2, 20
See also CA 85-88

Van Vechten, Carl 1880-1964......CLC 33
See also obituary CA 89-92
See also DLB 4, 9

Van Vogt, A(lfred) E(lton)
1912-......................CLC 1
See also CA 21-24R
See also SATA 14
See also DLB 8

Varda, Agnès 1928-..............CLC 16
See also CA 116

Vargas Llosa, (Jorge) Mario (Pedro)
1936-.......... CLC 3, 6, 9, 10, 15, 31
See also CA 73-76

Vassilikos, Vassilis 1933- .... CLC 4, 8
See also CA 81-84

Verga, Giovanni 1840-1922....... TCLC 3
See also CA 104

Verhaeren, Émile (Adolphe Gustave)
1855-1916.................. TCLC 12
See also CA 109

Verlaine, Paul (Marie)
1844-1896.................. NCLC 2

Verne, Jules (Gabriel)
1828-1905.................. TCLC 6
See also CA 110
See also SATA 21

Very, Jones 1813-1880.......... NCLC 9
See also DLB 1

Vian, Boris 1920-1959 .... TCLC 9
See also CA 106

Viaud, (Louis Marie) Julien 1850-1923
See Loti, Pierre
See also CA 107

Vicker, Angus 1916-
See Felsen, Henry Gregor

Vidal, Eugene Luther, Jr. 1925-
See Vidal, Gore

Vidal, Gore
1925-........CLC 2, 4, 6, 8, 10, 22, 33
See also CANR 13
See also CA 5-8R
See also DLB 6
See also AITN 1

Viereck, Peter (Robert Edwin)
1916-......................CLC 4
See also CANR 1
See also CA 1-4R
See also DLB 5

Vigny, Alfred (Victor) de
1797-1863.................. NCLC 7

Villiers de l'Isle Adam, Jean Marie Mathias Philippe Auguste, Comte de,
1838-1889.................. NCLC 3

Vinge, Joan (Carol) D(ennison)
1948-......................CLC 30
See also CA 93-96
See also SATA 36

Visconti, Luchino 1906-1976.......CLC 16
See also CA 81-84
See also obituary CA 65-68

Vittorini, Elio 1908-1966 ..... CLC 6, 9, 14
See also obituary CA 25-28R

Vliet, R(ussell) G. 1929-...........CLC 22
See also CA 37-40R

Voigt, Cynthia 1942-..............CLC 30
See also CA 106
See also SATA 33

Voinovich, Vladimir (Nikolaevich)
1932-......................CLC 10
See also CA 81-84

Von Daeniken, Erich 1935-
See Von Däniken, Erich
See also CANR 17
See also CA 37-40R
See also AITN 1

Von Däniken, Erich 1935-.........CLC 30
See also Von Daeniken, Erich

Vonnegut, Kurt, Jr.
1922-.... CLC 1, 2, 3, 4, 5, 8, 12, 22
See also CANR 1
See also CA 1-4R
See also DLB 2, 8
See also DLB-Y 80
See also DLB-DS 3
See also AITN 1

Vorster, Gordon 1924-............CLC 34

Voznesensky, Andrei 1933- ..... CLC 1, 15
See also CA 89-92

Waddington, Miriam 1917-........CLC 28
See also CANR 12
See also CA 21-24R

Wagman, Fredrica 1937-..........CLC 7
See also CA 97-100

Wagner, Richard 1813-1883 ...... NCLC 9

Wagoner, David (Russell)
1926-..................CLC 3, 5, 15
See also CAAS 3
See also CANR 2
See also CA 1-4R
See also SATA 14
See also DLB 5

Wahlöö, Per 1926-1975 ....CLC 7
See also CA 61-64

Wahlöö, Peter 1926-1975
See Wahlöö, Per

Wain, John (Barrington)
1925-.................. CLC 2, 11, 15
See also CA 5-8R
See also DLB 15, 27

Wajda, Andrzej 1926-.............CLC 16
See also CA 102

Wakefield, Dan 1932-.............CLC 7
See also CA 21-24R

Wakoski, Diane
1937-............ CLC 2, 4, 7, 9, 11
See also CAAS 1
See also CANR 9
See also CA 13-16R
See also DLB 5

Walcott, Derek (Alton)
1930-............. CLC 2, 4, 9, 14, 25
See also CA 89-92
See also DLB-Y 81

Waldman, Anne 1945- ....CLC 7
See also CA 37-40R
See also DLB 16

Waldo, Edward Hamilton 1918-
See Sturgeon, Theodore (Hamilton)

Walker, Alice
1944-............. CLC 5, 6, 9, 19, 27
See also CANR 9
See also CA 37-40R
See also SATA 31
See also DLB 6, 33

Walker, David Harry 1911-........CLC 14
See also CANR 1
See also CA 1-4R
See also SATA 8

Walker, Edward Joseph 1934-
See Walker, Ted
See also CA 21-24R

Walker, Joseph A. 1935-..........CLC 19
See also CA 89-92
See also DLB 38

Walker, Margaret (Abigail)
1915-...................... CLC 1, 6
See also CA 73-76

Walker, Ted 1934-................CLC 13
See also Walker, Edward Joseph
See also DLB 40

Wallace, Irving 1916- .... CLC 7, 13
See also CAAS 1
See also CANR 1
See also CA 1-4R
See also AITN 1

Wallant, Edward Lewis
1926-1962................. CLC 5, 10
See also CA 1-4R
See also DLB 2, 28

Walpole, Horace 1717-1797.........LC 2
See also DLB 39

Walpole, (Sir) Hugh (Seymour)
1884-1941.................. TCLC 5
See also CA 104
See also DLB 34

Walser, Martin 1927-.............CLC 27
See also CANR 8
See also CA 57-60

Walser, Robert 1878-1956 . . . . **TCLC 18**

Walsh, Gillian Paton 1939-
See Walsh, Jill Paton
See also CA 37-40R
See also SATA 4

Walsh, Jill Paton 1939- . . . .**CLC 35**
See also CLR 2

Wambaugh, Joseph (Aloysius, Jr.)
1937- . . . . **CLC 3, 18**
See also CA 33-36R
See also DLB 6
See also DLB-Y 83
See also AITN 1

Ward, Douglas Turner 1930- . . . .**CLC 19**
See also CA 81-84
See also DLB 7, 38

Warhol, Andy 1928- . . . .**CLC 20**
See also CA 89-92

Warner, Francis (Robert le Plastrier)
1937- . . . .**CLC 14**
See also CANR 11
See also CA 53-56

Warner, Sylvia Townsend
1893-1978 . . . . **CLC 7, 19**
See also CANR 16
See also CA 61-64
See also obituary CA 77-80
See also DLB 34

Warren, Robert Penn
1905- . . . .**CLC 1, 4, 6, 8, 10, 13, 18**
See also CANR 10
See also CA 13-16R
See also DLB 2
See also DLB-Y 80
See also AITN 1

Washington, Booker T(aliaferro)
1856-1915 . . . . **TCLC 10, CLC 34**
See also CA 114
See also SATA 28

Wassermann, Jakob
1873-1934 . . . . **TCLC 6**
See also CA 104

Wasserstein, Wendy 1950- . . . .**CLC 32**

Waters, Roger 1944-
See Pink Floyd

Wa Thiong'o, Ngugi
1938- . . . .**CLC 3, 7, 13, 36**
See also Ngugi, James (Thiong'o)
See also Ngugi wa Thiong'o

Waugh, Auberon (Alexander)
1939- . . . .**CLC 7**
See also CANR 6
See also CA 45-48
See also DLB 14

Waugh, Evelyn (Arthur St. John)
1903-1966 . . . . . . **CLC 1, 3, 8, 13, 19, 27**
See also CA 85-88
See also obituary CA 25-28R
See also DLB 15

Waugh, Harriet 1944- . . . .**CLC 6**
See also CA 85-88

Webb, Charles (Richard) 1939- . . . . .**CLC 7**
See also CA 25-28R

Webb, James H(enry), Jr.
1946- . . . .**CLC 22**
See also CA 81-84

Webb, Phyllis 1927- . . . .**CLC 18**
See also CA 104

Webber, Andrew Lloyd 1948-
See Rice, Tim and Webber, Andrew Lloyd

Weber, Lenora Mattingly
1895-1971 . . . .**CLC 12**
See also CAP 1
See also CA 19-20
See also obituary CA 29-32R
See also SATA 2
See also obituary SATA 26

Wedekind, (Benjamin) Frank(lin)
1864-1918 . . . . **TCLC 7**
See also CA 104

Weidman, Jerome 1913- . . . .**CLC 7**
See also CANR 1
See also CA 1-4R
See also DLB 28
See also AITN 2

Weinstein, Nathan Wallenstein 1903?-1940
See West, Nathanael
See also CA 104

Weir, Peter 1944- . . . .**CLC 20**
See also CA 113

Weiss, Peter (Ulrich)
1916-1982 . . . . **CLC 3, 15**
See also CANR 3
See also CA 45-48
See also obituary CA 106

Weiss, Theodore (Russell)
1916- . . . . **CLC 3, 8, 14**
See also CAAS 2
See also CA 9-12R
See also DLB 5

Welch, James 1940- . . . . **CLC 6, 14**
See also CA 85-88

Weldon, Fay
1933- . . . . **CLC 6, 9, 11, 19, 36**
See also CANR 16
See also CA 21-24R
See also DLB 14

Wellek, René 1903- . . . .**CLC 28**
See also CANR 8
See also CA 5-8R

Weller, Michael 1942- . . . .**CLC 10**
See also CA 85-88

Weller, Paul 1958- . . . .**CLC 26**

Welles, (George) Orson
1915-1985 . . . .**CLC 20**
See also CA 93-96

Wells, H(erbert) G(eorge)
1866-1946 . . . .**TCLC 6, 12, 19**
See also CA 110
See also SATA 20
See also DLB 34

Wells, Rosemary . . . .**CLC 12**
See also CA 85-88
See also SAAS 1
See also SATA 18

Welty, Eudora (Alice)
1909- . . . . **CLC 1, 2, 5, 14, 22, 33**
See also CA 9-12R
See also DLB 2

Werfel, Franz (V.) 1890-1945 . . . . . **TCLC 8**
See also CA 104

Wergeland, Henrik Arnold
1808-1845 . . . . **NCLC 5**

Wersba, Barbara 1932- . . . .**CLC 30**
See also CLR 3
See also CA 29-32R
See also SATA 1

Wertmüller, Lina 1928- . . . .**CLC 16**
See also CA 97-100

Wescott, Glenway 1901- . . . .**CLC 13**
See also CA 13-16R
See also DLB 4, 9

Wesker, Arnold 1932- . . . .**CLC 3, 5**
See also CANR 1
See also CA 1-4R
See also DLB 13

Wesley, Richard (Errol) 1945- . . . .**CLC 7**
See also CA 57-60
See also DLB 38

West, Jessamyn 1907-1984 . . . . . . **CLC 7, 17**
See also CA 9-12R
See also obituary SATA 37
See also DLB 6
See also DLB-Y 84

West, Morris L(anglo)
1916- . . . . **CLC 6, 33**
See also CA 5-8R

West, Nathanael
1903?-1940 . . . .**TCLC 1, 14**
See Weinstein, Nathan Wallenstein
See also DLB 4, 9, 28

West, Paul 1930- . . . . **CLC 7, 14**
See also CA 13-16R
See also DLB 14

West, Rebecca 1892-1983 . . . . . **CLC 7, 9, 31**
See also CA 5-8R
See also obituary CA 109
See also DLB 36
See also DLB-Y 83

Westall, Robert (Atkinson)
1929- . . . .**CLC 17**
See also CA 69-72
See also SATA 23

Westlake, Donald E(dwin)
1933- . . . . **CLC 7, 33**
See also CANR 16
See also CA 17-20R

Whalen, Philip 1923- . . . . **CLC 6, 29**
See also CANR 5
See also CA 9-12R
See also DLB 16

Wharton, Edith (Newbold Jones)
1862-1937 . . . .**TCLC 3, 9**
See also CA 104
See also DLB 4, 9, 12

Wharton, William 1925- . . . . **CLC 18, 37**
See also CA 93-96
See also DLB-Y 80

Wheatley (Peters), Phillis
1753?-1784 . . . .**LC 3**
See also DLB 31

Wheelock, John Hall
1886-1978 . . . .**CLC 14**
See also CANR 14
See also CA 13-16R
See also obituary CA 77-80
See also DLB 45

Whelan, John 1900-
See O'Faoláin, Seán

Author Index

Whitaker, Rodney 1925-
See Trevanian
See also CA 29-32R

White, E(lwyn) B(rooks)
1899-1985 . . . . CLC 10, 34
See also CLR 1
See also CANR 16
See also CA 13-16R
See also obituary CA 116
See also SATA 2, 29
See also DLB 11, 22
See also AITN 2

White, Edmund III 1940- . . . . CLC 27
See also CANR 3
See also CA 45-48

White, Patrick (Victor Martindale)
1912- . . . . CLC 3, 4, 5, 7, 9, 18
See also CA 81-84

White, T(erence) H(anbury)
1906-1964 . . . . CLC 30
See also CA 73-76
See also SATA 12

White, Walter (Francis)
1893-1955 . . . . TCLC 15
See also CA 115

Whitehead, E(dward) A(nthony)
1933- . . . . CLC 5
See also CA 65-68

Whitman, Walt 1819-1892 . . . . NCLC 4
See also SATA 20
See also DLB 3

Whitemore, Hugh 1936- . . . . .CLC 37

Whittemore, (Edward) Reed (Jr.)
1919- . . . . CLC 4
See also CANR 4
See also CA 9-12R
See also DLB 5

Whittier, John Greenleaf
1807-1892 . . . . NCLC 8
See also DLB 1

Wicker, Thomas Grey 1926-
See Wicker, Tom
See also CA 65-68

Wicker, Tom 1926- . . . . .CLC 7
See also Wicker, Thomas Grey

Wideman, John Edgar
1941- . . . . CLC 5, 34, 36
See also CANR 14
See also CA 85-88
See also DLB 33

Wiebe, Rudy (H.) 1934- . . . . . CLC 6, 11, 14
See also CA 37-40R

Wieners, John 1934- . . . . .CLC 7
See also CA 13-16R
See also DLB 16

Wiesel, Elie(zer)
1928- . . . . .CLC 3, 5, 11, 37
See also CANR 8
See also CA 5-8R
See also AITN 1

Wight, James Alfred 1916-
See Herriot, James
See also CA 77-80

Wilbur, Richard (Purdy)
1921- . . . . .CLC 3, 6, 9, 14
See also CANR 2
See also CA 1-4R
See also SATA 9
See also DLB 5

Wild, Peter 1940- . . . . .CLC 14
See also CA 37-40R
See also DLB 5

Wilde, Oscar (Fingal O'Flahertie Wills)
1854-1900 . . . . TCLC 1, 8
See also CA 104
See also SATA 24
See also DLB 10, 19, 34

Wilder, Billy 1906- . . . . .CLC 20
See also Wilder, Samuel
See also DLB 26

Wilder, Samuel 1906-
See Wilder, Billy
See also CA 89-92

Wilder, Thornton (Niven)
1897-1975 . . . . . . CLC 1, 5, 6, 10, 15, 35
See also CA 13-16R
See also obituary CA 61-64
See also DLB 4, 7, 9
See also AITN 2

Wilhelm, Kate 1928- . . . . .CLC 7
See also CANR 17
See also CA 37-40R
See also DLB 8

Willard, Nancy 1936- . . . . CLC 7, 37
See also CLR 5
See also CANR 10
See also CA 89-92
See also SATA 30, 37
See also DLB 5

Williams, C(harles) K(enneth)
1936- . . . . .CLC 33
See also CA 37-40R
See also DLB 5

Williams, Charles (Walter Stansby)
1886-1945 . . . . TCLC 1, 11
See also CA 104

Williams, (George) Emlyn
1905- . . . . .CLC 15
See also CA 104
See also DLB 10

Williams, John A(lfred)
1925- . . . . CLC 5, 13
See also CAAS 3
See also CANR 6
See also CA 53-56
See also DLB 2, 33

Williams, Jonathan (Chamberlain)
1929- . . . . .CLC 13
See also CANR 8
See also CA 9-12R
See also DLB 5

Williams, Joy 1944- . . . . .CLC 31
See also CA 41-44R

Williams, Paulette 1948-
See Shange, Ntozake

Williams, Tennessee
1911-1983 . . . . . . CLC 1, 2, 5, 7, 8, 11,
15, 19, 30
See also CA 5-8R
See also obituary CA 108
See also DLB 7
See also DLB-Y 83
See also DLB-DS 4
See also AITN 1, 2

Williams, Thomas (Alonzo)
1926- . . . . .CLC 14
See also CANR 2
See also CA 1-4R

Williams, Thomas Lanier 1911-1983
See Williams, Tennessee

Williams, William Carlos
1883-1963 . . . . . . CLC 1, 2, 5, 9, 13, 22
See also CA 89-92
See also DLB 4, 16

Williamson, Jack 1908- . . . . .CLC 29
See also Williamson, John Stewart
See also DLB 8

Williamson, John Stewart 1908-
See Williamson, Jack
See also CA 17-20R

Willingham, Calder (Baynard, Jr.)
1922- . . . . .CLC 5
See also CANR 3
See also CA 5-8R
See also DLB 2, 44

Wilson, A(ndrew) N(orman)
1950- . . . . .CLC 33
See also CA 112
See also DLB 14

Wilson, Andrew 1948-
See Wilson, Snoo

Wilson, Angus (Frank Johnstone)
1913- . . . . CLC 2, 3, 5, 25, 34
See also CA 5-8R
See also DLB 15

Wilson, Brian 1942- . . . . .CLC 12

Wilson, Colin 1931- . . . . CLC 3, 14
See also CANR 1
See also CA 1-4R
See also DLB 14

Wilson, Edmund
1895-1972 . . . . CLC 1, 2, 3, 8, 24
See also CANR 1
See also CA 1-4R
See also obituary CA 37-40R

Wilson, Ethel Davis (Bryant)
1888-1980 . . . . .CLC 13
See also CA 102

Wilson, John 1785-1854 . . . . NCLC 5

Wilson, John (Anthony) Burgess 1917-
See Burgess, Anthony
See also CANR 2
See also CA 1-4R

Wilson, Lanford 1937- . . . . . . CLC 7, 14, 36
See also CA 17-20R
See also DLB 7

Wilson, Robert (M.) 1944- . . . . CLC 7, 9
See also CANR 2
See also CA 49-52

Wilson, Sloan 1920- . . . . .CLC 32
See also CANR 1
See also CA 1-4R

Wilson, Snoo 1948- . . . . .CLC **33**
See also CA 69-72

Winchilsea, Anne (Kingsmill) Finch, Countess
of 1661-1720 . . . . LC **3**

Winters, (Arthur) Yvor
1900-1968 . . . . CLC **4, 8, 32**
See also CAP 1
See also CA 11-12
See also obituary CA 25-28R

Wiseman, Frederick 1930- . . . . .CLC **20**

Witkiewicz, Stanislaw Ignacy
1885-1939 . . . . TCLC **8**
See also CA 105

Wittig, Monique 1935?- . . . . .CLC **22**
See also CA 116

Wittlin, Joseph 1896-1976 . . . . .CLC **25**
See also Wittlin, Józef

Wittlin, Józef 1896-1976
See Wittlin, Joseph
See also CANR 3
See also CA 49-52
See also obituary CA 65-68

Wodehouse, P(elham) G(renville)
1881-1975 . . . . CLC **1, 2, 5, 10, 22**
See also CANR 3
See also CA 45-48
See also obituary CA 57-60
See also SATA 22
See also DLB 34
See also AITN 2

Woiwode, Larry (Alfred)
1941- . . . . CLC **6, 10**
See also CANR 16
See also CA 73-76
See also DLB 6

Wojciechowska, Maia (Teresa)
1927- . . . . .CLC **26**
See also CLR 1
See also CANR 4
See also CA 9-12R
See also SAAS 1
See also SATA 1, 28

Wolf, Christa 1929- . . . . CLC **14, 29**
See also CA 85-88

Wolfe, Gene (Rodman) 1931- . . . . . .CLC **25**
See also CANR 6
See also CA 57-60
See also DLB 8

Wolfe, Thomas (Clayton)
1900-1938 . . . . TCLC **4, 13**
See also CA 104
See also DLB 9
See also DLB-DS 2

Wolfe, Thomas Kennerly, Jr. 1931-
See Wolfe, Tom
See also CANR 9
See also CA 13-16R

Wolfe, Tom 1931- . . . . . CLC **1, 2, 9, 15, 35**
See also Wolfe, Thomas Kennerly, Jr.
See also AITN 2

Wolitzer, Hilma 1930- . . . . .CLC **17**
See also CA 65-68
See also SATA 31

Wonder, Stevie 1950- . . . . .CLC **12**
See also Morris, Steveland Judkins

Wong, Jade Snow 1922- . . . . .CLC **17**
See also CA 109

Woodcott, Keith 1934-
See Brunner, John (Kilian Houston)

Woolf, (Adeline) Virginia
1882-1941 . . . . .TCLC **1, 5, 20**
See also CA 104
See also DLB 36

Woollcott, Alexander (Humphreys)
1887-1943 . . . . TCLC **5**
See also CA 105
See also DLB 29

Wordsworth, William
1770-1850 . . . . NCLC **12**

Wouk, Herman 1915- . . . . CLC **1, 9**
See also CANR 6
See also CA 5-8R
See also DLB-Y 82

Wright, Charles 1935- . . . . . . CLC **6, 13, 28**
See also CA 29-32R
See also DLB-Y 82

Wright, James (Arlington)
1927-1980 . . . . .CLC **3, 5, 10, 28**
See also CANR 4
See also CA 49-52
See also obituary CA 97-100
See also DLB 5
See also AITN 2

Wright, Judith 1915- . . . . .CLC **11**
See also CA 13-16R
See also SATA 14

Wright, Richard (Nathaniel)
1908-1960 . . . . . . CLC **1, 3, 4, 9, 14, 21**
See also CA 108
See also DLB-DS 2

Wright, Richard B(ruce) 1937- . . . . . .CLC **6**
See also CA 85-88

Wright, Rick 1945-
See Pink Floyd

Wright, Stephen 1946- . . . . .CLC **33**

Wu Ching-tzu 1701-1754 . . . . LC **2**

Wurlitzer, Rudolph
1938?- . . . . CLC **2, 4, 15**
See also CA 85-88

Wylie (Benét), Elinor (Morton Hoyt)
1885-1928 . . . . TCLC **8**
See also CA 105
See also DLB 9, 45

Wyndham, John 1903-1969 . . . . . . .CLC **19**
See also Harris, John (Wyndham Parkes
Lucas) Beynon

Wyss, Johann David
1743-1818 . . . . NCLC **10**
See also SATA 27, 29

Yanovsky, Vassily S(emenovich)
1906- . . . . CLC **2, 18**
See also CA 97-100

Yates, Richard 1926- . . . . CLC **7, 8, 23**
See also CANR 10
See also CA 5-8R
See also DLB 2
See also DLB-Y 81

Yeats, William Butler
1865-1939 . . . . .TCLC **1, 11, 18**
See also CANR 10
See also CA 104
See also DLB 10, 19

Yehoshua, Abraham B.
1936- . . . . CLC **13, 31**
See also CA 33-36R

Yep, Laurence (Michael) 1948- . . . . .CLC **35**
See also CLR 3
See also CANR 1
See also CA 49-52
See also SATA 7

Yerby, Frank G(arvin)
1916- . . . . CLC **1, 7, 22**
See also CANR 16
See also CA 9-12R

Yevtushenko, Yevgeny (Aleksandrovich)
1933- . . . . CLC **1, 3, 13, 26**
See also CA 81-84

Yglesias, Helen 1915- . . . . CLC **7, 22**
See also CANR 15
See also CA 37-40R

Yorke, Henry Vincent 1905-1974
See Green, Henry
See also CA 85-88
See also obituary CA 49-52

Young, Al 1939- . . . . .CLC **19**
See also CA 29-32R
See also DLB 33

Young, Andrew 1885-1971 . . . . .CLC **5**
See also CANR 7
See also CA 5-8R

Young, Edward 1683-1765 . . . . LC **3**

Young, Neil 1945- . . . . .CLC **17**
See also CA 110

Yourcenar, Marguerite 1913- . . . . . .CLC **19**
See also CA 69-72

Yurick, Sol 1925- . . . . .CLC **6**
See also CA 13-16R

Zamyatin, Yevgeny Ivanovich
1884-1937 . . . . TCLC **8**
See also CA 105

Zangwill, Israel 1864-1926 . . . . TCLC **16**
See also CA 109
See also DLB 10

Zappa, Francis Vincent, Jr. 1940-
See Zappa, Frank
See also CA 108

Zappa, Frank 1940- . . . . .CLC **17**
See also Zappa, Francis Vincent, Jr.

Zaturenska, Marya
1902-1982 . . . . CLC **6, 11**
See also CA 13-16R
See also obituary CA 105

Zelazny, Roger 1937- . . . . .CLC **21**
See also CA 21-24R
See also SATA 39
See also DLB 8

Zhdanov, Andrei A(lexandrovich)
1896-1948 . . . . TCLC **18**

Zimmerman, Robert 1941-
See Dylan, Bob

Zindel, Paul 1936- . . . . .CLC **6, 26**
See also CLR 3
See also CA 73-76
See also SATA 16
See also DLB 7

Zinoviev, Alexander 1922- . . . . .CLC **19**
See also CA 116

Author Index

Zola, Émile 1840-1902 . . . . **TCLC 1, 6**
  See also CA 104

Zorrilla y Moral, José
    1817-1893 . . . . **NCLC 6**

Zoshchenko, Mikhail (Mikhailovich)
    1895-1958 . . . . **TCLC 15**
  See also CA 115

Zuckmayer, Carl 1896-1977 . . . . **CLC 18**
  See also CA 69-72

Zukofsky, Louis
    1904-1978 . . . . . . **CLC 1, 2, 4, 7, 11, 18**
  See also CA 9-12R
  See also obituary CA 77-80
  See also DLB 5

Zweig, Paul 1935-1984 . . . . **CLC 34**
  See also CA 85-88
  See also obituary CA 113

Zweig, Stefan 1881-1942 . . . . **TCLC 17**
  See also CA 112

Cumulative Index to Nationalities

AMERICAN

Adams, Henry **4**
Agee, James **1, 19**
Anderson, Maxwell **2**
Anderson, Sherwood **1, 10**
Atherton, Gertrude **2**
Barry, Philip **11**
Baum, L. Frank **7**
Beard, Charles A. **15**
Belasco, David **3**
Benchley, Robert **1**
Benét, Stephen Vincent **7**
Bierce, Ambrose **1, 7**
Bourne, Randolph S. **16**
Bromfield, Louis **11**
Burroughs, Edgar Rice **2**
Cabell, James Branch **6**
Cable, George Washington **4**
Cather, Willa **1, 11**
Chandler, Raymond **1, 7**
Chapman, John Jay **7**
Chesnutt, Charles Waddell **5**
Chopin, Kate **5, 14**
Comstock, Anthony **13**
Crane, Hart **2, 5**
Crane, Stephen **11, 17**
Crawford, F. Marion **10**
Crothers, Rachel **19**
Cullen, Countee **4**
Davis, Rebecca Harding **6**
Dreiser, Theodore **10, 18**
Dunbar, Paul Laurence **2, 12**
Fisher, Rudolph **11**
Fitzgerald, F. Scott **1, 6, 14**
Forten, Charlotte L. **16**
Freeman, Douglas Southall **11**
Freeman, Mary Wilkins **9**
Futrelle, Jacques **19**
Gale, Zona **7**

Garland, Hamlin **3**
Gilman, Charlotte Perkins **9**
Glasgow, Ellen **2, 7**
Goldman, Emma **13**
Grey, Zane **6**
Harper, Frances Ellen
 Watkins **14**
Harris, Joel Chandler **2**
Harte, Bret **1**
Hearn, Lafcadio **9**
Henry, O. **1, 19**
Hergesheimer, Joseph **11**
Howard, Robert E. **8**
Howells, William Dean **7, 17**
James, Henry **2, 11**
James, William **15**
Jewett, Sarah Orne **1**
Johnson, James Weldon **3, 19**
Kornbluth, C. M. **8**
Kuttner, Henry **10**
Lardner, Ring **2, 14**
Lewis, Sinclair **4, 13**
Lewisohn, Ludwig **19**
Lindsay, Vachel **17**
London, Jack **9, 15**
Lovecraft, H. P. **4**
Lowell, Amy **1, 8**
Marquis, Don **7**
Masters, Edgar Lee **2**
McKay, Claude **7**
Mencken, H. L. **13**
Millay, Edna St. Vincent **4**
Mitchell, Margaret **11**
Monroe, Harriet **12**
Nathan, George Jean **18**
O'Neill, Eugene **1, 6**
Rawlings, Majorie Kinnan **4**
Reed, John **9**
Robinson, Edwin Arlington **5**

Rogers, Will **8**
Rölvaag, O. E. **17**
Rourke, Constance **12**
Runyon, Damon **10**
Saltus, Edgar **8**
Sherwood, Robert E. **3**
Slesinger, Tess **10**
Steffens, Lincoln **20**
Stein, Gertrude **1, 6**
Sterling, George **20**
Stevens, Wallace **3, 12**
Tarkington, Booth **9**
Teasdale, Sara **4**
Thurman, Wallace **6**
Twain, Mark **6, 12, 19**
Van Doren, Carl **18**
Washington, Booker T. **10**
West, Nathanael **1, 14**
Wharton, Edith **3, 9**
White, Walter **15**
Wolfe, Thomas **4, 13**
Woollcott, Alexander **5**
Wylie, Elinor **8**

ARGENTINIAN

Lugones, Leopoldo **15**
Storni, Alfonsina **5**

AUSTRALIAN

Brennan, Christopher John **17**
Franklin, Miles **7**
Richardson, Henry Handel **4**

AUSTRIAN

Broch, Hermann **20**
Hofmannsthal, Hugo von **11**
Kafka, Franz **2, 6, 13**
Kraus, Karl **5**
Musil, Robert **12**

Schnitzler, Arthur **4**
Steiner, Rudolf **13**
Trakl, Georg **5**
Werfel, Franz **8**
Zweig, Stefan **17**

BELGIAN

Bosschère, Jean de **19**
Maeterlinck, Maurice **3**
Verhaeren, Émile **12**

BRAZILIAN

Machado de Assis, Joaquim
 Maria **10**

CANADIAN

Campbell, Wilfred **9**
Carman, Bliss **7**
Garneau, Hector Saint-
 Denys **13**
Grove, Frederick Philip **4**
Leacock, Stephen **2**
McCrae, John **12**
Nelligan, Émile **14**
Roberts, Charles G. D. **8**
Scott, Duncan Campbell **6**
Service, Robert W. **15**

CHILEAN

Mistral, Gabriela **2**

CHINESE

Liu E **15**
Lu Hsün **3**

CZECHOSLOVAKIAN

Capek, Karel **6**
Hašek, Jaroslav **4**

DANISH
Brandes, Georg   10

DUTCH
Couperus, Louis   15
Frank, Anne   17

ENGLISH
Baring, Maurice   8
Beerbohm, Max   1
Belloc, Hilaire   7, 18
Bennett, Arnold   5, 20
Benson, Stella   17
Bentley, E. C.   12
Besant, Annie   9
Blackwood, Algernon   5
Bridges, Robert   1
Brooke, Rupert   2, 7
Butler, Samuel   1
Chesterton, G. K.   1, 6
Conrad, Joseph   1, 6, 13
Coppard, A. E.   5
Crowley, Aleister   7
De la Mare, Walter   4
Dowson, Ernest   4
Doyle, Arthur Conan   7
Eddison, E. R.   15
Ellis, Havelock   14
Firbank, Ronald   1
Ford, Ford Madox   1, 15
Galsworthy, John   1
Gilbert, W. S.   3
Gissing, George   3
Granville-Barker, Harley   2
Gray, John   19
Haggard, H. Rider   11
Hall, Radclyffe   12
Hardy, Thomas   4, 10, 18
Henley, William Ernest   8
Hodgson, William Hope   13
Housman, A. E.   1, 10
Housman, Laurence   7
James, M. R.   6
Johnson, Lionel   19
Kaye-Smith, Sheila   20
Kipling, Rudyard   8, 17
Lawrence, D. H.   2, 9, 16
Lawrence, T. E.   18
Lee, Vernon   5
Leverson, Ada   18
Lewis, Wyndham   2, 9
Lindsay, David   15
Lowndes, Marie Belloc   12
Lowry, Malcolm   6
Macaulay, Rose   7
Meredith, George   17
Mew, Charlotte   8
Meynell, Alice   6
Milne, A. A.   6
Murry, John Middleton   16
Noyes, Alfred   7
Orwell, George   2, 6, 15
Owen, Wilfred   5
Powys, T. F.   9
Richardson, Dorothy   3
Rolfe, Frederick   12
Rosenberg, Isaac   12
Ruskin, John   20
Saki   3
Sayers, Dorothy L.   2, 15
Shiel, M. P.   8
Sinclair, May   3, 11
Strachey, Lytton   12

Summers, Montague   16
Sutro, Alfred   6
Swinburne, Algernon
  Charles   8
Symons, Arthur   11
Thomas, Edward   10
Thompson, Francis   4
Van Druten, John   2
Walpole, Hugh   5
Wells, H. G.   6, 12, 19
Williams, Charles   1, 11
Woolf, Virginia   1, 5, 20
Zangwill, Israel   16

FRENCH
Alain-Fournier   6
Apollinaire, Guillaume   3, 8
Artaud, Antonin   3
Barbusse, Henri   5
Bernanos, Georges   3
Bourget, Paul   12
Claudel, Paul   2, 10
Colette   1, 5, 16
Daumal, René   14
Dujardin, Édouard   13
Éluard, Paul   7
Fargue, Léon-Paul   11
France, Anatole   9
Gide, André   5, 12
Giraudoux, Jean   2, 7
Gourmont, Remy de   17
Huysmans, Joris-Karl   7
Jacob, Max   6
Jarry, Alfred   2, 14
Larbaud, Valéry   9
Loti, Pierre   11
Moréas, Jean   18
Péguy, Charles   10
Péret, Benjamin   20
Proust, Marcel   7, 13
Renard, Jules   17
Rostand, Edmond   6
Roussel, Raymond   20
Saint-Exupéry, Antoine de   2
Schwob, Marcel   20
Teilhard de Chardin, Pierre   9
Valéry, Paul   4, 15
Verne, Jules   6
Vian, Boris   9
Zola, Émile   1, 6

GERMAN
Benn, Gottfried   3
Borchert, Wolfgang   5
Brecht, Bertolt   1, 6, 13
Döblin, Alfred   13
Ewers, Hanns Heinz   12
Feuchtwanger, Lion   3
George, Stefan   2, 14
Hauptmann, Gerhart   4
Heym, Georg   9
Heyse, Paul   8
Huch, Ricarda   13
Kaiser, Georg   9
Liliencron, Detlev von   18
Mann, Heinrich   9
Mann, Thomas   2, 8, 14
Morgenstern, Christian   8
Nietzsche, Friedrich   10, 18
Rilke, Rainer Maria   1, 6, 19
Sternheim, Carl   8
Sudermann, Hermann   15
Toller, Ernst   10

Wassermann, Jakob   6
Wedekind, Frank   7

GREEK
Cafavy, C. P.   2, 7
Kazantzakis, Nikos   2, 5
Palamas, Kostes   5

HAITIAN
Roumain, Jacques   19

HUNGARIAN
Ady, Endre   11
Babits, Mihály   14
Csáth, Géza   13
Molnár, Ferenc   20
Radnóti, Miklós   16

INDIAN
Chatterji, Saratchandra   13
Tagore, Rabindranath   3

IRISH
A. E.   3, 10
Cary, Joyce   1
Dunsany, Lord   2
Gogarty, Oliver St. John   15
Gregory, Lady   1
Joyce, James   3, 8, 16
Moore, George   7
O'Grady, Standish   5
Shaw, Bernard   3, 9
Stephens, James   4
Stoker, Bram   8
Synge, J. M.   6
Tynan, Katharine   3
Wilde, Oscar   1, 8
Yeats, William Butler   1, 11,
  18

ITALIAN
Betti, Ugo   5
Brancati, Vitaliano   12
Campana, Dino   20
D'Annunzio, Gabriel   6
Giacosa, Giuseppe   7
Lampedusa, Giuseppe Tomasi
  di   13
Marinetti, F. T.   10
Pavese, Cesare   3
Pirandello, Luigi   4
Svevo, Italo   2
Verga, Giovanni   3

JAMAICAN
De Lisser, H. G.   12
Mais, Roger   8

JAPANESE
Akutagawa Ryūnosuke   16
Dazai Osamu   11
Ishikawa Takuboku   15
Masaoka Shiki   18
Mori Ōgai   14
Natsume, Sōseki   2, 10
Shimazaki, Tōson   5

LEBANESE
Gibran, Kahlil   1, 9

MEXICAN
Azuela, Mariano   3
Nervo, Amado   11

Romero, José Rubén   14

NEW ZEALAND
Mansfield, Katherine   2, 8

NICARAGUAN
Darío, Rubén   4

NORWEGIAN
Bjørnson, Bjørnstjerne   7
Grieg, Nordhal   10
Hamsun, Knut   2, 14
Ibsen, Henrik   2, 8, 16
Kielland, Alexander   5
Lie, Jonas   5
Undset, Sigrid   3

PERUVIAN
Vallejo, César   3

POLISH
Borowski, Tadeusz   9
Reymont, Wladyslaw
  Stanislaw   5
Schulz, Bruno   5
Sienkiewitz, Henryk   3
Witkiewicz, Stanislaw
  Ignacy   8

RUSSIAN
Andreyev, Leonid   3
Annensky, Innokenty   14
Babel, Isaak   2, 13
Balmont, Konstantin
  Dmitriyevich   11
Bely, Andrey   7
Blok, Aleksandr   5
Bryusov, Valery   10
Bulgakov, Mikhail   2, 16
Bunin, Ivan   6
Chekhov, Anton   3, 10
Esenin, Sergei   4
Gorky, Maxim   8
Hippius, Zinaida   9
Khlebnikov, Velimir   20
Khodasevich, Vladislav   15
Kuprin, Aleksandr   5
Mandelstam, Osip   2, 6
Mayakovsky, Vladimir   4, 18
Platonov, Andrei   14
Sologub, Fyodor   9
Tolstoy, Alexey
  Nikolayevich   18
Tolstoy, Leo   4, 11, 17
Tsvetaeva, Marina   7
Zamyatin, Yevgeny
  Ivanovich   8
Zhdanov, Andrei   18
Zoshchenko, Mikhail   15

SCOTTISH
Barrie, J. M.   2
Bridie, James   3
Gibbon, Lewis Grassic   4
Graham, R. B.
  Cunninghame   19
Lang, Andrew   16
MacDonald, George   9
Muir, Edwin   2
Tey, Josephine   14

SOUTH AFRICAN
Campbell, Roy   5
Schreiner, Olive   9

SPANISH
Barea, Arturo 14
Baroja, Pío 8
Benavente, Jacinto 3
Blasco Ibáñez, Vicente 12
Echegaray, José 4
García Lorca, Federico 1, 7
Jiménez, Juan Ramón 4
Machado, Antonio 3
Martínez Sierra, Gregorio 6
Miró, Gabriel 5
Ortega y Gasset, José 9
Pereda, José María de 16
Salinas, Pedro 17
Unamuno, Miguel de 2, 9
Valera, Juan 10
Valle-Inclán, Ramón del 5

SWEDISH
Dagerman, Stig 17
Heidenstam, Verner von 5
Lagerlöf, Selma 4
Strindberg, August 1, 8

SWISS
Spitteler, Carl 12
Walser, Robert 18

URUGUAYAN
Quiroga, Horacio 20

WELSH
Davies, W. H. 5
Lewis, Alun 3
Machen, Arthur 4
Thomas, Dylan 1, 8

YIDDISH
Aleichem, Sholom 1
Asch, Sholem 3
Peretz, Isaac Leib 16

Nationality Index

Cumulative Index to Critics

A. E.
See also **Russell, George William**
Oliver St. John Gogarty **15**:101
Standish O'Grady **5**:348, 349
James Stephens **4**:407
Leo Tolstoy **4**:459
Katharine Tynan **3**:505
William Butler Yeats **11**:516

Aaron, Daniel
Nathanael West **1**:485

Abbott, Lyman
Booker T. Washington **10**:522

Abcarian, Richard
Sherwood Anderson **1**:59

Abel, Lionel
Bertolt Brecht **1**:109
Henrik Ibsen **2**:232

Abercrombie, Lascelles
Thomas Hardy **4**:153

Abrams, Ivan B.
Sholom Aleichem **1**:24

Abramson, Doris E.
Rudolph Fisher **11**:207
Wallace Thurman **6**:449

Abril, Xavier
César Vallejo **3**:526

Achebe, Chinua
Joseph Conrad **13**:130

Adams, B. S.
Miklós Radnóti **16**:412

Adams, Elsie Bonita
Israel Zangwill **16**:461

Adams, Francis
Thomas Hardy **18**:84

Adams, Henry
William Dean Howells **7**:363
Mark Twain **12**:428

Adams, J. Donald
Theodore Dreiser **10**:177
F. Scott Fitzgerald **1**:239

Adams, Leonie
George Sterling **20**:376

Adams, Marion
Gottfried Benn **3**:111

Adams, Phoebe-Lou
Malcolm Lowry **6**:237

Adams, Richard P.
Mark Twain **19**:375

Adams, Robert M.
Gabriele D'Annunzio **6**:140
James Joyce **16**:234
Franz Kafka **13**:268
Tess Slesinger **10**:441

Adams, Robert Martin
Hermann Broch **20**:70
Alfred Döblin **13**:179
James Joyce **3**:273

Adams, Samuel Hopkins
Alexander Woollcott **5**:524

Adams, Walter S.
Thomas Wolfe **4**:506

Adcock, A. St. John
Wilfred Campbell **9**:31
O. Henry **1**:347
Joseph Hergesheimer **11**:274
William Hope Hodgson **13**:230
Sheila Kaye-Smith **20**:100
Bernard Shaw **3**:386

Adell, Alberto
Ramón del Valle-Inclán **5**:484

Adereth, M.
Charles Péguy **10**:413

Adler, Jacob H.
Henrik Ibsen **16**:180

Adler, Ruth
Isaac Leib Peretz **16**:405

Adrian, John
Paul Heyse **8**:123

Ady, Endre
Endre Ady **11**:12

Aguirre, Ángel Manuel
Juan Ramón Jiménez **4**:223

Aguinaga, Carlos Blanco
Miguel de Unamuno **2**:561

Aiken, Conrad
Sherwood Anderson **1**:37
Jean de Bosschère **19**:56
Robert Bridges **1**:127
James Branch Cabell **6**:62
Walter de la Mare **4**:71
F. Scott Fitzgerald **1**:237
Ford Madox Ford **15**:71
John Galsworthy **1**:296
Federico García Lorca **1**:308
Oliver St. John Gogarty **15**:102
Thomas Hardy **4**:155
Joseph Hergesheimer **11**:262
A. E. Housman **10**:241
Henry James **11**:329
D. H. Lawrence **2**:344
Wyndham Lewis **9**:236
Edgar Lee Masters **2**:460
Harriet Monroe **12**:216
Eugene O'Neill **1**:383
Charles Péguy **10**:415
Dorothy Richardson **3**:349
Rainer Maria Rilke **1**:414

Edwin Arlington Robinson **5**:403
Gertrude Stein **6**:406
Dylan Thomas **1**:466
H. G. Wells **12**:499
Virginia Woolf **1**:529

Aiken, Henry David
Friedrich Nietzsche **10**:383

Akhsharumov, N. D.
Leo Tolstoy **4**:446

Alcott, Louisa May
Rebecca Harding Davis **6**:148

Aldington, Richard
Rémy de Gourmont **17**:130
T. E. Lawrence **18**:149
Oscar Wilde **1**:499

Aldiss, Brian W.
Henry Kuttner **10**:271
Jules Verne **6**:497
H. G. Wells **19**:450

Aldridge, John
F. Scott Fitzgerald **1**:246

Alexander, Calvert
Sheila Kaye-Smith **20**:108

Alexander, Gary T.
William James **15**:184

Alexander, Holmes
Margaret Mitchell **11**:373

Alexandrova, Vera
Sergei Esenin **4**:113
Alexey Nikolayevich Tolstoy **18**:370

Alford, Norman
Lionel Johnson **19**:253

Allen, Clifford
Radclyffe Hall **12**:190

Allen, M. D.
T. E. Lawrence **18**:180

Allen, Mary
Jack London **15**:273

Allen, Paul
Hanns Heinz Ewers **12**:135

Allen, Paul Marshall
Rudolf Steiner **13**:447, 448
Jakob Wassermann **6**:520

Allen, Priscilla
Kate Chopin **14**:70

Allen, Walter
Arnold Bennett **5**:40
Wyndham Lewis **2**:394
Dorothy Richardson **3**:358

Allison, J. E.
Heinrich Mann **9**:331

Alpers, Antony
Katherine Mansfield **8**:291

Alpert, Hollis
O. Henry **1**:350

Alsen, Eberhard
Hamlin Garland **3**:200

Alter, Robert
Hermann Broch **20**:65

Altrocchi, Rudolph
Gabriele D'Annunzio **6**:135

Al'tshuler, Anatoly
Mikhail Bulgakov **16**:80

Alvarez, A.
Hart Crane **2**:118
Thomas Hardy **10**:221
D. H. Lawrence **2**:364
Wallace Stevens **3**:454
William Butler Yeats **1**:564

Alworth, E. Paul
Will Rogers **8**:336

Amann, Clarence A.
James Weldon Johnson **3**:247

Amis, Kingsley
G. K. Chesterton **1**:185
C. M. Kornbluth **8**:213
David Lindsay **15**:218
Jules Verne **6**:493

Ammons, Elizabeth
Edith Wharton **9**:552

Amoia, Alba della Fazia
Edmond Rostand **6**:381

Amon, Frank
D. H. Lawrence **9**:220

Anders, Gunther
Franz Kafka **2**:302

Anderson, C. G.
James Joyce **16**:208

Anderson, David D.
Sherwood Anderson **1**:52
Louis Bromfield **11**:85, 87
Sinclair Lewis **13**:351

Anderson, Frederick
Mark Twain **12**:445

Anderson, Isaac
Raymond Chandler **7**:167
Rudolph Fisher **11**:204

Anderson, Margaret C.
Anthony Comstock **13**:90
Emma Goldman **13**:210

Anderson, Maxwell
Sherwood Anderson **10**:31
Vicente Blasco Ibáñez **12**:32
Joseph Hergesheimer **11**:261
Edna St. Vincent Millay **4**:306

Anderson, Quentin
Willa Cather **1**:163

Anderson, Rachel
Sheila Kaye-Smith **20**:117

Anderson, Sherwood
Sherwood Anderson **10**:31
Stephen Crane **11**:133
Theodore Dreiser **10**:169
Ring Lardner **14**:291
Sinclair Lewis **13**:333
Vachel Lindsay **17**:233
Gertrude Stein **6**:407
Mark Twain **6**:459

Andreas, Osborn
Henry James **11**:330

Andrews, William L.
Charles Waddel Chesnutt **5**:136

Angenot, Marc
Jules Verne **6**:501

Angoff, Charles
Havelock Ellis **14**:116
George Jean Nathan **18**:318

Angus, Douglas
Franz Kafka **13**:264

Annan, Gabriele
Colette **16**:135

Annenkov, P. V.
Leo Tolstoy **4**:444

Annensky, Innokenty
Innokenty Annensky **14**:16

Anninsky, L.
Andrei Platonov **14**:403

Anouilh, Jean
Jean Giraudoux **7**:320

Anthony, Edward
Don Marquis **7**:443

Anthony, G. F. Penn
Pierre Teilhard de Chardin **9**:501

Antoine, Jacques C.
Jacques Roumain **19**:333

Antoninus, Brother
Hart Crane **2**:119

Appignanesi, Lisa
Robert Musil **12**:257

Apter, T. E.
Thomas Mann **14**:359
Virginia Woolf **20**:424

Aptheker, Herbert
Booker T. Washington **10**:530

Aquilar, Helene J.F. de
Federico García Lorca **7**:302

Aragon, Louis
Paul Eluard **7**:249

Aratari, Anthony
Federico García Lorca **1**:316

Arce de Vazquez, Margot
Gabriela Mistral **2**:477

Archer, William
Bliss Carman **7**:135
W. S. Gilbert **3**:207
A. E. Housman **10**:239
Laurence Housman **7**:352
Henrik Ibsen **2**:224
Selma Lagerlöf **4**:229
Alice Meynell **6**:294
Duncan Campbell Scott **6**:385
Arthur Symons **11**:428
Francis Thompson **4**:434
Mark Twain **12**:427
William Butler Yeats **11**:510

Arden, Eugene
Paul Laurence Dunbar **12**:113

Arendt, Hannah
Bertolt Brecht **1**:114
Franz Kafka **2**:301
Stefan Zweig **17**:429

Arms, George
Kate Chopin **5**:149

Armstrong, Martin
Katherine Mansfield **2**:446

Arner, Robert D.
Kate Chopin **5**:155; **14**:63, 65

Arnold, Matthew
Leo Tolstoy **11**:458

Aron, Albert W.
Jakob Wassermann **6**:509

Arrowsmith, William
Cesare Pavese **3**:334
Dylan Thomas **1**:468

Arvin, Newton
Henry Adams **4**:12

Ashbery, John
Raymond Roussel **20**:238
Gertrude Stein **1**:442

Ashworth, Arthur
Miles Franklin **7**:264

Asimov, Isaac
George Orwell **15**:314

Asselineau, Roger
Theodore Dreiser **18**:51

Aswell, Edward C.
Thomas Wolfe **4**:515

Atheling, William Jr.
See also **Blish, James**
Henry Kuttner **10**:266

Atherton, Gertrude
Ambrose Bierce **7**:88
May Sinclair **3**:434

Atherton, Stanley S.
Robert W. Service **15**:406

Atkins, Elizabeth
Edna St. Vincent Millay **4**:311

Atkins, John
Walter de la Mare **4**:75; **15**:352
George Orwell **6**:341; **15**:352

Atkinson, Brooks
Rudolph Fisher **11**:204
Ring Lardner **14**:293

Atlas, James
Gertrude Stein **1**:442
Thomas Wolfe **4**:538

Atlas, Marilyn Judith
Sherwood Anderson **10**:54

Attebery, Brian
L. Frank Baum **7**:25

Atterbury, Rev. Anson P.
Annie Besant **9**:13

Auchincloss, Louis
Paul Bourget **12**:72
Willa Cather **1**:164
Ellen Glasgow **2**:188
Henry James **2**:275
Sarah Orne Jewett **1**:367
Edith Wharton **3**:570

Auden, W. H.
James Agee **19**:19
Max Beerbohm **1**:72
Hilaire Belloc **7**:41
C. P. Cavafy **2**:90
Raymond Chandler **7**:168
G. K. Chesterton **1**:184, 186
Walter de la Mare **4**:81
Hugo von Hofmannsthal **11**:310
A. E. Housman **1**:358
Rudyard Kipling **8**:189
George MacDonald **9**:295
George Orwell **2**:512
Rainer Maria Rilke **6**:359
Frederick Rolfe **12**:268
Bernard Shaw **3**:389
Paul Valéry **4**:499
Nathanael West **1**:480
Oscar Wilde **1**:504, 507
Charles Williams **1**:516
Virginia Woolf **1**:546
William Butler Yeats **1**:562; **18**:443

Auernheimer, Raoul
Stefan Zweig **17**:431

Austin, Henry
Charlotte Gilman **9**:96

Austin, James C.
Rebecca Harding Davis **6**:151

Avery, George C.
Robert Walser **18**:420, 426

Avins, Carol
Mikhail Bulgakov **16**:107

Avseenko, V. G.
Leo Tolstoy **4**:446

Ayer, A. J.
William James **15**:186

Azorín
Ramón del Valle-Inclán **5**:479

Bab, Julius
Alfred Döblin **13**:158

Babbitt, Irving
H. L. Mencken **13**:371

Babel, Isaac
Isaac Babel **13**:17

Bacigalupo, Mario Ford
José María de Pereda **16**:382

Bacon, Leonard
Alexander Woollcott **5**:522

Bailey, Joseph W.
Arthur Schnitzler **4**:391

Bailey, Mabel Driscoll
Maxwell Anderson **2**:7

Baird, James
Wallace Stevens 3:471

Baker, Carlos
Sherwood Anderson 1:64
Edwin Muir 2:483

Baker, George P.
Philip Barry 11:45

Baker, Houston A., Jr.
Countee Cullen 4:52
Paul Laurence Dunbar 12:128
James Weldon Johnson 19:214
Booker T. Washington 10:533

Baker, I. L.
E. C. Bentley 12:16

Baker, Joseph E.
O. E. Rölvaag 17:330

Bakewell, Charles M.
William James 15:148

Balakian, Anna
Guillaume Apollinaire 8:19
Paul Claudel 10:131
Paul Eluard 7:257

Baldanza, Frank
Mark Twain 19:373

Baldwin, Charles C.
Louis Bromfield 11:71
Booth Tarkington 9:458

Baldwin, James Mark
William James 15:137

Baldwin, Richard E.
Charles Waddell Chesnutt
5:135

Baldwin, Roger N.
Emma Goldman 13:216

Ball, Clive
Benjamin Péret 20:203

Ball, Robert Hamilton
David Belasco 3:88

Balmforth, Ramsden
Laurence Housman 7:355

Balogh, Eva S.
Emma Goldman 13:223

Baltrušaitis, Jurgis
Emile Verhaeren 12:467

Bander, Elaine
Dorothy L. Sayers 2:537

Bandyopadhyay, Manik
Saratchandra Chatterji 13:83

Bangerter, Lowell A.
Hugo von Hofmannsthal 11:311

Banks, Nancy Huston
Charles Waddell Chesnutt
5:130

Bannister, Winifred
James Bridie 3:134

Baranov, Vadim
Alexey Nikolayevich Tolstoy
18:377

Barbour, Ian G.
Pierre Teilhard de Chardin
9:488

Barbusse, Henri
Henri Barbusse 5:14

Barclay, Glen St John
H. Rider Haggard 11:252
H. P. Lovecraft 4:273
Bram Stoker 8:399

Barea, Arturo
Miguel de Unamuno 2:559

Barea, Ilsa
Miguel de Unamuno 2:559

Bareham, Terence
Malcolm Lowry 6:251

Barfield, Owen
Rudolf Steiner 13:453

Baring, Maurice
Maurice Baring 8:32
Hilaire Belloc 7:32
Anton Chekhov 3:145
Anatole France 9:40
W. S. Gilbert 3:211
Saki 3:363
Leo Tolstoy 11:459

Barker, Dudley
G. K. Chesterton 6:101

Barker, Frank Granville
Joseph Conrad 1:219

Barker, John
H. G. Wells 12:515

Barker, Murl G.
Fyodor Sologub 9:445

Barksdale, Richard K.
Charlotte L. Forten 16:148
Claude McKay 7:466

Barltrop, Robert
Jack London 15:260

Barnard, Ellsworth
Edwin Arlington Robinson
5:411

Barnard, Marjorie
Miles Franklin 7:270

Barnes, Clive
August Strindberg 8:420

Barnsley, John H.
George Orwell 15:324

Barnstone, Willis
C. P. Cavafy 7:163
Edgar Lee Masters 2:472

Barooshian, Vahan D.
Velimir Khlebnikov 20:137

Barrett, Francis X.
Wallace Thurman 6:450

Barrett, William
F. Scott Fitzgerald 1:246
William James 15:182
Friedrich Nietzsche 10:378

Barrow, Leo L.
Pío Baroja 8:57
Machado de Assis 10:293

Barson, Alfred T.
James Agee 19:31

Barthes, Roland
Bertolt Brecht 1:102
Pierre Loti 11:363
Jules Verne 6:491

Bartkovich, Jeffrey
Maxim Gorky 8:89

Baruch, Elaine Hoffmann
George Orwell 15:344

Barzun, Jacques
E. C. Bentley 12:20
Raymond Chandler 7:171, 176
John Jay Chapman 7:195
William James 15:188
Malcolm Lowry 6:236
Friedrich Nietzsche 10:371
Bernard Shaw 3:398

Basdekis, Demetrios
Miguel de Unamuno 2:566

Baskervill, William Malone
George Washington Cable 4:24
Joel Chandler Harris 2:209

Baskett, Sam S.
Jack London 9:267

Basney, Lionel
Dorothy L. Sayers 15:382

Bates, Ernest Sutherland
Ludwig Lewisohn 19:271

Bates, H. E.
A. E. Coppard 5:179
Radclyffe Hall 12:188
Thomas Hardy 4:161
Katherine Mansfield 8:278

Bates, Scott
Guillaume Apollinaire 3:37

Battiscombe, Georgina
Stella Benson 17:24

Baudouin, Charles
Carl Spitteler 12:335
Emile Verhaeren 12:472

Baugh, Edward
Arthur Symons 11:445

Bauland, Peter
Bertolt Brecht 13:58
Gerhart Hauptmann 4:209

Baum, L. Frank
L. Frank Baum 7:12, 15

Baxandall, Lee
Bertolt Brecht 1:119

Bayerschmidt, Carl F.
Sigrid Undset 3:525

Bayley, John
Thomas Hardy 4:177
Bruno Schulz 5:427
Virginia Woolf 1:550

Beach, Joseph Warren
Joseph Conrad 1:199
Theodore Dreiser 10:175
Thomas Hardy 4:154; 18:92
James Joyce 3:257
D. H. Lawrence 2:350
Ludwig Lewisohn 19:264
George Meredith 17:266
Hugh Walpole 5:498
Edith Wharton 3:562
Emile Zola 1:588

Beadle, Gordon
George Orwell 15:354

Beals, Carleton
Mariano Azuela 3:74

Beard, Charles A.
Charles A. Beard 15:19

Beard, William
Charles A. Beard 15:33

Beards, Richard D.
D. H. Lawrence 16:317

Beauchamp, Gorman
George Orwell 15:361

Beaumont, E. M.
Paul Claudel 10:132

Beaumont, Keith S.
Alfred Jarry 14:278

Bechhofer, C. E.
Randolph S. Bourne 16:48

Beckelman, June
Paul Claudel 2:104

Becker, Carl
Charles A. Beard 15:20

Becker, George J.
D. H. Lawrence 16:320

Becker, May Lamberton
Marie Belloc Lowndes 12:203

Beckett, Samuel
James Joyce 3:255
Marcel Proust 7:525

Beckley, Richard
Carl Sternheim 8:371
Ernst Toller 10:486

Bédé, Jean-Albert
Emile Zola 1:596

Bedell, R. Meredith
Stella Benson 17:26

Bedient, Calvin
D. H. Lawrence 2:370

Beebe, Maurice
James Joyce 8:163

Beer, Gillian
George Meredith 17:285

Beer, J. B.
John Middleton Murry 16:344

Beer, Thomas
Stephen Crane 11:131
T. F. Powys 9:362

Beerbohm, Max
Maurice Baring 8:31
J. M. Barrie 2:39
Joseph Conrad 1:195
F. Marion Crawford 10:144
Arthur Conan Doyle 7:217
José Echegaray 4:98
John Galsworthy 1:301
W. S. Gilbert 3:209
Maxim Gorky 8:70
Harley Granville-Barker 2:192
William Ernest Henley 8:99
Laurence Housman 7:353
Henrik Ibsen 8:143
Rudyard Kipling 8:180
Andrew Lang 16:253
Edmond Rostand 6:372, 376
Bernard Shaw 3:378
Lytton Strachey 12:404
Alfred Sutro 6:419, 420
Arthur Symons 11:429
John Millington Synge 6:425
Israel Zangwill 16:443

Beharriell, S. Ross
Stephen Leacock 2:382

Critic Index

Behrman, S. N.
Ferenc Molnár 20:161
Robert E. Sherwood 3:414

Beichman, Janine
Masaoka Shiki 18:224

Beicken, Peter U.
Franz Kafka 2:309

Bell, Aubrey F. G.
Juan Ramón Jiménez 4:212
Gregorio Martinez Sierra and
  Maria Martinez Sierra 6:278

Bell, Clive
Marcel Proust 7:521

Bell, David F.
Alfred Jarry 2:286

Bellman, Samuel I.
Marjorie Kinnan Rawlings
  4:365
Constance Rourke 12:330

Belloc, Hilaire
Maurice Baring 8:34
G. K. Chesterton 1:178
Dorothy L. Sayers 15:373
H. G. Wells 6:530; 12:490

Belloni, Manuel
Leopoldo Lugones 15:290

Bellow, Saul
Sholom Aleichem 1:23
James Joyce 8:168
Rudolf Steiner 13:463

Bellquist, John Eric
August Strindberg 8:418

Bely, Andrei
Zinaida Hippius 9:154
Vladislav Khodasevich 15:199

Benamou, Michel
Wallace Stevens 3:457

Benavente, Jacinto
Ramón del Valle-Inclán 5:479

Benchley, Robert C.
Ring Lardner 14:291

Bender, Bert
Kate Chopin 5:157

Benediktsson, Thomas E.
George Sterling 20:382

Benet, Mary Kathleen
Colette 5:171

Benét, Stephen Vincent
Stephen Vincent Benét 7:69
Douglas Southall Freeman
  11:217, 220
Margaret Mitchell 11:371
Constance Rourke 12:317
Elinor Wylie 8:526

Benét, William Rose
Hart Crane 5:185
F. Scott Fitzgerald 1:236
Alfred Noyes 7:505
Elinor Wylie 8:526

Benjamin, Walter
Marcel Proust 7:538

Benn, Gottfried
Friedrich Nietzsche 10:371

Bennett, Arnold
Maurice Baring 8:31
Joseph Conrad 1:196
Theodore Dreiser 10:172
Ford Madox Ford 15:68
Anatole France 9:44
John Galsworthy 1:292
George Gissing 3:223
Joris-Karl Huysmans 7:408
George Meredith 17:264
Olive Schreiner 9:396
H. G. Wells 12:487; 19:421

Bennett, Charles A.
John Millington Synge 6:427

Bennett, D.R.M.
Anthony Comstock 13:86

Bennett, E. K.
Stefan George 14:202
Paul Heyse 8:120

Bennett, George N.
William Dean Howells 17:162

Bennett, Warren
F. Scott Fitzgerald 14:181

Benoit, Leroy J.
Paul Eluard 7:247

Bensen, Alice R.
Rose Macaulay 7:430

Benson, Eugene
Gabriele D'Annunzio 6:127

Benson, Ruth Crego
Leo Tolstoy 4:481

Benson, Stella
Stella Benson 17:22

Benstock, Bernard
James Joyce 8:165

Bentley, C. F.
Bram Stoker 8:388

Bentley, D.M.R.
Wilfred Campbell 9:33
Bliss Carman 7:149

Bentley, E. C.
Hilaire Belloc 18:25
E. C. Bentley 12:15
Damon Runyon 10:423

Bentley, Eric
Stephen Vincent Benét 7:78
Bertolt Brecht 1:98, 99; 6:40;
  13:47
James Bridie 3:134
Anton Chekhov 3:156
Federico García Lorca 1:310
Stefan George 14:198
Henrik Ibsen 2:225
Friedrich Nietzsche 10:377
Eugene O'Neill 1:392
Luigi Pirandello 4:337, 340
August Strindberg 1:446
Frank Wedekind 7:578
Oscar Wilde 1:499
William Butler Yeats 1:562

Berberova, Nina
Vladislav Khodasevich 15:201

Berendsohn, Walter A.
Selma Lagerlöf 4:231

Beresford, J. D.
Dorothy Richardson 3:349
H. G. Wells 19:424

Bereza, Henryk
Bruno Schulz 5:421

Berger, Dorothea
Ricarda Huch 13:251

Berger, Harold L.
C. M. Kornbluth 8:218

Bergin, Thomas Goddard
Giovanni Verga 3:540

Bergmann, S. A.
Stig Dagerman 17:85

Bergon, Frank
Stephen Crane 11:161

Bergonzi, Bernard
Hilaire Belloc 7:39
Rupert Brooke 7:127
G. K. Chesterton 1:180
Ford Madox Ford 1:289
John Galsworthy 1:302
John Gray 19:144
Wyndham Lewis 9:250
Wilfred Owen 5:371
Isaac Rosenberg 12:301
H. G. Wells 6:541

Bergson, Henri
William James 15:158

Berkman, Sylvia
Katherine Mansfield 2:452

Berlin, Isaiah
Osip Mandelstam 6:259
Leo Tolstoy 4:463

Berman, Paul
Emma Goldman 13:223
John Reed 9:390

Bermel, Albert
Guillaume Apollinaire 8:22
Antonin Artaud 3:61

Bernhard, Svea
Verner von Heidenstam 5:250

Bernstein, Melvin H.
John Jay Chapman 7:198

Bernstein, Rabbi Philip S.
Anne Frank 17:106

Berryman, John
Isaak Babel 2:36
Stephen Crane 11:139
F. Scott Fitzgerald 1:240
Anne Frank 17:116
Ring Lardner 2:334
Dylan Thomas 8:449
William Butler Yeats 11:513

Bersani, Leo
D. H. Lawrence 2:374

Bertaux, Felix
Alfred Döblin 13:160
Heinrich Mann 9:316
Jakob Wassermann 6:512

Berthoff, Warner
Ambrose Bierce 1:94
Willa Cather 1:165
Gertrude Stein 1:434

Bertocci, Angelo P.
Charles Péguy 10:417

Besant, Annie
Annie Besant 9:12

Best, Alan
Frank Wedekind 7:590

Besterman, Theodore
Annie Besant 9:17

Bethea, David M.
Vladislav Khodasevich 15:210

Bettany, F. G.
Arnold Bennett 5:22

Bettelheim, Bruno
Anne Frank 17:111

Bettinson, Christopher
André Gide 5:244

Bettman, Dane
Marcel Proust 13:406

Beucler, André
Léon-Paul Fargue 11:198

Bevington, Helen
Laurence Housman 7:360

Bewley, Marius
F. Scott Fitzgerald 1:260
Isaac Rosenberg 12:304
Wallace Stevens 3:450

Beyer, Edvard
Henrik Ibsen 16:189

Beyer, Harald
Bjørnstjerne Bjørnson 7:112
Nordahl Grieg 10:207
Alexander Kielland 5:279

Bhattacharya, Bhabani
Rabindranath Tagore 3:494

Bhattacharyya, Birendra Kumar
Saratchandra Chatterji 13:78

Biagi, Shirley
Tess Slesinger 10:444

Biasin, Gian-Paolo
Giuseppe Tomasi di Lampedusa
  13:296

Bien, Peter
C. P. Cavafy 2:91
Nikos Kazantzakis 2:315, 321;
  5:268

Bier, Jesse
Ambrose Bierce 1:96

Bierce, Ambrose
William Dean Howells 7:367
Jack London 9:254
George Sterling 20:369

Bierstadt, Edward Hale
Lord Dunsany 2:138

Bigelow, Gordon E.
Marjorie Kinnan Rawlings
  4:362

Billington, Ray Allen
Charlotte L. Forten 16:145

Bilton, Peter
Saki 3:372

Binion, Rudolph
Franz Kafka 6:221

Birchby, Sid
William Hope Hodgson 13:233

Birchenough, M. C.
Israel Zangwill 16:440

Birkerts, Sven
Robert Walser 18:436

Birmingham, George A.
John Millington Synge 6:425

Birnbaum, Marianna D.
Géza Csáth **13**:146

Birnbaum, Martin
Miklós Radnóti **16**:415
Arthur Schnitzler **4**:385

Birrell, Francis
Alfred Sutro **6**:422

Birstein, Ann
Anne Frank **17**:106

Bishop, Charles
Christian Morgenstern **8**:308

Bishop, Ferman
Sarah Orne Jewett **1**:365

Bishop, John Peale
Sherwood Anderson **10**:33
Stephen Vincent Benét **7**:69
F. Scott Fitzgerald **6**:160
A. E. Housman **10**:245
Margaret Mitchell **11**:371
Thomas Wolfe **4**:511

Bithell, Jethro
Ricarda Huch **13**:251
Detlev von Liliencron **18**:212
Christian Morgenstern **8**:307
Emile Verhaeren **12**:463

Bittleston, Adam
Rudolf Steiner **13**:447

Bixler, Julius Seelye
William James **15**:167

Björkman, Edwin
Knut Hamsun **14**:220
Selma Lagerlöf **4**:229
Maurice Maeterlinck **3**:323
Władysław Stanisław Reymont
5:391
Arthur Schnitzler **4**:388
Sigrid Undset **3**:510
Edith Wharton **3**:556

Bjørnson, Bjørnstjerne
Georg Brandes **10**:59
Jonas Lie **5**:325

Black, Hugo
Charles A. Beard **15**:32

Blackmur, R. P.
Henry Adams **4**:9
Samuel Butler **1**:135
Hart Crane **2**:113
Ford Madox Ford **15**:77
Thomas Hardy **4**:165
Henry James **2**:252, 258, 263
D. H. Lawrence **2**:351
T. E. Lawrence **18**:141
Wyndham Lewis **9**:235
Thomas Mann **2**:421
Edwin Muir **2**:484
Wallace Stevens **3**:445
Leo Tolstoy **4**:471
Carl Van Doren **18**:401
William Butler Yeats **1**:565

Blackstone, Bernard
Virginia Woolf **20**:395

Blair, Hector
Mikhail Zoshchenko **15**:507

Blair, Walter
Robert Benchley **1**:77, 79
Will Rogers **8**:333
Mark Twain **6**:463

Blake, Caesar R.
Dorothy Richardson **3**:355

Blake, George
J. M. Barrie **2**:46

Blake, Nicholas
See also **Day Lewis, C.**
E. C. Bentley **12**:15

Blake, Patricia
Vladimir Mayakovsky **4**:298

Blake, Warren Barton
Lafcadio Hearn **9**:123

Blankenagel, John C.
Jakob Wassermann **6**:513, 517

Blankner, Frederick V.
Luigi Pirandello **4**:330

Bleiler, E. F.
Algernon Blackwood **5**:77
Arthur Conan Doyle **7**:237
Jacques Futrelle **19**:94, 95
M. R. James **6**:211
H. P. Lovecraft **4**:271

Bligh, John
A. E. Housman **10**:262

Blish, James
See also **Atheling, William Jr.**
Henry Kuttner **10**:270

Blissett, William
Thomas Mann **2**:428

Bliven, Naomi
Jules Renard **17**:309

Bloch, Adèle
Nikos Kazantzakis **2**:319

Blok, Alexander
Innokenty Annensky **14**:16
Fyodor Sologub **9**:440

Bloom, Edward A.
Willa Cather **11**:103
Thomas Wolfe **13**:484

Bloom, Harold
David Lindsay **15**:240
Isaac Rosenberg **12**:309
John Ruskin **20**:288
Wallace Stevens **3**:476
Oscar Wilde **8**:498
William Butler Yeats **11**:529

Bloom, Lillian D.
Willa Cather **11**:103

Bloom, Robert
H. G. Wells **6**:548

Bloomfield, Paul
R. B. Cunninghame Graham
19:113

Bluestein, Gene
Constance Rourke **12**:324

Blunden, Allan
Georg Heym **9**:149

Blunden, Edmund
Robert Bridges **1**:128
W. H. Davies **5**:202
Wilfred Owen **5**:360

Blunt, Wilfrid Scawen
Charlotte Mew **8**:295

Bly, Robert
Knut Hamsun **14**:238

Boas, Guy
Lytton Strachey **12**:401

Boatwright, James
Margaret Mitchell **11**:381

Bockstahler, O. L.
Hermann Sudermann **15**:429

Bodelsen, C. A.
Rudyard Kipling **8**:202

Bodenheim, Maxwell
Eugene O'Neill **1**:382

Boewe, Charles
O. E. Rölvaag **17**:332

Bogan, Louise
Colette **1**:190
Paul Eluard **7**:244
Federico García Lorca **1**:308
James Joyce **3**:261
Jules Renard **17**:305
Edwin Arlington Robinson
5:410
Wallace Stevens **12**:359
Sara Teasdale **4**:427

Bogard, Carley Rees
Kate Chopin **5**:158

Bogart, E. L.
Charles A. Beard **15**:18

Bohn, Willard
Guillaume Apollinaire **8**:25

Bóka, László
Endre Ady **11**:19

Bold, Alan
Wyndham Lewis **2**:397

Boll, Theophilus E. M.
May Sinclair **3**:440

Bolles, Edwin C.
Sheila Kaye-Smith **20**:111

Bond, Tonette L.
Ellen Glasgow **7**:344

Bondanella, Peter E.
Italo Svevo **2**:553

Bone, Robert A.
Charles Waddell Chesnutt
5:133
Countee Cullen **4**:49
Paul Laurence Dunbar **2**:131;
12:117
Rudolph Fisher **11**:208
Frances Ellen Watkins Harper
14:258
James Weldon Johnson **3**:242
Claude McKay **7**:458
Wallace Thurman **6**:449
Walter White **15**:483

Bonheim, Helmut
James Joyce **3**:277

Bonnell, Peter H.
Aleksandr Kuprin **5**:301

Bonnerjea, René
Endre Ady **11**:14

Bonwit, Marianne
Wolfgang Borchert **5**:102

Böök, Fredrik
Verner von Heidenstam **5**:251

Booker, John Manning
Henri Barbusse **5**:13

Booth, Wayne C.
Anatole France **9**:54
James Joyce **16**:222

Borelli, Mary
Ramón del Valle-Inclán **5**:476

Borges, Jorge Luis
G. K. Chesterton **1**:181
Friedrich Nietzsche **10**:385;
18:332
Bernard Shaw **9**:420
H. G. Wells **6**:545
Oscar Wilde **1**:498

Borker, David
Innokenty Annensky **14**:29, 33

Borland, Hal
Louis Bromfield **11**:81

Borning, Bernard C.
Charles A. Beard **15**:34

Borras, F. M.
Maxim Gorky **8**:85

Borrello, Alfred
H. G. Wells **6**:545

Bort, Barry D.
Sherwood Anderson **10**:50

Bose, Buddhadeva
Rabindranath Tagore **3**:495

Bosmajian, Hamida
Tadeusz Borowski **9**:23

Bosschère, Jean de
Jean de Bosschère **19**:59

Bottome, Phyllis
Olive Schreiner **9**:395

Bouché, H. P.
Léon-Paul Fargue **11**:201

Boucher, Anthony
Josephine Tey **14**:450

Boulby, M.
Stefan George **14**:207

Bouraoui, H. A.
Georges Bernanos **3**:128

Bourget, Paul
Joris-Karl Huysmans **7**:403

Bourne, Randolph
Randolph S. Bourne **16**:42
George Washington Cable **4**:25
Vachel Lindsay **17**:222
Dorothy Richardson **3**:346
H. G. Wells **12**:495

Bovary, Claude
Willa Cather **1**:151

Bovey, John
Thomas Mann **14**:330

Bowen, Elizabeth
Rose Macaulay **7**:424
Katherine Mansfield **8**:279
Henry Handel Richardson **4**:374

Bowen, Robert O.
Sheila Kaye-Smith **20**:111

Bowie, Malcolm
René Daumal **14**:92
Paul Eluard **7**:258

Critic Index

Bowra, C. M.
  Guillaume Apollinaire **3**:34
  Aleksandr Blok **5**:85
  C. P. Cavafy **2**:87
  Federico García Lorca **1**:309
  Stefan George **2**:150
  Velimir Khlebnikov **20**:128
  Vladimir Mayakovsky **4**:293
  Rainer Maria Rilke **1**:409, 414
  Algernon Charles Swinburne
    8:435
  Paul Valéry **4**:490
  William Butler Yeats **1**:560

Bowring, Richard John
  Mori Ōgai **14**:381

Boxill, Anthony
  H. G. de Lisser **12**:99

Boyd, Ernest A.
  A. E. **3**:3
  Lord Dunsany **2**:136
  Thomas Hardy **10**:217
  Lionel Johnson **19**:240
  Gregorio Martínez Sierra and
    María Martínez Sierra **6**:278
  H. L. Mencken **13**:367
  George Jean Nathan **18**:303
  Standish O'Grady **5**:349
  Władysław Stanisław Reymont
    5:392
  Carl Spitteler **12**:336
  Lytton Strachey **12**:397
  Katharine Tynan **3**:504
  Miguel de Unamuno **9**:512

Boyd, Ian
  G. K. Chesterton **6**:103

Boyd, Thomas
  Ring Lardner **14**:291
  John Reed **9**:383

Boyer, James
  Thomas Wolfe **13**:491, 494

Boyesen, Hjalmar Hjorth
  Bjørnstjerne Bjørnson **7**:100
  Georg Brandes **10**:60
  George Washington Cable **4**:23
  Alexander Kielland **5**:275
  Jonas Lie **5**:324
  Friedrich Nietzsche **10**:358
  Hermann Sudermann **15**:417

Boynton, H. W.
  Marie Belloc Lowndes **12**:202
  Don Marquis **7**:434

Boynton, Percy H.
  Sherwood Anderson **1**:38
  Ambrose Bierce **1**:84
  Lafcadio Hearn **9**:126
  Sinclair Lewis **4**:247
  O. E. Rölvaag **17**:323
  Booth Tarkington **9**:457

Brachfeld, Georges I.
  André Gide **5**:234

Bradbrook, M. C.
  Henrik Ibsen **2**:238

Bradbury, Malcolm
  Malcolm Lowry **6**:249
  Virginia Woolf **1**:546

Bradbury, Ray
  L. Frank Baum **7**:20
  Edgar Rice Burroughs **2**:86
  Henry Kuttner **10**:271

Bradley, F. H.
  William James **15**:153

Braeman, John
  Charles A. Beard **15**:36

Bragdon, Claude
  Kahlil Gibran **1**:326

Bragman, Louis J.
  Arthur Symons **11**:436

Braithwaite, William Stanley
  Countee Cullen **4**:44
  Claude McKay **7**:455
  Sara Teasdale **4**:424

Braley, Berton
  George Jean Nathan **18**:299

Branch, Douglas
  Zane Grey **6**:179

Brand, Alice Glarden
  Mary Wilkins Freeman **9**:77

Brande, Dorothea
  Ludwig Lewisohn **19**:269

Brandes, Georg
  Bjørnstjerne Bjørnson **7**:101
  Paul Heyse **8**:113
  Henrik Ibsen **2**:218; **16**:155
  Friedrich Nietzsche **10**:356
  Emile Verhaeren **12**:458

Brathwaite, Edward [Kamau]
  Roger Mais **8**:246

Bratsas, Dorothy
  Amado Nervo **11**:404

Braun, Lucille V.
  Miguel de Unamuno **2**:570

Braun, Wilhelm
  Robert Musil **12**:239

Brawley, Benjamin
  Countee Cullen **4**:41
  Paul Laurence Dunbar **12**:106
  Frances Ellen Watkins Harper
    14:256
  Claude McKay **7**:457

Braybrooke, Neville
  George Orwell **2**:498

Braybrooke, Patrick
  J. M. Barrie **2**:43
  Thomas Hardy **18**:94
  Sheila Kaye-Smith **20**:104
  Alfred Noyes **7**:513
  Katharine Tynan **3**:505
  Hugh Walpole **5**:497
  H. G. Wells **6**:531

Brazil, John
  Jack London **9**:280

Brecher, Edward M.
  Havelock Ellis **14**:129

Brecht, Bertolt
  Bernard Shaw **9**:418

Brée, Germaine
  Georges Bernanos **3**:119
  André Gide **5**:221; **12**:165
  Jean Giraudoux **2**:162
  Marcel Proust **7**:529
  Jules Renard **17**:306

Brégy, Katharine
  Ernest Dowson **4**:87
  Katharine Tynan **3**:503

Bremner, Robert
  Anthony Comstock **13**:95

Brenan, Gerald
  Juan Ramón Jiménez **4**:213

Brennan, Joseph Payne
  H. P. Lovecraft **4**:270

Brennan, Joseph X.
  Edith Wharton **3**:568

Brenner, Rica
  Alfred Noyes **7**:512

Bresky, Dushan
  Anatole France **9**:52

Bresnahan, Roger J.
  Booker T. Washington **10**:541

Breton, André
  Benjamin Péret **20**:181

Breunig, Leroy C.
  Guillaume Apollinaire **3**:42;
    8:16

Brewster, Dorothy
  Emma Goldman **13**:216
  Virginia Woolf **1**:531

Bridges, Robert
  Mark Twain **19**:352

Briggs, A.D.P.
  Leo Tolstoy **4**:482

Briggs, Julia
  Algernon Blackwood **5**:78
  M. R. James **6**:211
  Vernon Lee **5**:320

Brink, André
  George Orwell **15**:357

Brink, Louise
  Henrik Ibsen **16**:157

Brinnin, John Malcolm
  Gertrude Stein **1**:431
  Dylan Thomas **1**:473

Bristol, Evelyn
  Konstantin Dmitriyevich
    Balmont **11**:42
  Fyodor Sologub **9**:443

Britten, Florence Haxton
  Stephen Vincent Benét **7**:73
  Alfred Döblin **13**:158

Brittin, Norman A.
  Edna St. Vincent Millay **4**:318
  Stefan Zweig **17**:426

Broadus, Edmund Kemper
  Robert Bridges **1**:125

Brockway, James
  O. Henry **1**:352

Brod, Max
  Franz Kafka **2**:304

Brodie, A. H.
  John McCrae **12**:209

Brodin, Pierre
  Pierre Loti **11**:361

Brodsky, Joseph
  Velimir Khlebnikov **20**:152
  Andrei Platonov **14**:415

Brome, Vincent
  Havelock Ellis **14**:141

Bronner, Milton
  Lionel Johnson **19**:234

Bronowski, Jacob
  Pierre Teilhard de Chardin
    9:488
  A. E. Housman **10**:243

Brook, Stephen
  Radclyffe Hall **12**:197

Brooks, Cleanth
  Ivan Bunin **6**:47
  F. Scott Fitzgerald **6**:163
  O. Henry **19**:185
  A. E. Housman **1**:355; **10**:249
  Ring Lardner **14**:299
  William Butler Yeats **1**:571;
    11:517

Brooks, Van Wyck
  Ambrose Bierce **1**:89
  Randolph S. Bourne **16**:45
  Willa Cather **1**:160
  Kate Chopin **14**:58
  F. Marion Crawford **10**:152
  Havelock Ellis **14**:113
  Emma Goldman **13**:219
  Bret Harte **1**:342
  O. Henry **1**:350
  Henry James **11**:324
  Vernon Lee **5**:311
  Jack London **9**:262
  Amy Lowell **8**:231
  H. L. Mencken **13**:382
  Constance Rourke **12**:317
  Edgar Saltus **8**:351
  Gertrude Stein **1**:430
  Booth Tarkington **9**:462
  Mark Twain **6**:461; **19**:362

Brophy, Brigid
  Colette **1**:192
  Ronald Firbank **1**:229
  Thomas Hardy **10**:223
  David Lindsay **15**:218
  Francis Thompson **4**:441

Brosman, Catherine Savage
  Alain-Fournier **6**:22

Brotherston, Gordon
  Rubén Darío **4**:68

Broun, Heywood
  Ring Lardner **14**:295
  Damon Runyon **10**:422
  Booth Tarkington **9**:454

Brouta, Julius
  Jacinto Benavente **3**:93

Brower, Reuben Arthur
  Virginia Woolf **20**:399
  William Butler Yeats **18**:445

Brower, Robert H.
  Masaoka Shiki **18**:220

Brown, Alec
  Mikhail Zoshchenko **15**:497

Brown, Clarence
  Osip Mandelstam **2**:401; **6**:260,
    262

Brown, Daniel R.
  Sinclair Lewis **4**:261
  Nathanael West **1**:491

Brown, E. K.
  Bliss Carman **7**:144
  Willa Cather **11**:99
  Emile Nelligan **14**:390
  Duncan Campbell Scott **6**:389
  Thomas Wolfe **4**:514

Brown, Edward J.
Isaac Babel **13**:39
Velimir Khlebnikov **20**:141
Vladislav Khodasevich **15**:209
Vladimir Mayakovsky **18**:258
Andrei A. Zhdanov **18**:478
Mikhail Zoshchenko **15**:514

Brown, G. G.
Gabriel Miró **5**:339

Brown, Ivor
Lewis Grassic Gibbon **4**:122
Alfred Sutro **6**:422

Brown, J. F.
Aleister Crowley **7**:211

Brown, John L.
Valéry Larbaud **9**:205

Brown, John Mason
Philip Barry **11**:48
Anton Chekhov **10**:103
Ada Leverson **18**:191
Eugene O'Neill **1**:394
Bernard Shaw **9**:419
Robert E. Sherwood **3**:416
Josephine Tey **14**:449
John Van Druten **2**:573, 575
Alexander Woollcott **5**:525

Brown, Leonard
Harriet Monroe **12**:219

Brown, Malcolm
George Moore **7**:486

Brown, Morrison
Louis Bromfield **11**:81

Brown, Sterling
Charles Waddell Chesnutt **5**:132
Paul Laurence Dunbar **12**:109, 110
Rudolph Fisher **11**:205
James Weldon Johnson **3**:241
Wallace Thurman **6**:447

Brown, Stuart Gerry
John Jay Chapman **7**:192

Brownell, William Crary
George Meredith **17**:262

Brownstein, Michael
Max Jacob **6**:203

Broyde, Steven
Osip Mandelstam **6**:267

Bruckner, D.J.R.
Charles Williams **11**:502

Bruehl, Charles P.
Georges Bernanos **3**:117

Bruffee, Kenneth A.
Joseph Conrad **13**:122

Bruford, W. H.
Anton Chekhov **10**:107

Brushwood, John S.
Amado Nervo **11**:403
Horacio Quiroga **20**:222
José Rubén Romero **14**:443

Brustein, Robert
Antonin Artaud **3**:50
Bertolt Brecht **1**:111
Henrik Ibsen **8**:149
Eugene O'Neill **1**:400
Luigi Pirandello **4**:345

Bernard Shaw **3:404
August Strindberg **1**:451

Bryant, Joseph G.
Paul Laurence Dunbar **12**:104

Bryusov, Valery
Konstantin Dmitriyevich
Balmont **11**:29

Buber, Martin
Franz Kafka **2**:295

Bucco, Martin
Robert W. Service **15**:403

Buchan, A. M.
Sarah Orne Jewett **1**:363

Buchan, John
T. E. Lawrence **18**:131

Buchanan, Robert
Rudyard Kipling **8**:178
Algernon Charles Swinburne **8**:423

Buck, Philo M., Jr.
Henrik Ibsen **2**:224
Jack London **9**:254
Eugene O'Neill **1**:388
Emile Zola **1**:588

Buckley, J. M.
Anthony Comstock **13**:87

Buckley, Jerome Hamilton
William Ernest Henley **8**:104

Buckley, Vincent
Henry Handel Richardson **4**:377

Budd, Louis J.
William Dean Howells **7**:380
Mark Twain **6**:473
Thomas Wolfe **4**:525

Büdel, Oscar
Luigi Pirandello **4**:351

Budyonny, Semyon
Isaac Babel **13**:14

Bufkin, E. C.
F. Scott Fitzgerald **14**:163

Bump, Jerome
D. H. Lawrence **9**:229

Bunche, Ralph J.
Walter White **15**:481

Bunin, Ivan
Ivan Bunin **6**:44
Aleksandr Kuprin **5**:298
Alexey Nikolayevich Tolstoy **18**:364

Buning, M.
T. F. Powys **9**:375

Burbank, Rex
Sherwood Anderson **1**:55

Burch, Charles Eaton
Paul Laurence Dunbar **12**:105

Burdett, Osbert
John Gray **19**:142
Alice Meynell **6**:300

Burgess, Anthony
C. P. Cavafy **7**:162
John Galsworthy **1**:305
James Joyce **8**:164

Burgess, C. F.
Joseph Conrad **13**:121

Burgin, Diana L.
Mikhail Bulgakov **16**:91

Burke, Kenneth
Rémy de Gourmont **17**:151
Gertrude Stein **1**:425

Burkhard, Arthur
Stefan George **14**:194

Burkhart, Charles
Ada Leverson **18**:198, 200
George Moore **7**:493

Burlyuk, David
Velimir Khlebnikov **20**:123

Burnam, Tom
F. Scott Fitzgerald **14**:153

Burne, Glenn S.
Rémy de Gourmont **17**:157

Burnshaw, Stanley
Rainer Maria Rilke **1**:418

Burpee, Lawrence J.
Wilfred Campbell **9**:29

Burroughs, John
Charles G. D. Roberts **8**:315

Büscher, Gustav
Friedrich Nietzsche **10**:368

Bush, Douglas
Robert Bridges **1**:130

Bush, William
Georges Bernanos **3**:127

Butcher, Philip
George Washington Cable **4**:29

Butler, E. M.
Rainer Maria Rilke **6**:360; **19**:303
Carl Spitteler **12**:342

Butler, John Davis
Jean Moréas **18**:285

Butor, Michel
Guillaume Apollinaire **3**:37

Buttel, Robert
Wallace Stevens **12**:384
William Butler Yeats **18**:463

Butter, Peter H.
Edwin Muir **2**:486
Francis Thompson **4**:439

Buttry, Dolores
Knut Hamsun **14**:248

Butts, Mary
M. R. James **6**:206

Buxton, Richard
Jean Moréas **18**:280

Byalik, Boris
Maxim Gorky **8**:87

Bynner, Witter
Robert W. Service **15**:399

Byrne, J. Patrick
A. E. **10**:17

Byrne, Madge E. Coleman
Rémy de Gourmont **17**:154

Byrns, Richard
Innokenty Annensky **14**:31

Cabell, James Branch
James Branch Cabell **6**:61
Theodore Dreiser **10**:173
Ellen Glasgow **7**:337
Joseph Hergesheimer **11**:265
Sinclair Lewis **13**:335
H. L. Mencken **13**:376
Booth Tarkington **9**:454
Elinor Wylie **8**:523

Cady, Edwin H.
Stephen Crane **11**:163
William Dean Howells **7**:381; **17**:165, 235

Cahan, Abraham
Sholem Asch **3**:65
Anton Chekhov **10**:100

Cahill, Daniel J.
Harriet Monroe **12**:224

Cairns, Christopher
Ugo Betti **5**:66

Calder, Jenni
George Orwell **2**:509

Calder-Marshall, Arthur
Louis Bromfield **11**:79
Wyndham Lewis **2**:384
Montague Summers **16**:434

Caldwell, Erskine
Louis Bromfield **11**:77

Caldwell, Helen
Machado de Assis **10**:297

Calisher, Hortense
Henry James **2**:274

Calista, Donald J.
Booker T. Washington **10**:528

Callan, Richard J.
Machado de Assis **10**:289

Calvin, Judith S.
Jean Giraudoux **7**:321

Cambon, Glauco
Hart Crane **2**:121
Gabriele D'Annunzio **6**:139

Camino, Berta Gamboa de
José Rubén Romero **14**:432

Cammell, Charles Richard
Aleister Crowley **7**:205
Montague Summers **16**:429

Campana, Dino
Dino Campana **20**:82

Campbell, Ian
Lewis Grassic Gibbon **4**:129, 130

Campbell, Joseph
James Joyce **3**:261

Campbell, Roy
Federico García Lorca **1**:311

Campbell, T. M.
Gerhart Hauptmann **4**:198

Camus, Albert
Franz Kafka **2**:297
Friedrich Nietzsche **10**:375

Canaday, Nicholas
James Weldon Johnson **19**:223

Canario, John W.
Joseph Conrad **13**:124

Canby, Henry Seidel
Gertrude Atherton 2:15
Stephen Vincent Benét 7:71
F. Scott Fitzgerald 1:235
Joseph Hergesheimer 11:267
T. E. Lawrence 18:139
John Millington Synge 6:430
Mark Twain 6:470

Cancalon, Elaine D.
Alain-Fournier 6:24

Canetti, Elias
Isaac Babel 13:35
Franz Kafka 6:222

Cantor, Jay
William Butler Yeats 11:539

Cantwell, Robert
Kate Chopin 5:147

Capetanakis, Demetrios
Stefan George 2:148

Cappon, James
Bliss Carman 7:141

Carden, Patricia
Isaak Babel 2:23, 25

Cardinal, Roger
Benjamin Péret 20:203

Carens, James F.
Oliver St. John Gogarty
15:113, 115

Cargill, Oscar
Sherwood Anderson 1:41
Sholem Asch 3:68
James Branch Cabell 6:69
Havelock Ellis 14:122
F. Scott Fitzgerald 1:239
Henry James 2:269
Ludwig Lewisohn 19:277
George Moore 7:483
Eugene O'Neill 1:387
Bernard Shaw 3:388
Lincoln Steffens 20:341
Gertrude Stein 1:427
August Strindberg 1:445
Sara Teasdale 4:428
Emile Zola 1:589

Carlsson, P. Allan
William James 15:180

Carlyle, Thomas
John Ruskin 20:265

Carman, Bliss
Charles G. D. Roberts 8:314

Carmer, Carl
Philip Barry 11:47

Carner, Mosco
Guiseppe Giacosa 7:313

Caron, James E.
Mark Twain 12:449

Carpenter, Humphrey
Charles Williams 11:497

Carpenter, Margaret Haley
Sara Teasdale 4:429

Carpenter, Richard
Thomas Hardy 18:99

Carpenter, William H.
Alexander Kielland 5:277

Carr, John Dickson
Raymond Chandler 1:169

Carr, W. I.
T. F. Powys 9:373

Carrington, C. E.
Rudyard Kipling 8:195

Carroll, Lewis
George MacDonald 9:287

Carruth, Hayden
Edwin Muir 2:484
William Butler Yeats 1:575

Carter, Angela
Géza Csáth 13:152

Carter, Eunice Hunton
Wallace Thurman 6:446

Carter, Lawson A.
Emile Zola 6:567

Carter, Lin
E. R. Eddison 15:57
William Hope Hodgson 13:233, 234
Henry Kuttner 10:271

Carus, Paul
Friedrich Nietzsche 10:363

Cary, Lucian
Joseph Hergesheimer 11:260

Cary, Richard
Sarah Orne Jewett 1:365
Vernon Lee 5:313

Casey, John
John Middleton Murry 16:347

Casey, T. J.
Georg Trakl 5:460

Cass, Colin S.
F. Scott Fitzgerald 14:186

Cassavant, Sharron Greer
John Middleton Murry 16:353

Cassidy, John A.
Algernon Charles Swinburne
8:438

Cassirer, Sidonie
Hermann Broch 20:54

Cassity, Turner
James Agee 1:12

Castagnaro, R. Anthony
José Rubén Romero 14:433

Cate, Hollis
Stephen Crane 17:75

Cather, Willa
Kate Chopin 5:142
Stephen Crane 11:134
Sarah Orne Jewett 1:361
Thomas Mann 2:417
Katherine Mansfield 2:450

Cavaliero, Glen
Sheila Kaye-Smith 20:113
T. F. Powys 9:375
Charles Williams 11:499

Caws, Mary Ann
Paul Eluard 7:255
Benjamin Péret 20:182, 185

Cecchetti, Giovanni
Giovanni Verga 3:546

Cecil, David
Max Beerbohm 1:71
Walter de la Mare 4:80
W. S. Gilbert 3:213
Virginia Woolf 5:508

Cerf, Bennett
O. Henry 1:350

Cevasco, G. A.
John Gray 19:160
Joris-Karl Huysmans 7:416

Chakravarty, Amiya
Thomas Hardy 4:163

Chamberlain, John
Charles Waddell Chesnutt
5:131
Claude McKay 7:456
Tess Slesinger 10:439
Thomas Wolfe 4:506

Chambers, Edmund K.
Lionel Johnson 19:227
Alice Meynell 6:293

Chambers, Jessie
D. H. Lawrence 16:286

Chambers, Ross
Raymond Roussel 20:244

Champigny, Robert
Alain-Fournier 6:14

Chandler, Frank W.
José Echegaray 4:102
Guiseppe Giacosa 7:312
Ferenc Molnár 20:158

Chandler, Raymond
Raymond Chandler 7:167, 168
A. A. Milne 6:311
Dorothy L. Sayers 15:375

Chapman, C. A.
Jaroslav Hasek 4:181

Chapman, Edward M.
Sarah Orne Jewett 1:360

Chapman, Esther
H. G. de Lisser 12:95

Chapman, John Jay
G. K. Chesterton 1:177

Chapman, Raymond
Samuel Butler 1:138

Chapman, Robert T.
Wyndham Lewis 9:241

Charlesworth, Barbara
Lionel Johnson 19:246

Chase, Richard
George Washington Cable 4:27
F. Scott Fitzgerald 14:162

Chatterton, Wayne
Alexander Woollcott 5:526

Chattopadhyay, Saratchandra
Saratchandra Chatterji 13:73

Chaudhuri, Nirad C.
Rudyard Kipling 8:197

Chauvin, R.
Emile Nelligan 14:391

Chekhov, Anton Pavlovich
See also **Tchekhov, Anton**
Leo Tolstoy 4:449

Chernyshevsky, N. G.
Leo Tolstoy 4:444

Chesnutt, Charles W.
Booker T. Washington 10:515

Chesterton, Cecil
Hilaire Belloc 7:31

Chesterton, G. K.
Maurice Baring 8:37
Hilaire Belloc 7:37; 18:23
Paul Claudel 10:124
Aleister Crowley 7:203, 204
Walter de la Mare 4:75
Arthur Conan Doyle 7:217
Theodore Dreiser 10:173
Anatole France 9:45
R. B. Cunninghame Graham
19:112
Bret Harte 1:339
William Ernest Henley 8:100
Henrik Ibsen 2:221
Rudyard Kipling 8:181
Andrew Lang 16:256
Vachel Lindsay 17:232
George MacDonald 9:289
H. L. Mencken 13:372
George Meredith 17:263
Alice Meynell 6:295
George Moore 7:475
John Middleton Murry 16:335
Bernard Shaw 3:380; 9:413
Francis Thompson 4:439
Leo Tolstoy 4:452
Mark Twain 12:428
H. G. Wells 6:524; 12:503;
19:422

Chevalier, Haakon M.
Marcel Proust 13:410

Chevalley, Abel
May Sinclair 3:439

Chiappelli, Fred
Dino Campana 20:86

Chiari, Joseph
Paul Claudel 2:103
Paul Eluard 7:250
Edmond Rostand 6:380

Chiaromonte, Nicola
Luigi Pirandello 4:353

Childs, Herbert Ellsworth
Edgar Lee Masters 2:466

Chisolm, A. R.
Christopher John Brennan
17:44, 50

Chisolm, Lawrence W.
Lu Hsün 3:298

Christ, Carol P.
Kate Chopin 14:77

Christgau, Robert
George Orwell 15:342

Christian, R. F.
Leo Tolstoy 4:470; 11:474

Chukovsky, Korney
Vladimir Mayakovsky 4:288

Church, Dan M.
Alfred Jarry 2:281

Church, Richard
Maurice Baring 8:36
Laurence Housman 7:357

Churchill, Kenneth
F. Marion Crawford 10:157
Frederick Rolfe 12:283

Chyet, Stanley F.
Ludwig Lewisohn 19:288

Ciancio, Ralph
Sherwood Anderson 1:64

Ciardi, John
Roy Campbell 5:122
Edna St. Vincent Millay 4:316

Ciecierska, Joanna
T. F. Powys 9:377

Ciholas, Karin Nordenhaug
André Gide 5:241

Cioran, E. M.
Leo Tolstoy 11:471
Paul Valéry 4:500

Cioran, Samuel D.
Andrey Bely 7:57

Ciruti, Joan E.
Leopoldo Lugones 15:292

Cismaru, Alfred
Boris Vian 9:533

Clark, Axel
Christopher John Brennan
17:58

Clark, Barrett H.
Maxwell Anderson 2:1
Booth Tarkington 9:461

Clark, David Ridgley
Oliver St. John Gogarty 15:111

Clark, Earl John
James Joyce 3:278

Clark, Emily
Joseph Hergesheimer 11:273

Clark, Sir Kenneth
John Ruskin 20:284

Clark, Tom
Damon Runyon 10:434

Clarke, Arthur C.
Jules Verne 6:492

Clarke, H. A.
Charlotte Gilman 9:98

Clarke, Helen A.
Bliss Carman 7:134

Claudel, Paul
Paul Claudel 10:120

Cleman, John
George Washington Cable 4:36

Clemens, S. L.
See also **Twain, Mark**
Mark Twain 6:454; 12:426

Clements, Clyde C., Jr.
Thomas Wolfe 4:533

Clever, Glenn
Duncan Campbell Scott 6:398,
400

Closs, August
Stefan George 2:149
Christian Morgenstern 8:305

Clurman, Harold
Bertolt Brecht 1:108, 109, 115,
122; 13:51
Henrik Ibsen 8:152
Eugene O'Neill 1:395

Cobb, Carl W.
Antonio Machado 3:311

Coblentz, Stanton A.
Sinclair Lewis 4:246

Cock, Albert A.
Francis Thompson 4:436

Cocking, J. M.
Marcel Proust 13:427

Cockshut, A.O.J.
Havelock Ellis 14:138
Radclyffe Hall 12:196
Thomas Hardy 10:229
Algernon Charles Swinburne
8:442

Cocteau, Jean
Colette 5:163
Raymond Roussel 20:225
Paul Valéry 4:493

Coffin, Robert P. Tristram
Pedro Salinas 17:353

Coffman, Stanley K., Jr.
Hart Crane 5:187

Cogswell, Fred
Duncan Campbell Scott 6:399

Cohen, Arthur A.
Osip Mandelstam 2:406

Cohen, J. M.
Georg Trakl 5:460

Cohen, Joseph
Isaac Rosenberg 12:295

Cohen, M. A.
Bertolt Brecht 13:60

Cohen, Morton
H. Rider Haggard 11:243

Cohen, Robert
Jean Giraudoux 2:167

Cohn, Ruby
Bertolt Brecht 1:116; 13:59

Colbron, Grace Isabel
Algernon Blackwood 5:70

Colby, Elbridge
F. Marion Crawford 10:147

Colby, Frank Moore
Gabriele D'Annunzio 6:130
Rudyard Kipling 8:180

Colby, Vineta
Vernon Lee 5:316

Colcord, Lincoln
O. E. Rölvaag 17:321

Cole, Leo R.
Juan Ramón Jiménez 4:220

Coleman, Charles W.
Lafcadio Hearn 9:118

Coleman, John D.
Liu E 15:248

Collier, Eugenia W.
James Weldon Johnson 3:242

Collier, S. J.
Max Jacob 6:191

Collignon, Jean
André Gide 12:151

Collin, W. E.
Hector Saint-Denys Garneau
13:196

Collingwood, R. G.
John Ruskin 20:273

Collins, Christopher
Yevgeny Ivanovich Zamyatin
8:557

Collins, Harold R.
Joseph Conrad 13:104

Collins, Joseph
Stella Benson 17:20
Edna St. Vincent Millay 4:309
Booth Tarkington 9:459

Collins, Thomas Lyle
Thomas Wolfe 13:472

Collis, John Stewart
Havelock Ellis 14:124
John Middleton Murry 16:357

Colombo, J. R.
Malcolm Lowry 6:237

Colum, Mary M.
Havelock Ellis 14:119
Paul Valéry 15:446

Colum, Padraic
A. E. 3:6; 10:13
Lord Dunsany 2:142
Kahlil Gibran 1:328
Lady Gregory 1:333
Edna St. Vincent Millay 4:306
George Moore 7:478
James Stephens 4:414

Colvert, James B.
Stephen Crane 11:146

Combs, Robert
Hart Crane 2:125

Comeau, Paul
Willa Cather 11:113

Comerchero, Victor
Nathanael West 1:482

Commager, Henry Steele
Henry Adams 4:6
Charles A. Beard 15:30
Stephen Vincent Benét 7:75
Willa Cather 1:155
F. Scott Fitzgerald 1:245
O. E. Rölvaag 17:322
Carl Van Doren 18:407, 408

Comstock, Anthony
Anthony Comstock 13:88

Connell, Allison
Valéry Larbaud 9:204

Connolly, Cyril
Stella Benson 17:23
Nordahl Grieg 10:205
A. E. Housman 1:354
James Joyce 3:276
D. H. Lawrence 2:369
Thomas Mann 14:326
Gertrude Stein 1:434
Thomas Wolfe 13:481

Connolly, Francis X.
Willa Cather 1:156

Connolly, Julian W.
Ivan Bunin 6:58

Connolly, Thomas E.
James Joyce 16:214

Conquest, Robert
Charles Williams 11:490

Conrad, Joseph
Joseph Conrad 6:112
Stephen Crane 11:132
Ford Madox Ford 15:67
Anatole France 9:43
R. B. Cunninghame Graham
19:101
Henry James 2:245
H. L. Mencken 13:365
Marcel Proust 7:520
Hugh Walpole 5:495
H. G Wells 6:523

Constable, W. G.
Wyndham Lewis 9:234

Cook, Bruce
Bertolt Brecht 13:67
Raymond Chandler 1:175

Cook, Mercer
Jacques Roumain 19:331

Cooke, Alistair
H. L. Mencken 13:392
Will Rogers 8:334

Cooke, Judy
May Sinclair 11:421

Cooke, Michael G.
H. G. de Lisser 12:98

Cooley, John R.
Stephen Crane 17:76

Coombes, H.
T. F. Powys 9:371
Edward Thomas 10:458

Cooper, Frederic Taber
See also **Winter, Calvin**
Gertrude Atherton 2:13
Arnold Bennett 5:23
Willa Cather 11:92
F. Marion Crawford 10:146
Theodore Dreiser 10:164
Anatole France 9:41
Zona Gale 7:277
Ellen Glasgow 2:175; 7:332
Zane Grey 6:176
Knut Hamsun 14:220
Jack London 9:253
Marie Belloc Lowndes 12:201,
202
May Sinclair 11:408

Cope, Jackson I.
James Joyce 8:169

Corbett, Edward P. J.
Margaret Mitchell 11:375

Cord, William O.
José Rubén Romero 14:437,
438

Cordle, Thomas
André Gide 5:222

Corke, Hilary
Charlotte Mew 8:298

Corkery, Daniel
John Millington Synge 6:432

Corn, Alfred
Andrey Bely 7:66
Wallace Stevens 12:385

Cornford, Frances
Rupert Brooke 7:123

Correa, Gustavo
Federico García Lorca 7:294

Critic Index

Corrigan, Matthew
Malcolm Lowry 6:244

Corrigan, Robert W.
Bertolt Brecht 1:119
Federico García Lorca 1:324
Henrik Ibsen 2:239
Gregorio Martínez Sierra and
María Martínez Sierra 6:284

Corrin, Jay P.
Hilaire Belloc 18:36

Cortissoz, Royal
Hamlin Garland 3:190

Cosman, Max
Joyce Cary 1:141

Costa, Richard Haver
Malcolm Lowry 6:246

Costello, Peter
Jules Verne 6:499

Costich, Julia Field
Antonin Artaud 3:62
Benjamin Péret 20:198

Cournos, John
Fyodor Sologub 9:434
Mikhail Zoshchenko 15:491

Coustillas, Pierre
George Gissing 3:236

Coward, Noël
Saki 3:373

Cowley, Malcolm
Sherwood Anderson 1:51
Guillaume Apollinaire 3:33
Henri Barbusse 5:13
A. E. Coppard 5:176
Hart Crane 2:117
Theodore Dreiser 10:179
F. Scott Fitzgerald 1:238, 272;
6:166; 14:155
Lafcadio Hearn 9:130
Sheila Kaye-Smith 20:96
Amy Lowell 1:371, 378
Katherine Mansfield 2:445
H. L. Mencken 13:380
Margaret Mitchell 11:372
Arthur Schnitzler 4:392
Carl Van Doren 18:408
H. G. Wells 12:502
Thomas Wolfe 13:467
Virginia Woolf 1:533

Cox, C. B.
Joseph Conrad 1:218

Cox, James M.
Mark Twain 19:369
Booker T. Washington 10:538

Cox, James Trammell
Ford Madox Ford 1:286

Cox, Oliver C.
Booker T. Washington 10:526

Coxe, Louis O.
Edith Wharton 3:567

Coxhead, Elizabeth
Lady Gregory 1:335

Craig, Cairns
William Butler Yeats 18:461

Craig, G. Dundas
Rubén Darío 4:63
Amado Nervo 11:395

Craig, Gordon
George Jean Nathan 18:294

Craige, Betty Jean
Federico García Lorca 7:297

Cramer, Carter M.
Nathanael West 14:477

Crane, Hart
Sherwood Anderson 10:32
Hart Crane 5:184

Crane, Stephen
Stephen Crane 11:123

Crankshaw, Edward
Jakob Wassermann 6:511

Crawford, F. Marion
F. Marion Crawford 10:141

Crawford, John
Will Rogers 8:332

Crawford, John W.
Emile Verhaeren 12:472

Crawford, Virginia M.
Joris-Karl Huysmans 7:407
Edmond Rostand 6:373

Creary, Jean
Roger Mais 8:241

Creelman, James
Booker T. Washington 10:514

Creese, Robb
Rudolf Steiner 13:456

Crews, Frederick C.
Joseph Conrad 1:216
Henry James 11:332

Crick, Bernard
George Orwell 15:321

Crispin, Edmund
C. M. Kornbluth 8:217

Crispin, John
Pedro Salinas 17:363

Crites
See also **Eliot, T. S.**
Bernard Shaw 9:417

Croce, Arlene
Eugene O'Neill 1:404

Croce, Benedetto
Emile Zola 1:588

Cross, Richard K.
Malcolm Lowry 6:253

Cross, Wilbur
Arnold Bennett 5:33
John Galsworthy 1:297

Crowley, Aleister
James Branch Cabell 6:65
Aleister Crowley 7:205, 208

Cruse, Harold
James Weldon Johnson 3:246
Booker T. Washington 10:531

Cuénot, Claude
Pierre Teilhard de Chardin
9:481

Cukierman, Walenty
Andrei Platonov 14:425

Cullen, Countee
James Weldon Johnson 3:240

Cunliffe, J. W.
Jean Moréas 18:284

Cunliffe, John W.
A. E. Housman 1:354

Cunningham, J. V.
Wallace Stevens 3:454

Cuppy, Will
Raymond Chandler 7:167
Ricarda Huch 13:243
Marie Belloc Lowndes 12:203
Dorothy L. Sayers 15:370

Current-Garcia, Eugene
O. Henry 19:193

Currey, R. N.
Alun Lewis 3:289

Curry, Steven S.
André Gide 12:180

Curti, Merle
Booker T. Washington 10:523

Curtis, Penelope
Anton Chekhov 3:170

Curtius, Ernst Robert
José Ortega y Gasset 9:339

Cushing, G. F.
Mihály Babits 14:41

Cushman, Keith
Ernest Dowson 4:93

Dabney, Virginius
Douglas Southall Freeman
11:224
Ellen Glasgow 7:337

Daemmrich, Horst S.
Thomas Mann 2:441

Dahlberg, Edward
Sherwood Anderson 1:56
F. Scott Fitzgerald 1:256

Dahlie, Hallvard
Nordahl Grieg 10:211

Daiches, David
Willa Cather 1:157
Joseph Conrad 1:211
A. E. Housman 1:355
James Joyce 3:258
Katherine Mansfield 2:449
Wilfred Owen 5:362
Isaac Rosenberg 12:291
Dylan Thomas 1:469
Virginia Woolf 1:539; 20:408
William Butler Yeats 1:558

Dale, Alzina Stone
Dorothy L. Sayers 15:384

Daleski, H. M.
Joseph Conrad 1:220
Thomas Hardy 18:116

Dalphin, Marcia
A. A. Milne 6:309

Damon, S. Foster
Amy Lowell 1:374

Dane, Clemence
Hugh Walpole 5:497

Daniel, John
Henri Barbusse 5:16

Daniels, Jonathan
Marjorie Kinnan Rawlings
4:359

Danielson, Larry W.
Selma Lagerlöf 4:242

Danto, Arthur C.
Friedrich Nietzsche 10:382

Darío, Rubén
F. T. Marinetti 10:310

Darrow, Clarence
Theodore Dreiser 10:171
Walter White 15:476

Darton, F. J. Harvey
Arnold Bennett 5:25

Dash, J. Michael
Jacques Roumain 19:343

Dathorne, Oscar R.
Roger Mais 8:244

Daumal, René
René Daumal 14:87

Dauner, Louise
Joel Chandler Harris 2:212

Davenport, Basil
Lewis Grassic Gibbon 4:120,
121

Daviau, Donald G.
Hugo von Hofmannsthal 11:307
Karl Kraus 5:282
Stefan Zweig 17:440

Davidow, Mary C.
Charlotte Mew 8:299

Davidson, Donald
Louis Bromfield 11:76
Joseph Conrad 6:114
Harriet Monroe 12:218

Davie, Donald
D. H. Lawrence 2:373
Wallace Stevens 3:449

Davies, A. Emil
Laurence Housman 7:354

Davies, Barrie
Wilfred Campbell 9:33

Davies, J. C.
André Gide 5:237

Davies, John
Alun Lewis 3:289

Davies, Laurence
R. B. Cunninghame Graham
19:131

Davies, Margaret
Colette 5:165

Davies, Norman
Isaac Babel 13:28

Davies, Robertson
Stephen Leacock 2:381

Davies, Ruth
Leonid Andreyev 3:27
Anton Chekhov 3:168

Davis, Arthur P.
Countee Cullen 4:44
Rudolph Fisher 11:207
Wallace Thurman 6:450

Davis, Beatrice
Miles Franklin 7:267

Davis, Cynthia
Dylan Thomas 1:475

Davis, Dick
Miklós Radnóti 16:416

Davis, Dorothy Salisbury
Josephine Tey **14**:453

Davis, Elmer
Anthony Comstock **13**:94

Davis, Richard Harding
Stephen Crane **11**:124

Davis, Robert Bernard
A. E. **10**:20

Davis, Robert Murray
F. Scott Fitzgerald **6**:167
Katherine Mansfield **8**:282

Davis, Oswald H.
Arnold Bennett **5**:45

Davison, Edward
A. E. **10**:16
Robert Bridges **1**:125
Walter de la Mare **4**:74
Alfred Noyes **7**:507
Saki **3**:365

Day, A. Grove
Vicente Blasco Ibáñez **12**:48

Day, Douglas
Malcolm Lowry **6**:241, 247

Day Lewis, C.
See also **Blake, Nicholas**
Wilfred Owen **5**:368
Dylan Thomas **8**:450
Edward Thomas **10**:456

D'Costa, Jean
Roger Mais **8**:247

Dean, James L.
William Dean Howells **7**:394

De Bacourt, Pierre
Jean Moréas **18**:284

Debicki, Andrew P.
César Vallejo **3**:530

De Bosschere, Jean
May Sinclair **3**:437

De Camp, L. Sprague
E. R. Eddison **15**:58
Robert E. Howard **8**:130

De Casseres, Benjamin
Pierre Loti **11**:356
Arthur Symons **11**:430

De Castris, A. L.
Luigi Pirandello **4**:342

Decavalles, A.
C. P. Cavafy **7**:162

Decker, Donald M.
Machado de Assis **10**:290

DeCoster, Cyrus
Juan Valera **10**:507

De Feo, Ronald
Robert Walser **18**:431

De Fornaro, Sofia
Giuseppe Giacosa **7**:305

Degler, Carl N.
Charlotte Gilman **9**:103

Dehon, Claire L.
Emile Verhaeren **12**:479

DeKoven, Marianne
Gertrude Stein **6**:415

De la Mare, Walter
Rupert Brooke **2**:53
Edward Thomas **10**:451

Delany, Paul
Katherine Mansfield **8**:286

De la Selva, Salomón
Rubén Darío **4**:55

Del Caro, Andrea
Stefan Zweig **17**:448

Deleuze, Gilles
Friedrich Nietzsche **18**:349

Dell, Floyd
Randolph S. Bourne **16**:43
Charlotte Gilman **9**:100
Emma Goldman **13**:209
Olive Schreiner **9**:395
Lincoln Steffens **20**:339
Carl Van Doren **18**:394

De Loss, John
Anthony Comstock **13**:97

De Muth, James
Ring Lardner **14**:314

Dennis, Scott A.
William Dean Howells **7**:397

De Onis, Federico
Pío Baroja **8**:47

De Ónis, Harriet
Mariano Azuela **3**:80

Derleth, August
Zona Gale **7**:282
H. P. Lovecraft **4**:266

De Selincourt, E.
Robert Bridges **1**:129

Desmond, John
Walter White **15**:479

Desmond, Shaw
Lord Dunsany **2**:143

Des Pres, Terrence
Bertolt Brecht **6**:38

Deutsch, Babette
Stephen Vincent Benét **7**:69
A. E. Coppard **5**:177
Hart Crane **5**:186
Countee Cullen **4**:40
Oliver St. John Gogarty **15**:100
Charlotte Mew **8**:299
Edna St. Vincent Millay **4**:311
Christian Morgenstern **8**:304
Wilfred Owen **5**:365
Rainer Maria Rilke **19**:300
Edwin Arlington Robinson **5**:413
Sara Teasdale **4**:426, 427

Deutsch, Leonard J.
Rudolph Fisher **11**:211

Deutscher, Isaac
George Orwell **2**:500

Devlin, John
Arturo Barea **14**:51
Vicente Blasco Ibáñez **12**:45

DeVoto, Bernard
Havelock Ellis **14**:120
Douglas Southall Freeman **11**:221
Don Marquis **7**:440
Margaret Mitchell **11**:374
Eugene O'Neill **6**:328
Mark Twain **6**:465; **19**:358
Carl Van Doren **18**:398

Thomas Wolfe **4**:509; **13**:470

Dewey, John
William James **15**:162

Dick, Kay
Colette **1**:192; **16**:137

Dick, Susan
George Moore **7**:495

Dickey, James
Stephen Crane **11**:159; **17**:82
Vachel Lindsay **17**:245
Jack London **15**:265
Edwin Arlington Robinson **5**:414

Dickinson, Patric
Charlotte Mew **8**:297

Dickinson, Peter
Dorothy L. Sayers **15**:377

Dickman, Adolphe-Jacques
André Gide **5**:213

Dickson, Lovat
Radclyffe Hall **12**:194

Didier, Pierre
Georges Bernanos **3**:117

Diggory, Terence
Vachel Lindsay **17**:247

Dilla, Geraldine P.
Emile Verhaeren **12**:470

Dillon, E. J.
Maxim Gorky **8**:69

Dillon, George
Oliver St. John Gogarty **15**:106

Dilworth, David A.
Mori Ōgai **14**:377

Dimnet, Ernest
T. F. Powys **9**:363

Dimock, Edward C., Jr.
Rabindranath Tagore **3**:493

Disch, Thomas M.
Rose Macaulay **7**:432

D'Itri, Patricia Ward
Damon Runyon **10**:435

Dixon, Melvin
Jacques Roumain **19**:337

Dobie, Ann B.
Gerhart Hauptmann **4**:207

Dobrée, Bonamy
Rudyard Kipling **8**:204
D. H. Lawrence **2**:345
John Middleton Murry **16**:334

Dobson, A.
Miguel de Unamuno **2**:569

Dobzhansky, Theodosius
Pierre Teilhard de Chardin **9**:489

Doggett, Frank
Wallace Stevens **3**:469; **12**:384

Dombroski, Robert
Vitaliano Brancati **12**:83, 90

Donceel, Joseph F., S.J.
Pierre Teilhard de Chardin **9**:487

Donchin, Georgette
Valery Bryusov **10**:81
Maxim Gorky **8**:92

Donnelly, John
Leo Tolstoy **11**:476

Donnelly, Mabel Collins
George Gissing **3**:233

Donoghue, Denis
Malcolm Lowry **6**:239
George MacDonald **9**:301
Eugene O'Neill **1**:404
Dorothy L. Sayers **2**:533
Wallace Stevens **3**:473
William Butler Yeats **1**:580

Dorofeyev, Victor
Andrei Platonov **14**:412

Dorosz, Kristofer
Malcolm Lowry **6**:251

Dos Passos, John
Pío Baroja **8**:48
Jacinto Benavente **3**:96
Vicente Blasco Ibáñez **12**:36
F. Scott Fitzgerald **1**:240
Miguel de Unamuno **9**:512

Dostoievsky, F. M.
Leo Tolstoy **4**:447

Doud, Robert E.
Pierre Teilhard de Chardin **9**:505

Douglas, Alfred
Oscar Wilde **8**:491, 495

Douglas, D. B.
Stefan Zweig **17**:446

Douglas, Frances
Gregorio Martinez Sierra and Maria Martinez Sierra **6**:276
Gabriel Miró **5**:337

Douglas, William O.
Carl Van Doren **18**:410

Dowling, Linda C.
John Gray **19**:151

Downer, Alan S.
Harley Granville-Barker **2**:195
Eugene O'Neill **1**:393

Downey, Fairfax
Rebecca Harding Davis **6**:150

Downs, Brian W.
Bjørnstjerne Bjørnson **7**:115
Henrik Ibsen **8**:146; **16**:167
August Strindberg **8**:408

Doyle, Arthur Conan
Rudyard Kipling **8**:182

Doyle, Peter
Mikhail Bulgakov **16**:100

Drake, Robert
Saki **3**:367, 368

Drake, Robert Y., Jr.
Margaret Mitchell **11**:376

Drake, William A.
Karel Čapek **6**:38
Ricarda Huch **13**:243
Georg Kaiser **9**:172
Detlev von Liliencron **18**:212
Charles Péguy **10**:404
Carl Sternheim **8**:368
Ramón del Valle-Inclán **5**:474
Jakob Wassermann **6**:509

Draper, Ronald P.
D. H. Lawrence **9**:222; **16**:293

Critic Index

Drayson, Pauline
Benjamin Péret **20**:203

Drayton, Arthur D.
Claude McKay **7**:463

Dreiser, Theodore
Sherwood Anderson **10**:41
Stephen Crane **11**:126
Theodore Dreiser **10**:173
Ford Madox Ford **15**:70
Ludwig Lewisohn **19**:265
H. L. Mencken **13**:365
George Jean Nathan **18**:314
George Sterling **20**:375
Mark Twain **12**:436

Drew, Elizabeth A.
Arnold Bennett **5**:31
Joseph Conrad **1**:212
James Joyce **3**:276
Sheila Kaye-Smith **20**:103
D. H. Lawrence **2**:368
Saki **3**:366

Drinkwater, John
Rupert Brooke **7**:121
William Ernest Henley **8**:101
Amy Lowell **8**:227
Alice Meynell **6**:298

Drinnon, Richard
Emma Goldman **13**:220

Driver, Tom F.
Eugene O'Neill **1**:397

DuBois, W. E. Burghardt
Rudolph Fisher **11**:204
Frances Ellen Watkins Harper **14**:256
Claude McKay **7**:455
Wallace Thurman **6**:446
Booker T. Washington **10**:520
Walter White **15**:473

Duchamp, Marcel
Raymond Roussel **20**:229

Ducharme, Edward
Elinor Wylie **8**:535

Duclaux, Mary
Charles Péguy **10**:403

Dudek, Louis
Emile Nelligan **14**:390

Dudley, W. E.
Jacques Futrelle **19**:95

Duffey, Bernard
Sherwood Anderson **1**:46

Duffin, Henry Charles
Walter de la Mare **4**:78

Duke, Maurice
James Branch Cabell **6**:78

Dukes, Ashley
Karel Capek **6**:81
Anton Chekhov **3**:147
Gerhart Hauptmann **4**:195
Hugo von Hofmannsthal **11**:291
Georg Kaiser **9**:172
A. A. Milne **6**:307
Dorothy L. Sayers **15**:372
Arthur Schnitzler **4**:390
Bernard Shaw **3**:381
Ernst Toller **10**:475
Leo Tolstoy **4**:453
Frank Wedekind **7**:575

Dukore, Bernard F.
Ernst Toller **10**:488
Stanisław Ignacy Witkiewicz **8**:512

Dunbar, Olivia Howard
Alice Meynell **6**:296

Dunham, Barrows
Lincoln Steffens **20**:347

Dunkle, Harvey I.
Stefan Zweig **17**:440

Dunleavy, Janet Egleston
George Moore **7**:497

Dupee, F. W.
Henry James **2**:274

Durant, Ariel
James Joyce **8**:167

Durant, Will
James Joyce **8**:167

Duranty, Walter
Mikhail Bulgakov **16**:73

Durbach, Errol
Henrik Ibsen **16**:194

Durkin, Mary Brian, O.P.
Dorothy L. Sayers **15**:387

Dusenbury, Winifred L.
Robert E. Sherwood **3**:414

Dussert, Pierre
Vachel Lindsay **17**:239

Dust, Patrick, H.
José Ortega y Gasset **9**:351

Duus, Louise
Rebecca Harding Davis **6**:155

Dyboski, Roman
Władysław Stanisław Reymont **5**:392
Henryk Sienkiewicz **3**:425

Dyrenforth, Harald O.
Georg Brandes **10**:67

Dyson, A. E.
F. Scott Fitzgerald **1**:252
Thomas Mann **14**:350
Mark Twain **19**:397
Oscar Wilde **1**:504
William Butler Yeats **18**:455

Eagle, Solomon
See also **Squire, J. C.**
Maurice Baring **8**:32
D. H. Lawrence **9**:212
F. T. Marinetti **10**:315

Eagleson, Harvey
Dorothy Richardson **3**:352

Eaker, J. Gordon
John Galsworthy **1**:300

Eakin, Paul John
Sarah Orne Jewett **1**:368

Eames, Ninetta
Jack London **9**:253

Early, L. R.
Charles G. D. Roberts **8**:327

Eastman, Max
Stephen Vincent Benét **7**:72
Oliver St. John Gogarty **15**:105
John Reed **9**:384
Yevgeny Ivanovich Zamyatin **8**:545

Eaton, G. D.
Pío Baroja **8**:50

Eaton, Walter Prichard
David Belasco **3**:87
Rachel Crothers **19**:70

Eberhart, Richard
Edwin Muir **2**:481
Wallace Stevens **3**:475

Eble, Kenneth
Kate Chopin **5**:147
William Dean Howells **17**:177

Echegaray, José
José Echegaray **4**:97

Eckstein, George
Tadeusz Borowski **9**:22

Economou, George
C. P. Cavafy **7**:164

Eddison, E. R.
E. R. Eddison **15**:53

Edel, Leon
Willa Cather **1**:161
Édouard Dujardin **13**:185
Ford Madox Ford **1**:287
Henry James **2**:271, 274
Dorothy Richardson **3**:354
Lytton Strachey **12**:417
Dylan Thomas **1**:473
Virginia Woolf **1**:540

Edgar, Pelham
Sherwood Anderson **1**:40
Bliss Carman **7**:145
Henry James **11**:325
Charles G. D. Roberts **8**:318
Duncan Campbell Scott **6**:386
Virginia Woolf **1**:530

Edman, Irwin
A. E. **3**:5

Edmonds, Dale
Malcolm Lowry **6**:240

Edwards, George Clifton
Maxim Gorky **8**:68

Edwards, Gwynne
Federico García Lorca **7**:300

Eggleston, Wilfrid
Frederick Philip Grove **4**:137

Eglinton, John
A. E. **3**:6; **10**:18

Ehre, Milton
Isaac Babel **13**:36
Valery Bryusov **10**:96
Yevgeny Ivanovich Zamyatin **8**:558

Ehrenburg, Ilya
Anne Frank **17**:113
Alexey Nikolayevich Tolstoy **18**:364

Eikenbaum, Boris M.
O. Henry **19**:182
Leo Tolstoy **4**:456; **11**:461

Eiland, Howard
Friedrich Nietzsche **18**:350

Eisinger, Erica M.
Colette **16**:121

Ejxenbaum, B. M.
See **Eikenbaum, Boris M.**

Ekström, Kjell
George Washington Cable **4**:27

Elder, Donald
Ring Lardner **2**:335

Eldershaw, M. Barnard
Henry Handel Richardson **4**:373

Elimimian, Isaac
Oscar Wilde **8**:502

Eliot, George
John Ruskin **20**:261

Eliot, T. S.
See also **Crites**
Henry Adams **4**:5
Hilaire Belloc **18**:22
Gottfried Benn **3**:105
Arthur Conan Doyle **7**:218
F. Scott Fitzgerald **14**:149
Thomas Hardy **4**:161
Henry James **2**:250
James Joyce **3**:252
Rudyard Kipling **8**:190
D. H. Lawrence **9**:219
Wyndham Lewis **9**:234
Edwin Muir **2**:487
John Middleton Murry **16**:331, 341
Edmond Rostand **6**:378
May Sinclair **11**:410
Algernon Charles Swinburne **8**:429
Arthur Symons **11**:439
Mark Twain **6**:468
Paul Valéry **4**:495; **15**:449
H. G. Wells **12**:504
Charles Williams **11**:485
William Butler Yeats **1**:557

Ellin, Stanley
Rudolph Fisher **11**:207

Elliot, Walter
James Bridie **3**:134

Elliott, George P.
Edgar Rice Burroughs **2**:76
Raymond Chandler **1**:169
George Orwell **6**:346

Elliott, John R., Jr.
Dorothy L. Sayers **15**:388

Ellis, Havelock
Alain-Fournier **6**:12
Vicente Blasco Ibáñez **12**:29
Paul Bourget **12**:57
Havelock Ellis **14**:102
Miles Franklin **7**:264
Rémy de Gourmont **17**:144
Radclyffe Hall **12**:184
Thomas Hardy **4**:147
Joris-Karl Huysmans **7**:404
Henrik Ibsen **16**:154
Friedrich Nietzsche **18**:331
Olive Schreiner **9**:395
Miguel de Unamuno **9**:508
Juan Valera **10**:499
H. G. Wells **12**:488
Emile Zola **6**:560

Ellis, Mrs. Havelock [Edith Lees Ellis]
Havelock Ellis **14**:105

Ellis, Keith
Machado de Assis **10**:286

Ellis-Fermor, Una
John Millington Synge **6**:438

Ellison, Ralph
Mark Twain **19**:381

Ellmann, Mary
Colette **1**:193

Ellmann, Richard
James Joyce **3**:267; **8**:171;
16:245
John Ruskin **20**:292
Wallace Stevens **12**:363
Italo Svevo **2**:550
Arthur Symons **11**:444
Oscar Wilde **1**:506; **8**:497
William Butler Yeats **1**:572

Eloesser, Arthur
Ricarda Huch **13**:245
Carl Spitteler **12**:341
Carl Sternheim **8**:369
Jakob Wassermann **6**:510
Frank Wedekind **7**:577

Elsworth, John
Andrey Bely **7**:58

Elwin, Malcolm
Andrew Lang **16**:260

Emery, Clark
Dylan Thomas **8**:454

Empson, William
Franz Kafka **13**:260

Emrich, Wilhelm
Franz Kafka **2**:309

Enck, John J.
Wallace Stevens **12**:370

Eng, Steve
Robert E. Howard **8**:137
Montague Summers **16**:435

Engel, Edwin A.
Eugene O'Neill **1**:399

Engle, Paul
Stephen Vincent Benét **7**:75

Englekirk, John Eugene
Mariano Azuela **3**:75, 79
Leopoldo Lugones **15**:284
Amado Nervo **11**:394
Horacio Quiroga **20**:209

Enright, D. J.
Bertolt Brecht **1**:121
Hermann Broch **20**:58
Rupert Brooke **7**:129
Aleister Crowley **7**:207
Stefan George **14**:200
Knut Hamsun **2**:208
D. H. Lawrence **2**:371
Thomas Mann **2**:427
Georg Trakl **5**:461

Ensor, R. C. K.
Detlev von Liliencron **18**:205

Eoff, Sherman H.
Pío Baroja **8**:54
Vicente Blasco Ibáñez **12**:44
José María de Pereda **16**:373,
375
José Rubén Romero **14**:436
Juan Valera **10**:504

Epstein, Perle S.
Malcolm Lowry **6**:242

Erickson, John D.
Joris-Karl Huysmans **7**:414

Ericson, Edward E., Jr.
Mikhail Bulgakov **2**:69

Erlich, Victor
Innokenty Annensky **14**:29
Aleksandr Blok **5**:94
Valery Bryusov **10**:88
Velimir Khlebnikov **20**:129
Vladimir Mayakovsky **18**:246

Erskine, John
Lafcadio Hearn **9**:123
Marcel Schwob **20**:323
Mark Twain **19**:355

Ervine, St. John G.
A. E. **10**:15
G. K. Chesterton **1**:178
John Galsworthy **1**:293
Bernard Shaw **3**:385
William Butler Yeats **1**:552

Erwin, John F., Jr.
Paul Claudel **2**:108

Eshleman, Clayton
César Vallejo **3**:527

Eskin, Stanley G.
Giuseppi Tomasi di Lampedusa
13:293

Esslin, Martin
Antonin Artaud **3**:59
Bertolt Brecht **1**:102, 117
Henrik Ibsen **2**:237
Alfred Jarry **2**:285
George Orwell **15**:349
Luigi Pirandello **4**:352
Arthur Schnitzler **4**:401
Boris Vian **9**:530
Frank Wedekind **7**:588
Stanisław Ignacy Witkiewicz
8:511

Etkind, Efim
Mikhail Bulgakov **16**:99

Etō, Jun
Sōseki Natsume **2**:492

Etulain, Richard W.
Zane Grey **6**:182
George MacDonald **9**:281

Evans, Calvin
Maurice Maeterlinck **3**:330

Evans, Elizabeth
Ring Lardner **14**:311

Evans, I. O.
Jules Verne **6**:494

Evans, Ifor
George MacDonald **9**:300

Evans, Robert O.
Joseph Conrad **13**:110

Evans, Walter
O. Henry **19**:197

Ewart, Gavin
E. C. Bentley **12**:24

Ewen, Frederic
Bertolt Brecht **13**:52

Ewers, John K.
Miles Franklin **7**:267

Fabrizi, Benedetto
Valéry Larbaud **9**:201

Fackler, Herbert V.
A. E. **3**:12

Fadiman, Clifton P.
Ambrose Bierce **1**:87
Louis Bromfield **11**:76
Willa Cather **11**:94
Oliver St. John Gogarty **15**:105
Knut Hamsun **14**:228
Joseph Hergesheimer **11**:276
Ricarda Huch **13**:242
Ring Lardner **2**:328
T. E. Lawrence **18**:138
Marie Belloc Lowndes **12**:204
T. F. Powys **9**:360
O. E. Rölvaag **17**:323
Dorothy L. Sayers **15**:374
May Sinclair **11**:412
Leo Tolstoy **4**:466; **11**:466
Mark Twain **19**:362
Carl Van Doren **18**:399
Thomas Wolfe **4**:513

Fagin, N. Bryllion
Anton Chekhov **3**:151

Faguet, Émile
Andrew Lang **16**:254

Fain, John Tyree
Joseph Hergesheimer **11**:278

Faiq, Salah
Benjamin Péret **20**:203

Fairchild, Hoxie Neale
Charlotte Mew **8**:299
Alice Meynell **6**:302
Charles Williams **1**:521

Fairlie, Henry
Randolph S. Bourne **16**:65

Falen, James E.
Isaak Babel **2**:32

Falk, Doris V.
Eugene O'Neill **6**:332

Fallis, Richard
Standish O'Grady **5**:357

Fanger, Donald
Mikhail Bulgakov **2**:64

Fant, Åke
Rudolf Steiner **13**:455

Farber, Manny
James Agee **1**:6

Fargue, Léon-Paul
Léon-Paul Fargue **11**:199

Farnsworth, Robert M.
Charles Waddell Chesnutt
5:134

Farrar, John
Robert Benchley **1**:77

Farrell, James T.
Sherwood Anderson **1**:45
Anton Chekhov **10**:104
Theodore Dreiser **10**:180
James Joyce **16**:205
Ring Lardner **14**:297
Jack London **9**:262
H. L. Mencken **13**:384
Leo Tolstoy **4**:461

Farren, Robert
John Millington Synge **6**:435

Farrison, W. Edward
Booker T. Washington **10**:524

Farrow, Anthony
George Moore **7**:498

Farson, Daniel
Bram Stoker **8**:394

Farwell, Marilyn R.
Virginia Woolf **1**:549

Fast, Howard
Franz Kafka **13**:262

Faulhaber, Uwe Karl
Lion Feuchtwanger **3**:184

Faulkner, William
Sherwood Anderson **1**:45; **10**:35
Mark Twain **6**:471
Thomas Wolfe **4**:521

Fauset, Jessie
Countee Cullen **4**:40

Featherstone, Joseph
Randolph S. Bourne **16**:63

Feder, Lillian
Joseph Conrad **13**:106
William Butler Yeats **1**:583

Fedin, Konstantin
Alexey Nikolayevich Tolstoy
18:364

Feger, Lois
Willa Cather **11**:105

Feibleman, James
Will Rogers **8**:332

Fein, Richard J.
Isaac Leib Peretz **16**:403

Feld, Ross
Guillaume Apollinaire **8**:27

Feldman, A. Bronson
Lionel Johnson **19**:244

Fen, Elisaveta
Mikhail Zoshchenko **15**:494

Fender, Stephen
Eugene O'Neill **6**:337

Fennimore, Keith J.
Booth Tarkington **9**:473

Ferenczi, László
Endre Ady **11**:24

Fergusson, Francis
Anton Chekhov **3**:158
Federica García Lorca **1**:315
James Joyce **3**:262
D. H. Lawrence **2**:351
Robert E. Sherwood **3**:413
Paul Valéry **4**:496

Ferlinghetti, Lawrence
John Reed **9**:388

Festa-McCormick, Diana
Andrey Bely **7**:65
Rainer Maria Rilke **19**:316

Feuchtwanger, Lion
Lion Feuchtwanger **3**:178, 180
Frank Wedekind **7**:578

Feuerlight, Ignace
Thomas Mann **8**:260

Fickert, Kurt J.
Wolfgang Borchert **5**:110

Ficowski, Jerzy
Bruno Schulz **5**:425

Critic Index

Fiedler, Leslie A.
James Agee **1**:1
Ronald Firbank **1**:228
F. Scott Fitzgerald **1**:249, 263
Jaroslav Hasek **4**:181
Nikos Kazantzakis **5**:260
Ludwig Lewisohn **19**:281
Margaret Mitchell **11**:385
Cesare Pavese **3**:335
Isaac Leib Peretz **16**:394
Mark Twain **6**:467; **12**:439
Nathanael West **1**:485

Field, Andrew
Fyodor Sologub **9**:437, 438

Field, Frank
Henri Barbusse **5**:17

Field, Leslie
Thomas Wolfe **13**:495

Field, Louise Maunsell
Algernon Blackwood **5**:71
Vicente Blasco Ibáñez **12**:36
F. Scott Fitzgerald **1**:235
Sheila Kaye-Smith **20**:99
Montague Summers **16**:425, 426

Field, Norma Moore
Sōseki Natsume **10**:338

Fife, Robert Herndon
Georg Brandes **10**:63

Figgis, Darrell
A. E. **3**:4

Figh, Margaret Gillis
Marjorie Kinnan Rawlings **4**:362

Filler, Louis
Randolph S. Bourne **16**:52

Firkins, Oscar W.
William Dean Howells **7**:372
Edgar Lee Masters **2**:463
Ferenc Molnár **20**:156
Sara Teasdale **4**:425

First, Ruth
Olive Schreiner **9**:405

Fisher, H.A.L.
Paul Valéry **15**:444

Fishtine, Edith
Juan Valera **10**:503

Fitts, Dudley
Arturo Barea **14**:50
Dorothy L. Sayers **15**:375

Fitzgerald, F. Scott
Sherwood Anderson **10**:34
F. Scott Fitzgerald **14**:147, 150
Ring Lardner **2**:330
H. L. Mencken **13**:362
Thomas Wolfe **13**:468

Fitzgerald, Penelope
Ada Leverson **18**:202

Fitzgerald, Robert
James Agee **19**:23

Fitzgibbon, Constantine
Dylan Thomas **1**:474

Fitzmaurice-Kelly, James
Vicente Blasco Ibáñez **12**:35
José María de Pereda **16**:367
Juan Valera **10**:498

Flanagan, John T.
Edgar Lee Masters **2**:468

Flandreau, Audrey
Ricarda Huch **13**:248

Flanner, Hildegarde
Edna St. Vincent Millay **4**:313

Flanner, Janet
Colette **1**:192

Flatin, Kjetil A.
Alexander Kielland **5**:279

Flaubert, Gustave
Leo Tolstoy **4**:448

Flautz, John T.
Edgar Rice Burroughs **2**:81

Flay, Joseph C.
Nikos Kazantzakis **2**:319

Fleishman, Avrom
D. H. Lawrence **16**:231

Fleming, Robert E.
James Weldon Johnson **3**:247

Fletcher, Ian
Lionel Johnson **19**:243
Arthur Symons **11**:450

Fletcher, John Gould
William Ernest Henley **8**:106
Amy Lowell **1**:370
George Sterling **20**:374

Flexner, Eleanor
Philip Barry **11**:55
Rachel Crothers **19**:76
Robert E. Sherwood **3**:410

Flexner, James Thomas
Carl Van Doren **18**:411

Flint, F. Cudworth
Amy Lowell **1**:379

Flint, F. S.
Jean de Bosschère **19**:59

Flint, R. W.
James Agee **1**:7
F. T. Marinetti **10**:320
Cesare Pavese **3**:340

Flora, Joseph M.
William Ernest Henley **8**:107

Flores, Angel
Arturo Barea **14**:50
Ricarda Huch **13**:244

Flournoy, Th.
William James **15**:144

Fogelquist, Donald F.
Juan Ramón Jiménez **4**:224

Folsom, James K.
Hamlin Garland **3**:199
Zane Grey **6**:180

Foltin, Lore B.
Arthur Schnitzler **4**:401
Franz Werfel **8**:482

Forbes, Esther
Carl Van Doren **18**:410

Forbes, Helen Cady
A. A. Milne **6**:307, 309

Ford, Ford Madox
Joseph Conrad **1**:202
Stephen Crane **11**:135
John Galsworthy **1**:299
Henry James **2**:245
H. G. Wells **6**:532

Ford, Julia Ellsworth
A. E. **3**:1

Forman, Henry James
Kahlil Gibran **1**:327
O. Henry **1**:347
Carl Van Doren **18**:393

Forster, E. M.
Samuel Butler **1**:136
C. P. Cavafy **2**:87; **7**:154
Joseph Conrad **1**:196
Gabriele D'Annunzio **6**:134
Ronald Firbank **1**:225
Anatole France **9**:48
Stefan George **14**:197
André Gide **12**:151
Thomas Hardy **4**:156
Henrik Ibsen **2**:221
Henry James **2**:252
Giuseppe Tomasi di Lampedusa **13**:292
T. E. Lawrence **18**:128, 136
George Orwell **6**:340
Marcel Proust **7**:523
Lytton Strachey **12**:406
Montague Summers **16**:426
Rabindranath Tagore **3**:484
Leo Tolstoy **4**:457
Edith Wharton **9**:543
Virginia Woolf **1**:527, 533; **5**:506

Forster, S.
William Dean Howells **17**:167

Fortebus, Thos.
Maurice Maeterlinck **3**:318

Forten, Charlotte L.
Charlotte L. Forten **16**:142

Fortin, René E.
Virginia Woolf **20**:415

Foster, Edward
Mary Wilkins Freeman **9**:68

Foster, George Burman
Friedrich Nietzsche **10**:366

Foster, John Wilson
A. E. **10**:23

Foster, Richard
F. Scott Fitzgerald **1**:264, 267
William Dean Howells **7**:384

Foucault, Michel
Raymond Roussel **20**:229

Fowler, Carolyn
Jacques Roumain **19**:338

Fowles, John
Stefan Zweig **17**:453

Fowlie, Wallace
Guillaume Apollinaire **3**:35
Antonin Artaud **3**:47
Paul Claudel **2**:103; **10**:125
Paul Eluard **7**:246
Léon-Paul Fargue **11**:200
André Gide **5**:233
Jean Giraudoux **2**:159
Max Jacob **6**:193
Charles Péguy **10**:409
Marcel Proust **7**:543
Paul Valéry **4**:492; **15**:447

Fox, W. H.
Franz Werfel **8**:478

Fox-Genovese, Elizabeth
Margaret Mitchell **11**:389

Fraiberg, Louis
Ludwig Lewisohn **19**:282

Fraiberg, Selma
Franz Kafka **2**:299

France, Anatole
Paul Bourget **12**:58, 59
Pierre Loti **11**:354
Jean Moréas **18**:275
Marcel Proust **7**:518
Marcel Schwob **20**:318

France, Peter
Vladimir Mayakovsky **18**:265

Francke, Kuno
Hermann Sudermann **15**:418

Franco, Jean
Horacio Quiroga **20**:214
Ramón del Valle-Inclán **5**:477
César Vallejo **3**:534

Frank, Bruno
Thomas Mann **8**:253

Frank, Joseph
José Ortega y Gasset **9**:348

Frank, Otto
Anne Frank **17**:115

Frank, Waldo
Mariano Azuela **3**:75
Randolph S. Bourne **16**:44
Hermann Broch **20**:50
Hart Crane **2**:112
Theodore Dreiser **10**:170
Emma Goldman **13**:217
Jack London **9**:258
Machado de Assis **10**:283
Mark Twain **19**:354

Frankenberg, Lloyd
James Stephens **4**:414

Franklin, Miles
Miles Franklin **7**:266

Franz, Thomas R.
Ramón del Valle-Inclán **5**:489

Fraser, G. S.
Roy Campbell **5**:118, 121
Wallace Stevens **3**:451
Dylan Thomas **1**:472
Oscar Wilde **1**:505
William Butler Yeats **1**:563

Fraser, Howard M.
Rubén Darío **4**:67

Fraser, Keath
F. Scott Fitzgerald **14**:172

Freccero, John
Italo Svevo **2**:543

Freeborn, Richard
Alexey Nikolayevich Tolstoy **18**:375

Freedley, George
Lady Gregory **1**:335

Freedman, Benedict
Jacques Futrelle **19**:92

Freedman, Morris
Federico García Lorca **1**:324
Luigi Pirandello **4**:344

Freeman, Douglas Southall
Lytton Strachey **12**:406

Freeman, John
Robert Bridges 1:124
Joseph Conrad 1:196
Maurice Maeterlinck 3:326
George Moore 7:477
Bernard Shaw 3:384
Edward Thomas 10:450

Freeman, Kathleen
Katherine Mansfield 2:447

Freeman, Mary
D. H. Lawrence 2:358

Freeman, Mary E. Wilkins
Mary Wilkins Freeman 9:64

French, Donald G.
John McCrae 12:208

French, Warren
Stephen Crane 17:71
Hamlin Garland 3:203

Frenz, Horst
Georg Kaiser 9:175

Freud, Sigmund
Havelock Ellis 14:103
Arthur Schnitzler 4:391
Lytton Strachey 12:397
Stefan Zweig 17:425

Friar, Kimon
C. P. Cavafy 7:155
Nikos Kazantzakis 2:311

Frick, Constance
George Jean Nathan 18:316

Friedberg, Maurice
Andrei Platonov 14:410

Friedenthal, Richard
Ricarda Huch 13:246

Friedman, Alan
Joseph Conrad 1:215

Friedman, Eva Merrett
Rainer Maria Rilke 19:324

Friedman, Lawrence J.
Booker T. Washington 10:535

Friedman, Melvin
Édouard Dujardin 13:189
Valéry Larbaud 9:199

Friedman, Norman
Franz Kafka 13:269

Friedman, Thomas
Rudolph Fisher 11:210

Friedrich, Otto
Ring Lardner 2:340

Frierson, William C.
Rose Macaulay 7:424
George Moore 7:484
May Sinclair 11:412

Frohock, W. M.
James Agee 1:2
F. Scott Fitzgerald 1:253
Thomas Wolfe 4:522

Fromm, Gloria G.
Arnold Bennett 20:33

Frost, Robert
James Agee 19:17
Edwin Arlington Robinson 5:406
Edward Thomas 10:452

Fruchter, Moses Joseph
Georg Kaiser 9:173

Frye, Northrop
Bliss Carman 7:147
Frederick Philip Grove 4:135
Wyndham Lewis 9:238
Charles G. D. Roberts 8:319
Wallace Stevens 3:452
Paul Valéry 15:453
Charles Williams 11:488

Frynta, Emanuel
Jaroslav Hašek 4:183

Fuchs, Daniel
Wallace Stevens 3:462

Fuerst, Norbert
Rainer Maria Rilke 19:305

Fuller, Edmund
Sholem Asch 3:68
James Joyce 3:271
Nikos Kazantzakis 5:259
Charles Williams 1:522

Fuller, Henry Blake
Louis Bromfield 11:74
Hanns Heinz Ewers 12:134
William Dean Howells 7:364
Hermann Sudermann 15:429

Fuller, Roy
Thomas Hardy 4:176

Furbank, P. N.
G. K. Chesterton 1:186
Italo Svevo 2:547

Furnas, J. C.
Mark Twain 19:410

Furness, Edna Lue
Alfonsina Storni 5:446

Fussell, D. H.
Thomas Hardy 10:232

Fussell, Edwin
Sherwood Anderson 1:51
F. Scott Fitzgerald 1:248

Fussell, Paul
John McCrae 12:211

Fyvcl, T. R.
George Orwell 15:329

Gagey, Edmond M.
Rachel Crothers 19:80
Eugene O'Neill 6:329

Gaillard, Dawson
Margaret Mitchell 11:382
Dorothy L. Sayers 15:389

Gaines, Francis Pendleton
Joel Chandler Harris 2:210

Gaither, Frances
Charlotte L. Forten 16:148

Gakov, Vladimir
Alexey Nikolayevich Tolstoy 18:383

Galassi, Frank S.
Stanisław Ignacy Witkiewicz 8:515

Gale, Zona
Zona Gale 7:278
Charlotte Gilman 9:101
James Weldon Johnson 19:208
Carl Van Doren 18:397

Galloway, David D.
Nathanael West 1:481

Galsworthy, John
Anton Chekhov 10:102
Joseph Conrad 1:199
Anatole France 9:47
R. B. Cunninghame Graham 19:111
Leo Tolstoy 4:457

Gamble, George
Edgar Saltus 8:343

Ganz, Arthur
Jean Giraudoux 2:173

García Lorca, Federico
Rubén Darío 4:63

Gardiner, Elaine
Kate Chopin 14:82

Gardner, Martin
L. Frank Baum 7:19

Gardner, May
Gregorio Martinez Sierra and Maria Martinez Sierra 6:279

Gardner, Monica M.
Henryk Sienkiewicz 3:425

Garis, Robert
Boris Vian 9:529

Garland, Hamlin
Stephen Crane 11:121
Zona Gale 7:281
Zane Grey 6:180

Garneau, Saint-Denys
Hector Saint-Denys Garneau 13:194, 195

Garnett, Constance
Leo Tolstoy 4:450

Garnett, David
T. E. Lawrence 18:136
Virginia Woolf 1:526

Garnett, Edward
Roy Campbell 5:115
Anton Chekhov 3:152
Joseph Conrad 1:198
Stephen Crane 11:126
R. B. Cunninghame Graham 19:111
Sarah Orne Jewett 1:359
James Joyce 16:201
D. H. Lawrence 2:343
T. E. Lawrence 18:134
Leo Tolstoy 4:450

Garret, Naomi M.
Jacques Roumain 19:333

Garrett, George
Horacio Quiroga 20:220

Garrett, Marvin P.
James Weldon Johnson 19:212

Garrigan, Kristine Ottesen
John Ruskin 20:297

Garrigue, Jean
Dylan Thomas 1:471

Garrison, William Lloyd
Frances Ellen Watkins Harper 14:254

Garten, F.
Gerhart Hauptmann 4:203, 205

Garvey, Marcus
Booker T. Washington 10:522

Garzilli, Enrico
Paul Valéry 15:461

Gascoigne, Bamber
Eugene O'Neill 1:403

Gascoyne, David
Ernst Toller 10:478

Gass, William H.
Bertolt Brecht 6:33
Colette 5:172
Ford Madox Ford 15:93
Malcolm Lowry 6:244
Marcel Proust 7:549
Rainer Maria Rilke 19:325
Gertrude Stein 1:438
Paul Valéry 4:502

Gassner, John
Maxwell Anderson 2:3
Philip Barry 11:60
Bertolt Brecht 1:100
Anton Chekhov 3:167
Federico García Lorca 7:294
Jean Giraudoux 2:160
Lady Gregory 1:334
Eugene O'Neill 1:389
August Strindberg 1:460
John Van Druten 2:576
Oscar Wilde 1:498

Gates, Norman T.
William Ernest Henley 8:109

Gatt-Rutter, John
Giuseppe Tomasi di Lampedusa 13:318

Gayle, Addison, Jr.
Paul Laurence Dunbar 12:121

Geddes, Gary
Duncan Campbell Scott 6:395

Geduld, Harry M.
J. M. Barrie 2:47

Geismar, Maxwell
Sherwood Anderson 1:50
Willa Cather 1:153
F. Scott Fitzgerald 1:244
Ellen Glasgow 2:179
Knut Hamsun 14:231
Henry James 11:335
Ring Lardner 2:330, 339
Sinclair Lewis 4:253
Jack London 9:263

Gekle, William Francis
Arthur Machen 4:280

Gelfant, Blanche H.
Margaret Mitchell 11:386

Genette, Gerard
Marcel Proust 7:550

Genovese, Eugene D.
Booker T. Washington 10:529

George, Emery
Miklós Radnóti 16:417

George, Ralph W.
Sholem Asch 3:69

George, W. L.
Sheila Kaye-Smith 20:94
Edgar Saltus 8:349

Gerber, Helmut E.
George Moore 7:489

Gerber, Philip L.
Theodore Dreiser 10:190

Gergely, Emro Joseph
Ferenc Molnár **20**:166

Gerhardi, William
Anton Chekhov **3**:153

Gerould, Daniel
Ernst Toller **10**:488
Stanisław Ignacy Witkiewicz **8**:510, 512

Gerould, Gordon Hall
F. Marion Crawford **10**:152

Gerould, Katherine Fullerton
O. Henry **19**:171

Gersh, Gabriel
Lytton Strachey **12**:412

Gershman, Herbert S.
Paul Eluard **7**:254
Benjamin Péret **20**:188

Gerson, Villiers
C. M. Kornbluth **8**:213

Getlein, Frank
Machado de Assis **10**:283

Getsi, Lucia
Georg Trakl **5**:464

Ghiselin, Brewster
James Joyce **3**:266

Ghose, Sisirkumar
Rabindranath Tagore **3**:486

Ghosh, Shibdas
Saratchandra Chatterji **13**:76

Gibbon, Monk
A. E. **3**:7

Gibbons, Stella
H. Rider Haggard **11**:243

Gibbons, Tom
Havelock Ellis **14**:132

Gibbs, Wolcott
Robert Benchley **1**:78
George Jean Nathan **18**:317
John Van Druten **2**:574

Gibson, Anne L.
Boris Vian **9**:537

Gibson, Robert
Alain-Fournier **6**:25

Gibson, William M.
William Dean Howells **7**:391

Gide, André
Paul Bourget **12**:66
Paul Claudel **10**:120
Jean Giraudoux **7**:317
Henry James **11**:328
Charles Péguy **10**:401
Marcel Proust **7**:525
Antoine de Saint-Exupéry **2**:515
Paul Valéry **15**:443
Oscar Wilde **1**:501

Gielgud, Sir John
Josephine Tey **14**:450

Giergielewicz, Mieczyslaw
Henryk Sienkiewicz **3**:430

Gifford, Henry
Osip Mandelstam **2**:409; **6**:269

Gignilliat, John L.
Douglas Southall Freeman **11**:231

Gilbert, Elliot L.
Jacques Futrelle **19**:96

Gilbert, Mary E.
Hugo von Hofmannsthal **11**:303

Gilbert, Sandra M.
D. H. Lawrence **9**:224

Gilbert, Stuart
Algernon Blackwood **5**:73
James Joyce **3**:265

Gilder, Rosamund
Montague Summers **16**:427

Giles, James R.
Claude McKay **7**:470

Gilkes, Michael
H. G. de Lisser **12**:99

Gill, Brendan
Eugene O'Neill **1**:407

Gillen, Charles H.
Saki **3**:373

Gillespie, Diane F.
May Sinclair **11**:417

Gillis, Adolph
Ludwig Lewisohn **19**:271

Gilman, Charlotte Perkins
Charlotte Gilman **9**:102

Gilman, Richard
Sholom Aleichem **1**:26
Bertolt Brecht **1**:121
Anton Chekhov **3**:173
Henrik Ibsen **2**:233
Eugene O'Neill **1**:399
Bernard Shaw **3**:402
August Strindberg **1**:461
Italo Svevo **2**:546

Gilroy, James P.
Marcel Schwob **20**:329

Gindin, James
F. Scott Fitzgerald **1**:265
Virginia Woolf **1**:544

Gingrich, Arnold
F. Scott Fitzgerald **1**:238

Ginsburg, Mirra
Mikhail Bulgakov **16**:82

Ginzburg, Lidija
Osip Mandelstam **2**:407

Ginzburg, Natalia
Cesare Pavese **3**:337

Giovanni, Nikki
Paul Laurence Dunbar **12**:124

Gippius, Zinaida
Fyodor Sologub **9**:433

Gittleman, Sol
Carl Sternheim **8**:378
Frank Wedekind **7**:583

Gladstone, W. E.
Annie Besant **9**:14

Glasgow, Ellen
Ellen Glasgow **7**:336
Joseph Hergesheimer **11**:269

Glassco, John
Hector Saint-Denys Garneau **13**:202

Glatstein, Jacob
Isaac Leib Peretz **16**:392

Glenny, Michael V.
Mikhail Bulgakov **16**:75, 91

Glicksberg, Charles I.
John Middleton Murry **16**:339
Carl Van Doren **18**:404

Gloster, Hugh M.
Rudolph Fisher **11**:205
Frances Ellen Watkins Harper **14**:257
James Weldon Johnson **3**:242
Wallace Thurman **6**:448
Walter White **15**:479

Goble, Danney
Zane Grey **6**:184

Godwin, A. H.
W. S. Gilbert **3**:211

Godwin, Murray
Damon Runyon **10**:422

Goes, Albrecht
Anne Frank **17**:104

Goetz, T. H.
Paul Bourget **12**:75

Gogarty, Oliver St. John
Lord Dunsany **2**:144
Oscar Wilde **1**:501

Goist, Park Dixon
Zona Gale **7**:287
Booth Tarkington **9**:474

Gold, Herbert
Sherwood Anderson **1**:49

Gold, Joseph
Charles G. D. Roberts **8**:322

Goldberg, Isaac
Sholem Asch **3**:65
Jacinto Benavente **3**:97
Vicente Blasco Ibáñez **12**:31
Rubén Darío **4**:59
Havelock Ellis **14**:110
Machado de Assis **10**:278
George Jean Nathan **18**:306
Amado Nervo **11**:393

Goldberg, S. L.
James Joyce **8**:160

Golden, Bruce
Ford Madox Ford **1**:285

Golding, William
Jules Verne **6**:492

Goldman, Emma
Emma Goldman **13**:211, 212

Goldsmith, Ulrich K.
Stefan George **2**:154; **14**:208

Goldstein, Sanford
Ishikawa Tabuboku **15**:125

Golffing, Francis
Gottfried Benn **3**:104
C. P. Cavafy **7**:155

Golino, Carlo L.
Dino Campana **20**:89

Gomme, Andor
Giuseppe Tomasi di Lampedusa **13**:302

Gömöri, George
Miklós Radnóti **16**:413

Goodman, Anne L.
Walter White **15**:479

Goodman, Paul
Franz Kafka **13**:260

Gordon, Ambrose, Jr.
Ford Madox Ford **1**:280, 286

Gordon, Caroline
James Joyce **3**:266

Gordon, Ian A.
Katherine Mansfield **2**:456; **8**:281

Gordon, Jan B.
Arthur Symons **11**:447

Gordon, Lyndall
Virginia Woolf **20**:428

Gorky, Maxim
Leonid Andreyev **3**:25
Isaac Babel **13**:15
Anton Chekhov **3**:145
Sergei Esenin **4**:107
Alexey Nikolayevich Tolstoy **18**:359

Gorman, Herbert S.
Sholem Asch **3**:66
James Joyce **16**:203
Katharine Tynan **3**:504

Gosse, Edmund
Bjørnstjerne Bjørnson **7**:105
Paul Claudel **10**:122
Anatole France **9**:42
André Gide **5**:213
Thomas Hardy **4**:149
Henrik Ibsen **8**:141; **16**:154
Henry James **11**:321
Andrew Lang **16**:255
Jonas Lie **5**:323
Pierre Loti **11**:354
George Moore **7**:478
Henryk Sienkiewicz **3**:421
Lytton Strachey **12**:391
Emile Zola **1**:585

Gottlieb, Annie
Tess Slesinger **10**:442

Gottlieb, Lois C.
Rachel Crothers **19**:82, 85

Gould, George M.
Lafcadio Hearn **9**:120

Gould, Gerald
May Sinclair **3**:438

Gould, Jean
Amy Lowell **8**:234

Gourmont, Rémy de
André Gide **12**:142
Joris-Karl Huysmans **7**:412
Jean Moréas **18**:278
Jules Renard **17**:301
Emile Verhaeren **12**:458

Grabowski, Zbigniew A.
Stanisław Ignacy Witkiewicz **8**:506

Graff, W. L.
Rainer Maria Rilke **19**:304

Graham, Eleanor
A. A. Milne **6**:313

Graham, Kenneth
Henry James **11**:342

Graham, Stephen
Valery Bryusov **10**:78
Aleksandr Kuprin **5**:296

Gramont, Sanche de
Antonin Artaud **3**:54

Grandgent, Charles Hall
John Jay Chapman **7**:187

Grant, Patrick
Rudolf Steiner **13**:460

Granville-Barker, Harley
Laurence Housman **7**:355

Granville-Barker, Helen
Gregorio Martínez Sierra and
María Martínez Sierra **6**:275

Grass, Günter
Alfred Döblin **13**:180

Grattan, C. Hartley
Ambrose Bierce **1**:85
Jack London **9**:259
H. G. Wells **12**:500

Graver, Lawrence
Ronald Firbank **1**:232

Graves, Robert
Samuel Butler **1**:134
T. E. Lawrence **18**:134
Alun Lewis **3**:284
George Moore **7**:488

Gray, Donald P.
Pierre Teilhard de Chardin
9:495

Gray, J. M.
Arthur Symons **11**:426

Gray, James
Edna St. Vincent Millay **4**:318

Gray, Ronald D.
Bertolt Brecht **6**:35
Henrik Ibsen **16**:186
Franz Kafka **6**:222; **13**:279
Thomas Mann **14**:344
Rainer Maria Rilke **19**:310

Gray, Simon
Tadeusz Borowski **9**:20

Gray, Thomas A.
Elinor Wylie **8**:532

Grayburn, William Frazer
Rebecca Harding Davis **6**:152

Greacen, Robert
Oliver St. John Gogarty **15**:105

Grebstein, Sheldon Norman
Sinclair Lewis **4**:256

Green, Benny
Damon Runyon **10**:434

Green, Dorothy
Henry Handel Richardson **4**:380

Green, Ellin
Laurence Housman **7**:360

Green, Julian
Charles Péguy **10**:406

Green, Martin
Dorothy L. Sayers **2**:532

Green, Roger Lancelyn
Andrew Lang **16**:263
David Lindsay **15**:217

Greenberg, Clement
Bertolt Brecht **1**:97

Greenberg, Eliezer
Isaac Leib Peretz **16**:401

Greenberg, Martin
Franz Kafka **13**:273

Greene, Anne
James Bridie **3**:139

Greene, Graham
George Bernanos **3**:126
Louis Bromfield **11**:78
Samuel Butler **1**:135
Havelock Ellis **14**:124
Ford Madox Ford **1**:282; **15**:75
Henry James **2**:256
Dorothy Richardson **3**:353
Frederick Rolfe **12**:270
Saki **3**:366
Hugh Walpole **5**:501
H. G. Wells **12**:505

Greene, Henry Copley
Marcel Schwob **20**:321

Greene, Naomi
Antonin Artaud **3**:54

Greenslet, Ferris
Ernest Dowson **4**:85
Lafcadio Hearn **9**:121

Gregg, Richard A.
Yevgeny Ivanovich Zamyatin
8:549

Gregor, Ian
Thomas Hardy **4**:170
D. H. Lawrence **9**:216
Oscar Wilde **1**:505

Gregory, Alyse
Sherwood Anderson **1**:36
Paul Valéry **4**:487

Gregory, Horace
James Agee **19**:17
Sherwood Anderson **10**:43
Vernon Lee **5**:318
Amy Lowell **1**:378
Harriet Monroe **12**:221

Grey, Zane
Zane Grey **6**:177

Griffin, Ernest G.
John Middleton Murry **16**:350

Griffin, Gerald
Oliver St. John Gogarty **15**:104

Griffith, John
Stephen Vincent Benét **7**:82

Griffith, Marlene
Ford Madox Ford **1**:284

Griffiths, Richard
Paul Claudel **2**:105

Grigson, Geoffrey
John Gray **19**:146
Wyndham Lewis **2**:386
A. A. Milne **6**:319
Dylan Thomas **1**:467; **8**:462

Grimm, Clyde L.
Mark Twain **12**:446

Grose, Kenneth
James Joyce **16**:241

Gross, Barry
F. Scott Fitzgerald **14**:165

Gross, Harvey
Thomas Mann **8**:264

Gross, John
William Ernest Henley **8**:106
Israel Zangwill **16**:451

Gross, Seymour L.
Ivan Bunin **6**:52

Gross, Theodore L.
F. Scott Fitzgerald **1**:269
Booker T. Washington **10**:532

Grosshut, F. S.
Lion Feuchtwanger **3**:178

Grosskurth, Phyllis
Havelock Ellis **14**:142

Grossman, Joan Delaney
Valery Bryusov **10**:95
Mikhail Bulgakov **16**:89

Grossman, Manual L.
Alfred Jarry **2**:284; **14**:274

Grossman, William L.
Machado de Assis **10**:282, 288

Grossvogel, David I.
Guillaume Apollinaire **8**:13
Bertolt Brecht **1**:106
Alfred Jarry **14**:271

Grubbs, Henry A.
Alfred Jarry **2**:278

Gruening, Martha
Wallace Thurman **6**:447

Grumbach, Doris
Colette **16**:116

Grummann, Paul H.
Gerhart Hauptmann **4**:197

Guerard, Albert J.
Joseph Conrad **6**:115; **13**:103,
104
André Gide **5**:224
Thomas Hardy **4**:171

Guest, Boyd
Mark Twain **12**:438

Guha-Thakurta, P.
Rabindranath Tagore **3**:485

Guicharnaud, Jacques
Paul Claudel **2**:104

Guillen, Claudio
Juan Ramón Jiménez **4**:214

Guillén, Jorge
Pedro Salinas **17**:358

Guiney, Louise Imogen
Lionel Johnson **19**:230

Guiton, Margaret
Georges Bernanos **3**:119

Gullace, Giovanni
Gabrielle D'Annunzio **6**:136

Gullason, Thomas A.
Stephen Crane **11**:148

Gullón, Ricardo
Miguel de Unamuno **9**:516
Ramón del Valle-Inclán **5**:482

Gulstad, Daniel E.
José Rubén Romero **14**:444

Gumilev, Nikolai
Innokenty Annensky **14**:17
Konstantin Dmitriyevich
Balmont **11**:30
Andrey Bely **7**:46
Valery Bryusov **10**:77
Vladislav Khodasevich **15**:197

Gunn, James
Henry Kuttner **10**:272

Gunn, Peter
Vernon Lee **5**:313

Gunther, John
Arthur Machen **4**:279

Günther, Werner
Carl Spitteler **12**:349

Gurko, Leo
Sinclair Lewis **4**:251

Gurko, Miriam
Sinclair Lewis **4**:251

Gustafson, Alrik
Bjørnstjerne Bjørnson **7**:111
Stig Dagerman **17**:88
Nordahl Grieg **10**:206
Knut Hamsun **2**:205; **14**:228
Verner von Heidenstam **5**:253
Selma Lagerlöf **4**:236
Jonas Lie **5**:325
August Strindberg **1**:448
Sigrid Undset **3**:516

Guthke, Karl S.
Henrik Ibsen **16**:172

Guthrie, William Norman
Gerhart Hauptmann **4**:192

Gwynn, Stephen
Henri Barbusse **5**:11
W. H. Davies **5**:198

Györgyey, Clara
Ferenc Molnár **20**:173

Habegger, Alfred
William Dean Howells **17**:175

Haber, Edythe C.
Mikhail Bulgakov **2**:71

Haber, Tom Burns
A. E. Housman **10**:258

Hackett, Francis
Henri Barbusse **5**:12
Rachel Crothers **19**:71
O. Henry **1**:349
James Joyce **16**:202
Walter White **15**:478

Hadfield, Alice Mary
Charles Williams **1**:516

Hadgraft, Cecil
Miles Franklin **7**:268

Hafley, James
Virginia Woolf **20**:403

Haggard, H. Rider
H. Rider Haggard **11**:242

Hahn, Steve
O. E. Rölvaag **17**:337

Hahn, Werner G.
Andrei A. Zhdanov **18**:482

Haight, Gordon
Marie Belloc Lowndes **12**:204

Hakutani, Yoshinobu
Theodore Dreiser **10**:197

Hale, Edward Everett, Jr.
John Jay Chapman **7**:186
Edmond Rostand **6**:376

Hall, J. C.
Edwin Muir **2**:483

Hall, James
Joyce Cary 1:142

Hall, Robert A., Jr.
W. S. Gilbert 3:213

Hall, Trevor H.
Arthur Conan Doyle 7:228

Hall, Vernon, Jr.
René Daumal 14:90

Hall, Wayne E.
A. E. 10:26
George Moore 7:499

Hallam-Hipwell, Hermine
Horacio Quiroga 20:208

Hallet, David
Louis Couperus 15:45

Hallett, Charles A.
Henrik Ibsen 16:182

Hallett, Richard
Isaac Babel 13:29

Halline, Allan G.
Maxwell Anderson 2:5

Halls, W. D.
Maurice Maeterlinck 3:328

Halperin, John
Lytton Strachey 12:418

Halpern, Joseph
Joris-Karl Huysmans 7:417

Haman, Aleš
Karel Čapek 6:90

Hamblen, Abigail Ann
Mary Wilkins Freeman 9:71

Hamburger, Michael
Gottfried Benn 3:105
Hugo von Hofmannsthal 11:305
Friedrich Nietzsche 18:338
Georg Trakl 5:457

Hamilton, Clayton
Alfred Sutro 6:420
Leo Tolstoy 4:453
Alexander Woollcott 5:520

Hamilton, G. Rostrevor
E. R. Eddison 15:54
Alice Meynell 6:302

Hammelmann, H. A.
Hugo von Hofmannsthal 11:299

Hammond, Josephine
Lord Dunsany 2:142

Hammond, Paul
Benjamin Péret 20:203

Hampshire, Stuart N.
Oscar Wilde 8:498

Hamsun, Knut
Knut Hamsun 14:232

Hanaford, Phebe A.
Frances Ellen Watkins Harper 14:255

Hanan, Patrick
Lu Hsün 3:300

Hankin, Cherry
Katherine Mansfield 2:458

Hankin, Robert M.
Andrei A. Zhdanov 18:471

Hankin, St. John
Oscar Wilde 1:495

Hanna, Suhail Ibn-Salim
Kahlil Gibran 9:85

Hannigan, D. F.
Thomas Hardy 18:88

Hannum, Hunter G.
Arthur Schnitzler 4:398

Hansen, Chadwick
Mark Twain 19:388

Hansen, Harry
Sherwood Anderson 1:37

Hanser, Richard
Karl Kraus 5:287

Hapgood, Hutchins
Emma Goldman 13:208

Hapke, Laura
Stephen Crane 17:79

Hardaway, R. Travis
Heinrich Mann 9:319

Hardin, James
Hermann Broch 20:68

Harding, D. W.
Isaac Rosenberg 12:287

Hardison, Felicia
Ramón del Valle-Inclán 5:480

Hardwick, Elizabeth
Henrik Ibsen 2:240
Leo Tolstoy 4:480

Hardy, Barbara
George Meredith 17:290

Hardy, Evelyn
Thomas Hardy 10:220

Hardy, Thomas
Havelock Ellis 14:101
Thomas Hardy 4:152; 10:216; 18:79

Hare, Humphrey
Algernon Charles Swinburne 8:436

Harkins, William E.
Karel Čapek 6:87, 88
Alexey Nikolayevich Tolstoy 18:368

Harlan, Louis R.
Booker T. Washington 10:532

Harman, H. E.
Joel Chandler Harris 2:210
John McCrae 12:208

Harmer, Ruth
Henrik Ibsen 16:178

Harper, Allanah
Léon-Paul Fargue 11:197

Harpham, Geoffrey Galt
Thomas Mann 14:362

Harris, Austin
Francis Thompson 4:437

Harris, Frank
Paul Bourget 12:65
Lord Dunsany 2:142
John Gray 19:141
H. L. Mencken 13:366
Oscar Wilde 1:508

Harris, Harold J.
George Orwell 15:306

Harris, William J.
Stephen Vincent Benét 7:84

Harrison, Barbara Grizzuti
Dorothy L. Sayers 2:536

Harrison, James
Rudyard Kipling 17:207

Harrison, John R.
Wyndham Lewis 9:240

Harrison, Stanley R.
Hamlin Garland 3:202

Hart, Francis Russell
George MacDonald 9:308

Hart, James D.
Margaret Mitchell 11:374

Hart, Jeffrey
F. Scott Fitzgerald 1:274

Hart, Pierre
Andrey Bely 7:55

Hart, Pierre R.
Mikhail Bulgakov 2:67

Hart, Walter Morris
Rudyard Kipling 8:182

Hart-Davis, Rupert
Dorothy L. Sayers 15:373

Harte, Bret
Mark Twain 6:453

Hartley, L. P.
Stella Benson 17:21
E. R. Eddison 15:52
Sheila Kaye-Smith 20:99
T. E. Lawrence 18:146
Marie Belloc Lowndes 12:202
Saki 3:364

Hartnett, Edith
Joris-Karl Huysmans 7:417

Harwell, Richard
Douglas Southall Freeman 11:230

Hasley, Louis
Don Marquis 7:446

Hassall, Christopher
Rupert Brooke 2:56; 7:124

Hassan, Ihab
Alfred Jarry 14:285
Franz Kafka 2:306
Edwin Muir 2:485

Hastings, Michael
Rupert Brooke 7:128

Hastings, R.
Gabriele D'Annunzio 6:141

Hatch, Robert
George Orwell 15:303

Hatfield, Henry
Thomas Mann 2:435
Robert Musil 12:255

Hathaway, R. H.
Bliss Carman 7:136

Hatvary, George Egon
James Stephens 4:412

Hatzantonis, Emmanuel
Nikos Kazantzakis 5:260

Haugen, Einar
O. E. Rölvaag 17:343

Havel, Hippolyte
Emma Goldman 13:208

Hawi, Khalil S.
Kahlil Gibran 9:87

Hawk, Affable
See also **MacCarthy, Desmond**
Andrew Lang 16:258
Marcel Proust 7:520

Hawkins, Desmond
Franz Kafka 13:257

Haworth, David
Andrei Platonov 14:412

Hawthorn, Jeremy
Virginia Woolf 20:418

Hay, Eloise Knapp
Rudyard Kipling 17:211

Haycraft, Howard
E. C. Bentley 12:18
Jacques Futrelle 19:90
Dorothy L. Sayers 2:529

Hayes, Richard
James Agee 1:4
Colette 5:163

Haymaker, Richard E.
R. B. Cunninghame Graham 19:123

Haynes, Reneé
Hilaire Belloc 7:38

Haynes, Roslynn D.
H. G. Wells 6:553

Hays, H. R.
Robert E. Howard 8:129

Hays, Michael
Carl Sternheim 8:381

Hayward, Max
Marina Tsvetaeva 7:565

Hazlitt, Henry
George Jean Nathan 18:312
Rainer Maria Rilke 19:301

Hazo, Samuel
Hart Crane 2:119
Wilfred Owen 5:366

Heaney, Seamus
William Butler Yeats 11:532

Heard, Gerald
Kahlil Gibran 1:328

Hearn, Lafcadio
Bjørnsterne Bjørnson 7:108
Paul Bourget 12:57
Anatole France 9:39
Pierre Loti 11:351
Leo Tolstoy 4:455
Emile Zola 6:559

Hebblethwaite, Peter, S.J.
Georges Bernanos 3:122

Hecht, Ben
Sholom Aleichem 1:22

Hedges, Elaine R.
Charlotte Gilman 9:105

Hedrick, Joan D.
Jack London 15:270

Heermance, J. Noel
Charles Waddell Chesnutt 5:137

Heidegger, Martin
Friedrich Nietzsche 10:380;
18:335
Georg Trakl 5:459

Heidenreich, Rev. Alfred
Rudolf Steiner 13:448

Heilburn, Carolyn
Dorothy L. Sayers 2:535

Heiney, Donald
Cesare Pavese 3:341
Boris Vian 9:536

Heller, Erich
Knut Hamsun 14:246
Franz Kafka 6:225
Karl Kraus 5:288
Thomas Mann 2:442; 14:338
Rainer Maria Rilke 1:419

Heller, Otto
Gerhart Hauptmann 4:193
Ricarda Huch 13:240
August Strindberg 1:443
Hermann Sudermann 15:421

Heller, Peter
Friedrich Nietzsche 18:342

Hellersberg-Wendriner, Anna
Thomas Mann 8:257

Helsinger, Elizabeth K.
John Ruskin 20:308

Hemingway, Ernest
Sherwood Anderson 10:35
Joseph Conrad 6:113
Stephen Crane 11:143
Ring Lardner 14:296
Marie Belloc Lowndes 12:205
Mark Twain 6:463

Hemmings, F.W.J.
Emile Zola 6:561, 570

Henderson, Alice Corbin
Edgar Lee Masters 2:460

Henderson, Archibald
John Galsworthy 1:295
Harley Granville-Barker 2:193
Henrik Ibsen 16:166
Maurice Maeterlinck 3:322
Bernard Shaw 3:382
August Strindberg 1:444
Mark Twain 6:458
Oscar Wilde 1:496

Henderson, Harold G.
Masaoka Shiki 18:220

Henderson, Harry III
John Reed 9:386

Henderson, Philip
Algernon Charles Swinburne
8:441
Alexey Nikolayevich Tolstoy
18:361

Hendricks, Frances Kellam
Mariano Azuela 3:79

Henighan, Tom
Edgar Rice Burroughs 2:83

Henkle, Roger B.
Wyndham Lewis 9:248

Henley, William Ernest
H. Rider Haggard 11:238
Andrew Lang 16:251
Mark Twain 12:426
Oscar Wilde 8:490
William Butler Yeats 18:452

Henn, Thomas Rice
A. E. 10:18

Hennelly, Mark M., Jr.
Bram Stoker 8:395

Henshaw, N. W.
W. S. Gilbert 3:216

Heppenstall, Rayner
Paul Claudel 2:99
John Middleton Murry 16:337
Raymond Roussel 20:240

Hepworth, James B.
Thomas Mann 14:342

Herdman, John
David Lindsay 15:227

Hergesheimer, Joseph
Gabriele D'Annunzio 6:131
Joseph Hergesheimer 11:261
Hugh Walpole 5:494

Herrick, Robert
Henri Barbusse 5:12
Carl Van Doren 18:391

Herring, Hubert
Charles A. Beard 15:23

Herron, Ima Honaker
Zona Gale 7:281

Herskovits, Melville J.
Walter White 15:477

Heseltine, Harry
Miles Franklin 7:273

Hesford, Walter
Rebecca Harding Davis 6:156

Hesse, Hermann
André Gide 12:143, 160
José Ortega y Gasset 9:337
Rainer Maria Rilke 1:409
Rabindranath Tagore 3:493

Hewett-Thayer, Harvey W.
Gerhart Hauptmann 4:199

Hewitt, Douglas
Joseph Conrad 6:122

Heymann, C. David
Amy Lowell 8:235

Hibberd, Dominic
Wilfred Owen 5:372

Hibberd, J. L.
Frank Wedekind 7:590

Hibbett, Howard
Akutagawa Ryūnosuke 16:18

Hicks, Granville
Henry Adams 4:6
Sherwood Anderson 10:40
George Washington Cable 4:26
Willa Cather 11:96
Theodore Dreiser 10:176
Ford Madox Ford 1:275
George Gissing 3:230
O. Henry 19:186
William Dean Howells 7:375
Henry James 2:255
Sarah Orne Jewett 1:362

Sinclair Lewis 13:337
Ludwig Lewisohn 19:268
Vachel Lindsay 17:238
Jack London 9:260
George Moore 7:495
George Jean Nathan 18:313
Eugene O'Neill 1:385
John Reed 9:383
Lincoln Steffens 20:344
Franz Werfel 8:467
Oscar Wilde 1:497

Higginbotham, Virginia
Federico García Lorca 7:296

Higgins, F. R.
William Butler Yeats 1:556

Higgins, Ian
Emile Verhaeren 12:476

Higgins, James
César Vallejo 3:531

Highet, Gilbert
A. E. Housman 1:357
James Joyce 3:264
Carl Spitteler 12:343

Highsmith, James Milton
Ambrose Bierce 7:92

Hijiya, Yukihito
Ishikawa Takuboku 15:127

Hilfer, Anthony Channell
Zona Gale 7:286
Sinclair Lewis 13:343

Hill, Claude
Bertolt Brecht 13:64
Arthur Schnitzler 4:397
Frank Wedekind 7:579

Hill, Hamlin L.
Don Marquis 7:442

Hill, Leslie
Raymond Roussel 20:252

Hill, Patricia Liggins
Frances Ellen Watkins Harper
14:262

Hillegas, Mark R.
H. G. Wells 19:427

Hillyer, Robert
Kahlil Gibran 1:327; 9:84

Hilton, Ian
Gottfried Benn 3:109

Hilton, James
George Orwell 15:299

Hind, Charles Lewis
G. K. Chesterton 1:177
Laurence Housman 7:353

Hinde, Thomas
Thomas Hardy 18:114

Hinden, Michael
Friedrich Nietzsche 10:396

Hindus, Milton
F. Scott Fitzgerald 1:243
Marcel Proust 13:415
Israel Zangwill 16:448

Hingley, Ronald
Anton Chekhov 3:165
Andrei A. Zhdanov 18:480

Hinton, Norman D.
Hart Crane 5:194

Hirsch, Edward
Robert W. Service 15:408

Hirsch, Jerrold
Ludwig Lewisohn 19:289

Hirschbach, Frank Donald
Thomas Mann 14:333

Hitchman, Janet
Dorothy L. Sayers 15:380

Hively, Evelyn T. Helmick
Elinor Wylie 8:531

Hobbs, Gloria L.
Marcel Schwob 20:327

Hobman, D. L.
Olive Schreiner 9:397

Hobson, J. A.
Olive Schreiner 9:394

Hochfield, George
Henry Adams 4:16

Hochman, Stanley
Jules Renard 17:313

Hockey, Lawrence
W. H. Davies 5:208

Hodson, W. L.
Marcel Proust 7:538

Hofacker, Erich P.
Christian Morgenstern 8:309

Hoffman, Charles G.
Joyce Cary 1:143

Hoffman, Daniel
Edwin Muir 2:488

Hoffman, Frederick J.
Sherwood Anderson 1:48, 53
Willa Cather 1:159, 161
Hart Crane 2:117
F. Scott Fitzgerald 1:255, 256;
14:152
James Joyce 3:263
Franz Kafka 2:293
D. H. Lawrence 2:354
Thomas Mann 2:420
Gertrude Stein 1:432

Hofmannsthal, Hugo von
Hugo von Hofmannsthal 11:290
Eugene O'Neill 6:325
Arthur Schnitzler 4:392

Hofstadter, Richard
Charles A. Beard 15:34

Hogan, Robert
Bernard Shaw 9:422

Hoggart, Richard
George Orwell 2:506

Holbrook, David
Dylan Thomas 8:452

Holden, Inez
Ada Leverson 18:187

Holdheim, William W.
André Gide 5:230

Holl, Karl
Gerhart Hauptmann 4:196

Hollingdale, R. J.
Thomas Mann 8:266; 14:353
Friedrich Nietzsche 10:387

Hollis, Christopher
George Orwell 2:502

Critic Index

Holloway, John
Wyndham Lewis 2:393

Holman, C. Hugh
Ellen Glasgow 7:348
Sinclair Lewis 13:346
Thomas Wolfe 4:526, 528;
13:489

Holmes, H. H.
C. M. Kornbluth 8:212

Holmes, John Haynes
Kahlil Gibran 9:82

Holoch, Donald
Liu E 15:251

Holroyd, Michael
Lytton Strachey 12:413

Holroyd, Stuart
Rainer Maria Rilke 1:416
Dylan Thomas 1:470
William Butler Yeats 1:564

Honig, Edwin
Federico García Lorca 1:318

Hook, Sidney
Charles A. Beard 15:25

Hooker, Brian
George Sterling 20:371

Hooker, Jeremy
Edward Thomas 10:460

Hope, A. D.
Henry Handel Richardson 4:376

Hope, John
Booker T. Washington 10:515

Hopkins, Kenneth
Walter de la Mare 4:81

Hopkins, Mary Alden
Anthony Comstock 13:90

Horgan, Paul
Maurice Baring 8:40

Hough, Graham
Wallace Stevens 3:457

Houston, Ralph
Alun Lewis 3:287

Hovey, Richard B.
John Jay Chapman 7:196, 200

Howard, Richard
Marcel Proust 13:423
Jules Renard 17:309

Howard, Robert E.
Robert E. Howard 8:128

Howard, Thomas
Dorothy L. Sayers 15:378

Howarth, Herbert
A. E. 3:8
Ford Madox Ford 1:291
James Joyce 3:270

Howe, Irving
Sholom Aleichem 1:23, 26
Sherwood Anderson 1:43
Isaac Babel 13:19
Arturo Barea 14:46
Mikhail Bulgakov 16:79
Stig Dagerman 17:87
Theodore Dreiser 10:187
George Gissing 3:235
Thomas Hardy 18:102
Sarah Orne Jewett 1:364

Rudyard Kipling 8:207
Sinclair Lewis 4:256
H. L. Mencken 13:385
George Orwell 2:512; 15:337
Isaac Leib Peretz 16:401
Luigi Pirandello 4:341
Isaac Rosenberg 12:306
Wallace Stevens 3:464
Leo Tolstoy 4:472
Edith Wharton 3:574
Emile Zola 1:595

Howe, M. A. DeWolfe
John Jay Chapman 7:189

Howe, Marguerite
José Ortega y Gasset 9:350

Howe, P. P.
John Millington Synge 6:428

Howell, Elmo
George Washington Cable 4:34

Howells, Bernard
Paul Claudel 2:106

Howells, William Dean
Arnold Bennett 20:17
Bjørnsterne Bjørnson 7:105
Vicente Blasco Ibáñez 12:33
George Washington Cable 4:25
Charles Waddell Chesnutt
5:130
Stephen Crane 11:126
Paul Laurence Dunbar 2:127;
12:103
Mary Wilkins Freeman 9:60
Hamlin Garland 3:190
Charlotte Gilman 9:101
Thomas Hardy 4:150
William Dean Howells 7:368
Henrik Ibsen 2:218; 16:155
Henry James 11:319
Sinclair Lewis 13:325
Vachel Lindsay 17:222
Booth Tarkington 9:452
Leo Tolstoy 4:450
Mark Twain 6:456; 12:424
Juan Valera 10:497
Giovanni Verga 3:538
Booker T. Washington 10:516
Edith Wharton 9:54
Emile Zola 1:586

Hsia, T. A.
Lu Hsün 3:296

Hsueh-Feng, Feng
Lu Hsün 3:295

Hubbard, Elbert
Edgar Saltus 8:344

Hubben, William
Franz Kafka 2:296

Hudson, Lynton
·Ferenc Molnár 20:170

Hueffer, Ford Madox
See **Ford, Ford Madox**

Hueffer, Oliver Madox
Jack London 9:256

Huffman, Claire Licari
Vitaliano Brancati 12:86

Huggins, Nathan Irvin
Claude McKay 7:465

Hughes, Glenn
David Belasco 3:88

Hughes, Helen Sard
May Sinclair 3:440

Hughes, Langston
Jacques Roumain 19:331
Wallace Thurman 6:447
Mark Twain 6:474

Hughes, Merritt Y.
Luigi Pirandello 4:329

Hughes, Randolph
Christopher John Brennan
17:36

Hughes, Riley
F. Scott Fitzgerald 1:247

Hughes, Robert P.
Vladislav Khodasevich 15:208

Hughes, Ted
Wilfred Owen 5:370

Hulbert, Ann
W. H. Davies 5:210

Hull, Keith N.
T. E. Lawrence 18:159

Hume, Robert A.
Henry Adams 4:10

Humphries, Rolfe
Federico García Lorca 1:309
Lady Gregory 1:334

Huneker, James
Georg Brandes 10:63
Maxim Gorky 8:71
Rémy de Gourmont 17:131
Lafcadio Hearn 9:124
Joris-Karl Huysmans 7:411
Henrik Ibsen 2:222
Maurice Maeterlinck 3:319
Friedrich Nietzsche 10:361
Bernard Shaw 3:381
Hermann Sudermann 15:418
Leo Tolstoy 4:453
Edith Wharton 9:541

Hunt, Elizabeth R.
José Echegaray 4:99

Hunt, Peter R.
G. K. Chesterton 6:107

Hunter, William
T. F. Powys 9:364

Huntington, Christopher
Alfred Döblin 13:163

Huntington, John
H. G. Wells 19:442

Husni, Khalil
Stephen Crane 17:74

Hutchison, Percy
E. R. Eddison 15:52
Marjorie Kinnan Rawlings
4:360

Hutchinson, Percy A.
Alfred Noyes 7:506

Hutman, Norma Louise
Antonio Machado 3:311

Hutton, Richard Holt
George Meredith 17:253
John Ruskin 20:270
H. G. Wells 6:523

Huxley, Aldous
Hermann Broch 20:49
Ernest Dowson 4:86
Maxim Gorky 8:76
D. H. Lawrence 2:352
Katherine Mansfield 2:447
H. L. Mencken 13:360
Edward Thomas 10:453
Emile Verhaeren 12:470

Huxley, Julian
Pierre Teilhard de Chardin
9:479

Huysmans, J. K.
Joris-Karl Huysmans 7:409

Huxley, Aldous
George Orwell 15:306

Hyde, Fillmore
Kahlil Gibran 1:325

Hyde, Lawrence
Dorothy Richardson 3:348

Hyman, Frieda Clark
Isaac Rosenberg 12:292

Hyman, Stanley Edgar
F. Scott Fitzgerald 1:263
Constance Rourke 12:320

Hynes, Samuel
James Agee 19:26
G. K. Chesterton 1:183
Joseph Conrad 1:213
Ford Madox Ford 1:278
Thomas Hardy 4:168

Hytier, Jean
André Gide 5:214

Ibsen, Henrik
Henrik Ibsen 16:153

Iggers, Wilma Abeles
Karl Kraus 5:285

Ilie, Paul
Miguel de Unamuno 2:565

Illiano, Antonio
Ugo Betti 5:65

Inge, William Ralph
Havelock Ellis 14:121

Innes, Christopher
Paul Claudel 10:134
Alfred Jarry 14:282

Ireland, G. W.
André Gide 12:176

Iribarne, Louis
Stanisław Ignacy Witkiewicz
8:516

Iron, Ralph
See also **Schreiner, Olive**
Olive Schreiner 9:393

Irvine, William
Bernard Shaw 3:394

Irwin, W. R.
Rose Macaulay 7:425
Charles Williams 1:523

Isaacs, Edith J. R.
Robert E. Sherwood 3:411

Isherwood, Christopher
Arthur Conan Doyle 7:228
H. G. Wells 12:506

Isitt, Yvonne
Robert Musil 12:244

Isola, Pietro
Gabriele D'Annunzio 6:130

Ivanov, Vyacheslav
Innokenty Annensky 14:17

Jack, Peter Monro
Federico García Lorca 1:307
Lewis Grassic Gibbon 4:121

Jackson, Blyden
Countee Cullen 4:51

Jackson, David
James Agee 1:16

Jackson, Elizabeth R.
Benjamin Péret 20:193

Jackson, Holbrook
Maurice Maeterlinck 3:322
Israel Zangwill 16:444

Jackson, Robert Louis
Aleksandr Kuprin 5:298

Jackson, Rosemary
George MacDonald 9:310
Bram Stoker 8:402

Jackson, Thomas H.
Nathanael West 14:483

Jacob, Max
Max Jacob 6:190

Jacobson, Dan
Olive Schreiner 9:402

Jaffe, Don
Don Marquis 7:450

Jahn, Werner
Lion Feuchtwanger 3:183

Jakobson, Roman
Vladimir Mayakovsky 4:291

Jaloux, Edmond
Valéry Larbaud 9:196

James, Clive
Arthur Conan Doyle 7:232

James, Henry
Arnold Bennett 20:19
Paul Bourget 12:64
Rupert Brooke 2:51; 7:120, 121
John Jay Chapman 7:185
Joseph Conrad 6:113
F. Marion Crawford 10:139
George Gissing 3:221
Thomas Hardy 4:156; 18:90
William Dean Howells 7:365
Henrik Ibsen 2:218
Henry James 2:244
Andrew Lang 16:257
Pierre Loti 11:352
Edmond Rostand 6:375
Hugh Walpole 5:492
H. G. Wells 6:525, 526; 12:493
Edith Wharton 3:555, 557
Emile Zola 1:586

James, M. R.
M. R. James 6:206

James, Stuart B.
Mark Twain 19:402

James, William
William James 15:155

Jameson, Fredric
Raymond Chandler 7:170
Wyndham Lewis 9:247

Jameson, Storm
Jacinto Benavente 3:95
Walter de la Mare 4:71
José Echegaray 4:100

Janeway, Elizabeth
Joyce Cary 1:140

Janouch, Gustav
Alfred Döblin 13:158
Franz Kafka 13:256

Janson, Kristofer
Bjørnstjerne Bjørnson 7:101

Jarrell, Randall
Ellen Glasgow 7:334
A. E. Housman 10:242
Rudyard Kipling 8:201
Walter de la Mare 4:79
Wallace Stevens 3:449

Jarry, Alfred
Alfred Jarry 14:268

Jaspers, Karl
Friedrich Nietzsche 10:370

Jean-Aubry, G.
Edmond Rostand 6:377

Jeffares, A. Norman
Oliver St. John Gogarty 15:107

Jeffers, Robinson
George Sterling 20:377

Jelliffe, Smith Ely
Henrik Ibsen 16:157

Jennings, Elizabeth
Wallace Stevens 3:459

Jensen, Emily
Virginia Woolf 20:426

Jerome, Joseph
Montague Summers 16:430

Jerrold, Walter
Alfred Noyes 7:508

Jiménez, Juan Ramón
Antonio Machado 3:306

Joad, C.E.M.
Samuel Butler 1:134
Havelock Ellis 14:116
H. L. Mencken 13:377

Johannesson, Eric O.
Selma Lagerlöf 4:241

John, Alun
Alun Lewis 3:291

Johns, Marilyn
August Strindberg 8:416

Johnson, Abby Arthur
Harriet Monroe 12:225

Johnson, Charles
Raymond Roussel 20:251

Johnson, Diane
Colette 5:173

Johnson, Gerald W.
Walter White 15:481

Johnson, James Weldon
Countee Cullen 4:41
Paul Laurence Dunbar 12:105
James Weldon Johnson 19:205
Claude McKay 7:456

Johnson, Lionel
Rudyard Kipling 8:176
William Butler Yeats 11:507

Johnson, Pamela Hansford
Marcel Proust 13:418

Johnson, R. Brimley
Stella Benson 17:18
Sheila Kaye-Smith 20:97
Rose Macaulay 7:421
May Sinclair 3:435

Johnson, Robert Underwood
George Washington Cable 4:26

Johnson, Roberta
Gabriel Miró 5:342

Johnson, Talmage C.
Kahlil Gibran 9:83

Johnson, Walter
August Strindberg 8:417

Joll, James
F. T. Marinetti 10:316

Jonas, Ilsedore B.
Thomas Mann 14:348

Jones, Anne Goodwyn
Kate Chopin 14:80

Jones, D. G.
Bliss Carman 7:149
Charles G. D. Roberts 8:325

Jones, Ernest
Ronald Firbank 1:225

Jones, Frank
Stephen Vincent Benét 7:75

Jones, G. P.
Frederick Rolfe 12:279

Jones, John Bush
W. S. Gilbert 3:215

Jones, Llewellyn
Joseph Hergesheimer 11:274

Jones, P. Mansell
Emile Verhaeren 12:474

Jones, Robert A.
Frank Wedekind 7:587

Jones, Sonia
Alfonsina Storni 5:451

Jong, Erica
Colette 1:193, 194

Jordan, Marion
Andrei Platonov 14:416

Jordy, William H.
Henry Adams 4:13

Jorgenson, Theodore
O. E. Rölvaag 17:327

Josephson, Matthew
Lafcadio Hearn 9:128

Josipovici, Gabriel
Bruno Schulz 5:427

Joyce, James
Henrik Ibsen 2:219
Bernard Shaw 3:381
Oscar Wilde 1:494

Juhnke, Janet
L. Frank Baum 7:23

Jullian, Philipe
Gabriele D'Annunzio 6:143
Oscar Wilde 8:496

Jung, C. G.
William James 15:165
James Joyce 3:257

Jung, Claire
George Heym 9:145

Jussem-Wilson, N.
Charles Péguy 10:410

Justice, Donald
A. E. Housman 1:357

Justus, James H.
Kate Chopin 14:72
Joseph Hergesheimer 11:282
Katherine Mansfield 8:283

Kafka, Franz
Endre Ady 11:12
Alfred Döblin 13:158
Franz Kafka 6:219; 13:256
Christian Morgenstern 8:304
Rudolf Steiner 13:435
Franz Werfel 8:466

Kahler, Erich
Hermann Broch 20:63
Franz Werfel 8:471

Kahn, Coppélia
Rebecca Harding Davis 6:155

Kahn, Lothar
Lion Feuchtwanger 3:183, 187

Kaiser, Ernst
Robert Musil 12:232

Kallet, Marilyn
Paul Eluard 7:260

Kallich, Martin
Lytton Strachey 12:409

Kam, Rose Salberg
Joseph Conrad 1:220

Kanfer, Stefan
Anne Frank 17:120
Kahlil Gibran 1:329

Kanin, Garson
Anne Frank 17:120

Kantra, Robert A.
Hilaire Belloc 18:30

Kaplan, Sydney Janet
Dorothy Richardson 3:359
May Sinclair 11:414

Karl, Frederick R.
Joyce Cary 1:146
Joseph Conrad 6:117; 13:126
George Orwell 6:349

Karlinsky, Simon
Innokenty Annensky 14:28
Zinaida Hippius 9:168
Andrei Platonov 14:422
Marina Tsvetaeva 7:559

Kauffmann, Stanley
James Agee 1:5
Kate Chopin 14:59
Knut Hamsun 14:242

Kaufmann, R. J.
John Middleton Murry 16:342
August Strindberg 1:454

Kaufmann, Walter
Friedrich Nietzsche 10:391

Kaun, Alexander S.
Leonid Andreyev 3:21
Georg Brandes 10:62
Sergei Esenin 4:110
Vladimir Mayakovsky 18:241

Kayden, Eugene M.
  Leonid Andreyev **3**:20
Kaye-Smith, Sheila
  Sheila Kaye-Smith **20**:109
Kayser, Wolfgang
  Hanns Heinz Ewers **12**:136
  Christian Morgenstern **8**:306
Kazin, Alfred
  James Agee **1**:4
  Sholom Aleichem **1**:25
  Sherwood Anderson **1**:47; **10**:41
  Charles A. Beard **15**:24
  Hilaire Belloc **18**:25
  Randolph S. Bourne **16**:51
  James Branch Cabell **6**:69
  Willa Cather **11**:98
  John Jay Chapman **7**:194
  Stephen Crane **11**:136
  Theodore Dreiser **10**:184; **18**:63
  Édouard Dujardin **13**:183
  F. Scott Fitzgerald **1**:250;
    14:151
  Anne Frank **17**:106
  Hamlin Garland **3**:195
  André Gide **12**:164
  Ellen Glasgow **2**:176
  Maxim Gorky **8**:82
  Joseph Hergesheimer **11**:278
  William Dean Howells **7**:378;
    17:191
  William James **15**:172
  James Joyce **3**:259
  Franz Kafka **2**:296
  D. H. Lawrence **2**:365; **16**:298
  Sinclair Lewis **4**:250
  Ludwig Lewisohn **19**:279
  Jack London **9**:261
  Rose Macaulay **7**:423
  Thomas Mann **8**:272
  H. L. Mencken **13**:378
  George Orwell **15**:357
  Marcel Proust **7**:532
  Constance Rourke **12**:319
  Gertrude Stein **1**:431
  H. G. Wells **12**:508
  Edith Wharton **3**:565
  Thomas Wolfe **4**:516; **13**:486
  Elinor Wylie **8**:530
Kedourie, Elie
  T. E. Lawrence **18**:169
Keefer, L. B.
  Gerhart Hauptmann **4**:199
Keeley, Edmund
  C. P. Cavafy **2**:93, 94
Keene, Donald
  Akutagawa Ryūnosuke **16**:33
  Dazai Osamu **11**:173
  Ishikawa Tabuboku **15**:124
  Masaoka Shiki **18**:233
  Toson Shimazaki **5**:433
Keith, W. J.
  Charles G. D. Roberts **8**:323
  Edward Thomas **10**:465
Kejzlarov, Ingeborg
  Joseph Hergesheimer **11**:284
Kelleher, John V.
  James Joyce **16**:216
Kelley, James
  Akutagawa Ryūnosuke **16**:19
  Josephine Tey **14**:450

Kelly, H. A., S.J.
  Édouard Dujardin **13**:187
Kelly, Robert Glynn
  Dorothy Richardson **3**:353
Kemelman, H. G.
  Eugene O'Neill **6**:326
Kendrick, Walter
  George Orwell **15**:344
Keniston, R. H.
  Vicente Blasco Ibáñez **12**:28
Kennedy, Andrew K.
  Bernard Shaw **3**:406
Kennedy, Edwin J. Jr.
  Virginia Woolf **5**:517
Kennedy, Eileen **7**:274
Kennedy, Gail
  William James **15**:176
Kennedy, P. C.
  Virginia Woolf **5**:506
Kennedy, Richard S.
  Thomas Wolfe **13**:482
Kennedy, Ruth Lee
  José Echegaray **4**:100
Kennelly, Brendan
  George Moore **7**:491
Kenner, Hugh
  Roy Campbell **5**:120
  F. Scott Fitzgerald **1**:273
  Ford Madox Ford **1**:278
  James Joyce **3**:268; **16**:229
  Wyndham Lewis **2**:388, 389
  Wallace Stevens **3**:474
  William Butler Yeats **1**:566
Kenny, John M., Jr.
  F. Scott Fitzgerald **14**:149
Kent, George E.
  Claude McKay **7**:467
Kenworthy, B. J.
  Georg Kaiser **9**:179
Kercheville, F. M.
  Rubén Darío **4**:62
Keresztury, Dezső
  Endre Ady **11**:22
Kermode, Frank
  Christopher John Brennan
    17:42
  Ernest Dowson **4**:90
  Giuseppe Tomasi di Lampedusa
    13:292
  D. H. Lawrence **2**:372; **16**:308
  Robert Musil **12**:251
  Wallace Stevens **3**:458
  Arthur Symons **11**:442
Kern, Gary
  Mikhail Zoshchenko **15**:510
Kernahan, Coulson
  Sheila Kaye-Smith **20**:106
Kerrigan, Anthony
  Pío Baroja **8**:53
  Miguel de Unamuno **2**:568
Kessler, Jascha
  Miklós Radnóti **16**:421
Kessler, Martin
  George Orwell **15**:303

Kestner, Joseph
  Antoine de Saint-Exupéry **2**:523
Kettle, Arnold
  Arnold Bennett **5**:48
  Joyce Cary **1**:141
  Joseph Conrad **1**:206
  John Galsworthy **1**:301
  Henry James **2**:264
Keylor, William R.
  Charles Péguy **10**:416
Khlebnikov, Velimir
  Velimir Khlebnikov **20**:123
Khodasevich, Vladislav
  Valery Bryusov **10**:79
  Zinaida Hippius **9**:155
  Vladislav Khodasevich **15**:198
Kidder, Rushworth M.
  Dylan Thomas **8**:458
Kiddle, Lawrence B.
  Mariano Azuela **3**:75
Kilmer, Joyce
  Havelock Ellis **14**:104
  Lafcadio Hearn **9**:125
  Lionel Johnson **19**:232
  Don Marquis **7**:434
  Rabindranath Tagore **3**:482
  Sara Teasdale **4**:424
Kilpatrick, James J.
  H. L. Mencken **13**:395
Kimball, Sidney Fiske
  Henry Adams **4**:4
Kimball, Sue L.
  Stephen Crane **17**:70
Kinahan, Frank
  F. Scott Fitzgerald **1**:267
Kindilien, Carlin T.
  Hamlin Garland **3**:197
King, C. D.
  Édouard Dujardin **13**:183
King, Edmund L.
  Gabriel Miró **5**:345
King, Henry Safford
  Paul Heyse **8**:121
King, J. Marin
  Marina Tsvetaeva **7**:570
King, Jonathan
  Henri Barbusse **5**:18
King, Martin Luther, Jr.
  Booker T. Washington **10**:530
King, Richard H.
  James Agee **19**:45
Kinnaird, Clark
  Damon Runyon **10**:428
Kinnamon, Keneth
  Charlotte L. Forten **16**:148
Kipling, Rudyard
  H. Rider Haggard **11**:241
Kirby, Michael
  F. T. Marinetti **10**:317
Kirchwey, Freda
  Walter White **15**:473
Kirk, Russell
  Hilaire Belloc **18**:30
  George Orwell **15**:309

Kirkconnell, Watson
  Endre Ady **11**:13
  Mihály Babits **14**:37
Klarmann, Adolf D.
  Wolfgang Borchert **5**:103
  Franz Werfel **8**:472
Klibbe, Lawrence H.
  José María de Pereda **16**:379
Klieneberger, H. R.
  Rainer Maria Rilke **19**:314
Klinck, Carl F.
  Wilfred Campbell **9**:31
  Robert W. Service **15**:411
Klingborg, Arne
  Rudolf Steiner **13**:455
Klingopulus, G. D.
  Rémy de Gourmont **17**:150
Klotz, Martin B.
  Isaak Babel **2**:31
Knapp, Bettina L.
  Antonin Artaud **3**:52
  Paul Claudel **10**:134
  Maurice Maeterlinck **3**:331
Knaust, Rebecca
  Giuseppe Giacosa **7**:315
Knecht, Loring D.
  André Gide **12**:172
Knickerbocker, Conrad
  Malcolm Lowry **6**:238
Knight, Damon
  C. M. Kornbluth **8**:216
  Henry Kuttner **10**:269
Knight, G. Wilson
  Henrik Ibsen **16**:171
  John Middleton Murry **16**:345
  Oscar Wilde **1**:503
Knight, Max
  Christian Morgenstern **8**:308
Knister, Raymond
  Duncan Campbell Scott **6**:385
Knodel, Arthur
  Jules Renard **17**:304
  Pierre Teilhard de Chardin
    9:478
Knowlton, Edgar C., Jr.
  Vicente Blasco Ibáñez **12**:48
Knox, Ronald A.
  Maurice Baring **8**:37
  G. K. Chesterton **6**:99
Kobler, J. F.
  Katherine Mansfield **8**:289
Koch, Stephen
  Antonin Artaud **3**:51
Kocmanova, Jessie
  R. B. Cunninghame Graham
    19:118
Koestler, Arthur
  George Orwell **2**:498
Koht, Halvdan
  Nordahl Grieg **10**:205
Kolb, Philip
  Marcel Proust **7**:547
Königsberg, I.
  Alfred Jarry **2**:283

Korg, Jacob
George Gissing 3:235

Kornbluth, C. M.
C. M. Kornbluth 8:213
George Orwell 15:307

Kort, Wolfgang
Alfred Döblin 13:173

Kosove, Joan Pataky
Maurice Maeterlinck 3:330

Kossman, Rudolf R.
Henry James 11:338

Kostelanetz, Richard
Gertrude Stein 6:414

Kostka, Edmund
Heinrich Mann 9:329

Kott, Jan
Tadeusz Borowski 9:23
Stanisław Ignacy Witkiewicz
8:507

Kotzamanidou, M.
Innokenty Annensky 14:31

Kozlenko, Vladimar
George Jean Nathan 18:311

Kramer, Leonie
Henry Handel Richardson 4:380

Kramer, Victor A.
James Agee 1:16; 19:36

Krans, Horatio Sheafe
William Butler Yeats 11:512

Kraus, Michael
Douglas Southall Freeman
11:224

Kreuter, Gretchen
F. Scott Fitzgerald 1:252

Kreuter Kent
F. Scott Fitzgerald 1:252

Kreymborg, Alfred
Edgar Lee Masters 2:465
Thomas Wolfe 4:518

Kridl, Manfred
Władysław Stanisław Reymont
5:393
Henryk Sienkiewicz 3:429

Krige, Uys
Olive Schreiner 9:397

Krispyn, Egbert
Georg Heym 9:145
Carl Sternheim 8:374

Kronenberger, Louis
Henry Adams 4:6
Max Beerbohm 1:67
Vicente Blasco Ibáñez 12:40
W. H. Davies 5:204
Ronald Firbank 1:225
Jean Giraudoux 7:317
George Jean Nathan 18:321
Carl Van Doren 18:402
Franz Werfel 8:468
Virginia Woolf 5:507
Alexander Woollcott 5:523

Krook, Dorothea
Henry James 2:272

Kroth, Anya M.
Marina Tsvetaeva 7:567

Krouse, Agate Nesaule
Dorothy L. Sayers 15:379

Kruchonykh, Alexey
Velimir Khlebnikov 20:123

Krutch, Joseph Wood
Maxwell Anderson 2:6
Philip Barry 11:46
Louis Bromfield 11:78
Ivan Bunin 6:44
Anton Chekhov 10:105
Colette 1:192
Rachel Crothers 19:76
Havelock Ellis 14:117
Zona Gale 7:280
Ellen Glasgow 7:335
Rémy de Gourmont 17:140
Joseph Hergesheimer 11:270
Henrik Ibsen 2:230
Sinclair Lewis 4:255
Ludwig Lewisohn 19:266
Rose Macaulay 7:423
Arthur Machen 4:277
George Jean Nathan 18:316
Eugene O'Neill 1:396
Marcel Proust 13:403
Władysław Stanisław Reymont
5:390
Frederick Rolfe 12:267
Constance Rourke 12:318
Bernard Shaw 3:397
Robert E. Sherwood 3:412
May Sinclair 3:438; 11:411
August Strindberg 1:450
Carl Van Doren 18:395, 399
Jakob Wassermann 6:508
Oscar Wilde 1:502
Virginia Woolf 20:391
Alexander Woollcott 5:521

Krzyzanowski, Jerzy R.
Władysław Stanisław Reymont
5:395
Stanisław Ignacy Witkiewicz
8:509

Kuhns, Richard F.
Giuseppe Tomasi di Lampedusa
13:307

Kunitomo, Tadao
Mori Ōgai 14:369

Kunst, Arthur E.
Lafcadio Hearn 9:135

Kurrick, Maire Jaanus
Georg Trakl 5:466

Kustow, Michael
Bertolt Brecht 1:122

Kuttner, Alfred Booth
D. H. Lawrence 16:277

Kuttner, Henry
Henry Kuttner 10:265

Kwiat, Joseph J.
Stephen Crane 11:142
Theodore Dreiser 10:200

LaBelle, Maurice M.
H. L. Mencken 13:388

Labor, Earle
Jack London 9:272; 15:256

Laffitte, Sophie
Anton Chekov 10:111

Lafourcade, Georges
Arnold Bennett 5:38

La France, Marston
Stephen Crane 11:156

Lagerkvist, Pär
August Strindberg 1:456

Lagerroth, Erland
Selma Lagerlöf 4:241

Lago, Mary M.
Rabindranath Tagore 3:498,
499

Lainoff, Seymour
Ludwig Lewisohn 19:292

Lakshin, Vladimir
Mikhail Bulgakov 2:73

Lalou, René
Rémy de Gourmont 17:137
Valéry Larbaud 9:196
Jules Renard 17:302
Marcel Schwob 20:322

Lambasa, Frank
Franz Werfel 8:474

Lambert, J. W.
John Galsworthy 1:304
Saki 3:369

Lamm, Martin
Federico García Lorca 1:314
August Strindberg 1:444

Lampan, Archibald
Charles G. D. Roberts 8:313

Landis, Joseph C.
Sholem Asch 3:70

Landsberg, Paul L.
Franz Kafka 13:258

Lane, Ann J.
Charlotte Gilman 9:108, 112

Lane, Lauriat, Jr.
Mark Twain 12:441

Lang, Andrew
Anatole France 9:44
H. Rider Haggard 11:237
Thomas Hardy 18:78, 85
Rudyard Kipling 8:176
George MacDonald 9:288
Mark Twain 12:427
Emile Zola 6:559

Lang, Cecil Y.
Charles Swinburne 8:439

Langbaum, Robert
Thomas Hardy 10:233

Lange, Victor
Georg Kaiser 9:184

Langer, Lawrence L.
Tadeusz Borowski 9:25

Langford, Walter M.
José Rubén Romero 14:444

Langland, Elizabeth
Theodore Dreiser 18:73

Langstaff, Eleanor De Selms
Andrew Lang 16:269

Lapp, John C.
Emile Zola 6:568

Lardner, John
Damon Runyon 10:427

Lardner, Ring
Ring Lardner 14:295

Lardner, Ring, Jr.
Ring Lardner 14:302

Larsen, Erling
James Agee 1:16

Larsen, Hanna Astrup
Knut Hamsun 2:202
Selma Lagerlöf 4:234
Sigrid Undset 3:511

Larson, Harold
Charles A. Beard 15:32
Bjørnstjerne Bjørnson 7:109

Lasch, Christopher
Lincoln Steffens 20:350

Lask, Thomas
George Jean Nathan 18:320

Laski, Harold J.
Randolph S. Bourne 16:44

Laski, Marghanita
Radclyffe Hall 12:192

Last, R. W.
Georg Kaiser 9:185

Latané, John H.
Charles A. Beard 15:17

Lauterbach, Charles E.
W. S. Gilbert 3:212

Lavrin, Janko
Leonid Andreyev 3:26
Andrey Bely 7:49
Aleksandr Blok 5:98
Sergei Esenin 4:110
Maxim Gorky 8:76
Knut Hamsun 2:203
Fyodor Sologub 9:436

Lawler, James R.
Paul Claudel 2:109

Lawrence, D. H.
R. B. Cunninghame Graham
19:106
Thomas Hardy 4:162; 18:90
D. H. Lawrence 9:217; 16:275
Thomas Mann 14:323
F. T. Marinetti 10:314
Frederick Rolfe 12:268
Giovanni Verga 3:539, 543
H. G. Wells 6:529
Walter White 15:475

Lawrence, Frieda
D. H. Lawrence 16:286

Lawrence, Margaret
Radclyffe Hall 12:189
Rose Macaulay 7:423

Lawrence, Thomas Edward
T. E. Lawrence 18:133, 137
Charlotte Mew 8:296

Lawry, Jon S.
Sherwood Anderson 10:46

Lawson, Henry
Miles Franklin 7:264

Lawson, John Howard
Robert E. Sherwood 3:410

Lawson, Richard H.
Edith Wharton 3:579

Lawson, Robb
Algernon Blackwood 5:70

Lawson, Victor
Paul Laurence Dunbar 12:110

Layton, Susan
Yevgeny Ivanovich Zamyatin
8:555

Lea, F. A.
John Middleton Murry 16:341

Lea, Henry A.
Franz Werfel 8:481

Leach, Henry Goddard
Selma Lagerlöf 4:230

Leacock, Stephen
O. Henry 1:346
Mark Twain 12:434

Leal, Luis
Mariano Azuela 3:80

Leary, Lewis
Kate Chopin 5:150
Lafcadio Hearn 9:134
Mark Twain 6:475

Leaska, Mitchell A.
Virginia Woolf 5:512

Leavis, F. R.
Joseph Conrad 1:204; 13:102
Thomas Hardy 4:164
Henry James 2:262
D. H. Lawrence 2:360
Isaac Rosenberg 12:290
Edward Thomas 10:454
Leo Tolstoy 11:473
Mark Twain 19:363
William Butler Yeats 18:441

Leavis, Q. D.
Dorothy L. Sayers 2:528
Edith Wharton 3:564

Leblanc-Maeterlinck, Georgette
Maurice Maeterlinck 3:320

Lebowitz, Naomi
Italo Svevo 2:554

Lederman, Marie Jean
Katherine Mansfield 2:456

Lednicki, Waclaw
Henryk Sienkiewicz 3:427

Leduc, Renato
John Reed 9:386

Lee, Alan
John Ruskin 20:304

Lee, Alice
Isaak Babel 2:23

Lee, Lynn
Don Marquis 7:450

Lee, Vernon
John Ruskin 20:265

Leftwich, Joseph
Israel Zangwill 16:449
Stefan Zweig 17:437

Le Gallienne, Richard
Rudyard Kipling 8:179
Don Marquis 7:435
George Meredith 17:260
Alfred Noyes 7:504
Montague Summers 16:427
Arthur Symons 11:426

Leggett, B. J.
A. E. Housman 10:259

Legh-Jones, J.
Guillaume Apollinaire 3:40

Lehan, Richard
F. Scott Fitzgerald 1:267
Ford Madox Ford 1:287

Lehmann, John
Rupert Brooke 7:129
Lewis Grassic Gibbon 4:121
Alun Lewis 3:287
Edward Thomas 10:455
Virginia Woolf 1:538

Lehnert, Herbert
Georg Heym 9:151

Leiber, Fritz, Jr.
Robert E. Howard 8:130
H. P. Lovecraft 4:267

Leibowitz, Herbert A.
Hart Crane 2:122

Leiris, Michel
Raymond Roussel 20:234

Lemaitre, Georges
André Gide 5:216
Jean Giraudoux 2:169

Lemaître, Jules
Paul Bourget 12:65
Anatole France 9:46
Pierre Loti 11:357

LeMoyne, Jean
Hector Saint-Denys Garneau
13:197

Lenin, Nikolai
See also **Lenin, V. I.**
Vladimir Mayakovsky 4:289

Lenin, V. I.
See also **Lenin, Nikolai**
John Reed 9:382
Leo Tolstoy 4:452

Lentricchia, Frank
Wallace Stevens 12:374

Leon, Derrick
Marcel Proust 7:527

Lerner, Max
Charles A. Beard 15:28
Randolph S. Bourne 16:49

Lerner, Michael G.
Pierre Loti 11:368
Boris Vian 9:535

LeSage, Laurent
Jean Giraudoux 2:163

Leslie, Shane
Frederick Rolfe 12:266

Lessing, Doris
A. E. Coppard 5:181
Olive Schreiner 9:400

Lessing, Otto
Heinrich Mann 9:314
Detlev von Liliencron 18:208

Levey, Michael
Thomas Hardy 10:223
Francis Thompson 4:441

Levi, Louise Landes
René Daumal 14:91

Levin, Harry
James Joyce 3:272; 16:219
José Ortega y Gasset 9:339
Charles Péguy 10:407
Marcel Proust 7:540; 13:412
Emile Zola 6:566

Levin, Meyer
Anne Frank 17:102

Levine, Robert T.
Franz Kafka 6:229

Levinson, Ronald B.
William James 15:170

Levitt, Morton P.
Nikos Kazantzakis 2:318

Le Vot, André
F. Scott Fitzgerald 14:176

Levy, Babette May
Mary Wilkins Freeman 9:67

Levy, Diane Wolfe
Anatole France 9:57

Levy, Karen D.
Alain-Fournier 6:28

Levy, Kurt L.
Mariano Azuela 3:82

Levy, Leo B.
Mark Twain 19:391

Lewis, Allan
Federico García Lorca 7:296
Maxim Gorky 8:88

Lewis, C. S.
Hilaire Belloc 18:20
G. K. Chesterton 6:99
E. R. Eddison 15:54, 57
H. Rider Haggard 11:246
Rudyard Kipling 8:192
David Lindsay 15:216, 217
George MacDonald 9:293
George Orwell 2:501
Dorothy L. Sayers 15:376
H. G. Wells 12:496
Charles Williams 1:511; 11:485

Lewis, Charlton M.
Francis Thompson 4:437

Lewis, Patricia M.
Akutagawa Ryūnosuke 16:24

Lewis, Paula Gilbert
Emile Nelligan 14:400

Lewis, Peter
Charlotte Gilman 9:115

Lewis, R. W. B.
Joseph Conrad 1:210
Hart Crane 5:191
F. Scott Fitzgerald 1:245
Henry James 2:267
Edith Wharton 3:575; 9:546

Lewis, Sinclair
Sherwood Anderson 10:34
Willa Cather 1:151
Theodore Dreiser 10:164
Hamlin Garland 3:194
Joseph Hergesheimer 11:260
William Dean Howells 7:374
Sinclair Lewis 13:325
Carl Van Doren 18:401

Lewis, Theophilus
Wallace Thurman 6:445

Lewis, Wyndham
Sherwood Anderson 10:38
James Joyce 3:253
H. L. Mencken 13:374
Virginia Woolf 20:393

Lewisohn, Adèle
Hanns Heinz Ewers 12:133

Lewisohn, Ludwig
A. E. Coppard 5:176
Zona Gale 7:278
John Galsworthy 1:295
Rémy de Gourmont 17:136
Gerhart Hauptmann 4:197
William Dean Howells 7:374
Georg Kaiser 9:171
Ludwig Lewisohn 19:262
Detlev von Liliencron 18:211
Ferenc Molnár 20:158
Luigi Pirandello 4:327
Rainer Maria Rilke 1:408
Hermann Sudermann 15:426
Ernst Toller 10:475

Leys, Gwen
Radclyffe Hall 12:189

Lid, R. W.
Raymond Chandler 7:168

Liddell, Robert
C. P. Cavafy 7:152

Liddiard, Jean
Isaac Rosenberg 12:308

Light, James F.
Nathanael West 1:486

Light, Martin
Sinclair Lewis 13:348

Lima, Robert
Federico García Lorca 1:321
Ramón del Valle-Inclán 5:485

Lindbergh, Anne Morrow
Antoine de Saint-Exupéry 2:516

Lindenberger, Herbert
Georg Trakl 5:462

Lindsay, (Nicholas) Vachel
O. Henry 19:168

Linklater, Eric
James Bridie 3:131

Linn, Rolf N.
Heinrich Mann 9:320

Lippett, Noriko Mizuta
Akutagawa Ryūnosuke 16:31

Lippman, Monroe
Philip Barry 11:61

Lippmann, Walter
Charles A. Beard 15:18
Sinclair Lewis 13:329
Amy Lowell 8:223
H. L. Mencken 13:369
George Jean Nathan 18:307
John Reed 9:381

Liptzin, Solomon
Arthur Schnitzler 4:393
Stefan Zweig 17:432

Liszt, Franz
Friedrich Nietzsche 10:353

Littell, Robert
Ambrose Bierce 1:83
Carl Van Doren 18:396

Little, Roger
Guillaume Apollinaire 3:45

Littlefield, Hazel
Lord Dunsany 2:145

Littlefield, Henry M.
L. Frank Baum 7:17

Littlejohn, David
F. Scott Fitzgerald **1**:254
James Weldon Johnson **19**:208

Livingston, Dennis
C. M. Kornbluth **8**:217

Livingstone, Angela
Marina Tsvetaeva **7**:563

Livingstone, L.
Miguel de Unamuno **2**:558

Lloyd-Jones, Hugh
Friedrich Nietzsche **10**:385

Lo Cicero, Donald
Paul Heyse **8**:122

Locke, Alain
James Weldon Johnson **19**:207

Locke, Frederick W.
Alain-Fournier **6**:17

Lockerbie, S. I.
Max Jacob **6**:197

Lockert, Lacy
Henryk Sienkiewicz **3**:423

Locklin, Gerald
Nathanael West **1**:489

Lockwood, William J.
Rose Macaulay **7**:428

Lodge, David
Maurice Baring **8**:38
Hilaire Belloc **18**:33
Arnold Bennett **20**:30
G. K. Chesterton **1**:181
Gertrude Stein **1**:442

Lodge, Oliver
Alfred Noyes **7**:506

Loftus, Richard J.
A. E. **3**:9
James Stephens **4**:415

Logan, J. D.
John McCrae **12**:208
Charles G. D. Roberts **8**:315

Loggins, Vernon
Paul Laurence Dunbar **12**:107
Amy Lowell **1**:378
Gertrude Stein **1**:427

Lohner, Edgar
Gottfried Benn **3**:104

Lohrke, Eugene
Ricarda Huch **13**:242

London, Jack
Jack London **9**:256

London, Kurt
Alexey Nikolayevich Tolstoy **18**:361

Long, Richard A.
James Weldon Johnson **19**:209

Long, Robert Emmet
F. Scott Fitzgerald **14**:176

Longaker, Mark
Ernest Dowson **4**:89
Sheila Kaye-Smith **20**:111

Longford, Elizabeth
Arthur Conan Doyle **7**:232

Longhurst, C. A.
Miguel de Unamuno **9**:523

Loomis, Emerson Robert
Bertolt Brecht **6**:30

Loram, Ian C.
Georg Kaiser **9**:177

Lott, Robert E.
Juan Valera **10**:506

Love, Debra Harper
Miguel de Unamuno **9**:522

Lovecraft, H. P.
Ambrose Bierce **7**:90
Algernon Blackwood **5**:72
F. Marion Crawford **10**:149
E. R. Eddison **15**:52
William Hope Hodgson **13**:231
Robert E. Howard **8**:129
M. R. James **6**:206
M. P. Shiel **8**:359
Bram Stoker **8**:386

Loveman, Samuel
Ambrose Bierce **7**:89

Lovett, Robert Morss
Sherwood Anderson **1**:35, 37, 41
Radclyffe Hall **12**:186
May Sinclair **3**:435, 440
Edith Wharton **3**:559

Loving, Pierre
Carl Sternheim **8**:367
Ernst Toller **10**:476

Lowell, Amy
Stephen Crane **11**:129
Rémy de Gourmont **17**:127
Vachel Lindsay **17**:226
Amy Lowell **8**:223
Edgar Lee Masters **2**:462
Edwin Arlington Robinson **5**:401
Emile Verhaeren **12**:465

Lowell, James Russell
William Dean Howells **7**:363
Algernon Charles Swinburne **8**:425

Lowell, Robert
Wallace Stevens **3**:448

Lowenthal, Leo
Knut Hamsun **14**:233

Lowes, John Livingston
Amy Lowell **8**:226

Lowry, Malcolm
Malcolm Lowry **6**:235

Lubbock, Percy
Henry James **11**:322
Leo Tolstoy **4**:454
Edith Wharton **3**:557

Lucas, Frank L.
Rupert Brooke **7**:123
Roy Campbell **5**:116
W. H. Davies **5**:202
A. E. Housman **10**:240
Isaac Rosenberg **12**:287
Algernon Charles Swinburne **8**:434

Lucas, John
Arnold Bennett **5**:50

Luciani, Vincent
Guiseppe Giacosa **7**:313

Lucie-Smith, Edward
Paul Claudel **2**:107

Lüdeke, H.
Elinor Wylie **8**:527

Luft, David S.
Robert Musil **12**:261

Lukács, Georg
Endre Ady **11**:23
Lion Feuchtwanger **3**:179
Maxim Gorky **8**:77
Heinrich Mann **9**:318
Thomas Mann **2**:419
Leo Tolstoy **4**:462

Lukashevich, Olga
Bruno Schulz **5**:422

Luker, Nicholas
Aleksandr Kuprin **5**:303

Lumley, Frederick
James Bridie **3**:137
Jean Giraudoux **2**:157

Lundquist, James
Theodore Dreiser **10**:193
Sinclair Lewis **4**:261

Lundwall, Sam J.
C. M. Kornbluth **8**:218

Lupoff, Richard A.
Edgar Rice Burroughs **2**:77

Luquiens, Frederick Bliss
Henry Adams **4**:5

Lurie, Alison
A. A. Milne **6**:320

Luyben, Helen L.
James Bridie **3**:140

Lyell, William, Jr.
Lu Hsün **3**:302

Lynch, Hannah
José María de Pereda **16**:362

Lynd, Robert
John Millington Synge **6**:431

Lynes, Carlos, Jr.
André Gide **12**:147

Lyngstad, Sverre
Jonas Lie **5**:330

Lynn, Kenneth S.
Theodore Dreiser **10**:181
Emma Goldman **13**:222
William Dean Howells **17**:161
Constance Rourke **12**:323
Mark Twain **6**:482; **19**:382

Lyon, Melvin
Henry Adams **4**:19

Lyons, Charles R.
Bertolt Brecht **13**:55

Lyons, J. B.
Oliver St. John Gogarty **15**:116

Lyons, Phyllis I.
Dazai Osamu **11**:190

Lytton, The Earl of
A. E. **10**:12

Mabbott, T. O.
H. P. Lovecraft **4**:265

MacAdam, Alfred J.
Machado de Assis **10**:303

MacAndrew, Andrew R.
Aleksandr Kuprin **5**:299

Macaree, David
Lewis Grassic Gibbon **4**:124

MacArthur, James
Bram Stoker **8**:385

Macauley, Robie
Ford Madox Ford **15**:79

MacCampbell, Donald
T. F. Powys **9**:367

MacCann, Donnarae
Mark Twain **19**:407

MacCarthy, Desmond
See also **Hawk, Affable**
Hilaire Belloc **18**:27
Paul Claudel **10**:122
Radclyffe Hall **12**:186
Vernon Lee **5**:312
Gregorio Martínez Sierra and María Martínez Sierra **6**:281
Gertrude Stein **6**:403
August Strindberg **8**:407
Ernst Toller **10**:476

MacClintock, Lander
Guiseppe Giacosa **7**:308
Luigi Pirandello **4**:338

MacDiarmid, Hugh
Lewis Grassic Gibbon **4**:122
R. B. Cunninghame Graham **19**:116

Macdonald, Dwight
James Agee **1**:7; **19**:22
Hilaire Belloc **18**:26
Randolph S. Bourne **16**:53
George Orwell **2**:505

MacDonald, George
George MacDonald **9**:288

MacDonald, Greville
George MacDonald **9**:291

Macdonald, Ian R.
Gabriel Miró **5**:342

MacDonald, William
Charles A. Beard **15**:17

MacGillivray, Royce
Bram Stoker **8**:390

Machen, Arthur
Mary Wilkins Freeman **9**:66

MacInnes, Colin
Ada Leverson **18**:191

Mack, John E.
T. E. Lawrence **18**:166

Mackail, J. W.
Maurice Maeterlinck **3**:317

MacKay, L. A.
Bliss Carman **7**:144

Mackenzie, Compton
Joseph Conrad **1**:201
John Galsworthy **1**:298

MacKenzie, Kenneth D.
Rudolf Steiner **13**:441

Mackridge, Peter
Nikos Kazantzakis **5**:272

Maclaren, Hamish
A. E. Coppard **5**:177

Maclaren-Ross, J.
M. P. Shiel **8**:363

Maclean, H.
Carl Sternheim **8**:374

MacLean, Hugh N.
John Millington Synge **6**:437

MacLeish, Archibald
James Agee **19**:17
Amy Lowell **1**:373
Elinor Wylie **8**:522
William Butler Yeats **1**:560

MacNeice, Louis
George MacDonald **9**:298
Dylan Thomas **8**:449
William Butler Yeats **11**:521

Macris, Peter J.
Stefan Zweig **17**:451

MacShane, Frank
Raymond Chandler **7**:172
Ford Madox Ford **15**:90

Macy, John
D. H. Lawrence **16**:282

Madariaga, Salvador de
Pío Baroja **8**:49
Gabriel Miró **5**:334
Miguel de Unamuno **9**:508
Paul Valéry **15**:455
Ramón del Valle-Inclán **5**:471

Maddocks, Melvin
Jules Renard **17**:310

Maddox, Conroy
Benjamin Péret **20**:203

Madeleva, Sister M.
Edna St. Vincent Millay **4**:309

Madison, Charles A.
Sholom Aleichem **1**:28
Sholem Asch **3**:70
Randolph S. Bourne **16**:54
Isaac Leib Peretz **16**:398

Magalaner, Marvin
Katherine Mansfield **2**:454

Magarshack, David
Anton Chekhov **3**:161

Magny, Claude-Edmonde
Franz Kafka **2**:292

Maguire, Robert A.
Andrey Bely **7**:62

Mahlendorf, Ursula R.
Georg Heym **9**:142

Mahony, Patrick
Maurice Maeterlinck **3**:328

Mainland, William F.
Hermann Sudermann **15**:436

Malin, Irving
Nathanael West **14**:486

Mall, Rita S.
Jules Renard **17**:314

Mallarmé, Stéphane
Jean Moréas **18**:277
Emile Verhaeren **12**:457
Emile Zola **6**:558

Mallinson, Jean
Charles G. D. Roberts **8**:326

Malmstad, John E.
Andrey Bely **7**:62

Malone, Andrew W.
Lord Dunsany **2**:143

Malone, Dumas
Douglas Southall Freeman
11:223, 225

Mandelstam, Nadezhda
Osip Mandelstam **2**:403; **6**:265
Mikhail Zoshchenko **15**:510

Mandelstam, Osip
Velimir Khlebnikov **20**:125

Manganiello, Dominic
Guiseppe Giacosa **7**:314

Mangione, Jerre
Hanns Heinz Ewers **12**:136

Manierre, William R.
Mark Twain **19**:394

Mankin, Paul A.
Ugo Betti **5**:57
Jean Giraudoux **2**:172

Mankowitz, Wolf
Israel Zangwill **16**:448

Manley, Norman Washington
Roger Mais **8**:241

Mann, Erika
Thomas Mann **8**:254

Mann, Heinrich
Heinrich Mann **9**:316

Mann, Klaus
Thomas Mann **8**:254

Mann, Thomas
Anton Chekhov **3**:160
Joseph Conrad **1**:200
Franz Kafka **2**:291
Ludwig Lewisohn **19**:263
Heinrich Mann **9**:322
Thomas Mann **8**:256; **14**:324,
326
Friedrich Nietzsche **10**:373
Bernard Shaw **3**:396
Leo Tolstoy **4**:459
Frank Wedekind **7**:576
Oscar Wilde **1**:503

Manning, Clarence Augustus
Sergei Esenin **4**:108

Mansfield, Katherine
Stella Benson **17**:18
John Galsworthy **1**:293
H. Rider Haggard **11**:242
Knut Hamsun **14**:222
Joseph Hergesheimer **11**:262
Sheila Kaye-Smith **20**:95
Jack London **9**:258
Rose Macaulay **7**:421
George Moore **7**:476
John Middleton Murry **16**:332
Dorothy Richardson **3**:347
Hugh Walpole **5**:492
Edith Wharton **3**:558

Manship, J. P.
Paul Claudel **10**:129

Marble, Annie Russell
Verner von Heidenstam **5**:253
Władysław Stanisław Reymont
5:391

March, George
Thomas Mann **2**:412

March, Harold
André Gide **12**:160
Marcel Proust **13**:412

Marcotte, Gilles
Hector Saint-Denys Garneau
13:99

Marcus, Jane
Olive Schreiner **9**:404

Marcus, Phillip L.
Standish O'Grady **5**:354

Marcus, Roxanne B.
Juan Valera **10**:509

Marcus, Steven
Isaac Babel **13**:20
O. Henry **1**:351

Marder, Herbert
Isaak Babel **2**:30

Marias, Julian
José Ortega y Gasset **9**:346
Miguel de Unamuno **2**:563

Marinetti, F. T.
F. T. Marinetti **10**:309, 312

Markel, Michael H.
Hilaire Belloc **18**:38

Marker, Lise-Lone
David Belasco **3**:90

Markert, Lawrence W.
Arthur Symons **11**:453

Markham, Edwin
E. R. Eddison **15**:51
George Sterling **20**:372

Markish, Simon
Isaac Babel **13**:31

Markov, Vladimir
Konstantin Dmitriyevich
Balmont **11**:35
Velimir Khlebnikov **20**:130,
136
Vladislav Khodasevich **15**:207

Marks, Elaine
Colette **5**:164

Markus, Liselotte
Anatole France **9**:51

Marlow, Norman
A. E. Housman **10**:254, 261

Marquerie, Alfredo
Jacinto Benavente **3**:101

Marquis, Don
Don Marquis **7**:438

Marrow, Arminel
Guillaume Apollinaire **8**:17

Marsden, Kenneth
Thomas Hardy **10**:223

Marsh, E.
Rupert Brooke **2**:50

Marsh, Fred T.
Hermann Broch **20**:49
Damon Runyon **10**:424
Nathanael West **14**:469

Marshall, Herbert
Vladimir Mayakovsky **18**:244

Marshall, Margaret
James Bridie **3**:132

Martin, Edward A.
Don Marquis **7**:448

Martin, Jay
Hamlin Garland **3**:200
Nathanael West **14**:481

Martin, Ronald E.
Theodore Dreiser **18**:58
Joseph Hergesheimer **11**:279

Marx, Leo
F. Scott Fitzgerald **6**:172
Mark Twain **19**:364

Masing-Delic, Irene
Valery Bryusov **10**:91

Maskaleris, Thanasis
Kostes Palamas **5**:382

Maslenikov, Oleg A.
Konstantin Dmitriyevich
Balmont **11**:32
Hilaire Belloc **7**:49
Zinaida Hippius **9**:155

Mason, Eudo C.
Rainer Maria Rilke **6**:364

Mason, Lawrence
Robert Benchley **1**:76

Massa, Ann
Vachel Lindsay **17**:236

Massingham, Harold
D. H. Lawrence **16**:276

Masson, David I.
C. M. Kornbluth **8**:221

Masters, Edgar Lee
Theodore Dreiser **10**:164
Harriet Monroe **12**:215
Mark Twain **19**:361

Materer, Timothy
Wyndham Lewis **9**:243

Mathew, Ray
Miles Franklin **7**:269

Mathews, Jackson
Paul Valéry **4**:492; **15**:451

Mathewson, Rufus W., Jr.
Maxim Gorky **8**:90
Alexey Nikolayevich Tolstoy
18:366

Mathewson, Ruth
Raymond Chandler **1**:176

Matich, Olga
Zinaida Hippius **9**:164, 165

Matsui, Sakuko
Sōseki Natsume **10**:331

Matthews, Brander
James Weldon Johnson **3**:239
H. L. Mencken **13**:359
John Ruskin **20**:272
Mark Twain **6**:454; **19**:351

Matthews, J. H.
Paul Eluard **7**:253
Benjamin Péret **20**:190
Raymond Roussel **20**:249

Matthews, John F.
Bernard Shaw **3**:405

Matthews, T. S.
James Agee **1**:9
Sheila Kaye-Smith **20**:108

Matthiessen, Francis Otto
Mary Wilkins Freeman 9:66
Henry James 2:259
William James 15:173
Sarah Orne Jewett 1:362

Maude, Aylmer
Leo Tolstoy 4:458

Maugham, W. Somerset
Arnold Bennett 5:34
Aleister Crowley 7:207
Rudyard Kipling 8:193
H. G. Wells 12:507

Mauriac, François
Jean Giraudoux 7:321

Maurice, Arthur Bartlett
Arthur Conan Doyle 7:216

Maurois, André
Paul Claudel 10:124
Anatole France 9:49
André Gide 12:171
Rudyard Kipling 8:186
D. H. Lawrence 9:218
Katherine Mansfield 8:277
Marcel Proust 7:530
Antoine de Saint-Exupéry 2:516
Lytton Strachey 12:402

Mautner, Franz H.
Karl Kraus 5:292

Maxwell, William
Samuel Butler 1:138

May, Charles E.
Ring Lardner 14:302

May, Frederick
Luigi Pirandello 4:349

May, Georges
Jean Giraudoux 2:156

May, Rollo
Friedrich Nietzsche 10:389

Mayakovsky, Vladimir
Velimir Khlebnikov 20:123

Mayne, Richard
Wyndham Lewis 2:398

Mays, Maurine
José María de Pereda 16:369

McArthur, Peter
Stephen Leacock 2:377

McAuley, James
Christopher John Brennan
17:55

McCarthy, Clare
Robert W. Service 15:413

McCarthy, Justin Huntly
August Strindberg 8:406

McCarthy, Mary
Henrik Ibsen 2:230
Eugene O'Neill 1:389, 393
Dorothy L. Sayers 15:370
John Van Druten 2:575

McCarthy, Patrick
Alice Meynell 6:303

McCarty, Mari
Colette 16:120

McClellan, Edwin
Sōseki Natsume 2:490; 10:330,
338
Tōson Shimazaki 5:434

McClintock, James I.
Jack London 9:273; 15:259

McClure, J. Derrick
David Lindsay 15:221, 222

McClure, John A.
Rudyard Kipling 17:203

McComas, J. Francis
C. M. Kornbluth 8:212
Henry Kuttner 10:265

McConnell, Frank
H. G. Wells 19:437

McCormick, John
Sherwood Anderson 1:62
F. Scott Fitzgerald 1:270

McCourt, Edward A.
Rupert Brooke 2:55

McDonald, E. Cordel
José Ortega y Gasset 9:344

McDowell, D.
Boris Vian 9:537

McDowell, Frederick P. W.
Ellen Glasgow 2:185

McDowell, Margaret B.
Edith Wharton 3:578

McElderry, Bruce R., Jr.
Max Beerbohm 1:73
Thomas Wolfe 4:522

McElrath, Joseph R., Jr.
Mary Wilkins Freeman 9:78

McFarland, Timothy
Géza Csáth 13:151

McFarlane, Brian
Henry Handel Richardson 4:381

McFarlane, James Walter
Bjørnstjerne Bjørnson 7:113
Georg Brandes 10:73
Knut Hamsun 2:206
Jonas Lie 5:330
Sigrid Undset 3:525

McFate, Patricia
Ford Madox Ford 1:285
James Stephens 4:418

McGreivey, John C.
Hamlin Garland 3:204

McHaffie, Margaret
Carl Spitteler 12:345, 352

McIlwaine, Shields
Kate Chopin 14:57

McKay, D. F.
Dylan Thomas 1:475

McKee, Mary J.
Edna St. Vincent Millay 4:317

McKenna, Stephen
Louis Couperus 15:44

McKeon, Joseph T.
Antone de Saint-Exupéry 2:526

McKilligan, K. M.
Édouard Dujardin 13:189

McKitrick, Eric
Edgar Saltus 8:350

McLaren, Moray
John Gray 19:143

McLaughlin, Ann L.
Katherine Mansfield 2:456

McLean, Andrew M.
Alfred Döblin 13:171

McLean, Hugh
Mikhail Zoshchenko 15:505

McLean, Robert C.
Ambrose Bierce 7:94

McLeod, Addison
Guiseppe, Giacosa 7:305

McLouth, Lawrence A.
Paul Heyse 8:118

McLuhan, Herbert Marshall
Wyndham Lewis 2:387
G. K. Chesterton 6:107

McMahon, Dorothy
Leopoldo Lugones 15:286

McMichael, Barbara
Charles Williams 11:493

McMillin, A. B.
Aleksandr Kuprin 5:300

McMurray, William
William Dean Howells 7:390

McNamara, Eugene
Thomas Mann 14:341

McVay, Gordon
Sergei Esenin 4:117

McVittie, John
Akutagawa Ryūnosuke 16:20,
21

McWilliam, G. H.
Ugo Betti 5:55, 59, 61

McWilliams, J. R.
Thomas Mann 14:345

Mechem, Rose Mary
Bertolt Brecht 1:121

Medina, Jeremy T.
Vicente Blasco Ibáñez 12:50

Meeker, Richard K.
Ellen Glasgow 7:342

Meier, August
Booker T. Washington 10:527

Meixner, John A.
Ford Madox Ford 1:283

Melcher, Edith
Paul Claudel 10:128

Melmoth
Benjamin Péret 20:203

Meloney, William Brown V
Marcel Schwob 20:324

Mencken, H. L.
Sherwood Anderson 10:37
Arnold Bennett 20:21
Ambrose Bierce 1:85; 7:90
James Branch Cabell 6:66
Willa Cather 11:92
Anthony Comstock 13:92, 93
Joseph Conrad 1:197; 13:101
Stephen Crane 11:129
Theodore Dreiser 10:163, 168,
178
Havelock Ellis 14:105, 107
F. Scott Fitzgerald 6:159;
14:147
Ford Madox Ford 15:72
Anatole France 9:45

Douglas Southall Freeman
11:220
Jacques Futrelle 19:90
Hamlin Garland 3:191
Ellen Glasgow 7:333
Emma Goldman 13:214
H. Rider Haggard 11:241
Joseph Hergesheimer 11:274
William Dean Howells 7:369
Henry James 2:151
James Weldon Johnson 19:204
Ring Lardner 2:328; 14:292
Sinclair Lewis 4:246; 13:325
Ludwig Lewisohn 19:261
Vachel Lindsay 17:234
Jack London 9:257
Marie Belloc Lowndes 12:200
H. L. Mencken 13:360
John Middleton Murry 16:335
George Jean Nathan 18:296,
299
José Ortega y Gasset 9:337
Edgar Saltus 8:349
Bernard Shaw 3:378; 9:415
Lincoln Steffens 20:336
George Sterling 20:378
August Strindberg 8:406
Hermann Sudermann 15:427
Montague Summers 16:424
Mark Twain 6:459; 12:429
Carl Van Doren 18:389, 398
H. G. Wells 6:528; 12:497
Edith Wharton 9:54
Walter White 15:477

Menes, Bonnie
Arthur Conan Doyle 7:240

Menninger, Karl
Havelock Ellis 14:118

Merchant, W. Moelwyn
Bertolt Brecht 1:113

Mercier, Vivian
Édouard Dujardin 13:188
Oliver St. John Gogarty 15:106
Standish O'Grady 5:353
James Stephens 4:411

Meredith, G. E.
F. Marion Crawford 10:139

Meredith, George
Thomas Hardy 18:81
Alice Meynell 6:293

Merrill, James
C. P. Cavafy 7:162

Mersand, Joseph
Rachel Crothers 19:78

Merwin, W. S.
Edwin Muir 2:482

Meserve, Walter J.
Philip Barry 11:65
William Dean Howells 7:386
Robert E. Sherwood 3:417

Mesher, David R.
Sherwood Anderson 10:52

Messenger, Christian K.
Ring Lardner 14:317

Metzger, Erika A.
Stefan George 14:211

Metzger, Michael M.
Stefan George 14:211

Critic Index

Meyerhoff, Hans
Robert Musil 12:237

Meyers, Jeffrey
Giuseppe Tomasi di Lampedusa 13:298
T. E. Lawrence 18:171
Thomas Mann 14:356
John Middleton Murry 16:352
Robert Musil 12:260
George Orwell 6:350

Mezei, Kathy
Hector Saint-Denys Garneau 13:204
Emile Nelligan 14:394, 396

Michael, D.P.M.
Arthur Machen 4:285

Michaels, Leonard
Raymond Chandler 1:175

Michaels, Walter Benn
Theodore Dreiser 18:68

Michaud, Regis
Léon-Paul Fargue 11:194
André Gide 12:143
Max Jacob 6:191

Michelson, Bruce
Mark Twain 6:485

Michie, James A.
James Bridie 3:142

Mickelson, Anne Z.
Thomas Hardy 4:176

Middleton, Christopher
Robert Walser 18:415, 416, 429

Middleton, George
John Middleton Murry 16:330

Mihaslovich, Vasa D.
Mikhail Zoshchenko 15:508

Mikes, George
Stephen Leacock 2:379

Miles, David H.
Hugo von Hofmannsthal 11:310
Rainer Maria Rilke 19:312

Miles, Hamish
Arthur Machen 4:278

Millay, Edna St. Vincent
Elinor Wylie 8:521

Miller, Arthur M.
Ambrose Bierce 7:91

Miller, Dickinson S.
William James 15:141

Miller, Henry
Knut Hamsun 14:228, 245
James Joyce 3:272
D. H. Lawrence 2:366
Marcel Proust 7:526
Jakob Wassermann 6:519

Miller, J. Hillis
Joseph Conrad 1:213
Thomas Hardy 4:174; 18:120
Friedrich Nietzsche 18:346
Wallace Stevens 3:468
Dylan Thomas 1:474
William Butler Yeats 1:575

Miller, James E., Jr.
Willa Cather 1:167
F. Scott Fitzgerald 1:257; 14:168

Miller, Perry
Douglas Southall Freeman 11:223

Miller, Richard F.
Henry Adams 4:11

Miller, Walter James
Jules Verne 6:498

Miller, William Lee
Robert Benchley 1:79

Millett, Kate
D. H. Lawrence 16:305

Millgate, Michael
Thomas Hardy 18:107

Millichap, Joseph R.
Thomas Wolfe 13:487

Milligan, E. E.
Antoine de Saint-Exupéry 2:519

Millner, Curtis
Pío Baroja 8:64

Mills, Gordon
Jack London 9:275

Mills, Ralph J., Jr.
W. H. Davies 5:207

Milne, A. A.
George Jean Nathan 18:303
A. A. Milne 6:311
Saki 3:363

Milne, Gordon
Edith Wharton 9:549

Miłosz, Czesław
Tadeusz Borowski 9:22
Joseph Conrad 1:207

Miner, Earl
Lafcadio Hearn 9:131
Dazai Osamu 11:172

Mirsky, D. S.
Leonid Andreyev 3:27
Innokenty Annensky 14:18
Isaac Babel 13:13
Konstantin Dmitriyevich Balmont 11:32
Andrey Bely 7:47
Aleksandr Blok 5:83
Valery Bryusov 10:80
Anton Chekhov 3:154
Sergei Esenin 4:111
Maxim Gorky 8:73
Zinaida Hippius 9:155
Vladislav Khodasevich 15:199
Aleksandr Kuprin 5:298
Vladimir Mayakovsky 18:240
Fyodor Sologub 9:435
Lytton Strachey 12:393
Alexey Nikolayevich Tolstoy 18:358
Leo Tolstoy 11:462, 464
Marina Tsvetaeva 7:556
Yevgeny Ivanovich Zamyatin 8:543

Mitchell, Bonner
Antoine de Saint-Exupéry 2:521

Mitchell, David
F. T. Marinetti 10:321

Mitchell, Julian
Aleister Crowley 7:207
Ada Leverson 18:196

Miyoshi, Masao
Dazai Osamu 11:177
Mori Ōgai 14:372
Sōseki Natsume 2:494

Mizener, Arthur
F. Scott Fitzgerald 1:241, 261
Ford Madox Ford 15:91
Thomas Hardy 10:218

Mochulsky, Konstantin
Andrey Bely 7:53

Moers, Ellen
F. Scott Fitzgerald 1:254

Moestrup, Jørn
Luigi Pirandello 4:353

Molina, Roderick A., O.F.M.
Amado Nervo 11:400

Mollinger, Robert N.
Wallace Stevens 12:381

Molnar, Thomas
Georges Bernanos 3:118

Monahan, Michael
Gabriele D'Annunzio 6:132

Monas, Sidney
Andrey Bely 7:53
Osip Mandelstam 2:404; 6:267
Mikhail Zoshchenko 15:502

Mondelli, Rudolph J.
Paul Bourget 12:69

Monkhouse, Cosmo
Vernon Lee 5:309

Monkshood, G. F.
Edgar Saltus 8:343

Monod, G.
Anatole France 9:38

Monro, Harold
Charlotte Mew 8:295, 297

Monroe, Harriet
Stephen Vincent Benét 7:73
Randolph S. Bourne 16:41
Robert Bridges 1:127
Hart Crane 5:184
Thomas Hardy 4:157
James Weldon Johnson 19:206
Amy Lowell 8:229
Edgar Lee Masters 2:462
Vachel Lindsay 17:228, 230
John McCrae 12:208
George Meredith 17:272
Edna St. Vincent Millay 4:307
John Reed 9:382
Edwin Arlington Robinson 5:405
Robert W. Service 15:399
May Sinclair 11:410
George Sterling 20:373
Wallace Stevens 12:356
Sara Teasdale 4:427

Monroe, N. Elizabeth
Selma Lagerlöf 4:239
Sigrid Undset 3:520

Montague, C. E.
John Millington Synge 6:426

Montale, Eugenio
Dino Campana 20:82

Montefiero, Janet
Sheila Kaye-Smith 20:116

Monteiro, George
O. Henry 19:196

Montenegro, Ernesto
Horacio Quiroga 20:206

Moody, A. D.
Virginia Woolf 5:509

Mooney, Harry J., Jr.
Leo Tolstoy 4:477

Moore, Marianne
Laurence Housman 7:355
Vachel Lindsay 17:228
Wallace Stevens 3:446

Moore, Raylyn
L. Frank Baum 7:21

Moore, Virginia
Charlotte Mew 8:297
Alice Meynell 6:301

Moorman, Charles
Charles Williams 1:519

Mora, José Ferrater
Miguel de Unamuno 2:560

Moran, Carlos Alberto
Raymond Chandler 1:174

Moran, John C.
F. Marion Crawford 10:157
Montague Summers 16:435

More, Paul Elmer
James Branch Cabell 6:66
Lafcadio Hearn 9:119
William James 15:156
Lionel Johnson 19:231
Friedrich Nietzsche 10:361
José Ortega y Gasset 9:335
Arthur Symons 11:430

Moreau, Geneviève
James Agee 19:39

Moreau, John Adam
Randolph S. Bourne 16:56

Moreland, David Allison
Jack London 9:282

Moreno, Janice Sanders
Leopoldo Lugones 15:289

Morgan, A. E.
Harley Granville-Barker 2:194

Morgan, Bayard Quincy
Christian Morgenstern 8:304
Arthur Schnitzler 4:386

Morgan, Charles
Mikhail Bulgakov 16:75
George Moore 7:481

Morgan, Edwin
Edwin Muir 2:489

Morgan, Florence A. H.
Charles Waddell Chesnutt 5:129

Morgan, H. Wayne
Hart Crane 2:122
Hamlin Garland 3:198

Morgan, John H.
Pierre Teilhard de Chardin 9:504

Morita, James R.
Tōson Shimazaki 5:438

Morley, Christopher
Arthur Conan Doyle **7**:219
Havelock Ellis **14**:108
Don Marquis **7**:434, 439
Saki **3**:365

Morley, S. Griswold
Rubén Darío **4**:57

Morris, C. B.
Pedro Salinas **17**:361

Morris, Irene
Georg Trakl **5**:456

Morris, Ivan
Akutagawa Ryūnosuke **16**:19

Morris, Lloyd
Sherwood Anderson **1**:42
Willa Cather **1**:12
F. Scott Fitzgerald **1**:244
Emma Goldman **13**:219
O. Henry **1**:349
Eugene O'Neill **1**:391
Marjorie Kinnan Rawlings
4:361
Edwin Arlington Robinson
5:405
Alexey Nikolayevich Tolstoy
18:357
Franz Werfel **8**:466

Morris, Virginia B.
Dorothy L. Sayers **15**:390

Morris, Wright
F. Scott Fitzgerald **1**:251
Ring Lardner **14**:310
Thomas Wolfe **13**:480

Morrow, Carolyn
Antonio Machado **3**:306

Morrow, Felix
Montague Summers **16**:429

Morrow, Patrick D.
O. E. Rölvaag **17**:340

Morsberger, Robert E.
Edgar Rice Burroughs **2**:85

Morse, A. Reynolds
M. P. Shiel **8**:360

Morse, J. Mitchell
James Joyce **3**:272

Morse, Samuel French
Wallace Stevens **3**:477

Morshead, E.D.A.
Andrew Lang **16**:250

Mortensen, Brita M. E.
August Strindberg **8**:408

Mortimer, Raymond
Marie Belloc Lowndes **12**:204
Lytton Strachey **12**:392

Morton, Frederic
Arturo Barea **14**:47
Anne Frank **17**:108

Morton, J. B.
Hilaire Belloc **7**:37

Moseley, Edwin M.
F. Scott Fitzgerald **1**:264

Moser, Thomas
Joseph Conrad **1**:208; **13**:113

Moses, Edwin
F. Scott Fitzgerald **14**:170

Moses, Montrose J.
Philip Barry **11**:54
David Belasco **3**:85

Mosig, Dirk
H. P. Lovecraft **4**:272

Moskowitz, Sam
Arthur Conan Doyle **7**:224
William Hope Hodgson **13**:234
Henry Kuttner **10**:266
M. P. Shiel **8**:361

Moss, Howard
Anton Chekhov **3**:175
Carl Van Doren **18**:409

Moss, Robert F.
Rudyard Kipling **17**:209

Motion, Andrew
Edward Thomas **10**:464

Motofugi, Frank T.
Mori Ōgai **14**:370

Mott, Frank Luther
Zane Grey **6**:180

Moynahan, Julian
D. H. Lawrence **16**:301

Muchnic, Helen
Andrey Bely **7**:61
Aleksandr Blok **5**:93
Mikhail Bulgakov **2**:65
Maxim Gorky **8**:78
Vladimir Mayakovsky **4**:296
Yevgeny Ivanovich Zamyatin
8:551

Muddiman, Bernard
Duncan Campbell Scott **6**:396

Mudrick, Marvin
Joseph Conrad **13**:119
D. H. Lawrence **2**:366
Wyndham Lewis **2**:386
Frederick Rolfe **12**:271
Bernard Shaw **3**:402

Mueller, Dennis
Lion Feuchtwanger **3**:185

Mueller, Gustave
Carl Spitteler **12**:343

Mueller, Janel M.
Henrik Ibsen **16**:175

Muggeridge, Malcolm
Havelock Ellis **14**:128

Muir, Edwin
Hermann Broch **20**:46
Joseph Conrad **1**:198
Knut Hamsun **14**:225
Thomas Hardy **4**:173
Hugo von Hofmannsthal **11**:295
Franz Kafka **6**:219
Marie Belloc Lowndes **12**:203
Lytton Strachey **12**:396
Virginia Woolf **1**:527; **5**:507
William Butler Yeats **18**:451

Muirhead, James F.
Carl Spitteler **12**:340

Mukoyama, Yoshihiko
Akutagawa Ryūnosuke **16**:28

Muller, Herbert J.
Thomas Wolfe **4**:519

Mumford, Lewis
Charles A. Beard **15**:28
Randolph S. Bourne **16**:48
Heinrich Mann **9**:318

Munk, Erika
George Orwell **15**:340

Munro, Ian S.
Lewis Grassic Gibbon **4**:126

Munro, John M.
Arthur Symons **11**:450

Munson, Gorham B.
Hart Crane **2**:111
Edgar Saltus **8**:347
Wallace Stevens **3**:445
Emile Zola **1**:590

Murch, A. E.
E. C. Bentley **12**:17
Cesare Pavese **3**:340
Dorothy L. Sayers **2**:531

Murfin, Ross C.
Algernon Charles Swinburne
8:445

Murray, Edward
F. Scott Fitzgerald **1**:272

Murray, Les
Isaac Rosenberg **12**:312

Murry, John Middleton
Arnold Bennett **20**:24
Ivan Bunin **6**:43
Anton Chekhov **3**:150
Paul Claudel **10**:121
Anatole France **9**:45
George Gissing **3**:233
Aleksandr Kuprin **5**:296
D. H. Lawrence **2**:346; **9**:214,
215; **16**:283
Katherine Mansfield **2**:451;
8:281
Wilfred Owen **5**:359
Marcel Proust **13**:401
Edward Thomas **10**:451
Hugh Walpole **5**:493

Muzzey, Annie L.
Charlotte Gilman **9**:99

Myers, David
Carl Sternheim **8**:377

Myers, Doris T.
Charles Williams **11**:496

Nabokov, Vladimir
See also Sirin, Vladimir
Andrey Bely **7**:55
James Joyce **8**:158
Franz Kafka **6**:230
Vladislav Khodasevich **15**:200
Marcel Proust **7**:552

Nadeau, Maurice
Alfred Jarry **14**:271

Nadel, Ira Bruce
Lytton Strachey **12**:420

Naess, Harald S.
Nordahl Grieg **10**:208
Knut Hamsun **14**:239

Naff, William E.
Tōson Shimazaki **5**:441

Nagel, James
Stephen Crane **11**:166

Nagy, Moses M.
Paul Claudel **2**:109

Naimy, Mikhail
Kahlil Gibran **9**:82

Naimy, N.
Kahlil Gibran **9**:90

Naipaul, V. S.
Joyce Cary **1**:142

Nakai Yoshiyuki
Mori Ōgai **14**:384

Nalbantian, Suzanne
Stefan George **14**:212

Naravane, Vishwanath S.
Saratchandra Chatterji **13**:74

Naremore, James
Virginia Woolf **5**:514

Nash, Berta
Arthur Machen **4**:284

Nash, Suzanne
Paul Valéry **15**:467

Nassaar, Christopher S.
John Gray **19**:150

Nassar, Eugene Paul
Kahlil Gibran **9**:93

Natan, Alex
Carl Sternheim **8**:370
Frank Wedekind **7**:580

Nathan, George Jean
Philip Barry **11**:58
David Belasco **3**:87
Jacinto Benavente **3**:96
Ugo Betti **5**:54
Ambrose Bierce **1**:87
Bertolt Brecht **13**:43
James Bridie **3**:132
Karel Čapek **6**:87
Ring Lardner **14**:294
H. L. Mencken **13**:361
A. A. Milne **6**:306
George Jean Nathan **18**:300
Eugene O'Neill **1**:386
Luigi Pirandello **4**:331
Bernard Shaw **3**:387
John Van Druten **2**:573
Franz Werfel **8**:469
Oscar Wilde **1**:500
Alexander Woolcott **5**:520
Israel Zangwill **16**:446

Neale-Silva, Eduardo
César Vallejo **3**:529

Neff, Rebeccah Kinnamon
May Sinclair **11**:419

Neider, Charles
Franz Kafka **13**:261
Thomas Mann **14**:332

Nejdefors-Frisk, Sonya
George Moore **7**:486

Nelson, Donald F.
Wolfgang Borchert **5**:112

Nelson, Hilda
René Daumal **14**:95

Nelson, James G.
John Gray **19**:148
Lionel Johnson **19**:252

Nelson, Lowry, Jr.
Italo Svevo **2**:539

Nemerov, Howard
  James Joyce **3**:280
  Thomas Mann **2**:431
  Wallace Stevens **3**:453

Nemes, Graciela P.
  Juan Ramón Jiménez **4**:215

Nersoyan, H. J.
  André Gide **12**:174

Neruda, Pablo
  Rubén Darío **4**:63

Nettelbeck, C. W.
  Georges Bernanos **3**:124

Nevins, Allan
  Ring Lardner **2**:327

Nevius, Blake
  Edith Wharton **3**:566

Newberry, Wilma
  José Echegaray **4**:104

Newcombe, Josephine M.
  Leonid Andreyev **3**:29

Newton, Nancy A.
  Antonio Machado **3**:314

Nicholls, Roger A.
  Heinrich Mann **9**:322

Nichols, Wallace B.
  Alfred Noyes **7**:508

Nicoll, Allardyce
  Maurice Baring **8**:33
  Henrik Ibsen **2**:228
  Eugene O'Neill **1**:391
  Bernard Shaw **3**:395
  August Strindberg **1**:450

Niebuhr, Reinhold
  Hilaire Belloc **18**:24
  Ludwig Lewisohn **19**:274

Nietzsche, Friedrich
  Friedrich Nietzsche **10**:354
  August Strindberg **8**:405

Nieuwenhuys, Rob
  Louis Couperus **15**:47

Niger, Shmuel
  Sholom Aleichem **1**:20

Nilsson, Nils Ake
  Osip Mandelstam **6**:257

Nims, John Frederick
  Dino Campana **20**:88

Nin, Anaïs
  D. H. Lawrence **2**:348

Nissenson, Hugh
  Ivan Bunin **6**:54

Noble, David W.
  F. Scott Fitzgerald **1**:264

Noble, James Ashcroft
  Israel Zangwill **16**:439

Nock, Albert J.
  Bret Harte **1**:341

Nolin, Bertil
  Georg Brandes **10**:71

Nolte, William H.
  George Jean Nathan **18**:324

Noon, William T., S.J.
  James Joyce **16**:237

Nordau, Max
  Friedrich Nietzsche **10**:357

Nordon, Pierre
  Arthur Conan Doyle **7**:226

Noreng, Harald
  Bjørnstjerne Bjørnson **7**:114

Norman, Henry
  F. Marion Crawford **10**:138
  Olive Schreiner **9**:393

Norman, W.H.H.
  Akutagawa Ryūnosuke **16**:18

Normand, Guessler
  Henri Barbusse **5**:19

Norris, Frank
  Stephen Crane **11**:123

Norris, Margot
  James Joyce **3**:281

Norton, David L.
  René Daumal **14**:91

Notopoulos, James A.
  T. E. Lawrence **18**:154

Novak, Barbara
  A. A. Milne **6**:313

Noyes, Alfred
  William Ernest Henley **8**:103
  Algernon Charles Swinburne **8**:431

Noyes, Henry
  Alfred Noyes **7**:515

Nozick, Martin
  Miguel de Unamuno **2**:568

Nugent, Robert
  Paul Eluard **7**:257

Nye, Russel
  L. Frank Baum **7**:15
  Zane Grey **6**:182

Oates, Joyce Carol
  Géza Csáth **13**:149
  Henry James **11**:340
  Thomas Mann **2**:441
  Andrei Platonov **14**:411
  Virginia Woolf **1**:540
  William Butler Yeats **1**:582

O'Brien, James
  Dazai Osamu **11**:180

O'Brien, Justin
  André Gide **12**:157
  Valéry Larbaud **9**:197
  Marcel Proust **7**:528

O'Casey, Sean
  George Jean Nathan **18**:316
  Bernard Shaw **3**:399

O'Connor, Frank
  A. E. **3**:8
  Anton Chekhov **3**:161
  A. E. Coppard **5**:180
  Lady Gregory **1**:336
  Thomas Hardy **4**:168
  James Stephens **4**:416

O'Connor, Patricia Walker
  Gregorio Martínez Sierra and
    María Martínez Sierra **6**:282, 284

O'Connor, Ulick
  Oliver St. John Gogarty **15**:110

O'Connor, William Van
  Joyce Cary **1**:145
  Wallace Stevens **3**:464
  Mark Twain **12**:443

O'Conor, Norreys Jepson
  Standish O'Grady **5**:353

O'Donnell, J. P.
  Bertolt Brecht **1**:116

O'Donnell, Thomas J.
  T. E. Lawrence **18**:163

O'Faolain, Sean
  A. E. **3**:8
  George Moore **7**:482
  Leo Tolstoy **4**:461

O'Hagan, Thomas
  John Millington Synge **6**:431

O'Hara, John
  Robert Benchley **1**:78

Ohlin, Peter H.
  James Agee **1**:10

Okeke-Ezigbo, Emeka
  Paul Laurence Dunbar **12**:127

Olgin, Moissaye J.
  Leonid Andreyev **3**:21
  Konstantin Dmitriyevich Balmont **11**:31
  Aleksandr Kuprin **5**:297

Oliphant, Margaret
  Thomas Hardy **4**:150; **18**:81
  Andrew Lang **16**:251

Oliver, Edith
  Maxim Gorky **8**:93

Olivero, Federico
  Rainer Maria Rilke **19**:299
  Emile Verhaeren **12**:460

Olsen, Tillie
  Rebecca Harding Davis **6**:153

Olson, Elder
  Dylan Thomas **1**:470
  William Butler Yeats **18**:448

Olson, Julius
  O. E. Rölvaag **17**:320

Olson, Paul A.
  O. E. Rölvaag **17**:342

Olson, Paul R.
  Juan Ramón Jiménez **4**:218

Olson, Stanley
  Elinor Wylie **8**:537

O'Neill, Eugene
  George Jean Nathan **18**:298
  Mark Twain **12**:439

O'Neill, Tom
  Giuseppe Tomasi di Lampedusa **13**:312

Opdahl, Keith M.
  Mark Twain **19**:403

Orage, A. R.
  A. E. **10**:14
  Ernest Dowson **4**:87

O'Reilly, Robert F.
  André Gide **12**:168

Orel, Harold
  Jacques Futrelle **19**:91

O'Rell, Max
  Paul Bourget **12**:64

Ormerod, Beverly
  Jacques Roumain **19**:335

Ornstein, Robert
  F. Scott Fitzgerald **1**:250

O'Rourke, David
  F. Scott Fitzgerald **14**:184
  Thomas Wolfe **13**:493

Orr, John
  Henrik Ibsen **16**:193

Ortega y Gasset, José
  José Ortega y Gasset **9**:334
  Marcel Proust **7**:536
  Ramón del Valle-Inclán **5**:479

Ortiz-Vargas, A.
  Gabriela Mistral **2**:475

Orwell, George
  Arturo Barea **14**:44
  Rudyard Kipling **17**:197
  D. H. Lawrence **2**:354
  George Orwell **15**:298, 301
  Jules Verne **6**:491
  H. G. Wells **6**:533

Osborne, Charles
  Thomas Hardy **10**:223
  Francis Thompson **4**:411

O'Sheel, Shaemas
  Lady Gregory **1**:333

Ossar, Michael
  Ernst Toller **10**:491

O'Sullivan, Maurice J., Jr.
  James Weldon Johnson **19**:220

O'Sullivan, Susan
  Gabriel Miró **5**:337

Oswald, Victor A., Jr.
  Hugo von Hofmannsthal **11**:297

Ouida
  F. Marion Crawford **10**:140

Ouimette, Victor
  José Ortega y Gasset **9**:354

Ould, Hermon
  Rudolf Steiner **13**:437

Overmyer, Janet
  Saki **3**:371

Ozick, Cynthia
  Bruno Schulz **5**:424

Pacey, Desmond
  Bliss Carman **7**:145
  Frederick Philip Grove **4**:140
  Charles G. D. Roberts **8**:319
  Duncan Campbell Scott **6**:393

Pachmuss, Temira
  Zinaida Hippius **9**:160, 166
  Franz Werfel **8**:475

Pacifici, Sergio
  Vitaliano Brancati **12**:90
  Giuseppe Tomasi di Lampedusa **13**:320
  Giovanni Verga **3**:545

Pack, Robert
  Wallace Stevens **3**:455

Page, Alex
  Virginia Woolf **20**:411

Paine, Albert Bigelow
  Mark Twain **19**:353

Painter, George D.
  Marcel Proust **7**:537

Pal, Bepin Chandra
Annie Besant **9**:15

Palamari, Demetra
Emile Zola **6**:569

Palamas, Kostes
Kostes Palamas **5**:377

Palermo, Patrick F.
Lincoln Steffens **20**:355

Palley, Julian
Pedro Salinas **17**:354, 357

Palmer, Nettie
Henry Handel Richardson **4**:375

Panek, LeRoy
E. C. Bentley **12**:22

Paolucci, Anne
Luigi Pirandello **4**:356

Papini, Giovanni
Rémy de Gourmont **17**:126

Param, Charles
Horacio Quiroga **20**:216

Parker, Alexander A.
Miguel de Unamuno **2**:565

Parker, Dorothy
See also **Reader, Constant**
Theodore Dreiser **10**:174
George Jean Nathan **18**:308

Parker, H. T.
Karl Čapek **6**:82

Parker, W. M.
R. B. Cunninghame Graham **19**:104

Parks, Edd Winfield
Edna St. Vincent Millay **4**:310

Parrinder, Patrick
H. G. Wells **19**:452

Parrington, Vernon Louis
James Branch Cabell **6**:63
Hamlin Garland **3**:193

Parrot, Louis
Paul Eluard **7**:249

Parrott, Cecil
Jaroslav Hašek **4**:189

Parry, I. F.
Franz Kafka **13**:263

Parry, Idris
Rainer Maria Rilke **1**:422
Robert Walser **18**:432

Parry, M.
Antoine de Saint-Exupéry **2**:524

Parsons, Ian
Isaac Rosenberg **12**:310

Partridge, Ralph
Josephine Tey **14**:449

Pasternak, Boris
Vladimir Mayakovsky **4**:298
Marina Tsvetaeva **7**:558

Pater, Walter
Arthur Symons **11**:426
Oscar Wilde **1**:495

Paterson, Gary H.
John Gray **19**:154
Lionel Johnson **19**:249

Paterson, Isabel
Ford Madox Ford **15**:73

Patmore, Coventry
Alice Meynell **6**:290
Francis Thompson **4**:433
Juan Valera **10**:498

Paton, Alan
Walter White **15**:482

Patrick, Walton R.
Ring Lardner **2**:338

Patt, Beatrice P.
Pío Baroja **8**:60

Pattee, Fred Lewis
Gertrude Atherton **2**:17
Kate Chopin **5**:144; **14**:57
Rebecca Harding Davis **6**:150
Mary Wilkins Freeman **9**:65
Bret Harte **1**:340
Lafcadio Hearn **9**:127
O. Henry **1**:348; **19**:177
Edith Wharton **3**:560

Patterson, Rodney L.
Konstantin Dmitriyevich
Balmont **11**:39

Patteson, Richard F.
H. Rider Haggard **11**:249

Pattison, Mark
George Meredith **17**:255

Pattison, Walter T.
Juan Ramón Jiménez **4**:212

Paul, David
Alain-Fournier **6**:12

Paul, Sherman
John Jay Chapman **7**:197

Paulson, Kristoffer
O. E. Rölvaag **17**:338

Pavese, Cesare
Edgar Lee Masters **2**:473

Payne, Ladell
James Weldon Johnson **19**:217

Payne, Robert
T. E. Lawrence **18**:157
Vladimir Mayakovsky **18**:252

Payne, William Morton
Arnold Bennett **5**:22
Bjørnstjerne Bjørnson **7**:109
Georg Brandes **10**:61
Wilfred Campbell **9**:29
Arthur Conan Doyle **7**:216
Mary Wilkins Freeman **9**:61
Ellen Glasgow **7**:332
Zane Grey **6**:177
Selma Lagerlöf **4**:229
Ludwig Lewisohn **19**:261
Harriet Monroe **12**:214, 215
Duncan Campbell Scott **6**:385
Leo Tolstoy **4**:449
Edith Wharton **3**:551
Israel Zangwill **16**:443

Paz, Octavio
Guillaume Apollinaire **3**:44
Rubén Darío **4**:64
Amado Nervo **11**:402

Peabody, A. P.
George MacDonald **9**:288

Peacock, Ronald
Hugo von Hofmannsthal **11**:295
Henrik Ibsen **2**:227
Georg Kaiser **9**:176
Bernard Shaw **3**:389
William Butler Yeats **1**:561

Pearsall, Robert Brainard
Rupert Brooke **2**:58

Pearsall, Ronald
Arthur Conan Doyle **7**:236

Pearson, Hesketh
Arthur Conan Doyle **7**:221
Bernard Shaw **3**:395

Pearson, Norman Holmes
Sherwood Anderson **1**:42

Peck, Harry Thurston
Charlotte Gilman **9**:97
William Dean Howells **7**:367
Joris-Karl Huysmans **7**:407
Edith Wharton **3**:551

Peckham, Morse
Edgar Saltus **8**:355
Algernon Charles Swinburne
8:440

Peden, William
Horacio Quiroga **20**:221

Peel, Donald F.
O. Henry **19**:189

Peers, E. Allison
Rubén Darío **4**:64
José Echegaray **4**:103

Péguy, Charles
Charles Péguy **10**:401

Pehrson, Elsa
Selma Lagerlöf **4**:240

Peirce, Charles Sanders
William James **15**:138

Pellizzi, Camillo
Eugene O'Neill **6**:327

Peña, Carlos González
Amado Nervo **11**:402

Pendo, Stephen
Raymond Chandler **7**:174

Pendry, E. P.
Sheila Kaye-Smith **20**:112

Penzoldt, Peter
Algernon Blackwood **5**:74
F. Marion Crawford **10**:153
M. R. James **6**:208
H. P. Lovecraft **4**:269

Péret, Benjamin
Benjamin Péret **20**:182

Perkins, George
William Dean Howells **7**:395

Perkins, Maxwell E.
F. Scott Fitzgerald **6**:159
Douglas Southall Freeman
11:219
Ring Lardner **14**:296
Thomas Wolfe **4**:518

Perkins, Michael
Guillaume Apollinaire **8**:25

Perlmutter, Elizabeth P.
Edna St. Vincent Millay **4**:321

Perosa, Sergio
Frederick Rolfe **12**:273

Perry, Henry Ten Eyck
W. S. Gilbert **3**:212

Perry, Ralph Barton
William James **15**:168

Perry, T. S.
Jean Moréas **18**:277

Persky, Serge
Leonid Andreyev **3**:17

Person, Leland S., Jr.
F. Scott Fitzgerald **6**:164

Peters, H. F.
Rainer Maria Rilke **6**:363

Peters, Margot
Dorothy L. Sayers **15**:379

Peterson, Dale E.
Vladimir Mayakovsky **4**:300

Petry, Alice Hall
Stephen Crane **17**:81

Peyre, Henri
Paul Claudell **2**:100
Colette **5**:170
Paul Eluard **7**:252
André Gide **5**:219, 227
Marcel Proust **7**:548
Jules Renard **17**:312
Paul Valéry **15**:463

Pfohl, Russell
Italo Svevo **2**:542

Phelan, Kappo
Bertolt Brecht **13**:43
Federico García Lorca **1**:309

Phelps, Arthur L.
Frederick Philip Grove **4**:132
Robert W. Service **15**:403

Phelps, Donald
Ring Lardner **14**:309

Phelps, Robert
Colette **16**:115, 125
Jules Renard **17**:312

Phelps, William Lyon
Sherwood Anderson **10**:31
Leonid Andreyev **3**:16
Maurice Baring **8**:33
J. M. Barrie **8**:33
Bjørnstjerne Bjørnson **7**:107
Rupert Brooke **7**:122
Anton Chekhov **3**:146
Stephen Crane **11**:130
Theodore Dreiser **10**:172
Zona Gale **7**:280
Maxim Gorky **8**:71
O. Henry **1**:346
Paul Heyse **8**:119
William Dean Howells **7**:371
Aleksandr Kuprin **5**:296
Jack London **9**:256
Amy Lowell **8**:224
Harriet Monroe **12**:217
George Jean Nathan **18**:300
Alfred Noyes **7**:502
Bernard Shaw **3**:384
Henryk Sienkiewicz **3**:422
May Sinclair **3**:433; **11**:410
Fyodor Sologub **9**:435
Lytton Strachey **12**:392
Hermann Sudermann **15**:423
Booth Tarkington **9**:453
Mark Twain **19**:353

Carl Van Doren 18:390
H. G. Wells 12:494
Edith Wharton 3:557

Phillips, Ewart E.
José Rubén Romero 14:440

Phillips, Klaus
Rainer Maria Rilke 6:369

Phillips, Rachel
Alfonsina Storni 5:447

Phillipson, John S.
James Agee 19:19

Philmus, Robert M.
H. G. Wells 12:511

Phoutrides, Aristides E.
Kostes Palamas 5:378

Pick, J. B.
David Lindsay 15:219

Pick, Lies Goslar
Anne Frank 17:105

Pickford, John
Wolfgang Borchert 5:112

Pickman, Hester
Rainer Maria Rilke 6:357

Picon, Gaëtan
André Gide 5:218

Pierce, Lorne
Frederick Philip Grove 4:136
Charles G. D. Roberts 8:318
Robert W. Service 15:402

Pike, Burton
Robert Musil 12:241

Pikoulis, John
Alun Lewis 3:291

Pilkington, John, Jr.
F. Marion Crawford 10:154

Pinchin, Jane Lagoudis
C. P. Cavafy 2:98

Pinkerton, Jan
Wallace Stevens 3:474

Pinsker, Sanford
Sholom Aleichem 1:30

Pinto, Vivian De Sola
William Ernest Henley 8:106
A. E. Housman 1:358
D. H. Lawrence 2:367
William Butler Yeats 11:526

Piper, D.G.B.
Mikhail Bulgakov 16:85

Pirandello, Luigi
Bernard Shaw 9:416
Giovanni Verga 3:542

Pisarev, Dmitri
Leo Tolstoy 4:466

Piscator, Erwin
Ernst Toller 10:488

Pitcher, Harvey
Anton Chekhov 3:172

Pitt, Valerie
Charles Williams 11:492

Pittock, Malcolm
Ernst Toller 10:489

Pizer, Donald
Stephen Crane 11:152; 17:81
Theodore Dreiser 18:52
Hamlin Garland 3:197, 198
William Dean Howells 7:385

Plant, Richard
Arthur Schnitzler 4:395

Platzner, Robert L.
H. G. Wells 19:431

Plomer, William
Lewis Grassic Gibbon 4:120
George Gissing 3:231

Podhoretz, Norman
Sholom Aleichem 1:23
George Orwell 15:333
John Millington Synge 6:436
Nathanael West 1:478

Poggioli, Renato
Innokenty Annensky 14:19
Isaak Babel 2:20
Konstantin Dmitriyevich
    Balmont 11:33
Aleksandr Blok 5:90
Valery Bryusov 10:86
Ivan Bunin 6:49
C. P. Cavafy 7:158
Sergei Esenin 4:112
Zinaida Hippius 9:158
Velimir Khlebnikov 20:134
Vladislav Khodasevich 15:203
Osip Mandelstam 2:400
Vladimir Mayakovsky 4:299
Fyodor Sologub 9:436
Marina Tsvetaeva 7:558

Pohl, Frederik
C. M. Kornbluth 8:215, 221

Pohl, Joy
David Lindsay 15:234

Politis, Linos
Kostes Palamas 5:384

Politzer, Heinz
Bertolt Brecht 6:31
Franz Kafka 13:275
Arthur Schnitzler 4:400
Franz Werfel 8:471

Pollard, Percival
Kate Chopin 5:143
Detlev von Liliencron 18:207
Rainer Maria Rilke 6:357
Edgar Saltus 8:345
Arthur Schnitzler 4:385
Frank Wedekind 7:574

Pollock, John
A. A. Milne 6:306

Pommer, Henry F.
Anne Frank 17:109

Poncé, Juan García
Robert Musil 12:254

Ponomareff, Constantin V.
Sergei Esenin 4:116

Popkin, Henry
Ferenc Molnár 20:171

Popper, Hans
Wolfgang Borchert 5:108

Porter, Katherine Anne
Max Beerbohm 1:69
Willa Cather 1:160
Colette 1:191
Ford Madox Ford 1:277
D. H. Lawrence 2:367
Katherine Mansfield 2:450
Gertrude Stein 1:428
Virginia Woolf 1:534

Porter, Laurence M.
Guillaume Apollinaire 8:18

Porter, Richard N.
Ivan Bunin 6:55

Porter, Thomas E.
Eugene O'Neill 1:404

Posin, J. A.
Mikhail Zoshchenko 15:498

Poster, William
H. P. Lovecraft 4:265

Potoker, Edward Martin
Ronald Firbank 1:230

Poulakidas, Andreas K.
Nikos Kazantzakis 2:320

Poulet, George
Marcel Proust 7:541

Pound, Ezra
Jean de Bosschère 19:58
W. H. Davies 5:199
Ford Madox Ford 15:69, 76
Rémy de Gourmont 17:134
Thomas Hardy 4:174
Henry James 2:249
Lionel Johnson 19:237
James Joyce 3:252; 16:201
Wyndham Lewis 2:386
Harriet Monroe 12:219, 220
Algernon Charles Swinburne
    8:429
Rabindranath Tagore 3:481

Povey, John
Roy Campbell 5:126

Powell, Anthony
George Orwell 2513

Powell, F. York
Charles A. Beard 15:17

Powell, Kerry
Arthur Symons 11:452

Powell, Lawrence Clark
Gertrude Atherton 2:18
Raymond Chandler 1:172

Powys, John Cowper
Edgar Lee Masters 2:464
T. F. Powys 9:361
Dorothy Richardson 3:350

Prater, Donald
Stefan Zweig 17:457

Praz, Mario
Luigi Pirandello 4:326

Predmore, Michael P.
Juan Ramón Jiménez 4:221,
    225

Prescott, Orville
Joyce Cary 1:141
Sinclair Lewis 13:338

Preston, Harriet Waters
Vernon Lee 5:309

Prevelakis, Pandelis
Nikos Kazantzakis 2:313

Price, Lucien
John Jay Chapman 7:188

Price, Martin
Joyce Cary 1:141

Price, Nancy
Lord Dunsany 2:144

Priestley, J. B.
J. M. Barrie 2:45
Arnold Bennett 5:29
James Bridie 3:137
Walter de la Mare 4:72
Anatole France 9:51
Henrik Ibsen 2:231
Stephen Leacock 2:380
Sinclair Lewis 4:255
George Meredith 17:268
August Strindberg 1:451
Hugh Walpole 5:495
William Butler Yeats 1:567
Emile Zola 1:594

Primeau, Ronald
Countee Cullen 4:52

Pringle, Mary Beth
Charlotte Gilman 9:110

Prioleau, Elizabeth Stevens
William Dean Howells 17:188

Pritchard, William H.
Edwin Arlington Robinson
    5:417

Pritchett, V. S.
Isaac Babel 13:26
Maurice Baring 8:33
Arnold Bennett 5:44
Stella Benson 17:21
Mikhail Bulgakov 16:82
Samuel Butler 1:136, 137
Karel Čapek 6:86
Anton Chekhov 3:155
Colette 16:126
Joseph Conrad 1:203, 206
Stephen Crane 11:150
Havelock Ellis 14:114
Ronald Firbank 1:229
Ford Madox Ford 15:84
Anatole France 9:50
George Gissing 3:232
H. Rider Haggard 11:256
Radclyffe Hall 12:191
Thomas Hardy 4:165
O. Henry 19:188
Giuseppe Tomasi di Lampedusa
    13:295
Ring Lardner 14:308
D. H. Lawrence 2:355
T. E. Lawrence 18:144
Ada Leverson 18:196
Wyndham Lewis 2:387
Machado de Assis 10:306
Katherine Mansfield 2:451
H. L. Mencken 13:378
George Meredith 17:282
John Middleton Murry 16:338
Robert Musil 12:247
George Orwell 2:497; 15:301
Marcel Proust 13:425
Dorothy Richardson 3:358
Saki 3:366
Bruno Schulz 5:425

Critic Index

Lytton Strachey **12**:400
John Millington Synge **6**:434
Giovanni Verga **3**:545
H. G. Wells **6**:534
Nathanael West **14**:473
Edith Wharton **9**:545
Emile Zola **1**:594
Mikhail Zoshchenko **15**:493

Proffer, Carl R.
Mikhail Bulgakov **16**:83
Aleksandr Kuprin **5**:301

Proffer, Ellendea
Mikhail Bulgakov **16**:83, 108

Proust, Marcel
Marcel Proust **13**:401
Jules Renard **17**:302
Leo Tolstoy **4**:466

Prusek, Jaroslav
Lu Hsün **3**:299

Pryce-Jones, Alan
Alain-Fournier **6**:18
Bertolt Brecht **1**:107
Robert Musil **12**:238

Puckett, Hugh W.
Robert Musil **12**:235

Punter, David
Ambrose Bierce **7**:98

Purdom, C. B.
Harley Granville-Barker **2**:196

Purser, John Thibaut
Ivan Bunin **6**:47

Pusch, Hans
Rudolf Steiner **13**:456

Putnam, Samuel
Machado de Assis **10**:281
Jean de Bosschère **19**:61

Pyatkovsky, A. Ya.
Leo Tolstoy **4**:445

Pyke, Rafford
Jacques Futrelle **19**:89

Pyne-Timothy, Helen
Claude McKay **7**:468

Qualtiere, Michael
Jack London **15**:267

Queen, Ellery
Dorothy L. Sayers **15**:375

Quennell, Peter
Radclyffe Hall **12**:188

Quiller-Couch, Arthur
Andrew Lang **16**:252
George Moore **7**:474

Quinn, Arthur Hobson
James Branch Cabell **6**:67
F. Marion Crawford **10**:149
Rachel Crothers **19**:72
Rebecca Harding Davis **6**:150
Joel Chandler Harris **2**:210
Bret Harte **1**:342

Quinn, Sister M. Bernetta
Wallace Stevens **12**:360

Quinn, Vincent
Hart Crane **5**:188

Quiroga, Horacio
Horacio Quiroga **20**:208

Raab, Rex
Rudolf Steiner **13**:455

Raban, Jonathan
Hilaire Belloc **18**:42

Rabinovich, Isaiah
Sholom Aleichem **1**:29
Isaac Leib Peretz **16**:395

Rabinowitz, Peter J.
Raymond Chandler **7**:177

Rabinowitz, Stanley J.
Fyodor Sologub **9**:447

Rabkin, Eric S.
George MacDonald **9**:307

Ragusa, Olga
Giuseppe Tomasi di Lampedusa
  13:314

Ragussis, Michael
D. H. Lawrence **2**:373

Rahv, Philip
Franz Kafka **2**:289
George Orwell **6**:340
Tess Slesinger **10**:439
Leo Tolstoy **11**:468
Virginia Woolf **5**:509

Rainey, Brian E.
Alfred Jarry **14**:277

Rainwater, Catherine
H. G. Wells **19**:446

Rajan, Tilottama
Friedrich Nietzsche **18**:344

Raknes, Ola
Jonas Lie **5**:325

Raleigh, John Henry
F. Scott Fitzgerald **1**:251
Eugene O'Neill **6**:335

Ralston, W.R.S.
Leo Tolstoy **4**:447

Ramchand, Kenneth
H. G. de Lisser **12**:95, 96
Roger Mais **8**:243
Claude McKay **7**:464

Ramsey, Warren
Guillaume Apollinaire **3**:36
Paul Valéry **4**:493

Randall, John H., III
Willa Cather **11**:101

Rankin, Daniel S.
Kate Chopin **5**:144

Ransom, John Crowe
Thomas Hardy **4**:164
Edna St. Vincent Millay **4**:314
Wallace Stevens **12**:366
Alexey Nikolayevich Tolstoy
  18:360
Edith Wharton **3**:563

Ransome, Arthur
Rémy de Gourmont **17**:138
Oscar Wilde **8**:492

Raper, J. R.
Ellen Glasgow **2**:189; **7**:345

Rapf, Joanna E.
Nathanael West **14**:493

Rapin, René
Willa Cather **11**:93

Rascoe, Burton
Zane Grey **6**:180
Don Marquis **7**:455
George Jean Nathan **18**:310
Thomas Wolfe **13**:472

Rashdall, H.
William James **15**:146

Raskin, Jonah
Rudyard Kipling **17**:202

Raven, Charles E.
Pierre Teilhard de Chardin
  9:486

Raven, Simon
Joyce Cary **1**:142

Rawson, Judy
F. T. Marinetti **10**:324

Ray, Gordon N.
H. G. Wells **6**:540

Ray, Robert J.
Ford Madox Ford **1**:285

Raybould, A. N.
Stefan George **14**:196

Rayfield, Donald
Anton Chekhov **10**:114
Osip Mandelstam **6**:266

Read, Herbert
Robert Bridges **1**:126
T. E. Lawrence **18**:131
George Moore **7**:479

Reader, Constant
See also **Parker, Dorothy**
Ford Madox Ford **15**:74
Sinclair Lewis **13**:332

Reavey, George
Alexey Nikolayevich Tolstoy
  18:367

Reck, Rima Drell
Georges Bernanos **3**:121

Redding, J. Saunders
Charles Waddell Chesnutt
  5:132
Countee Cullen **4**:42
Paul Laurence Dunbar **2**:128;
  12:113
Frances Ellen Watkins Harper
  14:256
James Weldon Johnson **3**:241

Reding, Katherine
Vicente Blasco Ibáñez **12**:38

Redman, Ben Ray
Georges Bernanos **3**:116
Georg Brandes **10**:64
Frances Ellen Watkins Harper
  14:261

Reed, F. A.
Nikos Kazantzakis **5**:267

Reed, John
John Reed **9**:381

Reed, John R.
H. G. Wells **6**:551

Reed, T. J.
Thomas Mann **14**:354

Rees, Richard
John Middleton Murry **16**:348

Reese, Ilse Meissner
Rudolf Steiner **13**:450

Reeve, F. D.
Aleksandr Blok **5**:88
Fyodor Sologub **9**:441
Mikhail Zoshchenko **15**:506

Reeves, Paschal
Thomas Wolfe **13**:485

Rehder, R. M.
Thomas Hardy **4**:177

Reichert, Herbert W.
Robert Musil **12**:248

Reid, James H.
Alfred Döblin **13**:164

Reid, John T.
Pío Baroja **8**:51

Reid, Randall
Nathanael West **14**:474

Reiger, C. C.
Lincoln Steffens **20**:336

Reilly, John H.
Jean Giraudoux **7**:324

Reilly, Joseph J.
Maurice Baring **8**:34
Kate Chopin **5**:146
Alice Meynell **6**:300

Reilly, Patrick
George Orwell **15**:325

Reinert, Otto
Henrik Ibsen **16**:170
August Strindberg **1**:458

Reinhard, Joakim
José María de Pereda **16**:364

Reis, Richard H.
George MacDonald **9**:304

Reisiger, Hans
Stefan Zweig **17**:424

Reiss, H. S.
Arthur Schnitzler **4**:394

Reményi, Joseph
Endre Ady **11**:15
Mihály Babits **14**:37
Ferenc Molnár **20**:163

Repplier, Agnes
Laurence Housman **7**:358
Alice Meynell **6**:295

Revell, Peter
Paul Laurence Dunbar **12**:125

Revitt, Paul J.
W. S. Gilbert **3**:215

Rexroth, Kenneth
Roy Campbell **5**:124
Anton Chekhov **10**:110
Arthur Conan Doyle **7**:229
Ford Madox Ford **1**:290
Lafcadio Hearn **9**:138
Wallace Stevens **3**:459
H. G. Wells **12**:508

Reynolds, Barbara
E. C. Bentley **12**:20
Dorothy L. Sayers **15**:392

Rhodenizer, V. B.
John McCrae **12**:209
Robert W. Service **15**:402

Rhodes, Anthony
Gabriele D'Annunzio **6**:137

Rhodes, S. A.
Guillaume Apollinaire **8**:12
Léon-Paul Fargue **11**:194
Marcel Schwob **20**:325

Rhys, Brian
Henri Barbusse **5**:14

Rhys, Ernest
Lionel Johnson **19**:228
Rabindranath Tagore **3**:483

Ribbans, Geoffrey
Miguel de Unamuno **2**:564

Rice, Martin P.
Valery Bryusov **10**:94

Rice, Wallace
Harriet Monroe **12**:215

Rich, Amy C.
Zona Gale **7**:277
Isaac Leib Peretz **16**:390

Richards, D. J.
Yevgeny Ivanovich Zamyatin
8:546

Richards, I. A.
George Moore **7**:494

Richardson, Jack
Eugene O'Neill **1**:406

Richardson, Maurice
M. R. James **6**:209
Bram Stoker **8**:386

Richardson, Michael
Benjamin Péret **20**:203

Richey, Elinor
Gertrude Atherton **2**:18

Richings, G. F.
Frances Ellen Watkins Harper
14:255

Richler, Mordecai
Jack London **9**:269

Richman, Robert
René Daumal **14**:92
Edward Thomas **10**:468

Ricks, Christopher
A. E. Housman **10**:257

Riddel, Joseph N.
Wallace Stevens **3**:466

Rideout, Walter B.
Sherwood Anderson **1**:54; **10**:47

Ridge, George Ross
Joris-Karl Huysmans **7**:413
Emile Zola **6**:565

Ridge, Lola
Henri Barbusse **5**:13

Riemer, Svend
Damon Runyon **10**:425

Riewald, J. G.
Max Beerbohm **1**:69

Rifkind, Donna
Colette **16**:138

Riley, Anthony W.
Alfred Döblin **13**:177
Frederick Philip Grove **4**:142,
144

Rilke, Rainer Maria
Thomas Mann **8**:252
Rainer Maria Rilke **19**:298

Rimanelli, Giose
Cesare Pavese **3**:339

Rimer, J. Thomas
Dazai Osamu **11**:188
Mori Ōgai **14**:375
Sōseki Natsume **10**:341

Ringe, Donald A.
George Washington Cable **4**:35

Rinsler, Norma
Guillaume Apollinaire **8**:21

Río, Amelia A. de del
Miguel de Unamuno **9**:513

Río, Ángel del
Federico García Lorca **7**:291
Miguel de Unamuno **9**:513

Ritchie, J. M.
Gottfried Benn **3**:113
Georg Kaiser **9**:189
Carl Spitteler **12**:345
Carl Sternheim **8**:375

Rittenhouse, Jessie B.
Edna St. Vincent Millay **4**:305
Sara Teasdale **4**:425

Rizzo, Gino
Ugo Betti **5**:57, 62

Roback, A. A.
Sholem Asch **3**:67
Isaac Leib Peretz **16**:390

Robb, Nesca A.
A. E. Housman **10**:249

Robbe-Grillet, Alain
Raymond Roussel **20**:232

Roberts, Charles G. D.
Bliss Carman **7**:136
Charles G. D. Roberts **8**:315

Roberts, David
Heinrich Mann **9**:326

Roberts, R. Ellis
Ernst Toller **10**:478

Roberts, S. C.
Arthur Conan Doyle **7**:223

Roberts, W. Adolphe
H. G. de Lisser **12**:95

Robertson, J. G.
Henry Handel Richardson **4**:371
Carl Spitteler **12**:347

Robinson, Christopher
Kostes Palamas **5**:385

Robinson, Henry Morton
James Joyce **3**:261

Robinson, Lennox
Lady Gregory **1**:333

Robinson, Paul
Havelock Ellis **14**:135

Robinson, W. R.
Edwin Arlington Robinson
5:416

Robinson, William H., Jr.
Rudolph Fisher **11**:206

Robson, W. W.
G. K. Chesterton **1**:188

Roby, Kinley E.
Arnold Bennett **20**:27

Rocks, James E.
Kate Chopin **14**:67

Rodgers, Lise
Hart Crane **5**:194

Roditi, Edouard
Oscar Wilde **1**:500

Rodman, Selden
James Agee **19**:18

Rodrigue, Elizabeth M.
André Gide **12**:146

Rogers, Timothy
Rupert Brooke **2**:57

Rogers, W. G.
Gertrude Stein **1**:429

Rogers, Will, Jr.
Will Rogers **8**:340

Roggendorf, Joseph
Tōson Shimazaki **5**:430

Rohrmoser, Günter
Bertolt Brecht **13**:44

Rolland, Romain
Carl Spitteler **12**:336

Rolleston, James L.
Franz Werfel **8**:482

Rollins, Hyder E.
O. Henry **19**:169

Rollins, Peter C.
Will Rogers **8**:338

Romains, Jules
Stefan Zweig **17**:429

Romein, Jan
Anne Frank **17**:100

Romein-Vershoor, Annie
Anne Frank **17**:101

Ronald, Ann
Zane Grey **6**:185

Ronay, Gabriel
Hanns Heinz Ewers **12**:137

Roosevelt, Eleanor
Anne Frank **17**:101

Roosevelt, Theodore
H. Rider Haggard **11**:241

Roppolo, Joseph Patrick
Philip Barry **11**:63

Rose, Marilyn Gaddis
Katharine Tynan **3**:506

Rose, Mark
Henry Kuttner **10**:276
Jules Verne **6**:504

Rose, Phyllis
Colette **16**:128

Rose, Shirley
Dorothy Richardson **3**:358

Rose, William
Rainer Maria Rilke **19**:301

Rosemont, Franklin
Benjamin Péret **20**:189

Rosen, Norma
Rebecca Harding Davis **6**:154

Rosenbaum, Belle
Margaret Mitchell **11**:373

Rosenbaum, Sidonia Carmen
Gabriela Mistral **2**:476
Alfonsina Storni **5**:444

Rosenberg, Harold
James Weldon Johnson **3**:241

Rosenberg, Isaac
Isaac Rosenberg **12**:286, 287

Rosenberg, John D.
John Ruskin **20**:285

Rosenberg, Samuel
Arthur Conan Doyle **7**:230

Rosenblatt, Roger
James Weldon Johnson **19**:215
John Millington Synge **6**:442

Rosenfeld, Paul
Sherwood Anderson **1**:34

Rosenheim, Richard
Rudolf Steiner **13**:443

Rosenstone, Robert A.
John Reed **9**:388

Rosenthal, M. L.
Vladimir Mayakovsky **18**:245
César Vallejo **3**:529
William Butler Yeats **1**:567;
11:533

Rosenthal, Michael
Joyce Cary **1**:147

Rosenthal, Raymond
Isaac Babel **13**:17
Mikhail Bulgakov **16**:78
Leo Tolstoy **4**:469
Giovanni Verga **3**:544

Ross, Alan
Nathanael West **1**:478

Ross, Stephen M.
James Weldon Johnson **3**:249

Rossetti, W. M.
George Meredith **17**:253

Rosten, Norman
Stephen Vincent Benét **7**:77

Rostropowicz, Joanna
Bruno Schulz **5**:424

Roth, Philip
Géza Csáth **13**:154

Roth, Phyllis A.
Bram Stoker **8**:396

Rothberg, Abraham
Jack London **15**:262

Roudiez, Leon S.
René Daumal **14**:90
Raymond Roussel **20**:248

Rountree, Benjamin
Jean de Bosschère **19**:66

Rountree, Mary
Jean de Bosschère **19**:66

Rourke, Constance Mayfield
Zona Gale **7**:277
Ring Lardner **14**:294
Sinclair Lewis **13**:336

Rouse, Blair
Ellen Glasgow **7**:339

Roussel, Raymond
Raymond Roussel **20**:227

Routley, Erik
E. C. Bentley **12**:19

Rowe, Anne
Lafcadio Hearn **9**:138

Rowse, A. L.
Alun Lewis **3**:285

Roy, Dilip Kumar
Saratchandra Chatteji **13**:73

Roy, Sandra
Josephine Tey **14**:458

Royal, Robert
Hilaire Belloc **18**:46

Royce, Josiah
William James **15**:160

Rozhdestvensky, Vsevolod
Sergei Esenin **4**:113

Rubens, Philip M.
Ambrose Bierce **7**:95

Rubin, Joan Shelley
Constance Rourke **12**:327

Rubin, Louis D., Jr.
James Agee **19**:40
George Washington Cable **4**:32
Countee Cullen **4**:51
Ellen Glasgow **2**:184
Thomas Wolfe **4**:536

Rudnitsky, Konstantin
Mikhail Bulgakov **16**:93

Rudwin, Maximilian J.
Paul Heyse **8**:119

Ruehlen, Petroula Kephala
C. P. Cavafy **2**:92

Ruggles, Alice McGuffey
Vachel Lindsay **17**:234

Ruhm, Herbert
Raymond Chandler **1**:171

Ruihley, Glenn Richard
Amy Lowell **8**:232

Rule, Jane
Radclyffe Hall **12**:192
Gertrude Stein **6**:413

Rumbold, Richard
Antoine de Saint-Exupéry **2**:518

Runciman, James
H. Rider Haggard **11**:239

Runyon, Damon
Damon Runyon **10**:425

Runyon, Damon, Jr.
Damon Runyon **10**:429

Ruoff, Gene W.
James Agee **19**:28

Russell, Bertrand
Joseph Conrad **1**:207
Havelock Ellis **14**:115
Henrik Ibsen **2**:231
William James **15**:151
Friedrich Nietzsche **10**:373
Bernard Shaw **3**:400
May Sinclair **3**:436
H. G. Wells **6**:538

Russell, D. C.
Raymond Chandler **1**:168

Russell, Frances Theresa
Edith Wharton **3**:561

Russell, Francis
Gertrude Stein **6**:410

Russell, Franklin
Jules Renard **17**:311

Russell, George William
See also **A. E.**
Kahlil Gibran **1**:327

Russell, Richard K.
George Jean Nathan **18**:326

Ryan, Don
Hanns Heinz Ewers **12**:134

Ryf, Robert S.
Joseph Conrad **1**:218

Sachs, Murray
Anatole France **9**:54

Sackville-West, Edward
Joseph Conrad **1**:204
Stefan George **2**:147
Henry James **2**:261
Emile Zola **1**:589

Sackville-West, V.
Hilaire Belloc **7**:36
Selma Lagerlöf **4**:230

Saddlemyer, Ann
Lady Gregory **1**:336

Sadleir, Michael
Alfred Döblin **13**:159

Sadler, Glenn Edward
George MacDonald **9**:303
Charles Williams **11**:495

Sagar, Keith
D. H. Lawrence **2**:371

St. Martin, Hardie
Antonio Machado **3**:307

Saintsbury, George
H. Rider Haggard **11**:237
Andrew Lang **16**:259
John Ruskin **20**:265
Juan Valera **10**:497
Israel Zangwill **16**:442
Emile Zola **6**:560

Sakanishi, Shio
Ishikawa Takuboku **15**:123

Sale, Roger
L. Frank Baum **7**:24
Ford Madox Ford **1**:288
Andrew Lang **16**:272
A. A. Milne **6**:321

Salinas, Pedro
Pedro Salinas **17**:351
Ramón del Valle-Inclán **5**:476

Salmon, Eric
Ugo Betti **5**:63

Salmonson, Jessica Amanda
Robert E. Howard **8**:137

Salomon, I. L.
Dino Campana **20**:89

Salomon, Louis B.
Nathanael West **14**:469

Samarin, Roman
O. Henry **19**:192

Sampley, Arthur M.
Maxwell Anderson **2**:6

Samuel, Maurice
Sholom Aleichem **1**:21
Isaac Leib Peretz **16**:393

Samuel, Richard
Carl Sternheim **8**:369

Samuels, Ernest
Henry Adams **4**:15

Sánchez, José
José María de Pereda **16**:371

Sanchez, Roberto G.
Jacinto Benavente **3**:100

Sandburg, Carl
See also **Sandburg, Charles A.**
Arturo Barea **14**:47
Stephen Vincent Benét **7**:77
Douglas Southall Freeman
11:219
Jack London **9**:254
Harriet Monroe **12**:216
Robert E. Sherwood **3**:412
Lincoln Steffens **20**:339

Sandburg, Charles A.
See also **Sandburg, Carl**
Jack London **9**:254

Sanders, Charles Richard
Lytton Strachey **12**:408

Sanders, Ivan
Géza Csáth **13**:151

Sanders, Scott
D. H. Lawrence **9**:225; **16**:310

Sandison, Alan
H. Rider Haggard **11**:248

Sandoe, James
Josephine Tey **14**:449, 451

Sandwell, B. K.
Frederick Philip Grove **4**:135

San Juan, E., Jr.
André Gide **5**:232

Sankrityayan, Kamala
Saratchandra Chatteji **13**:79

Santas, Joan Foster
Ellen Glasgow **2**:186

Santayana, George
William James **15**:163
Lionel Johnson **19**:241
Friedrich Nietzsche **10**:364
Marcel Proust **7**:523

Sapir, Edward
A. E. Housman **1**:353

Sargent, Daniel
Charles Péguy **10**:405

Saroyan, William
H. L. Mencken **13**:373
George Jean Nathan **18**:308

Sartre, Jean-Paul
Jean Giraudoux **7**:318

Sarvan, C. P.
Joseph Conrad **13**:141

Sassoon, Siegfried
Wilfred Owen **5**:358
Isaac Rosenberg **12**:290

Saul, George Brandon
A. E. Coppard **5**:178, 181
Lord Dunsany **2**:145
James Stephens **4**:416
Sara Teasdale **4**:428

Saunders, Thomas
Frederick Philip Grove **4**:137

Saurat, Denis
Rémy de Gourmont **17**:150
Pierre Loti **11**:360

Savage, D. S.
F. Scott Fitzgerald **1**:248
Virginia Woolf **20**:397

Savage, George
David Belasco **3**:88

Saveth, Edward N.
Henry Adams **4**:14

Sayers, Dorothy L.
Arthur Conan Doyle **7**:219
Dorothy L. Sayers **15**:371
Charles Williams **11**:486

Sayers, Raymond S.
Machado de Assis **10**:284

Scalia, S. E.
Vitaliano Brancati **12**:80

Scannell, Vernon
Edward Thomas **10**:459

Scarborough, Dorothy
Arthur Machen **4**:277

Scarfe, Francis
Dylan Thomas **1**:465
Paul Valéry **15**:540

Schacht, Richard
Friedrich Nietzsche **10**:386

Schade, George D.
Horacio Quiroga **20**:218

Scheffauer, Herman George
Ernst Toller **10**:474

Scheick, William J.
Arnold Bennett **20**:35
H. G. Wells **12**:513

Schevill, James
Eugene O'Neill **1**:405

Schickel, Richard
Raymond Chandler **1**:170

Schier, Donald
Alain-Fournier **6**:14

Schiller, F.C.S.
William James **15**:140

Schilling, Bernard N.
Israel Zangwill **16**:457

Schlant, Ernestine
Hermann Broch **20**:73

Schlegel, Dorothy B.
James Branch Cabell **6**:72

Schlesinger, Arthur M., Jr.
Charles A. Beard **15**:26
George Orwell **2**:497

Schlochower, Harry
Thomas Mann **2**:413

Schlueter, Paul
Arthur Schnitzler **4**:403

Schmidt, Michael
Walter de la Mare **4**:82
Charlotte Mew **8**:301

Schmidt, Paul
Velimir Khlebnikov **20**:149

Schmitt, Hans
Charles Péguy **10**:407

Schneider, Daniel J.
Henry James **11**:344
Wallace Stevens **12**:379

Schneider, Judith Morganroth
Max Jacob **6**:201

Schneider, Sister Lucy
Willa Cather **1**:165

Schnurer, Herman
Alfred Jarry **14**:270

Scholes, Robert
James Joyce **16**:225

Schöpp-Schilling, Beate
Charlotte Gilman **9**:107

Schorer, Mark
Sherwood Anderson **1**:60
F. Scott Fitzgerald **1**:239
Ford Madox Ford **1**:277
James Joyce **16**:207
D. H. Lawrence **16**:288
Sinclair Lewis **4**:259; **13**:340
Malcolm Lowry **6**:236
George Orwell **15**:300
Gertrude Stein **1**:437
H. G. Wells **6**:535
Thomas Wolfe **4**:521

Schorr, Daniel
Anne Frank **17**:104

Schreiner, Olive
See also **Iron, Ralph**
Olive Schreiner **9**:393

Schubert, P. Z.
Jaroslav Hašek **4**:189

Schultheiss, John
George Jean Nathan **18**:322

Schultz, Robert
Joseph Conrad **6**:123

Schultze, Sydney
Mikhail Bulgakov **16**:97
Leo Tolstoy **11**:478

Schumacher, Ernst
Bertolt Brecht **13**:53

Schumann, Detlev W.
Detlev von Liliencron **18**:213

Schürer, Ernst
Georg Kaiser **9**:190

Schwartz, Delmore
Ring Lardner **2**:334
Edna St. Vincent Millay **4**:314
Wallace Stevens **3**:451
William Butler Yeats **1**:556

Schwartz, Kessel
Antonio Machado **3**:309

Schwartz, William Leonard
Amy Lowell **8**:228

Schwarz, Egon
Hugo von Hofmannsthal **11**:306

Schweitzer, Albert
Rudolf Steiner **13**:450

Schweitzer, Darrell
Robert E. Howard **8**:133
H. P. Lovecraft **4**:274

Scott, Ann
Olive Schreiner **9**:405

Scott, Clement
John Gray **19**:141

Scott, Dixon
Lionel Johnson **19**:236
George Bernard Shaw **3**:382

Scott, J. A.
Ugo Betti **5**:54

Scott, J. D.
André Gide **5**:217

Scott, Kenneth W.
Zane Grey **6**:181

Scott, Nathan A., Jr.
D. H. Lawrence **2**:357

Scott, Robert Ian
Christopher John Brennan
17:41

Scott, Winfield Townley
H. P. Lovecraft **4**:265
Amy Lowell **8**:230
Edna St. Vincent Millay **4**:315
Booth Tarkington **9**:472

Scott-Craig, T.S.K.
A. E. Housman **10**:248

Scott-James, R. A.
Lytton Strachey **12**:407

Scrimgeour, Gary J.
F. Scott Fitzgerald **1**:262
John Galsworthy **1**:303

Searles, Stanhope
O. Henry **19**:168

Seaton, Beverly
John Ruskin **20**:312

Seaton, Jerome F.
Lu Hsün **3**:300

Seccombe, Thomas
George Gissing **3**:223

Secor, Walter Todd
Paul Bourget **12**:67

Sedgewick, G. G.
Stephen Leacock **2**:378

Sedgewick, Henry Dwight
Edith Wharton **3**:551

Sedgwick, H. D., Jr.
Gabriele D'Annunzio **6**:129

Seeley, Carol
Paul Eluard **7**:245

Seelye, John D.
Booth Tarkington **9**:470
Mark Twain **12**:451

Seferis, George
C. P. Cavafy **7**:159

Segall, Brenda
Rubén Darío **4**:66

Segel, Harold B.
Leonid Andreyev **3**:29
Aleksandr Blok **5**:99
Zinaida Hippius **9**:167
Vladimir Mayakovsky **4**:301

Sehmsdorf, Henning K.
Bjørnstjerne Bjørnson **7**:117

Seib, Kenneth
James Agee **1**:12
Dylan Thomas **8**:462

Seidensticker, Edward G.
Dazai Osamu **11**:171

Seidlin, Oskar
Georg Brandes **10**:64
Gerhart Hauptmann **4**:201
Thomas Mann **2**:423

Seldes, Gilbert
Max Beerbohm **1**:66
F. Scott Fitzgerald **1**:237
Ring Lardner **2**:333
Eugene O'Neill **1**:383

Sellin, Bernard
David Lindsay **15**:236

Seltzer, Alvin J.
Joyce Cary **1**:149
Joseph Conrad **1**:219
Franz Kafka **6**:224
Virginia Woolf **1**:548

Seltzer, Thomas
Leonid Andreyev **3**:18

Sendak, Maurice
George MacDonald **9**:300

Sender, Ramon
Arturo Barea **14**:47
Federico García Lorca **1**:317

Senf, Carol A.
Bram Stoker **8**:400

Sergeant, Howard
Roy Campbell **5**:122
Wilfred Owen **5**:365

Setchkarev, Vsevolod
Innokenty Annensky **14**:20
Valery Bryusov **10**:83

Sewell, Brocard
John Gray **19**:142

Sewell, Elizabeth
Paul Valéry **4**:494

Seyersted, Per
Kate Chopin **5**:150; **14**:59

Seymour, Alan
Antonin Artaud **3**:49

Seymour-Smith, Martin
Wyndham Lewis **2**:396

Shadick, Harold
Liu E **15**:246

Shafer, Robert
Lionel Johnson **19**:239
Ludwig Lewisohn **19**:275
James Stephens **4**:408

Shafer, Yvonne B.
Rachel Crothers **19**:81

Shain, Charles E.
F. Scott Fitzgerald **1**:259; **6**:161

Shane, Alex M.
Yevgeny Ivanovich Zamyatin
8:551

Shanks, Edward
M. P. Shiel **8**:360
Hermann Sudermann **15**:428

Shapiro, Karl
Dylan Thomas **1**:476
William Butler Yeats **1**:568

Sharistanian, Janet
Tess Slesinger **10**:446

Sharp, Dennis
Rudolf Steiner **13**:451

Sharp, Francis Michael
Georg Heym **9**:150

Sharp, William
Bliss Carman **7**:133

Shattuck, Roger
Guillaume Apollinaire **3**:33
Antonin Artaud **3**:59
René Daumal **14**:87
Alfred Jarry **2**:278, 283
Marcel Proust **7**:542
Paul Valéry **4**:501; **15**:459

Shaw, Bernard
Maurice Baring **8**:31
David Belasco **3**:84
Hilaire Belloc **7**:36; **18**:21
Samuel Butler **1**:136
G. K. Chesterton **6**:97
Anthony Comstock **13**:88
W. H. Davies **5**:198
José Echegaray **4**:96
Havelock Ellis **14**:103
R. B. Cunninghame Graham
19:102
William Ernest Henley **8**:98
William Dean Howells **7**:367
Henrik Ibsen **2**:220; **8**:143;
16:156
Henry James **11**:318
Andrew Lang **16**:259
T. E. Lawrence **18**:129
Friedrich Nietzsche **10**:360
Edmond Rostand **6**:372
John Ruskin **20**:278
Bernard Shaw **9**:410
Leo Tolstoy **11**:465
Mark Twain **12**:432
H. G. Wells **12**:489
Oscar Wilde **8**:489

Shaw, Donald L.
Pío Baroja **8**:56
José Echegaray **4**:105
José María de Pereda **16**:377

Shaw, Glenn W.
Akutagawa Ryūnosuke **16**:17

Shaw, Irwin
Bertolt Brecht **13**:43

Shaw, Leroy R.
Georg Kaiser **9**:187

Shaw, Priscilla Washburn
Paul Valéry **4**:498

Shaw, Vivian
F. Scott Fitzgerald **1**:236

Sheean, Vincent
Sinclair Lewis **4**:252

Sheed, Wilfrid
James Agee **19**:24
Hilaire Belloc **18**:45
G. K. Chesterton **1**:182

Shenker, Israel
E. C. Bentley **12**:25

Shepard, Odell
Bliss Carman **7**:137
Alexander Woollcott **5**:523

Shepherd, A. P.
Rudolf Steiner **13**:444

Sherard, Robert H.
H. G. Wells **19**:423

Sherburne, James Clark
John Ruskin **20**:293

Sherman, Joan R.
Charlotte L. Forten **16**:149
Frances Ellen Watkins Harper
14:259

Sherman, Stuart P.
Arnold Bennett **5**:27
Louis Bromfield **11**:72
Theodore Dreiser **10**:165
Sinclair Lewis **13**:327
Pierre Loti **11**:359
Don Marquis **7**:437
H. L. Mencken **13**:358
George Meredith **17**:265

Sherrard, Philip
C. P. Cavafy **7**:155

Sherwood, Margaret
Marie Belloc Lowndes **12**:200

Sherwood, Robert Emmet
Philip Barry **11**:58
Robert Sherwood **3**:409

Shestov, Lev
Anton Chekhov **3**:147
Leo Tolstoy **4**:478

Shiel, M. P.
M. P. Shiel **8**:360

Shinoda, Seishi
Ishikawa Takuboku **15**:125

Shivers, Albert S.
Maxwell Anderson **2**:9

Shklovsky, Victor
Mikhail Zoshchenko **15**:490

Sholokov, Mikhail
Andrei A. Zhdanov **18**:470

Short, Clarice
James Stephens **4**:413

Shostakovich, Dmitri
Andrei A. Zhdanov **18**:481

Showalter, Elaine
Dorothy Richardson **3**:360
Olive Schreiner **9**:403

Shreffler, Philip A.
H. P. Lovecraft **4**:272

Shulman, Alix Kates
Emma Goldman **13**:224

Shulman, Robert
Stephen Crane **17**:65, 79

Shumaker, Wayne
George Moore **7**:495

Shuman, R. Baird
Robert E. Sherwood **3**:414

Shumsky, Neil Larry
Israel Zangwill **16**:467

Shuttleworth, Martin
Henri Barbusse **5**:16

Sibley, Agnes
Charles Williams **11**:498

Sichel, Walter
W. S. Gilbert **3**:209

Sidney-Fryer, Donald
Ambrose Bierce **7**:96

Sievers, W. David
Philip Barry **11**:58

Silk, Dennis
Isaac Rosenberg **12**:298

Sillen, Samuel
George Orwell **15**:302

Silver, Arnold
Bernard Shaw **9**:426

Silvi, Margherita M.
Vitaliano Brancati **12**:80

Silz, Walter
Paul Heyse **8**:122

Simmons, Ernest J.
Konstantin Dmitriyevich
Balmont **11**:32
Leo Tolstoy **4**:473

Simon, Anne
F. T. Marinetti **10**:315

Simon, Irene
Virginia Woolf **20**:405

Simon, John
Henrik Ibsen **2**:232
Bernard Shaw **3**:405

Simon, John Kenneth
Valéry Larbaud **9**:202

Simonson, Harold P.
Zona Gale **7**:284
O. E. Rölvaag **17**:334

Simpson, Donald H.
Lytton Strachey **12**:415

Simpson, Lesley Byrd
Mariano Azuela **3**:79

Sinclair, May
Jean de Bosschère **19**:51
Sinclair Lewis **13**:327
Dorothy Richardson **3**:345
Edwin Arlington Robinson
5:400

Sinclair, Upton
Sherwood Anderson **10**:37
Vicente Blasco Ibáñez **12**:34
Emma Goldman **13**:213
Joseph Hergesheimer **11**:272
Jack London **9**:256
H. L. Mencken **13**:368
Mark Twain **12**:433
H. G. Wells **12**:492

Sinden, Margaret
Gerhart Hauptmann **4**:201

Singer, Armand E.
Paul Bourget **12**:73

Singer, David F.
Ludwig Lewisohn **19**:286

Singer, Isaac Bashevis
Knut Hamsun **14**:236
Bruno Schulz **5**:420, 426

Singh, Amritjit
Wallace Thurman **6**:450

Singh, Bhupal
Rudyard Kipling **8**:184

Sinyavsky, Andrey
Isaac Babel **13**:24

Sirin, Vladimir
See also **Nabokov, Vladimir**
Rupert Brooke **2**:54

Sisson, C. H.
Ford Madox Ford **15**:95
Edward Thomas **10**:468

Sitwell, Edith
W. H. Davies **5**:203
A. E. Housman **10**:240
D. H. Lawrence **2**:369
Gertrude Stein **6**:403
William Butler Yeats **1**:555

Sitwell, Sir Osbert
Ronald Firbank **1**:227
Ada Leverson **18**:187
Alfred Noyes **7**:514

Sizemore, Christine W.
Franz Kafka **6**:227

Skaggs, Merrill Maguire
Willa Cather **11**:115

Skelton, Isabel
Frederick Philip Grove **4**:133

Skelton, Robin
John Millington Synge **6**:439

Skinner, B. F.
Gertrude Stein **6**:404

Skinner, Richard Dana
Philip Barry **11**:51
Wallace Thurman **6**:445
Alexander Woollcott **5**:522

Slate, Tom
Edgar Rice Burroughs **2**:82

Slater, Candace
César Vallejo **3**:534

Slesinger, Tess
Tess Slesinger **10**:440

Slochower, Harry
Sholem Asch **3**:67
Alfred Döblin **13**:162
Heinrich Mann **9**:317
Arthur Schnitzler **4**:393
Ernst Toller **10**:483
Sigrid Undset **3**:515
Franz Werfel **8**:469

Slonim, Marc
Innokenty Annensky **14**:19
Isaak Babel **2**:37
Konstantin Dmitriyevich
Balmont **11**:33
Andrey Bely **7**:52
Aleksandr Blok **5**:87
Ivan Bunin **6**:51
Maxim Gorky **8**:79
Giuseppe Tomasi di Lampedusa
13:291
Vladimir Mayakovsky **18**:261
Andrei Platonov **14**:421
Alexey Nikolayevich Tolstoy
18:373
Marina Tsvetaeva **7**:557, 566
Andrei A. Zhdanov **18**:477
Mikhail Zoshchenko **15**:500

Smertinko, Johan J.
Sholem Asch **3**:65

Smirnova, Ludmilla
Alexey Nikolayevich Tolstoy
18:379

Smith, A.J.M.
Duncan Campbell Scott **6**:390
Emile Nelligan **14**:391

Smith, C. Alphonso
O. Henry **19**:172

Smith, Clark Ashton
William Hope Hodgson **13**:232
George Sterling **20**:377

Smith, George N.
Booker T. Washington **10**:514

Smith, Grover
Ford Madox Ford **1**:288

Smith, Harrison
Joyce Cary **1**:141
Heinrich Mann **9**:315

Smith, Hazel Littlefield
See **Littlefield, Hazel**

Smith, Henry James
O. Henry **1**:345

Smith, Henry Nash
Theodore Dreiser **10**:190
William Dean Howells **17**:172
Mark Twain **6**:478; **19**:384

Smith, Hugh Allison
Edmond Rostand **6**:379

Smith, James Steel
R. B. Cunninghame Graham
19:128

Smith, Marcus
George Orwell **15**:311

Smith, Maxwell A.
Antoine de Saint-Exupéry **2**:520

Smith, M. J.
Josephine Tey **14**:457

Smith, Nora Archibald
José Echegaray **4**:98

Smith, R. B.
Pierre Teilhard de Chardin
9:500

Smith, Robert A.
Claude McKay **7**:457

Smith, Rowland
Roy Campbell **5**:125
Wyndham Lewis **2**:399

Smith, Stanley Astredo
Guiseppe Giacosa **7**:306, 312

Smith, Sybille
Christopher John Brennan
17:46

Smith, Timothy d'Arch
Montague Summers **16**:430

Smith, Verity
Ramón del Valle-Inclán **5**:487

Smith, Virginia Llewellyn
Anton Chekhov **10**:112

Smith, William Jay
Valéry Larbaud **9**:200

Smith, Winifred
Arthur Schnitzler **4**:387

Smuts, J. C.
Olive Schreiner **9**:396

Snell, George
Ambrose Bierce **1**:88

Snider, Clifton
Virginia Woolf **5**:516

Snodgrass, Chris
Oscar Wilde **1**:509

Snodgrass, W. D.
Gottfried Benn **3**:108

Snow, C. P.
Ronald Firbank **1**:227
Ada Leverson **18**:189

Sochen, June
Zona Gale **7**:286

Critic Index

Sokel, Walter H.
Gottfried Benn **3**:107
Georg Heym **9**:142
Franz Kafka **2**:305; **13**:265, 285
Georg Kaiser **9**:182, 183
Robert Musil **12**:253
Rainer Maria Rilke **19**:318
Carl Sternheim **8**:369, 370
Ernst Toller **10**:485
Frank Wedekind **7**:579
Franz Werfel **8**:473

Sologub, Fyodor
Fyodor Sologub **9**:432

Solomon, Eric
Stephen Crane **11**:154

Solovyov, Vladimir
Valery Bryusov **10**:77

Solum, Nora O.
O. E. Rölvaag **17**:327

Sonnerfeld, Albert
Georges Bernanos **3**:120, 123

Sonstroem, David
John Ruskin **20**:309

Sontag, Susan
Antonin Artaud **3**:56
Cesare Pavese **3**:338
Robert Walser **18**:437

Sorensen, Otto M.
Bertolt Brecht **13**:50

Sorley, Charles Hamilton
Rupert Brooke **7**:120

Soskin, William
Marjorie Kinnan Rawlings **4**:360

Sőter, István
Miklós Radnóti **16**:409

Southerington, F. R.
Thomas Hardy **10**:225

Southworth, James Granville
Hart Crane **2**:117
Thomas Hardy **4**:166
Elinor Wylie **8**:530

Spacks, Patricia Meyer
Charles Williams **1**:524

Spalek, John M.
Franz Werfel **8**:482

Spalter, Max
Karl Kraus **5**:283

Spangler, George M.
Kate Chopin **5**:154

Spann, Meno
Franz Kafka **13**:282

Spanos, William V.
Dorothy L. Sayers **2**:534

Speaight, Robert
Pierre Teilhard de Chardin **9**:491

Spear, Allan H.
James Weldon Johnson **3**:246

Spears, Monroe K.
Hart Crane **2**:119

Spector, Ivar
Leonid Andreyev **3**:25

Speir, Jerry
Raymond Chandler **7**:179

Spell, Jefferson Rea
Mariano Azuela **3**:76
Horacio Quiroga **20**:211

Spencer, Benjamin T.
Sherwood Anderson **1**:61

Spencer, Theodore
William Butler Yeats **1**:554

Spender, Natasha
Raymond Chandler **1**:176

Spender, Stephen
Wolfgang Borchert **5**:106
Robert Bridges **1**:131
C. P. Cavafy **2**:93
Henry James **2**:253
James Joyce **3**:277
Franz Kafka **13**:257
D. H. Lawrence **2**:369
Wyndham Lewis **2**:385
Malcolm Lowry **6**:238
Wilfred Owen **5**:361
Bernard Shaw **3**:393
Dylan Thomas **8**:451
Charles Williams **11**:484
William Butler Yeats **1**:555
Stefan Zweig **17**:455

Sperber, Murray
George Orwell **6**:353; **15**:317

Spettigue, Douglas O.
Frederick Philip Grove **4**:138, 143, 144

Spilka, Mark
D. H. Lawrence **16**:289

Spiller, Robert E.
Henry Adams **4**:11
Hamlin Garland **3**:195

Spindler, Michael
Theodore Dreiser **18**:70
William Dean Howells **17**:186

Spinner, Jonathan Harold
Jack London **15**:255

Spitteler, Carl
Carl Spitteler **12**:334

Spivey, Ted R.
Oscar Wilde **8**:501

Sprague, Claire
Edgar Saltus **8**:352
Virginia Woolf **1**:545

Sprague, Rosemary
Sara Teasdale **4**:431

Sprinchorn, Evert
Henrik Ibsen **16**:191

Spring, Powell
Rudolf Steiner **13**:442

Squire, J. C.
See also **Eagle, Solomon**
Maurice Baring **8**:32
Robert Bridges **1**:125
G. K. Chesterton **6**:97
W. H. Davies **5**:201
Walter de la Mare **4**:72
A. E. Housman **1**:353
D. H. Lawrence **9**:212
Katherine Mansfield **8**:275
Alice Meynell **6**:297
Bernard Shaw **3**:385
William Butler Yeats **1**:553

Stafford, Jean
Anthony Comstock **13**:96

Stafford, John
Joel Chandler Harris **2**:211

Stafford, Tony J.
George Sterling **20**:387

Stahl, E. L.
Rainer Maria Rilke **1**:411

Stahlberger, Lawrence Leo
Vladimir Mayakovsky **18**:249

Stallman, Robert Wooster
Stephen Crane **11**:137
F. Scott Fitzgerald **14**:158

Stamm, Rudolf
Eugene O'Neill **1**:390

Stanford, Derek
Havelock Ellis **14**:130
Lionel Johnson **19**:248
Alfred Noyes **7**:515
Arthur Symons **11**:446
Dylan Thomas **8**:455

Stanford, W. B.
Nikos Kazantzakis **2**:314

Stanislavski, Constantin
Anton Chekhov **10**:101

Stansbury, Milton H.
Jean Giraudoux **2**:155

Stanton, Edward F.
Federico García Lorca **7**:298

Stanton, Ruth
José Rubén Romero **14**:433

Starck, Taylor
Stefan George **14**:193

Starkie, Enid
André Gide **12**:163

Starkie, Walter
Jacinto Benavente **3**:97
Vicente Blasco Ibáñez **12**:40
Federico García Lorca **1**:317
Gregorio Martinez Sierra and Maria Martinez Sierra **6**:277

Starr, Kevin
George Sterling **20**:381

Starr, Nathan Comfort
Charles Williams **11**:488

Starrett, Vincent
Ambrose Bierce **7**:89
Arthur Conan Doyle **7**:220
Arthur Machen **4**:278

Stavrou, C. N.
Nikos Kazantzakis **5**:261

Stead, W. T.
H. G. Wells **19**:421

Stearns, Harold
John Reed **9**:382

Stearns, Monroe M.
Thomas Wolfe **13**:474

Steele, Elizabeth
Hugh Walpole **5**:502

Steen, Marguerite
Hugh Walpole **5**:499

Steene, Birgitta
August Strindberg **8**:413

Steffens, Lincoln
Lincoln Steffens **20**:333

Stegner, Wallace
Willa Cather **1**:167
Bret Harte **1**:343
Thomas Wolfe **13**:477

Stein, Allen F.
Ring Lardner **2**:340

Stein, Gertrude
F. Scott Fitzgerald **14**:149
Henry James **2**:261

Stein, Paul
Jack London **9**:278

Stein, Richard L.
John Ruskin **20**:302

Steinbrink, Jeffrey
F. Scott Fitzgerald **14**:179

Steiner, George
Ford Madox Ford **1**:288
Henrik Ibsen **8**:148
Raymond Roussel **20**:237
Leo Tolstoy **4**:467

Steiner, Marie
Rudolf Steiner **13**:442

Steiner, Rudolf
Friedrich Nietzsche **10**:358
Rudolf Steiner **13**:438

Steiner, T. R.
Nathanael West **14**:488

Steinmann, Martin Jr.
T. F. Powys **9**:369

Stempel, Daniel
Lafcadio Hearn **9**:129

Stender-Petersen, Adolph
Władysław Stanisław Reymont **5**:390

Stenerson, Douglas C.
H. L. Mencken **13**:390

Stephen, James Kenneth
H. Rider Haggard **11**:240

Stephens, Donald
Bliss Carman **7**:147

Stephens, James
A. E. **10**:17
William Butler Yeats **11**:525; **18**:444

Stephensen, P. R.
Aleister Crowley **7**:210

Sterling, George
Ambrose Bierce **7**:88, 91
George Sterling **20**:376

Stern, Alfred
José Ortega y Gasset **9**:341

Stern, G. B.
Anne Frank **17**:114
Sheila Kaye-Smith **20**:101

Stern, Guy
Bertolt Brecht **13**:62

Stern, J. P.
Jaroslav Hašek **4**:186
Thomas Mann **2**:438
Friedrich Nietzsche **10**:394
Rainer Maria Rilke **1**:424

Stern, Philip Van Doren
Arthur Machen **4**:279

Stevens, Wallace
Harriet Monroe **12**:220
Wallace Stevens **12**:357
Paul Valéry **4**:494

Stevenson, Lionel
Gertrude Atherton **2**:16
John McCrae **12**:209
M. P. Shiel **8**:364
May Sinclair **11**:412
George Sterling **20**:378

Stevenson, Robert Louis
Thomas Hardy **18**:89
Marcel Schwob **20**:320

Stewart, Allegra
Gertrude Stein **1**:434

Stewart, Annette
Christopher John Brennan
17:53

Stewart, Desmond
T. E. Lawrence **18**:174

Stewart, Donald Ogden
Robert Benchley **1**:78
Robert W. Service **15**:400

Stewart, J.I.M.
James Joyce **3**:274
Rudyard Kipling **8**:197
D. H. Lawrence **2**:368
William Butler Yeats **1**:569

Stewart, Joan Hinde
Colette **16**:129

Stewart, Lady Margaret
Antoine de Saint-Exupéry **2**:518

Still, William
Frances Ellen Watkins Harper
14:255

Stillman, Linda Klieger
Alfred Jarry **14**:285

Stine, Peter
Franz Kafka **6**:232

Stinson, Robert
Lincoln Steffens **20**:360

Stirling, Monica
Colette **1**:191

Stock, Irvin
André Gide **12**:154

Stock, Michael O. P.
Pierre Teilhard de Chardin
9:484

Stockinger, Jacob
Colette **16**:118

Stone, Albert E., Jr.
Mark Twain **6**:471

Stone, Donald D.
Arnold Bennett **20**:37

Stone, Geoffrey
Roy Campbell **5**:117
Oscar Wilde **8**:499

Stonesifer, Richard J.
W. H. Davies **5**:205

Storer, Edward
Luigi Pirandello **4**:325

Stork, Charles Wharton
Sigrid Undset **3**:511
Verner von Heidenstam **5**:248,
249, 256
Hugo von Hofmannsthal **11**:294

Stott, William
James Agee **19**:33

Stouck, David
Willa Cather **11**:107, 112
Sarah Orne Jewett **1**:369

Stout, Joseph A., Jr.
Will Rogers **8**:338

Strachey, James
Lytton Strachey **12**:407

Strachey, John
George Orwell **2**:505

Strachey, Lytton
Thomas Hardy **4**:154
Lytton Strachey **12**:391

Strakhov, Nikolai N.
Leo Tolstoy **4**:449

Strakhovsky, Leonid I.
Osip Mandelstam **6**:257

Strauss, Harold
Jakob Wassermann **6**:512

Strauss, Walter A.
Marcel Proust **7**:533

Stream, George G.
Ugo Betti **5**:63

Striedter, Jurij
Vladimir Mayakovsky **18**:263
Alexey Nikolayevich Tolstoy
18:385

Strier, Richard
Hart Crane **2**:125

Strindberg, August
Friedrich Nietzsche **10**:353

Strizhevskaya, L
Saratchandra Chatterji **13**:81

Strong, Kenneth
Toson Shimazaki **5**:440

Strong, L.A.G.
Lewis Grassic Gibbon **4**:120
Radclyffe Hall **12**:188
Hugh Walpole **5**:501

Stroud, Parry
Stephen Vincent Benét **7**:78

Struc, Roman S.
Fyodor Sologub **9**:444

Struve, Gleb
Isaac Babel **13**:27
Mikhail Bulgakov **2**:63, 65
Ivan Bunin **6**:44
Maxim Gorky **8**:75
Alexey Nikolayevich Tolstoy
18:359
Yevgeny Ivanovich Zamyatin
8:545
Mikhail Zoshchenko **15**:492

Stuart, John
John Reed **9**:384

Stubbs, Marcia C.
Alain-Fournier **6**:15

Stuckey, W. J.
Margaret Mitchell **11**:377
Marjorie Kinnan Rawlings
4:365

Sturgeon, Mary C.
James Stephens **4**:409

Sturrock, John
Marcel Proust **13**:421

Sturtevant, Albert Morey
Alexander Kielland **5**:278

Styan, J. L.
Bertolt Brecht **13**:67
Georg Kaiser **9**:193

Styron, William
Thomas Wolfe **4**:535

Suckow, Ruth
Ricarda Huch **13**:241

Sukenick, Ronald
Wallace Stevens **12**:372

Sullivan, Jack
Algernon Blackwood **5**:78
Hanns Heinz Ewers **12**:139
M. R. James **6**:214

Sullivan, Kevin
Lady Gregory **1**:335
Oscar Wilde **1**:507

Sullivan, Zohreh T.
Rudyard Kipling **17**:214

Summer, Ed
Robert E. Howard **8**:138

Summers, Montague
Bram Stoker **8**:385
Montague Summers **16**:428

Sussex, Ronald
Emile Verhaeren **12**:473

Sutherland, Cynthia
Rachel Crothers **19**:83

Sutherland, Donald
Gertrude Stein **6**:407

Sutherland, Ronald
Frederick Philip Grove **4**:140

Sutton, Graham
Harley Granville-Barker **2**:195
A. A. Milne **6**:308
Alfred Sutro **6**:421

Sutton, Max Keith
W. S. Gilbert **3**:217

Suvin, Darko
Karel Čapek **6**:930
H. G. Wells **12**:510; **19**:434
Yevgeny Ivanovich Zamyatin
8:554

Swain, J. O.
Vicente Blasco Ibáñez **12**:43

Swales, Martin
Thomas Mann **8**:268; **14**:361
Arthur Schnitzler **4**:402

Swallow, Alan
Hart Crane **2**:116

Swan, Michael
Max Beerbohm **1**:71

Swann, Thomas Burnett
Ernest Dowson **4**:90
A. A. Milne **6**:315

Swanson, Roy Arthur
Kostes Palamas **5**:382

Sweetser, Wesley D.
Arthur Machen **4**:282

Swinburne, Algernon Charles
George Meredith **17**:254
Algernon Charles Swinburne
8:424

Swinnerton, Frank
Hilaire Belloc **7**:40
Arnold Bennett **5**:43
Robert Bridges **1**:130
Joseph Conrad **1**:201
Ford Madox Ford **1**:277
John Galsworthy **1**:298
George Gissing **3**:226
Wyndham Lewis **9**:237
Rose Macaulay **7**:426
Charlotte Mew **8**:298
A. A. Milne **6**:310
George Moore **7**:480
Wilfred Owen **5**:360
Dorothy Richardson **3**:352
Dorothy L. Sayers **2**:527
Bernard Shaw **3**:388
James Stephens **4**:411
H. G. Wells **6**:536
Virginia Woolf **1**:532

Sykes, Christopher
Frederick Rolfe **12**:272

Sykes, W. J.
Duncan Campbell Scott **6**:387

Symes, Gordon
Alun Lewis **3**:286

Symonds, John
Aleister Crowley **7**:211

Symonds, John Addington
Vernon Lee **5**:309
Algernon Charles Swinburne
8:426

Symons, A.J.A.
Frederick Rolfe **12**:269

Symons, Arthur
Gabriele D'Annunzio **6**:128
Ernest Dowson **4**:85
Havelock Ellis **14**:107
Thomas Hardy **4**:154
William Ernest Henley **8**:97
Joris-Karl Huysmans **7**:410
Alfred Jarry **2**:277
James Joyce **8**:158
Maurice Maeterlinck **3**:327
George Meredith **17**:256
George Moore **7**:474
Edgar Saltus **8**:348
Olive Schreiner **9**:393
Arthur Symons **11**:427
Sara Teasdale **4**:423
Emile Verhaeren **12**:468
William Butler Yeats **11**:509

Symons, Julian
E. C. Bentley **12**:18
Raymond Chandler **1**:173;
7:175
Arthur Conan Doyle **7**:238
Jacques Futrelle **19**:91
George Orwell **15**:298
Dorothy L. Sayers **15**:378
Josephine Tey **14**:454
Nathanael West **14**:471

Szabolcsi, Miklós
Endre Ady **11**:21
Mihály Babits **14**:42

Critic Index

Szczesny, Gerhard
Bertolt Brecht 6:32

Szogyi, Alex
Marcel Schwob 20:329

Tabachnick, Stephen Ely
T. E. Lawrence 18:177

Tagore, Rabindranath
Saratchandra Chatterji 13:72

Taine, H.
Friedrich Nietzsche 10:353

Talamantes, Florence
Alfonsina Storni 5:446

Talburt, Nancy Ellen
Josephine Tey 14:461

Tanner, Tony
Thomas Hardy 18:104
Jack London 9:269
George MacDonald 9:297

Taplin, Gardner B.
Andrew Lang 16:268

Tarkington, Booth
Booth Tarkington 9:462
Mark Twain 12:437

Tarn, Adam
Stanisław Ignacy Witkiewicz 8:508

Tarrant, Desmond
James Branch Cabell 6:76
Theodore Dreiser 10:196

Tate, Allen
Stephen Vincent Benét 7:70
Roy Campbell 5:117
Hart Crane 2:114, 117
Douglas Southall Freeman 11:222
Edwin Muir 2:481
Edwin Arlington Robinson 5:405
Paul Valéry 15:456
Charles Williams 11:484
William Butler Yeats 11:523

Taubman, Jane Adelman
Marina Tsvetaeva 7:566

Taupin, René
Rémy de Gourmont 17:141

Tayler, G. M.
Liu E 15:245

Taylor, A.J.P.
John Reed 9:390

Taylor, Alexander
Franz Kafka 13:272

Taylor, Colleen M.
Bruno Schulz 5:423

Taylor, Desmond Shaw
Lady Gregory 1:338

Taylor, Douglas
F. Scott Fitzgerald 14:156

Taylor, Martin C.
Gabriela Mistral 2:480

Taylor, Simon Watson
Alfred Jarry 14:276

Taylor, Una
Maurice Maeterlinck 3:324

Taylor, Wendell Hertig
E. C. Bentley 12:20

Tchekhov, Anton
See also **Chekhov, Anton Pavlovich**
Maxim Gorky 8:67, 68

Tchukovsky, K.
Valery Bryusov 10:78

Teilhard de Chardin, Pierre
Pierre Teilhard de Chardin 9:477

Teller, Gertrude E.
Stefan Zweig 17:434

Temple, Ruth Zabriskie
John Gray 19:155
Arthur Symons 11:440

Tenenbaum, Louis
Vitaliano Brancati 12:80, 82
Cesare Pavese 3:337

Tennyson, Alfred
Algernon Charles Swinburne 8:423

Terras, Victor
Isaak Babel 2:21
Osip Mandelstam 2:402; 6:262
Vladimir Mayakovsky 18:267

Terwilliger, Thomas
Hanns Heinz Ewers 12:135

Test, George A.
Karel Čapek 6:92

Thale, Jerome
Joseph Conrad 13:108

Thau, Annette
Max Jacob 6:195, 199

Theis, O. F.
Frank Wedekind 7:576

Theroux, Paul
Andrei Platonov 14:421

Thibaudet, Albert
Rémy de Gourmont 17:147

Thomas, David
Henrik Ibsen 8:154

Thomas, Dylan
Wilfred Owen 5:363
Dylan Thomas 8:451

Thomas, Hugh
Arturo Barea 14:52

Thomas, Lawrence
André Gide 5:219

Thomas, R. George
Edward Thomas 10:463

Thomas, R. Hinton
Thomas Mann 14:338

Thompson, Charles Miner
Mary Wilkins Freeman 9:61

Thompson, Edward J.
Rabindranath Tagore 3:484, 490

Thompson, Ewa M.
Aleksandr Blok 5:97

Thompson, Francis
Hilaire Belloc 18:18
Bliss Carman 7:133
Gabriele D'Annunzio 6:128
Ernest Dowson 4:90
A. E. Housman 10:238
Alice Meynell 6:291

John Ruskin 20:271
Algernon Charles Swinburne 8:428
William Butler Yeats 11:508

Thompson, Laurie
Stig Dagerman 17:89, 91

Thompson, Vance
Marcel Schwob 20:320

Thompson, William Irwin
A. E. 3:12

Thomson, Boris
Velimir Khlebnikov 20:144
Andrei Platonov 14:421

Thomson, H. Douglas
E. C. Bentley 12:13

Thomson, Paul van Kuykendall
Francis Thompson 4:440

Thomson, R.D.B.
Vladimir Mayakovsky 18:255

Thorndike, Lynn
Montague Summers 16:423

Thornton, R.K.R.
Lionel Johnson 19:254

Thorp, Willard
Sherwood Anderson 1:52

Thuente, Mary Helen
William Butler Yeats 11:537

Thurber, James
L. Frank Baum 7:14
Robert Benchley 1:80

Thurley, Geoffrey
Sergei Esenin 4:114

Thurman, Wallace
Countee Cullen 4:41
Claude McKay 7:456

Thurston, Henry W.
Henry Adams 4:4

Tiefenbrun, Ruth
Franz Kafka 13:280

Tietjens, Eunice
Willa Cather 11:93

Tikhonov, Nikolay
Sergei Esenin 4:113

Tilles, Solomon H.
Rubén Darío 4:65

Tillotson, Geoffrey
Ernest Dowson 4:88

Tillyard, E.M.W.
Joseph Conrad 1:209
James Joyce 3:269

Timberlake Craig
David Belasco 3:89

Timms, Edward
Karl Kraus 5:291

Tindall, Gillian
George Gissing 3:237

Tindall, William York
Joseph Conrad 13:117
James Joyce 16:212
D. H. Lawrence 2:356
Wallace Stevens 3:460
William Butler Yeats 1:578

Titche, Leon L., Jr.
Alfred Döblin 13:169
Robert Musil 12:250

Titiev, Janice Geasler
Alfonsina Storni 5:450

Tobin, Patricia
James Joyce 3:278

Toksvig, Signe
Sigrid Undset 3:510

Tolkien, J.R.R.
E. R. Eddison 15:57
Andrew Lang 16:266
Charles Williams 11:493

Toller, Ernst
Ernst Toller 10:479

Tolstoy, Leo
Leonid Andreyev 3:16

Tolton, C.D.E.
André Gide 5:243

Tomlin, E.W.F.
Wyndham Lewis 2:391

Topping, Gary
Zane Grey 6:183, 186

Torma, J.
René Daumal 14:86

Torres-Ríoseco, Arturo
José Rubén Romero 14:442

Toth, Susan Allen
Mary Wilkins Freeman 9:74

Tougas, Gerard
Hector Saint-Denys Garneau 13:200
Emile Nelligan 14:393

Toumanova, Nina Andronikova
Anton Chekhov 3:155

Townsend, Guy M.
Josephine Tey 14:454

Townsend, R. D.
Vicente Blasco Ibáñez 12:38
Sinclair Lewis 13:325

Towson, M. R.
Gottfried Benn 3:110

Toynbee, Philip
André Gide 5:228
James Joyce 3:264

Traschen, Isadore
Thomas Mann 2:436

Treece, Henry
Dylan Thomas 1:467

Tremper, Ellen
A. A. Milne 6:320

Trend, J. B.
Antonio Machado 3:305

Trensky, Paul I.
Karel Čapek 6:90

Trent, William P.
F. Marion Crawford 10:142
Thomas Hardy 18:87
Edwin Arlington Robinson 5:400

Trickett, Rachel
Dorothy Richardson 3:355

Trilling, Lionel
Willa Cather 1:162
Eugene O'Neill 1:402
George Orwell 2:499

Trollope, Anthony
John Ruskin 20:263

Trombly, Albert Edmund
W. H. Davies 5:200
Vachel Lindsay 17:232

Trotsky, Leon
Andrey Bely 7:46
Aleksandr Blok 5:83
Maxim Gorky 8:75
Zinaida Hippius 9:154
Jack London 9:260
Vladimir Mayakovsky 4:289
Frank Wedekind 7:589

Trotter, William Monroe
Booker T. Washington 10:517

Troy, William
F. Scott Fitzgerald 14:151
James Joyce 3:259
Virginia Woolf 1:534

Trueblood, Charles K.
John Galsworthy 1:296

Tsvetaeva, Marina
Valery Bryusov 10:79

Tucker, Carll
Eugene O'Neill 1:407

Tucker, Janet Grace
Innokenty Annensky 14:25

Tuell, Anne Kimball
Alice Meynell 6:297

Tull, J. F., Jr.
Miguel de Unamuno 9:517

Turgenev, Ivan
Leo Tolstoy 4:448, 460

Turk, F. A.
Pierre Teilhard de Chardin
9:497

Turnell, Martin
Alain-Fournier 6:19
Guillaume Apollinaire 3:40
Paul Claudel 10:130
Rémy de Gourmont 17:147

Turner, Arlin
George Washington Cable 4:28

Turner, Darwin T.
Countee Cullen 4:49
Paul Laurence Dunbar 2:129
Joel Chandler Harris 2:216

Turner, Henry M.
Booker T. Washington 10:518

Turner, Matthew Freke
Mark Twain 12:425

Turner, Sheila
Kahlil Gibran 1:328

Turpin, Waters E.
Rudolph Fisher 11:206

Turquet-Milnes, G.
Jean Moréas 18:282
Paul Valéry 4:490

Turrell, Charles Alfred
Gregorio Martinez Sierra and
Maria Martinez Sierra 6:273

Twain, Mark
See also **Clemens, S. L.**
Paul Bourget 12:61
William Dean Howells 7:368

Tyler, Robert L.
Arthur Machen 4:281

Tynan, Katherine
Lionel Johnson 19:232
Rose Macaulay 7:421
William Butler Yeats 11:506

Tynan, Kenneth
Bertolt Brecht 1:102

Tynyanov, Yury
Velimir Khlebnikov 20:125

Tytell, John
Frederick Rolfe 12:277

Ueda, Makoto
Dazai Osamu 11:185
Ishikawa Takuboku 15:129
Masaoka Shiki 18:229
Sōseki Natsume 2:495

Uitti, Karl D.
Rémy de Gourmont 17:156

Ullmann, Christiane
Paul Heyse 8:123

Ullmann, Stephen
Alain-Fournier 6:19

Umphrey, George W.
Rubén Darío 4:58
Amado Nervo 11:398

Underhill, John Garrett
Jacinto Benavente 3:93, 95
Gregorio Martinez Sierra and
Maria Martinez Sierra 6:273

Undset, Sigrid
D. H. Lawrence 2:353

Unterecker, John
Hart Crane 2:123

Untermeyer, Louis
W. H. Davies 5:205
Lion Feuchtwanger 3:178
F. Scott Fitzgerald 1:250
Vachel Lindsay 17:223
Amy Lowell 1:371
Edna St. Vincent Millay 4:307
Robert W. Service 15:401
George Sterling 20:374
Wallace Stevens 12:376
Sara Teasdale 4:425, 426
Thomas Wolfe 13:478

Updike, John
James Agee 1:6
Max Beerbohm 1:71, 72
Colette 16:116
Knut Hamsun 14:250
Alfred Jarry 14:273
Franz Kafka 13:283
Sōseki Natsume 10:347
Bruno Schulz 5:428

Urban, G. R.
Stefan George 2:152

Ureña, Pedro Henriquez
Rubén Darío 4:56

Uroff, M. D.
Hart Crane 2:124

Usmiani, Renate
Gerhart Hauptmann 4:208

Valency, Maurice
Anton Chekhov 3:163
Jean Giraudoux 7:327

Valera, Juan
Juan Valera 10:495

Vallery-Radot, Robert
Charles Péguy 10:403

Vandervelde, Lalla
Jean Moréas 18:278

Van Doren, Carl
Charles A. Beard 15:21
James Branch Cabell 6:64
Willa Cather 1:150
F. Scott Fitzgerald 1:236
Zona Gale 7:279
John Galsworthy 1:300
Hamlin Garland 3:192
O. Henry 19:174
Joseph Hergesheimer 11:263
Ring Lardner 2:326
Ludwig Lewisohn 19:267
Vachel Lindsay 17:231
Don Marquis 7:436
Edgar Lee Masters 2:461
Edna St. Vincent Millay 4:308
Gertrude Stein 1:427
Booth Tarkington 9:455
Mark Twain 12:430; 19:355
Carl Van Doren 18:392
Elinor Wylie 8:525

Van Doren, Mark
Rachel Crothers 19:73
Havelock Ellis 14:110
John Galsworthy 1:300
Thomas Hardy 4:167
Thomas Mann 2:425
Luigi Pirandello 4:333
Constance Rourke 12:316
Sara Teasdale 4:425
Miguel de Unamuno 9:512

Van Gelder, Robert
Stefan Zweig 17:427

Van Ghent, Dorothy
Dazai Osamu 11:172
Thomas Hardy 18:96
Henry James 11:331

Van Horne, John
Jacinto Benavente 3:94
José María de Pereda 16:368

Van Kranendonk, A. G.
Katherine Mansfield 2:448
T. F. Powys 9:368

Van Nostrand, Albert
Booth Tarkington 9:464

Van Vechten, Carl
Gertrude Atherton 2:15
Countee Cullen 4:39
Ronald Firbank 1:224
James Weldon Johnson 3:240
Edgar Saltus 8:346
M. P. Shiel 8:359
Walter White 15:474
Elinor Wylie 8:524

Vass, George, S. J.
Pierre Teilhard de Chardin
9:483

Vedder, Henry C.
George Washington Cable 4:24

Venable, Vernon
Thomas Mann 14:327

Vendler, Helen Hennessy
Wallace Stevens 12:377
William Butler Yeats 1:570

Ventura, L. D.
Guiseppe Giacosa 7:305

Verne, Jules
Jules Verne 6:490
H. G. Wells 6:524

Verschoyle, Derek
Malcolm Lowry 6:235

Versluys, Kristiaan
Emile Verhaeren 12:482

Vessey, David
Arthur Machen 4:286

Vezér, Erzsébet
Endre Ady 11:26

Vial, Fernand
Paul Claudel 2:102

Vickery, Walter N.
Andrei A. Zhdanov 18:475

Vidal, Gore
L. Frank Baum 7:21
Edgar Rice Burroughs 2:76
F. Scott Fitzgerald 6:167
William Dean Howells 17:180
Bernard Shaw 9:420
Edith Wharton 9:551

Viereck, Peter
Stefan George 14:213
Vachel Lindsay 17:241

Vigar, Penelope
Thomas Hardy 4:174

Vigliemo, V. H.
Sōseki Natsume 10:333

Vigneault, Robert
Hector Saint-Denys Garneau
13:204

Villa, Jose Garcia
Pedro Salinas 17:353

Villars, Jean Beraud
T. E. Lawrence 18:147

Villaseñor, José Sánchez, S. J.
José Ortega y Gasset 9:338

Vinde, Victor
Sigrid Undset 3:513

Virgillo, Carmelo
Machado de Assis 10:295

Visiak, E. H.
David Lindsay 15:220

Vislov, Alexander
Alexey Nikolayevich Tolstoy
18:382

Vitelli, James R.
Randolph S. Bourne 16:59

Vitins, Ieva
Anton Chekhov 10:115

Vittorini, Domenico
Gabriele D'Annunzio 6:132
Luigi Pirandello 4:331, 333

Vivas, Eliseo
D. H. Lawrence 16:294

Vlach, Robert
Jaroslav Hašek 4:181

Critic Index

Voelker, Joseph C.
D. H. Lawrence **9**:227

Vogt Gapp, Samuel
George Gissing **3**:229

Völker, Klaus
Bertolt Brecht **6**:34

Volpe, Edmond L.
Nathanael West **1**:479

Von Ende, A.
Detlev von Liliencron **18**:205

Von Ende, Amelia
Stefan Zweig **17**:423

Von Gronicka, André
Thomas Mann **14**:334

Von Mohrenschildt, D. S.
Valery Bryusov **10**:81

Vonnegut, Kurt, Jr
H. L. Mencken **13**:392
Mark Twain **6**:482

Von Wiren, Vera
Mikhail Zoshchenko **15**:503

Voronskij, Aleksandr
Isaac Babel **13**:12

Voronsky, A. K.
Yevgeny Ivanovich Zamyatin
8:541

Vortriede, Werner
Georg Heym **9**:163

Voss, Arthur
Bret Harte **1**:344
O. Henry **1**:351

Vroon, Ronald
Velimir Khlebnikov **20**:146

Waal, Carla
Knut Hamsun **14**:243

Wadlington, Warwick
Nathanael West **1**:489

Wadsworth, Frank W.
Ugo Betti **5**:56

Wadsworth, Philip A.
Antoine de Saint-Exupéry **2**:516

Wagenknecht, Edward
L. Frank Baum **7**:13
Walter de la Mare **4**:77
Ellen Glasgow **2**:178
Henry James **11**:346
Katherine Mansfield **2**:447
George Meredith **17**:274
Margaret Mitchell **11**:375

Waggoner, Hyatt Howe
Edwin Arlington Robinson
5:409

Wagner, Geoffrey
Lewis Grassic Gibbon **4**:123
Thomas Hardy **18**:110
Wyndham Lewis **2**:391

Wagner, Jean
Countee Cullen **4**:46
Paul Laurence Dunbar **12**:114
Frances Ellen Watkins Harper
14:258
James Weldon Johnson **3**:243
Claude McKay **7**:459
Damon Runyon **10**:430

Wagner, Philip
H. L. Mencken **13**:386

Wagstaff, Christopher
F. T. Marinetti **10**:321

Wahr, F. B.
Gerhart Hauptmann **4**:200

Waidson, H. M.
Robert Walser **18**:422

Wain, John
Arnold Bennett **5**:47
George Orwell **6**:343
Dylan Thomas **1**:471

Wake, Clive
Pierre Loti **11**:364

Walbrook, H. M.
J. M. Barrie **2**:42

Walcutt, Charles Child
Sherwood Anderson **1**:48
Stephen Crane **11**:143
Hamlin Garland **3**:196

Wald, Alan M.
Tess Slesinger **10**:442

Waldron, Edward E.
Walter White **15**:483

Walker, Dorothea
Sheila Kaye-Smith **20**:115

Walkley, A. B.
Harley Granville-Barker **2**:192
George Jean Nathan **18**:304

Wallace, Henry A.
Charles A. Beard **15**:22

Wallace, Jack E.
Theodore Dreiser **18**:54

Wallace, Margaret
Thomas Wolfe **13**:467

Wallace, William
George Moore **7**:473

Walpole, Hugh
James Branch Cabell **6**:63
F. Marion Crawford **10**:147
Knut Hamsun **14**:226
Joseph Hergesheimer **11**:269

Walser, Richard
Thomas Wolfe **4**:530

Walsh, Chad
Charles Williams **11**:487

Walsh, William
Katherine Mansfield **2**:453

Walter, Elisabeth
Hugo von Hofmannsthal **11**:293

Walters, Jennifer
Boris Vian **9**:531

Walters, Ray
Robert E. Howard **8**:133

Walton, Alan Hull
Havelock Ellis **14**:126

Walton, Edith H.
Tess Slesinger **10**:440

Walton, Geoffrey
Edith Wharton **9**:548

Ward, A. C.
Rupert Brooke **7**:125
George Gissing **3**:233

Ward, J. A.
Henry James **11**:336

Ward, J. P.
Edward Thomas **10**:461

Ward, Susan
Jack London **9**:276

Wardropper, Bruce W.
Antonio Machado **3**:309

Ware, Martin
Duncan Campbell Scott **6**:399

Warncke, Wayne
George Orwell **6**:346

Warner, Beverley E.
Edgar Saltus **8**:342

Warner, Rex
C. P. Cavafy **7**:153

Warnock, Mary
Friedrich Nietzsche **18**:340

Warren, Austin
Henry Adams **4**:19
M. R. James **6**:210
Franz Kafka **2**:295

Warren, L. A.
Jacinto Benavente **3**:99
Gregorio Martinez Sierra and
Maria Martinez Sierra **6**:280
Juan Valera **10**:501
Ramón del Valle-Inclán **5**:476

Warren, Robert Penn
Ivan Bunin **6**:47
Joseph Conrad **1**:205
O. Henry **19**:185
Ring Lardner **14**:299
Mark Twain **6**:480; **12**:448
Franz Werfel **8**:469
Thomas Wolfe **4**:507

Washington, Booker T.
Booker T. Washington **10**:513,
519

Wasson, Richard
Bram Stoker **8**:387

Waters, Brian
W. H. Davies **5**:205

Watkins, Floyd C.
Margaret Mitchell **11**:379
Thomas Wolfe **4**:524

Watson, Barbara Bellow
Bernard Shaw **3**:402

Watson, Charles N., Jr.
Jack London **15**:276

Watson, E. H. Lacon
Edgar Rice Burroughs **2**:75

Watson, George
Alice Meynell **6**:303

Watson, Harold
Paul Claudel **2**:108

Watson, William
Thomas Hardy **18**:79
George Meredith **17**:258
William Butler Yeats **11**:507

Watt, Ian
Joseph Conrad **13**:134
George Orwell **15**:347

Watters, R. E.
Stephen Leacock **2**:381

Watts, Cedric
Joseph Conrad **13**:132
R. B. Cunninghame Graham
19:136

Watts, Emily Stipes
Elinor Wylie **8**:536

Watts, Harold H.
Maxwell Anderson **2**:4
Ugo Betti **5**:65

Watts, Theodore
See also **Watts-Dunton,
Theodore**
Algernon Charles Swinburne
8:426

Watts-Dunton, Theodore
See also **Watts, Theodore**
Theodore Dreiser **10**:163

Waugh, Arthur
Robert Bridges **1**:128
Rupert Brooke **2**:54
Samuel Butler **1**:133
D. H. Lawrence **2**:344
Arthur Symons **11**:433

Waugh, Evelyn
Hilaire Belloc **18**:28
H. G. Wells **12**:503

Waxman, Meyer
Israel Zangwill **16**:446

Way, Brian
F. Scott Fitzgerald **6**:168

Weales, Gerald
James Bridie **3**:138
Harley Granville-Barker **2**:199
Laurence Housman **7**:358
Dorothy L. Sayers **2**:531
Charles Williams **1**:521

Webb, Charles Henry
Mark Twain **6**:453

Webb, Howard W., Jr.
Ring Lardner **2**:336; **14**:299

Weber, Brom
Sherwood Anderson **1**:56
Hart Crane **2**:115

Webster, Harvey Curtis
Countee Cullen **4**:43
Thomas Hardy **4**:166

Webster, Wentworth
José Echegaray **4**:97

Weeks, Jeffrey
Havelock Ellis **14**:140

Weideli, Walter
Bertolt Brecht **13**:48

Weidle, Wladimir
Paul Claudel **10**:126
Vladislav Khodasevich **15**:205

Weigand, Hermann J.
Hermann Broch **20**:51
Gerhart Hauptmann **4**:202
Henrik Ibsen **8**:144; **16**:162
Thomas Mann **2**:414

Weightman, John
Colette **5**:170
Marcel Proust **13**:430
Jules Renard **17**:307

Weil, Irwin
Maxim Gorky **8**:83

Weimar, Karl S.
Wolfgang Borchert 5:106
Bertolt Brecht 13:50

Weinstein, Arnold L.
Joseph Conrad 1:219
Ford Madox Ford 1:290
James Joyce 3:279
Franz Kafka 2:308

Weinstein, Bernard
Stephen Crane 11:159; 17:68

Weinstein, Norman
Gertrude Stein 1:439

Weintraub, Rodelle
T. E. Lawrence 18:162

Weintraub, Stanley
T. E. Lawrence 18:162
Bernard Shaw 3:400

Weir, Charles, Jr.
F. Scott Fitzgerald 1:239

Weiss, Beno
Italo Svevo 2:552

Weisstein, Ulrich
Heinrich Mann 9:323
Robert Walser 18:431

Welby, T. Earle
Algernon Charles Swinburne
8:432
Arthur Symons 11:434

Welland, Dennis
Wilfred Owen 5:373

Wellek, René
Hermann Broch 20:76
Georg Brandes 10:69
Karel Čapek 6:84
William Dean Howells 7:388
Henry James 2:268
Paul Valéry 15:464

Wellman, Esther Turner
Amado Nervo 11:396

Wells, Arvin B.
James Branch Cabell 6:73

Wells, H. G.
Hilaire Belloc 7:34; 18:19
Arnold Bennett 5:23
Stephen Crane 11:124
Ford Madox Ford 15:72
George Gissing 3:222
Henry James 2:247
James Joyce 3:252
Rudyard Kipling 8:184
Dorothy Richardson 3:345
Bernard Shaw 9:419
Jules Verne 6:491
Booker T. Washington 10:518
H. G. Wells 6:531; 12:492
Israel Zangwill 16:441

Wells, Henry W.
Stephen Vincent Benét 7:76
Wallace Stevens 12:369

Wells, Linton
Jacques Roumain 19:331

Wellwarth, G. E.
Antonin Artaud 3:48
Alfred Jarry 2:280

Welson, John
Benjamin Péret 20:203

Welty, Eudora
Willa Cather 11:110

Wertheim, Albert
Philip Barry 11:68

Wescott, Glenway
F. Scott Fitzgerald 6:160
Thomas Mann 8:258

Wesling, Donald
Vachel Lindsay 17:247

West, Anthony
Arturo Barea 14:46
Joyce Cary 1:142
Nikos Kazantzakis 5:259
Ada Leverson 18:190
Sinclair Lewis 13:338
Machado de Assis 10:286
Robert Musil 12:236
George Orwell 2:504
H. G. Wells 6:538

West, Donald
C. M. Kornbluth 8:219

West, Geoffrey
Arnold Bennett 5:35
Annie Besant 9:16

West, Herbert Faulkner
R. B. Cunninghame Graham
19:108

West, Nathanael
Nathanael West 14:468

West, Paul
José Ortega y Gasset 9:343

West, Rebecca
Sherwood Anderson 1:39
Maurice Baring 8:32
Arnold Bennett 5:32; 20:25
Willa Cather 1:153
Colette 1:191
F. Scott Fitzgerald 14:149
Ford Madox Ford 1:275
Emma Goldman 13:215
Radclyffe Hall 12:187
Knut Hamsun 14:225
Henry James 2:248
Franz Kafka 2:298
Wyndham Lewis 2:397
Katherine Mansfield 8:275
John Middleton Murry 16:333
Olive Schreiner 9:394
May Sinclair 3:436
H. G. Wells 6:525; 12:493
Edith Wharton 9:542
Virginia Woolf 1:530

Westbrook, Perry D.
Mary Wilkins Freeman 9:72

Wexelblatt, Robert
Leo Tolstoy 11:476

Weygandt, Cornelius
A. E. 3:2
Oliver St. John Gogarty 15:103
George Moore 7:476
James Stephens 4:410
Edward Thomas 10:454

Weyhaupt, Angela Evonne
Stanisław Ignacy Witkiewicz
8:514

Wharton, Edith
F. Marion Crawford 10:145
F. Scott Fitzgerald 6:160
Marcel Proust 7:520
Edith Wharton 9:543

Wharton, Lewis
John McCrae 12:208

Whatley, W. A.
Robert W. Service 15:400

Whay, R. A.
Jacques Futrelle 19:89

Wheatley, Dennis
William Hope Hodgson 13:237

Wheatley, Elizabeth D.
Arnold Bennett 5:36

Wheelwright, John
Federico García Lorca 1:307

Whipple, T. K.
Sherwood Anderson 1:39
Willa Cather 1:151
Zane Grey 6:178
Sinclair Lewis 4:248
Eugene O'Neill 1:384

Whitaker, Paul K.
Hermann Sudermann 15:432,
434

White, Antonia
Arturo Barea 14:44
Anne Frank 17:101

White, D. Fedotoff
Alexey Nikolayevich Tolstoy
18:361

White, David
José Ortega y Gasset 9:342

White, E. B.
Louis Bromfield 11:79
Don Marquis 7:441

White, Edmund
James Agee 19:47

White, George Leroy, Jr.
O. E. Rölvaag 17:325

White, Gertrude M.
Hilaire Belloc 7:42

White, Greenough
Bliss Carman 7:134
Francis Thompson 4:434

White, Ray Lewis
Sherwood Anderson 1:58

White, Walter F.
James Weldon Johnson 19:205

Whitman, Walt
John Ruskin 20:258

Whitney, Blair
Vachel Lindsay 17:244

Whittemore, Reed
Joseph Conrad 1:212
Ford Madox Ford 15:82
Bernard Shaw 3:401

Whittock, Trevor
Bernard Shaw 9:423

Widdows, P. F.
Emile Nelligan 14:392

Widmer, Kingsley
Nathanael West 14:490

Wiehr, Joseph
Knut Hamsun 14:222

Wiener, Leo
Isaac Leib Peretz 16:388

Wiesel, Elie
Isaac Leib Peretz 16:402

Wiggins, Robert A.
Ambrose Bierce 1:90

Wilbur, Richard
A. E. Housman 10:256

Wilcox, Earl
Jack London 9:271

Wilde, Oscar
William Ernest Henley 8:96
Rudyard Kipling 8:175
Algernon Charles Swinburne
8:427
Oscar Wilde 8:488
William Butler Yeats 11:507

Wilden, Anthony
Italo Svevo 2:550

Wildiers, N. M.
Pierre Teilhard de Chardin
9:493

Wilenski, R. H.
John Ruskin 20:282

Wiley, Paul L.
Ford Madox Ford 15:87

Wilkes, G. A.
Christopher John Brennan
17:38

Wilkins, Eithne
Robert Musil 12:232

Wilkins, Ernest Hatch
Gabriele D'Annunzio 6:136

Wilkinson, Louis U.
T. F. Powys 9:359

Wilkinson, Marguerite
Charlotte Mew 8:295

Wilks, Ronald
Maxim Gorky 8:83

Will, Frederic
Nikos Kazantzakis 5:264
Kostes Palamas 5:381-82

Willard, Nancy
Rainer Maria Rilke 1:421

Williams, C. E.
Robert Musil 12:258
Stefan Zweig 17:444

Williams, Charles
Hilaire Belloc 18:26
E. C. Bentley 12:14
Ford Madox Ford 15:75
Rudyard Kipling 17:195
John Middleton Murry 16:340
Dorothy L. Sayers 15:374

Williams, Cratis D.
Sherwood Anderson 1:55

Williams, Ellen
Harriet Monroe 12:223

Williams, Harold
W. H. Davies 5:200
Harley Granville-Barker 2:193
Laurence Housman 7:353
Katharine Tynan 3:504

Williams, I. M.
George Meredith 17:279

Williams, John Stuart
Alun Lewis 3:288

Williams, Kenny J.
Paul Laurence Dunbar 12:119
Frances Ellen Watkins Harper
14:258

Williams, Orlo
Luigi Pirandello 4:327

Williams, Raymond
Bertolt Brecht 1:105; 13:66
George Orwell 6:348
August Strindberg 1:457; 8:411
Ernst Toller 10:484

Williams, Rhys W.
Carl Sternheim 8:379

Williams, T. Harry
Douglas Southall Freeman
11:227

Williams, William Carlos
Ford Madox Ford 15:81
Federico García Lorca 7:290
Wallace Stevens 3:451
Nathanael West 14:468

Williams-Ellis, A.
Charlotte Mew 8:296

Williamson, Audrey
James Bridie 3:133

Williamson, Edward
Dino Campana 20:85

Williamson, Hugh Ross
Alfred Sutro 6:423

Williamson, Karina
Roger Mais 8:240, 250

Willibrand, William Anthony
Ernst Toller 10:480

Willoughby, L. A.
Christian Morgenstern 8:304

Wills, Garry
Hilaire Belloc 18:32

Willson, A. Leslie
Wolfgang Borchert 5:110

Wilmer, Clive
Miklós Radnóti 16:413

Wilshire, Bruce
William James 15:178

Wilson, A. N.
Hilaire Belloc 18:43, 45

Wilson, Angus
Arnold Bennett 5:43
Samuel Butler 1:137
Rudyard Kipling 8:205
Bernard Shaw 3:398
Emile Zola 1:591

Wilson, Christopher P.
Lincoln Steffens 20:364

Wilson, Clotilde
Machado de Assis 10:281

Wilson, Colin
Henri Barbusse 5:14
Arthur Conan Doyle 7:233
F. Scott Fitzgerald 1:251
M. R. James 6:210
Nikos Kazantzakis 2:317

T. E. Lawrence 18:152
David Lindsay 15:225, 230
H. P. Lovecraft 4:270
Rainer Maria Rilke 1:417
Bernard Shaw 3:400; 9:425
August Strindberg 8:411

Wilson, Daniel J.
Zane Grey 6:186

Wilson, Donald
André Gide 5:240

Wilson, Edmund
Henry Adams 4:13
Maxwell Anderson 2:3
Sherwood Anderson 1:35, 50
Maurice Baring 8:43
Philip Barry 11:46, 51
Charles A. Beard 15:22
Max Beerbohm 1:68, 73
Robert Benchley 1:76
Ambrose Bierce 1:89
Louis Bromfield 11:80
Samuel Butler 1:134
James Branch Cabell 6:70
George Washington Cable 4:29
Willa Cather 1:152
John Jay Chapman 7:187, 190
Anton Chekhov 3:159
Kate Chopin 5:148
Hart Crane 5:185
Arthur Conan Doyle 7:222
Theodore Dreiser 10:178
Ronald Firbank 1:226, 228
F. Scott Fitzgerald 1:233;
6:159; 14:147
Anatole France 9:48
A. E. Housman 10:252
James Weldon Johnson 3:240
James Joyce 3:256, 260
Franz Kafka 2:294
Rudyard Kipling 8:187
Giuseppe Tomasi di Lampedusa
13:301
Ring Lardner 2:325
D. H. Lawrence 2:345
H. P. Lovecraft 4:268
H. L. Mencken 13:363
Edna St. Vincent Millay 4:317
Ferenc Molnár 20:172
George Jean Nathan 18:310
Emile Nelligan 14:392
Marcel Proust 7:524
Jacques Roumain 19:332
Dorothy L. Sayers 2:530
Bernard Shaw 3:391, 396
Gertrude Stein 1:426; 6:404
Wallace Stevens 3:444
Lytton Strachey 12:398
Algernon Charles Swinburne
8:443
Leo Tolstoy 4:480
Paul Valéry 4:487; 15:442
H. G. Wells 12:500
Nathanael West 14:470
Edith Wharton 3:558, 579;
9:544
Elinor Wylie 8:523
William Butler Yeats 1:554

Wilson, H. Schütz
Emile Zola 6:558

Wilson, Sharon
E. R. Eddison 15:61

Wilt, Judith
George Meredith 17:295

Winchell, Walter
Damon Runyon 10:423

Winebaum, B. V.
William Hope Hodgson 13:232

Wing, George Gordon
César Vallejo 3:527

Winkler, R.O.C.
Franz Kafka 2:288

Winner, Anthony
Anton Chekhov 10:116
Joris-Karl Huysmans 7:415

Winship, George P., Jr.
Charles Williams 1:523

Winsnes, A. H.
Sigrid Undset 3:521

Winter, Calvin
See also **Cooper, Frederic
Taber**
Edith Wharton 3:553

Winter, Ella
Lincoln Steffens 20:349

Winter, William
David Belasco 3:86
Paul Heyse 8:118
Hermann Sudermann 15:425

Winterich, John T.
Will Rogers 8:334

Winters, Yvor
Henry Adams 4:8
Robert Bridges 1:131
Hart Crane 2:112
Henry James 2:257
Edwin Arlington Robinson
5:407
Wallace Stevens 3:447

Wirth, Andrzej
Tadeusz Borowski 9:20

Wisse, Ruth R.
Sholom Aleichem 1:32

Wister, Owen
John Jay Chapman 7:189

Witkiewicz, Stanisław Ignacy
Stanisław Ignacy Witkiewicz
8:505

Witte, W.
Christian Morgenstern 8:305

Wittig, Kurt
Lewis Grassic Gibbon

Wohlgelernter, Maurice
Israel Zangwill 16:452

Wolf, Leonard
Bram Stoker 8:392

Wolfe, Bernard
Joel Chandler Harris 2:214

Wolfe, Bertram D.
John Reed 9:385

**Wolfe, Deborah Cannon
Partridge**
Booker T. Washington 10:544

Wolfe, Thomas
Thomas Wolfe 4:510; 13:469

Wolff, Cynthia Griffin
Kate Chopin 5:156; 14:76

Wolff, Robert Lee
George MacDonald 9:296

Wolstenholme, Susan
Theodore Dreiser 18:64

Wood, Clement
Edgar Lee Masters 2:464

Wood, Frank
Rainer Maria Rilke 19:307

Wood, Michael
René Daumal 14:93

Woodard, Frederick
Mark Twain 19:407

Woodburn, John
Thomas Wolfe 4:521

Woodcock, George
Alain-Fournier 6:23
Wyndham Lewis 2:395
Malcolm Lowry 6:236
George Meredith 17:281
George Orwell 2:508; 15:364
Oscar Wilde 1:502

Woodford, Arthur B.
Charlotte Gilman 9:98

Woodress, James
Booth Tarkington 9:466

Woodring, Carl
Virginia Woolf 1:542

Woodruff, Bertram L.
Countee Cullen 4:42

Woodruff, Stuart C.
Ambrose Bierce 1:92

Woodson, C. G.
Douglas Southall Freeman
11:221

Woodward, James B.
Leonid Andreyev 3:27
Aleksandr Blok 5:96
Ivan Bunin 6:56

Woolf, D.
Giovanni Verga 3:546

Woolf, Leonard S.
Hilaire Belloc 7:33
Anton Chekhov 3:149
R. B. Cunninghame Graham
19:108
Radclyffe Hall 12:185
T. E. Lawrence 18:130
Amy Lowell 8:225
Constance Rourke 12:316
Mark Twain 6:460
H. G. Wells 12:498

Woolf, Virginia
Hilaire Belloc 7:34
Arnold Bennett 5:28; 20:24
Stella Benson 17:23
Rupert Brooke 2:53
Anton Chekhov 10:101
Joseph Conrad 1:198
George Gissing 3:228
Thomas Hardy 4:160
Henry James 2:251
Ring Lardner 2:326
D. H. Lawrence 9:213
Sinclair Lewis 4:247
Katherine Mansfield 8:276
George Meredith 17:272
George Moore 7:483

John Middleton Murry **16**:330
Dorothy Richardson **3**:347
John Ruskin **20**:281
Olive Schreiner **9**:395
Lytton Strachey **12**:403
Leo Tolstoy **4**:456
H. G. Wells **6**:527; **12**:496
Virginia Woolf **20**:392

Woollcott, Alexander
Theodore Dreiser **10**:170
Zona Gale **7**:278
George Jean Nathan **18**:295
Eugene O'Neill **1**:381
Bernard Shaw **3**:387

Worsley, T. C.
James Bridie **3**:133

Worster, W. W.
Knut Hamsun **2**:201

Wright, A. Colin
Mikhail Bulgakov **16**:104

Wright, Barbara
Alfred Jarry **14**:278

Wright, Charles
Frederick Rolfe **12**:277

Wright, Cuthbert
Thomas Mann **14**:326

Wright, Ellen F.
William Dean Howells **17**:183

Wright, Judith
Christopher John Brennan
17:47

Wright, Richard
H. L. Mencken **13**:381

Wright, Walter F.
Arnold Bennett **5**:49
George Meredith **17**:276

Wyatt, David
James Agee **19**:41

Wycherley, H. Alan
F. Scott Fitzgerald **1**:261

Wyers, Frances
Miguel de Unamuno **9**:520

Wyndham, Francis
Philip Barry **11**:67

Wyndham, George
Stephen Crane **11**:121

Yakushev, Henryka
Andrei Platonov **14**:427

Yamanouchi, Hisaaki
Sōseki Natsume **10**:343

Yand, H. Y.
Liu E **15**:245

Yardley, Jonathan
Ring Lardner **14**:303

Yarmolinsky, Avrahm
Innokenty Annensky **14**:24
Christian Morgenstern **8**:304

Yates, May
George Gissing **3**:224

Yates, Norris W.
Robert Benchley **1**:80
Don Marquis **7**:443
Will Rogers **8**:334

Yatron, Michael
Edgar Lee Masters **2**:470

Ybarra, T. R.
Vicente Blasco Ibáñez **12**:35

Yeats, William Butler
A. E. **3**:5; **10**:12, 16
Robert Bridges **1**:123
Ernest Dowson **4**:87
Lord Dunsany **2**:135
Oliver St. John Gogarty **15**:100
Lady Gregory **1**:331
William Ernest Henley **8**:101
Alfred Jarry **14**:270
Lionel Johnson **19**:229
George Moore **7**:482
Standish O'Grady **5**:347
Wilfred Owen **5**:362
Bernard Shaw **9**:412
Arthur Symons **11**:427
John Millington Synge **6**:425
Rabindranath Tagore **3**:501
Katharine Tynan **3**:502
Oscar Wilde **8**:490
Elinor Wylie **8**:527
William Butler Yeats **11**:515

Yevtushenko, Yevgeny
Andrei Platonov **14**:408

York, Lamar
Marjorie Kinnan Rawlings
4:367

Yoshie, Okazaki
Sōseki Natsume **10**:328

Young, Alfred
Booker T. Washington **10**:536

Young, Beatrice
Anatole France **9**:51

Young, Douglas F.
Lewis Grassic Gibbon **4**:126

Young, Howard T.
Federico García Lorca **1**:321
Juan Ramón Jiménez **4**:216
Antonio Machado **3**:307
Miguel de Unamuno **2**:562

Young, Kenneth
H. G. Wells **6**:547

Young, Stark
David Belasco **3**:89
Louis Bromfield **11**:75
Federico García Lorca **7**:290
Gregorio Martínez Sierra and
María Martínez Sierra **6**:281
Eugene O'Neill **1**:385; **6**:324
Luigi Pirandello **4**:327
Bernard Shaw **3**:390
Robert E. Sherwood **3**:410
Franz Werfel **8**:467

Youngberg, Karin
G. K. Chesterton **6**:105

Yourcenar, Marguerite
Thomas Mann **2**:433

Yu, Beongcheon
Akutagawa Ryūnosuke **16**:25
Lafcadio Hearn **9**:133
Sōseki Natsume **2**:493; **10**:336

Yuill, W. E.
Lion Feuchtwanger **3**:181, 186
Heinrich Mann **9**:324

Yutang, Lin
Lu Hsün **3**:294

Zabel, Morton Dauwen
Stephen Vincent Benét **7**:74
Joseph Conrad **1**:202
A. E. Coppard **5**:177
Oliver St. John Gogarty **15**:101
A. E. Housman **10**:247
James Joyce **3**:255
Harriet Monroe **12**:222
Wallace Stevens **12**:355

Zamyatin, Yevgeny
Andrey Bely **7**:48
Anatole France **9**:47
O. Henry **9**:180
Yevgeny Ivanovich Zamyatin
8:543

Zangana, Haifa
Benjamin Péret **20**:203

Zangwill, Israel
H. G. Wells **12**:487

Zaturenska, Marya
Amy Lowell **1**:378
Harriet Monroe **12**:221
Sara Teasdale **4**:430

Zavalishin, Vyacheslav
Mikhail Bulgakov **2**:64

Zegger, Hrisey Dimitrakis
May Sinclair **3**:441

Zempel, Solveig
O. E. Rölvaag **17**:346

Zhdanov, Andrei A.
Andrei A. Zhdanov **18**:467,
468
Mikhail Zoshchenko **15**:495

Ziff, Larzer
Ambrose Bierce **1**:94
John Jay Chapman **7**:199
Kate Chopin **5**:148
F. Marion Crawford **10**:156
Hamlin Garland **3**:199
Sarah Orne Jewett **1**:368

Zilboorg, Gregory
Yevgeny Ivanovich Zamyatin
8:542

Zimmerman, Dorothy
Virginia Woolf **1**:543

Zinman, Toby Silverman
Katherine Mansfield **2**:457

Ziolkowski, Theodore
Hermann Broch **20**:59
Alfred Döblin **13**:166
Rainer Maria Rilke **6**:366

Zlobin, Vladimir
Zinaida Hippius **9**:158

Zohn, Harry
Karl Kraus **5**:290

Zola, Emile
Joris-Karl Huysmans **7**:403

Zorn, Marilyn
Katherine Mansfield **8**:288

Zoshchenko, Mikhail
Mikhail Zoshchenko **15**:489

Zweig, Stefan
Maxim Gorky **8**:74
Thomas Mann **2**:418
Friedrich Nietzsche **10**:365
Leo Tolstoy **4**:458
Emile Verhaeren **12**:459
Stefan Zweig **17**:427

Critic Index